The United States Government Manual 2009/2010

Office of the Federal Register
National Archives and Records Administration

Revised September 15, 2009

Raymond A. Mosley,
Director of the Federal Register.

Adrienne C. Thomas,
Acting Archivist of the United States.

On the cover: This edition of *The United States Government Manual* marks the 75th anniversary of the National Archives and celebrates its important mission to ensure access to the essential documentation of Americans' rights and the actions of their Government. The cover displays an image of the Rotunda and the Declaration Mural, one of the 1936 Faulkner Murals in the Rotunda at the National Archives and Records Administration (NARA) Building in Washington, DC.

The National Archives Rotunda is the permanent home of the Declaration of Independence, the Constitution of the United States, and the Bill of Rights. These three documents, known collectively as the Charters of Freeedom, have secured the the rights of the American people for more than two and a quarter centuries. In 2003, the National Archives completed a massive restoration effort that included conserving the parchment of the Declaration of Independence, the Constitution, and the Bill of Rights, and re-encasing the documents in state-of-the-art containers.

In 1936, Barry Faulkner created two large-scale murals in the Rotunda depicting fictional scenes of the presentation of the Declaration of Independence and the Constitution. Each mural is about 13 feet high and 34 feet long. In September 2003, the murals were restored and also recreated as an interactive feature on NARA's Web site: www.archives.gov/nae/visit/rotunda.html. Flanking the permanent display of the Charters and the murals is the exhibit, "A New World Is At Hand," a selection of documents from the National Archives' holdings that chronicle milestones toward the creation of the Charters and their impact on United States and world history. Each year more than a million visitors come to the Rotunda of the National Archives to see the Charters of Freedom and the Faulkner Murals, which adorn its walls.

The Office of the Federal Register, publisher of *The United States Government Manual*, was established as a division of the National Archives in 1935 and moved into the new National Archives building with the other four divisions of the new agency on November 8, 1935.

We extend special thanks to the Creative and Digital Media Services at the Government Printing Office for its artistic contributions in designing the cover.

For sale by the Superintendent of Documents, U.S. Government Printing Office
Internet: bookstore.gpo.gov   Phone: toll free (866) 512–1800; DC area (202) 512–1800
Fax: (202) 512–2250   Mail: Stop SSOP, Washington, DC 20402–0001

ISBN 978–0–16–083949–8

Preface

As the official handbook of the Federal Government, *The United States Government Manual* provides comprehensive information on the agencies of the legislative, judicial, and executive branches. The *Manual* also includes information on quasi-official agencies; international organizations in which the United States participates; and boards, commissions, and committees.

A typical agency description includes a list of principal officials, a summary statement of the agency's purpose and role in the Federal Government, a brief history of the agency, including its legislative or executive authority, a description of its programs and activities, and a "Sources of Information" section. This last section provides information on consumer activities, contracts and grants, employment, publications, and many other areas of public interest.

The 2009/2010 *Manual* was prepared by the Presidential and Legislative Publications Unit, Office of the Federal Register. Alfred W. Jones was Managing Editor; Matthew R. Regan was Chief Editor, assisted by Heather McDaniel, Lois Davis, and Joseph Frankovic.

THE FEDERAL REGISTER AND ITS SPECIAL EDITIONS

The *Manual* is published as a special edition of the *Federal Register* (*see* 1 CFR 9.1). Its focus is on programs and activities. Persons interested in detailed organizational structure, the regulatory documents of an agency, or Presidential documents should refer to the *Federal Register* or one of its other special editions, described below.

Issued each Federal working day, the *Federal Register* provides a uniform system for publishing Presidential documents, regulatory documents with general applicability and legal effect, proposed rules, notices, and documents required to be published by statute.

The *Code of Federal Regulations* is an annual codification of the general and permanent rules published in the *Federal Register*. The *Code* is divided into 50 titles that represent broad areas subject to Federal regulation. The *Code* is kept up to date by the individual issues of the *Federal Register*.

The *Weekly Compilation of Presidential Documents* serves as a timely, up-to-date reference source for the public policies and activities of the President. It contains remarks, news conferences, messages, statements, and other Presidential material of a public nature issued by the White House during the week reported.

A companion publication to the *Weekly Compilation* is the *Public Papers of the Presidents,* which contains public Presidential documents and speeches in convenient book form. Volumes of the *Public Papers* have been published for every President since Herbert Hoover, with the exception of Franklin D. Roosevelt, whose papers were published privately.

OTHER OFFICE OF THE FEDERAL REGISTER PUBLICATIONS

The Office of the Federal Register publishes slip laws, which are pamphlet prints of each public and private law enacted by Congress. Slip laws are compiled annually as the *United States Statutes at Large*. The *Statutes* volumes contain all public and private laws and concurrent resolutions enacted during a session of Congress;

recommendations for executive, legislative, and judicial salaries; reorganization plans; proposed and ratified amendments to the Constitution; and Presidential proclamations. Included with many of these documents are sidenotes, U.S. Code and statutes citations, and a summary of their legislative histories.

PUBLICATION AVAILABILITY

The publications of the Office of the Federal Register are available for sale by writing to the following address:

Superintendent of Documents
P.O. Box 371954
Pittsburgh, PA 15250–7954

Publications are also available for sale through the Government Printing Office online bookstore at http://bookstore.gpo.gov, the Government Printing Office bookstore located in Washington, DC, and the retail sales outlet in Laurel, MD. Telephone inquiries should be directed to 202–512–1800.

ELECTRONIC SERVICES

The Office of the Federal Register maintains an Internet site for public law numbers, the Federal Register's public inspection list, and information on the Office and its activities at www.archives.gov/federal-register. This site also contains links to the texts of *The United States Government Manual*, public laws, the *Weekly Compilation of Presidential Documents*, the *Federal Register*, and the *Code of Federal Regulations* (both as officially published on a quarterly basis and a new unofficial, daily updated version, the e-CFR) in electronic format through *GPO Access*. For more information about these online publications, contact Electronic Information Dissemination Services, U.S. Government Printing Office. Phone, 202–512–1530, or 888–293–6498. Internet, www.gpoaccess.gov. Email, gpoaccess@gpo.gov.

FURTHER INFORMATION

Information on *The United States Government Manual* and other publications of the Office of the Federal Register may be obtained by writing to the following address:

Office of the Federal Register
National Archives and Records Administration
Washington, DC 20408

Inquiries should be directed by phone to 202–741–6000, faxed to 202–741–6012, or emailed to fedreg.info@nara.gov.

Contents

DECLARATION OF INDEPENDENCE 1

CONSTITUTION OF THE UNITED STATES 5

Chart: The Government of the United States 21

LEGISLATIVE BRANCH
Congress 25
Architect of the Capitol 43
United States Botanic Garden 45
Government Accountability Office 47
Government Printing Office 50
Library of Congress 53
Congressional Budget Office 60

JUDICIAL BRANCH
The Supreme Court of the United States 65
Lower Courts 66
Special Courts 73
Administrative Office of the United States Courts 75
Federal Judicial Center 79
United States Sentencing Commission 80

EXECUTIVE BRANCH
The President of the United States 85
The Vice President of the United States 85
Executive Office of the President 86
The White House Office 86
Office of the Vice President of the United States 88
Council of Economic Advisers 89
Council on Environmental Quality 89
National Security Council 90
Office of Administration 91
Office of Management and Budget 92
Office of National Drug Control Policy 94
Office of Policy Development 96
Office of Science and Technology Policy 97
Office of the United States Trade Representative 98

Executive Agencies

Departments
Department of Agriculture 103
Department of Commerce 127
Department of Defense 146
Department of the Air Force 156
Department of the Army 161
Department of the Navy 170

v

Defense Agencies   181
Joint Service Schools   191
Department of Education   195
Department of Energy   203
Department of Health and Human Services   212
Department of Homeland Security   225
Department of Housing and Urban Development   231
Department of the Interior   237
Department of Justice   253
Department of Labor   273
Department of State   289
Department of Transportation   304
Department of the Treasury   327
Department of Veterans Affairs   343

Independent Establishments and Government Corporations
African Development Foundation   351
Broadcasting Board of Governors   352
Central Intelligence Agency   355
Commodity Futures Trading Commission   356
Consumer Product Safety Commission   358
Corporation for National and Community Service   362
Defense Nuclear Facilities Safety Board   366
Environmental Protection Agency   366
Equal Employment Opportunity Commission   372
Export-Import Bank of the United States   377
Farm Credit Administration   379
Federal Communications Commission   382
Federal Deposit Insurance Corporation   388
Federal Election Commission   392
Federal Housing Finance Agency   393
Federal Labor Relations Authority   395
Federal Maritime Commission   398
Federal Mediation and Conciliation Service   401
Federal Mine Safety and Health Review Commission   402
Federal Reserve System   404
Federal Retirement Thrift Investment Board   409
Federal Trade Commission   410
General Services Administration   415
Inter-American Foundation   422
Merit Systems Protection Board   423
National Aeronautics and Space Administration   425
National Archives and Records Administration   431
National Capital Planning Commission   440
National Credit Union Administration   441
National Foundation on the Arts and the Humanities   445
National Endowment for the Arts   445
National Endowment for the Humanities   447
Institute of Museum and Library Services   449
National Labor Relations Board   451
National Mediation Board   456
National Railroad Passenger Corporation (Amtrak)   459
National Science Foundation   461
National Transportation Safety Board   466
Nuclear Regulatory Commission   470
Occupational Safety and Health Review Commission   473

Office of the Director of National Intelligence   476
Office of Government Ethics   478
Office of Personnel Management   479
Office of Special Counsel   483
Overseas Private Investment Corporation   484
Peace Corps   486
Pension Benefit Guaranty Corporation   489
Postal Regulatory Commission   492
Railroad Retirement Board   493
Securities and Exchange Commission   496
Selective Service System   501
Small Business Administration   503
Social Security Administration   513
Tennessee Valley Authority   517
Trade and Development Agency   519
United States Agency for International Development   522
United States Commission on Civil Rights   527
United States International Trade Commission   529
United States Postal Service   534

Guide to Boards, Commissions, and Committees   539

Quasi-Official Agencies
Legal Services Corporation   543
Smithsonian Institution   545
State Justice Institute   559
United States Institute of Peace   560

Selected Multilateral Organizations   563

Selected Bilateral Organizations   573

Appendix A: Commonly Used Abbreviations and Acronyms   575

Appendix B: Terminated and Transferred Agencies   597

**Appendix C: Agencies Appearing in the
Code of Federal Regulations**   657

NAME INDEX   667

AGENCY/SUBJECT INDEX   687

The Declaration of Independence

IN CONGRESS, JULY 4, 1776.

THE UNANIMOUS DECLARATION of the thirteen united STATES OF AMERICA,

WHEN in the Course of human events, it becomes necessary for one people to dissolve the political bands which have connected them with another, and to assume among the powers of the earth, the separate and equal station to which the Laws of Nature and of Nature's God entitle them, a decent respect to the opinions of mankind requires that they should declare the causes which impel them to the separation.—We hold these truths to be self-evident, that all men are created equal, that they are endowed by their Creator with certain unalienable Rights, that among these are Life, Liberty and the pursuit of Happiness.—That to secure these rights, Governments are instituted among Men, deriving their just powers from the consent of the governed,—That whenever any Form of Government becomes destructive of these ends, it is the Right of the People to alter or to abolish it, and to institute new Government, laying its foundation on such principles and organizing its powers in such form, as to them shall seem most likely to effect their Safety and Happiness. Prudence, indeed, will dictate that Governments long established should not be changed for light and transient causes; and accordingly all experience hath shown, that mankind are more disposed to suffer, while evils are sufferable, than to right themselves by abolishing the forms to which they are accustomed. But when a long train of abuses and usurpations, pursuing invariably the same Object evinces a design to reduce them under absolute Despotism, it is their right, it is their duty, to throw off such Government, and to provide new Guards for their future security.— Such has been the patient sufferance of these Colonies; and such is now the necessity which constrains them to alter their former Systems of Government. The history of the present King of Great Britain is a history of repeated injuries and usurpations, all having in direct object the establishment of an absolute Tyranny over these States. To prove this, let Facts be submitted to a candid world.—He has refused his Assent to Laws, the most wholesome and necessary for the public good.—He has forbidden his Governors to pass Laws of immediate and pressing importance, unless suspended in their operation till his Assent should be obtained; and when so suspended, he has utterly neglected to attend to them.—He has refused to pass other Laws for the accommodation of large districts of people, unless those people would relinquish the right of Representation in the Legislature, a right inestimable to them and formidable to tyrants only.—He has called together legislative bodies at places unusual, uncomfortable, and distant from the depository of their public Records, for the sole purpose of fatiguing them into compliance with his measures.—He has dissolved Representative Houses repeatedly, for opposing with manly firmness his invasions on the rights of the people.—He has refused for a long time, after such dissolutions, to cause others to be elected; whereby the Legislative powers, incapable of Annihilation, have returned to the People at large for their exercise; the State

1

remaining in the mean time exposed to all the dangers of invasion from without, and convulsions within.—He has endeavored to prevent the population of these States; for that purpose obstructing the Laws for Naturalization of Foreigners; refusing to pass others to encourage their migration hither, and raising the conditions of new Appropriations of Lands.—He has obstructed the Administration of Justice, by refusing his Assent to Laws for establishing Judiciary powers.—He has made Judges dependent on his Will alone, for the tenure of their offices, and the amount and payment of their salaries.—He has erected a multitude of New Offices, and sent hither swarms of Officers to harrass our people, and eat out their substance.—He has kept among us, in times of peace, Standing Armies, without the Consent of our legislatures.—He has affected to render the Military independent of and superior to the Civil power.—He has combined with others to subject us to a jurisdiction foreign to our constitution, and unacknowledged by our laws; giving his Assent to their Acts of pretended Legislation:—For quartering large bodies of armed troops among us:— For protecting them, by a mock Trial, from punishment for any Murders which they should commit on the Inhabitants of these States:—For cutting off our Trade with all parts of the world:—For imposing Taxes on us without our Consent:—For depriving us in many cases, of the benefits of Trial by Jury:—For transporting us beyond Seas to be tried for pretended offences:—For abolishing the free System of English Laws in a neighbouring Province, establishing therein an Arbitrary government, and enlarging its Boundaries so as to render it at once an example and fit instrument for introducing the same absolute rule into these Colonies:—For taking away our Charters, abolishing our most valuable Laws, and altering fundamentally the Forms of our Governments:—For suspending our own Legislatures, and declaring themselves invested with power to legislate for us in all cases whatsoever.—He has abdicated Government here, by declaring us out of his Protection and waging War against us.—He has plundered our seas, ravaged our Coasts, burnt our towns, and destroyed the lives of our people.—He is at this time transporting large Armies of foreign Mercenaries to compleat the works of death, desolation and tyranny, already begun with circumstances of Cruelty & perfidy scarcely paralleled in the most barbarous ages, and totally unworthy the Head of a civilized nation.—He has constrained our fellow Citizens taken Captive on the high Seas to bear Arms against their Country, to become the executioners of their friends and Brethren, or to fall themselves by their Hands.—He has excited domestic insurrections amongst us, and has endeavoured to bring on the inhabitants of our frontiers, the merciless Indian Savages, whose known rule of warfare, is an undistinguished destruction of all ages, sexes and conditions. In every stage of these Oppressions We have Petitioned for Redress in the most humble terms: Our repeated Petitions have been answered only by repeated injury. A Prince, whose character is thus marked by every act which may define a Tyrant, is unfit to be the ruler of a free people. Nor have We been wanting in attentions to our Brittish brethren. We have warned them from time to time of attempts by their legislature to extend an unwarrantable jurisdiction over us. We have reminded them of the circumstances of our emigration and settlement here. We have appealed to their native justice and magnanimity, and we have conjured them by the ties of our common kindred to disavow these usurpations, which, would inevitably interrupt our connections and correspondence. They too have been deaf to the voice of justice and of consanguinity. We must, therefore, acquiesce in the necessity, which denounces our Separation, and hold them, as we hold the rest of mankind, Enemies in War, in Peace Friends.—

   WE, THEREFORE, the Representatives of the UNITED STATES OF AMERICA, in General Congress, Assembled, appealing to the Supreme Judge of the world for the rectitude of our intentions, do, in the Name, and by Authority of the good People of these Colonies, solemnly publish and declare, That these United Colonies are, and of Right ought to be FREE AND INDEPENDENT STATES; that they are Absolved from all Allegiance to the British Crown, and that all political connection between them and the State of Great Britain, is and ought to be totally disolved; and that as Free and

Independent States, they have full Power to levy War, conclude Peace, contract Alliances, establish Commerce, and to do all other Acts and Things which Independent States may of right do.—And for the support of this Declaration, with a firm reliance on the protection of Divine Providence, we mutually pledge to each other our Lives, our Fortunes and our sacred Honor.

John Hancock
Button Gwinnett
Lyman Hall
Geo. Walton
Wm. Hooper
Joseph Hewes
John Penn
Edward Rutledge
Thos. Heyward, Jr.
Thomas Lynch, Jr.
Arthur Middleton
Samuel Chase
Wm. Paca
Thos. Stone
Charles Carroll of
    Carrollton
George Wythe
Richard Henry Lee
Th. Jefferson

Benj. Harrison
Thos. Nelson, Jr.
Francis Lightfoot Lee
Carter Braxton
Robt. Morris
Benjamin Rush
Benj. Franklin
John Morton
Geo. Clymer
Jas. Smith
Geo. Taylor
James Wilson
Geo. Ross
Caesar Rodney
Geo. Read
Tho. M: Kean
Wm. Floyd
Phil. Livingston
Frans. Lewis

Lewis Morris
Richd. Stockton
Jno. Witherspoon
Fras. Hopkinson
John Hart
Abra. Clark
Josiah Bartlett
Wm. Whipple
Saml. Adams
John Adams
Robt. Treat Paine
Elbridge Gerry
Step. Hopkins
William Ellery
Roger Sherman
Sam. Huntington
Wm. Williams
Oliver Wolcott
Matthew Thornton

The Constitution of the United States

WE THE PEOPLE of the United States, in Order to form a more perfect Union, establish Justice, insure domestic Tranquility, provide for the common defence, promote the general Welfare, and secure the Blessings of Liberty to ourselves and our Posterity, do ordain and establish this Constitution for the United States of America.

Article I

Section 1. All legislative Powers herein granted shall be vested in a Congress of the United States, which shall consist of a Senate and House of Representatives.

Section 2. The House of Representatives shall be composed of Members chosen every second Year by the People of the several States, and the Electors in each State shall have the Qualifications requisite for Electors of the most numerous Branch of the State Legislature.

No Person shall be a Representative who shall not have attained to the Age of twenty five Years, and been seven Years a Citizen of the United States, and who shall not, when elected, be an Inhabitant of that State in which he shall be chosen.

Representatives and direct Taxes shall be apportioned among the several States which may be included within this Union, according to their respective Numbers, which shall be determined by adding to the whole Number of free Persons, including those bound to Service for a Term of Years, and excluding Indians not taxed, three fifths of all other Persons. The actual Enumeration shall be made within three Years after the first Meeting of the Congress of the United States, and within every subsequent Term of ten Years, in such Manner as they shall by Law direct. The Number of Representatives shall not exceed one for every thirty Thousand, but each State shall have at Least one Representative; and until such enumerations shall be made, the State of New Hampshire shall be entitled to chuse three, Massachusetts eight, Rhode-Island and Providence Plantations one, Connecticut five, New-York six, New Jersey four, Pennsylvania eight, Delaware one, Maryland six, Virginia ten, North Carolina five, South Carolina five, and Georgia three.

When vacancies happen in the Representation from any State, the Executive Authority thereof shall issue Writs of Election to fill such Vacancies.

The House of Representatives shall chuse their speaker and other Officers; and shall have the sole Power of Impeachment.

Section 3. The Senate of the United States shall be composed of two Senators from each State, chosen by the Legislature thereof, for six Years; and each Senator shall have one Vote.

Immediately after they shall be assembled in Consequence of the first Election, they shall be divided as equally as may be into three Classes. The Seats of the

Senators of the first Class shall be vacated at the Expiration of the second Year, of the second Class at the Expiration of the fourth Year, and of the third Class at the Expiration of the sixth Year, so that one third may be chosen every second Year; and if Vacancies happen by Resignation, or otherwise, during the Recess of the Legislature of any State, the Executive thereof may make temporary Appointments until the next Meeting of the Legislature, which shall then fill such Vacancies.

No Person shall be a Senator who shall not have attained to the Age of thirty Years, and been nine Years a Citizen of the United States, and who shall not, when elected, be an Inhabitant of that State for which he shall be chosen.

The Vice President of the United States shall be President of the Senate, but shall have no Vote, unless they be equally divided.

The Senate shall chuse their other Officers, and also a President pro tempore, in the Absence of the Vice President, or when he shall exercise the Office of President of the United States.

The Senate shall have the sole Power to try all Impeachments. When sitting for that Purpose, they shall be on Oath or Affirmation. When the President of the United States is tried, the Chief Justice shall preside: And no Person shall be convicted without the concurrence of two thirds of the Members present. Judgment in Cases of Impeachment shall not extend further than to removal from Office, and disqualification to hold and enjoy any Office of honor, Trust or Profit under the United States: but the Party convicted shall nevertheless be liable and subject to Indictment, Trial, Judgment and Punishment, according to law.

Section 4. The Times, Places and Manner of holding Elections for Senators and Representatives, shall be prescribed in each State by the Legislature thereof; but the Congress may at any time by Law make or alter such Regulations, except as to the Places of chusing Senators.

The Congress shall assemble at least once in every Year, and such Meeting shall be on the first Monday in December, unless they shall by Law appoint a different Day.

Section 5. Each House shall be the Judge of the Elections, Returns and Qualifications of its own Members, and a Majority of each shall constitute a Quorum to do business; but a smaller Number may adjourn from day to day, and may be authorized to compel the Attendance of absent Members, in such Manner, and under such Penalties as each House may provide.

Each House may determine the Rules of its Proceedings, punish its Members for disorderly Behaviour, and, with the Concurrence of two thirds, expel a Member.

Each House shall keep a Journal of its Proceedings, and from time to time publish the same, excepting such Parts as may in their Judgment require Secrecy; and the yeas and Nays of the Members of either House on any question shall, at the Desire of one fifth of those Present, be entered on the Journal.

Neither House, during the Session of Congress, shall, without the Consent of the other, adjourn for more than three days, nor to any other place than that in which the two Houses shall be sitting.

Section 6. The Senators and Representatives shall receive a Compensation for their Services, to be ascertained by Law, and paid out of the Treasury of the United States. They shall in all Cases, except Treason, Felony and Breach of the Peace, be privileged from Arrest during their Attendance at the Session of their respective Houses, and in going to and returning from the same; and for any Speech or Debate in either House, they shall not be questioned in any other Place.

No Senator or Representative shall, during the Time for which he was elected, be appointed to any civil Office under the Authority of the United States, which shall have been created, or the Emoluments whereof shall have been encreased during such time; and no Person holding any Office under the United States, shall be a Member of either House during his Continuance in Office.

Section 7. All Bills for raising Revenue shall originate in the House of Representatives; but the Senate may propose or concur with Amendments as on other Bills.

Every Bill which shall have passed the House of Representatives and the Senate, shall, before it become a Law, be presented to the President of the United States; If he approve he shall sign it, but if not he shall return it, with his Objections to that House in which it shall have originated, who shall enter the Objections at large on their Journal, and proceed to reconsider it. If after such Reconsideration two thirds of that House shall agree to pass the Bill, it shall be sent, together with the Objections, to the other House, by which it shall likewise be reconsidered, and if approved by two thirds of that House, it shall become a Law. But in all such Cases the Votes of both Houses shall be determined by yeas and Nays, and the Names of the Persons voting for and against the Bill shall be entered on the Journal of each House respectively. If any Bill shall not be returned by the President within ten Days (Sundays excepted) after it shall have been presented to him, the Same shall be a Law, in like Manner as if he had signed it, unless the Congress by their Adjournment prevent its Return, in which Case it shall not be a Law.

Every Order, Resolution, or Vote to which the Concurrence of the Senate and House of Representatives may be necessary (except on a question of Adjournment) shall be presented to the President of the United States; and before the Same shall take Effect, shall be approved by him, or being disapproved by him, shall be repassed by two thirds of the Senate and House of Representatives, according to the Rules and Limitations prescribed in the Case of a Bill.

Section 8. The Congress shall have Power To lay and collect Taxes, Duties, Imposts and Excises, to pay the Debts and provide for the common Defence and general Welfare of the United States; but all duties, Imposts and Excises shall be uniform throughout the United States;

To borrow Money on the Credit of the United States;

To regulate Commerce with foreign Nations, and among the several States, and with the Indian Tribes;

To establish an uniform Rule of Naturalization, and uniform Laws on the subject of Bankruptcies throughout the United States;

To coin Money, regulate the Value thereof, and of foreign Coin, and fix the Standard of Weights and Measures;

To provide for the Punishment of counterfeiting the Securities and current Coin of the United States;

To establish Post Offices and post Roads;

To promote the Progress of Science and useful Arts, by securing for limited Times to Authors and Inventors exclusive Right to their respective Writings and Discoveries;

To constitute Tribunals inferior to the supreme Court;

To define and punish Piracies and Felonies committed on the high Seas, and Offences against the Law of Nations;

To declare War, grant Letters of Marque and Reprisal, and make rules concerning Captures on Land and Water;

To raise and support Armies, but no Appropriation of Money to that Use shall be for a longer Term than two Years;

To provide and maintain a Navy;

To make rules for the Government and Regulation of the land and naval Forces;

To provide for calling forth the Militia to execute the Laws of the Union, suppress Insurrections and repel Invasions;

To provide for organizing, arming, and disciplining, the Militia, and for governing such Part of them as may be employed in the Service of the United States, reserving to the States respectively, the Appointment of the Officers, and the Authority of training the Militia according to the discipline prescribed by Congress;

To exercise exclusive Legislation in all Cases whatsoever, over such District (not exceeding ten Miles square), as may, by Cession of particular States, and the Acceptance of Congress, become the Seat of the Government of the United States, and to exercise like Authority over all Places purchased by the Consent of the Legislature of the State in which the Same shall be for the Erection of Forts, Magazines, Arsenals, dock-Yards, and other needful Buildings;—And

To make all Laws which shall be necessary and proper for carrying into Execution the foregoing Powers, and all other Powers vested by this Constitution in the Government of the United States, or in any Department or Officer thereof.

Section 9. The Migration or Importation of such Persons as any of the States now existing shall think proper to admit, shall not be prohibited by the Congress prior to the Year one thousand eight hundred and eight, but a Tax or duty may be imposed on such Importation, not exceeding ten dollars for each Person.

The Privilege of the Writ of Habeas Corpus shall not be suspended, unless when in Cases of Rebellion or Invasion the public Safety may require it.

No Bill of Attainder or ex post facto Law shall be passed.

No Capitation, or other direct, Tax shall be laid, unless in Proportion to the Census or Enumeration herein before directed to be taken.

No Tax or Duty shall be laid on Articles exported from any State.

No Preference shall be given by any Regulation of Commerce or Revenue to the Ports of one State over those of another: nor shall Vessels bound to, or from, one State, be obliged to enter, clear, or pay Duties in another.

No money shall be drawn from the Treasury, but in Consequence of Appropriations made by Law; and a regular Statement and Account of the Receipts and Expenditures of all public Money shall be published from time to time.

No Title of Nobility shall be granted by the United States: And no Person holding any Office of Profit or Trust under them, shall, without the Consent of the Congress, accept of any present, Emolument, Office, or Title, of any kind whatever, from any King, Prince, or foreign State.

Section 10. No State shall enter into any Treaty, Alliance, or Confederation; grant Letters of Marque and Reprisal; coin Money; emit Bills of Credit; make any Thing but gold and silver Coin a Tender in Payment of Debts; pass any Bill of Attainder, ex post facto Law, or Law impairing the Obligation of Contracts, or grant any Title of Nobility.

No State shall, without the Consent of the Congress, lay any Imposts or Duties on Imports or Exports, except what may be absolutely necessary for executing it's inspection Laws: and the net Produce of all Duties and Imposts, laid by any State on Imports or Exports, shall be for the Use of the Treasury of the United States; and all such Laws shall be subject to the Revision and Controul of the Congress.

No State shall, without the Consent of Congress, lay any Duty of Tonnage, keep Troops, or Ships of War in time of Peace, enter into any Agreement or Compact with another State, or with a foreign Power, or engage in War, unless actually invaded, or in such imminent Danger as will not admit of delay.

Article II

Section 1. The executive Power shall be vested in a President of the United States of America. He shall hold his Office during the Term of four Years, and, together with the Vice President, chosen for the same Term, be elect d, as follows

Each State shall appoint, in such Manner as the Legislature thereof may direct, a Number of Electors, equal to the whole Number of Senators and Representatives to which the State may be entitled in the Congress: but no Senator or Representative, or Person holding an Office of Trust or Profit under the United States, shall be appointed an Elector.

The Electors shall meet in their respective States, and vote by Ballot for two Persons, of whom one at least shall not be an Inhabitant of the same State with themselves. And they shall make a List of all the Persons voted for, and of the Number of Votes for each; which List they shall sign and certify, and transmit sealed to the Seat of the Government of the United States, directed to the President of the Senate. The President of the Senate shall, in the Presence of the Senate and House of Representatives, open all the Certificates, and the Votes shall then be counted. The Person having the greatest Number of Votes shall be the President, if such Number be a Majority of the whole Number of Electors appointed; and if there be more than one who have such Majority, and have an equal Number of Votes, then the House of Representatives shall immediately chuse by Ballot one of them for President: and if no Person have a Majority, then from the five highest on the List the said House shall in like Manner chuse the President. But in chusing the President, the Votes shall be taken by States, the Representation from each State having one Vote; A quorum for this Purpose shall consist of a Member or Members from two thirds of the States, and a Majority of all the States shall be necessary to a Choice. In every Case, after the Choice of the President, the Person having the greatest Number of Votes of the Electors shall be the Vice President. But if there should remain two or more who have equal Votes, the Senate shall chuse from them by Ballot the Vice President.

The Congress may determine the Time of chusing the Electors, and the Day on which they shall give their Votes; which Day shall be the same throughout the United States.

No Person except a natural born Citizen, or a Citizen of the United States, at the time of the Adoption of this Constitution, shall be eligible to the Office of President; neither shall any Person be eligible to that Office who shall not have attained to the Age of thirty five Years, and been fourteen Years a Resident within the United States.

In Case of the Removal of the President from Office, or of his Death, Resignation, or Inability to discharge the Powers and Duties of the said Office, the Same shall devolve on the Vice President, and the Congress may by Law provide for the Case of Removal, Death, Resignation or Inability, both of the President and Vice President, declaring what Officer shall then act as President, and such Officer shall act accordingly, until the Disability be removed, or a President shall be elected.

The President shall, at stated Times, receive for his Services, a Compensation, which shall neither be encreased nor diminished during the Period for which he shall have been elected, and he shall not receive within that Period any other Emolument from the United States, or any of them.

Before he enter on the Execution of his Office, he shall take the following Oath or Affirmation:—"I do solemnly swear (or affirm) that I will faithfully execute the Office of President of the United States, and will to the best of my Ability, preserve, protect and defend the Constitution of the United States."

Section 2. The President shall be Commander in Chief of the Army and Navy of the United States, and of the Militia of the several States, when called into the actual

Service of the United States; he may require the Opinion, in writing, of the principal Officer in each of the executive Departments, upon any Subject relating to the Duties of their respective Offices, and he shall have Power to grant Reprieves and Pardons for Offences against the United States, except in Cases of Impeachment.

He shall have Power, by and with the Advice and Consent of the Senate, to make Treaties, provided two thirds of the Senators present concur; and he shall nominate, and by and with the Advice and Consent of the Senate, shall appoint Ambassadors, other public Ministers and Consuls, Judges of the supreme Court, and all other Officers of the United States, whose Appointments are not herein otherwise provided for, and which shall be established by Law: but the Congress may by Law vest the Appointment of such inferior Officers, as they think proper, in the President alone, in the Courts of Law, or in the Heads of Departments.

The President shall have Power to fill up all Vacancies that may happen during the Recess of the Senate, by granting Commissions which shall expire at the End of their next Session.

Section 3. He shall from time to time give to the Congress Information of the State of the Union, and recommend to their Consideration such Measures as he shall judge necessary and expedient; he may, on extraordinary Occasions, convene both Houses, or either of them, and in Case of Disagreement between them, with Respect to the Time of Adjournment, he may adjourn them to such Time as he shall think proper; he shall receive Ambassadors and other public Ministers; he shall take Care that the Laws be faithfully executed, and shall Commission all the Officers of the United States.

Section 4. The President, Vice President and all civil Officers of the United States, shall be removed from Office on Impeachment for, and Conviction of, Treason, Bribery, or other High Crimes and Misdemeanors.

Article III

Section 1. The judicial Power of the United States, shall be vested in one supreme Court, and in such inferior Courts as the Congress may from time to time ordain and establish. The Judges, both of the supreme and inferior Courts, shall hold their Offices during good Behaviour, and shall, at stated Times, receive for their Services, a Compensation, which shall not be diminished during their Continuance in Office.

Section 2. The judicial Power shall extend to all Cases, in Law and Equity, arising under this Constitution, the Laws of the United States, and Treaties made, or which shall be made, under their Authority;—to all Cases affecting Ambassadors, other public Ministers and Consuls;—to all Cases of admiralty and maritime Jurisdiction;— to Controversies to which the United States shall be a Party;—to Controversies between two or more States; between a State and Citizens of another State;— between Citizens of different States;—between Citizens of the same State claiming Lands under Grants of different States, and between a State, or the Citizens thereof, and foreign States, Citizens or Subjects.

In all Cases affecting Ambassadors, other public Ministers and Consuls, and those in which a State shall be Party, the supreme Court shall have original Jurisdiction. In all the other Cases before mentioned, the supreme Court shall have appellate Jurisdiction, both as to Law and Fact, with such Exceptions, and under such Regulations as the Congress shall make.

The Trial of all Crimes, except in Cases of Impeachment, shall be by Jury; and such Trial shall be held in the State where the said Crimes shall have been committed; but when not committed within any State, the Trial shall be at such Place or Places as the Congress may by Law have directed.

Section 3. Treason against the United States, shall consist only in levying War against them, or in adhering to their Enemies, giving them Aid and Comfort. No Person shall be convicted of Treason unless on the Testimony of two Witnesses to the same overt Act, or on Confession in open Court.

The Congress shall have Power to declare the Punishment of Treason, but no Attainder of Treason shall work Corruption of Blood, or Forfeiture except during the Life of the Person attainted.

Article IV

Section 1. Full Faith and Credit shall be given in each State to the public Acts, Records, and judicial Proceedings of every other State. And the Congress may by general Laws prescribe the Manner in which such Acts, Records and Proceedings shall be proved, and the Effect thereof.

Section 2. The Citizens of each State shall be entitled to all Privileges and Immunities of Citizens in the several States.

A Person charged in any State with Treason, Felony, or other Crime, who shall flee from Justice, and be found in another State, shall on Demand of the executive Authority of the State from which he fled, be delivered up, to be removed to the State having Jurisdiction of the Crime.

No person held to Service or Labour in one State, under the Laws thereof, escaping into another, shall, in Consequence of any Law or Regulation therein, be discharged from such Service or Labour, but shall be delivered up on Claim of the Party to whom such Service or Labour may be due.

Section 3. New States may be admitted by the Congress into this Union; but no new State shall be formed or erected within the Jurisdiction of any other State; nor any State be formed by the Junction of two or more States, or Parts of States, without the Consent of the Legislatures of the States concerned as well as of the Congress.

The Congress shall have Power to dispose of and make all needful Rules and Regulations respecting the Territory or other Property belonging to the United States; and nothing in this Constitution shall be so construed as to Prejudice any Claims of the United States, or of any particular State.

Section 4. The United States shall guarantee to every State in this Union a Republican Form of Government, and shall protect each of them against Invasion; and on Application of the Legislature, or of the Executive (when the Legislature cannot be convened) against domestic Violence.

Article V

The Congress, whenever two thirds of both Houses shall deem it necessary, shall propose Amendments to this Constitution, or, on the Application of the Legislatures of two thirds of the several States, shall call a Convention for proposing Amendments, which, in either Case, shall be valid to all Intents and Purposes, as Part of this Constitution, when ratified by the Legislatures of three fourths of the several States, or by Conventions in three fourths thereof, as the one or the other Mode of Ratification may be proposed by the Congress; Provided that no Amendment which may be made prior to the Year One thousand eight hundred and eight shall in any Manner affect the first and fourth Clauses in the Ninth Section of the first Article; and that no State, without its Consent, shall be deprived of its equal Suffrage in the Senate.

Article VI

All Debts contracted and Engagements entered into, before the Adoption of this Constitution, shall be as valid against the United States under this Constitution, as under the Confederation.

This Constitution, and the Laws of the United States which shall be made in Pursuance thereof; and all Treaties made, or which shall be made, under the Authority of the United States, shall be the supreme Law of the Land; and the Judges in every State shall be bound thereby, any Thing in the Constitution or Laws of any State to the Contrary notwithstanding.

The Senators and Representatives before mentioned, and the Members of the several State Legislatures, and all executive and judicial Officers, both of the United States and of the several States, shall be bound by Oath or Affirmation, to support this Constitution; but no religious Test shall ever be required as a Qualification to any Office or public Trust under the United States.

Article VII

The Ratification of the Conventions of nine States, shall be sufficient for the Establishment of this Constitution between the States so ratifying the Same.

done in Convention by the Unanimous Consent of the States present the Seventeenth Day of September in the Year of our Lord one thousand seven hundred and Eighty seven and of the Independence of the United States of America the Twelfth *In witness whereof We have hereunto subscribed our Names,*

G^o Washington—Presid^t
and deputy from Virginia

New Hampshire	John Langdon
	Nicholas Gilman
Massachusetts	Nathaniel Gorham
	Rufus King
Connecticut	Wm Saml Johnson
	Roger Sherman
New York	Alexander Hamilton
New Jersey	Wil: Livingston
	David Brearley.
	Wm Paterson.
	Jona: Dayton
Pennsylvania [1]	B Franklin
	Thomas Mifflin
	Robt Morris
	Geo. Clymer
	Thos FitzSimons
	Jared Ingersoll

---

[1] Spelled with one "n" on the original document.

	James Wilson
	Gouv Morris
Delaware	Geo: Read
	Gunning Bedford jun
	John Dickinson
	Richard Bassett
	Jaco: Broom
Maryland	James McHenry
	Dan of St Thos Jenifer
	Danl Carroll
Virginia	John Blair—
	James Madison Jr.
North Carolina	Wm Blount
	Richd Dobbs Spaight.
	Hu Williamson
South Carolina	J. Rutledge
	Charles Cotesworth Pinckney
	Charles Pinckney
	Pierce Butler.
Georgia	William Few
	Abr Baldwin

Amendments

(The first 10 Amendments were ratified December 15, 1791, and form what is known as the Bill of Rights)

Amendment 1

Congress shall make no law respecting an establishment of religion, or prohibiting the free exercise thereof; or abridging the freedom of speech, or of the press; or the right of the people peaceably to assemble, and to petition the Government for a redress of grievances.

Amendment 2

A well regulated Militia, being necessary to the security of a free State, the right of the people to keep and bear Arms, shall not be infringed.

Amendment 3

No Soldier shall, in time of peace be quartered in any house, without the consent of the Owner, nor in time of war, but in a manner to be prescribed by law.

Amendment 4

The right of the people to be secure in their persons, houses, papers, and effects, against unreasonable searches and seizures, shall not be violated, and no Warrants shall issue, but upon probable cause, supported by Oath or affirmation, and particularly describing the place to be searched, and the persons or things to be seized.

Amendment 5

No person shall be held to answer for a capital, or otherwise infamous crime, unless on a presentment or indictment of a Grand Jury, except in cases arising in the land or naval forces, or in the Militia, when in actual service in time of War or public danger; nor shall any person be subject for the same offence to be twice put in jeopardy of life or limb; nor shall be compelled in any criminal case to be a witness against himself, nor be deprived of life, liberty, or property, without due process of law; nor shall private property be taken for public use, without just compensation.

Amendment 6

In all criminal prosecutions, the accused shall enjoy the right to a speedy and public trial, by an impartial jury of the State and district wherein the crime shall have been committed, which district shall have been previously ascertained by law, and to be informed of the nature and cause of the accusation; to be confronted with the witnesses against him; to have compulsory process for obtaining witnesses in his favor, and to have the Assistance of Counsel for his defence.

Amendment 7

In Suits at common law, where the value in controversy shall exceed twenty dollars, the right of trial by jury shall be preserved, and no fact tried by a jury, shall be otherwise re-examined in any Court of the United States, than according to the rules of the common law.

Amendment 8

Excessive bail shall not be required, nor excessive fines imposed, nor cruel and unusual punishments inflicted.

Amendment 9

The enumeration in the Constitution, of certain rights, shall not be construed to deny or disparage others retained by the people.

Amendment 10

The powers not delegated to the United States by the Constitution, nor prohibited by it to the States, are reserved to the States respectively, or to the people.

Amendment 11

(*Ratified February 7, 1795*)

The Judicial power of the United States shall not be construed to extend to any suit in law or equity, commenced or prosecuted against one of the United States by Citizens of another State, or by Citizens or Subjects of any Foreign State.

Amendment 12

(*Ratified July 27, 1804*)

The Electors shall meet in their respective states, and vote by ballot for President and Vice-President, one of whom, at least, shall not be an inhabitant of the same state with themselves; they shall name in their ballots the person voted for as President, and in distinct ballots the person voted for as Vice-President, and they shall make distinct lists of all persons voted for as President, and of all persons voted for as Vice-President, and of the number of votes for each, which lists they shall sign and certify, and transmit sealed to the seat of the government of the United States, directed to the President of the Senate;—The President of the Senate shall, in the presence of the Senate and House of Representatives, open all the certificates and the votes shall then be counted;—The person having the greatest number of votes for President, shall be the President, if such number be a majority of the whole number of Electors appointed; and if no person have such majority, then from the persons having the highest numbers not exceeding three on the list of those voted for as President, the House of Representatives shall choose immediately, by ballot, the President. But in choosing the President, the votes shall be taken by states, the representation from each state having one vote; a quorum for this purpose shall consist of a member or members from two-thirds of the states, and a majority of all the states shall be necessary to a choice. And if the House of Representatives shall not choose a President whenever the right of choice shall devolve upon them, before the fourth day of March next following, then the Vice-President shall act as President, as in the case of the death or other constitutional disability of the President.—The person having the greatest number of votes as Vice-President, shall be the Vice-President, if such number be a majority of the whole number of Electors appointed, and if no person have a majority, then from the two highest numbers on the list, the Senate shall choose the Vice-President; a quorum for the purpose shall consist of two-thirds of the whole number of Senators, and a majority of the whole number shall be necessary to a choice. But no person constitutionally ineligible to the office of President shall be eligible to that of Vice-President of the United States.

Amendment 13

(Ratified December 6, 1865)

Section 1. Neither slavery nor involuntary servitude, except as a punishment for crime whereof the party shall have been duly convicted, shall exist within the United States, or any place subject to their jurisdiction.

Section 2. Congress shall have power to enforce this article by appropriate legislation.

Amendment 14

(Ratified July 9, 1868)

Section 1. All persons born or naturalized in the United States, and subject to the jurisdiction thereof, are citizens of the United States and of the State wherein they reside. No State shall make or enforce any law which shall abridge the privileges or immunities of citizens of the United States; nor shall any State deprive any person of life, liberty, or property, without due process of law; nor deny to any person within its jurisdiction the equal protection of the laws.

Section 2. Representatives shall be apportioned among the several States according to their respective numbers, counting the whole number of persons in each State, excluding Indians not taxed. But when the right to vote at any election for the choice of electors for President and Vice President of the United States, Representatives in Congress, the Executive and Judicial officers of a State, or the members of the Legislature thereof, is denied to any of the male inhabitants of such State, being twenty-one years of age, and citizens of the United States, or in any way abridged, except for participation in rebellion, or other crime, the basis of representation therein shall be reduced in the proportion which the number of such male citizens shall bear to the whole number of male citizens twenty-one years of age in such State.

Section 3. No person shall be a Senator or Representative in Congress, or elector of President and Vice President, or hold any office, civil or military, under the United States, or under any State, who, having previously taken an oath, as a member of Congress, or as an officer of the United States, or as a member of any State legislature, or as an executive or judicial officer of any State, to support the Constitution of the United States, shall have engaged in insurrection or rebellion against the same, or given aid or comfort to the enemies thereof. But Congress may by a vote of two-thirds of each House, remove such disability.

Section 4. The validity of the public debt of the United States, authorized by law, including debts incurred for payment of pensions and bounties for services in suppressing insurrection or rebellion, shall not be questioned. But neither the United States nor any State shall assume or pay any debt or obligation incurred in aid of insurrection or rebellion against the United States, or any claim for the loss or emancipation of any slave; but all such debts, obligations and claims shall be held illegal and void.

Section 5. The Congress shall have power to enforce, by appropriate legislation, the provisions of this article.

Amendment 15

(Ratified February 3, 1870)

Section 1. The right of citizens of the United States to vote shall not be denied or abridged by the United States or by any State on account of race, color, or previous condition of servitude.

Section 2. The Congress shall have power to enforce this article by appropriate legislation.

Amendment 16

(Ratified February 3, 1913)

The Congress shall have power to lay and collect taxes on incomes, from whatever source derived, without apportionment among the several States, and without regard to any census or enumeration.

Amendment 17

(Ratified April 8, 1913)

The Senate of the United States shall be composed of two Senators from each State, elected by the people thereof for six years; and each Senator shall have one vote. The electors in each State shall have the qualifications requisite for electors of the most numerous branch of the State legislatures.

When vacancies happen in the representation of any State in the Senate, the executive authority of such State shall issue writs of election to fill such vacancies: *Provided,* That the legislature of any State may empower the executive thereof to make temporary appointments until the people fill the vacancies by election as the legislature may direct.

This amendment shall not be so construed as to affect the election or term of any Senator chosen before it becomes valid as part of the Constitution.

Amendment 18

(Ratified January 16, 1919. Repealed December 5, 1933 by Amendment 21)

Section 1. After one year from the ratification of this article the manufacture, sale, or transportation of intoxicating liquors within, the importation thereof into, or the exportation thereof from the United States and all territory subject to the jurisdiction thereof for beverage purposes is hereby prohibited.

Section 2. The Congress and the several States shall have concurrent power to enforce this article by appropriate legislation.

Section 3. This article shall be inoperative unless it shall have been ratified as an amendment to the Constitution by the legislatures of the several States as provided in the Constitution, within seven years from the date of the submission hereof to the States by the Congress.

Amendment 19

(Ratified August 18, 1920)

The right of citizens of the United States to vote shall not be denied or abridged by the United States or by any State on account of sex.

Congress shall have power to enforce this article by appropriate legislation.

Amendment 20

(Ratified January 23, 1933)

Section 1. The terms of the President and Vice President shall end at noon on the 20th day of January, and the terms of Senators and Representatives at noon on the 3d day of January, of the years in which such terms would have ended if this article had not been ratified; and the terms of their successors shall then begin.

Section 2. The Congress shall assemble at least once in every year, and such meeting shall begin at noon on the 3d day of January, unless they shall by law appoint a different day.

Section 3. If, at the time fixed for the beginning of the term of the President, the President elect shall have died, the Vice President elect shall become President. If a President shall not have been chosen before the time fixed for the beginning of his term, or if the President elect shall have failed to qualify, then the Vice President elect shall act as President until a President shall have qualified; and the Congress may by law provide for the case wherein neither a President elect nor a Vice President elect shall have qualified, declaring who shall then act as President, or the manner in which one who is to act shall be selected, and such person shall act accordingly until a President or Vice President shall have qualified.

Section 4. The Congress may by law provide for the case of the death of any of the persons from whom the House of Representatives may choose a President whenever the right of choice shall have devolved upon them, and for the case of the death of any of the persons from whom the Senate may choose a Vice President whenever the right of choice shall have devolved upon them.

Section 5. Sections 1 and 2 shall take effect on the 15th day of October following the ratification of this article.

Section 6. This article shall be inoperative unless it shall have been ratified as an amendment to the Constitution by the legislatures of three-fourths of the several States within seven years from the date of its submission.

Amendment 21

(Ratified December 5, 1933)

Section 1. The eighteenth article of amendment to the Constitution of the United States is hereby repealed.

Section 2. The transportation or importation into any State, Territory, or possession of the United States for delivery or use therein of intoxicating liquors, in violation of the laws thereof, is hereby prohibited.

Section 3. This article shall be inoperative unless it shall have been ratified as an amendment to the Constitution by conventions in the several States, as provided in the Constitution, within seven years from the date of the submission hereof to the States by the Congress.

Amendment 22

(Ratified February 27, 1951)

Section 1. No person shall be elected to the office of the President more than twice, and no person who has held the office of President, or acted as President, for more than two years of a term to which some other person was elected President shall be elected to the office of the President more than once. But this Article shall not apply to any person holding the office of President when this Article was proposed by the Congress, and shall not prevent any person who may be holding the office of President, or acting as President, during the term within which this Article becomes operative from holding the office of President or acting as President during the remainder of such term.

Section 2. This article shall be inoperative unless it shall have been ratified as an amendment to the Constitution by the legislatures of three-fourths of the several States within seven years from the date of its submission to the States by the Congress.

Amendment 23

(Ratified March 29, 1961)

Section 1. The District constituting the seat of Government of the United States shall appoint in such manner as the Congress may direct:
    A number of electors of President and Vice President equal to the whole number of Senators and Representatives in Congress to which the District would be entitled if it were a State, but in no event more than the least populous State; they shall be in addition to those appointed by the States, but they shall be considered, for the purposes of the election of President and Vice President, to be electors appointed by a State; and they shall meet in the District and perform such duties as provided by the twelfth article of amendment.

Section 2. The Congress shall have power to enforce this article by appropriate legislation.

Amendment 24

(Ratified January 23, 1964)

Section 1. The right of citizens of the United States to vote in any primary or other election for President or Vice President, for electors for President or Vice President, or for Senator or Representative in Congress, shall not be denied or abridged by the United States or any State by reason of failure to pay any poll tax or other tax.

Section 2. The Congress shall have power to enforce this article by appropriate legislation.

Amendment 25

(Ratified February 10, 1967)

Section 1. In case of the removal of the President from office or of his death or resignation, the Vice President shall become President.

Section 2. Whenever there is a vacancy in the office of the Vice President, the President shall nominate a Vice President who shall take office upon confirmation by a majority vote of both Houses of Congress.

Section 3. Whenever the President transmits to the President pro tempore of the Senate and the Speaker of the House of Representatives his written declaration that he is unable to discharge the powers and duties of his office, and until he transmits to them a written declaration to the contrary, such powers and duties shall be discharged by the Vice President as Acting President.

Section 4. Whenever the Vice President and a majority of either the principal officers of the executive departments or of such other body as Congress may by law provide, transmit to the President pro tempore of the Senate and the Speaker of the House of Representatives their written declaration that the President is unable to discharge the powers and duties of his office, the Vice President shall immediately assume the powers and duties of the office as Acting President.

Thereafter, when the President transmits to the President pro tempore of the Senate and the Speaker of the House of Representatives his written declaration that no inability exists, he shall resume the powers and duties of his office unless the Vice President and a majority of either the principal officers of the executive department or of such other body as Congress may by law provide, transmit within four days to the President pro tempore of the Senate and the Speaker of the House of Representatives their written declaration that the President is unable to discharge the powers and duties of his office. Thereupon Congress shall decide the issue, assembling within forty-eight hours for that purpose if not in session. If the Congress, within twenty-one days after receipt of the latter written declaration, or, if Congress is not in session, within twenty-one days after Congress is required to assemble, determines by two-thirds vote of both Houses that the President is unable to discharge the powers and duties of his office, the Vice President shall continue to discharge the same as Acting President; otherwise, the President shall resume the powers and duties of his office.

Amendment 26

(Ratified July 1, 1971)

Section 1. The right of citizens of the United States, who are eighteen years of age or older, to vote shall not be denied or abridged by the United States or by any State on account of age.

Section 2. The Congress shall have the power to enforce this article by appropriate legislation.

Amendment 27

(Ratified May 7, 1992)

No law, varying the compensation for the services of the Senators and Representatives, shall take effect, until an election of Representatives shall have intervened.

THE GOVERNMENT OF THE UNITED STATES

THE CONSTITUTION

LEGISLATIVE BRANCH

THE CONGRESS

SENATE   HOUSE

ARCHITECT OF THE CAPITOL
UNITED STATES BOTANIC GARDEN
GOVERNMENT ACCOUNTABILITY OFFICE
GOVERNMENT PRINTING OFFICE
LIBRARY OF CONGRESS
CONGRESSIONAL BUDGET OFFICE

EXECUTIVE BRANCH

THE PRESIDENT

THE VICE PRESIDENT

EXECUTIVE OFFICE OF THE PRESIDENT

WHITE HOUSE OFFICE
OFFICE OF THE VICE PRESIDENT
COUNCIL OF ECONOMIC ADVISERS
COUNCIL ON ENVIRONMENTAL QUALITY
NATIONAL SECURITY COUNCIL
OFFICE OF ADMINISTRATION

OFFICE OF MANAGEMENT AND BUDGET
OFFICE OF NATIONAL DRUG CONTROL POLICY
OFFICE OF POLICY DEVELOPMENT
OFFICE OF SCIENCE AND TECHNOLOGY POLICY
OFFICE OF THE UNITED STATES
TRADE REPRESENTATIVE

JUDICIAL BRANCH

THE SUPREME COURT OF THE UNITED STATES

UNITED STATES COURTS OF APPEALS
UNITED STATES DISTRICT COURTS
TERRITORIAL COURTS
UNITED STATES COURT OF INTERNATIONAL TRADE
UNITED STATES COURT OF FEDERAL CLAIMS
UNITED STATES COURT OF APPEALS FOR THE ARMED FORCES
UNITED STATES TAX COURT
UNITED STATES COURT OF APPEALS FOR VETERANS CLAIMS
ADMINISTRATIVE OFFICE OF THE UNITED STATES COURTS
FEDERAL JUDICIAL CENTER
UNITED STATES SENTENCING COMMISSION

DEPARTMENT OF AGRICULTURE

DEPARTMENT OF COMMERCE

DEPARTMENT OF DEFENSE

DEPARTMENT OF EDUCATION

DEPARTMENT OF ENERGY

DEPARTMENT OF HEALTH AND HUMAN SERVICES

DEPARTMENT OF HOMELAND SECURITY

DEPARTMENT OF HOUSING AND URBAN DEVELOPMENT

DEPARTMENT OF THE INTERIOR

DEPARTMENT OF JUSTICE

DEPARTMENT OF LABOR

DEPARTMENT OF STATE

DEPARTMENT OF TRANSPORTATION

DEPARTMENT OF THE TREASURY

DEPARTMENT OF VETERANS AFFAIRS

INDEPENDENT ESTABLISHMENTS AND GOVERNMENT CORPORATIONS

AFRICAN DEVELOPMENT FOUNDATION
BROADCASTING BOARD OF GOVERNORS
CENTRAL INTELLIGENCE AGENCY
COMMODITY FUTURES TRADING COMMISSION
CONSUMER PRODUCT SAFETY COMMISSION
CORPORATION FOR NATIONAL AND COMMUNITY SERVICE
DEFENSE NUCLEAR FACILITIES SAFETY BOARD
ENVIRONMENTAL PROTECTION AGENCY
EQUAL EMPLOYMENT OPPORTUNITY COMMISSION
EXPORT-IMPORT BANK OF THE UNITED STATES
FARM CREDIT ADMINISTRATION
FEDERAL COMMUNICATIONS COMMISSION
FEDERAL DEPOSIT INSURANCE CORPORATION
FEDERAL ELECTION COMMISSION

FEDERAL HOUSING FINANCE AGENCY
FEDERAL LABOR RELATIONS AUTHORITY
FEDERAL MARITIME COMMISSION
FEDERAL MEDIATION AND CONCILIATION SERVICE
FEDERAL MINE SAFETY AND HEALTH REVIEW COMMISSION
FEDERAL RESERVE SYSTEM
FEDERAL RETIREMENT THRIFT INVESTMENT BOARD
FEDERAL TRADE COMMISSION
GENERAL SERVICES ADMINISTRATION
INTER-AMERICAN FOUNDATION
MERIT SYSTEMS PROTECTION BOARD
NATIONAL AERONAUTICS AND SPACE ADMINISTRATION
NATIONAL ARCHIVES AND RECORDS ADMINISTRATION
NATIONAL CAPITAL PLANNING COMMISSION

NATIONAL CREDIT UNION ADMINISTRATION
NATIONAL FOUNDATION ON THE ARTS AND THE HUMANITIES
NATIONAL LABOR RELATIONS BOARD
NATIONAL MEDIATION BOARD
NATIONAL RAILROAD PASSENGER CORPORATION (AMTRAK)
NATIONAL SCIENCE FOUNDATION
NATIONAL TRANSPORTATION SAFETY BOARD
NUCLEAR REGULATORY COMMISSION
OCCUPATIONAL SAFETY AND HEALTH REVIEW COMMISSION
OFFICE OF THE DIRECTOR OF NATIONAL INTELLIGENCE
OFFICE OF GOVERNMENT ETHICS
OFFICE OF PERSONNEL MANAGEMENT
OFFICE OF SPECIAL COUNSEL
OVERSEAS PRIVATE INVESTMENT CORPORATION

PEACE CORPS
PENSION BENEFIT GUARANTY CORPORATION
POSTAL REGULATORY COMMISSION
NATIONAL RAILROAD RETIREMENT BOARD
SECURITIES AND EXCHANGE COMMISSION
SELECTIVE SERVICE SYSTEM
SMALL BUSINESS ADMINISTRATION
SOCIAL SECURITY ADMINISTRATION
TENNESSEE VALLEY AUTHORITY
TRADE AND DEVELOPMENT AGENCY
UNITED STATES AGENCY FOR INTERNATIONAL DEVELOPMENT
UNITED STATES COMMISSION ON CIVIL RIGHTS
UNITED STATES INTERNATIONAL TRADE COMMISSION
UNITED STATES POSTAL SERVICE

Legislative Branch

LEGISLATIVE BRANCH

CONGRESS
One Hundred and Eleventh Congress, First Session

The Senate

The Capitol, Washington, DC 20510
Phone, 202–224–3121. Internet, www.senate.gov.

President of the Senate (Vice President of the United States)	JOSEPH R. BIDEN, JR.
President pro tempore	ROBERT C. BYRD
Majority Leader	HARRY REID
Minority Leader	MITCH McCONNELL
Secretary of the Senate	NANCY ERICKSON
Sergeant at Arms	TERRANCE GAINER
Secretary for the Majority	LULA JOHNSON DAVIS
Secretary for the Minority	DAVID J. SCHIAPPA
Chaplain	BARRY BLACK

The House of Representatives

The Capitol, Washington, DC 20515
Phone, 202–225–3121. Internet, www.house.gov.

The Speaker	NANCY PELOSI
Clerk	LORRAINE C. MILLER
Sergeant at Arms	WILSON L. LIVINGOOD
Chief Administrative Officer	DANIEL BEARD
Chaplain	REV. DANIEL P. COUGHLIN

The Congress of the United States was created by Article I, section 1, of the Constitution, adopted by the Constitutional Convention on September 17, 1787, providing that "All legislative Powers herein granted shall be vested in a Congress of the United States, which shall consist of a Senate and House of Representatives."

The first Congress under the Constitution met on March 4, 1789, in the Federal Hall in New York City. The membership then consisted of 20[1] Senators and 59 Representatives.

---

[1] New York ratified the Constitution on July 26, 1788, but did not elect its Senators until July 15 and 16, 1789. North Carolina did not ratify the Constitution until November 21, 1789; Rhode Island ratified it on May 29, 1790.

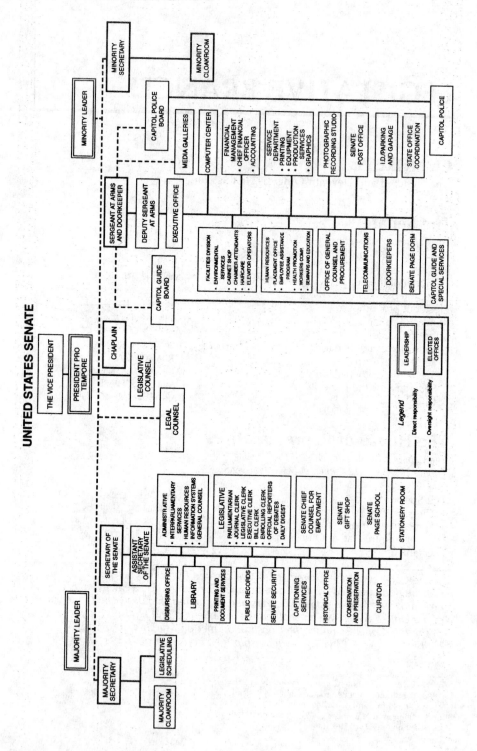

UNITED STATES SENATE

HOUSE OF REPRESENTATIVES

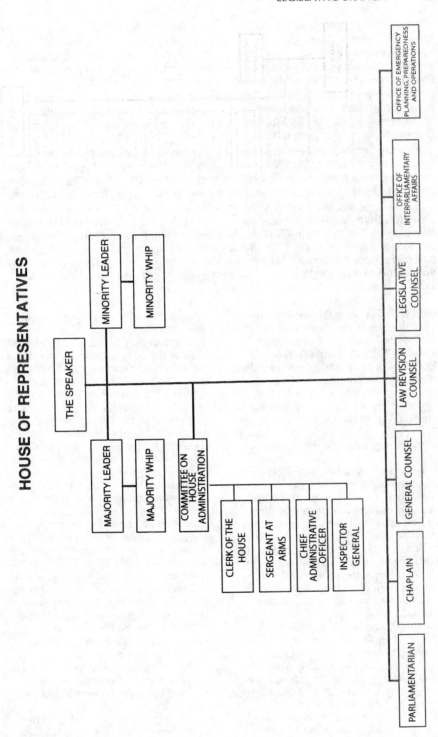

The Senate is composed of 100 Members, 2 from each State, who are elected to serve for a term of 6 years. Senators were originally chosen by the State legislatures. This procedure was changed by the 17th amendment to the Constitution, adopted in 1913, which made the election of Senators a function of the people. There are three classes of Senators, and a new class is elected every 2 years.

The House of Representatives comprises 435 Representatives. The number representing each State is determined by population, but every State is entitled to at least one Representative. Members are elected by the people for 2-year terms, all terms running for the same period.

Both the Senators and the Representatives must be residents of the State from which they are chosen. In addition, a Senator must be at least 30 years of age and must have been a citizen of the United States for at least 9 years; a Representative must be at least 25 years of age and must have been a citizen for at least 7 years.

A Resident Commissioner from Puerto Rico (elected for a 4-year term) and Delegates from American Samoa, the District of Columbia, Guam, and the Virgin Islands complete the composition of the Congress of the United States. Delegates are elected for a term of 2 years. The Resident Commissioner and Delegates may take part in the floor discussions but have no vote in the full House. They do, however, vote in the committees to which they are assigned and in the Committee of the Whole House on the State of the Union.

Officers The Vice President of the United States is the Presiding Officer of the Senate. In the Vice President's absence, the duties are taken over by a President pro tempore, elected by that body, or someone designated by the President pro tempore. The Presiding Officer of the House of Representatives, the Speaker, is elected by the House. The Speaker may designate any Member of the House to act in the Speaker's absence.

The positions of Senate majority and minority leader have been in existence only since the early years of the 20th century. Leaders are elected at the beginning of each new Congress by a majority vote of the Senators in their political party. In cooperation with their party organizations, leaders are responsible for the design and achievement of a legislative program. This involves managing the flow of legislation, expediting noncontroversial measures, and keeping Members informed regarding proposed action on pending business. Each leader serves as an ex officio member of his party's policymaking and organizational bodies and is aided by an assistant floor leader (whip) and a party secretary.

The House leadership is structured essentially the same as the Senate, with the Members in the political parties responsible for the election of their respective leader and whips.

The Secretary of the Senate, elected by vote of the Senate, performs the duties of the Presiding Officer of the Senate in the absence of the Vice President and pending the election of a President pro tempore. The Secretary is the custodian of the seal of the Senate, draws requisitions on the Secretary of the Treasury for moneys appropriated for the compensation of Senators, officers, and employees, and for the contingent expenses of the Senate, and is empowered to administer oaths to any officer of the Senate and to any witness produced before it. The Secretary's executive duties include certification of extracts from the Journal of the Senate; the attestation of bills and joint, concurrent, and Senate resolutions; in impeachment trials, issuance, under the authority of the Presiding Officer, of all orders, mandates, writs, and precepts authorized by the Senate; and certification to the President of the United States of the advice and consent of the Senate to ratification of treaties and the names of persons confirmed or rejected upon the nomination of the President.

The Sergeant at Arms, elected by vote of the Senate, serves as the executive, chief law enforcement, and protocol officer and is the principal administrative manager for most support services in the Senate. As executive officer, the Sergeant at Arms has custody of the Senate gavel; enforces Senate rules and regulations as they pertain to the Senate Chamber, the Senate wing of the Capitol, and the Senate Office Buildings; and subject to the Presiding Officer, maintains order on the Senate floor, chamber, and galleries. As chief law enforcement officer of the Senate, the Sergeant at Arms is authorized to maintain security in the Capitol and all Senate buildings, as well as to protect Senators; to arrest and detain any person violating Senate rules; and to locate absentee Senators for a quorum. The Sergeant at Arms serves as a member of the Capitol Police Board and as its chairman each odd year. As protocol officer, the Sergeant at Arms escorts the President and other heads of state or official guests of the Senate who are attending official functions in the Capitol; makes arrangements for funerals of Senators who die in office; and assists in planning the inauguration of the President and organizing the swearing-in and orientation programs for newly elected Senators.

The elected officers of the House of Representatives include the Clerk, the Sergeant at Arms, the Chief Administrative Officer, and the Chaplain.

The Clerk is custodian of the seal of the House and administers the primary legislative activities of the House. These duties include accepting the credentials of the Members-elect and calling the Members to order at the commencement of the first session of each Congress; keeping the Journal; taking all votes and certifying the passage of bills; and processing all legislation. Through various departments, the Clerk is also responsible for floor and committee reporting services; legislative information and reference services; the administration of House reports pursuant to House rules and certain legislation including the Ethics in Government Act and the Lobbying Disclosure Act of 1995; the distribution of House documents; and administration of the House Page Program. The Clerk is also charged with supervision of the offices vacated by Members due to death, resignation, or expulsion.

The Sergeant at Arms maintains the order of the House under the direction of the Speaker and is the keeper of the Mace. As a member of the U.S. Capitol Police Board, the Sergeant at Arms is the chief law enforcement officer for the House and serves as Board Chairman each even year. The ceremonial and protocol duties parallel those of the Senate Sergeant at Arms and include arranging the inauguration of the President of the United States, Joint Sessions of Congress, visits to the House of heads of state, and funerals of Members of Congress. The Sergeant at Arms enforces the rules relating to the privileges of the Hall of the House, including admission to the galleries, oversees garage and parking security of the House, and distributes all House staff identification cards.

Committees   The work of preparing and considering legislation is done largely by committees of both Houses of Congress. There are 16 standing committees in the Senate and 19 in the House of Representatives. The standing committees of the Senate and the House of Representatives are shown in the list below. In addition, there are two select committees in each House and various congressional commissions and joint committees composed of Members of both Houses. Each House may also appoint special investigating committees. The membership of the standing committees of each House is chosen by a vote of the entire body; members of other committees are appointed under the provisions of the measure establishing them.

Each bill and resolution is usually referred to the appropriate committee, which may report a bill out in its original form, favorably or unfavorably, recommend amendments, report original measures, or allow the proposed legislation to die in committee without action.

Standing Committees of the Congress

House Committee	Room[1]	Senate Committee	Room[2]
Agriculture	1301	Agriculture, Nutrition, and Forestry	SR–328A
Appropriations	H218	Appropriations	S–128
Armed Services	2120	Armed Services	SR–228
Budget	207	Banking, Housing, and Urban Affairs	SD–534
Education and Labor	2181	Budget	SD–624
Energy and Commerce	2125	Commerce, Science, and Transportation	SD–508
Financial Services	2129	Energy and Natural Resources	SD–304
Foreign Affairs	2170	Environment and Public Works	SD–410
Homeland Security	H2–176		
House Administration	1309		
Franking Commission:			
Majority	1216		
Minority	1216A	Finance	SD–219
Judiciary	2138	Foreign Relations	SD–446
Publications	B29 Cannon		
Natural Resources	1324		
Oversight and Government Reform	2157	Health, Education, Labor, and Pensions	SD–428
Rules	H312	Homeland Security and Governmental Affairs	SD–340
Minority	1627		
Science and Technology	2321		
Small Business	2361		
Standards of Official Conduct	HT2	Judiciary	SD–224
Office of Advice and Education	HT2		
Transportation and Infrastructure	2165	Rules and Administration	SR–305
Veterans' Affairs	335	Small Business and Entrepreneurship	SR–428A
Ways and Means	1102	Veterans' Affairs	SR–412

[1] Room numbers with three digits are in the Cannon House Office Building, four digits beginning with 1 are in the Longworth House Office Building, and four digits beginning with 2 are in the Rayburn House Office Building. Room numbers preceded by H or HT are in the House wing of the Capitol Building. Rooms preceded by an LA are in the John Adams Building of the Library of Congress.

[2] Room numbers preceded by S are in the Senate wing of the Capitol Building; those preceded by SD are in the Dirksen Office Building; those preceded by SR are in the Russell Office Building; and those preceded by SH are in the Hart Office Building.

Congressional Record Proceedings of Congress are published in the *Congressional Record,* which is issued each day when Congress is in session. Publication of the *Record* began March 4, 1873. It was the first record of debate officially reported, printed, and published directly by the Federal Government. The Daily Digest of the *Congressional Record,* printed in the back of each issue of the *Record,* summarizes the proceedings of that day in each House and each of their committees and subcommittees, respectively. The Digest also presents the legislative program for each day and, at the end of the week, gives the program for the following week. Its publication was begun March 17, 1947.

Sessions Section 4 of Article I of the Constitution makes it mandatory that "The Congress shall assemble at least once in every Year. . . ." Under this provision, also, the date for convening Congress was designated originally as the first Monday in December, "unless they shall by Law appoint a different Day." Eighteen acts were passed, up to 1820, providing for the meeting of Congress on other days of the year. From 1820 to 1934, however, Congress met regularly on the first Monday in December. In 1934 the Twentieth Amendment changed the convening of Congress to January 3, unless Congress "shall by law appoint a different day." In addition, the President, according to Article II, section 3, of the Constitution "may, on extraordinary Occasions, convene both Houses, or either of them, and in Case of Disagreement between them, with Respect to the Time of Adjournment, he may adjourn them to such Time as he shall think proper. . . ."

Powers of Congress Article I, section 8, of the Constitution defines the powers of Congress. Included are the powers to assess and collect taxes—called the chief power; to regulate commerce, both interstate and foreign; to coin money; to establish post offices and post roads; to establish courts inferior to the Supreme Court; to declare war; and to raise and maintain an army and navy. Congress is further empowered "To provide for calling forth the Militia to execute the Laws of the Union, suppress Insurrections and repel Invasions;" and "To make all Laws which shall be necessary and proper for carrying into Execution the foregoing Powers, and all other Powers vested by this Constitution in the Government of the United States, or in any Department or Officer thereof."

Amendments to the Constitution

Another power vested in the Congress is the right to propose amendments to the Constitution, whenever two-thirds of both Houses shall deem it necessary. Should two-thirds of the State legislatures demand changes in the Constitution, it is the duty of Congress to call a constitutional convention. Proposed amendments shall be valid as part of the Constitution when ratified by the legislatures or by conventions of three-fourths of the States, as one or the other mode of ratification may be proposed by Congress.

Special Powers of the Senate Under the Constitution, the Senate is granted certain powers not accorded to the House of Representatives. The Senate approves or disapproves certain Presidential appointments by majority vote, and treaties must be concurred in by a two-thirds vote.

Special Powers of the House of Representatives The House of Representatives is granted the power of originating all bills for the raising of revenue. Both Houses of Congress act in impeachment proceedings, which, according to the Constitution, may be instituted against the President, Vice President, and all civil officers of the United States. The House of Representatives has the sole power of impeachment, and the Senate has the sole power to try impeachments.

Prohibitions Upon Congress Section 9 of Article I of the Constitution also imposes prohibitions upon Congress. "The Privilege of the Writ of Habeas Corpus shall not be suspended, unless when in Cases of Rebellion or Invasion the public Safety may require it." A bill of attainder or an ex post facto law cannot be passed. No export duty can be imposed. Ports of one State cannot be given preference over those of another State. "No money shall be drawn from the Treasury, but in Consequence of Appropriations made by Law. . . ." No title of nobility may be granted.

Rights of Members According to section 6 of Article I, Members of Congress are granted certain privileges. In no case, except in treason, felony, and breach of the peace, can Members be arrested while attending sessions of Congress "and in going to and returning from the same. . . ." Furthermore, the Members cannot be questioned in any other place for remarks made in Congress. Each House may expel a Member of its body by a two-thirds vote.

Enactment of Laws All bills and joint resolutions must pass both the House of Representatives and the Senate and must be signed by the President, except those proposing a constitutional amendment, in order to become law, or be passed over the President's veto by a two-thirds vote of both Houses of Congress. Section 7 of Article I states: "If any Bill shall not be returned by the President within ten Days (Sundays excepted) after it shall have been presented to him, the Same shall be a Law, in like Manner as if he had signed it, unless the Congress by their Adjournment prevent its Return, in which Case it shall not be a Law." When a bill or joint resolution is introduced in the House, the usual procedure for its enactment into law is as follows:

—assignment to House committee having jurisdiction;

—if favorably considered, it is reported to the House either in its original form or with recommended amendments;

—if the bill or resolution is passed by the House, it is messaged to the Senate and referred to the committee having jurisdiction;

—in the Senate committee the bill, if favorably considered, may be reported in the form as received from the House, or with recommended amendments;

—the approved bill or resolution is reported to the Senate, and if passed by that body, is returned to the House;

—if one body does not accept the amendments to a bill by the other body, a conference committee comprised of Members of both bodies is usually appointed to effect a compromise;

—when the bill or joint resolution is finally approved by both Houses, it is signed by the Speaker (or Speaker pro tempore) and the Vice President (or President pro tempore or acting President pro tempore) and is presented to the President; and

—once the President's signature is affixed, the measure becomes a law. If the President vetoes the bill, it cannot become a law unless it is re-passed by a two-thirds vote of both Houses.

Electronic Access Specific information and legislation can be found on the Internet at http://thomas.loc.gov, http://clerk.house.gov, or www.senate.gov.

Publications The *Congressional Directory,* the *Senate Manual,* telephone directories for the U.S. Senate and the House of Representatives, and the *House Rules and Manual* may be obtained from the Superintendent of Documents, Government Printing Office, Washington, DC 20402. Internet, www.gpoaccess.gov/databases.html.

Senators

[Democrats in roman (57); Republicans in italic (40); Independents in bold (2); vacancy (1); total, 100]. Members who have died or resigned appear in bold brackets [ ].

Room numbers preceded by SR are in the Russell Office Building (Delaware and Constitution Avenues); those preceded by SD are in the Dirksen Office Building (First Street and Constitution Avenue); and those preceded by SH are in the Hart Office Building (Second and C Streets). Members' offices may be reached by phone at 202–224–3121.

Name	State	Room
Akaka, Daniel K	Hawaii	SH141
Alexander, Lamar	Tennessee	SD455
Barrasso, John	Wyoming	SD307
Baucus, Max	Montana	SH511
Bayh, Evan	Indiana	SR131
Begich, Mark	Alaska	SR144
Bennet, Michael F	Colorado	SH702
Bennett, Robert F	Utah	SD431
Bingaman, Jeff	New Mexico	SH703
Bond, Christopher S	Missouri	SR274
Boxer, Barbara	California	SH112
Brown, Sherrod	Ohio	SH713
Brownback, Sam	Kansas	SH303
Bunning, Jim	Kentucky	SH316
Burr, Richard	North Carolina	SR217
Burris, Roland W	Illinois	SR387
Byrd, Robert C	West Virginia	SH311
Cantwell, Maria	Washington	SD511
Cardin, Benjamin L.	Maryland	SH509
Carper, Thomas R	Delaware	SH513
Casey, Robert P., Jr	Pennsylvania	SR393
Chambliss, Saxby	Georgia	SR416
Coburn, Tom	Oklahoma	SR172
Cochran, Thad	Mississippi	SD113
Collins, Susan M	Maine	SD413
Conrad, Kent	North Dakota	SH530
Corker, Bob	Tennessee	SD185
Cornyn, John	Texas	SH517
Crapo, Mike	Idaho	SD239
DeMint, Jim	South Carolina	SR340
Dodd, Christopher J	Connecticut	SR448
Dorgan, Byron L	North Dakota	SH322
Durbin, Richard J	Illinois	SH309

Senators—Continued

[Democrats in roman (57); Republicans in italic (40); Independents in bold (2); vacancy (1); total, 100].
Members who have died or resigned appear in bold brackets **[ ]**.

Room numbers preceded by SR are in the Russell Office Building (Delaware and Constitution Avenues); those preceded by SD are in the Dirksen Office Building (First Street and Constitution Avenue); and those preceded by SH are in the Hart Office Building (Second and C Streets). Members' offices may be reached by phone at 202–224–3121.

Name	State	Room
Ensign, John	Nevada	SR119
Enzi, Mike	Wyoming	SR379A
Feingold, Russell D	Wisconsin	SH506
Feinstein, Dianne	California	SH331
Franken, Al	Minnesota	SH320
Gillibrand, Kristen E	New York	SR478
Graham, Lindsey O	South Carolina	SR290
Grassley, Charles E	Iowa	SH135
Gregg, Judd	New Hampshire	SR201
Hagan, Kay R	North Carolina	SD521
Harkin, Tom	Iowa	SH731
Hatch, Orrin G	Utah	SH104
Hutchison, Kay Bailey	Texas	SR284
Inhofe, James M	Oklahoma	SR453
Inouye, Daniel K	Hawaii	SH722
Isakson, Johnny	Georgia	SR120
Johanns, Mike	Nebraska	SR404
Johnson, Tim	South Dakota	SH136
Kaufman, Edward E	Delaware	SR383
[Kennedy, Edward M]	Massachusetts	SR317
Kerry, John F	Massachusetts	SR218
Klobuchar, Amy	Minnesota	SH302
Kohl, Herb	Wisconsin	SH330
Kyl, Jon	Arizona	SH730
Landrieu, Mary L	Louisiana	SH328
Lautenberg, Frank	New Jersey	SH324
Leahy, Patrick J	Vermont	SR433
LeMieux, George S	Florida	SR356
Levin, Carl	Michigan	SR269
Lieberman, Joseph I	Connecticut	SH706
Lincoln, Blanche L	Arkansas	SD355
Lugar, Richard G	Indiana	SH306
Merkley, Jeff	Oregon	SR107
McCain, John	Arizona	SR241
McCaskill, Claire	Missouri	SH717
McConnell, Mitch	Kentucky	SR361A
Menendez, Robert	New Jersey	SH528
Mikulski, Barbara A	Maryland	SH503
Murkowski, Lisa	Alaska	SH709
Murray, Patty	Washington	SR173
Nelson, Bill	Florida	SH716
Nelson, Ben	Nebraska	SH720
Pryor, Mark	Arkansas	SD255
Reed, Jack	Rhode Island	SH728
Reid, Harry	Nevada	SH522
Risch, James E	Idaho	SR483
Roberts, Pat	Kansas	SH109
Rockefeller, John D., IV	West Virginia	SH531
Sanders, Bernard	Vermont	SD332
Schumer, Charles E	New York	SH313
Sessions, Jeff	Alabama	SR335
Shaheen, Jeanne	New Hampshire	SH520

Senators—Continued

[Democrats in roman (57); Republicans in italic (40); Independents in bold (2); vacancy (1); total, 100].
Members who have died or resigned appear in bold brackets [ ].

Room numbers preceded by SR are in the Russell Office Building (Delaware and Constitution Avenues); those preceded by SD are in the Dirksen Office Building (First Street and Constitution Avenue); and those preceded by SH are in the Hart Office Building (Second and C Streets). Members' offices may be reached by phone at 202–224–3121.

Name	State	Room
Shelby, Richard C	Alabama	SH304
Snowe, Olympia J	Maine	SR154
Specter, Arlen	Pennsylvania	SH711
Stabenow, Debbie	Michigan	SH133
Tester, Jon	Montana	SH724
Thune, John	South Dakota	SR493
Udall, Mark	Colorado	SH317
Udall, Tom	New Mexico	SH110
Vitter, David	Louisiana	SH516
Voinovich, George V	Ohio	SH524
Warner, Mark R	Virginia	SR459A
Webb, Jim	Virginia	SR248
Whitehouse, Sheldon	Rhode Island	SH502
Wicker, Roger F	Mississippi	SD555
Wyden, Ron	Oregon	SD223

Representatives

[Democrats in roman (256); Republicans in italic (178); vacancy (1); total, 435]. Members who have resigned appear in bold brackets [ ].

Room numbers with three digits are in the Cannon House Office Building (New Jersey and Independence Avenues), four digits beginning with 1 are in the Longworth House Office Building (between South Capitol Street and New Jersey Avenue on Independence Avenue), and four digits beginning with 2 are in the Rayburn House Office Building (between First and South Capitol Streets on Independence Avenue). Members' offices may be reached by phone at 202–225–3121. The most current listing of House Members can be found on the Internet at http://clerk.house.gov.

Name	State (District)	Room
Abercrombie, Neil	Hawaii (1)	1502
Ackerman, Gary L	New York (5)	2243
Aderholt, Robert B	Alabama (4)	1433
Adler, John	New Jersey (3)	1223
Akin, W. Todd	Missouri (2)	117
Alexander, Rodney	Louisiana (5)	316
Altmire, Jason	Pennsylvania (4)	332
Andrews, Robert E	New Jersey (1)	2265
Arcuri, Michael A	New York (24)	127
Austria, Steve	Ohio (7)	1641
Baca, Joe	California (43)	2245
Bachmann, Michele	Minnesota (6)	107
Bachus, Spencer	Alabama (6)	2246
Baird, Brian	Washington (3)	2350
Baldwin, Tammy	Wisconsin (2)	2446
Barrett, J. Gresham	South Carolina (3)	439
Barrow, John	Georgia (12)	213
Bartlett, Roscoe G	Maryland (6)	2412
Barton, Joe	Texas (6)	2109
Bean, Melissa L	Illinois (8)	318
Becerra, Xavier	California (31)	1119
Berkley, Shelley	Nevada (1)	405
Berman, Howard L	California (28)	2221
Berry, Marion	Arkansas (1)	2305

Representatives—Continued

[Democrats in roman (256); Republicans in italic (178); vacancy (1); total, 435]. Members who have resigned appear in bold brackets [ ].

Room numbers with three digits are in the Cannon House Office Building (New Jersey and Independence Avenues), four digits beginning with 1 are in the Longworth House Office Building (between South Capitol Street and New Jersey Avenue on Independence Avenue), and four digits beginning with 2 are in the Rayburn House Office Building (between First and South Capitol Streets on Independence Avenue). Members' offices may be reached by phone at 202–225–3121. The most current listing of House Members can be found on the Internet at http://clerk.house.gov.

Name	State (District)	Room
Biggert, Judy	Illinois (13)	1034
Bilbray, Brian P	California (50)	227
Bilirakis, Gus M	Florida (9)	1124
Bishop, Rob	Utah (1)	123
Bishop, Sanford D., Jr	Georgia (2)	2429
Bishop, Timothy H	New York (1)	306
Blackburn, Marsha	Tennessee (7)	509
Blumenauer, Earl	Oregon (3)	2267
Blunt, Roy	Missouri (7)	217
Boccieri, John A	Ohio (16)	1516
Boehner, John A	Ohio (8)	1011
Bonner, Jo	Alabama (1)	2236
Bono Mack, Mary	California (45)	104
Boozman, John	Arkansas (3)	1519
Boren, Dan	Oklahoma (2)	216
Boswell, Leonard L	Iowa (3)	1427
Boucher, Rick	Virginia (9)	2187
Boustany, Charles W., Jr	Louisiana (7)	1117
Boyd, Allen	Florida (2)	1227
Brady, Kevin	Texas (8)	301
Brady, Robert A	Pennsylvania (1)	206
Braley, Bruce L	Iowa (1)	1019
Bright, Bobby	Alabama (2)	1205
Broun, Paul C	Georgia (10)	2104
Brown, Corrine	Florida (3)	2336
Brown, Henry E., Jr	South Carolina (1)	103
Brown-Waite, Ginny	Florida (5)	414
Buchanan, Vern	Florida (13)	218
Burgess, Michael C	Texas (26)	229
Burton, Dan	Indiana (5)	2308
Butterfield, G.K	North Carolina (1)	413
Buyer, Steve	Indiana (4)	2230
Calvert, Ken	California (44)	2201
Camp, Dave	Michigan (4)	314
Campbell, John	California (48)	1507
Cantor, Eric	Virginia (7)	329
Cao, Joseph	Louisiana (2)	2113
Capito, Shelley Moore	West Virginia (2)	2443
Capps, Lois	California (23)	1110
Capuano, Michael E	Massachusetts (8)	1414
Cardoza, Dennis A	California (18)	1224
Carnahan, Russ	Missouri (3)	1710
Carney, Christopher P	Pennsylvania (10)	416
Carson, André	Indiana (7)	425
Carter, John R	Texas (31)	409
Cassidy, Bill	Louisiana (6)	506
Castle, Michael N	Delaware (At Large)	1233
Castor, Kathy N	Florida (11)	317
Chaffetz, Jason	Utah (3)	1032
Chandler, Ben	Kentucky (6)	1504
Childers, Travis W	Mississippi (1)	1708

Representatives—Continued

[Democrats in roman (256); Republicans in italic (178); vacancy (1); total, 435]. Members who have resigned appear in bold brackets [ ].

Room numbers with three digits are in the Cannon House Office Building (New Jersey and Independence Avenues), four digits beginning with 1 are in the Longworth House Office Building (between South Capitol Street and New Jersey Avenue on Independence Avenue), and four digits beginning with 2 are in the Rayburn House Office Building (between First and South Capitol Streets on Independence Avenue). Members' offices may be reached by phone at 202–225–3121. The most current listing of House Members can be found on the Internet at http://clerk.house.gov.

Name	State (District)	Room
Chu, Judy	California (32)	2421
Clarke, Yvette D	New York (11)	1029
Clay, William Lacy	Missouri (1)	2418
Cleaver, Emanuel	Missouri (5)	1027
Clyburn, James E	South Carolina (6)	2135
Coble, Howard	North Carolina (6)	2468
Coffman, Mike	Colorado (6)	1508
Cohen, Steve	Tennessee (9)	1005
Cole, Tom	Oklahoma (4)	2458
Conaway, K. Michael	Texas (11)	1527
Connolly, Gerry	Virginia (11)	327
Conyers, John, Jr	Michigan (14)	2426
Cooper, Jim	Tennessee (5)	1536
Costa, Jim	California (20)	1314
Costello, Jerry F	Illinois (12)	2408
Courtney, Joe	Connecticut (2)	215
Crenshaw, Ander	Florida (4)	440
Crowley, Joseph	New York (7)	2404
Cuellar, Henry	Texas (28)	336
Culberson, John Abney	Texas (7)	1514
Cummings, Elijah E	Maryland (7)	2235
Dahlkemper, Kathy	Pennsylvania (3)	516
Davis, Artur	Alabama (7)	208
Davis, Danny K	Illinois (7)	2159
Davis, Geoff	Kentucky (4)	1108
Davis, Lincoln	Tennessee (4)	410
Davis, Susan A	California (53)	1526
Deal, Nathan	Georgia (9)	2133
DeFazio, Peter A	Oregon (4)	2134
DeGette, Diana	Colorado (1)	2335
Delahunt, William D	Massachusetts (10)	2454
DeLauro, Rosa L	Connecticut (3)	2413
Dent, Charles W	Pennsylvania (15)	1009
Diaz-Balart, Lincoln	Florida (21)	2244
Diaz-Balart, Mario	Florida (25)	328
Dicks, Norman D	Washington (6)	2467
Dingell, John D	Michigan (15)	2328
Doggett, Lloyd	Texas (25)	201
Donnelly, Joe	Indiana (2)	1530
Doyle, Michael F	Pennsylvania (14)	401
Dreier, David	California (26)	233
Dreihaus, Steve	Ohio (1)	408
Duncan, John J., Jr	Tennessee (2)	2207
Edwards, Chet	Texas (17)	2369
Edwards, Donna	Maryland (4)	318
Ehlers, Vernon J	Michigan (3)	2182
Ellison, Keith	Minnesota (5)	1122
Ellsworth, Brad	Indiana (8)	513
Emerson, Jo Ann	Missouri (8)	2440
Engel, Eliot L	New York (17)	2161
Eshoo, Anna G	California (14)	205

Representatives—Continued

[Democrats in roman (256); Republicans in italic (178); vacancy (1); total, 435]. Members who have resigned appear in bold brackets [ ].

Room numbers with three digits are in the Cannon House Office Building (New Jersey and Independence Avenues), four digits beginning with 1 are in the Longworth House Office Building (between South Capitol Street and New Jersey Avenue on Independence Avenue), and four digits beginning with 2 are in the Rayburn House Office Building (between First and South Capitol Streets on Independence Avenue). Members' offices may be reached by phone at 202–225–3121. The most current listing of House Members can be found on the Internet at http://clerk.house.gov.

Name	State (District)	Room
Etheridge, Bob	North Carolina (2)	1533
Fallin, Mary	Oklahoma (5)	1432
Farr, Sam	California (17)	1126
Fattah, Chaka	Pennsylvania (2)	2301
Filner, Bob	California (51)	2428
Flake, Jeff	Arizona (6)	240
Fleming, John	Louisiana (4)	1023
Forbes, J. Randy	Virginia (4)	2438
Fortenberry, Jeff	Nebraska (1)	1535
Foster, Bill	Illinois (14)	1339
Foxx, Virginia	North Carolina (5)	1230
Frank, Barney	Massachusetts (4)	2252
Franks, Trent	Arizona (2)	2435
Frelinghuysen, Rodney P	New Jersey (11)	2442
Fudge, Marcia	Ohio (11)	1513
Gallegly, Elton	California (24)	2309
Garrett, Scott	New Jersey (5)	137
Gerlach, Jim	Pennsylvania (6)	308
Giffords, Gabrielle	Arizona (8)	1728
Gillibrand, Kirsten E	New York (20)	120
Gingrey, Phil	Georgia (11)	119
Gohmert, Louie	Texas (1)	511
Gonzalez, Charles A	Texas (20)	303
Goodlatte, Bob	Virginia (6)	2240
Gordon, Bart	Tennessee (6)	2306
Granger, Kay	Texas (12)	320
Graves, Sam	Missouri (6)	1415
Grayson, Alan	Florida (8)	1605
Green, Al	Texas (9)	236
Green, Gene	Texas (29)	2372
Griffith, Parker	Alabama (5)	417
Grijalva, Raúl M	Arizona (7)	1440
Guthrie, S. Brett	Kentucky (2)	510
Gutierrez, Luis V	Illinois (4)	2266
Hall, John J	New York (19)	1217
Hall, Ralph M	Texas (4)	2405
Halvorson, Debbie	Illinois (11)	1541
Hare, Phil	Illinois (17)	428
Harman, Jane	California (36)	2400
Harper, Gregg	Michigan (3)	307
Hastings, Alcee L	Florida (23)	2353
Hastings, Doc	Washington (4)	1203
Heinrich, Martin	New Mexico (1)	1505
Heller, Dean	Nevada (2)	125
Hensarling, Jeb	Texas (5)	129
Herger, Wally	California (2)	242
Herseth Sandlin, Stephanie	South Dakota (At Large)	331
Higgins, Brian	New York (27)	431
Hill, Baron P	Indiana (9)	223
Himes, Jim	Connecticut (4)	214
Hinchey, Maurice D	New York (22)	2431

Representatives—Continued

[Democrats in roman (256); Republicans in italic (178); vacancy (1); total, 435]. Members who have resigned appear in bold brackets [ ].

Room numbers with three digits are in the Cannon House Office Building (New Jersey and Independence Avenues), four digits beginning with 1 are in the Longworth House Office Building (between South Capitol Street and New Jersey Avenue on Independence Avenue), and four digits beginning with 2 are in the Rayburn House Office Building (between First and South Capitol Streets on Independence Avenue). Members' offices may be reached by phone at 202–225–3121. The most current listing of House Members can be found on the Internet at http://clerk.house.gov.

Name	State (District)	Room
Hinojosa, Rubén	Texas (15)	2463
Hirono, Mazie K	Hawaii (2)	1524
Hodes, Paul W	New Hampshire (2)	1317
Hoekstra, Peter	Michigan (2)	2234
Holden, Tim	Pennsylvania (17)	2417
Holt, Rush D	New Jersey (12)	1214
Honda, Michael M	California (15)	1713
Hoyer, Steny H	Maryland (5)	1705
Hunter, Duncan	California (52)	1429
Inglis, Bob	South Carolina (4)	100
Inslee, Jay	Washington (1)	403
Israel, Steve	New York (2)	2457
Issa, Darrell E	California (49)	2347
Jackson, Jesse L., Jr	Illinois (2)	2419
Jackson-Lee, Sheila	Texas (18)	2160
Jenkins, Lynn	Kansas (2)	130
Johnson, Eddie Bernice	Texas (30)	1511
Johnson, Henry C. (Hank), Jr	Georgia (4)	1133
Johnson, Sam	Texas (3)	1211
Johnson, Timothy V	Illinois (15)	1207
Jones, Walter B	North Carolina (3)	2333
Jordan, Jim	Ohio (4)	515
Kagan, Steve	Wisconsin (8)	1232
Kanjorski, Paul E	Pennsylvania (11)	2188
Kaptur, Marcy	Ohio (9)	2186
Kennedy, Patrick J	Rhode Island (1)	407
Kildee, Dale E	Michigan (5)	2107
Kilpatrick, Carolyn C	Michigan (13)	2264
Kilroy, Mary Jo	Ohio (15)	1237
Kind, Ron	Wisconsin (3)	1406
King, Peter T	New York (3)	339
King, Steve	Iowa (5)	1139
Kingston, Jack	Georgia (1)	2368
Kirk, Mark Steven	Illinois (10)	1030
Kirkpatrick, Ann	Arizona (1)	1123
Kissell, Larry	North Carolina (8)	512
Klein, Ron	Florida (22)	313
Kline, John	Minnesota (2)	1210
Kosmas, Suzanne	Florida (24)	238
Kratovil, Frank M., Jr	Maryland (1)	314
Kucinich, Dennis J	Ohio (10)	2445
Lamborn, Doug	Colorado (5)	437
Lance, Leonard	New Jersey (7)	114
Langevin, James R	Rhode Island (2)	109
Larsen, Rick	Washington (2)	108
Larson, John B	Connecticut (1)	106
Latham, Tom	Iowa (4)	2217
LaTourette, Steven C	Ohio (14)	2371
Latta, Robert E	Ohio (5)	1531
Lee, Barbara	California (9)	2444
Lee, Christopher	New York (26)	1711

Representatives—Continued

[Democrats in roman (256); Republicans in italic (178); vacancy (1); total, 435]. Members who have resigned appear in bold brackets [ ].

Room numbers with three digits are in the Cannon House Office Building (New Jersey and Independence Avenues), four digits beginning with 1 are in the Longworth House Office Building (between South Capitol Street and New Jersey Avenue on Independence Avenue), and foi: digits beginning with 2 are in the Rayburn House Office Building (between First and South Capitol Streets on Independence Avenue). Members' offices may be reached by phone at 202–225–3121. The most current listing of House Members can be found on the Internet at http://clerk.house.gov.

Name	State (District)	Room
Levin, Sander M	Michigan (12)	1236
Lewis, Jerry	California (41)	2112
Lewis, John	Georgia (5)	343
Linder, John	Georgia (7)	1026
Lipinski, Daniel	Illinois (3)	1717
LoBiondo, Frank A	New Jersey (2)	2427
Loebsack, David	Iowa (2)	1221
Lofgren, Zoe	California (16)	102
Lowey, Nita M	New York (18)	2329
Lucas, Frank D	Oklahoma (3)	2311
Luetkemeyer, Blaine	Missouri (9)	1118
Lujan, Ben R	New Mexico (3)	502
Lummis, Cynthia M	Wyomin (At Large)	1004
Lungren, Daniel E	California (3)	2262
Lynch, Stephen F	Massachusetts (9)	221
McCarthy, Carolyn	New York (4)	2346
McCarthy, Kevin	California (22)	1523
McCaul, Michael T	Texas (10)	131
McClintock, Tom	California (4)	508
McCollum, Betty	Minnesota (4)	1714
McCotter, Thaddeus G	Michigan (11)	1632
McDermott, Jim	Washington (7)	1035
McGovern, James P	Massachusetts (3)	438
McHenry, Patrick T	North Carolina (10)	224
McHugh, John M	New York (23)	2366
McIntyre, Mike	North Carolina (7)	2437
McKeon, Howard P. (Buck)	California (25)	2184
McMahon, Michael E	New York (13)	323
McMorris Rodgers, Cathy	Washington (5)	1323
McNerney, Jerry	California (11)	312
Mack, Connie	Florida (14)	115
Maffei, Daniel B	New York (25)	1630
Maloney, Carolyn B	New York (14)	2331
Manzullo, Donald A	Illinois (16)	2228
Marchant, Kenny	Texas (24)	227
Markey, Betsy	Colorado (4)	1229
Markey, Edward J	Massachusetts (7)	2108
Marshall, Jim	Georgia (8)	504
Massa, Eric J	New York (29)	1208
Matheson, Jim	Utah (2)	2434
Matsui, Doris O	California (5)	222
Meek, Kendrick B	Florida (17)	1039
Meeks, Gregory W	New York (6)	2342
Melancon, Charlie	Louisiana (3)	404
Mica, John L	Florida (7)	2313
Michaud, Michael H	Maine (2)	1724
Miller, Brad	North Carolina (13)	1127
Miller, Candice S	Michigan (10)	228
Miller, Gary G	California (42)	2349
Miller, George	California (7)	2205
Miller, Jeff	Florida (1)	2439

Representatives—Continued

[Democrats in roman (256); Republicans in italic (178); vacancy (1); total, 435]. Members who have resigned appear in bold brackets [ ].

Room numbers with three digits are in the Cannon House Office Building (New Jersey and Independence Avenues), four digits beginning with 1 are in the Longworth House Office Building (between South Capitol Street and New Jersey Avenue on Independence Avenue), and four digits beginning with 2 are in the Rayburn House Office Building (between First and South Capitol Streets on Independence Avenue). Members' offices may be reached by phone at 202–225–3121. The most current listing of House Members can be found on the Internet at http://clerk.house.gov.

Name	State (District)	Room
Minnick, Walt	Idaho (1)	1517
Mitchell, Harry E	Arizona (5)	1410
Mollohan, Alan B	West Virginia (1)	2302
Moore, Dennis	Kansas (3)	1727
Moore, Gwen	Wisconsin (4)	1239
Moran, James P	Virginia (8)	2239
Moran, Jerry	Kansas (1)	2202
Murphy, Christopher S	Connecticut (5)	412
Murphy, Patrick J	Pennsylvania (8)	1609
Murphy, Scott	New York (20)	120
Murphy, Tim	Pennsylvania (18)	322
Murtha, John P	Pennsylvania (12)	2423
Myrick, Sue Wilkins	North Carolina (9)	230
Nadler, Jerrold	New York (8)	2334
Napolitano, Grace F	California (38)	1610
Neal, Richard E	Massachusetts (2)	2208
Neugebauer, Randy	Texas (19)	429
Nunes, Devin	California (21)	1013
Nye, Glenn C., III	Virginia (2)	116
Oberstar, James L	Minnesota (8)	2365
Obey, David R	Wisconsin (7)	2314
Olson, Pete	Texas (22)	514
Olver, John W	Massachusetts (1)	1111
Ortiz, Solomon P	Texas (27)	2110
Pallone, Frank, Jr	New Jersey (6)	237
Pascrell, Bill, Jr	New Jersey (8)	2464
Pastor, Ed	Arizona (4)	2465
Paul, Ron	Texas (14)	203
Paulsen, Erik	Minnesota (3)	126
Payne, Donald M	New Jersey (10)	2310
Pelosi, Nancy	California (8)	235
Pence, Mike	Indiana (6)	1431
Perlmutter, Ed	Colorado (7)	415
Perriello, Tom	Virginia (5)	1520
Peters, Gary	Michigan (9)	1130
Peterson, Collin C	Minnesota (7)	2211
Petri, Thomas E	Wisconsin (6)	2462
Pingree, Chellie	Maine (1)	1037
Pitts, Joseph R	Pennsylvania (16)	420
Platts, Todd Russell	Pennsylvania (19)	2455
Poe, Ted	Texas (2)	430
Polis, Jared	Colorado (2)	501
Pomeroy, Earl	North Dakota (At Large)	1501
Posey, Bill	Florida (15)	132
Price, David E	North Carolina (4)	2162
Price, Tom	Georgia (6)	424
Putnam, Adam H	Florida (12)	442
Quigley, Mike	Illinois (5)	1319
Radanovich, George	California (19)	2410
Rahall, Nick J., II	West Virginia (3)	2307
Rangel, Charles B	New York (15)	2354

Representatives—Continued

[Democrats in roman (256); Republicans in italic (178); vacancy (1); total, 435]. Members who have resigned appear in bold brackets [ ].

Room numbers with three digits are in the Cannon House Office Building (New Jersey and Independence Avenues), four digits beginning with 1 are in the Longworth House Office Building (between South Capitol Street and New Jersey Avenue on Independence Avenue), and four digits beginning with 2 are in the Rayburn House Office Building (between First and South Capitol Streets on Independence Avenue). Members' offices may be reached by phone at 202–225–3121. The most current listing of House Members can be found on the Internet at http://clerk.house.gov.

Name	State (District)	Room
Rehberg, Dennis R	Montana (At Large)	2448
Reichert, David G	Washington (8)	1703
Reyes, Silvestre	Texas (16)	2433
Richardson, Laura	California (37)	1725
Rodriguez, Ciro D	Texas (23)	2351
Roe, Phil	Tennessee (1)	419
Rogers, Harold	Kentucky (5)	2406
Rogers, Mike	Alabama (3)	133
Rogers, Mike	Michigan (8)	324
Rohrabacher, Dana	California (46)	2300
Rooney, Tom	Florida (16)	1529
Roskam, Peter J	Illinois (6)	507
Ros-Lehtinen, Ileana	Florida (18)	2470
Ross, Mike	Arkansas (4)	2436
Rothman, Steven R	New Jersey (9)	2303
Roybal-Allard, Lucille	California (34)	2330
Royce, Edward R	California (40)	2185
Ruppersberger, C.A. (Dutch)	Maryland (2)	2453
Rush, Bobby L	Illinois (1)	2416
Ryan, Paul	Wisconsin (1)	1113
Ryan, Tim	Ohio (17)	1421
Salazar, John T	Colorado (3)	326
Sánchez, Linda T	California (39)	1222
Sanchez, Loretta	California (47)	1114
Sarbanes, John P	Maryland (3)	426
Scalise, Steve	Louisiana (1)	429
Schakowsky, Janice D	Illinois (9)	2367
Schauer, Mark	Michigan (7)	1408
Schiff, Adam B	California (29)	2447
Schmidt, Jean	Ohio (2)	418
Shock, Aaron	Illinois (18)	509
Schrader, Kurt	Oregon (5)	1419
Schwartz, Allyson Y	Pennsylvania (13)	330
Scott, David	Georgia (13)	225
Scott, Robert C. (Bobby)	Virginia (3)	1201
Sensenbrenner, F. James, Jr	Wisconsin (5)	2449
Serrano, José E	New York (16)	2227
Sessions, Pete	Texas (32)	2233
Sestak, Joe	Pennsylvania (7)	1022
Shadegg, John B	Arizona (3)	436
Shea-Porter, Carol	New Hampshire (1)	1330
Sherman, Brad	California (27)	2242
Shimkus, John	Illinois (19)	2452
Shuler, Heath	North Carolina (11)	422
Shuster, Bill	Pennsylvania (9)	204
Simpson, Michael K	Idaho (2)	2312
Sires, Albio	New Jersey (13)	1024
Skelton, Ike	Missouri (4)	2206
Slaughter, Louise McIntosh	New York (28)	2469
Smith, Adam	Washington (9)	2402
Smith, Adrian	Nebraska (3)	503

Representatives—Continued

[Democrats in roman (256); Republicans in italic (178); vacancy (1); total, 435]. Members who have resigned appear in bold brackets [ ].

Room numbers with three digits are in the Cannon House Office Building (New Jersey and Independence Avenues), four digits beginning with 1 are in the Longworth House Office Building (between South Capitol Street and New Jersey Avenue on Independence Avenue), and four digits beginning with 2 are in the Rayburn House Office Building (between First and South Capitol Streets on Independence Avenue). Members' offices may be reached by phone at 202–225–3121. The most current listing of House Members can be found on the Internet at http://clerk.house.gov.

Name	State (District)	Room
Smith, Christopher H	New Jersey (4)	2373
Smith, Lamar	Texas (21)	2409
Snyder, Vic	Arkansas (2)	2210
Souder, Mark E	Indiana (3)	2231
Space, Zachary T	Ohio (18)	315
Speier, Jackie	California (12)	211
Spratt, John M., Jr	South Carolina (5)	1401
Stark, Fortney Pete	California (13)	239
Stearns, Cliff	Florida (6)	2370
Stupak, Bart	Michigan (1)	2268
Sullivan, John	Oklahoma (1)	434
Sutton, Betty	Ohio (13)	1721
Tanner, John S	Tennessee (8)	1226
[Tauscher, Ellen O]	California (10)	2459
Taylor, Gene	Mississippi (4)	2269
Teague, Harry	New Mexico (2)	1007
Terry, Lee	Nebraska (2)	2331
Thompson, Bennie G	Mississippi (2)	2432
Thompson, Glenn W	Pennsylvania (5)	124
Thompson, Mike	California (1)	231
Thornberry, Mac	Texas (13)	2209
Tiahrt, Todd	Kansas (4)	2441
Tiberi, Patrick J	Ohio (12)	113
Tierney, John F	Massachusetts (6)	2238
Titus, Dina	Nevada (3)	319
Tonko, Paul	New York (21)	128
Towns, Edolphus	New York (10)	2232
Tsongas, Niki	Massachusetts (5)	1607
Turner, Michael R	Ohio (3)	1740
Upton, Fred	Michigan (6)	2183
Van Hollen, Chris	Maryland (8)	1707
Velázquez, Nydia M	New York (12)	2466
Visclosky, Peter J	Indiana (1)	2256
Walden, Greg	Oregon (2)	2352
Walz, Timothy J	Minnesota (1)	1722
Wamp, Zach	Tennessee (3)	1436
Wasserman Schultz, Debbie	Florida (20)	118
Waters, Maxine	California (35)	2344
Watson, Diane E	California (33)	2430
Watt, Melvin L	North Carolina (12)	2304
Waxman, Henry A	California (30)	2204
Weiner, Anthony D	New York (9)	2104
Welch, Peter	Vermont (At Large)	1404
Westmoreland, Lynn A	Georgia (3)	1213
Wexler, Robert	Florida (19)	2241
Whitfield, Ed	Kentucky (1)	2411
Wilson, Charles A	Ohio (6)	226
Wilson, Joe	South Carolina (2)	212
Wittman, Rob	Virginia (1)	1318
Wolf, Frank R	Virginia (10)	241
Woolsey, Lynn C	California (6)	2263

Representatives—Continued

[Democrats in roman (256); Republicans in italic (178); vacancy (1); total, 435]. Members who have resigned appear in bold brackets [ ].

Room numbers with three digits are in the Cannon House Office Building (New Jersey and Independence Avenues), four digits beginning with 1 are in the Longworth House Office Building (between South Capitol Street and New Jersey Avenue on Independence Avenue), and four digits beginning with 2 are in the Rayburn House Office Building (between First and South Capitol Streets on Independence Avenue). Members' offices may be reached by phone at 202–225–3121. The most current listing of House Members can be found on the Internet at http://clerk.house.gov.

Name	State (District)	Room
Wu, David	Oregon (1)	2338
Yarmuth, John A	Kentucky (3)	319
Young, C.W. (Bill)	Florida (10)	2407
Young, Don	Alaska (At Large)	2111
Delegates		
BORDALLO, MADELEINE Z	Guam	427
CHRISTENSEN, DONNA M	Virgin Islands	1510
FALEOMAVAEGA, ENI F.H	American Samoa	2422
NORTON, ELEANOR HOLMES	District of Columbia	2136
SABLAN, GREGORIO KILILI CAMACHO	Northern Mariana Islands	423
Resident Commissioner		
PIERLUISI, PEDRO	Puerto Rico	1218

For further information concerning the United States Senate, contact the Secretary of the Senate, The Capitol, Washington, DC 20510. Phone, 202–224–2115. Internet, www.senate.gov. For further information concerning the House of Representatives, contact the Clerk, The Capitol, Washington, DC 20515. Phone, 202–225–7000. Internet, http://clerk.house.gov.

ARCHITECT OF THE CAPITOL

U.S. Capitol Building, Washington, DC 20515
Phone, 202–228–1793. Internet, www.aoc.gov.

ARCHITECT OF THE CAPITOL	STEPHEN T. AYERS, *Acting*
DEPUTY ARCHITECT/CHIEF OPERATING OFFICER	STEPHEN T. AYERS
Special Assistant to the Architect of the Capitol	MICHAEL G. TURNBULL
Director, Planning and Project Management	ANNA FRANZ
Director, Architecture Division	(VACANCY)
Director, Construction Division	MICHAEL FENN
Director of Facilities Planning and Programming	TERRELL EMMONS
Director of Design Services	BRUCE ARTHUR
Director of Congressional and External Relations	MIKE CULVER
Chief Administrative Officer	DAVID FERGUSON
Deputy Chief Administrative Officer	DAN CASSIL
Director, Human Resources Management Division	REBECCA TISCIONE
Director, Equal Employment Opportunity	TERESA BAILEY
Director, Information Resources Management	JAMES GETTER
Curator	BARBARA WOLANIN
Communications Officer	EVA MALECKI
Director, Procurement Division	CYNTHIA BENNETT
Inspector General	CAROL BATES

Director of Safety, Fire, and Environmental Programs	SUSAN ADAMS
Director, Safety and Environmental Division	BURL KELLER
Safety and Occupational Health Manager	CHARLES BOWMAN
Chief Financial Officer	PAULA LETTICE
Budget Officer	LAURI SMITH
Accounting Officer	JEFF REED
Director, Financial Management Systems Division	(VACANCY)
General Counsel	PETER KUSHNER
Chief Operating Officer	STEPHEN T. AYERS
Director, Labor Relations and Collective Bargaining	MARGARET COX
Superintendent, House Office Buildings	FRANK TISCIONE
Superintendent, Senate Office Buildings	ROBIN MOREY
Superintendent, Library of Congress Buildings and Grounds	GREGORY SIMMONS
Superintendent, U.S. Capitol	CARLOS ELIAS
Superintendent, Capitol Grounds	TED BECHTOL
Director, U.S. Botanic Garden	HOLLY H. SHIMIZU
Superintendent, U.S. Supreme Court	JAMES YELLMAN
Director of Utilities, U.S. Capitol Power Plant	MARK WEISS

The Architect of the Capitol is responsible for the care and maintenance of the U.S. Capitol and the buildings and grounds of the Capitol complex. The agency implements construction, renovation, conservation, and landscape improvement projects as authorized by the Congress.

The Architect of the Capitol is charged with operating and maintaining the buildings of the Capitol complex committed to his care by Congress. Permanent authority for the care and maintenance of the Capitol was established by the act of August 15, 1876 (40 U.S.C. 162, 163). The Architect's duties include the mechanical and structural maintenance of the Capitol, the conservation and care of works of art in the building under the Architect's jurisdiction, the upkeep and improvement of the Capitol grounds, and the arrangement of inaugural and other ceremonies held in the building or on the grounds.

In addition to the Capitol, the Architect is responsible for the upkeep of all of the congressional office buildings, the Library of Congress buildings, the U.S. Supreme Court building, the Thurgood Marshall Federal Judiciary Building, the Capitol Power Plant, the Capitol Police headquarters, and the Robert A. Taft Memorial. The Architect performs his duties in connection with

the Senate side of the Capitol and the Senate office buildings subject to the approval of the Senate Committee on Rules and Administration. In matters of general policy in connection with the House office buildings, his activities are subject to the approval and direction of the House Office Building Commission. The Architect is under the direction of the Speaker in matters concerning the House side of the Capitol. He is subject to the oversight of the Committee on House Administration with respect to many administrative matters affecting operations on the House side of the Capitol complex. In addition, the Architect of the Capitol serves as the Acting Director of the U.S. Botanic Garden under the Joint Committee on the Library.

The position of Architect of the Capitol was historically filled by Presidential appointment for an indefinite term. Legislation enacted in 1989 provides that the Architect is to be appointed for a term of 10 years by the President, with the advice and consent of the Senate, from a list of three candidates recommended by a congressional commission. Upon confirmation by the Senate, the Architect becomes an official of the legislative branch as an officer and agent of Congress. He is eligible for reappointment after completion of his term.

Recent and ongoing projects carried out by the Architect of the Capitol include construction of the Capitol Visitor Center; conservation of murals and decorative paintings in the Capitol; improvement of speech-reinforcement, electrical, and fire-protection systems in the Capitol and congressional office buildings; work on security improvements within the Capitol complex; renovation, restoration, and modification of the interiors and exteriors of the Thomas Jefferson and John Adams Buildings of the Library of Congress and provision of off-site book storage facilities for the Library; and facility management of the Thurgood Marshall Federal Judiciary Building.

For further information, contact the Office of the Architect of the Capitol, U.S. Capitol Building, Washington, DC 20515. Phone, 202–228–1793. Internet, www.aoc.gov.

UNITED STATES BOTANIC GARDEN

Office of Executive Director, 245 First Street SW., Washington, DC 20024
Phone, 202–225–6670. Internet, www.usbg.gov.

Conservatory, 100 Maryland Avenue SW., Washington, DC 20001
Phone, 202–226–8333.

Production Facility, 4700 Shepherd Parkway SW., Washington, DC 20032
Phone, 202–226–4780

DIRECTOR (Architect of the Capitol)   STEPHEN T. AYERS, *Acting*
EXECUTIVE DIRECTOR   HOLLY H. SHIMIZU

The United States Botanic Garden informs visitors about the importance and value of plants to the well-being of humankind and earth's ecosystems.

The United States Botanic Garden (USBG) is one of the oldest botanic gardens in North America. The Garden highlights the diversity of plants worldwide, as well as their aesthetic, cultural, economic, therapeutic, and ecological significance. The USBG encourages plant appreciation and the growth of botanical knowledge through artistic plant displays, exhibits, educational programs, and curation of a large collection of plants. It fosters plant conservation by serving as a repository for endangered species. Uniquely situated at the heart of the U.S. Government, the Garden seeks to promote the exchange of ideas and information relevant to its mission among national and international visitors and policymakers.

The Garden's collections include orchids, epiphytes, bromeliads, carnivorous plants, ferns, cycads, cacti, succulents, medicinal plants, rare and endangered plants, and plants valued as sources of food, beverages, fibers, cosmetics, and industrial products.

The U.S. Botanic Garden's facilities include the Conservatory, the National Garden, Bartholdi Park, an administration building, and an off-site production facility. The Conservatory, one of the largest structures of its kind in this country, reopened on December 11, 2001, after undergoing major renovation that required more than 4 years to complete. In addition to upgraded amenities for visitors, it features 12 exhibit and plant display areas.

The National Garden opened on October 1, 2006. Located on three acres adjacent to the west side of the Conservatory, the National Garden comprises a First Ladies Water Garden, a Butterfly Garden, a Rose Garden celebrating our national flower, a Lawn Terrace, a Regional Garden of native Mid-Atlantic plants, and an amphitheater where visitors may relax and enjoy the stunning views of the U.S. Capitol.

Outdoor plantings are also showcased in Bartholdi Park, a home landscape demonstration area located across from the Conservatory. Each of the displays is sized and scaled for suitability in an urban or suburban setting. The gardens display ornamental plants that perform well in this region arrayed in a variety of styles and themes. Also located in this park is Bartholdi Fountain, created by Frédéric Auguste Bartholdi (1834–1904), sculptor of the Statue of Liberty.

The U.S. Botanic Garden's staff is organized into horticulture, operations, administration, and public programs divisions. Programs for the public are listed in a quarterly calendar of events and also on the Garden's Web site. A horticultural hotline and Email address are available to answer questions from the public.

The U.S. Botanic Garden was founded in 1820 under the auspices of the Columbian Institute for the Promotion of Arts and Sciences, an organization that was the outgrowth of an association known as the Metropolitan Society, which received its charter from Congress on April 20, 1818. The Garden continued under the direction of the Institute until 1837, when the Institute ceased to exist as an active organization.

In June 1842, the U.S. Exploring Expedition under the command of Captain Charles Wilkes returned from its 4-year voyage with a wealth of information, artifacts, pressed-plant specimens, and living plants from around the world. The living plants were temporarily placed on exhibit on a lot behind the old Patent Office under the care of William D. Brackenridge, the Expedition's botanist. By November 1842, the plants were moved into a greenhouse built there with funds appropriated by Congress. Subsequently, the greenhouse was expanded with two additions and a small growing area to care for the burgeoning collection. In 1843, stewardship of the collection was placed under the direction and control of the Joint Committee on the Library, which had also assumed responsibility for publication of the results of the Expedition. Expansion of the Patent Office in 1849 necessitated finding a new location for the botanical collections.

The act of May 15, 1850 (9 Stat. 427) provided for the relocation of the Botanic Garden under the direction of the Joint Committee on the Library. The site selected was on the National Mall at the west end of the Capitol Grounds, practically the same site the Garden occupied during the period it functioned under the Columbian Institute. This site was later enlarged, and the main area continued to serve as the principal Garden site from 1850 to 1933, when the Garden was relocated to its present site.

Although the Government had assumed responsibility for the maintenance and stewardship of the plant collection in 1842, the two functions were divided between the Commissioner of Public Buildings and the Joint Committee on the Library, respectively. In 1856, in recognition of their increasing stature, the collections and their associated operations and facilities were officially named the United States Botanic Garden, and the Joint Committee on the Library assumed jurisdiction over both its direction and maintenance (11 Stat. 104). An annual appropriation has been provided by Congress since 1856.

Presently, the Joint Committee on the Library has supervision over the U.S. Botanic Garden through the Architect of the Capitol, who has held the title of Acting Director since 1934.

For further information concerning the United States Botanic Garden, contact the Public Programs Division, 245 First Street SW., Washington, DC 20024. Phone, 202–225–8333. Plant Hotline, 202–226–4785. Internet, www.usbg.gov. Email, usbg@aoc.gov.

GOVERNMENT ACCOUNTABILITY OFFICE

441 G Street NW., Washington, DC 20548
Phone, 202–512–3000. Internet, www.gao.gov.

COMPTROLLER GENERAL OF THE UNITED STATES	GENE L. DODARO, *Acting*
CHIEF OPERATING OFFICER	GENE L. DODARO
Chief Administrative Officer	SALLYANNE HARPER
Deputy Chief Administrative Officer	CHERYL WHITAKER
General Counsel	GARY L. KEPPLINGER
Inspector General	FRANCES GARCIA
Chief Human Capital Officer	CYNTHIA C. HECKMANN
Chief Information Officer	JOSEPH KRAUS
Controller/Administrative Services Office	GEORGE STRADER
Managing Director, Acquisition and Sourcing Management	KATHERINE SCHINASI
Managing Director, Applied Research and Methods	NANCY KINGSBURY
Managing Director, Defense Capabilities and Management	JANET ST. LAURENT
Managing Director, Congressional Relations	RALPH DAWN
Managing Director, Education, Workforce, and Income Security	CYNTHIA M. FAGNONI
Managing Director, Field Offices	DENISE HUNTER
Managing Director, Financial Management and Assurance	JEANETTE M. FRANZEL
Managing Director, Forensic Audits and Special Investigations	GREGORY D. KUTZ
Managing Director, Financial Markets and Community Investments	RICHARD J. HILLMAN
Managing Director, Health Care	MARJORIE KANOFF
Managing Director, Homeland Security and Justice	CATHLEEN BERRICK
Managing Director, International Affairs and Trade	JACQUELYN WILLIAMS-BRIDGERS
Managing Director, Information Technology	JOEL WILLEMSSEN
Managing Director, Knowledge Services	CATHERINE TETI
Managing Director, Natural Resources and Environment	PATRICIA DALTON
Managing Director, Opportunity and Inclusiveness	CAROLYN TAYLOR, *Acting*
Managing Director, Physical Infrastructure	KATHERINE SIGGERUD
Managing Director, Professional Development Program	DAVID CLARK
Managing Director, Public Affairs	CHARLES YOUNG
Managing Director, Quality and Continuous Improvement	TIMOTHY BOWLING
Managing Director, Strategic Issues	J. CHRISTOPHER MIHM

Managing Director, Strategic Planning and   HELEN HSING
    External Liaison

The Government Accountability Office is the investigative arm of the Congress and is charged with examining all matters relating to the receipt and disbursement of public funds.

The Government Accountability Office (GAO) is an independent, nonpartisan Agency that works for Congress. GAO is often called the "congressional watchdog" because it investigates how the Federal Government spends taxpayer dollars. The GAO was established as the General Accounting Office by the Budget Accounting Act of 1921 (31 U.S.C. 702). It was renamed the Government Accountability Office pursuant to the GAO Capital Reform Act of 2004 (31 U.S.C. 702 note).

Activities

GAO gathers information to help Congress determine how effectively executive branch agencies are doing their jobs. GAO's work routinely answers such basic questions as whether Government programs are meeting their objectives or providing good service to the public. Ultimately, GAO ensures that Government is accountable to the American people. To that end, GAO provides Senators and Representatives with the best information available to help them arrive at informed policy decisions—information that is accurate,

timely, and balanced. GAO supports congressional oversight by:
    —evaluating how well Government policies and programs are working;
    —auditing Agency operations to determine whether Federal funds are being spent efficiently, effectively, and appropriately;
    —investigating allegation of illegal and improper activities; and
    —issuing legal decisions and opinions.
    With virtually the entire Federal Government subject to its review, GAO issues a steady stream of products—more than 1,000 reports and hundreds of testimonies by GAO officials each year. GAO's familiar "blue book" reports meet short-term immediate needs for information on a wide range of Government operations. These reports also help Congress better understand issues that are newly emerging, long term in nature, and with more far-reaching impacts. GAO's work translates into a wide variety of legislative actions, improvements in Government operations, and billions of dollars in financial benefits for the American people.

For further information, contact the Office of Public Affairs, Government Accountability Office, 441 G Street NW., Washington, DC 20548. Phone, 202–512–4800. Internet, www.gao.gov.

GOVERNMENT ACCOUNTABILITY OFFICE

INDICATES A SUPPORT OR ADVISORY RELATIONSHIP WITH THE TEAMS/UNITS RATHER THAN A DIRECT REPORTING RELATIONSHIP

EDITORIAL NOTE: The Government Printing Office did not meet the publication deadline for submitting updated information of its activities, functions, and sources of information as required by the automatic disclosure provisions of the Freedom of Information Act (5 U.S.C. 552(a)(1)(A)).

GOVERNMENT PRINTING OFFICE

732 North Capitol Street NW., Washington, DC 20401
Phone, 202–512–0000. Internet, www.gpo.gov.

PUBLIC PRINTER	ROBERT C. TAPELLA
DEPUTY PUBLIC PRINTER AND CHIEF OPERATING OFFICER	PAUL ERICKSON
Chief of Staff	MARIA S. LEFEVRE
Superintendant of Documents	RICHARD G. DAVIS, *Acting*
Chief Management Officer	JANET SANSONE
Chief Technology Officer	REYNOLD SCHWEICKHARDT
Director, Congressional Relations	ANDREW M. SHERMAN
General Counsel	DREW SPALDING, *Acting*
Director, Communcations Office	(VACANCY)
Inspector General	J. ANTHONY OGDEN
Director, Office of Equal Employment Opportunity	NADINE L. ELZY
Director, Quality Assurance	BEN MEYER
Director, Public Relations	(VACANCY)
Managing Director, Library Services and Content Management	RICHARD G. DAVIS
Managing Director, Publication and Information Sales	DAVITA VANCE-COOKS
Managing Director, Official Journals of Government	JAMES C. BRADLEY
Director, Operations Support	MICHAEL BRADY
Managing Director, Plant Operations	OLIVIER A. GIROD
Managing Director, Security and Intelligence Documents	STEPHEN G. LEBLANC
Managing Director, Agency Accounts and Marketing	WILLIAM KURTZ
Managing Director, Print Procurement	RICK GARCIA
Chief Human Capital Officer	WILLIAM T. HARRIS
Chief Acquisition Officer	HERBERT JACKSON
Chief Financial Officer	STEVEN T. SHEDD
Chief Information Officer	MICHAEL WASH
Director, Environmental Services	(VACANCY)
Director, Labor Relations	T. MICHAEL FRAZIER

The Government Printing Office produces, procures, and disseminates printed and electronic publications of the Congress, executive departments, and establishments of the Federal Government.

The Government Printing Office (GPO) opened for business on March 4, 1861. GPO's duties are defined in title 44 of the U.S. Code. The Public Printer, who serves as the head of GPO, is appointed by the President and confirmed by the Senate.

Activities
Headquartered in Washington, DC, with a total employment of approximately 2,500, GPO is responsible for the production and distribution of information products and services for all three branches of the Federal

GOVERNMENT PRINTING OFFICE

PUBLIC PRINTER
CHIEF EXECUTIVE OFFICER

CHIEF MANAGEMENT OFFICER

HUMAN CAPITAL
CHIEF HUMAN CAPITAL OFFICER

ACQUISITIONS
CHIEF ACQUISITION OFFICER

FINANCE AND ADMINISTRATION
CHIEF FINANCIAL OFFICER

INFORMATION TECHNOLOGY AND SYSTEMS
CHIEF INFORMATION OFFICER

DEPUTY PUBLIC PRINTER
CHIEF OPERATING OFFICER

PLANT OPERATIONS
MANAGING DIRECTOR

SECURITY AND INTELLIGENT DOCUMENTS
MANAGING DIRECTOR

CUSTOMER SERVICES
MANAGING DIRECTOR

SUPERINTENDENT OF DOCUMENTS

LIBRARY SERVICES AND CONTENT MANAGEMENT
DIRECTOR

PUBLICATION AND INFORMATION SALES
DIRECTOR

INSPECTOR GENERAL

EQUAL EMPLOYMENT OPPORTUNITY
DIRECTOR

QUALITY ASSURANCE
DIRECTOR

CHIEF OF STAFF

CHIEF TECHNOLOGY OFFICER

CONGRESSIONAL RELATIONS
DIRECTOR

GENERAL COUNSEL

PUBLIC RELATIONS
DIRECTOR

Government. GPO is the Federal Government's primary centralized resource for gathering, cataloging, producing, providing, authenticating, and preserving published information in all its forms. GPO's 1.5-million-square-foot complex is the largest information processing, printing, and distribution facility in the world.

While many of our Nation's most important products, such as the *Congressional Record* and *Federal Register,* are produced at GPO's main plant, the majority of the Government's printing needs are met through a long-standing partnership with America's printing industry. GPO procures between 600 and 1,000 print-related projects a day through private sector vendors across the country, competitively buying products and services from thousands of private sector companies in all 50 States. The contracts cover the entire spectrum of printing and publishing services and are available to fit almost any firm from the largest to the smallest.

GPO disseminates Federal information products through a sales program, distribution network of more than 1,250 Federal libraries nationwide, and via GPO Access. More than 286,000 Federal Government document titles are available to the public at www.gpoaccess.gov.

Printed copies of many documents, ranging from Supreme Court opinions to reports from the Bureau of Labor Statistics, may also be purchased as follows:

—To order in person, please visit the GPO Main Bookstore at 710 North Capitol Street NW., Washington, DC, (corner of North Capitol and H Streets) from 8 a.m. to 4 p.m., eastern standard time.

—To order online, visit the GPO Online Bookstore at http://bookstore.gpo.gov.

—To order by phone or inquire about an order, call 866–512–1800 or, in the Washington, DC, metro area, call 202–512–1800 from 7 a.m. to 9 p.m., eastern standard time.

—To order by fax, dial 202–512–2104.

—To order by email, send inquiries to contactcenter@gpo.gov.

—To order by mail, write to Information Dissemination (Superintendent of Documents), P.O. Box 371954, Pittsburgh, PA 15250–7954.

All orders require prepayment by VISA, MasterCard, American Express, or Discover/NOVUS credit cards, check, or SOD deposit account.

Sources of Information

Congressional Relations Congressional relations matters, phone, 202–512–1991.
Public Relations Public relations inquiries, phone, 202–512–1957. Fax, 202–512–1998.
Contracts Commercial printers interested in Government printing contract opportunities should direct inquiries to Customer Services, Government Printing Office, Washington, DC 20401. Phone, 202–512–0111. Internet, www.gpo.gov/procurement/index.html.
GPO Access User Support Phone, 202–512–1530.

GPO Offices Nationwide

Office	Address	Telephone
Atlanta, GA	Suite 110, 1888 Emery St., 30318	404–605–9160
Charleston, SC	2825 Noisette Blvd., 29405	843–743–2036
Boston, MA	28 Court Square, 02108	617–720–3680
Chicago, IL	Suite 810, 200 N. LaSalle St., 60601	312–353–3916
Columbus, OH	Suite 112–B, 1335 Dublin Rd., 43215	614–488–4616
Dallas, TX	Rm. 731, 1100 Commerce St., 75242	214–767–0451
Oklahoma City, OK	Suite 100, 3420 D Ave., Tinker AFB, OK 73145	405–610–4146
San Antonio, TX	Suite 2, 1531 Connally St., Lackland AFB, TX 78236	210–675–1480
Denver, CO	Rm. D–1010, Bldg. 53, Denver Federal Center, 80225	303–236–5292
Hampton, VA	Suite 400, 11836 Canon Blvd., Newport News, VA 23606	757–873–2800
San Diego, CA	Suite 109, 2221 Camino Del Rio S., 92108	619–497–6050
New York, NY	Rm. 2930, 26 Federal Plaza, 10278	212–264–2252
Philadelphia, PA	Suite A–190, 928 Jaymore Rd., Southampton, PA 18966	215–364–6465
Pittsburgh, PA	Rm. 501, 1000 Liberty Ave., 15222	412–395–6929
RAPID RESPONSE CENTER	GPO Regional Printing Procurement Office, Rm. C825, Stop RRC, 732 North Capitol St. NW., Washington, DC 20401.	202–512–2240
San Francisco, CA	Suite I, 536 Stone Rd., Benicia, CA 94510	707–748–1970
Seattle, WA	4735 E. Marginal Way S., Federal Center South, 98134	206–764–3726

LIBRARY OF CONGRESS

101 Independence Avenue SE., Washington, DC 20540
Phone, 202–707–5000. Internet, www.loc.gov.

The Library of Congress is the national library of the United States, offering diverse materials for research including the world's most extensive collections in many areas such as American history, music, and law.

The Library of Congress was established by act of April 24, 1800 (2 Stat. 56), appropriating $5,000 "for the purchase of such books as may be necessary for the use of Congress . . . ." The Library's scope of responsibility has been widened by subsequent legislation (2 U.S.C. 131–168d). The Librarian, appointed by the President with the advice and consent of the Senate, directs the Library.

The Library's first responsibility is service to Congress. As the Library has developed, its range of service has expanded to include the entire governmental establishment and the public at large, making it a national library for the United States and a global resource through its Web site at www.loc.gov.

Activities

Collections The Library's extensive collections are universal in scope. They

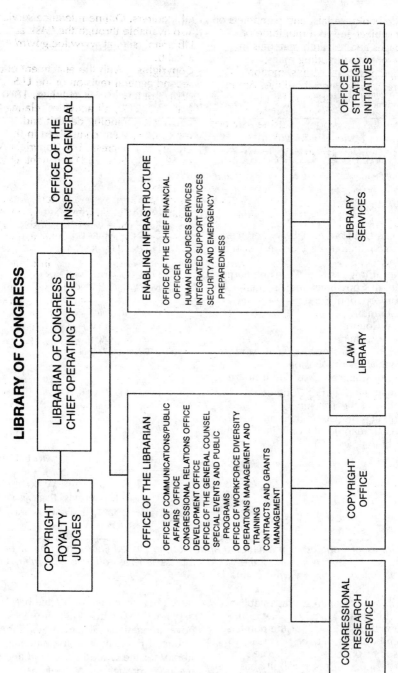

LIBRARY OF CONGRESS

OFFICE OF THE INSPECTOR GENERAL

LIBRARIAN OF CONGRESS CHIEF OPERATING OFFICER

COPYRIGHT ROYALTY JUDGES

ENABLING INFRASTRUCTURE

OFFICE OF THE CHIEF FINANCIAL OFFICER
HUMAN RESOURCES SERVICES
INTEGRATED SUPPORT SERVICES
SECURITY AND EMERGENCY PREPAREDNESS

OFFICE OF THE LIBRARIAN

OFFICE OF COMMUNICATIONS/PUBLIC AFFAIRS OFFICE
CONGRESSIONAL RELATIONS OFFICE
DEVELOPMENT OFFICE
OFFICE OF THE GENERAL COUNSEL
SPECIAL EVENTS AND PUBLIC PROGRAMS
OFFICE OF WORKFORCE DIVERSITY
OPERATIONS MANAGEMENT AND TRAINING
CONTRACTS AND GRANTS MANAGEMENT

CONGRESSIONAL RESEARCH SERVICE

COPYRIGHT OFFICE

LAW LIBRARY

LIBRARY SERVICES

OFFICE OF STRATEGIC INITIATIVES

include books, serials, and pamphlets on every subject and in a multitude of languages and research materials in many formats, including maps, photographs, manuscripts, motion pictures, and sound recordings. Among them are the most comprehensive collections of Chinese, Japanese, and Russian language books outside Asia and the former Soviet Union; volumes relating to science and legal materials outstanding for American and foreign law; the world's largest collection of published aeronautical literature; and the most extensive collection in the Western Hemisphere of books printed before 1501 A.D.

The manuscript collections relate to manifold aspects of American history and civilization and include the personal papers of most of the Presidents from George Washington through Calvin Coolidge. The music collections contain volumes and pieces—manuscript and published—from classic works to the newest popular compositions. Other materials available for research include maps and views; photographic records from the daguerreotype to the latest news photo; recordings, including folksongs and other music, speeches, and poetry readings; prints, drawings, and posters; government documents, newspapers, and periodicals from all over the world; and motion pictures, microforms, audio and video tapes, and digital products.

Reference Resources   Admission to the various research facilities of the Library is free. No introduction or credentials are required for persons over high school age. Readers must register by presenting valid photo identification with a current address, and for certain collections there are additional requirements. As demands for service to Congress and Federal Government agencies increase, reference service available through correspondence has become limited. The Library must decline some requests and refer correspondents to a library within their area that can provide satisfactory assistance. While priority is given to inquiries pertaining to its holdings of special materials or to subjects in which its resources are unique, the Library does attempt to provide helpful responses to all inquirers. Online reference service is also available through the ''Ask a Librarian'' site, at www.loc.gov/rr/askalib.

Copyrights   With the enactment of the second general revision of the U.S. copyright law by Act of July 8, 1870 (16 Stat. 212–217), all activities relating to copyright, including deposit and registration, were centralized in the Library of Congress. The Copyright Act of 1976 (90 Stat. 2541) brought all forms of copyrightable authorship, both published and unpublished, under a single statutory system which gives authors protection immediately upon creation of their works. Exclusive rights granted to authors under the statute include the right to reproduce and prepare derivative works, distribute copies or phonorecords, perform and display the work publicly, and in the case of sound recordings, to perform the work publicly by means of a digital audio transmission. Works eligible for copyright include literary works (books and periodicals), musical works, dramatic works, pantomimes and choreographic works, pictorial, graphic, and sculptural works, motion pictures, sound recordings, vessel hull designs, mask works, and architectural works. Serving in its capacity as a national registry for creative works, the Copyright Office registers more than 500,000 claims to copyright annually (representing more than 800,000 works) and is a major source of acquisitions for the universal collections of the Library of Congress. Most of the information available on paper is also accessible online, at www.loc.gov/copyright.

Extension of Service   The Library extends its service through the following:
  —an interlibrary loan system;
  —the photoduplication, at reasonable cost, of books, manuscripts, maps, newspapers, and prints in its collections;
  —the sale of sound recordings, which are released by its Recording Laboratory;
  —the exchange of duplicates with other institutions;
  —the sale of CD–ROM cataloging tools and magnetic tapes and the publication in book format or microform of cumulative catalogs, which make available the results of the expert

bibliographical and cataloging work of its technical personnel;

—a centralized cataloging program whereby the Library of Congress acquires material published all over the world, catalogs it promptly, and distributes cataloging information in machine-readable form and other means to the Nation's libraries;

—a cooperative cataloging program whereby the cataloging of data, by name authority and bibliographic records, prepared by other libraries becomes part of the Library of Congress database and is distributed through the Cataloging Distribution Service;

—a cataloging-in-publication program in cooperation with American publishers for printing cataloging information in current books;

—the National Serials Data Program, a national center that maintains a record of serial titles to which International Standard Serial Numbers have been assigned and serves, with this file, as the United States Register; and

—the development of general schemes of classification (Library of Congress and Dewey Decimal), subject headings, and cataloging, embracing the entire field of printed matter.

Furthermore, the Library provides for the following:

—the preparation of bibliographical lists responsive to the needs of Government and research;

—the maintenance and the publication of cooperative publications;

—the publication of catalogs, bibliographical guides, and lists, and of texts of original manuscripts and rare books in the Library of Congress;

—the circulation in traveling exhibitions of items from the Library's collections;

—the provision of books in braille, electronic access to braille books on the Internet, "talking books," and books on tape for the blind and the physically handicapped through 134 cooperating libraries throughout the Nation;

—the distribution of its electronic materials via the Internet; and

—the provision of research and analytical services on a fee-for-service basis to agencies in the executive and judicial branches.

Congressional Research Service The Congressional Research Service (CRS) provides confidential and nonpartisan policy analysis exclusively to the United States Congress. CRS assists Congress in the legislative process by identifying and clarifying current policy problems, exploring potential implications of proposed policies, monitoring and assessing program implementation and oversight, and helping congressional staff understand legislative procedures and processes.

For further information, call 202–707–5700.

American Folklife Center The Center was established in the Library of Congress by Act of January 2, 1976 (20 U.S.C. 2102 et seq.). It supports, preserves, and presents American folklife by receiving and maintaining folklife collections, scholarly research, field projects, performances, exhibitions, festivals, workshops, publications, and audiovisual presentations. The Center has conducted projects in many locations across the country, such as the ethnic communities of Chicago, IL; southern Georgia; a ranching community in northern Nevada; the Blue Ridge Parkway in southern Virginia and northern North Carolina; and the States of New Jersey, Rhode Island, and Montana. The projects have provided large collections of recordings and photographs for the Archive of Folk Culture. The Center administers the Federal Cylinder Project, which is charged with preserving and disseminating music and oral traditions recorded on wax cylinders dating from the late 1800s to the early 1940s. A cultural conservation study was developed at the Center, in cooperation with the Department of the Interior, pursuant to a congressional mandate. Various conferences, workshops, and symposia are given throughout the year.

The American Folklife Center maintains and administers the Archive of Folk Culture, an extensive collection of ethnographic materials from this country and around the world. It is the national repository for folk-related recordings, manuscripts, and other unpublished materials. The Center administers the Veterans History Project, which records and preserves the first-person accounts of war veterans. It also participates in Storycorps, a program to record and collect oral histories from people from all walks of life. This collection also resides in the American Folklife Center. The Center's reading room contains over 3,500 books and periodicals; a sizable collection of magazines, newsletters, unpublished theses, and dissertations; field notes; and many textual and some musical transcriptions and recordings.

The *Folklife Center News,* a quarterly newsletter, and other informational publications are available upon request. Many Center publications and a number of collections are available online through the Internet, at www.loc.gov/folklife.

For further information, call 202–707–5510.

Center for the Book   The Center was established in the Library of Congress by an act of October 13, 1977 (2 U.S.C. 171 *et seq.*), to stimulate public interest in books, reading, and libraries, and to encourage the study of books and print culture. The Center is a catalyst for promoting and exploring the vital role of books, reading, and libraries, nationally and internationally. As a partnership between the Government and the private sector, the Center for the Book depends on tax-deductible contributions from individuals and corporations to support its programs.

The Center's activities are directed toward the general public and scholars. The overall program includes reading promotion projects with television and radio networks, symposia, lectures, exhibitions, special events, and publications. More than 90 national educational and civic organizations participate in the Center's annual reading promotion campaign.

All 50 States and the District of Columbia have established statewide book centers that are affiliated with the Center for the Book in the Library of Congress. State centers plan and fund their own projects, involving members of the State's "community of the book," including authors, readers, prominent citizens, and public officials who serve as honorary advisers.

For further information, contact the Center for the Book. Phone, 202–707–5221. Fax, 202–707–0269. Email, cfbook@loc.gov.

National Film Preservation Board   The National Film Preservation Board, established by the National Film Preservation Act of 1992 (2 U.S.C. 179) and reauthorized by the National Film Preservation Act of 2005 (2 U.S.C. 179n), serves as a public advisory group to the Librarian of Congress. The Board works to ensure the survival, conservation, and increased public availability of America's film heritage, including advising the Librarian on the annual selection of films to the National Film Registry and counseling the Librarian on development and implementation of the national film preservation plan. Key publications are *Film Preservation 1993: A Study of the Current State of American Film Preservation, Redefining Film Preservation: A National Plan,* and *Television and Video Preservation 1997: A Study of the Current State of American Television and Video Preservation.*

For further information, call 202–707–5912.

National Sound Recording Preservation Board   The National Sound Recording Preservation Board, established by the National Recording Preservation Act of 2000 (2 U.S.C. 1701 note), includes three major components: a National Recording Preservation Advisory Board, which brings together experts in the field, a National Recording Registry, and a fundraising foundation, all of which are conducted under the auspices of the Library of Congress. The purpose of the Board is to create and implement a national plan for the long-term preservation and accessibility of the Nation's audio heritage. It also advises the Librarian on the selection of culturally, aesthetically, or historically significant sound recordings to be included on the National Recording Registry. The national recording preservation program will set standards for future private and public preservation efforts and will be conducted in conjunction with the Library's Packard Campus for Audio-Visual Conservation in Culpeper, VA.

For further information, call 202–707–5856.

Preservation   The Library provides technical information related to the preservation of library and archival material. A series of handouts on various preservation and conservation topics has been prepared by the Preservation Office. Information and publications are available from the Office of the Director for Preservation, Library of Congress, Washington, DC 20540–4500. Phone, 202–707–1840.

Sources of Information

Books for the Blind and Physically Handicapped   Talking and braille books and magazines are distributed through 134 regional and subregional libraries to blind and physically handicapped residents of the United States and its territories. Qualified users can also register for Web-Braille, an Internet-based service. Information is available at public libraries throughout the United States and from the headquarters office, National Library Service for the Blind and Physically Handicapped, Library of Congress, 1291 Taylor Street NW., Washington, DC 20542–4960. Phone, 202–707–5100.

Cataloging Data Distribution Cataloging and bibliographic information in the form of microfiche catalogs, book catalogs, magnetic tapes, CD–ROM cataloging tools, bibliographies, and other technical publications is distributed to libraries and other institutions. Information about ordering materials is available from the Cataloging Distribution Service, Library of Congress, Washington, DC 20541–4910. Phone, 202–707–6100. TDD, 202–707–0012. Fax, 202–707–1334. Email, cdsinfo@mail.loc.gov.

Library of Congress card numbers for new publications are assigned by the Cataloging in Publication Division. Direct inquiries to CIP Division, Library of Congress, Washington, DC 20540–4320. Phone, 202–707–6372.

Contracts   Persons seeking information about conducting business with the Library of Congress should visit the Library's Web site at www.loc.gov/about/business.

Copyright Services   Information about the copyright law (title 17 of the U.S. Code), the method of securing copyright, and copyright registration procedures may be obtained by writing to the Copyright Office, Library of Congress, 101 Independence Avenue SE., Washington, DC 20559–6000. Phone, 202–707–3000. Copyright information is also available through the Internet at www.loc.gov/copyright. Registration application forms may be ordered by calling the forms hotline at 202–707–9100. Copyright records may be researched and reported by the Copyright Office for a fee; for an estimate, call 202–707–6850. Members of the public may use the copyright card catalog in the Copyright Office without charge. The database of Copyright Office records cataloged from January 1, 1978, to the present is available through the Internet at www.loc.gov/copyright/rb.html. The Copyright Information Office is located in Room LM–401, James Madison Memorial Building, 101 Independence Avenue SE., Washington, DC 20559–6000. It is open to the public Monday through Friday, 8:30 a.m. to 5 p.m., except for Federal holidays.

Employment   Employment inquiries should be directed to Human Resources Services, Library of Congress, 101 Independence Avenue SE., Washington, DC 20540–2200. Vacancy announcements and applications are also available from the Employment Office, Room LM–107, 101 Independence Avenue SE. Phone, 202–707–4315. Internet, www.loc.gov/hr/employment.

Photoduplication Service   Copies of manuscripts, prints, photographs, maps, and book material not subject to copyright and other restrictions are available for a fee. Order forms for photo reproduction and price schedules are available from the Photoduplication Service, Library of Congress, 101 Independence Avenue SE., Washington,

DC 20540–4570. Phone, 202–707–5640.

Exhibitions Throughout the year, the Library offers free exhibitions featuring items from its collections. The new interactive Library of Congress Experience may be viewed Monday through Saturday, 10 a.m. to 5 p.m., in the Thomas Jefferson Building. This exhibit may be accessed online at www.myloc.gov. For more information, call 202–707–4604. To view current and past exhibitions, go to www.loc.gov/exhibits.

Publications Library of Congress publications are available through the Internet at www.loc.gov/shop. A monthly calendar of events listing programs and exhibitions at the Library of Congress, can be mailed regularly to persons within 100 miles of Washington, DC. It is also available online at www.loc.gov/loc/events. Send requests to Office Systems Services, Mail and Distribution Management Section, Library of Congress, 101 Independence Avenue SE., Washington, DC 20540–9441.

Reference and Bibliographic Services Guidance is offered to readers in identifying and using the material in the Library's collections, and reference service is provided to those with inquiries who have exhausted local, State, and regional resources. Persons requiring services that cannot be performed by the Library staff can be supplied with names of private researchers who work on a fee-for-service basis. Requests for information should be directed to the Reference Referral Service, Library of Congress, 101 Independence Avenue SE.,

Washington, DC 20540–4720. Phone, 202–707–5522. Fax, 202–707–1389.

Research and Reference Services in Science and Technology Reference specialists in the Science, Technology, and Business Division provide a free service in answering brief technical inquiries entailing a bibliographic response. Requests for reference services should be directed to the Science, Technology, and Business Division, Library of Congress, Science Reference Section, 101 Independence Avenue SE., Washington, DC 20540–4750. Phone, 202–707–5639. Internet, www.loc.gov/rr/scitech.

Research Services in General Topics Federal Government agencies can procure directed research and analytical products on foreign and domestic topics using the collections of the Library of Congress through the Federal Research Division. Science, technology, humanities, and social science topics of research are conducted by staff specialists exclusively on behalf of Federal agencies on a fee-for-service basis. Requests for service should be directed to the Federal Research Division, Marketing Office, Library of Congress, Washington, DC 20540–4840. Phone, 202–707–3909. Fax, 202–245–3920.

Visiting the Library of Congress Guided tours of the Library are offered to the public Monday through Friday at 10:30 and 11:30 a.m. and 1:30, 2:30, and 3:30 p.m. and on Saturday at 10:30 and 11:30 a.m. and 1:30 and 2:30 p.m. For more information about scheduling tours for groups of 10 or more, contact the Visitor Services Office at 202–707–0919.

For further information, contact the Public Affairs Office, Library of Congress, 101 Independence Avenue SE., Washington, DC 20540–8610. Phone, 202–707–2905. Fax, 202–707–9199. Email, pao@loc.gov. Internet, www.loc.gov.

CONGRESSIONAL BUDGET OFFICE

Second and D Streets SW., Washington, DC 20515
Phone, 202–226–2600. Internet, www.cbo.gov.

DIRECTOR	DOUGLASS W. ELMENDORF
DEPUTY DIRECTOR	ROBERT A. SUNSHINE
Associate Director for Legislative Affairs	EDWARD DAVIS
General Counsel	MARK P. HADLEY
Assistant Director for Management, Business, and Information Services	RODERICK GOODWIN
Associate Director for Communications	MELISSA MERSON
Assistant Director for Budget Analysis	PETE FONTAINE
Assistant Director for Health and Human Resources	BRUCE VAVRICHEK
Assistant Director for Macroeconomic Analysis	ROBERT A. DENNIS
Assistant Director for Microeconomic Studies	JOSEPH KILE
Assistant Director for National Security	J. MICHAEL GILMORE
Assistant Director for Tax Analysis	FRANK SAMMARTINO, *Acting*

The Congressional Budget Office provides the Congress with economic analyses of alternative fiscal, budgetary, and programmatic policy issues, and with information and estimates required for the congressional budget process.

The Congressional Budget Office (CBO) was established by the Congressional Budget Act of 1974 (2 U.S.C. 601), which also created a procedure by which the United States Congress considers and acts upon the annual Federal budget. This process enables the Congress to have an overview of the Federal budget and to make overall decisions regarding spending and taxing levels and the deficit or surplus these levels incur.

Activities

Economic Forecasting and Fiscal Policy Analysis The Federal budget affects and is affected by the national economy. The Congressional Budget Office provides the Congress with biannual forecasts of the economy and analyses of economic trends and alternative fiscal policies.

Scorekeeping Under the budget process, the Congress establishes (by concurrent resolution), targets for overall expenditures, budget authority and budget outlays, and broad functional categories. The Congress also establishes targets for the levels of revenues, the deficit or surplus, and the public debt. The Office "keeps score" for the Congress by monitoring the results of

congressional action on individual authorization, appropriation, and revenue bills against the targets specified in the concurrent resolution.

Cost Projections The Office prepares multiyear cost estimates for carrying out any public bill or resolution reported by congressional committees. As soon as practicable after the beginning of each fiscal year, CBO also provides multiyear projections on the costs of continuing current Federal spending and taxation policies.

Annual Report on the Budget The Office is responsible for submitting to the House and Senate Budget Committees each year a report on fiscal policy that includes alternative spending and revenue levels and baseline projections of the Federal budget.

Federal Mandates To better assess the impact of laws on State, local, and tribal governments and the private sector, the Congress passed the Unfunded Mandates Reform Act of 1995. The act amends the Congressional Budget Act to require CBO to give authorizing committees a statement about whether reported bills contain Federal mandates. If the 5-year direct costs of an intergovernmental or private-sector mandate exceed specified

CONGRESSIONAL BUDGET OFFICE

DIRECTOR

DEPUTY DIRECTOR

ASSOCIATE DIRECTOR FOR LEGISLATIVE AFFAIRS

GENERAL COUNSEL

ASSOCIATE DIRECTOR COMMUNICATIONS

ASSISTANT DIRECTOR MANAGEMENT, BUSINESS, AND INFORMATION SERVICES

ASSISTANT DIRECTOR MACROECONOMIC ANALYSIS

ASSISTANT DIRECTOR TAX ANALYSIS

ASSISTANT DIRECTOR BUDGET ANALYSIS

ASSISTANT DIRECTOR MICROECONOMIC STUDIES

ASSISTANT DIRECTOR HEALTH AND HUMAN RESOURCES

ASSISTANT DIRECTOR NATIONAL SECURITY

thresholds, CBO must provide an estimate of those costs (if feasible) and the basis of the estimate.

Budget-Related Studies The Office undertakes studies requested by the Congress on budget-related areas. This service is provided to the House and Senate Budget Committees, House and Senate Appropriations Committees, Senate Finance Committee, House Ways and Means Committee, and all other congressional committees.

For further information, contact the Management, Business, and Information Services Division, Congressional Budget Office, Second and D Streets SW., Washington, DC 20515. Phone, 202–226–2600. Fax, 202–226–2714. Internet, www.cbo.gov.

Judicial Branch

JUDICIAL BRANCH

THE SUPREME COURT OF THE UNITED STATES

United States Supreme Court Building
One First Street NE., Washington, DC 20543
Phone, 202–479–3000. Internet, www.supremecourtus.gov.

Members:

CHIEF JUSTICE OF THE UNITED STATES	JOHN G. ROBERTS, JR.
ASSOCIATE JUSTICES	JOHN PAUL STEVENS, ANTONIN SCALIA, ANTHONY M. KENNEDY, CLARENCE THOMAS, RUTH BADER GINSBURG, STEPHEN G. BREYER, SAMUEL A. ALITO, JR., SONIA SOTOMAYOR

Officers:

Counselor to the Chief Justice	JEFFREY P. MINEAR
Clerk	WILLIAM K. SUTER
Court Counsel	SCOTT S. HARRIS
Curator	CATHERINE E. FITTS
Director of Data Systems	DONNA CLEMENT
Librarian	JUDITH GASKELL
Marshal	PAMELA TALKIN
Public Information Officer	KATHLEEN L. ARBERG
Reporter of Decisions	FRANK D. WAGNER

Article III, section 1, of the Constitution of the United States provides that "[t]he judicial Power of the United States, shall be vested in one supreme Court, and in such inferior Courts as the Congress may from time to time ordain and establish."

The Supreme Court of the United States was created in accordance with this provision and by authority of the Judiciary Act of September 24, 1789 (1 Stat. 73). It was organized on February 2, 1790. Article III, section 2 of the Constitution defines the jurisdiction of the Supreme Court.

The Supreme Court is comprised of the Chief Justice of the United States and such number of Associate Justices as may be fixed by Congress, which is currently fixed at eight (28 U.S.C. 1). The President nominates the Justices with the advice and consent of the Senate. Article III, section 1, of the Constitution further provides that "[t]he Judges, both of the supreme and inferior Courts, shall hold their Offices during good Behaviour, and shall, at stated Times, receive for their Services, a Compensation, which shall not be diminished during their Continuance in Office."

Court officers assist the Court in the performance of its functions. They include the Administrative Assistant to the Chief Justice, the Clerk, the Reporter

65

of Decisions, the Librarian, the Marshal, the Director of Budget and Personnel, the Court Counsel, the Curator, the Director of Data Systems, and the Public Information Officer.

Appellate Jurisdiction   Appellate jurisdiction has been conferred upon the Supreme Court by various statutes under the authority given Congress by the Constitution. The basic statute effective at this time in conferring and controlling jurisdiction of the Supreme Court may be found in 28 U.S.C. 1251, 1253, 1254, 1257–1259, and various special statutes. Congress has no authority to change the original jurisdiction of this Court.

Rulemaking Power   Congress has from time to time conferred upon the Supreme Court power to prescribe rules of procedure to be followed by the lower courts of the United States.

Court Term   The term of the Court begins on the first Monday in October and lasts until the first Monday in October of the next year. Approximately 8,000 cases are filed with the Court in the course of a term, and some 1,000 applications of various kinds are filed each year that can be acted upon by a single Justice.

Access to Facilities   The Supreme Court is open to the public from 9 a.m. to 4:30 p.m., Monday through Friday, except on Federal holidays. Unless the Court or Chief Justice orders otherwise, the Clerk's office is open from 9 a.m. to 5 p.m., Monday through Friday, except on Federal legal holidays. The library is open to members of the bar of the Court, attorneys for the various Federal departments and agencies, and Members of Congress.

For further information concerning the Supreme Court, contact the Public Information Office, United States Supreme Court Building, One First Street NE., Washington, DC 20543. Phone, 202–479–3211. Internet, www.supremecourtus.gov.

Lower Courts

Article III of the Constitution declares, in section 1, that the judicial power of the United States shall be invested in one Supreme Court and in "such inferior Courts as the Congress may from time to time ordain and establish." The Supreme Court has held that these constitutional courts ". . . share in the exercise of the judicial power defined in that section, can be invested with no other jurisdiction, and have judges who hold office during good behavior, with no power in Congress to provide otherwise."

United States Courts of Appeals   The courts of appeals are intermediate appellate courts created by act of March 3, 1891 (28 U.S.C. ch. 3), to relieve the Supreme Court of considering all appeals in cases originally decided by the Federal trial courts. They are empowered to review all final decisions and certain interlocutory decisions (18 U.S.C. 3731; 28 U.S.C. 1291, 1292) of district courts.

They also are empowered to review and enforce orders of many Federal administrative bodies. The decisions of the courts of appeals are final except as they are subject to review on writ of certiorari by the Supreme Court.

The United States is divided geographically into 12 judicial circuits, including the District of Columbia. Each circuit has a court of appeals (28 U.S.C. 41, 1294). Each of the 50 States is assigned to one of the circuits. The territories and the Commonwealth of Puerto Rico are assigned variously to the first, third, and ninth circuits. There is also a Court of Appeals for the Federal Circuit, which has nationwide jurisdiction defined by subject matter. At present each court of appeals has from 6 to 28 permanent circuit judgeships (179 in all), depending upon the amount of judicial work in the circuit. Circuit judges hold their offices during good behavior as provided by Article III, section 1, of the Constitution. The judge senior in commission who is under 70 years of age (65 at inception of term), has been in office at least 1 year, and has not previously been chief judge, serves as the chief judge of the circuit for a 7-year term. One of the justices of the Supreme Court is assigned as circuit justice for each of the 13 judicial circuits. Each court of appeals normally hears cases in panels consisting of three judges but may sit *en banc* with all judges present.

The judges of each circuit (except the Federal Circuit) by vote determine the size of the judicial council for the circuit, which consists of the chief judge and an equal number of circuit and district judges. The council considers the state of Federal judicial business in the circuit and may "make all necessary and appropriate orders for [its] effective and expeditious administration . . ." (28 U.S.C. 332). The chief judge of each circuit may summon periodically a judicial conference of all judges of the circuit, including members of the bar, to discuss the business of the Federal courts of the circuit (28 U.S.C. 333). The chief judge of each circuit and a district judge elected from each of the 12 geographical circuits, together with the chief judge of the Court of International Trade, serve as members of the Judicial Conference of the United States, over which the Chief Justice of the United States presides. This is the governing body for the administration of the Federal judicial system as a whole (28 U.S.C. 331).
United States Court of Appeals for the Federal Circuit This court was

established under Article III of the Constitution pursuant to the Federal Courts Improvement Act of 1982 (28 U.S.C. 41, 44, 48), as successor to the former United States Court of Customs and Patent Appeals and the United States Court of Claims. The jurisdiction of the court is nationwide (as provided by 28 U.S.C. 1295) and includes appeals from the district courts in patent cases; appeals from the district courts in contract, and certain other civil actions in which the United States is a defendant; and appeals from final decisions of the U.S. Court of International Trade, the U.S. Court of Federal Claims, and the U.S. Court of Appeals for Veterans Claims. The jurisdiction of the court also includes the review of administrative rulings by the Patent and Trademark Office, U.S. International Trade Commission, Secretary of Commerce, agency boards of contract appeals, and the Merit Systems Protection Board, as well as rulemaking of the Department of Veterans Affairs; review of decisions of the U.S. Senate Select Committee on Ethics concerning discrimination claims of Senate employees; and review of a final order of an entity to be designated by the President concerning discrimination claims of Presidential appointees.

The court consists of 12 circuit judges. It sits in panels of three or more on each case and may also hear or rehear a case *en banc.* The court sits principally in Washington, DC, and may hold court wherever any court of appeals sits (28 U.S.C. 48).

Judicial Circuits—United States Courts of Appeals

Circuit	Judges	Official Station
	District of Columbia Circuit (11)	
(*Clerk*: Mark J. Langer; *Circuit Executive*: Elizabeth H. Paret; Washington, DC)	*Circuit Justice* Chief Justice John G. Roberts, Jr.	
	Circuit Judges	
	David Bryan Sentelle, *Chief Judge*	Washington, DC
	Douglas H. Ginsburg	Washington, DC
	Karen LeCraft Henderson	Washington, DC
	Judith W. Rogers	Washington, DC
	David S. Tatel	Washington, DC
	Merrick B. Garland	Washington, DC
	Janice Rogers Brown	Washington, DC
	Thomas B. Griffith	Washington, DC
	Brett M. Kavanaugh	Washington, DC

Judicial Circuits—United States Courts of Appeals—Continued

Circuit	Judges	Official Station
	(2 vacancies)	

First Circuit (6)

Districts of Maine, New Hampshire, Massachusetts, Rhode Island, and Puerto Rico (*Clerk:* Richard C. Donovan; *Circuit Executive:* Gary Wente;	*Circuit Justice* Justice Stephen G. Breyer	
	Circuit Judges	
	Sandra L. Lynch, *Chief Judge*	Boston, MA
	Juan R. Torruella	San Juan, PR
	Michael Boudin,	Boston, MA
	Kermit V. Lipez	Portland, ME
	Jeffrey R. Howard	Concord, NH
	(vacancy)	

Second Circuit (13)

Districts of Vermont, Connecticut, northern New York, southern New York, eastern New York, and western New York (*Clerk:* Catherine O'Hagan Wolfe; *Circuit Executive:* Karen Greve Milton; New York, NY)	*Circuit Justice* Justice Ruth Bader Ginsburg	
	Circuit Judges	
	Dennis G. Jacobs, *Chief Judge*	New York, NY
	Jose A. Cabranes	New Haven, CT
	Rosemary S. Pooler	Syracuse, NY
	Robert A. Katzmann	New York, NY
	Barrington D. Parker, Jr.	New York, NY
	Reena Raggi	Brooklyn, NY
	Richard C. Wesley	Geneseo, NY
	Peter W. Hall	Rutland, VT
	Debra Ann Livingston	New York, NY
	(4 vacancies)	

Third Circuit (14)

Districts of New Jersey, eastern Pennsylvania, middle Pennsylvania, western Pennsylvania, Delaware, and the Virgin Islands (*Clerk:* Marcia M. Waldron; *Circuit Executive:* Toby D. Slawsky; Philadelphia, PA)	*Circuit Justice* Justice Samuel A. Alito, Jr.	
	Circuit Judges	
	Anthony J. Scirica, *Chief Judge*	Philadelphia, PA
	Dolores Korman Sloviter	Philadelphia, PA
	Theodore A. McKee	Philadelphia, PA
	Marjorie O. Rendell	Philadelphia, PA
	Maryanne Trump Barry	Newark, NJ
	Thomas L. Ambro	Wilmington, DE
	Julio M. Fuentes	Newark, NJ
	D. Brooks Smith	Duncansville, PA
	D. Michael Fisher	Pittsburg, PA
	Michael A. Chagares	Newark, NJ
	Kent A. Jordan	Wilmington, DE
	Thomas M. Hardiman	Pittsburgh, PA
	(2 vacancies)	

Fourth Circuit (15)

Districts of Maryland, northern West Virginia, southern West Virginia, eastern Virginia, western Virginia, eastern North Carolina, western North Carolina, middle North Carolina, and South Carolina (*Clerk:* Patricia S. Connor; *Circuit Executive:* Samuel W. Phillips; Richmond, VA)	*Circuit Justice* Chief Justice John G. Roberts, Jr.	
	Circuit Judges	
	William B. Traxler, Jr., *Chief Judge*	Greenville, SC
	James Harvie Wilkinson III	Charlottesville, VA
	Paul V. Niemeyer	Baltimore, MD
	M. Blane Michael	Charleston, WV
	Diana Gribbon Motz	Baltimore, MD
	Robert B King	Charleston, WV
	Roger L Gregory	Richmond, VA
	Dennis W. Shedd	Columbia, SC
	Allyson K. Duncan	Raleigh, NC
	G. Steven Agee	Salem, VA
	(5 vacancies)	

Judicial Circuits—United States Courts of Appeals—Continued

Circuit	Judges	Official Station
	Fifth Circuit (17)	
Districts of northern Mississippi, southern Mississippi, eastern Louisiana, middle Louisiana, western Louisiana, northern Texas, southern Texas, eastern Texas, and western Texas (*Clerk*: Charles R. Fulbruge III; *Circuit Executive*: Gregory A. Nussel; New Orleans, LA)	*Circuit Justice* Justice Antonin Scalia *Circuit Judges* Edith Hollan Jones, *Chief Judge* Carolyn Dineen King E. Grady Jolly W. Eugene Davis Jerry Edwin Smith Jacques L. Wiener, Jr. Emilio M. Garza Fortunado P. Benavides Carl E. Stewart James L. Dennis Edith Brown Clement Edward C. Prado Priscilla Richman Owen Jennifer Walker Elrod Leslie H. Southwick Catharina Haynes (vacancy)	Houston, TX Houston, TX Jackson, MS Lafayette, LA Houston, TX New Orleans, LA San Antonio, TX Austin, TX Shreveport, LA New Orleans, LA New Orleans, LA San Antonio, TX Austin, TX Houston, TX Jackson, MS Dallas, TX
	Sixth Circuit (16)	
Districts of northern Ohio, southern Ohio, eastern Michigan, western Michigan, eastern Kentucky, western Kentucky, eastern Tennessee, middle Tennessee, and western Tennessee (*Clerk*: Leonard Green; *Circuit Executive*: Clarence G. Maddox II; Cincinnati, OH)	*Circuit Justice* Justice John Paul Stevens *Circuit Judges* Danny J. Boggs, *Chief Judge* Boyce F. Martin, Jr. Alice M. Batchelder Karen Nelson Moore Ransey Guy Cole, Jr. Eric L. Clay Ronald Lee Gilman Julia Smith Gibbons John M. Rogers Jeffrey S. Sutton Deborah L. Cook David W. McKeague Richard A. Griffin Raymond M. Kethledge Helene N. White (vacancy)	Louisville, KY Louisville, KY Medina, OH Cleveland, OH Columbus, OH Detroit, MI Memphis, TN Memphis, TN Lexington, KY Columbus, OH Akron, OH Lansing, MI Traverse City, MI Detroit, MI Detroit, MI
	Seventh Circuit (11)	
Districts of northern Indiana, southern Indiana, northern Illinois, central Illinois, southern Illinois, eastern Wisconsin, and western Wisconsin (*Clerk*: Gino J. Agnello; *Circuit Executive*: Collins T. Fitzpatrick; Chicago, IL)	*Circuit Justice* Justice John Paul Stevens *Circuit Judges* Frank H. Easterbrook, *Chief Judge* Richard A. Posner Joel M. Flaum Michael S. Kanne Ilana Diamond Rovner Diane P. Wood Terence T. Evans Ann C. Williams Diane S. Sykes John Daniel Tinder (vacancy)	Chicago, IL Chicago, IL Chicago, IL Lafayette, IN Chicago, IL Chicago, IL Milwaukee, WI Chicago, IL Milwaukee, WI Indianapolis, IN
	Eighth Circuit (11)	
Districts of Minnesota, northern Iowa, southern Iowa, eastern Missouri, western Missouri, eastern Arkansas, western Arkansas, Nebraska, North Dakota,	*Circuit Justice* Justice Samuel A. Alito, Jr. *Circuit Judges* James B. Loken, *Chief Judge* Roger L. Wollman	Minneapolis, MN Sioux Falls, SD

Judicial Circuits—United States Courts of Appeals—Continued

Circuit	Judges	Official Station
and South Dakota	Diana E. Murphy	Minneapolis, MN
(*Clerk:* Michael Ellis Gans;	Kermit E. Bye	Fargo, ND
Circuit Executive:	William Jay Riley	Omaha, NE
Millie B. Adams;	Michael J. Melloy	Cedar Rapids, IA
St. Louis, MO)	Lavenski R. Smith	Little Rock, AR
	Steven M. Colloton	Des Moines, IA
	Raymond W. Gruender	St. Louis, MO
	William Duane Benton	Kansas City, MO
	Bobby E. Shepherd	El Dorado, AR

Ninth Circuit (29)

Circuit	Judges	Official Station
Districts of northern	*Circuit Justice*	
California, eastern	Justice Anthony M. Kennedy	
California, central California,		
southern California, Oregon,	*Circuit Judges*	
Nevada, Montana, eastern	Alex Kozinski, *Chief Judge*	Pasadena, CA
Washington, western	Mary M. Schroeder	Phoenix, AZ
Washington, Idaho, Arizona,	Harry Pregerson	Woodland Hills, CA
Alaska, Hawaii, Territory	Stephen Reinhardt	Los Angeles, CA
of Guam, and District	Diarmuid F. O'Scannlain	Portland, OR
Court for the Northern	Pamela Ann Rymer	Pasadena, CA
Mariana Islands	Andrew J. Kleinfeld	Fairbanks, AK
(*Clerk:* Molly Dwyer;	Michael Daly Hawkins	Phoenix, AZ
Circuit Executive:	Sidney R. Thomas	Billings, MT
Cathy A. Catterson;	Barry G. Silverman	Phoenix, AZ
San Francisco, CA)	Susan P. Graber	Portland, OR
	M. Margaret McKeown	San Diego, CA
	Kim M. Wardlaw	Pasadena, CA
	William A. Fletcher	San Francisco, CA
	Raymond C. Fisher	Pasadena, CA
	Ronald M. Gould	Seattle, WA
	Richard A. Paez	Pasadena, CA
	Marsha S. Berzon	San Francisco, CA
	Richard C. Tallman	Seattle, WA
	Johnnie B. Rawlinson	Las Vegas, NV
	Richard R. Clifton	Honolulu, HI
	Jay S. Bybee	Las Vegas, NV
	Consuelo Maria Callahan	Sacramento, CA
	Carlos T. Bea	San Francisco, CA
	Milan D. Smith, Jr.	El Segundo, CA
	Sandra S. Ikuta	Pasadena, CA
	Norman Randy Smith	Pocatello, ID
	(2 vacancies)	

Tenth Circuit (12)

Circuit	Judges	Official Station
Districts of Colorado,	*Circuit Justice*	
Wyoming, Utah, Kansas,	Justice Stephen G. Breyer	
eastern Oklahoma, western		
Oklahoma, northern	*Circuit Judges*	
Oklahoma, and New	Robert H. Henry, *Chief Judge*	Oklahoma City, OK
Mexico	Deanell Reece Tacha	Lawrence, KS
(*Clerk:* Elisabeth A. Shumaker;	Paul J. Kelly, Jr.	Santa Fe, NM
Circuit Executive:	Mary Beck Briscoe	Lawrence, KS
David J. Tighe;	Carlos F. Lucero	Denver, CO
Denver, CO)	Michael R. Murphy	Salt Lake City, UT
	Harris L. Hartz	Albuquerque, NM
	Terrence L. O'Brien	Cheyenne, WY
	Michael W. McConnell	Salt Lake City, UT
	Timothy M. Tymkovich	Denver, CO
	Neil M. Gorusch	Denver, CO
	Jerome A. Holmes	Oklahoma City, OK

Eleventh Circuit (12)

Circuit	Judges	Official Station
Districts of northern	*Circuit Justice*	
Georgia, middle Georgia,	Justice Clarence Thomas	
southern Georgia, northern		
Florida, middle Florida,	*Circuit Judges*	
southern Florida, northern	Joel F. Dubina, *Chief Judge*	Montgomery, GA
Alabama, middle Alabama,	Gerald B. Tjoflat	Jacksonville, FL
southern Alabama	James Larry Edmondson	Atlanta, GA

Judicial Circuits—United States Courts of Appeals—Continued

Circuit	Judges	Official Station
(*Clerk:* Thomas K. Kahn; *Circuit Executive:* James P. Gerstenlauer; Atlanta, GA)	Stanley F. Birch, Jr.	Atlanta, GA
	Susan H. Black	Jacksonville, FL
	Edward E. Carnes	Montgomery, AL
	Rosemary Barkett	Miami, FL
	Frank Mays Hull	Atlanta, GA
	Stanley Marcus	Miami, FL
	Charles R. Wilson	Tampa, FL
	William H. Pryor, Jr.	Birmingham, Al
	(vacancy)	

Federal Circuit (12)		
(Clerk: Jan Horbaly)	*Circuit Justice* Chief Justice John G. Roberts, Jr.	
	Judges	
	Paul R. Michel, *Chief Judge*	Washington, DC
	Pauline Newman	Washington, DC
	Haldane Robert Mayer	Washington, DC
	Alan D. Lourie	Washington, DC
	Randall R. Rader	Washington, DC
	Alvin A. Schall	Washington, DC
	William C. Bryson	Washington, DC
	Arthur J. Gajarsa	Washington, DC
	Richard Linn	Washington, DC
	Timothy B. Dyk	Washington, DC
	Sharon Prost	Washington, DC
	Kimberly Moore	Washington, DC

United States District Courts   The district courts are the trial courts of general Federal jurisdiction. Each State has at least one district court, while the larger States have as many as four. Altogether there are 89 district courts in the 50 States, plus the one in the District of Columbia. In addition, the Commonwealth of Puerto Rico has a district court with jurisdiction corresponding to that of district courts in the various States.

At present, each district court has from 2 to 28 Federal district judgeships, depending upon the amount of judicial work within its territory. Only one judge is usually required to hear and decide a case in a district court, but in some limited cases it is required that three judges be called together to comprise the court (28 U.S.C. 2284). The judge senior in commission who is under 70 years of age (65 at inception of term), has been in office for at least 1 year, and has not previously been chief judge, serves as chief judge for a 7-year term. There are altogether 645 permanent district judgeships in the 50 States and 15 in the District of Columbia. There are 7 district judgeships in Puerto Rico. District judges hold their offices during good behavior as provided by Article III, section 1, of the Constitution. However, Congress may create temporary judgeships for a court with the provision that when a future vacancy occurs in that district, such vacancy shall not be filled. Each district court has one or more United States magistrate judges and bankruptcy judges, a clerk, a United States attorney, a United States marshal, probation officers, court reporters, and their staffs. The jurisdiction of the district courts is set forth in title 28, chapter 85, of the United States Code and at 18 U.S.C. 3231.

Cases from the district courts are reviewable on appeal by the applicable court of appeals.

Territorial Courts   Pursuant to its authority to govern the Territories (art. IV, sec. 3, clause 2, of the Constitution), Congress has established district courts in the territories of Guam and the Virgin Islands. The District Court of the Canal Zone was abolished on April 1, 1982, pursuant to the Panama Canal Act of 1979 (22 U.S.C. 3601 note). Congress has also established a district court in the Northern Mariana Islands, which presently is administered by the United States under a trusteeship agreement with the United Nations. These Territorial courts have jurisdiction not only over the subjects described in the judicial article of the Constitution but also over many local matters that, within the States, are decided in State courts. The district court of Puerto Rico, by contrast, is established under Article III, is classified like other "district courts," and is called a "court of the United States" (28 U.S.C. 451). There is one judge each in Guam and the Northern Mariana Islands, and two in the Virgin Islands. The judges in these courts are appointed for terms of 10 years.

For further information concerning the lower courts, contact the Administrative Office of the United States Courts, Thurgood Marshall Federal Judiciary Building, One Columbus Circle NE., Washington, DC 20544. Phone, 202–502–2600.

United States Court of International Trade   This court was originally established as the Board of United States General Appraisers by act of June 10, 1890, which conferred upon it jurisdiction theretofore held by the district and circuit courts in actions arising under the tariff acts (19 U.S.C. ch. 4). The act of May 28, 1926 (19 U.S.C. 405a), created the United States Customs Court to supersede the Board; by acts of August 7, 1939, and June 25, 1948 (28 U.S.C. 1582, 1583), the court was integrated into the United States court structure, organization, and procedure. The act of July 14, 1956 (28 U.S.C. 251), established the court as a court of record of the United States under Article III of the Constitution. The Customs Court Act of 1980 (28 U.S.C. 251) constituted the court as the United States Court of International Trade.

The Court of International Trade has jurisdiction over any civil action against the United States arising from Federal laws governing import transactions. This includes classification and valuation cases, as well as authority to review certain agency determinations under the Trade Agreements Act of 1979 (19 U.S.C. 2501) involving antidumping and countervailing duty matters. In addition, it has exclusive jurisdiction of civil actions to review determinations as to the eligibility of workers, firms, and

communities for adjustment assistance under the Trade Act of 1974 (19 U.S.C. 2101). Civil actions commenced by the United States to recover customs duties, to recover on a customs bond, or for certain civil penalties alleging fraud or negligence are also within the exclusive jurisdiction of the court.

The court is composed of a chief judge and eight judges, not more than five of whom may belong to any one political party. Any of its judges may be temporarily designated and assigned by the Chief Justice of the United States to sit as a court of appeals or district court judge in any circuit or district. The court has a clerk and deputy clerks, a librarian, court reporters, and other supporting personnel. Cases before the court may be tried before a jury. Under the Federal Courts Improvement Act of 1982 (28 U.S.C. 1295), appeals are taken to the U.S. Court of Appeals for the Federal Circuit, and ultimately review may be sought in appropriate cases in the Supreme Court of the United States.

The principal offices are located in New York, NY, but the court is empowered to hear and determine cases arising at any port or place within the jurisdiction of the United States.

For further information, contact the Clerk, United States Court of International Trade, One Federal Plaza, New York, NY 10278–0001. Phone, 212–264–2814.

Judicial Panel on Multidistrict Litigation   The Panel, created by act of April 29, 1968 (28 U.S.C. 1407), and consisting of seven Federal judges designated by the Chief Justice from the courts of appeals and district courts, is authorized to temporarily transfer to a single district, for coordinated or consolidated pretrial proceedings, civil actions pending in different districts that involve one or more common questions of fact.

For further information, contact the Clerk, Judicial Panel on Multidistrict Litigation, Room G–255, Thurgood Marshall Federal Judiciary Building, One Columbus Circle NE., Washington, DC 20002–8041. Phone, 202–502–2800.

Special Courts

The Supreme Court has held that
". . . Article III [of the Constitution]
does not express the full authority of
Congress to create courts, and that other
Articles invest Congress with powers in
the exertion of which it may create
inferior courts and clothe them with
functions deemed essential or helpful in
carrying those powers into execution."
Such courts, known as legislative courts,
have functions which ". . . are directed
to the execution of one or more of such
powers and are prescribed by Congress
independently of section 2 of Article III;
and their judges hold office for such
term as Congress prescribes, whether it
be a fixed period of years or during good
behavior." Appeals from the decisions of
these courts, with the exception of the
U.S. Tax Court and the U.S. Court of
Appeals for the Armed Forces, may be
taken to the U.S. Court of Appeals for
the Federal Circuit. Appeals from the
decisions of the Tax Court may be taken
to the court of appeals in which judicial
circuit the case was initially heard.
Certain decisions of the U.S. Court of
Appeals for the Armed Forces are
reviewable by writ of certiorari in the
Supreme Court.

United States Court of Federal Claims
The U.S. Court of Federal Claims has
jurisdiction over claims seeking money
judgments against the United States. A
claim must be founded upon the United
States Constitution; an act of Congress;
the regulation of an executive
department; an express or implied-in-fact
contract with the United States; or
damages, liquidated or unliquidated, in
cases not sounding in tort. Judges in the
U.S. Court of Federal Claims are
appointed by the President for 15-year
terms, subject to Senate confirmation.
Appeals are to the U.S. Court of Appeals
for the Federal Circuit.

For further information, contact the Clerk's Office,
United States Court of Federal Claims, 717 Madison
Place NW., Washington, DC 20005–1086. Phone,
202–357–6400. Internet, www.uscfc.uscourts.gov.

**United States Court of Appeals for the
Armed Forces**   This court was

established under Article I of the
Constitution of the United States
pursuant to act of May 5, 1950, as
amended (10 U.S.C. 867). Subject only
to certiorari review by the Supreme
Court of the United States in a limited
number of cases, the court serves as the
final appellate tribunal to review court-
martial convictions of all the Armed
Forces. It is exclusively an appellate
criminal court, consisting of five civilian
judges who are appointed for 15-year
terms by the President with the advice
and consent of the Senate. The court is
called upon to exercise jurisdiction to
review the record in all cases:
—extending to death;
—certified to the court by a Judge
Advocate General of an armed force or
by the General Counsel of the
Department of Transportation, acting for
the Coast Guard; or
—petitioned by accused who have
received a sentence of confinement for 1
year or more, and/or a punitive
discharge.
   The court also exercises authority
under the All Writs Act (28 U.S.C. 1651
(a)).
   In addition, the judges of the court are
required by law to work jointly with the
senior uniformed lawyer from each
armed force, the Chief Counsel of the
Coast Guard, and two members of the
public appointed by the Secretary of
Defense, to make an annual
comprehensive survey and to report
annually to the Congress on the
operation and progress of the military
justice system under the Uniform Code
of Military Justice, and to recommend
improvements wherever necessary.

For further information, contact the Clerk, United
States Court of Appeals for the Armed Forces, 450
E Street NW., Washington, DC 20442–0001. Phone,
202–761–1448. Fax, 202–761–4672. Internet,
www.armfor.uscourts.gov.

United States Tax Court   The United
States Tax Court is a court of record
under Article I of the Constitution of the
United States (26 U.S.C. 7441). The
court was created as the United States
Board of Tax Appeals by the Revenue

Act of 1924 (43 Stat. 336). The name was changed to the Tax Court of the United States by the Revenue Act of 1942 (56 Stat. 957). The Tax Reform Act of 1969 (83 Stat. 730) established the court under Article I and then changed its name to the United States Tax Court.

The court comprises 19 judges who are appointed by the President to 15-year terms and subject to Senate confirmation. The court also has varying numbers of both senior judges (who may be recalled by the chief judge to perform further judicial duties) and special trial judges (who are appointed by the chief judge and may hear and decide a variety of cases). The court's jurisdiction is set forth in various sections of title 26 of the U.S. Code.

The offices of the court and its judges are in Washington, DC. However, the court has national jurisdiction and schedules trial sessions in more than 70 cities in the United States. Each trial session is conducted by one judge, senior judge, or special trial judge. Court proceedings are open to the public and are conducted in accordance with the court's Rules of Practice and Procedure and the rules of evidence applicable in trials without a jury in the U.S. District Court for the District of Columbia. A fee of $60 is charged for the filing of a petition. Practice before the court is limited to practitioners admitted under the court's Rules of Practice and Procedure.

Decisions entered by the court, other than decisions in small tax cases, may be appealed to the regional courts of appeals and, thereafter, upon the granting of a writ of certiorari, to the Supreme Court of the United States. At the option of petitioners, simplified procedures may be used in small tax cases. Small tax cases are final and not subject to review by any court.

For further information, contact the Administrative Office, United States Tax Court, 400 Second Street NW., Washington, DC 20217–0002. Phone, 202–521–0700. Internet, www.ustaxcourt.gov.

United States Court of Appeals for Veterans Claims The United States Court of Veterans Appeals was established on November 18, 1988 (102 Stat. 4105, 38 U.S.C. 7251) pursuant to Article I of the Constitution, and given exclusive jurisdiction to review decisions of the Board of Veterans Appeals. The court was renamed the United States Court of Appeals for Veterans Claims by the Veterans Programs Enhancement Act of 1998 (38 U.S.C. 7251 note). The court may not review the schedule of ratings for disabilities or actions of the Secretary in adopting or revising that schedule. Decisions of the Court of Appeals for Veterans Claims may be appealed to the United States Court of Appeals for the Federal Circuit.

The court consists of seven judges appointed by the President, with the advice and consent of the Senate, for 15-year terms. One of the judges serves as chief judge.

The court's principal office is in the District of Columbia, but the court can also act at any place within the United States.

For further information, contact the Clerk, United States Court of Appeals for Veterans Claims, Suite 900, 625 Indiana Avenue NW., Washington, DC 20004–2950. Phone, 202–501–5970. Internet, www.vetapp.gov.

Other Courts There have also been created two courts of local jurisdiction for the District of Columbia: the District of Columbia Court of Appeals and the Superior Court.

Business of the Federal Courts

The business of all the Federal courts described here, except the Court of Appeals for the Armed Forces, the Tax Court, the Court of Appeals for Veterans Claims, and the District of Columbia courts, is discussed in detail in the text and tables of the *Annual Report of the Director of the Administrative Office of the United States Courts (1940–2001)*.

EDITORIAL NOTE: The Administrative Office of the United States Courts did not meet the publication deadline for submitting updated information of its activities, functions, and sources of information.

ADMINISTRATIVE OFFICE OF THE UNITED STATES COURTS

One Columbus Circle NE., Washington, DC 20544
Phone, 202–502–2600

DIRECTOR	JAMES C. DUFF
DEPUTY DIRECTOR	JILL C. SAYENGA
Associate Director and General Counsel	WILLIAM R. BURCHILL, JR.
Deputy Associate Director	ROBERT K. LOESCHE
Assistant Director, Office of Judicial Conference Executive Secretariat	LAURA C. MINOR
Deputy Assistant Directors, Office of Judicial Conference Executive Secretariat	JEFFREY A. HENNEMUTH, WENDY JENNIS
Assistant Director, Office of Legislative Affairs	CORDIA A. STROM
Deputy Assistant Director, Office of Legislative Affairs	DANIEL CUNNINGHAM
Assistant Director, Office of Public Affairs	DAVID A. SELLERS
Assistant Director, Office of Court Administration	NOEL J. AUGUSTYN
Deputy Assistant Director, Office of Court Administration	GLEN K. PALMAN
Assistant Director, Office of Defender Services	THEODORE J. LIDZ
Deputy Assistant Director, Office of Defender Services	STEVEN G. ASIN
Assistant Director, Office of Facilities and Security	ROSS EISENMAN
Deputy Assistant Director, Office of Facilities and Security	WILLIAM J. LEHMAN
Assistant Director, Office of Finance and Budget	GEORGE H. SCHAFER
Deputy Assistant Director, Office of Finance and Budget	(VACANCY)
Assistant Director, Office of Human Resources	CHARLOTTE G. PEDDICORD
Deputy Assistant Director, Office of Human Resources	NANCY E. WARD
Assistant Director, Office of Information Technology	HOWARD J. GRANDIER
Deputy Assistant Director, Office of Information Technology	JOSEPH R. PETERS, JR.
Assistant Director, Office of Internal Services	DOREEN G.B. BYDUME
Assistant Director, Office of Judges Programs	PETER G. MCCABE
Deputy Assistant Director, Office of Judges Programs	R. TOWNSEND ROBINSON
Assistant Director, Office of Probation and Pretrial Services	JOHN M. HUGHES
Deputy Assistant Director, Office of Probation and Pretrial Services	MATTHEW ROWLAND

The Administrative Office of the United States Courts is charged with the nonjudicial, administrative business of the United States Courts, including the maintenance of workload statistics and the disbursement of funds appropriated for the maintenance of the U.S. judicial system.

The Administrative Office of the United States Courts was created by act of August 7, 1939 (28 U.S.C. 601). The Office was established November 6, 1939. Its Director and Deputy Director are appointed by the Chief Justice of the United States after consultation with the Judicial Conference.

Administering the Courts The Director is the administrative officer of the courts of the United States (except the Supreme Court). Under the guidance of the Judicial Conference of the United States the Director is required, among other things, to do the following:

—supervise all administrative matters relating to the offices of clerks and other clerical and administrative personnel of the courts;

—examine the state of the dockets of the courts, secure information as to the courts' need of assistance, and prepare and transmit quarterly to the chief judges of the circuits statistical data and reports as to the business of the courts;

—submit to the annual meeting of the Judicial Conference of the United States, at least 2 weeks prior thereto, a report of the activities of the Administrative Office and the state of the business of the courts;

—fix the compensation of employees of the courts whose compensation is not otherwise fixed by law;

—regulate and pay annuities to widows and surviving dependent children of judges;

—disburse moneys appropriated for the maintenance and operation of the courts;

—examine accounts of court officers;

—regulate travel of judicial personnel;

—provide accommodations and supplies for the courts and their clerical and administrative personnel;

—establish and maintain programs for the certification and utilization of court interpreters and the provision of special interpretation services in the courts; and

—perform such other duties as may be assigned by the Supreme Court or the Judicial Conference of the United States.

The Director is also responsible for the preparation and submission of the budget of the courts, which shall be transmitted by the Office of Management and Budget to Congress without change.

Probation Officers The Administrative Office exercises general supervision of the accounts and practices of the Federal probation offices, subject to primary control by the respective district courts that they serve. The Office publishes quarterly, in cooperation with the Bureau of Prisons of the Department of Justice, a magazine entitled *Federal Probation,* which is a journal "of correctional philosophy and practice."

The Director also has responsibility with respect to the establishment of pretrial services in the district courts under the Pretrial Services Act of 1982 (18 U.S.C. 3152). These offices report to their respective courts information concerning pretrial release of persons charged with Federal offenses and supervise such persons who are released to their custody.

Bankruptcy The Bankruptcy Amendments and Federal Judgeship Act of 1984 (28 U.S.C. 151) provided that the bankruptcy judges for each judicial district shall constitute a unit of the district court to be known as the bankruptcy court. Bankruptcy judges are appointed by the courts of appeals in such numbers as authorized by Congress and serve for a term of 14 years as judicial officers of the district courts.

This act placed jurisdiction in the district courts over all cases under title 11, United States Code, and all proceedings arising in or related to cases under that title (28 U.S.C. 1334). The district court may provide for such cases and proceedings to be referred to its bankruptcy judges (as authorized by 28 U.S.C. 157).

ADMINISTRATIVE OFFICE OF THE UNITED STATES COURTS

The Director of the Administrative Office recommends to the Judicial Conference the official duty stations and places of holding court of bankruptcy judges, surveys the need for additional bankruptcy judgeships to be recommended to Congress, and determines the staff needs of bankruptcy judges and the clerks of the bankruptcy courts.

Federal Magistrate Judges   The Director of the Administrative Office exercises general supervision over administrative matters in offices of U.S. magistrate judges, compiles and evaluates statistical data relating to such offices, and submits reports thereon to the Judicial Conference. The Director reports annually to Congress on the business that has come before U.S. magistrate judges and also prepares legal and administrative manuals for the use of the magistrate judges. The act provides for surveys to be conducted by the Administrative Office of the conditions in the judicial districts in order to make recommendations as to the number, location, and salaries of magistrate judges, which are determined by the Judicial Conference subject to the availability of appropriated funds.

Federal Defenders   The Criminal Justice Act (18 U.S.C. 3006A) establishes the procedure for the appointment of private panel attorneys in Federal criminal cases for individuals who are unable to afford adequate representation, under plans adopted by each district court. The act also permits the establishment of Federal public defender or Federal community defender organizations by the district courts in districts where at least 200 persons annually require the appointment of counsel. Two adjacent districts may be combined to reach this total.

Each defender organization submits to the Director of the Administrative Office an annual report of its activities along with a proposed budget or, in the case of community defender organizations, a proposed grant for the coming year. The Director is responsible for the submission of the proposed budgets and grants to the Judicial Conference for approval. The Director also makes payments to the defender organizations out of appropriations in accordance with the approved budgets and grants, as well as compensating private counsel appointed to defend criminal cases in the United States courts.

Sources of Information

Information may be obtained from the following sources:

Bankruptcy Judges Division. Phone, 202–502–1900.

Budget Division. Phone, 202–502–2100.

Defender Services Division. Phone, 202–502–3030.

General Counsel. Phone, 202–502–1100.

Human Resources Division. Phone, 202–502–3100.

Judicial Conference Executive Secretariat. Phone, 202–502–2400.

Legislative Affairs Office. Phone, 202–502–1700.

Magistrate Judges Division. Phone, 202–502–1830.

Office of Probation and Pretrial Services. Phone, 202–502–1610.

Public Affairs Office. Phone, 202–502–2600.

Statistics Division. Phone, 202–502–1440.

For further information, contact the Administrative Office of the United States Courts, Thurgood Marshall Federal Judiciary Building, One Columbus Circle NE., Washington, DC 20544. Phone, 202–502–2600. Internet, www.uscourts.gov.

FEDERAL JUDICIAL CENTER

Thurgood Marshall Federal Judiciary Building,
One Columbus Circle NE., Washington, DC 20002–8003
Phone, 202–502–4000. Internet, www.fjc.gov.

DIRECTOR	BARBARA J. ROTHSTEIN
DEPUTY DIRECTOR	JOHN S. COOKE
Director, Education Division	BRUCE M. CLARKE
Director, Systems Innovation and Development Office	TED E. COLEMAN
Director, Research Division	JAMES B. EAGLIN
Director, International Judicial Relations Office	MIRA GUR-ARIE
Director, Federal Judicial History Office	BRUCE A. RAGSDALE
Director, Communications Policy and Design Office	SYLVAN A. SOBEL

The Federal Judicial Center is the judicial branch's agency for policy research and continuing education.

The Federal Judicial Center was created by act of December 20, 1967 (28 U.S.C. 620), to further the development and adoption of improved judicial administration in the courts of the United States.

The Center's basic policies and activities are determined by its Board, which is composed of the Chief Justice of the United States, who is permanent Chair of the Board by statute, and two judges of the U.S. courts of appeals, three judges of the U.S. district courts, one bankruptcy judge, and one magistrate judge, all of whom are elected for 4-year terms by the Judicial Conference of the United States. The Director of the Administrative Office of the United States Courts is also a permanent member of the Board.

Pursuant to statute, the Center carries out the following duties:

—develops and administers orientation and continuing education programs for Federal judges, Federal defenders, and nonjudicial court personnel, including probation officers, pretrial services officers, and clerks' office employees;

—conducts empirical and exploratory research and evaluation on Federal judicial processes, court management, and sentencing and its consequences, usually for the committees of the Judicial Conference or the courts themselves;

—produces research reports, training manuals, satellite broadcasts, video programs, computer based training, and periodicals about the Federal courts;

—provides guidance and advice and maintains data and records to assist those interested in documenting and conserving the history of the Federal courts; and

—cooperates with and assists other agencies and organizations in providing advice to improve the administration of justice in the courts of foreign countries.

Sources of Information

Information may be obtained from the following divisions and offices:

Director. Phone, 202–502–4160, or 202–502–4164. Fax, 202–502–4099.

Research. Phone, 202–502–4070. Fax, 202–502–4199.

Automation and Web Programs. Phone, 202–502–4139. Fax, 202–502–4088.

Clerk's Office Programs. Phone, 202–502–4148. Fax, 202–502–4088.

Judges and Attorneys Programs. Phone, 202–502–4050. Fax, 202–502–4299.

Management Programs. Phone, 202–502–4101. Fax, 202–502–4088.

Media Production. Phone, 202–502–4101. Fax, 202–502–4088.

Probation and Pretrial Services Programs. Phone, 502–202–4115. Fax, 202–502–4088.

Television and Video Programs. Phone, 202–502–4266. Fax, 202–502–4088.

Communications Policy and Design. Phone, 202–502–4250. Fax, 202–502–4077.

Federal Judicial History. Phone, 202–502–4180. Fax, 202–502–4077.

Information Services. Phone, 202–502–4153. Fax, 202–502–4077.

International Judicial Relations. Phone, 202–502–

4160. Fax, 202–502–4099.

Human Resources. Phone, 202–502–4165. Fax, 202–502–4099.

Systems Innovation and Development. Phone, 202–502–4223. Fax, 202–502–4288.

Electronic Access Selected Federal Judicial Center publications, Federal

judicial history databases, and various educational resources are available at www.fjc.gov.

Publications Single copies of most Federal Judicial Center publications are available free of charge. Phone, 202–502–4153. Fax, 202–502–4077.

For further information, contact the Federal Judicial Center, Thurgood Marshall Federal Judiciary Building, One Columbus Circle NE., Washington, DC 20002–8003. Phone, 202–502–4000. Internet, www.fjc.gov.

UNITED STATES SENTENCING COMMISSION

Suite 2–500, South Lobby, One Columbus Circle NE., Washington, DC 20002–8002
Phone, 202–502–4500. Internet, www.ussc.gov.

CHAIR	RICARDO H. HINOJOSA, *Acting*
VICE CHAIRS	WILLIAM B. CARR, JR., RUBEN CASTILLO, WILLIAM K. SESSIONS III
Commissioners	DABNEY L. FRIEDRICH, MICHAEL E. HOROWITZ, BERYL A. HOWELL
Commissioners (*ex officio*)	KELLI H. FERRY, EDWARD F. REILLY, JR.
Staff Director	JUDITH W. SHEON
General Counsel	KENNETH P. COHEN
Public Affairs Officer	MICHAEL COURLANDER
Director of Administration and Planning	SUSAN M. BRAZEL
Director and Chief Counsel of Training	PAMELA G. MONTGOMERY
Director of Legislative and Governmental Affairs	(VACANCY)
Director of Research and Data	GLENN R. SCHMITT

The United States Sentencing Commission develops sentencing guidelines and policies for the Federal court system.

The United States Sentencing Commission was established as an independent agency in the judicial branch of the Federal Government by the Sentencing Reform Act of 1984 (28 U.S.C. 991 *et seq.* and 18 U.S.C. 3551 *et seq.*). The Commission establishes sentencing guidelines and policies for the Federal courts, advising them of the appropriate form and severity of punishment for offenders convicted of Federal crimes.

The Commission is composed of seven voting members appointed by the President with the advice and consent of the Senate for 6-year terms, and two

nonvoting members. One of the voting members is appointed Chairperson.

The Commission evaluates the effects of the sentencing guidelines on the criminal justice system, advises Congress regarding the modification or enactment of statutes relating to criminal law and sentencing matters, establishes a research and development program on sentencing issues, and performs other related duties.

In executing its duties, the Commission promulgates and distributes to Federal courts and to the U.S. probation system guidelines to be consulted in determining sentences to be imposed in criminal cases, general policy statements regarding the application of guidelines, and policy statements on the appropriate use of probation and supervised release revocation provisions. These sentencing guidelines and policy statements are designed to further the purposes of just punishment, deterrence, incapacitation, and rehabilitation; provide fairness in meeting the purposes of sentencing; avoid unwarranted disparity; and reflect advancement in the knowledge of human behavior as it relates to the criminal justice process.

In addition, the Commission provides training, conducts research on sentencing-related issues, and serves as an information resource for Congress, criminal justice practitioners, and the public.

Sources of Information

Electronic Access   Commission information and materials may be obtained through the Internet at www.ussc.gov.

Guideline Application Assistance Helpline   Phone, 202–502–4545.

Public Information   Information concerning Commission activities is available from the Office of Publishing and Public Affairs. Phone, 202–502–4590.

For further information, contact the Office of Publishing and Public Affairs, United States Sentencing Commission, Suite 2–500, South Lobby, One Columbus Circle NE., Washington, DC 20002–8002. Phone, 202–502–4590. Internet, www.ussc.gov.

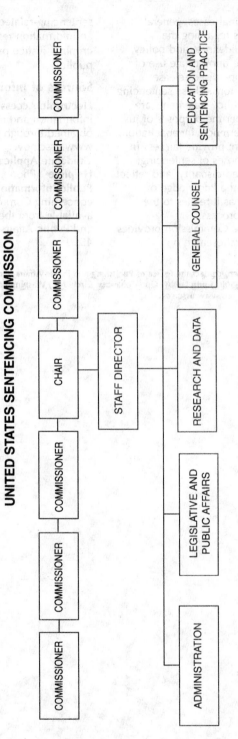

UNITED STATES SENTENCING COMMISSION

Executive Branch

EXECUTIVE BRANCH

THE PRESIDENT OF THE UNITED STATES

THE PRESIDENT OF THE UNITED STATES   Barack H. Obama

Article II, section 1, of the Constitution provides that "[t]he executive Power shall be vested in a President of the United States of America. He shall hold his Office during the Term of four Years, . . . together with the Vice President, chosen for the same Term . . . ." In addition to the powers set forth in the Constitution, the statutes have conferred upon the President specific authority and responsibility covering a wide range of matters (United States Code Index).

The President is the administrative head of the executive branch of the Government, which includes numerous agencies, both temporary and permanent, as well as the 15 executive departments.

The Cabinet

The Cabinet, a creation of custom and tradition dating back to George Washington's administration, functions at the pleasure of the President. Its purpose is to advise the President upon any subject, relating to the duties of the respective offices, on which he requests information (pursuant to Article II, section 2, of the Constitution).

The Cabinet is composed of the Vice President and the heads of the 15 executive departments—the Secretaries of Agriculture, Commerce, Defense, Education, Energy, Health and Human Services, Homeland Security, Housing and Urban Development, Interior, Labor, State, Transportation, Treasury, and Veterans Affairs, and the Attorney General. Additionally, in the Bush administration, Cabinet-level rank has been accorded to the Chief of Staff to the President; the Administrator, Environmental Protection Agency; the Director, Office of Management and Budget; the Director, Office of National Drug Control Policy; and the U.S. Trade Representative.

THE VICE PRESIDENT OF THE UNITED STATES

THE VICE PRESIDENT   Joseph R. Biden, Jr.

Article II, section I, of the Constitution provides that the President "shall hold his Office during the Term of four Years . . . together with the Vice President . . . ." In addition to his role as President of the Senate, the Vice President is empowered

85

to succeed to the Presidency, pursuant to Article II and the 20th and 25th amendments to the Constitution.

The executive functions of the Vice President include participation in Cabinet meetings and, by statute, membership on the National Security Council and the Board of Regents of the Smithsonian Institution.

EXECUTIVE OFFICE OF THE PRESIDENT

Under authority of the Reorganization Act of 1939 (5 U.S.C. 133–133r, 133t note), various agencies were transferred to the Executive Office of the President by the President's Reorganization Plans I and II of 1939 (5 U.S.C. app.), effective July 1, 1939. Executive Order 8248 of September 8, 1939, established the divisions of the Executive Office and defined their functions. Subsequently, Presidents have used Executive orders, reorganization plans, and legislative initiatives to reorganize the Executive Office to make its composition compatible with the goals of their administrations.

The White House Office

1600 Pennsylvania Avenue NW., Washington, DC 20500
Phone, 202–456–1414. Internet, www.whitehouse.gov.

ASSISTANT TO THE PRESIDENT AND CHIEF OF STAFF	RAHM I. EMANUEL
Assistant to the President and Deputy Chief of Staff for Operations	JAMES A. MESSINA
Assistant to the President and Deputy Chief of Staff for Policy	MONA K. SUTPHEN
Assistant to the President and Senior Advisor	DAVID M. AXELROD
Assistant to the President and Senior Advisor	PETER M. ROUSE
National Security Advisor	JAMES L. JONES, JR.
Assistant to the President and Deputy National Security Advisor	THOMAS E. DONLION
Assistant to the President and Deputy National Security Advisor for Counterterrorism and Homeland Security	JOHN O. BRENNAN
Assistant to the President and Cabinet Secretary	CHRISTOPHER P. LU
Assistant to the President and Counsel to the President	GREGORY B. CRAIG
Assistant to the President and Director of Legislative Affairs	PHILIP M. SCHILIRO
Assistant to the President and Director of Presidential Personnel	DONALD H. GIPS
Assistant to the President and Director of Political Affairs	PATRICK H. GASPARD
Assistant to the President and Director of Scheduling and Advance	ALYSSA M. MASTROMONACO
Assistant to the President and Director of Speechwriting	JONATHAN E. FAVREAU
Assistant to the President and Press Secretary	ROBERT L. GIBBS
Assistant to the President and Staff Secretary	ELIZABETH M. BROWN
Assistant to the President for Communications	ANITA B. DUNN

Assistant to the President for Energy and Climate Change	CAROL M. BROWNER
Assistant to the President for Intergovernmental Affairs and Public Engagement and Senior Advisor	VALERIE B. JARRETT
Assistant to the President for Management and Administration	BRADLEY J. KILEY
Assistant to the President, Chief of Staff to the First Lady and Counsel	SUSAN S. SHER
Deputy Assistant to the President and Chief of Staff for National Security Operations	MARK W. LIPPERT
Deputy Assistant to the President and Deputy Cabinet Secretary	ELIZABETH S. SMITH
Deputy Assistant to the President and Deputy Counsel to the President	CASSANDRA Q. BUTTS
Deputy Assistant to the President and Deputy Counsel to the President	MARY B. DEROSA
Deputy Assistant to the President and Deputy Director of Communications for Production	HOWARD D. PFEIFFER
Deputy Assistant to the President and Deputy Director of Presidential Personnel	KENNETH F. WILLIAMS-BENNETT
Deputy Assistant to the President and Deputy Staff Secretary	PETER F. RUNDLET
Deputy Assistant to the President and Director of Advance and Operations	EMMETT S. BELIVEAU
Deputy Assistant to the President and Director of Appointments and Scheduling	DANIELLE M. CRUTCHFIELD
Deputy Assistant to the President and Director of Intergovernmental Affairs	CECILIA MUÑOZ
Deputy Assistant to the President and Director of Policy and Projects for the First Lady	JOCELYN C. FRYE
Deputy Assistant to the President and Director of the Office of Public Engagement	CHRISTINA M. TCHEN
Deputy Assistant to the President and Director of the Office of Urban Affairs	ADOLFO CARRION, JR.
Deputy Assistant to the President and National Security Spokesperson	DENIS R. MCDONOUGH
Deputy Assistant to the President and Principal Deputy Counsel to the President	DANIEL J. MELTZER
Deputy Assistant to the President for Energy and Climate Change	HEATHER R. ZICHAL
Deputy Assistant to the President for Legislative Affairs	LISA M. KONWINSKI
Deputy Assistant to the President for Legislative Affairs and House Liaison	DANIEL A. TURTON
Deputy Assistant to the President for Legislative Affairs and Senate Liaison	SHAWN P. MAHER
Deputy Assistant to the President for Management and Administration	HENRY F. DE SIO, JR.

The White House Office serves the President in the performance of the many detailed activities incident to his immediate office.

The President's staff facilitates and maintains communication with the Congress, the heads of executive agencies, the press and other information media, and the general public.

The various Assistants to the President aid the President in such matters as he may direct.

Office of the Vice President of the United States

Eisenhower Executive Office Building, Washington, DC 20501
Phone, 202–456–7549

Assistant to the President and Chief of Staff to the Vice President	RON KLAIN
Deputy Assistant to the President and Deputy Chief of Staff to the Vice President	ALAN HOFFMAN
Deputy Assistant to the President and National Security Affairs Advisor to the Vice President	TONY BLINKEN
Deputy Assistant to the President and Domestic Policy Advisor to the Vice President	TERRELL MCSWEENY
Deputy Assistant to the President and Economic Advisor to the Vice President	JARED BERNSTEIN
Special Assistant to the President and Intergovernmental Affairs Advisor to the Vice President	EVAN RYAN
Assistant to the Vice President and Counselor	MIKE DONILON
Assistant to the Vice President and Counsel to the Vice President	CYNTHIA HOGAN
Assistant to the Vice President for Communications	JAY CARNEY
Press Secretary for the Vice President	ELIZABETH ALEXANDER
Assistant to the Vice President for Legislative Affairs	SUDAFI HENRY
Assistant to the Vice President for Management and Administration	MOE VELA
Assistant to the Vice President and Director of Scheduling	ELISABETH HIRE
Assistant to the Vice President and Director of Advance	PETE SELFRIDGE
Chief of Staff to Dr. Jill Biden	CATHY RUSSELL
Executive Assistants to the Vice President	MICHELE SMITH, NANCY ORLOFF

The Office of the Vice President serves the Vice President in the performance of the many detailed activities incident to his immediate office.

Council of Economic Advisers

1800 G Street NW., Washington, DC 20502
Phone, 202–395–5084. Internet, www.whitehouse.gov/cea.

CHAIR	CHRISTINA D. ROMER
Members	AUSTAN D. GOOLSBEE, CECILIA E. ROUSE
Chief of Staff	KAREN L. ANDERSON

The Council of Economic Advisers primarily performs an analysis and appraisal of the national economy for the purpose of providing policy recommendations to the President.

The Council of Economic Advisers (CEA) was established in the Executive Office of the President by the Employment Act of 1946 (15 U.S.C. 1023). It now functions under that statute and Reorganization Plan No. 9 of 1953 (5 U.S.C. app.), effective August 1, 1953.

The Council consists of three members appointed by the President with the advice and consent of the Senate. One of the members is designated by the President as Chairman.

The Council analyzes the national economy and its various segments; advises the President on economic developments; appraises the economic programs and policies of the Federal Government; recommends to the President policies for economic growth and stability; assists in the preparation of the economic reports of the President to the Congress; and prepares the Annual Report of the Council of Economic Advisers.

For further information, contact the Council of Economic Advisers, 1800 G Street NW., Washington, DC 20502. Phone, 202–395–5084. Internet, www.whitehouse.gov/cea.

Council on Environmental Quality

722 Jackson Place NW., Washington, DC 20503
Phone, 202–395–5750 or 202–456–6224. Fax, 202–456–2710. Internet, www.whitehouse.gov/ceq.

CHAIR	NANCY SUTLEY
Chief of Staff	JOHN CARSON
Deputy Chief of Staff	NICOLE BUFFA
General Counsel	EDWARD A. BOLING
Deputy General Counsel	(VACANCY)
Associate Director for Climate Change	JASON BORDOFF
Associate Director for Communications	CHRISTINE GLUNZ
Associate Director for Community Protection and Climate Solutions	ANTHONY JONES
Associate Director for International Affairs and Climate Change	LANDON VAN DYKE
Associate Director for Lands and Water Ecosystems	MICHAEL BOOTS
Associate Director for Legislative Affairs	JESSICA MAHER
Associate Director for Natural Resources	TERRENCE BREYMAN
Associate Director for NEPA Oversight	HORST GRECZMIEL

Associate Director for Policy Outreach	AMELIA SALZMAN
Associate Director for Ocean and Coastal Policy	HARDY PEARCE

The Council on Environmental Quality formulates and recommends national policies and initiatives to improve the environment.

The Council on Environmental Quality (CEQ) was established within the Executive Office of the President by the National Environmental Policy Act of 1969 (NEPA) (42 U.S.C. 4321 *et seq.*). The Environmental Quality Improvement Act of 1970 (42 U.S.C. 4371 *et seq.*) established the Office of Environmental Quality (OEQ) to provide professional and administrative support for the Council. The Council and OEQ are collectively referred to as the Council on Environmental Quality, and the CEQ Chair, who is appointed by the President and confirmed by the Senate, serves as the Director of OEQ.

The Council develops policies which bring together the Nation's social, economic, and environmental priorities, with the goal of improving Federal decisionmaking. As required by NEPA, CEQ evaluates, coordinates, and mediates Federal activities. It advises and assists the President on both national and international environmental policy matters. CEQ also oversees Federal agency and department implementation of NEPA.

For further information, contact the Information Office, Council on Environmental Quality, 722 Jackson Place NW., Washington, DC 20503. Phone, 202–395–5750. Fax, 202–456–2710. Internet, www.whitehouse.gov/ceq.

National Security Council

Eisenhower Executive Office Building, Washington, DC 20504
Phone, 202–456–1414. Internet, www.whitehouse.gov/nsc.

Members:

THE PRESIDENT	BARACK H. OBAMA
THE VICE PRESIDENT	JOSEPH R. BIDEN, JR.
The Secretary of State	HILLARY RODHAM CLINTON
The Secretary of Defense	ROBERT M. GATES

Statutory Advisers:

Director of National Intelligence	DENNIS C. BLAIR
Chairman, Joint Chiefs of Staff	ADM. MICHAEL G. MULLEN, USN

Standing Participants:

The Secretary of the Treasury	TIMOTHY F. GEITHNER
Chief of Staff to the President	RAHM I. EMANUEL
Counsel to the President	GREGORY B. CRAIG
National Security Advisor	JAMES L. JONES, JR.
Assistant to the President for Economic Policy	LAWRENCE H. SUMMERS

Officials:

Assistant to the President for National Security Affairs	JAMES L. JONES, JR.

Assistant to the President for National Security Affairs and Deputy National Security Adviser	THOMAS E. DONLION

The National Security Council was established by the National Security Act of 1947, as amended (50 U.S.C. 402). The Council was placed in the Executive Office of the President by Reorganization Plan No. 4 of 1949 (5 U.S.C. app.).

The National Security Council is chaired by the President. Its statutory members, in addition to the President, are the Vice President and the Secretaries of State and Defense. The Chairman of the Joint Chiefs of Staff is the statutory military adviser to the Council, and the Director of the Central Intelligence Agency is its intelligence adviser. The Secretary of the Treasury, the U.S. Representative to the United Nations, the Assistant to the President for National Security Affairs, the Assistant to the President for Economic Policy, and the Chief of Staff to the President are invited to all meetings of the Council. The Attorney General and the Director of National Drug Control Policy are invited to attend meetings pertaining to their jurisdictions; other officials are invited, as appropriate.

The Council advises and assists the President in integrating all aspects of national security policy as it affects the United States—domestic, foreign, military, intelligence, and economic—in conjunction with the National Economic Council.

For further information, contact the National Security Council, Old Executive Office Building, Washington, DC 20504. Phone, 202–456–1414. Internet, www.whitehouse.gov/nsc.

Office of Administration

Eisenhower Executive Office Building
1650 Pennsylvania Avenue, NW., Washington, DC 20503
Phone, 202–456–2861. Internet, www.whitehouse.gov/oa.

DIRECTOR	CAMERON MOODY
DEPUTY DIRECTOR	(VACANCY)
Chief Financial Officer	ALLYSON LAACKMAN
Chief Information Officer	BROOK COLANGELO
Chief Procurement and Contract Management Officer	ALTHEA KIREILIS
Director for Equal Employment Opportunity	CLARA PATTERSON
Director for Office of Security and Emergency Preparedness	JOHN GILL
General Counsel	DENISE MAES

The Office of Administration was formally established within the Executive Office of the President by Executive Order 12028 of December 12, 1977. The Office provides administrative support services to all units within the Executive Office of the President. The services provided include information, personnel, technology, and financial management; data processing; library and research services; security; legislative liaisons; and general office operations such as mail, messenger, printing, procurement, and supply services.

For further information, contact the Office of the Director, Office of Administration, Washington, DC 20503. Phone, 202–456–2861. Internet, www.whitehouse.gov/oa.

Office of Management and Budget

Executive Office Building, Washington, DC 20503
Phone, 202–395–3080. Internet, www.whitehouse.gov/omb.

DIRECTOR	PETER ORSZAG
DEPUTY DIRECTOR	ROBERT NABORS
Deputy Director for Management	(VACANCY)
Chief of Staff	JILL BLICKSTEIN
Administrator, Office of Federal Procurement Policy	(VACANCY)
Administrator, Office of Information and Regulatory Affairs	(VACANCY)
Assistant Director for Management and Operations	LAUREN E. WRIGHT
Assistant Director for Budget	ELIZABETH M. ROBINSON
Assistant Director for Legislative Reference	JAMES J. JUKES
Associate Director for Communications	KENNETH BAER
Associate Director for Economic Policy	JEFFREY LIEBMAN
Associate Director for Education, Income Maintenance and Labor	ROBERT GORDON
Associate Director for General Government Programs	XAVIER BRIGGS
Associate Director for Information Technology and E-Government	VIVEK KUNDRA
Associate Director for Legislative Affairs	KATHERINE ELTRICH
Associate Director for National Security Programs	STEVE KOSIAK
Associate Director for Natural Resource Programs	SALLY ERICSSON
Controller, Office of Federal Financial Management	DANIEL I. WERFEL, *Acting*
General Counsel	PREETA BANSAL
Associate Director for Health	KEITH FONTENOT
Executive Associate Director	JEFFREY LIEBMAN

The Office of Management and Budget evaluates, formulates, and coordinates management procedures and program objectives within and among Federal departments and agencies. It also controls the administration of the Federal budget, while routinely providing the President with recommendations regarding budget proposals and relevant legislative enactments.

The Office of Management and Budget (OMB), formerly the Bureau of the Budget, was established in the Executive Office of the President pursuant to Reorganization Plan No. 1 of 1939 (5 U.S.C. app.).

The Office's primary functions are:

—to assist the President in developing and maintaining effective government by reviewing the organizational structure and management procedures of the executive branch to ensure that the intended results are achieved;

OFFICE OF MANAGEMENT AND BUDGET

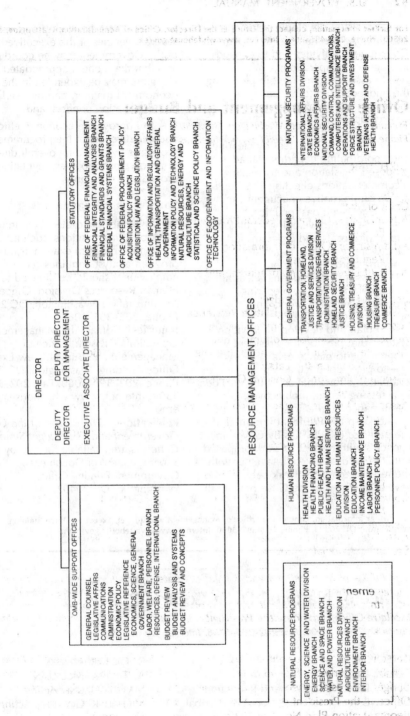

DIRECTOR
DEPUTY DIRECTOR FOR MANAGEMENT

DEPUTY DIRECTOR

EXECUTIVE ASSOCIATE DIRECTOR

OMB-WIDE SUPPORT OFFICES

GENERAL COUNSEL
LEGISLATIVE AFFAIRS
COMMUNICATIONS
ADMINISTRATION
ECONOMIC POLICY
LEGISLATIVE REFERENCE
ECONOMICS, SCIENCE, GENERAL GOVERNMENT BRANCH
LABOR, WELFARE, PERSONNEL BRANCH
RESOURCES, DEFENSE, INTERNATIONAL BRANCH

BUDGET REVIEW
BUDGET ANALYSIS AND SYSTEMS
BUDGET REVIEW AND CONCEPTS

STATUTORY OFFICES

OFFICE OF FEDERAL FINANCIAL MANAGEMENT
FINANCIAL INTEGRITY AND ANALYSIS BRANCH
FINANCIAL STANDARDS AND GRANTS BRANCH
FEDERAL FINANCIAL SYSTEMS BRANCH

OFFICE OF FEDERAL PROCUREMENT POLICY
ACQUISITION POLICY BRANCH
ACQUISITION LAW AND LEGISLATION BRANCH

OFFICE OF INFORMATION AND REGULATORY AFFAIRS
HEALTH, TRANSPORTATION AND GENERAL GOVERNMENT
INFORMATION POLICY AND TECHNOLOGY BRANCH
NATURAL RESOURCES, ENERGY AND AGRICULTURE BRANCH
STATISTICAL AND SCIENCE POLICY BRANCH

OFFICE OF E-GOVERNMENT AND INFORMATION TECHNOLOGY

RESOURCE MANAGEMENT OFFICES

NATURAL RESOURCE PROGRAMS

ENERGY, SCIENCE AND WATER DIVISION
ENERGY BRANCH
SCIENCE AND SPACE BRANCH
WATER AND POWER BRANCH
NATURAL RESOURCES DIVISION
AGRICULTURE BRANCH
ENVIRONMENT BRANCH
INTERIOR BRANCH

HUMAN RESOURCE PROGRAMS

HEALTH DIVISION
HEALTH FINANCING BRANCH
PUBLIC HEALTH BRANCH
HEALTH AND HUMAN SERVICES BRANCH
EDUCATION AND HUMAN RESOURCES DIVISION
EDUCATION BRANCH
INCOME MAINTENANCE BRANCH
LABOR BRANCH
PERSONNEL POLICY BRANCH

GENERAL GOVERNMENT PROGRAMS

TRANSPORTATION, HOMELAND, JUSTICE AND SERVICES DIVISION
TRANSPORTATION/GENERAL SERVICES ADMINISTRATION BRANCH
HOMELAND SECURITY BRANCH
JUSTICE BRANCH
HOUSING, TREASURY AND COMMERCE DIVISION
HOUSING BRANCH
TREASURY BRANCH
COMMERCE BRANCH

NATIONAL SECURITY PROGRAMS

INTERNATIONAL AFFAIRS DIVISION
STATE BRANCH
ECONOMICS AFFAIRS BRANCH
NATIONAL SECURITY DIVISION
COMMAND, CONTROL, COMMUNICATIONS, COMPUTERS AND INTELLIGENCE BRANCH
OPERATIONS AND SUPPORT BRANCH
FORCE STRUCTURE AND INVESTMENT BRANCH
VETERANS AFFAIRS AND DEFENSE HEALTH BRANCH

—to assist in developing efficient coordinating mechanisms to implement Government activities and to expand interagency cooperation;

—to assist the President in preparing the budget and in formulating the Government's fiscal program;

—to supervise and control the administration of the budget;

—to assist the President by clearing and coordinating departmental advice on proposed legislation and by making recommendations effecting Presidential action on legislative enactments, in accordance with past practice;

—to assist in developing regulatory reform proposals and programs for paperwork reduction, especially reporting burdens of the public;

—to assist in considering, clearing, and, where necessary, preparing proposed Executive orders and proclamations;

—to plan and develop information systems that provide the President with program performance data;

—to plan, conduct, and promote evaluation efforts that assist the President in assessing program objectives, performance, and efficiency;

—to keep the President informed of the progress of activities by Government agencies with respect to work proposed, initiated, and completed, together with the relative timing of work between the several agencies of the Government, all to the end that the work programs of the several agencies of the executive branch of the Government may be coordinated and that the moneys appropriated by the Congress may be expended in the most economical manner, barring overlapping and duplication of effort; and

—to improve the economy, efficiency, and effectiveness of the procurement processes by providing overall direction of procurement policies, regulations, procedures, and forms.

Sources of Information

Employment   Delegated examining is used for filling positions, such as economist, program examiners, and program analyst. Inquiries on employment should be directed to the Human Resources Division, Office of Administration, Washington, DC 20500. Phone, 202–395–1088.

Inquiries   Contact the Management and Operations Division, Office of Management and Budget, New Executive Office Building, Washington, DC 20503. Phone, 202–395–3080. Fax, 202–395–3504. Internet, www.whitehouse.gov/omb.

Publications   The Budget of the U.S. Government and The Budget System and Concepts are available for sale by the Superintendent of Documents, Government Printing Office, Washington, DC 20402.

For further information, contact the Office of Management and Budget, Executive Office Building, Washington, DC 20503. Phone, 202–395–3080. Internet, www.whitehouse.gov/omb.

Office of National Drug Control Policy

Executive Office of the President, Washington, DC 20503
Phone, 202–395–6700. Fax, 202–395–6708. Internet, www.ondcp.gov.

DIRECTOR	R. GIL KERLIKOWSKE
DEPUTY DIRECTOR	A. THOMAS MCLELLAN
Deputy Director for Demand Reduction	MARTHA GAGNE, Acting
Deputy Director for State, Local, and Tribal Affairs	MICHAEL K. GOTTLIEB, Acting
Deputy Director for Supply Reduction	PATRICK M. WARD, Acting
Associate Director, Performance and Budget	JON E. RICE

Associate Director, Legislative Affairs
Associate Director, Management and
Administration
Associate Director, Public Affairs
General Counsel
Chief Scientist, Counter-Drug Technology
Assessment Center
Associate Director, National Youth Anti-Drug
Media Campaign

DEBORAH J. WALKER, *Acting*
MICHELE C. MARX

RAFAEL LEMAITRE, *Acting*
DANIEL R. PETERSEN, *Acting*
DAVID W. MURRAY

ROBERT W. DENNISTON

The Office of National Drug Control Policy assists the President in establishing policies, priorities, and objectives in the National Drug Control Strategy. It also provides budget, program, and policy recommendations on the efforts of National Drug Control Program agencies.

The Office of National Drug Control Policy was established by the National Narcotics Leadership Act of 1988 (21 U.S.C. 1501 *et seq.*), effective January 29, 1989, reauthorized through the Office of National Drug Control Policy Reauthorization Act of 1988 (21 U.S.C. 1701 *et seq.*), and again reauthorized through the Office of National Drug Control Policy Reauthorization Act of 2006 (21 U.S.C. 1701 *et seq.*).

The Director of National Drug Control Policy is appointed by the President with the advice and consent of the Senate. The Director is assisted by a Deputy Director, a Deputy Director for Demand Reduction, a Deputy Director for Supply Reduction, and a Deputy Director for State, Local, and Tribal Affairs.

The Director is responsible for establishing policies, objectives, priorities, and performance measurements for the national drug control program, as well as for annually promulgating drug control strategies and supporting reports and a program budget, which the President submits to Congress. The Director advises the President regarding necessary changes in the organization, management,

budgeting, and personnel allocation of Federal agencies enforcing drug activities. The Director also notifies Federal agencies if their policies do not comply with their responsibilities under the National Drug Control Strategy. Additionally, the Office has direct programmatic responsibility for the Drug-Free Communities Program, the National Youth Anti-Drug Media Campaign, the various programs under the Counter-Drug Technology Assessment Center, and the High Intensity Drug Trafficking Areas Program.

Sources of Information

Employment Inquiries regarding employment should be directed to the Personnel Section, Office of National Drug Control Policy. Phone, 202–395–6695.

Publications To receive publications on drugs and crime, access specific drug-related data, obtain customized bibliographic searches, and learn more about data availability and other information resources, contact the Drugs and Crime Clearinghouse. Phone, 800–666–3332. Fax, 301–519–5212. Internet, www.ondcp.gov.

For further information, contact the Office of National Drug Control Policy, Executive Office of the President, Washington, DC 20503. Phone, 202–395–6700. Fax, 202–395–6708. Internet, www.ondcp.gov.

Office of Policy Development

Domestic Policy Council

Room 469, Eisenhower Executive Office Building, Washington, DC 20502
Phone, 202–456–5594. Internet, www.whitehouse.gov/dpc.

Assistant to the President and Director of the Domestic Policy Council	MELODY C. BARNES
Deputy Assistant to the President and Deputy Director of the Domestic Policy Council	HEATHER A. HIGGINBOTTOM
Deputy Assistant to the President and Director, Office of Social Innovation and Civic Participation	SONAL R. SHAH

National Economic Council

Room 235, Eisenhower Executive Office Building, Washington, DC 20502
Phone, 202–456–2800. Internet, www.whitehouse.gov/nec

Assistant to the President for Economic Policy and Director of the National Economic Council	LAWRENCE H. SUMMERS
Deputy Assistants to the President for Economic Policy	DIANA L. FARRELL, JASON L. FURMAN

The Office of Policy Development is comprised of the Domestic Policy Council and the National Economic Council, which are responsible for advising and assisting the President in the formulation, coordination, and implementation of domestic and economic policy. The Office of Policy Development also provides support for other policy development and implementation activities as directed by the President.

Domestic Policy Council

The Domestic Policy Council was established on August 16, 1993, by Executive Order 12859. The Council oversees development and implementation of the President's domestic policy agenda and ensures coordination and communication among the heads of relevant Federal offices and agencies.

National Economic Council

The National Economic Council was created on January 25, 1993, by Executive Order 12835, to coordinate the economic policymaking process and provide economic policy advice to the President. The Council also ensures that economic policy decisions and programs are consistent with the President's stated goals, and monitors the implementation of the President's economic goals.

Office of Science and Technology Policy

New Executive Office Building, 725 17th Street NW., Washington, DC 20502
Phone, 202–456–7116. Fax, 202–456–6021. Internet, www.ostp.gov.

DIRECTOR	JOHN HOLDREN
Chief of Staff	JIM KOHLENBERGER
Assistant Director At-Large	STEVE FETLER
General Counsel	RACHAEL LEONARD, *Acting*
Assistant Director, Federal Research and Development	KEI KOIZUMI
Assistant Director, Strategic Communicators / Senior Policy Analyst	RICK WEISS
Assistant Director, International Relations	JOAN ROLF
Assistant Director, Social and Behavioral Science	DIANE DIEULLIS, *Acting*
Assistant Director, Physical Sciences and Engineering	JEAN COTTAM ALLEN
Assistant Director, Life Sciences	DIANE DIEULLIS
Assistant Director, Biotechnology	MIKE STEBBINS
Associate Director and Chief Technology Officer	ANEESH CHOPRA
Assistant Director, Space and Aeronautics	ROBIE SAMANTA ROY
Assistant Director, Technology R&D	KEVIN HURST
Assistant Director, National Security and Emergency Preparedness	MIKE LEBLANC
Associate Director, Energy and Environment	SHERE ABBOTT
Operations Manager, Budget and Administration	DAVID HODGE
Executive Director, President's Council of Advisors on Science and Technology	DEBORAH STINE
Co-Chair, President's Council of Advisors on Science and Technology	ERIC LANDER
Co-Chair, President's Council of Advisors on Science and Technology	HAROLD VARMUS
Executive Director, National Science and Technology Council	CHRISTY JOHNSON
Director, National Coordination Office for the National Nanotechnology Initiative	CLAYTON TEAGUE
Director, National Coordination Office for Networking and Information Technology Research and Development	CHRIS GREER

The Office of Science and Technology Policy was established within the Executive Office of the President by the National Science and Technology Policy, Organization, and Priorities Act of 1976 (42 U.S.C. 6611).

The Office serves as a source of scientific, engineering, and technological analysis and judgment for the President with respect to major policies, plans, and programs of the Federal Government. In carrying out this mission, the Office advises the President of scientific and technological considerations involved in areas of national concern, including the economy, national security, health, foreign relations, and the environment; evaluates the scale, quality, and effectiveness of the Federal effort in science and technology; provides advice and assistance to the President, the Office of Management and Budget, and Federal agencies throughout the Federal budget development process; and assists the President in providing leadership and coordination for the research and development programs of the Federal Government.

For further information, contact the Office of Science and Technology Policy, New Executive Office Building, 725 17th Street NW., Washington, DC 20502. Phone, 202–456–7116. Fax, 202–456–6021. Internet, www.ostp.gov.

Office of the United States Trade Representative

600 Seventeenth Street NW., Washington, DC 20508
Phone, 202–395–3230. Internet, www.ustr.gov.

UNITED STATES TRADE REPRESENTATIVE	AMBASSADOR RONALD KIRK
Deputy U.S. Trade Representative (Washington)	DEMETRIOS MARANTIS
Deputy U.S. Trade Representative (Geneva)	PETER F. ALLGEIER
Chief of Staff	JULIANNA SMOOT
General Counsel	TIMOTHY REIF
Senior Counsel	PETER COWHEY
Assistant U.S. Trade Representative for Administration	FRED AMES
Assistant U.S. Trade Representative for Agricultural Affairs	JAMES MURPHY
Assistant U.S. Trade Representative for Southeast Asia and the Pacific	BARBARA WEISEL
Assistant U.S. Trade Representative for Congressional Affairs	DANIEL SEPULVEDA
Assistant U.S. Trade Representative for Economic Affairs	DAVID A. WALTERS
Assistant U.S. Trade Representative for Environment and Natural Resources	MARK LINSCOTT
Assistant U.S. Trade Representative for Europe and the Middle East	CHRISTOPHER WILSON
Assistant U.S. Trade Representative for Market Access & Industrial Competitiveness	JAMES SANFORD
Assistant U.S. Trade Representative for Intergovernmental Affairs and Public Liaison	LISA GARCIA
Assistant U.S. Trade Representative for Japan, Korea, and Asia Pacific Economic Cooperation Affairs	WENDY CUTLER
Assistant U.S. Trade Representative for China	TIMOTHY STRATFORD
Assistant U.S. Trade Representative for Central & South Asian Affairs	MICHAEL DELANEY
Assistant U.S. Trade Representative for Monitoring and Enforcement	DANIEL BRINZA
Assistant U.S. Trade Representative for Africa	FLORIE LISER

Assistant U.S. Trade Representative for Policy Coordination	CARMEN SURO-BREDIE
Assistant U.S. Trade Representative for Services and Investment	CHRISTINE BLISS
Assistant U.S. Trade Representative for Intellectual Property and Innovation	STANFORD MCCOY
Assistant U.S. Trade Representative for Labor	LEWIS KARESH
Assistant U.S. Trade Representative for World Trade Organization (WTO) and Multilateral Affairs	MATTHEW ROHDE
Assistant U.S. Trade Representative for the Americas	EVERETT EISSENSTAT
Assistant U.S. Trade Representative for Public and Media Affairs	CAROL GUTHRIE
Assistant U.S. Trade Representative for Trade & Development	MARY RYCKMAN
Deputy Chief of Mission (Geneva)	DAVID SHARK

The United States Trade Representative is responsible for directing all trade negotiations of and formulating trade policy for the United States.

The Office of the United States Trade Representative was created as the Office of the Special Representative for Trade Negotiations by Executive Order 11075 of January 15, 1963. The Trade Act of 1974 (19 U.S.C. 2171) established the Office as an agency of the Executive Office of the President charged with administering the trade agreements program.

The Office is responsible for setting and administering overall trade policy. It also provides that the United States Trade Representative shall be chief representative of the United States for the following:

—all activities concerning the General Agreement on Tariffs and Trade;

—discussions, meetings, and negotiations in the Organization for Economic Cooperation and Development when such activities deal primarily with trade and commodity issues;

—negotiations in the U.N. Conference on Trade and Development and other multilateral institutions when such negotiations deal primarily with trade and commodity issues;

—other bilateral and multilateral negotiations when trade, including East-West trade, or commodities is the primary issue;

—negotiations under sections 704 and 734 of the Tariff Act of 1930 (19 U.S.C. 1671c and 1673c); and

—negotiations concerning direct investment incentives and disincentives and bilateral investment issues concerning barriers to investment.

The Omnibus Trade and Competitiveness Act of 1988 codified these prior authorities and added additional authority, including the implementation of section 301 actions (regarding enforcement of U.S. rights under international trade agreements).

The Office is headed by the United States Trade Representative, a Cabinet-level official with the rank of Ambassador, who is directly responsible to the President. There are three Deputy United States Trade Representatives, who also hold the rank of Ambassador—two located in Washington and one in Geneva. The Chief Agricultural Negotiator also holds the rank of Ambassador.

The United States Trade Representative serves as an *ex officio* member of the Boards of Directors of the Export-Import Bank and the Overseas Private Investment Corporation, and serves on the National Advisory Council for International Monetary and Financial Policy.

OFFICE OF THE UNITED STATES TRADE REPRESENTATIVE

For further information, contact the Office of Public Affairs, Office of the United States Trade Representative, 600 Seventeenth Street NW., Washington, DC 20506. Phone, 202–395–3230. Internet, www.ustr.gov.

Departments

DEPARTMENT OF AGRICULTURE

1400 Independence Avenue SW., Washington, DC 20250
Phone, 202–720–4623. Internet, www.usda.gov.

SECRETARY OF AGRICULTURE	TOM VILSACK
DEPUTY SECRETARY	KATHLEEN MERRIGAN
Under Secretary for Farm and Foreign Agricultural Services	JAMES MILLER
Administrator, Farm Service Agency	JONATHAN COPPESS
Administrator, Foreign Agricultural Service	MICHAEL MICHNER
Administrator, Risk Management Agency	WILLIAM MURPHY, *Acting*
Under Secretary for Food, Nutrition, and Consumer Services	KEVIN CONCANNON
Administrator, Food and Nutrition Service	JULIE PARADIS
Director, Center for Nutrition Policy and Promotion	ROBERT POST, *Acting*
Under Secretary for Food Safety	(VACANCY)
Administrator, Food Safety and Inspection Service	ALFRED V. ALMANZA
Under Secretary for Natural Resources and Environment	(VACANCY)
Chief, Forest Service	ABIGAIL KIMBELL
Chief, Natural Resources Conservation Service	DAVID WHITE, *Acting*
Under Secretary for Research, Education, and Economics	(VACANCY)
Administrator, Agricultural Research Service	EDWARD B. KNIPLING
Administrator, Cooperative State Research, Education, and Extension Service	COLIEN HEFFERAN
Administrator, Economic Research Service	JOHN KORT
Administrator, National Agricultural Statistics Service	CYNTHIA CLARK
Under Secretary for Rural Development	(VACANCY)
Administrator, Rural Business and Cooperative Programs	JUDY CANALES
Administrator, Rural Housing and Community Facilities Programs	(VACANCY)
Administrator, Rural Utilities Programs	(VACANCY)
Assistant Secretary for Congressional Relations	(VACANCY)
Under Secretary for Marketing and Regulatory Programs	(VACANCY)
Administrator, Agricultural Marketing Service	RAYNE PEGG
Administrator, Animal and Plant Health Inspection Service	KEVIN SHEA, *Acting*

103

Administrator, Grain Inspection, Packers, and Stockyards Administration	J. DUDLEY BUTLER
Assistant Secretary for Administration	PEARLIE REED
Judicial Officer	WILLIAM G. JENSON
Chief Judge, Administrative Law Judges	MARC HILLSON
Director, Office of Ethics	RAYMOND SHEEHAN
Director, Office of Human Capital Management	JILL M. CRUMPACKER
Director, Office of Management Services	JEANNETTE CHIARI
Director, Office of Operations	JOHN CREW
Director, Office of Procurement and Property Management	DENISE HAYES, *Acting*
Director, Office of Security Services	MARY BALE, *Acting*
Director, Office of Small and Disadvantaged Business Utilization	(VACANCY)
Assistant Secretary for Civil Rights	JOE LEONARD
Director, Conflict Resolution and Prevention Center	SHEILA WALCOTT, *Acting*
Director, Office of Adjudication and Compliance	MICHAEL G. WATTS
Director, Office of Outreach and Diversity	CARL-MARTIN RUIZ
Chief Information Officer	CHRIS SMITH, *Acting*
Chief Financial Officer	JON HOLLADAY, *Acting*
General Counsel	J. MICHAEL KELLY, *Acting*
Inspector General	PHYLLIS K. FONG
Director, Office of Communications	CHRIS MATHER
Chief Economist	JOSEPH GLAUBER
Director, Office of Risk Assessment and Cost-Benefit Analysis	JAMES SCHAUB
Chairman, World Agricultural Outlook Board	GERALD BANGE
Director, Global Change Program Office	WILLIAM HOHENSTEIN
Director, Office of Energy Policy and New Uses	ROGER CONWAY
Director, National Appeals Division	ROGER J. KLURFELD
Director, Office of Budget and Program Analysis	SCOTT STEELE
Director, Office of the Executive Secretariat	BRUCE BUNDICK

[For the Department of Agriculture statement of organization, see the *Code of Federal Regulations*, Title 7, Part 2]

The Department of Agriculture works to improve and maintain farm income and to develop and expand markets abroad for agricultural products. The Department helps to curb and cure poverty, hunger, and malnutrition. It works to enhance the environment and to maintain production capacity by helping landowners protect the soil, water, forests, and other natural resources. The Department, through inspection and grading services, safeguards and ensures standards of quality in the daily food supply.

The Department of Agriculture (USDA) was created by act of May 15, 1862 (7 U.S.C. 2201).

In carrying out its work in the program mission areas, USDA relies on the support of departmental administration staff, as well as the Office of the Chief Financial Officer, Office of the Chief Information Officer, Office of Communications, Office of Congressional and Intergovernmental Relations, Office of the Inspector General, and the Office of the General Counsel.

DEPARTMENT OF AGRICULTURE

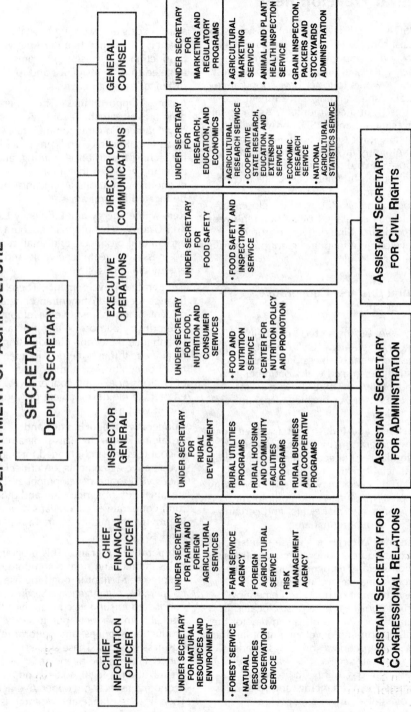

SECRETARY
DEPUTY SECRETARY

CHIEF INFORMATION OFFICER

CHIEF FINANCIAL OFFICER

INSPECTOR GENERAL

EXECUTIVE OPERATIONS

DIRECTOR OF COMMUNICATIONS

GENERAL COUNSEL

UNDER SECRETARY FOR NATURAL RESOURCES AND ENVIRONMENT
- FOREST SERVICE
- NATURAL RESOURCES CONSERVATION SERVICE

UNDER SECRETARY FOR FARM AND FOREIGN AGRICULTURAL SERVICES
- FARM SERVICE AGENCY
- FOREIGN AGRICULTURAL SERVICE
- RISK MANAGEMENT AGENCY

UNDER SECRETARY FOR RURAL DEVELOPMENT
- RURAL UTILITIES PROGRAMS
- RURAL HOUSING AND COMMUNITY FACILITIES PROGRAMS
- RURAL BUSINESS AND COOPERATIVE PROGRAMS

UNDER SECRETARY FOR FOOD, NUTRITION AND CONSUMER SERVICES
- FOOD AND NUTRITION SERVICE
- CENTER FOR NUTRITION POLICY AND PROMOTION

UNDER SECRETARY FOR FOOD SAFETY
- FOOD SAFETY AND INSPECTION SERVICE

UNDER SECRETARY FOR RESEARCH, EDUCATION, AND ECONOMICS
- AGRICULTURAL RESEARCH SERVICE
- COOPERATIVE STATE RESEARCH, EDUCATION, AND EXTENSION SERVICE
- ECONOMIC RESEARCH SERVICE
- NATIONAL AGRICULTURAL STATISTICS SERVICE

UNDER SECRETARY FOR MARKETING AND REGULATORY PROGRAMS
- AGRICULTURAL MARKETING SERVICE
- ANIMAL AND PLANT HEALTH INSPECTION SERVICE
- GRAIN INSPECTION, PACKERS AND STOCKYARDS ADMINISTRATION

ASSISTANT SECRETARY FOR CONGRESSIONAL RELATIONS

ASSISTANT SECRETARY FOR ADMINISTRATION

ASSISTANT SECRETARY FOR CIVIL RIGHTS

Rural Development

USDA's rural development mission is to assist rural Americans to increase their economic opportunities and improve their quality of life. To accomplish this, USDA works to foster new cooperative relationships among Government, industry, and communities. As a capital investment bank, USDA provides financing for rural housing and community facilities, business and cooperative development, telephone and high-speed Internet access, electric, water, and sewer infrastructure. Approximately 800 rural development field offices, staffed by 7,000 employees, provide frontline delivery of rural development loan and grant programs at the local level.

Rural Business-Cooperative Programs

To meet business credit needs in underserved areas, USDA rural development business programs are usually leveraged with commercial, cooperative, or other private sector lenders. USDA's business programs are as follows:

Business and Industry Guaranteed Loans This program helps create jobs and stimulates rural economies by providing financial backing for rural businesses. Loan proceeds may be used for working capital, machinery and equipment, buildings and real estate, and certain types of debt refinancing.

Business Enterprise These grants help public bodies, nonprofit corporations, and federally recognized Indian tribal groups finance and facilitate development of small and emerging private business enterprises located in rural areas. Grant funds can pay for the acquisition and development of land and the construction of buildings, plants, equipment, access streets and roads, parking areas, utility and service extensions, refinancing, and fees for professional services, as well as technical assistance and related training,

startup costs and working capital, financial assistance to a third party, production of television programs targeted to rural residents, and rural distance learning networks.

Business Opportunities This program promotes sustainable economic development in rural communities with exceptional needs. Funds are provided for technical assistance, training, and planning activities that improve economic conditions. Applicants must be located in rural areas.

Renewable Energy and Efficiency Loans and Grants This program encourages agricultural producers and small rural businesses to create renewable and energy-efficient systems.

Cooperative Development These grants finance the establishment and operation of centers for cooperative development. The primary purpose of this program is to enhance the economic condition of rural areas through the development of new cooperatives and improving operations of existing cooperatives, and encourage the development of value-added ventures.

Cooperative Opportunities and Problems Research This program encourages research, funded through cooperative agreements, on critical issues vital to the development and sustainability of agricultural and other rural cooperatives as a means of improving the quality of life in America's rural communities.

Cooperative Program This program helps farmers and rural communities become self-reliant through the use of cooperative organizations. Studies are conducted to support cooperatives that market farm products, purchase production supplies, and perform related business services. These studies concentrate on the financial, organizational, legal, social, and economic aspects of cooperative activity. Technical assistance and research is provided to improve cooperative performance in organizing new cooperatives, merging existing cooperatives, changing business structures, and developing strategies for growth. Applied research is conducted to give farmers and rural communities expert assistance pertaining to their cooperatives. The program also collects and publishes statistics regarding the role and scope of cooperative activity in U.S. agriculture. A bimonthly magazine, *Rural Cooperatives*, reports current developments and research for cooperative management leadership.

Economic Development These loans and grants finance economic development and job creation projects based on sound economic plans in rural areas. Loans and grants are available to any eligible USDA electric or telecommunications borrower to assist in developing rural areas from an economic standpoint, to create new job opportunities, and to help retain existing employment. Loans at zero interest are made primarily to finance business startup ventures and business expansion projects. Grants are made to eligible telephone and electric utilities to establish revolving loan programs operated at the local level. The revolving loan program provides capital to nonprofit entities and municipal organizations to finance business or community facilities which promote job creation in rural areas, for facilities which extend or improve medical care to rural residents, and for facilities which promote education and training to enhance marketable job skills for rural residents.

Intermediary Relending These loans finance business facilities and community development projects in rural areas. The Service lends these funds to intermediaries, which in turn provide loans to recipients who are developing business facilities or community development projects.

Sheep Industry The National Sheep Industry Improvement Center promotes strategic development activities to strengthen and enhance the production and marketing of sheep and goat products in the United States. It works to improve infrastructure and business development, market and environmental research, and designs unique responses to the needs of the industries for their long-term sustainable development. The Center's board of directors oversees its activities and operates a revolving fund for loans and grants.

Technology Transfer This program provides information to farmers and other rural users on a variety of sustainable agricultural practices that include both cropping and livestock operations. It offers reliable, practical information on production techniques and practices that reduce costs and that are environmentally friendly. Farmers can request such information by telephone at 800–346–9140.

For further information, contact the Rural Development, Legislative and Public Affairs Staff, Stop 0705, Department of Agriculture, 1400 Independence Avenue SW., Washington, DC 20250–0320. Phone, 202–720–4323.

Rural Housing Programs

Rural Development provides affordable rental housing, homeownership opportunities, and essential community facilities to rural Americans through a broad array of direct loan, guarantee, and grant programs. Rural residents and communities may inquire about any of these programs through local and State rural development offices. It also provides financial and management assistance through the following services:

—guaranteed single-family housing (SFH) loans which guarantee loans made by commercial lenders to moderate-income rural residents with sufficient income and acceptable credit, who may lack the downpayment to secure a loan without assistance;

—direct SFH loans made available to people with incomes less than 80 percent of area median, to build, purchase, and repair rural homes;

—home improvement and repair loans and grants for owner-occupants to remove health and safety hazards from a home;

—mutual self-help housing technical assistance grants for nonprofit organizations and public bodies to help groups of six to eight very low- and low-income families to build their own homes by providing "sweat equity" which reduces the families' mortgages;

—rural housing site loans for private or public nonprofit organizations to purchase sites for the development of housing for very low- and low-income families;

—direct and guaranteed multi-family housing loans for private nonprofit corporations, consumer cooperatives, State or local public agencies, and individuals or organizations operating on a nonprofit or limited profit basis to provide rental or cooperative housing in rural areas for persons of very low, low, and moderate income;

—farm labor housing loans and grants enabling farmers, public or private nonprofit organizations, or units of local government to build, buy, or rehabilitate farm labor housing;

—housing preservation grants made to a public body or public/private nonprofit organization to provide assistance to homeowners and landlords to repair and rehabilitate housing for very low- and low-income families in rural areas;

—housing for the homeless, SFH real estate-owned (REO) property to nonprofit organizations or public bodies for transitional housing for the homeless and to the Federal Emergency Management Agency to house families affected by natural disasters; and

—community program loans, direct and guaranteed loans and grants for public and quasi-public bodies, nonprofit associations, and Indian tribes for essential community facilities such as health care centers, public safety buildings and vehicles, and child care centers.

For further information, contact the Rural Development, Legislative and Public Affairs Staff, Stop 0705, Department of Agriculture, 1400 Independence Avenue SW., Washington, DC 20250–0320. Phone, 202–720–4323.

Rural Utilities Programs

Rural Development helps finance rural electric and telecommunications utilities in obtaining financing and administers a nationwide water and waste loan and grant program to improve the quality of life and promote economic development in rural America. A total of 890 rural electric and 800 rural telecommunications utilities in 47 States, Puerto Rico, the Virgin Islands, Guam, the Republic of the Marshall Islands, the Northern Mariana Islands, and the Federated States of Micronesia have received financial assistance. It also provides assistance through the following programs:

—The electric program provides loans for improving electric service to persons in rural areas, including construction of electric generating plants and transmission and distribution lines to provide reliable electric service.

—The telecommunications program provides loans and grants to improve telecommunications service and high-speed Internet access in rural areas.

—The water and waste direct and guaranteed loan program provides assistance to develop water and wastewater systems, including solid waste disposal and storm drainage in rural areas, cities, and towns.

—Water and waste disposal grants assist in reducing water and waste disposal costs to a reasonable level for users of the system.

—Emergency community water assistance grants provide assistance to rural communities experiencing a significant decline in quantity or quality of drinking water.

—Technical assistance and training grants are available to nonprofit organizations to provide rural water and waste system officials with technical assistance and training on a wide range of issues relating to the delivery of water and waste service to rural residents.

—Solid waste management grants are available for nonprofit organizations and public bodies to provide technical assistance and training to rural areas and towns to reduce or eliminate pollution of water resources and improve planning and management of solid waste facilities.

—The rural water circuit rider technical assistance program provides technical assistance to rural water systems to solve operational, financial, and management challenges.

—The distance learning and telemedicine program provides financing to help rural schools and health care providers purchase or improve telecommunications facilities and equipment to bring educational and medical resources to rural areas that otherwise might be unavailable.

—Rural Development also guarantees loans from the Department of the Treasury's Federal Financing Bank (FFB), which lends to borrowers, primarily for large-scale electric and telecommunication facilities. It may also guarantee electric and telecommunications loans from private sources.

For further information, contact the Rural Development Legislative and Public Affairs Staff, Department of Agriculture, Stop 0705, 1400 Independence Avenue SW., Washington, DC 20250–0320. Phone, 202–720–4323.

Marketing and Regulatory Programs

This mission area includes marketing and regulatory programs other than those concerned with food safety.

Agricultural Marketing Service

The Agricultural Marketing Service (AMS) was established by the Secretary of Agriculture on April 2, 1972, under the authority of Reorganization Plan No. 2 of 1953 (5 U.S.C. app.) and other authorities. The Service administers standardization, grading, certification, market news, marketing orders, research and promotion, and regulatory programs.

Market News The Service provides current, unbiased information to producers, processors, distributors, and others to assist them in the orderly marketing and distribution of farm commodities. Information is collected on supplies, shipments, prices, location, quality, condition, and other market data on farm products in specific markets and marketing areas. The data is disseminated nationally via the Internet and other electronic means and is shared with several countries. The Service also assists other countries in developing their own marketing information systems.

Standardization, Grading, and Classing Nearly 600 grade standards have been established for some 230 agricultural commodities to help buyers and sellers trade on agreed-upon quality levels. Standards are developed with the benefit of views from those in the industries

directly affected and others interested. The Service also participates in developing international commodity standards to facilitate trade.

Grading and classing services are provided to certify the grade and quality of products. These grading services are provided to buyers and sellers of live cattle, swine, sheep, meat, poultry, eggs, rabbits, fruits, vegetables, tree nuts, peanuts, dairy products, and tobacco. Classing services are provided to buyers and sellers of cotton and cotton products. These services are mainly voluntary and are provided upon request and for a fee. The Service is also responsible for testing seed.

Laboratory Testing The Service provides microbiological, chemical, and other scientific laboratory support to its commodity and food procurement programs, testing peanuts for aflatoxin, and testing seeds for germination and purity. The Agency also carries out quality assurance and safety oversight activities for its milk market laboratories, resident grading programs, and State and private laboratory programs.

The Service also administers the Pesticide Data Program which, in cooperation with States, samples and analyzes 33 agricultural commodities for pesticides residue. It shares residue test results with the Environmental Protection Agency and other public agencies.

Food Quality Assurance   Under a governmentwide quality assurance program, AMS is responsible for the development and revision of specifications used by Federal agencies in procuring food for military and civilian uses. The Service coordinates and approves certification programs designed to ensure that purchased products conform to the specification requirements.

Regulatory Programs   The Service administers several regulatory programs designed collectively to protect producers, handlers, and consumers of agricultural commodities from financial loss or personal injury resulting from careless, deceptive, or fraudulent marketing practices. Such regulatory programs encourage fair trading practices in the marketing of fruits and vegetables, require truth in seed labeling and in advertising. The Service provides voluntary laboratory analyses of egg products, and monitors the disposition of restricted shell eggs—eggs that are a potential health hazard.

Marketing Agreements and Orders   The Service administers marketing agreements and orders to establish and maintain orderly marketing conditions for certain commodities. Milk marketing orders establish minimum prices that handlers or distributors are required to pay producers. Programs for fruits, vegetables, and related specialty crops like nuts and spearmint oil promote product quality control and help stabilize supplies and market prices. In some cases, they also authorize research and market development activities, including advertising supported by assessments that handlers pay. Through the orderly marketing of commodities facilitated by these programs, the interests of both producers and consumers are protected.

Plant Variety Protection Program   The Service administers a program that provides for the issuance of certificates of plant variety protection. These certificates afford developers of novel varieties of sexually reproduced plants exclusive rights to sell, reproduce, import, or export such varieties, or use

them in the production of hybrids or different varieties for a period of 20 years for nonwoody plants and 25 years for woody plants.

Research and Promotion Programs   The Service monitors certain industry-sponsored research, promotion, and information programs authorized by Federal laws. These programs provide farmers and processors with a means to finance and operate various research, promotion, and information activities for cotton, potatoes, eggs, milk and dairy products, beef, pork, honey, watermelon, mushrooms, soybeans, blueberries, avocados, peanuts, and popcorn.

Transportation Programs   The Service is also responsible for the promotion of an efficient transportation system for rural America that begins at the farm gate and moves agricultural and other rural products through the Nation's highways, railroads, airports, and waterways, and into the domestic and international marketplace. To accomplish this, AMS conducts economic studies and analyses of these systems, and represents agricultural and rural transportation interests in policy and regulatory forums. To provide direct assistance to the transportation community, AMS supplies research and technical information to producers, producer groups, shippers, exporters, rural communities, carriers, governmental agencies, and universities.

Organic Standards   The Service, with the assistance of the National Organic Standards Board, develops national organic standards.

Other Programs   Other marketing service activities include financial grants to States for marketing improvement projects. The Agency also has responsibility for the conduct of studies of the facilities and methods used in the physical distribution of food and other farm products; for research designed to improve the handling of all agricultural products as they move from farm to consumers; for increasing marketing efficiency by developing improved operating methods and facilities; and for certifying equipment for processing, handling, and distributing dairy, poultry, and meat products.

Pesticide Recordkeeping Program The Agricultural Marketing Service manages the Pesticide Recordkeeping Program in coordination with State agencies, the National Agricultural Statistics Service, and the Environmental Protection Agency. The Service has developed educational programs and works with State agencies in inspecting applicator records.

For further information, contact the Public Affairs Staff, Agricultural Marketing Service, Department of Agriculture, Room 3510, South Agriculture Building, Stop 0273, Washington, DC 20250. Phone, 202–720–8998 or visit the Web site at www.ams.usda.gov.

Animal and Plant Health Inspection Service

[For the Animal and Plant Health Inspection Service statement of organization, see the *Code of Federal Regulations,* Title 7, Part 371]

The Animal and Plant Health Inspection Service was reestablished by the Secretary of Agriculture on March 14, 1977, pursuant to authority contained in 5 U.S.C. 301 and Reorganization Plan No. 2 of 1953 (5 U.S.C. app.).

The Service was established to conduct regulatory and control programs to protect and improve animal and plant health for the benefit of man and the environment. In cooperation with State governments, the agency administers Federal laws and regulations pertaining to animal and plant health and quarantine, humane treatment of animals, and the control and eradication of pests and diseases. Regulations to prevent the introduction or interstate spread of certain animal or plant pests or diseases are also enforced by the Service. It also carries out research and operational activities to reduce crop and livestock depredation caused by birds, rodents, and predators.

Biotechnology Regulatory Services Biotechnology regulatory officials are responsible for regulating the importation, movement, and field release of genetically engineered plants, insects, microorganisms, and any other known organism or potential plant pest.

Biotechnology regulations are designed to ensure that genetically engineered organisms, such as herbicide-tolerant cotton or virus-resistant papayas, are just as safe for agriculture and the environment as traditionally bred crop varieties. In regulating biotechnology, the Service works in concert with the Environmental Protection Agency and the Food and Drug Administration, agencies that also play important roles in protecting agriculture, a safe food supply, and the environment. Its involvement begins when a person or organization wishes to import, move across a State line, or field-test a genetically engineered plant. These activities are subject to the Service's permitting and notification system.

Plant Protection and Quarantine Plant protection officials are responsible for programs to control or eradicate plant pests and diseases. These programs are carried out in cooperation with the States involved, other Federal agencies, farmers, and private organizations. Pest control programs use a single tool or a combination of pest control techniques, both chemical and nonchemical, which are both effective and safe.

Plant protection officials develop Federal regulations and policies that prohibit or restrict the entry of foreign pests and plants, plant products, animal products and byproducts, and other materials that may harbor pests or diseases. These regulations and policies help protect agricultural production and natural resources from pests and diseases. The Service continues to take regulatory action on prohibited or restricted products.

Veterinary Services Animal health officials are responsible for programs to protect and improve the health, quality, and marketability of U.S. animals and animal products. The programs are carried out through cooperative links with States, foreign governments, livestock producers, and other Federal agencies.

Service officials exclude, control, and eradicate animal pests and diseases by carrying out eradication and control programs for certain diseases, providing diagnostic services, and gathering and disseminating information regarding animal health in the United States through land, air, and ocean ports. They also certify as to the health status of animals and animal products being exported to other countries, and respond to animal disease incursions or epidemics which threaten the health status of U.S. livestock and poultry.

The Service also administers a Federal law intended to ensure that all veterinary biological products, whether developed by conventional or new biotechnological procedures, used in the diagnosis, prevention, and treatment of animal disease are safe, pure, potent, and effective. The Service regulates firms that manufacture veterinary biological products subject to the act, including licensing the manufacturing establishment and its products, inspecting production facilities and production methods, and testing products under a surveillance program.

Animal Care   The Service administers Federal laws concerned with the humane care and handling of all warm-blooded animals bought, sold, and transported in commerce and used or intended for use as pets at the wholesale level, or used or intended for use in exhibitions or for research purposes. The agency also enforces the Horse Protection Act of 1970, which prohibits the soring of horses at shows and sales.

International Services   Service activities in the international arena include conducting cooperative plant and animal pest and disease control, eradication, and surveillance programs in foreign countries. These programs provide a first line of defense for the United States against threats such as screwworm, medfly, foot-and-mouth disease, and other exotic diseases and pests. The Service also provides international representation concerning sanitary and phytosanitary technical trade issues, and manages programs for overseas preclearance of commodities, passengers, and U.S. military activities.

Wildlife Services   Wildlife services officials cooperate with States, counties, local communities, and agricultural producer groups to reduce crop and livestock depredations caused by birds, rodents, and predators. Using methods and techniques that are biologically sound, environmentally acceptable, and economically feasible, they participate in efforts to educate and advise farmers and ranchers on proper uses of control methods and techniques; suppress serious nuisances and threats to public health and safety caused by birds, rodents, and other wildlife in urban and rural communities; and work with airport managers to reduce risks of bird strikes. In addition, they conduct research into predator-prey relationships, new control methods, and more efficient and safe uses of present methods such as toxicants, repellants and attractants, biological controls, scare devices, and habitat alteration.

For further information, contact Legislative and Public Affairs, Animal and Plant Health Inspection Service, Department of Agriculture, Washington, DC 20250. Phone, 202–720–2511.

Grain Inspection, Packers, and Stockyards Administration

The Grain Inspection, Packers, and Stockyards Administration (GIPSA) was established in 1994 to facilitate the marketing of livestock, poultry, meat, cereals, oilseeds, and related agricultural products, and to promote fair and competitive trading practices for the overall benefit of consumers and American agriculture. The Agency's mission is carried out in two different segments of American agriculture. The Federal Grain Inspection Service provides the U.S. grain market with Federal quality standards and a uniform system for applying them. The Packers and Stockyards Programs (P&SP) enforces the Packers and Stockyards Act of 1921 (P&S Act), 7 U.S.C. 181 *et seq.*, to promote fair and competitive marketing environments for the livestock, meat, and poultry industries. GIPSA also certifies State central filing systems for notification of liens against farm products. GIPSA is responsible for establishing official U.S. standards for grain and other assigned commodities, and for administering a nationwide official inspection and weighing system.

Inspection   The United States Grain Standards Act requires that, with some exceptions, all U.S. export grain be officially inspected. At export port locations, inspection is performed by GIPSA or by State agencies that have been delegated export inspection authority by the Administrator. For domestic grain marketed at inland locations, the Administrator designates private and State agencies to provide official inspection services upon request. Both export and domestic services are provided on a fee-for-service basis.

Weighing Official weighing of U.S. export grain is performed at port locations by GIPSA or by State agencies that have been delegated export weighing authority by the Administrator. For domestic grain marketed at inland locations, the weighing services may be provided by GIPSA or by designated private or State agencies. Weighing services are provided on a fee-for-service basis, upon request.

Standardization The Administration is responsible for establishing, maintaining, and revising official U.S. standards for corn, wheat, rye, oats, barley, flaxseed, sorghum, soybeans, triticale, sunflower seed, canola, and mixed grain. It is authorized to perform applied research to develop methods to improve accuracy and uniformity in grading grain. It is also responsible for standardization and inspection activities for rice, dry beans, peas, lentils, hay, straw, hops, and related processed grain commodities. Although standards no longer exist for hay, straw, and hops, GIPSA maintains inspection procedures for and retains authority to inspect these commodities.

Methods Development The Administration's methods development activities include applied research or tests that produce new or improved techniques for measuring grain quality. Examples include new knowledge gained through study of how to establish the framework for real-time grain inspection and develop reference methods to maintain consistency and standardization in the grain inspection system, and the comparison of different techniques for evaluation of end-use quality in wheat.

Packers and Stockyards Activities The P&S Act prohibits unfair, deceptive, anti-competitive, and fraudulent practices by market agencies, dealers, packers, swine contractors, and live poultry dealers in those particular industries. The P&S Act protects producers and poultry growers by requiring most regulated entities to obtain bonds and meet strict payment requirements. To protect unpaid cash sellers of livestock, packers are subject to trust provisions which require that livestock and related investments or proceeds from meat, meat food products, or livestock products derived from them be held in trust for unpaid sellers until payment is made in full. A similar provision exists for live poultry dealers to protect growers. P&SP analyzes all trust and bond claims as a courtesy to the regulated industries. It is also responsible for the Truth-in-Lending Act and the Fair Credit Reporting Act as each relates to persons and firms subject to the P&S Act. P&SP carries out the Secretary's responsibilities under section 1324 of the Food Security Act of 1985 pertaining to State-established central filing systems to pre-notify buyers, commission merchants, and selling agents of security interests against farm products. GIPSA administers the section of the statute commonly referred to as the "Clear Title" provision, and certifies qualifying State systems.

For further information, contact the Grain Inspection, Packers, and Stockyards Administration, Department of Agriculture, Washington, DC 20250. Phone, 202–720–0219.

Food Safety

Food Safety and Inspection Service

The Food Safety and Inspection Service (FSIS) was established by the Secretary of Agriculture on June 17, 1981, pursuant to authority contained in 5 U.S.C. 301 and Reorganization Plan No. 2 of 1953 (5 U.S.C. app.). FSIS is responsible for ensuring that the nation's commercial supply of meat, poultry, and egg products is safe, wholesome, and correctly labeled and packaged.

Meat, Poultry, and Egg Products Inspection Federal meat and poultry inspection is mandatory for cattle, calves, swine, goats, sheep, lambs, horses (and other equines), chickens, turkeys, ducks, geese, and guineas used for human food. FSIS provides for the inspection of each animal or bird at slaughter and processed products during various stages of production.

FSIS inspects all raw meat and poultry sold in interstate and foreign commerce, including imported products. It monitors meat and poultry products after they leave federally inspected plants. FSIS tests samples of egg products and meat and poultry products for microbial and chemical contaminants to monitor trends for enforcement purposes.

FSIS provides inspection at Federal facilities for meat, poultry, and egg products, as well as voluntary inspection for animals not covered under mandatory inspection regulations such as buffalo, rabbit, and deer. It monitors meat and poultry products in storage, distribution, and retail channels; and takes necessary compliance actions to protect the public, including detention of products, voluntary product recalls, court-ordered seizures of products, administrative withdrawal of inspection, and referral for criminal prosecution. FSIS also monitors state inspection programs which inspect meat and poultry products sold only within the state in which they were produced.

FSIS maintains a toll-free meat and poultry hotline (phone, 888–674–6854, TTY, 800–256–7072) to answer questions in English and Spanish about the safe handling of meat, poultry, and egg products. The hotline's hours are Monday through Friday, from 10 a.m. to 4 p.m., eastern time, year-round. An extensive selection of food safety messages, in English and Spanish, is also available at the same number 24 hours a day.

"Ask Karen" is a Web-based virtual representative tool that provides answers to consumer questions about food safety. "Ask Karen" is available 24 hours a day, 7 days a week, at www.askkaren.gov.

For further information, contact the Director, Food Safety Education Staff, Food Safety and Inspection Service, Department of Agriculture, Beltsville, Maryland 20705. Phone, 301–344–4755. Fax, 301–504–0203. Internet, www.fsis.usda.gov. Email, MPHotline.fsis@usda.gov.

Food, Nutrition, and Consumer Services

The mission of Food, Nutrition, and Consumer Services is to reduce hunger and food insecurity, in partnership with cooperating organizations, by providing access to food, a healthful diet, and nutrition education to children and needy people in a manner that supports American agriculture.

Food and Nutrition Service

The Food and Nutrition Service (FNS) administers the USDA food assistance programs. These programs, which serve one in six Americans, represent our Nation's commitment to the principle that no one in this country should fear hunger or experience want. They provide a Federal safety net to people in need. The goals of the programs are to provide needy persons with access to a more nutritious diet, to improve the eating habits of the Nation's children, and to help America's farmers by providing an outlet for distributing foods purchased under farmer assistance authorities.

The Service works in partnership with the States in all its programs. State and local agencies determine most administrative details regarding distribution of food benefits and eligibility of participants, and FNS provides commodities and funding for additional food and to cover administrative costs. FNS administers the following food assistance programs:

—The Food Stamp Program provides food benefits through State and local welfare agencies to needy persons to increase their food purchasing power. The benefits are used by program participants to buy food in retail stores approved by the Food and Nutrition Service to accept and redeem the benefits.

—The Special Supplemental Nutrition Program for Women, Infants, and Children (WIC) improves the health of low-income pregnant, breastfeeding, and nonbreastfeeding postpartum women, and infants and children up to 5 years of age by providing them with specific nutritious food supplements, nutrition education, and health care referrals.

—The WIC Farmers' Market Nutrition Program provides WIC participants with increased access to fresh produce. WIC participants receive coupons to purchase fresh fruits and vegetables from authorized farmers.

—The Commodity Supplemental Food Program provides a package of foods monthly to low-income pregnant, postpartum, and breastfeeding women, their infants and children under age 6, and the elderly. Nutrition education is also provided through this program.

—The National School Lunch Program supports nonprofit food services in elementary and secondary schools and in residential child-care institutions. More than half of the meals served through these institutions are free or at reduced cost.

—The School Breakfast Program supplements the National School Lunch Program by supporting schools in providing needy children with free or low-cost breakfasts that meet established nutritional standards.

—The Special Milk Program for Children provides milk for children in those schools, summer camps, and child-care institutions that have no federally supported meal programs.

—The Child and Adult Care Food Program provides cash and commodities for meals for preschool and school-age children in child-care facilities and for functionally impaired adults in facilities that provide nonresidential care for such individuals.

—The Summer Food Service Program for Children helps various organizations get nutritious meals to needy preschool and school-age children during the summer months and during school vacations.

—The Emergency Food Assistance Program provides State agencies with commodities for distribution to food banks, food pantries, soup kitchens, and other charitable institutions throughout the country, with administrative funds to assist in distribution.

—The Food Distribution Program on Indian Reservations and the Trust Territories provides an extensive package of commodities monthly to low-income households on or near Indian reservations in lieu of food stamps. This program is administered at the local level by Indian tribal organizations or State agencies.

—The Nutrition Program for the Elderly provides cash and commodities to States for meals for senior citizens. The food is delivered through senior citizen centers or meals-on-wheels programs.

—The Nutrition Assistance Programs for Puerto Rico and the Northern Marianas are block grant programs that replace the Food Stamp Programs in these two territories and provide cash and coupons to resident participants.

—The Nutrition Education and Training Program grants funds to States for the development and dissemination of nutrition information and materials to children and for training of food service and teaching personnel.

For further information, contact the Public Information Officer, Food and Nutrition Service, Department of Agriculture, Alexandria, VA 22302. Phone, 703–305–2286. Internet, www.usda.gov/fns.htm.

Center for Nutrition Policy and Promotion

The Center coordinates nutrition policy in USDA and provides overall leadership in nutrition education for the American public. It also coordinates with the Department of Health and Human Services in the review, revision, and dissemination of the *Dietary Guidelines for Americans*, the Federal Government's statement of nutrition policy formed by a consensus of scientific and medical professionals.

For further information, contact the Office of Public Information, Center for Nutrition Policy and Promotion, Suite 200, 1120 20th Street NW., Washington, DC 20036–3406. Phone, 202–418–2312. Internet, www.cnpp.usda.gov.

Farm and Foreign Agricultural Services

Farm Service Agency

The Farm Service Agency (FSA) administers farm commodity, disaster, and conservation programs for farmers and ranchers, and makes and guarantees farm emergency, ownership, and operating loans through a network of State and county offices.

Farm Commodity Programs FSA manages commodity programs such as the direct and countercyclical program, commodity and livestock disaster programs, marketing assistance loan programs, noninsured crop disaster assistance programs, and the tobacco transition payment program. It administers commodity loan programs for wheat, rice, corn, grain sorghum, barley, oats, oilseeds, peanuts, upland and extra-long-staple cotton, and sugar. FSA provides operating personnel for the Commodity Credit Corporation (CCC), a Government-owned and -operated organization. CCC provides short-term loans using the commodity as collateral. These loans provide farmers with interim financing and facilitate orderly marketing of farm commodities throughout the year.

Farm Loan Programs FSA makes and guarantees loans to family farmers and ranchers to purchase farmland and finance agricultural production. These programs help farmers who are temporarily unable to obtain private commercial credit. These may be beginning farmers who have insufficient net worth to qualify for commercial credit, who have suffered financial setbacks from natural disasters, or who have limited resources with which to establish and maintain profitable farming operations.

Noninsured Crop Disaster Assistance Program (NAP) NAP provides catastrophic crop loss protection for crops not covered by Federal crop insurance. Crops that are eligible include commercial crops grown for food and fiber, floriculture, ornamental nursery products, Christmas tree crops, turfgrass sod, seed crops, aquaculture (including ornamental fish such as goldfish), and industrial crops. Losses resulting from natural disasters not covered by the crop insurance policy may also be eligible for NAP assistance. NAP does not include trees grown for wood, paper, or pulp products.

Other Emergency Assistance There are FSA programs to assist farmers who encounter natural disasters from drought, flood, freeze, tornadoes, and other natural calamities. Eligible producers can be compensated for crop losses, livestock feed losses, and tree damage, and for the cost of rehabilitating eligible farmlands damaged by natural disaster. Low-interest loans for eligible farmers can help cover production and physical losses in counties declared disaster areas.

The largest component of USDA disaster assistance is the Crop Disaster

Program (CDP), which has provided more than $3 billion in financial relief to farmers, ranchers, foresters, and other agricultural producers who incurred losses because of recent adverse weather conditions.

Conservation Programs FSA's conservation programs include enhancement of wildlife habitat and water and air quality. The Conservation Reserve Program is the Federal Government's single-largest environmental improvement program on private lands. It safeguards millions of acres of topsoil from erosion, improves air quality, increases wildlife habitat, and protects ground and surface water by reducing water runoff and sedimentation. In return for planting a protective cover of grass or trees on vulnerable property, the owner receives a rental payment each year of a multi-year contract. Cost-share payments are also available to help establish permanent areas of grass, legumes, trees, windbreaks, or plants that improve water quality and give shelter and food to wildlife.

Commodity Operations FSA's commodity operations system facilitates the storage, management, and disposition of commodities used to meet humanitarian needs abroad. It administers the United States Warehouse Act (USWA), which authorizes the Secretary of Agriculture to license warehouse operators who store agricultural products. Warehouse operators that apply must meet the USDA standards established within the USWA and its regulations. Under the milk price support program, the Commodity Credit Corporation buys surplus butter, cheese, and nonfat dry milk from processors at announced prices to support the price of milk. These purchases help maintain market prices at the legislated support level, and the surplus commodities are used for hunger relief both domestically and internationally. FSA's commodity operations system also coordinates with other Government agencies to provide surplus commodities for various programs and also purchases commodities for the National School Lunch Program and other domestic feeding programs.

For further information, contact the Public Affairs Branch, Farm Service Agency, Department of Agriculture, Stop 0506, 1400 Independence Avenue SW., Washington, DC 20250. Phone, 202–720–5237. Internet, www.fsa.usda.gov.

Commodity Credit Corporation

The Commodity Credit Corporation (CCC) stabilizes, supports, and protects farm income and prices, assists in maintaining balanced and adequate supplies of agricultural commodities and their products, and facilitates the orderly distribution of commodities.

CCC carries out assigned foreign assistance activities, such as guaranteeing the credit sale of U.S. agricultural commodities abroad. Major emphasis is also being directed toward meeting the needs of developing nations. Agricultural commodities are supplied and exported to combat hunger and malnutrition and to encourage economic development in developing countries. In addition, under the Food for Progress Program, CCC supplies commodities to provide assistance to developing democracies.

For further information, contact the Information Division, Foreign Agricultural Service, Department of Agriculture, Stop 1004, 1400 Independence Avenue SW., Washington, DC 20250. Phone, 202–720–7115. Fax, 202–720–1727.

Risk Management Agency

The Risk Management Agency (RMA), via the Federal Crop Insurance Corporation (FCIC), oversees and administers the crop insurance program under the Federal Crop Insurance Act.

Crop insurance is offered to qualifying producers through 16 private sector crop insurance companies. Under the new Standard Reinsurance Agreement (SRA), RMA provides reinsurance, pays premium subsidies, reimburses insurers for administrative and operating costs and oversees the financial integrity and operational performance of the delivery system. RMA bears much of the noncommercial insurance risk under the SRA, allowing insurers to retain commercial insurance risks or reinsure those risks in the private market.

In 2006, the Federal crop insurance program is expected to provide producers with more than $44 billion in protection on approximately 246 million acres through about 1.2 million policies. There are 22 insurance plans available and 26 active pilot programs in various stages of development.

RMA is also working closely with the private sector to find new and innovative ways to provide expanded coverage. This includes risk protection for specialty crops, livestock and forage, and rangeland and pasture. Thus, RMA is able to reduce the need for ad hoc disaster bills and available coverage caused by long-term production declines that result from extended drought in many areas.

Additional information about RMA can be found on its Web site (www.rma.usda.gov), including agency news, State profiles, publications, announcements on current issues, summaries of insurance sales, pilot programs, downloadable crop policies, and agency-sponsored events. The site also features online tools, calculators, and applications.

For further information, contact the Office of the Administrator, Risk Management Agency, Department of Agriculture, Stop 0801, 1400 Independence Avenue SW., Washington, DC 20250. Phone, 202–690–2803. Internet, www.rma.usda.gov.

Foreign Agricultural Service

The Foreign Agricultural Service (FAS) works to improve foreign market access for U.S. products, to build new markets, to improve the competitive position of U.S. agriculture in the global marketplace, and to provide food aid and technical assistance to foreign countries.

FAS has the primary responsibility for USDA's activities in the areas of international marketing, trade agreements and negotiations, and the collection and analysis of international statistics and market information. It also administers the USDA's export credit guarantee and food aid programs. FAS helps increase income and food availability in developing nations by mobilizing expertise for agriculturally led economic growth.

FAS also enhances U.S. agricultural competitiveness through a global network of agricultural economists, marketing experts, negotiators, and other specialists. FAS agricultural counselors, attachés, trade officers, and locally employed FAS staff stationed in over 90 countries support U.S. agricultural interests and cover 140 countries.

In addition to agricultural affairs offices in U.S. embassies, agricultural trade offices also have been established in a number of key foreign markets and function as service centers for U.S. exporters and foreign buyers seeking market information.

Reports prepared by our overseas offices cover changes in policies and other developments that could affect U.S. agricultural exports. FAS staff in U.S. embassies around the world assess U.S. export marketing opportunities and respond to the daily informational needs of those who develop, initiate, monitor, and evaluate U.S. food and agricultural policies and programs.

In addition to data collection, FAS also maintains a worldwide agricultural reporting system based on information from U.S. agricultural traders, remote sensing systems, and other sources. Analysts in Washington, DC, prepare production forecasts, assess export marketing opportunities, and track changes in policies affecting U.S. agricultural exports and imports.

FAS programs help U.S. exporters develop and maintain markets for hundreds of food and agricultural products, from bulk commodities to brand name items. Formal market promotion activities are carried out chiefly in cooperation with agricultural trade associations, State-regional trade groups, small businesses, and cooperatives that plan, manage, and contribute staff resources and funds to support these efforts. FAS also provides guidance to help exporters locate buyers and provides assistance through a variety of other methods. This includes supporting U.S. participation in several major trade shows and a number of single-industry exhibitions each year.

For further information, contact the Public Affairs Division, Foreign Agricultural Service, Stop 1004, 1400 Independence Avenue, SW., Department of Agriculture, Washington, DC 20250-1004. Phone, 202–720–7115. Fax, 202–720–1727. Internet, http://www.fas.usda.gov.

Research, Education, and Economics

This mission area's main focus is to create, apply, and transfer knowledge and technology to provide affordable food and fiber, ensure food safety and nutrition, and support rural development and natural resource needs of people by conducting integrated national and international research, information, education, and statistical programs and services that are in the national interest.

Agricultural Research Service

The Agricultural Research Service (ARS) conducts research to develop and transfer solutions to agricultural problems of high national priority. It provides information access and dissemination to ensure high-quality, safe food and other agricultural products; assess the nutritional needs of Americans; sustain a competitive agricultural economy; enhance the natural resource base and the environment; and provide economic opportunities for rural citizens, communities, and society as a whole.

Research activities are carried out at 103 domestic locations (including Puerto Rico and the U.S. Virgin Islands) and 5 overseas locations. Much of this research is conducted in cooperation with partners in State universities and experiment stations, other Federal agencies, and private organizations. National Programs, headquartered in Beltsville, MD, is the focal point in the overall planning and coordination of ARS' research programs. Day-to-day management of the respective programs for specific field locations is assigned to eight area offices.

ARS also includes the National Agricultural Library (NAL), which is the primary resource in the United States for information about food, agriculture, and natural resources, and serves as an electronic gateway to a widening array of scientific literature, printed text, and agricultural images. NAL serves USDA and a broad customer base including policymakers, agricultural specialists, research scientists, and the general public. NAL works with other agricultural libraries and institutions to advance open and democratic access to information about agriculture and the Nation's agricultural knowledge.

For further information, contact the Agricultural Research Service, Department of Agriculture, 1400 Independence Avenue SW., Washington, DC 20250. Phone, 202–720–3656. Fax, 202–720–5427 Internet, www.ars.usda.gov.

Cooperative State Research, Education, and Extension Service

The Cooperative State Research, Education, and Extension Service (CSREES) links the research and education resources and activities of USDA and works with academic and land-grant institutions throughout the Nation. In cooperation with its partners and customers, CSREES advances a global system of research, extension, and higher education in the food and agricultural sciences and related environmental and human sciences to benefit people, communities, and the Nation.

CSREES's programs increase and provide access to scientific knowledge; strengthen the capabilities of land-grant and other institutions in research, extension, and higher education; increase access to and use of improved communication and network systems; and promote informed decisionmaking by producers, consumers, families, and community leaders to improve social conditions in the United States and around the world. These conditions include improved agricultural and other economic enterprises; safer, cleaner water, food, and air; enhanced stewardship and management of natural resources; healthier, more responsible and more productive individuals, families, and communities; and a stable, secure, diverse, and affordable national food supply.

CSREES provides research, extension, and education leadership through programs in plant and animal systems; natural resources and environment; economic and community systems; families, 4–H, and nutrition; competitive research and integrated research, education, and extension programs and awards management; science and education resources development; and information systems and technology management.

CSREES's partnership with the land-grant universities is critical to the effective shared planning, delivery, and accountability for research, higher education, and extension programs.

For further information, contact the Communications Staff, Cooperative State Research, Education, and Extension Service, Department of Agriculture, 1400 Independence Avenue SW., Washington, DC 20250–2207. Phone, 202–720–4651. Fax, 202–690–0289. Email, CSREES@csrees.usda.gov. Internet, www.csrees.usda.gov.

Economic Research Service

The mission of the Economic Research Service (ERS) is to inform and enhance public and private decisionmaking on economic and policy issues related to agriculture, food, the environment, and rural development.

Activities to support this mission and the following goals involve research and development of economic and statistical indicators on a broad range of topics including, but not limited to, global agricultural market conditions, trade restrictions, agribusiness concentration, farm and retail food prices, foodborne illnesses, food labeling, nutrition, food assistance programs, worker safety, agrichemical usage, livestock waste management, conservation, sustainability, genetic diversity, technology transfer, rural infrastructure,

and rural employment. Research results and economic indicators on such important agricultural, food, natural resource, and rural issues are fully disseminated to public and private decisionmakers through published and electronic reports and articles; special staff analyses, briefings, presentations, and papers; databases; and individual contacts. Through such activities, ERS provides public and private decisionmakers with economic and related social science information and analysis in support of the Department's goals of enhancing economic opportunities for agricultural producers; supporting economic opportunities and quality of life in rural America; enhancing the protection and safety of U.S. agriculture and food; improving U.S. nutrition and health; and enhancing the natural resource base and environment. More information on ERS's program is contained on the ERS Web site (www.ers.usda.gov).

For further information, contact the Information Services Division, Economic Research Service, Department of Agriculture, Washington, DC 20036–5831. Phone, 202–694–5100. Fax, 202–694–5641.

National Agricultural Statistics Service

The National Agricultural Statistics Service (NASS) prepares estimates and reports on production, supply, price, chemical use, and other items necessary for the orderly operation of the U.S. agricultural economy.

The reports include statistics on field crops, fruits and vegetables, dairy, cattle, hogs, sheep, poultry, aquaculture, and related commodities or processed products. Other estimates concern farm numbers, farm production expenditures, agricultural chemical use, prices received by farmers for products sold, prices paid for commodities and services, indexes of prices received and paid, parity prices, farm employment, and farm wage rates.

The Service prepares these estimates through a complex system of sample surveys of producers, processors, buyers, and others associated with agriculture. Information is gathered by mail, telephone, personal interviews, and field visits.

NASS is responsible for conducting the Census of Agriculture. The Census of Agriculture is taken every 5 years and provides comprehensive data on the agricultural economy down to the county level. Periodic reports are also issued on aquacultures, irrigation, and horticultural specialties.

The Service performs reimbursable survey work and statistical consulting services for other Federal and State agencies and provides technical assistance for developing agricultural data systems in other countries.

For further information, contact the Executive Assistant to the Administrator, National Agricultural Statistics Service, Department of Agriculture, Washington, DC 20250–2000. Phone, 202–720–2707. Fax, 202–720–9013.

Natural Resources and Environment

This mission area is responsible for fostering sound stewardship of 75 percent of the Nation's total land area. Ecosystems are the underpinning for the Department's operating philosophy in this area in order to maximize stewardship of our natural resources. This approach ensures that products, values, services, and uses desired by people are produced in ways that sustain healthy, productive ecosystems.

Forest Service

[For the Forest Service statement of organization, see the *Code of Federal Regulations,* Title 36, Part 200.1]

The Forest Service was created by the Transfer Act of February 1, 1905 (16 U.S.C. 472), which transferred the Federal forest reserves and the responsibility for their management from the Department of the Interior to the Department of Agriculture. The mission of the Forest Service is to achieve quality land management under the sustainable, multiple-use management concept to meet the diverse needs of people. It's objectives include:

—advocating a conservation ethic in promoting the health, productivity, diversity, and beauty of forests and associated lands;

—listening to people and responding to their diverse needs in making decisions;

—protecting and managing the national forests and grasslands to best

demonstrate the sustainable, multiple-use management concept;

—providing technical and financial assistance to State and private forest landowners, encouraging them toward active stewardship and quality land management in meeting their specific objectives;

—providing technical and financial assistance to cities and communities to improve their natural environment by planting trees and caring for their forests;

—providing international technical assistance and scientific exchanges to sustain and enhance global resources and to encourage quality land management;

—assisting States and communities in using the forests wisely to promote rural economic development and a quality rural environment;

—developing and providing scientific and technical knowledge, improving our capability to protect, manage, and use forests and rangelands; and

—providing work, training, and education to the unemployed, underemployed, elderly, youth, and the disadvantaged.

National Forest System The Service manages 155 national forests, 20 national grasslands, and 8 land utilization projects on over 191 million acres in 44 States, the Virgin Islands, and Puerto Rico under the principles of multiple-use and sustained yield. The Nation's tremendous need for wood and paper products is balanced with the other vital, renewable resources or benefits that the national forests and grasslands provide: recreation and natural beauty, wildlife habitat, livestock forage, and water supplies. The guiding principle is the greatest good to the greatest number in the long run.

These lands are protected as much as possible from wildfire, epidemics of disease and insect pests, erosion, floods, and water and air pollution. Burned areas get emergency seeding treatment to prevent massive erosion and stream siltation. Roads and trails are built where needed to allow for closely regulated timber harvesting and to give the public access to outdoor recreation areas and provide scenic drives and hikes. Picnic, camping, water-sport, skiing, and other areas are provided with facilities for public convenience and enjoyment. Timber harvesting methods are used that will protect the land and streams, assure rapid renewal of the forest, provide food and cover for wildlife and fish, and have minimum impact on scenic and recreation values. Local communities benefit from the logging and milling activities. These lands also provide needed oil, gas, and minerals. Rangelands are improved for millions of livestock and game animals. The national forests provide a refuge for many species of endangered birds, animals, and fish. Some 34.6 million acres are set aside as wilderness and 175,000 acres as primitive areas where timber will not be harvested.

Forest Research The Service performs basic and applied research to develop the scientific information and technology needed to protect, manage, use, and sustain the natural resources of the Nation's forests and rangelands. The Service's forest research strategy focuses on three major program components: understanding the structure and functions of forest and range ecosystems; understanding how people perceive and value the protection, management, and use of natural resources; and determining which protection, management, and utilization practices are most suitable for sustainable production and use of the world's natural resources.

Manpower Programs The Service operates the Youth Conservation Corps and the Volunteers in the National Forests programs and participates with the Department of Labor on several human resource programs that involve the Nation's citizens, both young and old, in forestry-related activities. Included in these programs are the Job Corps and the Senior Community Service Employment Program. These programs annually accomplish millions of dollars worth of conservation work, while providing participants with such benefits as training, paid employment, and meaningful outdoor experience.

For further information, contact the Office of Communications, Forest Service, Department of Agriculture, P.O. Box 96090, Washington, DC 20090–6090. Phone, 202–205–8333.

Field Offices—Forest Service

Region/Station/Area	Address
National Forest System Regions—Regional Forester	
1. Northern	Federal Bldg. (P.O. Box 7669), Missoula, MT 59807
2. Rocky Mountain	740 Simms St., P.O. Box 25127, Lakewood, CO 80225
3. Southwestern	517 Gold Ave. SW., Albuquerque, NM 87102
4. Intermountain	324 25th St., Ogden, UT 84401
5. Pacific Southwest	630 Sansome St., San Francisco, CA 94111
6. Pacific Northwest	333 SW. 1st Ave., P.O. Box 3623, Portland, OR 97208
8. Southern	1720 Peachtree Rd. NW., Atlanta, GA 30367
9. Eastern	310 W. Wisconsin Ave., Milwaukee, WI 53203
10. Alaska	Federal Office Bldg. (P.O. Box 21628), Juneau, AK 99802
Research Stations—Director	
Forest Products Laboratory	1 Gifford Pinchot Dr., Madison, WI 53705
North Central	1992 Folwell Ave., St. Paul, MN 55108
Northeastern	Suite 200, 100 Matson Ford Rd., P.O. Box 6775, Radnor, PA 19087–4585
Pacific Northwest	333 SW. 1st Ave., P.O. Box 3890, Portland, OR 97208
Pacific Southwest	800 Buchanan St., P.O. Box 245, Albany, CA 94710
Rocky Mountain	240 W. Prospect Ave., Fort Collins, CO 80526
Southern	200 Weaver Blvd., P.O. Box 2860, Asheville, NC 28802

Field Offices—Forest Service—Continued

Region/Station/Area	Address
	National Forest System Regions—Regional Forester
	State and Private Forestry Areas—Director
Northeastern	Suite 200, 100 Matson Ford Rd., P.O. Box 6775, Radnor, PA 19087–4585
International Institute of Tropical Forestry	UPR Experimental Station Grounds, Botanical Garden, Call Box 25000, Rio Piedras, PR 00928

Natural Resources Conservation Service

[For the Natural Resources Conservation Service statement of organization, see the *Code of Federal Regulations,* Title 7, Parts 600 and 601]

The Natural Resources Conservation Service (NRCS), formerly the Soil Conservation Service, has national responsibility for helping America's farmers, ranchers, and other private landowners develop and carry out voluntary efforts to conserve and protect our natural resources.

Conservation Technical Assistance   This is the foundation program of NRCS. Under this program, NRCS provides technical assistance to land users and units of government for the purpose of sustaining agricultural productivity and protecting and enhancing the natural resource base. This assistance is based on the voluntary cooperation of private landowners and involves comprehensive approaches to reduce soil erosion, improve soil and water quantity and quality, improve and conserve wetlands, enhance fish and wildlife habitat, improve air quality, improve pasture and range condition, reduce upstream flooding, and improve woodlands.

Emergency Watershed Protection Program   This program provides emergency assistance to safeguard lives and property in jeopardy due to sudden watershed impairment by natural disasters. Emergency work includes quickly establishing a protective plant cover on denuded land and stream banks; opening dangerously restricted channels; and repairing diversions and levees. An emergency area need not be declared a national disaster area to be eligible for help under this program.

Environmental Quality Incentive Program   This program assists producers with environmental and natural resource conservation improvements on their agricultural lands. One-half of the available funds are for conservation activities related to livestock production. Technical assistance, cost-share payments, incentive payments, and education focus on priority areas and natural resource concerns identified in cooperation with State technical committees, including such areas as nutrient management, pest management, and grazing land management.

Farmland Protection Program   This program protects soil by encouraging landowners to limit conversion of their farmland to nonagricultural uses. States, Indian tribes, or local governments administer all aspects of acquiring lands that are in the program, except when it is more effective and efficient for the Federal Government to do so.

Forestry Incentives Program   This program helps to increase the Nation's supply of products from nonindustrial private forest lands. This also ensures more effective use of existing forest lands and, over time, helps to prevent shortages and price increases for forest products. The program shares the cost incurred by landowners for tree planting and timberstand improvement.

National Cooperative Soil Survey   The National Cooperative Soil Survey provides the public with local information on the uses and capabilities of their soils. The published soil survey for a county or other designated area includes maps and interpretations that are the foundation for farm planning and other private land use decisions as well as for resource planning and policy by Federal, State, and local governments. The surveys are conducted cooperatively with other Federal, State, and local agencies and land grant universities. The Service is the national and world leader in soil classification and soil mapping, and is now expanding its work in soil quality.

Plant Materials Program At 26 plant materials centers across the country, NRCS tests, selects, and ensures the commercial availability of new and improved conservation plants for erosion reduction, wetland restoration, water quality improvement, streambank and riparian area protection, coastal dune stabilization, biomass production, carbon sequestration, and other needs. The Plant Materials Program is a cooperative effort with conservation districts, other Federal and State agencies, commercial businesses, and seed and nursery associations.

Resource Conservation and Development Program This is a locally driven program—an opportunity for civic-oriented groups to work together sharing knowledge and resources in solving common problems facing their region. The program offers aid in balancing the environmental, economic, and social needs of an area. A USDA coordinator helps each designated RC&D council plan, develop, and carry out programs for resource conservation, water management, community development, and environmental enhancement.

Rural Abandoned Mine Program This program helps protect people and the environment from the adverse effects of past coal-mining practices and promotes the development of soil and water resources on unreclaimed mine land. It provides technical and financial assistance to land users who voluntarily enter into 5- to 10-year contracts for the reclamation of eligible land and water.

Small Watersheds Program The program helps local sponsoring groups to voluntarily plan and install watershed protection projects on private lands. These projects include flood prevention, water quality improvement, soil erosion and sediment reduction, rural and municipal water supply, irrigation water management, fish and wildlife habitat enhancement, and wetlands restoration. The Service helps local community groups, government entities, and private landowners working together using an integrated, comprehensive watershed approach to natural resource planning.

Snow Survey and Water Supply Forecasting Program This program collects snowpack moisture data and forecasts seasonal water supplies for streams that derive most of their water from snowmelt. It helps farm operators, rural communities, and municipalities manage water resources through water supply forecasts. It also provides hydrometeorological data for regulating reservoir storage and managing streamflow. The Snow Supply Program is conducted in the Western States and Alaska.

Watershed Surveys and Planning This program assists Federal, State, and local agencies and tribal governments in protecting watersheds from damage caused by erosion, floodwater, and sediment and conserves and develops water and land resources. Resource concerns addressed by the program include water quality, water conservation, wetland and water storage capacity, agricultural drought problems, rural development, municipal and industrial water needs, upstream flood damages, and water needs for fish, wildlife, and forest-based industries. Types of surveys and plans include watershed plans, river basin surveys and studies, flood hazard analysis, and flood plain management assistance. The focus of these plans is to identify solutions that use land treatment and nonstructural measures to solve resource problems.

Wetlands Reserve Program Under this program, USDA purchases easements from agricultural land owners who voluntarily agree to restore and protect wetlands. Service employees help these owners develop plans to retire critical wetland habitat from crop production. The primary objectives are to preserve and restore wetlands, improve wildlife habitat, and protect migratory waterfowl.

Wildlife Habitat Incentives Program This program provides financial incentives to develop habitats for fish and wildlife on private lands. Participants agree to implement a wildlife habitat development plan, and USDA agrees to provide cost-share assistance for the initial implementation of wildlife habitat development practices. USDA and program participants enter into a cost-share agreement for wildlife habitat development, which generally lasts a

minimum of 10 years from the date that the contract is signed.

For further information, contact the Management Services Division, Natural Resources Conservation Service, Department of Agriculture, P.O. Box 2890, Washington, DC 20013. Phone, 202–690–4811.

Graduate School

600 Maryland Avenue SW., Suite 300, Washington, DC 20024–2520
Phone, 888–744–4723

Executive Director	JERRY ICE
Deputy Executive Director	LYNN EDWARDS

The Graduate School was established by act of May 15, 1862 (7 U.S.C. 2201). It is a continuing education school offering career-related training to adults. Courses are planned with the assistance of Government professionals and specialists. The Graduate School's objective is to improve Government services by providing needed continuing education and training opportunities for Government employees and agencies.

The faculty is mostly part-time and is drawn from throughout Government and the community at large. They are selected because of their professional and specialized knowledge and experience and thus bring a practicality and experience to their classrooms.

The school does not grant degrees but does provide planned sequences of courses leading to certificates of accomplishment in a number of occupational and career fields important to government. Training areas include management, auditing, computer science, communications, foreign language, procurement, financial management, and others.

For further information, contact the Communications Office, Graduate School, Room 270, 600 Maryland Avenue SW., Washington, DC 20024. Phone, 888–744–4723.

Sources of Information

Consumer Activities Educational, organizational, and financial assistance is offered to consumers and their families in such fields as rural housing and farm operating programs, improved nutrition, family living and recreation, food stamp, school lunch, donated foods, and other food programs.

Contracts and Small Business Activities To obtain information about contracting or subcontracting opportunities, attending small business outreach activities, or how to do business with USDA, contact the Office of Small and Disadvantaged Business Utilization.

Phone, 202–720–7117. Internet, www.usda.gov/da/smallbus.html.
Employment Most jobs in the Department are in the competitive service and are filled by applicants who have established eligibility under an appropriate examination administered by the Office of Personnel Management or Department Special Examining Units. General employment information is available at www.usajobs.opm.gov.
Whistleblower Hotline Persons wishing to register complaints of alleged improprieties concerning the Department should contact one of the regional offices or the Inspector General's

whistleblower hotline. Phone, 800–424–9121 (toll free, outside Washington, DC); 202–690–1622 (within the Washington, DC, metropolitan area); or 202–690–1202 (TDD). Fax, 202–690–2474.

Reading Rooms Located at each USDA agency at addresses indicated in the preceding text.

Speakers Contact the nearest Department of Agriculture office or county Extension agent. In the District of Columbia, contact the Office of Public Liaison, Office of Communications, Department of Agriculture, Washington, DC 20250. Phone, 202–720–2798.

For further information concerning the Department of Agriculture, contact the Office of Communications, Department of Agriculture, Washington, DC 20250. Phone, 202–720–4623. Internet, www.usda.gov.

DEPARTMENT OF COMMERCE

Fourteenth Street and Constitution Avenue NW., Washington, DC 20230
Phone, 202–482–2000. Internet, www.commerce.gov.

SECRETARY OF COMMERCE	GARY F. LOCKE
DEPUTY SECRETARY	DENNIS F. HIGHTOWER
Chief of Staff	ELLEN MORAN
Senior Advisor and Deputy Chief of Staff	RICK WADE
Deputy Chief of Staff	JAY REICH
Assistant Secretary for Legislative and Intergovernmental Affairs	APRIL S. BOYD
Chief Financial Officer and Assistant Secretary for Administration	(VACANCY)
Chief Information Officer	SUZANNE E. HILDING
General Counsel	CAMERON F. KERRY
Inspector General	TODD J. ZINSER
Director, Office of Business Liaison	N. ANNE OLAIMEY
Director, Office of Policy and Strategic Planning	TRAVIS SULLIVAN
Director, Office of Public Affairs	KEVIN GRIFFIS
Director, Executive Secretariat	TENE DOLPHIN
Director, Office of White House Liaison	FREDERICK C. SIGER
Senior Advisor for Recovery Act Implementation	ELLEN HERBST
International Intellectual Property Rights Coordinator	(VACANCY)
Director, Office of Small and Disadvantaged Business Utilization	LAJUENE DESMUKES
Deputy Assistant Secretary for Administration	JOHN FRANT CHARLES
Director for Security	ALFRED BROADBENT
Director, Office of Budget	NEIL K. SHAPIRO
Director for Management and Organization	JOHN J. PHELANN III
Director, Office of Civil Rights	SUZAN J. ARAMAKI
Director for Financial Management and Deputy Chief Financial Officer	LISA CASIAS
Director for Human Resources Management	DEBORAH JEFFERSON
Director for Administrative Services	FRED E. FANNING
Director for Acquisition Management	HELEN M. HURVCOMBE
Director for Intergovernmental Affairs	COURTNEY O. GREGOIRE
Press Secretary	PSRITS SHAH SELFRIDGE

BUREAU OF INDUSTRY AND SECURITY

Department of Commerce, Washington, DC 20230
Phone, 202–482–2721. Internet, www.bis.doc.gov.

Under Secretary for Industry and Security	DANIEL O. HILL, *Acting*
Deputy Under Secretary	DANIEL O. HILL
Assistant Secretary for Export Administration	MATTHEW S. BORMAN, *Acting*
Assistant Secretary for Export Enforcement	KEVIN DELLI-COLLI, *Acting*

ECONOMIC DEVELOPMENT ADMINISTRATION

Department of Commerce, Washington, DC 20230
Phone, 202–482–2309. Internet, www.eda.gov.

Assistant Secretary for Economic Development	(VACANCY)
Deputy Assistant Secretary	(VACANCY)
Chief Financial Office and Director of Administration	SANDRA WALTERS

ECONOMICS AND STATISTICS ADMINISTRATION

Department of Commerce, Washington, DC 20230
Phone, 202–482–3727. Internet, www.esa.doc.gov.

Under Secretary for Economic Affairs	REBECCA M. BLANK
Deputy Under Secretary	(VACANCY)
Associate Under Secretary for Management	KIM WHITE
Chief Economist	(VACANCY)
Director, Bureau of the Census	THOMAS MESENBOURG, *Acting*
Director, Bureau of Economic Analysis	J. STEVEN LANDEFELD

INTERNATIONAL TRADE ADMINISTRATION

Department of Commerce, Washington, DC 20230
Phone, 202–482–3917. Internet, ww.trade.gov.

Under Secretary for International Trade	MICHELLE O'NEILL, *Acting*
Deputy Under Secretary	MICHELLE O' NEILL
Assistant Secretary for Import Administration	DAVID SPOONER
Assistant Secretary for Market Access and Compliance	STEPHEN JACOBS, *Acting*
Assistant Secretary for Manufacturing and Services	MARY SAUNDERS, *Acting*
Assistant Secretary for Trade Promotion and Director of the U.S. and Foreign Commercial Service	ROCHELLE LIPSITZ, *Acting*
Chief Financial Officer and Director of Administration	DAVID M. ROBINSON
Chief Information Officer	RENEE MACKLIN

MINORITY BUSINESS DEVELOPMENT AGENCY

Department of Commerce, Washington, DC 20230
Phone, 202–482–5061. Internet, www.mbda.gov.

National Director, Minority Business Development Agency	(VACANCY)
Deputy Director	(VACANCY)
Associate Director for Management	EDITH J. MCCLOUD

NATIONAL OCEANIC AND ATMOSPHERIC ADMINISTRATION

Department of Commerce, Washington, DC 20230
Phone, 202–482–2985. Internet, www.noaa.gov.

Under Secretary for Oceans and Atmosphere and Administrator	JANE LUBCHENCO
Assistant Secretary for Oceans and Atmosphere and Deputy Administrator	(VACANCY)

Deputy Assistant Secretary for Oceans and Atmosphere	(VACANCY)
Deputy Assistant Secretary for International Affairs	(VACANCY)
Deputy Under Secretary for Oceans and Atmosphere	MARY M. GLACKIN
General Counsel	JANE H. CHALMERS, *Acting*
Director, Office of Communications	JUSTIN KENNEY
Director, Office of Legislative Affairs	JOHN GRAY
Chief Financial Officer	MAUREEN E. WYLIE
Chief Administrative Officer	WILLIAM F. BROGLIE
Assistant Administrator for Fisheries Service	JAMES W. BALSIGER, *Acting*
Assistant Administrator for Ocean Services and Coastal Zone Management	JOHN H. DUNNIGAN
Assistant Administrator for National Environmental Satellite, Data, and Information Services	MARY E. KICZA
Assistant Administrator for Weather Services	JOHN L. HAYES
Assistant Administrator for Oceanic and Atmospheric Research	RICHARD W. SPINRAD
Assistant Administrator for Program Planning and Integration	LAURA FURGIONE

NATIONAL TELECOMMUNICATIONS AND INFORMATION ADMINISTRATION

Department of Commerce, Washington, DC 20230
Phone, 202–428–1840. Internet, www.ntia.doc.gov.

Assistant Secretary for Communications and Information	(VACANCY)
Deputy Assistant Secretary	ANNA M. GOMEZ
Chief Counsel	KATHY D. SMITH
Associate Administrator for Spectrum Management	KARL NEBBIA
Associate Administrator for Policy Analysis and Development	(VACANCY)
Associate Administrator for International Affairs	FIONA ALEXANDER
Associate Administrator for Telecommunications and Information Applications	BERNADETTE A. MCGUIRE-RIVERA
Associate Administrator for Telecommunication Sciences and Director, Institute for Telecommunication Sciences	ALAN VINCENT

NATIONAL INSTITUTE OF STANDARDS AND TECHNOLOGY

100 Bureau Drive, Gaithersburg, MD 20899
Phone, 301–975–6478. TTY, 800–877–8339. Internet, www.nist.gov.

Director	(VACANCY)
Deputy Director	PATRICK D. GALLAGHER

NATIONAL TECHNICAL INFORMATION SERVICE

5301 Shawnee Road, Alexandria, VA 22312
Phone, 703–605–6050 or 888–584–8332. Internet, www.ntis.gov.

Director	ELLEN HERBST

UNITED STATES PATENT AND TRADEMARK OFFICE

600 Dulany Street, Arlington, VA 22313
Phone, 571–272–8400. Internet, www.uspto.gov.

Under Secretary for Intellectual Property and Director	JOHN J. DOLL, *Acting*
Deputy Under Secretary for Intellectual Property and Deputy Director	JOHN J. DOLL
Commissioner for Patents	MARGARET A. FOCARINO, *Acting*
Commissioner for Trademarks	LYNNE G. BERESFORD

The Department of Commerce encourages, serves, and promotes the Nation's international trade, economic growth, and technological advancement. The Department provides a wide variety of programs through the competitive free enterprise system. It offers assistance and information to increase America's competitiveness in the world economy; administers programs to prevent unfair foreign trade competition; provides social and economic statistics and analyses for business and government planners; provides research and support for the increased use of scientific, engineering, and technological development; works to improve our understanding and benefits of the Earth's physical environment and oceanic resources; grants patents and registers trademarks; develops policies and conducts research on telecommunications; provides assistance to promote domestic economic development; and assists in the growth of minority businesses.

The Department was designated as such by act of March 4, 1913 (15 U.S.C. 1501), which reorganized the Department of Commerce and Labor, created by act of February 14, 1903 (15 U.S.C. 1501), by transferring all labor activities into a new, separate Department of Labor.

Office of the Secretary

Secretary   The Secretary is responsible for the administration of all functions and authorities assigned to the Department of Commerce and for advising the President on Federal policy and programs affecting the industrial and commercial segments of the national economy. The Secretary is served by the offices of Deputy Secretary, Inspector General, General Counsel, and the Assistant Secretaries of Administration, Legislative and Intergovernmental Affairs, and Public Affairs. Other offices whose public purposes are widely administered are detailed below.

Business Liaison   The Office of Business Liaison directs the business community to the offices and policy experts who can best respond to their needs by promoting proactive, responsive, and effective outreach programs and relationships with the business community. It also informs the Secretary and Department officials of the critical issues facing the business community, informs the business community of Department and administration initiatives and priorities, as well as information regarding Department resources, policies, and programs, and provides general assistance to the business community.

For further information, call 202–482–1360.

DEPARTMENT OF COMMERCE

SECRETARY

DEPUTY SECRETARY

CHIEF OF STAFF

GENERAL COUNSEL

INSPECTOR GENERAL

CHIEF FINANCIAL OFFICER AND ASSISTANT SECRETARY FOR ADMINISTRATION

ASSISTANT SECRETARY FOR LEGISLATIVE AND INTERGOVERNMENTAL AFFAIRS

CHIEF INFORMATION OFFICER

OFFICE OF PUBLIC AFFAIRS

OFFICE OF BUSINESS LIAISON

EXECUTIVE SECRETARIAT

OFFICE OF WHITE HOUSE LIAISON

OFFICE OF POLICY AND STRATEGIC PLANNING

UNDER SECRETARY FOR INTELLECTUAL PROPERTY AND DIRECTOR
UNITED STATES PATENT AND TRADEMARK OFFICE

DIRECTOR
NATIONAL INSTITUTE OF STANDARDS AND TECHNOLOGY

DIRECTOR
NATIONAL TECHNICAL INFORMATION SERVICE

UNDER SECRETARY FOR ECONOMIC AFFAIRS
ECONOMICS AND STATISTICS ADMINISTRATION

DIRECTOR
BUREAU OF THE CENSUS

CHIEF ECONOMIST

DIRECTOR
BUREAU OF ECONOMIC ANALYSIS

ASSISTANT SECRETARY FOR COMMUNICATIONS AND INFORMATION
NATIONAL TELECOMMUNICATIONS AND INFORMATION ADMINISTRATION

NATIONAL DIRECTOR
MINORITY BUSINESS DEVELOPMENT AGENCY

ASSISTANT SECRETARY FOR ECONOMIC DEVELOPMENT
ECONOMIC DEVELOPMENT ADMINISTRATION

UNDER SECRETARY FOR INDUSTRY AND SECURITY
BUREAU OF INDUSTRY AND SECURITY

ASSISTANT SECRETARY FOR EXPORT ENFORCEMENT

ASSISTANT SECRETARY FOR EXPORT ADMINISTRATION

UNDER SECRETARY FOR INTERNATIONAL TRADE
INTERNATIONAL TRADE ADMINISTRATION

ASSISTANT SECRETARY FOR IMPORT ADMINISTRATION

ASSISTANT SECRETARY FOR MARKET ACCESS AND COMPLIANCE

ASSISTANT SECRETARY FOR MANUFACTURING AND SERVICES

ASSISTANT SECRETARY FOR TRADE PROMOTION AND DIRECTOR GENERAL UNITED STATES AND FOREIGN COMMERCIAL SERVICE

UNDER SECRETARY AND ADMINISTRATOR
NATIONAL OCEANIC AND ATMOSPHERIC ADMINISTRATION

ASSISTANT SECRETARY FOR OCEANS AND ATMOSPHERE AND DEPUTY ADMINISTRATOR

Bureau of Industry and Security

[For the Bureau of Industry and Security statement of organization, see the *Federal Registers* of June 7, 1988, 53 FR 20881, and April 26, 2002, 67 FR 20630]

The mission of the Bureau of Industry and Security (BIS) is to advance U.S. national security, foreign policy, and economic objectives by ensuring an effective export control and treaty compliance system and promoting continued U.S. strategic technology leadership. BIS activities include regulating the export of sensitive goods and technologies in an effective and efficient manner; enforcing export control, antiboycott, and public safety laws; cooperating with and assisting other countries on export control and strategic trade issues; assisting U.S. industry to comply with international arms control agreements; and monitoring the viability of the U.S. defense industrial base and seeking to ensure that it is capable of satisfying U.S. national and homeland security needs.

Export Administration   The Office of the Assistant Secretary for Export Administration is responsible for export licenses, treaty compliance, treaty obligations relating to weapons of mass destruction, and the defense industrial and technology base. The Office regulates the export of dual-use items requiring licenses for national security, nonproliferation, foreign policy, and short supply; ensures that approval or denial of license applications is consistent with economic and security concerns; promotes an understanding of export control regulations within the business community; represents the Department in interagency and international forums relating to export controls, particularly in multilateral regimes; monitors the availability of industrial resources of national defense; analyzes the impact of export controls on strategic industries; and assesses the security consequences of certain foreign investments.

Export Enforcement   The Office of the Assistant Secretary for Export Enforcement enforces dual-use export controls. This enables exporters to take advantage of legal export opportunities while ensuring that illegal exports will be detected and either prevented or investigated and sanctioned. The Office also ensures prompt, aggressive action against restrictive trade practices; reviews visa applications of foreign nationals to prevent illegal technology transfers; and conducts cooperative enforcement activities on an international basis.

Management and Policy Coordination   The Management and Policy Coordination (MPC) unit establishes and evaluates the Bureau's overall policy agenda, priorities, goals, unit objectives, and key metrics. MPC performs oversight of program operations and expenditures; executes or supervises the President's Management Agenda; and adjudicates appeals of licensing and enforcement decisions as part of an extended legal process involving administrative law judges and the Office of General Counsel. MPC provides guidance and coordination for the Bureau's participation in the Export Control and Related Border Security Assistance Program, which provides technical assistance to strengthen the export and transit control systems of nations that are identified as potential locations for the exporting of weapons of mass destruction, missile delivery systems, or the commodities, technologies, and equipment that can be used to design and build them.

Field Offices—Bureau of Industry and Security

Field Area	Address
Export Enforcement	
Boston, MA	Rm. 253, 10 Causeway St., 02222
Dallas, TX	Suite 622, 525 S. Griffin St., 75202
Hillside, IL	Suite 530, 4415 W. Harrison St., 60162
Houston, TX	Suite 250, 15355 Vantage Pkwy. West, 77032

Field Offices—Bureau of Industry and Security—Continued

Field Area	Address
Fort Lauderdale, FL	Suite 2060, 200 E. Las Olas Blvd., 33301
Herndon, VA	Suite 1125, 381 Elden St., 20170
Irvine, CA	Suite 310, 2601 Main St., 92614–6299
San Jose, CA	Suite 725, 160 W. Santa Clara St., 95113
Staten Island, NY	Suite 104, 1200 South Ave., 10314
Export Administration	
Newport Beach, CA	Suite 345, 300 Irvine Ave., 92660
San Jose, CA	Suite 725, 160 W. Santa Clara St., 95113

For further information, contact the Bureau of Industry and Security, Office of Public Affairs, Room 3897, Fourteenth Street and Constitution Avenue NW., Washington, DC 20230. Phone, 202–482–2721. Internet, www.bis.doc.gov.

Economic Development Administration

The Economic Development Administration (EDA) was created in 1965 under the Public Works and Economic Development Act (42 U.S.C. 3121) as part of an effort to target Federal resources to economically distressed areas and to help develop local economies in the United States. It was mandated to assist rural and urban communities that were outside the mainstream economy and that lagged in economic development, industrial growth, and personal income.

EDA provides grants to States, regions, and communities across the Nation to help create wealth and minimize poverty by promoting a favorable business environment to attract private capital investment and higher skill, higher wage jobs through capacity building, planning, infrastructure, research grants, and strategic initiatives. Through its grant program, EDA utilizes public sector resources to create an environment where the private sector risks capital and job opportunities are created.

Public works and development facilities grants support infrastructure projects that foster the establishment or expansion of industrial and commercial businesses, supporting the retention and creation of jobs.

Planning grants support the design and implementation of effective economic development policies and programs, by local development organizations, in States and communities. EDA funds a network of over 350 planning districts throughout the country.

Technical assistance provides for local feasibility and industry studies, management and operational assistance, natural resource development, and export promotion. In addition, EDA funds a network of university centers that provide technical assistance.

Research, evaluation, and demonstration funds are used to support studies about the causes of economic distress and to seek solutions to counteract and prevent such problems.

Economic adjustment grants help communities adjust to a gradual erosion or sudden dislocation of their local economic structure. This assistance provides funding for both planning and implementation to address economic change.

The Trade Adjustment Assistance program helps U.S. firms and industries injured as the result of economic globalization. A nationwide network of Trade Adjustment Assistance Centers offers low-cost, effective professional assistance to certified firms to develop and implement recovery strategies.

Regional Offices—Economic Development Administration

Region (Areas Served)	Address
Atlanta, GA (AL, FL, GA, MS, NC, SC, TN)	Suite 1820, 401 W. Peachtree St. NW., 30308

Regional Offices—Economic Development Administration—Continued

Region (Areas Served)	Address
Austin, TX (AR, LA, NM, OK, TX)	Suite 1100, 504 Lavaca St., 78701
Chicago, IL (IL, IN, MI, MN, OH, WI)	Suite 855, 111 N. Canal St., 60606
Denver, CO (CO, IA, KS, MO, MT, ND, NE, SD, UT, WY).	Suite 250, 410 17th St., 80202
Philadelphia, PA (CT, DE, DC, MA, MD, ME, NH, NJ, NY, PA, RI, VT, VA, WV; PR, VI).	Suite 140, S. 601 Walnut St., 19106
Seattle, WA (AK, AZ, CA, HI, ID, NV, OR, WA; AS, NMI, GU, FSM, RMI, RP).	Rm. 1890, 915 2d Ave., 98174

For further information, contact the Economic Development Administration, Department of Commerce, Washington, DC 20230. Phone, 202–482–2309. Fax, 202–273–4723. Internet, www.eda.gov.

Economics and Statistics Administration

The Economics and Statistics Administration (ESA) provides broad and targeted economic data, analyses, and forecasts for use by Government agencies, businesses, and others, as well as develops domestic and international economic policy. The Under Secretary is the chief economic adviser to the Secretary and provides leadership and executive management of the Bureau of the Census and the Bureau of Economic Analysis.

ESA provides key business, economic, and international trade information products that American business and the public can use to make informed decisions through STAT.USA®.

Bureau of the Census

[For the Bureau of the Census statement of organization, see the *Federal Register* of Sept. 16, 1975, 40 FR 42765]

The Bureau of the Census was established as a permanent office by act of March 6, 1902 (32 Stat. 51). The major functions of the Census Bureau are authorized by the Constitution, which provides that a census of population shall be taken every 10 years, and by laws codified as title 13 of the United States Code. The law also provides that the information collected by the Census Bureau from individual persons, households, or establishments be kept strictly confidential and be used only for statistical purposes. The Census Bureau is responsible for:

—the decennial censuses of population and housing;

—the quinquennial censuses of State and local governments, manufacturers, mineral industries, distributive trades, construction industries, and transportation;

—current surveys that provide information on many of the subjects covered in the censuses at monthly, quarterly, annual, or other intervals;

—compilation of current statistics on U.S. foreign trade, including data on imports, exports, and shipping;

—special censuses at the request and expense of State and local government units;

—publication of estimates and projections of the population;

—publication of current data on population and housing characteristics; and

—current reports on manufacturing, retail and wholesale trade, services, construction, imports and exports, State and local government finances and employment, and other subjects.

The Census Bureau makes available statistical results of its censuses, surveys, and other programs to the public through printed reports, CD–ROMs and DVDs, the Internet and other media, and prepares special tabulations sponsored and paid for by data users. It also produces statistical compendia, catalogs, guides, and directories that are useful in locating information on specific subjects. Upon request, the Bureau makes searches of decennial census records and furnishes certificates to individuals for use as evidence of age, relationship, or place of birth. A fee is charged for searches.

For further information, contact the Marketing Service Office, Bureau of the Census, Department of Commerce, Washington, DC 20233. Phone, 301–763–4636. Fax, 301–457–3842. Internet, www.census.gov.

Field Organization—Bureau of the Census

Regional Office (Areas Served)	Address
Atlanta, GA (AL, FL, GA)	Suite 3200, 101 Marietta St. NW., 30303–2700
Boston, MA (CT, MA, ME, NH, NY (all counties not listed under the New York Regional Office), PR, RI, VI, and VT)	Suite 301, 4 Copley Pl., 02117–9108
Charlotte, NC (KY, NC, SC, TN, VA)	Suite 106, 901 Center Park Dr., 28217–2935
Chicago, IL (IL, IN, WI)	Suite 5501, 2255 Enterprise Dr., Westchester, IL 60154
Dallas, TX (LA, MS, TX)	Suite 800S, 8585 Stemmons N. Fwy., 75237–3836
Denver, CO (AZ, CO, MT, NE, ND, NM, NV, SD, UT, and WY)	Suite 100, 6900 W. Jefferson Ave., Lakewood, CO 80235–2032
Detroit, MI (MI, OH, WV)	Suite 100, 1395 Brewery Park Blvd., 48207–2635
Kansas City, KS (AR, IA, KS, MN, MO, OK)	1211 N. 8th St., 66101–2129
Los Angeles, CA (CA (counties of Fresno, Imperial, Inyo, Kern, Kings, Los Angeles, Madera, Mariposa, Merced, Monterey, Orange, Riverside, San Benito, San Bernardino, San Diego, San Luis Obispo, Santa Barbara, Tulare, and Ventura), HI)	Suite 300, 15350 Sherman Way, Van Nuys, CA 91406–4224
New York, NY (NJ (counties of Bergen, Essex, Hudson, Middlesex, Morris, Passaic, Somerset, Sussex, Union, and Warren), NY (counties of Bronx, Kings, Nassau, New York, Queens, Richmond, Rockland, Suffolk, and Westchester))	Suite 800, 395 Hudson St., 10014
Philadelphia, PA (DC, DE, MD, NJ (all counties not listed under the New York Regional Office), PA)	Suite 504, 833 Chestnut St., 19107–4405
Seattle, WA (AK, CA (all counties not listed under the Los Angeles Regional Office), ID, OR, WA)	Suite 3800, 601 Union St., 98101–1074

Bureau of Economic Analysis

[For the Bureau of Economic Analysis statement of organization, see the *Federal Register* of Dec. 29, 1980, 45 FR 85496]

The Bureau of Economic Analysis (BEA) promotes a better understanding of the U.S. economy by providing the most timely, relevant, and accurate economic accounts data in an objective and cost-effective manner. BEA's economic statistics are closely watched and provide a comprehensive picture of the U.S. economy. BEA prepares national, regional, industry, and international accounts that present essential information on such issues in the world economy.

BEA's national economic statistics provide a comprehensive look at U.S. production, consumption, investment, exports and imports, and income and saving. The international transactions accounts provide information on trade in goods and services (including the balance of payments and trade), investment income, and government and private finances. In addition, the accounts measure the value of U.S. international assets and liabilities and direct investment by multinational companies.

The regional accounts provide data on total and per capita personal income by region, State, metropolitan area, and county, and on gross State product. The industry economic account provides a detailed view of the interrelationships between U.S. producers and users and the contribution to production across industries.

For further information, contact the Public Information Office, Bureau of Economic Analysis, Department of Commerce, Washington, DC 20230. Phone, 202–606–9900. Fax, 202–606–5310. Email, customerservice@bea.gov. Internet, www.bea.gov.

For further information, contact the Economics and Statistics Administration, Department of Commerce, Washington, DC 20230. Phone, 202–482–3727. Internet, www.esa.doc.gov.

International Trade Administration

[For the International Trade Administration statement of organization, see the *Federal Register* of Jan. 25, 1980, 45 FR 6148]

The International Trade Administration (ITA) was established on January 2, 1980, by the Secretary of Commerce to promote world trade and to strengthen the international trade and investment position of the United States.

ITA is headed by the Under Secretary for International Trade, who coordinates all issues concerning trade promotion, international commercial policy, market access, and trade law enforcement. The Administration is responsible for nonagricultural trade operations of the U.S. Government and supports the trade policy negotiation efforts of the U.S. Trade Representative.

Import Administration   The Office of Import Administration defends American industry against injurious and unfair trade practices by administering efficiently, fairly, and in a manner consistent with U.S. international trade obligations the antidumping and countervailing duty laws of the United States. The Office ensures the proper administration of foreign trade zones and advises the Secretary on establishment of new zones; oversees the administration of the Department's textiles program; and administers programs governing watch assemblies, and other statutory import programs.

Market Access and Compliance   The Office of Market Access and Compliance advises on the analysis, formulation, and implementation of U.S. international economic policies and carries out programs to promote international trade, improve access by U.S. companies to overseas markets, and strengthen the international trade and investment position of the United States. The Office analyzes and develops recommendations for region- and country-specific international economic, trade, and investment policy strategies and objectives. In addition, the Office is responsible for implementing, monitoring, and enforcing foreign compliance with bilateral and multilateral trade agreements.

Manufacturing and Services   The Manufacturing and Services unit advises on domestic and international trade and investment policies affecting the competitiveness of U.S. industry and carries on a program of research and analysis on manufacturing and services. Based on this analysis and interaction with U.S. industry, the unit Secretary develops strategies, policies, and programs to strengthen the competitive position of U.S. industries in the United States and world markets. The unit manages an integrated program that includes both industry and economic analysis, trade policy development and multilateral, regional, and bilateral trade agreements for manufactured goods and services; administers trade arrangements (other than those involving AD/CVD proceedings) with foreign governments in product and service areas; and develops and provides business information and assistance to the United States on its rights and opportunities under multilateral and other agreements.

Trade Promotion and U.S. and Foreign Commercial Service   The Trade Promotion and U.S. and Foreign Commercial Service unit directs ITA's export promotion programs, develops and implements a unified goal-setting and evaluation process to increase trade assistance to small- and medium-sized businesses, directs a program of international trade events, market research, and export-related trade information products and services; and directs programs to aid U.S. firms to compete successfully for major projects and procurements worldwide. ITA provides a comprehensive platform of export assistance services to support U.S. firms who enter or expand their presence in overseas markets, including counseling, trade events, and outreach services through 109 export assistance centers located in the United States and 158 posts located in 83 countries

throughout the world. For a complete listing of ITA's export assistance centers, both in the United States and abroad, consult the Web site at www.export.gov/ eac or call the Trade Information Center at 1–800–872–8723.

For further information, contact the International Trade Administration, Department of Commerce, Washington, DC 20230. Phone, 202–482–3917. Internet, www.trade.gov.

Minority Business Development Agency

[For the Minority Business Development Agency statement of organization, see the *Federal Register* of Mar. 17, 1972, 37 FR 5650, as amended]

The Minority Business Development Agency was established by Executive order in 1969. The Agency develops and coordinates a national program for minority business enterprise.

The Agency was created to assist minority businesses in achieving effective and equitable participation in the American free enterprise system and in overcoming social and economic disadvantages that have limited their participation in the past. The Agency provides national policies and leadership in forming and strengthening a partnership of business, industry, and government with the Nation's minority businesses.

Business development services are provided to the minority business community through three vehicles: the minority business opportunity

committees which disseminate information on business opportunities; the minority business development centers that provide management and technical assistance and other business development services; and electronic commerce which includes a Web page on the Internet that will show how to start a business and use the service to electronically match business with contract opportunities.

The Agency promotes and coordinates the efforts of other Federal agencies in assisting or providing market opportunities for minority business. It coordinates opportunities for minority firms in the private sector. Through such public and private cooperative activities, the Agency promotes the participation of Federal, State, and local governments, and business and industry in directing resources for the development of strong minority businesses.

National Enterprise Centers—Minority Business Development Agency

Region	Address	Director	Telephone
Atlanta, GA	Suite 1715, 401 W. Peachtree St. NW., 30308–3516	Patricia Hanes	404–730–3300
Chicago, IL	Suite 1406, 55 E. Monroe St., 60603	Eric Dobyne	312–353–0182
Dallas, TX	Suite 726, 1100 Commerce St., 75242	John Iglehart	214–767–8001
El Monte, CA	Suite 455, 9660 Flair Dr., 91713	Maria Acosta	818–453–8636
New York, NY	Suite 3720, 26 Federal Plz., 10278	Heyward Davenport	212–264–3262
San Francisco, CA	Rm. 1280, 221 Main St., 94105	Linda Marmolejo	415–744–3001

Regional Enterprise Centers—Minority Business Development Agency

Area	Address	Director	Telephone
Boston, MA	Suite 414, One Gateway Ctr., 02458	Dick Torborg	617–527–2186
Miami, FL	Suite 1314, 51 SW. First Ave., 33130	Augusto Guzman	305–536–5054
Pasadena, CA	Suite 460, Pasadena Office Towers, 150 S. Los Robles Ave., 91101.	Maria Acosta	818–453–8636
Philadelphia, PA	Suite 10128, 600 Arch St., 19106	Alfonso Jackson	215–597–9236

For further information, contact the Office of the Director, Minority Business Development Agency, Department of Commerce, Washington, DC 20230. Phone, 202–482–5061. Internet, www.mbda.gov.

National Oceanic and Atmospheric Administration

[For the National Oceanic and Atmospheric Administration statement of organization, see the *Federal Register* of Feb. 13, 1978, 43 FR 6128]

The National Oceanic and Atmospheric Administration (NOAA) was formed on October 3, 1970, by Reorganization Plan No. 4 of 1970 (5 U.S.C. app.).

NOAA's mission entails environmental assessment, prediction, and stewardship. It is dedicated to monitoring and assessing the state of the environment in order to make accurate and timely forecasts to protect life, property, and natural resources, as well as to promote the economic well-being of the United States and to enhance its environmental security. NOAA is committed to protecting America's ocean, coastal, and living marine resources while promoting sustainable economic development.

For a complete listing of NOAA facilities and activities in your State or Territory, consult the Web site at www.legislative.noaa.gov/NIYS0107/noaainyourstate.html.

National Weather Service

The National Weather Service (NWS) provides weather, water and climate warnings, forecasts and data for the United States, its territories, adjacent waters, and ocean areas. NWS data and products form a national information database and infrastructure used by Government agencies, the private sector, the public, and the global community to protect life and property and to enhance the national economy. Working with partners in Government, academic and research institutions and private industry, NWS strives to ensure their products and services are responsive to the needs of the American public. NWS data and information services support aviation and marine activities, wildfire suppression, and many other sectors of the economy.

NWS supports national security efforts with long- and short-range forecasts, air quality and cloud dispersion forecasts, and broadcasts of warnings and critical information over the 800-station NOAA Weather Radio network.

For further information, contact the National Weather Service, Attention: Executive Affairs, 1325 East-West Highway, Silver Spring, MD 20910–3283. Phone, 301–713–0675. Fax, 301–713–0049. Internet, www.nws.noaa.gov.

National Environmental Satellite, Data, and Information Service

The National Environmental Satellite, Data, and Information Service (NESDIS) operates the Nation's civilian geostationary and polar-orbiting environmental satellites. It also manages the largest collection of atmospheric, climatic, geophysical, and oceanographic data in the world. From these sources, NESDIS develops and provides, through various media, environmental data for forecasts, national security, and weather warnings to protect life and property. This data is also used to assist in energy distribution, the development of global food supplies, the management of natural resources, and in the recovery of downed pilots and mariners in distress.

For further information, contact the National Environmental Satellite, Data, and Information Service, 1335 East-West Highway, Silver Spring, MD 20910–3283. Phone, 301–713–3578. Fax, 301–713–1249. Internet, www.noaa.gov/nesdis/nesdis.html.

National Marine Fisheries Service

The National Marine Fisheries Service (NMFS) supports the management, conservation, and sustainable development of domestic and international living marine resources and the protection and restoration of healthy ecosystems. NMFS is involved in the stock assessment of the Nation's multi-billion-dollar marine fisheries, protecting marine mammals and threatened species, habitat conservation operations, trade and industry assistance, and fishery enforcement activities.

For further information, contact the National Marine Fisheries Service, 1315 East-West Highway, Silver Spring, MD 20910. Phone, 301–713–2239. Fax, 301–713–2258. Internet, www.nmfs.noaa.gov.

National Ocean Service

The National Ocean Service (NOS) works to balance the Nation's use of coastal resources through research, management, and policy. NOS monitors the health of U.S. coasts by examining how human use and natural events impact coastal ecosystems. Coastal communities rely on NOS for information about natural hazards so they can more effectively reduce or eliminate the destructive effects of coastal hazards. NOS assesses the damage caused by hazardous material spills and works to restore or replace the affected coastal resources. Through varied programs, NOS protects wetlands, water quality, beaches, and wildlife. In addition, NOS provides a wide range of navigational products and data that assist vessels' safe movement through U.S. waters and provides the basic set of information that establishes the latitude, longitude, and elevation framework necessary for the Nation's surveying, navigation, positioning, and mapping activities.

For further information, contact the National Ocean Service, Room 13231, SSMC 4, 1305 East-West Highway, Silver Spring, MD 20910. Phone, 301–713–3070. Fax, 301–713–4307. Internet, www.nos.noaa.gov.

Office of Oceanic and Atmospheric Research

The Office of Oceanic and Atmospheric Research (OAR) carries out research on weather, air quality and composition, climate variability and change, and ocean, coastal, and Great Lakes ecosystems. OAR conducts and directs its research programs in coastal, marine, atmospheric, and space sciences through its own laboratories and offices, as well as through networks of university-based programs across the country.

For further information, contact the Office of Oceanic and Atmospheric Research, Room 11458, 1315 East-West Highway, Silver Spring, MD 20910. Phone, 301–713–2458. Fax, 301–713–0163. Internet, www.oar.noaa.gov.

Office of Marine and Aviation Operations

The Office of Marine and Aviation Operations maintains a fleet of ships and aircraft, and manages several safety programs. Ships and aircraft are used for operational data collection and research in support of NOAA's mission, the Global Earth Observation System, and the Integrated Ocean Observing System. This includes flying "hurricane hunter" aircraft into nature's most turbulent storms to collect data critical to hurricane research.

For further information, contact Office of Marine and Aviation Operations, Suite 500, 8403 Colesville Rd., Silver Spring, MD 20910. Phone, 301–713–1045.

For further information, contact the Office of Public Affairs, National Oceanic and Atmospheric Administration, Department of Commerce, Washington, DC 20230. Phone, 202–482–4190. Internet, www.noaa.gov.

National Telecommunications and Information Administration

[For the National Telecommunications and Information Administration statement of organization, see the *Federal Register* of June 5, 1978, 43 FR 24348]

The National Telecommunications and Information Administration (NTIA) was established in 1978 by Reorganization Plan No. 1 of 1977 (5 U.S.C. app.) and Executive Order 12046 of March 27, 1978 (3 CFR, 1978 Comp., p. 158), by combining the Office of Telecommunications Policy of the Executive Office of the President and the Office of Telecommunications of the Department of Commerce to form a new agency reporting to the Secretary of Commerce. NTIA operates under the authority of the National Telecommunications and Information Administration Organization Act (47 U.S.C. 901).

NTIA's principal responsibilities and functions include:

—serving as the principal executive branch adviser to the President on telecommunications and information policy;

—developing and presenting U.S. plans and policies at international communications conferences and related meetings;

—prescribing policies for and managing Federal use of the radio frequency spectrum;

—serving as the principal Federal telecommunications research and engineering laboratory, through NTIA's Institute for Telecommunication Sciences, headquartered in Boulder, CO;

—administering Federal programs to assist telecommunication facilities, public safety organizations, and the general public with the transition to digital broadcasting;

—providing grants through the Broadband Technology Opportunities Program to increase broadband accessibility in underserved areas of the United States; and

—providing grants through the Public Telecommunications Facilities Program to extend delivery or public telecommunications services to U.S. citizens, to increase ownership and management by women and minorities, and to strengthen the capabilities of existing public broadcasting stations to provide telecommunications services.

For further information, contact the National Telecommunications and Information Administration, Department of Commerce, Washington, DC 20230. Phone, 202–482–1551. Internet, www.ntia.doc.gov.

National Institute of Standards and Technology

The National Institute of Standards and Technology (NIST) operates under the authority of the National Institute of Standards and Technology Act (15 U.S.C. 271), which amends the Organic Act of March 3, 1901 (ch. 872), that created the National Bureau of Standards (NBS) in 1901. In 1988, Congress renamed NBS as NIST and expanded its activities and responsibilities.

NIST is a nonregulatory Federal agency within the Commerce Department. Its mission is to promote measurement science, standards, and technology to enhance productivity, facilitate trade, and improve the quality of life. NIST carries out its mission through the NIST laboratories, which conduct research to advance the U.S. technological infrastructure; the Baldrige National Quality Program, which helps U.S. businesses and other organizations improve the performance and quality of their operations; the Hollings Manufacturing Extension Partnership, which helps smaller firms adopt new manufacturing and management technologies; and the Technology Innovative Program, which provides cost-shared awards to industry and other

institutions for high-risk, high-reward research in areas of critical national need.

For further information, contact the National Institute of Standards and Technology, 100 Bureau Drive, Gaithersburg, MD. Phone, 301–975–6478. Fax, 301–926–1630. Email, inquiries@nist.gov. Internet, www.nist.gov.

National Technical Information Service

The National Technical Information Service (NTIS) operates a central clearinghouse of scientific and technical information that is useful to U.S. business and industry. NTIS collects scientific and technical information; catalogs, abstracts, indexes, and permanently archives the information; disseminates products in the forms and formats most useful to its customers; develops electronic and other media to disseminate information; and provides information processing services to other Federal agencies. NTIS receives no appropriations. Its revenue comes from two sources: the sale of technical reports to business and industry, schools and universities, State and local government offices, and the public at large and from services to Federal agencies that help them communicate more effectively with their employees and constituents.

The NTIS collection of approximately 2.5 million works covers a broad array

of subjects and includes reports on the results of research and development and scientific studies on manufacturing processes, current events, and foreign and domestic trade; business and management studies; social, economic, and trade statistics; computer software and databases; health care reports, manuals, and data; environmental handbooks, regulations, economic studies, and applied technologies; directories to Federal laboratory and technical resources; and global competitive intelligence. The collection also includes audiovisual training materials in such areas as foreign languages, workplace safety and health, law enforcement, and fire services.

The *NTIS Bibliographic Database* is available online through commercial vendors and on CD–ROM from NTIS. Database entries since 1964 are available at the NTIS Web site. Internet, www.ntis.gov.

For further information, contact the National Technical Information Service Administration, 5301 Shawnee Road, Arlington, VA 22312. Phone, 703–605–6050 or 888–584–8332. Internet, www.ntis.gov.

United States Patent and Trademark Office

[For the Patent and Trademark Office statement of organization, see the *Federal Register* of Apr. 14, 1975, 40 FR 16707]

The United States Patent and Trademark Office (USPTO) was established by the act of July 19, 1952 (35 U.S.C. 1) "to promote the progress of science and the useful arts by securing for limited times to inventors the exclusive right to their respective discoveries for a certain

period of time" (Article I, Section 8 of the United States Constitution). The registration of trademarks is based on the commerce clause of the U.S. Constitution.

USPTO examines and issues patents. There are three major patent categories: utility patents, design patents, and plant patents. USPTO also issues statutory invention registrations and processes international patent applications.

Through the registration of trademarks, USPTO assists businesses in protecting their investments, promoting goods and services, and safeguarding consumers against confusion and deception in the marketplace. A trademark includes any distinctive word, name, symbol, device, or any combination thereof adopted and used or intended to be used by a manufacturer or merchant to identify his goods or services and distinguish them from those manufactured or sold by others. Trademarks are examined by the Office for compliance with various statutory requirements to prevent unfair competition and consumer deception.

In addition to the examination of patent and trademark applications, issuance of patents, and registration of trademarks, USPTO advises and assists government agencies and officials in matters involving all domestic and global aspects of intellectual property. USPTO also promotes an understanding of intellectual property protection.

USPTO provides public access to patent, trademark, and related scientific and technical information. Patents and trademarks may be freely reviewed and searched online at www.uspto.gov or at designated Patent and Trademark Depository Libraries. There are 80 Patent and Trademark Depository Libraries located within the United States and the territory of Puerto Rico. Additionally, USPTO's Scientific and Technical Information Center in Alexandria, VA, houses over 120,000 volumes of scientific and technical books in various languages; 90,000 bound volumes of periodicals devoted to science and technology; the official journals of 77 foreign patent organizations; and over 40 million foreign patents on paper, microfilm, microfiche, and CD-ROM.

For further information, contact the Office of Public Affairs, United States Patent and Trademark Office, 600 Dulaney Street, Alexandria, VA 22314. Phone, 571–272–8400. Internet, www.uspto.gov.

Sources of Information

Age and Citizenship Age search and citizenship information is available from the Personal Census Search Unit, Bureau of the Census, National Processing Center, P.O. Box 1545, Jeffersonville, IN 47131. Phone, 812–218–3046.

Economic Development Information Clearinghouse The EDA will host on its Web site the Economic Development Information Clearinghouse, an online depository of information on economic development (Internet, www.doc.gov/eda).

Contracting and Small Business For information regarding contract opportunities, contact the Office of Small and Disadvantaged Business Utilization. Phone, 202–482–1472. Internet, www.doc.gov/osdbu.

Employment Information is available electronically through the Internet, at www.doc.gov/ohrm. Phone, 202–482–5138.

The National Oceanic and Atmospheric Administration has field employment offices at the Western Administrative Support Center, Bin C15700, 7600 Sand Point Way NE., Seattle, WA 98115 (phone, 206–526–6294); 325 Broadway, Boulder, CO 80303 (phone, 303–497–6332); 601 East Twelfth Street, Kansas City, MO 64106 (phone, 816–426–2056); and 200 World Trade Center, Norfolk, VA 23510–1624 (phone, 757–441–6516).

Environment The National Oceanic and Atmospheric Administration conducts research and gathers data about the oceans, atmosphere, space, and Sun, and applies this knowledge to science and service in ways that touch the lives of all Americans, including warning of dangerous weather, charting seas and skies, guiding our use and protection of ocean and coastal resources, and improving our understanding and stewardship of the environment which sustains us all. For further information, contact the Office of Public and Constituent Affairs, National Oceanic and Atmospheric Administration, Room 6013, Fourteenth Street and Constitution Avenue NW., Washington, DC 20230. Phone, 202–482–6090. Fax, 202–482–3154. Internet, www.noaa.gov.

Inspector General Hotline The Office of Inspector General works to promote economy, efficiency, and effectiveness and to prevent and detect fraud, waste, abuse, and mismanagement in departmental programs and operations. Contact the Hotline, Inspector General, P.O. Box 612, Ben Franklin Station, Washington, DC 20044. Phone, 202–482–2495, or 800–424–5197 (toll free). TTD, 202–482–5923, or 800–854–8407 (toll free). Fax, 202–789–0522. Internet, www.oig.doc.gov. Email, hotline@oig.doc.gov.

Patents The United States Patent and Trademark Office has priority programs for advancement of examination of certain patent applications where the invention could materially enhance the quality of the environment of mankind. For further information, contact the Commissioner for Patents, Office of Petitions, Washington, DC 20231. Phone, 703–305–9282.

Publications The titles of selected publications are printed below with the operating units responsible for their issuance. These and other publications dealing with a wide range of business, economic, environmental, scientific, and technical matters are announced in the weekly *Business Service Checklist,* which may be purchased from the Superintendent of Documents, Government Printing Office, Washington, DC 20402. Phone, 202–512–1800.

Bureau of the Census Numerous publications presenting statistical information on a wide variety of subjects are available from the Government Printing Office, including the following: *Statistical Abstract of the U.S.; Historical Statistics of the United States, Colonial Times to 1970; County and City Data Book, 1994;* and *State and Metropolitan Area Data Book, 1997–1998.*

Employment opportunities, data highlights, large data files, access tools, and other material are available on the World Wide Web. Internet, www.census.gov. Email, webmaster@census.gov.

Bureau of Economic Analysis The *Survey of Current Business* (Monthly Journal) is available from the Government Printing Office. Current and historical estimates, general information, and employment opportunities are available on BEA's Web site at www.bea.gov. For more information, contact the Public Information Office. Phone, 202–606–9900. Email, webmaster@bea.gov.

Bureau of Industry and Security The Bureau's Web site (Internet, www.bis.doc.gov) provides information for the U.S. business community, including export news, general, subject and policy fact sheets, updates to the Export Administration regulations, Bureau program information, e-FOIA information, and export seminar event schedules. Publications available on the site include the Bureau's annual report, foreign policy controls report, and international diversification and defense market assessment guides. The Government Printing Office, in conjunction with the Bureau, has created a Web site that contains an up-to-date database of the entire export administration regulations, including the commerce control list, the commerce country chart, and the denied persons list (Internet, www.access.gpo.gov/bis/index.html). The Outreach and Educational Services Division has offices in Washington, DC (phone, 202–482–4811; fax, 202–482–2927) and on the West Coast (phone 949–660–0144, or 408–351–3378; fax, 949–660–9347, or 408–351–3355). For enforcement-related questions, contact the partnership-in-security hotline (phone, 800–424–2980).

International Trade Administration The Administration maintains a Web site, (Internet, www.trade.gov), which offers the single best place for individuals or firms seeking reports, documents, import case/regulations, texts of international agreements like NAFTA and GATT, market research, and points of contact for assistance in exporting, obtaining remedies from unfair trading practices, or receiving help with market access problems. Customers are able to review comprehensive information on how to export, search for trade information by either industry or by country, learn how to petition against unfairly priced imports, and obtain information on a number of useful international trade-related products like overseas trade leads and agent distributor reports. The Web site also features email addresses and locations for trade contacts in Washington, overseas, in major exporting centers in the United States, and in other parts of the Federal Government.

Minority Business Development Agency Copies of *Minority Business Today* and the *BDC Directory* may be obtained by contacting the Office of Business Development. Phone, 202–482–6022. Comprehensive information about programs, policy, centers, and access to the job matching database is available through the Internet at www.mbda.gov.

National Institute of Standards and Technology *Journal of Research; Publications of the Advanced Technology Program and Manufacturing Extension Partnership Program; Handbook of Mathematical Functions; Experimental Statistics; International System of Units (SI); Standard Reference Materials Catalog; Specifications, Tolerances, and Other Technical Requirements for Weighing and Measuring Devices Handbook;* and *Uniform Laws and Regulations Handbook* are available from the Government Printing Office.

National Oceanic and Atmospheric Administration The Administration provides technical memoranda, technical reports, monographs, nautical and aeronautical charts, coastal zone maps, data tapes, and a wide variety of raw and processed environmental data. Information on NOAA products is available through the Internet at www.noaa.gov. Contact the Office of Public and Constituent Affairs, Fourteenth Street and Constitution Avenue NW., Washington, DC 20230. Phone, 202–482–6090. Fax, 202–482–3154.

National Technical Information Service For general inquiries, to place an order, or to request the *Catalog of NTIS Products and Services,* contact the NTIS Sales Desk from 8 a.m. to 6 p.m. (eastern standard time). Phone, 800–553–6847. TDD, 703–487–4639. Fax, 703–605–6900. Email, info@ntis.gov. Internet, www.ntis.gov.

To inquire about NTIS information services for other Federal agencies, call 703–605–6540.

National Telecommunications and Information Administration Since 1970, several hundred technical reports and memoranda, special publications, contractor reports, and other information products have been published by NTIA or its predecessor agency. The publications are available from the National Telecommunications and Information Administration, Department of Commerce, Washington, DC 20230 (phone, 202–482–1551); or the National Telecommunications and Information Administration, Institute for Telecommunication Sciences, Department of Commerce, Boulder, CO 80302 (phone, 303–497–3572). Electronic information can be obtained at www.ntia.doc.gov.

United States Patent and Trademark Office *General Information Concerning Patents, Basic Facts About Trademarks, Official Gazette of the United States Patent and Trademark Office,* and *Attorneys and Agents Registered To Practice Before the U.S. Patent and Trademark Office* are available from the Government Printing Office. Publications can be accessed through the Internet at www.uspto.gov. Phone, 703–308–4357, or 800–786–9199.

For further information concerning the Department of Commerce, contact the Office of Public Affairs, Department of Commerce, Fourteenth Street and Constitution Avenue NW., Room 5040, Washington, DC 20230. Phone, 202–482–3263. Internet, www.doc.gov.

DEPARTMENT OF DEFENSE

Office of the Secretary, The Pentagon, Washington, DC 20301–1155
Phone, 703–545–6700. Internet, www.defenselink.mil.

SECRETARY OF DEFENSE	ROBERT M. GATES
DEPUTY SECRETARY OF DEFENSE	WILLIAM LYNN III
Under Secretary of Defense for Acquisition, Technology, and Logistics	ASHTON B. CARTER
Deputy Under Secretary of Defense (Business Transformation)	PAUL A. BRINKLEY
Deputy Under Secretary of Defense (Installations and Environment)	LOUIS W. ARNY III
Under Secretary of Defense for Policy	MICHELE FLOURNOY
Principal Deputy Under Secretary of Defense for Policy	JAMES N. MILLER, JR.
Assistant Secretary of Defense (International Security Affairs)	ALEXANDER R. VERSHBOW
Assistant Secretary of Defense (Special Operations and Low-Intensity Conflict)	MICHAEL VICKERS
Assistant Secretary of Defense (Homeland Defense and America's Security)	(VACANCY)
Assistant Secretary of Defense (Global Strategic Affairs	JOSEPH BENKERT
Assistant Secretary of Defense (Asian and Pacific Security Affairs)	(VACANCY)
Deputy Assistant Secretary of Defense (Plans)	JANINE DAVIDSON
Deputy Under Secretary of Defense (Technology Security Policy/Counter Proliferation)	(VACANCY)
Deputy Under Secretary of Defense (Strategy, Plans and Forces)	KATHLEEN HICKS
Deputy Under Secretary of Defense (Policy Integration and Chief of Staff)	PETER VERGA
Principal Deputy Under Secretary of Defense for Personnel and Readiness	WILLIAM J. CARR, *Acting*
Assistant Secretary of Defense (Reserve Affairs)	DAVID L. MCGINNIS, *Acting*
Deputy Assistant Secretary of Defense (Reserve Affairs)	JENNIFER C. BUCK
Deputy Under Secretary of Defense (Program Integration)	JEANNE FITES
Deputy Under Secretary of Defense (Readiness)	SAMUEL D. KLEINMAN
Deputy Under Secretary of Defense (Military Personnel Policy)	WILLIAM J. CARR
Deputy Under Secretary of Defense (Military Community and Family Policy)	ARTHUR J. MYERS, *Acting*
Deputy Under Secretary of Defense (Plans)	GAIL H. MCGINN
Under Secretary of Defense (Comptroller)/Chief Financial Officer	ROBERT F. HALE

146

Principal Deputy Under Secretary of Defense (Comptroller)	MICHAEL J. MCCORD
Under Secretary of Defense (Intelligence)	JAMES R. CLAPPER, JR.
Assistant Secretary of Defense (Networks and Information Integration)/Chief Information Officer	JOHN G. GRIMES
Assistant Secretary of Defense (Legislative Affairs)	(VACANCY)
Assistant Secretary of Defense (Public Affairs)	ROBERT L. HASTINGS, *Acting*
General Counsel	JEH C. JOHNSON
Director, Operational Test and Evaluation	CHARLES E. MCQUEARY
Principal Deputy Director for Operational Test and Evaluation	DAVID W. DUMA
Inspector General	GORDON S. HEDDELL, *Acting*
Director of Administration and Management	MICHAEL L. RHODES, *Acting*

Joint Chiefs of Staff

Chairman	ADM. MICHAEL G. MULLEN, USN
Vice Chairman	GEN. JAMES E. CARTWRIGHT, USMC
Chief of Staff, Army	GEN. GEORGE W. CASEY, JR., USA
Chief of Naval Operations	ADM. GARY ROUGHEAD, USN
Chief of Staff, Air Force	GEN. NORTON A. SCHWARTZ, USAF
Commandant, Marine Corps	GEN. JAMES T. CONWAY, USMC

[For the Department of Defense statement of organization, see the *Code of Federal Regulations,* Title 32, Chapter I, Subchapter R]

The Department of Defense is responsible for providing the military forces needed to deter war and protect the security of our country.

The major elements of these forces are the Army, Navy, Marine Corps, and Air Force, consisting of about 1.3 million men and women on active duty. They are backed, in case of emergency, by the 825,000 members of the Reserve and National Guard. In addition, there are about 600,000 civilian employees in the Defense Department.

Under the President, who is also Commander in Chief, the Secretary of Defense exercises authority, direction, and control over the Department, which includes the separately organized military departments of Army, Navy, and Air Force, the Joint Chiefs of Staff providing military advice, the combatant commands, and defense agencies and field activities established for specific purposes.

The National Security Act Amendments of 1949 redesignated the National Military Establishment as the Department of Defense and established it as an executive department (10 U.S.C. 111), headed by the Secretary of Defense.

Structure

The Department of Defense is composed of the Office of the Secretary of Defense; the military departments and the military services within those departments; the Chairman of the Joint Chiefs of Staff and the Joint Staff; the combatant commands; the defense agencies; DOD field activities; and such other offices, agencies, activities, and commands as may be established or designated by law, or by the President or the Secretary of Defense.

Each military department is separately organized under its own Secretary and functions under the authority, direction, and control of the Secretary of Defense. The Secretary of each military department is responsible to the Secretary of Defense for the operation and efficiency of his department. Orders

DEPARTMENT OF DEFENSE

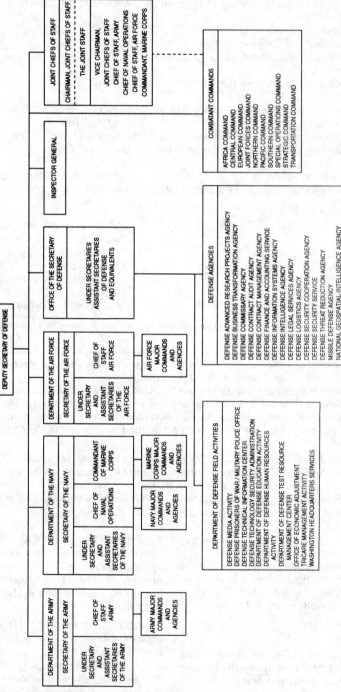

to the military departments are issued through the Secretaries of these departments or their designees, by the Secretary of Defense, or under authority specifically delegated in writing by the Secretary of Defense or provided by law.

The commanders of the combatant commands are responsible to the President and the Secretary of Defense for accomplishing the military missions assigned to them and exercising command authority over forces assigned to them. The operational chain of command runs from the President to the Secretary of Defense to the commanders of the combatant commands. The Chairman of the Joint Chiefs of Staff functions within the chain of command by transmitting the orders of the President or the Secretary of Defense to the commanders of the combatant commands.

Office of the Secretary of Defense

Secretary of Defense The Secretary of Defense is the principal defense policy adviser to the President and is responsible for the formulation of general defense policy and policy related to DOD, and for the execution of approved policy. Under the direction of the President, the Secretary exercises authority, direction, and control over the Department of Defense.

Acquisition, Technology, and Logistics The Under Secretary of Defense for Acquisition, Technology, and Logistics is the principal staff assistant and adviser to the Secretary of Defense for all matters relating to the DOD Acquisition System; research and development; modeling and simulation; systems engineering; advanced technology; developmental test and evaluation; production; systems integration; logistics; installation management; military construction; procurement; environment, safety, and occupational health management; utilities and energy management; business management modernization; document services; and nuclear, chemical, and biological defense programs.

Intelligence The Under Secretary of Defense for Intelligence is the principal staff assistant and adviser to the Secretary and Deputy Secretary of Defense for intelligence, intelligence-related matters, counterintelligence, and security. The Under Secretary of Defense for Intelligence supervises all intelligence and intelligence-related affairs of DOD.

Networks and Information Integration The Assistant Secretary of Defense (Networks and Information Integration) is the principal staff assistant and adviser to the Secretary and Deputy Secretary of Defense for achieving and maintaining information superiority in support of DOD missions, while exploiting or denying an adversary's ability to do the same. The Assistant Secretary of Defense also serves as the Chief Information Officer.

Personnel and Readiness The Under Secretary of Defense for Personnel and Readiness is the principal staff assistant and adviser to the Secretary of Defense for policy matters relating to the structure and readiness of the total force. Functional areas include readiness; civilian and military personnel policies, programs, and systems; civilian and military equal opportunity programs; health policies, programs, and activities; Reserve component programs, policies, and activities; family policy, dependents' education, and personnel support programs; mobilization planning and requirements; language capabilities and programs; and the Federal Voting Assistance Program. The Under Secretary of Defense (Personnel and Readiness) also serves as the Chief Human Capital Officer.

Policy The Under Secretary of Defense for Policy is the principal staff assistant and adviser to the Secretary of Defense for policy matters relating to overall international security policy and political-military affairs and represents the Department at the National Security Council and other external agencies regarding national security policy. Functional areas include homeland defense; NATO affairs; foreign military sales; arms limitation agreements; international trade and technology security; regional security affairs; special operations and low-intensity conflict; stability operations; integration of departmental plans and policies with overall national security objectives; drug control policy, requirements, priorities, systems, resources, and programs; and issuance of policy guidance affecting departmental programs.

Additional Staff In addition, the Secretary and Deputy Secretary of Defense are assisted by a special staff of assistants, including the Assistant Secretary of Defense for Legislative Affairs; the General Counsel; the Inspector General; the Assistant Secretary of Defense for Public Affairs; the Assistant to the Secretary of Defense (Intelligence Oversight); the Director of Administration and Management; the Under Secretary of Defense (Comptroller)/Chief Financial Officer; the Director of Operational Test and Evaluation; Director, Force Transformation; Director, Net Assessment; Director, Program Analysis and Evaluation; and such other officers as the Secretary of Defense establishes to assist him in carrying out his duties and responsibilities.

Joint Chiefs of Staff

Joint Chiefs of Staff

The Joint Chiefs of Staff consist of the Chairman; the Vice Chairman; the Chief of Staff of the Army; the Chief of Naval Operations; the Chief of Staff of the Air Force; and the Commandant of the Marine Corps. The Chairman of the Joint Chiefs of·Staff is the principal military adviser to the President, the National Security Council, and the Secretary of Defense. The other members of the Joint Chiefs of Staff are military advisers who may provide additional information upon request from the President, the National Security Council, or the Secretary of Defense. They may also submit their advice when it does not agree with that of the Chairman. Subject to the authority of the President and the Secretary of Defense, the Chairman of the Joint Chiefs of Staff is responsible for:

—assisting the President and the Secretary of Defense in providing for the strategic direction and planning of the Armed Forces;

—allocating resources to fulfill strategic plans;

—making recommendations for the assignment of responsibilities within the Armed Forces in accordance with and in support of those logistic and mobility plans;

—comparing the capabilities of American and allied Armed Forces with those of potential adversaries;

—preparing and reviewing contingency plans that conform to policy guidance from the President and the Secretary of Defense;

—preparing joint logistic and mobility plans to support contingency plans; and

—recommending assignment of logistic and mobility responsibilities to the Armed Forces to fulfill logistic and mobility plans.

The Chairman, while so serving, holds the grade of general or admiral and outranks all other officers of the Armed Forces.

The Vice Chairman of the Joint Chiefs performs duties assigned by the Chairman, with the approval of the Secretary of Defense. The Vice Chairman acts as Chairman when there is a vacancy in the office of the Chairman, or in the absence or disability of the Chairman. The Vice Chairman, while so serving, holds the grade of general or admiral and outranks all other officers of the Armed Forces except the Chairman of the Joint Chiefs of Staff.

Joint Staff

The Joint Staff, under the Chairman of the Joint Chiefs of Staff, assists the Chairman and the other members of the Joint Chiefs of Staff in carrying out their responsibilities.

The Joint Staff is headed by a Director who is selected by the Chairman in consultation with the other members of the Joint Chiefs of Staff and with the approval of the Secretary of Defense. Officers assigned to serve on the Joint Staff are selected by the Chairman in approximate equal numbers from the Army, Navy, Marine Corps, and Air Force.

Combatant Commands

The combatant commands are military commands with broad continuing missions maintaining the security and defense of the United States against attack; supporting and advancing the national policies and interests of the United States and discharging U.S. military responsibilities in their assigned areas; and preparing plans, conducting operations, and coordinating activities of the forces assigned to them in accordance with the directives of higher authority. The operational chain of command runs from the President to the Secretary of Defense to the commanders of the combatant commands. The Chairman of the Joint Chiefs of Staff serves as the spokesman for the commanders of the combatant commands, especially on the administrative requirements of their commands.

Combatant Commands

Command	Address	Commander
Central	USCENTCOM, 7115 S. Boundary Blvd., MacDill AFB, FL 33621–5101.	Gen. David H. Petraeus, USA
European	USEUCOM, APO AE 09131	Adm. James G. Stavridis, USN
Joint Forces	USJFCOM, Suite 200, 1562 Mitscher Ave., Norfolk, VA 23551–2488.	Gen. James N. Mattis, USMC
Pacific	USPACCOM, Box 64028, Camp H.M. Smith, HI 96861–4028.	Adm. Timothy J. Keating, USN
Southern	USSOUTHCOM, 3511 NW. 91st Ave., Miami, FL 33172	Gen. Douglas M. Fraser, USAF
Northern	USNORTHCOM, Suite 116, 250 S. Peterson Blvd., Peterson AFB, CO 80914–3010.	Gen. Victor E. Renuart, USAF
Africa	USAFRICOM, APO AE 09107	Gen. William E. Ward, USA
Special Operations	USSOCOM, 7701 Tampa Point Blvd., MacDill AFB, FL 33621–5323.	Gen. Bryan D. Brown, USAF
Strategic	USSTRATCOM, Suite 2A1, 901 SAC Blvd., Offutt AFB, NE 68113–6000.	Gen. Kevin P. Chilton, USAF
Transportation	USTRANSCOM, Rm. 339, 508 Scott Dr., Scott AFB, IL 62225–5357.	Gen. Duncan J. McNabb, USAF

Field Activities

American Forces Information Service

The American Forces Information Service (AFIS) provides internal communications program support to U.S. military forces worldwide to promote and sustain military unit and individual readiness, situational awareness, quality of life, and morale; trains public affairs, broadcast, and visual information professionals for DOD; and provides military commanders and combat forces with news, features, photography, videography, news clippings, and other internal command information products and services. AFIS provides internal communications policy guidance and oversight for departmental periodicals and pamphlets, military command newspapers, the broadcast elements of the military departments, DOD audiovisual matters, and public affairs and visual information training.

For further information, contact the American Forces Information Service, Department of Defense, Suite 300, 601 North Fairfax Street, Alexandria, VA 22314–2007. Phone, 703–428–1200. Internet, www.defenselink.mil/afis.

Counterintelligence Field Activity The DOD Counterintelligence Field Activity was established in 2002 to build a Defense counterintelligence (CI) system that is informed by national goals and objectives and supports the protection of DOD personnel and critical assets from foreign intelligence services, foreign terrorists, and other clandestine or covert threats. The desired end is a transformed Defense CI system which integrates and synchronizes the counterintelligence activities of the Military Departments, Defense Agencies, Joint Staff, and Combatant Commands.

For further information, contact the Department of Defense Counterintelligence Field Activity, Crystal Square 5, Suite 1200, 1755 Jefferson Davis Highway, Arlington, VA 22202–3537. Phone, 703–699–7799.

Defense Technical Information Center
The Defense Technical Information Center (DTIC) is a field activity in the Office of the Under Secretary of Defense (Acquisition, Technology, and Logistics). It operates under the authority, direction, and control of the Director, Defense Research and Engineering. DTIC provides defense scientific and technical information, offers controlled access to defense information, and designs and hosts more than 100 DOD Web sites. DTIC's collections include technical reports, summaries of research in progress, independent research and development material, defense technology transfer agreements, and DOD planning documents.

For further information, contact the Defense Technical Information Center, 8725 John J. Kingman Rd., Fort Belvoir, VA 22060–6218. Phone, 800–225–3842. Internet, www.dtic.mil/dtic/index.html.

Defense Technology Security Administration The Defense Technology Security Administration (DTSA) is the central DOD point of contact for development and implementation of technology security policies governing defense articles and services and dual-use commodities. DTSA administers the development and implementation of DOD technology security policies on international transfers of defense-related goods, services, and technologies to ensure that critical U.S. military technological advantages are preserved; transfers that could prove detrimental to U.S. security interests are controlled and limited; proliferation of weapons of mass destruction and their means of delivery is prevented; diversion of defense-related goods to terrorists is prevented; legitimate defense cooperation with foreign friends and allies is supported; and the health of the defense industrial base is assured.

For further information, contact the Director, Defense Technology Security Administration, 2900 Defense Pentagon, Washington, DC 20301–2900. Phone, 703–325–3294. Fax, 703–325–6467. Internet, www.dod.mil/policy/sections/policy_offices/dtsa/index.html.

Education Activity The Department of Defense Education Activity (DODEA) was established in 1992. It consists of two subordinate organizational entities: the Department of Defense Dependents Schools (DODDS) and the Department of Defense Domestic Dependent Elementary and Secondary Schools (DDESS). DODEA formulates, develops, and implements policies, technical guidance, and standards for the effective management of Defense dependents education activities and programs. It also plans, directs, coordinates, and manages the education programs for eligible dependents of U.S. military and civilian personnel stationed overseas and stateside; evaluates the programmatic and operational policies and procedures for DODDS and DDESS; and provides education activity representation at meetings and deliberations of educational panels and advisory groups.

For further information, contact the Department of Defense Education Activity, 4040 North Fairfax Drive, Arlington, VA 22203–1635. Phone, 703–588–3200. Internet, www.dodea.edu.

Human Resources Field Activity The Department of Defense Human Resources Activity enhances the operational effectiveness and efficiency of a host of dynamic and diverse programs supporting the Office of the Under Secretary of Defense for Personnel and Readiness. The Field Activity supports policy development, performs cutting-edge research and expert analysis, supports readiness and reengineering efforts, manages the largest automated personnel data repositories in the world, prepares tomorrow's leaders through robust developmental programs, supports recruiting and retaining the best and brightest, and delivers both benefits and critical services to warfighters and their families.

For further information, contact the Department of Defense Human Resources Activity Headquarters, Suite 200, 4040 Fairfax Drive, Arlington, VA 22203–1613. Phone, 703–696–1036. Internet, www.dhra.mil.

TRICARE Management Activity The TRICARE Management Activity (TMA) was formed in 1998 from the consolidation of the TRICARE Support Office (formerly Civilian Health and Medical Program of the Uniformed Services (CHAMPUS) headquarters), the Defense Medical Programs Activity, and the integration of health management program functions formerly located in the Office of the Assistant Secretary of Defense for Health Affairs. The mission of TMA is to manage TRICARE; manage the Defense Health Program appropriation; provide operational direction and support to the Uniformed Services in the management and administration of the TRICARE program; and administer CHAMPUS.

For further information, contact the TRICARE Management Activity, Suite 810, Skyline 5, 5111 Leesburg Pike, Falls Church, VA 22041–3206. Phone, 703–681–1730. Fax, 703–681–3665. Internet, www.tricare.osd.mil.

Test Resource Management The Test Resource Management Center (TRMC) is a DOD field activity under the authority, direction, and control of the Under Secretary of Defense for Acquisition, Technology, and Logistics. The Center develops policy, plans for, and assesses the adequacy of the major range and test facility base to provide adequate testing in support of development, acquisition, fielding, and sustainment of defense systems. TRMC develops and maintains the test and evaluation resources strategic plan, reviews the proposed DOD test and evaluation budgets, and certifies the adequacy of the proposed budgets and if they provide balanced support of the strategic plan. TRMC manages the Central Test and Evaluation Investment Program, the Test and Evaluation Science and Technology Program, and the Joint Mission Environment Test Capability Program.

Defense Prisoners of War and Missing Personnel Office The Defense Prisoner of War/Missing Personnel Office (DPMO) was established in 1993 to provide centralized management of prisoner of war/missing personnel affairs within the DOD. DPMO's primary responsibilities include leadership for and policy oversight over all efforts to account for Americans still missing from past conflicts and the recovery of and accounting for those who may become isolated in hostile territory in future conflicts. The Office also provides administrative and logistical support to the U.S.-Russia Joint Commission on POW/MIAs; conducts research and analysis to help resolve cases of those unaccounted for; examines DOD documents for possible public disclosure; and, through periodic consultations and other appropriate measures, maintains viable channels of communications on POW/MIA matters between DOD and Congress, the families of the missing, and the American public.

For further information, contact the Defense Prisoner of War/Missing Personnel Office, 2400 Defense Pentagon, Washington, DC 20301–2400. Phone, 703–699–1160. Fax, 703–602–4375. Internet, www.dtic.mil/dpmo.

Office of Economic Adjustment The Office of Economic Adjustment (OEA) assists communities that are adversely affected by base closures, expansions, or realignments and Defense contract or program cancellations. OEA provides technical and financial assistance to those communities and coordinates other Federal agencies' involvement through the Defense Economic Adjustment Program.

For further information, contact the Office of Economic Adjustment, Department of Defense, Suite 200, 400 Army Navy Drive, Arlington, VA 22202–4704. Phone, 703–604–6020.

Washington Headquarters Services
Washington Headquarters Services (WHS), established as a DOD Field Activity on October 1, 1977, is under the authority, direction, and control of the Director of Administration and Management. WHS provides a wide range of administrative and operational services to the Office of the Secretary of Defense, specified DOD components, select Federal Government activities, and the general public. This support includes contracting and procurement; Defense facilities management; Pentagon renovation and construction; directives and records management; financial management; library service; human resource services for executive, political, military, and civilian personnel; personnel security services; support for advisory boards and commissions; legal services and advice; information technology and data systems support; enterprise information technology

infrastructure services; and planning and evaluation functions.

For further information, contact the Administration and Program Support Directorate, Washington Headquarters Services, 1155 Defense Pentagon, Washington, DC 20301–1155. Phone, 703–601–6138. Internet, www.whs.pentagon.mil.

Defense Media Agency Defense Media Activity (DMA) gathers and reports defense news and information from all levels in the department to the DOD family worldwide through the Armed Forces Radio and Television Network, the Internet, and printed publications. DMA reports news about individual soldiers, sailors, marines, airmen, and defense civilian employees to the American public through the Hometown News Service. DMA provides World Wide Web infrastructure and services for DOD organizations. It collects, processes, and stores DOD imagery products created by the department and makes them available to the American public. It trains the department's public affairs and visual information military and civilian professionals. DMA also operates *Stars and Stripes*, a news and information organization, free of government editorial control and censorship for military audiences overseas.

For further information, contact the Defense Media Agency, Department of Defense, Suite 300, 601 North Fairfax Street, Alexandria, VA 22314–2007. Phone, 703–428–1200. Internet, www.dma.mil.

Sources of Information

News Organizations Newspapers and radio and television stations may subscribe to receive news releases about individual military members and Defense Department civilian employees at no cost. Phone, 210–925–6541. Email, hometown@dma.mil. Internet, www1.dmasa.dma.mil/hometown/.
Audiovisual Products Certain Department of Defense productions on film and videotapes, CD–ROMs, and other audiovisual products such as stock footage and still photographs are

available to the public. An up-to-date, full-text searchable listing of the Department's inventory of film, videotape, and interactive multimedia titles is available on the Internet. There may be a fee charged for the Department's audiovisual and multimedia products. For information, contact the following sources:
   —For newer productions, contact the National Technical Information Service, 5285 Port Royal Road, Springfield, VA 22161 (phone, 800–553–6847 or 703–605–6000), or the defense visual

information site (Internet, dodimagery.afis.osd.mil).

—For older productions, contact the Motion Picture, Sound, and Video Branch, National Archives and Records Administration, 8601 Adelphi Road, College Park, MD 20740–6001. Phone, 301–713–7050. For general inquiries, phone 800–234–8861 or 301–713–6800 or email inquiry@nara.gov.

—For still and motion images of operations, exercises, and historical events or for interactive training materials, contact the Defense Imagery Management Center. Phone, 888–743–4662. Internet, www.defenseimagery.mil. Email, askdimoc@hq.afis.osd.mil.

Contracts and Small Business Activities Contact the Director, Small and Disadvantaged Business Utilization, Office of the Secretary of Defense, 3061 Defense Pentagon, Washington, DC 20301–3061. Phone, 703–588–8631.

DOD Directives and Instructions Contact the Executive Services and Communications Directorate, Washington Headquarters Services, 1155 Defense Pentagon, Washington, DC 20301–1155. Phone, 703–601–4722.

Electronic Access Information about the following offices is available as listed below:

Office of the Secretary of Defense: www.defenselink.mil.

Joint Chiefs of Staff: www.jcs.mil.

Central Command: www.centcom.mil.

Combatant commands: www.defenselink.mil/pubs/almanac/unified.html.

European Command: www.eucom.mil.

Joint Forces Command: www.jfcom.mil.

Pacific Command: www.pacom.mil.

Northern Command: www.northcom.mil.

Southern Command: www.southcom.mil.

Special Operations Command: www.socom.mil.

Strategic Command: www.stratcom.mil.

Transportation Command: www.transcom.mil.

Employment Positions are filled by a variety of sources. Information concerning current vacancies and how to apply for positions may be found at https://storm.psd.whs.mil/. Assistance in applying for positions is also available from our Human Resources Services Center Help Desk at 703–604–6219, 7:30 a.m. to 5:00 p.m. weekdays or by writing to Washington Headquarters Services, 2521 South Clark Street, Suite 4000, Arlington, VA 22202.

Speakers Civilian and military officials from the U.S. Department of Defense are available to speak to numerous public and private sector groups interested in a variety of defense-related topics, including the global war on terrorism. Requests for speakers should be addressed to the Director for Community Relations and Public Liaison, 1400 Defense Pentagon, Room 2C546, Washington, DC 20310–1400, or by calling 703–695–2733.

Pentagon Tours Information on guided tours of the Pentagon may be obtained by writing to the Director, Pentagon Tours, 1400 Defense Pentagon, Room 2C546, Washington, DC 20310–1400 or calling 703–695–7778 or by sending an email to tourschd.pa@osd.mil. Internet, www.defenselink.mil/pubs/pentagon.

Defend America Web Site The Defend America Web site, which can be found at http://defendamerica.mil, is produced by the Department of Defense and devoted to educating people on the global war on terrorism. This site features up-to-date news, photographs, briefings and more information from authoritative Defense Department sources.

For further information concerning the Department of Defense, contact the Director, Directorate for Public Inquiry and Analysis, Office of the Assistant Secretary of Defense for Public Affairs, 1400 Defense Pentagon, Washington, DC 20301–1400. Phone, 703–428–0711. Internet, www.defenselink.mil and www.defendamerica.mil.

EDITORIAL NOTE: The Department of the Air Force did not meet the publication deadline for submitting updated information of its activities, functions, and sources of information as required by the automatic disclosure provisions of the Freedom of Information Act (5 U.S.C. 552(a)(1)(A)).

DEPARTMENT OF THE AIR FORCE

1690 Air Force Pentagon, Washington, DC 20330–1670
Phone, 703–697–6061. Internet, www.af.mil.

SECRETARY OF THE AIR FORCE	MICHAEL B. DONLEY
Chief of Staff	GEN. NORTON A. SCHWARTZ
Vice Chief of Staff	GEN. WILLIAM M. FRASER III
Chief Master Sergeant	CMSGT. JAMES A. ROY
Administrative Assistant	WILLIAM A. DAVIDSON
Auditor General	THEODORE J. WILLIAMS
Acquisition	DAVID M. VAN BUREN, *Acting*
Financial Management and Comptroller	JAMIE M. MORIN
General Counsel	CHARLES A. BLANCHARD
International Affairs	BRUCE S. LEMKIN
Installations, Environment and Logistics	(VACANCY)
Inspector General	LT. GEN. MARC E. ROGERS
Legislative Liaison	MAJ. GEN. HERBERT J. CARLISLE
Manpower and Reserve Affairs	(VACANCY)
Public Affairs	COL. LES A. KODLICK
Small Business Programs	RONALD A. POUSSARD
Warfighting Integration and Chief Information Officer	LT. GEN. WILLIAM L. SHELTON
Manpower and Personnel	LT. GEN. RICHARD Y. NEWTON III
Intelligence, Surveillance and Reconnaissance	LT. GEN. DAVID A. DEPTULA
Air, Space and Information Operations, Plans and Requirements	LT. GEN. DANIEL J. DARNELL
Logistics, Installation and Mission Support	LT. GEN. LOREN M. RENO
Strategic Plans and Programs	LT. GEN. RAYMOND E. JOHNS, JR.
Analyses, Assessments and Lessons Learned	JACQUELINE R. HENNINGSEN
Strategic Deterrence and Nuclear Integration Office	MAJ. GEN. C. DONALD ALSTON
Chief of Chaplains	MAJ. GEN. CECIL R. RICHARDSON
Air Force Historian	CLARENCE R. ANDEREGG
Judge Advocate General	LT. GEN. JACK L. RIVES
Chief, Air Force Reserve	LT. GEN. CHARLES E. STENNER, JR.
Safety	MAJ. GEN. FREDERICK F. ROGGERO.
Surgeon General	LT. GEN. JAMES G. ROUDEBUSH
Chief Scientist	WERNER J.A. DAHM
Test and Evaluation	JOHN T. MANCLARK
Chief, National Guard Bureau	GEN. CRAIG R. MCKINLEY
Director, Air National Guard	LT. GEN. HARRY M. WYATT III

The Department of the Air Force is responsible for defending the United States through control and exploitation of air and space.

The Department of the Air Force (USAF) was established as part of the National Military Establishment by the National Security Act of 1947 (61 Stat. 502) and came into being on September 18, 1947. The National Security Act Amendments of 1949 redesignated the National Military Establishment as the Department of Defense, established it as an executive department, and made the Department of the Air Force a military department within the Department of Defense (63 Stat. 578). The Department of the Air Force is separately organized under the Secretary of the Air Force. It operates under the authority, direction, and control of the Secretary of Defense (10 U.S.C. 8010). The Department consists of the Office of the Secretary of the Air Force, the Air Staff, and field organizations.

Secretary The Secretary is responsible for matters pertaining to organization, training, logistical support, maintenance, welfare of personnel, administrative, recruiting, research and development, and other activities prescribed by the President or the Secretary of Defense.

Air Staff The mission of the Air Staff is to furnish professional assistance to the Secretary, the Under Secretary, the Assistant Secretaries, and the Chief of Staff in executing their responsibilities.

Field Organizations The major commands, field operating agencies, and direct reporting units together represent the field organizations of the Air Force. These are organized primarily on a functional basis in the United States and on an area basis overseas. These commands are responsible for accomplishing certain phases of the worldwide activities of the Air Force. They also are responsible for organizing, administering, equipping, and training their subordinate elements for the accomplishment of assigned missions.

Major Commands

The Continental U.S. Commands

Air Combat Command This Command operates Air Force bombers and CONUS-based, combat-coded fighter and attack aircraft. It organizes, trains, equips, and maintains combat-ready forces for rapid deployment and employment while ensuring strategic air defense forces are ready to meet the challenges of peacetime air sovereignty and wartime air defense.

Air Force Materiel Command This Command advances, integrates, and uses technology to develop, test, acquire, and sustain weapons systems. It also performs single-manager continuous product and process improvement throughout a product's life cycle.

Air Mobility Command This Command provides airlift, air refueling, special air mission, and aeromedical evacuation for U.S. forces. It also supplies forces to theater commands to support wartime tasking.

Air Force Reserve Command This Command supports the Air Force mission of defending the Nation through control and exploitation of air and space. It plays an integral role in the day-to-day Air Force mission and is not a force held in reserve for possible war or contingency operations.

Air Force Space Command This Command operates space and ballistic missile systems, including ballistic missile warning, space control, spacelift, and satellite operations.

Air Force Special Operations Command This Command provides the air component of U.S. Special Operations Command, deploying specialized air power and delivering special operations combat power.

Air Education and Training Command
This Command recruits, assesses, commissions, educates, and trains Air Force enlisted and officer personnel. It provides basic military training, initial and advanced technical training, flying training, and professional military and degree-granting professional education. The Command also conducts joint, medical service, readiness, and Air Force security assistance training.

Major Commands

Command	Address	Commander
Air Combat	Langley AFB, VA 23665–2788	Gen. John D.W. Corley
Air Education and Training	Randolph AFB, TX 78150–4324	Gen. Stephen R. Lorenz
Air Force Materiel	Wright-Patterson AFB, OH 45433–5001	Gen. Donald J. Hoffman
Air Force Reserve	Robins AFB, GA 31098–1635	Lt. Gen. Charles E. Stenner, Jr.
Air Force Space	Peterson AFB, CO 80914–4020	Gen. C. Robert Kehler
Air Force Special Operations	Hurlburt Field, FL 32544–5273	Lt. Gen. Donald C. Wurster
Air Mobility	Scott AFB, IL 62225–5310	Gen. Arthur J. Lichte

Overseas Commands

Pacific Air Forces The Command is responsible for planning, conducting, and coordinating offensive and defensive air operations in the Pacific and Asian theaters.

United States Air Forces in Europe The Command plans, conducts, controls, coordinates, and supports air and space operations to achieve United States national and NATO objectives.

Overseas Commands

Command	Address	Commander
Pacific Air Forces	Hickam AFB, HI 96853–5420	Gen. Carrol H. Chandler
U.S. Air Forces in Europe	APO AE 09094–0501	Gen. Roger A. Brady

Field Activities

Air National Guard The Center performs the operational and technical tasks associated with manning, equipping, and training Air National Guard units to required readiness levels.
Base Closures The Agency serves as the Federal real property disposal agent and provides integrated executive management for Air Force bases in the United States as they are closed under the delegated authorities of the Base Closure and Realignment Act of 1988 and the Defense Base Closure and Realignment Act of 1990.
Communications The Agency ensures that command, control, communications, and computer systems used by USAF warfighters are integrated and interoperable. It develops and validates C[4] architectures, technical standards, technical reference codes, policies, processes and procedures, and technical solutions, supporting information superiority through technical excellence.
Emergency Preparedness The Office is responsible for Air Force-related national security emergency preparedness functions, including military support to civil authorities, civil defense, and law enforcement agencies and planning for continuity of operations during emergencies.
Engineering The Agency maximizes Air Force civil engineers' capabilities in base and contingency operations by providing tools, practices, and professional support for readiness, training, technical support, management practices, automation support, vehicles and equipment, and research, development, and acquisition consultation.
Environmental Quality The Center provides the Air Force with services in environmental remediation, compliance, planning, and pollution prevention, as

well as construction management and facilities design.

Flight Standards The Agency performs worldwide inspection of airfields, navigation systems, and instrument approaches. It provides flight standards to develop Air Force instrument requirements, and certifies procedures and directives for cockpit display and navigation systems. It also provides air traffic control and airlift procedures and evaluates air traffic control systems and airspace management procedures.

Historic Publications The Office researches, writes, and publishes books and other studies on Air Force history and provides historical support to Air Force headquarters.

Historical Research The Agency serves as a repository for Air Force historical records and provides research facilities for scholars and the general public.

Intelligence The Agency provides intelligence services to support Air Force operations through flexible collection, tailored air and space intelligence, weapons monitoring, and information warfare products and services.

Medical Operations The Agency assists the USAF Surgeon General in developing plans, programs, and policies for the medical service, aerospace medicine, clinical investigations, quality assurance, health promotion, family advocacy, bioenvironmental engineering, military public health, and radioactive material management.

Modeling and Simulation The Agency implements policies and standards and supports field operations in the areas of modeling and simulation.

News The Agency gathers information and packages and disseminates electronic and printed news and information products. It manages and operationally controls Air Force Internal Information, the Army and Air Force Hometown News Service, the Air Force Broadcasting Service, and the Air Force Armed Forces Radio and Television outlets worldwide; operates the Air Force hotline; and provides electronic information through the Air Force bulletin board and the Internet.

Nuclear Weapons Monitoring The Air Force Technical Applications Center monitors compliance with various nuclear treaties. It provides real-time reporting of nuclear weapons tests and operates a global network of sensors and analytical laboratories to monitor foreign nuclear activity. It conducts research and development of proliferation detection technologies for all weapons of mass destruction.

Real Estate The Agency acquires, manages, and disposes of land for the Air Force worldwide and maintains a complete land and facilities inventory.

Weather Services The Service provides centralized weather services to the Air Force, Army joint staff, designated unified commands, and other agencies, ensuring standardization of procedures and interoperability within the USAF weather system and assessing its technical performance and effectiveness.

Direct Reporting Units

Air Force Communication and Information Center The Center applies information technology to improve operations processes and manages all Air Force information technology systems.

Air Force District of Washington The Air Force District of Washington (AFDW) provides support for Headquarters Air Force and other Air Force units in the National Capital Region.

Curtis E. LaMay Center for Doctrine Development and Education The LeMay Center leads in the development of Air Force operational-level doctrine and establishes the Air Force's position in Joint and multinational doctrine. The Center assists in the development, analysis, and wargaming of air, space, and cyberspace power concepts, doctrine, and strategy. Through wargames and military education, it also educates Air Force, Joint Defense, and multinational communities on warfighting doctrine.

Air Force Operational Test and Evaluation Center The Center plans and conducts test and evaluation procedures to determine operational effectiveness and suitability of new or modified USAF systems and their capacity to meet mission needs.

Air Force Security Forces Center The Center ensures quick and effective security responses to protect U.S. personnel around the globe.

U.S. Air Force Academy The Academy provides academic and military instruction and experience to prepare future USAF career officers. Graduates receive Bachelor of Science degrees in 1 of 26 academic majors and commissions as second lieutenants.

Direct Reporting Units

Unit	Address	Commander
Air Force District of Washington	Andrews AFB, MD 20762–7001	Maj. Gen. Ralph J. Jodice II
LeMay Center for Doctrine Development and Education	Maxwell AFB, AL 36112–6335	Maj. Gen. Stephen J. Miller
Air Force Operational Test and Evaluation Center	Kirtland AFB, NM 87117–5558	Maj. Gen. Stephen T. Sargeant
Air Force Security Forces Center	Lackland AFB, TX 78236–0119	Col. Steven W. Robinette
U.S. Air Force Academy	USAF Academy, CO 80840–5000	Lt. Gen. Michael C. Gould

For further information concerning the Department of the Air Force, contact the Office of the Director of Public Affairs, Department of the Air Force, 1690 Air Force Pentagon, Washington, DC 20330–1670. Phone, 703–697–6061. Internet, www.af.mil.

DEPARTMENT OF THE ARMY

The Pentagon, Washington, DC 20310
Phone, 703–695–6518. Internet, www.army.mil.

SECRETARY OF THE ARMY	PRESTON M. GEREN
UNDER SECRETARY OF THE ARMY	(VACANCY)
Assistant Secretary of the Army (Acquisition, Logistics, and Technology)	DEAN G. POPPS, *Acting*
Assistant Secretary of the Army (Civil Works)	TERRENCE SALT, *Acting*
Assistant Secretary of the Army (Financial Management)	(VACANCY)
Assistant Secretary of the Army (Installations and Environment)	(VACANCY)
Assistant Secretary of the Army (Manpower and Reserve Affairs)	RONALD J. JAMES
General Counsel	(VACANCY)
Administrative Assistant to the Secretary of the Army	JOYCE E. MORROW
Chief Information Officer/G–6	LT. GEN. JEFFREY A. SORENSON
Inspector General	LT. GEN. R. STEVEN WHITCOMB
Auditor General	PATRICK J. FITZGERALD
Deputy Under Secretary of the Army	THOMAS E. KELLY III
Deputy Under Secretary of the Army (Business Transformation)	(VACANCY)
Chief of Legislative Liaison	MAJ. GEN. BERNARD CHAMPOUX
Chief of Public Affairs	MAJ. GEN. KEVIN J. BERNER
Director, Small Business Programs	TRACEY L. PINSON
Office of the Chief of Staff:	
Chief of Staff, United States Army	GEN. GEORGE W. CASEY, JR.
Vice Chief of Staff	GEN. PETER W. CHIARELLI
Director of the Army Staff	LT. GEN. DAVID H. HUNTOON
Vice Director of the Army Staff	JAMES B. GUNLICKS
Army Staff:	
Deputy Chief of Staff, G–1	LT. GEN. MICHAEL D. ROCHELLE
Deputy Chief of Staff, G–2	LT. GEN. RICHARD P. ZAHNER
Deputy Chief of Staff, G–3/5/7	LT. GEN. JAMES D. THURMAN
Deputy Chief of Staff, G–4	LT. GEN. MITCHELL STEVENSON
Deputy Chief of Staff, G–8	LT. GEN. STEPHEN M. SPEAKES
Chief, Army Reserve	LT. GEN. JACK C. STULTZ
Chief, National Guard Bureau	GEN. CRAIG R. MCKINLEY
Chief of Engineers	LT. GEN. ROBERT L. VAN ANTWERP, JR.
Surgeon General	LT. GEN. ERIC B. SCHOOMAKER
Assistant Chief of Staff for Installation Management	LT. GEN. ROBERT WILSON
Chief of Chaplains	MAJ. GEN. DOUGLAS L. CARVER
Provost Marshall General	BRIG. GEN. RODNEY L. JOHNSON
Judge Advocate General	LT. GEN. SCOTT C. BLACK

Director, Army National Guard	LT. GEN. CLYDE A. VAUGHN

Commands:

Commanding General, U.S. Army Forces Command	GEN. CHARLES C. CAMPBELL
Commanding General, U.S. Army Training and Doctrine Command	GEN. MARTIN E. DEMPSEY
Commanding General, U.S. Army Material Command	GEN. ANN DUNWOODY

Army Service Component Commands:

Commanding General, USARCENT	LT. GEN. JAMES J. LOVELACE
Commanding General, USARNORTH	LT. GEN. THOMAS R. TURNER II
Commanding General, U.S. Army South	MAJ. GEN. KEITH M. HUBER
Commanding General, U.S. Army Europe	GEN. CARTER F. HAM
Commanding General, U.S. Army Pacific	LT. GEN. BENJAMIN R. MIXON
Commanding General, Eighth U.S. Army	LT. GEN. JOSEPH F. FIL, JR.
Commanding General, U.S. Army Special Operations Command	LT. GEN. JOHN F. MULHOLLAND, JR.
Commanding General, U.S. Army Military Surface Deployment and Distribution Command	MAJ. GEN. JAMES L. HODGE
Commanding General, U.S. Army Space and Missile Defense Command/Army Strategic Command	LT. GEN. KEVIN T. CAMPBELL

Direct Reporting Units:

Commanding General, U.S. Army Network Enterprise Technology Command/9th Signal Command	MAJ. GEN. SUSAN LAWRENCE
Commanding General, U.S. Army Medical Command	LT. GEN. ERIC B. SCHOOMAKER
Commanding General, U.S. Army Intelligence and Security Command	MAJ. GEN. DAVID P. LACQUEMENT
Commanding General, U.S. Army Criminal Investigation Command	BRIG. GEN. RODNEY L. JOHNSON
Commanding General, U.S. Army Corps of Engineers	LT. GEN. ROBERT L. VAN ANTWERP, JR.
Commanding General, U.S. Army Military District of Washington	MAJ. GEN. RICHARD A. ROWE, JR.
Commanding General, Army Test and Evaluation Command	MAJ. GEN. ROGER A. NADEAU
Superintendent, U.S. Military Academy	LT. GEN. FRANKLIN L. HAGENBECK
Commanding General, U.S. Army Reserve Command	LT. GEN. JACK C. STULTZ
Director, U.S. Army Acquisition Support Center	CRAIG SPISAK
Commanding General, U.S. Army Installation Management Command	LT. GEN. ROBERT WILSON

The mission of the Department of the Army is to organize, train, and equip active duty and reserve forces for the preservation of peace, security, and the defense of our Nation. As part of our national military team, the Army focuses on land operations; its soldiers must be trained with modern arms and equipment and be ready to respond quickly. The Army also administers programs aimed at protecting the environment, improving waterway navigation, flood and beach erosion control, and water resource development. It provides military assistance to Federal, State, and local government agencies, including natural disaster relief assistance.

The American Continental Army, now called the United States Army, was established by the Continental Congress on June 14, 1775, more than a year before the Declaration of Independence. The Department of War was established as an executive department at the seat of government by act approved August 7, 1789 (1 Stat. 49). The Secretary of War was established as its head. The National Security Act of 1947 (50 U.S.C. 401) created the National Military Establishment, and the Department of War was designated the Department of the Army. The title of its Secretary became Secretary of the Army (5 U.S.C. 171). The National Security Act Amendments of 1949 (63 Stat. 578) provided that the Department of the Army be a military department within the Department of Defense.

Secretary The Secretary of the Army is the senior official of the Department of the Army. Subject to the direction, authority, and control of the President as Commander in Chief and of the Secretary of Defense, the Secretary of the Army is responsible for and has the authority to conduct all affairs of the Department of the Army, including its organization, administration, operation, efficiency, and such other activities as may be prescribed by the President or the Secretary of Defense as authorized by law.

For further information, call 703–695–7922.

Army Staff Presided over by the Chief of Staff, the Army Staff is the military staff of the Secretary of the Army. It is the duty of the Army Staff to perform the following functions:

—prepare for deployment of the Army and for such recruiting, organizing, supplying, equipping, training, mobilizing, and demobilizing of the Army as will assist the execution of any power, duty, or function of the Secretary or the Chief of Staff;

—investigate and report upon the efficiency of the Army and its preparation for military operations;

—act as the agent of the Secretary of the Army and the Chief of Staff in coordinating the action of all organizations of the Department of the Army; and

—perform such other duties not otherwise assigned by law as may be prescribed by the Secretary of the Army.

Program Areas

Civil Functions Civil functions of the Department of the Army include the Civil Works Program, the Nation's major Federal water resources development activity involving engineering works such as major dams, reservoirs, levees, harbors, waterways, locks, and many other types of structures; the administration of Arlington and Soldiers' Home National Cemeteries; and other related matters.

History This area includes advisory and coordination service provided on historical matters, including historical properties; formulation and execution of the Army Historical Program; and preparation and publication of histories required by the Army.

Installations This area consists of policies, procedures, and resources for management of installations to ensure the availability of efficient and affordable base services and infrastructure in support of military missions. It includes the review of facilities requirements and stationing, identification and validation of resource requirements, and program and budget development and justification. Other activities include support for base operations; morale, welfare, and recreation; real property maintenance and repair; environmental programs; military construction; housing;

DEPARTMENT OF THE ARMY

base realignment and closure; and competitive sourcing.

Intelligence This area includes management of Army intelligence with responsibility for policy formulation, planning, programming, budgeting, evaluation, and oversight of intelligence activities. The Army staff is responsible for monitoring relevant foreign intelligence developments and foreign disclosure; imagery, signals, human, open-source, measurement, and signatures intelligence; counterintelligence; threat models and simulations; and security countermeasures.

Medical This area includes management of health services for the Army and, as directed for other services, agencies, and organizations; health standards for Army personnel; health professional education and training; career management authority over commissioned and warrant officer personnel of the Army Medical Department; medical research, materiel development, testing and evaluation; policies concerning health aspects of Army environmental programs and prevention of disease; and planning, programming, and budgeting for Army-wide health services.

Military Operations and Plans This includes Army forces strategy formation; mid-range, long-range, and regional strategy application; arms control, negotiation, and disarmament; national security affairs; joint service matters; net assessment; politico-military affairs; force mobilization and demobilization; force

planning, programming structuring, development, analysis, requirements, and management; operational readiness; overall roles and missions; collective security; individual and unit training; psychological operations; information operations; unconventional warfare; counterterrorism; operations security; signal security; special plans; table of equipment development and approval; nuclear and chemical matters; civil affairs; military support of civil defense; civil disturbance; domestic actions; command and control; automation and communications programs and activities; management of the program for law enforcement, correction, and crime prevention for military members of the Army; special operations forces; foreign language and distance learning; and physical security.

Reserve Components This area includes management of individual and unit readiness and mobilization for Reserve Components, comprised of the Army National Guard and the U.S. Army Reserve.

Religious This area includes management of religious and moral leadership and chaplain support activities throughout the Department; religious ministrations, religious education, pastoral care, and counseling for Army military personnel; liaison with the ecclesiastical agencies; chapel construction requirements and design approval; and career management of clergymen serving in the Chaplains Branch.

Army Commands

U.S. Army Forces Command The U.S. Army Forces Command (FORSCOM) trains, mobilizes, deploys, sustains, transforms, and reconstitutes conventional forces, providing relevant and ready land power to combatant commanders worldwide in defense of the Nation at home and abroad.

For further information, contact FORSCOM. Phone, 404–464–5023. Internet, www.forscom.army.mil.

U.S. Army Training and Doctrine Command Headquartered in Fort Monroe, Virginia, the U.S. Army Training and Doctrine Command (TRADOC) recruits, trains, and educates the Army's soldiers; develops leaders; supports training in units; develops doctrine; establishes standards; and builds the future Army. TRADOC operates schools and centers at Army installations. TRADOC's priorities are recruiting a quality all-volunteer force; providing rigor and relevance in training and leader development; fostering innovation; preparing the Army for joint operations; and developing the future forces.

For further information, contact TRADOC. Phone, 757–788–4465. Internet, www.tradoc.army.mil.

U.S. Army Materiel Command The U.S. Army Materiel Command (AMC) is the Army's principal materiel developer. AMC's missions include the

development of weapon systems, advanced research on future technologies, and maintenance and distribution of spare parts and equipment. AMC works closely with Program Executive Offices, industry, academia, and other military services and Government agencies to develop, test, and acquire equipment that soldiers and units need to accomplish their missions.

For further information, contact AMC. Phone, 703–806–8010. Internet, www.amc.army.mil.

Army Service Component Commands

U.S. Army Central The U.S. Army Central (USARCENT) conducts operations to attack, disrupt, and defeat terrorism; deter and defeat adversaries; deny access to weapons of mass destruction; assure regional access; strengthen regional stability; build the self-reliance of partner nations' security forces; and protect the vital interests of the United States.

For further information, contact the USARCENT Public Affairs Office. Phone, 813–827–5895. Email, pao@centcom.mil. Internet, www.arcent.army.mil.

U.S. Army North The U.S. Army North (USARNORTH) was established to support the U.S. Northern Command. USARNORTH provides training to all units in the country and helps maintain readiness to support homeland defense and civil support missions.

For further information, contact USARNORTH Public Affairs Office. Phone, 210–221–0015. Email, 5aopao@arnorth.army.mil. Internet, www.arnorth.army.mil.

U.S. Army South The U.S. Army South (USARSO) is a major subordinate command of the U.S. Army Forces Command, Fort McPherson, Georgia, and is the Army Service Component Command of the U.S. Southern Command. USARSO executes and is responsible for all Army operations within the U.S. Southern Command's area (Central and South America and the Caribbean Islands). USARSO seeks to

build regional cooperative security and increase hemispheric cooperation by planning and executing multilateral exercises and carrying out humanitarian aid, peacekeeping, engineering, and medical assistance exercises. USARSO maintains a deployable headquarters at Fort Sam Houston, Texas, where they conduct strategic and operational planning.

For further information, contact the USARSO Public Affairs Office. Phone, 210–295–6388. Email, usarsowebmaster@samhouston.army.mil. Internet, www.usarso.army.mil.

U.S. Army Europe The U.S. Army Europe provides the principal land component for the U.S. European Command (EUCOM). U.S. Army Europe (USAREUR) forms, trains, and projects expeditionary forces and JTF-capable headquarters to prosecute joint and combined operations throughout a 91 country area. As the U.S. Army's largest forward-deployed expeditionary force, USAREUR supports NATO and U.S. bilateral, multinational, and unilateral objectives. It supports U.S. Army forces in the European command area; receives and assists in the reception, staging, and onward movement and integration of U.S. forces; establishes, operates, and expands operational lines of communication; ensures regional security, access, and stability through presence and security cooperation; and supports U.S. combatant commanders and joint and combined commanders.

For further information, contact USAREUR. Phone, 011–49–6221–39–4100. Internet, www.hqusareur.army.mil.

U.S. Army Pacific The U.S. Army Pacific (USARPAC) provides trained and ready forces in support of military operations and peacetime engagements in the Asia-Pacific area. USARPAC carries out a cooperative engagement strategy known as the Theater Security Cooperation Program with the 43 Asian and Pacific nations within or bordering its area of responsibility. These countries include the Philippines, Thailand, Vietnam, Japan, Mongolia, Russia, China, South Korea, India, Bangladesh, Australia, New Zealand, Marshall Islands, and Papua New Guinea.

For further information, contact USARPAC. Phone, 808–438–1393. Internet, www.usarpac.army.mil.

Eighth U.S. Army Eighth U.S. Army provides forces to the commander of the U.S. Forces Korea who in turn provides them to the commander of the Republic of Korea/U.S. Combined Forces Command.

For further information, contact Eighth U.S. Army. Phone, 011–82–279–13–6544. Internet, http:// 8tharmy.korea.army.mil.

U.S. Army Special Operations Command The U.S. Army Special Operations Command (USASOC) trains, equips, deploys, and sustains Army special operations forces for worldwide special operations supporting regional combatant commanders and country ambassadors. USASOC soldiers deploy to numerous countries conducting missions such as peacekeeping, humanitarian assistance, demining, and foreign internal defense. USASOC includes special forces, rangers, civil affairs, psychological operations, special operations aviation, and signal and support.

For further information, contact USASOC. Phone, 910–432–3000. Internet, www.usasoc.soc.mil.

U.S. Army Military Surface Deployment and Distribution Command The U.S. Army Military Surface Deployment and

Distribution Command (SDDC) provides global surface deployment command and control and distribution operations to meet national security objectives for the Department of Defense (DOD). This requires a presence in 24 ports worldwide as DOD's single-port manager, transportation, traffic-management services, deployment planning and engineering, and development of new technologies. SDDC is also the link between DOD shippers and the commercial surface transportation industry.

For further information, contact SDDC. Phone, 703–428–3207. Internet, www.sddc.army.mil.

U.S. Army Space and Missile Defense Command/Army Strategic Command The U.S. Army Space and Missile Defense Command (SMDC) serves as the Army's specified proponent for space and national missile defense and operational integrator for theater missile defense. SMDC coordinates, integrates, and/or executes combat development, materiel development, technology, and advanced research and development for missile defense and space programs. It also serves as the Army Service Component Command, the primary land component for the U.S. Strategic Command. SMDC's mission includes space operations, information operations, global strike, integrated missile defense, and command and control, communications, computers, intelligence, surveillance, and reconnaissance. In addition, SMDC serves as a primary research and development organization for the Missile Defense Agency. From its headquarters in Arlington, Virginia, SMDC also oversees a number of Army elements around the globe, ensuring missile defense protection for the Nation and deployed forces, and facilitates access to space assets and products.

For further information, contact SMDC. Phone, 703–607–1873. Internet, www.smdc.army.mil.

Sources of Information

Arlington and Soldiers' and Airmen's Home National Cemeteries   For information write to the Superintendent, Arlington National Cemetery, Arlington, VA 22211–5003. Phone, 703–607–8545.

Army Historical Program   For information concerning the Army Historical Program, write to the U.S. Army Center of Military History, Collins Hall, 103 Third Avenue, Fort Lesley J. McNair, Washington, DC 20319–5058. Phone, 202–685–2714. Fax, 202–685–4570. Internet, www.army.mil/cmh. Information on historic buildings preservation and reuse is available through the Office of Historic Properties. Phone, 703–692–9892.

Civilian Employment   For information, visit the Army civilian personnel Web site (Internet, www.cpol.army.mil) or contact the civilian personnel advisory center at the desired Army installation.

Contracts   Contract procurement policies and procedures are the responsibility of the Deputy for Procurement, Office of the Assistant Secretary of the Army (Acquisition, Logistics, and Technology), The Pentagon, Washington, DC 20310–0103. Phone, 703–695–6154.

Environment   Contact the Public Affairs Office, Office of the Chief of Public Affairs, Headquarters, Department of the Army, Washington, DC 20314–1000 (Phone, 202–761–0010); U.S. Army Environmental Command (Internet, http://aec.army.mil/usaec/); or the Army Environmental Policy Institute (Internet, www.aepi.army.mil).

Films, Videotapes, and Videodiscs   Requests for loan of Army-produced films should be addressed to the Visual Information Support Centers of Army installations. Unclassified Army productions are available for sale from the National Audiovisual Center, National Technical Information Service, 5285 Port Royal Road, Springfield, VA 22161. Phone, 800–553–NTIS. Internet, www.ntis.gov/Index.aspx.

Freedom of Information and Privacy Act Requests   Requests should be addressed to the Information Management Officer of the Army installation or activity responsible for the requested information.

Military Surface Deployment and Distribution Command   Information concerning military transportation news and issues is available electronically through the Internet, www.sddc.army.mil/Public/Home.

Public Affairs and Community Relations   For official Army information and community relations, contact the Office of the Chief of Public Affairs, Department of the Army, Washington, DC 20310–1508. Phone, 703–697–5081. During nonoffice hours, call 703–697–4200.

Publications   Requests should be addressed to either the proponent listed on the title page of the document or the Information Management Officer of the Army activity that publishes the requested publication. Official texts published by Headquarters, Department of the Army, are available from the National Technical Information Service, Department of Commerce, Attn: Order Preprocessing Section, 5285 Port Royal Road, Springfield, VA 22161–2171. Phone, 703–487–4600. Internet, www.ntis.gov. If it is uncertain which Army activity published the document, forward the request to the Publishing Division, Army Publishing Directorate, Room 1050, 2461 Eisenhower Avenue, Alexandria, VA 22331–0301. Phone, 703–325–6292. Internet, www.apd.army.mil.

Research   Information on long-range research and development plans concerning future materiel requirements and objectives may be obtained from the Commander, U.S. Army Research Development and Engineering Command, Attn: AMSRD–PA, Bldg. E5101, 5183 Blackhawk Road, Aberdeen Proving Ground, MD 21010–5424.

Small Business Activities   Assistance for small businesses and minority educational institutions to enhance their ability to participate in the Army contracting program is available through the Office of Small Business Programs,

Office of the Secretary of the Army, 106 Army Pentagon, Washington, DC 20310–0106. Phone, 703–697–2868.

Speakers Civilian organizations desiring an Army speaker may contact a nearby Army installation or write or call the Community Relations Division, Office of the Chief of Public Affairs, Department of the Army, Washington, DC 20310–1508. Phone, 703–697–5081. Requests for Army Reserve speakers may be addressed to HQDA (DAAR–PA), Washington, DC 20310–2423, or the local Army Reserve Center.

Organizations in the Washington, DC, area desiring chaplain speakers may contact the Chief of Chaplains, Department of the Army, Washington, DC 20310–2700. Phone, 703–601–1140. Information on speakers may be obtained by contacting the Public Affairs Office, Office of the Chief of Engineers, Washington, DC 20314, or the nearest Corps of Engineer Division or District Office.

Military Career and Training Opportunities Information on all phases of Army enlistments and specialized training is available by writing to the U.S. Army Recruiting Command, 1307 Third Avenue, Fort Knox, KY 40121–2725. For information about career and training opportunities, contact the appropriate office listed below:

Army health professions: Headquarters U.S. Army Recruiting Command, Health Services Directorate (RCHS–OP), 1307 Third Avenue, Fort Knox, KY 40121–2725. Phone, 502–626–0367. Email, Tanya.Beecher@usarec.army.mil. Internet, www.healthcare.goarmy.com.

Army National Guard training opportunities: Army National Guard, NGB–ASM, 1411 Jefferson Davis Highway, Arlington, VA 22202–3231. Phone, 703–607–5834. Internet, www.arng.army.mil.

Army Reserve training opportunities for enlisted personnel and officers: Army Reserve Personnel Command, One Reserve Way, St. Louis, MO 63132–5200. Phone, 314–592–0000 or 800–318–5298. Internet, www.goarmyreserve.com.

Army Reserve Officers' Training Corps (ROTC): U.S. Army Cadet Command, Recruiting, Retention and Operations Directorate, ATCC–OP, 55 Patch Road, Fort Monroe, VA 23651. Phone, 757–788–3770. Or, contact a professor of military science or Army ROTC Advisor at the nearest college or university offering the program in your area. Internet, www.armyrotc.com.

Chaplain Recruiting Branch HQ: U.S. Army Recruiting Command, Attn: RCRO- SM-CH, 1307 Third Avenue, Fort Knox, KY 40121–2726. Phone, 502–626–0722 or 866–684–1571. Fax, 502–626–1213. Internet, www.chaplain.goarmy.com.

Judge Advocate General's Corps: Department of the Army, Judge Advocate Recruiting Office, 1777 North Kent Street, Suite 5200, Rosslyn, VA 20124–2194. Phone, 866–ARMY–JAG. Internet, www.law.goarmy.com.

U.S. Military Academy: Director of Admissions, United States Military Academy, Building 606, West Point, NY 10996. Phone, 845–938–4041. Internet, www.usma.edu.

For further information concerning the Department of the Army, contact the Office of the Chief of Public Affairs, Headquarters, Department of the Army, Washington, DC 20310–1508. Phone, 703–697–5081. Internet, www.army.mil.

DEPARTMENT OF THE NAVY

The Pentagon, Washington, DC 20350
Phone, 703–697–7391. Internet, www.navy.mil.

SECRETARY OF THE NAVY	RAYMOND E. MAYBUS
UNDER SECRETARY OF THE NAVY	ROBERT O. WORK
Director, Office of Program and Process Assessment	JO A. DECKER
Special Assistant for Acquisition and Business Reform	(VACANCY)
Deputy Under Secretary of the Navy	BRUCE STUBBS, *Acting*
Deputy Chief Management Officer/Director of Business Transformation	ANNE NEUBERGER
Director, Small Business Programs	TIMOTHY FOREMAN
Auditor General of the Navy	RICHARD A. LEACH
Director, Naval Criminal Investigative Service	THOMAS A. BETRO
Chief of Information	REAR ADM. FRANK THORPE, IV, USN
Chief Information Officer	ROBERT J. CAREY
Chief of Legislative Affairs	REAR ADM. MICHAEL H. MILLER, USN
General Counsel	ANNE M. BRENNAN, *Acting*
Principal Deputy General Counsel	(VACANCY)
Deputy General Counsel	ANNE M. BRENNAN
Naval Inspector General	VICE ADM. ANTHONY L. WINNS, USN
Judge Advocate General of the Navy	VICE ADM. BRUCE MACDONALD, JAGC, USN
Deputy Judge Advocate General	REAR ADM. JAMES W. HOUCK, JAGC, USN
Assistant Secretary of the Navy (Financial Management and Comptroller)	JOHN W. MCNAIR, JR.
Deputy	(VACANCY)
Director, Office of Budget	REAR ADM. STANLEY D. BOZIN, USN
Director, Office of Financial Operations	MARK E. EASTON
Assistant Secretary of the Navy (Manpower and Reserve Affairs)	(VACANCY)
Deputy Assistant Secretary (Reserve Affairs)	(VACANCY)
Deputy Assistant Secretary (Total Force Transformation)	(VACANCY)
Deputy Assistant Secretary (Civilian Human Resources)	PATRICIA C. ADAMS
Deputy Assistant Secretary (Military Personnel Policy)	(VACANCY)
Director, Secretary of the Navy Council of Review Boards	COL. MARK D. FRANKLIN, USMC
Director, Board for Correction of Naval Records	W. DEAN PFEIFFER

Assistant Secretary of the Navy (Installations and Environment)	B.J. PENN
Principal Deputy	HOWARD SNOW
Deputy Assistant Secretary (Installations and Facilities)	HOWARD SNOW
Deputy Assistant Secretary (Infrastructure Strategy and Analysis)	DENNIS BIDDICK
Deputy Assistant Secretary (Safety)	THOMAS A. ROLLOW
Deputy Assistant Secretary (Environment)	DONALD SCHREGARDUS
Assistant Secretary of the Navy (Research, Development, and Acquisition)	SEAN J. STACKLEY
Principal Deputy	VICE ADM. DAVID ARCHITZEL, USN
Principal Civilian Deputy	JIM THOMSEN
Chief of Naval Research	REAR ADM. NEVIN P. CARR, JR., USN
Deputy Assistant Secretary (Air Programs)	THOMAS LAUX
Deputy Assistant Secretary (C41/Space Programs)	GARY A. FEDERICI
Deputy Assistant Secretary (Expeditionary Warfare Programs)	ROGER SMITH
Deputy Assistant Secretary (Ship/Integrated Warfare Systems Programs)	ALLISON STILLER
Deputy Assistant Secretary (Management and Budget)	CAPT. FRANCIS TISAK, USN, *Acting*
Deputy Assistant Secretary (Acquisition and Logistics Mangement)	REAR ADM. SEAN CREAN
Deputy Assistant Secretary (International Programs)	REAR ADM. STEVE VOETSH

U.S. Navy

Chief of Naval Operations	ADM. GARY ROUGHEAD, USN
Vice Chief of Naval Operations	ADM. PATRICK M. WALSH, USN
Deputy Chief, Manpower, Personnel, Training and Education	VICE ADM. MARK E. FERGUSON III, USN
Director of Naval Intelligence	REAR ADM. TONY L. COTHRON, USN
Deputy Chief, Fleet Readiness and Logistics	VICE ADM. MICHAEL K. LOOSE, USN
Deputy Chief, Plans, Policy, and Operations	VICE ADM. WILLIAM DOUGLAS CROWDER, USN
Deputy Chief, Warfare Requirements and Programs	PAT MCGLAUGHLIN
Deputy Chief, Communication Networks	VICE ADM. HARRY B. HARRIS, JR., USN
Deputy Chief, Resources, Requirements, and Assessments	VICE ADM. BERNARD MCCULLOUGH, USN
Director, Navy Staff	VICE ADM. JOHN C. HARVEY, JR., USN
Director of Naval Nuclear Propulsion Program	ADM. KIRKLAND H. DONALD, USN
Director of Test and Evaluation and Technology Requirements	REAR ADM. DAVID DUNAWAY, USN
Surgeon General of the Navy	VICE ADM. ADAM M. ROBINSON, JR., MC, USN
Director of Naval Reserve	VICE ADM. DIRK DEBBINK, USN
Chief of Chaplains of the Navy/Director of Religious Ministries	REAR ADM. ROBERT BURT, CHC, USN

Assistant Chief, Information Technology	VICE ADM. WILLIAM DOUGLAS CROWDER, USN

Major Shore Commands:

Commander, Naval Air Systems Command	VICE ADM. DAVID J. VENLET, USN
Commander, Naval Network and Space Operations Command	REAR ADM. H. DENBY STARLING II, USN
Commander, Naval Facilities Engineering Command	REAR ADM. WAYNE SHEAR, JR., USN
Commander, Naval Legal Service Command	REAR ADM. JAMES W. HOUCK, JAGC, USN
Commander, Naval Meteorology and Oceanography Command	REAR ADM. DAVID W. TITLEY, USN
Commander, Naval Sea Systems Command	VICE ADM. KEVIN M. MCCOY, USN
Commander, Naval Supply Systems Command	REAR ADM. MICHAEL J. LYDEN, SC, USN
Commander, Space and Naval Warfare Systems Command	REAR ADM. MICHAEL L. BACHMANN, USN
Commander, Naval Warfare Development Command	REAR ADM. WENDI B. CARPENTER, USN
Chief, Bureau of Medicine and Surgery	VICE ADM. ADAM M. ROBINSON, JR., MC, USN
Commander, Naval Education and Training Command	REAR ADM. GARY JONES, USN
Chief of Naval Personnel	VICE ADM. MARK E. FERGUSON III, USN
Commander, Office of Naval Intelligence	VICE ADM. DAVID J. DORSETT, USN
Director, Strategic Systems Program	REAR ADM. STEPHEN E. JOHNSON, USN
Commander, Navy Installations Command	VICE ADM. MICHAEL C. VITALE, USN

Major Fleet Commands:

Commander, U.S. Atlantic Fleet	ADM. JONATHAN W. GREENERT, USN
Commander, U.S. Pacific Fleet	ADM. ROBERT F. WILLARD, USN
Commander, U.S. Naval Forces Europe	ADM. MARK FITZGERALD, USN
Commander, Military Sealift Command	REAR ADM. ROBERT D. REILLY, JR., USN
Commander, Naval Forces Central Command	VICE ADM. WILLIAM E. GORTNEY, USN
Commander, Naval Reserve Forces Command	REAR ADM. JOHN G. MESSERSCHMIDT, USN
Commander, Naval Special Warfare Command	REAR ADM. EDWARD G. WINTERS, USN
Commander, Operational Test and Evaluation Force	REAR ADM. STEPHEN S. VOETSCH, USN

U.S. Marine Corps

Commandant of the Marine Corps	GEN. JAMES T. CONWAY, USMC
Assistant Commandant of the Marine Corps	GEN. JAMES AMOS, USMC
Sergeant Major of the Marine Corps	SGT. MAJ. CARLTON KENT, USMC
Director, Marine Corps Staff	LT. GEN. RICHARD KRAMLICH, USMC
Director, Command, Control, Communications, and Computers	BRIG. GEN. GEORGE ALLEN, USMC

Deputy Commandant for Aviation	LT. GEN. GEORGE J. TRAUTMAN, USMC
Deputy Commandant for Installations and Logistics	LT. GEN. EDWARD G. USHER III, USMC
Deputy Commandant for Manpower and Reserve Affairs	LT. GEN. RONALD COLEMAN, USMC
Deputy Commandant for Plans, Policies, and Operations	LT. GEN. JOSEPH F. DUNFORD, JR., USMC
Deputy Commandant for Programs and Resources	LT. GEN. DUANE THISEN, USMC
Counsel for the Commandant	ROBERT D. HOGUE
Director of Administration and Resource Management	ALBERT A. WASHINGTON
Deputy Director of Human Intelligence, Defense Intelligence Agency	BRIG. GEN. RICHARD LAKE, USMC
Director of Marine Corps History and Museums	CHARLES P. NEIMEYER
Director of Public Affairs	COL. BRIAN F. SALAS, USMC
Director, Special Projects Directorate	TOM DAWSON
Legislative Assistant to the Commandant	BRIG. GEN. MICHAEL R. REGNERS, USMC
Chaplain of the Marine Corps	REAR ADM. ALAN BAKER, CHC, USN
Marine Corps Dental Officer	KENNETH R. WRIGHT
Medical Officer of the Marine Corps	REAR ADM. RICHARD R. JEFFRIES, USN
President, Permanent Marine Corps Uniform Board	COL. ROYAL MORTENSON, USMC
Commanding General, Marine Corps Recruiting Command	MAJ. GEN. ROBERT E. MILSTEAD, JR., USMC
Commanding General, Marine Corps Combat Development Command	LT. GEN. GEORGE FLYNN, USMC
Commander, Marine Corps Systems Commands	BRIG. GEN. MICHAEL BROGAN, USMC
Commander, Marine Corps Base, Quantico	COL. CHARLES A. DALLACHIE, USMC

[For the Department of the Navy statement of organization, see the *Code of Federal Regulations,* Title 32, Part 700]

The primary mission of the Department of the Navy is to protect the United States, as directed by the President or the Secretary of Defense, by the effective prosecution of war at sea including, with its Marine Corps component, the seizure or defense of advanced naval bases; to support, as required, the forces of all military departments of the United States; and to maintain freedom of the seas.

The United States Navy was founded on October 13, 1775, when Congress enacted the first legislation creating the Continental Navy of the American Revolution. The Department of the Navy and the Office of Secretary of the Navy were established by act of April 30, 1798 (10 U.S.C. 5011, 5031). For 9 years prior to that date, by act of August 7, 1789 (1 Stat. 49), the conduct of naval affairs was under the Secretary of War.

The National Security Act Amendments of 1949 provided that the Department of the Navy be a military department within the Department of Defense (63 Stat. 578).

The Secretary of the Navy is appointed by the President as the head of the

DEPARTMENT OF THE NAVY

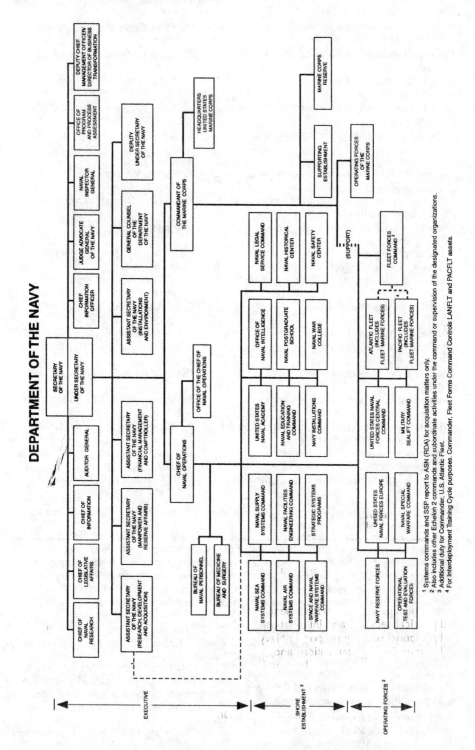

1 Systems commands and SSP report to ASN (RDA) for acquisition matters only.
2 Also includes other Echelon 2 commands and subordinate activities under the command or supervision of the designated organizations.
3 Additional duty for Commander, U.S. Atlantic Fleet.
4 For Interdeployment Training Cycle purposes. Commander, Fleet Forms Command Controls LANFLT and PACFLT assets.

Department of the Navy and is responsible to the Secretary of Defense for the operation and efficiency of the Navy (10 U.S.C. 5031). The Department of the Navy includes the U.S. Coast Guard when it is operating as a Service in the Navy.

Secretary   The Secretary of the Navy is the head of the Department of the Navy, responsible for the policies and control of the Department of the Navy, including its organization, administration, functioning, and efficiency. The members of the Secretary's executive administration assist in the discharge of the responsibilities of the Secretary of the Navy.

Legal   The Office of the Judge Advocate General provides all legal advice and related services throughout the Department of the Navy, except for the advice and services provided by the General Counsel. It also provides legal and policy advice to the Secretary of the Navy on military justice, ethics, administrative law, claims, environmental law, operational and international law and treaty interpretation, and litigation involving these issues. The Judge Advocate General provides technical supervision for the Naval Justice School at Newport, RI.

For further information, contact the Office of the Judge Advocate General, Department of the Navy, Washington Navy Yard, Suite 3000, 1322 Patterson Avenue SE., Washington, DC 20374–5066. Phone, 202–685–5190.

Criminal Investigations   The Naval Criminal Investigative Service provides criminal investigative, counterintelligence, law enforcement and physical security, and information and personnel security support to Navy and Marine Corps organizations and personnel worldwide, both ashore and afloat. The Naval Criminal Investigative Service is comprised of law enforcement professionals who are investigators, crime laboratory technicians, technical investigative specialists, security

specialists, and administrative support personnel.

For further information, contact the Director, Naval Criminal Investigative Service, Department of the Navy, 716 Sicard Street SE., Building 111, Washington Navy Yard, Washington, DC 20388–5000 (phone, 202–433–8800) or the Operations Control Center/Headquarters Duty Officer (phone, 202–433–9323).

Research   The Office of Naval Research encourages, promotes, plans, initiates, and coordinates naval research; coordinates naval research and development conducted by other agencies and offices of the Department of the Navy; and supervises, manages, and controls activities within or for the Department of the Navy relating to patents, inventions, trademarks, copyrights, and royalty payments.

For further information, contact the Public Affairs Office, Office of Naval Research, Ballston Tower One, 800 North Quincy Street, Arlington, VA 22217–5660. Phone, 703–696–5031.

Operating Forces   The operating forces of the Navy are responsible for naval operations necessary to carry out the Department of the Navy's role in upholding and advancing the national policies and interests of the United States. The operating forces of the Navy include the several fleets, seagoing forces, fleet marine forces and other assigned Marine Corps forces, the Military Sealift Command, Naval Reserve forces, and other forces and activities as may be assigned by the President or the Secretary of the Navy. The Chief of Naval Operations is responsible for the command and administration of the operating forces of the Navy.

The Atlantic Fleet is composed of ships, submarines, and aircraft that operate throughout the Atlantic Ocean and Mediterranean Sea.

The Naval Forces, Europe, includes forces assigned by the Chief of Naval Operations or made available from either the Pacific or Atlantic Fleet to operate in the European theater.

The Pacific Fleet is composed of ships, submarines, and aircraft operating throughout the Pacific and Indian Oceans.

The Military Sealift Command provides ocean transportation for personnel and cargo of all components of the Department of Defense and, as authorized, for other Federal agencies; operates and maintains underway replenishment ships and other vessels providing mobile logistic support to elements of the combatant fleets; and operates ships in support of scientific projects and other programs for Federal agencies.

Other major commands of the operating forces of the Navy are the Naval Forces Central Command, Operational Test and Evaluation Force, Naval Special Warfare Command, and Naval Reserve Force.

Activities

Air Systems   The Naval Air Systems Command provides material support to the Navy and Marine Corps for aircraft, airborne weapons systems, avionics, related photographic and support equipment, ranges, and targets.

For further information, contact the Commander, Naval Air Systems Command, 47123 Buse Road, Patuxent River, MD 20670–1547. Phone, 301–757–1487.

Coast Guard   The Commandant of the Coast Guard reports to the Secretary of the Navy and the Chief of Naval Operations when the Coast Guard is operating as a service in the Navy, and represents the Coast Guard before the Joint Chiefs of Staff. During such service, Coast Guard operations are integrated and uniform with Department of the Navy operations to the maximum extent possible. The Commandant of the Coast Guard organizes, trains, prepares, and maintains the readiness of the Coast Guard for the performance of national defense missions, as directed. The Commandant also maintains a security capability; enforces Federal laws and regulations on and under the high seas and waters subject to the jurisdiction of the United States; and develops, establishes, maintains, and operates aids to maritime navigation and ice breaking and rescue facilities, with due regard to the requirements of national defense.

Computers and Telecommunications
The Naval Network and Space Operations Command (NNSOC) was formed in July 2002 by the merger of elements of Naval Space Command and Naval Network Operations Command. The command operates and maintains the Navy's space and global telecommunications systems and services, directly supports war fighting operations and command and control of naval forces, and promotes innovative technological solutions to war fighting requirements. NNSOC enables naval forces to use information and space technologies and expertise to achieve and maintain knowledge superiority essential for dominating the battle space.

For further information, contact the Commander, Naval Network and Space Operations Command, 5280 Fourth Street, Dahlgren, VA 22448–5300. Phone, 540–653–6100.

Education and Training   The Naval Education and Training Command provides shore-based education and training for Navy, certain Marine Corps, and other personnel; develops specifically designated education and training afloat programs for the fleet; provides voluntary and dependents education; and participates with research and development activities in the development and implementation of the most effective teaching and training systems and devices for optimal education and training.

For further information, contact the Commander, Naval Education and Training Command, Department of the Navy, Naval Air Station Pensacola, 250 Dallas Street, Pensacola, FL 32508–5220. Phone, 850–452–2713.

Facilities   The Naval Facilities Engineering Command provides material and technical support to the Navy and Marine Corps for shore facilities, real property and utilities, fixed ocean systems and structures, transportation and construction equipment, energy, environmental and natural resources management, and support of the naval construction forces.

For further information, contact the Commander, Naval Facilities Engineering Command and Chief of Civil Engineers, Washington Navy Yard, 1322 Patterson Avenue SE., Suite 1000, Washington, DC 20374–5065. Phone, 202–685–1423.

Intelligence The Office of Naval Intelligence ensures the fulfillment of the intelligence requirements and responsibilities of the Department of the Navy.

For further information, contact the Commander, Office of Naval Intelligence, Department of the Navy, 4251 Suitland Road, Washington, DC 20395–5720. Phone, 301–669–3001.

Manpower The Bureau of Naval Personnel directs the procurement, distribution, administration, and career motivation of the military personnel of the regular and reserve components of the U.S. Navy to meet the quantitative and qualitative manpower requirements determined by the Chief of Naval Operations.

For further information, contact the Bureau of Naval Personnel, Department of the Navy, Federal Office Building 2, Washington, DC 20370–5000. Phone, 703–614–2000.

Medicine The Bureau of Medicine and Surgery directs the provision of medical and dental services for Navy and Marine Corps personnel and their dependents; administers the execution and implementation of contingency support plans and programs to provide effective medical and dental readiness capability; provides professional and technical medical and dental service to the fleet, fleet marine force, and shore activities of the Navy; and ensures cooperation with civil authorities in matters pertaining to public health disasters and other emergencies.

For further information, contact the Bureau of Medicine and Surgery, Department of the Navy, 2300 E Street NW., Washington, DC 20373–5300. Phone, 202–762–3211.

Oceanography The Naval Meteorology and Oceanography Command and the Naval Observatory are responsible for the science, technology, and engineering operations which are essential to explore the ocean and the atmosphere and to provide astronomical data and time for naval and related national objectives. To that end, the naval oceanographic program studies astrometry, hydrography, meteorology, oceanography, and precise time.

For further information, contact the following offices: Oceanographer of the Navy, U.S. Naval Observatory, 3450 Massachusetts Avenue NW., Washington, DC 20392–1800. Phone, 202–762–1026; Commander, Naval Meteorology and Oceanography Command, 1100 Balch Blvd., Stennis Space Center, MS 39529–5005. Phone, 228–688–4188; and Superintendent, Naval Observatory, 3450 Massachusetts Avenue NW., Washington, DC 20392–5100. Phone, 202–762–1438.

Sea Systems The Naval Sea Systems Command provides material support to the Navy and Marine Corps and to the Departments of Defense and Transportation for ships, submarines, and other sea platforms, shipboard combat systems and components, other surface and undersea warfare and weapons systems, and ordnance expendables not specifically assigned to other system commands.

For further information, contact the Commander, Naval Sea Systems Command, 1333 Isaac Hull Avenue SE., Washington Navy Yard, DC 20376–1010. Phone, 202–781–1973.

Space and Naval Warfare The Space and Naval Warfare Systems Command provides technical and material support to the Department of the Navy for space systems; command, control, communications, and intelligence systems; and electronic warfare and undersea surveillance.

For further information, contact the Commander, Space and Naval Warfare Systems Command, 4301 Pacific Highway, San Diego, CA 92110–3127. Phone, 619–524–3428.

Strategic Systems The Office of Strategic Systems Programs provides development, production, and material support to the Navy for fleet ballistic missile and strategic weapon systems, security, training of personnel, and the installation and direction of necessary supporting facilities.

For further information, contact the Director, Strategic Systems Programs, Department of the Navy, Nebraska Avenue Complex, 287 Somers Court NW., Suite 10041, Washington, DC 20393–5446. Phone, 202–764–1608.

Supply Systems The Naval Supply Systems Command provides supply management policies and methods and administers related support service systems for the Navy and Marine Corps.

For further information, contact the Commander, Naval Supply Systems Command, 5450 Carlisle Pike, P.O. Box 2050, Mechanicsburg, PA 17055–0791. Phone, 717–605–3565.

Warfare Development The Navy Warfare Development Command plans and coordinates experiments employing emerging operational concepts; represents the Department of the Navy in joint and other service laboratories and facilities and tactical development commands; and publishes and disseminates naval doctrine.

For further information, contact the Commander, Navy Warfare Development Command, 686 Cushing Road, Sims Hall, Newport, RI 02841. Phone, 401–841–2833.

United States Marine Corps

Commandant of the Marine Corps,
Headquarters, U.S. Marine Corps, 2 Navy Annex, Washington, DC 20380–1775
Phone, 703–614–1034. Internet, www.usmc.mil.

The United States Marine Corps was established on November 10, 1775, by resolution of the Continental Congress. Marine Corps composition and functions are detailed in 10 U.S.C. 5063.

The Marine Corps, which is part of the Department of the Navy, is the smallest of the Nation's combat forces and is the only service specifically tasked by Congress to be able to fight in the air, on land, and at sea. Although marines fight in each of these dimensions, they are primarily a maritime force, inextricably linked with the Navy to move from the sea to fight on land.

The Marine Corps conducts entry-level training for its enlisted marines at two bases, Marine Corps Recruit Depot, Parris Island, SC, and Marine Corps Recruit Depot, San Diego, CA. Officer candidates are evaluated at Officer Candidate School at Marine Corps

Combat Development Command, Quantico, VA. Marines train to be first on the scene to respond to attacks on the United States or its interests, acts of political violence against Americans abroad, disaster relief, humanitarian assistance, or evacuation of Americans from foreign countries.

Marine Corps Districts

District	Address
1st	1605 Stewart Ave., Garden City, NY 11530–4761
4th	Bldg. 54, Suite 3, New Cumberland, PA 17072–0806
6th	Marine Corps Recruit Depot, P.O. Box 19201, Parris Island, SC 29905–9201
8th	Bldg. 10, Naval Support Activity, New Orleans, LA 70142
9th	3805 E. 155th St., Kansas City, MO 64147–1309
12th	3704 Hochmuth Ave., San Diego, CA 92140–5191

For further information, contact the Division of Public Affairs, Headquarters, U.S. Marine Corps, 2 Navy Annex, Washington, DC 20380–1775. Phone, 703–614–1034. Internet, www.usmc.mil.

United States Naval Academy

Annapolis, MD 21402–5018
Phone, 410–293–1500. Internet, www.usna.edu.

The United States Naval Academy is the undergraduate college of the naval service. Through its comprehensive 4-

year program, which stresses excellence in academics, physical education, professional training, conduct, and honor, the Academy prepares young men and women morally, mentally, and physically to be professional officers in the Navy and Marine Corps. All graduates receive a bachelor of science degree in 1 of 19 majors.

For further information concerning the United States Naval Academy, contact the Superintendent, United States Naval Academy, 121 Blake Road, Annapolis, MD 21402–5018.

Sources of Information

Civilian Employment   Information about civilian employment with the Department of the Navy can be obtained from the Office of the Deputy Assistant Secretary of the Navy for Civilian Human Resources Web site, www.donhr.navy.mil. Information about civilian employment opportunities in the Washington, DC, metropolitan area can be obtained from the Secretariat/ Headquarters Human Resources Office, Navy Annex, Room 2510, Washington, DC 20370–5240. Phone, 703–693–0888.

Consumer Activities   Research programs of the Office of Naval Research cover a broad spectrum of scientific fields, primarily for the needs of the Navy, but much information is of interest to the public. Inquiries on specific research programs should be directed to the Office of Naval Research (Code 10), 800 North Quincy Street, Arlington, VA 22217–5660. Phone, 703–696–5031.

Contracts and Small Business Activities   Information about small businesses, minority-owned businesses, and labor surplus activities can be obtained from the Office of Small and Disadvantaged Business Utilization (SADBU), 720 Kennon Street SE., Room 207, Washington Navy Yard, DC 20374–5015. Phone, 202–685–6485.

Environment   For information on environmental protection and natural resources management programs of the Navy and Marine Corps, contact the Assistant Secretary of the Navy (Installations and Environment), Environment and Safety, 1000 Navy Pentagon, Room 4A686, Washington, DC 20350–1000. Phone, 703–693–5080.

General Inquiries   Navy and Marine Corps recruiting offices, installation commanders, and Commanding Officers of Marine Corps Districts (see listing in the preceding text) can answer general inquiries concerning the Navy and Marine Corps and their community and public information programs.

The Department of the Navy Office of Information provides accurate and timely information about the Navy so that the general public, the press, and Congress may understand and assess the Navy's programs, operations, and needs. The Office also coordinates Navy participation in community events and supervises the Navy's internal information programs, 1200 Navy Pentagon, Room 4B463, Washington, DC 20350–1200. Phone, 703–695–0965.

Speakers and Films   Information can be obtained on speakers, films, and the Naval Recruiting Exhibit Center. For information on the above Navy items, contact the Office of Information, Department of the Navy, 1200 Navy Pentagon, Room 4B463, Washington, DC 20350–1200. Phone, 703–695–0965. For information on above Marine Corps items, contact the Commandant of the Marine Corps, Headquarters, U.S. Marine Corps (PHC), Room 5E774, The Pentagon, Washington, DC 20380–1775. Phone, 703–614–4309.

Tours   To broaden the understanding of the mission, functions, and programs of the Naval Observatory, regular night tours and special group day tours are conducted. The night tours are by reservation only and are given on alternating Monday nights. Information concerning activities of the observatory and public tours may be obtained by writing to the Superintendent, United

States Naval Observatory, 3450 Massachusetts Avenue NW., Washington, DC 20392–5420. Phone, 202–762–1438.

Marine Corps Military Career and Training Opportunities   The Marine Corps conducts enlisted personnel and officer training programs; provides specialized skill training; participates in the Naval Reserve Officers Training Corps Program for commissioning officers in the Marine Corps; provides the Platoon Leaders Class program for commissioning officers in the Marine Corps Reserve to college freshmen, sophomores, or juniors and the Officer Candidate Class program for college graduates or seniors.

Information about these programs is available at most civilian educational institutions and Navy and Marine Corps recruiting stations. Interested persons also may write directly to the Marine Corps Recruiting Command, 3280 Russell Road, Quantico, VA 22134–5103. Phone, 703–784–9454.

Information about Marine Corps Reserve opportunities can be obtained from local Marine Corps recruiting stations or Marine Corps Reserve drill centers. Interested persons may also write directly to the Director, Reserve Affairs, 3280 Russell Road, Suite 507, Quantico, VA 22134–5103. Phone, 703–784–9100.

For further information concerning the Navy, contact the Office of Information, Department of the Navy, 1200 Navy Pentagon, Washington, DC 20350–1200. For press inquiries, phone 703–697–7391 or 703–697–5342. Internet, www.navy.mil. For further information regarding the Marine Corps, contact the Director of Public Affairs, Headquarters, U.S. Marine Corps, 2 Navy Annex (Pentagon 5D773), Washington, DC 20380–1775. Phone, 703–614–1492.

DEFENSE AGENCIES

Defense Advanced Research Projects Agency

3701 North Fairfax Drive, Arlington, VA 22203–1714
Phone, 703–526–6630. Internet, www.darpa.mil.

Director	REGINA E. DUGAN
Deputy Director	ROBERT LEHENY

The Defense Advanced Research Projects Agency is a separately organized agency within Department of Defense and is under the authority, direction, and control of the Under Secretary of Defense (Acquisition, Technology & Logistics). The Agency serves as the central research and development organization of the Department of Defense with a primary responsibility to maintain U.S. technological superiority over potential adversaries. It pursues imaginative and innovative research and development projects and conducts demonstration projects that embody technology appropriate for joint programs, programs in support of deployed forces, or selected programs of the military departments. To this end, the Agency arranges, manages, and directs the performance of work connected with assigned advanced projects by the military departments, other Government agencies, individuals, private business entities, and educational or research institutions, as appropriate.

For further information, contact the Defense Advanced Research Projects Agency, 3701 North Fairfax Drive, Arlington, VA 22203–1714. Phone, 703–526–6630. Internet, www.darpa.mil.

Defense Business Transformation Agency

1851 South Bell Street, Suite 1000, Arlington, VA 22240
Phone, 703–607–2110. Internet, www.bta.mil.

Director	DAVID M. FISHER
Deputy Director	DOUGLAS W. WEBSTER

The Defense Business Transformation Agency (BTA) was established on October 7, 2005. Its mission is to guide the transformation of business operations throughout DOD and to deliver enterprise-level capabilities that align to warfighter needs. BTA directs improvement in business operations

181

across DOD. The BTA strives to improve business operations across the

Department of Defense and attract talented, dedicated professionals.

For further information, please contact the Defense Business Transformation Agency. Phone, 703–607–2110. Internet, www.dod.mil/dbt/contact.html.

Defense Commissary Agency

1300 E Avenue, Fort Lee, VA 23801
Phone, 804–734–8253. Internet, www.commissaries.com.

Director and Chief Executive Officer	PHILIP E. SAKOWITZ, JR.
Chief Operating Officer	THOMAS E. MILKS

The Defense Commissary Agency was established in 1990 and is under the authority, direction, and control of the Under Secretary of Defense for Personnel and Readiness and the operational supervision of the Defense Commissary Agency Board of Directors. The Agency provides an efficient and effective worldwide system of commissaries that sell quality groceries and household supplies at low prices to members of the Armed Services community. This benefit satisfies customer demand for quality products and delivers exceptional savings while enhancing the military community's quality of life. This Agency supports the morale and peace of mind of deployed combat personnel, who know their families have secure and affordable access to American products. It works closely with its employees, customers, and civilian business partners to satisfy its customers and to promote the commissary benefit. The benefit fosters recruitment, retention, and readiness of skilled and trained personnel.

Sources of Information

Employment The following information is available on the Defense Commissary Agency's Web site at www.commissaries.com or by calling the following telephone numbers: employment (703–603–1600); small business activities (804–734–8000, extension 4–8015/4–8529); contracting for resale items (804–734–8000, extension 4–8884/4–8885); and contracting for operations support and equipment (804–734–8000, extension 4–8391/4–8830). Also the publication *A Business Guide for Marketing to the Defense Commissary Agency* is available online at www.commissaries.com/business/documents/business_guide.pdf.

For further information, contact the Defense Commissary Agency, 1300 E Avenue, Fort Lee, VA 23801–1800. Phone, 800–699–5063, extension 4–8998. Internet, www.commissaries.com.

Defense Contract Audit Agency

8725 John J. Kingman Road, Suite 2135, Fort Belvoir, VA 22060–6219
Phone, 703–767–3200. Internet, www.dcaa.mil.

Director	APRIL STEPHENSON
Deputy Director	FRANCIS P. SUMMERS, JR.

The Defense Contract Audit Agency was established in 1965 and is under the authority, direction, and control of the Under Secretary of Defense (Comptroller)/Chief Financial Officer. The Agency performs all necessary contract audit functions for DOD and provides accounting and financial advisory services to all Defense components responsible for procurement and contract administration. These services are provided in connection with the negotiation, administration, and settlement of contracts and subcontracts to ensure taxpayer dollars are spent on fair and reasonable contract prices. They include evaluating the acceptability of costs claimed or proposed by contractors and reviewing the efficiency and economy of contractor operations. Other Government agencies may request the Agency's services under appropriate arrangements.

The Agency manages its operations through 5 regional offices responsible for approximately 104 field audit offices throughout the United States and overseas. Each region is responsible for the contract auditing function in its assigned area.

Regional Offices—Defense Contract Audit Agency

Region	Address	Director	Telephone
Central	6321 E. Campus Circle, Irving, TX 75063–2742	Ed Nelson	972–753–2513
Eastern	Suite 300, 2400 Lake Park Dr., Smyrna, GA 30080–7644.	Paul Phillips	770–319–4400
Mid-Atlantic	Suite 1000, 615 Chestnut St., Philadelphia, PA 19106–4498.	David Eck	215–597–7451
Northeastern	Suite 300, 59 Composite Way, Lowell, MA 01851–5150	Ron Meldonian	978–551–9710
Western	Suite 300, 16700 Valley View Ave., La Mirada, CA 90638–5830.	Christopher Andrezze	714–228–7001

For further information, contact the Executive Officer, Defense Contract Audit Agency, 8725 John J. Kingman Road, Suite 2135, Fort Belvoir, VA 22060–6219. Phone, 703–767–3265. Internet, www.dcaa.mil.

Defense Contract Management Agency

6350 Walker Lane, Alexandria, VA 22310–3241
Phone, 703–428–1700. Internet, www.dcma.mil.

Director	CHARLES E. WILLIAMS, JR., *Acting*
Deputy Director	JIM RUSSELL

The Defense Contract Management Agency was established by the Deputy Secretary of Defense in 2000 and is under the authority, direction, and control of the Under Secretary of Defense (Acquisition, Technology, and Logistics). It is responsible for DOD contract management in support of the military departments, other DOD components, the National Aeronautics and Space Administration, other designated Federal and State agencies, foreign governments, and international organizations, as appropriate.

For further information, contact the Public Affairs Office, Defense Contract Management Agency, 6350 Walker Lane, Alexandria, VA 22310–3241. Phone, 703–428–1969. Internet, www.dcma.mil.

Defense Finance and Accounting Service

Crystal Mall 3, Room 920, Arlington, VA 22240–5291
Phone, 703–607–2616. Internet, www.dfas.mil.

Director	TERESA A. MCKAY
Principal Deputy Director	RICHARD GUSTAFSON

The Defense Finance and Accounting Service was established in 1991 under the authority, direction, and control of the Under Secretary of Defense (Comptroller)/Chief Financial Officer to strengthen and reduce costs of financial management and operations within DOD. The Service is responsible for all payments to servicemembers, employees, vendors, and contractors. It provides business intelligence and finance and accounting information to DOD decisionmakers. It is also responsible for preparing annual financial statements for DOD and for the consolidation, standardization, and modernization of finance and accounting requirements, functions, processes, operations, and systems in the Department.

For further information, contact Defense Finance and Accounting Service Corporate Communications, Room 924, Crystal Mall 3, Arlington, VA 22240–5291. Phone, 703–607–0122. Internet, www.dfas.mil.

Defense Information Systems Agency

P.O. Box 4502, Arlington, VA 22204–4502
Phone, 703–607–6900. Internet, www.disa.mil.

Director	LT. GEN. CARROLL F. POLLETT, USA
Vice Director	REAR ADM. ELIZABETH HIGHT, USN

Established originally as the Defense Communications Agency in 1960, the Defense Information Systems Agency (DISA) is under the authority, direction, and control of the Assistant Secretary of Defense (Networks and Information Integration). DISA is a combat support agency responsible for planning, engineering, acquiring, fielding, operating, and supporting global net-centric solutions to serve the needs of the President, Vice President, Secretary of Defense, and other DOD components under all conditions of peace and war.

For further information, contact the Public Affairs Office, Defense Information Systems Agency, P.O. Box 4502, Arlington, VA 22204–4502. Phone, 703–607–6900. Internet, www.disa.mil.

Defense Intelligence Agency

The Pentagon, Washington, DC 20340–5100
Phone, 703–695–0071. Internet, www.dia.mil.

Director	Lt. Gen. Ronald L. Burgess, Jr., USA
Deputy Director	Letitia A. Long

The Defense Intelligence Agency (DIA) was established in 1961 and is under the authority, direction, and control of the Under Secretary of Defense for Intelligence. Its mission is to provide timely, objective, and cogent military intelligence to warfighters, force planners, and defense and national security policymakers. DIA obtains and reports information through its field sites worldwide and the Defense Attaché System; provides timely all-source intelligence analysis; directs Defense Human Intelligence programs; operates the Joint Intelligence Task Force for Combating Terrorism and the Joint Military Intelligence College; coordinates and facilitates Measurement and Signature Intelligence activities; manages and plans collection from specialized technical sources; manages secure DOD intelligence networks; and coordinates required intelligence support for the Secretary of Defense, Joint Chiefs of Staff, Combatant Commanders, and Joint Task Forces.

For further information, contact the Public Affairs Office, Defense Intelligence Agency, Washington, DC 20340–5100. Phone, 703–695–0071. Internet, www.dia.mil.

Defense Legal Services Agency

The Pentagon, Washington, DC 20301–1600
Phone, 703–695–3341. Internet, www.dod.mil/dodgc.

Director (General Counsel)	Jeh Charles Johnson
Deputy Director (Deputy General Counsel)	Robert S. Taylor

The Defense Legal Services Agency was established in 1981 and is under the authority, direction, and control of the General Counsel of the Department of Defense, who also serves as its Director.

The Agency provides legal advice and services for specified DOD components and adjudication of personnel security cases for DOD and other assigned Federal agencies and departments. It also provides technical support and assistance for development of the Department's legislative program; coordinates positions on legislation and Presidential Executive orders; provides a centralized legislative and congressional document reference and distribution point for the Department; maintains the Department's historical legislative files; and administers programs governing standards of conduct and alternative dispute resolution.

For further information, contact the Administrative Office, Defense Legal Services Agency, Room 3A734, Washington, DC 20301–1600. Phone, 703–697–8343. Internet, www.dod.mil/dodgc.

Defense Logistics Agency

Suite 2533, 8725 John J. Kingman Road, Fort Belvoir, VA 22060–6221
Phone, 703–767–6200. Internet, www.dla.mil.

Director	VICE ADM. ALAN S. THOMPSON, USN
Vice Director	MAJ. GEN. ARTHUR B. MORRILL III, USAF

The Defense Logistics Agency (DLA) is under the authority, direction, and control of the Under Secretary of Defense for Acquisition, Technology, and Logistics. It supports both the logistics requirements of the military services and their acquisition of weapons and other materiel. The Agency provides logistics support and technical services to all branches of the military and to a number of Federal agencies. Agency supply centers consolidate the requirements of the military services and procure the supplies in sufficient quantities to meet their projected needs. The Agency manages supplies in eight commodity areas: fuel, food, clothing, construction material, electronic supplies, general supplies, industrial supplies, and medical supplies.

Field Activities—Defense Logistics Agency

Activity	Commander
Defense Distribution Center	Brig. Gen. Peter Talleri, USMC
Defense Energy Support Center	Kim Huntley
Defense Logistics Information Service	Col. Laura Sampsel, USMC
Defense National Stockpile Center	Cornel A. Holder
Defense Reutilization and Marketing Service	Twila Gonzales
Defense Supply Centers:	
Columbus	Brig. Gen. Patricia E. McQuistion, USA
Philadelphia	Brig. Gen. Gus Perna, USA
Richmond	Rear Adm. Vincent Griffith, USN
Document Automation and Production Service	Stephen Sherman
Europe	Col. Derek Smith, USA
Pacific	Col. Bill McCarver, USA
Central	Col. Keith Kodalen, USA

Sources of Information

DOD Surplus Sales Program Questions concerning this program should be addressed to DOD Surplus Sales, International Sales Office, 74 Washington Avenue North, Battle Creek, MI 49017–3092. Phone, 877–352–2255.

Employment For the Washington, DC, metropolitan area, all inquiries and applications concerning the Agency's job recruitment program should be addressed to Human Resources, Customer Support Office, 3990 East Broad Street, Building 11, Section 3, Columbus, OH, 43213–0919. Phone, 877–352–4762.

Environment For information concerning the Agency's program, contact the Staff Director, Environmental and Safety, Defense Logistics Agency, Attn: DSS–E, 8725 John J. Kingman Road, Fort Belvoir, VA 22060–6221. Phone, 703–767–6278.

Procurement and Small Business Activities For information, contact the Director, Small and Disadvantaged Business Utilization, Defense Logistics Agency, Attn: DB, 8725 John J. Kingman Road, Fort Belvoir, VA 22060–6221. Phone, 703–767–0192.

For further information, contact the Defense Logistics Agency, Suite 2533, 8725 John J. Kingman Road, Fort Belvoir, VA 22060–6221. Phone, 703–767–5200. Internet, www.dla.mil.

Defense Security Cooperation Agency

2800 Defense Pentagon, Washington, DC 20301–2800
Phone, 703–601–3700. Internet, www.dsca.mil.

Director	VICE ADM. JEFFREY WIERINGA, USN
Deputy Director	RICHARD MILLIES

The Defense Security Cooperation Agency was established in 1971 and is under the authority, direction, and control of the Under Secretary of Defense (Policy). The Agency executes the traditional security assistance functions such as military assistance, international military education and training, and foreign military sales, as well as program management responsibilities for humanitarian assistance, demining, and other DOD programs.

For further information, contact the Defense Security Cooperation Agency, 2800 Defense Pentagon, Washington, DC 20301–2800. Phone, 703–601–3700. Email, lpa-web@dsca.mil. Internet, www.dsca.mil.

Defense Security Service

1340 Braddock Place, Alexandria, VA 22314–1651
Phone, 703–325–9471. Internet, www.dss.mil.

Director	KATHLEEN WATSON
Deputy Director	(VACANCY)

The Defense Security Service (DSS) is under the authority, direction, and control of the Under Secretary of Defense for Intelligence. DSS ensures the safeguarding of classified information used by contractors on behalf of the Department of Defense and 22 other executive branch agencies under the National Industrial Security Program; oversees the protection of conventional arms, munitions, and explosives in the custody of DOD contractors; evaluates the protection of selected private sector critical assets and infrastructures (physical and cyber-based systems) and recommends measures needed to maintain operations identified as vital to DOD; makes clearance determinations for industry and provides support services for DOD Central Adjudicative Facilities; and provides security education, training, and proactive awareness programs for military, civilian, and cleared industry to enhance their proficiency and awareness of DOD security policies and procedures. DSS also has a counterintelligence office to integrate counterintelligence principles into security countermeasures missions and to support the national counterintelligence strategy.

Operating Locations and Centers—Defense Security Service

Region/Center	Director
Regional Headquarters	
Northern (495 Summer St., Boston, MA 02210)	Alfred Buccigrosso
Capital (241 18th St., Suite 100–A, Arlington, VA 22202)	Christopher Forrest
Southern (Pembroke 5, Suite 525, 293 Independence Blvd., Virginia Beach, VA 23462')	Alfred Sanchez
Western (11770 Bernardo Plaza, Suite 450, San Diego, CA 92128)	Karl Hellman
Security Education Training and Awareness (881 Elkridge Landing Rd., Linthicum, MD 21090)	Kevin Jones
Defense Industrial Security Clearance Office (Suite 400, 2780 Airport Square, Columbus, OH 43219)	John W. Faulkner

For further information, contact the Defense Security Service, Office of Congressional and Public Affairs, 1340 Braddock Place, Alexandria, VA 22314–1651. Phone, 703–325–9471. Internet, www.dss.mil.

Defense Threat Reduction Agency

8725 John J. Kingman Road, MS 6201, Ft. Belvoir, VA 22260–5916
Phone, 703–325–2102. Internet, www.dtra.mil.

Director	JAMES A. TEGNELIA
Deputy Director	MAJ. GEN. RANDAL R. CASTRO, USA

The Defense Threat Reduction Agency (DTRA) was established in 1998 and is under the authority, direction, and control of the Under Secretary of Defense for Acquisition, Technology, and Logistics. DTRA's mission is to reduce the threat posed by weapons of mass destruction (WMDs). DTRA covers the full range of WMD threats (chemical, biological, nuclear, radiological, and high explosive), bridges the gap between the warfighters and the technical community, sustains the nuclear deterrent, and provides both offensive and defensive technology and operational concepts to the warfighters. DTRA reduces the threat of WMDs by implementing arms control treaties and executing the Cooperative Threat Reduction Program. It uses combat support, technology development, and chemical-biological defense to deter the use and reduce the impact of such weapons. It prepares for future threats by developing the technology and concepts needed to counter the new weapons of mass destruction threats and adversaries.

For further information, contact the Public Affairs Office, Defense Threat Reduction Agency, 8725 John J. Kingman Road, MS 6201, Fort Belvoir, VA 22060–5916. Phone, 703–767–5870. Internet, www.dtra.mil.

Missile Defense Agency

The Pentagon, Washington, DC 20301–7100
Phone, 703–695–6420. Internet, www.mda.mil.

Director	LT. GEN. PATRICK J. O'REILLY, USA
Deputy Director	REAR ADM. JOSEPH A. HORN, JR., USN
Executive Director	DAVID ALTWEGG
Chief of Staff	COL. DAVID BAGNATI, USA

[For the Missile Defense Agency statement of organization, see the *Code of Federal Regulations*, Title 32, Part 388]

The Missile Defense Agency's (MDA) mission is to establish and deploy a layered ballistic missile defense system to intercept missiles in all phases of their flight and against all ranges of threats. This capability will provide a defense of the United States, deployed forces, allies, and friends. MDA is under the authority, direction, and control of the Under Secretary of Defense for Acquisition, Technology, and Logistics. MDA manages and directs DOD's ballistic missile defense acquisition programs and enables the Services to field elements of the overall system as soon as practicable. MDA will develop and test technologies and, if necessary, use prototype and test assets to provide early capability. Additionally, MDA will improve the effectiveness of deployed capabilities by implementing new technologies as they become available or when the threat warrants an accelerated capability.

For further information, contact the Human Resources Directorate, Missile Defense Agency, Washington, DC 20301–7100. Phone, 703–614–8740. Internet, www.mda.mil.

National Geospatial-Intelligence Agency

4600 Sangamore Road, Bethesda, MD 20816–5003
Phone, 301–227–7300. Internet, www.nga.mil.

Director	VICE ADM. ROBERT B. MURRETT, USN
Deputy Director	LLOYD B. ROWLAND

The National Geospatial-Intelligence Agency (NGA), formerly the National Imagery and Mapping Agency, was established in 1996 and is under the authority, direction, and control of the Under Secretary of Defense for Intelligence. NGA is a DOD combat support agency and a member of the national intelligence community. NGA's mission is to provide timely, relevant, and accurate geospatial intelligence in support of our national security. Geospatial intelligence means the use and analysis of imagery to describe, assess, and visually depict physical features and geographically referenced activities on the Earth. Headquartered in Bethesda, MD, NGA has major facilities in the Washington, DC, Northern Virginia, and St. Louis, MO, areas with NGA support teams worldwide.

For further information, contact the Public Affairs Office, National Geospatial-Intelligence Agency, 4600 Sangamore Road, Bethesda, MD 20816–5003. Phone, 301–227–2057. Fax, 301–227–3920. Internet, www.nga.mil.

National Security Agency/Central Security Service

Fort George G. Meade, MD 20755–6248
Phone, 301–688–6524. Internet, www.nsa.gov.

Director	LT. GEN. KEITH B. ALEXANDER, USA
Deputy Director	JOHN C. INGLIS

The National Security Agency (NSA) was established in 1952, and the Central Security Service (CSS) was established in 1972. NSA/CSS is under the authority, direction, and control of the Under Secretary of Defense for Intelligence. As the Nation's cryptologic organization, NSA/CSS employs the Nation's premier codemakers and codebreakers. It ensures an informed, alert, and secure environment for U.S. warfighters and policymakers. The cryptologic resources of NSA/CSS unite to provide U.S. policymakers with intelligence information derived from America's adversaries while protecting U.S. Government signals and information systems from exploitation by those same adversaries.

For further information, contact the Public Affairs Office, National Security Agency/Central Security Service, Fort George G. Meade, MD 20755–6248. Phone, 301–688–6524. Internet, www.nsa.gov.

Pentagon Force Protection Agency

Washington, DC 20301
Phone, 703–693–3685. Internet, www.pfpa.mil.

Director	STEVEN E. CALVERY
Deputy Director	JONATHAN H. COFER

The Pentagon Force Protection Agency (PFPA) was established in May 2002 in response to the events of September 11, 2001, and subsequent terrorist threats facing the DOD workforce and facilities in the National Capital Region (NCR). PFPA is under the authority, direction, and control of the Director, Administration and Management, in the Office of the Secretary of Defense. PFPA provides force protection, security, and law enforcement for the people, facilities, infrastructure, and other resources at the Pentagon Reservation and for DOD activities and facilities within the NCR that are not under the jurisdiction of a military department. Consistent with the national strategy on combating terrorism, PFPA addresses the full spectrum of threats, including chemical, biological, and radiological agents, through a strategy of prevention, preparedness, detection, and response to ensure that the DOD workforce and facilities in the NCR are secure and protected.

For further information, contact the Pentagon Force Protection Agency, Washington, DC 20301. Phone, 703–693–3685. Internet, www.pfpa.mil.

JOINT SERVICE SCHOOLS

Defense Acquisition University

Fort Belvoir, VA 22060–5565
Phone, 703–805–3360. Internet, www.dau.mil.

President   FRANK J. ANDERSON, JR.

The Defense Acquisition University, established pursuant to the Defense Acquisition Workforce Improvement Act of 1990 (10 U.S.C. 1701 note), serves as the DOD center for acquisition, technology, and logistics training; performance support; continuous learning; and knowledge sharing. The University is a unified structure with five regional campuses and the Defense Systems Management College-School of Program Managers, which provides executive and international acquisition training. The University's mission is to provide the training, career management, and services that enable the acquisition, technology, and logistics community to make smart business decisions and deliver timely and affordable capabilities to warfighters.

For further information, contact the Director, Operations Support Group, Defense Acquisition University, Fort Belvoir, VA 22060–5565. Phone, 800–845–7606. Internet, www.dau.mil.

National Defense Intelligence College

Defense Intelligence Analysis Center, Washington, DC 20340–5100
Phone, 202–231–5466. Internet, www.ndic.edu.

President   A. DENIS CLIFT

The National Defense Intelligence College (previously the Joint Military Intelligence College) was established in 1962. It is a joint service interagency educational institution serving the intelligence community and operates under the authority of the Director, Defense Intelligence Agency. Its mission is to educate military and civilian intelligence professionals, conduct and disseminate relevant intelligence research, and perform academic outreach regarding intelligence matters. The College is authorized by Congress to award the bachelor of science in intelligence and master of science of strategic intelligence. Courses are offered to full-time students in a traditional daytime format and for part-time students in the evening, on Saturday, and in an executive format (one weekend per month and a 2-week intensive summer period).

For further information, contact the Admissions Office, MCA–2, National Defense Intelligence College, Defense Intelligence Analysis Center, Washington, DC 20340–5100. Phone, 202–231–5466 or 202–231–3319. Internet, www.ndic.edu.

National Defense University

300 Fifth Avenue, Building 62, Fort McNair, Washington, DC 20319–5066
Phone, 202–685–3922. Internet, www.ndu.edu.

President   VICE ADM. ANN E. RONDEAU, USN

THE NATIONAL WAR COLLEGE

300 D Street, Building 61, Fort McNair, Washington, DC 20319–5078
Phone, 202–685–3674. Fax, 202–685–6461. Internet, www.ndu.edu/ndu/nwc/nwchp.html.

Commandant   MAJ. GEN. ROBERT STEEL, USAF

INDUSTRIAL COLLEGE OF THE ARMED FORCES

408 Fourth Avenue, Building 59, Fort McNair, Washington, DC 20319–5062
Phone, 202–685–4337. Internet, www.ndu.edu/ndu/icaf.

Commandant   REAR ADM. GARRY HALL, USN

JOINT FORCES STAFF COLLEGE

Norfolk, VA 23511–1702
Phone, 757–443–6200. Internet, www.jfsc.ndu.edu.

Commandant   BRIG. GEN. KATHERINE P. KASUN,
                                                                              USA

INFORMATION RESOURCES MANAGEMENT COLLEGE

300 Fifth Avenue, Building 62, Fort McNair, Washington, DC 20319–5066
Phone, 202–685–6300. Internet, www.ndu.edu/irmc.

Director   ROBERT D. CHILDS

COLLEGE OF INTERNATIONAL SECURITY AFFAIRS

260 Fifth Avenue, Building 64, Fort McNair, Washington, DC 20319–5066
Phone, 202–685–2290. Internet, www.ndu.edu/cisa.

Director   R. JOSEPH DeSUTTER

National Defense University

The National Defense University was established in 1976 and incorporates the following colleges and programs: the Industrial College of the Armed Forces, the National War College, the Joint Forces Staff College, the Information Resources Management College, the College of International Security Affairs, the Institute for National Strategic Studies, the Center for the Study of Weapons of Mass Destruction, the Center for Technology and National Security Policy, the International Student Management Office, the Joint Reserve Affairs, Capstone, the Security of Defense Corporate Fellows Program, the NATO Education Center, the Institute for National Security Ethics and Leadership, the Center for Joint Strategic Logistics Excellence, the Center for Applied Strategic Leaders, and the Center for Complex Operations.

The mission of the National Defense University is to prepare military and civilian leaders from the United States and other countries to evaluate national and international security challenges through multidisciplinary educational and research programs, professional exchanges, and outreach.

For further information, contact the Human Resources Directorate, National Defense University, Building 62, 300 Fifth Avenue, Fort McNair, Washington, DC 20319–5066. Phone, 202–685–2169. Internet, www.ndu.edu.

The National War College

The National War College provides education in national security policy to selected military officers and career civil service employees of Federal departments and agencies concerned with national security. It is the only senior service college with the primary mission of offering a course of study that emphasizes national security policy formulation and the planning and implementation of national strategy. Its 10-month academic program is an issue-centered study in U.S. national security. The elective program is designed to permit each student to tailor his or her academic experience to meet individual professional development needs.

For further information, contact the Department of Administration, The National War College, Building 61, Room G20, 300 D Street, Fort McNair, Washington, DC 20319–5078. Phone, 202–685–3674. Internet, www.ndu.edu/nwc.

Industrial College of the Armed Forces

The Industrial College of the Armed Forces is an educational institution that prepares selected military and civilians for strategic leadership and success in developing our national security strategy and in evaluating, marshalling, and managing resources in the execution of that strategy. The College offers an education in the understanding of the importance of industry to our national security strategy, and more importantly the resource component of national security. The rigorous, compressed curriculum, completed in two semesters, leads to a master of science degree in national resource strategy.

For further information, contact the Director of Operations, Industrial College of the Armed Forces, Building 59, 408 Fourth Avenue, Fort McNair, Washington, DC 20319–5062. Phone, 202–685–4333. Internet, www.ndu.edu/icaf.

Joint Forces Staff College

The Joint Forces Staff College (JFSC) is an intermediate- and senior-level joint college in the professional military education system dedicated to the study of the principles, perspectives, and techniques of joint operational-level planning and warfare. The mission of JFSC is to educate national security professionals in the planning and execution of joint, multinational, and interagency operations in order to instill a primary commitment to joint, multinational, and interagency teamwork, attitudes, and perspectives. The College accomplishes this mission through four schools: the Joint Advanced Warfighters School, the Joint and Combined Warfighting School, the Joint Continuing and Distance Education School, and the Joint Command, Control, and Information Operations School.

For further information, contact the Public Affairs Officer, Joint Forces Staff College, 7800 Hampton Boulevard, Norfolk, VA 23511–1702. Phone, 757–443–6212. Fax, 757–443–6210. Internet, www.jfsc.ndu.edu.

Information Resources Management College

The Information Resources Management College provides graduate-level courses in information resources management. The College prepares leaders to direct the information component of national power by leveraging information and information technology for strategic advantage. The College's primary areas of concentration include policy, strategic planning, leadership/management, process improvement, capital planning and investment, performance- and results-based management, technology assessment, architecture, information assurance and security, acquisition, domestic preparedness, transformation, e-Government, and information operations.

For further information, contact the Registrar, Information Resources Management College, Building 62, 300 Fifth Avenue, Fort McNair, Washington, DC 20319–5066. Phone, 202–685–6300. Internet, www.ndu.edu/irmc.

Uniformed Services University of the Health Sciences

4301 Jones Bridge Road, Bethesda, MD 20814–4799
Phone, 301–295–3770. Internet, www.usuhs.mil.

President   CHARLES L. RICE

Authorized by act of September 21, 1972 (10 U.S.C. 2112), the Uniformed Services University of the Health Sciences was established to educate career-oriented medical officers for the Military Departments and the Public Health Service. The University currently incorporates the F. Edward Hebert School of Medicine (including graduate and continuing education programs) and the Graduate School of Nursing.

Students are selected by procedures recommended by the Board of Regents and prescribed by the Secretary of Defense. The actual selection is carried out by a faculty committee on admissions and is based upon motivation and dedication to a career in the uniformed services and an overall appraisal of the personal and intellectual characteristics of the candidates without regard to sex, race, religion, or national origin. Applicants must be U.S. citizens.

Medical school matriculants will be commissioned officers in one of the uniformed services. They must meet the physical and personal qualifications for such a commission and must give evidence of a strong commitment to serving as a uniformed medical officer. The graduating medical student is required to serve a period of obligation of not less than 7 years, excluding graduate medical education.

Students of the Graduate School of Nursing must be commissioned officers of the Army, Navy, Air Force, or Public Health Service prior to application. Graduate nursing students must serve a commitment determined by their respective service.

For further information, contact the President, Uniformed Services University of the Health Sciences, 4301 Jones Bridge Road, Bethesda, MD 20814–4799. Phone, 301–295–3770. Internet, www.usuhs.mil.

DEPARTMENT OF EDUCATION

400 Maryland Avenue SW., Washington, DC 20202
Phone, 202–401–2000 or 800–872–5327 (toll free). TTY, 800–437–0833. Internet, www.ed.gov.

SECRETARY OF EDUCATION	ARNE DUNCAN
DEPUTY SECRETARY	TONY MILLER
Chief of Staff	MARGOT ROGERS
Assistant Secretary for Communication and Outreach	PETER CUNNINGHAM
Assistant Secretary for Planning, Evaluation and Policy Development	CARMEL MARTIN
General Counsel	CHARLES P. ROSE
Inspector General	MARY MITCHELSON, *Acting*
Director, Institute of Education Sciences	JOHN EASTON
Assistant Secretary for Civil Rights	RUSSLYNN ALI
Chief Financial Officer	THOMAS SKELLY, *Acting*
Assistant Secretary for Management	JOANN RYAN, *Acting*
Assistant Secretary for Legislation and Congressional Affairs	GABRIELLA GOMEZ
Director, Center for Faith-Based and Neighborhood Partnerships	PETER GROFF
Assistant Deputy Secretary, Office of Safe and Drug-Free Schools	KEVIN JENNINGS
Assistant Deputy Secretary, Office of Innovation and Improvement	JAMES H. SHELTON
Assistant Secretary for Special Education and Rehabilitative Services	ANDY PEPIN, *Acting*
Assistant Deputy Secretary and Director, Office of English Language Acquisition, Language Enhancement, and Academic Achievement for Limited English Proficient Students	RICHARD SMITH, *Acting*
Assistant Secretary for Elementary and Secondary Education	THELMA MELENDEZ
Executive Director, White House Initiative on Educational Excellence for Hispanic Americans	JUAN SEPULVEDA
Under Secretary	MARTHA KANTER
Chief Operating Officer for Federal Student Aid	WILLIAM J. TAGGART
Assistant Secretary for Postsecondary Education	DANIEL T. MADZELAN, *Acting*
Assistant Secretary for Vocational and Adult Education	DENNIS BERRY, *Acting*
Executive Director, White House Initiative on Historically Black Colleges and Universities	JOHN WILSON
Executive Director, White House Initiative on Tribal Colleges and Universities	(VACANCY)

The Department of Education establishes policy for, administers, and coordinates most Federal assistance to education. Its mission is to ensure equal access to education and to promote educational excellence throughout the Nation.

The Department of Education was created by the Department of Education Organization Act (20 U.S.C. 3411) and is administered under the supervision and direction of the Secretary of Education.

Secretary The Secretary of Education advises the President on education plans, policies, and programs of the Federal Government and serves as the chief executive officer of the Department, coordinating and overseeing all Department activities, providing support and encouragement to States and localities on matters related to education, and focusing the resources of the Department and the attention of the country on ensuring equal access to education and promoting educational excellence throughout the Nation.

Activities

Institute of Education Sciences The Institute of Education Sciences was formally established by the Education Sciences Reform Act of 2002. The Institute includes national education centers focused on research, special education research, statistics, and evaluation, and is the mechanism through which the Department supports the research activities needed to improve education policy and practice.

Elementary and Secondary Education The Office of Elementary and Secondary Education directs, coordinates, and formulates policy relating to early childhood, elementary, and secondary education. Included are grants and contracts to State educational agencies and local school districts, postsecondary schools, and nonprofit organizations for disadvantaged, migrant, and Indian children; enhancement of State student achievement assessment systems; improvement of reading instruction; impact aid; technology; and after-school learning programs. The Office also focuses on improving K–12 education, providing children with language and cognitive development, early reading, and other readiness skills and support, and improving the quality of teachers and other instructional staff.

English Language Acquisition The Office of English Language Acquisition, Language Enhancement, and Academic Achievement for Limited English Proficient Students helps children who are limited in their English, including immigrant children and youth, attain English proficiency, develop high levels of academic attainment in English, and meet the same challenging State academic content and student academic achievement standards that all children are expected to meet.

Federal Student Aid Federal Student Aid partners with postsecondary schools and financial institutions to deliver programs and services that help students finance their education beyond high school. This includes administering postsecondary student financial assistance programs authorized under Title IV of the Higher Education Act of 1965, as amended. The Title IV programs collectively represent the Nation's largest source of financial aid for postsecondary students, providing $73 billion in aid to over 10 million students attending more than 6,000 institutions in fiscal year 2005.

Innovation and Improvement The Office of Innovation and Improvement (OII) oversees competitive grant programs that support innovations in the educational system and disseminates the lessons learned from these innovative practices. OII also helps coordinate policies related to parental options and choice. OII administers, coordinates, and recommends programs and policy for improving the quality of activities designed to support and test innovations throughout the K–12 system in areas such as parental choice, teacher quality, use of technology in education, and arts in education. OII encourages the establishment of charter schools through

DEPARTMENT OF EDUCATION

OFFICE OF THE
SECRETARY

OFFICE OF THE
DEPUTY SECRETARY

OFFICE OF
COMMUNICATIONS
AND OUTREACH

OFFICE OF THE
UNDER SECRETARY

OFFICE OF SAFE AND
DRUG-FREE SCHOOLS

OFFICE OF THE
GENERAL COUNSEL

FEDERAL STUDENT
AID

OFFICE OF INNOVATION
AND IMPROVEMENT

OFFICE OF
INSPECTOR GENERAL

OFFICE OF
POSTSECONDARY
EDUCATION

OFFICE OF SPECIAL
EDUCATION AND
REHABILITATIVE
SERVICES

INSTITUTE OF
EDUCATION SCIENCES

OFFICE OF
VOCATIONAL AND
ADULT EDUCATION

OFFICE OF ENGLISH
LANGUAGE ACQUISITION

OFFICE FOR
CIVIL RIGHTS

OFFICE OF ELEMENTARY
AND SECONDARY
EDUCATION

OFFICE OF LEGISLATION
AND CONGRESSIONAL
AFFAIRS

OFFICE OF THE CHIEF
FINANCIAL OFFICER

OFFICE OF
MANAGEMENT

OFFICE OF THE CHIEF
INFORMATION
OFFICER

OFFICE OF PLANNING,
EVALUATION AND
POLICY DEVELOPMENT

planning, start-up funding, and approaches to credit enhancement for charter school facilities. OII also encourages the expansion of parental options and information in the public schools through magnet schools, public school choice, and supplemental educational services, and by working with community organizations to inform parents of their school choice options. OII serves as the Department's liaison and resource to the nonpublic education community, oversees the Family Policy Compliance Office, and manages the Fund for the Improvement of Education.

Postsecondary Education   The Office of Postsecondary Education (OPE) formulates Federal postsecondary education policy and administers programs that address critical national needs in support of their mission to increase access to quality postsecondary education. To increase access to postsecondary education, OPE develops policy for Federal student financial programs and support programs that reach out to low-income, first-generation college students and communities. OPE also supports programs that strengthen the capacity of colleges and universities serving a high percentage of disadvantaged students and improve teacher quality. OPE recognizes accrediting agencies that monitor academic quality, promote innovation in higher education, and improve and expand American educational resources for international studies and services.

Safe and Drug-Free Schools   The Office of Safe and Drug-Free Schools (OSDFS) administers, coordinates, and recommends policy for improving drug and violence prevention programs. OSDFS, in partnership with State and local educational agencies and public and private nonprofit organizations, supports and provides funding for efforts to create safe schools, respond to crises, prevent drug and alcohol abuse, ensure the health and well-being of students, and teach students good citizenship and character. The Office coordinates Department efforts in these areas with other Federal agencies and also leads the Department of Education's homeland

security efforts. OSDFS also participates in the formulation and development of program policy, legislative proposals, and developing administration policies related to violence and drug prevention. The Office drafts program regulations, advises the Secretary on the formulation of comprehensive school health education policy, and develops a national research agenda with other Federal agencies. OSDFS also administers the Department's character, citizenship, and civic education programs.

Special Education and Rehabilitative Services   The Office of Special Education and Rehabilitative Services (OSERS) provides leadership and resources to help ensure that people with disabilities have equal opportunities to learn, work, and live as fully integrated and contributing members of society. OSERS has three components. The Office of Special Education Programs administers the Individuals with Disabilities Education Act legislation, which helps States meet the early intervention and educational needs of infants, toddlers, children, and youth with disabilities. The Rehabilitation Services Administration supports State vocational rehabilitation, independent living, and assistive technology programs that provide people with disabilities the services, technology, and job training and placement assistance they need to gain meaningful employment and lead independent lives. The National Institute on Disability and Rehabilitation Research supports research and development programs that improve the ability of individuals with disabilities to work and live in a barrier-free, inclusive society. OSERS supports Gallaudet University, the National Technical Institute for the Deaf, the American Printing House for the Blind, and the Helen Keller National Center.

Vocational and Adult Education   The Office of Vocational and Adult Education (OVAE) administers grant, contract, and technical assistance programs for vocational-technical education and for adult education and literacy. OVAE promotes programs that enable adults to acquire the basic literacy skills necessary to function in today's society. OVAE also helps students acquire challenging academic and technical skills and prepare for high-skill, high-wage, and high-demand occupations in the 21st century global economy. OVAE provides national leadership and works to strengthen the role of community colleges in expanding access to postsecondary education for youth and adults in advancing workforce development.

Regional Offices   Each regional office serves as a center for the dissemination of information and provides technical assistance to State and local educational agencies and other institutions and individuals interested in Federal educational activities. Offices are located in Boston, MA; New York, NY; Philadelphia, PA; Atlanta, GA; Chicago, IL; Dallas, TX; Kansas City, MO; Denver, CO; San Francisco, CA; and Seattle, WA.

Federally Aided Corporations

American Printing House for the Blind

P.O. Box 6085, Louisville, KY 40206
Phone, 502–895–2405. Internet, www.aph.org.

President   TUCK TINSLEY III
Chairman of the Board   W. JAMES LINTNER, JR.

Founded in 1858 as a nonprofit organization, the American Printing House for the Blind (APH) received its Federal charter in 1879 when Congress passed the Act to promote Education of the Blind. This Act designates APH as the official supplier of educational materials adapted for students who are legally blind and who are enrolled in formal educational programs below the college level. Materials produced and distributed by APH include textbooks in Braille and large type, educational tools such as Braille typewriters and microcomputer software and hardware, teaching aides such as tests and performance measures, and other special supplies. The materials are distributed through allotments to the States to programs serving individuals who are blind.

For further information, contact the American Printing House for the Blind, P.O. Box 6085, Louisville, KY 40206. Phone, 502–895–2405. Internet, www.aph.org.

Gallaudet University

800 Florida Avenue NE., Washington, DC 20002
Phone, 202–651–5000. Internet, www.gallaudet.edu.

President, Gallaudet University   ROBERT R. DAVILA
Chair, Board of Trustees   BENJAMIN J. SOUKUP, JR.

Gallaudet University received its Federal charter in 1864 and is currently authorized by the Education of the Deaf Act of 1986, as amended. Gallaudet is a private, nonprofit education institution providing elementary, secondary, undergraduate, and continuing education programs for persons who are deaf. The University offers a traditional liberal arts curriculum for students who are deaf, and graduate programs in fields related to deafness for students who are deaf and students who are hearing. Gallaudet also conducts a wide variety of basic and applied deafness research and provides public service programs for persons who are deaf and for professionals who work with persons who are deaf.

Gallaudet University is accredited by a number of accrediting bodies, among which are the Middle States Association of Colleges and Secondary Schools, the National Council for Accreditation of Teacher Education, and the Conference of Educational Administrators of Schools and Programs for the Deaf.

Laurent Clerc National Deaf Education Center   Gallaudet's Laurent Clerc National Deaf Education Center operates elementary and secondary education programs that are federally funded, on the main campus of the University—the Kendall Demonstration Elementary School and the Model Secondary School for the Deaf. These programs are authorized by the Education of the Deaf Act of 1986 (20 U.S.C. 4304, as amended) for the primary purpose of developing, evaluating, and disseminating model curricula, instructional techniques and strategies, and materials that can be used in a variety of educational environments serving individuals throughout the Nation who are deaf or hard of hearing. The Education of the Deaf Act requires the programs to include students preparing for postsecondary opportunities other than college and students with a broad spectrum of needs, such as students who are lower achieving academically, come from non-English-speaking homes, have secondary disabilities, are members of minority groups, or are from rural areas.

Model Secondary School for the Deaf The school was established by act of October 15, 1966 (20 U.S.C. 693), which was superseded by the Education of the Deaf Act of 1986. The school provides day and residential facilities for secondary-age students from across the United States from grades 9 to 12, inclusively.

Kendall Demonstration Elementary School The school became the Nation's first demonstration elementary school for the deaf by act of December 24, 1970 (20 U.S.C. 695). This act was superseded by the Education of the Deaf Act of 1986. The school is a day program for students from the Washington, DC, metropolitan area from the age of onset of deafness to age 15, inclusively, but not beyond the eighth grade or its equivalent.

For further information, contact the Public Relations Office, Gallaudet University, 800 Florida Avenue NE., Washington, DC 20002. Phone, 202–651–5505. Internet, www.gallaudet.edu.

Howard University

2400 Sixth Street NW., Washington, DC 20059
Phone, 202–806–6100. Internet, www.howard.edu.

President	SIDNEY A. RIBEAU

Howard University was established by act of March 2, 1867 (14 Stat. 438). It offers instruction in 12 schools and colleges, as follows: the colleges of arts and sciences; dentistry; engineering, architecture, and computer sciences; medicine; pharmacy, nursing, and allied health sciences; the graduate school; the schools of business; communications; divinity; education; law; and social work. In addition, Howard University has research institutes, centers, and special programs in the following areas: cancer, child development, computational science and engineering, international affairs, sickle cell disease, and the national human genome project.

For further information, contact the Office of University Communications, Howard University, 2400 Sixth Street NW., Washington, DC 20059. Phone, 202–806–0970. Internet, www.howard.edu.

National Institute for Literacy

1775 I Street NW., Suite 730, Washington, DC 20006
Phone, 202–233–2025

Director	DANIEL MILLER, *Acting*

The National Institute for Literacy provides leadership on literacy issues, including the improvement of reading instruction for children, youth, and adults. The Institute serves as a national resource on current and comprehensive literacy research, practice, and policy.

National Technical Institute for the Deaf/Rochester Institute of Technology

52 Lomb Memorial Drive, Rochester, NY 14623
Phone, 716–475–6853 (voice/TDD). Internet, www.ntid.edu.

President, Rochester Institute of Technology	WILLIAM W. DESTLER
Vice President, National Technical Institute for the Deaf	T. ALAN HURWITZ

The National Technical Institute for the Deaf (NTID) was established by act of June 8, 1965 (20 U.S.C. 681) to promote the employment of persons who are deaf, by providing technical and professional education. The National Technical Institute for the Deaf Act was superseded by the Education of the Deaf Act of 1986 (20 U.S.C. 4431, as amended). The U.S. Department of Education maintains a contract with the Rochester Institute of Technology (RIT) for the operation of a residential facility for postsecondary technical training and education for individuals who are deaf. The purpose of the special relationship with the host institution is to give NTID's faculty and students access to more facilities, institutional services, and career preparation options than could be otherwise provided by a national technical institute for the deaf standing alone.

NTID offers a variety of technical programs at the certificate, diploma, and associate degree levels. Degree programs include majors in business, engineering, science, and visual communications. In addition, NTID students may participate in approximately 200 educational programs available through the Rochester Institute of Technology. Students who are deaf that enroll in NTID or RIT programs are provided a wide range of support services and special programs to assist them in preparing for their careers, including tutoring, counseling, interpreting, specialized educational media, cooperative work experience, and specialized job placement. RIT and NTID are both accredited by the Middle States Association of Colleges and Secondary Schools.

NTID also conducts applied research in occupational- and employment-related aspects of deafness, communication assessment, demographics of NTID's target population, and learning processes in postsecondary education. In addition, NTID conducts training workshops and seminars related to deafness. These workshops and seminars are offered to professionals throughout the Nation who employ, work with, teach, or otherwise serve persons who are deaf.

For further information, contact the Rochester Institute of Technology, National Technical Institute for the Deaf, Department of Recruitment and Admissions, Lyndon Baines Johnson Building, 52 Lomb Memorial Drive, Rochester, NY 14623–5604. Phone, 716–475–6700. Internet, www.ntid.edu.

Sources of Information

Inquiries on the following information may be directed to the specified office, Department of Education, 400 Maryland Avenue SW., Washington, DC 20202. **Contracts and Small Business Activities** Call or write the Office of Small and Disadvantaged Business Utilization. Phone, 202–245–6301.

Employment Inquiries and applications for employment, and inquiries regarding the college recruitment program, should be directed to the Human Resources Group. Phone, 202–401–0553.
Organization Contact the Executive Office, Office of Management. Phone, 202–401–0690. TDD, 202–260–8956.

For further information, contact the Information Resources Center, Department of Education, Room 5E248 (FB–6), 400 Maryland Avenue SW., Washington, DC 20202. Phone, 800–USA–LEARN. Internet, www.ed.gov.

DEPARTMENT OF ENERGY

1000 Independence Avenue SW., Washington, DC 20585
Phone, 202–586–5000. Internet, www.energy.gov.

SECRETARY OF ENERGY	STEVEN CHU
DEPUTY SECRETARY	DANIEL PONEMAN
Under Secretary for Science	STEVEN KOONIN
Under Secretary of Energy	KRISTINA JOHNSON
Assistant Secretary, Fossil Energy	VICTOR DER, *Acting*
Assistant Secretary, Energy Efficiency and Renewable Energy	CATHY ZOI
Assistant Secretary, Nuclear Energy	WARREN F. MILLER, JR.
Administrator, Energy Information Administration	RICHARD NEWELL
Director of Science	WILLIAM BRINKMAN
Assistant Secretary, Environmental Management	INES R. TRIAY, *Acting*
Director of Civilian Radioactive Waste Management	CHRISTOPHER A. KOUTS, *Acting*
Under Secretary for Nuclear Security and Administrator for National Nuclear Security Administration	THOMAS P. D'AGOSTINO
Deputy Administrator for Defense Programs	BRIG. GEN. JONATHAN GEORGE, USAF, *Acting*
Deputy Administrator for Defense Nuclear Nonproliferation	KENNETH E. BAKER, *Acting*
Deputy Administrator for Naval Reactors	ADM. KIRKLAND H. DONALD, USN
Deputy Under Secretary for Counterterrorism	STEVEN AOKI
Chief Financial Officer	STEVEN J. ISAKOWITZ
Chief Human Capital Officer	RITA FRANKLIN, *Acting*
Chief Information Officer	THOMAS N. PYKE
General Counsel	SCOTT BLAKE HARRIS
Inspector General	GREGORY H. FRIEDMAN
Assistant Secretary, Congressional and Intergovernmental Affairs	ELIZABETH A. NOLAN, *Acting*
Assistant Secretary, Policy and International Affairs	DAVID SANDALOW
Director, Public Affairs	DAN LEISTIKOW
Director of Economic Impact and Diversity	ANNIE WHATLEY, *Acting*
Director of Hearings and Appeals	POLI A. MARMOLEJOS
Director of Intelligence and Counterintelligence	STANLEY BORGIA, *Acting*
Director of Management	INGRID KOLB
Director of Health, Safety, and Security	GLENN S. PODONSKY
Director of Legacy Management	DAVID GEISER, *Acting*
Assistant Secretary, Electricity Delivery and Energy Reliability	PATRICIA HOFFMAN, *Acting*

FEDERAL ENERGY REGULATORY COMMISSION

888 First Street NE., Washington, DC 20426
Phone, 202–502–8055. Internet, www.ferc.gov.

Chairman	JOHN WELLINGHOFF
Commissioners	SUEDEEN G. KELLY, PHILIP D. MOELLER, MARC L. SPITZER, (VACANCY)

The Department of Energy's mission is to foster a secure and reliable energy system that is environmentally and economically sustainable; to be a responsible steward of the Nation's nuclear weapons; to clean up the Department's facilities; to lead in the physical sciences and advance the biological, environmental, and computational sciences; and to provide premier scientific instruments for the Nation's research enterprise.

The Department of Energy (DOE) was established by the Department of Energy Organization Act (42 U.S.C. 7131), effective October 1, 1977, pursuant to Executive Order 12009 of September 13, 1977. The act consolidated the major Federal energy functions into one Cabinet-level Department.

Secretary The Secretary decides major energy policy and planning issues; acts as the principal spokesperson for the Department; and ensures the effective communication and working relationships with Federal, State, local, and tribal governments and the public. The Secretary is the principal adviser to the President on energy policies, plans, and programs.

Intelligence and Counterintelligence The Office of Intelligence and Counterintelligence ensures that all departmental intelligence information requirements are met and that the Department's technical, analytical, and research expertise is made available to support U.S. intelligence efforts. The Office develops and implements programs to identify, neutralize, and deter foreign government or industrial intelligence activities directed at or involving Department programs, personnel, facilities, technologies, classified information, and sensitive information. The Office ensures effective use of the U.S. Government's intelligence apparatus in support of DOE's need for information on foreign energy situations and hostile threats, information on global nuclear weapons

development, nonproliferation, and foreign hydrocarbon, nuclear, and other energy production and consumption. The Office formulates all DOE intelligence and counterintelligence policy and coordinates all investigative matters with the Federal Bureau of Investigation.

For further information, contact the Office of Intelligence and Counterintelligence. Phone, 202–586–2610.

Health, Safety, and Security The Office of Health, Safety, and Security develops policies to protect national security and other critical assets entrusted to the Department of Energy. It also manages security operations for departmental facilities in the national capital area.

For further information, contact the Office of Health, Safety, and Security. Phone, 301–903–3777.

Energy Programs

Renewable Energy The Office of Energy Efficiency and Renewable Energy is responsible for formulating and directing programs designed to increase the production and utilization of renewable energy (solar, biomass, wind, geothermal, alcohol fuels, etc.) and hydrogen, and improving the energy efficiency of the transportation, buildings, industrial, and utility sectors through support of research and development and technology transfer activities. It also has responsibility for administering programs that provide financial assistance for State energy planning; the weatherization of housing

DEPARTMENT OF ENERGY

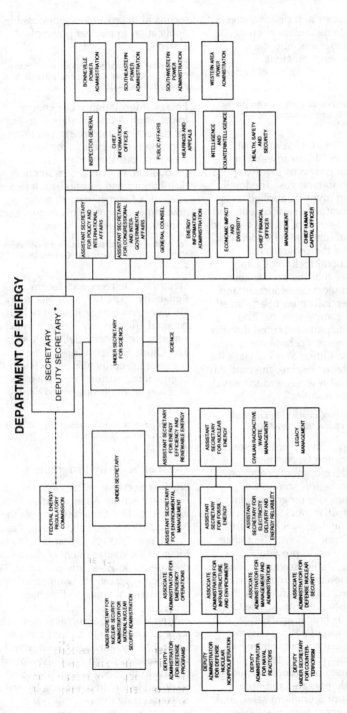

* The Deputy Secretary also serves as the Chief Operating Officer.

owned by the poor and disadvantaged; implementing State and local energy conservation programs; and the promotion of energy efficient construction and renovation of Federal facilities.

For further information, contact the Director of Information and Business Management Systems. Phone, 202–586–9290.

Fossil Energy   The Office of Fossil Energy is responsible for research and development of programs involving coal, petroleum, and natural gas. The fossil energy program involves applied research, exploratory development, and limited proof-of-concept testing targeted to high-risk and high-payoff endeavors. The objective of the program is to provide the general technology and knowledge base that the private sector can use to complete development and initiate commercialization of advanced processes and energy systems. The program is principally executed through the National Energy Technology Laboratory. The Office also manages the strategic petroleum reserve, the northeast home heating oil reserve, and the naval petroleum shale reserves.

For further information, contact the Office of Communications. Phone, 202–586–6803.

Nuclear Energy   The Office of Nuclear Energy manages the Department's research and development programs associated with fission and fusion energy. This includes programs relating to naval and civilian nuclear reactor development, nuclear fuel cycle, and space nuclear applications. The Office manages a program to provide radioactive and stable isotope products to various domestic and international markets for medical research, health care, and industrial research. The Office also conducts technical analyses concerning nonproliferation; assesses alternative nuclear systems and new reactor and fuel cycle concepts; manages depleted uranium hexafluoride activities, highly enriched uranium downblend, natural uranium sales, and uranium enrichment legacy activities; and evaluates proposed advanced nuclear fission energy concepts and

technical improvements for possible application to nuclear powerplant systems.

For further information, contact the Director, Corporate Communications and External Affairs. Phone, 301–903–3796.

Energy Information   The Energy Information Administration is responsible for collecting, processing, publishing, and distributing data in the areas of energy resource reserves, energy production, demand, consumption, distribution, and technology. It performs analyses of energy data to assist government and nongovernment users in understanding energy trends.

For further information, contact the Director, National Energy Information Center. Phone, 202–586–6537.

Electricity Delivery and Energy Reliability   The Office of Electricity Delivery and Energy Reliability leads a national effort to modernize and expand America's electricity delivery system. The Office is responsible for the enhanced security and reliability of the energy infrastructure and facilitates the recovery from disruptions to energy supply.

For further information, contact the Office of the Director. Phone, 202–586–1411.

Nuclear Security Programs

Nuclear Security   The National Nuclear Security Administration (NNSA) was created by Congress through the National Defense Authorization Act for Fiscal Year 2000 (113 Stat. 512) to bring focus to the management of the Nation's defense nuclear security programs. Three existing organizations within the Department of Energy—Defense Programs, Defense Nuclear Nonproliferation, and Naval Reactors— were combined into a new, separately organized and managed agency within DOE, headed by an Administrator who reports to the Secretary. NNSA is responsible for strengthening United States security through military application of nuclear energy and by reducing the global threat from terrorism and weapons of mass destruction.

NNSA's service center and eight site offices provide operations oversight and contract administration for NNSA site activities, acting as the agency's risk acceptance for the site. The site offices are responsible for the following functions: the safe and secure operation of facilities under the purview of NNSA; supporting NNSA programs to ensure their success in accordance with their expectations; and ensuring the long-term viability of the site to support NNSA programs and projects.

For further information, contact the Associate Administrator for Management and Administration. Phone, 202–586–5753.

Site Offices—National Nuclear Security Agency

Office/Address	Telephone
NNSA Service Center (P.O. Box 5400, Albuquerque, NM 87185)	505–845–6202
Site Offices	
Kansas City, MO (P.O. Box 41020, 64141)	816–997–3341
Nevada (P.O. Box 98518, Las Vegas, NV 89193)	702–295–3521
Livermore, CA (P.O. Box 808, L–293, 94551)	925–422–2008
Los Alamos, NM (3747 W. Jemez Rd., 87544)	505–667–5491
Pantex, TX (P.O. Box 30030, Amarillo, TX 79120)	806–477–3000
Savannah River, SC (Attn: S. Green, HRM&DD, P.O. Box A, Aiken, SC 29802)	803–925–7697
Y–12 (P.O. Box 2050, Oak Ridge, TN 37831)	865–576–0885
Sandia, NM (P.O. Box 5400, Albuquerque, NM 87185)	505–845–5264

Defense Activities   The Office of the Deputy Administrator for Defense Programs directs the Nation's nuclear weapons research, development, testing, production, and surveillance program. It is also responsible for the production of the special nuclear materials used by the weapons program within the Department and the management of defense nuclear waste and byproducts. The Office ensures the technology base for the surety, reliability, military effectiveness, and credibility of the nuclear weapon stockpile. It also manages research in inertial confinement fusion.

For further information, contact the Associate Administrator for Management and Administration. Phone, 202–586–5753.

Naval Reactors   The Office of the Deputy Administrator for Naval Reactors manages and performs research, development, design, acquisition, specification, construction, inspection, installation, certification, testing overhaul, refueling, operations procedures, maintenance, supply support, and ultimate disposition of naval nuclear propulsion plants.

For further information, contact the Deputy Administrator for Naval Reactors. Phone, 202–781–6174.

Nuclear Nonproliferation   The Office of the Deputy Administrator for Defense Nuclear Nonproliferation directs the development of the Department's policy, plans, procedures, and research and development activities relating to arms control, nonproliferation, export controls, international nuclear safety and safeguard, and surplus fissile materials inventories elimination activities.

For further information, contact the Associate Administrator for Management and Administration. Phone, 202–586–5753.

Environmental Quality Programs

Civilian Radioactive Waste Management
The Office of Civilian Radioactive Waste Management is responsible for implementation of the Nuclear Waste Policy Act of 1982, as amended (42. U.S.C. 10101 *et seq.*), which provides for the development of a permanent, safe geologic repository for disposal of spent nuclear fuel and high-level radioactive waste.

For further information, contact the Director for Human Capital Division Resources. Phone, 202–586–8839.

Environmental Management   The Office of the Assistant Secretary for Environmental Management manages safe cleanup and closure of sites and facilities; directs a safe and effective waste management program, including storage and disposal of transuranic and mixed low- and high-level waste; and develops and implements an applied research program to provide innovative technologies that yield permanent cleanup solutions at reduced costs.

For further information, contact the Director of Communication/External Affairs. Phone, 202–586–7709.

Legacy Management The Office of Legacy Management manages the Department's post-closure responsibilities and ensures the future protection of human health and the environment. The Office has control and custody of legacy land, structures, and facilities and is responsible for maintaining them at levels suitable for long-term use.

For further information, contact the Director of Business Operations. Phone, 202–586–7388.

Science Program

The Office of Science supports basic research that underpins DOE missions in national security, energy, and environment; constructs and operates large scientific facilities for the U.S.

scientific community; and provides the infrastructure support for 10 national laboratories. In terms of basic research, the Office of Science provides over 40 percent of Federal support to the physical sciences (including 90 percent of Federal support for high energy and nuclear physics), the sole support to select sub-fields of national importance, such as nuclear medicine, heavy element chemistry, and magnetic fusion, and support for the research of scientists and graduate students located in universities throughout the Nation. Office of Science support for major scientific user facilities, including accelerators, synchrotron light sources, and neutron sources, means that more that 18,000 scientists per year are able to use these state-of-the-art facilities to conduct research in a wide range of fields, including biology, medicine, and materials.

For further information, contact the Director of Human Resources. Phone, 301–903–5705.

Site Offices—Office of Science

Office/Address	Telephone
Site Offices	
Ames, IA (No. 311 TASF, Iowa State Univ., 50011)	515–294–9557
Argonne, IL (9800 S. Cass Ave., 60439)	630–252–2000
Berkeley, CA (1 Cyclotron Rd., MS90–1023, 94720)	510–488–4000
Brookhaven, NY (53 Bell Ave., Bldg. 464, Upton, NY 11973)	631–344–5050
Fermi, IL (MS 118, P.O. Box 2000, Kirk Rd. and Pine St., Batavia, IL 60510)	630–840–3000
Pacific Northwest (P.O. Box 350, MS K942, Richland, WA 99352)	509–372–4365
Princeton, NJ (US Rt. 1, Forrestal Campus C Site, Rm. B290 LSB 08542)	609–243–3700
Stanford, CA (2575 Sand Hill Rd., B–41, MS 8–A, Menlo Park, CA 94025)	650–926–3300
Thomas Jefferson (12000 Jefferson Ave., Newport News, VA 23606)	757–269–7100
Support Centers	
Chicago, IL (9800 S. Cass Ave., Argonne, IL 60439)	630–252–2000
Oak Ridge, TN (P.O. Box 2001, 37831)	865–574–1000

Federal Energy Regulatory Commission

The Federal Energy Regulatory Commission (FERC) is an independent agency within the Department of Energy which regulates the interstate

transmission of electricity, natural gas, and oil. FERC has retained many of the functions of the Federal Power Commission, such as setting rates and charges for the transportation and sale of natural gas and the transportation of oil by pipelines, as well the valuation of such pipelines. FERC also reviews proposals to build liquefied natural gas terminals and interstate natural gas pipelines as well as licensing hydropower projects. FERC is composed of five members appointed by the President of the United States with the advice and consent of the Senate. FERC Commissioners serve 5-year terms and have an equal vote on regulatory matters. One member is designated by the President to serve as both Chairman and FERC's administrative head.

For further information, contact the Office of External Affairs. Phone, 202–502–8004 or 866–208–3372. Fax, 202–208–2106. Internet, www.ferc.gov.

Operations and Field Offices

The vast majority of the Department's energy and physical research and development, environmental restoration, and waste management activities are carried out by contractors who operate Government-owned facilities. Management and administration of Government-owned, contractor-operated facility contracts are the major responsibility of the Department's five operations offices and three field offices.

Department operations offices provide a formal link between Department headquarters and the field laboratories and other operating facilities. They also manage programs and projects as assigned from lead headquarters program offices. Routine management guidance, coordination, oversight of the operations, field and site offices, and daily specific program direction for the operations offices is provided by the appropriate Assistant Secretary, office director, or program officer.

Operations and Field Offices—Department of Energy

Office/Address	Telephone
Operations Offices	
Idaho Falls (850 Energy Dr., Idaho Falls, ID 83415)	208–526–5665
Richland (P.O. Box 550, 825 Jadwin Ave., Richland, WA 99352)	509–376–7395
Savannah River (P.O. Box A, Aiken, SC 29802)	803–925–7697
Field Offices	
Carlsbad (P.O. Box 3090, Carlsbad, NM 88221)	505–234–7200
Ohio (175 Tri-County Pkwy., Springdale, OH 45246)	513–246–0500
Golden (1617 Cole Blvd., Golden, CO 80401)	303–275–4700

Power Administrations

The marketing and transmission of electric power produced at Federal hydroelectric projects and reservoirs is carried out by the Department's four Power Administrations. Management oversight of the Power Administrations is the responsibility of the Deputy Secretary.

Bonneville Power Administration The Administration markets power produced by the Federal Columbia River Power System at the lowest rates, consistent with sound business practices, and gives preference to public entities.

In addition, the Administration is responsible for energy conservation, renewable resource development, and fish and wildlife enhancement under the provisions of the Pacific Northwest Electric Power Planning and Conservation Act of 1980 (16 U.S.C. 839 note).

For further information, contact the Bonneville Power Administration, 905 NE. Eleventh Avenue, Portland, OR 97232–4169. Phone, 503–230–3000.

Southeastern Power Administration The Administration is responsible for the transmission and disposition of surplus electric power and energy generated at reservoir projects in the States of West Virginia, Virginia, North Carolina, South Carolina, Georgia, Florida, Alabama, Mississippi, Tennessee, and Kentucky.

The Administration sets the lowest possible rates to consumers, consistent with sound business principles, and gives preference in the sale of such power and energy to public bodies and cooperatives.

For further information, contact the Southeastern Power Administration, 1166 Athens Tech Road, Elberton, GA 30635–4578. Phone, 706–213–3800.

Southwestern Power Administration
The Administration is responsible for the sale and disposition of electric power and energy in the States of Arkansas, Kansas, Louisiana, Missouri, Oklahoma, and Texas.

The Southwestern Power Administration transmits and disposes of the electric power and energy generated at Federal reservoir projects, supplemented by power purchased from public and private utilities, in such a manner as to encourage the most widespread and economical use. The Administration sets the lowest possible rates to consumers, consistent with sound business principles, and gives preference in the sale of power and energy to public bodies and cooperatives.

The Administration also conducts and participates in the comprehensive planning of water resource development in the Southwest.

For further information, contact the Southwestern Power Administration, Suite 1600, Williams Center Tower One, One West Third Street, Tulsa, OK 74103–3532. Phone, 918–595–6600.

Western Area Power Administration
The Administration is responsible for the Federal electric power marketing and transmission functions in 15 Central and Western States, encompassing a geographic area of 1.3 million square miles. The Administration sells power to cooperatives, municipalities, public utility districts, private utilities, Federal and State agencies, and irrigation districts. The wholesale power customers, in turn, provide service to millions of retail consumers in the States of Arizona, California, Colorado, Iowa, Kansas, Minnesota, Montana, Nebraska, Nevada, New Mexico, North Dakota, South Dakota, Texas, Utah, and Wyoming.

The Administration is responsible for the operation and maintenance of transmission lines, substations, and various auxiliary power facilities in the aforementioned geographic area and also for planning, construction, and operation and maintenance of additional Federal transmission facilities that may be authorized in the future.

For further information, contact the Western Area Power Administration, 12155 West Alameda Parkway, Lakewood, CO 80228–1213. Phone, 720–962–7000.

Sources of Information

Consumer Information   For information on the consumer impact of Department policies and operations and for other DOE consumer information, call 202–586–1908.
Contracts and Small and Disadvantaged Business Utilization Activities
Information on business opportunities with the Department and its contractors is available electronically through the Internet at www.pr.doe.gov. For information on existing DOE awards, call 202–586–9051.
Electronic Access   Information concerning the Department is available through the Internet at www.energy.gov.

Employment   Most jobs in the Department are in the competitive service. Positions are filled through hiring individuals with Federal civil service status, but may also be filled using lists of competitive eligibles from the Office of Personnel Management or the Department's special examining units. Contact the Office of Human Capital Management. Phone, 202–586–1234.
Freedom of Information Act   To obtain administrative and technical support in matters involving the Freedom of Information, Privacy, and Computer Matching Acts, call 202–586–5955 or email FOIA-Central@hq.doe.gov.

Inspector General Hotline Persons who wish to raise issues of concern regarding departmental operations, processes, or practices or who may be aware of or suspect illegal acts or noncriminal violations should contact the hotline. Phone, 202–586–4073 or 800–541–1625. Email ighotmail@hq.doe.gov.

Public Information Issuances, Press Releases, and Publications For media contacts, call 202–586–5575.

Public Reading Room For information materials on DOE and public access to DOE records, call 202–586–3142.

Scientific and Technical Information The Office manages a system for the centralized collection, announcement, and dissemination of and historical reference to the Department's scientific and technical information and worldwide energy information. Contact the Office of Scientific and Technical Information, 175 Oak Ridge Turnpike, Oak Ridge, TN 37830–7255. Phone, 423–576–1188.

Whistleblower Assistance Federal or DOE contractor employees wishing to make complaints of alleged wrongdoing against the Department or its contractors should call 202–586–4034.

For further information concerning the Department of Energy, contact the Office of Public Affairs, Department of Energy, 1000 Independence Avenue SW., Washington, DC 20585. Phone, 202–586–4940. Internet, www.energy.gov.

DEPARTMENT OF HEALTH AND HUMAN SERVICES

200 Independence Avenue SW., Washington, DC 20201
Phone, 202–619–0257. Internet, www.hhs.gov.

SECRETARY OF HEALTH AND HUMAN SERVICES	KATHLEEN SEBELIUS
DEPUTY SECRETARY	WILLIAM CORR
Chief of Staff	LAURA PETROU
Chair, Departmental Appeals Board	CONSTANCE B. TOBIAS
Director, Intergovernmental Affairs	PAUL DIOGUARDI
Director, Office for Civil Rights	(VACANCY)
Executive Secretary	(VACANCY)
Assistant Secretary for Health	(VACANCY)
Surgeon General	(VACANCY)
Assistant Secretary for Administration and Management	(VACANCY)
Assistant Secretary for Resources and Technology	(VACANCY)
Assistant Secretary for Legislation	(VACANCY)
Assistant Secretary for Planning and Evaluation	(VACANCY)
Assistant Secretary for Public Affairs	(VACANCY)
Assistant Secretary for Preparedness and Response	W. CRAIG VANDERWAGEN
General Counsel	(VACANCY)
Inspector General	DANIEL R. LEVINSON
National Coordinator, Health Information Technology	DAVID BLUMENTHAL
Chief Administrative Law Judge	(VACANCY)
Director, Office of Global Health Affairs	(VACANCY)

ADMINISTRATION ON AGING

1 Massachusetts Avenue, NW., Suite 4100, Washington, DC 20201
Phone, 202–401–4634. Internet, www.aoa.gov.

Assistant Secretary	(VACANCY)

ADMINISTRATION FOR CHILDREN AND FAMILIES

370 L'Enfant Promenade SW., Washington, DC 20447
Phone, 202–401–9200. Internet, www.acf.hhs.gov.

Assistant Secretary	(VACANCY)

AGENCY FOR HEALTHCARE RESEARCH AND QUALITY

540 Gaither Road, Rockville, MD 20850
Phone, 301–427–1889. Internet, www.ahrq.gov.

Director	CAROLYN CLANCY

AGENCY FOR TOXIC SUBSTANCES AND DISEASE REGISTRY

1600 Clifton Road NE., Atlanta, GA 30333
Phone, 404–639–0700. Internet, www.atsdr.cdc.gov.

Administrator   THOMAS FRIEDEN

CENTERS FOR DISEASE CONTROL AND PREVENTION

1600 Clifton Road NE., Atlanta, GA 30333
Phone, 404–639–3311. Internet, www.cdc.gov.

Director   THOMAS FRIEDEN

CENTERS FOR MEDICARE AND MEDICAID SERVICES

7500 Security Boulevard, Baltimore, MD 21244
Phone, 410–786–3000. Internet, www.cms.gov.

Administrator   (VACANCY)

FOOD AND DRUG ADMINISTRATION

5600 Fishers Lane, Rockville, MD 20857
Phone, 888–463–6332. Internet, www.fda.gov.

Commissioner   MARGARET HAMBURG

HEALTH RESOURCES AND SERVICES ADMINISTRATION

5600 Fishers Lane, Rockville, MD 20857
Phone, 301–443–2216. Internet, www.hrsa.gov.

Administrator   MARY K. WAKEFIELD

INDIAN HEALTH SERVICE

801 Thompson Avenue, Suite 400, Rockville, MD 20852
Phone, 301–443–1083. Internet, www.ihs.gov.

Director   YVETTE ROUBIDEAUX

NATIONAL INSTITUTES OF HEALTH

1 Center Drive, Bethesda, MD 20892
Phone, 301–496–4000. Internet, www.nih.gov.

Director   (VACANCY)

SUBSTANCE ABUSE AND MENTAL HEALTH SERVICES ADMINISTRATION

1 Choke Cherry Road, Rockville, MD 20857
Phone, 240–276–2130. Internet, www.samhsa.gov.

Administrator   (VACANCY)

The Department of Health and Human Services is the Cabinet-level department of the Federal executive branch most involved with the Nation's human concerns. In one way or another, it touches the lives of more Americans than any other Federal agency. It is a department of people serving people, from newborn infants to persons requiring health services to our most elderly citizens.

The Department of Health and Human Services (HHS) was created as the Department of Health, Education, and Welfare on April 11, 1953 (5 U.S.C. app.).

Secretary   The Secretary of Health and Human Services advises the President on health, welfare, and income security plans, policies, and programs of the Federal Government and directs Department staff in carrying out the approved programs and activities of the Department and promotes general public understanding of the Department's goals, programs, and objectives.

Public Health and Science   The Office serves as the Secretary's primary adviser on matters involving the Nation's public health. It provides assistance in implementing and coordinating Secretarial decisions for the Public Health Service and coordination of population-based health, clinical divisions; provides oversight of research conducted or supported by the Department; implements several programs to provide population-based public health services; and provides direction and policy oversight, through the Surgeon General, for the Public Health Service Commissioned Corps.

Regional Offices—Department of Health and Human Services

Area	Address/Areas Served	Telephone
Atlanta, GA	Atlanta Federal Ctr., 61 Forsyth St. SW., 30303 (AL, FL, GA, KY, MS, NC, SC, TN).	404–562–7888
Boston, MA	Government Ctr., 02203 (CT, MA, ME, NH, RI, VT)	617–565–1500
Chicago, IL	233 N. Michigan Ave., 60601 (IL, IN, MI, OH, WI)	312–353–5160
Dallas, TX	1301 Young St., 75202 (AR, LA, NM, OK, TX)	214–767–3301
Denver, CO	1961 Stout St., 80294 (CO, MT, ND, SD, UT, WY)	303–844–3372
Kansas City, MO	601 E. 12th St., 64106 (IA, KS, MO, NE)	816–426–2821
New York, NY	26 Federal Plz., 10278 (NJ, NY, PR, VI)	212–264–4600
Philadelphia, PA	150 S. Independence Mall W., 19106 (DC, DE, MD, PA, VA, WV)	215–861–4633
San Francisco, CA	90 7th St., Suite 5–100, 94103 (AS, AZ, CA, GU, HI, NV)	415–437–8500
Seattle, WA	2201 6th Ave., 98121 (AK, ID, OR, WA)	206–615–2010

Administration on Aging

The mission of the Administration on Aging is to help elderly individuals maintain their independence and dignity in their homes and communities through comprehensive, coordinated, and cost effective systems of long-term care and livable communities across the United States. The agency develops policies, plans, and programs designed to advance the concerns and interests of older people and their caregivers. The Administration works in partnership with the National Aging Network to promote the development of all-inclusive structures and home and community-based long-term care that is responsive to the needs and preferences of older people.

For further information, contact the Administration on Aging, 1 Massachusetts Avenue NW., Suite 4100, Washington, DC 20201. Phone, 202–401–4634. Internet, www.aoa.gov.

DEPARTMENT OF HEALTH AND HUMAN SERVICES

SECRETARY

DEPUTY SECRETARY

CHIEF OF STAFF

EXECUTIVE SECRETARY

DIRECTOR, INTERGOVERNMENTAL AFFAIRS AND SECRETARY'S REGIONAL REPRESENTATIVES

GENERAL COUNSEL

CHIEF ADMINISTRATIVE LAW JUDGE, OFFICE OF MEDICARE HEARINGS AND APPEALS

DIRECTOR, OFFICE FOR CIVIL RIGHTS

DIRECTOR, CENTER FOR FAITH-BASED AND COMMUNITY INITIATIVES

INSPECTOR GENERAL

CHAIR, DEPARTMENTAL APPEALS BOARD

DIRECTOR, OFFICE OF GLOBAL HEALTH AFFAIRS

NATIONAL COORDINATOR, OFFICE OF THE NATIONAL COORDINATOR FOR HEALTH INFORMATION TECHNOLOGY

ADMINISTRATOR, AGENCY FOR TOXIC SUBSTANCES AND DISEASE REGISTRY

COMISSIONER, FOOD AND DRUG ADMINISTRATION

ADMINISTRATOR, HEALTH AND RESOURCES AND SERVICES ADMINISTRATION

DIRECTOR, INDIAN HEALTH SERVICE

DIRECTOR, NATIONAL INSTITUTES OF HEALTH

ASSISTANT SECRETARY ADMINISTRATION FOR CHILDREN AND FAMILIES

ASSISTANT SECRETARY ADMINISTRATION ON AGING

ADMINISTRATOR, CENTERS FOR MEDICARE AND MEDICAID SERVICES

DIRECTOR, AGENCY FOR HEALTHCARE RESEARCH AND QUALITY

DIRECTOR, CENTERS FOR DISEASE CONTROL AND PREVENTION

ADMINISTRATOR, SUBSTANCE ABUSE AND MENTAL HEALTH SERVICES ADMINISTRATION

ASSISTANT SECRETARY FOR HEALTH

ASSISTANT SECRETARY FOR ADMINISTRATION AND MANAGEMENT

DIRECTOR, PROGRAM SUPPORT CENTER

ASSISTANT SECRETARY FOR RESOURCES AND TECHNOLOGY

ASSISTANT SECRETARY FOR PLANNING AND EVALUATION

ASSISTANT SECRETARY FOR PREPAREDNESS AND RESPONSE

ASSISTANT SECRETARY FOR LEGISLATION

ASSISTANT SECRETARY FOR PUBLIC AFFAIRS

Administration for Children and Families

The Administration for Children and Families provides advice to the Secretary on issues pertaining to children, youth, and families; child support enforcement; community services; developmental disabilities; family assistance; Native American assistance; refugee resettlement; and legalized aliens.

For further information, contact the Administration for Children and Families, 370 L'Enfant Promenade SW., Washington, DC 20447. Phone, 202–401–9200. Internet, www.acf.hhs.gov.

Agency for Healthcare Research and Quality

The Agency for Healthcare Research and Quality (AHRQ) is charged with improving the quality, safety, efficiency, and effectiveness of health care for all Americans. AHRQ supports health services research that will improve the quality of health care and promote evidence-based decisionmaking.

For further information, contact the Agency for Healthcare Research and Quality, 540 Gaither Road, Rockville, MD 20850. Phone, 301–427–1889. Internet, www.ahrq.gov. Email, info@ahrq.gov.

Agency for Toxic Substances and Disease Registry

The Agency for Toxic Substances and Disease Registry, as part of the Public Health Service, is charged with the prevention of exposure to toxic substances and the prevention of the adverse health effects and diminished quality of life associated with exposure to hazardous substances from waste sites, unplanned releases, and other sources of pollution present in the environment.

For further information, contact the Agency for Toxic Substances and Disease Registry, MS E–61, 4770 Buford Highway NE., Atlanta, GA 30341. Phone, 770–488–0604. Internet, www.atsdr.cdc.gov.

Centers for Disease Control and Prevention

The Centers for Disease Control and Prevention (CDC), as part of the Public Health Service, is charged with protecting the public health of the Nation by providing leadership and direction in the prevention of and control of diseases and other preventable conditions and responding to public health emergencies. Within the CDC, there are four coordinating centers, two coordinating offices, and the National Institute for Occupational Safety and Health.

Coordinating Center for Environmental Health and Injury Prevention   The Center plans, directs, and coordinates national and global public health research, programs, and laboratory sciences that improve health and eliminate illness, disability, and/or death caused by injuries or environmental exposure.

For further information, contact the Coordinating Center for Environmental Health and Injury Prevention, 4770 Buford Highway NE., Atlanta, GA 30341. Phone, 770–488–0608. Internet, www.cdc.gov.

Coordinating Center for Health Information and Service   The Center assures that the CDC provides high-quality information and programs in the most effective ways to help people, families, and communities protect their health and safety.

Coordinating Center for Health Promotion   The Center plans, directs, and coordinates national programs for the prevention of premature mortality, morbidity, and disability due to chronic diseases, genomics, disabilities (physical and developmental), and birth defects. The Center also is responsible for public health programs related to health promotion, reproductive health, and hereditary conditions, and genomics.

Coordinating Center for Infectious Diseases   The Center protects health and enhances the potential for full, satisfying, and productive living across the lifespan of all people in all communities related to infectious diseases.

Coordinating Office for Global Health   The Office provides leadership and works with partners around the globe to increase life expectancy and years of quality life, and increase global preparedness to prevent and control naturally occurring and man-made threats to health.

Coordinating Office for Terrorism Preparedness and Emergency Response   The Office helps the Nation prepare for and respond to urgent public health threats by providing strategic direction, support, and coordination for CDC's terrorism preparedness and emergency response activities. These activities enable the public health system to develop the building blocks needed to respond to public health threats.

National Institute for Occupational Safety and Health   The Institute plans, directs, and coordinates a national program to develop and establish recommended occupational safety and health standards and to conduct research, training, technical assistance, and related activities to assure safe and healthy working conditions for every working person.

For further information, contact the Centers for Disease Control and Prevention, 1600 Clifton Road NE., Atlanta, GA, 30333. Phone, 404–639–3311, Internet, www.cdc.gov.

Centers for Medicare and Medicaid Services

The Centers for Medicare and Medicaid Services, formerly known as the Health Care Financing Administration, was created to administer the Medicare, Medicaid, and related Federal medical care programs.

For further information, contact the Centers for Medicare and Medicaid Services, Department of Health and Human Services, 7500 Security Boulevard, Baltimore, MD 21244. Phone, 410–786–3000. Internet, www.cms.gov.

Food and Drug Administration

The Food and Drug Administration (FDA) is responsible for protecting the public health by ensuring the safety, efficacy, and security of human and veterinary drugs, biological products, medical devices, the Nation's food supply, cosmetics, and products that emit radiation. FDA is also responsible for advancing the public health by accelerating innovations to make medicines more effective and providing the public with accurate, science-based information on medicines and food to improve their health. FDA plays a significant role in addressing the Nation's counterterrorism capability and ensuring the security of the food supply.

For further information, contact the Food and Drug Administration, 5600 Fishers Lane, Rockville, MD 20857. Phone, 888–463–6332. Internet, www.fda.gov.

Health Resources and Services Administration

The Health Resources and Services Administration (HRSA) works to ensure the delivery of primary health care in thousands of medically underserved communities. More than 7,000 HRSA-supported community health center sites provide primary and preventive health care to 17 million people, regardless of their ability to pay. In an average year, HRSA awards 7,200 grants to 3,000 public and private organizations. Together, these grantees provide safety-net health care to 24 million people. HRSA programs seek to improve the diversity of the U.S. health care workforce and encourage the placement of health professionals in communities where health care is scarce. HRSA oversees a national organ and tissue transplantation system, manages vaccine injury compensation programs, and maintains a health care malpractice database. HRSA also provides support for clinics that provide life-sustaining care and medications to 50 percent of the U.S. population diagnosed with HIV/AIDS, essential services for mothers and children, and systems of care for rural areas.

For further information, contact the Office of Communications, Health Resources and Services Administration, 5600 Fishers Lane, Rockville, MD 20857. Phone, 301–443–3376. Internet, www.hrsa.gov.

Indian Health Service

The Indian Health Service, as part of the Public Health Service, provides a comprehensive health services delivery system for American Indians and Alaska Natives. It assists Native American tribes in developing their health programs; facilitates and assists tribes in coordinating health planning, obtaining and utilizing health resources available through Federal, State, and local programs, operating comprehensive health programs, and evaluating health programs; and provides comprehensive health care services including hospital and ambulatory medical care, preventive and rehabilitative services, and development of community sanitation facilities.

For further information, contact the Management Policy and Internal Control Staff, Indian Health Service, Suite 625A, 801 Thompson Avenue, Rockville, MD 20852. Phone, 301–443–2650. Internet, www.ihs.gov.

National Institutes of Health

The National Institutes of Health (NIH) supports biomedical and behavioral research domestically and abroad, conducts research in its own laboratories and clinics, trains research scientists, and develops and disseminates credible, science-based health information to the public.

Aging   The Institute conducts and supports research on the aging process, age-related diseases, and other special problems and needs of older Americans. It also provides information about aging to the scientific community, health care providers, and the public.

For further information, contact the National Institute on Aging. Phone, 301–496–1752. Internet, www.nia.nih.gov.

Alcohol Abuse and Alcoholism   The Institute leads the national effort to reduce alcohol-related problems by conducting and supporting biomedical and behavioral research into the causes, consequences, prevention, and treatment of alcohol-use disorders.

For further information, contact the National Institute on Alcohol Abuse and Alcoholism. Phone, 301–443–3885 or 301–443–3860. Internet, www.niaaa.nih.gov.

Allergy and Infectious Diseases   The Institute conducts and supports research, research training, and clinical evaluations on the causes, treatment, and prevention of a wide variety of infectious, allergic, and immunologic diseases.

For further information, contact the National Institute of Allergy and Infectious Diseases. Phone, 866–284–4107 (toll free) or 301–496–5717. Internet, www.niaid.nih.gov.

Arthritis and Musculoskeletal and Skin Diseases   The Institute supports research into the causes, treatment, and prevention of arthritis and musculoskeletal and skin diseases.

For further information, contact the National Institute of Arthritis and Musculoskeletal and Skin Diseases. Phone, 301–496–4353. Internet, www.niams.nih.gov.

Biomedical Imaging and Bioengineering   The Institute conducts, coordinates, and supports research, training, dissemination of health information, and other programs with respect to biomedical imaging, biomedical engineering, and associated technologies and modalities with biomedical applications.

For further information, contact the National Institute of Biomedical Imaging and Bioengineering. Phone, 301–451–6768. Internet, www.nibib.nih.gov.

Cancer   The Institute coordinates the National Cancer Program and conducts and supports research, training, and public education with regard to the cause, diagnosis, prevention, and treatment of cancer.

For further information, contact the Cancer Information Service. Phone, 800–422–6237 or 301–435–3848. Internet, www.cancer.gov.

Center for Information Technology   The Center provides, coordinates, and manages information technology to advance computational science.

For further information, contact the Center for Information Technology. Phone, 301–496–6203. Internet, www.cit.nih.gov.

Child Health and Human Development   The Institute conducts and supports laboratory, clinical, and epidemiological research on the reproductive, neurobiologic, developmental, and behavioral processes that determine and maintain the health of children, adults, families, and populations.

For further information, contact the Eunice Kennedy Shriver National Institute of Child Health and Human Development. Phone, 301–496–5133. Internet, www.nichd.nih.gov.

Clinical Center   The NIH Clinical Center is the clinical research hospital for NIH. Through clinical research, physician-investigators translate laboratory discoveries into better treatments, therapies, and interventions to improve the Nation's health. Clinical and laboratory research are both conducted at the Center. This tandem approach drives all aspects of its operations. More than 350,000 patients from across the Nation have participated in clinical research studies since the Center opened in 1953. About 1,500 clinical research studies are currently in progress.

For further information, contact the Clinical Center. Phone, 301–496–2563. Internet, http://clinicalcenter.nih.gov

Complementary and Alternative Medicine   The Center is dedicated to exploring complementary and alternative healing practices in the context of rigorous science; educating and training complementary and alternative medicine researchers; and disseminating authoritative information to the public and professionals. Through its programs, the Center seeks to facilitate the integration of safe and effective complementary and alternative practices into conventional medicine.

For further information, call 888–644–6226. Internet, http://nccam.nih.gov.

Deafness and Other Communication Disorders   The Institute conducts and supports biomedical and behavioral research and research training on normal and disordered processes of hearing, balance, smell, taste, voice, speech, and language, and provides health information, based on scientific discovery, to the public. The Institute conducts diverse research performed in its own laboratories and funds a program of research and research grants.

For further information, contact the National Institute on Deafness and Other Communication Disorders. Phone, 301–496–7243. Internet, www.nidcd.nih.gov.

Dental and Craniofacial Diseases   The Institute conducts and supports research and research training into the causes, prevention, diagnosis, and treatment of craniofacial, oral, and dental diseases and disorders.

For further information, contact the National Institute of Dental and Craniofacial Research. Phone, 301–496–4261. Internet, www.nidcr.nih.gov.

Diabetes and Digestive and Kidney Diseases   The Institute conducts, fosters, and supports basic and clinical research into the causes, prevention, diagnosis, and treatment of diabetes, endocrine, and metabolic diseases, digestive diseases and nutrition, kidney and urologic diseases, and blood diseases.

For further information, contact the National Institute of Diabetes and Digestive and Kidney Diseases. Phone, 301–496–3583. Internet, www.niddk.nih.gov.

Drug Abuse   The Institute's primary mission is to lead the Nation in bringing the power of science to bear on drug abuse and addiction through the strategic support and conduct of research across a broad range of disciplines and the rapid and effective dissemination and use of the results of that research to significantly improve drug abuse and addiction prevention, treatment, and policy.

For further information, contact the National Institute on Drug Abuse. Phone, 301–443–1124. Internet, www.nida.nih.gov.

Environmental Health Sciences   The Institute reduces the burden of human illnesses and disability by understanding how the environment influences the development and progression of human disease. To have the greatest impact on preventing disease and improving human health, the Institute focuses on basic science, disease-oriented research, global environmental health, and multidisciplinary training for researchers.

For further information, contact the National Institute of Environmental Health Sciences. Phone, 919–541–3345. Internet, www.niehs.nih.gov.

Fogarty International Center   The Center addresses global health challenges through innovative and collaborative research and training programs. It also supports and advances the NIH mission through international partnerships.

For further information, contact the Fogarty International Center. Phone, 301–496–2075. Internet, www.fic.nih.gov.

General Medical Sciences   The Institute supports basic biomedical research and research training in areas ranging from cell biology, chemistry, and biophysics to genetics, pharmacology, and systemic response to trauma.

For further information, contact the National Institute of General Medical Sciences. Phone, 301–496–7301. Internet, www.nigms.nih.gov.

Heart, Lung, and Blood Diseases   The Institute provides leadership for a global program in diseases of the heart, blood vessels, lung, and blood; sleep disorders; and blood resources. It conducts, fosters, and supports an integrated and coordinated program of basic research, clinical investigations and trials, observational studies, and demonstration and education projects.

For further information, contact the National Heart, Lung, and Blood Institute. Phone, 301–496–0554. Internet, www.nhlbi.nih.gov.

Human Genome Research The Institute, which helped lead the Human Genome Project, leads and supports a broad range of initiatives and studies aimed at understanding the structure and function of the human genome and its role in health and disease.

For further information, contact the National Human Genome Research Institute. Phone, 301– 496–0844. Internet, www.genome.gov.

Medical Library The Library of Medicine serves as the Nation's chief medical information source and is authorized to provide medical library services and online bibliographic search capabilities, such as MEDLINE and TOXLINE, to public and private agencies, organizations, institutions, and individuals.

For further information, contact the National Library of Medicine. Phone, 301–496–6308. Internet, www.nlm.nih.gov.

Mental Health The National Institute of Mental Health works to transform the understanding and treatment of mental illnesses through basic and clinical research to further the prevention, recovery, and cure of disabling mental conditions that affect millions of Americans.

For further information, contact the National Institute of Mental Health. Phone, 301–443–3673. Internet, www.nimh.nih.gov.

Minority Health and Health Disparities The Center advises the NIH Director and the Institute and Center Directors on the development of NIH-wide policy issues related to minority health disparities research, research on other health disparities, and related research training; develops a comprehensive strategic plan governing the conduct and support of all NIH minority health disparities research, research on other health disparities, and related research training activities; and administers funds for the support of that

research through grants and through leveraging the programs of NIH.

For further information, contact the National Center on Minority Health and Health Disparities. Phone, 301–402–1366. Internet, www.ncmhd.nih.gov.

Neurological Disorders and Stroke The Institute's mission is to reduce the burden of neurological diseases. It conducts, fosters, coordinates, and guides research on the causes, prevention, diagnosis, and treatment of neurological disorders and stroke, and supports basic, translational, and clinical research in related scientific areas.

For further information, contact the National Institute of Neurological Disorders and Strokes Brain Resources and Information Network, P.O. Box 5801, Bethesda, MD 20824. Phone, 800–352– 9424. Internet, www.ninds.nih.gov.

Nursing Research The Institute supports and conducts research to improve patient care across the life span. The research focuses on developing innovative techniques and interventions that prevent disease and disability, enhancing quality of life for patients and caregivers, and improving care at the end of life. The Institute addresses current workforce challenges in the research field by supporting new scientists and nursing faculty.

For further information, contact the National Institute of Nursing Research. Phone, 301–496– 0207. Internet, www.ninr.nih.gov.

Ophthalmological Diseases The Institute conducts, fosters, and supports research on the causes, natural history, prevention, diagnosis, and treatment of disorders of the eye and visual system. It also directs the National Eye Health Education Program.

For further information, contact the National Eye Institute. Phone, 301–496–5248. Internet, www.nei.nih.gov.

Research Resources The Center provides laboratory scientists and clinical investigators with the resources, tools, and training necessary to understand, detect, treat, and prevent a wide range of diseases. With this support, scientists engage in basic laboratory research, translate these findings to animal-based studies, and apply them to patient-oriented research. Through many collaborations, the Center supports all aspects of research, connecting researchers, patients, and communities across the Nation.

For further information, contact the National Center for Research Resources. Phone, 301–435–0888. Internet, www.ncrr.nih.gov.

Scientific Review The Center for Scientific Review (CSR) organizes the peer review groups that evaluate the majority of grant applications submitted to NIH. These groups include

experienced and respected researchers from across the country and abroad. Since 1946, CSR has ensured that NIH grant applications receive fair, independent, expert, and timely reviews—free from inappropriate influences—so NIH can fund the most promising research. CSR also receives all incoming applications and assigns them to the NIH Institutes and Centers that fund grants.

For further information, contact the Center for Scientific Review. Phone, 301–435–1111. Internet, www.csr.nih.gov.

For further information, contact the National Institutes of Health, 1 Center Drive, Bethesda, MD 20892. Phone, 301–496–4000. Internet, www.nih.gov.

Substance Abuse and Mental Health Services Administration

The Substance Abuse and Mental Health Services Administration (SAMHSA) funds and administers grant programs and contracts that support, expand, enhance, and improve the quality, availability, and range of substance abuse treatment and mental health services. SAMHSA has a matrix management system that outlines and guides its activities to improve the accountability, capacity, and effectiveness of the Nation's substance

abuse prevention, addictions treatment, and mental health service delivery systems. The system includes 11 program priority areas: co-occurring disorders, substance abuse treatment capacity, seclusion and restraint, children and families, mental health system transformation, suicide prevention, homelessness, older adults, HIV/AIDS and Hepatitis, criminal and juvenile, and workforce development.

For further information, contact the Substance Abuse and Mental Health Services Administration, 1 Choke Cherry Road, Rockville, MD 20857. Phone, 240–276–2130. Internet, www.samhsa.gov.

Sources of Information

Office of the Secretary
Direct inquiries to the appropriate office, Department of Health and Human Services, Hubert H. Humphrey Building, 200 Independence Avenue SW., Washington, DC 20201. Internet, www.hhs.gov.
Civil Rights For information on enforcement of civil rights laws, call 800–368–1019. TDD, 800–537–7697. Internet, www.hhs.gov/ocr. For information on medical records and health information privacy, call 800–

368–1019. TDD, 866–788–4989. Internet, www.hhs.gov/ocr/hipaa.
Contracts and Small Business Activities For information concerning programs, contact the Director, Office of Small and Disadvantaged Business Utilization. Phone, 202–690–7300.
Departmental Appeals Board For operations information, call 202–565–0200, or direct inquiries to Departmental Appeals Board Immediate Office, M.S. 6127, 330 Independence Avenue SW., Cohen Building, Room G–644,

Washington, DC 20201. Internet, www.hhs.gov/dab.

Inspector General   General inquiries may be directed to the Office of Inspector General, Wilbur J. Cohen Building, 330 Independence Avenue SW., Washington, DC 20201. Phone, 202–619–1142. Internet, www.oig.hhs.gov.

Inspector General Hotline   To report fraud, waste, or abuse against Department programs, contact the Office of Inspector General, HHS–TIPS Hotline, P.O. Box 23489, L'Enfant Plaza Station, Washington, DC 20026–3489. Phone, 800–447–8477. TTY, 800–377–4950. Fax, 800–223–8164.

Locator   For inquiries about the location and telephone numbers of HHS offices, call 202–619–0257.

Program Support   For information concerning fee-for-service activities in the areas of acquisitions, occupational health, information technology support, human resources, financial management, and administrative operations, contact the Program Support Center, 5600 Fishers Lane, Rockville, MD 20857. Phone, 301–443–0034. Internet, www.psc.gov.

Office of Public Health and Science
Contact the Assistant Secretary for Health, Room 716G, 200 Independence Avenue SW., Washington, DC 20201. Phone, 202–690–7694. Internet, www.hhs.gov/ash.

Surgeon General   Phone, 301–443–4000. Internet, www.surgeongeneral.gov.

Administration on Aging

Direct inquiries to the Administration on Aging, Washington, DC 20201. Internet, www.aoa.hhs.gov. Email, aoainfo@aoa.gov.

Aging   Contact the National Aging Information Center. Phone, 202–619–7501. Fax, 202–401–7620.

Elder Care Services   Contact the Elder Care Locator. Phone, 800–677–1116.

Administration for Children and Families

Direct inquiries to the appropriate office, Administration for Children and Families, 370 L'Enfant Promenade SW.,

Washington, DC 20447. Phone, 202–401–9215. Internet, www.acf.gov.

Agency for Healthcare Research and Quality

Direct inquiries to the appropriate office at the Agency for Healthcare Research and Quality, 540 Gaither Road, Rockville, MD 20850. Phone, 301–427–1200. Internet, www.ahrq.gov.

Agency for Toxic Substances and Disease Registry

Information regarding programs and activities is available electronically through the Internet at www.atsdr.cdc.gov.

Centers for Disease Control and Prevention

Direct inquiries to the appropriate office at the Centers for Disease Control and Prevention, Department of Health and Human Services, 1600 Clifton Road NE., Atlanta, GA 30333.

Electronic Access   Information regarding programs, films, publications, employment, and activities is available electronically through the Internet at www.cdc.gov.

Employment   The majority of scientific and technical positions are filled through the Commissioned Corps of the Public Health Service, a uniformed service of the U.S. Government.

Centers for Medicare and Medicaid Services

Direct inquiries to the appropriate office, Centers for Medicare and Medicaid Services, 7500 Security Boulevard, Baltimore, MD 21244–1850. Internet, www.cms.gov.

Electronic access   General information on Medicare/Medicaid is available on the Internet at www.cms.gov. Beneficiary-specific Medicare/Medicaid information is available at www.medicare.gov. General information on the Insure Kids Now! program is available at www.insurekidsnow.gov.

Food and Drug Administration

Direct inquiries to the appropriate office, Food and Drug Administration, 5600 Fishers Lane, Rockville, MD 20857.

Electronic Access Information on FDA is available through the Internet at www.fda.gov.

Employment FDA uses various civil service examinations and registers in its recruitment for positions. For more information, visit the Department's Web site at www.hhs.gov/careers/.

Health Resources and Services Administration

Direct inquiries to the appropriate office, Health Resources and Services Administration, 5600 Fishers Lane, Rockville, MD 20857. Internet, www.hrsa.gov.

Employment The majority of positions are in the Federal civil service. Some health professional positions are filled through the Commissioned Corps of the Public Health Service, a uniformed service of the U.S. Government.

Indian Health Service

Direct inquiries to the appropriate office, Indian Health Service, 801 Thompson Avenue, Rockville, MD 20852.

Electronic Access Information on IHS is available through the Internet at www.ihs.gov.

National Institutes of Health

Direct inquiries to the appropriate office, National Institutes of Health, 1 Center Drive, Bethesda, MD 20892. Phone, 301–496–4000. Internet, www.nih.gov.

Employment Information about employment opportunities is available at the National Institutes of Health employment Web site at www.jobs.nih.gov.

Public Health Service Commissioned Corps Officer Program Information on the Commissioned Corps Officer programs is available at NIH's Public Health Service Commissioned Corps Officer Web site at http://hr.od.nih.gov/corps/default.htm.

Substance Abuse and Mental Health Services Administration

Direct inquiries to the appropriate office, Substance Abuse and Mental Health Services Administration, 1 Choke Cherry Road, Rockville, MD 20857.

Electronic Access Information is available through the Internet at www.samhsa.gov, www.mentalhealth.org, or www.health.org.

For further information, contact the Locator, Department of Health and Human Services, 200 Independence Avenue SW., Washington, DC 20201. Phone, 202–619–0257. Internet, www.hhs.gov.

DEPARTMENT OF HOMELAND SECURITY

Washington, DC 20528
Phone, 202–282–8000. Internet, www.dhs.gov.

SECRETARY OF HOMELAND SECURITY	JANET NAPOLITANO
DEPUTY SECRETARY	JANE HOLL LUTE
Chief of Staff for Policy	NOAH KROLOFF
Chief of Staff for Operations	JAN LESHER

Directorates:

Federal Emergency Management Agency

Administrator	W. CRAIG FUGATE
Deputy Administrator/Chief Operating Officer	DAVID GARRATT, *Acting*
Deputy Administrator, National Preparedness	TIMOTHY MANNING
Assistant Administrator, Disaster Operations	CARWILE WILLIAMS
Assistant Administrator, Disaster Assistance	JAMES W. WALKE

Management

Under Secretary	ELAINE C. DUKE
Deputy Under Secretary	SHARIE BORBEAU
Chief Administrative Services Officer	DONALD G. BATHURST
Chief Human Capital Officer	JEFF NEAL
Chief Information Officer	MARGIE GRAVES, *Acting*
Chief Procurement Officer	RICHARD GUNDERSON, *Acting*
Chief Security Officer	JERRY WILLIAMS
Chief Financial Officer	PEGGY SHERRY, *Acting*

National Preparedness and Programs

Under Secretary	RAND BEERS
Deputy Under Secretary	PHILLIP REITINGER
Assistant Secretary, Infrastructure	JAMES SNYDER
Assistant Secretary, Cyber Security and Communications	GREGORY SCHAFFER
Assistant Secretary, Intergovernmental Programs	JULIETTE KAYYEM

Policy

Assistant Secretary	DAVID HAEYMAN
Deputy Assistant Secretary	ESTHER OLAVARRIA
Special Adviser, Asylum and Refugee Affairs	IGOR V. TIMOFEYEV
Executive Director, Homeland Security Advisory Council	REBECCA SHARP
Director, Immigration Statistics	MICHAEL HOEFER
Assistant Secretary, Office of International Affairs	ALAN BERSIN
Assistant Secretary, Private Sector Coordination	BRIDGER MCGAW, *Acting*
Assistant Secretary, Strategic Plans	(VACANCY)

Science and Technology

Under Secretary	BRADLEY BUSWELL, *Acting*

Director, Operations Analysis	ERVIN KAPOS
Director, Corporate Communications	DANIEL DAYTON
Director, Interagency Programs	RANDALL ZELLER
Director, International Cooperative	LILIA RAMIREZ

Program Office

Director, Strategy, Policy, and Budget	RICHARD WILLIAMS
Director, Test and Evaluation and Standards	GARY CARTER
Director, Business Operations, Services, and Human Capital	DOUGLAS M. SMITH
Director, Special Programs	KEVIN KIRSCH
Director, Innovation/Homeland Security Advanced Research Projects Agency	ROGER MCGINNIS
Director, Research	STARNES WALKER
Director, Transition	RICH KIKLA

Components:

Director, United States Citizenship and Immigration Services	MICHAEL AYTES, *Acting*
Ombudsman, United States Citizenship and Immigration Services	RICHARD FLOWERS, *Acting*
Civil Rights and Civil Liberties Officer	TIMOTHY J. KEEFER, *Acting*
Commandant, United States Coast Guard	THAD W. ALLEN
Director, Office of Counternarcotics Enforcement	JOHN LEECH, *Acting*
Commissioner, Customs and Border Protection	JAYSON AHERN, *Acting*
Director, Domestic Nuclear Detection Office	CHUCK GALLAWAY, *Acting*
Executive Secretary, Executive Secretariat	PHIL MCNAMARA
Director, Federal Law Enforcement Training Center	CONNIE L. PATRICK
General Counsel	IVAN K. FONG
Coordinator, Gulf Coast Region Recovery and Rebuilding	JANET WOODKA
Assistant Secretary, Office of Health Affairs and Chief Medical Officer	JON R. KROHMER
Assistant Secretary, United States Immigration and Customs Enforcement	JOHN T. MORTON
Inspector General	RICHARD L. SKINNER
Under Secretary, Office of Intelligence and Analysis	BART JOHNSON, *Acting*
Assistant Secretary, Office of Legislative Affairs	CHANI WIGGINS
Senior Military Adviser	CHARLIE RAY
Director, Office of Operations Coordination	ROGER T. RUFE, JR.
Chief Privacy Officer	MARY ELLEN CALLAHAN
Assistant Secretary, Office of Public Affairs	SEAN SMITH
Director, United States Secret Service	MARK J. SULLIVAN
Assistant Secretary, Transportation Security Administration	GALE ROSSIDES, *Acting*
White House Liaison	JACOB H. BRAUN

The Department of Homeland Security leads the unified national effort to secure America. It will prevent and deter terrorist attacks and protect against and respond to threats and hazards to the Nation. The Department will ensure safe and secure borders, welcome lawful immigrants and visitors, and promote the free-flow of commerce.

DEPARTMENT OF HOMELAND SECURITY

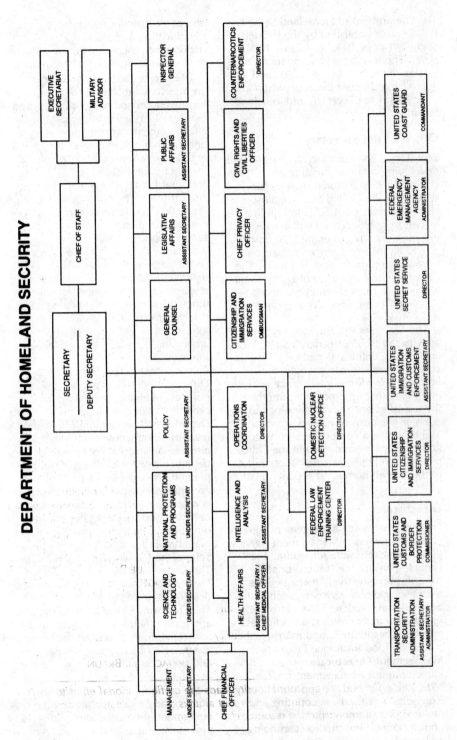

The Department of Homeland Security (DHS) was established by the Homeland Security Act of 2002, (6 U.S.C. 101 note). The Department came into existence on January 24, 2003, and is administered under the supervision and direction of the Secretary of Homeland Security.

Office of the Secretary

Secretary   The Secretary is charged with developing and coordinating a comprehensive national strategy to strengthen the United States against terrorist threats or attacks. In fulfilling this effort, the Secretary will advise the President on strengthening U.S. borders, providing for intelligence analysis and infrastructure protection, improving the use of science and technology to counter weapons of mass destruction, and creating a comprehensive response and recovery division.

The Office of the Secretary oversees activities with other Federal, State, local, and private entities as part of a collaborative effort to strengthen our borders, provide for intelligence analysis and infrastructure protection, improve the use of science and technology to counter weapons of mass destruction, and to create a comprehensive response and recovery system. Within the Office, there are multiple offices that contribute to the overall homeland security mission.

Directorates

Federal Emergency Management Agency
Federal Emergency Management Agency (FEMA) is responsible for leading the effort to prepare the Nation for all hazards and effectively manage Federal response and recovery efforts following any national incident. FEMA also initiates proactive mitigation activities, trains first responders, and manages the National Flood Insurance Program.

Management Directorate   The Directorate for Management is responsible for budget, appropriations, expenditure of funds, accounting and finance; procurement; human resources and personnel; information technology systems; facilities, property, equipment, and other material resources; and identification and tracking of performance measurements relating to the responsibilities of the Department.

The Directorate for Management ensures that the Department's employees have well-defined responsibilities and that managers and their employees have effective means of communicating with one another, with other governmental and nongovernmental bodies, and with the public they serve.

National Preparedness and Programs Directorate   The Directorate for National Protection and Programs safeguards our critical information systems, borders, seaports, bridges, and highways by working with State, local, and private sector partners to identify threats, determine vulnerabilities, and target resources toward the greatest risks. Its functions include strengthening national risk management efforts for critical infrastructure and defining and advancing homeland security protection initiatives.

Policy Directorate   The Policy Directorate develops and integrates policies, planning, and programs in order to better coordinate the Department's prevention, protection, response, and recovery missions. It is also responsible for coordinating departmentwide policies, programs, and planning; developing and communicating policies across multiple components of the homeland security network; and providing the basis and direction for departmentwide strategic planning and budget priorities.

Science and Technology Directorate
The Directorate for Science and Technology is the primary research and development arm of the Department. The Directorate provides Federal, State, and local officials with the technology and capabilities to protect the homeland. Its strategic objectives are to develop and deploy systems to prevent, detect, and mitigate the consequences of chemical, biological, radiological, nuclear, and explosive attacks; develop equipment, protocols, and training procedures for response to and recovery from those attacks; enhance the

Department's and other Federal, State, local, and tribal agencies technical capabilities to fulfill their homeland security-related functions; and develop technical standards and establish certified laboratories to evaluate homeland security and emergency responder technologies for SAFETY Act certification.

Components
United States Citizenship and Immigration Services United States Citizenship and Immigration Services is responsible for the administration of immigration and naturalization adjudication functions and establishing immigration policies and priorities.
Citizenship and Immigration Services Ombudsman The Ombudsman provides recommendations for resolving individual and employer problems with United States Citizenship and Immigration Services in order to ensure national security and the integrity of the legal immigration system, increase efficiencies in administering citizenship and immigration services, and improve customer service.
Office for Civil Rights and Civil Liberties The Office provides legal and policy advice to Department leadership on civil rights and civil liberties issues, investigates and resolves complaints, and provides leadership to DHS Equal Employment Opportunity Programs.
United States Coast Guard The Coast Guard protects the public, the environment, and U.S. economic interests in the Nation's ports and waterways, along the coast, on international waters, or in any maritime region, as required, to support national security.
Office of Counternarcotics Enforcement The Office coordinates Federal policy and operations on interdicting the entry of illegal drugs into the United States and tracking and severing connections between illegal drug trafficking and terrorism.
United States Customs and Border Protection United States Customs and Border Protection is responsible for protecting our Nation's borders in order

to prevent terrorists and terrorist weapons from entering the United States, while facilitating the flow of legitimate trade and travel.
Domestic Nuclear Detection Office The Office is responsible for developing a global nuclear detection architecture and acquiring and supporting the deployment of a domestic nuclear detection system to report any attempt to use nuclear or radiological material against the United States. The office also works to enhance the nuclear detection efforts of Federal, State, territorial, tribal, and local governments and the private sector to ensure a coordinated response to such threats.
Executive Secretariat The Executive Secretariat supports the Office of the Secretary, disseminates information and written communications within the Department, and develops, implements, and manages business processes for written communications and briefing materials. It also facilitates and manages communications with Federal agencies, the Homeland Security Council, the National Security Council, and other White House executive offices.
Federal Law Enforcement Training Center The Center provides career-long training to law enforcement professionals from 81 Federal agencies and State, local, and international law enforcement agencies to help them fulfill their responsibilities safely and proficiently.
Chief Financial Officer The Chief Financial Officer oversees all financial management activities relating to the programs and operations of DHS, develops and maintains an integrated accounting and financial management system, and is responsible for financial reporting and internal controls.
Office of General Counsel The Office of General Counsel provides legal services for homeland security-related matters and ensures that DHS activities comply with all legal requirements.
Office of the Federal Coordinator for Gulf Coast Rebuilding The Office assists the gulf coast region with long-term planning and coordinates the Federal Government's response to

rebuild the gulf coast region devastated by Hurricanes Katrina and Rita.

Office of Health Affairs   The Office is responsible for providing incident management guidance, coordinates the Department's bio defense activities, and ensures a unified approach to medical preparedness. The Office also develops and maintains workforce protection and occupational health standards for DHS employees.

United States Immigration and Customs Enforcement   Immigration and Customs Enforcement is the largest investigative arm of DHS. It is responsible for identifying and shutting down vulnerabilities on the Nation's border and for economic, transportation, and infrastructure security.

Office of Inspector General   The Inspector General is responsible for conducting and supervising audits, investigations, and inspections relating to the Department's programs and operations. It also recommends ways for the Department to carry out its responsibilities in the most effective, efficient, and economical manner possible.

Office of Intelligence and Analysis   The Office is responsible for using information and intelligence from multiple sources to identify and assess current and future threats to the United States.

Office of Legislative Affairs   The Office serves as the primary liaison to Members of Congress and their staffs, the White House and executive branch, and to other Federal agencies and governmental entities that have roles in assuring national security.

Senior Military Advisor   The Senior Military Advisor is responsible for providing counsel to the Secretary and department components relating to the facilitation, coordination, and execution of policy, procedures, and preparedness activities and operations between DHS and the Department of Defense.

Office of Operations Coordination   The Office coordinates operational issues throughout the Department, integrates internal and external operations, conducts incident management, and facilitates staff planning and execution.

Chief Privacy Officer   The Privacy Officer works to minimize the impact on the individual's privacy, particularly the individual's personal information and dignity, while achieving the Department's mission.

Office of Public Affairs   The Office develops and implements a communications strategy and advises the Secretary and other DHS officials on how to effectively communicate issues and priorities of public interest.

United States Secret Service   The Secret Service protects the President and other high-level officials and investigates counterfeiting and other financial crimes, including financial institution fraud, identity theft, and computer fraud and computer-based attacks on our Nation's financial, banking, and telecommunications infrastructure.

Transportation Security Administration   The Transportation Security Administration protects the Nation's transportation systems to ensure freedom of movement for people and commerce.

Sources of Information

Electronic Access   Additional information about the Department of Homeland Security is available electronically through the Internet at www.dhs.gov.

For further information concerning the Department of Homeland Security, contact the Office of Public Affairs, Department of Homeland Security, Washington, DC 20528. Phone, 202–282–8000. Internet, www.dhs.gov.

DEPARTMENT OF HOUSING AND URBAN DEVELOPMENT

451 Seventh Street SW., Washington, DC 20410
Phone, 202–708–1422. Internet, www.hud.gov.

SECRETARY OF HOUSING AND URBAN DEVELOPMENT	SHAUN DONOVAN
DEPUTY SECRETARY	ROY SIMS
Assistant Deputy Secretary for Field Policy and Management	(VACANCY)
General Counsel	HELEN R. KANOVSKY
Assistant Secretary for Housing/Federal Housing Commissioner	DAVID STEVENS
Assistant Secretary for Community Planning and Development	MERCEDES M. MARQUEZ
Assistant Secretary for Public and Indian Housing	SANDRA B. HENRIQUEZ
Assistant Secretary for Policy Development and Research	(VACANCY)
Assistant Secretary for Fair Housing and Equal Opportunity	JOHN TRASVIÑA
Assistant Secretary for Administration	(VACANCY)
Chief Financial Officer	(VACANCY)
General Deputy Assistant Secretary for Public Affairs	NEILL COLEMAN
Assistant Secretary for Congressional and Intergovernmental Relations	PETER KOVAR
President, Government National Mortgage Association	JOSEPH J. MURIN
Inspector General	KENNETH M. DONOHUE, SR.
Assistant Deputy Secretary for Field Policy and Management	(VACANCY)
Director, Office of Departmental Operations and Coordination	INEZ BANKS-DUBOSE
Chief Information Officer	JERRY E. WILLIAMS
Chief Procurement Officer	DAVE WILLIAMSON, *Acting*
Director, Office of Healthy Homes and Lead Hazard Control	JON GANT
Director, Office of Departmental Equal Employment Opportunity	LINDA BRADFORD-WASHINGTON
Director, Center for Faith-Based and Community Initiatives	MARK LINTON

The Department of Housing and Urban Development is the principal Federal agency responsible for programs concerned with the Nation's housing needs, fair housing opportunities, and improvement and development of the Nation's communities.

The Department of Housing and Urban Development (HUD) was established in 1965 by the Department of Housing and Urban Development Act (42 U.S.C. 3532–3537). It was created to:

—administer the principal programs that provide assistance for housing and for the development of the Nation's communities;

—encourage the solution of housing and community development problems through States and localities; and

—encourage the maximum contributions that may be made by vigorous private homebuilding and mortgage lending industries, both primary and secondary, to housing, community development, and the national economy.

Although HUD administers many programs, its major functions may be grouped into six categories:

—insuring mortgages for single-family and multi-family dwellings, and extending loans for home improvement and for purchasing mobile homes;

—channeling funds from investors into the mortgage industry through the Government National Mortgage Association;

—making direct loans for construction or rehabilitation of housing projects for the elderly and the handicapped;

—providing Federal housing subsidies for low- and moderate-income families;

—providing grants to States and communities for community development activities; and

—promoting and enforcing fair housing and equal housing opportunity.

Secretary   The Secretary formulates recommendations for basic policies in the fields of housing and community development; encourages private enterprise participation in housing and community development; promotes the growth of cities and States and the efficient and effective use of housing and community and economic development resources by stimulating private sector initiatives, public/private sector partnerships, and public entrepreneurship; ensures equal access to housing and affirmatively prevents discrimination in housing; and provides general oversight for the Federal National Mortgage Association.

Program Areas

Community Planning and Development The Office administers grant programs to help communities plan and finance their growth and development, increase their capacity to govern, and provide shelter and services for homeless people. The Office is responsible for implementing Community Development Block Grant (CDBG) programs for entitlement communities; State- and HUD-administered small cities programs; community development loan guarantees; special purpose grants for insular areas and historically black colleges and universities; Appalachian Regional Commission grants; Home Investment in Affordable Housing, which provides Federal assistance for housing rehabilitation, tenant-based assistance, assistance to first-time homebuyers, and new construction when a jurisdiction is determined to need new rental housing; the Department's programs to address homelessness; the John Heinz Neighborhood Development Program; community outreach partnerships; the joint community development plan, assisting institutions of higher education working in concert with State and local governments to undertake activities

DEPARTMENT OF HOUSING AND URBAN DEVELOPMENT

under the CDBG program; community adjustment and economic diversification planning grants; the YouthBuild Program, which provides opportunities and assistance to very low-income high school dropouts, ages 16–24; empowerment zones and enterprise communities; efforts to improve the environment; and community planning and development efforts with other departments and agencies, public and private organizations, private industry, financial markets, and international organizations.

For further information, contact the Office of Community Planning and Development. Phone, 202–708–2690.

Fair Housing and Equal Opportunity
The Office administers fair housing laws and regulations prohibiting discrimination in public and private housing; equal opportunity laws and regulations prohibiting discrimination in HUD-assisted housing and community development programs; the fair housing assistance grants program to provide financial and technical assistance to State and local government agencies to implement local fair housing laws and ordinances; and the Community Housing Resources Boards program to provide grants for fair housing activities such as outreach and education, identification of institutional barriers to fair housing, and complaint telephone hotlines.

For further information, contact the Office of Fair Housing and Equal Opportunity. Phone, 202–708–4252.

Federal Housing Enterprise Oversight
The Office oversees the financial safety and soundness of the Federal National Mortgage Association (Fannie Mae) and the Federal Home Loan Mortgage Corporation (Freddie Mac) to ensure that they are adequately capitalized and operating safely.

For further information, contact the Office of Federal Housing Enterprise Oversight. Phone, 202–414–3800.

Government National Mortgage Association (GNMA)
The mission of this Government corporation, also known as Ginnie Mae, is to support expanded affordable housing by providing an efficient Government-guaranteed secondary market vehicle to link the capital markets with Federal housing markets. Ginnie Mae guarantees mortgage-backed securities composed or FHA-insured or VA-guaranteed mortgage loans that are issued by private lenders and guaranteed by GNMA with the full faith and credit of the United States. Through these programs, Ginnie Mae increases the overall supply of credit available for housing by providing a vehicle for channeling funds from the securities market into the mortgage market.

For further information, contact the Government National Mortgage Association. Phone, 202–708–0926.

Housing
The Office of Housing is responsible for the Department's housing functions and oversees aid for construction and financing of new and rehabilitated housing and for preservation of existing housing. The Office underwrites single-family, multi-family, property improvement, and manufactured home loans; administers special purpose programs designed specifically for the elderly, the handicapped, and the chronically mentally ill; administers assisted housing programs for low-income families who are experiencing difficulties affording standard housing; administers grants to fund resident ownership of multi-family house properties; and protects consumers against fraudulent practices of land developers and promoters.

For further information, contact the Office of Housing. Phone, 202–708–3600.

Healthy Homes and Lead Hazard Control
This Office is responsible for lead hazard control policy development, abatement, training, regulations, and research. Activities of the Office include increasing public and building industry awareness of the dangers of lead-based paint poisoning and the options for detection, risk reduction, and abatement; encouraging the development of safer, more effective, and less costly methods for detection, risk reduction, and

abatement; and encouraging State and local governments to develop lead-based paint programs covering contractor certification, hazard reduction, financing, enforcement, and primary prevention, including public education.

For further information, contact the Office of Healthy Homes and Lead Hazard Control. Phone, 202–755–1785.

Public and Indian Housing   The Office administers public and Indian housing programs; provides technical and financial assistance in planning, developing, and managing low-income projects; provides operating subsidies for public housing agencies (PHAs) and Indian housing authorities (IHAs), including procedures for reviewing the management of public housing agencies; administers the comprehensive improvement assistance and comprehensive grant programs for modernization of low-income housing projects to upgrade living conditions, correct physical deficiencies, and achieve operating efficiency and economy; administers program for resident participation, resident management, homeownership, economic development and supportive services, and drug-free neighborhood programs; protects tenants from the hazards of lead-based paint poisoning by requiring PHAs and IHAs to comply with HUD regulations for the testing and removal of lead-based paint from low-income housing units; implements and monitors program requirements related to program eligibility and admission of families to public and assisted housing, and tenant income and rent requirements pertaining to continued occupancy; administers the HOPE VI and vacancy reduction programs; administers voucher and certificate programs and the Moderate Rehabilitation Program; coordinates all departmental housing and community development programs for Indian and Alaskan Natives; and awards grants to PHAs and IHAs for the construction, acquisition, and operation of public and Indian housing projects, giving priority to projects for larger families and acquisition of existing units.

For further information, contact the Office of Public and Indian Housing. Phone, 202–708–0950.

Regional Offices—Department of Housing and Urban Development

Region	Address	Deputy Regional Director	Telephone
CT, ME, MA, NH, RI, VT	Rm. 301, 10 Causeway St., Boston, MA 02222–1092	Kristine Foye	617–994–8200
NJ, NY	26 Federal Plz., New York, NY 10278–0068	JoAnna Aniello	212–264–8000
DE, DC, MD, PA, VA, WV	100 Penn Sq., Philadelphia, PA 19107–3380	Brenda Laroche	215–656–0600
AL, FL, GA, KY, MS, NC, SC, TN, PR	Five Points Plaza, 40 Marietta St. NW., Atlanta, GA 30303–2806	Pat Hoban-Moore	404–331–5001
IL, IN, MI, MN, OH, WI	77 W. Jackson Blvd., Chicago, IL 60604–3507	Beverly Bishop	312–353–5680
AR, LA, NM, OK, TX	801 Cherry St., Fort Worth, TX 76113–2905	C. Donald Babers	817–978–5540
IA, KS, MO, NE	Rm. 200, 400 State Ave., Kansas City, KS 66101–2406	Gene Lipscomb	913–551–5462
CO, MT, ND, SD, UT, WY	23d Fl., 1670 Broadway, Denver, CO 80202–4801	Deborah Griswold	303–672–5440
AZ, CA, HI, NV	3d Fl., 600 Harrison St., San Francisco, CA 94107–1300	Caroline H. Krewson	415–489–6400
AK, ID, OR, WA	Suite 200, 909 1st Ave., Seattle, WA 98104–1000	Martha Dilts	206–220–5101

Sources of Information

Inquiries on the following subjects should be directed to the nearest regional office or to the specified headquarters office, Department of Housing and Urban Development, 451 Seventh Street SW., Washington, DC 20410. Phone, 202–708–0614. TDD, 202–708–1455.

Contracts   Contact the Contracting Division. Phone, 202–708–1290.
Directory Locator   Phone, 202–708–0614. TDD, 202–708–1455.

Employment   Inquiries and applications should be directed to the headquarters Office of Human Resources (phone, 202–708–0408); or the Personnel Division at the nearest HUD regional office.

Freedom of Information Act (FOIA) Requests   Persons interested in inspecting documents or records under the Freedom of Information Act should contact the Freedom of Information Officer. Phone, 202–708–3054. Written requests should be directed to the Director, Executive Secretariat, Department of Housing and Urban Development, Room 10139, 451 Seventh Street SW., Washington, DC 20410.

HUD Hotline   The Hotline is maintained by the Office of the Inspector General as a means for individuals to report activities involving fraud, waste, or mismanagement. Phone, 202–708–4200, or 800–347–3735 (toll free). TDD, 202–708–2451.

Program Information Center   The Center provides viewing facilities for information regarding departmental activities, functions, and publications and other literature to headquarters visitors. Phone, 202–708–1420.

Property Disposition   For single-family properties, contact the Property Disposition Division (phone, 202–708–0614); or the Chief Property Officer at the nearest HUD regional office. For multifamily properties, contact the Property Disposition Division (phone, 202–708–0614); or the Regional Housing Director at the nearest HUD regional office.

For further information, contact the Office of Public Affairs, Department of Housing and Urban Development, 451 Seventh Street SW., Washington, DC 20410. Phone, 202–708–0980. Internet, www.hud.gov.

DEPARTMENT OF THE INTERIOR

1849 C Street NW., Washington, DC 20240
Phone, 202–208–3100. Internet, www.doi.gov.

SECRETARY OF THE INTERIOR	KENNETH L. SALAZAR
DEPUTY SECRETARY	DAVID HAYES
Chief of Staff	THOMAS STRICKLAND
Deputy Chief of Staff	R. RENEE STONE
Special Trustee for American Indians	(VACANCY)
Director of Congressional and Legislative Affairs	CHRISTOPHER MANSOUR
Counselor to the Secretary	STEVEN W. BLACK
White House Liaison	BRIAN SCRENAR
Science Adviser to the Secretary	KATHERINE M. BATTEN
Director, Office of Communications	BETSEY J. HILDEBRANDT
Director of External and Intergovernmental Affairs	RAYMOND RIVERA
Director, Office of the Executive Secretariat and Regulatory Affairs	FAY IUDICELLO
Senior Advisor to the Secretary for Alaskan Affairs	KIM S. ELTON
Solicitor	(VACANCY)
Deputy Solicitor	ARTHUR E. GARY
Counselor to the Solicitor	PAUL SMYTH
Associate Solicitor (Administration)	EDWARD KEABLE
Associate Solicitor (Parks and Wildlife)	BARRY ROTH
Associate Solicitor (Land and Water Resources)	LAURA B. BROWN
Associate Solicitor (General Law)	ARTHUR E. GARY
Associate Solicitor (Indian Affairs)	EDITH BLACKWELL
Associate Solicitor (Mineral Resources)	ROBERT D. COMER
Director, Office of Ethics	MELINDA J. LOFTIN
Inspector General	EARL E. DEVANEY
Deputy Inspector General	MARY KENDALL
Assistant Secretary for Water and Science	(VACANCY)
Deputy Assistant Secretary	DEANNA ARCHULETA
Director, U.S. Geological Survey	(VACANCY)
Commissioner, Bureau of Reclamation	MICHAEL CONNOR
Assistant Secretary for Fish and Wildlife and Parks	THOMAS STRICKLAND
Deputy Assistant Secretary	WILLIAM G. SHAFROTH
Director, U.S. Fish and Wildlife Service	(VACANCY)
Director, National Park Service	(VACANCY)
Assistant Secretary for Indian Affairs	LARRY ECHOHAWK
Principal Deputy Assistant Secretary	(VACANCY)
Deputy Assistant Secretary for Policy and Economic Development	GEORGE SKIBINE
Deputy Assistant Secretary for Management	(VACANCY)
Director, Bureau of Indian Affairs	JEROLD GIDNER
Director, Bureau of Indian Education	(VACANCY)

Assistant Secretary for Land and Minerals Management	(VACANCY)
Deputy Assistant Secretary	EDWARD FARQUHAR
Director, Minerals Management Service	(VACANCY)
Director, Bureau of Land Management	(VACANCY)
Director, Office of Surface Mining Reclamation and Enforcement	(VACANCY)
Assistant Secretary for Policy, Management, and Budget	RHEA S. SUH
Chief Information Officer	SANJEER BHAGOWALIA
Deputy Assistant Secretary for Policy and and Program Management	ROBERT STANTON
Director, Office of Environmental Policy and Compliance	WILLIE R. TAYLOR
Director, Office of Policy Analysis	(VACANCY)
Director, Office of Hawaiian Relations	KAIINI KALOI
Director, Office of Wildlife Coordination	KIRK ROWDABAUGH
Deputy Assistant Secretary for Budget and Business Management	PAMELA K. HAZE
Director, Office of Small and Disadvantaged Business Utilization	MARK OLIVER
Director, Office of Budget	(VACANCY)
Director, Office of Financial Management	DANIEL FLETCHER
Director, Office of Acquisition and Property Management	DEBRA SONDERMAN
Director, National Business Center	DOUGLAS BOURGEOIS
Deputy Assistant Secretary for Human Capital, Performance, and Partnerships	(VACANCY)
Deputy Chief Human Capital Officer	KATHLEEN J.H. WHEELER
Director, Office of Human Resources	SHARLYN GRIGSBY
Director, Office of Civil Rights	SHARON ELLER
Director, Office of Occupational Health and Safety	DIANE SCHMITZ
Director, Office of Strategic Employee Development	SANDRA WELLS
Director, Office of Collaborative Action and Dispute Resolution	ELENA GONZALEZ
Director, Office of Conservation, Partnerships, and Management Policy	OLIVIA FERRITER
Director, Office of Planning and Performance Management	RICHARD T. BECK
Director, Office of Hearings and Appeals	ROBERT S. MORE
Director, Office of Competition, Efficiency, and Analysis	ROBERT M. GORDON
Deputy Assistant Secretary for Law Enforcement, Security, and Emergency Management	LARRY R. PARKINSON
Director, Office of Law Enforcement and Security	KIMBERLY THORSEN
Director, Office of Emergency Management	LAURENCE BROUN
Deputy Assistant Secretary for Insular Affairs	(VACANCY)
Director, Office of Insular Affairs	NIKOLAO PULA

The Department of the Interior protects and provides access to our Nation's natural and cultural heritage and honors our trust responsibilities to tribes and our commitments to island communities.

The Department of the Interior was created by act of March 3, 1849 (43 U.S.C. 1451), which transferred to it the General Land Office, the Office of Indian Affairs, the Pension Office, and the Patent Office. It was reorganized by Reorganization Plan No. 3 of 1950, as amended (5 U.S.C. app.).

The Department manages the Nation's public lands and minerals, national parks, national wildlife refuges, and western water resources and upholds Federal trust responsibilities to Indian tribes and Alaskan natives. It is also responsible for migratory wildlife conservation; historic preservation; endangered species conservation; surface-mined lands protection and restoration; mapping geological, hydrological, and biological science for the Nation; and for financial and technical assistance for the insular areas.

Secretary The Secretary of the Interior reports directly to the President and is responsible for the direction and supervision of all operations and activities of the Department. Some areas where public purposes are broadly applied include:

Fish, Wildlife, and Parks The Office of the Assistant Secretary for Fish and Wildlife and Parks has responsibility for programs associated with the use, management and conservation of natural resources, lands and cultural facilities associated with the National Park and National Refuge Systems, and the conservation and enhancement of fish, wildlife, vegetation, and habitat. The Office represents the Department in the coordination of marine ecosystems and biological resources programs with other Federal agencies. It also exercises secretarial direction and supervision over the United States Fish and Wildlife Service and the National Park Service.

Water and Science The Office of the Assistant Secretary for Water and Science provides oversight to the U.S. Geological Survey, the Bureau of Reclamation and the Central Utah Project Completion Act Office. It provides policy direction and oversight in program areas related to water project operations, facility security and natural resource management as well as for geologic, hydrologic, cartographic, biologic, and technological research. It provides guidance in developing national water and science policies and environmental improvement.

Land and Minerals Management The Office of the Assistant Secretary for Land and Minerals Management has responsibility for programs associated with public land management; operations management and leasing for minerals on public lands, including the Outer Continental Shelf to the outer limits of the United States economic jurisdiction; minerals operations management on Indian lands; surface mining reclamation and enforcement functions; and management of revenues from Federal and Indian mineral leases.

Indian Affairs The Office of the Assistant Secretary for Indian Affairs is responsible for establishing and implementing Indian policy and programs; maintaining the Federal-tribal government-to-government relationship; assisting the Secretary of the Interior with carrying out the Department's Federal trust responsibilities; exercising direction and supervision of the Bureau of Indian Affairs and the Bureau of Indian Education; directly supervising the Federal acknowledgment of tribes, tribal self-determination and self-governance, Indian gaming, economic development, and all administrative, financial, and information resources management activities; and maintaining liaison coordination between the Department and other Federal agencies that provide services or funding to the federally recognized tribes and to the eligible American Indians and Alaska Natives.

The Office of the Special Trustee for American Indians (OST) oversees Indian

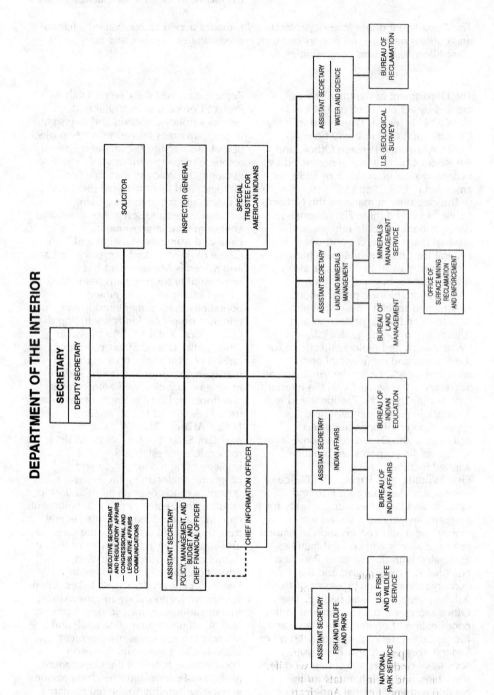

DEPARTMENT OF THE INTERIOR

trust reform efforts departmentwide to ensure the establishment of policies, procedures, systems, and practices to allow the Secretary to discharge the Government's fiduciary trust responsibilities to American Indians and tribes. OST also has programmatic responsibility for the management of financial trust assets, asset appraisals, and fiduciary trust beneficiary services.

Insular Affairs The Office of Insular Affairs (OIA) assists the territories of American Samoa, Guam, the U.S. Virgin Islands, and the Commonwealth of the Northern Mariana Islands in developing more efficient and effective government by providing financial and technical assistance, and serves as a focal point for the management of relations between the United States and the islands by developing and promoting appropriate Federal policies. OIA also carries out the Secretary's responsibilities that are related to the three freely associated states (the Federated States of Micronesia, the Republic of the Marshall Islands, and the Republic of Palau); the Palmyra Atoll excluded areas; and Midway Atoll's nonterrestrial areas.

For further information, contact the Department of the Interior, Washington, DC 20240. Phone, 202–208–3100. Internet, www.doi.gov.

Bureaus

United States Fish and Wildlife Service

[For the United States Fish and Wildlife Service statement of organization, see the Code of Federal Regulations, Title 50, Subchapter A, Part 2]

The United States Fish and Wildlife Service is the principal Federal agency dedicated to fish and wildlife conservation. The Service's history spans nearly 140 years, dating from the establishment of its predecessor agency, the Bureau of Fisheries, in 1871. First created as an independent agency, the Bureau of Fisheries was later placed in the Department of Commerce. A second predecessor agency, the Bureau of Biological Survey, was established in 1885 in the Department of Agriculture. In 1939, the two Bureaus and their functions were transferred to the Department of the Interior. In 1940, they were consolidated into one agency and redesignated the Fish and Wildlife Service by Reorganization Plan III (5 U.S.C. app.).

The United States Fish and Wildlife Service is responsible for conserving, protecting, and enhancing fish, wildlife, and plants and their habitats for the continuing benefit of the American people. The Service manages the 150-million-acre National Wildlife Refuge System, which encompasses 550 units, thousands of small wetlands, and other special management areas. It also operates 70 national fish hatcheries, 64 fishery resource offices, and 81 ecological services field stations. The Service enforces Federal wildlife laws, administers the Endangered Species Act, manages migratory bird populations, restores nationally significant fisheries, conserves and restores wildlife habitat such as wetlands, and assists foreign governments with their conservation efforts. It also oversees the Sport Fish and Wildlife Restoration Programs, which collect and distribute revenues from excise taxes on fishing and hunting equipment to State fish and wildlife agencies.

The Service is responsible for improving and maintaining fish and wildlife resources by proper management of wildlife and habitat. It also helps fulfill the public demand for recreational fishing while maintaining the Nation's fisheries at a level and in a condition that will ensure their continued survival.

Specific wildlife and fishery resources programs include:

—migratory birds (wildlife refuge management for production, migration, and wintering; law enforcement; game; and bird population, production, and harvest surveys);

—mammals and nonmigratory birds (refuge management of resident species, law enforcement, protection of certain marine mammals, and technical assistance);

—coastal anadromous fish (hatchery production and stocking);

—Great Lakes fisheries (hatchery production of lake trout and fishery management in cooperation with Canada and the States); and

—other inland fisheries (hatchery production and stocking of Indian lands, and technical assistance).

The Service provides national and international leadership in identifying, protecting, and restoring endangered species of fish, wildlife, and plants. This program includes:

—developing the Federal Endangered and Threatened Species List, conducting status surveys, preparing recovery plans, conducting Federal agency consultations and coordinating efforts nationally and internationally;

—operating national wildlife refuges;

—law enforcement;

—foreign importation enforcement; and

—consultation with foreign countries.

In the area of resource management, the Service provides leadership for the protection and improvement of land and water environments (habitat preservation) that directly benefit the living natural resources and add quality to human life. Activities include:

—administration of grant programs benefiting imperiled species and habitat on State, Federal, and tribal lands;

—operation of programs that provide technical and financial assistance to private landowners for habitat restoration and improvement;

—environmental impact assessment, including review of hydroelectric dams, wind and nuclear power sites, stream channelization, and dredge-and-fill permits;

—environmental impact statement review;

—management of the Coastal Barrier Resource System mapping;

—surveillance of pesticides, heavy metals, and other contaminants in wildlife; and

—surveys and studies of fish and wildlife populations.

Public use and information programs include preparing informational brochures and Web sites; coordinating environmental studies on Service lands; operating visitor centers, self-guided nature trails, observation towers, and display ponds; and providing recreational activities such as hunting, fishing, and wildlife photography.

The Service's Office of Federal Assistance apportions funds for projects designed to conserve and enhance the Nation's fish and wildlife resources. The funds for the projects are generated from excise taxes on sporting arms and fishing equipment.

Regional Offices—United States Fish and Wildlife Service

Region	Address	Telephone
ALBUQUERQUE—AZ, NM, OK, TX	P.O. Box 1306, Albuquerque, NM 87103–1306	505–248–6911
ANCHORAGE—AK	1011 E. Tudor Rd., Anchorage, AK 99503	907–786–3542
ATLANTA—AL, AR, FL, GA, KY, LA, MS, NC, PR, SC, TN, VI	1875 Century Blvd. NE., Atlanta, GA 30345–3301	404–679–4000
HADLEY—CT, DE, MA, ME, MD, NH, NJ, NY, PA, RI, VT, VA, WV	300 Westgate Ctr. Dr., Hadley, MA 01035–9589	413–253–8200
DENVER—CO, KS, MT, NE, ND, SD, UT, WY	P.O. Box 25486, Denver Federal Center, Denver, CO 80225	303–236–7920
PORTLAND—HI, ID, OR, WA, Pacific Islands	911 NE. 11th Ave., Portland, OR 97232–4181	503–231–6118
SACRAMENTO—CA, NV, Klamath Basin	Suite W–2606, 2800 Cottage Way, Sacramento, CA 95825–1846	916–414–6464
TWIN CITIES—IL, IN, IA, MI, MN, MO, OH, WI	Federal Bldg., Fort Snelling, Twin Cities, MN 55111–4056	612–713–5300

For further information, contact the Office of Public Affairs, Fish and Wildlife Service, Department of the Interior, 1849 C Street NW., Washington, DC 20240. Phone, 703–358–2220. Internet, www.fws.gov.

National Park Service

The National Park Service was established in the Department of the Interior on August 25, 1916 (16 U.S.C. 1).

The National Park Service is dedicated to conserving unimpaired the natural and cultural resources and values of the National Park System for the enjoyment, education, and inspiration of this and future generations. There are 391 units in the National Park System, including national parks, monuments and memorials, scenic parkways, preserves, reserves, trails, riverways, wild and scenic rivers, seashores, lakeshores, recreation areas, battlefields and battlefield parks and sites, national military parks, international historic sites, and historic sites associated with important movements, events, and personalities of the American past.

The National Park Service has a Service Center in Denver that provides planning, architectural, engineering, and other professional services. The Service is also responsible for managing a great variety of national and international programs designed to help extend the benefits of natural and cultural resource conservation and outdoor recreation throughout this country and the world.

Activities   The National Park Service develops and implements park management plans and staffs the areas under its administration. It relates the natural values and historical significance of these areas to the public through talks, tours, films, exhibits, publications, and other interpretive media. It operates campgrounds and other visitor facilities and provides lodging, food, and transportation services in many areas.

The National Park Service also administers the following programs: the State portion of the Land and Water Conservation Fund, nationwide outdoor recreation coordination and information, State comprehensive outdoor recreation planning, planning and technical assistance for the national wild and scenic rivers system, the national trails system, natural area programs, the National Register of Historic Places, national historic landmarks, historic preservation, technical preservation services, the historic American buildings survey, the historic American engineering record, and interagency archeological services.

Regional Offices—National Park Service

Regions	Address	Telephone
ALASKA—AK	Suite 114, 240 West 5th Ave., Anchorage, AK 99501	907–644–3510
INTERMOUNTAIN—AZ, CO, MT, NM, OK, TX, UT, WY	P.O. Box 25287, 12795 W. Alameda Pkwy., Denver, CO 80225–0287	303–969–2500
MIDWEST—AR, IL, IN, IA, KS, MI, MN, MO, ND, NE, OH, SD, WI	601 Riverfront Dr., Omaha, NE 68102–4226	402–661–1736
NATIONAL CAPITAL—Washington, DC, and nearby MD, VA, and WV	1100 Ohio Dr. SW., Washington, DC 20242–0001	202–619–7000
NORTHEAST—CT, DE, ME, MA, MD, NH, NJ, NY, PA, RI, VT, VA, WV	5th Fl., 200 Chestnut St., Philadelphia, PA 19106–2818	215–597–7013
PACIFIC WEST—CA, HI, ID, NV, OR, WA, American Samoa, Guam	Suite 700, 1111 Jackson St., Oakland, CA 94607–1372	510–817–1304
SOUTHEAST—AL, FL, GA, KY, LA, MS, NC, SC, TN, PR, VI	1924 Bldg., 100 Alabama St. SW., Atlanta, GA 30303	404–507–5600

For further information, contact the Chief, Office of Communications and Public Affairs, National Park Service, Department of the Interior, 1849 C Street NW., Washington, DC 20240. Phone, 202–208–6843. Internet, www.nps.gov.

United States Geological Survey

The U.S. Geological Survey (USGS) was established by the Organic Act of March 3, 1879 (43 U.S.C. 31). USGS classifies public lands, examines the geological structure, and assesses the energy, mineral, water, and biology resources and products within and outside the national domain.

USGS provides relevant, objective scientific studies and information used to help address issues and solve problems dealing with natural resources, natural hazards, and the environmental effects on human and wildlife health. It is responsible for:

—investigating and assessing the Nation's water, energy, biological, and mineral resources;

—conducting research on global change;

—providing information to land and resource managers in the Department to help them assess and manage the biological and environmental consequences of management practices;

—investigating natural hazards and providing real-time information about the Earth and minimizing loss of life and property from earthquakes, volcanoes, floods, droughts, landslides, coastal erosion, and wildland fires;

—maintaining an archive of land-remote sensing data for historical, scientific, and technical purposes, including long-term global environmental monitoring;

—ensuring production and availability of basic biologic, hydrologic, geologic, geographic, and geospatial data of the Nation; and

—maintaining and analyzing databases of natural resource information.

To attain these objectives, USGS prepares maps and digital and cartographic data; collects and interprets data on energy, mineral, and biological resources; conducts nationwide assessments of the quality, quantity, and use of the Nation's water resources; performs fundamental and applied research in the sciences and techniques involved; and publishes the results of its investigations through maps, technical reports, and fact sheets.

For further information, contact the U.S. Geological Survey, Department of the Interior, 12201 Sunrise Valley Drive, Reston, VA 20192. Phone, 703–648–4000. Internet, www.usgs.gov. Email, ASK@usgs.gov.

Office of Surface Mining Reclamation and Enforcement

The Office of Surface Mining Reclamation and Enforcement (OSM) was established in the Department of the Interior by the Surface Mining Control and Reclamation Act of 1977 (30 U.S.C. 1211).

The Office's primary goal is to assist States in operating a nationwide program that protects society and the environment from the adverse effects of coal mining, while ensuring that surface coal mining can be done without permanent damage to land and water resources. With most coal mining States responsible for regulating coal mining and reclamation activities within their borders, OSM's main objectives are to oversee State mining regulatory and abandoned-mine reclamation programs, assist States in meeting the objectives of the surface mining law, and regulate mining and reclamation activities on Federal and Indian lands, and in those States choosing not to assume primary responsibility.

Activities   The Office establishes national policy for the surface mining control and reclamation program provided for in the surface mining law, reviews and approves amendments to previously approved State programs, and reviews and recommends approval of new State program submissions. Other activities include:

—managing the collection, disbursement, and accounting for abandoned-mine land reclamation fees;

—administering civil penalties programs;

—establishing technical standards and regulatory policy for reclamation and enforcement efforts;

—providing guidance for environmental considerations, research, training, and technology transfer for State, tribal, and Federal regulatory and abandoned-mine land reclamation programs; and

—monitoring and evaluating State and tribal regulatory programs, cooperative agreements, and abandoned-mine land reclamation programs.

For further information, contact the Office of Communications, Office of Surface Mining Reclamation and Enforcement, Department of the Interior, Washington, DC 20240. Phone, 202–208–2565. TDD, 202–208–2694. Internet, www.osmre.gov.

Bureau of Indian Affairs

The Bureau of Indian Affairs (BIA) was created as part of the War Department in 1824 and transferred to the Department of the Interior when the latter was established in 1849. The mission of BIA is to fulfill its trust responsibilities and promote self-determination on behalf of federally recognized tribal governments, American Indians, and Alaska Natives. BIA provides services directly or through contracts, grants, or compacts to approximately 1.9 million American Indians and Alaska Natives, members of 562 federally recognized Indian tribes in the 48 contiguous United States and Alaska.

The scope of BIA's programs is extensive, covering virtually the entire range of State and local governmental services. The programs administered by either tribes or BIA include: management of natural resources on 56 million acres of trust land, fire protection, emergency natural disaster relief, economic development programs in some of the most isolated and economically depressed areas of the United States, law enforcement, administration of tribal courts and detention centers, implementation of legislated land and water claim settlements, building, repair, and maintenance of roads and bridges, repair and maintenance of high-hazard dams, and operation of irrigation systems and agricultural programs on Federal Indian lands.

BIA works with American Indian and Alaska Native tribal governments and organizations, other Federal agencies, State and local governments, and other groups interested in the development and implementation of effective programs.

Regional Offices—Bureau of Indian Affairs

Region	Address	Telephone
Alaska	P.O. Box 25520, Juneau, AK 99802–5520	800–645–8397
Eastern	545 Marriott Dr., Suite 700, Nashville, TN 37214	615–564–6700
Eastern Oklahoma	P.O. Box 8002, 3100 W. Peak Blvd., Muskogee, OK 74402–8002	918–781–4600
Great Plains	115 4th Ave. SE., Aberdeen, SD 57401–4382	605–226–7343
Midwest	One Federal Dr., Rm. 550, Ft. Snelling, MN 55111–4007	612–713–4400
Navajo	P.O. Box 1060, Gallup, NM 87305	505–863–8314
Northwest	911 NE. 11th Ave., Portland, OR 97232–4169	503–231–6702
Pacific	2800 Cottage Way, Sacramento, CA 95825	916–978–6000
Rocky Mountain	316 N. 26th St., Billings, MT 59101–1362	406–247–7943
Southern Plains	WCD Office Complex, P.O. Box 368, Anadarko, OK 73005–0368	405–247–6673
Southwest	P.O. Box 26567, 1001 Indian School Rd. NW., Albuquerque, NM 87104–2303.	505–563–3100
Western	2 Arizona Center, 12th Flr., 400 N. 5th St., Phoenix, AZ 85004–0010	602–379–6600

Bureau of Indian Education

The Bureau of Indian Education (BIE), formerly known as the Office of Indian Education Programs, provides quality educational opportunities for eligible American Indian and Alaska Native elementary, secondary, and post-secondary students from the federally recognized tribes. BIE is responsible for the direction and management of all education functions, including the formation of policies and procedures, the supervision of all program activities, and the approval of expenditure of funds appropriated for education functions.

There are 183 elementary and secondary schools within the BIE system serving approximately 48,000 students. Of these schools, 59 are BIE-operated and 124 are tribally controlled through BIE contracts or grants. BIE also supports 26 tribal colleges and universities in the continental U.S. and directly operates Haskell Indian Nations University in Lawrence, KS, and the Southwest Indian Polytechnic Institute in Albuquerque, NM.

For further information, contact the Office of the Assistant Secretary for Indian Affairs, Office of Public Affairs, Department of the Interior, 1849 C Street NW., MS–3658–MIB, Washington, DC 20240. Phone, 202–208–3710.

Minerals Management Service

The Minerals Management Service was established on January 19, 1982, by Secretarial order. The Service assesses the nature, extent, recoverability, and value of leasable minerals on the Outer Continental Shelf. It ensures the orderly and timely inventory and development and the efficient recovery of mineral resources; encourages utilization of the best available and safest technology; and safeguards against fraud, waste, and abuse.

Offshore Energy and Minerals Management The Service is responsible for resource assessment and evaluation; environmental review; leasing and permitting activities (including public liaison and planning functions), management of leases, easements, and rights-of-way; and inspection and enforcement programs for Outer Continental Shelf lands.

Programs are developed for energy, including renewable energy, mineral, and related activities on the Outer Continental Shelf in consultation with the Congress, affected States, local governments, environmental groups, industry, and the public.

The Service conducts extensive environmental studies and consultations with State officials prior to issuing leases, easements, or rights-of-way. Once permits or other approvals have been issued, inspectors conduct frequent inspections of offshore operations, and environmental studies personnel collect data to ensure that marine and coastal environments are kept free of pollutants.

Minerals Revenue Management The Service is responsible for collecting, accounting for, and disbursing revenues associated with minerals produced on Federal and Indian-leased lands. The Service also conducts a comprehensive compliance program to ensure that fair market value is received for the mineral assets and that royalties are timely and accurately paid.

The basic organization of the Service consists of a headquarters in Washington, DC, with program components located in Herndon, VA, and Lakewood, CO; three Outer Continental Shelf regional offices; and two administrative service centers.

Field Offices—Minerals Management Service

Office	Address	Telephone
Minerals Revenue Management	P.O. Box 25165, Denver, CO 80225–0165	303–231–3162
OCS Regional Offices		
Alaska Region	Suite 500, 3801 Centerpoint Dr., Anchorage, AK 99503–5820	907–334–5200
Gulf of Mexico Region	1201 Elmwood Park Blvd., New Orleans, LA 70123–2394	504–736–2589
Pacific Region	770 Paseo Camarillo, Camarillo, CA 93010–6064	805–389–7502
Administrative Service Centers		
Western Service Center	P.O. Box 25165, Denver, CO 80225–0165	303–231–3900
Southern Service Center	1201 Elmwood Park Blvd., New Orleans, LA 70123–2394	504–736–2616

For further information, contact the Chief, Public Affairs, Minerals Management Service, Department of the Interior, Room 5417, (MS 5438), 1849 C Street NW., Washington, DC 20240–7000. Phone, 202–208–3985. Internet, www.mms.gov.

Bureau of Land Management

The Bureau of Land Management was established July 16, 1946, by the consolidation of the General Land Office (created in 1812) and the Grazing Service (formed in 1934).

The Bureau manages more land—256 million surface acres—than any other Federal Government agency. Most of this public land is located in 12 western States, including Alaska. There are also small, scattered parcels in States east of the Mississippi River. The Bureau also administers more than 700 million acres of subsurface mineral estate throughout the Nation. These public lands make up about 13 percent of the total land surface of the United States and more than 40 percent of all land managed by the Federal Government. The Bureau preserves open space in the fast-growing, fast-changing West by managing the public lands for multiple uses and by conserving resources so that current and future generations may use and enjoy them.

Resources managed by the Bureau include timber, solid minerals, oil and gas, geothermal energy, wildlife habitat, endangered plant and animal species, rangeland vegetation, recreation and cultural values, wild and scenic rivers, designated conservation and wilderness areas, and open space. Bureau programs provide for the protection (including fire suppression), orderly development, and use of the public lands and resources under principles of multiple use and sustained yield. Land use plans are developed with public involvement to provide orderly use and development while maintaining and enhancing the quality of the environment. The Bureau also manages watersheds to protect soil and enhance water quality; develops recreational opportunities on public lands; administers programs to protect and manage wild horses and burros; and under certain conditions, makes land available for sale to individuals, organizations, local governments, and other Federal agencies when such transfer is in the public interest. Lands may be leased to State and local government agencies and to nonprofit organizations for certain purposes.

The Bureau oversees and manages the development of energy and mineral leases and ensures compliance with applicable regulations governing the extraction of these resources. It has responsibility to issue rights-of-way, leases, and permits.

The Bureau is also responsible for the survey of Federal lands and establishes and maintains public land records and mining claims records. It administers a program of payments in lieu of taxes based on the amount of federally owned lands in counties and other units of local government.

Field Offices—Bureau of Land Management

State Office	Address	Telephone
Alaska—AK	No. 13, 222 W. 7th Ave., Anchorage, 99513–7599	907–271–5080
Arizona—AZ	One N. Central Ave., Phoenix, 85004–4427	602–417–9200
California—CA	Suite W–1834, 2800 Cottage Way, Sacramento, 95825–0451.	916–978–4600
Colorado—CO	2850 Youngfield St., Lakewood, 80215–7093	303–239–3700
Eastern States—All States bordering on and east of the Mississippi River.	7450 Boston Blvd., Springfield, VA 22153–1711	703–440–1711
Idaho—ID	1387 S. Vinnell Way, Boise, 83709–1657	208–373–4001
Montana—MT, ND, SD	P.O. Box 36800, 5001 Southgate Dr., Billings, MT 59101–6800.	406–896–5012
Nevada—NV	P.O. Box 12000, 1340 Financial Way, Reno, 89502–0006	775–861–6590
New Mexico—KS, NM, OK, TX	P.O. Box 27115, 1474 Rodeo Rd., Santa Fe, NM 87502–0115.	505–438–7501
Oregon—OR, WA	P.O. Box 2965, 333 SW. 1st Ave., Portland, OR	503–808–6026
Utah—UT	P.O. Box 45155, Salt Lake City, 84145–0155	801–539–4001
Utah—UT	Suite 500, 440 W. 200 South, Salt Lake City, 84101	801–539–4001
Wyoming—NE, WY	P.O. Box 1828, 5353 Yellowstone Rd., Cheyenne, WY 82003.	307–775–6001
Service and Support Offices		
National Interagency Fire Center (NIFC)	3833 S. Development Ave., Boise, ID 83705–5354	208–387–5446
National Training Center	9828 N. 31st Ave., Phoenix, AZ 85051–2517	602–906–5500
National Operations Center	Bldg. 50, P.O. Box 25047, Denver, CO 80225–0047	303–236–8857
Washington Office Headquarters Directorate	1849 C St. NW., Washington, DC 20240	202–452–7732
National Law Enforcement Office	1849 C St. NW., Washington, DC 20240	202–208–3269

For further information, contact the Office of Public Affairs, **Bureau of Land Management, Department of the Interior**, LS–406, 1849 C Street NW., Washington, DC 20240. Phone, 202–452–5125. Internet, www.blm.gov.

Bureau of Reclamation

The Bureau of Reclamation was established pursuant to the Reclamation Act of 1902 (43 U.S.C. 371 *et seq.*). The Bureau is the largest wholesale water supplier and the second largest producer of hydroelectric power in the United States, with operations and facilities in the 17 Western States. Its facilities also provide substantial flood control, recreation, and fish and wildlife benefits.

Major Offices—Bureau of Reclamation

Office/Region	Address	Telephone
Commissioner	Rm. 7657, Dept. of the Interior, Washington, DC 20240–0001.	202–513–0575
Denver Office	Bldg. 67, Box 25007, Denver, CO 80225	303–445–2797
Great Plains Region	Box 36900, 316 N. 26th St., Billings, MT 59107	406–247–7610
Lower Colorado Region	Box 61470, Boulder City, NV 89006–1470	702–293–8421
Mid-Pacific Region	2800 Cottage Way, Sacramento, CA 95825	916–978–5100
Pacific Northwest Region	1150 N. Curtis Rd., Boise, ID 83706	208–378–5020
Upper Colorado Region	Rm. 6107, 125 S. State St., Salt Lake City, UT 84138	801–524–3793

For further information, contact the Public Affairs Office, Bureau of Reclamation, Department of the Interior, Washington, DC 20240–0001. Phone, 202–513–0575. Internet, www.usbr.gov.

Sources of Information

Inquiries on the following subjects should be directed to the specified office, Department of the Interior, Washington, DC 20240.

Contracts   Contact the Office of Acquisition and Property Management, Room 2607. Phone, 202–208–6352.

Electronic Access   Information is available electronically from the Department of the Interior. Internet, www.doi.gov (or see listings for specific Department components).

Employment   Direct general inquiries to the Personnel Liaison Staff, 202–208–6702, the personnel office of a specific bureau or office, or visit any of the field personnel offices.

Museum   The Interior Museum presents exhibits on the history and mission of the Department. Programs highlight Bureau management of cultural and natural resources. The museum staff coordinates tours of the art and architecture of the Interior building. For more information, contact the museum staff or visit our Web site. Phone, 202–208–4743. Internet, www.doi.gov/interiormuseum.

Library   The Interior Library is a research level collection that covers the broad range of matters related to the Department's mission. Specific collections include departmental publications, a selective depository of Federal documents, a wide array of electronic information sources available through the library Web site, a comprehensive law collection, an extensive periodical collection, and a rare book collection consisting of 19th-century monographs on Native Americans, American history, and zoology. For more information contact the library staff or visit our Web site. Phone, 202–208–5815. Internet, http://library.doi.gov.

Reading Room   Visit the Department of the Interior Library, Main Interior Building. Phone, 202–208–5815.

Employee Locator   To locate an employee of the Department of the Interior, call 202–208–3100.

United States Fish and Wildlife Service

Inquiries on the following subjects should be directed to the specified office, U.S. Fish and Wildlife Service, Department of the Interior, 1849 C Street NW., Washington, DC 20240.

Congressional/Legislative Services   Congressional staffers and persons seeking information about specific legislation should call the Congressional/Legislative Services Office. Phone, 703–358–2240.

Contracts   Contact the Washington, DC, headquarters Division of Contracting and General Services (phone, 703–358–1728) or any of the regional offices.

Electronic Access   The Fish and Wildlife Service offers a range of information through the Internet at www.fws.gov.

Employment For information regarding employment opportunities with the U.S. Fish and Wildlife Service, contact the Headquarters Personnel Office (phone, 703–358–1743) or the regional office within the area you are seeking employment.

Import/Export Permits To obtain CITES permits for importing and exporting wildlife, contact the Office of Management Authority. Phone, 800–358–2104 or 703–358–2104.

Law Enforcement To obtain information about the enforcement of wildlife laws or to report an infraction of those laws, contact the Division of Law Enforcement (phone, 703–358–1949) or the nearest regional law enforcement office.

National Wildlife Refuges For general information about the National Wildlife Refuge System, as well as information about specific refuges, contact the Division of Refuges (phone, 703–358–2029) or the nearest national wildlife refuge or regional refuge office.

News Media Inquiries Specific information about the U.S. Fish and Wildlife Service and its activities is available from the Office of Public Affairs (phone, 703–358–2220) or the public affairs officer in each of the Service's regional offices.

Publications The U.S. Fish and Wildlife Service has publications available on subjects ranging from the National Wildlife Refuge System to endangered species. Some publications are only available as sales items from the Superintendent of Documents, Government Printing Office, Washington, DC 20402. Further information is available from the Publications Unit, U.S. Fish and Wildlife Service, Mail Stop NCTC Washington, DC 20240. Phone, 800–344–9453.

National Park Service

Contracts Contact the nearest regional office; Administrative Services Division, National Park Service, 1849 C Street NW., Washington, DC 20240 (phone, 202–354–1950); or the Denver Service Center, P.O. Box 25287, 12795 West

Alameda Parkway, Denver, CO 80225 (phone, 303–969–2100).

Employment Employment inquiries and applications may be sent to the Human Resources Office, National Park Service, Department of the Interior, Washington, DC, and to the regional offices and individual parks. Applications for temporary employment should be sent to the Division of Human Resources, National Park Service, 1849 C Street NW., Washington, DC 20240. Phone, 202–354–1927. Schools interested in the recruitment program should write to: Chief Human Resources Officer, National Park Service, 1849 C Street NW., Washington, DC 20240. Phone, 202–354–1927.

Grants For information on grants authorized under the Land and Water Conservation Fund and the Urban Park and Recreation Recovery Program, contact the National Park Service, 1849 C Street NW., Washington, DC 20240. Phone, 202–354–6900. For information on grants authorized under the Historic Preservation Fund, contact the National Park Service, 1849 C Street NW., Washington, DC 20240. Phone, 202–354–2067.

Publications Items related to the National Park Service are available from the Superintendent of Documents, Government Printing Office, Washington, DC 20401. Phone, 202–512–1800. Items available for sale include the *National Park System Map and Guide* (stock no. 024–005–01135–8); *The National Parks: Index 2001–2003* (stock no. 024–005–01209–5); and *National Parks: Lesser Known Areas* (stock no. 024–005–01152–8). Contact the Consumer Information Center, Pueblo, CO 81009, for other publications about the National Park Service available for sale. For general park and camping information, write to the National Park Service, Office of Public Inquiries, 1849 C Street NW., Washington, DC 20240.

United States Geological Survey

Contracts, Grants, and Cooperative Agreements Write to the Office of Acquisition and Grants, 12201 Sunrise

Valley Drive, National Center, Mail Stop 205G, Reston, VA 20192. Phone, 703–648–7485.

Employment   Visit USGS Jobs at www.usgs.gov/ohr/oars/, or contact one of the following Personnel Offices:

USGS Headquarters Human Resources Office, 12201 Sunrise Valley Drive, Mail Stop 601, Reston, VA 20192. Phone, 703–648–7405.

USGS Eastern Region Human Resources Office, 12201 Sunrise Valley Drive, Mail Stop 157, Reston, VA 20192 (phone, 703–648–7470) or 3850 Holcomb Bridge Road, Suite 160, Norcross, GA 30092 (phone, 770–409–7750).

USGS Central Region Human Resources Office, Mail Stop 603, Box 25046, Denver, CO 80225. Phone, 303–236–9565.

USGS Western Region Human Resources Office, 3020 E. State University Drive, Suite 2001, Sacramento, CA 95819. Phone, 916–278–9400.

Communications   For news media and congressional inquiries, arranging interviews, and obtaining news releases and other informational products pertaining to USGS programs and activities, contact the Office of Communications at:

USGS Headquarters, Office of Communications, National Center, Mail Stop 119, Reston, VA 20192. Phone, 703–648–4460.

USGS Eastern Region, Office of Communications, National Center, Mail Stop 150, Reston, VA 20192. Phone, 703–648–4483.

USGS Central Region, Office of Communications, Box 25046, Denver Federal Center, Denver, CO 80225. Phone, 303–202–4744.

USGS Western Region, Office of Communications, 909 1st Avenue, Suite 704, Seattle, WA 98104. Phone, 206–220–4573.

General Inquiries, Maps, Publications, Scientific Reports, and Water Data   Contact USGS at 888–ASK–USGS, or email ASK@usgs.gov.

Publications and Thematic Maps   USGS scientific publications and thematic maps are available to the public through the USGS Publications Warehouse (pubs.usgs.gov), with more than 61,000 bibliographic citations for USGS reports and thematic maps. USGS technical and scientific reports and maps and nontechnical general interest publications are described in the quarterly online periodical *New Publications of the U.S. Geological Survey* at pubs.usgs.gov/publications.

Maps and Reports   Customers can now browse and purchase online thousands of USGS maps and reports. The USGS Store (store.usgs.gov) is an online catalog that presents thumbnail images of more than 58,000 topographic maps along with larger images of other selected maps.

Water Data   Information on the availability of and access to water data acquired by the USGS and other local, State, and Federal agencies can be obtained by calling USGS. Phone, 888–ASK–USGS. Internet, water.usgs.gov.

Maps, Aerial Photographs, Geodetic Control Data or Index Material, Digital Cartographic Data, and USGS Products Purchases   Write to or visit the following network of USGS Earth Science Information Centers:

Alaska—4230 University Drive, Rm. 101, Anchorage, 99508–4664. Phone, 907–786–7011.

California—345 Middlefield Road, Bldg. 3, Rm. 3128, Menlo Park, 94025. Phone, 650–329–4309.

Colorado—Denver Federal Center, Bldg. 810, Box 25286, Denver, 80225. Phone, 303–202–4200.

Missouri—1400 Independence Road, Mail Stop 231, Rolla, 65401. Phone, 573–308–3500.

South Dakota—EROS Data Center, Sioux Falls, 57198 (also for spacecraft and aircraft remote sensing data). Phone, 605–594–6151.

Virginia—12201 Sunrise Valley Drive, Rm. 1C100, Reston, 20192. Phone, 703–648–5953.

Libraries and Reading Rooms   Reports, maps, publications, and a variety of Earth and biological information resources and historical documents are available through the USGS library system. Locations, directions, and resources are available at www.usgs.gov/library. Online reference assistance is available through Ask-A-Librarian at http://library.usgs.gov/ext_request.html. The main USGS libraries are located in the following States:

Arizona—2255 N. Gemini Drive, Bldg. 6, Rm. 670, Flagstaff, 86001

California—345 Middlefield Road, Bldg. 15 Foyer, Menlo Park, 94025–3591.

Colorado—Denver Federal Center, Bldg. 20, Rm. C–2002, Denver, 80225–0046.

Virginia—12201 Sunrise Valley Drive, Rm. 1D100, Reston 20192.

Office of Surface Mining Reclamation and Enforcement

Contracts   Contact the Procurement Branch, Office of Surface Mining, Department of the Interior, 1951 Constitution Avenue NW., Washington, DC 20240. Phone, 202–208–2839. TDD, 202–208–2737.

Employment   For information on OSM employment opportunities throughout the United States, go to the jobs Web site, at https://jobs.quickhire.com/scripts/smart.exe.

Bureau of Indian Affairs and Bureau of Indian Education

Inquiries regarding Indian Affairs programs, including those of the Bureau of Indian Affairs and the Bureau of Indian Education, may be obtained from the Office of the Assistant Secretary for Indian Affairs, Office of Public Affairs, Department of the Interior, 1849 C Street NW., MS–3658–MIB, Washington, DC 20240. Phone, 202–208–3710.

Minerals Management Service

Information about the Minerals Management Service and its activities is available from the Chief, Public Affairs, Department of the Interior, 1849 C Street NW., Room 5417, MS 5438, Washington, DC 20240. Phone, 202–208–3985.

Bureau of Land Management

Contracts The Bureau of Land Management (BLM) and the Department of the Interior (DOI) are now acquiring goods and services through the Internet Web site at http://ideasec.nbc.gov. To take advantage of future business opportunities with BLM, you must (1) obtain a valid Dun & Bradstreet number from Dun & Bradstreet at www.dnb.com, or by calling them at 800–333–0505; or (2) register your firm on the Central Contractor Registration System at www.ccr.gov.

Also, for information about BLM's purchases, how to do business with BLM, and the BLM acquisition offices and contacts, visit the BLM National Acquisition Web site at www.blm.gov/natacq. You may also view BLM's projected purchases of goods and services, known as the Advanced Procurement Plan.

Employment Inquiries should be directed to the National Operations Center Division of Human Resources Services, any Bureau of Land Management State Office, or the Washington Office Human Resources Branch, Department of the Interior, Washington, DC. Phone, 202–452–5072.

General Inquiries For information about parcels of land that the Bureau occasionally sells, contact any of the State offices or the Bureau of Land Management, Office of Public Affairs, Department of the Interior, Washington, DC 20240. Phone, 202–452–5125. Fax, 202–452–5124.

Publications The annual publication *Public Land Statistics,* which relates to public lands, is available from the Superintendent of Documents, Government Printing Office, Washington, DC 20402.

Reading Rooms All State offices provide facilities for individuals who wish to examine status records, tract books, or other records relating to the public lands and their resources.

Small Business Activities The Bureau has three major buying offices that provide contacts for small business activities: the Headquarters Office in Washington, DC (phone, 202–452–5177); the national operations center in Lakewood, CO (phone, 303–236–9436); and the Oregon State office (phone, 503–808–6216). The acquisition plan and procurement office contacts are available through the Internet at www.blm.gov/natacq.

Speakers Local Bureau offices will arrange for speakers to explain Bureau programs upon request from organizations within their areas of jurisdiction.

Bureau of Reclamation

Contracts Information is available to contractors, manufacturers, and suppliers from Acquisition and Assistance Management Division, Building 67, Denver Federal Center, Denver, CO 80225. Phone, 303–445–2431. Internet, www.fedbizopps.gov.

Employment Information on engineering and other positions is available from the Diversity and Human Resources Office, Denver, CO (phone, 303–445–2684) or from the nearest regional office. Internet, www.usajobs.opm.gov.

Publications   Publications for sale are available through the National Technical Information Service. Phone, 703–605–6585.

For further information, contact the U.S. Department of the Interior, 1849 C Street NW., Washington, DC 20240. Phone, 202–208–3100. Internet, www.doi.gov.

DEPARTMENT OF JUSTICE

950 Pennsylvania Avenue NW., Washington, DC 20530
Phone, 202–514–2000. Internet, www.usdoj.gov.

THE ATTORNEY GENERAL	ERIC HOLDER
DEPUTY ATTORNEY GENERAL	DAVID W. OGDEN
Chief of Staff	KEVIN A. OHLSON
Associate Attorney General	THOMAS J. PERRELLI
Senior Counsel, Office of Dispute Resolution	JOANNA M. JACOBS, *Acting*
Solicitor General	ELENA KAGAN
Inspector General	GLENN A. FINE
Assistant Attorney General, Office of Legal Counsel	DAVID BARRON, *Acting*
Assistant Attorney General, Office of Legislative Affairs	FAITH BURTON, *Acting*
Assistant Attorney General, Office of Legal Policy	KEVIN JONES, *Acting*
Assistant Attorney General for Administration, Justice Management Division	LEE LOFTUS
Assistant Attorney General, Antitrust Division	CHRISTINE A. VARNEY
Assistant Attorney General, Civil Division	D. ANTHONY WEST
Assistant Attorney General, Civil Rights Division	LORETTA KING, *Acting*
Assistant Attorney General, Criminal Division	LANNY A. BREUER
Assistant Attorney General, National Security Division	DAVID KRIS
Assistant Attorney General, Environment and Natural Resources Division	JOHN CRUDEN, *Acting*
Assistant Attorney General, Tax Division	JOHN DICICCO, *Acting*
Assistant Attorney General, Office of Justice Programs	LAURIE ROBINSON, *Acting*
Director, Office of Public Affairs	MATTHEW MILLER
Director, Office of Information and Privacy	MELANIE ANN PUSTAY
Director, Office of Intergovernmental and Public Liaison	(VACANCY)
Director, Executive Office for U.S. Attorneys	H. MARSHALL JARRETT
Director, Bureau of Prisons	HARLEY G. LAPPIN
Director, Federal Bureau of Investigation	ROBERT S. MUELLER III
Director, United States Marshals Service	JOHN F. CLARK
Director, Bureau of Alcohol, Tobacco, Firearms, and Explosives	KENNETH E. MELSON, *Acting*
Director, Executive Office for Immigration Review	THOMAS G. SNOW, *Acting*
Director, Executive Office for United States Trustees	CLIFFORD J. WHITE III
Director, Community Relations Service	ONDRAY T. HARRIS
Director, Community Oriented Policing Services	TIMOTHY QUINN, *Acting*
Director, Office on Violence Against Women	CATHERINE PIERCE, *Acting*

253

Administrator, Drug Enforcement Administration	MICHELE LEONHART, *Acting*
Chairman, United States Parole Commission	EDWARD F. REILLY, JR.
Chairman, Foreign Claims Settlement Commission	MAURICIO J. TAMARGO
Chief, INTERPOL–U.S. National Central Bureau	MARTIN RENKIEWICZ
Counsel, Office of Professional Responsibility	MARY PATRICE BROWN, *Acting*
Director, Professional Responsibility Advisory Office	JERRI U. DUNSTON
Pardon Attorney	RONALD L. RODGERS
Director, National Drug Intelligence Center	MICHAEL F. WALTHER
Trustee, Office of the Federal Detention Trustee	STACIA HYLTON

[For the Department of Justice statement of organization, see the *Code of Federal Regulations,* Title 28, Chapter I, Part 0]

The Department of Justice serves as counsel for its citizens. It represents them in enforcing the law in the public interest. Through its thousands of lawyers, investigators, and agents, the Department plays the key role in protection against criminals and subversion, ensuring healthy business competition, safeguarding the consumer, and enforcing drug, immigration, and naturalization laws.

The Department of Justice was established by act of June 22, 1870 (28 U.S.C. 501, 503, 509 note), with the Attorney General as its head. The affairs and activities of the Department of Justice are generally directed by the Attorney General.

Attorney General   The Attorney General represents the United States in legal matters generally and gives advice and opinions to the President and to the heads of the executive departments of the Government when so requested. The Attorney General appears in person to represent the Government before the U.S. Supreme Court in cases of exceptional gravity or importance.

Community Relations Service   The Service offers assistance to communities in resolving disputes relating to race, color, or national origin and facilitates the development of viable agreements as alternatives to coercion, violence, or litigation. It also assists and supports communities in developing local mechanisms as proactive measures to prevent or reduce racial/ethnic tensions.

For further information, contact any regional office or the Director, Community Relations Service, Department of Justice, Suite 2000, 600 E Street NW., Washington, DC 20530. Phone, 202–305–2935.

Regional Offices—Community Relations Service

Address	Director	Phone/FTS
Atlanta, GA (75 Piedmont Ave. NE., 30303)	Thomas Battles	404–331–6883
Boston, MA (Suite 222, 308 Atlantic Ave., 02201)	Frank Amoroso	617–424–5715
Chicago, IL (230 S. Dearborn Ave., 60604)	Jesse Taylor	312–353–4391
Dallas, TX (1420 W. Mockingbird Ln., 75247)	Carmelita Freeman	214–655–8175
Denver, CO (1244 Speer Blvd., 80204–3584)	Philip Arreola	303–844–2973
Kansas City, MO (1100 Main St., 64105–2112)	Pascal Marquez	816–426–7434
Los Angeles, CA (888 S. Figuera St., 90017)	Ron Wakabayashi	213–894–2941
New York, NY (26 Federal Plz., 10278)	Reinaldo Rivera	212–264–0700
Philadelphia, PA (2d & Chestnut Sts., 19106)	(vacancy)	215–597–2344
Seattle, WA (915 2d Ave., 98101)	Rosa Melendez	206–220–6700

Pardon Attorney   The Office of the Pardon Attorney assists the President in the exercise of his pardon power under the Constitution. Generally, all requests for pardon or other forms of executive clemency, including commutation of

DEPARTMENT OF JUSTICE

ATTORNEY GENERAL

DEPUTY ATTORNEY GENERAL

SOLICITOR GENERAL

ASSOCIATE ATTORNEY GENERAL

OFFICE OF THE SOLICITOR GENERAL

OFFICE OF JUSTICE PROGRAMS

EXECUTIVE OFFICE FOR UNITED STATES TRUSTEES

OFFICE OF DISPUTE RESOLUTION

COMMUNITY ORIENTED POLICING SERVICES

OFFICE OF INFORMATION AND PRIVACY

FOREIGN CLAIMS SETTLEMENT COMMISSION

OFFICE ON VIOLENCE AGAINST WOMEN

CIVIL RIGHTS DIVISION

ANTITRUST DIVISION

TAX DIVISION

CIVIL DIVISION

ENVIRONMENT AND NATURAL RESOURCES DIVISION

COMMUNITY RELATIONS SERVICE

OFFICE OF LEGAL POLICY

OFFICE OF LEGISLATIVE AFFAIRS

OFFICE OF INTER-GOVERNMENTAL AND PUBLIC LIAISON

OFFICE OF PUBLIC AFFAIRS

OFFICE OF LEGAL COUNSEL

FEDERAL BUREAU OF INVESTIGATION

DRUG ENFORCEMENT ADMINISTRATION

EXECUTIVE OFFICE FOR UNITED STATES ATTORNEYS

UNITED STATES ATTORNEYS

BUREAU OF ALCOHOL, TOBACCO, FIREARMS, AND EXPLOSIVES

CRIMINAL DIVISION

BUREAU OF PRISONS

UNITED STATES MARSHALS SERVICE

U.S. NATIONAL CENTRAL BUREAU-INTERPOL

OFFICE OF THE FEDERAL DETENTION TRUSTEE

NATIONAL SECURITY DIVISION

OFFICE OF THE INSPECTOR GENERAL

JUSTICE MANAGEMENT DIVISION

EXECUTIVE OFFICE FOR IMMIGRATION REVIEW

OFFICE OF PROFESSIONAL RESPONSIBILITY

OFFICE OF THE PARDON ATTORNEY

UNITED STATES PAROLE COMMISSION

NATIONAL DRUG INTELLIGENCE CENTER

PROFESSIONAL RESPONSIBILITY ADVISORY OFFICE

sentences, are directed to the Pardon Attorney for investigation and review. The Pardon Attorney prepares the Department's recommendation to the President for final disposition of each application.

For further information, contact the Office of the Pardon Attorney, Department of Justice, Suite 1100, 1425 New York Avenue NW., Washington, DC 20530. Phone, 202–616–6070. Internet, www.usdoj.gov/pardon.

Solicitor General The Office of the Solicitor General represents the U.S. Government in cases before the Supreme Court. It decides what cases the Government should ask the Supreme Court to review and what position the Government should take in cases before the Court. It also supervises the preparation of the Government's Supreme Court briefs and other legal documents and the conduct of the oral arguments in the Court. The Solicitor General also decides whether the United States should appeal in all cases it loses before the lower courts.

For further information, contact the Executive Officer, Office of the Solicitor General, Room 5142, 950 Pennsylvania Avenue NW., RFK Justice Building (Main), Washington, DC 20530–0001.

U.S. Attorneys The Executive Office for U.S. Attorneys was created on April 6, 1953, to provide liaison between the Department of Justice in Washington, DC, and the U.S. attorneys. Its mission is to provide general executive assistance to the 94 offices of the U.S. attorneys and to coordinate the relationship between the U.S. attorneys and the organization components of the Department of Justice and other Federal agencies.

For further information, contact the Executive Office for United States Attorneys, Department of Justice, Room 2261, 950 Pennsylvania Avenue NW., Washington, DC 20530. Phone, 202–514–1020. Internet, www.usdoj.gov/usao/eousa.

U.S. Trustee Program The Program was established by the Bankruptcy Reform Act of 1978 (11 U.S.C. 101 *et seq.*) as a pilot effort in 10 regions encompassing 18 Federal judicial districts to promote the efficiency and protect the integrity of the bankruptcy system by identifying and helping to investigate bankruptcy fraud and abuse. It now operates nationwide except in Alabama and North Carolina. The Bankruptcy Abuse Prevention and Consumer Protection Act of 2005 (11 U.S.C. 101 note) significantly expanded the Program's responsibilities and provided additional tools to combat bankruptcy fraud and abuse. The Executive Office for U.S. Trustees provides day-to-day policy and legal direction, coordination, and control.

For further information, contact the Executive Office for U.S. Trustees, Department of Justice, Suite 8000, 20 Massachusetts Avenue NW., Washington, DC 20530. Phone, 202–307–1391. Internet, www.usdoj.gov/ust.

Divisions

Antitrust Division

The Assistant Attorney General in charge of the Antitrust Division is responsible for promoting and maintaining competitive markets by enforcing the Federal antitrust laws. This involves investigating possible antitrust violations, conducting grand jury proceedings, reviewing proposed mergers and acquisitions, preparing and trying antitrust cases, prosecuting appeals, and negotiating and enforcing final judgments. The Division prosecutes serious and willful violations of antitrust laws by filing criminal suits that can lead to large fines and jail sentences. Where criminal prosecution is not appropriate, the Division seeks a court order forbidding future violations of the law and requiring steps by the defendant to remedy the anticompetitive effects of past violations.

The Division also is responsible for acting as an advocate of competition within the Federal Government as well as internationally. This involves formal appearances in Federal administrative agency proceedings, development of legislative initiatives to promote deregulation and eliminate unjustifiable exemptions from the antitrust laws, and participation on executive branch policy task forces and in multilateral international organizations. The Division provides formal advice to other agencies on the competitive implications of proposed transactions requiring Federal approval, such as mergers of financial institutions.

For further information, contact the FOIA Unit, Antitrust Division, Department of Justice, 325 Seventh Street NW., Washington, DC 20530. Phone, 202–514–2692.

Civil Division

The Civil Division represents the United States, its departments and agencies, Members of Congress, Cabinet officers, and other Federal employees. Its litigation reflects the diversity of Government activities involving, for example, the defense of challenges to Presidential actions; national security issues; benefit programs; energy policies; commercial issues such as contract disputes, banking, insurance, fraud, and debt collection; all manner of accident and liability claims; and violations of the immigration and consumer protection laws. The Division confronts significant policy issues, which often rise to constitutional dimensions, in defending and enforcing various Federal programs and actions. Each year, Division attorneys handle thousands of cases that collectively involve billions of dollars in claims and recoveries.

The Division litigates cases in the following areas:

—Commercial litigation, litigation associated with the Government's diverse financial involvements including all monetary suits involving contracts, express or implied; actions to foreclose on Government mortgages and liens; bankruptcy and insolvency proceedings; suits against guarantors and sureties; actions involving fraud against the Government, including false or fraudulent claims for Federal insurance, loans, subsidies, and other benefits such as Medicare, false or fraudulent claims for payment under Federal contracts,

whistleblower suits, and Government corruption; patent, copyright, and trademark cases and suits arising out of construction, procurement, service contracts, and claims associated with contract terminations; claims for just compensation under the fifth amendment; claims for salary or retirement by civilian and military personnel; cases assigned by congressional reference or special legislation; and litigation involving interests of the United States in any foreign court, whether civil or criminal in nature.

—Consumer litigation, including civil and criminal litigation and related matters arising under various consumer protection and public health statutes.

—Federal programs, including constitutional challenges to statutes, suits to overturn Government policies and programs, challenges to the legality of Government decisions, allegations that the President has violated the Constitution or Federal law, suits to enforce regulatory statutes and to remedy or prevent statutory or regulatory violations. The areas of litigation include: suits against the heads of Federal departments and agencies and other government officials to enjoin official actions, as well as suits for judicial review of administrative decisions, orders, and regulations; suits involving national security, including suits to protect sensitive intelligence sources and materials; suits to prevent interference with Government operations; litigation concerning the constitutionality of Federal laws; and suits raising employment discrimination claims and Government personnel issues.

—Immigration litigation, involving civil litigation under the Immigration and Nationality Act and related laws; district court litigation, habeas corpus review and general advice; petitions for removal order review and immigration-related appellate matters; cases pertaining to the issuance of visas and passports; and litigation arising under the legalization and employer sanction provisions of the immigration laws.

—Torts, including the broad range of tort litigation arising from the operation of the Federal Government, constitutional tort claims against Federal Government officials throughout the Government, aviation disasters, environmental and occupational disease, and radiation and toxic substance exposure. It defends petitions filed pursuant to the Vaccine Injury Compensation Program and is responsible for administering the Radiation Exposure Compensation Program. It also handles maritime litigation and suits that seek personal monetary judgments against individual officers or employees.

—Appellate, having primary responsibility for the litigation of Civil Division cases in the courts of appeal, and on occasion, State appeal courts. The Appellate Staff prepares Government briefs and presents oral arguments for these cases. Additionally, the Appellate Staff works with the Solicitor General's office to prepare documents filed for these cases in the Supreme Court, including briefs on the merits, petitions for certiorari, and jurisdictional statements. The Appellate Staff also works with the Solicitor General's office to obtain authorization for appellate review.

For further information, contact the Office of the Assistant Attorney General, Civil Division, Department of Justice, Tenth Street and Pennsylvania Avenue NW., Washington, DC 20530. Phone, 202–514–3301.

Civil Rights Division

The Civil Rights Division, headed by an Assistant Attorney General, was established in 1957 to secure effective Federal enforcement of civil rights. The Division is the primary institution within the Federal Government responsible for enforcing Federal statutes prohibiting discrimination on the basis of race, sex, disability, religion, citizenship, and national origin. The Division has responsibilities in the following areas:

—Coordination and review of various civil rights statutes that prohibit discrimination on the basis of race, color, national origin, sex, and religion in programs and activities that receive Federal financial assistance by Federal agencies.

—Criminal cases involving conspiracies to interfere with federally protected rights; deprivation of rights under color of law; the use of force or threat of force to injure or intimidate someone in their enjoyment of specific rights (such as voting, housing, employment, education, public facilities, and accommodations); interference with the free exercise of religious beliefs or damage to religious property; the holding of a worker in a condition of slavery or involuntary servitude; and interference with persons seeking to obtain or provide reproductive services.

—Disability rights cases, achieving equal opportunity for people with disabilities in the United States by implementing the Americans with Disabilities Act (ADA). The section's enforcement, certification, regulatory, coordination, and technical assistance activities, combined with an innovative mediation program and a technical assistance grant program, provide an approach for carrying out the ADA's mandates. The section also carries out responsibilities under sections 504 and 508 of the Rehabilitation Act, the Help America Vote Act of 2002, the Small Business Regulatory Enforcement Fairness Act, and Executive Order 12250.

—Educational opportunities litigation, involving title IV of the Civil Rights Act of 1964, the Equal Educational Opportunities Act of 1974, and title III of the Americans with Disabilities Act. In addition, the section is responsible for enforcing other statutes such as title VI of the Civil Rights Act of 1964, title IX of the Education Amendments of 1972, section 504 of the Rehabilitation Act of 1973, title II of the Americans with Disabilities Act, and the Individuals with Disabilities Education Act upon referral from other governmental agencies.

—Employment litigation enforcing against State and local government employers the provisions of title VII of the Civil Rights Act of 1964, as amended, and other Federal laws prohibiting employment practices that discriminate on grounds of race, sex, religion, and national origin. The section also enforces against State and local government and private employers the provisions of the Uniformed Services Employment and Reemployment Rights Act of 1994, which prohibits employers from discriminating or retaliating against an employee or applicant for employment because of such person's past, current or future military obligation.

—Housing and Civil Enforcement statutes enforcing the Fair Housing Act, which prohibits discrimination in housing; the Equal Credit Opportunity Act, which prohibits discrimination in credit; title II of the Civil Rights Act of 1964, which prohibits discrimination in certain places of public accommodation, such as hotels, restaurants, nightclubs and theaters; title III of the Civil Rights Act of 1964, which prohibits discrimination in public facilities; and the Religious Land Use and Institutionalized Persons Act, which prohibits local governments from adopting or enforcing land use regulations that discriminate against religious assemblies and institutions or which unjustifiably burden religious exercise.

—Immigration-related unfair employment practices enforcing the antidiscrimination provisions of the Immigration and Nationality Act, which protect U.S. citizens and legal immigrants from employment discrimination based upon citizenship or immigration status and national origin, unfair documentary practices relating to the employment eligibility verification process, and retaliation.

—Special litigation protecting the constitutional and statutory rights of persons confined in certain institutions owned or operated by State or local governments, including facilities for individuals with mental and developmental disabilities, nursing homes, prisons, jails, and juvenile detention facilities where a pattern or practice of violations exist; civil enforcement of statutes prohibiting a pattern or practice of conduct by law enforcement agencies that violates Federal law; and protection against a threat of force and physical obstruction

that injures, intimidates, or interferes with a person seeking to obtain or provide reproductive health services, or to exercise the first amendment right of religious freedom at a place of worship.

—Voting cases enforcing the Voting Rights Act, the Help America Vote Act of 2002, the National Voter Registration Act, the Voting Accessibility for the Elderly and Handicapped Act, the Uniformed and Overseas Citizens Absentee Voting Act, and other Federal statutes designed to safeguard citizens' rights to vote. This includes racial and language minorities, illiterate persons, individuals with disabilities, overseas citizens, persons who change their residence shortly before a Presidential election, and persons 18 to 20 years of age.

For further information, contact the Executive Officer, Civil Rights Division, Department of Justice, 950 Pennsylvania Avenue NW., Washington, DC 20035. Phone, 202–514–4224. Internet, www.usdoj.gov/crt.

Criminal Division

The Criminal Division develops, enforces, and supervises the application of all Federal criminal laws, except those specifically assigned to other divisions. In addition to its direct litigation responsibilities, the Division formulates and implements criminal enforcement policy and provides advice and assistance, including representing the United States before the United States Courts of Appeal. The Division engages in and coordinates a wide range of criminal investigations and prosecutions, such as those targeting individuals and organizations that engage in international and national drug trafficking and money laundering systems or organizations and organized crime groups. The Division also approves or monitors sensitive areas of law enforcement such as participation in the Witness Security Program and the use of electronic surveillance; advises the Attorney General, Congress, the Office of Management and Budget, and the White House on matters of criminal law; provides legal advice, assistance, and training to Federal, State, and local prosecutors and investigative agencies;

provides leadership for coordinating international and national law enforcement matters; and provides training and development assistance to foreign criminal justice systems. Areas of responsibility include:

—Asset forfeiture and money laundering, including the prosecution of complex, sensitive, multidistrict and international cases; formulating policy and conducting training in the money laundering and forfeiture areas; developing legislation and regulations; ensuring the uniform application of forfeiture and money laundering statutes; participating in bilateral and multilateral initiatives to develop international forfeiture and money laundering policy and promote international cooperation; adjudicating petitions for remission or mitigation of forfeited assets; distributing forfeited funds and properties to appropriate domestic and foreign law enforcement agencies and community groups within the United States; and ensuring that such agencies comply with proper usage of received funds.

—Child exploitation and obscenity, including providing prosecutorial and forensic assistance to Federal prosecutors and law enforcement agents in investigating and prosecuting violators of Federal criminal statutes relating to the manufacture, distribution, receipt, or possession, of child pornography; selling, buying, or transporting women and children to engage in sexually explicit conduct; interstate or international travel to sexually abuse children; abusing children on Federal and Indian lands; transporting obscene materials in interstate or foreign commerce; international parental abduction; nonpayment of certain court-ordered child support; and contributing to the development of policy and legislative efforts related to these areas.

—Computer crime and intellectual property, including cyber-attacks on critical information systems, improving domestic and international infrastructure to pursue network criminals most effectively; and initiating and participating in international efforts to combat computer crime.

—Enforcement, overseeing the use of the most sophisticated investigative tools at the Department's disposal; reviewing all Federal electronic surveillance requests and requests to apply for court orders permitting the use of video surveillance; authorizing or denying the entry of applicants into the Federal Witness Security Program (WSP) and coordinating and administering matters relating to all aspects of the WSP among all program components; reviewing requests for witness immunity; transfer of prisoners to and from foreign countries to serve the remainder of their prison sentences; attorney and press subpoenas; applications for S-visa status; and disclosure of grand jury information.

—Fraud, including cases that focus on corporate and securities fraud schemes, financial institution fraud, insurance fraud, fraud involving Government programs such as Medicare, and international criminal activities including the bribery of foreign government officials in violation of the Foreign Corrupt Practices Act.

—International affairs, including requests for international extradition and foreign evidence on behalf of Federal, State, and local prosecutors and investigators, fulfilling foreign requests for fugitives and evidence, and negotiating and implementing law enforcement treaties.

—Narcotics and dangerous drugs, including statutes pertaining to controlled substances; developing and implementing domestic and international narcotics law enforcement policies and programs; developing and administering other cooperative drug enforcement strategies, such as the Bilateral Case Initiative, and projects conducted by the law enforcement and intelligence communities.

—Organized crime and racketeering efforts against traditional groups and emerging groups from Asia and Europe.

—Organized Crime Drug Enforcement Task Forces, combining the resources and expertise of several Federal agencies in cooperation with the Tax Division, U.S. attorneys offices, and State and local law enforcement to identify, disrupt, and dismantle major drug supply and money laundering organizations through coordinated, nationwide investigations targeting the entire infrastructure of these enterprises.

—Overseas prosecutorial development, assistance, and training for prosecutors and judicial personnel in other countries to develop and sustain democratic criminal justice institutions.

—Policy and legislation, developing legislative proposals and reviewing pending legislation affecting the Federal criminal justice system; reviewing and developing proposed changes to the Federal sentencing guidelines and rules; and analyzing crime policy and program issues.

—Public integrity efforts to combat corruption of elected and appointed public officials at all levels of Government.

—Special investigations of individuals who took part in Nazi-sponsored acts of persecution abroad before and during World War II and who subsequently entered or seek to enter the United States illegally and/or fraudulently, and interagency investigation into assets looted from victims of Nazi persecution.

—Terrorism, involving design, implementation, and support of law enforcement efforts, legislative initiatives, policies, and strategies relating to international and domestic terrorism.

—Domestic security, enforcing Federal criminal laws relating to violent crimes, the illegal use of firearms and explosives, and alien smuggling and other immigration-related offenses.

For further information, contact the Office of the Assistant Attorney General, Criminal Division, Department of Justice, Tenth Street and Pennsylvania Avenue NW., Washington, DC 20530. Phone, 202–514–2601.

Environment and Natural Resources Division

The Environment and Natural Resources Division is the Nation's environmental lawyer. The Division's responsibilities include enforcing civil and criminal environmental laws that protect America's health and environment. It also defends environmental challenges to Government activities and programs and ensures that environmental laws are implemented in a fair and consistent manner nationwide. It also represents the United States in all matters concerning the protection, use, and development of the Nation's natural resources and public lands, wildlife protection, Indian rights and claims, and the acquisition of Federal property. To carry out this broad mission, the Division litigates in the following areas:

—Environmental crimes, prosecuting individuals and corporate entities violating laws designed to protect the environment.

—Civil environmental enforcement, on behalf of EPA; claims for damages to natural resources filed on behalf of the Departments of the Interior, Commerce, and Agriculture; claims for contribution against private parties for contamination of public land; and recoupment of money spent to clean up certain oil spills on behalf of the U.S. Coast Guard.

—Environmental defense, representing the United States in suits challenging the Government's administration of Federal environmental laws including claims that regulations are too strict or lenient, and claims alleging that Federal agencies are not complying with environmental standards.

—Wildlife and marine resources protection, including prosecution of smugglers and black-market dealers in protected wildlife.

—Use and protection of federally owned public lands and natural resources across a broad spectrum of laws.

—Indian resources protection, including establishing water rights, establishing and protecting hunting and fishing rights, collecting damages for trespass on Indian lands, and establishing reservation boundaries and rights to land.

—Land acquisition for use by the Federal Government for purposes ranging from establishing public parks to building Federal courthouses.

For further information, contact the Office of the Assistant Attorney General, Environment and Natural Resources Division, Department of Justice, Tenth Street and Pennsylvania Avenue NW., Washington, DC 20530. Phone, 202–514–2701.

National Security Division

The National Security Division (NSD) develops, enforces, and supervises the application of all Federal criminal laws related to the national counterterrorism and counterespionage enforcement programs, except those specifically assigned to other divisions. NSD litigates and coordinates a wide range of prosecutions and criminal investigations involving terrorism and violations of the espionage, export control, and foreign agents registration laws. It administers the Foreign Intelligence Surveillance Act and other legal authorities for national security activities; approves and monitors the use of electronic surveillance; provides legal and policy advice regarding the classification of and access to national security information; performs prepublication review of materials written by present and former DOJ employees; trains the law enforcement and intelligence communities; and advises the Department and legislative and executive branches on all areas of national security law. NSD also serves as the Department's representative on interdepartmental boards, committees, and entities dealing with issues related to national security.

NSD also has some additional counterterrorism, counterespionage, and intelligence oversight responsibilities as follows:

—Promote and oversee national counterterrorism enforcement programs;

—Develop and implement counterterrorism strategies, legislation, and initiatives;

—Facilitate information sharing between and among the Department and other Federal agencies on terrorism threats;

—Share information with international law enforcement officials to assist with international threat information and litigation initiatives;

—Liaison with the intelligence, defense, and immigration communities and foreign governments on counterterrorism issues and cases;

—Supervise the investigation and prosecution of cases involving national

security, foreign relations, the export of military and strategic commodities and technology, espionage, sabotage, neutrality, and atomic energy;

—Coordinates cases involving the application for the Classified Information Procedures Act;

—Enforce the Foreign Agents Registration Act of 1938 and related disclosure laws;

—Supervise the preparation of certifications and applications for orders under the Foreign Intelligence Surveillance Act (FISA);

—Represent the United States before the Foreign Intelligence Surveillance Court;

—Participate in the development, implementation, and review of United States intelligence policies;

—Evaluate existing and proposed national security-related activities to determine their consistency with relevant policies and law;

—Monitor intelligence and counterintelligence activities of other agencies to ensure conformity with Department objectives;

—Prepare reports evaluating domestic and foreign intelligence and counterintelligence activities;

—Process requests to use FISA-derived information in criminal, civil, and immigration proceedings and to disseminate that information to foreign governments.

For further information, contact the Office of the Assistant Attorney General, National Security Division, Department of Justice, Tenth Street and Pennsylvania Avenue NW., Washington, DC 20530. Phone, 202–514–5600. Internet, www.usdoj.gov/nsd.

Tax Division

Tax Division ensures the uniform and fair enforcement of Federal tax laws in Federal and State courts. The Division conducts enforcement activities to deter specific taxpayers, as well as the taxpaying public at large, from conduct that deprives the Federal Government of its tax-related revenue. It represents the United States and its officers in all civil and criminal litigation arising under the internal revenue laws, other than proceedings in the United States Tax

Court. Tax Division attorneys frequently join with assistant U.S. attorneys in prosecuting tax cases. Some criminal tax grand jury investigations and prosecutions are handled solely by Tax Division prosecutors, while others are delegated to assistant U.S. attorneys. Division attorneys evaluate requests by the Internal Revenue Service or United States attorneys to initiate grand jury investigations or prosecutions of tax crimes.

The Division handles a wide array of civil tax litigation, including the following:

—Suits to enjoin the promotion of abusive tax shelters and to enjoin activities relating to aiding and abetting the understatement of tax liabilities of others;

—Suits to enforce Internal Revenue Service administrative summonses that seek information essential to determine and collect taxpayers' liabilities, including summonses for records of corporate tax shelters and offshore transactions;

—Suits brought by the United States to set aside fraudulent conveyances and to collect assets held by nominees and alter egos;

—Tax refund suits challenging the Internal Revenue Service's determination of taxpayers' Federal income, employment, excise, and estate liabilities;

—Bankruptcy litigation raising issues of the validity, dischargeability, and priority of Federal tax claims, and the feasibility of reorganization plans;

—Suits brought by taxpayers challenging determinations made in the collection due process proceedings before the Internal Revenue Service's Office of Appeals; and

—Suits against the United States for damages for the unauthorized disclosure of tax return information or for damages claimed because of alleged injuries caused by Internal Revenue Service employees in the performance of their official duties.

The Division also collects judgments in tax cases. To this end, the Division directs collection efforts and coordinates with, monitors the efforts of, and provides assistance to the various United States attorneys' offices in collecting outstanding judgments in tax cases.

The Division also works with the Internal Revenue Service, United States attorneys, and other Government agencies on policy and legislative proposals to enhance tax administration and handling tax cases assigned to those offices.

For further information, contact the Office of the Assistant Attorney General, Tax Division, Department of Justice, Tenth Street and Pennsylvania Avenue NW., Washington, DC 20530. Phone, 202–514–2901. Internet, www.usdoj.gov/tax.

Bureaus

Federal Bureau of Investigation

935 Pennsylvania Avenue NW., Washington, DC 20535. Phone, 202–324–3000. Internet, www.fbi.gov.

The Federal Bureau of Investigation (FBI) is the principal investigative arm of the United States Department of Justice. It is primarily charged with gathering and reporting facts, locating witnesses, and compiling evidence in cases involving Federal jurisdiction. It also provides law enforcement leadership and assistance to State and international law enforcement agencies.

The Federal Bureau of Investigation was established in 1908 by the Attorney General, who directed that Department of Justice investigations be handled by its own staff. The Bureau is charged with investigating all violations of Federal law except those that have been assigned by legislative enactment or otherwise to another Federal agency. Its jurisdiction includes a wide range of responsibilities in the national security, criminal, and civil fields. Priority has been assigned to areas such as counterterrorism, counterintelligence, cyber-crimes, internationally and nationally organized crime/drug matters, and financial crimes.

The FBI also offers cooperative services to local, State, and international law enforcement agencies. These services include fingerprint identification, laboratory examination, police training, the Law Enforcement Online communication and information service for use by the law enforcement community, the National Crime Information Center, and the National Center for the Analysis of Violent Crime.

For further information, contact the Office of Public and Congressional Affairs, Federal Bureau of Investigation, J. Edgar Hoover FBI Building, 935 Pennsylvania Avenue NW., Washington, DC 20535. Phone, 202–317–2727.

Bureau of Prisons

320 First Street NW., Washington, DC 20534. Phone, 202–307–3198. Internet, www.bop.gov.

The mission of the Bureau of Prisons is to protect society by confining offenders in the controlled environments of prisons and community-based facilities that are safe, humane, cost-efficient, and appropriately secure, and that provide work and other self-improvement opportunities to assist offenders in becoming law-abiding citizens. The Bureau has its headquarters also known as Central Office, in Washington, DC. The Central Office is divided into nine divisions, including the National Institute of Corrections.

The Correctional Programs Division (CPD) is responsible for inmate classification and programming, including psychology and religious services, substance abuse treatment, case management, and programs for special needs offenders. CPD provides policy direction and daily operational oversight of institution security, emergency preparedness, intelligence gathering, inmate discipline, inmate sentence computations, receiving and discharge, and inmate transportation, as well as coordinating international treaty transfers and overseeing the special security needs of inmates placed in the Federal

Witness Protection Program. CPD administers contracts and intergovernmental agreements for the confinement of offenders in community-based programs, community corrections centers, and other facilities, including privately managed facilities. CPD staff is also involved in the Bureau's privatization efforts.

The Industries, Education, and Vocational Training Division oversees Federal Prison Industries, or UNICOR, which is a wholly owned Government corporation that provides employment and training opportunities for inmates confined in Federal correctional facilities. Additionally, it is responsible for oversight of educational, occupational, and vocational training, and leisure-time programs, as well as those related to inmate release preparation.

The National Institute of Corrections (NIC) provides technical assistance, training, and information to State and local corrections agencies throughout the country, as well as the Bureau. It also provides research assistance and documents through the NIC Information Center.

For further information, contact the Public Information Office, Bureau of Prisons, 320 First Street NW., Washington, DC 20534. Phone, 202–514–6551.

United States Marshals Service

Washington, DC 20530. Phone, 202–307–9000

The United States Marshals Service is the Nation's oldest Federal law enforcement agency, having served as a vital link between the executive and judicial branches of the Government since 1789. The Marshals Service performs tasks that are essential to the operation of virtually every aspect of the Federal justice system. The Service has these responsibilities:

—providing support and protection for the Federal courts, including security for 800 judicial facilities and nearly 2,000 judges and magistrates, as well as countless other trial participants such as jurors and attorneys;

—apprehending the majority of Federal fugitives;

—operating the Federal Witness Security Program and ensuring the safety of endangered Government witnesses;

—maintaining custody of and transporting thousands of Federal prisoners annually;

—executing court orders and arrest warrants;

—managing and selling seized property forfeited to the Government by drug traffickers and other criminals and assisting the Justice Department's asset forfeiture program;

—responding to emergency circumstances, including civil disturbances, terrorist incidents, and other crisis situations through its Special Operations Group, and restoring order in riot and mob-violence situations; and

—operating the U.S. Marshals Service Training Academy.

For further information, contact the Office of Public Affairs, U.S. Marshals Service, Department of Justice, Washington, DC 20530. Phone, 202–307–9065. Internet, www.usmarshals.gov.

International Criminal Police Organization–United States National Central Bureau

Washington, DC 20530. Phone, 202–616–9000. Fax, 202–616–8400.

The U.S. National Central Bureau (USNCB) is the United States representative to INTERPOL, the International Criminal Police Organization. Also known as INTERPOL—Washington, the USNCB provides an essential communications link between the U.S. police community and their counterparts in the foreign member countries. The USNCB also serves as the United States point of contact for the European Police Office (EUROPOL), the European Union's law enforcement organization.

INTERPOL is an association of 182 countries dedicated to promoting mutual assistance among law enforcement authorities in the prevention and suppression of international crime. With no police force of its own, INTERPOL has no powers of arrest or search and seizure and therefore relies on the law enforcement authorities of its member countries. Each member country is required to have a national central bureau, such as the USNCB, to act as the primary point of contact for police matters. INTERPOL serves as a channel of communication for its member countries to cooperate in the investigation and prosecution of crime, provides a forum for discussions, working group meetings, and symposia to enable police to focus on specific areas of criminal activity affecting their countries, and issues and maintains information and databases on crime, fugitives, stolen passports and vehicles, missing persons, and humanitarian concerns, which are supplied by and can be used as a source by its member countries.

The USNCB is staffed by a permanent staff and detailed special agents from numerous Federal law enforcement agencies. The USNCB is organized into the Terrorism and Violent Crimes Division, the Economic Crimes Division, the Drug Division, the Fugitive Division, the Investigative Support Division, the Administrative Services Division, the Office of the General Counsel, and the State and Local Liaison Division (SLLD).

SLLD coordinates INTERPOL requests with 62 INTERPOL State liaison offices established in each State and the cities of New York, Boston, Chicago, Washington, DC, Miami-Dade, San Diego (city and county), Los Angeles, San Francisco, and Seattle. The USNCB has three sub-bureaus which serve to more effectively address the law enforcement needs of U.S. territories. The sub-bureaus are located in Puerto Rico, American Samoa, and the U.S. Virgin Islands. SLLD provides the primary means of communication between foreign law enforcement authorities and domestic State and local police for the purpose of pursuing international investigations. International leads developed in criminal investigations being conducted by a

State or local police entity can be pursued through their liaison office.

For further information, contact the INTERPOL–U.S. National Central Bureau, Department of Justice, Washington, DC 20530. Phone, 202–616–9000.

Drug Enforcement Administration

600–700 Army Navy Drive, Arlington, VA 22202. Phone, 202–307–1000. FTS, 367–1000

The Drug Enforcement Administration (DEA) is the lead Federal agency in enforcing narcotics and controlled substances laws and regulations. DEA also enforces the Federal money laundering and bulk currency smuggling statutes when the funds involved in the transactions or smuggling are derived from the sale of narcotics. It was created in July 1973 by Reorganization Plan No. 2 of 1973 (5 U.S.C. app.).

DEA enforces the provisions of the controlled substances and chemical diversion and trafficking laws and regulations of the United States, and operates on a worldwide basis. It presents cases to the criminal and civil justice systems of the United States—or any other competent jurisdiction—on those significant organizations and their members involved in cultivation, production, smuggling, distribution, laundering of proceeds, or diversion of controlled substances appearing in or destined for illegal traffic in the United States. DEA disrupts and dismantles these organizations by arresting their members, confiscating their drugs, and seizing their assets; and creates, manages, and supports enforcement-related programs—domestically and internationally—aimed at reducing the availability of and demand for illicit controlled substances.

DEA's responsibilities include:

—investigation of major narcotic, chemical, drug-money laundering, and bulk currency smuggling violators who operate at interstate and international levels;

—seizure and forfeiture of assets derived from, traceable to, or intended to be used for illicit drug trafficking;

—seizure and forfeiture of assets derived from or traceable to drug-money laundering or the smuggling of bulk currency derived from illegal drugs;

—enforcement of regulations governing the legal manufacture, distribution, and dispensing of controlled substances;

—management of an intelligence program that supports drug investigations, initiatives, and operations worldwide;

—coordination with Federal, State, and local law enforcement authorities and cooperation with counterpart agencies abroad;

—assistance to State and local law enforcement agencies in addressing their most significant drug and drug-related violence problems;

—leadership and influence over international counterdrug and chemical policy and support for institution building in host nations;

—training, scientific research, and information exchange in support of drug traffic prevention and control; and

—education and assistance to the public community on the prevention, treatment, and dangers of drugs.

DEA maintains liaison with the United Nations, INTERPOL, and other organizations on matters relating to international narcotics control programs. It has offices throughout the United States and in 62 foreign countries.

For further information, contact the Public Affairs Section, Drug Enforcement Administration, Department of Justice, Washington, DC 20537. Phone, 202–307–7977.

Office of Justice Programs

810 Seventh Street NW., Washington, DC 20531. Phone, 202–307–0703

The Office of Justice Programs (OJP) was established by the Justice Assistance Act of 1984 and reauthorized in 1994 to provide Federal leadership, coordination, and assistance needed to make the Nation's justice system more efficient and effective in preventing and controlling crime. OJP is responsible for collecting statistical data and conducting analyses; identifying emerging criminal justice issues; developing and testing promising approaches to address these issues; evaluating program results, and disseminating these findings and other information to State and local governments.

The Office is comprised of the following bureaus and offices:

—The Bureau of Justice Assistance provides funding, training, and technical assistance to State and local governments to combat violent and drug-related crime and help improve the criminal justice system.

—The Bureau of Justice Statistics is responsible for collecting and analyzing data on crime, criminal offenders, crime victims, and the operations of justice systems at all levels of government.

—The National Institute of Justice sponsors research and development programs, conducts demonstrations of innovative approaches to improve criminal justice, and develops new criminal justice technologies.

—The Office of Juvenile Justice and Delinquency Prevention provides grants and contracts to States to help them improve their juvenile justice systems and sponsors innovative research, demonstration, evaluation, statistics, replication, technical assistance, and training programs to help improve the Nation's understanding of and response to juvenile violence and delinquency.

—The Office for Victims of Crime administers victim compensation and assistance grant programs and provides funding, training, and technical assistance to victim service organizations, criminal justice agencies, and other professionals to improve the Nation's response to crime victims.

—The Drug Courts Program Office supports the development, implementation, and improvement of drug courts through technical assistance and training and grants to State, local, or tribal governments and courts.

—The Corrections Program Office provides financial and technical assistance to State and local governments to implement corrections-related programs including correctional facility construction and corrections-based drug treatment programs.

—The Executive Office for Weed and Seed helps communities build stronger, safer neighborhoods by implementing the weed and seed strategy, a community-based, multidisciplinary approach to combating crime.

—The Office for State and Local Domestic Preparedness Support is responsible for enhancing the capacity of State and local jurisdictions to prepare for and respond to incidents of domestic terrorism involving chemical and biological agents, radiological and explosive devices, and other weapons of mass destruction.

—The Office of the Police Corps and Law Enforcement Education provides college educational assistance to students who commit to public service in law enforcement, and scholarships with no service commitment to dependents of law enforcement officers who died in the line of duty.

For further information, contact the Department of Justice Response Center. Phone, 800–421–6770. Internet, www.ojp.usdoj.gov. Email, askojp@ojp.usdoj.gov.

Office on Violence Against Women

800 K Street NW., Washington, DC 20530. Phone, 202–307–6026

The Office on Violence Against Women (OVW) was established in 2005 to reduce violence against women through the implementation of the Violence Against Women Act. OVW is responsible for administering financial and technical assistance to communities that are developing programs, policies, and practices aimed at ending domestic and dating violence, sexual assault, and stalking.

For further information, contact the Office on Violence Against Women, Department of Justice, Washington, DC, 20530. Phone, 202–307–6026. Internet, www.ovw.usdoj.gov.

Bureau of Alcohol, Tobacco, Firearms and Explosives

650 Massachusetts Avenue NW., Washington, DC 20226. Phone, 202–927–8500

The Bureau of Alcohol, Tobacco, Firearms and Explosives (ATF) is responsible for enforcing Federal criminal laws and regulating the firearms and explosives industries. ATF, formerly known as the Bureau of Alcohol, Tobacco, and Firearms, was initially established by Department of Treasury Order No. 221, effective July 1, 1972, which transferred the functions, powers, and duties arising under laws relating to alcohol, tobacco, firearms, and explosives from the Internal Revenue Service to ATF. The Homeland Security Act of 2002 (6 U.S.C. 531) transferred certain functions and authorities of ATF to the Department of Justice and established it under its current name. ATF works, directly and through

partnerships, to investigate and reduce violent crime involving firearms and explosives, acts of arson, and illegal trafficking of alcohol and tobacco products. The Bureau provides training and support to its Federal, State, local, and international law enforcement partners and works primarily in 23 field divisions across the 50 States, Puerto Rico, the U.S. Virgin Islands, and Guam. It also has foreign offices in Mexico, Canada, Colombia, and France.

For further information, contact the Office of Public Affairs, Bureau of Alcohol, Tobacco, Firearms and Explosives. Phone, 202–927–8500. Internet, www.atf.gov.

Boards

Executive Office for Immigration Review

Falls Church, VA 22041. Phone, 703–305–0289. Internet, www.usdoj.gov/eoir.

The Executive Office for Immigration Review, under a delegation of authority from the Attorney General, is charged with adjudicating matters brought under various immigration statutes to its three administrative tribunals: the Board of Immigration Appeals, the Office of the Chief Immigration Judge, and the Office of the Chief Administrative Hearing Officer.

The Board of Immigration Appeals has nationwide jurisdiction to hear appeals from certain decisions made by immigration judges and by district directors of the Department of Homeland Security (DHS). In addition, the Board is responsible for hearing appeals involving disciplinary actions against attorneys and representatives before DHS and the Board.

Decisions of the Board are binding on all DHS officers and immigration judges unless modified or overruled by the Attorney General or a Federal court. All Board decisions are subject to judicial review in Federal court. The majority of appeals reaching the Board involve orders of removal and applications for relief from removal. Other cases before

the Board include the removal of aliens applying for admission to the United States, petitions to classify the status of alien relatives for the issuance of preference immigrant visas, fines imposed upon carriers for the violation of the immigration laws, and motions for reopening and reconsideration of decisions previously rendered.

The Office of the Chief Immigration Judge provides overall direction for more than 200 immigration judges located in 53 immigration courts throughout the Nation. Immigration judges are responsible for conducting formal administrative proceedings and act independently in their decisionmaking capacity. Their decisions are administratively final, unless appealed or certified to the Board.

In removal proceedings, an immigration judge determines whether an individual from a foreign country should be admitted or allowed to stay in the United States or be removed. Judges are located throughout the United States, and each judge has jurisdiction to consider various forms of relief available under the law, including applications for asylum.

The Office of the Chief Administrative Hearing Officer is responsible for the general supervision and management of administrative law judges who preside at hearings which are mandated by provisions of immigration law concerning allegations of unlawful employment of aliens, unfair immigration-related employment practices, and immigration document fraud.

For further information, contact the Office of Legislative and Public Affairs, Executive Office for Immigration Review, Department of Justice, Falls Church, VA 22041. Phone, 703–305–0289. Internet, www.usdoj.gov/eoir.

United States Parole Commission

Friendship Boulevard, Chevy Chase, MD 20815. Phone, 301–492–5990

The United States Parole Commission (USPC) makes parole release decisions for eligible Federal and District of Columbia prisoners; authorizes methods of release and conditions under which release occurs; prescribes, modifies, and monitors compliance with the terms and conditions governing offenders' behavior while on parole or mandatory or supervised release; issues warrants for violation of supervision; determines probable cause for the revocation process; revokes parole, mandatory, or supervised release; releases from supervision those offenders who are no longer a risk to public safety; and promulgates the rules, regulations, and guidelines for the exercise of USPC's authority and the implementation of a national parole policy.

USPC has sole jurisdiction over the following: Federal offenders who committed offenses before November 1, 1987; D.C. Code offenders who committed offenses before August 5, 2000; D.C. Code offenders sentenced to a term of supervised release; Uniform Code of Military Justice offenders who are in Bureau of Prison's custody; transfer treaty cases; and State probationers and parolees in the Federal Witness Protection Program.

For further information, contact the United States Parole Commission, Department of Justice, 5550 Friendship Boulevard, Chevy Chase, MD 20815. Phone, 301–492–5990. Internet, www.usdoj.gov/uspc/parole.htm.

Office of Community Oriented Policing Services

The Office of Community Oriented Policing Services (COPS) was established to assist law enforcement agencies in enhancing public safety through the implementation of community policing strategies. COPS does so by providing training to enhance law enforcement officers' problem-solving and community interaction skills; encouraging law enforcement and community members to develop initiatives to prevent crime; substantially increasing the number of law enforcement officers directly interacting with the community; and supporting the development of new technologies to shift law enforcement's focus to preventing crime and disorder within their communities.

The COPS Office includes the following program divisions:

—The grants administration division is responsible for developing and designing new programs to provide resources for the hiring of new officers and to further the adoption and implementation of community policing, reviewing grant applications, and assisting grantees in the implementation of their grants.

—The grants monitoring division is responsible for tracking grantees' compliance with the conditions of their grants. The Division conducts site visits and reviews grantee files to ensure that COPS funds are properly used to hire officers and implement community policing. The Division also provides onsite technical assistance to grantees, office-based grant reviews, alleged noncompliance reviews, audit resolution, and collects and disseminates examples of successful community policing strategies.

—The training and technical assistance division is responsible for coordinating the provision of training and technical assistance to advance the adoption, implementation, and sustaining of community policing in the thousands of communities served by the COPS Office.

—The compliance division is responsible for the monitoring and coordination of the Office of Inspector

General (OIG) audits and independent audits required by the Single Audit Act and serves as the liaison between grantees and auditors in the conduct and resolution of OIG audits.

For further information, contact the Office of Community Oriented Policing Services (COPS), Department of Justice, 1100 Vermont Avenue NW., Washington, DC 20530. Phone, 202–514–2058. Internet, www.cops.usdoj.gov.

Foreign Claims Settlement Commission of the United States

The Foreign Claims Settlement Commission of the United States is a quasi-judicial, independent agency within the Department of Justice which adjudicates claims of U.S. nationals against foreign governments, either under specific jurisdiction conferred by Congress or pursuant to international claims settlement agreements. The decisions of the Commission are final and are not reviewable under any standard by any court or other authority. Funds for payment of the Commission's awards are derived from congressional appropriations, international claims settlements, or the liquidation of foreign assets in the United States by the Departments of Justice and the Treasury.

The Commission also has authority to receive, determine the validity and amount, and provide for the payment of claims by members of the U.S. armed services and civilians held as prisoners of war or interned by a hostile force in Southeast Asia during the Vietnam conflict, or by the survivors of such service members and civilians.

The Commission is also responsible for maintaining records and responding to inquiries related to the various claims programs it has conducted against the Governments of Albania, Bulgaria, China, Cuba, Czechoslovakia, Egypt, Ethiopia, the Federal Republic of Germany, the German Democratic Republic, Hungary, Iran, Italy, Panama, Poland, Romania, the Soviet Union, Vietnam, and Yugoslavia, as well as those authorized under the War Claims Act of 1948 and other statutes.

For further information, contact the Office of the Chairman, Foreign Claims Settlement Commission of the United States, Department of Justice, Suite 6002, 600 E Street NW., Washington, DC 20579. Phone, 202–616–6975. Fax, 202–616–6993.

Sources of Information

Controlled Substances Act Registration Information about registration under the Controlled Substances Act may be obtained from the Registration Section of the Drug Enforcement Administration, P.O. Box 28083, Central Station, Washington, DC 20038. Phone, 202–307–7255.

Disability-Related Matters Contact the Civil Rights Division's ADA Hotline. Phone, 800–514–0301. TDD, 800–514–0383. Internet, www.usdoj.gov/crt/ada/adahom1.htm.

Drugs and Crime Clearinghouse Phone, 800–666–3332 (toll free).

Electronic Access Information concerning Department of Justice programs and activities is available electronically through the Internet at www.usdoj.gov.

The NCJRS Electronic Bulletin Board may be accessed by calling 301–738–8895 (modem).

Employment The Department maintains an agencywide job line. Phone, 202–514–3397.

Attorneys' applications: Director, Office of Attorney Personnel Management, Department of Justice, Room 6150, Tenth Street and Constitution Avenue NW., Washington, DC 20530. Phone, 202–514–1432. Assistant U.S. attorney applicants should apply to individual U.S. attorneys.

United States Marshals Service: Field Staffing Branch, United States Marshals Service, Department of Justice, 600 Army Navy Drive, Arlington, VA 22202–4210.

Federal Bureau of Investigation: Director, Washington, DC 20535, or any of the field offices or resident agencies whose addresses are listed in the front of most local telephone directories.

Drug Enforcement Administration: regional offices, laboratories, or Washington Headquarters Office of Personnel.

Bureau of Prisons: Central Office, 320 First Street NW., Washington, DC 20534 (phone, 202–307–3082); or any regional or field office.

Office of Justice Programs: 633 Indiana Avenue NW., Washington, DC 20531. Phone, 202–307–0730.

United States Trustee Program, Room 770, 901 E Street NW., Washington, DC 20530. Phone, 202–616–1000.

Foreign Claims Settlement Commission: Attorneys: Office of the Chief Counsel, Suite 6002, 600 E Street NW., Washington, DC 20579 (phone, 202–616–6975); Other: Administrative Officer, same address and phone.

Housing Discrimination Matters
Contact the Civil Rights Division's Housing and Civil Enforcement Section. Phone, 800–896–7743.

Immigration-Related Employment Matters The Civil Rights Division maintains a worker hotline. Phone, 800–255–7688. TDD, 800–237–2515. It also offers information for employers. Phone, 800–255–8155. TDD, 800–362–2735.

Publications and Films The *FBI Law Enforcement Bulletin* and *Uniform Crime Reports—Crime in the United States* are available from the Superintendent of Documents, Government Printing Office, Washington, DC 20402.

The Annual Report of the Attorney General of the United States is published each year by the Department of Justice, Washington, DC 20530.

Textbooks on citizenship consisting of teachers manuals and student textbooks at various reading levels are distributed free to public schools for applicants for citizenship and are on sale to all others from the Superintendent of Documents, Government Printing Office, Washington, DC 20402. Public schools or organizations under the supervision of public schools which are entitled to free textbooks should make their requests to the appropriate Immigration and Naturalization Service Regional Office.

For general information, call 202–514–3946.

The Freedom of Information Act Guide and Privacy Act Overview and the *Freedom of Information Case List,* both published annually, are available from the Superintendent of Documents, Government Printing Office, Washington, DC 20530.

FOIA Update (Stock No. 727–002–00000–6), published quarterly, is available free of charge to FOIA offices and other interested offices Governmentwide. This publication is also available from the Superintendent of Documents, Government Printing Office, Washington, DC 20402.

Guidelines for Effective Human Relations Commissions, Annual Report of the Community Relations Service, Community Relations Service Brochure, CRS Hotline Brochure, Police Use of Deadly Force: A Conciliation Handbook for Citizens and Police, Principles of Good Policing: Avoiding Violence Between Police and Citizens, Resolving Racial Conflict: A Guide for Municipalities, and *Viewpoints and Guidelines on Court-Appointed Citizens Monitoring Commissions in School Desegregation* are available upon request from the Public Information Office, Community Relations Service, Department of Justice, Washington, DC 20530.

A limited number of drug educational films are available, free of charge, to civic, educational, private, and religious groups.

A limited selection of pamphlets and brochures is available. The most widely requested publication is *Drugs of Abuse,* an identification manual intended for professional use. Single copies are free.

Copies of the Foreign Claims Settlement Commission's semiannual (through December 1966) and annual (from January 1967) reports to the Congress concerning its activities are available at the Commission in limited quantities.

Copies of the *Program Plan* and other Office of Justice Programs publications and documents are available by calling the National Criminal Justice Reference Service (phone, 303–251–5500 or 800–

851–3420 (toll free); Internet, www.ncjrs.org). Some documents are also available from the Office's Web site, (Internet, www.ojp.usdoj.gov).

Reading Rooms   Located in Washington, DC, at the following locations:

Department of Justice, Room 6505, Tenth Street and Constitution Avenue NW., Washington, DC 20530. Phone, 202–514–3775.

Bureau of Prisons, 320 First Street NW., 20534. Phone, 202–307–3029.

Foreign Claims Settlement Commission, 600 E Street NW., 20579. Phone, 202–616–6975.

U.S. Parole Commission, 5550 Friendship Boulevard, Chevy Chase, MD 20815. Phone, 301–492–5959.

Board of Immigration Appeals, Suite 2400, 5107 Leesburg Pike, Falls Church, VA 22041. Phone,

703–305–0168.

National Institute of Justice, 9th Floor, 633 Indiana Avenue NW., Washington, DC 20531 (phone, 202–307–5883).

Redress for Wartime Relocation/ Internment   Contact the Civil Rights Division's Office of Redress Administration. Helpline phone, 202–219–6900. TDD, 202–219–4710. Internet, www.usdoj.gov.

Small Business Activities   Contract information for small businesses can be obtained from the Office of Small and Disadvantaged Business Utilization, Department of Justice, Tenth Street and Pennsylvania Avenue NW., Washington, DC 20530. Phone, 202–616–0521.

For further information concerning the Department of Justice, contact the Office of Public Affairs, Department of Justice, Tenth Street and Constitution Avenue NW., Washington, DC 20530. Phone, 202–514–2007. TDD, 202–786–5731. Internet, www.usdoj.gov.

DEPARTMENT OF LABOR

200 Constitution Avenue NW., Washington, DC 20210
Phone, 202–693–5000. Internet, www.dol.gov.

SECRETARY OF LABOR	HILDA L. SOLIS
DEPUTY SECRETARY	SETH D. HARRIS
Chief of Staff	KATHERINE ARCHULETA
Executive Secretary	DEBORAH GREENFIELD
Chief Administrative Law Judge	JOHN M. VITTONE
Chief Administrative Appeals Judge, Benefits Review Board	NANCY S. DOLDER
Chief Economist	ALEXANDRE MAS
Chief Financial Officer	LISA FIELY, *Acting*
Chief Administrative Appeals Judge, Administrative Review Board	WAYNE C. BEYER
Chairman, Employees Compensation Appeals Board	ALEC J. KOROMILAS
Director, Office of Job Corps	ESTHER R. JOHNSON
Director, Office of Small Business Programs	JOSE A. LIRA
Director, Women's Bureau	(VACANCY)
Assistant Secretary for Administration and Management	T. MICHAEL KERR
Assistant Secretary for Congressional and Intergovernmental Affairs	BRIAN KENNEDY
Assistant Secretary for Employment and Training	(VACANCY)
Assistant Secretary for Employment Standards	SHELBY HALLMARK, *Acting*
Administrator, Wage and Hour	(VACANCY)
Assistant Secretary for Mine Safety and Health	MIKE DAVIS
Assistant Secretary of Disability Employment Policy	KATHLEEN MARTINEZ
Assistant Secretary for Occupational Safety and Health	JORDAN BARAB, *Acting*
Assistant Secretary for Employee Benefit Security Administration	MICHAEL L. DAVIS
Assistant Secretary for Policy	(VACANCY)
Assistant Secretary for Public Affairs	JAIME ZAPATA, *Acting*
Assistant Secretary for Veterans' Employment and Training	(VACANCY)
Commissioner of Labor Statistics	KEITH HALL
Deputy Under Secretary for International Affairs	SANDRA POLASKI
Inspector General	GORDON S. HEDDELL
Solicitor of Labor	(VACANCY)
Director, Center for Faith-Based and Community Initiatives	(VACANCY)
Director, Office of the 21st Century Workforce	(VACANCY)

The Department of Labor fosters and promotes the welfare of the job seekres, wage earners, and retirees of the United States, by improving their working conditions, advancing their opportunities for profitable employment, protecting their retirement and health care benefits, helping employers find workers, strengthening free collective bargaining, and tracking changes in employment, prices, and other national economic measurements. In carrying out this mission, the Department administers a variety of Federal labor laws including those that guarantee workers' rights to safe and healthful working conditions; a minimum hourly wage and overtime pay; freedom from employment discrimination; unemployment insurance; and other income support.

The Department of Labor (DOL) was created by act of March 4, 1913 (29 U.S.C. 551). A Bureau of Labor was first created by Congress by act of June 24, 1884, in the Interior Department. The Bureau of Labor later became independent as a Department of Labor without executive rank by act of June 13, 1888. It again returned to bureau status in the Department of Commerce and Labor, which was created by act of February 14, 1903 (15 U.S.C. 1501; 29 U.S.C. 1 note).

Secretary   The Secretary is the principal adviser to the President on the development and execution of policies and the administration and enforcement of laws relating to wage earners, their working conditions, and their employment opportunities.

Employees' Compensation Appeals Board   The Board is a three-member quasi-judicial body appointed by the Secretary which has been delegated exclusive jurisdiction by Congress to hear and make final decisions on workers' compensation appeals of Federal employees from determinations of the Office of Workers' Compensation Programs (Office) arising under the Federal Employees' Compensation Act. The Employees' Compensation Appeals Board (Board) was created by Reorganization Plan No. 2 of 1946 (60 Stat. 1095). The Board is independent of the Office, and its jurisdiction is strictly appellate and extends to questions of fact and law. The Board's decisions are not reviewable and are binding upon the Office.

For further information, call the Administrative Officer. Phone, 202–693–6234. Internet, www.dol.gov.

Administrative Review Board   The Board consists of a maximum of five members appointed by the Secretary. It adjudicates appeals cases under a wide range of Federal labor laws arising under the McNamara O'Hara Service Contract Act and the Davis Bacon Act. Board decisions may be appealed to Federal district or appellate courts.

For further information, call 202–693–6234.

Benefits Review Board   The Board consists of five members appointed by the Secretary. It adjudicates appeals cases under the Longshore and Harbor Workers' Compensation Act and the Black Lung Benefits Act. Board decisions may be appealed to the U.S. Courts of Appeals and to the U.S. Supreme Court.

For further information, call 202–693–6234.

Office of Small Business Programs   The Office of Small Business Programs ensures procurement opportunities for small businesses, disadvantaged businesses, women-owned businesses, HUBZone businesses, and businesses owned by service-disabled veterans. It serves as the Department's ombudsman under the Small Business Regulatory Enforcement Fairness Act (SBREFA) and is the Department's central referral point for inquiries and complaints arising under SBREFA. It is also active in the Department of Labor's compliance assistance activities. The Office manages the Department's programs for minority

DEPARTMENT OF LABOR

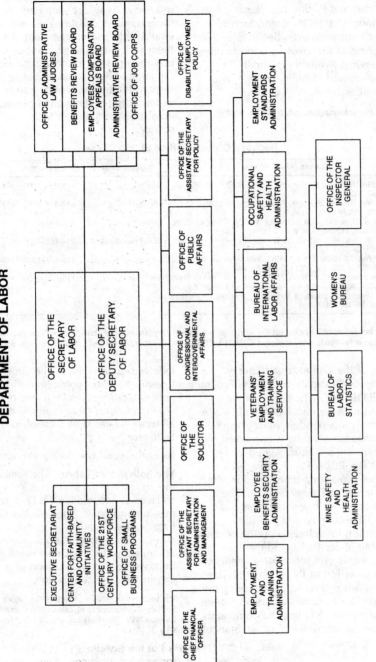

OFFICE OF THE SECRETARY OF LABOR

OFFICE OF THE DEPUTY SECRETARY OF LABOR

OFFICE OF ADMINISTRATIVE LAW JUDGES
BENEFITS REVIEW BOARD
EMPLOYEES' COMPENSATION APPEALS BOARD
ADMINISTRATIVE REVIEW BOARD
OFFICE OF JOB CORPS

EXECUTIVE SECRETARIAT
CENTER FOR FAITH-BASED AND COMMUNITY INITIATIVES
OFFICE OF THE 21ST CENTURY WORKFORCE
OFFICE OF SMALL BUSINESS PROGRAMS

OFFICE OF THE CHIEF FINANCIAL OFFICER
OFFICE OF THE ASSISTANT SECRETARY FOR ADMINISTRATION AND MANAGEMENT
OFFICE OF THE SOLICITOR
OFFICE OF CONGRESSIONAL AND INTERGOVERNMENTAL AFFAIRS
OFFICE OF PUBLIC AFFAIRS
OFFICE OF THE ASSISTANT SECRETARY FOR POLICY
OFFICE OF DISABILITY EMPLOYMENT POLICY

EMPLOYMENT AND TRAINING ADMINISTRATION
EMPLOYEE BENEFITS SECURITY ADMINISTRATION
VETERANS' EMPLOYMENT AND TRAINING SERVICE
BUREAU OF INTERNATIONAL LABOR AFFAIRS
OCCUPATIONAL SAFETY AND HEALTH ADMINISTRATION
EMPLOYMENT STANDARDS ADMINISTRATION

MINE SAFETY AND HEALTH ADMINISTRATION
BUREAU OF LABOR STATISTICS
WOMEN'S BUREAU
OFFICE OF THE INSPECTOR GENERAL

colleges and universities and Asian American and Pacific Islanders. Additionally, the Office conducts national outreach activities to raise awareness of the growing opportunities and services available to small businesses and minority colleges and universities.

For further information, call 202–693–6460.

Office of Job Corps   Job Corps's mission is to attract young adults, teach them relevant skills they need to become employable and independent, and help them secure meaningful jobs or opportunities for further education. The Office has six regional offices responsible for monitoring and oversight of Job Corps centers, outreach and admissions, and career transition services.

Regional Offices—Office of Job Corps

Address (Areas Served)	Regional Director	Telephone	Fax
Atlanta, GA (Rm. 6T9, 61 Forsyth St. SW., 30303) (AL, FL, GA, MS, NC, SC, TN).	Walt Hall	404–302–5400	404–302–4515
Boston, MA (Rm. E–350, JFK Federal Bldg., 02203) (CT, NJ, NY, MA, ME, NH, PR, RI, VI, VT).	Joe Semansky	617–788–0186	617–788–0189
Chicago, IL (Rm. 676, 230 S. Dearborn St., 60604) (IA, IL, IN, KS, MI, MN, MO, NE, OH, WI).	Donna Kay	312–596–5470	312–596–5471
Dallas, TX (Rm. 403, 525 Griffin St., 75202) (AR, CO, LA, MT, ND, NM, OK, SD, TX, UT, WY).	June Boswell	214–850–4100	214–850–4101
Philadelphia, PA (Suite 815 E., 170 S. Independence Mall West, 19106–3315) (DC, DE, MD, KY, PA, VA, WV).	Lynn Intrepidi	215–861–5500	215–861–5520
San Francisco, CA (Rm. 1050, 71 Stevenson St., 94119-3767) (AK, AZ, CA, HI, ID, NV, OR, WA, American Samoa, Saipan-CNMI, Federated States of Micronesia, Republic of Marshall Islands, Territory of Guam).	Brian Daher	415–625–2600	415–625–2590

For further information, contact the Office of Job Corps, Department of Labor, 200 Constitution Avenue NW., Room N–4463, Washington, DC 20210. Phone, 202–693–3000. Internet, http://jobcorps.dol.gov.

Office of the Ombudsman/Energy Employees Occupational Illness Program Act (EEOICPA)   The Office of the Ombudsman for Part E of the EEOICPA is a small, independent office, headed by the Ombudsman, who is appointed by the Secretary of Labor. Signed into law in October 2004, Part E replaced a previous program administered by the Department of Energy (Part D). The Office conducts town hall meetings around the country and provides information to claimants on the benefits available under Part E and the requirements and procedures applicable to the provision of those benefits. The Office advises the DOL concerning the location of Resource Centers and issues annual reports detailing the complaints, grievances, and requests for assistance received by the Office. The Office also assesses the most common difficulties encountered by claimants and potential claimants during that year and performs all other related duties specified by the Secretary.

For further information, call 202–693–5890.

The Solicitor of Labor   The Office of the Solicitor provides necessary legal services to accomplish the Department's mission and goals. The Solicitor directs a broad-scale litigation effort in the Federal courts pertaining to various labor statutes administered by the Department, ranging from workers' compensation to employment discrimination.

For further information, contact the Office of the Solicitor, Department of Labor, 200 Constitution Avenue NW., Washington, DC 20210. Phone, 202–693–5260.

Regional Offices—Office of the Solicitor
(RS: Regional Solicitor; ARS: Associate Regional Solicitor)

Region	Address	Solicitor
Atlanta, GA (AL, FL, GA, KY, MS, NC, SC, TN).	Rm. 7T10, 61 Forsyth St., 30303	Stanley E. Keen (RS)

Regional Offices—Office of the Solicitor—Continued
(RS: Regional Solicitor; ARS: Associate Regional Solicitor)

Region	Address	Solicitor
Branch Office	Suite 230, 618 Church St., Nashville, TN 37219–2440.	Theresa Ball (ARS)
Boston, MA (CT, ME, MA, NH, RI, VT)	Rm. E–375, JFK Federal Office Bldg., 02203.	Michael Felson, *Acting* (RS)
Chicago, IL (IL, IN, MI, MN, OH, WI).	Rm. 844, 230 S. Dearborn St., 60604–1502.	Joan Gestrin (RS)
Branch Office	Rm. 881, 1240 E. 9th St., Cleveland, OH 44199.	Benjamin Chinni (ARS)
Dallas, TX (AR, LA, NM, OK, TX)	Suite 501, 525 S. Griffin St., 75202–5020	James Culp (RS)
Kansas City, MO (CO, IA, KS, MO, MT, NE, ND, SD, UT, WY).	Suite 1020, 2300 Main St., 64108	Michael A. Stabler (RS)
Branch Office	Suite 1600, 1999 Broadway, Denver, CO 80202–6550.	(vacancy) (ARS)
New York, NY (NJ, NY, PR, VI)	Rm. 983, 201 Varick St., 10014	Patricia M. Rodenhausen (RS)
Philadelphia, PA (DE, DC, MD, PA, VA, WV).	Suite 630 E., 170 S. Independence Mall West, 19106–3306.	Catherine O. Murphy (RS)
Branch Office	1100 Wilson Blvd., 22d Floor West, Arlington, VA 22209–2247.	Douglas N. White (ARS)
San Francisco, CA (AK, AZ, CA, HI, ID, NV, OR, WA, GU, MP, AS).	Suite 3–700, 90 7th St. 94103	Lawrence Brewster (RS)
Branch Office	Suite 370, 350 S. Figueroa St., Los Angeles, CA 90071–1202.	Daniel Chasek, *Acting* (ARS)
Branch Office	Suite 945, 1111 3d Ave., Seattle, WA 98101–3212.	Bruce L. Brown (ARS)

Women's Bureau   The Women's Bureau is responsible for promoting the status of wage-earning women, improving their working conditions, increasing their efficiency, and advancing their opportunities for profitable employment.

For further information, call 202–693–6710.

Regional Offices—Women's Bureau

Address (Areas Served)	Administrator
Atlanta, GA (Suite 6B75, 61 Forsyth St. SW., 30303) AL, FL, GA, KY, MS, NC, SC, TN) ...	Paulette N. Lewis
Boston, MA (Rm. 525A, JFK Federal Bldg., 02203) (CT, MA, ME, NH, RI, VT)	Jacqueline Cooke
Chicago, IL (Rm. 1022, 230 S. Dearborn St., 60604) (IL, IN, MI, MN, OH, WI)	Nancy Chen
Dallas, TX (Suite 735, 525 Griffin St., 75202) (AR, LA, NM, OK, TX)	Beverly Lyle
Denver, CO (Suite 1620, 1999 Broadway, 80202–6550) (CO, MT, ND, SD, UT, WY)	Frances Jefferson
Kansas City, MO (Suite 1050, 2300 Main St., 64108) (IA, KS, MO, NE)	Dorothy A. Witherspoon
New York, NY (Rm. 708, 201 Varick St., 10014) (NJ, NY, PR, VI)	Grace Protos
Philadelphia, PA (Suite 631 E., 170 S. Independence Mall W., 19106–3318) (DC, DE, MD, PA, VA, WV).	Lucia Bruce
San Francisco, CA (Suite 2–650,90 7th St. 94103) (AZ, CA, GU, HI, NV)	Jenny Erwin
Seattle, WA (Rm. 925, 1111 3d Ave., 98101) (AK, ID, OR, WA)	Betty Lock

International Affairs   The Bureau of International Labor Affairs is mandated to carry out the Secretary's international responsibilities, develop departmental policy and programs relating to international activities, and coordinate departmental international activities involving other U.S. Government agencies, intergovernmental and nongovernmental organizations.

For further information, call 202–693–4770.

Office of Inspector General   The Office of Inspector General conducts audits and investigations to review the effectiveness, efficiency, economy, and integrity of all DOL programs and operations, including those performed by its contractors and grantees. The Office is unique among Inspectors General because it conducts labor racketeering investigations in employee benefit plans, labor-managemen t relations, and internal labor union affairs.

For further information, call 202–693–5100.

Employment and Training Administration

The Employment and Training Administration (ETA) provides quality job training, employment, labor market information, and income maintenance services primarily through State and local workforce development systems. ETA also administers programs to enhance employment opportunities and business prosperity.

Office of Workforce Investment   The Office of Workforce Investment (OWI) provides leadership, oversight, policy guidance, and technical assistance to the Nation's workforce investment system including the One-Stop Career Center systems, the youth and adult employment and training programs, and national programs for targeted populations. OWI oversees investments in innovative workforce solutions in high-growth sectors of the economy, including providing training through community colleges. OWI also oversees the development and dissemination of tools and information related to workforce and economic data, career guidance, and workforce skills and competencies.

For further information, call 202–693–3980.

Office of Workforce Security   The Office of Workforce Security provides national leadership, oversight, policy guidance, and technical assistance to Federal-State unemployment compensation system. The Office also interprets Federal legislative requirements.

For more information, call 202–693–3029. Internet, www.workforcesecurity.doleta.gov.

Office of National Response   The Office of National Response is responsible for national leadership, oversight, policy guidance, funding allocations, and technical assistance for Trade Adjustment Assistance and National Emergency Grant programs for dislocated workers.

For more information, call 202–693–3500.

Office of Apprenticeship   The Office of Apprenticeship administers the National

Registered Apprenticeship System. The Office promotes the adoption by employers, labor, and other organizers of formalized, structured training programs. It also enhances opportunities for women and minorities to participate in such programs.

For more information, call 202–693–2796. Internet, www.doleta.gov/oa.

Office of Foreign Labor Certification   The Office of Foreign Labor Certification provides national leadership and policy guidance to carry out the responsibilities of the Secretary of Labor, under the Immigration and Nationality Act, as amended, concerning foreign workers seeking admission to the United States for employment.

For more information, call 202–693–3010. Internet, www.foreignlaborcert.doleta.gov.

Office of Performance and Technology   The Office of Performance and Technology (PROTECH) is responsible for the construction, maintenance, and improvement of ETA's technology infrastructure for its national and regional offices. PROTECH provides executive leadership for the Agency in the development of its strategic plan, measurement of performance and results, and increased accountability of the workforce investment system to customers, partners, and stakeholders. PROTECH ensures that ETA has a 21st century information technology infrastructure supporting the Agency's mission and all its business lines.

For further information, call 202–693–3420.

Office of Policy Development and Research   The Office of Policy Development and Research (OPDR) supports ETA policies and investments to improve the public workforce. OPDR analyzes, formulates, and recommends legislative changes and options for policy initiatives and provides ETA with relevant research, demonstrations, and program evaluations.

For further information, call 202–693–3700.

Office of Financial and Administrative Management The Office of Financial and Administrative Management (OFAM) provides leadership and direction to ensure sound management of financial resources throughout the ETA and also budget, accounting, and data analysis services for the ETA. OFAM is responsible for planning, developing, promulgating, and executing policies, standards, and guidelines governing ETA management of information, budget, accounting, financial and procurement systems, personnel management, organizational analysis, technical training and life-long learning, and administrative and property management services. OFAM provides centralized services to ETA National Office components for procurement and for job training assistance management. The Office also plans and administers the ETA personnel and organizational management programs, which include staffing, position classification and management, employee development and utilization, and labor management and employee relations.

For further information, call 202–693–2800.

Office of Regional Innovation and Transformation The Office of Regional Innovation and Transformation, through its six regional offices, supports the development and operation of the workforce investment system through oversight of and assistance to States and other agency grant recipients. These activities protect Federal taxpayer investment, maximize program return-on-investment, improve the administration and outcome of ETA-funded grants and programs, and better meet the needs of businesses and workers in the 21st century economy.

For further information, call 202–693–3690.

The Employment and Training Administration has six regional offices responsible for the oversight and grants administration of employment and training programs operated by State governments.

Regional Offices—Employment and Training Administration

Address (Areas Served)	Administrator	Telephone	Fax
Atlanta, GA (Rm. 6M12, 61 Forsyth St. SW., 30303) (AL, FL, GA, KY, MS, NC, SC, TN).	Helen N. Parker	404–302–5300	404–302–5382
Boston, MA (Rm. E–350, JFK Federal Bldg., 02203) (CT, NJ, NY, MA, ME, NH, PR, RI, VI, VT).	Grace A. Kilbane	617–788–0170	617–788–0101
Chicago, IL (Rm. 628, 230 S. Dearborn St., 60604) (IA, IL, IN, KS, MI, MN, MO, NE, OH, WI).	Byron Zudiema	312–596–5400	312–596–5401
Dallas, TX (Rm. 317, 525 S. Griffin St., 75202) (AR, CO, LA, MT, ND, NM, OK, SD, TX, UT, WY).	Joseph C. Juarez	972–850–4600	972–850–4605
Philadelphia, PA (Suite 825 E., 170 S. Independence Mall West, 19106–3315) (DC, DE, MD, PA, VA, WV).	Lenita Jacobs-Simmons.	215–861–5201	215–861–5260
San Francisco, CA (Suite 17–300, 90 7th St., 94103) (AK, AZ, CA, HI, ID, NV, OR, WA, American Samoa, Saipan-CNMI, Federated States of Micronesia, Republic of Marshall Islands, Territory of Guam).	Richard Trigg	415–625–7900	415–625–7903

For further information, contact the Employment and Training Administration. Phone, 202–693–2700. Internet, www.doleta.gov.

Employee Benefits Security Administration

The Employee Benefits Security Administration (EBSA) promotes and protects the pension, health, and other benefits of the over 150 million participants and beneficiaries in over 6 million private sector employee benefit plans. In administering its responsibilities, EBSA assists workers in understanding their rights and protecting their benefits; facilitates compliance by plan sponsors, plan officials, service providers, and other members of the regulated community; encourages the growth of employment-based benefits;

and deters and corrects violations of the relevant statutes. The Employee Retirement Income Security Act (ERISA) is enforced through 15 EBSA field offices nationwide and the national office in Washington, DC.

Field Offices—Employee Benefits Security Administration

Area/Address	Director
Atlanta, GA (Suite 7B54, 61 Forsyth St. SW., 30303)	Rebecca Marshall
Boston, MA (Rm. 575, John F. Kennedy Bldg., 02203)	Jean Ackerman
Chicago, IL (Suite 1600, 200 W. Adams St., 60606)	Steve Haugen
Cincinnati, OH (Suite 210, 1885 Dixie Hwy., Fort Wright, KY 41011)	Paul Baumann
Detroit, MI (Suite 1310, 211 W. Fort St., 48226–3211)	Patrick Kawa (DS)
Dallas, TX (Rm. 900, 525 S. Griffin St., 75202)	Roger Hilburn
Kansas City, MO (Suite 1100, 2300 Main St., 64108)	Steve Eischen
Los Angeles, CA (Suite 200, 1055 E. Colorado Blvd., Pasadena, CA 91106–2341)	Crisanta Johnson
Miami, FL (Suite 104, Bldg. H, 8040 Peters Rd., Plantation, FL 33324)	Isabel Colon (DS)
New York, NY (Suite 1200, 33 Whitehall St., 10004)	Jonathan Kay
Philadelphia, PA (Suite 870 W., 170 S. Independence Mall W., 19106)	Mabel Capolongo
St. Louis, MO (Rm. 6310, Robert A. Young Federal Bldg., 1222 Spruce St., 63103–2818)	Gary Newman (DS)
San Francisco, CA (Suite 11–300, 90 7th St., 94103)	Billy Beaver
Seattle, WA (Suite 860, 1111 3d Ave., 98101–3212)	Duane Peterson (DS)
Washington, DC (Suite 200, 1335 East-West Highway, Silver Spring, MD 20910)	Elizabeth Bond (DS)

For further information, contact the Employee Benefits Security Administration. Phone, 866–444–3272. Internet, www.dol.gov/ebsa.

Employment Standards Administration

The Employment Standards Administration (ESA) manages and directs employment standards programs. It handles minimum wage and overtime standards; registration of farm labor contractors; determining prevailing wage rates to be paid on Government contracts and subcontracts; nondiscrimination and affirmative action for minorities, women, veterans, and handicapped Government contract and subcontract workers; and workers' compensation programs for Federal and certain private employers and employees. ESA also safeguards the financial integrity and internal democracy of labor unions and administers statutory programs to certify employee protection provisions for various federally sponsored transportation programs.

Contracts   The Office of Federal Contract Compliance Programs (OFCCP)

administers and enforces three equal opportunity mandates: Executive Order 11246, as amended; section 503 of the Rehabilitation Act of 1973, as amended; and the Vietnam Era Veterans' Readjustment Assistance Act of 1974, as amended, 38 U.S.C. 4212. These mandates prohibit Federal contractors and subcontractors from discriminating on the basis of race, color, religion, sex, national origin, disability, or veteran status. They also require Federal contractors and subcontractors to take affirmative steps to ensure equal opportunity in their employment processes. OFCCP also shares responsibility with the U.S. Equal Opportunity Employment Commission in enforcing Title I of the Americans with Disabilities Act.

For further information, contact the Office of Federal Contract Compliance Programs help desk. Phone, 800–397–6251. Internet, www.dol.gov/esa/ofccp/index.htm.

Regional Directors—Office of Federal Contract Compliance Programs

Address (Areas Served)	Director
Southeast (61 Forsyth St. SW., Atlanta, GA 30303) (AL, FL, GA, KY, MS, NC, SC, TN)	Evelyn Y. Teague
Midwest (230 S. Dearborn St., Chicago, IL 60604) (IA, IL, IN, KS, MI, MN, MO, NE, OH, WI).	Sandra S. Zeigler

Regional Directors—Office of Federal Contract Compliance Programs—Continued

Address (Areas Served)	Director
Southwest and Rocky Mtns. (525 S. Griffin St., Dallas, TX 75202) (AR, CO, LA, MT, ND, NM, OK, SD, TX, UT, WY).	Joan Sessoms-Ford
Northeast (201 Varick St., New York, NY 10014) (CT, MA, ME, NH, NJ, NY, PR, RI, VI, VT).	(vacancy)
Mid-Atlantic (170 S. Independence Mall West, Philadelphia, PA 19106) (DC, DE, MD, PA, VA, WV).	Michelle Hodge, *Acting*
Pacific (90 7th St., San Francisco, CA 94103) (AK, AZ, CA, HI, ID, NV, OR, WA)	William D. Smitherman

Wages The Wage and Hour Division is responsible for planning, directing, and administering programs dealing with a variety of Federal labor legislation. These programs are designed to protect low-wage incomes; safeguard the health and welfare of workers by discouraging excessively long work hours; safeguard the health and well-being of minors; prevent curtailment of employment and earnings for students, trainees, and handicapped workers; minimize losses of income and job rights caused by indebtedness; and direct a program of farm labor contractor registration designed to protect the health, safety, and welfare of migrant and seasonal agricultural workers.

For further information, contact the Office of the Administrator, Wage and Hour Division, Department of Labor, Room S–3502, 200 Constitution Avenue NW., Washington, DC 20210. Phone, 202–693–0051.

Regional Administrators—Wage and Hour Division

Address (Areas Served)	Regional Administrator
Northeast Region (850 W., 170 S. Independence Mall W., Philadelphia, PA 19106)	Corlis L. Sellers
Southeast Region (Rm. 7M40, 61 Forsyth St. SW., Atlanta, GA 30303)	Oliver Peebles III, *Acting*
Midwest Region (Rm. 530, 230 S. Dearborn St., Chicago, IL 60604–1591)	Karen Chaikin, *Acting*
Southwest Region (Rm. 800, 525 S. Griffin St., Dallas, TX 75202–5007)	Cynthia Watson
Western Region (Suite 13, 90 7th St., San Francisco, CA 94103–6714)	George Friday, Jr.

Labor-Management Standards The Office of Labor-Management Standards conducts criminal and civil investigations to safeguard the financial integrity of unions and to ensure union democracy, and conducts investigative audits of labor unions to uncover and remedy criminal and civil violations of the Labor-Management Reporting and Disclosure Act and related statutes.

For Labor-Management Reporting and Disclosure Act assistance, call 202–693–0123. For electronic forms software technical support, call 866–401–1109. For transit employee protections assistance, call 202–693–0126. Internet, www.dol.gov/esa/olms.

Regional Offices—Office of Labor-Management Standards

Region	Address	Director
Atlanta, GA	Suite 8B85, 61 Forsyth St. SW., 30303	L. Antoinette Dempsey
Chicago, IL	Suite 774, 230 S. Dearborn St., 60604	Ronald Lehman
Philadelphia, PA	Suite 775 W., 170 S. Independence Mall West, 19106	Eric Feldman
San Francisco, CA	Suite 18–300, 90 7th St., 94103	Dennis Eckert

Workers' Compensation The Office of Workers' Compensation Programs is responsible for programs providing workers' compensation for Federal employees, benefits to employees in private enterprise while engaged in maritime employment on navigable waters in the United States, and benefits to coal miners who are totally disabled due to pneumoconiosis, a respiratory disease contracted after prolonged inhalation of coal mine dust, and to their survivors when the miner's death is due to pneumoconiosis.

For further information, contact the Office of the Director, Office of Workers' Compensation Programs, Department of Labor, Room S–3524, 200 Constitution Avenue NW., Washington, DC 20210. Phone, 202–693–0031.

Regional Offices—Office of Workers' Compensation Programs

Region (Areas Served)	Address	Director
Chicago, IL (IL, IN, MI, OH, WI)	Rm. 800, 230 S. Dearborn St., 60604	Nancy Jenson
Dallas, TX (AR, LA, NM, OK, TX)	Rm. 407, 525 S. Griffin St., 75202	E. Martin Walker
Jacksonville, FL (AL, FL, GA, KY, MS, NC, SC, TN).	Rm. 943, 400 W. Bay St., 32202	Richard Brettell
New York, NY (CT, MA, ME, NH, PR, RI, NJ, NY, VI, VT).	201 Varick St., 10014	Robert Sullivan
Philadelphia, PA (DC, DE, MD, PA, VA, WV)	170 S. Independence Mall West, 19106	R. David Lotz
San Francisco, CA (AZ, CA, Guam, HI, NV)	Suite 15–100, 90 7th St., 94103	Sharon Tyler

District Offices
Division of Federal Employees' Compensation

Boston, MA	Rm. E–260, JFK Federal Bldg., 02203	Susan Morales
Chicago, IL	8th Fl., 230 S. Dearborn St., 60604	Joan Rosel
Cleveland, OH	Rm. 851, 1240 E. 9th St., 44199	Karen Spence
Dallas, TX	Rm. 100, 525 S. Griffin St., 75202	Frances Memmolo
Denver, CO	Suite 600, 1999 Broadway, 80202	Shirley Bridge
Jacksonville, FL	Rm. 826, 400 W. Bay St., 32202	Magdalena Fernandez
Kansas City, MO	Suite 1090, 2300 Main St., 64108	Lois Maxwell
New York, NY	201 Varick St., 10014	Zev Sapir
Philadelphia, PA	170 S. Independence Mall West, 19106	Jack McKenna
San Francisco, CA	90 7th St., 94103	Andrew Tharp
Seattle, WA	1111 3d Ave., 98101	Marcus Tapia
Washington, DC	Rm. 800, 800 N. Capitol St. NW., 20211	Linda DeCarlo

Division of Longshore and Harbor Workers' Compensation

Baltimore, MD	31 Hopkins Plz., 21201	Emma Riley
Boston, MA	Rm. E–260, JFK Federal Bldg., 02203	David B. Groeneveld
Honolulu, HI	300 Ala Moana Blvd., 96850	R. Todd Bruininks
Houston, TX	Suite 140, 8866 Gulf Freeway, 77017	Brad Soshea
Jacksonville, FL	Rm. 63A, 400 W. Bay St., 32202	Charles Lee
Long Beach, CA	Suite 720, 401 E. Ocean Blvd., 90802	Eric Richardson
New Orleans, LA	Suite 617, 600 S. Maestri Pl., 70130	David A. Duhon
New York, NY	201 Varick St., 10014	Richard V. Robilotti
Norfolk, VA	Rm. 212, 200 Granby Mall, 23510	Theresa Magyar
San Francisco, CA	Suite 15–100, 90 7th St., 94103	R. Todd Bruininks
Seattle, WA	Suite 620, 1111 3d Ave., 98101–3212	Karen Staats

Division of Coal Mine Workers' Compensation

Charleston, WV	Suite 110, 500 Quarrier St., 25301	Richard Hanna
Columbus, OH	Suite 300, 1160 Dublin Rd., 43215	Lorraine Rardain
Denver, CO	1999 Broadway, 80201	Deborah Brunger
Greensburg, PA	1225 S. Main St., 15601	Colleen Smalley
Johnstown, PA	Rm. 226, 319 Washington St., 15901	Stuart Glassman
Pikeville, KY	164 Main St., 41501	Roger Belcher
Wilkes-Barre, PA	Suite 300A, 100 N. Wilkes-Barre Blvd., 18702.	Maribeth Girton

District Offices—Division of Energy Employees Occupational Illness Compensation

Area	Address	Director
Cleveland, OH	Suite 350, 1001 Lakeside Ave., 44114	Annette Prindle
Denver, CO	Suite 1120, 1999 Broadway, 80201	Janet Kipsen
Jacksonville, FL	Suite 722, 440 W. Bay St., 32202	James Bibeault
Seattle, WA	Suite 601, 719 2d Ave., 98104	Joyce Vail

For further information, contact the Employment Standards Administration, Department of Labor, Room S–3524, 200 Constitution Avenue NW., Washington, DC 20210. Phone, 202–693–0031. Internet, www.dol.gov/esa/index.htm.

Occupational Safety and Health Administration

The Occupational Safety and Health Administration (OSHA) sets and enforces workplace safety and health standards and assists employers in complying with those standards. OSHA, created pursuant to the Occupational Safety and Health Act of 1970 (29 U.S.C. 651 *et seq.*), has established a fourfold focus:
—firm enforcement of workplace safety and health rules;

—swift promulgation of strong, protective health and safety standards;

—increased outreach and help for workers and their employers in their efforts to eliminate and control workplace hazards; and

—partnership with the States that are running their own OSHA-approved programs.

Regional Offices—Occupational Safety and Health Administration

Address (Areas Served)	Administrator	Telephone
Atlanta, GA (Rm. 6T50, 61 Forsyth St. SW., 30303) (AL, FL, GA, KY, MS, NC, SC, TN).	Cindy Coe Laseter	404–562–2300
Boston, MA (Rm. E–340, JFK Federal Bldg., 02203) (CT, MA, ME, NH, RI, VT)	Marthe Kent	617–565–9860
Chicago, IL (230 S. Dearborn St., 60604) (IL, IN, MI, MN, OH, WI)	Michael Connors	312–353–2220
Dallas, TX (Suite 602, 525 Griffin St., 75202) (AR, LA, NM, OK, TX)	Dean McDaniel	972–850–4145
Denver, CO (1999 Broadway, 80202) (CO, MT, ND, SD, UT, WY)	Greg Baxter	720–264–6550
Kansas City, MO (Suite 1010, 2300 Main St., 64108) (IA, KS, MO, NE	Charles Adkins	816–283–8745
New York, NY (Rm. 670, 201 Varick St., 10014) (NJ, NY, PR)	Robert Kulik, *Acting* ..	212–337–2378
Philadelphia, PA (Suite 740, 170 S. Independence Mall West, 19106) (DC, DE, MD, PA, VA, WV).	John Hermanson	215–861–4900
San Francisco, CA (Suite 18100, 90 7th St., 94103) (AZ, CA, HI, NV	Ken Atha	415–625–2555
Seattle, WA (Suite 715, 1111 3d Ave., 98101) (AK, ID, OR, WA)	Richard Terrill	206–553–5930

For further information, contact the Occupational Safety and Health Administration, Department of Labor, 200 Constitution Avenue NW., Washington, DC 20210. Phone, 202–693–1999.

Mine Safety and Health Administration

The Mine Safety and Health Administration (MSHA) is responsible for safety and health in the Nation's mines. MSHA develops and promulgates mandatory safety and health standards, ensures compliance with such standards, assesses civil penalties for violations, and investigates accidents. It cooperates with and provides assistance to the States in the development of effective State mine

safety and health programs; improves and expands training programs in cooperation with the States and the mining industry; and contributes to the improvement and expansion of mine safety and health research and development. All of these activities are aimed at preventing and reducing mine accidents and occupational diseases in the mining industry.

District Offices—Mine Safety and Health Administration (Coal Mine Safety and Health)

District/Address	Telephone
Barbourville, KY (3837 S. U.S. Hwy., 25 E, 40906)	606–546–5123
Birmingham, AL (Suite 213, 135 Gemini Cir., 35209–4896)	205–290–7300
Denver, CO (Bldg. 25, E–18, 6th & Kipling, 2d St., 80225)	303–231–5458
Mt. Pleasant, PA (Suite 100, 631 Excel Dr., 15666)	724–925–5150
Madisonville, KY (100 YMCA Dr., 42431–9019)	270–821–4180
Morgantown, WV (604 Cheat Rd., 26508)	304–225–6800
Mount Hope, WV (100 Bluestone Rd., 25880)	304–877–3900
Norton, VA (P.O. Box 560, 24273)	276–679–0230
Pikeville, KY (100 Fae Ramsey Ln., 41501)	606–432–0943
Vincennes, IN (Suite 200, 2300 Willow St., 47591)	812–882–7617
Wilkes-Barre, PA (Suite 034, 7 N. Wilkes-Barre Blvd., 18702)	570–826–6321
Metal/Nonmetal Mine Safety and Health	
Northeastern (547 Keystone Dr., Warrendale, PA 15086–7573)	724–772–2333

District Offices—Mine Safety and Health Administration (Coal Mine Safety and Health)—Continued

District/Address	Telephone
Southeastern (Suite 212, 135 Gemini Cir., Birmingham, AL 35209–4896)	205–290–7294
North Central (515 W. 1st St., Duluth, MN 55802–1302)	218–720–5448
South Central (Rm. 462, 1100 Commerce St., Dallas, TX 75242–0499)	214–767–8401
Rocky Mountain (P.O. Box 25367, Denver, CO 80225–0367)	303–231–5465
Western (Suite 610, 2060 Peabody Rd., Vacaville, CA 95687)	707–447–9844
Additional Offices	
Pittsburgh Safety and Health Technology Center (P.O. Box 18233, Pittsburgh, PA 15236)	412–386–6901
Approval and Certification Center (R.R. 1, Box 251, Triadelphia, WV 26059)	304–547–0400
National Mine Health and Safety Academy (1301 Airport Rd., Beaver, WV 25813–9426)	304–256–3100

For further information, contact the Office of Programs, Education and Outreach Services, Mine Safety and Health Administration, Department of Labor, Room 2317, 1100 Wilson Boulevard, Arlington, VA 22209–3939. Phone, 202–693–9400.

Office of Disability Employment Policy

The Office of Disability Employment Policy (ODEP) provides national disability employment policy leadership by developing and influencing the implementation of disability employment policies and practices affecting the employment of people with disabilities. ODEP's response to low employment rates among such a large group of Americans is unique, comprehensive, and aggressive, and includes the active involvement and cooperation of Federal, State, and local public and private entities, including employers. ODEP also leads efforts to achieve the employment-related goals of the President's New Freedom Initiative.

ODEP addresses the significant barriers to employment faced by individuals with disabilities by developing and disseminating national, State, and local disability employment policy; by fostering implementation of innovative strategies and practices among employers and throughout the various systems serving people with disabilities; by conducting disability-related research to build knowledge to inform policy development; and by providing technical assistance to service delivery systems and employers to increase employment opportunities and the recruitment, retention, and promotion of people with disabilities.

For further information, call 202–693–7880. TTY, 202–693–7881. Internet, www.dol.gov/odep.

Bureau of Labor Statistics

The Bureau of Labor Statistics (BLS) is the principal fact-finding agency of the Federal Government in the broad field of labor economics and statistics. The Bureau is an independent national statistical agency that collects, processes, analyzes, and disseminates essential statistical data to the American public, Congress, other Federal agencies, State and local governments, businesses, and labor. BLS also serves as a statistical

resource to the Department of Labor. Data are available relating to employment, unemployment, and other characteristics of the labor force; consumer and producer prices, consumer expenditures, and import and export prices; wages and employee benefits; productivity and technological change; employment projections; occupational illness and injuries; and international comparisons of labor statistics. Most of the data are collected in surveys conducted by the Bureau, the Bureau of the Census (on a contract basis), or on a cooperative basis with State agencies.

The Bureau strives to have its data satisfy a number of criteria, including: relevance to current social and economic issues, timeliness in reflecting today's rapidly changing economic conditions, accuracy and consistently high statistical quality, and impartiality in both subject matter and presentation.

The basic data are issued in monthly, quarterly, and annual news releases; bulletins, reports, and special publications; and periodicals. Data are also made available through an electronic news service, magnetic tape, diskettes, and microfiche, as well as on the Internet at stats.bls.gov. Regional offices issue additional reports and releases usually presenting locality or regional detail.

Regional Offices—Bureau of Labor Statistics

Region	Address	Commissioner
Atlanta, GA (AL, FL, GA, KY, MS, NC, SC, TN)	61 Forsyth St. SW., 30303	Janet S. Rankin
Boston, MA (CT, ME, MA, NH, NY, PR, RI, VT)	JFK Federal Bldg., 02203	Denis S. McSweeney
Chicago, IL (IA, IL, IN, MI, MN, ND, NE, OH, SD, WI)	230 S. Dearborn St., 60604	Jay Mousa
Dallas, TX (AR, CO, KS, LA, MO, MT, NM, OK, TX, UT, WY).	525 Griffin Sq. Bldg., 75202	Stan Suchman
Philadelphia, PA (DE, DC, MD, NJ, PA, VA, WV)	Suite 610E, 170 S. Independence Mall West, 19106.	Sheila Watkins
San Francisco, CA (AK, AS, AZ, CA, GU, HI, ID, NV, OR, Pacific Islands, WA).	71 Stevenson St., 94119–3766	Richard Holden

For further information, contact the Associate Commissioner, Office of Publications and Special Studies, Bureau of Labor Statistics, Department of Labor, Room 4110, 2 Massachusetts Avenue NE., Washington, DC 20212. Phone, 202–691–5200.

Veterans' Employment and Training Service

The Veterans' Employment and Training Service (VETS) is responsible for administering veterans' employment and training programs and activities to ensure that legislative and regulatory mandates are accomplished. The field staff works closely with and provides technical assistance to State employment security agencies and to Workforce Investment Act and Homeless Veterans Reintegration Programs grant recipients to ensure that veterans are provided the priority services required by law. They also coordinate with employers, labor unions, veterans service organizations, and community organizations through planned public information and outreach activities. VETS provides training to separating servicemembers through its

transition assistance program. Federal contractors are provided management assistance in complying with their veterans affirmative action and reporting obligations. VETS protects the employment and reemployment rights of servicemembers and veterans by investigating complaints received under the Uniformed Services Employment and Reemployment Rights Act concerning denial of veterans preference in Federal hiring and also complaints concerning job, seniority, and pension rights to veterans following absences from work for active military service. VETS also protects employment and reemployment rights of members of the Reserve and National Guard.

Regional Administrators/State Directors—Veterans' Employment and Training Service

(RA: Regional Administrator; D: Director)

Region/Address	Director	Telephone
Aberdeen, SD (420 S. Roosevelt St., 57402–4730)	Earl R. Schultz (D)	605–626–2325

Regional Administrators/State Directors—Veterans' Employment and Training Service—Continued

(RA: Regional Administrator; D: Director)

Region/Address	Director	Telephone
Albany, NY (Rm. 518, Bldg. 12, Harriman State Campus, 12240)	Barry Morgan (D)	518–457–7465
Albuquerque, NM (501 Mountain Rd. NE., 87102)	Sharon Mitchell (D)	505–346–7502
Atlanta, GA (Rm. 6T85, 61 Forsyth St. SW., 30303)	William Bolls (RA)	404–562–2305
Atlanta, GA (Suite 203, 151 Ellis St. NE., 30303)	Ed Gresham (D)	404–656–3127
Austin, TX (Suite 516–T, 1117 Trinity St., 78701)	John McKinny (D)	512–463–2814
Baltimore, MD (Rm. 205, 1100 N. Eutaw St., 21201)	Stan Seidel (D)	410–767–2110
Baton Rouge, LA (Rm. 184, 1001 N. 23d St., 70802)	Lester Parmenter (D)	225–389–0339
Bismarck, ND (1000 E. Divide Ave., 58501)	Jerry Meske (D)	701–250–4337
Boise, ID (Suite 101, 413 Idaho St., 83702)	Dale Langford (D)	208–332–8947
Boston, MA (1st Fl., 19 Staniford St., 02114–2502)	Paul Desmond (D)	617–626–6699
Boston, MA (Rm. E–315, JFK Federal Bldg., 02203)	David Houle (RA)	617–565–2080
Carson City, NV (1925 N. Carson St., 89701)	Darrol Brown (D)	775–687–4632
Casper, WY (100 W. Midwest Ave. 82602–2760)	David McNulty (D)	307–261–5454
Charleston, WV (Rm. 102, 112 California Ave., 25305–0112)	Charles Stores (D)	304–558–4001
Chicago, IL (Rm. 1064, 230 S. Dearborn St., 60604)	Heather Higgins (RA)	312–353–4932
Chicago, IL (Rm. 8174, 33 S. State St., 60603)	Patrick Winfrey (D)	312–793–3433
Columbia, SC (Suite 141, 631 Hampton St., 29201)	William C. Plowden, Jr. (D)	803–765–5195
Columbus, OH (P.O. Box 1618, 4020 East 5th Ave., 43219)	Rob Creel (D)	614–466–2768
Concord, NH (Rm. 3602, 53 Pleasant St., James C. Cleveland Federal Bldg., 03301).	Dennis Viola (D)	603–225–1424
Dallas, TX (Rm. 858, 525 Griffin St., 75202)	Lester L. Williams, Jr. (RA)	214–767–4987
Denver, CO (Suite 700, 633 17th St., 80202)	Milton Gonzales (D)	303–844–2151
Des Moines, IA (150 Des Moines St., 50309–5563)	Anthony Smithart (D)	515–281–9061
Detroit, MI (Suite 9–550, 3032 W. Grand Blvd., 48202)	Todd Kaminski (D)	313–456–3182
Frankfort, KY (2d. Fl. W., 275 E. Main St., 40621–2339)	Charles R. Netherton (D)	502–564–7062
Harrisburg, PA (Rm. 1106, 7th & Forster Sts., 17120)	Randall Wright (D)	717–787–5834
Hato Rey, PR (No. 198, Calle Guayama, 00917)	Angel Mojica (D)	787–754–5391
Helena, MT (301 South Park, No. 578, 59604)	Byron Erikson (D)	406–841–2005
Honolulu, HI (Rm. 315, 830 Punch Bowl St., 96813)	Tom Rosenswike (D)	808–522–8216
Indianapolis, IN (Rm. SE–103, 10 N. Senate Ave., 46204)	Gary Tyler (D)	317–232–6804
Jackson, MS (1235 Echelon Pkwy., 39213–1699)	Benjamin McCaffery (D)	601–321–6078
Jefferson City, MO (421 E. Dunklin St., 65101–3138)	Mickey J. Jones (D)	573–751–3921
Juneau, AK (1111 W. 8th St., 99802–5509)	Thomas Hall (D)	907–465–2723
Lewiston, ME (Suite 104, 5 Mollison Way, 04240)	Jon Guay (D)	207–753–9090
Lincoln, NE (550 South 16th St., 68508)	Stacy Destafano (D)	402–437–5289
Little Rock, AR (Rm. 237, No. 2 Capitol Mall, 72201)	Bryan Gallup (D)	501–682–3786
Madison, WI (Rm. G–201A, 201 E. Washington Ave., 53702)	Dan Schmitz (D)	608–266–3110
Montgomery, AL (Rm. 2218, 649 Monroe St., 36131–0001)	Thomas M. Karrh (D)	334–223–7677
Montpelier, VT (Rm. 303, 87 State St., 05602)	Richard Gray (D)	802–828–4441
Nashville, TN (Suite 406, 350 Pageant Ln., Clarksville, 37040)	Angela Mauldin (D)	931–572–1677
Oklahoma City, OK (Room 304–2, 2401 N. Lincoln Blvd., 73105)	Kenneth Allen (D)	405–231–5088
Olympia, WA (3d Fl., 605 Woodland Sq. Loop SE., 98503–1040)	Tom Pearson (D)	360–438–4600
Philadelphia, PA (770 W., 170 S. Independence Mall, 19106–3310)	Joseph W. Hortiz, Jr. (RA)	215–861–5390
Phoenix, AZ (1400 W. Washington St., 85005)	Michael Espinosa (D)	602–542–2515
Raleigh, NC (700 Wade Ave., 27605)	Evon Digregorio	919–856–4792
Richmond, VA (Rm. 118, 703 E. Main St., 23219)	Paul Hinkhouse (D)	804–786–7270
Sacramento, CA (Rm. W1142, 800 Capitol Mall, 94280–0001)	William F. Beal (D)	916–654–8178
St. Paul, MN (Suite 200, 332 Minnesota St., 55101)	Kevin Nagel (D)	651–296–3665
Salt Lake City, UT (Suite 209, 140 E. 300 South St., 84111–2333)	Dale Brockbank (D)	801–524–5703
San Francisco, CA (Suite 2–600, 90 7th St., 94103)	Christopher Still (RA)	415–975–4702
Tallahassee, FL (Suite B30, 107 E. Madison St., 32399)	Derek Taylor (D)	850–245–7199
Topeka, KS (Suite 509, 900 SW. Jackson St., 66612–1220)	Areon Kelvington (D)	785–296–5032
Trenton, NJ (11th Fl., CN–058, Labor Bldg., 08625)	Donna Scheel (D)	609–292–2930
Wakefield, RI (4808 Tower Hill Rd., 02879)	Steven Durst (D)	401–528–5134
Washington, DC (Rm. 3156, 64 New York Ave. NE., 20002)	Stanley Williams (D)	202–671–2143
Wethersfield, CT (200 Follybrook Blvd., 06109)	Louis Kennedy (D)	860–263–6490
Wilmington, DE (Rm. 108,4425 N. Market St., 19809–0828)	David Rich (D)	302–761–8138

For further information, contact the Assistant Secretary for Veterans' Employment and Training, Department of Labor, 200 Constitution Avenue NW., Washington, DC 20210. Phone, 202–693–4700.

Sources of Information

Contracts   General inquiries may be directed to the Procurement Services Center, Room S–4307, 200 Constitution Avenue NW., Washington, DC 20210. Phone, 202–693–4570.

Inquiries on doing business with the Job Corps should be directed to the Job Corps Regional Director in the appropriate Department of Labor regional office listed in this writeup.

Electronic Access Information concerning Department of Labor agencies, programs, and activities is available electronically through the Internet at www.dol.gov.

Employment The Department of Labor's Web site (www.dol.gov) provides detailed information about job opportunities with the Department, including the address and telephone numbers of the Department's personnel offices in the regions and in Washington, DC.

Publications The Office of Public Affairs distributes fact sheets which describe the activities of the major agencies within the Department.

The Employment and Training Administration issues periodicals such as *Area Trends in Employment and Unemployment* available by subscription through the Superintendent of Documents, Government Printing Office, Washington, DC 20402. Information about publications may be obtained from the Administration's Information Office. Phone, 202–219–6871.

The Office of Labor-Management Standards (OLMS) publishes the text of the Labor-Management Reporting and Disclosure Act and pamphlets that explain the reporting, election, bonding, and trusteeship provisions of the act. The pamphlets and reporting forms used by persons covered by the act are available free in limited quantities from the OLMS National Office at Room N–5616, 200 Constitution Avenue NW., Washington, DC 20210, and from OLMS field offices listed in the telephone directory under United States Government, Department of Labor.

The Employee Benefits Security Administration distributes fact sheets, pamphlets, and booklets on employer obligations and employee rights under ERISA. A list of publications is available by writing to the Office of Participant Assistance, Employee Benefit Security Administration, Room N–5623, 200 Constitution Avenue NW., Washington, DC 20210. Phone, 866–444–3272. Internet, www.dol.gov/ebsa.

The Bureau of Labor Statistics has an information office at 2 Massachusetts Avenue NE., Room 2850, Washington, DC 20212. Phone, 202–606–5886. Periodicals include the *Monthly Labor Review, Consumer Price Index, Producer Prices and Price Indexes, Employment and Earnings, Current Wage Developments, Occupational Outlook Handbook,* and *Occupational Outlook Quarterly.* Publications are both free and for sale, but for-sale items must be obtained from the Superintendent of Documents, Government Printing Office. Inquiries may be directed to the Washington Information Office or to the Bureau's regional offices.

Publications of the Employment Standards Administration, such as *Handy Reference Guide to the Fair Labor Standards Act,* and *OFCCP, Making Affirmative Action Work,* are available from the nearest area office. Single copies are free.

Reading Rooms Department of Labor Library, Room N2439, 200 Constitution Avenue NW., Washington, DC 20210. Phone, 202–219–6992.

The Office of Labor-Management Standards maintains a Public Disclosure Room at Room N–5616, 200 Constitution Avenue NW., Washington, DC 20210. Reports filed under the Labor-Management Reporting and Disclosure Act may be examined there and purchased for 15 cents per page. Reports also may be obtained by calling the Public Disclosure Room at 202–219–7393, or by contacting an Office field office listed in the telephone directory under United States Government, Department of Labor.

The Employee Benefits Security Administration maintains a Public Disclosure Room at Room N–1513, 200 Constitution Avenue NW., Washington, DC 20210. Reports filed under the Employee Retirement Income Security Act may be examined there and purchased for 15 cents per page or by calling the Public Disclosure Room at 202–693–8673.

The Office of Small Business Programs maintains a clearinghouse and inventory of compliance-assistance materials, which may be examined in Room C–2313, 200 Constitution Avenue NW., Washington, DC 20210. Phone, 888–972–7332. Internet, www.dol.gov/osbp.

For further information concerning the Department of Labor, contact the Office of Public Affairs, Department of Labor, Room S–1032, 200 Constitution Avenue NW., Washington, DC 20210. Phone, 202–693–4650. Internet, www.dol.gov.

DEPARTMENT OF STATE

2201 C Street NW., Washington, DC 20520
Phone, 202–647–4000. Internet, www.state.gov.

SECRETARY OF STATE	HILARY RODHAM CLINTON
DEPUTY SECRETARY OF STATE	JAMES B. STEINBERG
Deputy Secretary of State for Management and Resources	JACOB J. LEW
Ambassador-at-Large and Coordinator for Counterterrorism	(VACANCY)
U.S. Global AIDS Coordinator	MARK DYBUL
Assistant Secretary for Intelligence and Research	(VACANCY)
Assistant Secretary for Legislative Affairs	RICHARD R. VERMA
Chairman, Foreign Service Grievance Board	IRA F. JAFFE
Chief of Protocol	(VACANCY)
Counselor and Chief of Staff	CHERYL MILLS
Civil Service Ombudsman	(VACANCY)
Counselor of the Department of State	CHERYL MILLS
Director of the Office of Civil Rights	JOHN M. ROBINSON
Director, Policy Planning Staff	ANNE-MARIE SLAUGHTER
Inspector General	HAROLD W. GEISEL, *Acting*
Legal Adviser	HAROLD KOH
Special Assistant to the Secretary and Executive Secretary of the Department	DANIEL B. SMITH
Under Secretary for Arms Control and International Security Affairs	ROSE GOTTEMOELLER, *Acting*
Assistant Secretary for International Security and Nonproliferation	C.S. ELIOT KANG, *Acting*
Assistant Secretary for Political-Military Affairs	FRANK J. RUGGIERO, *Acting*
Assistant Secretary for Verification, Compliance, and Implementation	ROSE GOTTEMOELLER
Under Secretary for Economic, Energy, and Agricultural Affairs	(VACANCY)
Assistant Secretary for Economic, Energy, and Business Affairs	DAVID NELSON, *Acting*
Under Secretary for Democracy and Global Affairs	(VACANCY)
Assistant Secretary for Democracy, Human Rights, and Labor	KAREN B. STEWART, *Acting*
Assistant Secretary for Oceans and International Environmental and Scientific Affairs	RENO L. HARNISH III, *Acting*
Assistant Secretary for Population, Refugees, and Migration	SAMUEL M. WITTEN, *Acting*
Under Secretary for Management	PATRICK F. KENNEDY
Assistant Secretary for Administration	STEVEN J. RODRIQUEZ, *Acting*
Assistant Secretary for Consular Affairs	JANICE L. JACOBS

Assistant Secretary for Diplomatic Security and Director of the Office of Foreign Missions	ERIC J. BOSWELL
Assistant Secretary for Information Resource Management and Chief Information Officer	SUSAN SWART
Assistant Secretary for Resource Management and Chief Financial Officer	JAMES MILLETTE, *Acting*
Director and Chief Operating Officer of Overseas Buildings Operations	RICHARD SHINNICK, *Acting*
Director General of the Foreign Service and Director of Human Resources	HARRY K. THOMAS, JR.
Director of the Foreign Service Institute	RUTH A. WHITESIDE
Director, Office of Medical Services	THOMAS W. YUN
Under Secretary for Political Affairs	WILLIAM J. BURNS
Assistant Secretary for African Affairs	(VACANCY)
Assistant Secretary for East Asian and Pacific Affairs	(VACANCY)
Assistant Secretary for European and Eurasian Affairs	DANIEL FRIED
Assistant Secretary for International Narcotics and Law Enforcement Affairs	DAVID JOHNSON
Assistant Secretary for Western Hemisphere Affairs	THOMAS A. SHANNON, JR.
Assistant Secretary for Near Eastern Affairs	JEFFREY D. FELTMAN, *Acting*
Assistant Secretary for South and Central Asian Affairs	RICHARD A. BOUCHER
Deputy Assistant Secretary for Afghanistan and Pakistan	PAUL JONES
Assistant Secretary for International Organization Affairs	ESTHER BRIMMER
Under Secretary for Public Diplomacy and Public Affairs	(VACANCY)
Assistant Secretary for Public Affairs and Spokesman for the Department of State	IAN KELLY
Assistant Secretary for Educational and Cultural Affairs	(VACANCY)
Coordinator, International Information Programs	JEREMY CURTIN
Permanent Representative of the United States of America to the Organization of American States	HECTOR E. MORALES, JR.

United States Mission to the United Nations [1]

799 United Nations Plaza, New York, NY 10017

United States Permanent Representative to the United Nations and Representative in the Security Council	SUSAN E. RICE
Deputy United States Representative to the United Nations	ALEJANDRO DANIEL WOLFF
United States Representative for Special Political Affairs in the United Nations	ROSEMARY DICARLO
United States Representative on the Economic and Social Council	(VACANCY)
United States Representative for United Nations Management and Reform	(VACANCY)

[For the Department of State statement of organization, see the *Code of Federal Regulations*, Title 22, Part 5]

The Department of State advises the President in the formulation and execution of foreign policy and promotes the long-range security and well-being of the United States. The Department determines and analyzes the facts relating to American overseas interests, makes recommendations on policy and future action, and takes the necessary steps to carry out established policy. In so doing, the Department engages in continuous consultations with the American public, the Congress, other U.S. departments and agencies, and foreign governments; negotiates treaties and agreements with foreign nations; speaks for the United States in the United Nations and other international organizations in which the United States participates; and represents the United States at international conferences.

The Department of State was established by act of July 27, 1789, as the Department of Foreign Affairs and was renamed Department of State by act of September 15, 1789 (22 U.S.C. 2651 note).

Secretary of State The Secretary of State is responsible for the overall direction, coordination, and supervision of U.S. foreign relations and for the interdepartmental activities of the U.S. Government abroad. The Secretary is the first-ranking member of the Cabinet, is a member of the National Security Council, and is in charge of the operations of the Department, including the Foreign Service.

Regional Bureaus Foreign affairs activities worldwide are handled by the geographic bureaus, which include the Bureaus of African Affairs, European and Eurasian Affairs, East Asian and Pacific Affairs, Near East Affairs, South and Asian Affairs, and Western Hemisphere Affairs.

Administration The Bureau of Administration provides support programs and services to Department of State and U.S. embassies and consulates. These functions include administrative policy, domestic emergency management, and management of owned or leased facilities in the United States; procurement, supply, travel, and transportation support; diplomatic pouch, domestic mail, official records, publishing, library, and language services; support to the schools abroad that educate dependents of U.S. Government employees assigned to diplomatic and consular missions; and small and disadvantaged business utilization. Direct services to the public and other Government agencies include: authenticating documents used abroad for legal and business purposes; responding to requests under the

---

[1] A description of the organization and functions of the United Nations can be found under *Selected Multilateral Organizations* in this book.

DEPARTMENT OF STATE

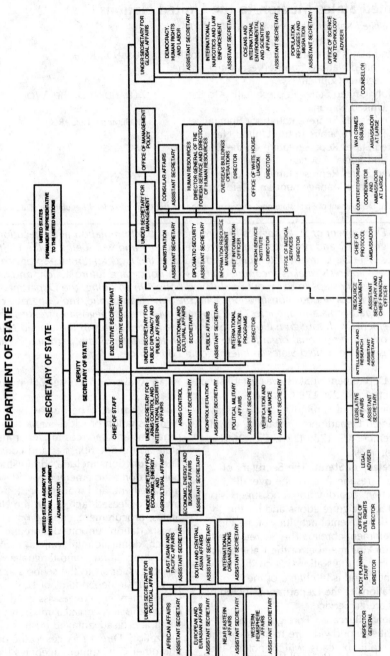

Freedom of Information and Privacy Acts and providing the electronic reading room for public reference to State Department records; and determining use of the diplomatic reception rooms of the Harry S Truman headquarters building in Washington, DC.

For further information, contact the Bureau of Administration at 703–875–7000.

Consular Affairs The Bureau of Consular Affairs is responsible for the protection and welfare of American citizens and interests abroad; the administration and enforcement of the provisions of the immigration and nationality laws insofar as they concern the Department of State and Foreign Service; and the issuance of passports and visas and related services. Approximately 18 million passports a year are issued by the Bureau's Office of Passport Services at the processing centers in Portsmouth, NH, and Charleston, SC, and the regional agencies in Boston, MA; Chicago, IL; Aurora, CO; Honolulu, HI; Houston, TX; Los Angeles, CA; Miami, FL; New Orleans, LA; New York, NY; Philadelphia, PA; San Francisco, CA; Seattle, WA; Norwalk, CT; Detroit, MI; Minneapolis, MN; and Washington, DC. In addition, the Bureau helps secure America's borders against entry by terrorists or narco-traffickers, facilitates international adoptions, and supports parents whose children have been abducted abroad.

For further information, visit the Bureau of Consular Affairs Web site at www.travel.state.gov.

Democracy, Human Rights, and Labor The Bureau of Democracy, Human Rights, and Labor (DRL) is responsible for developing and implementing U.S. policy on democracy, human rights, labor, and religious freedom. DRL dialogs with foreign governments and builds partnerships in multilateral organizations in order to build global consensus in support of democratic rule and human rights. It prepares the annual *Country Reports on Human Rights Practices* which are regarded as the most comprehensive and objective assessment of human rights conditions around the world. Through the Human Rights and Democracy Fund, DRL provides comprehensive technical and financial support for democracy and human rights, which helps prosecute war criminals, promote religious freedom, monitor free and fair elections, support workers' rights, encourage the establishment of the rule of law, and facilitate the growth of civil society. It participates in the Inter-Governmental Forum on Corporate Social Responsibility, encouraging governments and private industry to eliminate child labor. DRL also works to advance liberty in and access to electronic communication through the Secretary's Task Force on Global Internet Freedom.

For further information, contact the Bureau of Democracy, Human Rights, and Labor at 202–647–2126.

Diplomatic Security The Bureau of Diplomatic Security provides a secure environment to promote U.S. interests at home and abroad. The Bureau's mission includes the protection of the Secretary of State and other senior Government officials, resident and visiting foreign dignitaries, and foreign missions in the United States; the conduct of criminal, counterintelligence, and personnel security investigations; ensuring the integrity of international travel documents, sensitive information, classified processing equipment, and management information systems; the physical and technical protection of domestic and overseas facilities of the Department of State; providing professional law enforcement and security training to U.S. and foreign personnel; and a comprehensive, multifaceted overseas security program serving the needs of U.S. missions and the resident U.S. citizens and business communities. Through the Office of Foreign Missions, the Bureau regulates the domestic activities of the foreign diplomatic community in the areas of taxation, real property acquisitions, motor vehicle operation, domestic travel, and customs processing.

For further information, contact the Bureau of Diplomatic Security. Phone, 571–345–2507. Fax, 571–345–2527. Internet, www.diplomaticsecurity.state.gov.

Economic, Energy, and Business Affairs The Bureau of Economic, Energy, and Business Affairs has overall responsibility for formulating and implementing policy regarding international development and reconstruction, trade, investment, intellectual property enforcement, international energy issues, terrorism financing and economic sanctions, international communications and information policy, and aviation and maritime affairs.

For further information, contact the Bureau of Economic, Energy, and Business Affairs. Phone, 202–647–7971. Fax, 202–647–5713. Internet, www.state.gov/e/eeb.

Educational and Cultural Affairs The Bureau of Educational and Cultural Affairs administers the principal provisions of the Mutual Educational and Cultural Exchange Act (the Fulbright-Hays Act), including U.S. international educational and cultural exchange programs. These programs include the prestigious Fulbright Program for students, scholars, and teachers; the International Visitor Program, which brings leaders and future leaders from other countries to the United States for consultation with their professional colleagues; and citizen exchanges through cooperative relationships with U.S. nongovernmental organizations that support the Bureau's mission.

For further information, contact the Bureau of Educational and Cultural Affairs. Phone, 202–203–5118. Fax, 202–203–5115. Internet, http:// exchanges.state.gov/.

Foreign Missions The Office of Foreign Missions (OFM) operates the motor vehicles, tax, customs, real property, and travel programs to regulate and serve the 175 foreign missions in the United States and approximately 55,000 foreign mission members and dependents. The Office is also an advocate for improved treatment of U.S. missions and personnel abroad. It guards the U.S. public against abuses of diplomatic privilege and preserves U.S. security interests. OFM maintains regional offices in New York, Chicago, San Francisco, Los Angeles, Miami, Houston, and Honolulu.

For further information, contact the Office of Foreign Missions. Phone, 202–895–3500. Fax, 202–736–4145.

Foreign Service Institute The Foreign Service Institute of the Department of State is the Federal Government's primary training institution for foreign affairs-related training. In addition to the Department of State, the Institute provides training for more than 47 other governmental agencies. The Institute's more than 500 courses, including some 70 foreign language courses, range in length from 1 day to 2 years. The courses are designed to promote successful performance in each professional assignment, to ease the adjustment to other countries and cultures, and to enhance the leadership and management capabilities of the foreign affairs community.

For further information, contact the Foreign Service Institute. Phone, 703–302–6729. Fax, 703–302–7227.

Information Resource Management The Bureau of Information Resource Management (IRM) provides the Department with the information technology it needs to carry out U.S. diplomacy in the information age. The IRM Bureau is led by the Department's Chief Information Officer. IRM establishes effective information resource management planning and policies; ensures availability of information technology systems and operations, including information technology contingency planning, to support the Department's diplomatic, consular, and management operations; exercises management responsibility for ensuring that the Department's information resources meet the business requirements of the Department and provide an effective basis for knowledge sharing and collaboration within the Department and with other foreign affairs agencies and partners; exercises delegated approving authority for the Secretary of State for development and administration of the Department's computer and information security programs and policies.

Inspector General The Office of Inspector General (OIG) conducts independent audits, inspections, and investigations to promote effective management, accountability, and positive change in the Department of State, the Broadcasting Board of Governors (BBG), and the foreign affairs community. OIG provides leadership to promote integrity, efficiency, effectiveness, and economy; prevent and detect waste, fraud, abuse, and mismanagement; identify vulnerabilities and recommend constructive solutions; offer expert assistance to improve Department and BBG operations; communicate timely, useful information that facilitates decisionmaking and achieves measurable gains; and keep the Department, BBG, and Congress informed.

For further information, contact the Office of Inspector General. Phone, 202–663–0340. Internet, www.oig.state.gov.

Intelligence and Research The Bureau coordinates the activities of U.S. intelligence agencies to ensure that their overseas activities are consistent with U.S. foreign policy objectives and interests. It also provides all-source analysis which gives the Department insights and information to foreign policy questions. It organizes seminars on topics of high interest to policymakers and the intelligence community and monitors and analyzes foreign public and media opinion on key issues.

For further information, call 202–647–1080.

International Information Programs The Bureau of International Information Programs (IIP) informs, engages, and influences international audiences about U.S. policy and society to advance America's interests. IIP is a leader in developing and implementing public diplomacy strategies that measurably influence international audiences through quality programs and cutting-edge technologies. IIP provides localized contact for U.S. policies and messages, reaching millions worldwide in English, Arabic, Chinese, French, Persian, Russian, and Spanish. IIP delivers America's message to the world through a number of key products and services. These programs reach, and are created strictly for, key international audiences, such as U.S. diplomatic missions abroad, the media, government officials, opinion leaders, and the general public in more than 140 countries around the world. They include Web and print publications, speaker programs—both traveling (live) and electronic—and information resource services. IIP orchestrates the State Department's efforts to counter anti-American disinformation/propaganda and serves as the Department's chief link with other agencies in coordinating international public diplomacy programs.

For further information, contact the Bureau of International Information Programs. Phone, 202–453–8358. Fax, 202–453–8356. Internet, www.state.gov/r/iip/.

International Narcotics and Law Enforcement The Bureau of International Narcotics and Law Enforcement Affairs (INL) is responsible for developing policies and managing programs to combat and counter international narcotics production and trafficking, and to strengthen law enforcement and other rule of law institutional capabilities outside the United States. The Bureau also directs narcotics control coordinators at posts abroad and provides guidance on narcotics control, justice sector reform, and anticrime matters to the chiefs of missions. It supports the development of strong, sustainable criminal justice systems as well as training for capable police force and competent judicial officials. INL works closely with a broad range of other U.S. Government agencies.

For further information, contact the Bureau of International Narcotics and Law Enforcement Affairs. Phone, 202–647–2842. Fax, 202–736–4045.

International Organizations The Bureau of International Organization Affairs provides guidance and support for

U.S. participation in international organizations and conferences and formulates and implements U.S. policy toward international organizations, with particular emphasis on those organizations which make up the United Nations system. It provides direction in the development, coordination, and implementation of U.S. multilateral policy.

For further information, call 202–647–9326. Fax, 202–647–2175.

International Security and Nonproliferation   The Bureau of International Security and Nonproliferation (ISN), is responsible for managing a broad range of nonproliferation, counterproliferation, and arms control functions. ISN leads U.S. efforts to prevent the spread of weapons of mass destruction (nuclear, chemical, and biological weapons) and their delivery systems. It is also responsible for the following functions:
   —spearheading efforts to promote international consensus on weapons of mass destruction proliferation through bilateral and multilateral diplomacy;
   —addressing weapons of mass destruction proliferation threats posed by non-state actors and terrorist groups by improving physical security, using interdiction and sanctions, and actively participating in the Proliferation Security Initiative;
   —coordinating the implementation of key international treaties and arrangements, working to make them relevant to today's security challenges;
   —working closely with the UN, the G–8, NATO, the Organization for the Prohibition of Chemical Weapons, the International Atomic Energy Agency, and other international institutions and organizations to reduce and eliminate the threat posed by weapons of mass destruction; and
   —supporting efforts of foreign partners to prevent, protect against, and respond to the threat or use of weapons of mass destruction by terrorists.

For further information, contact the Bureau of International Security and Nonproliferation. Phone, 202–647–9868. Fax, 202–736–4863. Internet, www.state.gov/t/isn.

Legal Adviser   The Office of the Legal Adviser advises the Secretary of State and other Department officials on all domestic and international legal matters relating to the Department of State, Foreign Service, and diplomatic and consular posts abroad. The Office's lawyers draft, negotiate, and interpret treaties, international agreements, domestic statutes, departmental regulations, Executive orders, and other legal documents; provide guidance on international and domestic law; represent the United States in international organization, negotiation, and treaty commission meetings; work on domestic and foreign litigation affecting the Department's interests; and represent the United States before international tribunals, including the International Court of Justice.

For further information, contact the Office of the Legal Adviser. Phone, 202–647–9598. Fax, 202–647–7096. Internet, www.state.gov/s/l/.

Legislative Affairs   The Bureau of Legislative Affairs coordinates legislative activity for the Department of State and advises the Secretary, the Deputy, as well as the Under Secretaries and Assistant Secretaries on legislative strategy. The Bureau facilitates effective communication between State Department officials and the Members of Congress and their staffs. Legislative Affairs works closely with the authorizing, appropriations, and oversight committees of the House and Senate, as well as with individual Members that have an interest in State Department or foreign policy issues. The Bureau also manages Department testimony before House and Senate hearings, organizes Member and staff briefings, facilitates Congressional travel to overseas posts for Members and staff throughout the year, and reviews proposed legislation and coordinates Statements of Administration Policy on legislation affecting the conduct of U.S. foreign policy. Legislative Affairs staff advises individual Bureaus of the Department on legislative and outreach strategies and coorindates those strategies with the Secretary's priorities.

For further information, contact the Bureau of Legislative Affairs. Phone, 202–647–1714.

Medical Services The Office of Medical Services (MED) develops, manages, and staffs a worldwide primary health care system for U.S. Government employees and their eligible dependents residing overseas. In support of its overseas operations, MED approves and monitors the medical evacuation of patients, conducts pre-employment and in-service physical clearance examinations, and provides clinical referral and advisory services. MED also provides for emergency medical response in the event of a crisis at an overseas post.

For further information, contact the Office of Medical Services. Phone, 202–663–1649. Fax 202–663–1613.

Oceans and International Environmental, and Scientific Affairs

The Bureau of Oceans and International Environmental and Scientific Affairs (OES) serves as the foreign policy focal point for international oceans, environmental, and scientific efforts. OES projects, protects, and promotes U.S. global interests in these areas by articulating U.S. foreign policy, encouraging international cooperation, and negotiating treaties and other instruments of international law. The Bureau serves as the principal adviser to the Secretary of State on international environment, science, and technology matters and takes the lead in coordinating and brokering diverse interests in the interagency process, where the development of international policies or the negotiation and implementation of relevant international agreements are concerned. The Bureau seeks to promote the peaceful exploitation of outer space, develop and coordinate policy on international health issues, encourage government to government scientific cooperation, and prevent the destruction and degradation

of the planet's natural resources and the global environment.

For further information, contact the Bureau of Oceans and International Environmental and Scientific Affairs. Phone, 202–647–6961. Fax, 202–647–0217.

Overseas Building Operations The Bureau of Overseas Buildings Operations (OBO) directs the worldwide overseas buildings program for the Department of State and the U.S. Government community serving abroad under the authority of the chiefs of mission. Along with the input and support of other State Department bureaus, foreign affairs agencies, and Congress, OBO sets worldwide priorities for the design, construction, acquisition, maintenance, use, and sale of real properties and the use of sales proceeds. OBO also serves as the Single Real Property Manager of all overseas facilities under the authority of the chiefs of mission.

For further information, contact the Bureau of Overseas Buildings Operations. Phone, 703–875–4131. Fax, 703–875–5043. Internet, www.state.gov/obo.

Political-Military Affairs The Bureau of Political-Military Affairs is the principal link between the Departments of State and Defense and is the Department of State's lead on operational military matters. The Bureau provides policy direction in the areas of international security, security assistance, military operations, defense strategy and policy, counter-piracy measures, military use of space, and defense trade. Its responsibilities include securing base access to support the deployment of U.S. military forces overseas, negotiating status of forces agreements, coordinating participation in coalition combat and stabilization forces, promoting critical infrastructure protection, regulating arms transfers, directing military assistance to U.S. allies, combating illegal trafficking in small arms and light weapons, facilitating the education and training of international peacekeepers and foreign military personnel, managing humanitarian mine action programs, and assisting other countries in reducing the availability of man-portable air defense systems.

For further information, contact the Bureau of Political-Military Affairs. Phone, 202–647–5104. Fax, 202–736–4413. Internet, www.state.gov/t/pm.

Population, Refugees, and Migration The Bureau of Population, Refugees, and Migration directs the Department's population, refugee, and migration policy development. It administers U.S. contributions to international organizations for humanitarian assistance- and protection-related programs on behalf of refugees, conflict victims, and internally displaced persons and provides U.S. contributions to nongovernmental organizations which provide assistance and protection to refugees abroad. The Bureau oversees the annual admissions of refugees to the United States for permanent resettlement, working closely with the Department of Homeland Security, the Department of Health and Human Services, and various State and private voluntary agencies. It coordinates U.S. international population policy and promotes its goals through bilateral and multilateral cooperation. It works closely with the U.S. Agency for International Development, which administers U.S. international population programs. The Bureau also coordinates the Department's international migration policy through bilateral and multilateral diplomacy. The Bureau oversees efforts to encourage greater participation in humanitarian assistance and refugee resettlement on the part of foreign governments and uses humanitarian diplomacy to increase access and assistance to those in need in the absence of political solutions.

For further information, contact the Bureau of Population, Refugees, and Migration. Phone, 202–663–1071. Fax, 202–663–1002. Internet, www.state.gov/g/prm.

Protocol The Chief of Protocol is the principal adviser to the U.S. Government, the President, the Vice President, and the Secretary of State on matters of diplomatic procedure governed by law or international custom and practice. The Office is responsible for the following activities:

—arranging visits of foreign chiefs of state, heads of government, and other high officials to the United States;

—organizing credential presentations of newly arrived Ambassadors, as presented to the President and to the Secretary of State;

—operating the President's guest house, Blair House;

—organizing delegations representing the President at official ceremonies abroad;

—conducting official ceremonial functions and public events;

—interpreting the official order of precedence;

—conducting outreach programs of cultural enrichment and substantive briefings of the Diplomatic Corps;

—accrediting of over 103,000 embassy, consular, international organization, and other foreign government personnel, members of their families, and domestics throughout the United States;

—determining entitlement to diplomatic or consular immunity;

—publishing of diplomatic and consular lists;

—resolving problems arising out of diplomatic or consular immunity, such as legal and police matters; and

—approving the opening of embassy and consular offices in conjunction with the Office of Foreign Missions.

For further information, contact the Office of the Chief of Protocol. Phone, 202–647–2663. Fax, 202–647–1560.

Resource Management The Bureau of Resource Management integrates strategic planning, budgeting, and performance to secure departmental resources. The Bureau manages all departmental strategic and performance planning; budgeting and resource management for operation accounts; global financial services, including accounting, disbursing, and payroll; issuance of financial statements and oversight of the Department's management control program; coordination of national security resources and remediation of vulnerabilities within the Department's global critical infrastructure; and management of the International Cooperative Administrative Support Services Program.

For further information, contact the Bureau of Resource Management. Phone, 202–647–7490. Internet, www.state.gov/s/d/rm/.

Verification, Compliance, and Implementation The Bureau of Verification, Compliance, and Implementation is responsible for ensuring and verifying compliance with international arms control, nonproliferation, and disarmament agreements and commitments. The Bureau also ensures that U.S. intelligence capabilities to collect, analyze, and disseminate verification and compliance information are acquired, maintained, and enhanced. The Bureau is the principal policy representative to the intelligence community with regard to verification and compliance matters, and uses this role to promote, preserve, and enhance key collection and analytic capabilities and to ensure that intelligence verification, compliance, and implementation requirements are met. The Bureau staffs and manages treaty implementation commissions, creating negotiation and implementation policy for agreements and commitments, and developing policy for future arms control, nonproliferation, and disarmament arrangements. It also provides support to arms control, nonproliferation, and disarmament policymaking, including information technology support and secure government-to-government communication linkages with foreign treaty partners. The Bureau is also responsible for preparing verifiability assessments on proposals and agreements, and reporting these to Congress as required. The Bureau also prepares the President's Annual Report to Congress on Adherence to and Compliance With Arms Control, Nonproliferation, and Disarmament Agreements and Commitments, as well as the reports required by the Iran, North Korea, and Syria Nonproliferation Act.

For further information, contact the Bureau of Verification, Compliance, and Implementation. Phone, 202–647–5315. Fax, 202–647–1321. Internet, www.state.gov/t/vc.

Foreign Service To a great extent the future of our country depends on the relations we have with other countries, and those relations are conducted principally by the U.S. Foreign Service. Trained representatives stationed worldwide provide the President and the Secretary of State with much of the raw material from which foreign policy is made and with the recommendations that help shape it.

Ambassadors are the personal representatives of the President and report to the President through the Secretary of State. Ambassadors have full responsibility for implementation of U.S. foreign policy by any and all U.S. Government personnel within their country of assignment, except those under military commands. Their responsibilities include negotiating agreements between the United States and the host country, explaining and disseminating official U.S. policy, and maintaining cordial relations with that country's government and people.

A listing of Foreign Service posts, together with addresses and telephone numbers and key personnel, appears in *Key Officers of Foreign Service Posts— Guide for Business Representatives,* which is for sale by the Superintendent of Documents, Government Printing Office, Washington, DC 20402.

United States Diplomatic Offices— Foreign Service

(C: Consular Office; N: No Embassy or Consular Office)

Country/Capitol	Chief of Mission
Afghanistan/Kabul	William B. Wood
Albania/Tirana	John Withers
Algeria/Algiers	David D. Pearce
Andorra/Andorra La Vella	Eduardo Aguirre, Jr.
Angola/Luanda	Dan W. Mozena
Antigua and Barbuda/St. John's (N).	Brent Hardt (charge d'affaires)
Argentina/Buenos Aires	Earl Anthony Wayne
Armenia/Yerevan	Joseph Pennington (charge d'affaires)
Australia/Canberra	Robert M. McCallum
Austria/Vienna	Scott F. Kilner (charge d'affaires)
Azerbaijan/Baku	Anne E. Derse

United States Diplomatic Offices—
Foreign Service—Continued
(C: Consular Office; N: No Embassy or Consular Office)

Country/Capitol	Chief of Mission
Bahamas/Nassau	Timothy Zuniga-Brown (charge d'affaires)
Bahrain/Manama	J. Adam Ereli
Bangladesh/Dhaka	James Moriarty
Barbados/Bridgetown	Brent Hardt (charge d'affaires)
Belarus/Minsk	Karen B. Stewart
Belgium/Brussels	Sam Fox
Belize/Belmopan	J.A. Diffily (charge d'affaires)
Benin/Cotonou	Gayleatha B. Brown
Bolivia/La Paz	Krishna R. Urs (charge d'affaires)
Bosnia and Herzegovina/Sarajevo.	Charles L. English
Botswana/Gaborone	Stephen J. Nolan
Brazil/Brasilia	Clifford M. Sobel
Brunei Darussalam/Bandar Seri Begawan.	Emil M. Skodon
Bulgaria/Sofia	Jon Ross Beyrle
Burkina Faso/Ouagadougou	(vacancy)
Burma/Rangoon	Sharon E. Villarosa
Burundi/Bujumbura	Patricia Moller
Cambodia/Phnom Penh	Joseph A. Mussomeli
Cameroon/Yaounde	Janet E. Garvey
Canada/Ottawa	Terry Breese (charge d'affaires)
Cape Verde/Praia	Marianne M. Myles
Central African Republic/Bangui	Frederick B. Cook
Chad/N'Djamena	Louis J. Nigro, Jr.
Chile/Santiago	Paul E. Simons
China/Beijing	Clark T. Randt, Jr.
Colombia/Bogota	William R. Brownfield
Comoros/Moroni (N)	R. Niles Marquardt
Congo, Democratic Republic of the/Kinshasa.	William J. Garvelink
Congo, Republic of the/Brazzaville.	Alan W. Eastham
Costa Rica/San Jose	Peter Cianchette
Cote d'Ivoire/Abidjan	Wanda L. Nesbitt
Croatia/Zagreb	Robert A. Bradtke
Cuba/Havana (U.S. Interests Section).	Michael E. Parmly
Curacao/Willemstad	Timothy J. Dunn
Cyprus/Nicosia	Ronald L. Schlicher
Czech Republic/Prague	Richard W. Graber
Denmark/Copenhagen	James Cain
Djibouti, Republic of/Djibouti	James C. Swan
Dominican Republic/Santo Domingo.	Roland Bullen (charge d'affaires)
East Timor/Dili	Hans G. Klemm
Ecuador/Quito	Linda Jewell
Egypt/Cairo	Margaret Scobey
El Salvador/San Salvador	Robert Blau (charge d'affaires)
Equatorial Guinea/Malabo	Donald C. Johnson
Eritrea, State of/Asmara	Ronald K. McMullen
Estonia/Tallinn	Stanley Davis Phillips
Ethiopia/Addis Ababa	Donald Y. Yamamoto
Fiji Islands, Republic of/Suva	Larry Miles Dinger
Finland/Helsinki	Amy J. Hyatt (charge d'affaires)
France/Paris	Craig Roberts Stapleton
Gabonese Republic/Libreville	Eunice S. Reddick
Gambia/Banjul	Barry L. Wells
Georgia/Tbilisi	John F. Tefft
Germany/Berlin	William Robert Timken, Jr.
Ghana/Accra	Donald Teitelbaum
Greece/Athens	Daniel P. Speckhard
Grenada/St. George (N)	Karen McIssac (charge d'affaires)

United States Diplomatic Offices—
Foreign Service—Continued
(C: Consular Office; N: No Embassy or Consular Office)

Country/Capitol	Chief of Mission
Guatemala/Guatemala	Stephen McFarland
Guinea/Conakry	(vacancy)
Guinea-Bissau/Bissau (N)	Marcia S. Bernicat
Guyana/Georgetown	John Melvin Jones
Haiti/Port-au-Prince	Janet A. Sanderson
Holy See/Vatican City	Francis Rooney
Honduras/Tegucigalpa	Charles Ford
Hong Kong/Hong Kong (C)	James B. Cunningham
Hungary/Budapest	April H. Foley
Iceland/Reykjavik	Carol Van Voorst
India/New Delhi	(vacancy)
Indonesia/Jakarta	Cameron R. Hume
Iraq/Baghdad	Ryan C. Crocker
Ireland/Dublin	Thomas C. Foley
Israel/Tel Aviv	James Cunningham
Italy/Rome	Ronald Spogli
Jamaica/Kingston	Brenda La Grange Johnson
Japan/Tokyo	John Thomas Schieffer
Jerusalem (C)	Jacob Walles
Jordan/Amman	Robert S. Beecroft
Kazakhstan/Almaty	Richard Hoagland
Kenya/Nairobi	Michael E. Ranneberger
Kiribati/Tarawa (N)	Larry Miles Dinger
Korea/Seoul	Alexander R. Vershbow
Kosovo/Pristina	Tina S. Kaidanow
Kuwait/Kuwait	Deborah K. Jones
Kyrgyz Republic/Bishkek	Tatiana Gfoeller
Laos/Vientiane	Ravic Rolf Huso
Latvia/Riga	Catherine Todd Bailey
Lebanon/Beirut	Michelle Sison
Lesotho/Maseru	Robert B. Nolan
Liberia/Monrovia	Linda Thomas-Greenfield
Liechtenstein/Vaduz	Peter R. Coneway
Lithuania/Vilnius	John A. Cloud, Jr.
Luxembourg/Luxembourg	Ann Louise Wagner
Lybia/Tripoli	Gene Cretz
Macedonia/Skopje	Gillian Arlette Milovanovic
Madagascar/Antananarivo	R. Niles Marquardt
Malawi/Lilongwe	Peter W. Bodde
Malaysia/Kuala Lumpur	Christopher J. LaFleur
Maldives/Male (N)	Robert O. Blake, Jr.
Mali/Bamako	Gillian A. Milovanov
Malta/Valletta	Molly Hering Bordonaro
Marshall Islands/Majuro	Clyde Bishop
Mauritania/Nouakchott	Mark Boulware
Mauritius/Port Louis	(vacancy)
Mexico/Mexico City	Leslie Bassett (charge d'affaires)
Micronesia/Kolonia	Miriam K. Hughes
Moldova/Chisinau	Michael D. Kirby
Monaco/Monaco	Craig Roberts
Mongolia/Ulaanbaatar	Mark Clements Minton
Montenegro, Republic of/Podgorica.	Roderick W. Moore
Morocco/Rabat	(vacancy)
Mozambique/Maputo	(vacancy)
Namibia/Windhoek	Gail Dennise Mathieu
Nauru/Yaren (N)	Larry Miles Dinger
Nepal/Kathmandu	Nancy J. Powell
Netherlands/The Hague	Michael F. Gallagher (charge d'affaires)
New Zealand/Wellington	William Paul McCormick
Nicaragua/Managua	Robert Callahan
Niger/Niamey	Bernadette M. Allen
Nigeria/Abuja	Robin R. Sanders
Norway/Oslo	Benson K. Whitney
Oman/Muscat	Gary Grappo
Pakistan/Islamabad	Anne W. Patterson
Panama/Panama	Barbara Stephenson

United States Diplomatic Offices— Foreign Service—Continued

(C: Consular Office; N: No Embassy or Consular Office)

Country/Capitol	Chief of Mission
Papua New Guinea/Port Moresby.	Leslie V. Rowe
Paraguay/Asuncion	Liliana Ayalde
Peru/Lima	P. Michael McKinley
Philippines/Manila	Kristie A. Kenney
Poland/Warsaw	Victor Henderson Ashe
Portugal/Lisbon	Thomas F. Stephenson
Qatar/Doha	Joseph LeBaron
Romania/Bucharest	Nicholas F. Taubman
Russian Federation/Moscow	William J. Burns
Rwanda/Kigali	W. Stuart Symington IV
St. Kitts and Nevis/Basseterre (N).	Brent Hardt (charge d'affaires)
St. Lucia/Castries (N)	Brent Hardt (charge d'affaires)
St. Vincent and the Grenadines/ Kingstown (N).	Brent Hardt (charge d'affaires)
Samoa/Apia	William Paul McCormick
Sao Tome and Principe/Sao Tome (N).	Eunice S. Reddick
Saudi Arabia/Riyadh	Ford M. Fraker
Senegal/Dakar	(vacancy)
Serbia/Belgrade	Cameron P. Munter
Seychelles/Victoria	(vacancy)
Sierra Leone/Freetown	June Carter Perry
Singapore/Singapore	Patricia Louise Herbold
Slovak Republic/Bratislava	Vincent Obsitnik
Slovenia/Ljubljana	Maryruth Coleman (charge d'affaires)
Solomon Islands/Honiara	Leslie V. Rowe
South Africa/Pretoria, Cape Town.	(vacancy)
Spain/Madrid	Eduardo Aguirre, Jr.
Sri Lanka/Colombo	Robert O. Blake, Jr.
Sudan/Khartoum	Alberto M. Fernandez charge d'affaires
Suriname/Paramaribo	Lisa Bobbie Schreiber Hughes
Swaziland/Mbabane	Maurice S. Parker
Sweden/Stockholm	Michael M. Wood
Switzerland/Bern	Peter R. Coneway
Syrian Arab Republic/Damascus	Raymond D. Maxwell (charge d'affaires)
Tajikistan/Dushanbe	Tracey Jacobson
Tanzania/Dar es Salaam	(vacancy)
Thailand/Bangkok	Ralph Leo Boyce, Jr.
Togolese, Republic/Lome	Patricia M. Hawkins
Tonga/Nuku'alofa (N)	Larry Miles Dinger
Trinidad and Tobago/Port-of-Spain.	Len Kusnitz (charge d'affaires)

United States Diplomatic Offices— Foreign Service—Continued

(C: Consular Office; N: No Embassy or Consular Office)

Country/Capitol	Chief of Mission
Tunisia/Tunis	Robert F. Godec
Turkey/Ankara	Ross Wilson
Turkmenistan/Ashgabat	Richard Miles (charge d'affaires)
Tuvalu/Funafuti (N)	Larry Miles Dinger
Uganda/Kampala	Steven A. Browning
Ukraine/Kiev	William B. Taylor
United Arab Emirates/Abu Dhabi	Richard Olson
United Kingdom/London	Robert H. Tuttle
Uruguay/Montevideo	Robin Matthewman (charge d'affaires)
Uzbekistan/Tashkent	Richard Norland
Vanuatu/Port Vila (N)	Leslie V. Rowe
Venezuela/Caracas	John Caulfield (charge d'affaires)
Vietnam/Hanoi	Michael W. Marine
Yemen/Sanaa	Stephen Seche
Zambia/Lusaka	Donald E. Booth
Zimbabwe/Harare	James D. McGee

United States Permanent Diplomatic Missions to International Organizations

Organization	Ambassador
African Union/Addis Ababa	(vacancy)
European Union/Brussels	Chris Murray (charge d'affaires)
International Civil Aviation Organization.	(vacancy)
North Atlantic Treaty Organization/Brussels.	Victoria Nuland
Organization of American States/ Washington, DC.	Hector E. Morales, Jr.
Organization for Economic Co-operation and Development/ Paris.	(vacancy)
Organization for Security and Co-operation in Europe/Vienna.	Julie Finley
United Nations/Geneva	(vacancy)
United Nations/New York	Susan E. Rice
United Nations/Vienna	(vacancy)
U.S. Mission to United Nations Agencies for Food and Agriculture.	Tony P. Hall
U.S. Mission to United Nations Economic, Scientific and Cultural Organization/Paris.	Louise V. Oliver

Sources of Information

Contracts General inquiries may be directed to the Office of Acquisitions Management (A/LM/AQM), Department of State, P.O. Box 9115, Arlington, VA 22219. Phone, 703–516–1706. Fax, 703–875–6085.

Diplomatic and Official Passports Inquirers for these types of passports should contact their respective travel offices. The U.S. Government only issues these types of passports to individuals traveling abroad in connection with official employment. For additional information, please refer to the Consular Affairs web site. Internet, http://travel.state.gov.

Electronic Access The Department's Bureau of Public Affairs, Office of Public Communication, coordinates the dissemination of public electronic information for the Department. The main web site (Internet, www.state.gov) and the Secretary's web site (Internet, secretary.state.gov) provide comprehensive, up-to-date information on foreign policy, support for U.S. businesses and careers, and the counterterrorism rewards program and much more.

The Bureau of Consular Affairs web site (Internet, http://travel.state.gov) provides travel warnings and other information designed to help Americans travel safely abroad, as well as information on U.S. passports and visas and downloadable applications.

The State Department Electronic Reading Room at foia.state.gov uses new information technologies to enable access to unique historical records of international significance which have been made available to the public under the Freedom of Information Act or as a special collection.

Employment   Inquiries about employment in the Foreign Service should be directed to HR/REE, Room H–518, 2401 E Street NW., Washington, DC 20522. Phone, 202–261–8888. Internet, www.careers.state.gov. Information about civil service positions in the Department of State and copies of civil service job announcements can be accessed through the Internet at www.careers.state.gov. Individual questions may be directed to cspapps@state.gov. Job information staff is also available to answer questions from 8:30 a.m. to 4:30 p.m. eastern time on Federal workdays. Phone, 202–663–2176.

Freedom of Information Act and Privacy Act Requests   Requests from the public for Department of State records should be addressed to the Director, Office of Information Programs and Services, Department of State, SA–2, 515 Twenty-second Street NW., Washington, DC 20522–6001. Phone, 202–261–8300. Individuals are requested to indicate on the outside of the envelope the statute under which they are requesting access: FOIA REQUEST or PRIVACY REQUEST.

A public reading room, where unclassified and declassified documents may be inspected, is located in the Department of State, SA–2, 515 Twenty-second Street NW., Washington, DC 20522–6001. Phone, 202–261–8484. Directions to the reading room may be obtained from receptionists at public entrances to the Department.

Additional information about the Department's FOIA program can be found on the FOIA electronic reading room (Internet, foia.state.gov).

Missing Persons, Emergencies, Deaths of Americans Abroad   For information concerning missing persons, emergencies, travel warnings, overseas voting, judicial assistance, and arrests or deaths of Americans abroad, contact the Office of American Citizens Services and Crisis Management, Department of State. Phone, 888–407–4747 or 202–501–4444 (international). Internet, http://travel.state.gov. Correspondence should be directed to this address: Overseas Citizens Services, Bureau of Consular Affairs, Department of State, Washington, DC 20520.

Inquiries regarding international parental child abduction or adoption of foreign children by private U.S. citizens should be directed to the Office of Children's Issues, CA/OCS/CI, Department of State, SA–29, 2201 C Street NW., Washington, DC 20520–4818. Phone, 888–407–4747 or 202–501–4444 (international). Internet, http://travel.state.gov and http://adoption.state.gov.

Passports   Passport information is available through the Internet at http://travel.state.gov. For information on where to apply for a passport nationwide go to http://iafdb.travel.state.gov. For passport questions, travel emergencies, or to make an appoinment at any Regional Passport Agency, call the National Passport Information Center at 887–4–USA–PPT (887–487–2778) (TDD/TTY: 888–874–7793). Passport information is available 24 hours, 7 days a week; customer service representatives are available Monday-Friday 8 a.m. to 10 p.m., eastern standard time, excluding federal holidays. Correspondence can be submitted via Internet at http://travel.state.gov/passport/about/npic/npic__896.html or can be directed to the appropriate regional agency (Internet, http://travel.state.gov/passport/passport_4312.html) or the Correspondence Branch, Passport Services, Room 510, 1111 Nineteenth Street NW., Washington, DC 20524.

Public Affairs The Bureau of Public Affairs carries out the Secretary's foreign policy objectives and helps American and foreign audiences understand the importance of foreign affairs. Led by the Assistant Secretary, who also serves as Department spokesman, the Bureau pursues the State Department's mission to inform the American people and foreign audiences and to feed their concerns and comments back to policymakers. Phone, 202–647–6575.

Publications Publications that are produced on a regular basis include *Background Notes* and the *Foreign Relations* series. The Bureau of Public Affairs also occasionally publishes brochures and other publications to inform the public of U.S. diplomatic efforts. All publications are available on the Internet at www.state.gov.

Small Business Information Information about doing business with the Department of State is available from the Office of Small and Disadvantaged Business Utilization. The publication, *A Guide to Doing Business With the Department of State*, the current *Forecast of Contracting Opportunities*, and small business links are available from our Web site. Phone, 703–875–6822. Internet, www.state.gov/m/a.sdbu.

Telephone Directory The Department's telephone directory can be accessed at http://state.gov/m/a/gps/directory.

Tips for U.S. Travelers Abroad *Tips for Americans Traveling Abroad* contains extensive information about traveling and living in foreign countries. Internet, http://travel.state.gov/travel/living/living_1234.html. Additional information for travlers is available at http://travel.state.gov/travel/tips/brochures/brochures_1234.html.

Visas To obtain information on visas for foreigners wishing to enter the United States, call 202–663–1225. Internet, http://travel.state.gov/visa/visa_1750.html.

For further information, contact the Office of Public Communication, Public Information Service, Bureau of Public Affairs, Department of State, Washington, DC 20520. Phone, 202–647–6575. Internet, www.state.gov.

DEPARTMENT OF TRANSPORTATION

1200 New Jersey Avenue SE., Washington, DC 20590
Phone, 202–366–4000. Internet, www.dot.gov.

SECRETARY OF TRANSPORTATION	RAY LaHOOD
DEPUTY SECRETARY	THOMAS J. BARRETT
Chief of Staff	JOAN DEBOER
White House Liaison	NATE TURNBULL
Under Secretary for Policy	ROY KIENTIZ
Counselor to the Under Secretary for Policy	(VACANCY)
Director of Public Affairs	JILL ZUCKMAN
Chief Information Officer	JACKIE PATILLO, *Acting*
Director, Executive Secretariat	LISA F. FARMER, *Acting*
Director of Civil Rights	MARY WIGHAM-JONES, *Acting*
Director of Drug and Alcohol Policy and Compliance	JIM L. SWART
Director of Small and Disadvantaged Business Utilization	LEONARDO SAN ROMAN, *Acting*
Director, Office of Intelligence, Security, and Emergency Response	MICHAEL LOWDER
General Counsel	LINDY KNAPP, *Acting*
Inspector General	CAL SCOVEL
Assistant Secretary for Administration	LINDA J. WASHINGTON
Assistant Secretary for Aviation and International Affairs	CHRISTA FORNAROTTO, *Acting*
Assistant Secretary for Budget and Programs and Chief Financial Officer	LANA HURDLE, *Acting*
Assistant Secretary for Governmental Affairs	DANA GRESHAM
Assistant Secretary for Transportation Policy	DAVID MATSUDA, *Acting*

FEDERAL AVIATION ADMINISTRATION

800 Independence Avenue SW., Washington, DC 20591
Phone, 202–366–4000; 866–835–5322 (toll free). Internet, www.faa.gov.

Administrator	LYNNE A. OSMUS, *Acting*
Deputy Administrator	(VACANCY)
Associate Administrator for Airports	CATHERINE M. LANG, *Acting*
Chief Counsel	JAMES W. WHITLOW
Chief Operating Officer, Air Traffic Organization	HENRY P. KRAKOWSKI
Assistant Administrator for Information and Chief Information Officer	DAVID M. BOWEN
Assistant Administrator for Civil Rights	FANNY RIVERA
Associate Administrator for Commercial Space Transportation	GEORGE NIELD
Assistant Administrator for Government and Industry	MARY U. WALSH, *Acting*
Assistant Administrator for Financial Services/ Chief Financial Officer	RAMESH K. PUNWANI

304

Assistant Administrator for Human Resource Management	VENTRIS C. GIBSON
Assistant Administrator for Policy, Planning, and Environment	NANCY LOBUE, *Acting*
Assistant Administrator for Public Affairs	LAURA J. BROWN, *Acting*
Assistant Administrator for Region and Center Operations	PAULA LEWIS
Assistant Administrator for Security and Hazardous Materials	CLAUDIA MANNO, *Acting*
Associate Administrator for Aviation Safety	MARGARET GILLIGAN
Assistant Administrator for International Aviation	DI REIMOLD, *Acting*

FEDERAL HIGHWAY ADMINISTRATION

1200 New Jersey Avenue SE., Washington, DC 20590
Phone, 202–366–0650. Internet, www.fhwa.dot.gov.

Administrator	JAMES D. RAY, *Acting*
Deputy Administrator	(VACANCY)
Executive Director	JEFFERY F. PANIATI
Chief Counsel	THOMAS P. HOLIAN III, *Acting*
Associate Administrator for Administration	PATRICIA A. PROSPERI
Associate Administrator for Civil Rights	ALAN MASUDA
Associate Administrator for Policy and Governmental Affairs	JAMES A. CHEATHAM, *Acting*
Associate Administrator for Public Affairs	DOUG R. HECOX, *Acting*
Associate Administrator for Professional and Corporate Development	(VACANCY)
Associate Administrator for Research, Development, and Technology	MICHAEL F. TRENTACOSTE
Associate Administrator for Federal Lands Highway	JOHN R. BAXTER
Associate Administrator for Infrastructure	KING W. GEE
Associate Administrator for Operations	JEFFREY A. LINDLEY
Associate Administrator for Planning, Environment, and Realty	GLORIA M. SHEPHERD
Associate Administrator for Safety	JOSEPH S. TOOLE
Chief Financial Officer	ELISSA K. KONOVE

FEDERAL RAILROAD ADMINISTRATION

1120 Vermont Avenue NW., Washington, DC 20590
Phone, 202–493–6000. Internet, www.fra.dot.gov.

Administrator	KAREN RAE, *Acting*
Deputy Administrator	(VACANCY)
Special Assistant to the Administrator	MICHAEL HALLOCK
Director, Public Affairs	WARREN FLATAU, *Acting*
Associate Administrator for Financial Management/Chief Financial Officer and Administration	PEGGY REID
Director, Policy and Communication	TIMOTHY BARKLEY
Associate Administrator for Railroad Development	MARK YACHMETZ
Associate Administrator for Safety	JO STRANG

Chief Counsel	S. MARK LINDSEY
Director, Office of Civil Rights	CALVIN GIBSON

NATIONAL HIGHWAY TRAFFIC SAFETY ADMINISTRATION

1200 New Jersey Avenue SE., Washington, DC 20590
Phone, 202–366–9550; 888–327–4236 (toll free). Internet, www.nhtsa.gov.

Administrator	CHARLES HURLEY
Deputy Administrator	(VACANCY)
Director of Communications	MARK PAUSTENBACH
Chief Counsel	(VACANCY)
Director, Office of Civil Rights	ROSE TRUJILLO
Senior Associate Administrator for Policy and Operations	GREGORY WALTER
Supervisor, Executive Secretariat	BERNADETTE MILLINGS
Director, Office of Human Resources	DARLENE PEOPLES
Associate Administrator for Planning, Administrative, and Financial Management	REBECCA PENNINGTON
Associate Administrator, Communications and Consumer Information	SUSAN GORCOWSKI
Chief Information Officer	(VACANCY)
Associate Administrator, National Center for Statistics and Analysis	JOSEPH CARA
Senior Associate Administrator for Traffic Injury Control	BRIAN MCLAUGHLIN
Associate Administrator for Research and Program Development	JEFFREY MICHAEL
Associate Administrator for Regional Operations and Program Delivery	MARLENE MARKISON
Senior Associate Administrator for Vehicle Safety	RONALD MEDFORD
Associate Administrator for Rulemaking	STEPHEN R. KRATZKE
Associate Administrator for Enforcement	DANIEL SMITH
Associate Administrator for Applied Vehicle Safety Research	JOHN MADDOX
Associate Administrator, National Center for Statistics and Analysis	MARILENA AMONI
Director, Strategic Planning and Domestic and Global Integration for Vehicle Safety	JOSEPH CARRA

FEDERAL TRANSIT ADMINISTRATION

1200 New Jersey Avenue SE., Washington, DC 20590
Phone, 202–366–4043. Internet, www.fta.dot.gov.

Administrator	(VACANCY)
Deputy Administrator	(VACANCY)
Executive Director	MATTHEW J. WELBES
Associate Administrator for Administration	ANN LINNERTZ
Associate Administrator for Budget and Policy	ROBERT J. TUCCILLO
Associate Administrator for Planning	SUSAN BORINSKY
Associate Administrator for Program Management	SUSAN E. SCHRUTH
Associate Administrator for Research, Demonstration, and Innovation	VINCENT VALDES

Associate Administrator, Office of Communications and Congresional Affairs	(VACANCY)
Chief Counsel	(VACANCY)
Director, Office of Civil Rights	CHERYL HERSHEY

MARITIME ADMINISTRATION

1200 New Jersey Avenue SE., Washington, DC 20590
Phone, 202–366–5807; 800–996–2723 (toll free). Internet, www.marad.dot.gov.

Administrator	(VACANCY)
Deputy Administrator	JAMES E. CAPONITI, *Acting*
Assistant Administrator	JAMES E. CAPONITI
Associate Administrator for Administration/ Chief Information Officer	TAYLOR E. JONES II
Associate Administrator for National Security	KEVIN M. TOKARSKI
Associate Administrator for Intermodal, System Development	H. KEITH LESNICK
Associate Administrator for Environment and Compliance	JOSEPH A. BYRNE
Associate Administrator for Business and Workforce Development	JEAN E. MCKEEVER
Associate Administrator for Budget and Programs/Chief Financial Officer	DAVID J. RIVAIT
Chief Counsel	(VACANCY)
Director of Congressional and Public Affairs	(VACANCY)
Director of Civil Rights	DAVID J. ADAMS
Secretary, Maritime Subsidy Board	LEONARD SUTTER
Superintendent, United States Merchant Marine Academy	ALLEN B. WORLEY

SAINT LAWRENCE SEAWAY DEVELOPMENT CORPORATION

1200 New Jersey Avenue SE., Washington, DC 20590
Phone, 202–366–0091; 1–800–785–2779 (toll free). Fax, 202–366–7147. Internet, www.seaway.dot.gov.
180 Andrews Street, Massena, NY 13662
Phone, 315–764–3200

Administrator	COLLISTER JOHNSON, JR.
Deputy Administrator	CRAIG H. MIDDLEBROOK
Chief of Staff	ANITA K. BLACKMAN
Chief Counsel	CARRIE LAVIGNE
Director of Trade Development and Public Affairs	REBECCA A. MCGILL
Director of Congressional Affairs	NANCY ALCALDE
Director of Budget and Programs	KEVIN P. O'MALLEY
Associate Administrator	SALVATORE L. PISANI
Deputy Associate Administrator	CAROL A. FENTON
Human Resources Officer	JILL HAMILTON
Director of Engineering	THOMAS A. LAVIGNE
Chief Financial Officer	(VACANCY)
Director of Lock Operations and Marine Services	LORI K. CURRAN
Director of Maintenance	KARL J. LIVINGSTON

PIPELINE AND HAZARDOUS MATERIALS SAFETY ADMINISTRATION

1200 New Jersey Avenue SE., Washington, DC 20590
Phone, 202–366–4433. Internet, www.phmsa.dot.gov.

Administrator	(VACANCY)
Deputy Administrator	CYNTHIA DOUGLAS, *Acting*
Assistant Administrator/Chief Safety Officer	CYNTHIA DOUGLAS
Chief Counsel	(VACANCY)
Director, Office of Civil Rights	HELEN HAGIN
Associate Administrator for Management and Administration	(VACANCY)
Associate Administrator for Pipeline Safety	JEFFREY WIESE
Associate Administrator for Hazardous Materials Safety	THEODORE WILLKE
Director, Office of Governmental, International, and Public Affairs	(VACANCY)

RESEARCH AND INNOVATIVE TECHNOLOGY ADMINISTRATION

1200 New Jersey Avenue SE., Washington, DC 20590
Phone, 202–366–7582. Internet, www.rita.dot.gov. Email, info.rita@dot.gov.

Administrator	PETER H. APPEL
Deputy Administrator	STEVEN SMITH, *Acting*
Chief Counsel	ROBERT MONNIERE, *Acting*
Deputy Chief Counsel	ROBERT MONNIERE
Associate Administrator, Office of Government, International, and Public Affairs	THOMAS BOLLE, *Acting*
Associate Administrator for Administration	(VACANCY)
Public Affairs Contact	KIM RIDDLE
Associate Administrator for Research, Development and Technology	JAN BRECHT-CLARK
Deputy Associate Administrator for Research, Development and Technology	KELLY LEONE
Director, Bureau of Transportation Statistics	STEVEN DILLINGHAM
Deputy Director, Bureau of Transportation Statistics	DEBORAH JOHNSON, *Acting*
Director, Volpe National Transportation Systems Center	RICHARD JOHN, *Acting*
Director, Transportation Safety Institute	JOHN PHILLIPS
Associate Administrator, Intelligent Transportation Systems Joint Program Office	SHELLY ROW
Deputy Associate Administrator, Intelligent Transportation Systems Joint Program Office	JOHN AUGUSTINE
Director of Civil Rights	LINDA BOWMAN
Chief Financial Officer	KATHY MONTGOMERY

FEDERAL MOTOR CARRIER SAFETY ADMINISTRATION

1200 New Jersey Avenue SE., Washington, DC 20590
Phone, 202–366–2519. Internet, www.fmcsa.dot.gov.

Administrator	(VACANCY)
Deputy Administrator	(VACANCY)

Assistant Administrator (Chief Safety Officer)	ROSE A. MCMURRAY
Regulatory Ombudsman	STEVEN LAFRENIERE
Director for Administration/Chief Financial Officer	KATHLEEN O'SULLIVAN
Associate Administrator for Enforcement and Program Delivery	WILLIAM QUADE
Associate Administrator for Research and Information Technology, and Chief Information Officer	TERRY SHELTON
Associate Administrator of Field Operations	DAN HARTMAN
Associate Administrator for Policy and Program Development	LARRY MINOR
Chief Counsel	DAVE TOCHEN
Director, Office of Civil Rights	KENNIE MAY
Director, Office of Communications	CANDICE TOLLIVER

SURFACE TRANSPORTATION BOARD

395 E Street SW., Washington, DC 20423–0001
Phone, 202–245–0245. Internet, www.stb.dot.gov.

Chairman	FRANCIS P. MULVEY, *Acting*
Vice Chairman	CHARLES D. NOTTINGHAM
Commissioner	(VACANCY)
Director, Office of Public Assistance, Governmental Affairs and Compliance	MATTHEW T. WALLEN
Director, Office of Economics, Environmental Analysis, and Administration	LELAND L. GARDNER
Director, Office of Proceedings	RACHEL D. CAMPBELL
General Counsel	ELLEN D. HANSON
Secretary	ANNE K. QUINLAN

[For the Department of Transportation statement of organization, see the *Code of Federal Regulations*, Title 49, Part 1, Subpart A]

The U.S. Department of Transportation establishes the Nation's overall transportation policy. Under its umbrella are 11 administrations whose jurisdictions include highway planning, development, and construction; motor carrier safety; urban mass transit; railroads; aviation; and the safety of waterways, ports, highways, and oil and gas pipelines. Decisions made by the Department in conjunction with the appropriate State and local officials strongly affect other programs such as land planning, energy conservation, scarce resource utilization, and technological change.

The Department of Transportation (DOT) was established by act of October 15, 1966, as amended (49 U.S.C. 102 and 102 note), "to assure the coordinated, effective administration of the transportation programs of the Federal Government" and to develop "national transportation policies and programs conducive to the provision of fast, safe, efficient, and convenient transportation at the lowest cost consistent therewith." It became operational in April 1967 and was comprised of elements transferred from eight other major departments and agencies.

Secretary The Department of Transportation is administered by the Secretary of Transportation, who is the principal adviser to the President in all matters relating to Federal transportation programs.

Under Secretary The Under Secretary for Policy serves as a principal policy advisor to the Secretary and provides leadership in policy development for the Department.

DEPARTMENT OF TRANSPORTATION

Aviation and International Affairs The Office of the Assistant Secretary for Aviation and International Affairs has principal responsibility for the development, review, and coordination of policy for international transportation, and for development, coordination, and implementation of policy relating to economic regulation of the airline industry. The Office:

—licenses U.S. and foreign carriers to serve in international air transportation and conducts carrier fitness determinations for carriers serving the United States;

—develops policies to support the Department in aviation and maritime multilateral and bilateral negotiations with foreign governments and participates on the U.S. negotiating delegations;

—develops policies on a wide range of international transportation and trade matters;

—arranges and coordinates cooperative agreements with foreign governments for the exchange of state-of-the-art scientific and technical information;

—processes and resolves complaints concerning unfair competitive practices in domestic and international air transportation;

—establishes international and intra-Alaska mail rates;

—determines the disposition of requests for approval and immunization from the antitrust laws of international aviation agreements; and

—administers the essential air service program.

For further information, call 202–366–8822.

Drug and Alcohol Policy and Compliance The Office ensures that the national and international drug and alcohol policies and goals of the Secretary are developed and carried out in a consistent, efficient, and effective manner within the transportation industries. The Office provides expert advice, counsel, and recommendations to the Secretary regarding drugs and alcohol as they pertain to the Department of Transportation and testing within the transportation industry.

For further information, contact the Office of Drug and Alcohol Policy and Compliance. Phone, 202–366–3784.

Intelligence, Security, and Emergency Response The Office ensures development, coordination, and execution of plans and procedures for the Department of Transportation to balance transportation security requirements with safety, mobility, and economic needs of the Nation through effective intelligence, security, preparedness, and emergency reponse programs. The Office monitors the Nation's transportation network on a continuous basis; advises the Secretary on incidents affecting transportation systems; provides leadership on national preparedness, response, and transportation security matters; briefs the Secretary on intelligence relevant to the transportation sector; performs DOT's National Response Framework Emergency Support Function responsibilities; coordinates DOT participation in emergency preparedness and response exercises under the National Training and Exercise Program; administers DOT's Continuity of Government and Continuity of Operations programs; and serves as the DOT representative for emergency planning for civil aviation support to NATO and other allies.

For further information, contact the Office of Intelligence, Security, and Emergency Response. Phone, 202–366–6525.

Transportation Policy The Office of the Assistant Secretary for Transportation Policy has principal responsibility for analysis, development, articulation, and review of policies and plans for all modes of transportation. The Office:

—develops, coordinates, and evaluates public policy related to the transportation industries, and maintains policy and economic oversight of regulatory programs and legislative initiatives of the Department;

—reviews transportation matters involving the public and private sectors, analyzes current and emerging transportation policy issues, and assesses their economic and institutional implications;

—provides departmental policy leadership and coordination on safety, energy, and environmental initiatives which affect air, surface, marine, and pipeline transportation;

—provides leadership on questions involving the financing of transportation infrastructure projects, and provides economic analyses of new transportation technologies; and

—coordinates the development of intermodal transportation solutions that move people and goods in an energy-efficient manner, provide the foundation for improved productivity growth, strengthen the Nation's ability to compete in the global economy, and obtain the optimum yield from the Nation's transportation resources.

For further information, contact the Office of Transportation Policy. Phone, 202–366–4416.

Federal Aviation Administration

The Federal Aviation Administration (FAA), formerly the Federal Aviation Agency, was established by the Federal Aviation Act of 1958 (72 Stat. 731). The agency became a component of the Department of Transportation in 1967 pursuant to the Department of Transportation Act (49 U.S.C. 106). The mission of the FAA is to regulate civil aviation and U.S. commercial space transportation, maintain and operate air traffic control and navigation systems for both civil and military aircrafts, and develop and administer programs relating to aviation safety and the National Airspace System.

Activities

Air Navigation Facilities The agency is responsible for the location, construction or installation, maintenance, operation, and quality assurance of Federal visual and electronic aids to air navigation. The agency operates and maintains voice/data communications equipment, radar facilities, computer systems, and visual display equipment at flight service stations, airport traffic control towers, and air route traffic control centers.

Airport Programs The agency maintains a national plan of airport requirements, administers a grant program for development of public use airports to assure and improve safety and to meet current and future airport capacity needs, evaluates the environmental impacts of airport

development, and administers an airport noise compatibility program with the goal of reducing noncompatible uses around airports. It also develops standards and technical guidance on airport planning, design, safety, and operations and provides grants to assist public agencies in airport system and master planning and airport development and improvement.

Airspace and Air Traffic Management The safe and efficient utilization of the navigable airspace is a primary objective of the agency. To meet this objective, it operates a network of airport traffic control towers, air route traffic control centers, and flight service stations. It develops air traffic rules and regulations and allocates the use of the airspace. It also provides for the security control of air traffic to meet national defense requirements.

Civil Aviation Abroad Under the Federal Aviation Act of 1958 and the International Aviation Facilities Act (49 U.S.C. app. 1151), the agency encourages aviation safety and civil aviation abroad by exchanging aeronautical information with foreign aviation authorities; certifying foreign repair stations, airmen, and mechanics; negotiating bilateral airworthiness agreements to facilitate the import and export of aircraft and components; and providing technical assistance and training in all areas of the agency's expertise. It provides technical representation at international conferences, including participation in the International Civil Aviation Organization and other international organizations.

Commercial Space Transportation   The agency regulates and encourages the U.S. commercial space transportation industry. It licenses the private sector launching of space payloads on expendable launch vehicles and commercial space launch facilities. It also sets insurance requirements for the protection of persons and property and ensures that space transportation activities comply with U.S. domestic and foreign policy.

Registration   The agency provides a system for registering aircraft and recording documents affecting title or interest in the aircraft, aircraft engines, propellers, appliances, and spare parts.

Research, Engineering, and Development   The research, engineering, and development activities of the agency are directed toward providing the systems, procedures, facilities, and devices needed for a safe and efficient system of air navigation and air traffic control to meet the needs of civil aviation and the air defense system. The agency also performs an aeromedical research function to apply knowledge gained from its research program and the work of others to the safety and promotion of civil aviation and the health, safety, and efficiency of agency employees. The agency also supports development and testing of improved aircraft, engines, propellers, and appliances.

Safety Regulation   The Administration issues and enforces rules, regulations, and minimum standards relating to the manufacture, operation, and maintenance of aircraft, as well as the rating and certification (including medical) of airmen and the certification of airports serving air carriers. It performs flight inspection of air navigation facilities in the United States and, as required, abroad.

Test and Evaluation   The agency conducts tests and evaluations of specified items such as aviation systems, subsystems, equipment, devices, materials, concepts, or procedures at any phase in the cycle of their development from conception to acceptance and implementation, as well as assigned independent testing at key decision points.

Other Programs   The agency administers the aviation insurance program under the defense materials system with respect to priorities and allocation for civil aircraft and civil aviation operations. The agency develops specifications for the preparation of aeronautical charts. It publishes current information on airways and airport service and issues technical publications for the improvement of safety in flight, airport planning and design, and other aeronautical activities. It serves as the executive administration for the operation and maintenance of the Department of Transportation automated payroll and personnel systems.

Major Field Organizations—Federal Aviation Administration

Region/Field Office	Address	Administrator/Director
Alaskan—AK	No. 14, 222 W. 7th Ave., Anchorage, AK 99513	Robert N. Lewis
Central—IA, KS, MO, NE	901 Locust, Kansas City, MO 64106	Joseph N. Miniace
Eastern—DE, MD, NJ, NY, PA, VA, WV	1 Aviation Plz., Jamaica, NY 11434	Carmine Gallo
Great Lakes—IL, IN, MI, MN, ND, OH, SD, WI	2300 E. Devon Ave., Des Plaines, IL 600180	Barry Cooper
New England—CT, MA, ME, NH, RI, VT	12 New England Executive Park, Burlington, MA 01803	Amy Lind Corbett
Northwest Mountain—CO, ID, MT, OR, UT, WA, WY	1601 Lind Ave. SW., Renton, WA 98055	Kathryn Vernon
Southern—AL, FL, GA, KY, MS, NC, PR, SC, TN	1701 Columbia Ave., College Park, GA 30337	Douglas R. Murphy
Southwest—AR, LA, NM, OK, TX	2601 Meacham Blvd., Fort Worth, TX 76137–4298	Teresa Brunner
Western-Pacific—AZ, CA, HI, NV	15000 Aviation Blvd., Hawthorne, CA 90261	William C. Withycombe
Europe, Africa	15, Rue de la Loi B–1040, Brussels, Belgium	Anthony Fazio
Asia-Pacific	U.S. Embassy, FAA, Singapore	Christopher Metts

Major Field Organizations—Federal Aviation Administration—Continued

Region/Field Office	Address	Administrator/Director
Western Hemisphere	8600 NW. 36th St., Miami, FL 33166	Phyllis Preston, *Acting*
William J. Hughes Technical Center	Atlantic City, NJ 08405	Wilson Felder
Mike Monroney Aeronautical Center	6500 S. MacArthur, Oklahoma City, OK 73125	Lindy Ritz

For further information, contact the Office of Communications, Federal Aviation Administration, Department of Transportation, 800 Independence Avenue SW., Washington, DC 20591. Phone, 202–267–3883. Fax, 202–267–5039.

Federal Highway Administration

The Federal Highway Administration (FHWA) was established as an agency of the Department of Transportation by the Department of Transportation Act (49 U.S.C. 104). Title 23 of the United States Code and other supporting legislation authorize the Administration's various activities.

FHWA's mission is to improve mobility on our Nation's highways through national leadership, innovation, and program delivery. The Administration works with Federal, State, and local agencies as well as other stakeholders and partners to preserve and improve the National Highway System, which includes the Interstate System and other roads of importance for national defense and mobility. The FHWA works to improve highway safety and minimize traffic congestion on these and other key facilities. The FHWA bears the responsibility of ensuring that America's roads and highways remain safe, technologically up-to-date, and environmentally-friendly.

Through surface transportation programs, innovative and traditional financing mechanisms, and new types of pavement and operational technology, FHWA increases the efficiency by which people and goods move throughout the Nation. The Administration also works to improve the efficiency of highway and road connections to other modes of transportation. The Federal-aid Highway Program's budget is primarily divided between Federal-aid funding and the Federal Lands Highway Program.

Programs

Federal-aid Highway Program   FHWA manages the Federal-aid Highway Program, which provides financial and technical assistance to States for constructing and improving the Nation's transportation infrastructure. The program includes the provision of engineering standards and policies, technical expertise, and other assistance related to the maintenance of highways, rural and urban roads, bridges, tunnels, hydraulic/geotechnical structures, and other engineering activities. Projects associated with the Federal-aid highway program include the National Highway System, Surface Transportation Program, Highway Bridge Program, Congestion Mitigation and Air Quality Improvement Program, Intelligent Transportation Systems Program, Transportaton Infrastructure Finance and Innovation Act Program, the Emergency Relief Program, and the Federal Lands Highway Program.

Federal Lands Highway Program   The Federal Lands Highway Program (FLHP) funds and gives technical assistance to a coordinated program of public roads servicing the transportation needs of Federal and Indian lands. The Program provides funding for public roads and highways on Federal and tribal lands that are not a State or local government responsibility. The planning, construction, and improvement of highways and bridges in national forests and parks, other federally owned land, and tribal lands benefit from FLHP funding.

Organization The FHWA consists of a Headquarters office in Washington, DC; a Federal-aid division office in each State, the District of Columbia, and Puerto Rico; four metropolitan offices in New York City, Philadelphia, Chicago, and Los Angeles serving as extensions of the corresponding Federal-aid division offices; and three Federal Lands Highway division offices.

Field and Division Offices—Federal Highway Administration

Field Organization	Federal-Aid Division Offices
North	CT, IL, IA, IN, MA, ME, MI, MN, MO, NH, NJ, NY, OH, PA, RI, VT, WI, WV
South	AL, AR, DC, DE, FL, GA, KS, KY, LA, MD, MS, NC, OK, PR, SC, TN, TX, VA
West	AK, AZ, CA, CO, HI, ID, MT, ND, NE, NM, NV, OR, SD, UT, WA, WY

Federal Lands Highway Divisions

Division	Address	Phone
Eastern	Loudoun Technology Ctr., 21400 Ridgetop Cir., Sterling, VA 20166	703–404–6201
Central	Suite 390, 12300 W. Dakota Ave., Lakewood, CO 80228	720–963–3500
Western	610 E. Fifth St., Vancouver, WA 98661	360–619–7700

For further information, contact the Department of Transportation, Federal Highway Administration, Office of Information and Management Services, 1200 New Jersey Avenue, SE., Washington, DC 20590. Phone, 202–366–0534. Internet, www.fhwa.dot.gov.

Federal Railroad Administration

The Federal Railroad Administration was created pursuant to section 3(e)(1) of the Department of Transportation Act of 1966 (49 U.S.C. 103). The purpose of the Administration is to promulgate and enforce rail safety regulations, administer railroad financial assistance programs, conduct research and development in support of improved railroad safety and national rail transportation policy, provide for the rehabilitation of Northeast Corridor rail passenger service, and consolidate government support of rail transportation activities.

Activities

Passenger and Freight Services The Administration oversees and provides financial assistance to Amtrak and administers financial assistance programs to demonstrate high-speed rail technology, to reduce grade crossing hazards in high-speed rail corridors, to provide for investments in small freight railroads and other rail projects, to plan for high-speed rail projects, and to plan and deploy magnetic levitation technology.

Railroad Safety The Administration administers and enforces the Federal laws and related regulations designed to promote safety on railroads; exercises jurisdiction over all areas of rail safety under the Rail Safety Act of 1970, such as track maintenance, inspection standards, equipment standards, and operating practices. Railroad and related industry equipment, facilities, and records are inspected and required reports reviewed. In addition, the administration educates the public about safety at highway-rail grade crossings and the danger of trespassing on rail property.

Research and Development The Administration's ground transportation research and development program seeks to advance all aspects of intercity ground transportation and railroad safety pertaining to the physical sciences and engineering, in order to improve railroad safety and ensure that railroads continue to be a viable national transportation resource.

Transportation Test Center The Administration tests and evaluates conventional and advanced railroad systems and components at the Transportation Test Center near Pueblo, CO. Private sector companies and the Governments of the United States, Canada, and Japan use the facility to explore the operation of conventional and advanced systems under controlled conditions. It is used by Amtrak for the testing of new high-speed locomotives and trains and by the Federal Transit Administration for testing urban rapid transit vehicles.

For further information, contact the Transportation Technology Center, Pueblo, CO 81001. Phone, 719–584–0507.

Major Field Organizations—Federal Railroad Administration

Region	Address	Administrator	Telephone
Northeastern—CT, MA, ME, NH, NJ, NY, RI, VT	Rm. 1077, 55 Broadway, Cambridge, MA 02142	Les Fiorenzo	617–494–2302
Eastern—DC, DE, MA, OH, PA, VA, WV	Suite 660, 1510 Chester Pike, Crum Lynne, PA 19022	David R. Myers	610–521–8200
Southern—AL, FL, GA, KY, MS, NC, SC, TN	Suite 16T20, 61 Forsyth St. SW., Atlanta, GA 30303–3104	Fred Dennin II	404–562–3800
Central—IL, IN, MI, MN, WI	Suite 310, 200 W. Adam St., Chicago, IL 60606	Laurence A. Hasvold	312–353–6203
Southwestern—AR, LA, NM, OK, TX	Suite 450, 4100 International Plz., Fort Worth, TX, 76109–4820	Bonnie Murphy	817–862–2200
Midwestern—CO, IA, KS, MO, NE	Suite 464, 901 Locust St., Kansas City, MO 64106	Darrell J. Tisor	816–392–3840
Western—AZ, CA, NV, UT	Suite 466, 801 I St., Sacramento, CA 95814	Alvin Settje	916–498–6540
Northwestern—AK, ID, MT, ND, OR, SD, WA, WY	Suite 650, 703 Broadway, Vancouver, WA 98660	Dave Brooks	360–696–7536

For further information, contact the Office of Congressional and Public Affairs, Federal Railroad Administration, Department of Transportation, 1200 New Jersey Avenue SE., Washington, DC 20590. Phone, 202–493–6024. Internet, www.fra.dot.gov.

National Highway Traffic Safety Administration

[For the National Highway Traffic Safety Administration statement of organization, see the *Code of Federal Regulations,* Title 49, Part 501]

The National Highway Traffic Safety Administration (NHTSA) was established by the Highway Safety Act of 1970 (23 U.S.C. 401 note) to help reduce the number of deaths, injuries, and economic losses resulting from motor vehicle crashes on the Nation's highways.

The Administration carries out programs relating to the safety performance of motor vehicles and related equipment; administers the State and community highway safety program with the FHWA; regulates the Corporate Average Fuel Economy program; investigates and prosecutes odometer fraud; carries out the National Driver Register Program to facilitate the exchange of State records on problem drivers; conducts studies and operates programs aimed at reducing economic losses in motor vehicle crashes and repairs; performs studies, conducts demonstration projects, and promotes programs to reduce impaired driving, increase seat belt use, and reduce risky driver behaviors; and issues theft prevention standards for passenger and nonpassenger motor vehicles.

Activities

Research and Development The Administration provides a foundation for the development of motor vehicle and highway safety program standards by analyzing data and researching, developing, testing, and evaluating motor vehicles, motor vehicle equipment, and advanced technologies, and collecting and analyzing crash data. The research program covers numerous areas affecting safety and includes laboratory-testing facilities to obtain necessary basic data. NHTSA strives to encourage industry to adopt advanced motor vehicle safety designs, elevate public awareness of safety potentials, and provide a base for vehicle safety information.

Regional Operations and Program Delivery   The Administration administers State highway safety grant programs, authorized by the Safe, Accountable, Flexible, Efficient Transportation Equity Act: A Legacy for Users. The Highway Safety formula grant program provides funds to the States, Indian nations, and the territories each year to support safety programs, particularly in the following national priority areas: occupant protection, impaired driving, police traffic services, emergency medical services, data/traffic records, motorcycle safety, pedestrian and bicycle safety, speed control, and roadway safety. Incentive grants are also used to encourage States to implement effective impaired driving, occupant protection, motorcycle safety, and data improvement programs.

Rulemaking   The Administration issues Federal motor vehicle safety standards that prescribe safety features and levels of safety-related performance for vehicles and vehicular equipment. It conducts the New Car Assessment Program, under which passenger cars, light trucks, and vans are subjected to high-speed crashes in order to test their frontal and side impact safety performance. Seperate tests are conducted to assess the vehicles' resistance to rollovers. Results from these tests are made public in order to help consumers choose the safest motor vehicles. The Administration educates consumers on using vehicle safety features. To promote maximum feasible fuel economy, it manages a program establishing and revising fleet average fuel economy standards for passenger car and light truck manufacturers. The Administration also carries out an anti-theft program, which includes issuing rules requiring the designation of likely high-theft vehicles that must meet parts-marking requirements and calculating and publishing annual motor vehicle theft rates.

Enforcement   The Office of Enforcement identifies and investigates problems with motor vehicles and vehicular equipment. If the Office determines that a vehicle or equipment suffers from a safety-related defect or that it does not meet all applicable Federal motor vehicle safety standards, the Office will seek a recall, which requires manufactuers to notify owners and remedy the defect free of charge. The Office monitors recalls to ensure that owners are being notified in a timely manner and the scope of the recall and the remedy are adequate to correct the problem.

National Center for Statistics and Analysis   The Administration maintains a collection of scientific and technical information related to motor vehicle safety and operates the National Center for Statistics and Analysis, whose activities include the development and maintenance of national highway-crash data collection systems and related analysis efforts. These comprehensive motor vehicle safety information resources serve as documentary reference points for Federal, State, and local agencies, as well as industry, universities, and the public.

Communications and Consumer Information   The Administration develops, directs, and implements communications based on NHTSA policy and programs, including public awareness campaigns such as "Click It or Ticket" and "Over the Limit. Under Arrest." It also manages the toll-free Motor Vehicle Auto Safety Hotline to identify safety problems in motor vehicles and equipment. Consumers can call the hotline (phone, 888–327–4236; TDD, 800–424–9153 or 202–366–7800 in the Washington, DC area) 24 hours a day, 7 days a week, to report safety-related problems. English and Spanish speaking representatives are available between 8 a.m. and 10 p.m. eastern standard time, Monday through Friday, except Federal holidays. Consumers can also reach the hotline via the Internet at www.nhtsa.dot.gov/hotline. These calls form the basis for investigations and, ultimately, recalls if safety-related defects are identified. The hotline also provides information and literature to consumers about vehicle and child-seat recalls, New Car Assessment Program test results, and a variety of other highway safety information.

Regional Offices—National Highway Traffic Safety Administration

Region/Address	Administrator
Atlanta, GA (Rm. 17T30, 61 Forsyth St. SW., 30303–3104)	Terrance D. Schiavone
Baltimore, MD (Suite 6700, 10 S. Howard St., 21201)	Elizabeth A. Baker
Cambridge, MA (55 Broadway, Kendall Sq., Code 903, 02142)	Philip J. Weiser
Fort Worth, TX (Rm. 8a38, 819 Taylor St., 76102–6177)	Georgia S. Chakiris
Kansas City, MO (466 Locust St., 64106)	Romell W. Cooks
Lakewood, CO (Suite 140, 12300 W. Dakota Ave., 80228)	Bill Watada
Olympia Fields, IL (Suite 201, 19900 Governors Dr., 60461)	Michael Witter
San Francisco, CA (Suite 2230, 201 Mission St., 94105)	David Manning
Seattle, WA 98174 (3140 Jackson Federal Bldg., 915 2d Ave., 98174)	John Moffat
White Plains, NY (Suite 204, 222 Mamaroneck Ave., 10605)	Thomas M. Louizou

For further information, contact the Office of Communications and Consumer Information, National Highway Traffic Safety Administration, Department of Transportation, 1200 New Jersey Avenue SE., Washington, DC 20590. Phone, 202–366–9550. Internet, www.nhtsa.dot.gov.

Federal Transit Administration

[For the Federal Transit Administration statement of organization, see the *Code of Federal Regulations*, Title 49, Part 601]

The Federal Transit Administration (FTA) (formerly the Urban Mass Transportation Administration) was established as an operating administration of the Department of Transportation by section 1 of Reorganization Plan No. 2 of 1968 (5 U.S.C. app. 1), effective July 1, 1968. FTA's mission is to assist in developing improved mass transportation, encourage the planning and establishment of areawide mass transportation systems, and provide financial assistance to State and local governments to finance mass transportation systems and carry out national transit goals and policy.

Programs

Capital Investment   Grants are authorized to assist in financing the acquisition, construction, reconstruction, and improvement of facilities and equipment for use in mass transportation service in urban areas. There are three categories of funds available under the capital investment program: fixed guideway modernization, rolling stock renewal, safety-related improvements, and signal and power modernization; new starts funds for construction of new

fixed guideway service; and bus funds for acquiring buses and rolling stock, ancillary equipment, and the construction of bus facilities.

For further information, call 202–366–2053.

Elderly and Persons With Disabilities
The program provides financial assistance to private nonprofit agencies to meet the transportation needs of elderly persons and persons with disabilities where services provided by public operators are unavailable, insufficient, or inappropriate; to public bodies approved by the State to coordinate services for elderly persons or persons with disabilities; or to public bodies which certify to the Governor that no nonprofit corporation or association is readily available in an area to provide the service. Funds are allocated by formula to the States. Local organizations apply for funding through a designated State agency.

For further information, call 202–366–2053.

Job Access and Reverse Commute
Grants   The program makes funding available to public agencies and nonprofit organizations to pay the capital and operating costs of delivering new or expanded job access or reverse commute services, and to promote the

use of transit during nontraditional work hours, as well as encourage employer-based transportation strategies and use of transit pass programs. The program provides competitive grants for two kinds of projects:

—job access projects implementing new or expanded transportation services for transporting welfare recipients and low-income persons to and from jobs and needed employment support services such as child care; and

—reverse commute projects implementing new or expanded general-purpose public transportation services to transport residents of urban, rural, and suburban areas to suburban employment centers.

For further information, call 202–366–0176. Internet, www.fta.dot.gov/funding/grants/grants_financing_3623.html.

Non-Urbanized Area Assistance The Administration provides capital and operating assistance for public transportation in non-urbanized areas. Funds are allocated to the Governor, and the program is administered at the State level by the designated transportation agency. Assistance is provided for planning, administrative, and program development activities; coordination of public transportation programs; vehicle acquisition; and other capital investments in support of transit services tailored to the needs of elderly individuals and individuals with disabilities and other individuals who depend upon transit for their basic mobility.

Planning The program provides financial assistance in meeting the transportation planning needs of metropolitan planning organizations by allocating funds to States which, in turn, they allocate to the metropolitan planning organizations. Assistance is available for transportation planning, technical assistance studies, demonstrations, management training, and cooperative research.

For further information, call 202–366–6385.

Research and Technology The Administration seeks to improve public transportation for America's communities by delivering products and services that are valued by its customers and by assisting transit agencies in better meeting the needs of their customers. To accomplish these goals, it partners with the transportation industry to undertake research, development, and education that will improve the quality, reliability, and cost-effectiveness of transit in America and that leads to increases in transit ridership.

Transit research and technology efforts are categorized as follows:

—joint partnership agreements with both public and private research organizations, transit providers, and industry to promote the early deployment of innovation in public transportation services, management, operational practices, and technology of broad applicability.

—advanced technologies that assist the study, design, and demonstration of fixed-guideways, bus and rapid transit, fuel-cell-powered transit buses, advanced propulsion control for rail transit, and other types of technologies in development; and

—international mass transportation programs that promote American transit products and services overseas, cooperate with foreign public sector entities on research and development in the public transportation industries, enable American vendors to showcase their products and services, and facilitate technology transfer and information diffusion for developing nations through trade missions and other international venues.

For further information, call 202–366–4052. Internet, www.fta.dot.gov/research.

Rural Transportation Assistance The Rural Transportation Assistance Program allocates funds annually to the States to provide assistance for transit research, technical assistance, training, and related support activities for transit providers serving non-urbanized areas. Additional funds are used at the national level for developing training materials, developing and maintaining a national clearinghouse on rural transit activities and information, and providing technical assistance through peer practitioners to promote exemplary techniques and practices.

For further information, call 202–366–2053.

Safety The Administration's safety program supports State and local agencies in fulfilling their responsibility for the safety and security of urban mass transportation facilities and services, through the encouragement and sponsorship of safety and security planning, training, information collection and analysis, drug control programs, system/safety assurance reviews, generic research, and other cooperative government/industry activities.

For further information, call 202–366–4020.

Training and Technical Assistance Through the National Transit Institute (NTI), the Administration develops and offers training courses for improving transit planning, operations, workforce performance, and productivity. NTI courses are conducted at sites across the United States on a wide variety of subjects, ranging from multimodal planning to management development, third-party contracting, safety, and security. Current NTI course offerings are available online at www.ntionline.com.

For further information, call 202–366–6635.

Field Organization—Federal Transit Administration

Region/Address	Telephone
Atlanta, GA (Suite 800, 230 Peachtree NW., 30303)	404–865–5600
Cambridge, MA (Suite 920, 55 Broadway, 02142)	617–494–2055
Chicago, IL (Suite 320, 200 W. Adams St., 60606)	312–353–2789
Fort Worth, TX (Suite 8A36, 819 Taylor St., 76102)	817–978–0550
Kansas City, MO (Suite 404, 901 Locust St., 64106)	816–329–3920
Lakewood, CO (Suite 310, 12300 W. Dakota Ave., 80228)	720–963–3300
New York, NY (Suite 429, 1 Bowling Green, 10004–1415)	212–668–2170
Philadelphia, PA (Suite 500, 1760 Market St., 19103)	215–656–7100
San Francisco, CA (Suite 1650, 201 Mission St., 94105)	415–744–3133
Seattle, WA (Suite 3142, 915 2d Ave., 98174)	206–220–7954

Metropolitan Offices—Federal Transit Administration

Office/Address	Telephone
Chicago, IL (Suite 320, 200 W. Adams St., 60606–5232)	312–886–1616
Los Angeles, CA (Suite 1850, 888 S. Figueroa St., 90017)	213–202–3950
New York, NY (Suite 428, 1 Bowling Green, 10004–1415)	212–668–2201
Philadelphia, PA (Suite 500, 1760 Market St., 19103–4142)	215–656–7070
Washington, DC (Suite 510, 1990 K St. NW, 20006)	202–219–3562

For further information, contact the Office of Communications and Congressional Affairs, Federal Transit Administration, Department of Transportation, 1200 New Jersey Avenue SE., Washington, DC 20590. Phone, 202–366–4043. Internet, www.fta.dot.gov.

Maritime Administration

The Maritime Administration was established by Reorganization Plan No. 21 of 1950 (5 U.S.C. app.). The Maritime Act of 1981 (46 U.S.C. 1601) transferred the Maritime Administration to the Department of Transportation. The Administration manages programs to aid in the development, promotion, and operation of the U.S. merchant marine. It is also charged with organizing and directing emergency merchant ship operations.

The Maritime Administration administers subsidy programs to pay the difference between certain costs of operating ships under the U.S. flag and foreign competitive flags on essential services, and the difference between the costs of constructing ships in U.S. and foreign shipyards. It provides financing guarantees for the construction, reconstruction, and reconditioning of ships; and enters into capital construction fund agreements that grant tax deferrals on moneys to be used for the acquisition, construction, or reconstruction of ships.

The Administration constructs or supervises the construction of merchant-type ships for the Federal Government. It helps industry generate increased business for U.S. ships and conducts programs to develop ports, facilities, and intermodal transport, and to promote domestic shipping.

It conducts program and technical studies and administers a war risk insurance program that insures operators and seamen against losses caused by hostile action if domestic commercial insurance is not available.

Under emergency conditions the Maritime Administration charters Government-owned ships to U.S. operators, requisitions or procures ships owned by U.S. citizens, and allocates them to meet defense needs.

It maintains a national defense reserve fleet of Government-owned ships that it operates through ship managers and general agents when required in national defense interests. An element of this activity is the Ready Reserve force consisting of a number of ships available for quick-response activation.

The Administration regulates sales to aliens and transfers to foreign registry of ships that are fully or partially owned by U.S. citizens. It also disposes of Government-owned ships found nonessential for national defense.

The Administration operates the U.S. Merchant Marine Academy, Kings Point, NY, where young people are trained to become merchant marine officers, and conducts training in shipboard firefighting at Toledo, OH. It also administers a Federal assistance program for the maritime academies operated by the States of CA, ME, MA, MI, NY, and TX.

Field Organization—Maritime Administration

Field Office	Address	Director	Telephone
North Atlantic	Rm. 418, One Bowling Green, New York, NY 10004	Robert F. McKeon	212–668–3330
Mid Atlantic	Rm. 211, Bldg. 4D, 7737 Hampton Blvd, Norfolk, VA 23505	L. Frank Mach, *Acting*	757–441–6393
South Atlantic	51st SW First Ave., Miami, FL 33130	Lauren K. Brand	305–530–6420
Great Lakes	Suite 203, 1701 E. Woodfield Rd., Schaumburg, IL 60173	Doris J. Bautch	847–995–0122
Upper Mississippi	Suite 2.202F, 1222 Spruce St., St. Louis, MO 63103	Robert G. Goodwin, Jr..	314–539–6783
Eastern Gulf/ Lower Mississippi.	Rm. 1223, 500 Poydras St., New Orleans, LA 70130	James J. Murphy, *Acting*.	504–589–6658
Southern California.	Rm. 5190, 501 West Ocean Blvd., Long Beach, CA 90802	Alan T. Hicks	562–628–0246
Northern California.	Suite 1800, 201 Mission St., San Francisco, CA 94105	John Hummer	415–744–3125
Pacific Northwest	Rm. 3196, 915 2d Ave., Seattle, WA 98174	Randall D. Rogers	206–220–7717
Merchant Marine Academy.	300 Steamboat Rd., Kings Point, NY 11024	Allen B. Worley	516–773–5000

For further information, contact the Office of Congressional and Public Affairs, Maritime Administration, Department of Transportation, 1200 New Jersey Avenue SE., Washington, DC 20590. Phone, 202–366–5807 or 800–996–2723. Internet, www.marad.dot.gov.

Saint Lawrence Seaway Development Corporation

The Saint Lawrence Seaway Development Corporation was established by the Saint Lawrence Seaway Act of May 13, 1954 (33 U.S.C. 981–990), and became an operating administration of the Department of Transportation in 1966.

The Corporation, working cooperatively with the Saint Lawrence Seaway Management Corporation

(SLSMC) of Canada, is dedicated to operating and maintaining a safe, reliable, and efficient deep draft waterway between the Great Lakes and the Atlantic Ocean. It ensures the safe transit of commercial and noncommercial vessels through the two U.S. locks and the navigation channels of the Saint Lawrence Seaway System. The Corporation works jointly with SLSMC on all matters related to rules and regulations, overall operations, vessel inspections, traffic control, navigation aids, safety, operating dates, and trade development programs.

The Great Lakes/Saint Lawrence Seaway System extends from the Atlantic Ocean to the Lake Superior ports of Duluth/Superior, a distance of 2,342 miles. The Corporation's main customers are vessel owners and operators, Midwest States and Canadian provinces, Great Lakes port communities, shippers and receivers of domestic and international cargo, and the Great Lakes/ Saint Lawrence Seaway Systems maritime and related services industries. International and domestic commerce through the Seaway contributes to the economic prosperity of the entire Great Lakes region.

For further information, contact the Director of Trade Development and Public Affairs, Saint Lawrence Seaway Development Corporation, Department of Transportation, 1200 New Jersey Avenue SE., Washington, DC 20590. Phone, 202–366–0091. Fax, 202–366–7147. Internet, www.greatlakes-seaway.com.

Pipeline and Hazardous Materials Safety Administration

The Pipeline and Hazardous Materials Administration was established on February 20, 2005. It is responsible for hazardous materials transportation and pipeline safety.

Hazardous Materials The Office of Hazardous Materials Safety develops and issues regulations for the safe and secure transportation of hazardous materials by all modes, excluding bulk transportation by water. The regulations cover shipper and carrier operations, packaging and container specifications, and hazardous materials definitions. The Office provides training and outreach to help shippers and carriers meet the requirements of the hazardous material regulations. The Office is also responsible for the enforcement of regulations other than those applicable to a single mode of transportation. The Office manages a fee-funded grant program to assist States in planning for hazardous materials emergencies and to assist States and Indian tribes with training for hazardous materials emergencies. Additionally, the Office maintains a national safety program to safeguard food and certain other products from contamination during motor or rail transportation.

For further information, call 202–366–0656. Internet, hazmat.dot.gov.

Regional Offices—Office of Hazardous Materials Safety

Region	Address	Chief
Central—IA, IL, IN, KY, MI, MN, MO, ND, NE, OH, SD, WI	Suite 478, 2350 E. Devon Ave., Des Plaines, IL 60018	Kevin Boehne
Eastern—CT, DC, DE, MA, MD, ME, NH, NJ, NY, PA, RI, VA, VT, WV	Suite 306, 820 Bear Tavern Rd., W. Trenton, NJ 08628	Colleen Abbenhaus
Southern—AL, FL, GA, MS, NC, PR, SC, TN	Suite 602, 233 Peachtree St. NE., Atlanta, GA 30303	John Heneghan
Southwest—AR, CO, KS, LA, NM, OK, TX	Suite 1110, 8701 S. Gessner Rd., Houston, TX 77004	Billy Hines
Western—AK, AZ, CA, HI, ID, MT, NV, OR, UT, WA, WY	Suite 550B, 3401 Centrelake Dr., Ontario, CA 91761	Scott Simmons

Pipelines   The Office of Pipeline Safety's (OPS) mission is to ensure the safety, security, and environmental protection of the Nation's pipeline transportation system. The Office establishes and enforces safety and environmental standards for transportation of gas and hazardous liquids by pipeline. OPS also analyzes data, conducts education and training, promotes damage prevention, and conducts research and development for pipeline safety. Through OPS-administered grants-in-aid, States that voluntarily assume regulatory jurisdiction of pipelines can receive funding for up to 50 percent of the costs for their intrastate pipeline safety programs. OPS engineers inspect most interstate pipelines and other facilities not covered by the State programs. The Office also implements the Oil Pollution Act of 1990 by providing approval for and testing of oil pipeline spill response plans.

For further information, call 202–366–4595.

Regional Offices—Office of Pipeline Safety

Region	Address	Chief
Central—IA, IL, IN, KS, MI, MN, MO, ND, NE, OH, SD, WI	Rm. 462, 901 Locust St., Kansas City, MO 64106	Ivan Huntoon
Eastern—CT, DC, DE, MA, MD, ME, NH, NJ, NY, PA, RI, VA, VT, WV	Rm. 7128, 400 7th St. SW., Washington, DC 20590	William Gute
Southern—AL, AR, FL, GA, KY, MS, NC, PR, SC, TN	Suite 602, 223 Peachtree St. NE., Atlanta, GA 30303	Linda Daugherty
Southwest—AZ, LA, NM, OK, TX	Suite 1110, 8701 S. Gessner Rd., Houston, TX 77074	Rodrick M. Seeley
Western—AK, CA, CO, HI, ID, MT, NV, OR, UT, WA, WY	Suite 110, 12300 W. Dakota Ave., Lakewood, CO 80215	Chris Hoidal

For further information, contact the Office of Governmental, International and Public Affairs, Pipeline and Hazardous Materials Safety Administration, Department of Transportation, Suite 8406, 1200 New Jersey Avenue SE., Washington, DC 20590. Phone, 202–366–4831. Internet, www.phmsa.dot.gov.

Research and Innovative Technology Administration

The Research and Innovative Technology Administration (RITA) was created under the Norman Y. Mineta Research and Special Programs Improvement Act (49 U.S.C. 101 note). RITA coordinates, facilitates, and reviews the Department's research and development programs and activities; performs comprehensive transportation statistics research, analysis, and reporting; and promotes the use of innovative technologies to improve our Nation's transportation system. RITA brings together important DOT data, research, and technology transfer assets and provides strategic direction and oversight of DOT's Intelligent Transportation Systems Program.

RITA is composed of the staff from the Office of Research, Development, and Technology, the Volpe National Transportation Systems Center, the Transportation Safety Institute, and the Bureau of Transportation Statistics.

For further information, contact the Research and Innovative Technology Administration, Department of Transportation, 1200 New Jersey Avenue SE., Washington, DC 20590. Phone, 202–366–4180. Internet, www.rita.dot.gov. Email, info.rita@dot.gov.

Federal Motor Carrier Safety Administration

The Federal Motor Carrier Safety Administration was established within the Department of Transportation on January 1, 2000, pursuant to the Motor

Carrier Safety Improvement Act of 1999 (49 U.S.C. 113).

Formerly a part of the Federal Highway Administration, the Federal Motor Carrier Safety Administration's primary mission is to prevent commercial motor vehicle-related fatalities and injuries. Activities of the Administration contribute to ensuring safety in motor carrier operations through strong enforcement of safety regulations, targeting high-risk carriers and commercial motor vehicle drivers; improving safety information systems and commercial motor vehicle technologies; strengthening commercial motor vehicle equipment and operating standards; and increasing safety awareness. To accomplish these activities, the Administration works with Federal, State, and local enforcement agencies, the motor carrier industry, labor safety interest groups, and others.

Activities

Commercial Drivers' Licenses The Administration develops standards to test and license commercial motor vehicle drivers.

Data and Analysis The Administration collects and disseminates data on motor carrier safety and directs resources to improve motor carrier safety.

Regulatory Compliance and Enforcement The Administration operates a program to improve safety performance and remove high-risk carriers from the Nation's highways.

Research and Technology The Administration coordinates research and development to improve the safety of motor carrier operations and commercial motor vehicles and drivers.

Safety Assistance The Administration provides States with financial assistance for roadside inspections and other commercial motor vehicle safety programs. It promotes motor vehicle and motor carrier safety.

Other Activities The Administration supports the development of unified motor carrier safety requirements and procedures throughout North America. It participates in international technical organizations and committees to help share the best practices in motor carrier safety throughout North America and the rest of the world. It enforces regulations ensuring safe highway transportation of hazardous materials and has established a task force to identify and investigate those carriers of household goods which have exhibited a substantial pattern of consumer abuse.

Field Organization—Federal Motor Carrier Safety Administration Administration

Region	Address	Telephone
Eastern—AL, CT, DE, DC, ME, MD, MA, NH, NJ, NY, PA, PR, RI, VT, VA, WV.	Suite N, 802 Cromwell Park Dr., Glen Burnie, MD 21061–2819 ...	443–703–2240
Southern—AL, AR, FL, GA, KY, LA, MS, NM, NC, OK, SC, TN, TX.	Suite 1700, 1800 Century Blvd., Atlanta, GA 30345	404–327–7400
Midwestern—IL, IN, IA, KS, MI, MN, MO, NE, OH, WI.	Suite 210, 19900 Governors Dr., Olympia Fields, IL 60461–1021	708–283–3577
Western—AK, AZ, CA, CO, HI, ID, MT, NV, ND, OR, SD, UT, WA, WY.	B–300, Golden Hills Office Centre, 12600 W. Colfax Ave., Lakewood, CO 80215.	303–407–2350

For further information, contact the Federal Motor Carrier Safety Administration, 1200 New Jersey Avenue SE., Washington, DC 20590. Phone, 202–366–2519. Internet, www.fmcsa.dot.gov.

Surface Transportation Board

The Surface Transportation Board was established in 1996 by the Interstate Commerce Commission (ICC) Termination Act of 1995 (49 U.S.C.

10101 *et seq.*) as an independent adjudicatory body organizationally housed within the Department of Transportation with jurisdiction over certain surface transportation economic regulatory matters formerly under ICC jurisdiction. The Board consists of three members, appointed by the President with the advice and consent of the Senate for 5-year terms.

The Board adjudicates disputes and regulates interstate surface transportation through various laws pertaining to the different modes of surface transportation. The Board's general responsibilities include the oversight of firms engaged in transportation in interstate and foreign commerce to the extent that it takes place within the United States, or between or among points in the contiguous United States and points in Alaska, Hawaii, or U.S. territories or possessions. Surface transportation matters under the Board's jurisdiction in general include railroad rate and service issues, rail restructuring transactions (mergers, line sales, line construction, and line abandonments), and labor matters related thereto; certain trucking company, moving van, and noncontiguous ocean shipping company rate matters; certain intercity passenger bus company structure, financial, and

operational matters; and certain pipeline matters not regulated by the Federal Energy Regulatory Commission.

In performing its functions, the Board is charged with promoting, where appropriate, substantive and procedural regulatory reform and providing an efficient and effective forum for the resolution of disputes. Through the granting of exemptions from regulations where warranted, the streamlining of its decisionmaking process and the regulations applicable thereto, and the consistent and fair application of legal and equitable principles, the Board seeks to provide an effective forum for efficient dispute resolution and facilitation of appropriate market-based business transactions. Through rulemakings and case disposition, it strives to develop new and better ways to analyze unique and complex problems, to reach fully justified decisions more quickly, to reduce the costs associated with regulatory oversight, and to encourage private sector negotiations and resolutions to problems, where appropriate.

For further information, contact the Office of Public Assistance, Governmental Affairs, and Compliance, Surface Transportation Board, 395 E Street SW., Washington, DC, 20423–0001. Phone, 202–245–0230. Internet, www.stb.dot.gov.

Sources of Information

Inquiries for information on the following subjects should be directed to the specified office, Department of Transportation, Washington, DC 20590, or to the address indicated.

Civil Rights   For information on equal employment opportunity, nondiscrimination in DOT employment and transportation services, or DOT's Disadvantaged Business Enterprise certification appeals program, contact the Director, Departmental Office of Civil Rights. Phone, 202–366–4648. Internet, www.dot.gov/ost/docr.

Consumer Activities   For information about air travelers' rights or for assistance in resolving consumer problems with providers of commercial

air transportation services, contact the Consumer Affairs Division (phone, 202–366–2220).

To report vehicle safety problems, obtain information on motor vehicle and highway safety, or to request consumer information publications, call the National Highway Traffic Safety Administration's 24-hour auto safety hotline. Phone, 202–366–0123 (Washington, DC, area) or 800–424–9393 (toll free except Alaska and Hawaii).

Contracts   Contact the Office of the Senior Procurement Executive. Phone, 202–366–4263.

Employment   The principal occupations in the Department are air traffic controller, aviation safety specialist, electronics maintenance technician, engineer (civil, aeronautical, automotive, electronic, highway, and general), administrative/management, and clerical. For further information, contact the Transportation Administrative Service Center DOT Connection, Room PL–402, 1200 New Jersey Avenue SE., Washington, DC 20590. Phone, 202–366–9391 or 800–525–2878.

Environment Inquiries on environmental activities and programs should be directed to the Assistant Secretary for Transportation Policy, Office of Transportation Policy Development, Washington, DC 20590. Phone, 202–366–4416.

Films Many films on transportation subjects are available for use by educational institutions, community groups, private organizations, etc. Requests for specific films relating to a particular mode of transportation may be directed to the appropriate operating administration.

Fraud, Waste, and Abuse To report, contact the Office of Inspector General hotline, P.O. Box 23178, Washington, DC 20026–0178. Phone, 202–366–1461 or 800–424–9071.

Publications The Department and its operating agencies issue publications on a wide variety of subjects. Many of these publications are available from the issuing agency or for sale from the Government Printing Office and the National Technical Information Service, 5285 Port Royal Road, Springfield, VA 22151. Contact the Department or the specific agency at the addresses indicated in the text.

Reading Rooms Contact the Department of Transportation Dockets, PL–401, 400 Seventh Street SW., Washington, DC 20590. Phone, 800–647–5527. Administrations and their regional offices maintain reading rooms for public use. Contact the specific administration at the address indicated in the text.

Other reading rooms include: Department of Transportation Library, Room 2200, 1200 New Jersey Avenue SE., Washington, DC 20590 (phone, 202–366–0745); Department of Transportation/TASC Law Library, Room 2215, 1200 New Jersey Avenue SE., Washington, DC 20590 (phone, 202–366–0749); Department of Transportation Library, FB–10A Branch, Room 930, 800 Independence Avenue SW., Washington, DC 20591 (phone, 202–267–3115); and Department of Transportation Library, Transpoint Branch, B–726, 2100 Second Street SW., Washington, DC 20593 (phone, 202–267–2536).

Speakers The Department of Transportation and its operating administrations and regional offices make speakers available for civic, labor, and community groups. Contact the specific agency or the nearest regional office at the address indicated in the text.

Surface Transportation Board Proceedings and Public Records Requests for public assistance with pending or potential proceedings of the Board should be addressed to the Office of Public Assistance, Governmental Affairs, and Compliance, Surface Transportation Board, 395 E Street SW., Washington, DC 20423–0001. Phone, 202–245–0238.

Requests for access to the Board's public records should be made to the Office of the Secretary, Surface Transportation Board, 395 E Street SW., Washington, DC 20423–0001. Phone, 202–245–0232.

Telephone Directory The Department of Transportation telephone directory is available for sale by the Superintendent of Documents, Government Printing Office, Washington, DC 20402.

For further information concerning the Department of Transportation, contact the Office of Public Affairs, Department of Transportation, 1200 New Jersey Avenue SE., Washington, DC 20590. Phone, 202–366–5580. Internet, www.dot.gov.

DEPARTMENT OF THE TREASURY

1500 Pennsylvania Avenue NW., Washington, DC 20220
Phone, 202–622–2000. Internet, www.treas.gov.

SECRETARY OF THE TREASURY	TIMOTHY GEITHNER
DEPUTY SECRETARY	NEAL S. WOLIN
Chief of Staff	MARK PATTERSON
Executive Secretary	ANDREW MAYOCK
Inspector General	ERIC THORSON
Treasury Inspector General for Tax Administration	J. RUSSELL GEORGE
General Counsel	GEORGE W. MADISON
Deputy General Counsel	(VACANCY)
Assistant Secretary (Economic Policy)	ALAN B. KRUEGER
Deputy Assistant Secretary (Macroeconomics)	(VACANCY)
Deputy Assistant Secretary for Policy Coordination	AARON KLEIN
Deputy Assistant Secretary (Microeconomic Analysis)	JOHN WORTH, *Acting*
Assistant Secretary (Legislative Affairs)	KIM N. WALLACE
Deputy Assistant Secretary (Appropriation and Management)	(VACANCY)
Deputy Assistant Secretary (Business and Public Liaison)	(VACANCY)
Assistant Secretary for Management/Chief Financial Officer/Chief Performance Officer	DANIEL TANGHERLINI
Deputy Assistant Secretary for Chief Human Resources and Chief Human Capital Officer	ROCHELLE GRANAT
Deputy Chief Financial Officer	AL RUNNELS
Chief Information Officer	MIKE DUFFY
Deputy Assistant Secretary for Management and Budget	(VACANCY)
Senior Procurement Executive	TOM SHARPE
District of Columbia Pension	NANCY OSTROWSKI
Assistant Secretary (Public Affairs)	(VACANCY)
Deputy Assistant Secretary (Public Affairs)	ANDREW WILLIAMS
Assistant Secretary (Tax Policy)	(VACANCY)
Deputy Assistant Secretary (Tax Policy)	(VACANCY)
Deputy Assistant Secretary (International Tax Affairs)	MICHAEL MUNDACA
Treasurer of the United States	ROSIE RIOS
Under Secretary (Domestic Finance)	(VACANCY)
Deputy Assistant Secretary for Financial Education	DAN IANNICOLA
Deputy Assistant Secretary for Critical Infrastructure Protection and Compliance	D. SCOTT PARSONS

Director, Community Development Financial Institutions Fund	DONNA GAMBRELL
Assistant Secretary (Financial Institutions)	MICHAEL S. BARR
Deputy Assistant Secretary (Financial Institutions Policy)	(VACANCY)
Assistant Secretary (Financial Markets)	(VACANCY)
Deputy Assistant Secretary (Federal Finance)	SETH WHEELER
Deputy Assistant Secretary (Government Financial Policy)	(VACANCY)
Fiscal Assistant Secretary	KENNETH CARFINE
Deputy Assistant Secretary (Accounting Policy)	ROBERT N. REID
Deputy Assistant Secretary (Fiscal Operations and Policy)	GARY GRIPPO
Under Secretary (Terrorism and Financial Intelligence)	STUART LEVEY
Assistant Secretary (Terrorist Financing)	DAVID S. COHEN
Deputy Assistant Secretary (Terrorist Financing)	DANNY GLASER
Assistant Secretary (Financial Stability)	HERBERT M. ALLISON
Assistant Secretary (Intelligence and Analysis)	JANICE GARDNER
Deputy Assistant Secretary for Tax, Trade and Tariff Policy	TIMOTHY E. SKUD
Director, Office of Financial Crimes Enforcement Network (FinCEN)	JAMES FREIS
Under Secretary (International Affairs)	LAEL BRAINARD
Assistant Secretary (International Affairs)	ANDY BAUKOL
Deputy Assistant Secretary for International Monetary and Financial Policy	MARK SOBEL
Deputy Assistant Secretary for South and East Asia	ROBERT S. DOHNER
Deputy Assistant Secretary for Multilateral Development Bank and Specialized Development Institution	KAREN MATHIASEN, *Acting*
Deputy Assistant Secretary for Eurasia and Latin America	ERIC MEYER, *Acting*
Deputy Assistant Secretary for Technical Assistance Policy	W. LARRY MACDONALD
Deputy Assistant Secretary for Trade and Investment Policy	DAVID KAVANAUGH

ALCOHOL AND TOBACCO TAX AND TRADE BUREAU
1310 G Street NW., Washington, DC 20220
Phone, 202–927–5000. Fax, 202–927–5611. Internet, www.ttb.gov.

Administrator	JOHN MANFREDA
Deputy Administrator	VICKY MCDOWELL
Assistant Administrator (Field Operations)	MARY RYAN
Assistant Administrator (Headquarters)	BILL FOSTER
Associate Chief Counsel	ROBERT TOBIASSEN

OFFICE OF THE COMPTROLLER OF THE CURRENCY
250 E Street SW., Washington, DC 20219
Phone, 202–874–5000. Internet, www.occ.treas.gov.

| Comptroller | JOHN C. DUGAN |

Chief of Staff	JOHN G. WALSH
Chief Information Officer	BAJINDER N. PAUL
Deputy to the Federal Deposit Insurance Corporation Director (Comptroller of the Currency)	WILLIAM A. ROWE III
Ombudsman	LARRY HATTIX
First Senior Deputy Comptroller	JULIE L. WILLIAMS
Senior Deputy Comptroller for the Office of Management and Chief Financial Officer	THOMAS R. BLOOM
Senior Deputy Comptroller for Midsize Community Bank Supervision	JENNIFER C. KELLY
Senior Deputy Comptroller and Chief National Bank Examiner	TIMOTHY M. LONG
Senior Deputy Comptroller for International and Economic Affairs	MARK LEVONIAN
Senior Deputy Comptroller for Large Bank Supervision	DOUGLAS W. ROEDER

BUREAU OF ENGRAVING AND PRINTING

Fourteenth and C Streets SW., Washington, DC 20228
Phone, 202–874–3019. Internet, www.moneyfactory.com.

Director	LARRY R. FELIX
Deputy Director	PAMELA J. GARDINER
Associate Director (Chief Financial Officer)	LEONARD R. OLIJAR
Associate Director (Chief Information Officer)	PETER O. JOHNSON
Associate Director (Eastern Currency Facility)	JON J. CAMERON
Associate Director (Western Currency Facility)	CHARLENE WILLIAMS
Associate Director (Management)	SCOTT WILSON
Associate Director (Product and Technology Development)	JUDITH DIAZ MYERS
Chief Counsel	KEVIN RICE

FINANCIAL MANAGEMENT SERVICE

401 Fourteenth Street SW., Washington, DC 20227
Phone, 202–874–6740. Internet, www.fms.treas.gov.

Commissioner	DAVID A. LEBRYK, *Acting*
Deputy Commissioner	MARGARET MARQUETTE, *Acting*
Director, Legislative and Public Affairs	ALVINA A. MCHALE
Chief Counsel	MIKE COLLOTTA, *Acting*
Assistant Commissioner, Debt Management Services	SCOTT JOHNSON
Assistant Commissioner, Federal Finance	SHERYL MORROW
Assistant Commissioner, Governmentwide Accounting and Agency Services	D. JAMES STURGILL
Assistant Commissioner, Information Resources	JOHN KOPEC, *Acting*
Assistant Commissioner, Management (Chief Financial Officer)	DAVID REBICH, *Acting*
Assistant Commissioner, Regional Operations	RITA BRATCHER

INTERNAL REVENUE SERVICE

1111 Constitution Avenue NW., Washington, DC 20224
Phone, 202–622–5000. Internet, www.irs.gov.

Commissioner of Internal Revenue	DOUGLAS H. SHULMAN
Commissioner, Large and Midsize Business Division	STEVEN T. MILLER
Commissioner, Small Business/Self-Employed Division	CHRISTOPHER WAGNER
Commissioner, Tax Exempt and Government Entities Division	SARAH H. INGRAM
Commissioner, Wage and Investment Division	RICK BYRD
Deputy Commissioner Operations Support	MARK A. ERNST
Deputy Commissioner Services and Enforcement	LINDA STIFF
Chief Counsel	CLARISSA POTTER, *Acting*
Chief Financial Officer	ALISON DOONE
Chief, Agency-Wide Shared Services	DAVID GRANT, *Acting*
Chief, Appeals	DIANE RYAN
Chief, Communications and Liaison	FRANK M. KEITH
Chief, Criminal Investigation	EILEEN MAYER
Chief Technology Officer	TERRY V. MILHOLLAND
National Taxpayer Advocate	NINA E. OLSON
Director, Office of Research, Analysis and Statistics	MARK J. MAZUR
Chief Human Capitol Officer	JIM FALCONE
Director, Privacy, Information Protection and Data Security	DEBORAH G. WOLF
Director, Office of Professional Responsibility	KAREN L. HAWKINS
Director, Whistleblower Office	STEVE A. WHITLOCK

UNITED STATES MINT

801 Ninth Street NW., Washington, DC 20220
Phone, 202–354–7200. Internet, www.usmint.gov.

Director	EDMUND C. MOY
Deputy Director	ANDREW BRUNHART
Chief Counsel	DAN SHAVER
Associate Director, Finance	PATRICIA M. GREINER
Associate Director, Information Technology	ANDREW BRUNHART, *Acting*
Associate Director, Manufacturing	RICHARD PETERSON
Associate Director, Sales and Marketing	B.B. CRAIG
Associate Director, Protection	DENNIS O'CONNOR

BUREAU OF THE PUBLIC DEBT

999 E Street NW., Washington, DC 20239–0001
Phone, 202–504–3500. Internet, www.publicdebt.treas.gov

Commissioner	VAN ZECK
Deputy Commissioner	ANITA SHANDOR
Chief Counsel	PAUL WOLFTEICH
Director (Public and Legislative Affairs Staff)	KIM TREAT
Executive Director (Government Securities Regulation Staff)	LORI SANTAMORENA

Assistant Commissioner (Financing)	DARA SEAMAN
Assistant Commissioner (Information Technology)	KIMBERLY A. MCCOY
Assistant Commissioner (Public Debt Accounting)	DEBRA HINES
Assistant Commissioner (Retail Securities)	JOHN R. SWALES III
Assistant Commissioner (Management Services)	FRED PYATT
Executive Director (Administration Resource Center)	CYNTHIA Z. SPRINGER

OFFICE OF THRIFT SUPERVISION

1700 G Street NW., Washington, DC 20552
Phone, 202–906–6000. Internet, www.ots.treas.gov.

Director	JOHN E. BOWMAN, *Acting*
Deputy Director	SCOTT N. POLAKOFF
Chief Counsel	JOHN E. BOWMAN
Managing Director, Examinations, Supervision and Consumer Protection	TIMOTHY T. WARD
Managing Director, External Affairs	BARBARA L. SHYCOFF
Chief Information Officer and Chief Financial Officer	WAYNE G. LEISS
Managing Director, Human Resources and Administrative Services	(VACANCY)

The Department of the Treasury performs four basic functions: formulating and recommending economic, financial, tax, and fiscal policies; serving as financial agent for the U.S. Government; enforcing the law; and manufacturing coins and currency.

The Treasury Department was created by act of September 2, 1789 (31 U.S.C. 301 and 301 note). Many subsequent acts have figured in the development of the Department, delegating new duties to its charge and establishing the numerous bureaus and divisions that now comprise the Treasury.

Secretary   As a major policy adviser to the President, the Secretary has primary responsibility for formulating and recommending domestic and international financial, economic, and tax policy; participating in the formulation of broad fiscal policies that have general significance for the economy; and managing the public debt. The Secretary also oversees the activities of the Department in carrying out its major law enforcement responsibility; in serving as the financial agent for the U.S. Government; and in manufacturing coins, currency, and other products for customer agencies. The Secretary also

serves as the Government's chief financial officer.

Activities

Economic Policy   The Office of the Assistant Secretary for Economic Policy assists policymakers in the determination of economic policies. The Office:

—reviews and analyzes domestic and international economic issues and developments in the financial markets;

—assists in the development of official economic projections; and

—works closely with Federal Government agencies to develop economic forecasts underlying the yearly budget process.

Enforcement   The The Office of the Assistant Secretary for Enforcement coordinates Treasury law enforcement matters, including the formulation of policies for Treasury enforcement activities, and cooperates on law enforcement matters with other Federal

DEPARTMENT OF THE TREASURY

TREASURY BUREAUS

1 Assistant Secretary (Management) and Chief Financial Officer is Treasury's Chief Operating Officer.

agencies. It oversees the following branches of the Department:

—the Alcohol and Tobacco Tax and Trade Bureau, charged with collecting excise taxes on alcoholic beverages and tobacco products;

—the Office of Financial Enforcement, assisting in implementing the Bank Secrecy Act and administering related Treasury regulations; and

—the Office of Foreign Assets Control, controlling assets in the United States of "blocked" countries and the flow of funds and trade to them.

Financial Institutions   The Office of the Assistant Secretary for Financial Institutions exercises policy direction and control over Department activities relating to the substance of proposed legislation pertaining to the general activities and regulation of private financial intermediaries and relating to other Federal regulatory agencies.

Fiscal Affairs   The Office of the Fiscal Assistant Secretary supervises the administration of the Government's fiscal affairs. It manages the cash position of the Treasury and projects and monitors "debt subject-to-limit;" directs the performance of the fiscal agency functions of the Federal Reserve Banks; conducts governmentwide accounting and cash management activities; exercises supervision over depositories of the United States; and provides management overview of investment practices for Government trusts and other accounts.

International Affairs   The Office of the Assistant Secretary for International Affairs advises and assists policymakers in the formulation and execution of policies dealing with international financial, economic, monetary, trade, investment, environmental, and energy policies and programs. The work of the Office is organized into groups responsible for monetary and financial policy; international development, debt, and environmental policy; trade and investment policy; economic and financial technical assistance; and geographical areas (Asia, the Americas, Africa, Eurasia, and Latin America). The staff offices performing these functions:

—conduct financial diplomacy with industrial and developing nations and regions;

—work toward improving the structure and operations of the international monetary system;

—monitor developments in foreign exchange and other markets and official operations affecting those markets;

—facilitate structural monetary cooperation through the International Monetary Fund and other channels;

—oversee U.S. participation in the multilateral development banks and coordinate U.S. policies and operations relating to bilateral and multilateral development lending programs and institutions;

—formulate policy concerning financing of trade;

—coordinate policies toward foreign investments in the United States and U.S. investments abroad; and

—analyze balance of payments and other basic financial and economic data, including energy data, affecting world payment patterns and the world economic outlook.

Tax Policy   The Office of the Assistant Secretary for Tax Policy advises and assists the Secretary and the Deputy Secretary in the formulation and execution of domestic and international tax policies and programs. These functions include:

—analysis of proposed tax legislation and tax programs;

—projections of economic trends affecting tax bases;

—studies of effects of alternative tax measures;

—preparation of official estimates of Government receipts for the President's annual budget messages;

—legal advice and analysis on domestic and international tax matters;

—assistance in the development and review of tax legislation and domestic and international tax regulations and rulings; and

—participation in international tax treaty negotiations and in maintenance of relations with international organizations on tax matters.

Treasurer of the United States   The Office of the Treasurer of the United

States was established on September 6, 1777. The Treasurer was originally charged with the receipt and custody of Government funds, but many of these functions have been assumed by different bureaus of the Department of the Treasury. In 1981, the Treasurer was assigned responsibility for oversight of the Bureau of Engraving and Printing and the United States Mint. The Treasurer reports to the Secretary through the Assistant Secretary for Management/Chief Financial Officer.

Treasury Inspector General The Treasury Inspector General for Tax Administration (TIGTA) was established in January 1999, in accordance with the Internal Revenue Service Restructuring and Reform Act of 1998, to provide independent oversight of the Internal Revenue Service programs and activities. TIGTA is charged with monitoring the Nation's tax laws to ensure the IRS acts with efficiency, economy, and effectiveness toward program accomplishment; ensuring compliance with applicable laws and regulations, preventing, detecting, and deterring fraud, waste, and abuse; investigating activities or allegations related to fraud, waste, and abuse by IRS personnel; and protecting the IRS against attempts to corrupt or threaten its employees.

For further information concerning the departmental offices, contact the Public Affairs Office, Department of the Treasury, 1500 Pennsylvania Avenue NW., Washington, DC 20220. Phone, 202–622–2960.

Alcohol and Tobacco Tax and Trade Bureau

The Alcohol and Tobacco Tax and Trade Bureau (TTB) administers and enforces the existing Federal laws and Tax Code provisions related to the production and taxation of alcohol and tobacco products. TTB also collects all excise taxes on the manufacture of firearms and ammunition.

For further information, contact the Office of Public and Governmental Affairs, Alcohol and Tobacco Tax and Trade Bureau. Phone, 202–927–5000. Internet, www.ttb.gov.

Office of the Comptroller of the Currency

[For the Office of the Comptroller of the Currency statement of organization, see the *Code of Federal Regulations,* Title 12, Part 4]

The Office of the Comptroller of the Currency was created February 25, 1863 (12 Stat. 665), as a bureau of the Department of the Treasury. Its primary mission is to regulate national banks. The Office is headed by the Comptroller, who is appointed for a 5-year term by the President with the advice and consent of the Senate.

The Office regulates national banks by its power to examine banks; approves or denies applications for new bank charters, branches, or mergers; takes enforcement action—such as bank closures—against banks that are not in compliance with laws and regulations; and issues rules, regulations, and interpretations on banking practices.

The Office supervises approximately 2,100 national banks, including their trust activities and overseas operations. Each bank is examined annually through a nationwide staff of approximately 1,900 bank examiners supervised in 4 district offices. The Office is independently funded through assessments of the assets of national banks.

For further information, contact the Communications Division, Office of the Comptroller of the Currency, 250 E Street SW., Mail Stop 3–2, Washington, DC 20219. Phone, 202–874–4700.

Bureau of Engraving and Printing

The Bureau of Engraving and Printing operates on basic authorities conferred by act of July 11, 1862 (31 U.S.C. 303), and additional authorities contained in past appropriations made to the Bureau that are still in force. Operations are financed by a revolving fund established in 1950 in accordance with Public Law 81–656. The Bureau is headed by a Director who is selected by the Secretary of the Treasury.

The Bureau designs, prints, and finishes all of the Nation's paper currency and many other security documents, including White House invitations and military identification cards. It also is responsible for advising and assisting Federal agencies in the design and production of other Government documents that, because of their innate value or for other reasons, require security or counterfeit-deterrence characteristics.

The Bureau also operates a second currency manufacturing plant in Fort Worth, TX (9000 Blue Mound Road, 76131). Phone, 817–231–4000.

For further information, contact the Office of External Relations, Bureau of Engraving and Printing, Department of the Treasury, Room 533–M, Fourteenth and C Streets SW., Washington, DC 20228. Phone, 202–874–3019. Fax, 202–874–3177. Internet, www.moneyfactory.com.

Financial Management Service

The Financial Management Service (FMS) provides central payment services to Federal program agencies, operates the Federal Government's collections and deposit systems, provides governmentwide accounting and reporting services, and manages the collection of delinquent debt owed to the Federal Government. FMS has four regional financial centers located in Texas, Missouri, Pennsylvania, and California and one debt collection center in Alabama.

Accounting The Service gathers and publishes governmentwide financial information that is used by the public and private sectors to monitor the Government's financial status and establish fiscal and monetary policies. These publications include the *Daily Treasury Statement,* the *Monthly Treasury Statement,* the *Treasury Bulletin,* the *U.S. Government Annual Report,* and the *Financial Report of the U.S. Government.*

Collections FMS administers the world's largest collection system, gathering more than $2.2 trillion annually through a network of more than 10,000 financial institutions. It also manages the collection of Federal revenues such as individual and corporate income tax deposits, customs duties, loan repayments, fines, and proceeds from leases.

FMS and IRS launched the Electronic Federal Tax Payment System (www.eftps.gov), which allows individuals and businesses to pay Federal taxes through the Internet. EFTPS-OnLine also provides such features as an instant, printable acknowledgment for documenting each transaction, the ability to schedule advance payments, and access to payment history.

The Treasury Offset Program is one of the methods used to collect delinquent debt. FMS uses the program to withhold Federal payments, such as Federal income tax refunds, Federal salary payments, and Social Security benefits, to recipients with delinquent debts, including past-due child support obligations and State and Federal income tax debt.

Electronic Commerce Through its electronic money program, FMS tests new payments and collection technologies using the Internet and card technology, as well as related technologies such as digital signatures and biometrics. FMS has initiated electronic money pilot programs to help Federal agencies modernize their payments and collection activities. Examples include stored-value cards used on military bases and in Government hospitals, electronic checks, point-of-sale check truncations, and Internet credit card collection programs.

Payments   Each year, FMS disburses nearly one billion non-Defense payments, with a dollar value of more than $1.7 trillion, to a wide variety of recipients, such as those who receive Social Security, IRS tax refunds, and veterans benefits. For fiscal year 2008, nearly 79 percent of these transactions were issued by electronic funds transfer. The remainder of FMS payments is disbursed by check.

Regional Financial Centers—Financial Management Service

Center/Address	Director
Austin, TX (P.O. Box 149058, 78741)	Robert Mange
Kansas City, MO (P.O. Box 12599, 64116)	Gary Beets
Philadelphia, PA (P.O. Box 8676, 19101)	Betty Belinkski
San Francisco, CA (P.O. Box 193858, 94119)	Philip Belisle

For further information, contact the Office of Legislative and Public Affairs, Financial Management Service, Department of the Treasury, Room 555, 401 Fourteenth Street SW., Washington, DC 20227. Phone, 202–874–6740. Internet, www.fms.treas.gov.

Internal Revenue Service

The Office of the Commissioner of Internal Revenue was established by act of July 1, 1862 (26 U.S.C. 7802). The Internal Revenue Service (IRS) is responsible for administering and enforcing the internal revenue laws and related statutes, except those relating to alcohol, tobacco, firearms, and explosives. Its mission is to collect the proper amount of tax revenue, at the least cost to the public, by efficiently applying the tax law with integrity and fairness. To achieve that purpose, the IRS:

—strives to achieve the highest possible degree of voluntary compliance in accordance with the tax laws and regulations;

—advises the public of their rights and responsibilities;

—determines the extent of compliance and the causes of noncompliance;

—properly administers and enforces the tax laws; and

—continually searches for and implements new, more efficient ways of accomplishing its mission.

Basic activities include the following:

—ensuring satisfactory resolution of taxpayer complaints and providing taxpayer service and education;

—determining, assessing, and collecting internal revenue taxes;

—determining pension plan qualifications and exempt organization status; and

—preparing and issuing rulings and regulations to supplement the provisions of the Internal Revenue Code.

The source of most revenues collected is the individual income tax and the social insurance and retirement taxes. Other major sources are corporate income, excise, estate, and gift taxes. Congress first received authority to levy taxes on the income of individuals and corporations in 1913, pursuant to the 16th amendment of the Constitution.

For further information, contact the Internal Revenue Service, Department of the Treasury, 1111 Constitution Avenue NW., Washington, DC 20224. Phone, 202–622–5000.

United States Mint

The establishment of a mint was authorized by act of April 2, 1792 (1 Stat. 246). The Bureau of the Mint was established by act of February 12, 1873 (17 Stat. 424), and recodified on September 13, 1982 (31 U.S.C. 304, 5131). The name was changed to United States Mint by Secretarial order dated January 9, 1984.

The primary mission of the Mint is to produce an adequate volume of circulating coinage for the Nation to conduct its trade and commerce. The Mint also produces and sells numismatic coins, American Eagle gold and silver bullion coins, and national medals. In addition, the Fort Knox Bullion Depository is the primary storage facility for the Nation's gold bullion.

The U.S. Mint maintains sales centers at the Philadelphia and Denver Mints and at Union Station in Washington, DC. Public tours are conducted, with free admission, at the Philadelphia and Denver Mints.

Field Facilities
(PM: Plant Manager; O: Officer in Charge)

Facility/Address	Facility Head
Bullion Depository, Fort Knox, KY 40121	Bert Barnes (O)
Denver, CO 80204	David Croft (PM)
Philadelphia, PA 19106	Marc Landry (PM)
San Francisco, CA 94102	Larry Eckerman (PM)
West Point, NY 10996	Ellen McCullom (PM)

For further information, contact the United States Mint, Department of the Treasury, 801 Ninth Street NW., Washington, DC 20220. Phone, 202–354–7222.

Bureau of the Public Debt

The Bureau of the Public Debt was established on June 30, 1940, pursuant to the Reorganization Act of 1939 (31 U.S.C. 306).

The Bureau's mission is to borrow the money needed to operate the Federal Government, account for the resulting public debt, and provide reimbursable support to Federal agencies. The Bureau fulfills its mission through five programs: wholesale securities, Government agency investment, retail securities services, summary debt accounting, and franchise services.

The Bureau auctions and issues Treasury bills, notes, and bonds and manages the U.S. Savings Bond Program. It issues, services, and redeems bonds through a nationwide network of issuing and paying agents. It provides daily and other periodic reports to account for the composition and size of the debt. In addition, the Bureau implements the regulations for the Government securities market. These regulations provide for investor protection while maintaining a fair and liquid market for Government securities.

For more information, contact the Director, Public and Legislative Affairs, Office of the Commissioner, Bureau of the Public Debt, Washington, DC 20239–0001. Phone, 202–504–3502. Internet, www.publicdebt.treas.gov.

Office of Thrift Supervision

The Office of Thrift Supervision (OTS) regulates Federal- and State-chartered savings institutions. Created by the Financial Institutions Reform, Recovery, and Enforcement Act of 1989, its mission is to effectively and efficiently supervise Thrift institutions in a manner that encourages a competitive industry to meet housing and other credit and financial services needs and ensure access to financial services for all Americans.

OTS is headed by a Director appointed by the President, with the advice and consent of the Senate, for a 5-year term. The Director is responsible for the overall direction and policy of the agency. OTS is responsible for the following:

—examining and supervising thrift institutions in the four OTS regions to ensure the safety and soundness of the industry;

—ensuring that thrifts comply with consumer protection laws and regulations;

—conducting a regional quality assurance program to ensure consistent applications of policies and procedures;

—developing national policy guidelines to enhance statutes and regulations and to establish programs to implement new policy and law;

—issuing various financial reports, including the quarterly report on the financial condition of the thrift industry;

—preparing regulations, bulletins, other policy documents, congressional testimony, and official correspondence on matters relating to the condition of the thrift industry, interest rate risk, financial derivatives, and economic issues; and

—prosecuting enforcement actions relating to thrift institutions.

For further information, contact External Affairs, Office of Thrift Supervision, 1700 G Street NW., Washington, DC 20552. Phone, 202–906–6677. Fax, 202–906–7849. Internet, www.ots.treas.gov.

Sources of Information

Departmental Offices

Contracts   Write to the Director, Office of Procurement, Suite 400–W, 1310 G Street NW., Washington, DC 20220. Phone, 202–622–0203.

Environment   Environmental statements prepared by the Department are available for review in the Departmental Library. Information on Treasury environmental matters may be obtained from the Office of the Assistant Secretary of the Treasury for Management and Chief Financial Officer, Treasury Department, Washington, DC 20220. Phone, 202–622–0043.

General Inquiries   For general information about the Treasury Department, including copies of news releases and texts of speeches by high-level Treasury officials, write to the Office of the Assistant Secretary (Public Affairs and Public Liaison), Room 3430, Departmental Offices, Treasury Department, Washington, DC 20220. Phone, 202–622–2920.

Inspector General   For general information, contact the Assistant Inspector General for Management at 202–927–5200, or visit the Office of Inspector General Web site at www.treas.gov/inspector-general. To report the possible existence of a Treasury activity constituting a violation of law, rules, regulations, or mismanagement, gross waste of funds, abuse of authority, or a substantial and specific danger to the public health and safety (not including the Internal Revenue Service, which reports to the Treasury Inspector General for Tax Administration), phone, 800–359–3898; fax, 202–927–5799; email, Hotline@oig.treas.gov; or write to Treasury OIG Hotline, Office of

Inspector General, 1500 Pennsylvania Avenue NW., Washington, DC 20220. For Freedom of Information Act/Privacy Act requests, write to Freedom of Information Act Request, Treasury OIG, Office of Counsel, Suite 510, 740 15th Street NW., Washington, DC 20220.
Reading Room The Reading Room is located in the Treasury Library, Room 1428, Main Treasury Building, 1500 Pennsylvania Avenue NW., Washington, DC 20220. Phone, 202–622–0990.
Small and Disadvantaged Business Activities Write to the Director, Office of Small and Disadvantaged Business Utilization, Suite 400–W, 1310 G Street NW., Washington, DC 20220. Phone, 202–622–0530.
Tax Legislation Information on tax legislation may be obtained from the Assistant Secretary (Tax Policy), Departmental Offices, Treasury Department, Washington, DC 20220. Phone, 202–622–0050.
Telephone Directory The Treasury Department telephone directory is available for sale by the Superintendent of Documents, Government Printing Office, Washington, DC 20402.
Treasury Inspector General for Tax Administration Individuals wishing to report fraud, waste, or abuse against or by IRS employees should write to the Treasury Inspector General for Tax Administration, P.O. Box 589, Ben Franklin Station, Washington, DC 20044–0589. Phone, 800–366–4484. Email, complaints@tigta.treas.gov.
Comptroller of the Currency For Freedom of Information Act Requests, contact the Manager, Disclosure Services and Administrative Operations, Communications Division, 250 E Street SW., Mail Stop 3–2, Washington, DC 20219 (phone, 202–874–4700; fax, 202–874–5274). For information about contracts, contact the Acquisition Management Division at 250 E Street SW., Washington, DC 20219 (phone, 202–874–5040; fax, 202–874–5625). For information regarding national bank examiner employment opportunities (generally hired at the entry level through a college recruitment program), contact the Director for Human

Resources Operations, 250 E Street SW., Washington, DC 20219 (phone, 202–874–4500; fax, 202–874–4655). Publications are available from the Communications Division, 250 E Street SW., Washington, DC 20219 (phone, 202–874–4700; fax, 202–874–5263).

Bureau of Engraving and Printing

Address inquiries on the following subjects to the specified office, Bureau of Engraving and Printing.
Contracts and Small Business Activities Information relating to contracts and small business activity may be obtained by contacting the Office of Procurement. Phone, 202–874–1981.
Employment Information regarding employment opportunities and required qualifications is available from the Office of Human Resources. Phone, 202–874–2633.
Freedom of Information Act Requests Inquiries should be directed to 202–874–3733.
General Inquiries Requests for information about the Bureau, its products, or numismatic and philatelic interests should be directed to 202–874–3019.
Mail Order Sales Uncut sheets of currency, engraved Presidential portraits, historical engravings of national landmarks, and other souvenirs and mementos are available for purchase by phone at 800–456–3408 and the Internet at www.moneyfactory.com.
Tours Tours of the Bureau's facilities are provided throughout the year according to the schedules listed below.
Washington, DC:
Peak season, March through August, 9 a.m. until 10:45 a.m. and 12:30 p.m. until 2 p.m. Tickets are required for all tours. Tours begin every 15 minutes, with the last tour beginning at 2 p.m. The times between 11 a.m. and 12:15 p.m. are reserved for school and other groups. The ticket booth is located on Raoul Wallenberg Place (formerly Fifteenth Street) and opens at 8 a.m. Tour tickets are free. The ticket booth remains open for the morning and evening tours until all tickets have been distributed. Lines form early and tickets

go quickly, typically by 9 a.m. during peak season. Tickets are distributed on a first-come, first-served basis. Lines organize on Raoul Wallenberg Place.

Evening tours, April through August, 5 p.m. until 7 p.m. Tours are offered every 15 minutes.

Non-peak season, September through February, 9 a.m. until 2 p.m. No tickets are necessary for tours during this time. Lines organize on Fourteenth Street.

Fort Worth, TX:
Non-peak season, September through May, 9 a.m. until 2 p.m. The Visitors Center is open from 8:30 a.m. until 3:30 p.m.

June and July, 11 a.m. until 5 p.m. Tour hours are every 30 minutes, from 11 a.m. until 5 p.m. The Visitors Center is open from 10:30 a.m. until 6:30 p.m.

No tours are given at either facility on weekends, Federal holidays, or between Christmas and New Year's Day.

Up-to-the-minute tour information is available on the Bureau's Web site at www.moneyfactory.com. Information about the Washington, DC, tour and visitors center can also be obtained by calling 202–874–2330 or 866–874–2330. Information about the Fort Worth tour and visitor center can be obtained by calling 817–231–4000 or 866–865–1194.

Financial Management Service

Inquiries on the following subjects should be directed to the specified office, Financial Management Service, 401 Fourteenth Street SW., Washington, DC 20227. Fax, 202–874–7016.
Contracts   Write to the Director, Acquisition Management Division, Room 428 LCB. Phone, 202–874–6910.
Employment   Inquiries may be directed to the Human Resources Division, Room 170A, 3700 East-West Highway, Hyattsville, MD 20782. Phone, 202–874–8090. TDD, 202–874–8825.

Internal Revenue Service

Audiovisual Materials   Films providing information on the American tax system, examination and appeal rights, and the tax responsibilities of running a small business are available. Some of the films

are also available in Spanish. The films can be obtained by contacting any territory office.

Also available are audio and video cassette tapes that provide step-by-step instructions for preparing basic individual income tax forms. These tapes are available in many local libraries.
Contracts   Write to the Internal Revenue Service, 1111 Constitution Avenue NW. (OS:A:P), Washington, DC 20224. Phone, 202–283–1710.
Customer Service   The Internal Revenue Service provides year-round tax information and assistance to taxpayers, primarily through its Web site and toll-free telephone system, which also includes telephone assistance to deaf and hearing-impaired taxpayers who have access to a teletypewriter or television/phone. The toll-free numbers are listed in local telephone directories and in the annual tax form packages. Taxpayers may also visit agency offices for help with their tax problems. Individual preparation is available for handicapped or other individuals unable to use the group preparation method. Foreign language tax assistance is also available at many locations. The IRS encourages taxpayers to use the resources available at www.irs.gov for assistance with their tax questions or to locate electronic filing sources.
Educational Programs   The Service provides, free of charge, general tax information publications and booklets on specific tax topics. Taxpayer information materials also are distributed to major television networks and many radio and television stations, daily and weekly newspapers, magazines, and specialized publications. Special educational materials and films are provided for use in high schools and colleges. Individuals starting a new business are given specialized materials and information at small business workshops, and community colleges provide classes based on material provided by the Service. The community outreach tax assistance program provides assistance, through agency employees, to community groups.

Through the volunteer income tax assistance program and the tax counseling for the elderly program, the Service recruits, trains, and supports volunteers who offer free tax assistance to low-income, elderly, military, and non-English-speaking taxpayers.

Materials, films, and information on the educational programs can be obtained by contacting any territory office.

Employment   For information, write to the recruitment coordinator at any of the territory offices.

Publications   The *Annual Report— Commissioner of Internal Revenue*, the *Internal Revenue Service Data Book*, and periodic reports of statistics of income are available from the Superintendent of Documents, Government Printing Office, Washington, DC 20402.

Audit of Returns, Appeal Rights, and Claims for Refund, Your Federal Income Tax, Farmers Tax Guide, Tax Guide for Small Business, and other publications are available at Internal Revenue Service offices free of charge.

Reading Rooms   Public reading rooms are located in the national office and in each territory office.

Speakers   Arrangements for speakers on provisions of the tax law and operations of the Internal Revenue Service for professional and community groups may be made by writing to the Senior Commissioner's Representative or, for national organizations only, to the Communications Division at the IRS National Headquarters in Washington, DC.

Taxpayer Advocate   Each district has a problem resolution staff which attempts to resolve taxpayer complaints not satisfied through regular channels.

United States Mint

Contracts and Employment   Inquiries should be directed to the facility head of the appropriate field office or to the Director of the Mint.

Numismatic Services   The United States Mint maintains public exhibit and sales areas at the Philadelphia and Denver Mint, and at Union Station in Washington, DC. Brochures and order forms for official coins, medals, and other numismatic items are available through the Internet at www.usmint.gov.

Publications   The *CFO Annual Financial Report* is available from the United States Mint, Department of the Treasury, 801 Ninth Street NW., Washington, DC 20220. Phone, 202–354–7800.

Bureau of the Public Debt

Electronic Access   Information about the public debt, U.S. Savings Bonds, Treasury bills, notes, and bonds, and other Treasury securities is available through the Internet at www.treasurydirect.gov. Forms and publications may be ordered electronically at the same address.

Employment   General employment inquiries should be addressed to the Bureau of the Public Debt, Division of Human Resources, Recruitment, and Classification Branch, Parkersburg, WV 26106–1328. Phone, 304–480–6144.

Savings Bonds   Savings bonds are continuously on sale at more than 40,000 financial institutions and their branches in virtually every locality in the United States. Information about bonds is provided by such issuing agents. Savings bonds may also be purchased and held in an online account. Current rate information is available at www.treasurydirect.gov or toll free by calling 800–4US–BOND or 800–487–2663. Requests for information about all series of savings bonds, savings notes, and retirement plans or individual retirement bonds should be addressed to the Bureau of the Public Debt, Department of the Treasury, 200 Third Street, Parkersburg, WV 26106–1328. Phone, 304–480–7711.

Treasury Securities   Information inquiries regarding the purchase of Treasury bills, bonds, and notes should be addressed to a Treasury direct contact center, or to the Bureau of the Public Debt, 200 Third Street, Parkersburg, WV 26106–1328. Phone, 800–722–2678.

Office of Thrift Supervision

Electronic Access   Information about OTS and institutions regulated by OTS is available through the Internet at www.ots.treas.gov.

Employment   Inquiries about employment opportunities with the Office of Thrift Supervision should be directed to the Human Resources Office. Phone, 202–906–6061.

Freedom of Information Act/Privacy Act Requests   For information not readily available from the Web site, please submit to the Office of Thrift Supervision, Dissemination Branch, 1700 G Street NW., Washington, DC 20552. Email, publicinfo@ots.treas.gov. Fax, 202–906–7755.

General Information   General information about OTS may be obtained by calling 202–906–6000.

Publications   Publications that provide information and guidance regarding the thrift industry are available at the "Public Information" link on the Web site.

For further information, contact the Public Affairs Office, Department of the Treasury, 1500 Pennsylvania Avenue NW., Washington, DC 20220. Phone, 202–622–2960. Internet, www.treas.gov.

DEPARTMENT OF VETERANS AFFAIRS

810 Vermont Avenue NW., Washington, DC 20420
Phone, 202–273–4800. Internet, www.va.gov.

SECRETARY OF VETERANS AFFAIRS	ERIC K. SHINSEKI
DEPUTY SECRETARY	W. SCOTT GOULD
CHIEF OF STAFF	JOHN R. GINGRICH
General Counsel	JOHN H. THOMPSON, *Acting*
Chairman, Board of Veterans' Appeals	JAMES P. TERRY
Vice Chairman, Board of Veterans' Appeals	STEVE L. KELLER
Director, Office of Small and Disadvantaged Business Utilization	GAIL L. WEGNER, *Acting*
Advisory Committee Management Officer	E. PHILIP RIGGIN
Director, Center for Minority Veterans	LUCRETIA MCCLENNEY
Director, Center for Women Veterans	IRENE TROWELL-HARRIS
Director, Office of Employment Discrimination Complaint Adjudication	RAFAEL A. TORRES, *Acting*
Director, Center for Faith-Based and Community Initiatives	STEPHEN DILLARD, *Acting*
Inspector General	GEORGE J. OPFER
Veterans' Service Organizations Liaison	KEVIN SECOR
Under Secretary for Health, Veterans Health Administration	(VACANCY)
Deputy Under Secretary for Health	GERALD M. CROSS
Deputy Under Secretary for Health for Operations and Management	WILLIAM F. FEELEY
Under Secretary for Benefits, Veterans Benefits Administration	PATRICK DUNNE
Deputy Under Secretary for Benefits	MIKE WALCOFF
Under Secretary for Memorial Affairs, National Cemetery Administration	STEVE L. MURO, *Acting*
Deputy Under Secretary for Memorial Affairs	STEVE L. MURO
Assistant Secretary for Management	RITA A. REED, *Acting*
Principal Deputy Assistant Secretary	RITA A. REED
Deputy Assistant Secretary for Budget	DANIEL A. TUCKER
Deputy Assistant Secretary for Finance	EDWARD J. MURRAY
Executive Director for Office of Acquisition, Logistics and Construction	GLENN D. HAGGSTROM
Director, Office of Construction and Facilities Management	DONALD H. ORNDOFF
Deputy Assistant Secretary for Acquisitions	JAN R. FRYE
Assistant Secretary for Information and Technology	STEPHEN WARREN, *Acting*
Deputy Assistant Secretary for Information and Technology	STEPHEN WARREN
Deputy Chief Information Officer, IT Enterprise, Strategy, Policy, Plans and Programs	SCOTT CRAGG

Deputy Chief Information Officer, Enterprise Operations and Field Development	JEFF SHYSHKA
Deputy Chief Information Officer, Enterprise Development	PAUL TIBBITS
Deputy Assistant Secretary, IT Resource Development	ROM MASCETTI
Deputy Assistant Secretary, Information Protection and Risk Management	ADAIR MARTINEZ
Assistant Secretary for Policy and Planning	KAREN W. PANE, *Acting*
Principal Deputy Assistant Secretary for Policy and Planning	KAREN W. PANE
Deputy Assistant Secretary for Planning and Evaluation	JULIE ANDERSON
Deputy Assistant Secretary for Policy	MARK GORENFLO
Assistant Secretary for Operations, Security, and Preparedness	KEVIN HANRETTA, *Acting*
Deputy Assistant Secretary Emergency Management	KEVIN HANRETTA
Director, National Center for Veterans Analysis and Statistics	DAT TRAN
Deputy Assistant Secretary for Security and Law Enforcement	FREDERICK R. JACKSON
Assistant Secretary for Human Resources and Administration	WILLIE L. HENSLEY, *Acting*
Principal Deputy Assistant Secretary for Human Resources and Administration	WILLIE L. HENSLEY
Director, Office of Administration	CONSTANTINE G. VERENES
Deputy Assistant Secretary for Office Diversity and Inclusion	GEORGIA COFFEY
Deputy Assistant Secretary for Human Resources Management	VICKI BROOKS
Deputy Assistant Secretary for Labor Management Relations	SCOTT HOLLIDAY, *Acting*
Deputy Assistant Secretary for Resolution Management	RAFAEL A. TORRES
Assistant Secretary for Public and Intergovernmental Affairs	L. TAMMY DUCKWORTH
Deputy Assistant Secretary for Public Affairs	RANDALL K. STAGNER
Deputy Assistant Secretary for Intergovernmental and International Affairs	EMILY SMITH
Assistant Secretary for Congressional and Legislative Affairs	DANIEL C. DEVINE, *Acting*
Deputy Assistant Secretary for Congressional and Legislative Affairs	DANIEL C. DEVINE

The Department of Veterans Affairs operates programs to benefit veterans and members of their families. Benefits include compensation payments for disabilities or death related to military service; pensions; education and rehabilitation; home loan guaranty; burial; and a medical care program incorporating nursing homes, clinics, and medical centers.

The Department of Veterans Affairs (VA) was established as an executive department by the Department of Veterans Affairs Act (38 U.S.C. 201 note). It is comprised of three organizations that administer veterans programs: the Veterans Health Administration, the Veterans Benefits

DEPARTMENT OF VETERANS AFFAIRS

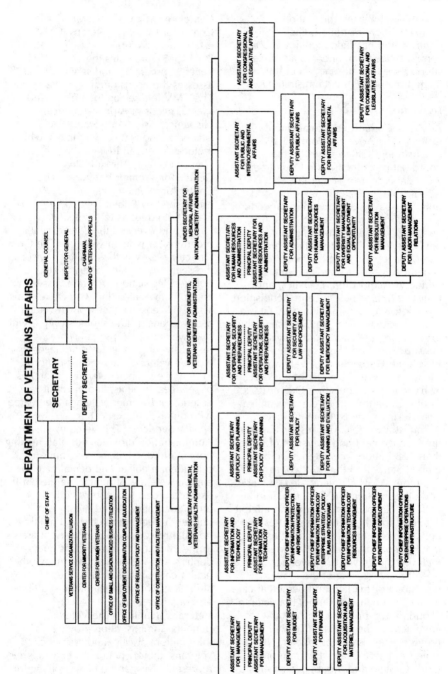

Administration, and the National Cemetery Administration. Each organization has field facilities and a central office component. Staff offices support the overall function of the Department and its Administrations.

Activities

Advisory Committee Management Office   The Advisory Committee Management Office serves as the coordinating office for the Department's 25 Federal advisory committees. It is responsible for establishing clear and uniform goals, standards, and procedures for advisory committee activities. It is also responsible for ensuring that VA advisory committee operations are in compliance with the provisions of the Federal Advisory Committee Act.

Office of Acquisition, Logistics, and Construction   The Office of Acquisition, Logistics, and Construction (OALC) is a multifunctional organization responsible for directing the acquisition, logistics, construction, and leasing functions within the Department of Veterans Affairs. The Executive Director, OALC, is also the Chief Acquisition Officer (CAO) for the Department of Veterans Affairs.

Cemeteries   The National Cemetery Administration (NCA) is responsible for the management and oversight of more than 128 national cemeteries in the United States and Puerto Rico, as well as 33 soldiers' lots, Confederate cemeteries, and other monument sites. Burial in a national cemetery is available to eligible veterans and their eligible spouses and dependent children. At no cost to the family, a national cemetery burial includes the gravesite, graveliner, opening and closing of the grave, headstone or marker, and perpetual care as part of a national shrine. If a veteran is buried in a private cemetery, anywhere in the world, NCA will provide a headstone or marker. NCA's State Cemetery Grants Program provides funds to State and tribal governments to establish, expand, or improve State-operated veterans' cemeteries. NCA issues Presidential Memorial Certificates to recognize the service of honorably discharged service members or veterans.

Center for Minority Veterans   The Center for Minority Veterans (CMV), established by Public Law 103–446 (108 Stat. 4645), promotes the use of VA benefits, programs, and services by and assesses the needs of minority veterans. The CMV focuses on the unique and special needs of African-Americans, Hispanics, Asian-Americans, Pacific Islanders, and Native Americans, which include American Indians, Native Hawaiians, and Alaska Natives.

Center for Women Veterans   The Center for Women Veterans (CWV), established by Public Law 103–446 (108 Stat. 4645), reports to the Secretary's Office and oversees the Department's programs for women veterans. The CwV Director serves as the primary advisor to the Secretary on all matters related to policies, legislation, programs, issues, and initiatives affecting women veterans. The CWV ensures that women veterans receive benefits and services on par with male veterans; VA programs are responsive to gender-specific needs of women veterans; outreach is performed to improve women veterans' awareness of services, benefits, and eligibility criteria; and women veterans are treated with dignity and respect.

Health Services   The Veterans Health Administration provides hospital, nursing home, and domiciliary care, and outpatient medical and dental care to eligible veterans of military service in the Armed Forces. It conducts both individual medical and health-care delivery research projects and multi-hospital research programs, and it assists in the education of physicians and dentists and with training of many other health care professionals through affiliations with educational institutions and organizations.

Veterans Benefits   The Veterans Benefits Administration provides information, advice, and assistance to veterans, their dependents, beneficiaries, representatives, and others applying for VA benefits. It also cooperates with the Department of Labor and other Federal, State, and local agencies in developing employment opportunities for veterans and referral for assistance in resolving socioeconomic, housing, and other related problems.

The Compensation and Pension Service is responsible for claims for disability compensation and pension, specially adapted housing, accrued benefits, adjusted compensation in death cases, and reimbursement for headstone or marker; allowances for automobiles and special adaptive equipment; special clothing allowances; emergency officers' retirement pay; survivors' claims for death compensation, dependency and indemnity compensation, death pension, and burial and plot allowance claims; forfeiture determinations; and a benefits protection program for minors and incompetent adult beneficiaries.

The Education Service administers the Montgomery GI Bill program and other programs which provide education benefits to qualified active-duty members, veterans, certain dependents of veterans, and members of the Selected and Ready Reserve. The Service also checks school records to ensure that they comply with the pertinent law, approves courses for the payment of educational benefits, and administers a work-study program. Additional details are available at www.gibill.va.gov.

The Insurance Service's operations for the benefit of service members, veterans, and their beneficiaries are available through the regional office and insurance center (phone, 800–669–8477) in Philadelphia, PA, which provides the full range of functional activities necessary for a national life insurance program. Activities include the complete maintenance of individual accounts, underwriting functions, life and death insurance claims awards, and any other insurance-related transactions. The agency also administers the Veterans Mortgage Life Insurance Program for those disabled veterans who receive a VA grant for specially adapted housing and supervises the Servicemembers' Group Life Insurance Program and the Veterans Group Life Insurance Program.

The Loan Guaranty Service is responsible for operations that include appraising properties to establish their values; approving grants for specially adapted housing; supervising the construction of new residential properties; establishing the eligibility of veterans for the program; evaluating the ability of a veteran to repay a loan and the credit risk; making direct loans to Native American veterans to acquire a home on trust land; servicing and liquidating defaulted loans; and disposing of real estate acquired as the consequence of defaulted loans.

The Vocational Rehabilitation and Employment Service provides outreach, motivation, evaluation, counseling, training, employment, and other rehabilitation services to service-connected disabled veterans. Vocational and educational counseling, as well as the evaluation of abilities, aptitudes, and interests are provided to veterans and servicepersons. Counseling, assessment, education programs, and, in some cases, rehabilitation services are available to spouses and children of totally and permanently disabled veterans as well as surviving orphans, widows, and widowers of certain deceased veterans.

Vocational training and rehabilitation services are available to children with spina bifida having one or both parents who served in the Republic of Vietnam during the Vietnam era, or served in certain military units in or near the demilitarized zone in Korea, between September 1, 1967 and August 31, 1971.

Veterans' Appeals   The Board of Veterans' Appeals (BVA) is responsible for entering the final appellate decisions in claims of entitlement to veterans' benefits and for deciding certain matters concerning fees charged by attorneys and agents for representation of veterans before VA and requests for revision of prior BVA decisions on the basis of clear and unmistakable error. Final Board decisions are appealable to the U.S. Court of Appeals for Veterans Claims.

Field Facilities   The Department's operations are handled through the following field facilities:

—cemeteries, providing burial services to veterans, their spouses, and dependent children;

—domiciliaries, providing the least intensive level of inpatient medical care including necessary ambulatory medical treatment, rehabilitation, and support services in a structured environment to veterans who are unable because of their disabilities to provide adequately for themselves in the community;

—medical centers, providing eligible beneficiaries with medical and other health care services equivalent to those provided by private-sector institutions, augmented in many instances by services to meet the special requirements of veterans;

—outpatient clinics to provide eligible beneficiaries with ambulatory care; and

—regional offices to grant benefits and services provided by law for veterans, their dependents, and beneficiaries within an assigned territory; furnish information regarding VA benefits and services; adjudicate claims and make awards for disability compensation and pension; conduct outreach and information dissemination and provide support and assistance to various segments of the veteran population to include former prisoners of war, minority veterans, homeless veterans, women veterans and elderly veterans; supervise payment of VA benefits to incompetent beneficiaries; provide vocational rehabilitation and employment training; administer educational benefits; guarantee loans for purchase, construction, or alteration of homes; process grants for specially adapted housing; process death claims; and assist veterans in exercising rights to benefits and services.

For a complete listing of the Department's field facilities, consult the Web site at www2.va.gov/directory/guide/home.asp.

Sources of Information

Audiovisuals Persons interested in the availability of VA video productions or exhibits for showing outside of VA may write to the Chief, Media Services Division (032B), Department of Veterans Affairs, 810 Vermont Avenue NW., Washington, DC 20420. Phone, 202–273–9781 or 9782.

Contracts Persons interested in business opportunities with the VA may contact the Director, Acquisition

Resources Service (049A5), 810 Vermont Avenue NW., Washington, DC 20420. Phone, 202–273–8815. Information on business opportunities with the VA can be found on the Internet at www.va.gov/oamm/busopp/doingbusiness.htm. Additional information is available at the Office of Acquisition and Material Management Web site at www.va.gov/oamm. Information on solicitations issued by VA is available at www.va.gov/oamm/busopp/index.htm.

Small Business Programs Persons seeking information on VA's small business programs may call 800–949–8387 or 202–565–8124. The Office of Small and Disadvantaged Business Utilization Web site (Internet, www.va.gov/osdbu) contains a considerable amount of information about these programs.

Veterans Business Ownership Services The Center for Veterans Enterprise assists veterans who want to open or expand a business. This Center is a component of the Office of Small and Disadvantaged Business Utilization. Phone, 866–584–2344. Internet, www.vetbiz.gov. Email, vacve@mail.va.gov.

Electronic Access Information concerning the Department of Veterans Affairs is available electronically through the Internet at www.va.gov.

Employment The Department of Veterans Affairs employs physicians, dentists, podiatrists, optometrists, nurses, nurse anesthetists, physician assistants, expanded-function dental auxiliaries, registered respiratory therapists, certified respiratory technicians, licensed physical therapists, occupational therapists, pharmacists, and licensed practical or vocational nurses under VA's excepted merit system. This system does not require civil service eligibility. Other professional, technical, administrative, and clerical occupations, such as veterans claims examiners, secretaries, and management analysts, exist in VA that do require civil service eligibility. Persons interested in employment should contact the human resources services office at their nearest VA facility or search the VA Web site at www.va.gov/jobs. All qualified applicants will receive consideration for appointments without regard to race, religion, color, national origin, sex, political affiliation, or any nonmerit factor.

Freedom of Information Act Requests Inquiries should be directed to the Assistant Secretary for Information and Technology, Information Management Service (045A4), 810 Vermont Avenue NW., Washington, DC 20420. Phone, 202–273–8135.

Inspector General Inquiries and Hotline Publicly available documents and information on the VA Office of Inspector General are available electronically through the Internet at www.va.gov/oig. Complaints may be sent by mail to the VA Inspector General (53E), P.O. Box 50410, Washington, DC 20091–0410. Hotline phone, 800–488–8244. Email, vaoighotline@va.gov.

Medical Center (Hospital) Design, Construction, and Related Services Construction projects for VA medical centers and other facilities in excess of $4 million are managed and controlled at the VA central office, located in Washington, DC. Projects requiring design, construction, and other related services are advertised on the Internet FirstGov site at www.firstgov.gov. Submit project-specific qualifications (SF 254 and SF 255) to the Director, A/E Evaluation and Program Support Team (181A), 810 Vermont Avenue NW., Washington, DC 20420. Phone, 202–565–4181. Additional information regarding the selection process can be found on the VA Office of Facilities Management Internet site at www.va.gov/facmgt.

Construction projects for VA medical centers and other facilities which are less than $4 million are managed and controlled at the individual medical centers. For information regarding these specific projects, contact the Acquisition and Materiel Management Office at each individual VA medical center. Addresses and additional information on VA medical centers can be found on the VA Internet site at www.va.gov/facilities.

News Media Representatives may contact VA through the nearest regional Office of Public Affairs:

Atlanta (404–929–5880)
Chicago (312–980–4235)
Dallas (817–385–3720)
Denver (303–914–5855)
Los Angeles (310–268–4207)
New York (212–807–3429)
Washington, DC (202–530–9360)

National media may contact the Office of Public Affairs in the VA Central Office, 810 Vermont Avenue NW., Washington, DC 20420. Phone, 202–273–6000.

Publications The *Annual Performance and Accountability Report* may be obtained (in single copies), without charge, from the Office of Budget (041H), 810 Vermont Avenue NW., Washington, DC 20420.

The 2005 VA pamphlet *Federal Benefits for Veterans and Dependents* (80–98–1) is available for sale by the Superintendent of Documents, Government Printing Office, Washington, DC 20402.

The *Board of Veterans Appeals Index* (I–01–1), an index to appellate decisions, is available on microfiche in annual cumulation from July 1977 through December 1994. The quarterly indexes may be purchased for $7 and annual cumulative indexes for $22.50. The VADEX/CITATOR of Appellate Research Materials is a complete printed quarterly looseleaf cumulation of research material which may be purchased for $175 with binder and for $160 without binder. The Vadex Infobase, a computer-searchable version of the VADEX, is also available on diskettes for $100 per copy. These publications may be obtained by contacting Promisel and Korn, Inc. Phone, 301–986–0650. Archived decisions of the Board of Veterans' Appeals are available through the VA Web site at www.va.gov.

A January 2000 VA pamphlet entitled *Understanding the Appeal Process* (01–00–1) is available for sale from the Superintendent of Documents, Government Printing Office, Washington, DC 20402.

The VA pamphlet, *A Summary of Department of Veteran Affairs Benefits* (27–82–2), may be obtained, without charge, from any VA regional office.

Interments in VA National Cemeteries, VA NCA–IS–1, details eligibility information and contains a list of both national and State veterans cemeteries. Copies may be obtained without charge from the National Cemetery Administration (41C1), 810 Vermont Avenue NW., Washington, DC 20420. Call 800–827–1000 or visit www.cem.va.gov for more information.

For further information, contact the Office of Public and Intergovernmental Affairs, Department of Veterans Affairs, 810 Vermont Avenue NW., Washington, DC 20420. Phone, 202–273–6000. Internet, www.va.gov/opa.

Independent Establishments and Government Corporations

AFRICAN DEVELOPMENT FOUNDATION

1400 I Street NW., Suite 1000, Washington, DC 20005
Phone, 202–673–3916. Fax, 202–673–3810. Internet, www.usadf.gov.

Board of Directors:

CHAIRMAN	JOHN O. AGWUNOBI
VICE CHAIRMAN	JOHN W. LESLIE
Board Members	JULIUS E. COLES, MORGAN M. DAVIS, (3 VACANCIES)

Staff:

President	LLOYD O. PIERSON
General Counsel	DORIS MASON MARTIN
Chief Financial Officer and Director for Strategic Planning	WILLIAM E. SCHUERCH
Chief Information Officer	LARRY P. BEVAN
Director of Management and Administration and Chief Human Capital Officer	M. CATHERINE GATES
Director of Legislative and Public Affairs	(VACANCY)

[For the African Development Foundation statement of organization, see the *Code of Federal Regulations,* Title 22, Part 1501]

The African Development Foundation's goals are to alleviate poverty and promote broad-based sustainable development and empowerment in Africa; to expand local capacity to promote and support grassroots, participatory development; and to enhance and strengthen U.S. relations with Africa through effective development assistance.

The African Development Foundation was established by the African Development Foundation Act (22 U.S.C. 290h) as a Government corporation to support the self-help efforts of the poor in Africa.

The Foundation invests in private and nongovernmental organizations in Africa to promote and support innovative enterprise development, create jobs, and increase incomes of the poor. It seeks to expand local institutional and financial capacities to foster entrepreneurship, ownership, and community-based economic development.

The Foundation also works within the United States, in African countries, and with other nation states to gather and expand resources for grassroots development. It achieves this through strategic partnerships with U.S. and

351

international private sector corporations, African host governments, U.S. and other government agencies, and philanthropic organizations.

For further information, contact the Director of Legislative and Public Affairs, African Development Foundation, 1400 I Street NW., Suite 1000, Washington, DC 20005–2248. Phone, 202–673–3916. Fax, 202–673–3810. Email, info@usadf.gov. Internet, www.usadf.gov.

BROADCASTING BOARD OF GOVERNORS

330 Independence Avenue SW., Washington, DC 20237
Phone, 202–203–4545. Internet, www.bbg.gov

CHAIRMAN	(VACANCY)
Board Members	JOAQUIN F. BLAYA, BLANQUITA WALSH CULLUM, D. JEFFREY HIRSCHBERG, STEVEN J. SIMMONS (4 VACANCIES)
(Secretary of State, *ex officio*)	HILLARY RODHAM CLINTON
Executive Director, Broadcasting Board of Governors	JEFFREY N. TRIMBLE
General Counsel	TIMI E. KENEALY, *Acting*
Chief Financial Officer	JANET K. STORMES
Director, Management Planning	JANICE H. BRAMBILLA
Director, Office of Public Affairs	LETITIA KING , *Acting*
Congressional Coordinator	SUSAN ANDROSS
Director, Office of Strategic Planning and Performance Measurement	BRUCE SHERMAN
Policy and Program Coordinator	JOHN GIAMBALVO
Special Projects Officer	OANH TRAN
Director, International Broadcasting Bureau	(VACANCY)
Deputy Director	DANFORTH W. AUSTIN, *Acting*
Chief of Staff	MARIE LENNON
Senior Advisor	JOHN WELCH
Director, New Media	REBECCA MCMENAMIN
Director, Office of Marketing and External Liaison	GARY THATCHER
Director, Marketing and Program Placement	DOUG BOYNTON
Director, Performance Review	KELU CHAO
Director, Office of Civil Rights	DELIA L. JOHNSON
Director, Contracts	VIVIAN B. GALLUPS
Director, Human Resources	DONNA GRACE
Director, Security	MICHAEL LAWRENCE, *Acting*
Director, Policy	CHARLES GOOLSBY, *Acting*
Director, Office of Engineering and Technical Services and Chief Information Officer	KEN BERMAN, *Acting*
Director, Voice of America	DANFORTH W. AUSTIN
Executive Editor	STEVE REDISCH
Chief of Staff	BARBARA BRADY, *Acting*
Senior Advisors	SHEILA GANDJI, WILLIAM MARSH
Director of Internet	MICHAEL MESSENGER
Broadcast Technology Officer	JOHN ROGERS
Director, Public Relations	JOAN MOWER, *Acting*
Associate Director for Language Programming	JOHN LENNON

Associate Director for Operations	MARK L. PRAHL
Director, Office of Cuba Broadcasting	PEDRO V. ROIG
Director, Technical Operations	MICHAEL PALLONE
Director, Administration	IRVIN RUBENSTEIN
Director, Broadcast Operations	JORGE HERNANDEZ
President, Radio Free Europe/Radio Liberty	JEFFREY GEDMIN
President, Radio Free Asia	LIBBY LIU
President, Middle East Broadcasting Networks (MBN)	BRIAN T. CONNIFF

The Broadcasting Board of Governors' mission is to promote freedom and democracy and to enhance understanding by broadcasting accurate, objective, and balanced news and information about the United States and the world to audiences abroad.

The Broadcasting Board of Governors (BBG) became an independent agency on October 1, 1999, by authority of the Foreign Affairs Reform and Restructuring Act of 1998 (22 U.S.C. 6501 note). It is composed of nine members. Eight members are appointed by the President and confirmed by the Senate; the ninth, an ex-officio member, is the Secretary of State.

The BBG serves as the governing body for all nonmilitary U.S. broadcasting and provides programming in 56 languages via radio, television, and the Internet. The BBG broadcast services include the Voice of America, the Office of Cuba Broadcasting, Radio Free Europe/Radio Liberty, Radio Free Asia, and the Middle East Broadcasting Networks.

All BBG broadcast services adhere to the broadcasting standards and principles of the International Broadcasting Act of 1994, which include reliable, accurate, and comprehensive news; balanced and comprehensive presentations of U.S. thought, institutions, and policies, as well as discussions about those policies; information about developments throughout the world; and a variety of opinions from nations around the world.

Activities

International Broadcasting Bureau   The International Broadcasting Bureau (IBB) provides human resource, EEO, procurement, security, information technology, public affairs, administrative, research, and program evaluation services to the Voice of America and Radio/TV Marti. It also provides marketing, program placement, and transmission services for all the BBG broadcast organizations, managing a global network of transmitting sites and an extensive system of leased satellite and fiber optic circuits, along with a rapidly growing Internet delivery system. The IBB Office of Policy produces U.S. government editorials broadcast daily on VOA. Internet, www.ibb.gov.

Voice of America   Voice of America (VOA) is an independent international multimedia broadcasting service of the U.S. government. VOA broadcasts more than 1,000 hours a week, which include U.S. and international news, features, and educational and cultural programs about the United States and the world, to more than 115 million people worldwide. VOA programs are produced and broadcast in 44 languages. More than 1,200 VOA affiliate radio and television stations around the world download programs through satellite and digital audio (MP3) technology. Internet, www.voanews.com.

Radio Free Europe/Radio Liberty   Radio Free Europe/Radio Liberty (RFE/RL) is an international communications service to Eastern Europe, the Caucasus, and Central and Southwestern Asia. Concentrating on domestic events and international news, RFE/RL has for more than 50 years provided its 35 million listeners with balanced and reliable information to bolster democratic development and civil society in countries struggling to overcome autocratic institutions, violations of human rights, centralized economies, ethnic and religious hostilities, regional

BROADCASTING BOARD OF GOVERNORS

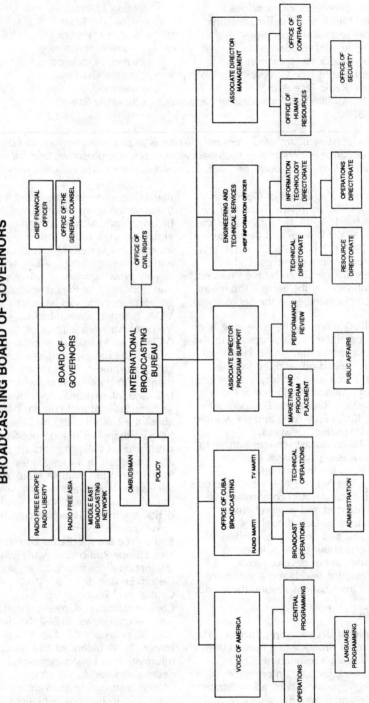

conflicts, and controlled media. A not-for-profit corporation, RFE/RL is funded by a Federal grant from the Broadcasting Board of Governors. Internet, www.rferl.org.

Radio Free Asia   Radio Free Asia (RFA) is an independent, nonprofit organization broadcasting and publishing information online in nine East Asian languages, including Burmese, Cantonese, Khmer, Korean, Lao, Mandarin, Tibetan, Uyghur, and Vietnamese. RFA provides news and information related specifically to the people in East Asia who are censored from officially sanctioned domestic media. All language services are staffed and directed by native speakers and maintain Web sites which offer podcasting, syndication, and feedback options, while several services also offer regular toll-free hotlines to callers in Asia. RFA is funded by an annual grant from the Broadcasting Board of Governors. Internet, www.rfa.org.

Middle East Broadcasting Networks The Middle East Broadcasting Networks, Inc., is a non-profit corporation that operates the Arabic-language Alhurra TV and Radio Sawa networks. Alhurra TV broadcasts to 22 countries in the Middle East via satellite. Its schedule includes up-to-the-minute newscasts, documentaries, discussion programs, and other programs on a variety of subjects. Radio Sawa broadcasts on FM and AM to major Middle Eastern countries. It also seeks to reach a significant portion of the under 30 population with a combination of news, opinion features, and a blend of mainstream Western and Arabic music. Internet, www.radiosawa.com and www.alhurra.com.

Office of Cuba Broadcasting   The Office of Cuba Broadcasting oversees Radio Marti and TV Marti. These two Spanish language services provide news about Cuba and the world, features, and entertainment programs aimed at Cuba. Based in Miami, these comprehensive and timely broadcasts offer Cubans the opportunity to receive unfiltered and accurate information. Radio and TV Marti are disseminated through medium wave (AM), shortwave, Internet, satellite, and special transmissions. Internet, www.martinoticias.org.

For further information, contact the Office of Public Affairs, Broadcasting Board of Governors, 330 Independence Avenue SW., Washington, DC 20237. Phone, 202–203–4959. Fax, 202–203–4960. Internet, www.bbg.gov. Email, publicaffairs@ibb.gov.

CENTRAL INTELLIGENCE AGENCY

Washington, DC 20505
Phone, 703–482–0623. Internet, www.cia.gov.

DIRECTOR   LEON PANETTA

[For the Central Intelligence Agency statement of organization, see the *Code of Federal Regulations,* Title 32, Part 1900]

The Central Intelligence Agency collects, evaluates, and disseminates vital information on political, military, economic, scientific, and other developments abroad needed to safeguard national security.

The Central Intelligence Agency was established by the National Security Act of 1947, as amended (50 U.S.C. 401 *et seq.*). It now functions under that statute, Executive Order 12333 of December 4, 1981, the Intelligence Reform and Terrorism Prevention Act of 2004 (50 U.S.C. 401 note), and other laws, Executive orders, regulations, and directives.

The Central Intelligence Agency is headed by a Director, who is appointed by the President with the advice and consent of the Senate.

The Central Intelligence Agency does the following:

—collects intelligence from human sources and other appropriate means, but, it does not carry out internal security functions nor exercise police, subpoena, or law enforcement powers;

—correlates, evaluates, and disseminates intelligence related to national security;

—provides overall direction for and coordination of intelligence collecting outside the United States by U.S. Intelligence Community elements authorized to engage in human source collection. In coordination with other departments, agencies, or authorized elements of the United States Government, it ensures that resources are used effectively and that adequate consideration is given to the risks to those involved in such collection and to the United States;

—carries out other intelligence-related functions and duties necessary for safeguarding national security as the President or the Director of National Intelligence (DNI) may direct; and

—coordinates, under the direction of the DNI and consistent with section 207 of the Foreign Service Act of 1980, relationships between elements of the U.S. Intelligence Community and the intelligence or security services of foreign governments or international organizations in matters of national security or intelligence that is acquired clandestinely.

For further information, contact the Central Intelligence Agency, Office of Public Affairs, Washington, DC 20505. Phone, 703–482–0623. Fax, 703–482–1739. Internet, www.cia.gov.

COMMODITY FUTURES TRADING COMMISSION

1155 Twenty-first Street NW., Washington, DC 20581
Phone, 202–418–5000. Fax, 202–418–5521. Internet, www.cftc.gov.

CHAIRMAN	GARY GENSLER
COMMISSIONERS	BARTHOLOMEW H. CHILTON, MICHAEL V. DUNN, JILL E. SOMMERS
General Counsel	TERRY S. ARBIT
Executive Director	MADGE BOLINGER
Director, Division of Market Oversight	RICHARD SHILTS
Director, Division of Clearing and Intermediary Oversight	ANANDA RADHAKRISHNAN
Director, Division of Enforcement	STEPHEN OBIE
Chief Economist	GEOFFREY PRICE

[For the Commodity Futures Trading Commission statement of organization, see the *Code of Federal Regulations*, Title 17, Part 140]

The mission of the Commodity Futures Trading Commission is to protect market users and the public from fraud, manipulation, and abusive practices related to the sale of commodity futures and options, and to foster open, competitive, and financially sound commodity futures and option markets.

The Commodity Futures Trading Commission, the Federal regulatory agency for futures trading, was established by the Commodity Futures Trading Commission Act of 1974 (7 U.S.C. 4a). The Commission began

COMMODITY FUTURES TRADING COMMISSION

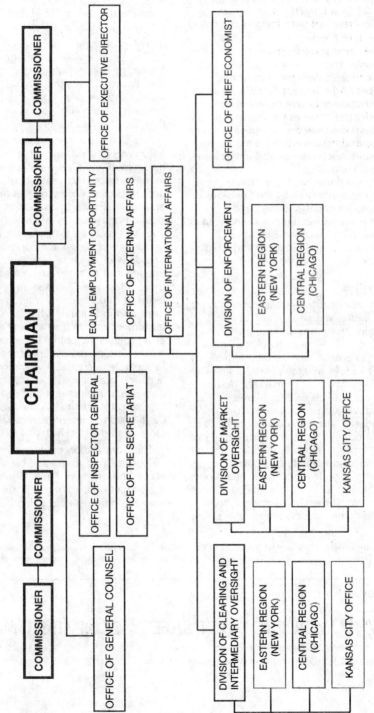

operation in April 1975, and its authority to regulate futures trading was renewed by Congress in 1978, 1982, 1986, 1992, 1995, and 2000.

The Commission consists of five Commissioners who are appointed by the President, with the advice and consent of the Senate. One Commissioner is designated by the President to serve as Chairman. The Commissioners serve staggered 5-year terms, and by law no more than three Commissioners can belong to the same political party.

The Commission has six major operating components: the Divisions of Market Oversight, Clearing and Intermediary Oversight, and Enforcement and the Offices of the Executive Director, General Counsel, and Chief Economist.

Activities

The Commission regulates trading on the U.S. futures markets, which offer commodity futures and options contracts. It regulates these markets in order to ensure the operational integrity of the futures markets. The Commission regulates two tiers of markets: designated contract markets and registered derivatives transaction execution facilities. It also exercises more limited regulatory or enforcement authority over other types of markets. Additionally, the Commission regulates derivatives clearing organizations. Each board of trade that operates a designated contract market must own or have a relationship with a derivatives clearing organization

which provides clearing services for each futures contract executed.

The Commission also regulates the activities of numerous commodity trading professionals, including brokerage houses (futures commission merchants), futures industry salespersons (associated persons), commodity trading advisers, commodity pool operators, and floor brokers and traders.

The Commission's regulatory and enforcement efforts are designed to foster transparent and financially sound markets, encourage market competition and efficiency, ensure market integrity, and protect market participants and the public from fraud, manipulation, and abusive practices. It oversees the rules under which designated contract markets and derivatives clearing organizations operate and monitors enforcement of those rules. The Commission reviews the terms of futures contracts and registers firms and individuals who handle customer funds or give trading advice. It also protects the public by enforcing rules that require customer funds be kept in separate accounts, away from accounts maintained by firms for their own use or maintained on behalf of the firm, and that such customer accounts be marked to present market value at the close of trading each day.

The Commission maintains regional offices in Chicago, IL, and New York, NY, where many of the Nation's designated contract markets are located. An additional regional office is located in Kansas City, MO.

For further information, contact the Office of External Affairs, Commodity Futures Trading Commission, 1155 Twenty-first Street NW., Washington, DC 20581. Phone, 202–418–5080. Internet, www.cftc.gov.

CONSUMER PRODUCT SAFETY COMMISSION

4330 East-West Highway, Bethesda, MD 20814
Phone, 301–504–7923. Internet, www.cpsc.gov.

CHAIR   INEZ TENEBAUM

COMMISSIONERS

ROBERT ADLER, THOMAS H. MOORE, NANCY NORD, ANNE NORTHUP

General Counsel	CHERYL A. FALVEY
Director, Office of Congressional Relations	JOHN HORNER
Director, Office of the Secretary	TODD A. STEVENSON
Freedom of Information Officer	ALBERTA MILLS
Director, Office of Equal Employment Opportunity and Minority Enterprise	KATHLEEN V. BUTTREY
Executive Director	PATRICIA M. SEMPLE
Deputy Executive Director	JACQUELINE ELDER
Inspector General	CHRISTOPHER W. DENTEL
Director, Office of Human Resources Management	DONNA M. SIMPSON
Director, Office of International Programs and Intergovernmental Affairs	RICHARD O'BRIEN
Assistant Executive Director, Office of Information and Technology Services	PATRICK D. WEDDLE
Director, Office of Information and Public Affairs	(VACANCY)
Director, Office of Financial Management, Planning and Evaluation	EDWARD E. QUIST
Assistant Executive Director for Compliance and Field Operations	JOHN GIBSON MULLAN
Deputy Assistant Executive Director, Office of Compliance	MARC J. SCHOEM
Assistant Executive Director for Hazard Identification and Reduction	ROBERT J. HOWELL
Associate Executive Director for Economics	GREGORY B. RODGERS
Associate Executive Director for Engineering Sciences	HUGH M. MCLAURIN
Associate Executive Director for Epidemiology	RUSSELL H. ROEGNER
Associate Executive Director for Health Sciences	MARY ANN DANELLO
Associate Executive Director for Laboratory Sciences	ANDREW G. STADNIK

[For the Consumer Product Safety Commission statement of organization, see the *Code of Federal Regulations*, Title 16, Part 1000]

The Consumer Product Safety Commission protects the public against unreasonable risks of injury from consumer products; assists consumers in evaluating the comparative safety of consumer products; develops uniform safety standards for consumer products and minimizes conflicting State and local regulations; and promotes research and investigation into the causes and prevention of product-related deaths, illnesses, and injuries.

The Consumer Product Safety Commission was established as an independent regulatory agency by the Consumer Product Safety Act (15 U.S.C. 2051 *et seq.*) in 1973 and reauthorized by the Consumer Product Safety Improvement Act of 2008. The Commission consists of up to five members, who are appointed by the President with the advice and consent of the Senate, for 7-year terms.

The Commission implements provisions of the Flammable Fabrics Act (15 U.S.C. 1191); Poison Prevention Packaging Act of 1970 (15 U.S.C. 1471); Federal Hazardous Substances Act (15

CONSUMER PRODUCT SAFETY COMMISSION

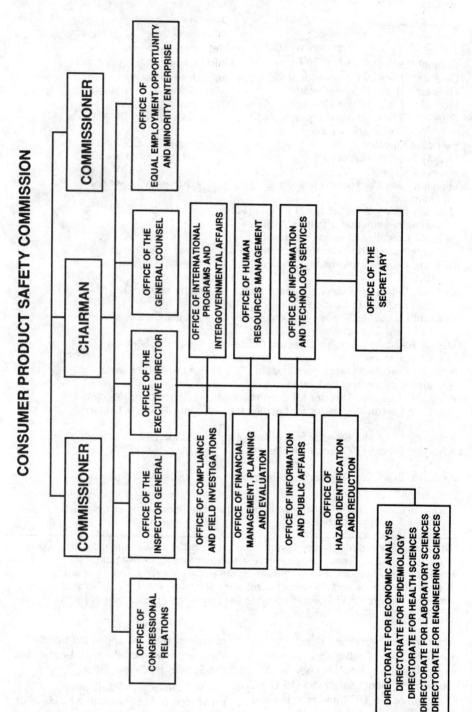

U.S.C. 1261); act of August 2, 1956 (15 U.S.C. 1211), prohibiting the transportation of refrigerators without door safety devices; Children's Gasoline Burn Prevention Act (15 U.S.C. 2056 note); and Virginia Graeme Baker Pool and Spa Safety Act (15 U.S.C. 8001 *et seq.*).

Activities

To help protect the public from unreasonable risks of injury associated with consumer products, the Commission performs the following functions:

—requires manufacturers to report defects in products that could create substantial hazards;

—requires, where appropriate, corrective action with respect to specific substantially hazardous consumer products already in commerce;

—collects information on consumer product-related injuries and maintains a comprehensive Injury Information Clearinghouse;

—conducts research on consumer product hazards;

—encourages and assists in the development of voluntary standards related to the safety of consumer products;

—establishes, where appropriate, mandatory consumer product standards;

—bans, where appropriate, hazardous consumer products; and

—conducts outreach programs for consumers, industry, and local governments.

The Commission also has a special project to reach as many Americans as possible with important, lifesaving safety information. The Neighborhood Safety Network is an effort to disseminate safety information too hard to reach populations by partnering with other organizations within these populations. Organizations may register for this program at www.cpsc.gov/nsn/nsn.html.

Offices

The Commission's headquarters is located at 4330 East-West Highway, Bethesda, MD 20814.

Sources of Information

Consumer Information   The Commission operates a toll-free Consumer Product Safety Hotline, 800–638–2772 (English and Spanish); and a teletypewriter for the hearing-impaired, 800–638–8270 (or in Maryland only, 800–492–8140). The Commission has several Web sites where additional safety information may be obtained. Information specific to recalls can be obtained at www.recalls.gov. Safety information related to All-Terrain Vehicles can be obtained at www.atvsafety.gov.

General Inquiries   Information on Commission activities may be obtained from the Office of Information and Public Affairs, Consumer Product Safety Commission, 4330 East-West Highway, Bethesda, MD 20814. Phone, 301–504–7923. Internet, www.cpsc.gov.

Reading Room   A public information room is maintained at the Commission's headquarters.

For further information, contact the Office of Information and Public Affairs, Consumer Product Safety Commission, 4330 East-West Highway, Bethesda, MD 20814. Phone, 301–504–7908. Email, info@cpsc.gov. Internet, www.cpsc.gov.

EDITORIAL NOTE: The Corporation for National and Community Service did not meet the publication deadline for submitting updated information of its activities, functions, and sources of information as required by the automatic disclosure provisions of the Freedom of Information Act (5 U.S.C. 552(a)(1)(A)).

CORPORATION FOR NATIONAL AND COMMUNITY SERVICE

1201 New York Avenue NW., Washington, DC 20525
Phone, 202–606–5000. Internet, www.nationalservice.gov.

Board of Directors:

CHAIR	ALAN SOLOMONT
VICE CHAIR	STEPHEN GOLDSMITH
Members	JULIE FISHER CUMMINGS, MARK D. GEARAN, HYEPIN IM, JAMES PALMER, STAN SOLOWAY, ERIC J. TANENBLATT, LAYSHA WARD, (6 VACANCIES)

Staff:

Chief Executive Officer	NICOLA GOREN, *Acting*
Inspector General	KENNETH BACH, *Acting*
Chief Financial Officer	WILLIAM ANDERSON, *Acting*
Chief Human Capital Officer	RAYMOND LIMON
Chief of Program Operations	KRISTIN MCSWAIN
Director, AmeriCorps*NCCC	MIKEL HERRINGTON, *Acting*
Director, AmeriCorps*State and National	LOIS NEMBHARD, *Acting*
Director, AmeriCorps*VISTA	PAUL DAVIS, *Acting*
Director, Civil Rights and Inclusiveness	LIZ A. HONNOLL
Director, Corporate Relations	RHONDA TAYLOR, *Acting*
Director, Emergency Management	COLLEEN CLAY
Director, Field Liaison	MICHAEL BERNING
Director, Financial Management	WILLIAM ANDERSON
Director, Government Relations	RHODA GLICKMAN
Director, Grants and Field Financial Management	ROCCO GAUDIO
Director, Grants Oversight and Monitoring	ALEDA ROBINSON
Director, Grants Policy and Operations	VIELKA GARIBALDI, *Acting*
Director, Information Technology	MARY CADAGIN
Director, Leadership Development and Training	GRETCHEN VAN DER VEER
Director, Learn and Serve America	ELSON NASH, *Acting*
Director, Public Affairs	RANIT SCHMELZER
Director, Research and Policy Development	ROBERT GRIMM
Director, Senior Corps	ANGELA ROBERTS, *Acting*
General Counsel	FRANK TRINITY
Strategic Advisor, Faith Based and Neighborhood Partnerships	JOHN KELLY

The Corporation for National and Community Service engages Americans of all ages and backgrounds in community-based service that addresses the Nation's educational, public safety, environmental, and other human needs to achieve direct and demonstrable results. In so doing, the Corporation fosters civic responsibility, strengthens the ties that bind us together as a people, and provides educational opportunity for those who make a substantial commitment to service.

CORPORATION FOR NATIONAL AND COMMUNITY SERVICE

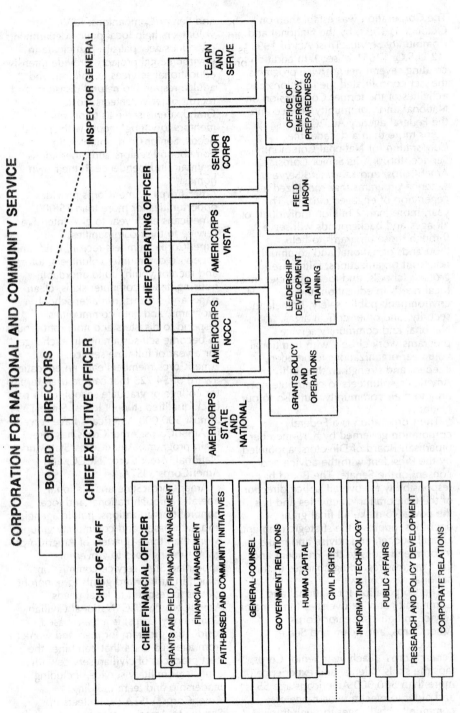

BOARD OF DIRECTORS

CHIEF EXECUTIVE OFFICER

INSPECTOR GENERAL

CHIEF OF STAFF

CHIEF OPERATING OFFICER

- AMERICORPS STATE AND NATIONAL
- AMERICORPS NCCC
- AMERICORPS VISTA
- SENIOR CORPS
- LEARN AND SERVE

- GRANTS POLICY AND OPERATIONS
- LEADERSHIP DEVELOPMENT AND TRAINING
- FIELD LIAISON
- OFFICE OF EMERGENCY PREPAREDNESS

CHIEF FINANCIAL OFFICER

- GRANTS AND FIELD FINANCIAL MANAGEMENT
- FINANCIAL MANAGEMENT

- FAITH-BASED AND COMMUNITY INITIATIVES
- GENERAL COUNSEL
- GOVERNMENT RELATIONS
- HUMAN CAPITAL
- CIVIL RIGHTS
- INFORMATION TECHNOLOGY
- PUBLIC AFFAIRS
- RESEARCH AND POLICY DEVELOPMENT
- CORPORATE RELATIONS

The Corporation was established on October 1, 1993, by the National and Community Service Trust Act of 1993 (42 U.S.C. 12651 *et seq.*). In addition to creating several new service programs, the Act consolidated the functions and activities of the former Commission on National and Community Service and the Federal agency ACTION.

For more than a decade, the Corporation for National Community Service, through its Senior Corps, AmeriCorps, and Learn and Serve America programs, has mobilized a new generation of engaged citizens. This year, more than 2 million individuals of all ages and backgrounds will serve through those programs to help thousands of national and community nonprofit organizations, faith-based groups, schools, and local agencies meet local needs in education, the environment, public safety, homeland security, and other critical areas. National and community service programs work closely with traditional volunteer organizations to broaden, deepen, and strengthen the ability of America's volunteers to contribute not only to their community, but also to our Nation.

The Corporation is a Federal corporation governed by a 15-member bipartisan Board of Directors, appointed by the President with the advice and consent of the Senate. The Board has responsibility for overall policy direction of the Corporation's activities and has the power to make all final grant decisions, approve the strategic plan and annual budget, and advise and make recommendations to the President and the Congress regarding changes in the national service laws.

The Corporation for National and Community Service oversees three major service initiatives: Senior Corps, AmeriCorps, and Learn and Serve America.

Senior Corps   Each year Senior Corps taps the skills, talents, and experience of more than 500,000 Americans age 55 and older to meet a wide range of community challenges through three programs: Retired and Senior Volunteers Program (RSVP), Foster Grandparents, and Senior Companions. RSVP volunteers help local police departments conduct safety patrols, participate in environmental projects, provide intensive educational services to children and adults, respond to natural disasters, and recruit other volunteers. Foster Grandparents serve as tutors and mentors to young people with special needs. Senior Companions help homebound seniors and other adults maintain independence in their own homes.

AmeriCorps   AmeriCorps provides opportunities for more than 75,000 Americans each year to give intensive service to their communities. AmeriCorps members recruit, train, and supervise community volunteers, tutor and mentor youth, build affordable housing, teach computer skills, clean parks and streams, run after-school programs, and help communities respond to disasters and nonprofit groups to become self-sustaining. In exchange for a year of full-time service, AmeriCorps members earn an education award of $4,725 that can be used to pay for college or graduate school, or to pay back qualified student loans. Since 1994 almost 500,000 Americans have served in AmeriCorps. AmeriCorps has three main programs: AmeriCorps*State and National, AmeriCorps*NCCC, and AmeriCorps*VISTA.

AmeriCorps*State and National operates through national and local nonprofit organizations, public agencies, and faith-based and community groups. More than three-quarters of AmeriCorps grant funding goes to Governor-appointed State service commissions, which in turn award grants to nonprofit groups to respond to local needs. AmeriCorps*NCCC (National Civilian Community Corps) is a team-based, residential program for men and women from ages 18 to 24 that combines the best practices of civilian service with aspects of military service, including leadership and team building. AmeriCorps*VISTA (Volunteers in Service to America) members serve full-time, for 1 year, in nonprofits, public agencies, and faith-based organizations to fight illiteracy, improve health services, create and expand business, increase housing opportunities, and bridge the digital divide.

Learn and Serve America Learn and Serve America engages more than one million students in community service linked to academic achievement and the development of civic skills. This type of learning, called service learning, improves communities while preparing young people for a lifetime of responsible citizenship.

Learn and Serve America provides grants to schools, colleges, and nonprofit groups to support its efforts. Grants are awarded through the Corporation and State educational agencies and commissions, nonprofit organizations, and higher education associations. School-based programs receive grants through State educational agencies or nonprofits, while community-based programs apply for funding through the same State commissions that coordinate AmeriCorps grants or through nonprofits. Higher education institutions and associations apply directly to the Corporation for grants. In addition to providing grants, Learn and Serve America serves as a resource on service and service-learning to teachers, faculty members, schools, and community groups and promotes student service through the Presidential Freedom Scholarships.

Other Initiatives Other programs and special initiatives administered by the Corporation's umbrella include: King Day of Service Grants, which support community organizations in their efforts to engage local citizens in service on the Martin Luther King, Jr., Federal holiday; and the President's Council on Service and Civic Participation, which presents the President's Volunteer Service Award to citizens of all ages and backgrounds

who have demonstrated a sustained commitment to service. The Corporation also provides extensive training and technical assistance to support and assist State service commissions and local service programs.

The Corporation and its programs work with the USA Freedom Corps, established on January 29, 2002, by Executive Order 13254. USA Freedom Corps is a White House initiative to foster a culture of citizenship, service, and responsibility, and help all Americans answer the President's call to service.

Sources of Information

Electronic Access Information regarding the Corporation's programs and activities is available on the Internet at www.nationalservice.gov. Information for persons interested in joining AmeriCorps is available at www.americorps.gov. Information for persons interested in joining Senior Corps is at www.seniorcorps.gov. Information on the USA Freedom Corps is available at www.usafreedomcorps.gov.

General Information To obtain additional information regarding AmeriCorps, call 800–942–2677. For Senior Corps programs, call 800–424–8867. TDD, 202–565–2799. For USA Freedom Corps, call 877–872–2677.

Grants All notices of available funds are made through the grants.gov Web site. State program offices and commissions on national and community service are located in most States and are the best source of information on programs in specific States or communities. To contact State offices or State commissions, visit www.nationalservice.gov/contactus.html.

For further information, contact the Corporation for National and Community Service, 1201 New York Avenue NW., Washington, DC 20525. Phone, 202–606–5000. Internet, www.nationalservice.gov.

DEFENSE NUCLEAR FACILITIES SAFETY BOARD

Suite 700, 625 Indiana Avenue NW., Washington, DC 20004
Phone, 202–694–7000. Fax, 202–208–6518. Internet, www.dnfsb.gov.

CHAIRMAN	(VACANCY)
VICE CHAIRMAN	JOHN E. MANSFIELD
Members	JOSEPH F. BADER, LARRY W. BROWN, PETER S. WINOKUR
General Counsel	RICHARD A. AZZARO
General Manager	BRIAN GROSNER
Technical Director	TIMOTHY DWYER

The Defense Nuclear Facilities Safety Board reviews and evaluates the content and implementation of standards relating to the design, construction, operation, and decommissioning of defense nuclear facilities of the Department of Energy.

The Defense Nuclear Facilities Safety Board was established as an independent agency on September 29, 1988, by the Atomic Energy Act of 1954, as amended (42 U.S.C. 2286–2286i).

The Board is composed of five members appointed by the President with the advice and consent of the Senate. Members of the Board are appointed from among United States citizens who are respected experts in the field of nuclear safety.

Activities

The Defense Nuclear Facilities Safety Board reviews and evaluates the content and implementation of standards for defense nuclear facilities of the Department of Energy (DOE); investigates any event or practice at these facilities which may adversely affect public health and safety; and reviews and monitors the design, construction, and operation of facilities. The Board makes recommendations to the Secretary of Energy concerning DOE defense nuclear facilities to ensure adequate protection of public health and safety. In the event that any aspect of operations, practices, or occurrences reviewed by the Board is determined to present an imminent or severe threat to public health and safety, the Board transmits its recommendations directly to the President.

For further information, contact the Defense Nuclear Facilities Safety Board, Suite 700, 625 Indiana Avenue NW., Washington, DC 20004. Phone, 202–694–7000. Internet, www.dnfsb.gov.

ENVIRONMENTAL PROTECTION AGENCY

1200 Pennsylvania Avenue NW., Washington, DC 20460–0001
Phone, 202–272–0167. Internet, www.epa.gov.

ADMINISTRATOR	LISA JACKSON
DEPUTY ADMINISTRATOR	SCOTT FULTON, *Acting*
Associate Administrator for Public Affairs	M. ALLYN BROOKS-LASURE, *Acting*
Associate Administrator for Congressional and Intergovernmental Relations	JOYCE FRANK, *Acting*

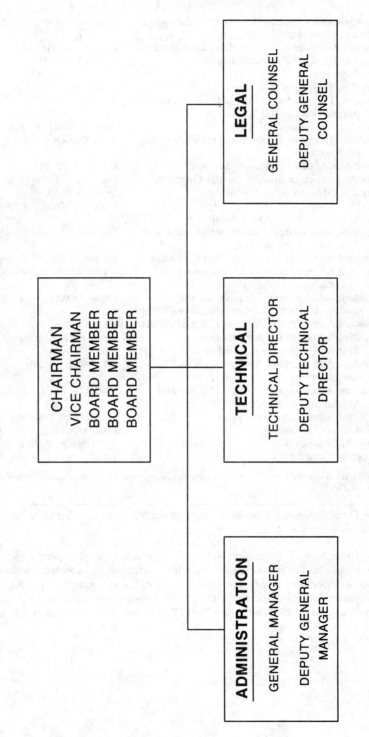

DEFENSE NUCLEAR FACILITIES SAFETY BOARD

CHAIRMAN
VICE CHAIRMAN
BOARD MEMBER
BOARD MEMBER
BOARD MEMBER

ADMINISTRATION
GENERAL MANAGER
DEPUTY GENERAL MANAGER

TECHNICAL
TECHNICAL DIRECTOR
DEPUTY TECHNICAL DIRECTOR

LEGAL
GENERAL COUNSEL
DEPUTY GENERAL COUNSEL

Associate Administrator for Policy, Economics, and Innovation	MARCIA MULKEY, *Acting*
Associate Administrator for Homeland Security	JUAN REYES, *Acting*
Chief Judge, Office of Administrative Law Judges	SUSAN L. BIRO
Director, Executive Secretariat	BRIAN HOPE, *Acting*
Director, Office of Children's Health Protection and Environmental Education	RUTH McCULLY
Director, Office of Civil Rights	KAREN D. HIGGINBOTHAM
Director, Office of Cooperative Environmental Management	RAFAEL DeLEON
Director, Office of Executive Services	DIANE N. BAZZLE
Director, Office of Small Business Programs	JEANETTE L. BROWN
Director, Science Advisory Board	VANESSA T. VU
Lead Environmental Appeals Judge, Environmental Appeals Board	EDWARD REICH
Assistant Administrator for Administration and Resources Management	CRAIG E. HOOKS, *Acting*
Assistant Administrator for Air and Radiation	ELIZABETH CRAIG, *Acting*
Assistant Administrator for Enforcement and Compliance Assurance	CATHY McCABE, *Acting*
Assistant Administrator for Environmental Information and Chief Information Officer	LINDA TRAVERS, *Acting*
Assistant Administrator for International Affairs	KATHY PETRUCCELLI, *Acting*
Assistant Administrator for Prevention, Pesticides, and Toxic Substances	JAMES JONES, *Acting*
Assistant Administrator for Research and Development	LEK KADELI, *Acting*
Assistant Administrator for Solid Waste and Emergency Response	BARRY N. BREEN, *Acting*
Assistant Administrator for Water	MICHEAL H. SHAPIRO, *Acting*
Chief Financial Officer	MARYANN FROEHLICH, *Acting*
General Counsel	PAT HIRSCH, *Acting*
Inspector General	BILL RODERICK, *Acting*

[For the Environmental Protection Agency statement of organization, see the *Code of Federal Regulations,* Title 40, Part 1]

The Environmental Protection Agency protects human health and safeguards the natural environment.

The Environmental Protection Agency was established in the executive branch as an independent agency pursuant to Reorganization Plan No. 3 of 1970 (5 U.S.C. app.), effective December 2, 1970. It was created to permit coordinated and effective governmental action on behalf of the environment. The Agency is designed to serve as the public's advocate for a livable environment.

ENVIRONMENTAL PROTECTION AGENCY

Core Functions

Air and Radiation   The Office of Air and Radiation activities of the Agency include the following:

—developing national programs, policies, regulations, and standards for air quality, emission standards for stationary and mobile sources, and emission standards for hazardous air pollutants;

—conducting research and providing information on indoor air pollutants to the public;

—providing technical direction, support, and evaluation of regional air activities;

—providing training in the field of air pollution control;

—providing technical assistance to States and agencies having radiation protection programs, including radon mitigation programs and a national surveillance and inspection program for measuring radiation levels in the environment; and

—providing technical support and policy direction to international efforts to reduce global and transboundary air pollution and its effects.

For further information, call 202–564–7400.

Water   The Agency's water quality activities represent a coordinated effort to keep the Nation's waters clean and safe for fishing, swimming, and drinking, including the following:

—development of national programs, technical policies, and regulations for water pollution control and water supply;

—ground water and drinking water source protection;

—marine and estuarine protection;

—control of polluted runoff;

—water quality standards and effluent guidelines development;

—support of regional water activities;

—development of programs for technical assistance and technology transfer; and

—training in the field of water quality.

For further information, call 202–564–5700.

Solid Waste and Emergency Response   The Office of Solid Waste and Emergency Response provides policy, guidance, and direction for the Agency's hazardous waste and emergency response programs, including these tasks:

—development of policies, standards, and regulations for hazardous waste treatment, storage, and disposal;

—national coordination of solid waste and materials management;

—national management of the Superfund toxic waste cleanup program;

—development, coordination, implementation, and management of agencywide chemical and oil spill accident prevention, emergency preparedness and response, and right-to-know programs;

—implementation of Title II of the Small Business Liability and Brownfields Revitalization Act;

—advocate for the reuse and revitalization of formerly contaminated land to achieve agency land reuse goals;

—management of environmental justice/public participation programs related to all waste programs;

—development and implementation of programs to prevent and detect leakage from underground storage tanks and to clean up contamination from leaks which have occurred;

—analysis of technologies and methods for the recovery of useful energy from solid waste;

—economic impact assessment of the Resource Conservation and Recovery Act and Comprehensive Environmental Response, Compensation, and Liability Act regulations;

—coordination with the Department of Defense on base closure environmental issues; and

—technical assistance in the development, management, and operation of waste management activities, including technical assistance to Federal facilities.

For further information, call 202–566–0200.

Prevention, Pesticides, and Toxic Substances   The Office of Prevention, Pesticides, and Toxic Substances is responsible for the following tasks:

—promoting the public's right to know about industrial chemicals;

—promoting pollution prevention through innovative strategies;

—evaluating and regulating pesticides and industrial chemicals to safeguard all Americans;

—reviewing and regulating emerging technology, including nanotechnology-derived products;

—developing, evaluating, and implementing science policies both domestically and internationally;

—establishing safe levels for pesticide residues on food;

—developing national strategies for control of persistent, bioaccumulative, and toxic substances;

—developing scientific criteria for assessing chemical substances, standards for test protocols for chemicals, rules and procedures for industry reporting, and scientific information for the regulation of pesticides and toxic chemicals to ensure protection of people or the environment; and

—evaluating and assessing the impact of existing chemicals, new chemicals, and chemicals with new uses to determine the hazard and develop appropriate restrictions.

The Office also coordinates its activities with States and other agencies during the assessment and control of toxic substances and pesticides.

For further information, call 202–564–2902.

Research and Development The Office of Research and Development (ORD) provides the scientific foundation for the Agency's environmental protection mission. ORD's chief role is to conduct and support high-quality research targeted to understanding and resolving the Nation's most serious environmental threats. In addition, ORD develops methods and technologies to reduce exposures to pollution and prevent its creation. The Office is also a major player in sharing information on technological innovations to protect people and the environment. ORD prepares health and ecological risk assessments and makes recommendations for sound risk management strategies in order to assure that highest risk pollution problems receive optimum remediation. The Office manages a vital extramural grants program entitled Science To Achieve Results, which awards research grants to scientists in universities and students in environmental science. All ORD extramural and intramural research is carefully aligned to support the Agency's environmental goals and strategic priorities.

For further information, call 202–564–6620.

Enforcement and Compliance Assurance The Office of Enforcement and Compliance Assurance (OECA) is the lead agency office for matters pertaining to the Agency's enforcement and compliance assurance programs. OECA manages a national criminal enforcement, forensics, and training program. OECA also manages the Agency's regulatory, site remediation, and Federal facilities enforcement and compliance assurance programs, as well as the Agency's environmental justice program, and Federal activities program responsibilities under the National Environmental Policy Act.

For further information, call 202–564–2440.

Regional Offices

The Agency's 10 regional offices represent its commitment to the development of strong local programs for pollution abatement. The Regional Administrators are responsible for accomplishing, within their regions, the national program objectives established by the Agency. They develop, propose, and implement an approved regional program for comprehensive and integrated environmental protection activities.

Regional Offices—Environmental Protection Agency

Region/Address/Areas Served	Regional Administrator
Region I (Suite 1100, 1 Congress St., Boston, MA 02114–2023) (CT, MA, ME, NH, RI, VT)	Robert W. Varney
Region II (290 Broadway, New York, NY 10007–1866) (NJ, NY, PR, VI)	George Palou, Acting
Region III (1650 Arch St., Philadelphia, PA 19103–2029) (DC, DE, MD, PA, VA, WV)	Donald S. Welsh
Region IV (61 Forsyth St. SW., Atlanta GA 30303–3104) (AL, FL, GA, KY, MS, NC, SC, TN)	Stan Meiburg, Acting
Region V (77 W. Jackson Blvd., Chicago, IL 60604–3507) (IL, IN, MI, MN, OH, WI)	Mary A. Gade
Region VI (Suite 1200, 1445 Ross Ave., Dallas, TX 75202–2733) (AR, LA, NM, OK, TX)	Richard E. Greene
Region VII (901 N. 5th St., Kansas City, KS 66101) (IA, KS, MO, NE)	John B. Askew
Region VIII (1595 Wynkoop St., Denver, CO 80202–1129) (CO, MT, ND, SD, UT, WY)	Carol Rushin, Acting
Region IX (75 Hawthorne St., San Francisco, CA 94105) (AZ, CA, HI, NV, and U.S. affiliated Pacific Islands).	Wayne H. Nastri
Region X (1200 6th Ave., Seattle, WA 98101) (AK, ID, OR, WA)	Elin D. Miller

Sources of Information

Information inquiries for the following subjects should be directed by telephone to the respective organization listed below; by mail to 1200 Pennsylvania Avenue NW., Washington, DC 20460; or through the Internet at www.epa.gov.
Contracts and Procurement Office of Acquisition Management. Phone, 202–564–4310.
Grants and Fellowships Office of Grants and Debarment. Internet, www.epa.gov/ogd.

Employment Office of Human Resources. Internet, www.epa.gov/careers.
Freedom of Information Act Requests Freedom of Information Officer. Phone, 202–566–1667. Email, hq.foia@epa.gov.
Information Resources Phone, 202–564–6665.
Telephone Directory Available for sale by the Superintendent of Documents, Government Printing Office, P.O. Box 37194, Pittsburgh, PA 15250–7954.

For further information, contact the Office of Public Affairs, Environmental Protection Agency, 1200 Pennsylvania Avenue NW., Washington, DC 20460–0001. Phone, 202–564–4355. Internet, www.epa.gov.

EQUAL EMPLOYMENT OPPORTUNITY COMMISSION

1801 L Street NW., Washington, DC 20507
Phone, 202–663–4900. TTY, 202–663–4494. Internet, www.eeoc.gov.

CHAIR	STUART J. ISHIMARU, *Acting*
VICE CHAIR	CHRISTINE M. GRIFFIN, *Acting*
Commissioners	CONSTANCE S. BARKER, (2 VACANCIES)
Executive Officer	STEPHEN LLEWELLYN
Chief Operating Officer	(VACANCY)
General Counsel	(VACANCY)
Inspector General	ALETHA L. BROWN
Director, Office of Communications and Legislative Affairs	(VACANCY)
Director, Office of Equal Opportunity	VERONICA VILLALOBOS
Director, Office of Federal Operations	CARLTON M. HADDEN
Legal Counsel	(VACANCY)
Director, Office of Field Programs	NICHOLAS INZEO
Chief Financial Officer	JEFFREY SMITH
Director, Office of Human Resources	MARA LOPEZ, *Acting*
Director, Office of Information Technology	KIMBERLY HANCHER
Director, Office of Research, Information, and Planning	DEIDRE FLIPPEN

The Equal Employment Opportunity Commission enforces laws prohibiting employment discrimination based on race, color, gender, religion, national origin, age, and disability in the Federal and private sectors.

The Equal Employment Opportunity Commission (EEOC) was created by title VII of the Civil Rights Act of 1964 (42 U.S.C. 2000e–4), and became

operational July 2, 1965. Laws under the EEOC's enforcement mission include title VII of the Civil Rights Act of 1964 (42 U.S.C. 2000e *et seq.*), the Age

EQUAL EMPLOYMENT OPPORTUNITY COMMISSION

Discrimination in Employment Act of 1967 (29 U.S.C. 621 et seq.), sections of the Rehabilitation Act of 1973 (29 U.S.C. 791 et seq.), the Equal Pay Act of 1963 (29 U.S.C. 206), title I of the Americans with Disabilities Act of 1990 (42 U.S.C. 12101 et seq.), and sections of the Civil Rights Act of 1991 (105 Stat. 1071). The EEOC is a bipartisan commission composed of five members appointed by the President, with the advice and consent of the Senate, for staggered 5-year terms. The President designates a Chairman and Vice Chairman. In addition to the members of the Commission, the President appoints a General Counsel, with the advice and consent of the Senate, to support the Commission and provide direction, coordination, and supervision of the EEOC's litigation program. The General Counsel serves for a term of 4 years.

Activities

Enforcement   The EEOC enforces its statutory, regulatory, policy, and program responsibilities through its headquarters-based Office of Field Programs, the Office of General Counsel, and 53 field offices. The field offices receive charges of discrimination from the public and use a variety of resolution methods, tailored to each charge, from voluntary mediation to full-scale. The field staff is responsible for achieving a wide range of objectives, focusing on the quality, timeliness, and appropriateness of individual, class, and systemic charges and for securing relief for victims of discrimination in accordance with Commission policies. The field staff also counsel individuals about their rights under the laws enforced by the EEOC and conduct outreach and technical assistance programs. The Office of General Counsel conducts the Commission's litigation in U.S. District Courts and Courts of Appeal.

Complaints Against the Federal Government   The EEOC establishes the procedures for Federal employees and job applicants to file complaints of employment discrimination or retaliation for having in engaged in protected EEO activity. The agency charged with discrimination is responsible for informal counseling, and, if a complaint is filed and that complaint is accepted, for investigating the claims raised therein. At the conclusion of the investigation, complainants may request a hearing before an EEOC administrative judge or that the agency issue a final decision on the matter. The agency's final decision or final action after a hearing may be appealed to the Commission.

In addition, the Office of Federal Operations provides oversight and technical assistance concerning EEO complaint adjudication and the maintenance of effective affirmative programs of equal employment opportunity throughout the Federal government. Using the guidance and principles contained in the EEOC's EEO Management Directive 715, the Commission monitors and evaluates Federal agencies' affirmative employment programs under title VII and section 501 of the Rehabilitation Act and ensures that all Federal employees compete on a fair and level playing field.

Other Activities   The Commission promotes voluntary compliance with equal employment opportunity statutes through a variety of educational and technical assistance activities. The Commission's outreach and education programs provide general information about the EEOC, its mission, rights and responsibilities under the statutes enforced by the Commission, and the charge/complaint process. EEOC representatives are available on a limited basis at no cost to make presentations and participate in meetings, conferences, and seminars with employee and employer groups, professional associations, students, nonprofit entities, community organizations, and other members of the general public.

The Commission also offers more in-depth training tailored to employers for a fee. This training is available to private employers and State, local, and Federal government personnel through the EEOC Training Institute. The EEOC Training Institute provides a wide variety of training to assist in educating managers and employees on the laws enforced by the EEOC and how to prevent and eliminate discrimination in the workplace. The EEOC develops policy guidance and provides technical assistance to employers and employees, and coordinates with other agencies and stakeholders regarding the statutes and regulations it enforces.

The Commission also publishes data on the employment status of minorities and women through six employment surveys covering private employers, apprenticeship programs, labor unions, State and local governments, elementary and secondary schools, and colleges and universities. This collection of data is shared with selected Federal agencies and is made available, in appropriate form, for public use.

Field Offices—Equal Employment Opportunity Commission

(DO: District Office; AO: Area Office; LO: Local Office; FO: Field Office)

Office	Address/Telephone	Director
Albuquerque, NM (AO)	Suite 900, 505 Marquette NW., 87102. Ph., 505–248–5176. Fax, 505–248–5239. TTY, 505–248–5240.	Georgia Marchbanks
Atlanta, GA (DO)	Suite 4R30, 100 Alabama St. SW., 30303. Ph., 404–562–6930. Fax, 404–562–6910. TTY, 404–562–6801.	Bernice Williams-Kimbrough
Baltimore, MD (FO)	3d Fl., City Crescent Bldg., 10 S. Howard St., 21201. Ph., 410–209–2245. Fax, 410–962–2817. TTY, 410–962–6065.	Gerald Kiel
Birmingham, AL (DO)	Suite 2000, 1130 22d St. S., 35205. Ph., 205–212–2089. Fax, 205–212–2105. TTY, 205–212–2112.	Delner Franklin-Thomas
Boston, MA (AO)	Rm. 475, John F. Kennedy Fed. Govt. Ctr., 02203–0506. Ph., 617–565–3191. Fax, 617–565–3196. TTY, 617–565–3204.	Robert L. Sanders
Buffalo, NY (LO)	Suite 350, 6 Fountain Plz., 14202. Ph., 716–551–4443. Fax, 716–551–4387. TTY, 716–551–5923.	Elizabeth Cadle
Charlotte, NC (DO)	Suite 400, 129 W. Trade St., 28202. Ph., 704–344–6744. Fax, 704–344–6734. TTY, 704–344–6684.	Reuben Daniels
Chicago, IL (DO)	Suite 2000, 500 W. Madison St., 60661. Ph., 312–353–8550. Fax, 312–886–1168 TTY, 312–353–2421.	John P. Rowe
Cincinnati, OH (AO)	Suite 10–019, 550 Main St., 45202. Ph., 513–684–2379. Fax, 513–684–2361. TTY, 513–684–2074.	Wilma L. Javey
Cleveland, OH (FO)	Suite 3001, 1240 E. 9th St., 44119. Ph., 216–522–7447. Fax, 216–522–7395. TTY, 216–522–8441.	Daniel Cabot
Dallas, TX (DO)	3d Fl., 207 S. Houston St., 75202. Ph., 214–253–2852. Fax, 214–253–2720. TTY, 214–253–2852.	Michael Fetzer
Denver, CO (FO)	Suite 410, 303 E. 17th Ave., 80203. Ph., 303–866–1311. Fax, 303–866–1085. TTY, 303–866–1950.	Nancy Sienko
Detroit, MI (FO)	Rm. 865, 477 Michigan Ave., 48226. Ph., 313–226–3347. Fax, 313–226–2778. TTY, 313–226–7599.	Gail Cober
El Paso, TX (AO)	Suite 500, 300 E. Main Dr., 79901. Ph., 915–534–6685. Fax, 915–534–6701. TTY, 915–534–6710.	Teresa Anchondo
Fresno, CA (LO)	2300 Tulare St., 93721. Ph., 559–487–5940. Fax, 559–487–5053. TTY, 559–487–5837.	Melissa Barrios
Greensboro, NC (LO)	Suite 201, 2303 W. Meadowview Rd., 27407. Ph., 336–547–4080. Fax, 336–547–4032. TTY, 336–547–4035.	Jose Rosenberg
Greenville, SC (LO)	Suite 1402, 301 N. Main St., 29601. Ph., 864–241–4410. Fax, 864–241–4416. TTY, 864–241–4403.	Patricia Fuller
Honolulu, HI (LO)	Rm. 7–127, 300 Ala Moana Blvd., P.O. Box 50082, 96850. Ph., 808–541–3722. Fax, 808–541–3390. TTY, 808–541–3722.	Timothy Riera
Houston, TX (DO)	7th Fl., 1919 Smith St., 77002. Ph., 713–209–3379. Fax, 713–209–3381. TTY, 713–209–3439.	Roy J. Ruff
Indianapolis, IN (DO)	Suite 1900, 101 W. Ohio St., 46204–4203. Ph., 317–226–6418. Fax, 317–226–7953. TTY, 317–226–5162.	Danny G. Harter
Jackson, MS (AO)	Suite 207, 100 W. Capitol St., 39269. Ph., 601–948–8400. Fax, 601–948–8401. TTY, 601–948–8469.	Wilma Scott
Kansas City, KS (AO)	Suite 905, 400 State Ave., 66101. Ph., 913–551–5655. Fax, 913–551–6956. TTY, 913–551–5657.	Billie Ashton
Las Vegas, NV (LO)	Suite 8112, 333 Las Vegas Blvd., 89101. Ph., 702–388–5054. Fax, 702–388–5094. TTY, 702–388–5098.	Lucy Orta
Little Rock, AR (AO)	Suite 200, 820 S. Louisiana St., 72201. Ph., 501–324–5066. Fax, 501–324–5991. TTY, 501–324–5481.	Wanda Milton
Los Angeles, CA (DO)	4th Fl., 255 E. Temple St., 90012. Ph., 213–894–1112. Fax, 213–894–1459. TTY, 213–894–1121.	Olophius Perry
Louisville, KY (AO)	Suite 268, 600 Dr. Martin Luther King Jr. Pl., 40202. Ph., 502–582–6744. Fax, 502–582–5895. TTY, 502–582–6285.	Marcia Hall-Craig
Memphis, TN (DO)	9th Fl., 1407 Union Ave., 38104. Ph., 901–544–0151. Fax, 901–544–0111. TTY, 901–544–0112.	Katherine Kores
Miami, FL (DO)	Suite 2700, 2 S. Biscayne Blvd., 33131. Ph., 305–808–1800. Fax, 305–808–1855. TTY, 305–808–1742.	Jacqueline McNair
Milwaukee, WI (AO)	Suite 800, 310 W. Wisconsin Ave., 53203. Ph., 414–297–1294. Fax, 414–297–3146. TTY, 414–297–1115.	Rosemary Fox, *Acting*

Field Offices—Equal Employment Opportunity Commission—Continued

(DO: District Office; AO: Area Office; LO: Local Office; FO: Field Office)

Office	Address/Telephone	Director
Minneapolis, MN (AO)	Suite 720, 330 S. 2d Ave., 55401. Ph., 612–335–4054. Fax, 612–335–4044. TTY, 612–335–4045.	Julie Schmid, *Acting*
Mobile, AL (LO)	Suite 504, 63 S. Royal St., 36602. Ph., 251–690–2585. Fax, 251–690–2581. TTY, 251–690–2579.	Erika La'Cour
Nashville, TN (AO)	Suite 202, 50 Vantage Way, 37228. Ph., 615–736–7481. Fax, 615–736–2107. TTY, 615–736–5870.	Sarah Smith
New Orleans, LA (FO)	Suite 1900, 1555 Poydras St., 70112. Ph., 504–595–2835. Fax, 504–595–2884. TTY, 504–595–2958.	Keith Hill
New York, NY (DO)	5th Fl., 33 Whitehall St., 10004. Ph., 212–336–3660. Fax, 212–336–3625. TTY, 212–336–3622.	Spencer H. Lewis, Jr.
Newark, NJ (AO)	21st Fl., One Newark Ctr., 07102. Ph., 973–645–5978. Fax, 973–645–4524. TTY, 973–645–3004.	Corrado Gigante
Norfolk, VA (AO)	Suite 739, 200 Granby St., 23510. Ph., 757–441–3470. Fax, 757–441–6720. TTY, 757–441–3578.	Herbert Brown
Oakland, CA (LO)	Suite 1170–N, 1301 Clay St., 94612. Ph., 510–637–3239. Fax, 510–637–3235. TTY, 510–637–3234.	Michelle Nardella
Oklahoma City, OK (AO)	Suite 524, 215 Dean A. McGee Ave., 73102. Ph., 405–231–4356. Fax, 405–231–4125.TTY, 405–231–5745.	Jack Vasquez, *Acting*
Philadelphia, PA (DO)	13th Fl., 801 Market St., 19103. Ph., 215–440–2620. Fax, 215–440–2632. TTY, 215–440–2610.	Marie Tomasso
Phoenix, AZ (DO)	Suite 690, 3300 N. Central Ave., 85012. Ph., 602–640–5011. Fax, 602–640–5071. TTY, 602–640–5072.	Chester Bailey
Pittsburgh, PA (AO)	Suite 1112, 1001 Liberty Ave., 15222. Ph., 412–395–5849. Fax, 412–395–5903. TTY, 412–395–5904.	Joseph Hardiman
Raleigh, NC (AO)	1309 Annapolis Dr., 27608–2129. Ph., 919–856–4085. Fax, 919–856–4151. TTY, 919–856–4296.	Thomas Colclough
Richmond, VA (LO)	Suite 600, 803 E. Main St., 23219. Ph., 804–771–2141. Fax, 804–771–2222. TTY, 804–771–2227.	Patricia Glisson
San Antonio, TX (FO)	Suite 200, 5410 Fredericksburg Rd., 78229–3555. Ph., 210–281–7642. Fax, 210–281–7690. TTY, 210–281–7610.	Pedro Esquivel
San Diego, CA (LO)	Suite 510, 401 B St., 92101. Ph., 619–557–7277. Fax, 619–557–7274. TTY, 619–557–5748.	Thomas McCammon
San Francisco, CA (DO)	Suite 500, 350 Embarcadero, 94105. Ph., 415–625–5611. Fax, 415–625–5609. TTY, 415–625–5610.	Michael Baldonando
San Jose, CA (LO)	Suite 200, 96 N. 3d St., 95112. Ph., 408–291–7447. Fax, 408–291–4539. TTY, 408–291–7374.	Hae Jung Atkins
San Juan, PR (LO)	Suite 1202, 525 F.D. Roosevelt Ave., Plz. Las Americas, 00918. Ph., 787–771–1428. Fax, 787–771–1485. TTY, 787–771–1484.	William Sanchez
Savannah, GA (LO)	Suite G, 410 Mall Blvd., 31406. Ph., 912–652–4077. Fax, 912–652–4248. TTY, 912–652–4439.	Mason Barrett
Seattle, WA (FO)	Suite 400, 909 First Ave., 98104. Ph., 206–220–6870. Fax, 206–220–6911. TTY, 206–220–6882.	Luis Lucero
St. Louis, MO (DO)	Rm. 8100, 1222 Spruce St., 63103. Ph., 314–539–7830. Fax, 314–539–7893. TTY, 314–539–7803.	James Neely, Jr.
Tampa, FL (FO)	Rm. 1000, 501 E. Polk St., 33602. Ph., 813–202–7905. Fax, 813–228–2841. TTY, 813–228–2003.	Manuel Zurita
Washington, DC (FO)	4th Fl., 131 M St. NE., 20507. Ph., 202–419–0770. Fax, 202–419–0739. TTY, 202–419–0702.	Mindy Weinstein, *Acting*

Sources of Information

Electronic Access   Information regarding the programs and activities of the Commission is available through the Internet at www.eeoc.gov. EEOC's most popular publications may be downloaded from that site in PDF format for easy reproduction.

Employment   The Commission hires in many different job categories, including information intake representatives, office automation assistants, investigators, paralegals, program analysts, attorneys, mediators, and social scientists. Employment opportunities are posted on www.usajobs.gov. Employment inquiries may also be directed to the Office of Human Resources, Equal Employment Opportunity Commission, 131 M Street NE, Washington, DC 20507 (phone, 202–663–4306) or the appropriate district office.

General Inquiries   A nationwide toll-free telephone number links callers with the appropriate field office where charges may be filed. Phone, 800–669–4000. TTY, 800–669–6820.

Information About Survey Forms (EEO–1, 2, 3, 4, 5, and 6) Phone, 202–663–3362. Publications not available on www.eeoc.gov may be obtained by

calling 800–669–3362. TTY, 800–800–3302. Fax, 513–489–8692.
Media Inquiries Office of Communications and Legislative Affairs, 131 M Street NE, Washington, DC 20507. Phone, 202–663–4191.
Publications Phone, 800–669–3362. TTY, 800–800–3302. Fax, 513–489–8692.

Reading Room EEOC Library, 131 M Street NE, Washington, DC 20507. Phone, 202–663–4630.
Speakers Office of the Executive Secretariat, 131 M Street NE, Washington, DC 20507. Phone, 202–663–4070. TTY, 202–663–4494.

For further information, contact the Equal Employment Opportunity Commission, 131 M Street NE, Washington, DC 20507. Phone, 202–663–4191. Internet, www.eeoc.gov.

EXPORT–IMPORT BANK OF THE UNITED STATES

811 Vermont Avenue NW., Washington, DC 20571
Phone, 202–565–3946 or 800–565–3946. Internet, www.exim.gov.

PRESIDENT AND CHAIRMAN	JAMES H. LAMBRIGHT
VICE CHAIRMAN	LINDA MYSLIWY CONLIN
Directors	DIANE FARRELL, J. JOSEPH GRANDMAISON, BIJAN R. KIAN
Chief Operating Officer and Senior Vice President, Export Finance	JOHN A. MCADAMS
Senior Vice President and Chief Financial Officer	JOHN F. SIMONSON
Vice President, Treasurer	DAVID SENA
Vice President, Controller	JOSEPH SORBERA
Vice President, Asset Management	FRANCES I. NWACHUKU
Vice President, Transportation Portfolio Management	B. MICHELE DIXEY
Senior Vice President and General Counsel	KAMIL P. COOK, *Acting*
Deputy General Counsel	KAMIL P. COOK
Vice President, Trade Finance and Insurance	JEFFREY ALAN ABRAMSON
Vice President, Business Credit	PAMELA S. BOWERS
Vice President, Strategic Initiatives	RAYMOND J. ELLIS
Vice President, Structured Finance	BARBARA A. O'BOYLE
Vice President, Transportation	ROBERT A. MORIN
Vice President, Short-Term Trade Finance	WALTER KOSCIOW
Vice President, Industry Sector Development	C. MICHAEL FORGIONE
Senior Vice President, Credit and Risk Management	KENNETH M. TINSLEY
Vice President, Credit Review and Compliance	WALTER HILL, JR.
Vice President, Engineering and Environment	JAMES A. MAHONEY, JR.
Vice President, Credit Underwriting	DAVID W. CARTER
Vice President, Country Risk and Economic Analysis	WILLIAM A. MARSTELLER
Senior Vice President, Small Business	JOHN RICHTER
Vice President, Domestic Business Development	WAYNE L. GARDELLA
Senior Vice President, Resource Management	MICHAEL CUSHING
Chief Information Officer	FERNANDA F. YOUNG
Director, Human Resources	NATASHA MCCARTHY
Director, Administration and Security	PAUL PEREZ

Chief Acquisition Officer	MARK PITRA
Director, Equal Employment and Diversity	PATREASE JONES-BROWN
Senior Vice President, Policy and Planning	JAMES C. CRUSE
Vice President, Policy Analysis	HELENE WALSH
Vice President, Operations and Data Quality	MICHELE A. KUESTER
Senior Vice President, Communications	PHILLIP S. COGAN, *Acting*
Deputy Head, Communications and Director, Public Affairs	PHILLIP S. COGAN
Senior Vice President, Congressional Affairs	WILLIAM E. HELLERT, *Acting*
Vice President, Congressional Affairs	WILLIAM E. HELLERT
Inspector General	MICHAEL W. TANKERSLEY

The Export-Import Bank of the United States helps the private sector to create and maintain U.S. jobs by financing exports of the Nation's goods and services. To accomplish this mission, the Bank offers a variety of loan, guarantee, and insurance programs to support transactions that would not be awarded to U.S. companies without the Bank's assistance.

The Export-Import Bank of the United States (Ex-Im Bank), established in 1934, operates as an independent agency of the U.S. Government under the authority of the Export-Import Bank Act of 1945, as amended (12 U.S.C. 635 *et seq.*). Its Board of Directors consists of a President and Chairman, a First Vice President and Vice Chair, and three other Directors, all are appointed by the President with the advice and consent of the Senate.

Ex-Im Bank's mission is to help American exporters meet government-supported financing competition from other countries, so that U.S. exports can compete for overseas business on the basis of price, performance, and service, and in doing so help create and sustain U.S. jobs. The Bank also fills gaps in the availability of commercial financing for creditworthy export transactions.

Ex-Im Bank is required to find a reasonable assurance of repayment for each transaction it supports. Its legislation requires it to meet the financing terms of competitor export credit agencies, but not to compete with commercial lenders. Legislation restricts the Bank's operation in some countries and its support for military goods and services.

Activities

Ex-Im Bank is authorized to have loans, guarantees, and insurance outstanding at any one time in aggregate amount not in excess of $100 billion. It supports U.S. exporters through a range of diverse programs, which are offered under four broad categories of export financing, including the following:

—working capital guarantees, provided to lender, so that they can provide creditworthy small- and medium-sized exporters with working capital they need to buy, build, or assemble products for export sale;

—export credit insurance which protects exporters and lenders against both the commercial and political risks of a foreign buyer defaulting on payment;

—loan guarantees which encourage sales to creditworthy foreign buyers by providing private sector lenders in medium- and long-term transactions with Ex-Im Bank guarantees against the political and commercial risks of nonpayment; and

—direct loans made to provide foreign buyers with competitive, fixed-rate medium- or long-term financing from Ex-Im Bank for their purchases from U.S. exporters.

Ex-Im Bank initiated several changes to enhance its support to small business. It created a new position, Senior Vice President for Small Business, who reports directly to the Bank's President and Chairman. In addition, the Bank's regional offices are now dedicated exclusively to small business outreach and support. The Bank also established a Small Business Committee to coordinate, evaluate, and make recommendations on Bank functions necessary for a successful small business strategy.

Regional Offices

The Export-Import Bank operates five regional offices.

Regional Offices—Export-Import Bank

Region	Address	Telephone	Fax
Regional Offices			
New York	33 Whitehall St., 22d Fl., Suite B, New York, NY 10004	212–809–2650	212–809–2687
Miami	Suite 203, 5835 Blue Lagoon Dr., Miami, FL 33126	305–526–7436	305–526–7435
Chicago	Suite 2450, 200 W. Adams St., Chicago, IL 60606	312–353–8081	312–353–8098
Houston	Suite 405, 1880 S. Dairy Ashford II, Houston, TX 77077 ...	281–721–0465	281–679–0156
Western Regional Offices			
Newport Beach	Suite 305, 3300 Irvine Ave., Newport Beach, CA 92660	562–980–4580	562–980–4590
San Francisco	14th Fl., 250 Montgomery St., San Francisco, CA 94104 ..	415–705–2285	415–705–1156
San Diego	Suite 230, 6363 Greenwich Dr., San Diego, CA 92122	619–557–7091	619–557–6176

For further information, contact the Export-Import Bank, Business Development Office, 811 Vermont Avenue NW., Washington, DC 20571. Phone, 202–565–3946 or 800–565–3946. Internet, www.exim.gov.

FARM CREDIT ADMINISTRATION

1501 Farm Credit Drive, McLean, VA 22102–5090
Phone, 703–883–4000. Fax, 703–734–5784. Internet, www.fca.gov.

CHAIRMAN and CHIEF EXECUTIVE OFFICER	LELAND A. STROM
Members of the Board	NANCY C. PELLETT, DALLAS P. TONSAGER
Secretary to the Board	ROLAND E. SMITH
Chief Operating Officer	WILLIAM J. HOFFMAN
Director, Office of Congressional and Public Affairs	MICHAEL A. STOKKE
General Counsel	CHARLES R. RAWLS
Inspector General	CARL A. CLINEFELTER
Director, Office of Examination and Chief Examiner	THOMAS G. MCKENZIE
Director, Office of Regulatory Policy	ANDREW D. JACOB
Director, Office of Secondary Market Oversight	S. ROBERT COLEMAN
Director, Office of Management Services	STEPHEN G. SMITH

[For the Farm Credit Administration statement of organization, see the *Code of Federal Regulations*, Title 12, Parts 600 and 611]

The Farm Credit Administration is responsible for ensuring the safe and sound operation of the banks, associations, affiliated service organizations, and other entities that collectively comprise what is known as the Farm Credit System, and for protecting the interests of the public and those who borrow from Farm Credit institutions or invest in Farm Credit securities.

The Farm Credit Administration (FCA) was established as an independent financial regulatory agency in the executive branch of the Federal Government by Executive Order 6084 on March 27, 1933. FCA carries out its responsibilities by conducting examinations of the various Farm Credit lending institutions, which are Farm Credit Banks, the Agricultural Credit Bank, Agricultural Credit Associations, and Federal Land Credit Associations.

FARM CREDIT ADMINISTRATION

* Reports to the Board for policy and to the Chief Executive Officer for administration.
** Maintains a confidential advisory relationship with each of the Board members.

FCA also examines the service organizations owned by the Farm Credit lending institutions, as well as the National Cooperative Bank.

FCA policymaking is vested in the Farm Credit Administration Board, whose three full-time members are appointed to 6-year terms by the President, with the advice and consent of the Senate. One member of the Board is designated by the President as Chairman and serves as the Administration's chief executive officer. The Board is responsible for approving rules and regulations, providing for the examination and regulation of and reporting by Farm Credit institutions, and establishing the policies under which the Administration operates. Board meetings are regularly held on the second Thursday of the month and are subject to the Government in the Sunshine Act. Public announcements of these meetings are published in the *Federal Register.*

The lending institutions of the Farm Credit System were established to provide adequate and dependable credit and closely related services to farmers, ranchers, and producers or harvesters of aquatic products; persons engaged in providing on-the-farm services; rural homeowners; and associations of farmers, ranchers, and producers or harvesters of aquatic products, or federations of such associations that operate on a cooperative basis and are engaged in marketing, processing, supply, or business service functions for the benefit of their members. Initially capitalized by the United States Government, the Farm Credit lending institutions are organized as cooperatives and are completely owned by their borrowers. The loan funds provided to borrowers by these institutions are obtained primarily through the sale of securities to investors in the Nation's capital markets.

The Agricultural Credit Act of 1987, as amended (12 U.S.C. 2279aa-1), established the Federal Agricultural Mortgage Corporation (commonly known as "Farmer Mac"). The Corporation, designated as part of the Farm Credit System, is a federally chartered instrumentality of the United States and promotes the development of a secondary market for agricultural real estate and rural housing loans. Farmer Mac also provides guarantees for the timely payment of principal and interest on securities, representing interests in or obligations backed by pools of agricultural real estate loans. The Administration is responsible for the examination and regulation of Farmer Mac to ensure the safety and soundness of its operations.

The Administration manages regulations under which Farm Credit institutions operate. These regulations implement the Farm Credit Act of 1971, as amended (12 U.S.C. 2001), and have the force and effect of law. Similar to other Federal regulators of financial institutions, the Administration's authorities include the power to issue cease-and-desist orders, to levy civil monetary penalties, to remove officers and directors of Farm Credit institutions, and to establish financial and operating reporting requirements. Although it is prohibited from participation in routine management or operations of Farm Credit institutions, the Administration is authorized to become involved in these institutions' management and operations when the Farm Credit Act or its regulations have been violated, when taking an action to correct an unsafe or unsound practice, or when assuming a formal conservatorship over an institution.

The Administration does not operate on funds appropriated by Congress; it derives income from assessments collected from the institutions that it regulates and examines. In addition to its headquarters in McLean, VA, the Administration maintains four field offices located in Aurora, CO; Bloomington, MN; Irving, TX; and Sacramento, CA.

Authority for the organization and activities of the institutions comprising the cooperative Farm Credit System which operate under the regulation of the Farm Credit Administration may be found in the Farm Credit Act of 1971, as amended.

Sources of Information

Inquiries for information on the following subjects may be directed to the specified office, Farm Credit Administration, 1501 Farm Credit Drive, McLean, VA 22102–5090.

Contracts and Procurement   Inquiries regarding the Administration's procurement and contracting activities should be directed in writing to the Office of Management Services. Phone, 703–883–4135. TTY, 703–883–4200. Requests for proposals, invitations for bids, and requests for quotations are posted when open on the Administration's Web site at www.fca.gov.

Employment   Inquiries regarding employment with the Administration should be directed to the Office of Management Services. Phone, 703–883–

4135. TTY, 703–883–4200. Vacancy announcements are posted on the Administration's Web site at www.fca.gov.

Freedom of Information Requests   Requests for agency records must be submitted in writing, clearly labeled "FOIA Request" and addressed to the Office of the General Counsel. Phone, 703–883–4020 (voice and TTY). Requests may be submitted through the Internet at www.fca.gov.

Publications   Publications and information on the Farm Credit Administration may be obtained by writing to the Office of Congressional and Public Affairs. They are also posted on the Farm Credit Administration's Web site at www.fca.gov. Phone, 703–883–4056 (voice and TTY). Fax, 703–790–3260. Email, info-line@fca.gov.

For further information, contact the Office of Congressional and Public Affairs, Farm Credit Administration, 1501 Farm Credit Drive, McLean, VA 22102–5090. Phone, 703–883–4056 (voice and TTY). Email, info-line@fca.gov. Internet, www.fca.gov.

FEDERAL COMMUNICATIONS COMMISSION

445 Twelfth Street SW., Washington, DC 20554
Phone, 888–225–5322 (toll free). TTY, 888–835–5322 (toll free). Internet, www.fcc.gov.

CHAIRMAN	JULIUS GENACHOWSKI
COMMISSIONERS	MEREDITH ATTWELL BAKER, MIGNON CLYBURN, MICHAEL J. COPPS, ROBERT M. MCDOWELL
Managing Director	(VACANCY)
General Counsel	MICHELE ELLISON, *Acting*
Inspector General	KENT NILSSON
Chief, Consumer and Governmental Affairs Bureau	CATHY SEIDEL
Chief, Enforcement Bureau	KRIS MONTEITH
Chief, International Bureau	JOHN GIUSTI, *Acting*
Chief, Media Bureau	MONICA DESAI
Chief, Office of Administrative Law Judges	RICHARD L. SIPPEL
Chief, Office of Engineering and Technology	JULIUS KNAPP
Chief, Office of Strategic Planning and Policy Analysis	ELIZABETH ANDRION, *Acting*
Chief, Wireless Telecommunications Bureau	JIM SCHLICHTING, *Acting*
Chief, Wireline Competition Bureau	JULIE VEACH, *Acting*
Chief, Public Safety and Homeland Security Bureau	DAVID FURTH, *Acting*

Director, Office of Communications Business Opportunities	CAROLYN FLEMING WILLIAMS
Director, Office of Legislative Affairs	MICHAEL J. PERKO, *Acting*
Director, Office of Media Relations	DAVID FISKE
Director, Office of Workplace Diversity	LAWRENCE SHAFFNER, *Acting*

[For the Federal Communications Commission statement of organization, see the *Code of Federal Regulations,* Title 47, Part 0]

The Federal Communications Commission regulates interstate and foreign communications by radio, television, wire, satellite, and cable. It is responsible for the orderly development and operation of broadcast services and the provision of rapid, efficient nationwide and worldwide telephone and telegraph services at reasonable rates. Its responsibilities also include the use of communications for promoting safety of life and property and for strengthening the national defense.

The Federal Communications Commission (FCC) was created by the Communications Act of 1934 (47 U.S.C. 151 *et seq.*) to regulate interstate and foreign communications by wire and radio in the public interest. The scope of FCC regulation includes radio and television broadcasting; telephone, telegraph, and cable television operation; two-way radio and radio operators; and satellite communication.

The Commission is composed of five members, who are appointed by the President with the advice and consent of the Senate. One of the members is designated by the President as Chairman.

Activities

Media The Media Bureau develops, recommends, and administers the policy and licensing programs for the regulation of media, including cable television, multichannel video programming distribution, broadcast television and radio, and satellite services in the United States and its territories. The Bureau's responsibilities include the following:

—conducting rulemaking proceedings concerning the legal, engineering, and economic aspects of electronic media services;

—resolving waiver petitions, declaratory rulings, and adjudications related to electronic media services; and

—processing applications for authorization, assignment, transfer, and renewal of media services, including AM, FM, TV, the cable TV relay service, and related matters.

For further information, contact the Media Bureau. Phone, 202–418–7200 or 888–225–5322.

Wireline Competition Bureau The Wireline Competition Bureau advises and makes recommendations to the Commission, or acts for the Commission under delegated authority, in all matters pertaining to the regulation and licensing of communications common carriers and ancillary operations (other than matters pertaining exclusively to the regulation and licensing of wireless telecommunications services and facilities). The Bureau carries out the following duties:

—ensures choice, opportunity, and fairness in the development of wireline telecommunications;

—assesses the present and future wireline telecommunications needs of the Nation and promotes the development and widespread availability of wireline telecommunications;

—promotes economically efficient investment in wireline telecommunications infrastructure; and

—reviews and coordinates orders, programs, and actions initiated by other bureaus and offices in matters affecting wireline telecommunications to ensure consistency with overall Commission policy.

For further information, contact the Wireline Competition Bureau. Phone, 202–418–1500 or 888–225–5322.

Consumer and Governmental Affairs The Consumer and Governmental Affairs

FEDERAL COMMUNICATIONS COMMISSION

Bureau develops and administers the Commission's consumer and governmental affairs policies and initiatives to enhance the public's understanding of the Commission's work and to facilitate its relationship with other governmental agencies and organizations. The Bureau is responsible for the following:

—facilitating public participation in the Commission's decisionmaking process;

—representing the Commission on consumer and government committees, working groups, task forces, and conferences;

—working with public, Federal, State, local, and tribal agencies to develop and coordinate policies;

—overseeing the Consumer Advisory Committee, Federal Advisory Committee, and the Local and State Government Advisory Committee, and providing expert advice and assistance regarding compliance with applicable disability and accessibility requirements, rules, and regulations;

—resolving informal complaints through mediation; and

—conducting consumer outreach and education programs.

For further information, contact the Consumer and Governmental Affairs Bureau. Phone, 202–418–1400 or 888–225–5322.

Enforcement The Enforcement Bureau serves as the Commission's primary entity responsible for the enforcement of the Communications Act and other communications statutes, the Commission's rules, Commission orders and authorizations, and other matters related to pending applications for a license or other authorization. The Bureau's responsibilities include investigating and resolving complaints regarding the following:

—acts or omissions of common carriers (wireline, wireless, and international);

—acts or omissions of noncommon carriers subject to the Commission's jurisdiction under Title II of the Communications Act;

—accessibility to communications services and equipment for persons with disabilities, when filed formally;

—noncompliance with the lighting and marking of radio transmitting towers, and pole attachment regulations;

—noncompliance with the broadcast and cable television children's television programming commercial limits; and

—unauthorized construction and operation of communications facilities and false distress signals.

For further information, contact the Enforcement Bureau. Phone, 202–418–7450 or 888–225–5322.

Regional and Field Offices—Enforcement Bureau

Office	Address	Director
Regional Offices		
Kansas City, MO	2d Fl., 520 NE. Colbern Rd., Lee's Summit, 64086	Dennis P. Carlton
Chicago, IL	Rm. 306, 1550 Northwest Hwy., 60068–1460	G. Michael Moffitt, *Acting*
San Francisco, CA	Suite 106, 5653 Stoneridge Dr., Pleasanton, 94588–8543	Rebecca Dorch
Field Offices		
Atlanta, GA	Rm. 320, 3575 Koger Blvd., Duluth, 30096–7577	Douglas Miller
Boston, MA	1 Batterymarch Pk., Quincy 02169–7495	Dennis Loria
Chicago, IL	Rm. 306, 1550 Northwest Hwy., Park Ridge, 60068–1460	James Roop
Columbia, MD	9200 Farm House Land, Columbia, 21046	James Higgins
Dallas, TX	Rm. 1170, 9330 LBJ Fwy., 75243–3429	James D. Wells
Denver, CO	Suite 303, 215 S. Wadsworth Blvd., Lakewood, 80226–1544.	Nikki Shears
Detroit, MI	24897 Hathaway St., Farmington Hills, 48335–1552	James A. Bridgewater
Kansas City, MO	2d Fl., 520 NE. Colbern Rd., Lee's Summit, 64086–4895	Robert C. McKinney
Los Angeles, CA	Rm. 660, 18000 Studebaker Rd., Cerritos, 90703–2692	Nader Haghighat
New Orleans, LA	Rm. 460, 2424 Edenborn Ave., Metairie, 70001	(vacancy)
New York, NY	Rm. 1151, 201 Varick St., 10014–7046	Daniel W. Noel
Philadelphia, PA	Rm. 404, 2300 E. Lincoln Hwy., Langhorne, 19047–1859	Gene Stanbro
San Francisco, CA	Suite 105, 5653 Stoneridge Dr., Pleasanton, 94588–8543	Thomas N. VanStavern
San Diego, CA	Rm. 370, 4542 Ruffner St., 92111–2216	Bill Zears
Seattle, WA	Rm. 312, 11410 NE. 122d Way, Kirkland, 98034–6927	Kristine McGowan
Tampa, FL	Rm. 1215, 2203 N. Lois Ave., 33607–2356	Ralph M. Barlow

International Bureau The International Bureau develops, recommends, and administers policies, standards, procedures, and programs for the regulation of international telecommunications facilities and services and the licensing of satellite facilities under its jurisdiction. The International Bureau assumes the principal representational role for Commission activities in international organizations. The Bureau also has the following duties and responsibilities:

—monitoring compliance with the terms and conditions of authorizations and licenses granted by the Bureau and pursues enforcement actions in conjunction with appropriate bureaus and offices;

—providing advice and technical assistance to U.S. trade officials in the negotiation and implementation of telecommunications trade agreements; and

—promoting the international coordination of spectrum allocation and frequency and orbital assignments in order to minimize cases of international radio interference involving U.S. licenses.

For further information, contact the International Bureau. Phone, 202–418–0437 or 888–225–5322.

Wireless Telecommunications The Wireless Telecommunications Bureau administers all domestic commercial and private wireless telecommunications programs and rules. The commercial wireless services include cellular, paging, personal communications, specialized mobile radio, air-ground, and basic exchange telecommunications services. The private wireless services generally serve the specialized internal communications needs of eligible users, and include the public safety, microwave, aviation, and marine services. Additionally, the Bureau:

—develops, recommends, administers, and coordinates policy matters for the assigned services, including rulemaking, interpretations, and equipment standards;

—explains and advises the public on rules and interpretations and provides rule interpretation material for the Enforcement Bureau;

—serves as the FCC's principal policy and administrative resource with regards to all spectrum auctions;

—implements the compulsory provisions of law and treaties covering the use of radio for the safety of life and property at sea and in the air;

—projects the demand for existing and possible new communications requirements and services; and

—processes applications and licensing for the assigned services.

For further information, contact the Wireless Telecommunications Bureau. Phone, 202–418–0600 or 888–225–5322.

Public Safety and Homeland Security Bureau

The Public Safety and Homeland Security Bureau is responsible for developing, recommending, and administering the agency's policies pertaining to public safety communications issues, including: 911 and E911; operability and interoperability of public safety communications; communications infrastructure protection and disaster response; and network security and reliability. The Bureau also serves as a clearinghouse for public safety communications information and issues requiring emergency responses:

—priority emergency communications programs;

—alert and warning of U.S. citizens;

—continuity of government operations (COG) and continuity of operations planning;

—public safety outreach (e.g. first responder organizations and hospitals);

—disaster management coordination and outreach;

—FCC 24/7 Communication Center; and

—studies and reports of public safety, homeland security, and disaster management issues.

For further information, contact the Public Safety and Homeland Security Bureau. Phone, 202–418–1300 or 888–225–5322. Email, pshsbinfo@fcc.gov.

Sources of Information

Inquiries for information on the special subjects listed in the following paragraphs and those concerning licensing/grant requirements in the various services may be directed to the person or office specified or to the Chief of the Bureau or Office listed below as having responsibility for the service, Federal Communications Commission, 445 Twelfth Street SW., Washington, DC 20554. Internet, www.fcc.gov.

Licensing/Grant Responsibility—Federal Communications Commission

Service	Bureau or Office
All broadcasting (except broadcast auxiliary services)	Media
Cable TV relay services (CARS)	
Cable signal leakage	
Registration of cable systems	
Interstate telecommunications services	Wireline Competition
Emergency Alert System	Public Safety and Homeland Security
Amateur radio	Wireless Telecommunications
Auxiliary broadcast services	
Aviation radio	
Commercial radio operators	
Common carrier microwave services	
Interactive video and data services	
Land mobile radio	
Marine radio	
Private microwave radio	
Broadband radio service	
Educational broadband service	
Direct broadcast satellites (DBS)	International
Foreign carrier affiliation notification	
International accounting rate change applications	
International high frequency broadcast stations	
International public fixed radio communication applications	
Permit to deliver programs to foreign broadcast stations (Section 325–C applications)	
Requests for data network identification code (DNIC) assignment	
Requests for international signaling point code (ISPC) assignment	
Recognized private operating agencies	
Satellite Earth stations	
Satellite space stations (GSO)	
Satellite space stations (NGSO)	
Submarine cable landing license applications	

Federal Advisory Committee Management Direct inquiries to the Office of Managing Director. Phone, 202–418–2178.

Consumer Assistance Inquiries concerning general information on Commission operations should be addressed to the Reference Center, Room CY–B523, 445 Twelfth Street SW., Washington, DC 20554. Phone, 888–225–5322. TTY, 888–835–5322.

Contracts and Procurement Direct inquiries to the Chief, Contracts and Purchasing Center. Phone, 202–418–1952.

Electronic Access Information regarding the Commission is also available electronically through the Internet at www.fcc.gov.

Employment and Recruitment The Commission's programs require attorneys, electronics engineers, economists, accountants, administrative management and computer specialists, and clerical personnel. Requests for employment information should be directed to the Recruitment and Staffing Service Center. Phone, 202–418–0130. To view or apply for job vacancies visit www.fcc.gov/jobs/fccjobs.html.

Equal Employment Practices by Industry Direct inquiries to the Portals Consumer Center. Phone, 888–225–5322.

Internal Equal Employment Practices Direct inquiries to the Office of Workplace Diversity. Phone, 202–418–1799.

Ex-Parte Presentations Information concerning ex-parte presentations should be directed to the Commission's Office of General Counsel. Phone, 202–418–1720.

Fees Information concerning the Commission's fee programs is available at www.fcc.gov/fees or by contacting the Commission Registration System/Fee Filer Help Desk at 1–877–480–3201 (option 4).

Freedom of Information Act Requests Requests should be directed to the FOIA Requester Service Center. Phone, 202–418–0212. Email, foia@fcc.gov.

Information Available for Public Inspection At the Commission's headquarters office in Washington, DC, dockets concerning rulemaking and adjudicatory matters, copies of applications for licenses and grants, and reports required to be filed by licensees and cable system operators are maintained in the public reference rooms (some reports are held

confidentially by law). The Library has Commission rules and regulations on file (phone, 202–418–0450). General information is also available through the Commission's fax-on-demand (phone, 202–418–2805).

In addition to the information available at the Commission, each broadcasting station makes available for public reference certain information pertaining to the operation of the station, a current copy of the application filed for license, and nonconfidential reports filed with the Commission.

Publications The Office of Media Relations distributes publications, public notices, and press releases. Phone, 202–418–0503.

For further information, contact the Consumer Center, Federal Communications Commission, 445 Twelfth Street SW., Washington, DC 20554. Phone, 888–225–5322. TTY, 888–835–5322. Internet, www.fcc.gov.

FEDERAL DEPOSIT INSURANCE CORPORATION

550 Seventeenth Street NW., Washington, DC 20429
Phone, 703–562–2222. Internet, www.fdic.gov.

CHAIRMAN	SHEILA C. BAIR
VICE CHAIRMAN	MARTIN J. GRUENBERG
Director, Appointive	THOMAS J. CURRY
Director, Comptroller of the Currency	JOHN C. DUGAN
Director, Office of Thrift Supervision	(VACANCY)
Deputy to the Chairman and Chief Operating Officer	JOHN F. BOVENZI
Deputy to the Chairman and Chief Financial Officer	STEVEN O. APP
Deputy to the Chairman for External Affairs	PAUL NASH
Chief of Staff	JESSE O. VILLARREAL, JR.
Deputy to the Vice Chairman	BARBARA A. RYAN
Deputy to the Director (Appointive)	LISA ROY
Deputy to the Director (Comptroller of the Currency)	WILLIAM A. ROWE III
Deputy to the Director (Office of Thrift Supervision)	(VACANCY)
General Counsel	ROBERTA MCINERNEY, *Acting*
Director, Division of Administration	ARLEAS UPTON KEA
Director, Division of Finance	BRET D. EDWARDS
Director, Division of Information Technology and Chief Information Officer	MICHAEL E. BARTELL
Director, Division of Insurance and Research	ARTHUR J. MURTON
Director, Division of Resolutions and Receiverships	MITCHELL L. GLASSMAN

Director, Division of Supervision and Consumer Protection	SANDRA L. THOMPSON
Director, Office of Diversity and Economic Opportunity	D. MICHAEL COLLINS
Director, Office of Enterprise Risk Management	JAMES H. ANGEL, JR.
Director, Office of International Affairs	FRED S. CARNS
Director, Office of Legislative Affairs	ERIC J. SPITLER
Ombudsman	COTTRELL L. WEBSTER
Director, Office of Public Affairs	ANDREW S. GRAY
Chief Learning Officer	THOM H. TERWILLIGER
Inspector General	JOHN T. RYMER

The Federal Deposit Insurance Corporation promotes and preserves public confidence in U.S. financial institutions by insuring bank and thrift deposits up to the legal limit of $100,000; by periodically examining State-chartered banks that are not members of the Federal Reserve System for safety and soundness as well as compliance with consumer protection laws; and by liquidating assets of failed institutions to reimburse the insurance funds for the cost of failures.

The Federal Deposit Insurance Corporation (FDIC) was established under the Banking Act of 1933 in response to numerous bank failures during the Great Depression. FDIC began insuring banks on January 1, 1934. As of April 1, 2006, the deposit insurance coverage on certain retirement accounts at a bank or savings institution was raised to $250,000. The basic insurance coverage for other deposit accounts remains at $100,000.

The FDIC does not operate on funds appropriated by Congress. Its income is derived from insurance premiums on deposits held by insured banks and savings associations and from interest on the required investment of the premiums in U.S. Government securities. It also has authority to borrow from the Treasury up to $30 billion for insurance purposes.

Management of the FDIC consists of a Board of Directors that includes the Chairman, Vice Chairman, and Appointive Director. The Comptroller of the Currency, whose office supervises national banks, and the Director of the Office of Thrift Supervision, which supervises federally or State-chartered savings associations, are also members of the Board. All five Board members are appointed by the President and confirmed by the Senate, with no more than three being from the same political party.

Activities

The FDIC insures about $4.2 trillion of U.S. bank and thrift deposits. The insurance fund is composed of insurance premiums paid by banks and savings associations and the interest on the investment of those premiums in U.S. Government securities, as required by law. Premiums are determined by an institution's level of capitalization and potential risk to the insurance fund.

The FDIC examines about 5,250 State-chartered commercial and savings banks that are not members of the Federal Reserve System, called State nonmember banks. The FDIC also has authority to examine other types of FDIC-insured institutions for deposit insurance purposes. The two types of examinations conducted are for safety and soundness and for compliance with applicable consumer laws such as the Truth in Lending Act, the Home Mortgage Disclosure Act, the Equal Credit Opportunity Act, the Fair Housing Act, and the Community Reinvestment Act. Examinations are performed on the institution's premises and off-site through computer data analysis.

A failed bank or savings association is generally closed by its chartering authority, and the FDIC is named receiver. The FDIC is required to resolve the closed institution in a manner that is least costly to the FDIC. Ordinarily, the FDIC attempts to locate a healthy

FEDERAL DEPOSIT INSURANCE CORPORATION

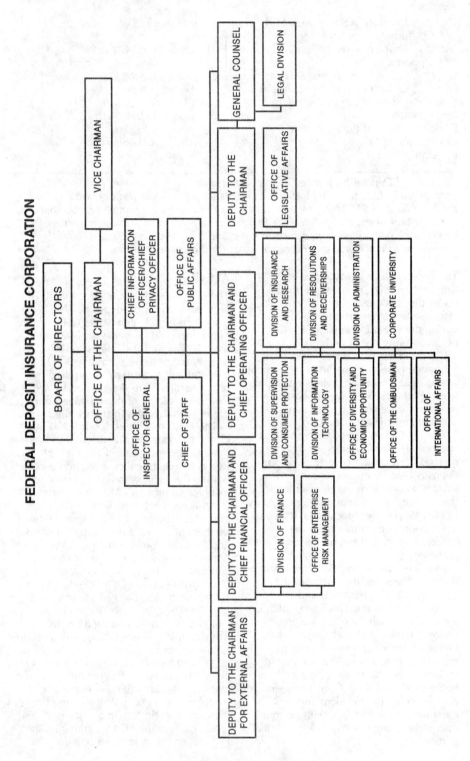

institution to acquire the failed entity. If such an entity cannot be found, the FDIC pays depositors the amount of their insured funds, usually by the next business day following the closing. Depositors with funds that exceed the insurance limit often receive an advance dividend, which is a portion of their uninsured funds that is determined by an estimate of the future proceeds from liquidating the failed institution's remaining assets. Depositors with funds in a failed institution that exceed the insurance limit receive a receivership certificate for those funds and partial payments of their uninsured funds as asset disposition permits.

As part of its insurance, supervisory, and receivership responsibilities, the FDIC also performs other functions relating to State nonmember banks, including:

—approval or disapproval of mergers, consolidations, and acquisitions where the resulting bank is an insured State nonmember;

—approval or disapproval of a proposal by a bank to establish and operate a new branch, close an existing branch, or move its main office from one location to another;

—approval or disapproval of requests to engage as principal in activities and investments that are not permissible for a national bank;

—issuance of enforcement actions, including cease-and-desist orders, for specific violations or practices requiring corrective action; and

—review of changes in ownership or control of a bank.

Regional Offices—Federal Deposit Insurance Corporation

Region/Address	Telephone
Atlanta, GA (Suite 800, 10 Tenth St. NE., 30309)	678–916–2200
Chicago, IL (Suite 3500, 500 W. Monroe St., 60661)	312–382–6000
Dallas, TX (1601 Bryan St., 75201)	214–754–0098
Kansas City, MO (Suite 1200, 2345 Grand Blvd., 64108)	816–234–8000
New York, NY (4th Fl., 20 Exchange Pl., 10005)	917–320–2500
San Francisco, CA (Suite 2300, 25 Jessie St., 94105)	415–546–0160

Sources of Information

Consumer Information Telephone inquiries about deposit insurance and other consumer matters can be directed to the Consumer Response Center at 877–275–3342, from 8 a.m. to 8 p.m. eastern standard time, Monday through Friday. For credit card complaints, call 800–378–9581, from 8:30 a.m. to 4:30 p.m. central standard time, Monday through Friday. Written inquiries may be sent to the Division of Supervision and Consumer Protection at the regional offices listed above or to FDIC headquarters. Email inquiries may be sent to the FDIC Web site at www.fdic.gov/deposit/deposits/index.html. The online FDIC customer assistance form for submitting an inquiry or a complaint is available at www.fdic.gov/starsmail/index.asp. A copy of a bank's quarterly Report of Condition is available from the call center at cost, or free from the FDIC Web site at www.fdic.gov/Call_TFR_Rpts/.

General Inquiries Written requests for general information may be directed to the FDIC's Public Information Center, 3501 Fairfax Drive, Room E–1002, Arlington, VA (telephone 703–562–2200 or 1–877–275–3342).

Public Records Many FDIC records are available on the FDIC Web site. Inquiries about other types of records available to the public, including records available under the Freedom of Information Act, should be directed to the Chief, FOIA/PA Group 550 17th St. NW., Washington, DC 20429, or any regional office.

Publications Publications, press releases, congressional testimony, directives to financial institutions, and other documents are available through the Public Information Center. Phone,

877–275–3342 (press 1; then press 5). Email, publicinfo@fdic.gov. Internet, www.fdic.gov/news/publications/index.html.

For further information, contact the Office of Public Affairs, Federal Deposit Insurance Corporation, 550 Seventeenth Street NW., Washington, DC 20429. Phone, 202–898–6993. Email, communications@fdic.gov. Internet, www.fdic.gov.

FEDERAL ELECTION COMMISSION

999 E Street NW., Washington, DC 20463
Phone, 202–694–1100 or 800–424–9530 (toll free). Internet, www.fec.gov.

CHAIRMAN	STEVEN T. WALTHER
VICE CHAIRMAN	MATTHEW S. PETERSEN
Commissioners	CYNTHIA L. BAUERLY, CAROLINE C. HUNTER, DONALD F. McGAHN II, ELLEN L. WEINTRAUB
Staff Director	ROBERT A. HICKEY
General Counsel	THOMASENIA P. DUNCAN
Inspector General	LYNNE A. McFARLAND
Chief Financial Officer	MARY G. SPRAGUE

The Federal Election Commission has exclusive jurisdiction in the administration and civil enforcement of laws regulating the acquisition and expenditure of campaign funds to ensure compliance by participants in the Federal election campaign process. Its chief mission is to provide public disclosure of campaign finance activities and effect voluntary compliance by providing the public with information on the laws and regulations concerning campaign finance.

The Federal Election Commission is an independent agency established by section 309 of the Federal Election Campaign Act of 1971, as amended (2 U.S.C. 437c). It is composed of six Commissioners appointed by the President with the advice and consent of the Senate. The act also provides for three statutory officers—the Staff Director, the General Counsel, and the Inspector General—who are appointed by the Commission.

Activities

The Commission administers and enforces the Federal Election Campaign Act of 1971, as amended (2 U.S.C. 431 et seq.), and the Revenue Act, as amended (26 U.S.C. 1 et seq.). These laws provide for the public funding of Presidential elections, public disclosure of the financial activities of political committees involved in Federal elections, and limitations and prohibitions on contributions and expenditures made to influence Federal elections (Presidency, Senate, and House of Representatives).

Public Funding of Presidential Elections The Commission oversees the public financing of Presidential elections by certifying Federal payments to primary candidates, general election nominees, and national nominating conventions. It also audits recipients of Federal funds and may require repayments to the U.S. Treasury if a committee makes nonqualified campaign expenditures.

Disclosure The Commission ensures the public disclosure of the campaign finance activities reported by political committees supporting Federal candidates. Committee reports, filed regularly, disclose where campaign money comes from and how it is spent.

The Commission places reports on the public record within 48 hours after they are received and computerizes the data contained in the reports.

Sources of Information

Congressional Affairs Office   This Office serves as primary liaison with Congress and executive branch agencies. The Office is responsible for keeping Members of Congress informed about Commission decisions and, in turn, for informing the Commission on legislative developments. For further information, call 202–694–1006 or 800–424–9530.

Employment   Inquiries regarding employment opportunities should be directed to the Director, Human Resources and Labor Relations. Phone, 202–694–1080 or 800–424–9530.

General Inquiries   The Information Services Division provides information and assistance to Federal candidates, political committees, and the general public. This division answers questions on campaign finance laws, conducts workshops and seminars on the law, and provides publications and forms. For information or materials, call 202–694–1100 or 800–424–9530.

Media Inquiries   The Press Office answers inquiries from print and broadcast media sources around the country, issues press releases on Commission actions and statistical data, responds to informational requests, and distributes other materials. All persons representing media should direct inquiries to the Press Office. Phone, 202–694–1220 or 800–424–9530.

Public Records   The Office of Public Records, located at 999 E Street NW., Washington, DC, provides space for public inspection of all reports and statements relating to campaign finance since 1972. It is open weekdays from 9 a.m. to 5 p.m. and has extended hours during peak election periods. The public is invited to visit the Office or obtain information by calling 202–694–1120 or 800–424–9530.

Reading Room   The library contains a collection of basic legal research resources, with emphasis on political campaign financing, corporate and labor political activity, and campaign finance reform. It is open to the public on weekdays between 9 a.m. and 5 p.m. For further information, call 202–694–1600 or 800–424–9530.

For further information, contact Information Services, Federal Election Commission, 999 E Street NW., Washington, DC 20463. Phone, 202–694–1100 or 800–424–9530. Internet, www.fec.gov.

FEDERAL HOUSING FINANCE AGENCY

1700 G Street NW., Washington, DC 20552
Phone, 866–796–5595. Internet, www.fhfa.gov.

DIRECTOR	EDWARD J. DeMARCO, *Acting*
Senior Deputy Director and Chief Operating Office	STEPHEN M. CROSS, *Acting*
Deputy Director for Enterprise Regulation	CHRIS DICKERSON
Deputy Director for Federal Home Loan Bank Regulation	STEPHEN M. CROSS
Inspector General	(VACANCY)
General Counsel	ALFRED M. POLLARD
Senior Associate Director and Chief Accountant	WANDA DELEO
Senior Associate Director for Conservatorship	JEFFREY SPOHN
Associate Director, Office of External Relations	PETER BRERETON

Associate Director and Chief Economist, Office of Policy Analysis and Research	PATRICK J. LAWLER
Associate Director, Office of Management Planning	MYRTLE S. HABERSHAM
Chief Administrative Officer	DAVID A. LEE
Chief Financial Officer	MARK KINSEY
Chief Human Capital Officer	JANET MURPHY
Chief Information Officer	KEVIN WINKLER
Chief Strategic Planning	(VACANCY)

The Federal Housing and Finance Agency works to promote a stable and liquid mortgage market, affordable housing, and community investment through safety and soundness oversight of Fannie Mae, Freddie Mac, and the Federal Home Loan Banks.

The Federal Housing and Finance Agency (FHFA) was established by the Federal Housing Finance Regulatory Reform Act of 2008 (12 U.S.C. 4501 *et seq.*) as an independent agency in the executive branch. The FHFA is the result from the merger of the Federal Housing Finance Board and the Office of Federal Housing Enterprise Oversight, as well as the transfer of the Department of Housing and Urban Development's government-sponsored enterprise mission team into the agency.

FHFA is managed by a Director who is appointed by the President and confirmed by the Senate. The FHFA Director also serves as the Chairman of the Federal Housing Oversight Board, a newly created advisory board that testifies before Congress on the status of the Federal housing market enterprises. The Secretary of the Treasury, the Secretary of Housing and Urban Development, and the Securities and Exchange Commission Chairman are also members of the Board.

FHFA was created to ensure the security and supervision of Fannie Mae, Freddie Mac, the 12 Federal Home Loan Banks, and the Office of Finance. The agency's increased regulatory powers and affordable housing goals were designed to restore confidence in the 14 government-sponsored loan enterprises, enabling these entities to provide more effective assistance to troubled mortgage markets.

Activities

In futherance of affordable housing and community investment goals, FHFA

practices prudential oversight to strengthen vital components of the Nation's secondary mortgage markets, ensuring:

—maintenance of adequate capital and internal controls;

—operations that foster efficient, competitive, and resilient national housing finance markets, including activities relating to mortgages on housing for low- and moderate-income families;

—compliance with the rules, regulations, guidelines, and orders issued by FHFA and the authorizing statutes; and

—lending practices consistent with the public interest.

Sources of Information

Employment   Inquiries and application for employment should be directed to the Office of Human Resources Management, FHFA, 1625 I Street NW., Washington, DC 20006 or through the agency Web site www.fhfa.gov.

Publications   Written requests for copies of publications may be directed to the Office of External Relations, FHFA, 1700 G Street NW., Washington, DC 20552 or emailed to fhfainfo@fhfa.gov.

Public Records   Many FHFA records are available on the FHFA Web site, www.fhfa.gov. Inquiries about other records available to the public, including those available under the Freedom of Information Act, should be directed by email to the Chief FOIA Officer at foia@fhfa.gov.

For further information, contact the Office of External Relations, Federal Housing Finance Agency, 1625 I Street NW., Washington, DC 20006. Phone, 866–796–5595. Internet, www.fhfa.gov. Email, fhfainfo@fhfa.gov.

EDITORIAL NOTE: The Federal Labor Relations Authority did not meet the publication deadline for submitting updated information of its activities, functions, and sources of information as required by the automatic disclosure provisions of the Freedom of Information Act (5 U.S.C. 552(a)(1)(A)).

FEDERAL LABOR RELATIONS AUTHORITY

1400 K Street NW., Washington, DC 20005
Phone, 202–218–7770. Internet, www.flra.gov.

CHAIR	CAROL WALLER POPE
EXECUTIVE DIRECTOR	CATHERINE V. EMERSON, *Acting*
Chief Counsel	SUE MCCLUSKEY
Director, Case Intake Office and Legal Publications	DONALD HARRIS
Solicitor	ROSA M. KOPPEL
Deputy Solicitor	WILLIAM TOBEY
Inspector General	FRANCINE C. EICHLER
Chief Administrative Law Judge	CHARLES CENTER
Members	THOMAS M. BECK, (VACANCY)
Chief Counsels	JAMES ABBOTT, (VACANCY)
General Counsel	(VACANCY)
Deputy General Counsel	(VACANCY)
Federal Service Impasses Panel	
Chairman	(VACANCY)
Members	(7 VACANCIES)
Executive Director	H. JOSEPH SCHIMANSKY
Foreign Service Labor Relations Board	
Chair	CAROL WALLER POPE
Members	(5 VACANCIES)
General Counsel	(VACANCY)

The Federal Labor Relations Authority oversees the Federal service labor-management relations program. It administers the law that protects the right of employees of the Federal Government to organize, bargain collectively, and participate through labor organizations of their own choosing in decisions affecting them. The Authority also ensures compliance with the statutory rights and obligations of Federal employees and the labor organizations that represent them in their dealings with Federal agencies.

The Federal Labor Relations Authority was created as an independent establishment by Reorganization Plan No. 2 of 1978 (5 U.S.C. app.), effective January 1, 1979, pursuant to Executive Order 12107 of December 28, 1978, to consolidate the central policymaking functions in Federal labor-management relations. Its duties and authority are specified in title VII (Federal Service Labor-Management Relations) of the Civil Service Reform Act of 1978 (5 U.S.C. 7101–7135).

FEDERAL LABOR RELATIONS AUTHORITY

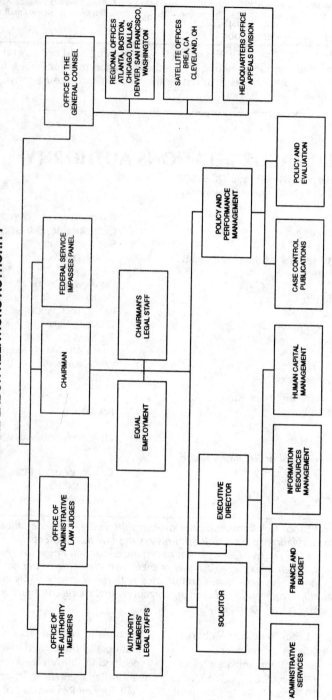

Activities

The Authority adjudicates disputes arising under the Federal labor-management relations program, deciding cases concerning the negotiability of collective bargaining agreement proposals, appeals concerning unfair labor practices and representation petitions, and exceptions to grievance arbitration awards. Consistent with its statutory charge to provide leadership in establishing policies and guidance to participants in the Federal labor-management relations program, it also assists Federal agencies and unions in understanding their rights and responsibilities under the program through training. The Chairman of the Authority serves as the chief executive and administrative officer. The Chairman also chairs the Foreign Service Labor Relations Board.

The General Counsel of the Authority investigates alleged unfair labor practices, files and prosecutes unfair labor practice complaints before the Authority, and exercises such other powers as the Authority may prescribe.

The Federal Service Impasses Panel, an entity within the Authority, is assigned the function of providing assistance in resolving negotiation impasses between agencies and unions. After investigating an impasse, the Panel can either recommend procedures to the parties for the resolution of the impasse or assist the parties in resolving the impasse through whatever methods and procedures it considers appropriate, including factfinding and recommendations. If the parties do not arrive at a settlement after assistance by the Panel, the Panel may hold hearings and take whatever action is necessary to resolve the impasse.

The Foreign Service Labor Relations Board and the Foreign Service Impasse Disputes Panel administer provisions of chapter 2 of the Foreign Service Act of 1980 (22 U.S.C. 3921) concerning labor-management relations. This chapter establishes a statutory labor-management relations program for Foreign Service employees of the U.S. Government. Administrative and staff support is provided by the Federal Labor Relations Authority and the Federal Service Impasses Panel.

Regional Offices—Federal Labor Relations Authority

City/Address	Director	Telephone
Atlanta, GA (Suite 701, 285 Peachtree Ctr. Ave., 30303–1270)	Richard S. Jones, *Acting*	404–331–5300
Boston, MA (Suite 472, Thomas P. O'Neill Federal Bldg., 10 Causeway St., 02222).	Philip T. Roberts	671–565–5100
Chicago, IL (Suite 1150, 55 W. Monroe, 60603–9729)	Peter A. Sutton	312–886–3465
Dallas, TX (Suite 926, LB–107, 525 S. Griffin St., 75202–1906)	James Petrucci	214–767–6266
Denver, CO (Suite 100, 1244 Speer Blvd., 80204–3581)	Matthew Jarvinen	303–844–5224
San Francisco, CA (Suite 220, 901 Market St., 94103–1791)	Gerald M. Cole	415–356–5000
Washington, DC (2d Fl., 1400 K St. NW., 20424-0001)	Robert P. Hunter	202–357–6029

Sources of Information

Employment Employment inquiries and applications may be sent to the Human Resources Division. Phone, 202–218–7963. Internet, www.flra.gov/29-jobs.html.

Public Information and Publications
The Authority will assist in arranging reproduction of documents and ordering transcripts of hearings. Requests for publications should be submitted to the Director, Case Control and Legal Publications. Phone, 202–218–7780. Internet, www.flra.gov.

For further information, contact the Office of the Executive Director, Federal Labor Relations Authority, 1400 K Street NW., Washington, DC 20005. Phone, 202–218–7949. Email, flraexecutivedirector@flra.gov. Internet, www.flra.gov.

FEDERAL MARITIME COMMISSION

800 North Capitol Street NW., Washington, DC 20573–0001
Phone, 202–523–5707. Internet, www.fmc.gov.

CHAIRMAN	RICHARD A. LIDINSKY, JR.
COMMISSIONERS	JOSEPH E. BRENNAN, REBECCA F. DYE, (2 VACANCIES)
General Counsel	PETER J. KING
Secretary	KAREN V. GREGORY
Director, Consumer Affairs and Dispute Resolution Services	RONALD D. MURPHY
Administrative Law Judge	CLAY G. GUTHRIDGE
Director, Office of Equal Employment Opportunity	KEITH I. GILMORE
Inspector General	ADAM R. TRZECIAK
Director, Office of Administration	(VACANCY)
Director, Office of Operations	AUSTIN L. SCHMITT
Director, Bureau of Certification and Licensing	SANDRA L. KUSUMOTO
Director, Bureau of Enforcement	VERN W. HILL
Director, Bureau of Trade Analysis	FLORENCE A. CARR

The Federal Maritime Commission regulates the waterborne foreign commerce of the United States. It ensures that U.S. oceanborne trades are open to all on fair and equitable terms and protects against concerted activities and unlawful practices.

The Federal Maritime Commission was established by Reorganization Plan No. 7 of 1961 (46 U.S.C. 301–307), effective August 12, 1961. It is an independent agency that regulates shipping under the following statutes: the Shipping Act of 1984, as amended (46 U.S.C. 40101–41309); Section 19 of the Merchant Marine Act, 1920 (46 U.S.C. 42101–42109); the Foreign Shipping Practices Act of 1988 (46 U.S.C. 42301–42307); and the act of November 6, 1966 (46 U.S.C. 44101–44106).

Activities

Agreements The Commission reviews agreements by and among ocean common carriers and/or marine terminal operators, filed under section 5 of the Shipping Act of 1984, for statutory compliance as well as for likely impact on competition. It also monitors activities under all effective agreements for compliance with the provisions of law and its rules, orders, and regulations.

Tariffs The Commission monitors and prescribes requirements to ensure accessibility and accuracy of electronic tariff publications of common carriers engaged in the foreign commerce of the United States. Special permission applications may be submitted for relief from statutory and/or Commission tariff requirements.

Service Contracts The Commission receives and reviews filings of confidential service contracts between shippers and ocean common carriers. The Commission also monitors publication of certain essential terms of those service contracts.

Non-Vessel-Operating Common Carrier Service Arrangements The Commission receives and reviews service arrangements entered into by non-vessel-operating common carriers and their customers. Cargo moving under these service arrangements are exempt from the tariff publication and adherence requirements of the Shipping Act, on the

FEDERAL MARITIME COMMISSION

COMMISSIONER · COMMISSIONER · CHAIRMAN · COMMISSIONER · COMMISSIONER

OFFICE OF EQUAL EMPLOYMENT OPPORTUNITY

OFFICE OF THE INSPECTOR GENERAL

OFFICE OF THE SECRETARY

OFFICE OF OPERATIONS

OFFICE OF ADMINISTRATION

OFFICE OF THE GENERAL COUNSEL

OFFICE OF ADMINISTRATIVE LAW JUDGES

OFFICE OF CONSUMER AFFAIRS AND DISPUTE RESOLUTION SERVICES

BUREAU OF CERTIFICATION AND LICENSING

BUREAU OF TRADE ANALYSIS

BUREAU OF ENFORCEMENT

AREA REPRESENTATIVES — HOUSTON, LOS ANGELES, NEW ORLEANS, NEW YORK, SEATTLE, SOUTH FLORIDA

OFFICE OF FINANCIAL MANAGEMENT

OFFICE OF HUMAN RESOURCES

OFFICE OF INFORMATION TECHNOLOGY

OFFICE OF MANAGEMENT SERVICES

condition that the service arrangements must be filed with the Commission.

Licenses The Commission issues licenses to those persons and entities in the United States who wish to carry out the business of providing freight forwarding services and nonvessel-operating common carrier services.

Passenger Indemnity The Commission administers the passenger indemnity provisions of the act of November 6, 1966, which require shipowners and operators to obtain certificates of financial responsibility to pay judgments for personal injury or death or to refund fares in the event of nonperformance of voyages.

Complaints The Commission reviews alleged or suspected violations of the shipping statutes and rules and regulations of the Commission and may take administrative action to institute formal proceedings, to refer matters to other governmental agencies, or to bring about voluntary agreement between the parties.

Formal Adjudicatory Procedures The Commission conducts formal investigations and hearings on its own motion and adjudicates formal complaints in accordance with the Administrative Procedure Act (5 U.S.C. note prec. 551).

Alternative Dispute Resolution The Commission reviews informal complaints and attempts to assist parties in resolving disputes. Mediation and other dispute resolution services are available in order to assist parties in achieving a more acceptable resolution to a dispute at less cost than may be possible in litigation. These services are available before and after the commencement of litigation.

The Commission also provides an informal process to adjudicate certain complaints involving less than $50,000 in damages.

Rulemaking The Commission promulgates rules and regulations to interpret, enforce, and ensure compliance with shipping and related statutes by common carriers and other persons subject to the Commission's jurisdiction.

Investigation and Economic Analyses The Commission prescribes and administers programs to ensure compliance with the provisions of the shipping statutes. These programs include: education and outreach activities; the collection of information relating to field investigation of activities and practices of ocean common carriers, terminal operators, agreements among ocean common carriers and/or marine terminal operators, ocean transportation intermediaries, passenger vessel operators, and other persons subject to the shipping statutes; and rate analyses, studies, and economic reviews of current and prospective trade conditions, including the extent and nature of competition in various trade areas.

International Affairs The Commission conducts investigations of foreign governmental and carrier practices that adversely affect the U.S. shipping trade. In consultation with other executive agencies, the Commission takes action to effect the elimination of discriminatory practices on the part of foreign governments against shipping in the United States foreign trade, and to achieve comity between the United States and its trading partners.

Area Representatives—Federal Maritime Commission

Area	Address/Phone/Fax/Email	Representative
Los Angeles	839 S. Beacon St., Rm. 320, San Pedro, CA 90733–0230.	
	Phone, 310–514–4905. Fax, 310–514–3931. Email, oclark@fmc.gov	Oliver E. Clark
South Florida	3475 Sheridan St., Hollywood, FL 33029–3659.	
	Phone, 954–963–5362. Fax, 954–963–5630. Email, amargolis@fmc.gov	Andrew Margolis
	Phone, 954–963–5284. Fax, 954–963–5630. Email, emintz@fmc.gov	Eric O. Mintz
New Orleans	1515 Poydras St., New Orleans, LA 70112.	
	Phone, 504–589–6662. Fax, 504–589–6663. Email, bjohnson@fmc.gov	Bruce N. Johnson, Sr.
New York	JFK Int'l Airport, Bldg. 75, Rm. 205B, Jamaica, NY 11430.	
	Phone, 718–553–2228. Fax, 718–553–2229. Email, emingione@fmc.gov	Emanuel J. Mingione
	Phone, 718–553–2223. Fax, 718–553–2229. Email, jcastellano@fmc.gov	Joseph A. Castellano
Seattle	7 S. Nevada St., Suite 100, Seattle, WA 98134.	
	Phone, 206–553–0221. Fax, 206–553–0222. Email, mmoneck@fmc.gov	Michael A. Moneck
Houston	650 N. Sam Houston Pkwy, Suite 230, Houston, TX 77060.	

Area	Address/Phone/Fax/Email	Representative
	Phone, 281–591–6088. Fax, 281–591–6099. Email, dzezima@fmc.gov	Debra A. Zezima

Sources of Information

Electronic Access Information about the Federal Maritime Commission is available in electronic form through the Internet at www.fmc.gov.

Employment Employment inquiries may be directed to the Office of Human Resources, Federal Maritime Commission, 800 North Capitol Street NW., Washington, DC 20573–0001. Phone, 202–523–5773.

Consumer Affairs and Dispute Resolution Services Phone, 202–523–5807. Email, complaints@fmc.gov.

Publications The *Performance and Accountability Report (2008)* and the *FY08 Management Discussion and Analysis Report* are recent publications of the Federal Maritime Commission.

For further information, contact the Office of the Secretary, Federal Maritime Commission, 800 North Capitol Street NW., Washington, DC 20573–0001. Phone, 202–523–5725. Fax, 202–523–0014. Internet, www.fmc.gov. Email, secretary@fmc.gov.

FEDERAL MEDIATION AND CONCILIATION SERVICE

2100 K Street NW., Washington, DC 20427
Phone, 202–606–8100. Internet, www.fmcs.gov.

DIRECTOR   SCOT L. BECKENBAUGH, *Acting*

The Federal Mediation and Conciliation Service assists labor and management in resolving disputes in collective bargaining contract negotiation through voluntary mediation and arbitration services.

The Federal Mediation and Conciliation Service (FMCS) was created by the Labor Management Relations Act, 1947 (29 U.S.C. 172). The Director is appointed by the President with the advice and consent of the Senate.

Activities

FMCS helps prevent disruptions in the flow of interstate commerce caused by labor-management disputes by providing mediators to assist disputing parties in the resolution of their differences. Mediators have no law enforcement authority and rely wholly on persuasive techniques.

FMCS offers its facilities in labor-management disputes to any industry affecting interstate commerce with employees represented by a union, either upon its own motion or at the request of one or more of the parties to the dispute, whenever in its judgment such dispute threatens to cause a substantial interruption of commerce. The Labor Management Relations Act requires that parties to a labor contract must file a dispute notice if agreement is not reached 30 days in advance of a contract termination or reopening date. The notice must be filed with FMCS and the appropriate State or local mediation agency. FMCS is required to avoid the mediation of disputes that would have only a minor effect on interstate commerce if State or other conciliation services are available to the parties.

Mediation Efforts of FMCS mediators are directed toward the establishment of sound and stable labor-management relations on a continuing basis, thereby helping to reduce the incidence of work stoppages. The mediator's basic function is to encourage and promote better day-to-day relations between labor and management, so that issues arising in negotiations may be faced as problems to be settled through mutual effort rather than issues in dispute.

Arbitration FMCS, on the joint request of employers and unions, will also assist in the selection of arbitrators from a roster of private citizens who are qualified as neutrals to adjudicate matters in dispute.

For further information, contact the Office of Arbitration Services. Phone, 202–606–5111.

For further information, contact the Public Affairs Office, Federal Mediation and Conciliation Service, 2100 K Street NW., Washington, DC 20427. Phone, 202–606–8100. Internet, www.fmcs.gov.

FEDERAL MINE SAFETY AND HEALTH REVIEW COMMISSION

601 New Jersey Avenue NW., Suite 9500, Washington, DC 20001–2021
Phone, 202–434–9900. Email, fmshrc@fmshrc.gov. Internet, www.fmshrc.gov.

CHAIRMAN	MARY LUCILLE JORDAN
COMMISSIONERS	ROBERT F. COHEN, JR., MICHAEL F. DUFFY, MICHAEL G. YOUNG, (VACANCY)
Chief Administrative Law Judge	ROBERT J. LESNICK
General Counsel	MICHAEL A. MCCORD
Executive Director	LISA M. BOYD

The Federal Mine Safety and Health Review Commission ensures compliance with occupational safety and health standards in the Nation's surface and underground coal, metal, and nonmetal mines.

The Federal Mine Safety and Health Review Commission is an independent, adjudicative agency established by the Federal Mine Safety and Health Act of 1977 (30 U.S.C. 801 *et seq.*), as amended. It provides administrative trial and appellate review of legal disputes arising from enforcement actions taken by the Department of Labor.

The Commission consists of five members who are appointed by the President with the advice and consent of the Senate and who serve staggered 6-year terms. The Chairman is appointed from among the Commissioners by the President.

The Commission and its Office of Administrative Law Judges are charged with deciding cases brought before it by the Mine Safety and Health

Administration, mine operators, and miners or their representatives. These cases generally involve review of the Administration's enforcement actions, including citations, mine-closure orders, and proposals for civil penalties issued for violations of the act or the mandatory safety and health standards promulgated by the Secretary of Labor. The Commission also has jurisdiction over discrimination complaints filed by miners or their representatives in connection with their safety and health, complaints for compensation filed on behalf of miners idled as a result of mine closure orders issued by the Administration, and disputes over mine emergency response plans.

FEDERAL MINE SAFETY AND HEALTH REVIEW COMMISSION

COMMISSIONER

COMMISSIONER

CHAIRMAN

COMMISSIONER

COMMISSIONER

CHIEF ADMINISTRATIVE LAW JUDGE

GENERAL COUNSEL

EXECUTIVE DIRECTOR

Activities

Cases brought before the Commission are assigned to the Office of Administrative Law Judges, and hearings are conducted pursuant to the requirements of the Administrative Procedure Act (5 U.S.C. 554, 556) and the Commission's procedural rules (29 CFR 2700).

A judge's decision becomes a final but nonprecedential order of the Commission 40 days after issuance unless the Commission has directed the case for review in response to a petition or on its own motion. If a review is conducted, a decision of the Commission becomes final 30 days after issuance unless a party adversely affected seeks review in the U.S. Circuit Court of Appeals for the District of Columbia or the Circuit within which the mine subject to the litigation is located.

As far as practicable, hearings are held at locations convenient to the affected mines. In addition to its Washington, DC, offices, the Office of Administrative Law Judges maintains an office in the Colonnade Center, Room 280, 1244 Speer Boulevard, Denver, CO 80204.

Sources of Information

Commission decisions are published bimonthly and are available through the Superintendent of Documents, U.S. Government Printing Office, Washington, DC 20402. The Commission's Web site includes recent decisions, a searchable database of previous decisions, procedural rules, audio recordings of recent public meetings, and other pertinent information.

Requests for Commission records should be submitted in accordance with the Commission's Freedom of Information Act regulations. Other information, including Commission rules of procedure and brochures explaining the Commission's functions, is available from the Executive Director, Federal Mine Safety and Health Review Commission, 601 New Jersey Avenue NW., Suite 9500, Washington, DC 20001–2021. Internet, www.fmshrc.gov. Email, fmshrc@fmshrc.gov.

For information on filing requirements, the status of cases before the Commission, or docket information, contact the Office of General Counsel or the Docket Office, Federal Mine Safety and Health Review Commission, 601 New Jersey Avenue NW., Suite 9500, Washington, DC 20001. Email, fmshrc@fmshrc.gov.

For further information, contact the Executive Director, Federal Mine Safety and Health Review Commission, 601 New Jersey Avenue NW., Suite 9500, Washington DC 20001–2021. Phone, 202–434–9905. Fax, 202–434–9906. Internet, www.fmshrc.gov. Email, fmshrc@fmshrc.gov.

FEDERAL RESERVE SYSTEM

Board of Governors of the Federal Reserve System
Twentieth Street and Constitution Avenue NW., Washington, DC 20551
Phone, 202–452–3000. Internet, www.federalreserve.gov.

Board of Governors

CHAIRMAN   BEN S. BERNANKE
VICE CHAIRMAN   DONALD L. KOHN
Members   ELIZABETH DUKE, DANIEL K. TARULLO, KEVIN M. WARSH, (2 VACANCIES)

Staff:

Director, Division of Board Members	MICHELLE A. SMITH
Congressional Liaison	LARICKE D. BLANCHARD
General Counsel	SCOTT G. ALVAREZ
Secretary	JENNIFER J. JOHNSON
Director, Division of Banking Supervision and Regulation	ROGER T. COLE
Director, Division of Consumer and Community Affairs	SANDRA F. BRAUNSTEIN
Director, Division of Federal Reserve Bank Operations and Payment Systems	LOUISE L. ROSEMAN
Director, Division of Information Technology	MAUREEN HANNAN
Director, Division of International Finance	D. NATHAN SHEETS
Director, Management Division	H. FAY PETERS
Director, Division of Monetary Affairs	BRIAN MADIGAN
Director, Division of Research and Statistics	DAVID J. STOCKTON
Staff Director, Office of Staff Director for Management	STEPHEN R. MALPHRUS
Inspector General	ELIZABETH A. COLEMAN

Officers of the Federal Reserve Banks

Federal Reserve Bank Chairmen:

Boston, MA	LISA M. LYNCH
New York, NY	STEPHEN FRIEDMAN
Philadelphia, PA	WILLIAM F. HECHT
Cleveland, OH	TANNY B. CRANE
Richmond, VA	LEMUEL E. LEWIS
Atlanta, GA	D. SCOTT DAVIS
Chicago, IL	JOHN A. CANNING, JR.
St. Louis, MO	STEVEN H. LIPSTEIN
Minneapolis, MN	JAMES J. HYNES
Kansas City, MO	LU M. CORDOVA
Dallas, TX	JAMES T. HACKETT
San Francisco, CA	T. GARY ROGERS

Presidents:

Atlanta, GA	DENNIS P. LOCKHART
Boston, MA	ERIC S. ROSENGREN
Chicago, IL	CHARLES L. EVANS
Cleveland, OH	SANDRA PIANALTO
Dallas, TX	RICHARD W. FISHER
Kansas City, MO	THOMAS M. HOENIG
Minneapolis, MN	GARY H. STERN
New York, NY	WILLIAM C. DUDLEY
Philadelphia, PA	CHARLES L. POSSER
Richmond, VA	JEFFERY M. LACKER
St. Louis, MO	JAMES B. BULLARD
San Francisco, CA	JANET L. YELLEN

Federal Open Market Committee

Chairman	BEN S. BERNANKE
Vice Chairman	WILLIAM C. DUDLEY
Members	CHARLES L. EVANS, DONALD L. KOHN, JEFFREY M. LACKER, DENNIS P. LOCKHART, KEVIN M. WARSH, JANET L. YELLEN, (VACANCY)

Staff:

Secretary and Economist	BRIAN MADIGAN
Deputy Secretary	DEBORAH DANKER
Assistant Secretaries	DAVID SKIDMORE, MICHELLE SMITH
General Counsel	SCOTT G. ALVAREZ
Economists	D. NATHAN SHEETS, DAVID J. STOCKTON

Federal Advisory Councils:

Secretary, Federal Advisory Council	WILLIAM DOWNE
Chairman, Consumer Advisory Council	EDNA R. SAWADY
President, Thrift Institutions Advisory Council	CURTIS L. HAGE

The Federal Reserve System, the central bank of the United States, is charged with administering and formulating the Nation's credit and monetary policy. Through its supervisory and regulatory banking functions, the Federal Reserve maintains the safety and soundness of the Nation's economy, responding to the Nation's domestic and international financial needs and objectives.

The Federal Reserve System was established by the Federal Reserve Act (12 U.S.C. 221), approved December 23, 1913. Its major responsibility is in the execution of monetary policy. It also performs other functions, such as the transfer of funds, handling Government deposits and debt issues, supervising and regulating banks, and acting as lender of last resort.

It is the responsibility of the Federal Reserve System to contribute to the strength and vitality of the U.S. economy. By influencing the lending and investing activities of depository institutions and the cost and availability of money and credit, the Federal Reserve System helps promote the full use of human and capital resources, the growth of productivity, relatively stable prices, and equilibrium in the Nation's international balance of payments. Through its supervisory and regulatory banking functions, the Federal Reserve System helps maintain a commercial banking system that is responsive to the Nation's financial needs and objectives.

The System consists of the Board of Governors in Washington, DC; the 12 Federal Reserve Banks and their 25 branches and other facilities situated throughout the country; the Federal Open Market Committee; the Federal Advisory Council; the Consumer Advisory Council; the Thrift Institutions Advisory Council; and the Nation's financial institutions, including commercial banks, savings and loan associations, mutual savings banks, and credit unions.

Board of Governors

The Board is composed of seven members appointed by the President with the advice and consent of the Senate. The Chairman of the Board of Governors is a member of the National Advisory Council on International Monetary and Financial Policies. The Board determines general monetary, credit, and operating policies for the System as a whole and formulates the rules and regulations necessary to carry out the purposes of the Federal Reserve Act. The Board's principal duties consist of monitoring credit conditions; supervising the Federal Reserve Banks, member banks, and bank holding companies; and regulating the implementation of certain consumer credit protection laws.

Power To Influence Credit Conditions The Board has the power, within statutory limitations, to fix the requirements concerning reserves to be maintained by depository institutions on transaction accounts or nonpersonal time deposits. The Board of Governors reviews and determines the discount rate charged by the Federal Reserve Banks. For the purpose of preventing excessive use of credit for the purchase or carrying of securities, the Board is authorized to regulate the amount of credit that may be initially extended and subsequently maintained on any security (with certain exceptions).

Supervision of Federal Reserve Banks

The Board is authorized to make examinations of the Federal Reserve Banks, to require statements and reports from such Banks, to supervise the issue and retirement of Federal Reserve notes, to require the establishment or discontinuance of branches of Reserve Banks, and to exercise supervision over all relationships and transactions of those Banks with foreign branches.

Supervision of Bank Holding Companies

The Federal Reserve has primary responsibility for supervising and regulating the activities of bank holding companies. The main objectives of this activity are to control the expansion of bank holding companies by avoiding the creation of monopoly or restraining trade in banking, and to limit the expansion of bank holding companies to those nonbanking activities that are closely related to banking, thus maintaining a separation between banking and commerce. A company that seeks to become a bank holding company must obtain the prior approval of the Federal Reserve. Any company that qualifies as a bank holding company must register with the Federal Reserve System and file reports with the System.

Supervision of Banking Organizations

The Federal Reserve is responsible for the supervision and regulation of domestic and international activities of U.S. banking organizations. It supervises State-chartered banks that are members of the System, all bank holding companies, and Edge Act and agreement corporations (corporations chartered to engage in international banking).

The Board has jurisdiction over the admission of State banks and trust companies to membership in the Federal Reserve System, the termination of membership of such banks, the establishment of branches by such banks, and the approval of bank mergers and consolidations where the resulting institution will be a State member bank. It receives copies of condition reports submitted to the Federal Reserve Banks. It has power to examine all member banks and the affiliates of member banks and to require condition reports from them. It has authority to require periodic and other public disclosure of information with respect to an equity security of a State member bank that is held by 500 or more persons. It establishes minimum standards with respect to installation, maintenance, and operation of security devices and procedures by State member banks. Also, it has authority to issue cease-and-desist orders in connection with violations of law or unsafe or unsound banking practices by State member banks and to remove directors or officers of such banks in certain circumstances, and it may suspend member banks from the use of the credit facilities of the Federal Reserve System for making undue use of bank credit for speculative purposes or for any other purpose inconsistent with the maintenance of sound credit conditions.

The Board may grant authority to member banks to establish branches in foreign countries or dependencies or insular possessions of the United States, to invest in the stocks of banks or corporations engaged in international or foreign banking, or to invest in foreign banks. It also charters, regulates, and supervises certain corporations that engage in foreign or international banking and financial activities.

The Board is authorized to issue general regulations permitting interlocking relationships in certain circumstances between member banks and organizations dealing in securities or between member banks and other banks.

The Board prescribes regulations to ensure a meaningful disclosure by lenders of credit terms so that consumers will be able to compare more readily the various credit terms available and will be informed about rules governing credit cards, including their potential liability for unauthorized use.

The Board has authority to impose reserve requirements and interest rate ceilings on branches and agencies of foreign banks in the United States, to grant loans to them, to provide them access to Federal Reserve services, and to limit their interstate banking activities.

Federal Open Market Committee

The Federal Open Market Committee is comprised of the Board of Governors and five of the presidents of the Reserve Banks. The Chairman of the Board of Governors is traditionally the Chairman of the Committee. The president of the Federal Reserve Bank of New York serves as a permanent member of the Committee. Four of the twelve Reserve Bank presidents rotate annually as members of the Committee.

Open market operations of the Reserve Banks are conducted under regulations adopted by the Committee and pursuant to specific policy directives issued by the Committee, which meets in Washington, DC, at frequent intervals. Purchases and sales of securities in the open market are undertaken to supply bank reserves to support the credit and money needed for long-term economic growth, to offset cyclical economic swings, and to accommodate seasonal demands of businesses and consumers for money and credit. These operations are carried out principally in U.S. Government obligations, but they also include purchases and sales of Federal agency obligations. All operations are conducted in New York, where the primary markets for these securities are located; the Federal Reserve Bank of New York executes transactions for the Federal Reserve System Open Market Account in carrying out these operations.

Under the Committee's direction, the Federal Reserve Bank of New York also undertakes transactions in foreign currencies for the Federal Reserve System Open Market Account. The purposes of these operations include helping to safeguard the value of the dollar in international exchange markets and facilitating growth in international liquidity in accordance with the needs of an expanding world economy.

Federal Reserve Banks

The 12 Federal Reserve Banks are located in Atlanta, GA; Boston, MA; Chicago, IL; Cleveland, OH; Dallas, TX; Kansas City, MO; Minneapolis, MN; New York, NY; Philadelphia, PA; Richmond, VA; San Francisco, CA; and St. Louis, MO. Branch banks are located in Baltimore, MD; Birmingham, AL; Buffalo, NY; Charlotte, NC; Cincinnati, OH; Denver, CO; Detroit, MI; El Paso, TX; Helena, MT; Houston, TX; Jacksonville, FL; Little Rock, AR; Los Angeles, CA; Louisville, KY; Memphis, TN; Miami, FL; Nashville, TN; New Orleans, LA; Oklahoma City, OK; Omaha, NE; Pittsburgh, PA; Portland, OR; Salt Lake City, UT; San Antonio, TX; and Seattle, WA.

Reserves on Deposit The Reserve Banks receive and hold on deposit the reserve or clearing account deposits of depository institutions. These banks are permitted to count their vault cash as part of their required reserve.

Extensions of Credit The Federal Reserve is required to open its discount window to any depository institution that is subject to Federal Reserve reserve requirements on transaction accounts or nonpersonal time deposits. Discount window credit provides for Federal Reserve lending to eligible depository institutions under two basic programs. One is the adjustment credit program; the other supplies more extended credit for certain limited purposes.

Short-term adjustment credit is the primary type of Federal Reserve credit. It is available to help borrowers meet temporary requirements for funds. Borrowers are not permitted to use adjustment credit to take advantage of any spread between the discount rate and market rates.

Extended credit is provided through three programs designed to assist depository institutions in meeting longer term needs for funds. One provides seasonal credit—for periods running up to 9 months—to smaller depository institutions that lack access to market funds. A second program assists institutions that experience special difficulties arising from exceptional circumstances or practices involving only that institution. Finally, in cases where more general liquidity strains are affecting a broad range of depository institutions—such as those whose portfolios consist primarily of longer term assets—credit may be provided to address the problems of particular institutions being affected by the general situation.

Currency Issue The Reserve Banks issue Federal Reserve notes, which constitute the bulk of money in circulation. These notes are obligations of the United States and are a prior lien upon the assets of the issuing Federal Reserve Bank. They are issued against a pledge by the Reserve Bank with the Federal Reserve agent of collateral security including gold certificates, paper discounted or purchased by the Bank, and direct obligations of the United States.

Other Powers The Reserve Banks are empowered to act as clearinghouses and as collecting agents for depository institutions in the collection of checks and other instruments. They are also authorized to act as depositories and fiscal agents of the United States and to exercise other banking functions specified in the Federal Reserve Act. They perform a number of important functions in connection with the issue and redemption of United States Government securities.

Sources of Information

Employment Written inquiries regarding employment should be addressed to the Director, Division of Personnel, Board of Governors of the Federal Reserve System, Washington, DC 20551.

Procurement Firms seeking business with the Board should address their inquiries to the Director, Division of Support Services, Board of Governors of the Federal Reserve System, Washington, DC 20551.

Publications Among the publications issued by the Board are *The Federal Reserve System—Purposes and Functions,* and a series of pamphlets including *Guide to Business Credit and the Equal Credit Opportunity Act; Consumer Handbook; Making Deposits: When Will Your Money Be Available;* and *When Your Home Is On the Line: What You Should Know About Home Equity Lines of Credit.* Copies of these pamphlets are available free of charge. Information regarding publications may be obtained in Room MP–510 (Martin Building) of the Board's headquarters. Phone, 202–452–3244.

Reading Room A reading room where persons may inspect records that are available to the public is located in Room B–1122 at the Board's headquarters, Twentieth Street and Constitution Avenue NW., Washington, DC 20551. Information regarding the availability of records may be obtained by calling 202–452–3684.

For further information, contact the Office of Public Affairs, Board of Governors, Federal Reserve System, Washington, DC 20551. Phone, 202–452–3204 or 202–452–3215. Internet, www.federalreserve.gov.

FEDERAL RETIREMENT THRIFT INVESTMENT BOARD

1250 H Street NW., Washington, DC 20005
Phone, 202–942–1600. Fax, 202–942–1676. Internet, www.tsp.gov.

CHAIRMAN	ANDREW M. SAUL
Members	TERRENCE A. DUFFY, THOMAS A. FINK, ALEJANDRO M. SANCHEZ, GORDON J. WHITING
Officials:	
Executive Director	GREGORY T. LONG
Chief Investment Officer	TRACEY A. RAY

Participant Services Director	PAMELA-JEANNE MORAN
Director of External Affairs	THOMAS J. TRABUCCO
General Counsel	THOMAS K. EMSWILER
Chief Information Officer	MARK A. HAGERTY
Chief Financial Officer	JAMES B. PETRICK
Director of Research and Strategic Planning	RENEE WILDER

The Federal Retirement Thrift Investment Board administers the Thrift Savings Plan, which provides Federal employees the opportunity to save for additional retirement security.

The Federal Retirement Thrift Investment Board was established as an independent agency by the Federal Employees' Retirement System Act of 1986 (5 U.S.C. 8351 and 8401–79). The act vests responsibility for the agency in six named fiduciaries: the five Board members and the Executive Director. The five members of the Board, one of whom is designated as Chairman, are appointed by the President with the advice and consent of the Senate and serve on the Board on a part-time basis. The members appoint the Executive Director, who is responsible for the management of the agency and the Plan.

Activities

The Thrift Savings Plan is a tax-deferred, defined contribution plan that was established as one of the three parts of the Federal Employees' Retirement System. For employees covered under the System, savings accumulated through the Plan make an important addition to the retirement benefits provided by Social Security and the System's Basic Annuity. Civil Service Retirement System employees and members of the Uniformed Services may also take advantage of the Plan to supplement their annuities.

The Board operates the Thrift Savings Plan and manages the investments of the Thrift Savings Fund solely for the benefit of participants and their beneficiaries. As part of these responsibilities, the Board maintains an account for each Plan participant, makes loans, purchases annuity contracts, and provides for the payment of benefits.

For further information, contact the Director of External Affairs, Federal Retirement Thrift Investment Board, 1250 H Street NW., Washington, DC 20005. Phone, 202–942–1640. Internet, www.tsp.gov.

FEDERAL TRADE COMMISSION

600 Pennsylvania Avenue NW., Washington, DC 20580
Phone, 202–326–2222. Internet, www.ftc.gov.

CHAIRMAN	JONATHAN LEIBOWITZ
COMMISSIONERS	PAMELA JONES HARBOUR, WILLIAM E. KOVACIC, J. THOMAS ROSCH, (VACANCY)
Chief of Staff	JONI LUPOVITZ
Executive Director	CHARLES SCHNEIDER
Chief Information Officer	STANLEY LOWE
Chief Financial Officer	STEVEN FISHER
Director, Bureau of Competition	RICH FEINSTEIN
Director, Bureau of Consumer Protection	DAVID VLADECK
Director, Bureau of Economics	JOE FARRELL

General Counsel	DAVID C. SHONKA, *Acting*
Director, Office of Congressional Relations	JEANNE BUMPUS
Director, Office of International Affairs	RANDOLPH W. TRITELL
Director, Office of Public Affairs	CLAUDIA FARRELL, *Acting*
Director, Office of Policy Planning	SUSAN DeSANTI
Secretary of the Commission	DONALD S. CLARK
Chief Administrative Law Judge	D. MICHAEL CHAPPELL
Inspector General	JOHN SEEBA

[For the Federal Trade Commission statement of organization, see the *Code of Federal Regulations,* Title 16, Part 0]

The Federal Trade Commission has jurisdiction to enhance consumer welfare and protect competition in broad sectors of the economy. The Commission enforces the laws that prohibit business practices that are anticompetitive, deceptive, or unfair to consumers; promotes informed consumer choice and public understanding of the competitive process; and seeks to accomplish its mission without impeding legitimate business activity.

The Federal Trade Commission was established in 1914 by the Federal Trade Commission Act (15 U.S.C. 41–58). The Commission is composed of five members appointed by the President, with the advice and consent of the Senate, for a term of 7 years. Not more than three of the Commissioners may be members of the same political party. One Commissioner is designated by the President as Chairman of the Commission and is responsible for its administrative management.

Activities

The Commission's principal functions include the following:

—promoting competition through the prevention of general trade restraints such as price-fixing agreements, boycotts, illegal combinations of competitors, and other unfair methods of competition;

—stopping corporate mergers, acquisitions, or joint ventures that may substantially lessen competition or tend to create a monopoly;

—preventing pricing discrimination, exclusive dealing, tying arrangements, and discrimination among competing customers by sellers;

—preventing interlocking directorates or officers' positions that may restrain competition;

—preventing the dissemination of false or deceptive advertisements of consumer products and services as well as other unfair or deceptive practices;

—promoting electronic commerce by stopping fraud on the Internet and working with other domestic and foreign agencies to develop and promote policies to safeguard online privacy of personal information;

—protecting the privacy of consumers' personal information to prevent illegal or unwanted use of financial or other data;

—stopping various fraudulent telemarketing schemes and protecting consumers from abusive, deceptive, or unwanted telephone tactics; and enforcing the National Do Not Call Registry;

—ensuring truthful labeling of textile, wool, and fur products;

—requiring creditors to disclose in writing certain cost information, such as the annual percentage rate, before consumers enter into credit transactions, as required by the Truth in Lending Act;

—protecting consumers against circulation of inaccurate or obsolete credit reports and ensuring that credit bureaus, consumer reporting agencies, credit grantors, and bill collectors exercise their responsibilities in a manner that is fair and equitable;

—educating consumers and businesses about their rights and responsibilities under Commission rules and regulations; and

—gathering factual data concerning economic and business conditions and

FEDERAL TRADE COMMISSION

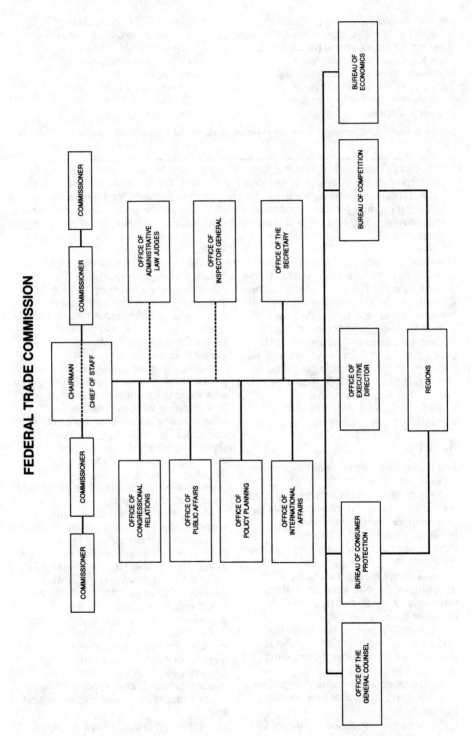

making it available to the Congress, the President, and the public.

Competition   One of the two major missions of the Commission is to encourage competition in the American economy. The Commission seeks to prevent unfair practices that undermine competition and attempts to prevent mergers or acquisitions of companies if the result may be to lessen competition. Under some circumstances, companies planning to merge must first give notice to the Commission and the Department of Justice's Antitrust Division and provide certain information concerning the operations of the companies involved.

The Commission also enforces the provisions of the Robinson-Patman Act, a part of the Clayton Act prohibiting companies from discriminating among their customers in terms of price or other services provided.

Consumer Protection   Consumer protection is the second of the two main missions of the Commission. The Commission, therefore, works to accomplish the following:

—increase the usefulness of advertising by ensuring that it is truthful and not misleading;

—reduce instances of fraudulent, deceptive, or unfair marketing practices;

—prevent creditors from using unlawful practices when granting credit, maintaining credit information, collecting debts, and operating credit systems; and

—educate the public about Commission activities.

The Commission initiates investigations in areas of concern to consumers. It has issued and enforces many trade regulation rules in areas important to consumers, including health and nutrition claims in advertising; environmental advertising and labeling; general advertising issues; health care, telemarketing and electronic commerce, business opportunity, and franchise and investment fraud; mortgage lending and discrimination; enforcement of Commission orders; and enforcement of credit statutes and trade regulation rules.

Competition and Consumer Advocacy
To promote competition, consumer protection, and the efficient allocation of resources, the Commission also advocates consumer interest in a competitive marketplace by encouraging courts, legislatures, and government administrative bodies to consider efficiency and consumer welfare as important elements in their deliberations. The Commission uses these opportunities to support procompetitive means of regulating the Nation's economy, including the elimination of anticompetitive restrictions that reduce the welfare of consumers and the implementation of regulatory programs that protect the public and preserve as much as possible the discipline of competitive markets.

Compliance Activities   Through systematic and continuous review, the Commission obtains and maintains compliance with its cease-and-desist orders. All respondents against whom such orders have been issued are required to file reports with the Commission to substantiate their compliance. In the event compliance is not obtained, or if the order is subsequently violated, civil penalty proceedings may be instituted.

Cooperative Procedures   In carrying out the statutory directive to prevent unfair methods of competition or unfair or deceptive practices, the Commission makes extensive use of voluntary and cooperative procedures. Through these procedures, business and industry may obtain authoritative guidance and a substantial measure of certainty as to what they may do under the laws administered by the Commission.

The Commission issues administrative interpretations in plain language of laws enforced by the Commission. Guides provide the basis for voluntary abandonment of unlawful practices by members of a particular industry or by an industry in general. Failure to comply with the guides may result in corrective action by the Commission under applicable statutory provisions.

Enforcement   The Commission's law enforcement work falls into two general categories: actions to foster voluntary compliance with the law, and formal administrative or Federal court litigation leading to mandatory orders against offenders.

Compliance with the law may be obtained through voluntary and cooperative action by private companies in response to nonbinding staff advice, formal advisory opinions by the Commission, and guides and policy statements delineating legal requirements as to particular business practices.

Formal litigation is instituted either by issuing an administrative complaint or by filing a Federal district court complaint charging a person, partnership, or corporation with violating one or more of the statutes administered by the Commission. If the charges in an administrative matter are not contested or if the charges are found to be true after an administrative hearing in a contested case, an order may be issued requiring discontinuance of the unlawful practices.

Investigations Investigations by the Commission may originate through complaint by a consumer or a competitor, the Congress, or from Federal, State, or municipal agencies. Also, the Commission itself may initiate an investigation into possible violations of the laws it administers. No formality is required in submitting a complaint. A letter or call giving the facts in detail, accompanied by all supporting evidence in possession of the complaining party, is sufficient. The Commission also maintains electronic complaint systems that are accessible through its Web site.

It is the general policy of the Commission not to disclose the identity of any complainant, except as required by law or Commission rules.

Upon receipt of a complaint, various criteria are applied in determining whether the particular matter should be investigated.

An order issued after an administrative proceeding that requires the respondent to cease and desist or take other corrective action may be appealed. Appeals processes may go as far as the Supreme Court.

In addition to or in lieu of the administrative proceeding initiated by a formal complaint, the Commission may request that a U.S. district court issue a preliminary or permanent injunction to halt the use of allegedly unfair or deceptive practices, to prevent an anticompetitive merger or unfair methods of competition from taking place, or to prevent violations of any statute enforced by the Commission.

Reports The Commission prepares studies of conditions and problems affecting the marketplace. Such reports may be used to inform legislative proposals in response to requests of the Congress and statutory directions, or for the information and guidance of the Commission, the executive branch of the Government, and the public. Such reports have provided the basis for significant legislation and have also led to voluntary changes in the conduct of business, with resulting benefits to the public.

Regional Offices—Federal Trade Commission

Region	Address	Director
East Central (DC, DE, MD, MI, OH, PA, VA, WV)	Suite 200, 1111 Superior Ave., Cleveland, OH 44114	John Mendenhall
Midwest (IA, IL, IN, KS, KY, MN, MO, ND, NE, SD, WI)	Suite 1860, 55 E. Monroe St., Chicago, IL 60603	C. Steven Baker
Northeast (CT, MA, ME, NH, NJ, NY, RI, VT, PR, VI)	Suite 318, One Bowling Green, New York, NY 10004	Leonard Gordon
Northwest (AK, ID, MT, OR, WA, WY)	Suite 2896, 915 2d Ave., Seattle, WA 98174	Charles A. Harwood
Southeast (AL, FL, GA, MS, NC, SC, TN)	Suite 1500, 225 Peachtree St. NE., Atlanta, GA 30303	Bradley Elbein
Southwest (AR, LA, NM, OK, TX)	Suite 2150, 1999 Bryan St., Dallas, TX 75201	Deanya T. Kueckelhan
Western (AZ, CA, CO, HI, NV, UT)	Suite 570, 901 Market St., San Francisco, CA 94103	Jeffrey A. Klurfeld
	Suite 700, 10877 Wilshire Blvd., Los Angeles, CA 90024	

Sources of Information

Contracts and Procurement Persons seeking to do business with the Federal Trade Commission should contact the Assistant Chief Financial Officer for Acquisitions, Federal Trade Commission, Washington, DC 20580. Phone, 202–326–2339. Fax, 202–326–3529. Internet, www.ftc.gov.

Employment Civil service registers are used in filling positions for economists, accountants, investigators, and other professional, administrative, and clerical personnel. The Federal Trade Commission employs a sizable number of attorneys under the excepted appointment procedure. All employment inquiries should be directed to the Director of Human Resources Management, Federal Trade Commission, Washington, DC 20580. Phone, 202–326–2021. Fax, 202–326–2328. Internet, www.ftc.gov.

General Inquiries Persons desiring information on consumer protection or restraint of trade questions, or to register a complaint, should contact the Federal Trade Commission (phone, 202–326–2222 or 877–382–4357) or the nearest regional office. Complaints may also be filed on the Internet at www.ftc.gov.

Publications Consumer and business education publications of the Commission are available through the Consumer Response Center, Federal Trade Commission, Washington, DC 20580. Phone, 877–382–4357. TTY, 866–653–4261. Internet, www.ftc.gov.

For further information, contact the Office of Public Affairs, Federal Trade Commission, 600 Pennsylvania Avenue NW., Washington, DC 20580. Phone, 202–326–2180. Fax, 202–326–3366. Internet, www.ftc.gov.

GENERAL SERVICES ADMINISTRATION

1800 F Street NW., Washington, DC 20405
Phone, 202–708–5082. Internet, www.gsa.gov.

ADMINISTRATOR	PAUL F. PROUTY, *Acting*
DEPUTY ADMINISTRATOR	BARNABY L. BRASSEUX
Chief of Staff	DANIELLE M. GERMAIN
Chairman, Civilian Board of Contract Appeals	STEPHEN M. DANIELS
Inspector General	BRIAN D. MILLER
General Counsel	LENNARD S. LOEWENTRITT, *Acting*
Associate Administrator for Civil Rights	MADELINE C. CALIENDO
Associate Administrator for Citizen Services and Communications	MARTHA A. DORRIS, *Acting*
Associate Administrator for Congressional and Intergovernmental Affairs	KEVIN A. MESSNER
Associate Administrator for Small Business Utilization	FELIPE MENDOZA
Associate Administrator for Performance Improvement	KIMBER H. BOYER, JR.
Chief Financial Officer	KATHLEEN M. TURCO
Chief Information Officer	CASEY COLEMAN
Chief Human Capital Officer	GAIL T. LOVELACE
Chief Acquisition Officer	DAVID A. DRABKIN, *Acting*
Chief Emergency Response and Recovery Officer	RICHARD A. REED

FEDERAL ACQUISITION SERVICE

2200 Crystal Drive, Room 1100, Arlington, VA 22202
Phone, 703–605–5400. Fax, 703–605–9955. Internet, www.gsa.gov/fsa.

Commissioner	JAMES A. WILLIAMS
Deputy Commissioner	TYREE VARNADO
Chief of Staff	BRUCE E. CAUGHMAN
Chief Information Officer	ELIZABETH L. DELNEGRO, *Acting*
Assistant Commissioner for Customer Accounts and Research	GARY FEIT
Assistant Commissioner for Acquisition Management	STEVEN J. KEMPF
Assistant Commissioner for Integrated Technology Services	EDWARD J. O'HARE
Assistant Commissioner for General Supplies and Services	JOSEPH H. JEU
Assistant Commissioner for Travel, Motor Vehicle, and Card Services	WILLIAM F. WEBSTER
Assistant Commissioner for Administration	KAREN J. HAMPEL
Controller	JON A. JORDAN
Assistant Commissioner for Strategic Business Planning and Process Improvement	AMANDA G. FREDRIKSEN, *Acting*
Assistant Commissioner for Assisted Acquisition Services	MARY A. DAVIE

PUBLIC BUILDINGS SERVICE

1800 F Street NW., Washington, DC 20405
Phone, 202–501–1100. Fax, 202–219–2310. Internet, www.gsa.gov/pbs.

Commissioner	DAVID L. WINSTEAD
Deputy Commissioner	ANTHONY COSTA
Chief of Staff	J. KENNETH SCHELBERT
Assistant Commissioner for Budget and Financial Management	LISA A. WARD
Assistant Commissioner for Organizational Resources	SEAN M. MILDREW
Assistant Commissioner for Real Property Asset Management	CATHLEEN C. KRONOPOLUS
Assistant Commissioner for Applied Science	GLENN S. HUNTER, JR.
Assistant Commissioner for National Customer Service Management	MARTHA BENSON, *Acting*
Chief Architect	LESLIE L. SHEPHERD
Assistant Commissioner for Capital Construction Program Management	WILLIAM J. GUERIN
Assistant Commissioner for Real Estate Acquisition	SAMUEL J. MORRIS III

OFFICE OF GOVERNMENTWIDE POLICY

1800 F Street NW., Washington, DC 20405
Phone, 202–501–8880. Internet, www.gsa.gov/ogp.

Associate Administrator for Governmentwide Policy	KEVIN A. MESSNER, *Acting*
Deputy Associate Administrator	STANLEY F. KACZMARCZYK

Director, Policy Initiatives	JAMES L. DEAN
Deputy Associate Administrator, Technology Strategy	STANLEY F. KACZMARCZYK, *Acting*
Director, Regulatory Information Service Center	JOHN C. THOMAS
Deputy Associate Administrator, Real Property Management	CAROLYN M. AUSTIN-DIGGS
Deputy Associate Administrator, Travel, Transportation, and Asset Management	REBECCA R. RHODES

[For the General Services Administration statement of organization, see the *Code of Federal Regulations,* Title 41, Part 105–53]

The General Services Administration establishes policy for and provides economical and efficient management of Government property and records, including construction and operation of buildings; procurement and distribution of supplies; utilization and disposal of real and personal property; transportation, travel, fleet, and communications management; and management of the governmentwide automatic data processing resources program.

The General Services Administration (GSA) was established by section 101 of the Federal Property and Administrative Services Act of 1949 (40 U.S.C. 751).

Contract Appeals The Civilian Board of Contract Appeals is responsible for resolving disputes arising out of contracts between the GSA and other Government agencies, excluding the Defense Department, Postal Service, and Tennessee Valley Authority. The Board also hears and decides requests for review of transportation audit rate determinations; claims by Federal civilian employees regarding travel and relocation expenses; claims for the proceeds of the sale of property of certain Federal civilian employees, and cases involving the Indian Self-Determination and Education Assistance Act and the Federal Crop Insurance Corporation.

In addition, the Board provides alternative dispute resolution services to executive agencies for contract disputes and other contract-related matters. Although the Board is located within the agency, it functions as an independent tribunal.

For further information, contact the Civilian Board of Contract Appeals, General Services Administration, Washington, DC 20405. Phone, 202–606–8800.

Governmentwide Policy The Office of Governmentwide Policy (OGP) collaborates with the Federal community to develop policies and guidelines for the management of Government property, technology, and administrative services. OGP's policymaking authority and policy support activities encompass the areas covering electronic government and information technology, real property and the workplace, travel, transportation, personal property, aircraft, Federal motor vehicle fleet, mail, regulatory information and use of Federal advisory committees. OGP also provides leadership to interagency groups and facilities governmentwide management reform through the effective use of performance measures and best practices.

The Office of Technology Strategy provides policy guidance on issues pertaining to electronic business and technology and coordinates information technology strategies to improve Government effectiveness and efficiency. The Office fosters interagency collaboration on IT management policies and assists agencies on IT policy matters such as IT accommodation, security, smart cards, and electronic signatures. For further information, call 202–501–0202.

The Office of Real Property Management provides policy guidance

GENERAL SERVICES ADMINISTRATION

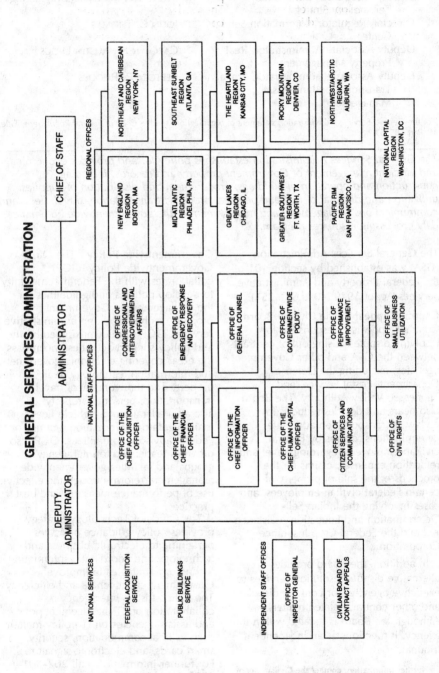

for the responsible management of the Federal Government's real property assets and the development of quality workplaces. It develops and issues governmentwide management regulations and standards that relate to real property asset management and workplace development. Real property programs include real estate management, acquisition, disposal, design, construction, performance standards, delegations, safety and environmental issues, and sustainable design. For further information, call 202–501–0856.

The Office of Travel, Transportation, and Asset Management develops governmentwide policies to ensure the economical and efficient management of Government assets, mail, travel, transportation, and relocation allowances. It develops regulations, collects and analyzes governmentwide data, manages interagency policy committees, and collaborates with customers and stakeholders to address and facilitate governmentwide improvements. For further information, call 202–501–1777.

The Regulatory Information Services Center compiles and analyzes data on governmentwide regulatory information and activities. The principal publication of the Center is the *Unified Agenda of Federal Regulatory and Deregulatory Actions*, which is published in the *Federal Register* every spring and fall and is available online at www.reginfo.gov. For further information, call 202–482–7340.

The Office of Policy Initiatives develops policy, training, evaluation, and performance metrics for the Federal Advisory Committee Program to maximize public participation in Federal decisionmaking through Federal Advisory Committees.

For further information, contact the Office of Governmentwide Policy. Phone, 202–501–8880.

Citizen Services and Communications

The Office of Citizen Services and Communications (OCSC) serves as a central Federal gateway for citizens, businesses, other governments, and the media to access information and services from the Government on the Web, in print, over the telephone, or by email. The work of OCSC is divided into two components: the Office of Citizen Services, which serves as the focal point for information and services distributed by the Federal Government, and the Office of Communications and Marketing, which conveys information about GSA services to Federal employees, agency customers and stakeholders, the news media, and the American public in general.

The Federal Citizen Information Center (FCIC) is a major component of OCSC's citizen services. The FCIC serves citizens, businesses, and other Government agencies by providing information and services via USA.gov, 1–800–333–4636, and print publications available through Pueblo, Colorado. It also develops and implements innovative technologies to improve the delivery of Government information and services to citizens. The FCIC manages:

—National Contact Center;
—Consumer Information Catalog;
—Consumer Action Handbook; and
—the following Government information Web sites: USA.gov, Kids.gov, Pueblo.gsa.gov, ConsumerAction.gov, GobiernoUSA.gov, and Consumidor.gov.

Citizen Services also collaborates with Federal, State, local, and foreign governments and intergovernmental organizations to promote more effective use of information technology and EGov solutions.

The communications and market component of OCSC plans, administers, and coordinates GSA media relations, as well as internal and external communications efforts. It also assists with GSA-wide strategic marketing activities, event planning, graphics and audiovisual production, and writing and editing support services for the entire agency.

For further information, contact the Office of Citizen Services and Communications. Phone, 202–501–0705.

Acquisitions   The Office of the Chief Acquisition Officer manages and strengthens both Federal and GSA acquisition policies. The Office provides Federal agencies with the goods, services, and support required while maintaining compliance and integrity in contracting. It also ensures compliance with applicable laws, regulations, and policies; fosters full and open competition; develops and trains the acquisition workforce; and promotes accountability for acquisition decisionmaking.

For further information, contact the Office of the Chief Acquisition Officer. Phone, 202–501–1043.

Small Business Utilization   The Office of Small Business Utilization focuses on programs, policy, and outreach to assist the small business community nationwide in doing business with GSA.

For further information, contact the Office of Small Business Utilization. Phone, 202–501–1021.

Small Business Centers—General Services Administration

Region	Address	Telephone
National Capital—Washington, DC	Rm. 1050, 7th & D Sts. SW., 20407	202–708–5804
New England—Boston, MA	Rm. 901, 10 Causeway St., 02222	617–565–8100
Northeast and Caribbean—New York, NY	Rm. 18–110, 26 Federal Plz., 10278	212–264–1234
Mid-Atlantic—Philadelphia, PA	9th Fl., 20 N. 8th St., 19107	215–466–4918
Southeast Sunbelt—Atlanta, GA	Suite 600, 77 Forsyth St., 30303	404–331–5103
Great Lakes—Chicago, IL	Rm. 3714, 230 S. Dearborn St., 60604	888–353–5383
Heartland—Kansas City, MO	Rm. 1161, 1500 E. Bannister Rd., 64131	816–926–7203
Southwest—Fort Worth, TX	Rm. 1E13A, 819 Taylor St., 76102	817–978–0800
Rocky Mountain—Denver, CO	Rm. 240, 1 Denver Federal Ctr., 80225	303–236–7409
Pacific Rim—San Francisco, CA	Rm. 5–6535, 450 Golden Gate Ave., 94102	415–522–2700
Satellite office—Los Angeles, CA	Rm. 3108, 300 N. Los Angeles St., 90012	213–894–3210
Northwest/Arctic—Auburn, WA	400 15th St. SW., 98001	253–931–7956

Federal Acquisition Service

The Federal Acquisition Service (FAS) offers services to customer agencies by providing innovative, compliant, and integrated solutions to today's acquisition challenges. Its mission is to provide excellent acquisition services for Federal agencies to increase overall Government efficiency. This includes acquisition of products and services and full-service programs in information technology, telecommunications, professional services, supplies, motor vehicles, travel and transportation, charge cards, and personal property utilization and disposal.

FAS offers numerous ways for customers to acquire products, services, and solutions. Key acquisition programs include multiple award schedules and governmentwide acquisition contracts that provide customers easy access to a wide range of information technology, telecommunications, and professional products and services. It also provides its customers with access to the products and services through online Web sites such as GSA *Advantage!*, eBuy,

Schedules eLibrary, GSA Auctions, Transportation Management Services Solutions, and other electronic tools.

For further information, contact the Office of the Commissioner, Federal Acquisition Service. Phone, 703–605–5400.

Public Buildings Service

The Public Buildings Service (PBS) serves as the landlord for the civilian Federal Government, providing workplaces for Federal agencies while maintaining cost-effectiveness and responsibility for the American taxpayer. PBS designs, builds, leases, manages, and maintains space in office buildings, courthouses, laboratories, border stations, data processing centers, warehouses, and child care centers. It repairs, alters, and renovates existing facilities and disposes of surplus Government properties. PBS is a leader in energy conservation, green building, and recycling. It also preserves and maintains more than 400 historic properties, conserves a substantial inventory of artwork, and commissions talented American artists to create original work for new Federal buildings.

PBS collects rent from Federal tenants, which is deposited into the Federal Buildings Fund, the principal funding mechanism for PBS.

For further information, contact the Office of the Commissioner, Public Buildings Service. Phone, 202–501–1100.

Regional Offices—General Services Administration

Region	Address	Administrator
New England	Boston, MA (10 Causeway St., 02222)	Glenn C. Rotondo, *Acting*
Northeast and Caribbean	New York, NY (26 Federal Plz., 10278)	Steve Ruggerio, *Acting*
Mid-Atlantic	Philadelphia, PA (20 N. 8th St., 19107–3191)	Linda C. Chero, *Acting*
Southeast Sunbelt	Atlanta, GA (Suite 600, 77 Forsyth St., 30303)	Jimmy H. Bridgeman, *Acting*
Great Lakes	Chicago, IL (230 S. Dearborn St., 60604)	James C. Handley
The Heartland	Kansas City, MO (1500 E. Bannister Rd., 64131)	Bradley Scott
Greater Southwest	Fort Worth, TX (819 Taylor St., 76102)	Scott Armey
Rocky Mountain	Denver, CO (Bldg. 41, Denver Federal Ctr., 80225–0006)	Timothy Horne, *Acting*
Pacific Rim	San Francisco, CA (5th Fl., 450 Golden Gate Ave., 94102)	Jeffrey E. Neely, *Acting*
Northwest/Arctic	Auburn, WA (GSA Ctr., 400 15th St. SW., 98002)	Robin G. Graf, *Acting*
National Capital	Washington, DC (301 7th St. SW., 20407)	Sharon J. Banks, *Acting*

Sources of Information

Contracts Individuals seeking to do business with the General Services Administration may obtain information through the Internet at www.gsa.gov.

Electronic Access Information about GSA is available electronically through the Internet at www.gsa.gov.

Employment Job announcements and applications for employment with GSA are located on the GSA Web site at www.gsa.gov. For inquiries regarding employment with GSA, contact the Office of Human Resources Services. Email, GSAjobs@gsa.gov.

Fraud and Waste Contact the Inspector General's hotline. Phone, 202–501–1780 or 800–424–5210.

Freedom of Information Act Requests Inquiries concerning policies pertaining to Freedom of Information Act matters should be addressed to the GSA FOIA Office, General Services Administration, Room 6001, Washington, DC 20405. Phone, 202–501–2262. Fax, 202–501–2727.

Privacy Act Requests Inquiries concerning policies pertaining to Privacy Act matters should be addressed to GSA Privacy Act Officer, Information Resources and Privacy Management Division (CIB), General Services Administration, Room 6224, Washington, DC 20405. Phone, 202–501–1452.

Property Disposal Inquiries about the redistribution or competitive sale of surplus real property should be directed to the Office of Real Property Disposal, Public Buildings Service, 1800 F Street NW., Washington, DC 20405. Phone, 202–501–0084.

Public and News Media Inquiries Inquiries from both the general public and news media should be directed to the Office of Communications, General Services Administration, 1800 F Street NW., Washington, DC 20405. Phone, 202–501–1231.

Publications Many GSA publications are available from the Government Printing Office bookstore at http://bookstore.gpo.gov. Orders and questions about publications and paid subscriptions should be directed to the Superintendent of Documents, Government Printing Office, Washington, DC 20401. Some subscriptions may be obtained free of charge or at cost from a Small Business Center or GSA's Centralized Mailing List Service (phone, 817–334–5215). If a publication is not available through any of these sources, contact a specific GSA staff office, regional office, or service. Addresses and phone numbers may be found at www.gsa.gov.

For a free copy of the *U.S. Government TTY Directory*, contact the Federal Citizen Information Center, Department TTY, Pueblo, CO 81009. Phone, 888–878–3256. Internet, www.gsa.gov/frs. For a free copy of the quarterly *Consumer Information Catalog*, including information on food, nutrition, employment, Federal benefits, the environment, fraud, privacy and Internet issues, investing and credit, and education, write to the Federal Citizen Information Center, Pueblo, CO 81009. Phone, 888–878–3256. Internet, www.pueblo.gsa.gov.

For information about Federal programs and services, call the Federal Citizen Information Center's National Contact Centers at 800–333–4636, Monday through Friday from 8 a.m. to 8 p.m. eastern standard time.

For a free copy of the *Federal Relay Service Brochure,* call 877–387–2001. TTY, 202–585–1840.

Small Business Activities Inquiries concerning programs to assist small businesses should be directed to one of the Small Business Centers listed in the preceding text.

Speakers Inquiries and requests for speakers should be directed to the Office of Citizen Services and Communications (X), General Services Administration, Washington, DC 20405 (phone, 202–501–0705); or contact the nearest regional office.

For further information concerning the General Services Administration, contact the Office of Citizen Services and Communications (X), General Services Administration, Washington, DC 20405. Phone, 202–501–0705.

INTER–AMERICAN FOUNDATION

901 North Stuart Street, Tenth Floor, Arlington, VA 22203
Phone, 703–306–4301. Internet, www.iaf.gov.

CHAIR	JOHN P. SALAZAR
VICE CHAIR	THOMAS J. DODD
Directors	KAY KELLEY ARNOLD, GARY C. BRYNER, THOMAS A. SHANNON, JR., JACK C. VAUGHN, JR., ROGER W. WALLACE, (VACANCY)
President	LARRY L. PALMER
General Counsel	JENNIFER HODGES
Vice President for Operations	LINDA B. KOLKO
Regional Director for South America and the Caribbean	JUDITH MORRISON
Regional Director for Central America and Mexico	JILL WHEELER

The Inter-American Foundation is an independent Federal agency that supports social and economic development in Latin America and the Caribbean. It makes grants primarily to private, local, and community organizations that carry out self-help projects.

The Inter-American Foundation (IAF) was created in 1969 (22 U.S.C. 290f) as an experimental U.S. foreign assistance program. IAF is governed by a nine-person Board of Directors appointed by the President with the advice and consent of the Senate. Six members are drawn from the private sector and three

from the Federal Government. The Board of Directors appoints the President of IAF.

IAF works in Latin America and the Caribbean to promote equitable, participatory, and sustainable self-help development by awarding grants directly to local organizations throughout the region. It also enters into partnerships with public and private sector entities to build support and mobilize local, national, and international resources for grassroots development.

For further information, contact the Office of the President, Inter-American Foundation, 901 North Stuart Street, Tenth Floor, Arlington, VA 22203. Phone, 703–306–4301. Internet, www.iaf.gov.

MERIT SYSTEMS PROTECTION BOARD

1615 M Street NW., Fifth Floor, Washington, DC 20419
Phone, 202–653–7200 or 800–209–8960. TDD, 800–877–8339. Fax, 202–653–7130. Internet,
www.mspb.gov.

CHAIRMAN	NEIL A. G. MCPHIE
VICE CHAIRMAN	MARY M. ROSE
Member	(VACANCY)
Chief of Staff	TRACEY D. WATKINS
Clerk of the Board	WILLIAM D. SPENCER
Director, Financial and Administrative Management	CHARLIE ROCHE
Director, Information Resources Management	TOMMY HWANG
Director, Office of Appeals Counsel	JAMES READ
Director, Office of Equal Employment Opportunity	CHARLENE PROCTOR, *Acting*
Director, Office of Policy and Evaluation	JOHN CRUM
Director, Office of Regional Operations	DEBORAH MIRON
General Counsel	B. CHAD BUNGARD

[For the Merit Systems Protection Board statement of organization, see the *Code of Federal Regulations*, Title 5, Part 1200]

The Merit Systems Protection Board protects the integrity of the Federal personnel merit systems and the rights of Federal employees. In overseeing the personnel practices of the Federal Government, the Board conducts special studies of the merit systems, hears and decides charges of wrongdoing and employee appeals of adverse agency actions, and orders corrective and disciplinary actions when appropriate.

The Merit Systems Protection Board is a successor agency to the United States Civil Service Commission, established by act of January 16, 1883 (22 Stat. 403). Reorganization Plan No. 2 of 1978 (5 U.S.C. app.) redesignated part of the Commission as the Merit Systems Protection Board.

Activities

The Board has responsibility for hearing and adjudicating appeals by Federal employees of adverse personnel actions, such as removals, suspensions, and demotions. It also resolves cases involving reemployment rights, the denial of periodic step increases in pay, actions against administrative law judges, and charges of prohibited personnel practices, including charges in connection with whistleblowing. The Board has the authority to enforce its decisions and to order corrective and disciplinary actions. An employee or applicant for employment involved in an appealable action that also involves an allegation of discrimination may ask the Equal Employment Opportunity Commission to review a Board decision. Final decisions and orders of the Board

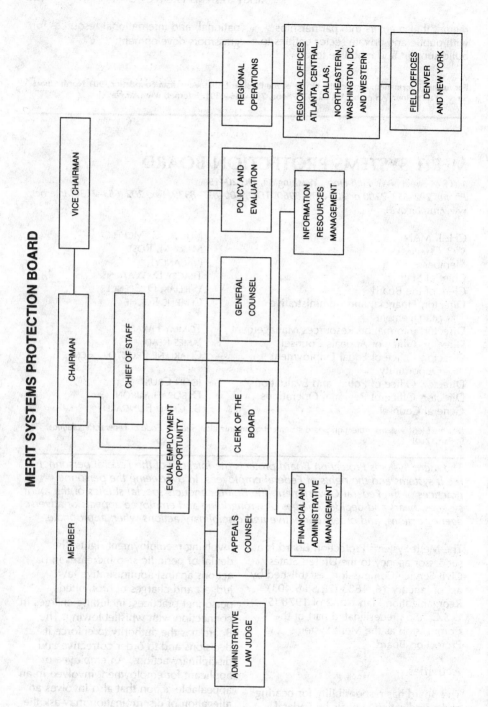

MERIT SYSTEMS PROTECTION BOARD

can be appealed to the U.S. Court of Appeals for the Federal Circuit.

The Board reviews regulations issued by the Office of Personnel Management and has the authority to require agencies to cease compliance with any regulation that could constitute a prohibited personnel practice. It also conducts special studies of the civil service and other executive branch merit systems and reports to the President and the Congress on whether the Federal work force is being adequately protected against political abuses and prohibited personnel practices.

Regional Offices—Merit Systems Protection Board

Region	Address	Director	Telephone
Atlanta	401 W. Peachtree St. NW., Atlanta, GA 30308	Thomas J. Lanphear	404–730–2755
Central	31st Fl., 230 S. Dearborn St., Chicago, IL 60604	Martin W. Baumgaertner	312–353–2923
Dallas	Rm. 620, 1100 Commerce St., Dallas, TX 75242	Sharon F. Jackson	214–767–0555
Northeastern	Suite 1700, 1601 Market St., Philadelphia, PA 19103.	William L. Boulden	215–597–9960
Washington, DC	Suite 205, 1800 Diagonal Rd., Alexandria, VA 22314.	Jeremiah Cassidy	703–756–6250
Western	Suite 2310, 201 Mission St., San Francisco, CA 94104.	Amy Dunning	415–904–6772

Field Offices—Merit Systems Protection Board

Region	Address	Chief Administrative Judge	Telephone
Denver	Suite 318, 165 S. Union Blvd., Lakewood, CO 80228.	Maxanne Witkin	303–969–5101
New York	Rm. 3137A, 26 Federal Plz., New York, NY 10278	Arthur S. Joseph	212–264–9372

For further information, contact the Merit Systems Protection Board, 1615 M Street NW., Washington, DC 20419. Phone, 202–653–7200 or 800–209–8960. TDD, 800–877–8339. Fax, 202–653–7130. Email, mspb@mspb.gov. Internet, www.mspb.gov.

NATIONAL AERONAUTICS AND SPACE ADMINISTRATION

300 E Street SW., Washington, DC 20546
Phone, 202–358–0000. Internet, www.nasa.gov.

ADMINISTRATOR	CHARLES F. BOLDEN, JR.
DEPUTY ADMINISTRTATOR	LORI B. GARVER
Associate Administrator	CHRISTOPHER SCOLESE
Associate Deputy Administrator	CHARLES SCALES
Chief of Staff	(VACANCY)
Deputy Chief of Staff/White House Liaison	DAVID L. NOBLE
Assistant Associate Administrator	CHRISTYL JOHNSON
Assistant Administrator for External Relations	MICHAEL F. O'BRIEN
Associate Administrator for Aeronautics Research Mission Directorate	JAIWON SHIN
Associate Administrator for Exploration Systems Mission Directorate	DOUGLAS COOKE
Associate Administrator for Institutions and Management	THOMAS S. LUEDTKE
Assistant Administrator for Diversity and Equal Opportunity	BRENDA R. MANUEL

Assistant Administrator for Human Capital Management	TONI DAWSEY
Assistant Administrator for Infrastructure and Administration	OLGA DOMINGUEZ
Assistant Administrator for Internal Controls and Management Systems	LOU BECKER
Assistant Administrator for Procurement	BILL MCNALLY
Assistant Administrator for Security and Program Protection	JACK FORSYTHE, *Acting*
Assistant Administrator for Small Business Programs	GLENN A. DELGADO
Executive Director, NASA Shared Services Center	RICHARD E. ARBUTHNOT
Associate Administrator for Program Analysis and Evaluation	WILLIAM M. HAWES
Headquarters Operations	CHRIS JEDREY
Associate Administrator for Science Mission Directorate	ED WEILER
Associate Administrator for Space Operations Mission Directorate	WILLIAM GERSTENMAIER
Chief Engineer	MICHAEL RYSCHKEWITSCH
Chief Financial Officer	RONALD R. SPOEHEL
Chief Health and Medical Officer	RICHARD S. WILLIAMS
Chief Information Officer	BOBBY GERMAN, *Acting*
Chief Safety and Mission Assurance Officer	BRYAN O'CONNOR
Chief of Strategic Communications/Assistant Administrator for Communications Planning	MARY D. KERWIN, *Acting*
Assistant Administrator for Education	JOYCE L. WINTERTON
Assistant Administrator for Legislative and Intergovernmental Affairs	MARY D. KERWIN, *Acting*
Assistant Administrator for Public Affairs	BOB JACOBS, *Acting*
Director, Innovative Partnerships Program	DOUGLAS A. COMSTOCK
Director, Office of Program and Institutional Integration	RICHARD J. KEEGAN
General Counsel	MICHAEL C. WHOLLEY
Inspector General	TOM HOWARD, *Acting*
Director, Ames Research Center	S. PETE WORDEN
Director, Dryden Flight Research Center	DAVID D. MCBRIDE, *Acting*
Director, John H. Glenn Research Center	WOODROW WHITLOW
Director, Goddard Space Flight Center	ROBERT D. STRAIN
Director, Lyndon B. Johnson Space Center	MICHAEL COATS
Director, John F. Kennedy Space Center	ROBERT D. CABANA
Director, Langley Research Center	LESA ROE
Director, George C. Marshall Space Flight Center	ROBERT M. LIGHTFOOT, *Acting*
Director, John C. Stennis Space Center	ARTHUR E. GOLDMAN
Director, Jet Propulsion Laboratory	CHARLES ELACHI

[For the National Aeronautics and Space Administration statement of organization, see the *Code of Federal Regulations,* Title 14, Part 1201]

The mission of the National Aeronautics and Space Administration is to pioneer the future in space exploration, scientific discovery, and aeronautics research.

NATIONAL AERONAUTICS AND SPACE ADMINISTRATION

* In accordance with law or regulation, the offices of Diversity and Equal Opportunity and Small Business Programs maintain reporting relationships to the Administrator and Deputy Administrator.

The National Aeronautics and Space Administration (NASA) was established by the National Aeronautics and Space Act of 1958, as amended (42 U.S.C. 2451 *et seq.*).

Activities

Aeronautics Research Directorate   The Aeronautics Research Mission Directorate conducts research and technology activities to develop the knowledge, tools, and technologies to support the development of future air and space vehicles and to support the transformation of the Nations's air transportation system. The Directorate's programs focus on cutting-edge, fundamental research in traditional aeronautical disciplines, as well as emerging fields with promising applications to aeronautics, and are conducted in conjunction with industry, academia, and other U.S. Government departments and agencies, including the Federal Aviation Administration and the Department of Defense.

For further information, call 202–358–2047.

Space Operations Mission Directorate The Space Operations Mission Directorate (SOMD) provides the foundation for NASA's space program—space travel for human and robotic missions, in-space laboratories, and the means to return data to Earth. SOMD is responsible for many critical enabling capabilities that make possible much of the science, research, and exploration achievements of the rest of NASA. This is done through three themes: the International Space Station, Space Shuttle, and Space and Flight Support.

The International Space Station is a complex of laboratories maintained to support scientific research, technology development, and the exploration of a permanent human presence in Earth's orbit.

The Space Shuttle, first launched in 1981, provides the only current capability in the United States for human access to space. The Shuttle's focus over the next several years will be the assembly of the International Space Station after which it will be phased out of service.

The Space and Flight Support theme encompasses space communications, launch services, and rocket propulsion testing. Space communications consists of five major elements: the Space Network or Tracking and Data Relay Satellite System, the Deep Space Network, the Near Earth Network, the NASA Integrated Services Network, and NASA Spectrum Management. The launch services program focuses on acquisition of commercial launch services for NASA's space and Earth science missions. The rocket propulsion testing program supports the flight readiness of various liquid propulsion engines and acts as a test bed for rocket engines of the future.

For further information, call 202–358–2015.

Science Mission Directorate   The Science Mission Directorate carries out the scientific exploration of the Earth, Moon, Mars, and beyond, charting the best route of discovery. The Directorate manages and sponsors research, flight missions, advanced technology development, and related activities. It works to expand our understanding of the Earth and the Sun and the Sun's effect on the solar system environments; explore the solar system with robots to study its origins and evolution including the origins of life within it; and explore the universe beyond, from the search for planets and life in other solar systems to the origin, evolution, and destiny of the universe itself.

For further information, call 202–358–3889 or visit www.nasascience.nasa.gov.

Exploration Systems Mission Directorate The Exploration Systems Mission Directorate (ESMD) is responsible for creating a suite of new human exploration capabilities called Constellation Systems. This system includes a crew exploration vehicle, transportation, lunar and planetary body exploration, in-space support, and ground-based support systems. The ESMD also includes robotic missions to the Moon and research payloads that use the International Space System, as well as ground-based facilities.

For further information, call 202–358–7246.

NASA Centers

Ames Research Center   The Ames Research Center, located in California's Silicon Valley, provides solutions to NASA's exploration questions through interdisciplinary scientific discovery and innovative technology systems. The Center provides leadership in astrobiology, information science, small spacecraft, advanced thermal protection systems, human factors, and the development of new tools for a safer and more efficient national airspace. It also develops unique partnerships and collaborations, exemplified by NASA's Astrobiology Institute, the NASA Research Park, and the University Affiliated Research Center.

Dryden Flight Research Center   The Dryden Flight Research Center, located at Edwards, CA, is NASA's primary installation for flight research. Since 1946, Dryden's researchers have led the way in major advancements to the design and capabilities of many civilian and military aircraft. Dryden's workforce expertise in aeronautics and in the development of flight research tools and techniques, coupled with the suite of specialized laboratories and facilities needed for flight validation, are key to the development and maturation of new vehicles.

Glenn Research Center   The Glenn Research Center, with two locations in Cleveland and Sandusky, Ohio, works with other NASA Centers to develop spaceflight systems and technologies to create a new, safer, and less expensive rocket system to return Americans to the moon and help humanity explore the universe. Glenn provides expertise in propulsion, power, communications, and testing for spacecraft and lunar systems. In aeronautics, Glenn scientists and engineers imagine and prove new technologies to make airplanes safer, quieter, and more environmentally friendly.

Goddard Space Flight Center   The Goddard Space Flight Center, located in Greenbelt, MD, expands the knowledge of Earth and its environment, the solar system, and the universe through observations from space. The Center also conducts scientific investigations, develops and operates space systems, and advances essential technologies.

Johnson Space Center   The Lyndon B. Johnson Space Center, located in Houston, TX, leads the United States in the human exploration of space. The Center has made major advances in science, technology, engineering, and medicine and has led the Nation's human space flight programs and projects. It strives to advance the Nation's exploration of the universe with its expertise in medical, biomedical, and life sciences, lunar and planetary geosciences, crew and mission operations, crew health and safety, project management, and space systems engineering. The Center also leads worldwide research in extraterrestrial materials curation and the interaction between humans and robotics, as well as the biology and physiology of humans in space.

Kennedy Space Center   The John F. Kennedy Center, located in Florida, is responsible for NASA's space launch operation and spaceport and range technologies. Home to the Space Shuttle fleet and the launch services program, it carries out its primary mission by managing the processing and launch of astronaut crews; the Space Shuttle and associated payloads; International Space Station elements, research experiments, and supplies; and enabling the payload processing of a wide variety of robotics payloads launched on commercial services into space. NASA is preparing to send humans back to the Moon as part of the Constellation Program, and the Kennedy Space Center is undergoing changes in support of this mission. NASA's next-generation spacecraft and launch vehicle system, the Orion crew exploration vehicle and Ares rockets, will launch from the Kennedy Space Center. The Center will carry out the ground processing for the new Ares rockets as well as the final assembly of the Orion crew exploration vehicle.

Langley Research Center The Langley Research Center, located in Hampton, VA, is renowned for its scientific and technological expertise in aerospace research, systems integration, and atmospheric science. Established 1917 as an aeronautics lab, the Center also has a rich heritage in space and science technologies. The Center conducts critical research in materials and structures; aerodynamics; and hypersonic, supersonic, and subsonic flight; and has developed and validated technologies to improve the effectiveness, capability, comfort, and efficiency of the Nation's air transportation system. It supports the space exploration program and space operations with systems analysis and engineering, aerosciences, materials and structures, and technology and systems development and testing. The Center continues to have a principal role in understanding and protecting our planet through atmospheric measurement, instruments, missions, and prediction algorithms. In 2003, NASA's Engineering and Safety Center was established at Langley to improve mission safety by performing independent engineering assessments, testing, analysis, and evaluation to determine appropriate preventative and corrective action for problems, trends, or issues across NASA programs and projects.

Marshall Space Flight Center The George C. Marshall Space Flight Center, located in Hunstville, AL, develops and integrates the transportation and space systems required for the Agency's exploration, operations, and scientific missions. It provides the engineering and scientific capabilities to deliver space transportation and propulsion systems, space systems development and integration, scientific and exploration instruments, and basic and applied research. The Center manages the Space Shuttle propulsion elements, life support systems and operations for scientific experiments aboard the International Space Station, the Ares I crew and Ares V cargo launch vehicles, the Chandra X-

ray Observatory, and the Lunar Precursor Robotic Program. Other programs and projects include the International Lunar Network, Discovery and New Frontiers Programs, and Michoud Assembly Facility.

Stennis Space Center The John C. Stennis Center, located near Bay St. Louis, MS, has served as NASA's rocket propulsion testing ground for more than four decades. Today, the Center provides test services not only for America's space program, but also for the Department of Defense and the private sector. Every space shuttle main engine is tested at Stennis. The Center will also test engines and stages for NASA's Constellation Program, designed to return astronauts to the moon with possible journeys beyond. The Center's Applied Science and Technology Project Office provides world class project management to support NASA's science and technology goals, and supports NASA's Applied Sciences Program through the Crosscutting Gulf of Mexico Coastal Program.

Jet Propulsion Laboratory The Laboratory, which is managed under contract by the California Institute of Technology in Pasadena, CA, develops spacecraft and space sensors and conducts mission operations and ground-based research in support of solar system exploration, Earth science and applications, Earth and ocean dynamics, space physics and astronomy, and information systems technology. It is also responsible for the management of the Deep Space Network in support of NASA projects.

Sources of Information

Contracts and Small Business Activities Inquiries regarding contracting for small business opportunities with NASA should be directed to the Assistant Administrator for Small Business Programs, Room 5C39, NASA Headquarters, 300 E Street SW., Washington, DC 20546. Phone, 202–358–2088.

Employment Direct all general inquiries to the NASA Shared Services Center, Stennis, MS 39529. Phone, 877–

677–2123. Email, nssc-contactcenter@nasa.gov.

OIG Hotline   An individual may report crimes, fraud, waste, and abuse in NASA programs and operations by calling the OIG Hotline (800–424–9183); by writing to the NASA Inspector General (P.O. Box 23089, L'Enfant Plaza Station, Washington, DC 20026); or by sending an electronic message from the OIG's Web site (www.hq.nasa.gov/office/oig/hq/cyberhotline.html).

Publications, Speakers, Films, and Exhibit Services   Several publications concerning these services can be obtained by contacting the Public Affairs Officer of the nearest NASA Center. Publications include *NASA Directory of Services for the Public, NASA Film List,* and *NASA Educational Publications List.*

The headquarters telephone directory and certain publications and picture sets are available for sale from the Superintendent of Documents, Government Printing Office, Washington, DC 20402. Telephone directories for NASA Centers are available only from the Centers. Publications and documents not available for sale from the Superintendent of Documents or the National Technical Information Service (Springfield, VA 22151) may be obtained from NASA Center's Information Center in accordance with the NASA regulation concerning freedom of information.

Reading Room   NASA Headquarters Information Center, Room 1H23, 300 E Street SW., Washington, DC 20546. Phone, 202–358–0000.

For further information, contact the Headquarters Information Center, National Aeronautics and Space Administration, Washington, DC 20546. Phone, 202–358–0000. Internet, www.nasa.gov.

NATIONAL ARCHIVES AND RECORDS ADMINISTRATION

8601 Adelphi Road, College Park, Maryland 20740
Phone, 866–272–6272. Internet, www.archives.gov.

ARCHIVIST OF THE UNITED STATES	ADRIENNE C. THOMAS, *Acting*
DEPUTY ARCHIVIST OF THE UNITED STATES	ADRIENNE C. THOMAS
Chief of Staff	DEBRA WALL
Assistant Archivist for Administration	RICHARD JUDSON, *Acting*
Assistant Archivist for Information Services	MARTHA MORPHY
Assistant Archivist for Presidential Libraries	SHARON K. FAWCETT
Assistant Archivist for Records Services— Washington, DC	MICHAEL J. KURTZ
Assistant Archivist for Regional Records Services	THOMAS E. MILLS
Director of the Federal Register	RAYMOND A. MOSLEY
Director of Public Affairs and Communications Staff	SUSAN COOPER
Director, Congressional Affairs	JOHN HAMILTON
Director, Equal Employment Opportunity and Diversity Programs	ROBERT JEW
Director, Information Security Oversight Office	WILLIAM J. BOSANKO
Office of Government Information Services	(VACANCY)
Director, Policy and Planning Staff	SUSAN M. ASHTIANIE
Executive Director, National Historical Publications and Records Commission	KATHLEEN M. WILLIAMS

General Counsel
Inspector General

GARY M. STERN
PAUL BRACHFELD

[For the National Archives and Records Administration statement of organization, see the *Federal Register* of June 25, 1985, 50 FR 26278]

The National Archives and Records Administration safeguards and preserves the records of our Government, ensuring that the people can discover, use, and learn from this documentary heritage; establishes policies and procedures for managing U.S. Government records; manages the Presidential Libraries system; and publishes the laws, regulations, and Presidential and other public documents.

The National Archives and Records Administration (NARA) is the successor agency to the National Archives Establishment, which was created in 1934 and subsequently incorporated into the General Services Administration as the National Archives and Records Service in 1949. NARA was established as an independent agency in the executive branch of the Government by act of October 19, 1984 (44 U.S.C. 2101 *et seq.*), effective April 1, 1985.

Activities

Archival Program   The National Archives and Records Administration maintains, as archival records, the historically valuable records of the U.S. Government, dating from the Revolutionary War era to the recent past; arranges and preserves records and prepares finding aids to facilitate their use; makes records available for use in research rooms in its facilities and via the Internet; answers written and oral requests for information contained in its holdings; and, for a fee, provides copies of records. These holdings include the records of the U.S. House of Representatives and the U.S. Senate, which are preserved and administered by the Center for Legislative Archives. Many important records are available on microfilm and on the NARA Web site at www.archives.gov. Archival records created in the Washington, DC area and in the custody of NARA are maintained in NARA facilities in the Washington, DC area. Archival records of high regional or local interest in the custody of NARA are maintained in NARA archives locations throughout the country. NARA also has nine affiliated archives that hold NARA-owned records on behalf of NARA and make them available to the public.

Records Management   To ensure proper documentation of the organization, policies, and activities of the Government, NARA develops standards and guidelines for the nationwide management and disposition of recorded information. It appraises Federal records and approves records disposition schedules. It also inspects agency records and records management practices, develops records management training programs, provides guidance and assistance on proper records management, and provides for storage of inactive records. For agencies headquartered in the Washington, DC vicinity, these functions are assigned to the Office of Records Services/ Washington, DC.

Office of Records Services (Washington, DC)

Modern Records Program   The Modern Records Program improves the life cycle management of Federal records in all media for Government agencies; provides formal training in Federal records management; preserves and makes available permanent electronic records; and coordinates technical assistance to Federal agencies on records creation, management, and disposition to agencies in the Washington, DC area. For more information, log on to www.archives.gov/records-mgmt.

The Washington National Records Center offers a wide range of records storage and servicing options as described below under Regional Records Services, and also offers customized

NATIONAL ARCHIVES AND RECORDS ADMINISTRATION

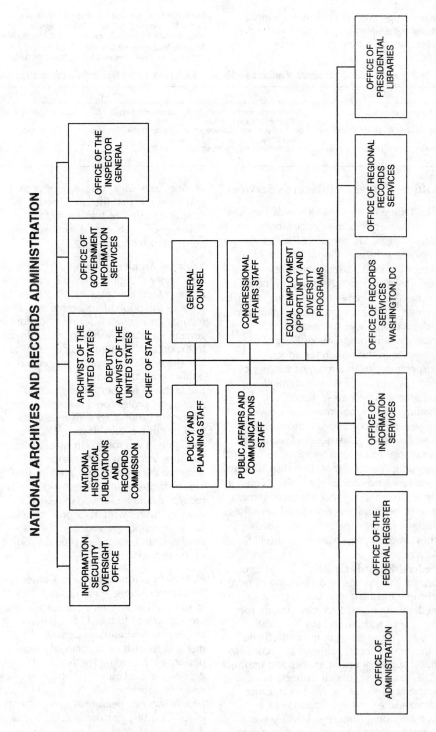

workshops and records management assistance upon request and will assist agencies with their records storage problems.

For further information on records center services in the Washington, DC area (West Virginia, Virginia, and Maryland), contact the Director of the Records Management Division, Washington National Records Center. Phone, 301–778–1650.

Washington Area Records Facilities—National Archives and Records Administration

Facility	Address	Director	Telephone
National Archives	700 Pennsylvania Ave. NW., Washington, DC 20408.	James Hastings	202–357–5393
National Archives at College Park	8601 Adelphi Rd., College Park, MD 20740.	Sharon Gibbs Thibodeau	301–837–3400
Washington National Records Center.	4205 Suitland Rd., Suitland, MD 20746.	Alan Kramer	301–778–1600

Office of Regional Records Services

The Office of Regional Records Services provides services to agencies outside the Washington, DC area. NARA has nine regions and the National Personnel Records Center. Each region operates a full life-cycle records program, including records management operations, records centers, and archives. NARA maintains information about the records management programs of Federal agencies in the region; conducts inspections, evaluations, or surveys of records and records management programs in agencies; reports on findings; and recommends improvements or necessary corrective actions. NARA also furnishes guidance and technical assistance to Federal agencies on records creation, management, and disposition; develops and conducts training aimed at improving agency records management and disposition practices; and appraises Federal records to determine whether they warrant preservation by the U.S. Government.

Federal Records Centers   These Centers are for the storage and servicing of non-current and certain active records of Federal agencies. Services include the storage of textual and special media records; storage for nonclassified and classified records; retrieval of records to fulfill statutory requirements and conduct daily business; special projects to respond to sudden shifts in customer demands; expedited response to congressional inquiries, litigation, and urgent business needs; and disposition

services, providing disposal for records that have reached their required retention period or transfer to the holdings of the National Archives for permanent records.

Regional Archives   Archival records of high regional significance are maintained in these facilities. Archives locations provide the public free access to these records, to Internet resources helpful for genealogical and historical research, and to expert staff available to guide visitors. On-site workshops teach the general public, educators, and students how to use archives for their hobby, school-related, or professional interests. Many important original records held in NARA facilities in the Washington, DC area are available in microform in most of these facilities. Archival staff arrange and preserve the records and prepare finding aids to facilitate their use; make the records available for use in research rooms; answer written or oral requests for information contained in the holdings; and, for a fee, provide copies of the records.

National Personnel Records Center

The Center stores, services, and disposes of the civilian personnel, medical, and pay records of former U.S. Civil Service employees and military personnel and medical records of discharged military personnel. Including the National Archives at St. Louis, the facility provides research rooms in which the public and Federal agency personnel can reference official military personnel folders and other related records. The Center also provides Federal agencies with services and technical advice relating to records disposition, filing and classification schemes, and protection of vital civilian and military records.

For further information, contact the Office of Regional Records Services. Phone, 301–837–2950. Fax, 301–837–1617. Internet, www.archives.gov/ locations/records-management.html.

Regional Records Services Facilities—National Archives and Records Administration

(HQ: Headquarters facility; A: Facility holding archival records)

City	Address	Director	Telephone
Northeast Region (HQ)	380 Trapelo Rd., Waltham, MA 02154–6399	Diane LeBlanc	781–663–0130
Boston, MA (A)	380 Trapelo Rd., Waltham, 02154–6399		781–663–0130
Pittsfield, MA	100 Conte Dr., 01201–8230		413–236–3600
New York City, NY (A)	201 Varick St., 10014–4811		866–840–1752
Mid-Atlantic Region (HQ)	900 Market St., Philadelphia, PA 19107–4292	V. Chapman Smith	215–606–0100
Center City Philadelphia, PA (A).	900 Market St., 19107–4292		215–606–0100
Northeast Philadelphia, PA	14700 Townsend Rd., 19154–1096		215–305–2000
Southeast Region (HQ) (A)	5780 Jonesboro Rd., Morrow, GA 30260–3806	James McSweeney	770–968–2100
Ellenwood, GA	4712 Southpark Blvd., 30294–3595		404–736–2820
Great Lakes Region (HQ)	7358 S. Pulaski Rd., Chicago, IL 60629–5898	David E. Kuehl	773–948–9001
Chicago, IL (A)	7358 S. Pulaski Rd., 60629–5898		773–948–9001
Dayton, OH	3150 Springboro Rd., 45439–1883		937–425–0672
Kingsridge, OH	8801 Kingsridge Dr., Miamisburg, OH 45458		937–425–0650
Central Plains Region (HQ)	2312 E. Bannister Rd., Kansas City, MO 64131– 3011.	R. Reed Whitaker	816–268–8000
Kansas City, MO (A)	2312 E. Bannister Rd., 64131–3011		816–268–8000
Lee's Summit, MO	200 Space Ctr. Dr., 64064–1182		816–268–8000
Lenexa, KS	17501 West 98th St., 66219–1735		913–268–8000
Southwest Region (HQ)	1400 John Burgess Dr., Fort Worth, TX 76140	Preston Huff	
Fort Worth, TX (A)	501 W. Felix St., Bldg. 1, P.O. Box 6216, 76115		817–831–5620
Rocky Mountain Region (HQ) (A).	Bldg. 48, Denver Federal Ctr., Denver, CO 80225–0307.	Barbara Voss	303–407–5740
Pacific Region (HQ)	1000 Commodore Dr., San Bruno, CA 94066	David Drake, *Acting*	650–238–3477
Laguna Niguel, CA (A)	1st Fl. E., 24000 Avila Rd., 92607–3497		949–360–2641
San Francisco, CA (A)	1000 Commodore Dr., San Bruno, 94066		415–238–3501
Riverside County, CA	23123 Cajalco Rd., Perris, 92570–7298		951–956–2000
Pacific Alaska Region (HQ)	6125 Sand Point Way NE., Seattle, WA 98115– 7999.	Candace Lein-Hayes	206–336–5142
Seattle, WA (A)	6125 Sand Point Way NE., 98115–7999		206–336–5142
Anchorage, AK (A)	654 W. 3d Ave., 99501–2145		907–261–7820
National Personnel Records Center (HQ).	9700 Page Ave., St. Louis, MO 63132	Ronald L. Hindman	314–801–0800

Affiliated Archives Facilities—National Archives and Records Administration

Facility	Address	Telephone	Fax
Library of Congress	Prints and Photographs Division, Rm. 339, James Madison Bldg., Washington, DC 20540–4730.	202–707–6399	202–707–6647
New Mexico State Records Center and Archives.	Archives and Historical Services Division, New Mexico Commission of Public Records, 1205 Camino Carlos Rey, Sante Fe, NM 87505.	505–476–7900	505–476–7909
Oklahoma Historical Society	Research Division, 2401 North Laird Ave., Oklahoma City, OK 73105.	405–522–5248	
Pennsylvania State Archives	Bureau of Archives and History, Pennsylvania Historical and Museum Commission, 350 North St., Harrisburg, PA 17120.	717–783–3281	
U.S. Government Printing Office	Superintendent of Documents, 732 N. Capitol St. NW., Washington, DC 20401.	202–512–1800	
U.S. Military Academy	Special Collections and Archives Division, U.S. Military Academy Library, Jefferson and Collum Rd., West Point, NY 10996–1711.	845–938–3259	845–938–4000
U.S. Naval Academy	William W. Jeffries Memorial Archives, Rm. 320, Nimitz Library, 589 McNair Rd., Annapolis, MD 21402.	410–293–6922	410–293–4926
Yellowstone National Park Archives.	P.O. Box 168, Yellowstone National Park, WY 82190	307–344–2563	307–344–2323
University of North Texas Libraries.	P.O. Box 305190, Denton, TX 76203	940–565–3269	

Presidential Libraries   Through the Presidential libraries, which are located at sites selected by the Presidents and built with private funds, NARA preserves and makes available the records and personal papers of a particular President's administration. In addition to providing reference services on Presidential documents, each library prepares documentary and descriptive publications and operates a museum to exhibit documents, historic objects, and other memorabilia of interest to the public.

The records of each President since Herbert Hoover are administered by NARA. While such records were once considered personal papers, all Presidential records created on or after January 20, 1981, are declared by law to be owned and controlled by the United States and are required to be transferred to NARA at the end of the administration, pursuant to the Presidential Records Act of 1978 (44 U.S.C. 2201 *et seq.*).

For further information, contact the Office of Presidential Libraries. Phone, 301–837–3250. Fax, 301–837–3199.

Presidential Libraries—National Archives and Records Administration

Library	City/Address	Director	Telephone
Herbert Hoover Library	West Branch, IA 52358–0488	Timothy G. Walch	319–643–5301
Franklin D. Roosevelt Library	Hyde Park, NY 12538–1999	Cynthia M. Koch	845–486–7770
Harry S. Truman Library	Independence, MO 64050–1798	Michael Devine	816–268–8200
Dwight D. Eisenhower Library	Abilene, KS 67410–2900	Karl Weissenbach	785–263–6700
John F. Kennedy Library	Boston, MA 02125–3398	Thomas J. Putnam	617–514–1600
Lyndon B. Johnson Library	Austin, TX 78705–5702	Tina Houston, *Acting*	512–721–0200
Richard Nixon Library	Yorba Linda, CA 92886–3903	Timothy Naftali	714–983–9120
Richard Nixon Library	College Park, MD 20740–6001	Timothy Naftali	301–837–3290
Gerald R. Ford Library	Ann Arbor, MI 48109–2114	Elaine K. Didier	734–205–0555
Gerald R. Ford Museum	Grand Rapids, MI 49504–5353	Elaine K. Didier	616–254–0400
Jimmy Carter Library	Atlanta, GA 30307–1498	Jay E. Hakes	404–865–7100
Ronald Reagan Library	Simi Valley, CA 93065–0666	R. Duke Blackwood	805–577–4000
George Bush Library	College Station, TX 77845–3906	Warren L. Finch, Jr.	979–691–4000
William J. Clinton Library	Little Rock, AR 72201–1749	Terri Garner	501–374–4242
George W. Bush Library	Lewisville, TX 75057–6409	Alan C.Lowe	972–353–8888
Presidential Materials Staff	Washington, DC 20408–0001	Nancy Kegan Smith	202–357–5200

The Office of the Federal Register   The Office of the Federal Register (OFR) prepares and publishes a wide variety of public documents. Upon issuance, acts of Congress are published in slip law (pamphlet) form and then cumulated and published for each session of Congress in the *United States Statutes at Large*.

Each Federal workday, the OFR publishes the *Federal Register*, which contains current Presidential proclamations and Executive orders, Federal agency regulations having general applicability and legal effect, proposed agency rules, and documents required by statute to be published. All Federal regulations in force are codified annually in the *Code of Federal Regulations*.

Presidential speeches, news conferences, messages, and other materials released by the White House Office of the Press Secretary are published online in the *Daily Compilation of Presidential Documents*

and annually in the *Public Papers of the Presidents*. The *Daily Compilation of Presidential Documents,* as well as electronic versions of the previous *Weekly Compilation of Presidential Documents* from 1993 onward, can be accessed at www.presidentialdocuments.gov.

The *United States Government Manual,* published annually, serves as the official handbook of the Federal Government, providing extensive information on the legislative, judicial, and executive branches.

All of the above publications are available in both paper editions and online in electronic formats at www.federalregister.gov.

For further information, contact Information Services, Office of the Federal Register. Phone, 202–741–6000. TTY, 202–741–6086. Fax, 202–741–6012. Email, fedreg.info@nara.gov. Internet, www.archives.gov/federal-register or www.federalregister.gov.

National Archives Trust Fund Board
The National Archives Trust Fund Board receives funds from the sale of reproductions of historic documents and publications about the records, as well as from gifts and bequests. The Board invests these funds and uses income to support archival functions such as the preparation of publications that make information about historic records more widely available. Members of the Board are the Archivist of the United States, the Secretary of the Treasury, and the Chairman of the National Endowment for the Humanities.

For further information, contact the Secretary, National Archives Trust Fund Board. Phone, 301–837–3550.

National Historical Publications and Records Commission
The National Historical Publications and Records Commission (NHPRC) is the grant-making affiliate of the National Archives and Records Administration. Its mission is to promote the preservation and use of America's documentary heritage essential to understanding our democracy, history, and culture. NHPRC grants help State and local archives, universities, historical societies, and other nonprofit organizations solve preservation problems dealing with electronic records, improve training and techniques, strengthen archival programs, preserve and process records collections, and provide access to them through the publication of finding aids and documentary editions of the papers of the Founding Era and other themes and historical figures in American history. The NHPRC works in partnership with a national network of State historical records advisory boards. It also provides Federal leadership in public policy for the preservation of, and access to, America's documentary heritage.

For further information, contact the National Historical Publications and Records Commission. Phone, 202–357–5010. Email, nhprc@archives.gov. Internet, www.archives.gov/nhprc.

Information Security Oversight Office
The Information Security Oversight Office (ISOO) oversees the security classification programs in both Government and industry and reports to the President annually on their status. Executive orders 12829 and 12958 serve as the authority for ISOO, and the Office receives its policy and program guidance from the National Security Council. An organizational component of the National Archives and Records Administration, ISOO's goals are to hold classification activity to the minimum necessary to protect the national security; to ensure the safeguarding of classified national security information in both Government and industry in a cost-effective and efficient manner; and to promote declassification and public access to information as soon as national security considerations permit.

For further information, contact the Information Security Oversight Office. Phone, 202–357–5250.

Office of Government Information Services
Established under the OPEN Government Act of 2007, the Office of Government Information Services (OGIS) reviews Freedom of Information Act (FOIA) activities throughout the Government. OGIS serves as liaison between individuals making FOIA requests and administrative agencies, establishing mediation services and resolving disputes as necessary. OGIS reviews and provides input on policies and procedures of administrative agencies under FOIA, reviews agency compliance with FOIA, and recommends policy changes to Congress and the President to improve administration of FOIA.

Sources of Information

Calendar of Events   To be added to the mailing list for the monthly *National Archives Calendar of Events* or for a recorded announcement of events at the National Archives locations in Washington, DC and College Park, MD, call 202–357–5000. TDD, 301–837–0482.

Congressional Affairs   The Congressional Affairs staff maintains contact with and responds to inquiries from congressional offices. Phone, 202–357–5100. Fax, 202–357–5959.

Contracts Information on business opportunities with NARA is available electronically at www.fedbizopps.gov.

Educational Opportunities NARA offers several courses on archival and records management principles and on using NARA resources for research and in the classroom. For information on public programs and workshops, contact the Center for the National Archives Experience Education Office at 202–357–5210. Fax, 202–357–5925.

For information about the "Modern Archives Institute," contact the Modern Archives Institute, Room 301, National Archives Building, 700 Pennsylvania Avenue NW., Washington, DC 20408–0001. Phone 202–357–5259.

For information about records management workshops, contact the National Records Management Training Program (phone, 301–837–0660), any regional records services facility, or the Office of Regional Records Services (phone, 301–837–2950). Internet, www.archives.gov/records-mgmt/training/index.html.

For information about "The Federal Register: What It Is and How To Use It," call 202–741–6000.

For information about the "Institute for the Editing of Historical Documents" at the University of Wisconsin, Madison, or fellowships in documentary editing and archival administration, contact NHPRC, National Archives and Records Administration, 700 Pennsylvania Avenue NW., Washington, DC 20408–0001. Phone, 202–357–5010. Email, nhprc@archives.gov. Internet, www.archives.gov/grants.

Electronic Access Information about NARA and its holdings and publications is available electronically. Internet, www.archives.gov. Email, inquire@nara.gov.

Employment For job opportunities nationwide, contact the nearest NARA facility or the Human Resources Operations Branch, Room 339, 9700 Page Avenue, St. Louis, MO 63132. Phone, 800–827–4898. TDD, 314–801–0886. Internet, www.archives.gov/careers/jobs.

Freedom of Information Act/Privacy Act Requests Requests should be directed as follows:

For operational records of the National Archives and Records Administration, contact the NARA Freedom of Information Act/Privacy Act Officer, General Counsel Staff, National Archives and Records Administration, 8601 Adelphi Road, College Park, MD 20740–6001. Phone, 301–837–3642. Fax, 301–837–0293.

For archival records in the custody of the Office of Records Services—Washington, DC contact the Special Access/FOIA Staff, National Archives and Records Administration, 8601 Adelphi Road, College Park, MD 20740–6001. Phone, 301–837–3190. Fax, 301–837–1864.

For archival records located at a NARA archives location outside the Washington, DC metropolitan area, contact the facility holding the records or the Office of Regional Records Services. Phone, 301–837–2950. Fax, 301–837–1617. To determine the location of records, search NARA's online Archival research catalog (ARC) at www.archives.gov/research/arc.

For archival records in the custody of a Presidential library, contact the library that has custody of the records (see the "Presidential Libraries" section).

For records in the physical custody of the Washington National Records Center or the regional Federal records centers, contact the Federal agency that transferred the records to the facility. Records stored in the records centers remain in the legal custody of the agency that created them.

Grants For NHPRC grants, contact NHPRC, National Archives and Records Administration, 700 Pennsylvania Avenue NW., Washington, DC 20408–0001. Phone, 202–357–5010. Email, nhprc@archives.gov. Internet, www.archives.gov/grants.

Museum Shops Publications, document facsimiles, and document-related souvenirs are available for sale at the National Archives Shop in Washington, DC, each Presidential library, and at the archives locations in Atlanta and Kansas City. Phone, 202–357–5271. Internet, www.estore.archives.gov.

Museum Programs Contact the Center for the National Archives Experience, National Archives and Records Àdministration, Washington, DC 20408. Phone, 202–357–5210. Fax, 202–357–5926.

Public Affairs The Public Affairs staff maintains contact with and responds to inquiries from the media, issues press releases and other literature, and maintains contact with organizations representing the archival profession, scholarly organizations, and other groups served by NARA. Phone, 202–357–5300.

Publications Agency publications, including facsimiles of certain documents, finding aids to records, and *Prologue*, a scholarly journal published quarterly, are available from the Customer Service Center (NWCC2), NARA, Room 1000, National Archives at College Park, 8601 Adelphi Road, College Park, MD 20740–6001. Phone, 800–234–8861. Fax, 301–837–0483. Internet, www.archives.gov/publications.

Most records management publications are available electronically on the NARA Web site. Limited quantities of some records management publications and posters are available in hard copy format from the Life Cycle Management Division, NARA, 8601 Adelphi Road, College Park, MD 20740–6001. Phone, 301–837–3560. Fax, 301–837–3699. Email, nara.recordsmgttraining@nara.gov

Information about laws, regulations, and Presidential documents is available from the Office of the Federal Register, NARA, Washington, DC 20408. Phone, 202–741–6000. Email, fedreg.info@nara.gov. Internet, www.archives.gov/federal-register or www.federalregister.gov. To subscribe to the *Federal Register* table of contents electronic mailing list, go to http://listserv.access.gpo.gov and select online mailing list archives, FEDREGTOC–L. To receive email notification of new public laws, subscribe to PENS (Public Law Electronic Notification Service) at www.archives.gov/federal-register, "New Public Laws."

NHPRC guidelines are available from the NHPRC, National Archives and Records Administration, 700 Pennsylvania Avenue NW., Washington, DC 20408–0001. Phone, 202–357–5010. Email, nhprc@archives.gov. Internet, www.archives.gov/grants.

Reference Services Records are available for research purposes in reading rooms at the National Archives building, 700 Pennsylvania Avenue NW., Washington, DC (phone, 202–357–5400); at the National Archives at College Park, 8601 Adelphi Road, College Park, MD (phone, 866–272–6272); and at each Presidential library, the National Personnel Records Center, and at NARA's 13 archives locations throughout the country. Written requests for information may be sent to any of these units, or they may be addressed to the Customer Services Division, National Archives at College Park, Room 1000, 8601 Adelphi Road, College Park, MD 20740–6001. Phone, 866–272–6272. Email, inquire@nara.gov.

The Public Inspection Desk of the Office of the Federal Register is open every Federal business day for public inspection of documents scheduled for publication in the next day's *Federal Register*, at Suite 700, 800 North Capitol Street NW., Washington, DC. Phone, 202–741–6000. In addition, the documents currently on public inspection may be viewed at: www.federalregister.gov.

Speakers and Presentations The National Archives conducts regular public programs featuring authors, films, and symposia related to National Archives holdings. For programs in the Washington, DC area, more information is available on the calendar update line. Phone, 202–357–5000. The calendar of events is also available by sending an email to reservations.nwe@nara.gov.

Teacher Workshops and Teaching Materials The National Archives education specialists have developed programs to train teachers in the use of primary source material in the classroom and can provide information on how to obtain documentary teaching materials for classroom use. For further information, contact the education staff of the Center for the National Archives Experience. Phone, 202–357–5210.

Tours Individuals or groups may request guided tours of the exhibitions at the National Archives building. Tours are given by reservation only and subject to availability. Individuals are requested to make arrangements at least 6 weeks in advance. Tours are scheduled for 9:45 a.m. Monday through Friday. Tours of the National Archives at College Park, MD, may also be arranged. Self-guided tours are available, through reservations, Monday through Friday from 10:15 a.m. until 90 minutes before closing. Groups are limited to 100 people. For more information and reservations, contact the Tour Office between 9 a.m. and 4 p.m., Monday through Friday. Phone, 202–357–5450. Email, visitorservices@nara.gov.

Volunteer Service Volunteer service opportunities are available at the National Archives Building and the National Archives at College Park, MD. Volunteers conduct tours, provide information in the exhibit halls, work with staff archivists in processing historic documents, and serve as genealogical aides in the genealogical orientation room.

For more information, contact the Volunteer Program Staff. Phone, 202–357–5272. Fax, 202–357–5925. Email, volunteer@nara.gov. Similar opportunities exist in the Presidential libraries and at NARA's 13 archives locations nationwide. Contact the facility closest to you for information about volunteer opportunities.

For further information, write or visit the National Archives and Records Administration, 700 Pennsylvania Avenue NW., Washington, DC 20408–0001. Phone, 202–357–5400. Internet, www.archives.gov. Email, inquire@nara.gov.

NATIONAL CAPITAL PLANNING COMMISSION

401 Ninth Street NW., Suite 500, Washington, DC 20004
Phone, 202–482–7200. Internet, www.ncpc.gov.

CHAIRMAN	JOHN V. COGBILL III
VICE CHAIRMAN	ROBERT E. MILLER
Members	HERBERT F. AMES, ARRINGTON DIXON, JOHN M. HART, STACIE S. TURNER
Ex Officio:	
(Secretary of the Interior)	KEN SALAZAR
(Secretary of Defense)	ROBERT M. GATES
(Administrator of General Services)	PAUL F. PROUTY, *Acting*
(Chairman, Senate Committee on Homeland Security and Governmental Affairs)	JOSEPH I. LIEBERMAN
(Chairman, House Committee on Oversight and Government Reform)	EDOLPHUS TOWNS
(Mayor of the District of Columbia)	ADRIAN M. FENTY
(Chairman, Council of the District of Columbia)	VINCENT C. GRAY
Staff:	
Executive Director	MARCEL ACOSTA, *Acting*
Deputy Executive Director	(VACANCY)
Chief Operating Officer	BARRY S. SOCKS

Director, Planning Research and Policy Division	JULIA A. KOSTER
Director, Plan and Project Implementation Division	WILLIAM G. DOWD
Director, Urban Design and Plan Review Division	DAVID W. LEVY
Chief of Staff to Executive Director	MICHAEL SHERMAN
Chief Urban Designer	CHRISTINE SAUM
General Counsel	LOIS J. SCHIFFER
Director, Office of Public Affairs	LISA N. MACSPADDEN
Secretariat	DEBORAH B. YOUNG

[For the National Capital Planning Commission statement of organization, see the Code of Federal Regulations, Title 1, Part 456.2]

The National Capital Planning Commission is the central agency for conducting planning and development activities for Federal lands and facilities in the National Capital Region. The region includes the District of Columbia and all land areas within the boundaries of Montgomery and Prince George's Counties in Maryland and Fairfax, Loudoun, Prince William, and Arlington Counties and the city of Alexandria in Virginia.

The National Capital Planning Commission was established as a park planning agency by act of June 6, 1924, as amended (40 U.S.C. 71 *et seq.*). Two years later its role was expanded to include comprehensive planning. In 1952, under the National Capital Planning Act, the Commission was designated the central planning agency for the Federal and District of Columbia governments.

In 1973, the National Capital Planning Act was amended by the District of Columbia Home Rule Act, which made the Mayor of the District of Columbia the chief planner for the District and gave the Commission specific authority for reviewing certain District decisions. The Commission continues to serve as the central planning agency for the Federal Government in the National Capital Region.

The Commission is composed of five appointed and seven *ex officio* members. Three citizen members, including the Chairman, are appointed by the President and two by the mayor of the District of Columbia. Presidential appointees include one resident each from Maryland and Virginia and one from anywhere in the United States. The two mayoral appointees must be District of Columbia residents.

For further information, contact the National Capital Planning Commission, 401 Ninth Street NW., Suite 500, Washington, DC 20004. Phone, 202–482–7200. Fax, 202–482–7272. Internet, www.ncpc.gov. Email, info@ncpc.gov.

NATIONAL CREDIT UNION ADMINISTRATION

1775 Duke Street, Alexandria, VA 22314
Phone, 703–518–6300. Internet, www.ncua.gov.

CHAIRMAN	MICHAEL E. FRYZEL
VICE CHAIRMAN	RODNEY E. HOOD
Member	GIGI HYLAND
Director, Public and Congressional Affairs	JOHN J. MCKECHNIE III

NATIONAL CAPITAL PLANNING COMMISSION

Executive Director	DAVID M. MARQUIS
General Counsel	ROBERT M. FENNER
Chief Financial Officer	MARY ANN WOODSON
Director, Office of Small Credit Union Initiatives	TAWANA Y. JAMES
Director, Office of Corporate Credit Unions	MARK TREICHEL
Director, Office of Examination and Insurance	MELINDA LOVE
Director, Office of Human Resources	KATHY SACHEN-GUTE
Director, Office of Capital Markets and Planning	OWEN COLE
Director, Office of Chief Information Officer	DOUG VERNER
Inspector General	WILLIAM DESARNO
President, Asset Management and Assistance Center	MIKE BARTON

[For the National Credit Union Administration statement of organization, see the *Code of Federal Regulations,* Title 12, Part 720]

The National Credit Union Administration is responsible for chartering, insuring, supervising, and examining Federal credit unions and administering the National Credit Union Share Insurance Fund. The Administration also administers the Community Development Revolving Loan Fund and manages the Central Liquidity Facility, a mixed-ownership Government corporation whose purpose is to supply emergency loans to member credit unions.

The National Credit Union Administration (NCUA) was established by act of March 10, 1970 (12 U.S.C. 1752), and reorganized by act of November 10, 1978 (12 U.S.C. 226), as an independent agency in the executive branch of the Federal Government. It regulates and insures all Federal credit unions and insures State-chartered credit unions that apply and qualify for share insurance.

Activities

Chartering The Administration grants Federal credit union charters to groups sharing a common bond of occupation or association or groups within a well-defined neighborhood, community, or rural district. A preliminary investigation is made to determine if certain standards are met before granting a Federal charter.

For further information, contact the appropriate regional office listed in the following table.

Examinations The Administration regularly examines Federal credit unions to determine their solvency and compliance with laws and regulations and to assist credit union management and operations.

For further information, contact the Director, Office of Examination and Insurance. Phone, 703–518–6360.

Share Insurance The act of October 19, 1970 (12 U.S.C. 1781 *et seq.*), provides for a program of share insurance. The insurance is mandatory for Federal credit unions. State-chartered credit unions in many States are required to have Federal share insurance, and it is optional for other State-chartered credit unions. Credit union members' accounts are insured up to $100,000. The National Credit Union Share Insurance Fund requires each insured credit union to place and maintain a 1-percent deposit of its insured savings with the Fund.

For further information, contact the Director, Office of Examination and Insurance. Phone, 703–518–6360.

Supervision   Supervisory activities are carried out through regular examiner contacts and through periodic policy and regulatory releases from the Administration. The Administration also identifies emerging problems and monitors operations between examinations.

Regional Offices—National Credit Union Administration

Region	Address	Director	Telephone	Fax
CT, MA, ME, NH, NV, NY, MI, RI, VT	9 Washington Sq., Washington Ave. Ext., Albany, NY 12205	Mark A. Treichel	518–862–7400	518–862–7420
AK, DC, DE, MD, NJ, PA, VA, WV	Suite 4206, 1775 Duke St., Alexandria, VA 22314	Robert Leonard, *Acting*	703–519–4600	703–519–4620
AL, FL, GA, IN, KY, MS, NC, OH, PR, SC, TN, VI	Suite 1600, 7000 Central Pkwy., Atlanta, GA 30328	Alonzo A. Swann III	678–443–3000	678–443–3020
AR, IA, IL, LA, KS, MN, MO, ND, NE, OK, SD, TX, WI	Suite 5200, 4807 Spicewood Springs Rd., Austin, TX 78759	C. Keith Morton	512–342–5600	512–342–5620
AS, AZ, CA, CO, GU, HI, ID, MT, NM, OR, WA, WY	Suite 301, 1230 W. Washington St., Tempe, AZ 85281	Jane Walters, *Acting*	602–302–6000	602–302–6024

Sources of Information

Consumer Assistance   Questions about credit union insurance and other consumer matters can be directed to NCUA's Consumer Assistance Center at 1–800–755–1030, from 9 a.m. to 4 p.m. eastern standard time, Monday through Friday. After business hours, consumers may leave a recorded message.

Consumer Complaints   The Administration investigates the complaints of members unable to resolve problems with their Federal credit unions. Complaints should be sent to the Regional Office in the State where the credit union is located.

Employment   Inquiries and applications for employment should be directed to the Office of Human Resources, National Credit Union Administration, 1775 Duke Street, Alexandria, VA 22314–3428.

Federally Insured Credit Unions   A list of federally insured credit union names, addresses, asset levels, and number of members is available for review at NCUA's central and regional offices. Copies of the listing are available at a nominal fee from NCUA, Publications, 1775 Duke Street, Alexandria, VA 22314–3428. Phone, 703–518–6340. A listing is also available electronically through the Internet at www.ncua.gov/indexdata.html.

Publications   A listing and copies of NCUA publications are available from NCUA, Publications, 1775 Duke Street, Alexandria, VA 22314–3428. Phone, 703–518–6340. Publications are also available electronically through the Internet at www.ncua.gov.

Starting a Federal Credit Union Groups interested in forming a Federal credit union may obtain free information by writing to the appropriate regional office.

For further information concerning the National Credit Union Administration, contact the Office of Public and Congressional Affairs, National Credit Union Administration, 1775 Duke Street, Alexandria, VA 22314–3428. Phone, 703–518–6330. Internet, www.ncua.gov.

NATIONAL FOUNDATION ON THE ARTS AND THE HUMANITIES

The purpose of the National Foundation on the Arts and the Humanities is to develop and promote a broadly conceived national policy of support for the humanities and the arts in the United States, and for institutions which preserve the cultural heritage of the United States.

The National Foundation on the Arts and the Humanities was created as an independent agency by the National Foundation on the Arts and the Humanities Act of 1965 (20 U.S.C. 951). The Foundation consists of the National Endowment for the Arts, the National Endowment for the Humanities, the Federal Council on the Arts and the Humanities, and the Institute of Museum and Library Services. The Federal Council on the Arts and the Humanities assists the Endowments in coordinating their programs and other activities with those of Federal agencies. Each Endowment is advised on its respective grantmaking and related policies, programs, and procedures by its own National Council, composed of the Endowment Chairman and other members appointed by the President and confirmed by the Senate. Members of Congress, appointed by the leadership of the House and the Senate, serve in an *ex officio*, non-voting capacity on the National Council on the Arts. The Federal Council's membership comprises the Chairmen of the two Endowments, the Director of Museum and Library Services, and other key Federal cultural officials. Excluding participation by certain of its members, the Federal Council makes agreements to indemnify—against loss or damage—items eligible under the Arts and Artifacts Indemnity Act (20 U.S.C. 971).

[For the National Foundation on the Arts and the Humanities statement of organization, see the *Code of Federal Regulations*, Title 45, Part 1100]

National Endowment for the Arts

1100 Pennsylvania Avenue NW., Washington, DC 20506
Phone, 202–682–5400. TDD, 202–682–5496. Internet, www.arts.gov.

CHAIRMAN	ROCCO LANDESMAN
SENIOR DEPUTY CHAIRMAN	JOAN SHEIGEKAWA
Deputy Chairman, Grants and Awards	ROBERT FRANKEL, *Acting*
Deputy Chairman, Management and Budget	LAURENCE M. BADEN
Deputy Chairman, States, Regions and Local Arts Agencies	PATRICE WALKER POWELL
AccessAbility Director	PAULA TERRY
Administrative Services Director	KATHLEEN M. EDWARDS
Arts Education Director	SARAH B. CUNNINGHAM
Budget Officer	JOHN SOTELO
Chief Information Officer	MICHAEL BURKE
Civil Rights, Equal Employment Opportunity Director	ANGELIA RICHARDSON
Communications Director	VICTORIA HUTTER, *Acting*

Council Operations Director and Deputy Director, Office of Government Affairs	MICHAEL FAUBION
Dance Director	DOUGLAS SONNTAG
Design Director	MAURICE COX
Federal Partnerships Coordinator	TONY TIGHE
Finance Officer	SANDRA STUECKLER
Folk/Traditional Arts Director	BARRY BERGEY
General Counsel	KAREN ELIAS, *Acting*
Government Affairs Director	ANITA DECKER
Grants and Contracts Officer	NICKI JACOBS
Guidelines and Panel Operations Director	JILLIAN L. MILLER
Human Resources Director	CRAIG M. MCCORD, SR.
Indemnity Program Administrator	ALICE M. WHELIHAN
Inspector General	AUVONETT JONES, *Acting*
International Activities Director	PENNIE OJEDA
Literature Grants Programs Director	JON P. PEEDE
Media Arts Director	TED LIBBEY
Museum/Visual Arts Director	ROBERT FRANKEL
Music/Opera Director	WAYNE BROWN
National Reading Initiatives Director	DAVID KIPEN
Presenting Director	MARIO GARCIA DURHAM
Research and Analysis Director	SUNIL IYENGAR
State and Regional Director	JOHN OSTROUT
Theater/Musical Theater Director	BILL O'BRIEN

The National Endowment for the Arts, established by Congress in 1965 as an independent Federal agency, is the official arts organization of the United States Government. It is dedicated to supporting excellence in the arts, both new and established; bringing the arts to all Americans; and providing leadership in arts education.

Through its grants and programs, the Arts Endowment brings great art to all 50 States and 6 U.S. jurisdictions including rural areas, inner cities, and military bases. The Arts Endowment awards competitive matching grants to nonprofit organizations, units of State or local government, and federally recognized tribal communities or tribes, for projects, programs, or activities in the fields of artist communities, arts education, dance, design, folk and traditional arts, literature, local arts agencies, media arts, museums, music, musical theater, opera, presenting, theater, and visual arts. In addition, it awards competitive nonmatching individual fellowships in literature and honorary fellowships in jazz, folk and traditional arts, and opera. Forty percent of the Arts Endowment's

grant funds go to the 56 State and jurisdictional arts agencies and their 6 regional arts organizations in support of arts projects in thousands of communities across the country.

Sources of Information

Grants For information about Arts Endowment funding opportunities, contact the Communications Office. Phone, 202–682–5400. TDD, 202–682–5496. Internet, www.arts.gov/grants.

Publications To obtain a copy of the Arts Endowment's annual report, funding guidelines, or other publications, contact the Communications Office. Phone, 202–682–5400. TDD, 202–682–5496. Internet, www.arts.gov.

For further information, contact the Communications Office, National Endowment for the Arts, 1100 Pennsylvania Avenue NW., Washington, DC 20506–0001. Phone, 202–682–5400. TDD, 202–682–5496. Internet, www.arts.gov.

EDITORIAL NOTE: The National Endowment for the Humanities did not meet the publication deadline for submitting updated information of its activities, functions, and sources of information as required by the automatic disclosure provisions of the Freedom of Information Act (5 U.S.C. 552(a)(1)(A)).

National Endowment for the Humanities

1100 Pennsylvania Avenue NW., Washington, DC 20506
Phone, 202–606–8400 or 800–634–1121 (toll free). TDD, 202–606–8282 or 866–372–2930 (toll free). Internet, www.neh.gov. Email, info@neh.gov.

CHAIR	JIM LEACH
DEPUTY CHAIRMAN	MICHAEL MCDONALD, *Acting*
Chief of Staff	(VACANCY)
Assistant Chairman for Planning and Operations	JEFF THOMAS
Assistant Chair for Partnership and National Affairs	CAROLE WATSON
Assistant Chairman for Programs	ADAM WOLFSON
Director, White House and Congressional Affairs	JEREMY BERNARD
Director, We the People Program	MICHAEL MCDONALD, *Acting*
Director, Communications	NOEL MILAN, *Acting*
General Counsel	MICHAEL MCDONALD
Inspector General	SHELDON BERNSTEIN
Director, Administrative Services	BARRY MAYNES
Chief Information Officer	BRETT BOBLEY
Director, Division of Education Programs	WILLIAM CRAIG RICE
Director, Division of Preservation and Access	NADINA GARDNER
Director, Division of Public Programs	THOMAS PHELPS
Director, Division of Research Programs	JANE AIKIN, *Acting*
Director, Office of Challenge Grants	STEPHEN M. ROSS
Director, Office of Digital Humanities	BRETT BOBLEY
Director, Federal/State Partnership	EDYTHE MANZA
Director, Office of Grant Management	SUSAN DAISEY
Director, Office of Human Resources	ANTHONY MITCHELL, *Acting*
Director, Office of Planning and Budget	LARRY MYERS
Director, Office of Publications	DAVID SKINNER

The National Endowment for the Humanities is an independent, grantmaking agency established by Congress in 1965 to support research, education, preservation, and public programs in the humanities.

According to the agency's authorizing legislation, the term "humanities" includes, but is not limited to, the study of the following: language, both modern and classical; linguistics; literature; history; jurisprudence; philosophy; archeology; comparative religion; ethics; the history, criticism, and theory of the arts; and those aspects of the social sciences that employ historical or philosophical approaches.

The Endowment makes grants to individuals, groups, or institutions—schools, colleges, universities, museums, public television stations, libraries, public agencies, and nonprofit private groups to increase understanding and appreciation of the humanities.

Challenge Grants Nonprofit institutions interested in developing new sources of long-term support for educational, scholarly, preservation, and public programs in the humanities may be-

NATIONAL ENDOWMENT FOR THE HUMANITIES

CHAIRMAN

DEPUTY CHAIRMAN

GENERAL COUNSEL

COMMUNICATIONS

WE THE PEOPLE

PUBLICATIONS

WHITE HOUSE AND CONGRESSIONAL AFFAIRS

INSPECTOR GENERAL

CHIEF INFORMATION OFFICER

ASSISTANT CHAIRMAN FOR PARTNERSHIP AND NATIONAL AFFAIRS

FEDERAL/STATE PARTNERSHIP

ASSISTANT CHAIRMAN FOR PLANNING AND OPERATIONS

ACCOUNTING
ADMINISTRATIVE SERVICES
GRANT MANAGEMENT
HUMAN RESOURCES
INFORMATION RESOURCES MANAGEMENT
LIBRARY
PLANNING AND BUDGET

ASSISTANT CHAIRMAN FOR PROGRAMS

CHALLENGE GRANTS
DIGITAL HUMANITIES
EDUCATION PROGRAMS
PRESERVATION AND ACCESS
PUBLIC PROGRAMS
RESEARCH PROGRAMS

assisted in these efforts by a challenge grant.

For further information, call 202–606–8309.

Digital Humanities The Office of Digital Humanities encourages and supports projects that use or study the impact of digital technology on education, preservation, public programming, and research in the humanities.

For further information, call 202–606–8401. Email, odh@neh.gov.

Education Through grants to educational institutions and fellowships to scholars and teachers, this division strengthens sustained thoughtful study of the humanities at all levels of education.

For further information, call 202–606–8500.

Federal/State Partnership Humanities committees in each of the 50 States, the Virgin Islands, Puerto Rico, the District of Columbia, the Northern Mariana Islands, American Samoa, and Guam receive grants from the Endowment, which they, in turn, grant to support humanities programs at the local level.

For further information, call 202–606–8254.

Preservation and Access This division supports projects that will create, preserve, and increase the availability of resources important for research, education, and public programming in the humanities.

For further information, call 202–606–8570.

Public Programs This division strives to fulfill the Endowment's mandate "to increase public understanding of the humanities" by supporting those institutions and organizations that develop and present humanities programming for general audiences.

For further information, call 202–606–8269.

Research This division promotes original research in the humanities by providing grants for significant research projects.

For further information, call 202–606–8200.

We the People Program This program is designed to encourage and enhance the teaching, study, and understanding of American history, culture, and democratic principles.

For further information, call 202–606–8337.

Sources of Information

Employment For employment information, contact the NEH Job Line. Phone, 202–606–8281.

Grants Those interested in applying for a grant in the humanities should visit www.neh.gov for information and guidelines related to grant programs offered by the National Endowment for the Humanities. For further information, call 202–606–8446. Applications for grants must be submitted through www.grants.gov.

Publications The bimonthly review of issues in the humanities, entitled *Humanities,* is available by subscription ($24 domestic, $33.60 foreign) through the Superintendent of Documents, P.O. Box 371954, Pittsburgh, PA 15250–7954, or by phone at 202-512-1800.

For further information, contact the Office of Communications, National Endowment for the Humanities, Room 510, 1100 Pennsylvania Avenue NW., Washington, DC 20506. Phone, 202–606–8400 or 800–634–1121. TDD, 202–606–8282 or 866–372–2930. Internet, www.neh.gov. Email, info@neh.gov.

Institute of Museum and Library Services

1800 M Street NW., 9th Floor, Washington, DC 20036
Phone, 202–653–4657. Internet, www.imls.gov. Email, imlsinfo@imls.gov.

DIRECTOR	ANNE-IMELDA M. RADICE
Deputy Director for Library Services	MARY L. CHUTE
Deputy Director for Museum Services	MARSHA SEMMEL

Deputy Director for Policy, Planning, Research, and Communications	MAMIE BITTNER
Chief of Staff	KATE FERNSTROM
Counselor to the Director	SCHROEDER CHERRY
Director, Strategic Partnerships	MARSHA SEMMEL
Associate Deputy Director for Library Services	JOYCE RAY
Associate Deputy Director, State Programs	LAURIE BROOKS
Associate Deputy Director for Museum Services	MARY ESTELLE KENNELLY
General Counsel	NANCY E. WEISS

The institute of Museum and Library Services is the primary source of Federal support for the Nation's 122,000 libraries and 17,000 museums. Its mission is to create strong libraries and museums that connect people to information and ideas. The Institute seeks to sustain heritage, culture, and knowledge; enhance learning and innovation; and support professional development.

The Institute of Museum and Library Services (IMLS) was established within the National Foundation on the Arts and the Humanities by the Museum and Library Services Act of September 30, 1996 (110 Stat. 3009–293), which amended the Museum Services Act (20 U.S.C. 961 *et seq.*). The Institute combines administration of Federal museum programs formerly carried out by the Institute of Museum Services and Federal library programs formerly carried out by the Department of Education. The Institute's director is appointed by the President with the advice and consent of the Senate and is authorized to make grants to museums and libraries. The Director receives policy advice on museum and library programs from the National Museum and Library Services Board, which is comprised of 20 members appointed by the President, the Director, the Deputy Director for the Office of Museum Services, and the Deputy Director for the Office of Library Services.

In addition to providing distinct programs of support for museums and libraries, IMLS encourages collaboration between these community resources. The Institute's library programs help libraries use new technologies to identify, preserve, and share library and information resources across institutional, local, and State boundaries and to reach those for whom library use requires extra effort or special materials. Museum programs strengthen museum

operations, improve care of collections, increase professional development opportunities, and enhance the community service role of museums.

IMLS awards grants to all types of museums and libraries. Eligible museums include art, history, general, children's, natural history, science and technology, as well as historic houses, zoos and aquariums, botanical gardens and arboretums, nature centers, and planetariums. Eligible libraries include public, school, academic, research, and special libraries. The Institute makes grants in 11 program categories. These grants improve electronic sharing of information and expand public access to an increasing wealth of information and services.

Native American Library Services   This program provides small grants to tribes and Alaska Native villages for core library operations, technical assistance, and enhancement grants to promote innovative practices.

Native Hawaiian Library Services   This program provides grants to nonprofit organizations that primarily serve and represent Native Hawaiians.

National Leadership Grants   This program provides grants to enhance the quality of library and museum services nationwide. Awarded projects demonstrate national impact and generate results—whether new tools, research, models, services, practices, or alliances—that can be widely adapted or replicated to extend the benefit of Federal support.

Museums for America This program provides funds to aid museums in advancing their capacity to serve a wider, more diverse public through education, partnerships, and technology.

Laura Bush 21st Century Librarians Program This program supports efforts to recruit and educate the next generation of librarians and the faculty who will prepare them for careers in library science.

21st Century Museum Professionals This program supports the preparation of museum professionals for the future by updating and expanding their knowledge and skills.

Native American/Native Hawaiian Museum Services This program enables Native American tribes and organizations that primarily serve Native Hawaiians to benefit their communities and audiences through strengthened museum services in the areas of programming, professional development, and enhancement of museum services.

Conservation Project Support This program awards matching grants to help museums identify conservation needs and priorities and perform activities to ensure the safekeeping of their collections.

Museum Grants for African American History and Culture This program enables African American museums to gain knowledge and abilities in the areas of management, operations, programming, collections care, and other museum skills.

Museum Assessment Program IMLS helps support the cost of the Museum Assessment Program through a cooperative agreement with the American Association of Museums. The program is designed to help museums assess their strengths and weaknesses and plan for the future.

Conservation Assessment Program IMLS helps support the cost of the Conservation Assessment Program through a cooperative agreement with Heritage Preservation. The program is designed to support a 2-day site visit by a conservation professional to perform the assessment and up to 3 days to write the report.

National Medals for Museum and Library Service This program recognizes outstanding museums and libraries that provide meaningful public service for their communities.

Sources of Information

Electronic Access Information about IMLS programs, application guidelines, and lists of grantees are available electronically. Internet, www.imls.gov. Email, imlsinfo@imls.gov.

Grants, Contracts, and Cooperative Agreements For information about applying for IMLS funding, contact the appropriate program office. Museums should contact the Office of Museum Services, Institute of Museum and Library Services, 1800 M Street NW., 9th Floor, Washington, DC 20036 (phone, 202–653–4798). Libraries should contact the Office of Library Services, Institute of Museum and Library Services, 1800 M Street NW., Washington, DC 20036 (phone, 202–653–4700).

For further information, contact the Office of Public and Legislative Affairs, Institute of Museum and Library Services, 1800 M Street NW., Washington, DC 20036. Phone, 202–653–4757. Internet, www.imls.gov. Email, imlsinfo@imls.gov.

NATIONAL LABOR RELATIONS BOARD

1099 Fourteenth Street NW., Washington, DC 20570
Phone, 202–273–1000. TDD, 202–273–4300. Internet, www.nlrb.gov.

CHAIRMAN   WILMA B. LIEBMAN

Members	PETER C. SCHAUMBER, (3 VACANCIES)
Executive Secretary	LESTER A. HELTZER
Deputy Executive Secretary	DAVID B. PARKER
Solicitor	WILLIAM B. COWEN
Inspector General	DAVID P. BERRY
Representation Appeals	LAFE E. SOLOMON
Associate Director, Division of Information	(VACANCY)
Chief Administrative Law Judge	ROBERT A. GIANNASI
Deputy Chief Administrative Law Judge	C. RICHARD. MISERENDINO
Chief, Information Technology	RICHARD WESTFIELD
Deputy Chief Information Officer	BRYAN BURNETT
General Counsel	RONALD MEISBURG
Deputy General Counsel	JOHN E. HIGGINS, JR.
Director, Equal Employment Opportunity	ROBERT J. POINDEXTER
Deputy Director	BRENDA VALENTINE HARRIS
Associate General Counsel, Division of Operations-Management	RICHARD A. SIEGEL
Deputy Associate General Counsel	ANNE G. PURCELL
Associate General Counsel, Division of Advice	BARRY J. KEARNEY
Deputy Associate General Counsel	ELLEN A. FARRELL
Associate General Counsel, Division of Enforcement Litigation	JOHN H. FERGUSON
Deputy Associate General Counsel	MARGERY E. LIEBER
Director of Administration	GLORIA J. JOSEPH
Deputy Director of Administration	KATHLEEN JAMES

[For the National Labor Relations Board statement of organization, see the *Federal Register* of June 14, 1979, 44 FR 34215]

The National Labor Relations Board is vested with the power to prevent and remedy unfair labor practices committed by private sector employers and unions and to safeguard employees' rights to organize and determine whether to have unions as their bargaining representative.

The National Labor Relations Board (NLRB) is an independent agency created by the National Labor Relations Act of 1935 (Wagner Act; 29 U.S.C. 167). The Board is authorized to designate appropriate units for collective bargaining and to conduct secret ballot elections to determine whether employees desire representation by a labor organization.

Activities

The NLRB has two principal functions: preventing and remedying unfair labor practices by employers and labor organizations or their agents and conducting secret ballot elections among employees in appropriate collective-bargaining units to determine whether or not they desire to be represented by a labor organization in bargaining with

employers about their wages, hours, and working conditions. The agency also conducts secret ballot elections among employees who have been covered by a union-security agreement to determine whether or not they wish to revoke their union's authority to make such agreements. In jurisdictional disputes between two or more unions, the Board determines which competing group of workers is entitled to perform the work involved.

The regional directors and their staffs process representation, unfair labor practice, and jurisdictional dispute cases. They issue complaints in unfair labor practice cases; seek settlement of unfair labor practice charges; obtain compliance with Board orders and court judgments; and petition district courts for injunctions to prevent or remedy unfair labor practices. The regional directors

NATIONAL LABOR RELATIONS BOARD

direct hearings in representation cases; conduct elections pursuant to the agreement of the parties or the decision-making authority delegated to them by the Board or pursuant to Board directions; and issue certifications of representatives when unions win or certify the results when unions lose employee elections. They process petitions for bargaining unit clarification, for amendment of certification, and for rescission of a labor organization's authority to make a union-shop agreement. They also conduct national emergency employee referendums.

Administrative law judges conduct hearings in unfair labor practice cases, make findings of fact and conclusions of law, and recommend remedies for violations found. Their decisions can be appealed to the Board for a final agency determination. The Board's decisions are subject to review in the U.S. courts of appeals.

Field Offices—National Labor Relations Board

(RO: Resident Office; SR: Subregion)

Office/Address	Director	Telephone	Fax
Region 1, Rm. 601, 10 Causeway St., Boston, MA 02222–1072	Rosemary Pye	617–565–6700	617–565–6725
Region 2, Rm. 3614, 26 Federal Plz., New York, NY 10278–0104.	Celeste J. Mattina	212–264–0300	212–264–2450
Region 3			
Suite 630, 130 S. Elmwood Ave., Buffalo, NY 14202	Rhonda P. Ley	716–551–4931	716–551–4972
Rm. 342, Clinton Ave. at N. Pearl St., Albany, NY 12207–2350 (RO).	Barnett Horowitz	518–431–4155	518–431–4157
Region 4, 7th Fl., 615 Chestnut St., Philadelphia, PA 19106–4404.	Dorothy L. Moore-Duncan	215–597–7601	215–597–7658
Region 5			
8th Fl., 103 S. Gay St., Baltimore, MD 21202–4026	Wayne R. Gold	410–962–2822	410–962–2198
Suite 5530, 1099 14th St., Washington, DC 20570–0001 (RO) ...	Mark Baptiste-Kalaris	202–208–3000	202–208–3013
Region 6, Rm. 904, 1000 Liberty Ave., Pittsburgh, PA 15219	Robert W. Chester	412–395–4400	412–395–5986
Region 7			
Rm. 300, 477 Michigan Ave., Detroit, MI 48226–2569	Stephen M. Glasser	313–226–3200	313–226–2090
Rm. 330, 82 Ionia NW., Grand Rapids, MI 49503–3022 (RO)	Chet H. Byerly, Jr.	616–456–2679	616–456–2596
Region 8, Rm. 1695, 1240 E. 9th St., Cleveland, OH 44199–2086.	Frederick Calatrello	216–522–3716	216–522–2418
Region 9, Rm. 3003, 550 Main St., Cincinnati, OH 45202–3271	Gary Muffley	513–684–3686	513–684–3946
Region 10			
Suite 1000, Harris Twr., 233 Peachtree St. NE., Atlanta, GA 30303.	Martin M. Arlook	404–331–2896	404–331–2858
Suite 3400, 1130 South 22d St., Birmingham, AL 35205–2870 (RO).	C. Douglas Marshall	205–731–1062	205–731–0955
Region 11, Suite 200, 4035 University Pkwy., Winston-Salem, NC 27106–3323.	Willie L. Clark, Jr.	336–631–5201	336–631–5210
Region 12			
Suite 530, 201 E. Kennedy Blvd., Tampa, FL 33602–5824	Rochelle Kentov	813–228–2641	813–228–2874
Suite 340, 550 Water St., Jacksonville, FL 32202–5177 (RO)	Nicholas Ohanesian	904–232–3768	904–232–3146
Rm. 1320, 51 SW. 1st Ave., Miami, FL 33130–1608 (RO)	Harold Maier	305–536–5391	305–536–5320
Region 13, Suite 900, The Rockery Bldg., 209 S. LaSalle St., Chicago, IL 60604–5208.	Joseph A. Barker	312–353–7570	312–886–1341
Region 14, Rm. 8.302, 1222 Spruce St., St. Louis, MO 63103–2829.	Ralph R. Tremain	314–539–7770	314–539–7794
Suite 200, 300 Hamilton Blvd., Peoria, IL 61602–1246 (SR 33) ..	Will Vance	309–671–7080	309–671–7095
Region 15, 7th Fl., 600 S. Maestri Pl., New Orleans, LA 70130–3413.	M. Kathleen McKinney	504–589–6361	504–589–4069
Region 16			
Rm. 8A24, 819 Taylor St., Fort Worth, TX 76102–6178	Martha Kinard	817–978–2921	817–978–2928
Suite 1545, 1919 Smith St., Houston, TX 77002 (RO)	Nadine Littles	713–209–4888	713–209–4890
Suite 705, 711 Navarro St., San Antonio, TX 78205–1711 (RO)	Steve E. Martinez	210–472–6140	210–472–6143
Region 17			
Suite 100, 8600 Farley St., Overland Park, KS 66212–4677	Daniel L. Hubbel	913–967–3000	913–967–3010
Rm. 318, 224 S. Boulder Ave., Tulsa, OK 74103–3027 (RO)	Charles T. Hoskin	918–581–7951	918–581–7970
Region 18			
Suite 790, 330 S. 2d Ave., Minneapolis, MN 55401–2221	(vacancy)	612–348–1757	612–348–1785
Rm. 439, 210 Walnut St., Des Moines, IA 50309–2103 (RO)	David T. Garza	515–284–4391	515–284–4713
Region 19			
Rm. 2948, 915 2d Ave., Seattle, WA 98174–1078	Richard L. Ahearn	206–220–6300	206–220–6305
Suite 210, 605 W. 4th Ave., Anchorage, AK 99501–1936 (RO) ...	Minoru N. Hayashi	907–271–5015	907–271–3055
Suite 1910, 601 SW. 2d Ave., Portland, OR 97204–3170 (SR 36).	Linda L. Davidson	503–326–3085	503–326–5387
Region 20			
Suite 400, 901 Market St., San Francisco, CA 94103–1735	Joseph P. Norelli	415–356–5130	415–356–5156
Rm. 7–245, 300 Ala Moana Blvd., Honolulu, HI 96850–4980 (SR 37).	Thomas W. Cestare	808–541–2814	808–541–2818

Field Offices—National Labor Relations Board—Continued
(RO: Resident Office; SR: Subregion)

Office/Address	Director	Telephone	Fax
Region 21			
9th Fl., 888 S. Figueroa St., Los Angeles, CA 90017–5449	James F. Small	213–894–5200	213–894–2778
Suite 418, 555 W. Beech St., San Diego, CA 92101–2939 (RO)	Steven J. Sorensen	619–557–6184	619–557–6358
Region 22, 5th Floor, 20 Washington Pl., Newark, NJ 07102–3110.	J. Michael Lightner	973–645–2100	973–645–3852
Region 24, Suite 1002, 525 F.D. Roosevelt Ave., Hato Rey, PR 00918–1002.	Marta Figueroa	787–766–5347	787–766–5478
Region 25, Rm. 238, 575 N. Pennsylvania St., Indianapolis, IN 46204–1577.	Rik Lineback	317–226–7381	317–226–5103
Region 26			
Suite 350, The Brinkley Plaza Bldg., 80 Monroe Ave., Memphis, TN 38103–2481.	Ronald K. Hooks	901–544–0018	901–544–0008
Suite 800, 425 W. Capitol Ave., Little Rock, AR 72201–3489 (RO).	Stacia Campbell	501–324–6311	501–324–5009
Suite 320, 810 Broadway, Nashville, TN 37203–3816 (RO)	Joseph H. Artilles	615–736–5921	615–736–7761
Region 27, 7th Fl. N. Twr., 600 17th St., Denver, CO 80202–5433.	Michael W. Josserand	303–844–3551	303–844–6249
Region 28			
Suite 1800, 2600 N. Central Ave., Phoenix, AZ 85004–3099	Cornele A. Overstreet	602–640–2160	602–640–2178
Suite 1820, 505 Marquette Ave. NW., Albuquerque, NM 87102–2181 (RO).	(vacancy)	505–248–5125	505–248–5134
P.O. Box 971187, El Paso, TX 79997–1187 (RO)	(vacancy)	915–592–6571	915–592–6572
Suite 400, 600 Las Vegas Blvd. S., Las Vegas, NV 89101–6637 (RO).	(vacancy)	702–388–6416	702–388–8248
Region 29, 10th Fl., Jay St. & Myrtle Ave., Brooklyn, NY 11201–4201.	Alvin B. Blyer	718–330–7713	718–330–7579
Region 30, Suite 700, 310 W. Wisconsin Ave., Milwaukee, WI 53203–2211.	Irving E. Gottschalk	414–297–3861	414–297–3880
Region 31, Suite 700, 11150 W. Olympic Blvd., Los Angeles, CA 90064–1824.	James J. McDermott	310–235–7351	310–235–7420
Region 32, Suite 300N, 1301 Clay St., Oakland, CA 94612–5211.	Alan B. Reichard	510–637–3300	510–637–3315
Region 34, 21st Fl., 280 Trumbull St., Hartford, CT 06103–3503	(vacancy)	860–240–3522	860–240–3564

Sources of Information

Contracts Prospective suppliers of goods and services may inquire about agency procurement and contracting practices by writing to the Chief, Procurement and Facilities Branch, National Labor Relations Board, Washington, DC 20570. Phone, 202–273–4040.

Electronic Access Information about the Board's programs and activities is available through the Internet at www.nlrb.gov.

Employment The Board appoints administrative law judges from a register established by the Office of Personnel Management. The agency hires attorneys, stenographers, and typists for all its offices; field examiners for its field offices; and administrative personnel for its Washington office. Inquiries regarding college and law school recruiting programs should be directed to the nearest regional office. Employment inquiries and applications may be sent to any regional office or the Washington human resources office.

Publications Anyone desiring to inspect formal case documents or read agency publications may use facilities of the Washington or field offices. The agency will assist in arranging reproduction of documents and order transcripts of hearings. The Board's offices offer free informational leaflets in limited quantities: *The National Labor Relations Board and YOU (Unfair Labor Practices), The National Labor Relations Board and YOU (Representation Cases), Your Government Conducts an Election for You on the Job,* and *The National Labor Relations Board—What It Is, What It Does.* The Superintendent of Documents, Government Printing Office, Washington, DC 20402, sells *A Guide to Basic Law and Procedures Under the NLRA,* the *Annual Report,* the *Classified Index of National Labor Relations Board Decisions and Related Court Decisions,* volumes of Board decisions, and a number of subscription services, including the *NLRB Casehandling Manual* (in three parts), the *Weekly Summary of NLRB Cases*, the *NLRB Election Report*, and *An Outline of Law and Procedure in Representation Cases.* Most NLRB publications are posted on the agency's Web site at www.nlrb.gov/publications.

Speakers   To give the public and persons appearing before the agency a better understanding of the National Labor Relations Act and the Board's policies, procedures, and services, Washington and regional office personnel participate as speakers or panel members before bar associations, labor, educational, civic, or management organizations, and other groups. Requests for speakers or panelists may be made to Washington officials or to the appropriate regional director.

For further information, contact the Division of Information, National Labor Relations Board, 1099 Fourteenth Street NW., Washington, DC 20570. Phone, 202–273–1991. Internet, www.nlrb.gov.

NATIONAL MEDIATION BOARD

1301 K Street NW., Suite 250 East, Washington, DC 20005
Phone, 202–692–5000. Internet, www.nmb.gov.

CHAIRMAN	READ VAN DE WATER
Members	ELIZABETH DOUGHERTY, HARRY R. HOGLANDER
Director, Mediation Services	LARRY GIBBONS
Director, Alternative Dispute Resolution	DANIEL RAINEY
General Counsel, Office of Legal Affairs	MARY JOHNSON
Director, Arbitration Services	ROLAND WATKINS
Director, Administration	JUNE KING

The National Mediation Board facilitates harmonious labor-management relations within two of the Nation's key transportation sectors: the railroads and the airlines. The Board handles mediation and employee representation disputes and provides administrative and financial support in adjusting grievances in the railroad industry.

The National Mediation Board (NMB) is an independent agency established by the 1934 amendments to the Railway Labor Act of 1926 (45 U.S.C. 151–158, 160–162, 1181–1188). The Board is composed of three members, appointed by the President and confirmed by the Senate. The board designates a Chairman on a yearly basis.

The Agency's dispute-resolution processes are designed to resolve disputes over the negotiation of new or revised collective bargaining agreements and the interpretation or application of existing agreements. It also effectuates employee rights of self-organization where a representation dispute exists.

Activities

Mediation   Following receipt of an application for meditation, the NMB assigns a mediator to assist the parties in reaching an agreement. The NMB is obligated to use its best efforts to bring about a peaceful resolution to the dispute. If such efforts do not settle the dispute, the NMB advises the parties and offers interest arbitration as an alternative approach to resolve the remaining issues. If either party rejects this offer, the NMB releases the parties from formal mediation. This release triggers a 30-day cooling off period. During this period, NMB continues to work with the parties to achieve a consensual resolution. If,

NATIONAL MEDIATION BOARD

however, an agreement is not reached by the end of the 30-day period, the parties are free to exercise lawful self-help, such as carrier-imposed working conditions or a strike by the union/organization.

Alternative Dispute Resolution   In addition to traditional mediation services, NMB also provides voluntary Alternative Dispute Resolution (ADR) services. ADR services include facilitation, training, grievance mediation, and an Online Dispute Resolution component, which applies technology to the dispute resolution process. The purpose of the ADR program is to assist the parties in learning and applying more effective, less confrontational methods for resolving their disputes, and to help them resolve more of their own disputes without outside intervention.

Presidential Emergency Board   If NMB determines that a dispute threatens to substantially deprive any section of the country of essential transportation service, it notifies the President. The President may, at his discretion, establish a Presidential Emergency Board (PEB) to investigate and report back within 30 days. After the PEB has been created and for 30 days after it has made its report to the President, neither party to the dispute may exercise self-help.

There are also special emergency procedures for unresolved disputes affecting publicly funded and operated commuter railroads and their employees. If the mediation procedures are exhausted, the parties to the dispute, or the Governor of any State where the railroad operates, may request that the President establish a PEB. The President is required to establish such a board if requested. If no settlement is reached within 60 days following the creation of the PEB, NMB is required to conduct a public hearing on the dispute. If there is no settlement within 120 days after the creation of the PEB, any party, or the Governor of any affected state, may request a second, final-offer PEB. No self-help is permitted pending the exhaustion of these emergency procedures.

Representation   When a labor organization or individual files an application with NMB to represent employees, the Agency assigns an investigator to conduct a representation investigation. Should the applicant meet the requirements, NMB continues the investigation, usually with a secret telephone or Internet election. NMB is responsible for ensuring that the requirements for a fair election process have been maintained. If the employees vote to be represented, NMB issues a certification which commences the carrier's statutory duty to bargain with the certified representative.

Arbitration   NMB provides both grievance arbitration and interest arbitration. Grievance arbitration is a process for resolving disputes regarding the interpretation or application of an existing collective bargaining agreement. Grievances must be handled through grievance arbitration if not otherwise resolved, and cannot be used by the parties to trigger self-help actions. NMB has significant administrative responsibilities for grievance arbitration in the railroad industry, which includes those before the National Railroad Adjustment Board (NRAB), as well as the two types of arbitration panels established by the labor-management parties at each railroad: public law boards (PLBs) and special boards of adjustment (SBAs). Grievance arbitration in the airline industry is accomplished at the various system boards of adjustment created jointly by labor and management at the parties' expense. NMB furnishes panels of prospective arbitrators for the parties' selection in both the airline and railroad industries. NMB also pays the salary and travel expenses of the arbitrators for railroad arbitration proceedings. Grievance arbitration decisions are final and binding with very limited grounds for judicial review.

Interest arbitration is a process to establish the terms of a new or modified collective bargaining agreement through arbitration, rather than through negotiations. Unlike grievance arbitration, its use is not statutorily required. NMB offers the parties the opportunity to use binding interest arbitration when the agency has determined that further mediation efforts will not be successful. In addition, the parties may directly agree to resolve their collective bargaining dispute or portions of their dispute through interest arbitration. NMB generally provides the parties with panels of potential arbitrators from which they select an individual to resolve their dispute. In some instances, however, the parties agree to allow NMB to directly appoint an arbitrator. Interest arbitration decisions are final and binding with very narrow grounds for judicial appeal.

Sources of Information

Electronic Access   Information pertaining to Board operations, including weekly case activity reports, representation determinations, press releases, and an agency directory, are available on the Internet at www.nmb.gov.

NMB Knowledge Store   The Knowledge Store contains over 100,000 documents in an easily searchable format, including arbitration awards, representation decisions, annual reports, PEB reports, industry contracts, and union constitutions and bylaws.

Publications   The *Annual Reports of the National Mediation Board* are available on the NMB Web site (www.nmb.gov) in the Knowledge Store. A limited supply of paper copies is also available for public distribution by calling 202–692–5031.

Virtual Reading Room   Copies of collective-bargaining agreements between labor and management of various rail and air carriers and NMB Determinations (back to at least October 1, 1998) are available on the NMB Web site (www.nmb.gov) in the Knowledge Store.

For further information, contact the Public Information Officer, National Mediation Board, Suite 250 East, 1301 K Street NW., Washington, DC 20005-7011. Phone, 202–692–5050. Internet, www.nmb.gov.

NATIONAL RAILROAD PASSENGER CORPORATION (AMTRAK)

60 Massachusetts Avenue NE., Washington, DC 20002
Phone, 202–906–3000. Internet, www.amtrak.com.

Board of Directors:

CHAIRMAN	TOM CARPER
Members	RAY LaHOOD (SECRETARY OF TRANSPORTATION), JOSEPH H. BOARDMAN (PRESIDENT), DONNA McLEAN, NANCY NAPLES, (4 VACANCIES)

Officers:

President and Chief Executive Officer	JOSEPH H. BOARDMAN
Chief Financial Officer	D. J. STADTLER
Vice President, Labor Relations	JOSEPH M. BRESS
Chief Operating Officer	WILLIAM L. CROSBIE
Vice President, Human Resources and Diversity Initiatives	LORRAINE A. GREEN
Vice President, Strategic Partnerships	(VACANCY)
Vice President, Government Affairs and Corporate Communications	JOSEPH H. McHUGH

Vice President, Marketing and Product Management	EMMETT FREMAUX
General Counsel and Corporate Secretary	ELEANOR D. ACHESON
Vice President, Security, Strategy and Special Operations	WILLIAM ROONEY
Chief Information Officer	ED TRAINOR
Inspector General	FRED E. WEIDERHOLD

[For the National Railroad Passenger Corporation statement of organization, see the *Code of Federal Regulations,* Title 49, Part 700]

The National Railroad Passenger Corporation was established by Congress to meet the Nation's intercity passenger transportation needs.

The National Railroad Passenger Corporation (Amtrak) was created by the Rail Passenger Service Act of 1970, as amended (49 U.S.C. 241), and was incorporated under the laws of the District of Columbia to provide a balanced national transportation system by developing, operating, and improving U.S. intercity rail passenger service.

Amtrak operates approximately 300 trains per day, serving over 500 stations in 46 States, over a system of 21,800 route miles. Of this route system, Amtrak owns about 530 route miles in the Northeast and several other small track segments elsewhere in the country.

Amtrak owns or leases its stations and owns its own repair and maintenance facilities. The Corporation employs a total workforce of approximately 19,000 and provides all reservation, station, and on-board service staffs, as well as train and engine operating crews. Outside the Northeast Corridor, Amtrak contracts with privately or publicly owned railroads for the right to operate over their track. Under contract, these railroads are responsible for the condition of the roadbed and for coordinating the flow of traffic.

In fiscal year 2008, Amtrak transported over 28 million people with 78,000 passengers traveling on Amtrak per day. Also, Amtrak runs commuter trains under contract with several commuter agencies.

Although Amtrak's basic route system was originally designated by the Secretary of Transportation in 1971, modifications have been made to the Amtrak system and to individual routes that have resulted in more efficient and cost-effective operations. Although capital funding has increased in recent years, operating budget constraints mean that new service will only be added if a State agrees to cover any operating losses.

For further information, contact the Government Affairs Department, Amtrak, 60 Massachusetts Avenue NE., Washington, DC 20002. Phone, 202–906–3918. Internet, www.amtrak.com.

EDITORIAL NOTE: The National Science Foundation did not meet the publication deadline for submitting updated information of its activities, functions, and sources of information as required by the automatic disclosure provisions of the Freedom of Information Act (5 U.S.C. 552(a)(1)(A)).

NATIONAL SCIENCE FOUNDATION

4201 Wilson Boulevard, Arlington, VA 22230
Phone, 703–292–5111. TDD, 800–281–8749. Internet, www.nsf.gov. Email, info@nsf.gov.

National Science Board

Chair	STEVEN C. BEERING
Vice Chairman	PATRICIA D. GALLOWAY
Members	MARK C. ABBOT, DAN E. ARVIZU, BARRY C. BARISH, CAMILLA P. BENBOW, RAY M. BOWEN, JOHN T. BRUER, G. WAYNE CLOUGH, FRANCE A. CORDOVA, KELVIN K. DROEGEMEIER, JOSÉ-MARIE GRIFFITHS, ESIN GULARI, KARL HESS, ELIZABETH HOFFMAN, LOUIS J. LANZEROTTI, ALAN I. LESHNER, GEORGE P. PETERSON, DOUGLAS D. RANDALL, ARTHUR K. REILLY, DIANE L. SOUVAINE, JON C. STRAUSS, KATHRYN D. SULLIVAN, THOMAS N. TAYLOR, RICHARD F. THOMPSON
(*Ex officio*)	ARDEN L. BEMENT, JR.
Executive Officer/Director	CRAIG R. ROBINSON, *Acting*

National Science Foundation

DIRECTOR	ARDEN L. BEMENT, JR.
DEPUTY DIRECTOR	CORA B. MARRETT, *Acting*
Assistant Director for Biological Sciences	JAMES COLLINS
Assistant Director for Computer and Information Science and Engineering	JEANNETTE M. WING
Assistant Director for Education and Human Resources	WANDA E. WARD, *Acting*
Assistant Director for Engineering	MICHAEL M. REISCHMAN, *Acting*
Assistant Director for Geosciences	TIMOTHY L. KILLEEN
Assistant Director for Mathematical and Physical Sciences	TONY F. CHAN
Assistant Director for Social, Behavioral, and Economic Sciences	DAVID W. LIGHTFOOT
Director, Office of Cyberinfrastructure	EDWARD SEIDEL
Director, Office of International Science and Engineering	LARRY H. WEBER
Director, Office of Polar Programs	KARL A. ERB
Director, Office of Equal Opportunity Programs	JAMES H. LIGHTBOURNE, *Acting*
General Counsel	LAWRENCE RUDOLPH
Inspector General	CHRISTINE C. BOESZ
Director, Office of Integrative Activities	W. LANCE HAWORTH
Director, Office of Legislative and Public Affairs	JEFF NESBIT
Chief Financial Officer and Director, Office of Budget, Finance, and Award Management	THOMAS N. COOLEY

Chief Human Capital Officer and Director,
    Office of Information and Resource
    Management   ANTHONY A. ARNOLIE

Chief Information Officer   GEORGE O. STRAWN
Affirmative Action Officer   (VACANCY)

[For the National Science Foundation statement of organization, see the *Federal Register* of February 8, 1993, 58 FR 7587–7595; May 27, 1993, 58 FR 30819; May 2, 1994, 59 FR 22690; and Oct. 6, 1995, 60 FR 52431]

The National Science Foundation promotes the progress of science and engineering through the support of research and education programs.

The National Science Foundation (NSF) is an independent agency created by the National Science Foundation Act of 1950, as amended (42 U.S.C. 1861–1875).

The purposes of the Foundation are to increase the Nation's base of scientific and engineering knowledge and strengthen its ability to conduct research in all areas of science and engineering; to develop and help implement science and engineering education programs that can better prepare the Nation for meeting the challenges of the future; and to promote international cooperation through science and engineering. In its role as a leading Federal supporter of science and engineering, the agency also has an important role in national policy planning.

The Director and the Deputy Director are appointed by the President, with the advice and consent of the Senate, to a 6-year term and an unspecified term, respectively. The Foundation's activities are guided by the National Science Board. The National Science Board is composed of 24 members and the Director *ex officio*. Members are appointed by the President with the advice and consent of the Senate for 6-year terms, with one-third appointed every 2 years. They are selected because of their records of distinguished service in science, engineering, education, research management, or public affairs to be broadly representative of the views of national science and engineering leadership. The Board also has a broad national policy responsibility to monitor and make recommendations to promote the health of U.S. science and engineering research and education.

The Foundation's Office of Inspector General is responsible for conducting and supervising audits, inspections, and investigations relating to the programs and operations of the Foundation, including allegations of misconduct in science.

Activities

The National Science Foundation initiates and supports fundamental, long-term, merit-selected research in all the scientific and engineering disciplines. This support is made through grants, contracts, and other agreements awarded to universities, colleges, academic consortia, and nonprofit and small business institutions. Most of this research is directed toward the resolution of scientific and engineering questions concerning fundamental life processes, natural laws and phenomena, fundamental processes influencing the human environment, and the forces affecting people as members of society as well as the behavior of society as a whole.

The Foundation encourages cooperative efforts by universities, industries, and government. It also promotes the application of research and development for better products and services that improve the quality of life and stimulate economic growth.

The Foundation promotes the development of research talent through support of undergraduate and graduate students, as well as postdoctoral researchers. It administers special programs to identify and encourage participation by groups underrepresented in science and technology and to strengthen research capability at smaller institutions, small businesses, undergraduate colleges, and universities.

The Foundation supports major national and international science and engineering activities, including the U.S. Antarctic Program, the Ocean Drilling

NATIONAL SCIENCE FOUNDATION

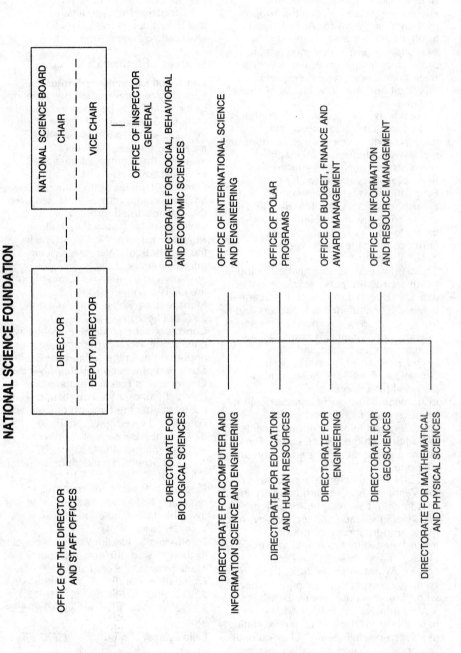

Program, global geoscience studies, and others. Cooperative scientific and engineering research activities support exchange programs for American and foreign scientists and engineers, execution of jointly designed research projects, participation in the activities of international science and engineering organizations, and travel to international conferences.

Support is provided through contracts and cooperative agreements with national centers where large facilities are made available for use by qualified scientists and engineers. Among the types of centers supported by the Foundation are astronomy and atmospheric sciences, biological and engineering research, science and technology, supercomputers, and long-term ecological research sites.

The Foundation's science and engineering education activities include grants for research and development activities directed to model instructional materials for students and teachers and the application of advanced technologies to education. Grants also are available for teacher preparation and enhancement and informal science education activities. Funding is also provided for college science instrumentation, course and curriculum improvement, faculty and student activities, and minority resource centers. In addition, studies of the status of math, science, and engineering education are supported.

The National Science Board presents the Vannevar Bush Award annually to a person who, through public service activities in science and technology, has made an outstanding contribution toward the welfare of mankind and the Nation. It also presents the Public Service Award to an individual and to a company, corporation, or organization who, through contributions to public service in areas other than research, have increased the public understanding of science or engineering. The National Science Foundation annually presents the Alan T. Waterman Award to an outstanding young scientist or engineer for support of research and study. The Foundation also provides administrative

support for the President's Committee on the National Medal of Science.

Information on these awards is available through the Internet at www.nsf.gov/home/nsb/start.htm.

Sources of Information

Board and Committee Minutes Summary minutes of the open meetings of the Board may be obtained from the National Science Board Office. Phone, 703–292–7000. Information on NSB meetings, minutes, and reports is available through the Internet at www.nsf.gov/home/nsb/start.htm. Summary minutes of the Foundation's advisory groups may be obtained from the contacts listed in the notice of meetings published in the *Federal Register* or under "News and Media" on the Foundation's Web site. General information about the Foundation's advisory groups may be obtained from the Division of Human Resource Management, Room 315, Arlington, VA 22230. Phone, 703–292–8180.

Contracts The Foundation publicizes contracting and subcontracting opportunities in the *Commerce Business Daily* and other appropriate publications. Organizations seeking to undertake contract work for the Foundation should contact either the Division of Contracts, Policy, and Oversight (phone, 703–292–8240) or the Division of Administrative Services (phone, 703–292–8190), National Science Foundation, Arlington, VA 22230.

Electronic Access Information regarding NSF programs and services is available through the Internet at www.nsf.gov.

Employment Inquiries may be directed to the Division of Human Resource Management, National Science Foundation, Room 315, Arlington, VA 22230. Phone, 703–292–8180. TDD, 703–292–8044. Internet, www.nsf.gov/jobs.

Fellowships Consult the *NSF Guide to Programs* and appropriate announcements and brochures for postdoctoral fellowship opportunities that may be available through some Foundation divisions. Beginning graduate and minority graduate students wishing to apply for fellowships should contact the Directorate for Education and Human Resources. Phone, 703–292–8601.

Freedom of Information Act Requests Requests for agency records should be submitted in accordance with the Foundation's FOIA regulation at 45 CFR 612. Such requests should be clearly identified with "FOIA REQUEST" and be addressed to the FOIA Officer, Office of General Counsel, National Science Foundation, Room 1265, Arlington, VA 22230. Phone, 703–292–8060. Fax, 703–292–9041. Email, foia@nsf.gov.

Grants Individuals or organizations who plan to submit grant proposals should refer to the *NSF Guide to Programs, Grant Proposal Guide* (NSF–01–2), and appropriate program brochures and announcements that may be obtained as indicated in the Publications section. Grant information is also available through the Internet at www.nsf.gov.

Office of Inspector General General inquiries may be directed to the Office of Inspector General, National Science Foundation, Room 1135, Arlington, VA 22230. Phone, 703–292–7100.

Privacy Act Requests Requests for personal records should be submitted in accordance with the Foundation's Privacy Act regulation at 45 CFR 613. Such requests should be clearly identified with "PRIVACY ACT REQUEST" and be addressed to the Privacy Act Officer, National Science Foundation, Room 1265, Arlington, VA 22230. Phone, 703–292–8060.

Publications The National Science Board assesses the status and health of science and its various disciplines, including such matters as human and material resources, in reports submitted to the President for submission to the Congress. The most recent report is *Science and Engineering Indicators, 2004* (NSB–04–04).

The National Science Foundation issues publications that announce and describe new programs, critical dates, and application procedures for competitions. Single copies of these publications can be ordered by writing to NSF Clearinghouse, P.O. Box 218, Jessup, MD 20794–0218. Phone, 301–947–2722. Email, pubinfo@nsf.gov. Internet, www.nsf.gov.

Other Foundation publications include: the *Grant Policy Manual* (NSF–01–2), which contains comprehensive statements of Foundation grant administration policy, procedures, and guidance; *Guide to Programs*, which summarizes information about support programs; the quarterly *Antarctic Journal of the United States* and its annual review issue; and the *NSF Annual Report*. These publications are available from the Superintendent of Documents, Government Printing Office, Washington, DC 20402. Internet, www.nsf.gov.

Reading Room A collection of Foundation policy documents and staff instructions, as well as current indexes, are available to the public for inspection and copying during regular business hours, 8:30 a.m. to 5 p.m., Monday through Friday, in the National Science Foundation Library, Room 225, Arlington, VA 22230. Phone, 703–292–7830.

Small Business Activities The Office of Small Business Research and Development provides information on opportunities for Foundation support to small businesses with strong research capabilities in science and technology. Phone, 703–292–8330. The Office of Small and Disadvantaged Business Utilization oversees agency compliance with the provisions of the Small Business Act and the Small Business Investment Act of 1958, as amended (15 U.S.C. 631, 661, 683). Phone, 703–292–8330.

For further information, contact the National Science Foundation Information Center, 4201 Wilson Boulevard, Arlington, VA 22230. Phone, 703–292–5111. TDD, 800–281–8749. Internet, www.nsf.gov. Email, info@nsf.gov.

NATIONAL TRANSPORTATION SAFETY BOARD

490 L'Enfant Plaza SW., Washington, DC 20594
Phone, 202–314–6000. Fax, 202–314–6110. Internet, www.ntsb.gov.

CHAIRMAN	DEBORAH A.P. HERSMAN
VICE CHAIRMAN	CHRISTOPHER A. HART
Members	ROBERT L. SUMWALT, (2 VACANCIES)
Managing Director	JOSEPH G. OSTERMAN
Chief Financial Officer	STEVEN GOLDBERG
Chief Administrative Law Judge	WILLIAM E. FOWLER, JR.
General Counsel	GARY HALBERT
Deputy General Counsel	WILLIAM LOVE
Director, Office of Aviation Safety	THOMAS E. HAUETER
Deputy Director, Office of Aviation Safety	JOHN DELISI
Chief, Major Investigations	DANA SCHULZE
Chief Advisor for International Safety Affairs	ROBERT MACINTOSH
Deputy Director, Regional Operations	JEFF GUZZETTI
Director, Office of Government and Industry Affairs	(VACANCY)
Deputy Director, Government Affairs	MILDRED STAREK
Director, Office of Transportation Disaster Assistance	SHARON BRYSON
Assistant Director, Office of Transportation Disaster Assistance	ERIC GROSOF
Associate Managing Director, Office of Public Affairs	TED LOPATKIEWICZ
Director, Office of Highway Safety	BRUCE MAGLADRY
Deputy Director, Operations	DWIGHT FOSTER
Deputy Director, Accident Investigations	BARBARA CZECH
Director, Office of Marine Safety	JOHN SPENCER
Deputy Director, Office of Marine Safety	MICHAEL ROSECRANS
Director, Office of Railroad, Pipeline, and Hazardous Materials Investigations	ROBERT J. CHIPKEVICH
Chief Technical Advisor	JAMES RITTER
Chief, Railroad Division	JAMES SOUTHWORTH
Chief, Pipeline and Hazardous Materials Division	ROBERT TRAINOR
Director, Office of Research and Engineering	(VACANCY)
Deputy Director, Office of Research and Engineering	JOSEPH KOLLY
Director, Office of Safety Recommendations and Communications	ELAINE WEINSTEIN
Deputy Director, Operations	DANIELLE ROEBER
Director, Training Center	PAUL SCHUDA

[For the National Transportation Safety Board statement of organization, see the *Code of Federal Regulations*, Title 49, Part 800]

The National Transportation Safety Board seeks to ensure that all types of transportation in the United States are conducted safely. The Board investigates accidents, conducts studies, and makes recommendations to Government agencies, the transportation industry, and others on safety measures and practices.

NATIONAL TRANSPORTATION SAFETY BOARD

The National Transportation Safety Board (NTSB) was established in 1967 and became totally independent on April 1, 1975, by the Independent Safety Board Act of 1974 (49 U.S.C. 1111).

NTSB consists of five Members appointed for 5-year terms by the President with the advice and consent of the Senate. The President designates two of these Members as Chairman and Vice Chairman of the Board for 2-year terms. The designation of the Chairman is made with the advice and consent of the Senate.

Activities

Accident Investigation   NTSB is responsible for investigating, determining probable cause, making safety recommendations, and reporting the facts and circumstances of incidents in the following areas:

—U.S. civil aviation and certain public-use aircraft accidents;

—railroad accidents in which there is a fatality or substantial property damage, or that involve a passenger train;

—pipeline accidents in which there is a fatality, substantial property damage, or significant injury to the environment;

—highway accidents, including railroad grade-crossing accidents, that the Board selects in cooperation with the States;

—major marine casualties and marine accidents involving a public vessel and a nonpublic vessel, in accordance with regulations prescribed jointly by the Board and the U.S. Coast Guard;

—certain accidents involving hazardous materials; and

—other transportation accidents that are catastrophic, involve problems of a recurring character, or otherwise should be investigated in the judgment of the Board.

Safety Problem Identification   NTSB makes recommendations on matters pertaining to transportation safety and is a catalyst for transportation accident prevention by conducting safety studies and special investigations; assessing techniques of accident investigation and publishing recommended procedures; establishing regulatory requirements for reporting accidents; evaluating the transportation safety consciousness and efficacy of other Government agencies in the prevention of accidents; evaluating the adequacy of safeguards and procedures concerning the transportation of hazardous materials and the performance of other Government agencies charged with ensuring the safe transportation of such materials; and reporting annually to the Congress on its activities.

Family Assistance for Aviation Disasters   NTSB coordinates the resources of the Federal Government and other organizations to support the efforts of local and State governments and airlines to meet the needs of aviation disaster victims and their families. It assists in making Federal resources available to local authorities and airlines.

Certificate, Civil Penalty, or License Appeal   On appeal, NTSB reviews the suspension, amendment, modification, revocation, or denial of certain certificates, licenses, and assessments of civil penalties issued by the Secretary of Transportation. NTSB also reviews on appeal from the orders of any administrative law judge, the decisions of the Commandant of the Coast Guard revoking, suspending, or denying certain licenses, certificates, documents, and registers.

Aviation Regional—National Transportation Safety Board

Regional Office	Address	Officer
EASTERN:		
Ashburn, VA	45065 Riverside Pkwy., 20147	David Muzio
Atlanta, GA	Suite 3M25, 60 Forsyth St. SW., 30303	Jeff Kennedy
Miami, FL	Suite 418, 8240 NW. 52d Ter., 33166	Jeff Kennedy

Aviation Regional—National Transportation Safety Board—Continued

Regional Office	Address	Officer
CENTRAL:		
Arlington, TX	Suite 150, 624 Six Flags Dr., 76011	Jeff Kennedy
Chicago, IL	31 W. 775 N. Ave., 60185	Carl Dinwiddie
Denver, CO	Suite 500, 4760 Oakland St., 80239	David Bowling
WESTERN:		
Gardena, CA	Suite 555, 1515 W. 190th St., 90248	Jeff Rich
Seattle, WA	Rm. 201, 19518 Pacific Hwy. S., 98188	Debra Eckrote, *Acting*
ALASKA:		
Anchorage, AK	Box 11, Rm. 216, 222 W. 7th Ave., 99513	James LaBelle

Railroad/Highway Field Offices—National Transportation Safety Board

Field Office	Address
RAILROAD:	
Eastern	Suite 3M25, 60 Forsyth St. SW., Atlanta, GA 30303
Central	31 W. 775 N. Ave., W. Chicago, IL 60185
Western	Suite 555, 1515 W. 190th St., Gardena, CA 90248
HIGHWAY:	
Eastern	Suite 3M25, 60 Forsyth St. SW., Atlanta, GA 30303
Central	Suite 150, 624 Six Flags Dr., Arlington, TX 76011
	Suite 500, 4760 Oakland St., Denver, CO 80239
Western	Suite 555, 1515 W. 190th St., Gardena, CA 90248

Sources of Information

Contracts and Procurement Inquiries regarding NTSB's procurement and contracting activities should be addressed to the Contracting Officer, National Transportation Safety Board, Washington, DC 20594. Phone, 202–314–6102.

Electronic Access Agency information, including aircraft accident data, synopses of aircraft accidents, speeches and congressional testimony given by Board members and staff, press releases, job vacancy announcements, and notices of Board meetings, public hearings, and other agency events, is available in electronic form through the Internet at www.ntsb.gov.

Employment Send applications for employment to the Human Resources Division, National Transportation Safety Board, Washington, DC 20594. Phone, 202–314–6230.

Publications Publications are provided free of charge to the following categories of subscribers: Federal, State, or local transportation agencies; international transportation organizations or foreign governments; educational institutions or public libraries; nonprofit public safety organizations; and the news media. Persons in these categories who are interested in receiving copies of Board publications should contact the Records Management Division, National Transportation Safety Board, Washington, DC 20594. Phone, 202–314–6551. All other persons interested in receiving publications must purchase them from the National Technical Information Service, 5285 Port Royal Road, Springfield, VA 22161. Orders may be placed by telephone to the Subscription Unit at 703–487–4630 or the sales desk at 703–487–4768.

Reading Room The Board's Public Reference Room is available for record inspection or photocopying. It is located in Room 6500 at the Board's Washington, DC, headquarters and is open from 8:45 a.m. to 4:45 p.m. every business day. Requests for access to public records should be made in person at Room 6500, or by writing to the Records Management Division, National Transportation Safety Board, Washington, DC 20594. Phone, 202–314–6551.

For further information, contact the Office of Public Affairs, National Transportation Safety Board, 490 L'Enfant Plaza SW., Washington, DC 20594. Phone, 202–314–6100. Fax, 202–314–6110. Internet, www.ntsb.gov.

NUCLEAR REGULATORY COMMISSION

Washington, DC 20555
Phone, 301–415–7000. Internet, www.nrc.gov. Email, opa.resource@nrc.gov.

CHAIRMAN	GREGORY B. JACZKO
COMMISSIONERS	DALE E. KLEIN, KRISTINE L. SVINICKI, (2 VACANCIES)
Chief Administrative Judge, Atomic Safety and Licensing Board Panel	E. ROY HAWKENS
Director, Office of Commission Appellate Adjudication	BROOKE D. POOLE, *Acting*
Director, Office of International Programs	MARGARET M. DOANE
General Counsel	STEPHEN G. BURNS
Secretary of the Commission	ANNETTE L. VIETTI-COOK
Executive Director, Advisory Committee on Reactor Safeguards	EDWIN M. HACKETT
Chief Financial Officer	JAMES E. DYER
Executive Director for Operations	R. WILLIAM BORCHARDT
Deputy Executive Director for Reactor and Preparedness Programs	BRUCE S. MALLETT
Deputy Executive Director for Materials, Waste, Research, State, Tribal, and Compliance Programs	MARTIN T. VIRGILIO
Deputy Executive Director for Corporate Management	DARREN B. ASH
Director, Office of Congressional Affairs	REBECCA L. SCHMIDT
Director, Office of Public Affairs	ELIOT B. BRENNER
Inspector General	HUBERT T. BELL, JR.

[For the Nuclear Regulatory Commission statement of organization, see the *Code of Federal Regulations,* Title 10, Part I]

The Nuclear Regulatory Commission licenses and regulates civilian use of nuclear energy to protect public health and safety and the environment.

The Nuclear Regulatory Commission (NRC) was established as an independent regulatory agency under the provisions of the Energy Reorganization Act of 1974 (42 U.S.C. 5801 *et seq.*) and Executive Order 11834 of January 15, 1975. All licensing and related regulatory functions formerly assigned to the Atomic Energy Commission were transferred to the Commission.

The Commission's major program components are the Office of Nuclear Reactor Regulation, the Office of New Reactors, the Office of Nuclear Material

Safety and Safeguards, the Office of Federal and State Materials and Environmental Management Programs, and the Office of Nuclear Regulatory Research. Headquarters offices are located in suburban Maryland, and there are four regional offices.

The Commission ensures that the civilian uses of nuclear materials and facilities are conducted in a manner consistent with the public health and safety, environmental quality, national security, and the antitrust laws. Most of the Commission's effort is focused on

NUCLEAR REGULATORY COMMISSION

THE COMMISSION

COMMISSIONER

COMMISSIONER

CHAIRMAN

COMMISSIONER

COMMISSIONER

OFFICE OF CHIEF FINANCIAL OFFICER

OFFICE OF THE GENERAL COUNSEL

DIRECTOR, OFFICE OF INTERNATIONAL PROGRAMS

OFFICE OF THE SECRETARY OF THE COMMISSION

OFFICE OF THE INSPECTOR GENERAL

DIRECTOR, OFFICE OF CONGRESSIONAL AFFAIRS

DIRECTOR, OFFICE OF PUBLIC AFFAIRS

EXECUTIVE DIRECTOR, ADVISORY COMMITTEE ON REACTOR SAFEGUARDS

CHIEF ADMINISTRATIVE JUDGE (CHAIRMAN), ATOMIC SAFETY AND LICENSING BOARD PANEL

DIRECTOR, OFFICE OF COMMISSION APPELLATE ADJUDICATION

EXECUTIVE DIRECTOR FOR OPERATIONS

ASSISTANT FOR OPERATIONS

DEPUTY EXECUTIVE DIRECTOR FOR CORPORATE MANAGEMENT

DEPUTY EXECUTIVE DIRECTOR FOR MATERIALS, WASTE, RESEARCH STATE, TRIBAL AND COMPLIANCE PROGRAMS

DEPUTY EXECUTIVE DIRECTOR FOR REACTOR AND PREPAREDNESS PROGRAMS

DIRECTOR, COMPUTER SECURITY OFFICE

DIRECTOR, OFFICE OF INFORMATION SERVICES

DIRECTOR, OFFICE OF ADMINISTRATION

DIRECTOR, OFFICE OF ENFORCEMENT

DIRECTOR, OFFICE OF NUCLEAR REGULATORY RESEARCH

DIRECTOR, OFFICE OF INVESTIGATIONS

DIRECTOR, OFFICE OF NUCLEAR MATERIAL SAFETY AND SAFEGUARDS

DIRECTOR, OFFICE OF FEDERAL AND STATE MATERIALS AND ENVIRONMENTAL MANAGEMENT PROGRAMS

DIRECTOR, OFFICE OF SMALL BUSINESS AND CIVIL RIGHTS

DIRECTOR, OFFICE OF HUMAN RESOURCES

REGIONAL ADMINISTRATOR REGION II

REGIONAL ADMINISTRATOR REGION IV

DIRECTOR, OFFICE OF NUCLEAR SECURITY AND INCIDENT RESPONSE

REGIONAL ADMINISTRATOR REGION I

REGIONAL ADMINISTRATOR REGION III

DIRECTOR, OFFICE OF NEW REACTORS

DIRECTOR, OFFICE OF NUCLEAR REACTOR REGULATION

regulating the use of nuclear energy to generate electric power.

Activities

The Nuclear Regulatory Commission is primarily responsible for the following functions:

—licensing the construction, operation, and closure of nuclear reactors and other nuclear facilities, such as nuclear fuel cycle facilities, low-level radioactive waste disposal sites under NRC jurisdiction, the geologic repository for high-level radioactive waste, and nonpower test and research reactors;

—licensing the possession, use, processing, handling, and export of nuclear material;

—licensing the operators of nuclear power and nonpower test and research reactors;

—inspecting licensed facilities and activities;

—conducting the U.S. Government research program on light-water reactor safety;

—developing and implementing rules and regulations that govern licensed nuclear activities;

—investigating nuclear incidents and allegations concerning any matter regulated by NRC;

—maintaining the NRC Incident Response Program;

—collecting, analyzing, and disseminating information about the operational safety of commercial nuclear power reactors and certain nonreactor activities; and

—developing effective working relationships with the States regarding reactor operations and the regulation of nuclear material, and assuring that adequate regulatory programs are maintained by those States that exercise regulatory control over certain nuclear materials in the State.

Sources of Information

Freedom of Information Act Requests
Requests for copies of records should be directed to the FOIA/Privacy Act Officer, Mail Stop T–5 F09, Nuclear Regulatory Commission, Washington, DC 20555–0001. Phone, 301–415–7169. Fax, 301–

415–5130. Requests may also be submitted using the form on our Web site at http://www.nrc.gov/reading-rm/foia/foia-submittal-form.html.

Publications   NRC publishes scientific, technical, and administrative information dealing with licensing and regulation of civilian nuclear facilities and materials, as well as periodic reports, including the annual *Report to Congress on Abnormal Occurrences*, the annual *Performance and Accountability Report*, the quarterly *Licensee, Contractor, and Vendor Inspection Status Report*, the annual *NRC Information Digest*, the *NRC Strategic Plan*, and *Nuclear Regulatory Commission Issuances*.

Some publications and documents are available on the Internet at www.nrc.gov. The U.S. Government Printing Office (GPO) and the National Technical Information Service (NTIS) sell single copies of, or subscriptions to, NRC publications. To obtain prices and order NRC publications, contact the Superintendent of Documents, GPO, Mail Stop SSOP, Washington, DC 20402–0001 (phone, 202–512–1800; Internet, bookstore.gpo.gov) or NTIS, Springfield, VA 22161–0002 (phone, 703–605–6000; Internet, www.ntis.gov).

Active Regulatory Guides may be obtained without charge at http://www.nrc.gov/reading-rm/doc-collections/reg-guides/, by faxed request to 301–415–2289, by email request to distribution.resource@nrc.gov, or by written request to the Reproduction and Distribution Services Section, U.S. Nuclear Regulatory Commission, Washington, DC 20555–0001. They may also be purchased, as they are issued, on standing orders from NTIS. These *Regulatory Guides* are published in 10 subject areas: power reactors, research and test reactors, fuels and materials facilities, environmental and siting, materials and plant protection, products, transportation, occupational health, antitrust and financial review, and general.

Draft Regulatory Guides are issued for public comment. These drafts may be downloaded through the Internet at http://www.nrc.gov/reading-rm/doc-collections/reg-guides. They may be commented on through the Internet using the form at http://www.nrc.gov/public-involve/doc-comment/form.html. Comments may also be emailed to nrcrep.resource@nrc.gov. *Draft Regulatory Guides* may also be obtained, to the extent of supply, by faxed request to 301–415–2289, by email request to distribution.resource@nrc.gov, or by written request to the Reproduction and Distribution Services Section, U.S. Nuclear Regulatory Commission, Washington, DC 20555–0001.

Reading Rooms The headquarters Public Document Room maintains an extensive collection of documents related to NRC licensing proceedings and other significant decisions and actions. Documents issued prior to October 1999 are available in paper or microfiche. Documents issued after October 1999 are also available from NRC's full-text document management system, which is accessible from the NRC Web site at www.nrc.gov/reading-rm/adams.html. The headquarters Public Document Room is located on the first floor at One White Flint North, 11555 Rockville Pike, Rockville, MD, and is open Monday through Friday from 7:45 a.m. to 4:15 p.m., except on Federal holidays.

Documents from the collection may be reproduced, with some exceptions, on paper, microfiche, or CD–ROM for a nominal fee. For additional information regarding the Public Document Room, go to www.nrc.gov/reading-rm/pdr.html or contact the Nuclear Regulatory Commission, Public Document Room, Washington, DC 20555–0001. Phone, 301–415–4737 (Washington, DC, area), or 800–397–4209. Email, pdr.resource@nrc.gov. Fax, 301–415–3548.

Selected regional libraries of the Government Printing Office Federal Depository Library Program maintain permanent microfiche collections of NRC documents released between January 1981 and October 1999. For further information, contact the Public Document Room at the phone number in preceeding text.

For further information, contact the Office of Public Affairs, Nuclear Regulatory Commission, Washington, DC 20555–0001. Phone, 301–415–8200. Internet, www.nrc.gov. Email, opa.resource@nrc.gov.

OCCUPATIONAL SAFETY AND HEALTH REVIEW COMMISSION

1120 Twentieth Street NW., Washington, DC 20036–3457
Phone, 202–606–5050. Fax, 202–418–3017. Internet, www.oshrc.gov.

CHAIRMAN	THOMASINA V. ROGERS
COMMISSIONERS	HORACE A. THOMPSON, (VACANCY)
General Counsel	NADINE N. MANCINI
Chief Administrative Law Judge	IRVING SOMMER
Director, Office of Administration	RICHARD C. LOEB
Executive Secretary	RAY H. DARLING, JR.

The Occupational Safety and Health Review Commission ensures the timely and fair resolution of cases involving the alleged exposure of American workers to unsafe or unhealthy working conditions.

The Occupational Safety and Health Review Commission is an independent, quasi-judicial agency established by the Occupational Safety and Health Act of 1970 (29 U.S.C. 651–678).

The Commission rules on cases when disagreements arise over the results of safety and health inspections performed by the Department of Labor's Occupational Safety and Health

OCCUPATIONAL SAFETY AND HEALTH REVIEW COMMISSION

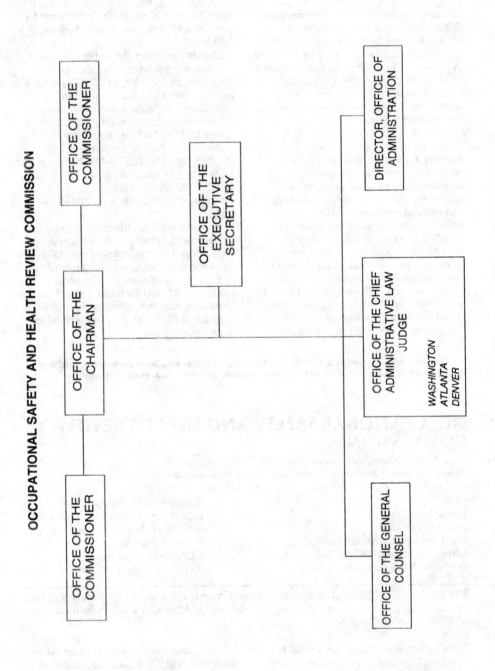

Administration (OSHA). Employers have the right to dispute any alleged job safety or health violation found during the inspection by OSHA, the penalties it proposes, and the time given to correct any hazardous situation.

The Occupational Safety and Health Act covers virtually every employer in the country. Its purpose is to reduce the incidence of personal injuries, illness, and deaths among working men and women in the United States that result from their employment. It requires employers to provide a working environment free from recognized hazards that are causing or likely to cause death or serious physical harm to the employees and to comply with occupational safety and health standards promulgated under the act.

Activities

The Commission was created to adjudicate enforcement actions initiated under the act when they are contested by employers, employees, or representatives of employees. A case arises when a citation, issued to an employer as the result of an OSHA inspection, is contested within 15 working days of receipt of the report.

There are two levels of adjudication within the Commission. All cases are first assigned to an administrative law judge. A hearing is generally held in the community or as close as possible to where the alleged violation occurred. After the hearing, the judge issues a decision, based on findings of fact and conclusions of law.

A substantial number of the judge's decisions become final orders of the Commission. However, if a party petitions the Commission members for review of the judge's decision and the petition is granted, Commission members will issue the final order.

After a final order is issued, any party to the case may seek a review of the decision in the United States Courts of Appeals.

The Commission's principal office is in Washington, DC. Administrative law judges are also located in two regional offices.

Regional Offices

City/Address	Telephone
Atlanta, GA (Rm. 2R90, Bldg. 1924, 100 Alabama St. SW., 30303–3104)	404–562–1640
Denver, CO (Rm. 407, 721 19th St., 80202–2517)	303–844–3409

Sources of Information

Publications Copies of the Commission's *Rules of Procedure, Guide to Review Commission Procedures, Guide to Simplified Proceedings,* and *Employee Guide to Review Commission Procedures: Supplement to the Guide to Review Commission Procedures,* and decisions are available from the Office of the Executive Secretary. Phone, 202–606–5400. Fax, 202–606–5050. Internet, www.oshrc.gov.

For further information, contact the Director, Office of Administration, Occupational Safety and Health Review Commission, 1120 Twentieth Street NW., Washington, DC 20036–3457. Phone, 202–606–5050. Fax, 202–418–3017. Internet, www.oshrc.gov.

EDITORIAL NOTE: The Office of the Director of National Intelligence did not meet the publication deadline for submitting updated information of its activities, functions, and sources of information as required by the automatic disclosure provisions of the Freedom of Information Act (5 U.S.C. 552(a)(1)(A)).

OFFICE OF THE DIRECTOR OF NATIONAL INTELLIGENCE

Washington, DC 20511
Phone, 703–733–8600. Internet, www.dni.gov.

DIRECTOR	DENNIS C. BLAIR
Director of the Intelligence Staff	LT. GEN. JOHN F. KIMMONS, USA
General Counsel	ROBERT S. LITT
Director, National Counterterrorism Center	MICHAEL LEITER
Deputy Director for Analysis	PETER LAVOY
Deputy Director for Policy, Plans and Requirements	DAVID R. SHEDD
Deputy Director for Collection	GLENN A. GAFFNEY
Deputy Director for Future Capabilities	ALDEN MUNSON
Director, National Counterproliferation Center	KENNETH BRILL
Program Manager, Information Sharing Environment	THOMAS E. MCNAMARA
Intelligence Community Chief Information Officer	PRISCILLA GUTHRIE
Chief Financial Officer	MARILYN A. VACCA
Chief Human Capital Officer	RONALD P. SANDERS
Director, Intelligence Advanced Research Projects Activity	LISA PORTER
Iran Mission Manager	(VACANCY)
North Korea Mission Manager	JOSEPH DeTRANI
Cuba/Venezuela Mission Manager	TIMOTHY LANGFORD
Civil Liberties Protection Officer	ALEXANDER W. JOEL
Inspector General	ROSLYN A. MAZER
Chancellor, National Intelligence University	TERESA DOMZAL
Director, Equal Employment Opportunity and Diversity	PATRICIA T. TAYLOR

As head of the Intelligence Community, the Director of National Intelligence oversees and coordinates the foreign and domestic activities of the Intelligence Community across the Federal Government.

The Director of National Intelligence (DNI) is a Cabinet-level post established by section 1011 of the Intelligence Reform and Terrorism Prevention Act of 2004 (50 U.S.C. 403). The DNI is responsible for overseeing and coordinating elements of the Intelligence Community and is the principal intelligence adviser to the President. The DNI reports directly to the President of the United States.

The DNI's responsibilities are:

—coordinating collection, processing, analysis, and dissemination of intelligence information required by the President, the National Security Council, the Secretaries of State and Defense, and other executive branch officials in performing their duties and responsibilities;

—ensuring the sharing of intelligence information within the Intelligence Community;

OFFICE OF THE DIRECTOR OF NATIONAL INTELLIGENCE

—establishing personnel policies and programs applicable to the Intelligence Community; and

—determining the annual National Intelligence Program budget and directing the expenditure of those funds.

For further information, contact the Office of the Director of National Intelligence, Washington, DC 20511. Phone, 703–733–8600. Internet, www.dni.gov.

OFFICE OF GOVERNMENT ETHICS

1201 New York Avenue NW., Suite 500, Washington, DC 20005–3917
Phone, 202–482–9300. TDD, 202–482–9293. Fax, 202–482–9237. Internet, www.usoge.gov.

DIRECTOR	ROBERT I. CUSICK
GENERAL COUNSEL	DON W. FOX
Deputy Director for the Office of International Assistance and Governance Initiatives	JANE S. LEY
Deputy Director for the Office of Agency Programs	JOSEPH E. GANGLOFF
Deputy Director for Administration	(VACANCY)
Deputy General Counsel	WALTER M. SHAUB, JR.

[For the Office of Government Ethics statement of organization, see the *Code of Federal Regulations*, Title 5, Part 2600]

The Office of Government Ethics directs executive branch policies related to preventing conflicts of interest on the part of Government employees and resolving those conflicts of interest that do occur.

The Office of Government Ethics (OGE) is an executive branch agency established under the Ethics in Government Act of 1978, as amended (5 U.S.C. app. 401).

The Director of OGE is appointed by the President with the advice and consent of the Senate for a 5-year term.

Activities

The chief responsibilities of OGE are as follows:

—developing appropriate ethics policies for the executive branch through the promulgation of regulations on Standards of Ethical Conduct, public and confidential financial disclosure of executive branch officials, ethics training programs, and the identification and resolution of conflicts of interest;

—reviewing for identification and resolution of actual or potential conflicts of interest, the financial disclosure reports of potential nominees to, the incumbents of, and those leaving executive branch positions requiring Presidential appointment with Senate confirmation;

—making the financial disclosure reports from individuals required to file with OGE available for public inspection;

—providing education and training to 6,000 ethics officials through instructor instructor-led and Web-based training programs;

—assessing the effectiveness of public and confidential financial disclosure systems maintained by over 130 executive branch agencies;

—maintaining an extensive program to provide advice on Standards of Ethical Conduct and conflict of interest laws;

—conducting onsite reviews of agency ethics programs;

—ordering corrective action on the part of agencies and employees, including orders to establish or modify an agency's ethics program;

—evaluating the effectiveness of the Ethics Act, the conflict of interest laws, and other related statutes and recommending appropriate changes; and

—providing technical assistance in support of U.S. international anticorruption and good governance initiatives.

Sources of Information

Electronic Access Information regarding OGE's services and programs is available in electronic format on the Internet at www.usoge.gov.

Publications The Office of Government Ethics periodically updates its publication, *The Informal Advisory Letters and Memoranda and Formal Opinions of the United States Office of Government Ethics,* available from the Government Printing Office. In addition, OGE has ethics publications and instructional resources available. Upon request, OGE also provides copies of executive branch public financial disclosure reports (SF 278s) in accordance with the Ethics Act and OGE's regulations.

For further information, contact the Office of Government Ethics, Suite 500, 1201 New York Avenue NW., Washington, DC 20005–3917. Phone, 202–482–9300. TTY, 800–877–8339. Fax, 202–482–9237. Email, contactoge@oge.gov. Internet, www.usoge.gov.

EDITORIAL NOTE: The Office of Personnel Management did not meet the publication deadline for submitting updated information of its activities, functions, and sources of information as required by the automatic disclosure provisions of the Freedom of Information Act (5 U.S.C. 552(a)(1)(A)).

OFFICE OF PERSONNEL MANAGEMENT

1900 E Street NW., Washington, DC 20415–0001
Phone, 202–606–1800. TTY, 202–606–2532. Internet, www.opm.gov.

DIRECTOR	JOHN BERRY
DEPUTY DIRECTOR	(VACANCY)
Chief of Staff and Director of External Affairs	ELIZABETH MONTOYA
Inspector General	PATRICK E. MCFARLAND
Chair, Federal Prevailing Rate Advisory Committee	(VACANCY)
General Counsel	ELAINE KAPLAN
Chief Financial Officer	MARK REGER
Director of Modernization	REGINALD BROWN
Associate Director, Strategic Human Resources Policy Division	NANCY H. KICHAK
Associate Director, Human Capital Leadership and Merit System Accountability Division	KEVIN E. MAHONEY
Associate Director, Management Services Division and Chief Human Capital Officer	RONALD FLOM
Associate Director, Federal Investigative Services Division	KATHY DILLAMAN
Associate Director, Human Resources Products and Services Division	KAY T. ELY
Director, Office of Communications and Public Liaison	SEDELTA VERBLE
Director, Office of Congressional Relations	TANIA SHAND

Executive Director, Chief Human Capital
Officer Council

SYDNEY SMITH-HEIMBROCK, *Acting*

[For the Office of Personnel Management statement of organization, see the *Federal Register* of Jan. 5, 1979, 44 FR 1501]

The Office of Personnel Management administers a merit system to ensure compliance with personnel laws and regulations and assists agencies in recruiting, examining, and promoting people on the basis of their knowledge and skills, regardless of their race, religion, sex, political influence, or other nonmerit factors.

The Office of Personnel Management (OPM) was created as an independent establishment by Reorganization Plan No. 2 of 1978 (5 U.S.C. app.), pursuant to Executive Order 12107 of December 28, 1978. Many of the functions of the former United States Civil Service Commission were transferred to OPM.

Activities

Employee Benefits OPM manages numerous activities that directly affect the well-being of the Federal employee and indirectly enhance employee effectiveness. These include health benefits, life insurance, and retirement benefits.

Examining and Staffing The Office of Personnel Management is responsible for providing departments and agencies with technical assistance and guidance in examining competitive positions in the Federal civil service for General Schedule grades 1 through 15 and Federal Wage system positions. In addition, OPM is responsible for the following duties:

—providing testing and examination services, at the request of an agency, on a reimbursable basis;

—establishing basic qualification standards for all occupations;

—certifying agency delegated examining units to conduct examining;

—providing employment information for competitive service positions; and

—providing policy direction and guidance on promotions, reassignments, appointments in the excepted and competitive services, reinstatements, temporary and term employment, veterans preference, workforce planning and reshaping, organizational design, career transition, and other staffing provisions.

Executive Resources OPM leads in the selection, management, and development of Federal executives. OPM provides policy guidance, consulting services, and technical support on Senior Executive Service (SES) recruitment, selection, succession planning, mobility performance, awards, and removals. It reviews agency nominations for SES career appointments and administers the Qualifications Review Boards that certify candidates' executive qualifications. It manages SES, senior-level, and scientific and professional space allocations to agencies, administers the Presidential Rank Awards program, and conducts orientation sessions for newly appointed executives. In addition, OPM manages three interagency residential development and training centers for executives and managers.

Investigations The Office of the Inspector General conducts comprehensive and independent audits, investigations, and evaluations relating to OPM programs and operations. It is responsible for administrative actions against health care providers who commit sanctionable offenses with respect to the Federal Employees' Health Benefits Program or other Federal programs.

For further information, contact the Office of the Inspector General. Phone, 202–606–1200.

Personnel Systems OPM provides leadership and guidance to agencies on systems to support the manager's personnel management responsibilities. These include the following:

—white- and blue-collar pay systems, including SES and special occupational pay systems; geographical adjustments and locality payments; special rates to address recruitment and retention

OFFICE OF PERSONNEL MANAGEMENT

problems; allowances and differentials, including recruitment and relocation bonuses, retention allowances, and hazardous duty/environmental pay; and premium pay;

—annual and sick leave, court leave, military leave, leave transfer and leave bank programs, family and medical leave, excused absence, holidays, and scheduling of work, including flexible and compressed work schedules;

—performance management, covering appraisal systems, performance pay and awards, and incentive awards for suggestions, inventions, and special acts;

—classification policy and standards for agencies to determine the series and grades for Federal jobs;

—labor-management relations, including collective bargaining, negotiability, unfair labor practices, labor-management cooperation, and consulting with unions on Governmentwide issues;

—systems and techniques for resolving disputes with employees;

—quality of worklife initiatives, such as employee health and fitness, work and family, AIDS in the workplace, and employee assistance programs;

—human resources development, including leadership and administration of the Human Resources Development Council and the Government Performance and Results Act interest group;

—the Training and Management Assistance program, to help agencies develop training and human resources management solutions, including workforce planning and succession management strategies, e-learning applications, traditional classroom training materials, compensation and performance management systems, and other customized products;

—information systems to support and improve Federal personnel management decisionmaking; and

—Governmentwide instructions for personnel processing and recordkeeping, and for release of personnel data under the Freedom of Information Act and the Privacy Act.

OPM also provides administrative support to special advisory bodies,

including the Federal Prevailing Rate Advisory Committee, the Federal Salary Council, and the Presidential Advisory Committee on Expanding Training Opportunities.

Oversight OPM assesses human capital management Governmentwide and within agencies to gather information for policy development and program refinement, ensure compliance with law and regulation, and enhance agency capability for human resources management accountability. Agency accountability systems help ensure that human capital decisions are consistent with merit principles and that human capital strategies are aligned with mission accomplishment. OPM also works with agencies to find better and more strategic ways to manage Federal human capital.

Workforce Diversity OPM provides leadership, direction, and policy for Governmentwide affirmative recruiting programs for women, minorities, individuals with disabilities, and veterans. It also provides leadership, guidance, and technical assistance to promote merit and equality in systemic workforce recruitment, employment, training, and retention. In addition, OPM gathers, analyzes, and maintains statistical data on the diversity of the Federal workforce, and prepares evaluation reports for Congress and others on individual agency and Governmentwide progress toward full workforce representation for all Americans in the Federal sector.

Other Personnel Programs OPM coordinates the temporary assignment of employees between Federal agencies and State, local, and Indian tribal governments; institutions of higher education; and other eligible nonprofit organizations for up to 2 years, for work of mutual benefit to the participating organizations. It administers the Presidential Management Intern Program, which provides 2-year, excepted appointments with Federal agencies to recipients of graduate degrees in appropriate disciplines. In addition, the Office of Personnel Management administers the Federal Merit System

Standards, which apply to certain grant-aided State and local programs.

Federal Executive Boards Federal Executive Boards (FEBs) were established by Presidential memorandum on November 10, 1961, to improve internal Federal management practices and to provide a central focus for Federal participation in civic affairs in major metropolitan centers of Federal activity. They carry out their functions under OPM supervision and control.

FEBs serve as a means for disseminating information within the Federal Government and for promoting discussion of Federal policies and activities of importance to all Federal executives in the field. Each Board is composed of heads of Federal field offices in the metropolitan area. A chairman is elected annually from among the membership to provide overall leadership to the Board's operations. Committees and task forces carry out interagency projects consistent with the Board's mission.

Federal Executive Boards are located in 28 metropolitan areas that are important centers of Federal activity. These areas are as follows: Albuquerque-Santa Fe, NM; Atlanta, GA; Baltimore, MD; Boston, MA; Buffalo, NY; Chicago, IL; Cincinnati, OH; Cleveland, OH; Dallas-Fort Worth, TX; Denver, CO; Detroit, MI; Honolulu, HI-Pacific; Houston, TX; Kansas City, MO; Los Angeles, CA; Miami, FL; New Orleans, LA; New York, NY; Newark, NJ; Oklahoma City, OK; Philadelphia, PA; Pittsburgh, PA; Portland, OR; St. Louis, MO; San Antonio, TX; San Francisco, CA; Seattle, WA; and the Twin Cities (Minneapolis-St. Paul, MN).

Federal Executive Associations or Councils have been locally organized in approximately 65 other metropolitan areas to perform functions similar to the Federal Executive Boards but on a lesser scale of organization and activity.

For further information, contact the Director for Federal Executive Board Operations, Office of Personnel Management, Room 5524, 1900 E Street NW., Washington, DC 20415–0001. Phone, 202–606–1000.

Sources of Information

Contracts For information, contact the Chief, Contracting Division, Office of Personnel Management, Washington, DC 20415–0071. Phone, 202–606–2240. Internet, www.opm.gov/procure/index.htm.
Employment Information about Federal employment and current job openings is available from USAJobs (phone, 478–757–3000; TTY, 478–744–2299; Internet, www.usajobs.opm.gov). Contact information for your local OPM office is available in the blue pages of the phone book under U.S. Government, Office of Personnel Management. For information about employment opportunities within the Office of Personnel Management, contact the Director of Human Resources. Phone, 202–606–2400.
Publications The Chief, Publications Services Division, can provide information about Federal personnel management publications. Phone, 202–606–1822. Internet, http://apps.opm.gov/publications.

For further information, contact the Office of Communications, Office of Personnel Management, 1900 E Street NW., Washington, DC 20415–0001. Phone, 202–606–1800. TTY, 202–606–2532. Internet, www.opm.gov.

OFFICE OF SPECIAL COUNSEL

1730 M Street NW., Suite 218, Washington, DC 20036–4505
Phone, 202–254–3600 or 800–872–9855. Fax, 202–653–5151. Internet, www.osc.gov.

SPECIAL COUNSEL
DEPUTY SPECIAL COUNSEL

WILLIAM REUKAUF, *Acting*
(VACANCY)

Associate Special Counsel for Investigation and Prosecution Division	LEONARD DRIBINSKY
Outreach Director	SHIRINE MOAZED, *Acting*
Associate Special Counsel for Legal Counsel and Policy Division	ERIN M. MCDONNELL
Director of Congressional Affairs	ANNE WOHLFELD, *Acting*
Director of Public Affairs	DARSHAN SHETH, *Acting*

The Office of Special Counsel investigates allegations of certain activities prohibited by civil service laws, rules, or regulations and litigates before the Merit Systems Protection Board.

Activities

The Office of Special Counsel (OSC) was established on January 1, 1979, by Reorganization Plan No. 2 of 1978 (5 U.S.C. app.). The Civil Service Reform Act of 1978 (5 U.S.C. 1101 note), which became effective on January 11, 1979, enlarged its functions and powers. Pursuant to provisions of the Whistleblower Protection Act of 1989 (5 U.S.C. 1211 *et seq.*), OSC functions as an independent investigative and prosecutorial agency within the executive branch which litigates before the Merit Systems Protection Board.

The primary role of OSC is to protect employees, former employees, and applicants for employment from prohibited personnel practices, especially reprisal for whistleblowing. Its basic areas of statutory responsibility are to do the following:

—receive and investigate allegations of prohibited personnel practices and other activities prohibited by civil service law, rule, or regulation and, if warranted, initiating corrective or disciplinary action;

—provide a secure channel through which information evidencing a violation of any law, rule, or regulation, gross mismanagement, gross waste of funds, abuse of authority, or substantial and specific danger to public health or safety may be disclosed without fear of retaliation and without disclosure of identity, except with the employee's consent; and

—enforce the provisions of the Hatch Act and the Uniformed Services Employment and Reemployment Rights Act.

Sources of Information

Field offices are located in Dallas, TX (525 Griffin Street, Room 824, Box 103, Dallas, TX 75202. Phone, 214–747–1519. Fax, 214–767–2764); Oakland, CA (1301 Clay Street, Suite 1220N, Oakland, CA 94612–5217. Phone, 510–637–3460. Fax, 510–637–3474); and Detroit, MI (477 Michigan Avenue, Suite 2340, Detroit, MI 48226. Phone, 313-226-4496. Fax, 313-226-5606).

For further information, contact the Office of Special Counsel, 1730 M Street NW., Suite 218, Washington, DC 20036–4505. Phone, 202–254–3600 or 800–872–9855. Fax, 202–653–5151. Internet, www.osc.gov.

OVERSEAS PRIVATE INVESTMENT CORPORATION

1100 New York Avenue NW., Washington, DC 20527
Phone, 202–336–8400. Fax, 202–336–7949. Internet, www.opic.gov.

PRESIDENT AND CHIEF EXECUTIVE OFFICER	LAWRENCE SPINELLI, *Acting*
EXECUTIVE VICE PRESIDENT	(VACANCY)
Vice President of External Affairs	LAWRENCE SPINELLI, *Acting*

Vice President of Investment Policy	BERTA M. HEYBEY, *Acting*
Vice President of Structured Finance	ROBERT B. DRUMHELLER
Vice President of Small and Medium Enterprise Finance	JAMES C. POLAN
Vice President of Insurance	ROD MORRIS
Vice President of Investment Funds	BARBARA K. DAY, *Acting*
Vice President and General Counsel	DEV JAGADESAN, *Acting*
Vice President and Chief Financial Officer	ROSEMARY G. ALLEN, *Acting*

[For the Overseas Private Investment Corporation statement of organization, see the *Code of Federal Regulations,* Title 22, Chapter VII]

The Overseas Private Investment Corporation is a self-sustaining Federal agency whose purpose is to promote economic growth in developing countries and emerging markets by encouraging U.S. private investment in those nations.

The Overseas Private Investment Corporation (OPIC) was established in 1971 as an independent agency by the Foreign Affairs Reform and Restructuring Act (112 Stat. 2681–790). OPIC helps U.S. businesses invest overseas, fosters economic development in new and emerging markets, complements the private sector in managing risks associated with foreign direct investment, and supports U.S. foreign policy. OPIC charges market-based fees for its products, and it operates on a self-sustaining basis at no net cost to taxpayers.

OPIC helps U.S. businesses compete in emerging markets when private sector support is not available. OPIC offers up to $250 million in long-term financing and/or political risk insurance to U.S. companies investing in over 150 emerging markets and developing countries. Backed by the full faith and credit of the U.S. Government, OPIC advocates for U.S. investment, offers experience in risk management, and draws on an outstanding record of success.

OPIC mobilizes America's private sector to advance U.S. foreign policy and development initiatives. Projects supported by OPIC expand economic development, which encourages political stability and free market reforms. Over the agency's 35 year history, OPIC has supported $177 billion worth of investments that have helped developing countries to generate over $13 billion in host government revenues and create over 800,000 host country jobs. OPIC projects have also generated $71 billion in U.S. exports and supported more than 271,000 American jobs. OPIC promotes U.S. best practices by requiring projects to adhere to international standards on the environment, worker rights, and human rights.

Activities

OPIC insures U.S. investors, contractors, exporters, and financial institutions against political violence, expropriation of assets by foreign governments, and the inability to convert local currencies into U.S. dollars. OPIC can insure up to $250 million per project and has no minimum investment size requirements. Insurance is available for investments in new ventures, expansions of existing enterprises, privatizations, and acquisitions with positive developmental benefits.

OPIC provides financing through direct loans and loan guaranties for medium- and long-term private investment. Loans range from $100,000 to $250 million for projects sponsored by U.S. companies, and financing can be provided on a project finance or corporate finance basis. In most cases, the U.S. sponsor is expected to contribute at least 25 percent of the project equity, have a track record in the industry, and have the means to contribute to the financial success of the project.

To address the lack of sufficient equity investment in emerging markets, OPIC has supported the creation of privately owned and managed investment funds that make direct equity and equity-related investments in new, expanding, or privatizing companies. These funds, which have a regional or sectoral focus, provide the long-term growth capital that can serve as a catalyst for private sector economic activity in developing countries and the creation of new markets and opportunities for American companies.

Helping America's small businesses grow through investments in emerging markets is an important OPIC priority. Any small business with annual revenues less than $35 million is eligible for small business center programs. For businesses with annual revenues over $35 million and under $250 million, OPIC's regular small business programs are available. OPIC provides direct loans to U.S. small businesses, and offers insurance products

to meet the special needs of small businesses. Other client services include streamlined applications and processing procedures, and online small business resources from our Web site at www.opic.gov.

Sources of Information

General Inquiries   Inquiries should be directed to the Information Officer, Overseas Private Investment Corporation, 1100 New York Avenue NW., Washington, DC 20527. Phone, 202–336–8799. Email, info@opic.gov. Internet, www.opic.gov.

Publications   OPIC programs are further detailed in the *Annual Report* and the *Program Handbook.* These publications are available free of charge and on the Web site.

For further information, contact the Overseas Private Investment Corporation, 1100 New York Avenue NW., Washington, DC 20527. Phone, 202–336–8400. Fax, 202–336–7949. Internet, www.opic.gov.

PEACE CORPS

1111 Twentieth Street NW., Washington, DC 20526
Phone, 202–692–2000 or 800–424–8580 (toll free). Fax, 202–692–2231. Internet,
www.peacecorps.gov.

DIRECTOR	AARON S. WILLIAMS
DEPUTY DIRECTOR	(VACANCY)
Chief of Staff/Operations	KATHY RULON, *Acting*
Deputy Chief of Staff/Operations	(VACANCY)
Director of Congressional Relations	SUZIE CARROLL, *Acting*
General Counsel	CARL SOSEBEE, *Acting*
Director of Communications	LINDA ISAAC, *Acting*
Director of Press Relations	LAURA LARTIGUE, *Acting*
Director of Office of Strategic Information, Research and Planning	(VACANCY)
American Diversity Program Manager	SHIRLEY EVEREST
Director of Private Sector Initiatives	BARBI BROADUS, *Acting*
Inspector General	KATHY BULLER
Director of Peace Corps Response	RICK MONTPELLIER, *Acting*
Regional Director/Africa Operations	LYNN FODEN, *Acting*
Regional Director/Europe, Mediterranean, and Asia Operations	DAVID BURGESS, *Acting*
Regional Director/Inter-American and the Pacific Operations	ROGER CONRAD, *Acting*
Director, Overseas Programming and Training Support	HOWARD ANDERSON, *Acting*
Chief Financial Officer	THOMAS BELLAMY, *Acting*

Associate Director for Management	GARRY STANBERRY, *Acting*
Associate Director for Volunteer Support	GLENN EGELMAN, *Acting*
Chief Information Officer	CHRIS SARANDOS, *Acting*
Associate Director for Volunteer Recruitment and Selection	ROSIE MAUK
Associate Director for Safety and Security	(VACANCY)
Chief Acquisition Officer	CAREY FOUNTAIN
Chief Compliance Officer	(VACANCY)
AIDS Relief Coordinator	PAM MARTIN
Director of Special Initiatives	(VACANCY)

The mission of the Peace Corps is to help the people of interested countries in meeting their need for trained men and women, and to help promote better mutual understanding between Americans and citizens of other countries.

The Peace Corps was established by the Peace Corps Act of 1961, as amended (22 U.S.C. 2501), and was made an independent agency by title VI of the International Security and Development Cooperation Act of 1981 (22 U.S.C. 2501–1).

The Peace Corps consists of a Washington, DC, headquarters; 9 area offices; and overseas operations in 76 countries, utilizing nearly 8,000 volunteers.

Activities

To fulfill the Peace Corps mandate, men and women are trained for a 9- to 14-week period in the appropriate local language, the technical skills necessary for their particular jobs, and the cross-cultural skills needed to adjust to a society with traditions and attitudes different from their own. Volunteers serve for a period of 2 years, living among the people with whom they work. Volunteers are expected to become a part of the community through their voluntary service.

Thousands of volunteers serve throughout the world, working in six program areas: education, health and HIV/AIDS, environment, youth development, agriculture, and business development. Community-level projects are designed to incorporate the skills of volunteers with the resources of host-country agencies and other international assistance organizations to help solve specific development problems, often in conjunction with private volunteer organizations.

In the United States, the Peace Corps is working to promote an understanding of people in other countries. Through its World Wise Schools Program, volunteers are matched with elementary and junior high schools in the United States to encourage an exchange of letters, pictures, music, and artifacts. Participating students increase their knowledge of geography, languages, and different cultures, while gaining an appreciation for volunteerism.

The Peace Corps offers other domestic programs involving former volunteers, universities, local public school systems, and private businesses and foundations in a partnership to help solve some of the United States' most pressing domestic problems.

The Peace Corps Office of Private Sector Initiatives works with schools, civic groups, businesses, and neighborhood and youth organizations in the United States to facilitate their support of Peace Corps initiatives here and abroad.

Area Offices—Peace Corps

Office	Address	Telephone
Atlanta, GA (AL, FL, GA, MS, PR, SC, TN)	Suite 2R70, Bldg. 1924, 100 Alabama St., 30303	404–562–3456
Boston, MA (MA, ME, NH, RI, VT)	Suite 450, 10 Causeway St., 02222	617–565–5555
Chicago, IL (IL, IN, KY, MI, MO, OH)	Suite 450, 55 W. Monroe St., 60603	312–353–4990
Dallas, TX (AR, LA, NM, OK, TX)	Rm. 427, 1100 Commerce St., 75242	214–767–5435

PEACE CORPS

GENERAL COUNSEL

AMERICAN DIVERSITY / EQUAL EMPLOYMENT OPPORTUNITY

DIRECTOR

DEPUTY DIRECTOR

OFFICE OF THE INSPECTOR GENERAL

CHIEF OF STAFF

DEPUTY CHIEF OF STAFF

EXECUTIVE SECRETARIAT

DIRECTOR OF SPECIAL INITIATIVES

CHIEF COMPLIANCE OFFICER

OFFICE OF STRATEGIC INFORMATION, RESEARCH AND PLANNING

OFFICE OF PRIVATE SECTOR INITIATIVES

OFFICE OF COMMUNICATIONS PRESS RELATIONS

OFFICE OF CONGRESSIONAL RELATIONS

OFFICE OF AIDS RELIEF

EUROPE, MEDITERRANEAN, AND ASIA REGION

OVERSEAS POSTS

INTER-AMERICA AND THE PACIFIC REGION

OVERSEAS POSTS

AFRICA REGION

OVERSEAS POSTS

OFFICE OF SAFETY AND SECURITY

OFFICE OF VOLUNTEER RECRUITMENT AND SELECTION

DOMESTIC PROGRAMS

OFFICE OF VOLUNTEER SUPPORT

OFFICE OF OVERSEAS PROGRAMMING AND TRAINING SUPPORT

OFFICE OF CHIEF FINANCIAL OFFICER *

OFFICE OF MANAGEMENT

OFFICE OF THE CHIEF INFORMATION OFFICER *

PEACE CORPS RESPONSE

OFFICE OF ACQUISITIONS AND CONTRACT MANAGEMENT *

* In their functions as Chief Financial Officer and Chief Information Officer, the incumbents report directly to the Director. The Office of Acquisitions and Contract Management reports to the Chief of Staff with a dotted line report to the Director.

Area Offices—Peace Corps—Continued

Office	Address	Telephone
Denver, CO (CO, KS, NE, UT, WY)	Suite 2205, 1999 Broadway, 80202	303–844–7020
Los Angeles, CA (AZ, southern CA)	Suite 155, 2361 Rosecrans Ave., El Segundo, CA 90245.	310–356–1100
Minneapolis, MN (IA, MN, ND, SD, WI)	Suite 420, 330 2d Ave. S., 55401	612–348–1480
New York, NY (CT, NJ, NY, PA)	Suite 1025, 201 Varick St., 10014	212–352–5440
Oakland, CA (northern CA, HI, NV)	Suite 620N, 1301 Clay St., 94612	510–637–1520
Seattle, WA (AK, ID, MT, OR, WA)	Westlake Building, Suite 605, 1601 5th Ave., 98101	206–553–5490
Washington, DC (DC, DE, MD, NC, VA, WV)	Suite 100, 1525 Wilson Blvd., Arlington, VA 22209	703–235–9191

Sources of Information

Becoming a Peace Corps Volunteer

Contact the nearest area office. Phone, 800–424–8580. Internet, www.peacecorps.gov.

Employment Contact the Peace Corps, Office of Human Resources Management, Washington, DC 20526.

Phone, 202–692–1200. Internet, www.peacecorps.gov.

For recorded employment opportunities, call 800–818–9579 (toll free).

General Inquiries Information or assistance may be obtained by contacting the Peace Corps Washington, DC, headquarters or any of its area offices.

For further information, contact the Press Office, Peace Corps, 1111 Twentieth Street NW., Washington, DC 20526. Phone, 202–692–2230 or 800–424–8580. Fax, 202–692–2201. Internet, www.peacecorps.gov.

EDITORIAL NOTE: The Pension Benefit Guaranty Corporation did not meet the publication deadline for submitting updated information of its activities, functions, and sources of information as required by the automatic disclosure provisions of the Freedom of Information Act (5 U.S.C. 552(a)(1)(A)).

PENSION BENEFIT GUARANTY CORPORATION

1200 K Street NW., Washington, DC 20005
Phone, 202–326–4400 or 800–736–2444 (toll free). Internet, www.pbgc.gov.

Board of Directors:

Chairman (Secretary of Labor)	HILDA L. SOLIS
Members:	
(Secretary of the Treasury)	TIMOTHY F. GEITHNER
(Secretary of Commerce)	GARY F. LOCKE

Officials:

DIRECTOR	VINCENT K. SNOWBARGER, *Acting*
Deputy Director, Operations	VINCENT K. SNOWBARGER
Director, Communications and Public Affairs	(VACANCY)
Director, Legislative and Regulatory	JOHN HANLEY
Director, Policy, Research and Analysis	DAVID GUSTAFSON
Deputy Director, Policy	(VACANCY)
Chief of Staff	(VACANCY)
Chief Information Officer	PATSY A. GARNETT
Chief Management Officer	STEPHEN E. BARBER
Director, Budget	EDGAR BENNETT
Director, Facilities and Services	PATRICIA DAVIS
Director, Human Resources	ARRIE ETHERIDGE
Director, Procurement	STEVE BLOCK, *Acting*

Director, Strategic Planning and Evaluation	WILMER GRAHAM
Chief Operating Officer	RICHARD MACY
Director, Benefits Administration and Payment	BENNIE L. HAGANS
Chief Investment Officer	JOHN H. GREENBERG
Chief Insurance Program Officer	TERRENCE M. DENEEN
Chief Counsel	ISRAEL GOLDOWITZ
Director, Insurance Supervision and Compliance	JOSEPH HOUSE
Chief Financial Officer	PATRICIA KELLY
Director, Contracts and Controls Review	MARTIN BOEHM
Director, Financial Operations	THEODORE J. WINTER, JR.
General Counsel	JUDITH STARR
Inspector General	REBECCA ANNE BATTS

The Pension Benefit Guaranty Corporation protects the pension benefits of nearly 44 million Americans who participate in defined-benefit pension plans sponsored by private-sector employees.

The Pension Benefit Guaranty Corporation (PBGC) is a self-financing, wholly owned Government corporation subject to the Government Corporation Control Act (31 U.S.C. 9101–9109). The Corporation, established by title IV of the Employee Retirement Income Security Act of 1974 (29 U.S.C. 1301–1461), operates in accordance with policies established by its Board of Directors, which consists of the Secretaries of Labor, Commerce, and the Treasury. The Secretary of Labor is Chairman of the Board. A seven-member Advisory Committee, composed of two labor, two business, and three public members appointed by the President, advises the agency on investment issues.

Activities

Coverage   The Corporation insures most private-sector defined-benefit pension plans, which provide a pension benefit based on factors such as age, years of service, and salary.

The Corporation administers two insurance programs separately covering single-employer and multiemployer plans. Nearly 44 million workers and retirees participate in about 30,330 covered plans.

Single-Employer Insurance   Under the single-employer program, the Corporation guarantees payment of basic pension benefits if an insured plan terminates without sufficient assets to pay those benefits. However, the law

limits the total monthly benefit that the agency may guarantee for one individual to $4,125 per month for a 65-year-old individual in a pension plan that terminates in 2007. The law also sets other restrictions on PBGC's guarantee, including limits on the insured amount of recent benefit increases. In certain cases, the Corporation may also pay some benefits above the guaranteed amount depending on the funding level of the plan and amounts recovered from employers.

A plan sponsor may terminate a single-employer plan in a standard termination if the plan has sufficient assets to purchase private annuities to cover all benefit liabilities. If a plan does not have sufficient assets, the sponsor may seek to transfer the pension liabilities to the PBGC by demonstrating that it meets the legal criteria for a distress termination. In either termination, the plan administrator must inform participants in writing at least 60 days prior to the date the administrator proposes to terminate the plan. Only a plan that has sufficient assets to pay all benefit liabilities may terminate in a standard termination. The Corporation also may institute termination of underfunded plans in certain specified circumstances.

Multiemployer Insurance   Under title IV, as revised in 1980 by the Multiemployer Pension Plan Amendments Act (29 U.S.C. 1001 note),

PENSION BENEFIT GUARANTY CORPORATION

which changed the insurable event from plan termination to plan insolvency, the Corporation provides financial assistance to multiemployer plans that are unable to pay nonforfeitable benefits. The plans are obligated to repay such assistance. The act also made employers withdrawing from a plan liable to the plan for a portion of its unfunded vested benefits.

Premium Collections   All defined-benefit pension plans insured by PBGC are required to pay premiums to the Corporation according to rates set by Congress. The annual premium per plan participant for multiemployer pension plans is $8. The basic premium for all single-employer plans is $31 per participant per year. Underfunded single-employer plans must also pay an additional premium equal to $9 per $1,000 of unfunded vested benefits. A termination premium of $1,250 per participant per year applies to certain distress and involuntary plan terminations occurring on or after January 1, 2006, payable for 3 years after the termination.

Sources of Information

Access to the Pension Benefit Guaranty Corporation is available through the Internet at www.pbgc.gov.

TTY/TDD users may call the Federal Relay Service toll free at 800–877–8339 and ask to be connected to 800–736–2444.

For further information, contact the Pension Benefit Guaranty Corporation, 1200 K Street NW., Washington, DC 20005–4026. Phone, 202–326–4400 or 800–736–2444. Internet, www.pbgc.gov.

POSTAL REGULATORY COMMISSION

901 New York Avenue NW., Suite 200, Washington, DC 20268–0001
Phone, 202–789–6800. Fax, 202–789–6861. Internet, www.prc.gov.

CHAIRMAN	DAN G. BLAIR
VICE CHAIRMAN	NANCI E. LANGLEY
Commissioners	MARK ACTON, RUTH Y. GOLDWAY, TONY HAMMOND
Executive Assistant to the Chairman	DIANE BAKER
Chief of Staff	TRICIA HOLLIS
Chief Administrative Officer and Secretary	STEVEN W. WILLIAMS
General Counsel	STEPHEN L. SHARFMAN
Director, Office of Accountability and Compliance	JOHN D. WALLER
Director, Office of Public Affairs and Government Relations	ANN FISHER
Deputy Chief Administrative Officer and Personnel Officer	GARRY SIKORA
Inspector General	JOHN F. CALLENDER

[For the Postal Regulatory Commission statement of organization, see the *Code of Federal Regulations*, Title 39, Part 3002]

The Postal Regulatory Commission develops and implements a modern system of postal rate regulation.

The Postal Regulatory Commission is the successor agency to the Postal Rate Commission, which was created by the Postal Reorganization Act, as amended (39 U.S.C. 3601–3604). The Commission was established as an independent agency in the executive branch of Government by the Postal Accountability and Enhancement Act (39 U.S.C. 101 note). It is composed of five Commissioners, appointed by the President with the advice and consent of the Senate, one of whom is designated as Chairman.

The Commission promulgates rules and regulations, establishes procedures, and takes other actions necessary to carry out its obligations. It considers complaints received from interested persons relating to United States Postal Service rates, regulations, and services. The Commission also has certain reporting obligations, including a report on universal postal service and the postal monopoly.

Sources of Information

Employment The Commission's programs require attorneys, economists, statisticians, accountants, industrial engineers, marketing specialists, and administrative and clerical personnel to fulfill its responsibilities. Requests for employment information should be directed to the Personnel Officer.

Electronic Access Electronic access to current docketed case materials is available through the Internet at www.prc.gov. Email can be sent to the Commission at prc-admin@prc.gov and prc-dockets@prc.gov.

Reading Room Facilities for inspection and copying of records, viewing automated daily lists of docketed materials, and accessing the Commission's Internet site are located at Suite 200, 901 New York Avenue NW., Washington, DC. The room is open from 8 a.m. to 4:30 p.m., Monday through Friday, except legal holidays.

Rules of Practice and Procedure The Postal Regulatory Commission's Rules of Practice and Procedure governing the conduct of proceedings before the Commission may be found in parts 3001, 3010, 3015, 3020, 3030, 3031, and 3060 of title 39 of the *Code of Federal Regulations.*

For further information, contact the Secretary, Postal Regulatory Commission, 901 New York Avenue NW., Suite 200, Washington, DC 20268–0001. Phone, 202–789–6840. Internet, www.prc.gov.

RAILROAD RETIREMENT BOARD

844 North Rush Street, Chicago, IL 60611–2092
Phone, 312–751–4777. Fax, 312–751–7154. Email, opa@rrb.gov. Internet, www.rrb.gov.

CHAIRMAN	MICHAEL S. SCHWARTZ
Labor Member	V.M. SPEAKMAN, JR.
Management Member	JEROME F. KEVER
Inspector General	MARTIN J. DICKMAN
Director, Administration and Senior Executive Officer	HENRY M. VALIULIS
Director, Equal Opportunity	LYNN E. COUSINS
Director, Human Resources	KEITH B. EARLEY
Supervisor, Public Affairs	ANITA J. ROGERS
Supervisor, Acquisition Management	PAUL T. AHERN
Facility Manager	SCOTT L. RUSH
General Counsel	STEVEN A. BARTHOLOW
Director, Legislative Affairs	MARGARET A. LINDSLEY
Director, Hearings and Appeals	KARL T. BLANK
Secretary to the Board	BEATRICE E. EZERSKI
Chief Actuary	FRANK J. BUZZI
Chief Information Officer	TERRI S. MORGAN

Chief Financial Officer	KENNETH P. BOEHNE
Director, Programs	DOROTHY A. ISHERWOOD
Director, Assessment and Training	CATHERINE A. LEYSER
Director, Field Service	MARTHA M. BARRINGER
Director, Operations	ROBERT J. DUDA
Director, Policy and Systems	RONALD RUSSO
Chief, Resource Management Center	JANET M. HALLMAN

[For the Railroad Retirement Board statement of organization, see the *Code of Federal Regulations,* Title 20, Part 200]

The Railroad Retirement Board administers comprehensive retirement-survivor and unemployment-sickness benefit programs for the Nation's railroad workers and their families.

The Railroad Retirement Board was originally established by the Railroad Retirement Act of 1934, as amended (45 U.S.C. 201—228z–1).

The Board derives statutory authority from the Railroad Retirement Act of 1974 (45 U.S.C. 231–231u) and the Railroad Unemployment Insurance Act (45 U.S.C. 351–369). It administers these acts and participates in the administration of the Social Security Act and the Health Insurance for the Aged Act insofar as they affect railroad retirement beneficiaries.

The Board is composed of three members appointed by the President with the advice and consent of the Senate—one upon recommendations of representatives of employees; one upon recommendations of carriers; and one, the Chairman, as a public member.

Activities

The Railroad Retirement Act provides for the payment of annuities to individuals who have completed at least 10 years of creditable railroad service, or 5 years if performed after 1995, and have ceased compensated service upon their attainment of specified ages, or at any age if permanently disabled for all employment. In some circumstances occupational disability annuities or supplemental annuities are provided for career employees.

A spouse's annuity is provided, under certain conditions, for the wife or husband of an employee annuitant. Divorced spouses may also qualify.

Survivor annuities are awarded to the qualified spouses, children, and parents of deceased career employees, and various lump-sum benefits are also available under certain conditions.

Benefits based upon qualifying railroad earnings in a preceding 1-year period are provided under the Railroad Unemployment Insurance Act to individuals who are unemployed in a benefit year, but who are ready and willing to work, and to individuals who are unable to work because of sickness or injury.

The Board maintains, through its field offices, a placement service for unemployed railroad personnel.

Sources of Information

Benefit Inquiries The Board maintains direct contact with railroad employees and railroad retirement beneficiaries through its field offices located across the country. Field personnel explain benefit rights and responsibilities on an individual basis, assist employees in applying for benefits, and answer questions related to the benefit programs. The Board also relies on railroad labor groups and employers for assistance in keeping railroad personnel informed about its benefit programs.

To locate the nearest field office, individuals should check with their rail employer or local union official. Information may also be obtained by calling the Board toll-free at 1–877–772–5772, or by visiting the Board's Web site at www.rrb.gov. Most offices are open to the public from 9 a.m. to 3:30 p.m., Monday through Friday.

RAILROAD RETIREMENT BOARD

The Inspector General reports administratively to the Chairman.

The Director of Equal Opportunity reports administratively to the Director of Administration and programmatically to the Board.

* Non-voting member of the Executive Committee.

** A member of the Executive Committee is designated by the Board to serve as Senior Executive Officer.

Electronic Access   Railroad Retirement Board information is available online at www.rrb.gov.

Employment   Employment inquiries should be directed to the Bureau of Human Resources, Railroad Retirement Board, 844 North Rush Street, Chicago, IL 60611–2092. Phone, 312–751–4580. Email, recruit@rrb.gov.

Congressional and Legislative Assistance Congressional offices making inquiries regarding constituents' claims should contact the Office of Administration, Congressional Inquiry Section. Phone, 312–751–4970. Fax, 312–751–7154. Email, opa@rrb.gov. For information regarding legislative matters, contact the Office of Legislative Affairs, Suite 500,

1310 G Street NW., Washington, DC 20005–3004. Phone, 202–272–7742. Fax, 202–272–7728. Email, ola@rrb.gov.

Publications   General information pamphlets on benefit programs may be obtained from the Board's field offices or Chicago headquarters. Requests for annual reports or statistical data should be directed to Public Affairs at the Chicago headquarters. Phone, 312–751–4777. Fax, 312–751–7154. Email, opa@rrb.gov.

Telecommunications Devices for the Deaf (TDD)   The Board provides TDD services. Phone 312–751–4701 for beneficiary inquiries or 312–751–4334 for equal opportunity inquiries.

For further information, contact Public Affairs, Railroad Retirement Board, 844 North Rush Street, Chicago, IL 60611–2092. Phone, 312–751–4777. Fax, 312–751–7154. Email, opa@rrb.gov. Internet, www.rrb.gov.

SECURITIES AND EXCHANGE COMMISSION

100 F Street NE., Washington, DC 20549
Phone, 202–551–7500. Internet, www.sec.gov.

CHAIRMAN	MARY L. SCHAPIRO
COMMISSIONERS	LUIS A. AGUILAR, KATHLEEN L. CASEY, TROY A. PAREDES, ELISSE B. WALTER
Senior Advisers to the Chairman	STEPHEN DEVINE, KAYLA J. GILLAN, DIDEM A. NISANCI
Director, Office of Legislative and Intergovernmental Affairs	WILLIAM SCHULZ
Director, Office of Public Affairs	JOHN NESTER
Director, Office of Investor Education and Advocacy	KRISTI J. KAEPPLEIN
Secretary	ELIZABETH M. MURPHY
Executive Director	DIEGO T. RUIZ
Associate Executive Director, Office of Human Resources	JEFFREY RISINGER
Associate Executive Director, Office of Administrative Services	SHARON SHEEHAN
Associate Executive Director, Office of Financial Management	KRISTINE CHADWICK
General Counsel	DAVID BECKER
Director, Division of Corporation Finance	MEREDITH CROSS
Director, Division of Enforcement	ROBERT KHUZAMI
Director, Division of Investment Management	ANDREW J. DONOHUE
Director, Division of Trading and Markets	ERIK R. SIRRI

Director, Office of Compliance Inspections and Examinations — LORI A. RICHARDS
Chief Accountant — JAMES L. KROEKER
Chief Administrative Law Judge — BRENDA P. MURRAY
Chief Economist — JAMES OVERDAHL
Chief Information Officer, Office of Information Technology — CHARLES BOUCHER
Director, Office of International Affairs — ETHIOPIS TAFARA
Director, Office of Equal Employment Opportunity — ALTA RODRIGUEZ
Director, Office of Risk Assessment — JONATHAN S. SOKOBIN
Inspector General — H. DAVID KOTZ
Director, Office of Interactive Disclosure — DAVID M. BLASZKOWSKY

[For the Securities and Exchange Commission statement of organization, see the *Code of Federal Regulations*, Title 17, Part 200]

The Securities and Exchange Commission administers Federal securities laws that seek to provide protection for investors; to ensure that securities markets are fair and honest; and, when necessary, to provide the means to enforce securities laws through sanctions.

The Securities and Exchange Commission (SEC) was created under authority of the Securities Exchange Act of 1934 (15 U.S.C. 78a–78jj) and was organized on July 2, 1934. The Commission serves as adviser to United States district courts in connection with reorganization proceedings for debtor corporations in which there is a substantial public interest. The Commission also has certain responsibilities under section 15 of the Bretton Woods Agreements Act of 1945 (22 U.S.C. 286k–1) and section 851(e) of the Internal Revenue Code of 1954 (26 U.S.C. 851(e)).

The Commission is vested with quasi-judicial functions. Persons aggrieved by its decisions in the exercise of those functions have a right of review by the United States courts of appeals.

Activities

Full and Fair Disclosure The Securities Act of 1933 (15 U.S.C. 77a) requires issuers of securities and their controlling persons making public offerings of securities in interstate commerce or through the mail to file with the Commission registration statements containing financial and other pertinent data about the issuer and the securities being offered. There are limited exemptions, such as government securities, nonpublic offerings, and intrastate offerings, as well as certain offerings not exceeding $1.5 million. The effectiveness of a registration statement may be refused or suspended after a public hearing if the statement contains material misstatements or omissions, thus barring sale of the securities until it is appropriately amended.

Regulation of Investment Advisers Persons who, for compensation, engage in the business of advising others with respect to securities must register with the Commission. The Commission is authorized to define what practices are considered fraudulent or deceptive and to prescribe means to prevent those practices.

Regulation of Mutual Funds and Other Investment Companies The Commission registers investment companies and regulates their activities to protect investors. The regulation covers sales load, management contracts, composition of boards of directors, and capital structure. The Commission must also determine the fairness of various transactions of investment companies before these actually occur.

The Commission may institute court action to enjoin the consummation of mergers and other plans of

SECURITIES AND EXCHANGE COMMISSION

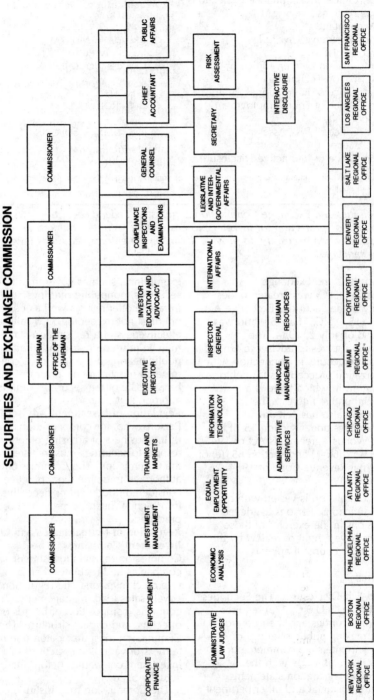

reorganization of investment companies if such plans are unfair to securities holders. It also may impose sanctions by administrative proceedings against investment company management for violations of the act and other Federal securities laws and file court actions to enjoin acts and practices of management officials involving breaches of fiduciary duty and personal misconduct and to disqualify such officials from office.

Regulation of Securities Markets The Securities Exchange Act of 1934 assigns to the Commission broad regulatory responsibilities over the securities markets, the self-regulatory organizations within the securities industry, and persons conducting a business in securities. Persons who execute transactions in securities generally are required to register with the Commission as broker-dealers. Securities exchanges and certain clearing agencies are required to register with the Commission, and associations of brokers or dealers are permitted to register with the Commission. The Act also provides for the establishment of the Municipal Securities Rulemaking Board to formulate rules for the municipal securities industry.

The Commission oversees the self-regulatory activities of the national securities exchanges and associations, registered clearing agencies, and the Municipal Securities Rulemaking Board. In addition, the Commission regulates industry professionals, such as securities brokers and dealers, certain municipal securities professionals, government securities brokers and dealers, and transfer agents.

Rehabilitation of Failing Corporations In cases of corporate reorganization proceedings administered in Federal courts, the Commission may participate as a statutory party. The principal functions of the Commission are to protect the interests of public investors involved in such cases through efforts to ensure their adequate representation, and to participate in legal and policy issues that are of concern to public investors generally.

Representation of Debt Securities Holders The Commission safeguards the interests of purchasers of publicly offered debt securities issued pursuant to trust indentures.

Enforcement Activities The Commission's enforcement activities are designed to secure compliance with the Federal securities laws administered by the Commission and the rules and regulations adopted thereunder. These activities include measures to do the following:

—compel compliance with the disclosure requirements of the registration and other provisions of the relevant acts;

—prevent fraud and deception in the purchase and sale of securities;

—obtain court orders enjoining acts and practices that operate as a fraud upon investors or otherwise violate the laws;

—suspend or revoke the registrations of brokers, dealers, investment companies, and investment advisers who willfully engage in such acts and practices;

—suspend or bar from association persons associated with brokers, dealers, investment companies, and investment advisers who have violated any provision of the Federal securities laws; and

—prosecute persons who have engaged in fraudulent activities or other willful violations of those laws.

In addition, attorneys, accountants, and other professionals who violate the securities laws face possible loss of their privilege to practice before the Commission.

To this end, private investigations are conducted into complaints or other indications of securities violations. Evidence thus established of law violations is used in appropriate administrative proceedings to revoke registration or in actions instituted in Federal courts to restrain or enjoin such activities. Where the evidence tends to establish criminal fraud or other willful violation of the securities laws, the facts are referred to the Attorney General for criminal prosecution of the offenders.

The Commission may assist in such prosecutions.

Regional Offices—Securities and Exchange Commission

City	Address	Director	Telephone
New York, NY	3 World Financial Ctr., 200 Vesey St., 10281–1022	Mark K. Schonfeld	212–336–1100
Boston, MA	23d Fl., 33 Arch St., 02110–1424	David Bergers	617–573–8900
Philadelphia, PA	Suite 2000, 701 Market St., 19106–1532	Daniel M. Hawke	215–597–3100
Miami, FL	Suite 1800, 801 Brickell Ave., 33131	David P. Nelson	305–982–6300
Atlanta, GA	Suite 1000, 3475 Lenox Rd. NE., 30326–1232	Katherine Addleman	404–842–7600
Chicago, IL	Suite 900, 175 W. Jackson Blvd., 60604	Merri Jo Gillette	312–353–7390
Denver, CO	Suite 1500, 1801 California St., 80202–2656	George Curtis	303–844–1000
Fort Worth, TX	Suite 1900, 801 Cherry St., 76102–6882	Rose Romero	817–978–3821
Salt Lake City, UT	Suite 1800, 15 W. South Temple St., 84101	Kenneth D. Israel, Jr.	801–524–5796
Los Angeles, CA	Suite 1100, 5670 Wilshire Blvd., 90036–3648	Rosalind Tyson	323–965–3998
San Francisco, CA	Suite 1100, 44 Montgomery St., 94104	Marc J. Fagel	415–705–2500

Sources of Information

Inquiries regarding the following matters should be directed to the appropriate office, Securities and Exchange Commission, 100 F Street NE., Washington, DC 20549.

Contracts   Inquiries regarding SEC procurement and contracting activities should be directed to the Office of Administrative Services. Phone, 202–551–7400.

Electronic Access   Information on the Commission is available through the Internet at www.sec.gov.

Employment   With the exception of the attorney category, positions are in the competitive civil service, which means applicants must apply for consideration for a particular vacancy and go through competitive selection procedures. The Commission operates a college and law school recruitment program, including on-campus visitations for interview purposes. Inquiries should be directed to the Office of Human Resources. Phone, 202–942–7500. Fax, 703–914–0592.

Investor Assistance and Complaints   The Office of Investor Education and Advocacy answers questions from investors, assists investors with specific problems regarding their relations with broker-dealers and companies, and advises the Commission and other offices and divisions regarding problems frequently encountered by investors and possible regulatory solutions to such problems. Phone, 202–551–6551. Consumer information line, 800–732–0330. Fax, 202–772–9295. Complaints and inquiries may also be directed to any regional or district office.

Publications   Blank copies of SEC forms and other publications are available in the Publications Unit. Phone, 202–551–4040.

Reading Rooms   The Commission maintains a public reference room in Washington, DC, where registration statements and other public documents filed with the Commission are available for public inspection Monday through Friday, except on holidays, between the hours of 10:00 a.m. and 3:00 p.m. Phone, 202–551–5850. Copies of public material may be purchased from the Commission's contract copying service at prescribed rates. The Commission also maintains a library where additional information may be obtained. Phone, 202–551–5450. Fax, 202–772–9326.

Small Business Activities   Information on securities laws that pertain to small businesses in relation to securities offerings may be obtained from the Commission. Phone, 202–551–3460.

For further information, contact the Office of Public Affairs, Securities and Exchange Commission, 100 F Street NE., Washington, DC 20549. Phone, 202–551–4120. Fax, 202–777–1026. Internet, www.sec.gov.

SELECTIVE SERVICE SYSTEM

National Headquarters, Arlington, VA 22209-2425
Phone, 703–605–4000. Internet, www.sss.gov.

DIRECTOR	ERNEST E. GARCIA, *Acting*
DEPUTY DIRECTOR	(VACANCY)
Executive Director	ERNEST E. GARCIA
Chief of Staff	(VACANCY)
Senior Advisor to Director	(VACANCY)
Special Assistant to the Director	(VACANCY)
General Counsel	RUDY G. SANCHEZ, JR.
Associate Director for Public and Intergovernmental Affairs	RICHARD S. FLAHAVAN
Associate Director for Operations and Chief Information Officer	SCOTT V. CAMPBELL
Associate Director for Support Services	EDWARD A. BLACKADAR, JR.
Comptroller	CARLO VERDINO

[For the Selective Service System statement of organization, see the *Code of Federal Regulations,* Title 32, Part 1605]

The Selective Service System provides manpower to the Armed Forces in an emergency and operates an Alternative Service Program during a draft for men classified as conscientious objectors.

The Selective Service System was established by the Military Selective Service Act (50 U.S.C. app. 451–471a). The act requires the registration of male citizens of the United States and all other male persons who are in the United States and who are ages 18 to 25. The act exempts members of the active Armed Forces and nonimmigrant aliens. Proclamation 4771 of July 20, 1980, requires male persons born on or after January 1, 1960, and who have attained age 18 but have not attained age 26 to register. Registration is conducted at post offices within the United States, at U.S. embassies and consulates outside the United States, and online at www.sss.gov.

The act imposes liability for training and service in the Armed Forces upon registrants who are ages 18 to 26, except those who are exempt or deferred. Persons who have been deferred remain liable for training and service until age 35. Aliens are not liable for training and service until they have remained in the United States for more than 1 year. Conscientious objectors who are found to be opposed to all service in the Armed Forces are required to perform civilian work in lieu of induction into the Armed Forces.

The authority to induct registrants, including doctors and allied medical specialists, expired July 1, 1973.

Regional Offices—Selective Service System

Region/Address	Director	Telephone
North Chicago, IL (Suite 276, 2834 Green Bay Rd., 60064–9983)	Thomas White	847–688–7985
Smyrna, GA (Suite 270, 2400 Lake Park Dr., 30080)	Keith A. Scragg	770–319–6036
Denver, CO (Suite 1014, 3401 Quebec St., 80207–2323)	Debbie Bielanski	720–941–1670

SELECTIVE SERVICE SYSTEM

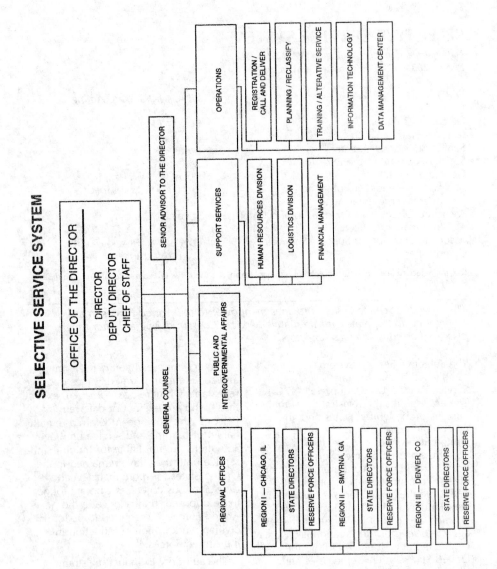

Sources of Information

Employment Inquiries and applications should be directed to the Director, Selective Service System, Attn: SPT/HR, Arlington, VA 22209–2425. Phone, 703–605–4056.

Procurement Inquiries should be directed to the Director, Selective Service System, Attn: STP/LO, Arlington, VA 22209–2425. Phone, 703–605–4064.

Publications Selective Service regulations appear in chapter XVI of title 32 of the *Code of Federal Regulations.*
Requirements of Law Persons desiring information concerning the requirements of the Military Selective Service Act should contact the National Headquarters of the Selective Service System. Phone, 703–605–4000.

For further information, contact the Office of Public and Intergovernmental Affairs, Selective Service System, Arlington, VA 22209–2425. Phone, 703–605–4100. Internet, www.sss.gov.

SMALL BUSINESS ADMINISTRATION

409 Third Street SW., Washington, DC 20416
Phone, 202–205–6600. Fax, 202–205–7064. Internet, www.sba.gov.

ADMINISTRATOR	KAREN MILLS
DEPUTY ADMINISTRATOR	(VACANCY)
Chief Counsel for Advocacy	SHAWNE MCGIBBON, *Acting*
Chief Financial Officer	(VACANCY)
Chief Information Officer	CHRISTINE RIDER
Chief of Staff	ANA MA
Counselor to the Administrator	GINGER LEW
General Counsel	SARA LIPSCOMB
Inspector General	PETER MCCLINTOCK, *Acting*
Associate Administrator for Disaster Assistance	HERBERT MITCHELL
Associate Administrator for Communications and Public Liaison	JONATHAN CARVER
Assistant Administrator for Congressional and Legislative Affairs	TIFFANI COOPER, *Acting*
Assistant Administrator for Equal Employment Opportunity and Civil Rights Compliance	MARGARETH BENNETT
Associate Administrator for Field Operations	TOBY MCGRATH
Assistant Administrator for Hearings and Appeals	DELORICE FORD
Assistant Administrator for Veterans Business Development	WILLIAM ELMORE
Associate Administrator for Capital Access	ERIC ZARNIKOW
Director of Financial Assistance	GRADY HEDGESPETH
Director of International Trade	LUZ HOPEWELL
Director of Investment	(VACANCY)
Director of Surety Guarantees	FRANK LALUMIERE
Assistant Administrator for Native American Affairs	HOLLY SCHICK, *Acting*
Associate Deputy Administrator for Entrepreneurial Development	PENNY PICKETT
Director of Business and Community Initiatives	ELLEN M. THRASHER
Director of Small Business Development Centers	ANTONIO DOSS

Director of Women's Business Ownership	(VACANCY)
Associate Administrator for Government Contracting and Business Development	JOSEPH JORDAN
Director of Government Contracting	KAREN HONTZ
Director of Business Development	JOSEPH LODDO
Director of HUBZone Empowerment Contracting	GUY TORRES
Associate Administrator for Management and Administration	DARRYL HAIRSTON
Director of Business Operations	AJOY SINHA, *Acting*
Chief Human Capital Officer	NAPOLEON AVERY
Director of Executive Secretariat	KIM BRADLEY

[For the Small Business Administration statement of organization, see the Code of Federal Regulations, Title 13, Part 101]

The Small Business Administration aids, counsels, assists, and protects the interests of small business; ensures that small business concerns receive a fair portion of Government purchases, contracts, and subcontracts, as well as of the sales of Government property; makes loans to small business concerns, State and local development companies, and the victims of floods or other catastrophes, or of certain types of economic injury; and licenses, regulates, and makes loans to small business investment companies.

The Small Business Administration (SBA) was created by the Small Business Act of 1953 and derives its present existence and authority from the Small Business Act (15 U.S.C. 631 *et seq.*) and the Small Business Investment Act of 1958 (15 U.S.C. 661).

Activities

Advocacy The Office of Advocacy is mandated by Congress to serve as an independent voice within the Federal Government for the approximately 27.2 million small businesses throughout the country. The Office is headed by the Chief Counsel for Advocacy, appointed by the President from the private sector with the advice and consent of the Senate, who advances the views, concerns, and interests of small business before the Congress, the White House, and Federal and State regulatory agencies.

The Office monitors and reports annually on Federal agency compliance with the Regulatory Flexibility Act (RFA), which requires agencies to analyze the impact of their regulations on small businesses and consider less burdensome alternatives. Small entities include small businesses, nonprofit organizations, and

governmental jurisdictions. Executive Order 13272 requires Federal agencies to take the Office's comments into consideration before proposed regulations are finalized and requires the Office to train Federal agencies on RFA compliance.

The Office is one of the leading national sources for information on the state of small business and the issues that affect small business success and growth. It conducts economic and statistical research into matters affecting the competitive strength of small business and jobs created by small business, and analyzes the impact of Federal laws, regulations, and programs on small businesses, making recommendations to policymakers for appropriate adjustments to meet the special needs of small business.

Additionally, regional advocates enhance communication between the small business community and the Chief Counsel. As the Chief Counsel's direct link to local business owners, State and local government agencies, State legislatures, and small business organizations, they help identify new issues and problems of small business by monitoring the effect of Federal and State regulations and policies on the

SMALL BUSINESS ADMINISTRATION

local business communities within their regions.

For further information, contact the Office of Advocacy. Phone, 202–205–6533. Email, advocacy@sba.gov.

Business and Community Initiatives
The Office of Business and Community Initiatives (OBCI) develops and cosponsors counseling, education, training, and information resources for small businesses. It has partnered with the private sector to promote entrepreneurial development. OBCI directs the national program of the Service Corps of Retired Executives (SCORE), a resource partner of SBA. SCORE provides free counseling, mentoring, training seminars, and specialized assistance to veterans and active military personnel. For more information, visit www.score.org. OBCI also offers young entrepreneurs a teen business site at www.sba.gov/teens.

The Office of International Visitors briefs foreign delegations, business organizations, and international nongovernmental organizations (NGOs) on the SBA model.

In addition to education and training events, SBA offers an online management series on business growth and sustainability at www.sba.gov/library/pubs.

For further information, contact the Office of Business and Community Initiatives. Phone, 202–205–6665.

Capital Access The Office of the Associate Administrator for Capital Access provides overall direction for SBA's financial programs. They offer a comprehensive array of debt and equity programs for startup and expanding businesses. In addition to lending to businesses which sell their products and services domestically, the Office provides financial assistance programs for small business exporters in the form of loan programs and technical assistance. The Office also oversees a surety bond guarantee program for small business contractors and SBA's lender oversight programs.

For further information, contact the Office of Capital Access. Phone, 202–205–6657.

Disaster Assistance The Administration serves as the Federal disaster bank for nonfarm, private sector losses. It lends money to help the victims of disasters repair or replace most disaster-damaged property. Direct loans with subsidized interest rates are made to assist individuals, homeowners, businesses of all sizes, and nonprofit organizations.

For further information, contact the Office of Disaster Assistance. Phone, 202–205–6734.

Financial Assistance SBA provides its guarantee to lending institutions and certified development companies which make loans to small-business concerns, which in turn use the loans for working capital and financing the acquisition of land and buildings; the construction, conversion, or expansion of facilities; and the purchase of machinery and equipment.

The Administration also provides small-scale financial and technical assistance to very small businesses through loans and grants to nonprofit organizations that act as intermediaries under SBA's microloan program.

For further information, contact the nearest Small Business Administration district office (listed at the end of this entry).

Government Contracting and Policy, Planning and Liaison SBA helps small businesses, including small disadvantaged businesses, women-owned small businesses, HUBZone-certified firms, and service-disabled veteran-owned small businesses obtain a fair share of Government procurement through a variety of programs and services. The contracting liaison helps small businesses secure an equitable share of natural resources sold by the Federal Government. It works closely with Federal agencies and the Office of Management and Budget to establish policy and regulations concerning small business access to Government contracts. It assists in the formulation of small business procurement policies as they relate to size standards, the Small Business Innovation Research Program, and the Small Business Technology Transfer Program.

For further information, contact the nearest Office of Government Contracting or visit our Web site. Phone, 202–205–6459. Internet, www.sba.gov/GC/ indexcontacts.html.

International Trade   The Office of International Trade (OIT) supports small business access to export markets and participates in broader U.S. Government activities related to trade policy and international commercial affairs to encourage an environment of trade and international economic policies favorable to small businesses. These activities are designed to facilitate both entrance and growth into the international marketplace, including educational initiatives, technical assistance programs and services, and risk management and trade finance products.

SBA's export promotion activities for small business combine financial and technical assistance through a nationwide delivery system. Export-finance products include long-term, short-term, and revolving lines of credit through SBA's 7(a) program administered by a staff of field-based export specialists located in U.S. Export Assistance Centers (USEACs). They work with the U.S. Department of Commerce and the Export Import Bank of the United States, and the effort is leveraged through close collaboration with commercial lenders, Small Business Development Centers, and local business development organizations.

Available financial assistance can provide a business with up to $1.25 million with terms up to 25 years for real estate and 15 years for equipment. Export Working Capital program loans generally provide 12 months of renewable financing. For smaller loan amounts, SBA Export Express has a streamlined, quick approval process for businesses needing up to $250,000. Technical assistance includes making available to current and potential small business exporters export training, export legal assistance, and collaboration with the 30 Small Business Development Centers with international trade expertise

and the Government's USA Trade Information Center.

SBA is required to work with the Government's international trade agencies to ensure that small business is adequately represented in bilateral and multilateral trade negotiations. OIT represents SBA and the Government on two official U.S. Government-sponsored multilateral organizations concerned with small business: the Organization for Economic Cooperation and Development and Asia-Pacific Economic Cooperation. SBA's trade policy involvement is carried out with the U.S. Trade Representative and the Commerce Department's International Trade Administration. Private sector input on trade policy is achieved through participation with the small business industry sector advisory committee on international trade. OIT also lends support to the Government's key trade initiatives such as Trade Promotion Authority, the Central American Free Trade Area, and the Free Trade Area of the Americas. The Commerce and State Departments, Agency for International Development, and the U.S. Trade Representative look to the SBA to share ideas and provide small business technical expertise to certain countries.

OIT's office in Washington, DC, coordinates SBA's participation/operation of USEACs, including budget, policy and administration. It participates in a variety of interagency trade efforts and financial programs. OIT provides representations to the cabinet-level Trade Promotion Coordinating Committee concerning trade and international economic policy. It also participates on the Industry Sector Advisory Council on Small Business International Trade and the congressionally sponsored Task Force on Small Business International Trade. SBA's Administrator is also a sitting member of the President's Export Council.

OIT's field offices provide a nationwide network of service delivery for small business exporters. Full-time SBA export specialists staff 16 USEACs. Their outreach efforts are supplemented by the 70 SBA district offices by employees with collateral duties as international trade officers.

For further information, contact the Office of International Trade. Phone, 202–205–6720. Internet, www.sba.gov/oit.

Venture Capital The Small Business Investment Company (SBIC) program was created in 1958 to fill the gap between the availability of venture capital and the needs of small businesses in startup and growth situations. The structure of the program is unique in that SBICs are privately owned and managed venture capital funds, licensed and regulated by the SBA, that use their own capital plus funds borrowed with an SBA guarantee to make equity and debt investments in qualifying small businesses. The New Markets Venture Capital (NMVC) program is a sister program focused on low-income areas, which augments the contribution made by SBICs to U.S. small businesses. In addition, NMVC companies may make technical assistance grants to potential portfolio companies.

The Government itself does not make direct investments or target specific industries in the SBIC program. Fund portfolio management and investment decisions are left to qualified private fund managers. To obtain an SBIC license, an experienced team of private equity managers must secure minimum commitments from private investors. SBICs may only invest in "small businesses" having net worth of less than $18 million and prior 2 years' average after-tax income of less than $6 million.

For further information, contact the Investment Division. Phone, 202–205–6510. Internet, www.sba.gov/inv.

HUBZone Program The HUBZone program provides Federal contracting assistance for qualified small businesses located in historically underutilized business zones in an effort to increase employment, capital investment, and economic development in these areas, including Indian reservations. The Office coordinates efforts with other Federal agencies and local municipal governments to leverage resources to assist qualified small businesses located in HUBZone areas. The program provides for set-asides, sole source awards, and price evaluation preferences for HUBZone small businesses and establishes goals for awards to such firms.

For further information, visit our Web site at www.sba.gov/hubzone. Phone, 202–205–6731.

Business Development The Office of Business Development is responsible for the 8(a) Business Development Program. The Office assists small businesses by providing access to capital and credit, business counseling, training workshops, technical guidance, and assistance with contracts and loans. Its primary business development tools are the Mentor-Protégé Program and the 7(j) Management and Technical Assistance Program.

For further information, visit our Web site at www.sba.gov/8abd. Phone, 202–205–5852.

Native American Affairs The Office of Native American Affairs was established to assist and encourage the creation, development, and expansion of Native American-owned small businesses by developing and implementing initiatives designed to address those difficulties encountered by Native Americans in their quest to start, develop, and expand small businesses. In addition, in an effort to address the unique conditions encountered by reservation-based entrepreneurs, the Office is developing a Web-based resource entitled the "Tribal Self Assessment Tool." It is intended to allow tribal nations to assess their vision and goals relative to their governance structure, culture, capabilities, and resources. The tool is free and will be available on the Internet.

For further information, contact the Office of Native American Affairs. Phone, 202–205–7364.

Regulatory Fairness Program Congress established the national ombudsman and 10 Regulatory Fairness Boards in 1996 as part of the Small Business Regulatory Enforcement Fairness Act (SBREFA). Section 222 of SBREFA was designed to ensure that small businesses, small government entities, and small nonprofit organizations that experience unfair regulatory enforcement action by Federal agencies have a means to register their comments about such actions. Comments from small business concerns are received by email, fax, regular mail, or by testifying at ombudsman hearings that are held across the country. The ombudsman acts as a neutral liaison between small business concerns and affected agencies to include comments for the report. Each of the Regulatory Fairness Boards (RegFair) has five volunteer members who are owners, operators, or officers of small business concerns that are appointed by the SBA Administrator for 3-year terms. Each RegFair Board meets at least annually with the ombudsman on matters of concern to small businesses relating to the enforcement or compliance activities of Federal agencies; report to the ombudsman on substantiated instances of excessive enforcement; and, prior to publication, provide comment on the annual report to Congress.

For further information, contact the Office of the National Ombudsman. Phone, 202–205–2417 or 888–734–3247. Internet, www.sba.gov/ ombudsman.

Small Business Development Centers

The Office of Small Business Development Centers (OSBDC) provides counseling and training to existing and prospective small business owners at more than 950 service locations in every State, Puerto Rico, the U.S. Virgin Islands, Guam, and American Samoa. OSBDC develops national policies and goals; establishes standards for the selection and performance of its Small Business Development Centers (SBDCs); monitors compliance with applicable Office of Management and Budget circulars and laws; and implements new approaches to improve existing centers. OSBDC also oversees 63 lead centers and maintains liaison with other Federal, State, and local agencies and private organizations whose activities relate to its centers. It also assesses how the program is affected by substantive developments and policies in other SBA areas, Government agencies, and the private sector.

The Small Business Development Center Program is a cooperative effort of the private sector, educational community, and Federal, State, and local governments. The Program enhances local economic development by providing small businesses with the management and technical assistance they need to succeed. It also provides services such as development of business plans, manufacturing assistance, financial packages, procurement contracts, and international trade assistance. Special areas include e-commerce; technology transfer; IRS, EPA, and OSHA regulatory compliance; research and development; defense economic transition assistance; disaster recovery assistance; and market research. Based on client needs assessments, business trends, and individual business requirements, SBDCs modify their services to meet the evolving needs of the small business community.

For further information, contact the Office of Small Business Development Centers. Phone, 202–205– 6766.

Surety Bonds   Through its Surety Bond Guarantee Program, SBA helps small and emerging contractors to obtain the bonding necessary for them to bid on and receive contracts up to $5 million. (The former $2 million threshold was increased to $5 million under the American Recovery and Reinvestment Act and is effective through September 30, 2010). SBA guarantees bonds that are issued by participating surety companies, and reimburses between 70% and 90% of losses and expenses incurred should a small business default on the contract. Construction, service, or supply contractors are eligible for the program if they, together with their affiliates, meet the size standard for the primary industry in which the small business is engaged, as defined by the North American Industry Classification System (NAICS).

For further information, contact the Office of Surety Guarantees. Phone, 202–205–6540. Internet, www.sba.gov/osg.

Technology   The Office of Technology has authority and responsibility for directing and monitoring the Governmentwide activities of the Small Business Innovation Research Program (SBIR) and the Small Business Technology Transfer Program (STTR). The Office develops and issues policy directives for the general conduct of the programs within the Federal Government and maintains a source file and information program to provide each interested and qualified small business concern with information on opportunities to compete for SBIR and STTR program awards. The Office also coordinates with each participating Federal agency in developing a master release schedule of all program solicitations; publishes the *Presolicitation Announcement* quarterly online, which contains pertinent facts on upcoming solicitations; and surveys and monitors program operations within the Federal Government and reports on the progress of the programs each year to Congress.

The Office has four main objectives: to expand and improve SBIR and STTR; to increase private sector commercialization of technology developed through Federal research and development; to increase small business participation in Federal research and development; and to improve the dissemination of information concerning SBIR and STTR, particularly with regard to participation by women-owned small business concerns and by socially and economically disadvantaged small business concerns.

For further information, contact the Office of Technology. Phone, 202–205–6450. Email, technology@sba.gov.

Veterans Affairs   The Office of Veterans Business Development (OVBD) is responsible for the formulation, execution, and promotion of policies and programs that provide assistance to small business concerns owned and controlled by veterans and service-disabled veterans. This includes reserve component members of the U.S. military. Additionally, OVBD serves as an ombudsman for the full consideration

of veterans in all programs of the Administration.

OVBD provides e-counseling and works with every SBA program to ensure that veterans receive special consideration in the operation of that program. OVBD also provides numerous tools such as the *VetGazette* veterans newsletter, the Reserve and Guard business assistance kits, program design assistance, and training events. Additionally, OVBD manages five Veterans Business Outreach Centers to provide outreach, directed referrals, and tailored entrepreneurial development services such as business training, counseling, and mentoring to veterans, including service-disabled veterans, and reservist-entrepreneurs. These centers provide an in-depth resource for existing and potential veteran entrepreneurs. The Office also coordinates SBA collaborative efforts with Veterans Service Organizations, the Departments of Defense, Labor, and Veterans Affairs, the National Veterans Business Development Corporation, State departments of veterans affairs, the National Committee for Employer Support of the Guard and Reserve, the Department of Defense Yellow Ribbon Reintegration Program and other public, civic, and private organizations to ensure that the entrepreneurial needs of veterans, service-disabled veterans, and self-employed members of the Reserve and National Guard are being met.

For further information, contact the Office of Veterans Business Development. Phone, 202–205–6773. Internet, www.sba.gov/vets or www.sba.gov/reservists.

Women's Business Ownership   The Office of Women's Business Ownership (OWBO) provides assistance to current and potential women business owners and acts as their advocate in the public and private sectors. OWBO assists women in becoming full partners in economic development by providing business training, counseling, mentoring, and other assistance through representatives in local SBA offices, Women's Business Centers (WBCs), and mentoring roundtables. Each WBC is tailored to meet the needs of its individual community and places a special emphasis on helping women who are socially and economically disadvantaged. Assistance covers every stage of business from startup to going public. There are WBCs in almost every State and U.S. territory.

OWBO works with other SBA programs, Federal agencies, and private sector organizations to leverage its resources and improve opportunities for women-owned businesses to access Federal procurement and international trade opportunities. OWBO also works with the National Women's Business Council and the Department of Labor to maintain the most current research on women's business ownership.

SBA has loan guaranty programs to help women access the credit and capital they need to start and grow successful businesses. The 7(a) Loan Guaranty Program offers a number of effective ways to finance business needs, including unsecured smaller loans and revolving lines of credit. The 504 Program provides long-term, fixed-rate financing for major fixed assets, such as land and buildings through certified development programs. Equity financing is available through the Small Business Investment Company Program. The Microloan Program offers direct small loans, combined with business assistance, through SBA-licensed intermediaries nationwide. The SBA does not offer grants for small businesses.

For further information, contact the Women's Business Ownership representative in your SBA district office. Phone, 202–205–6673. Email, owbo@sba.gov. Internet, www.sba.gov/aboutsba/sbaprograms/onlinewbc/index.html.

Field Operations The Office of Field Operations provides management direction and oversight to SBA's 10 regional and 68 district offices, acting as the liaison between the district offices, the Administration's program delivery system, and the headquarters administrative and program offices.

For further information, contact the Office of Field Operations. Phone, 202–205–6808.

Field Offices—Small Business Administration

(RO: Regional Office; DO: District Office; BO: Branch Office)

Office	Address	Officer in Charge	Telephone
ATLANTA, GA (RO)	Suite 1800, 233 Peachtree St. NE., 30303	Elliott Cooper, *Acting*	404–331–4999
Atlanta, GA (DO)	Suite 1900, 233 Peachtree St. NE., 30303	Terri Denison	404–331–0100
Birmingham, AL (DO)	Suite 201, 801 Tom Martin Dr., 35211	Thomas Todt, *Acting*	205–290–7101
Charlotte, NC (DO)	Suite 300, 6302 Fairview Rd., 28210–2227	Lee Cornelison	704–344–6563
Columbia, SC (DO)	Rm. 1425, 1835 Assembly St., 29201	Elliot Cooper	803–765–5377
Gulfport, MS (BO)	Suite 103, 2510 14th St., 39501	Judith Adcock	228–863–4449
Jackson, MS (DO)	210 E, 210 E. Capital St., 39201	Janita Stewart	601–965–4378
Jacksonville, FL (DO)	Suite 100–B, 7825 Baymeadows Way, 32256–7504.	Wilfredo Gonzalez	904–443–1970
Louisville, KY (DO)	Rm. 188, 600 Dr. M.L. King, Jr. Pl., 40202	Steve Ayers	502–582–5978
Miami, FL (DO)	7th Fl., 100 S. Biscayne Blvd., 33131	Francisco Marrero	305–536–5533
Nashville, TN (DO)	Suite 201, 50 Vantage Way, 37228–1500	Clint Smith	615–736–5850
BOSTON, MA (RO)	Suite 812, 10 Causeway St., 02222	Robert Nelson, *Acting*	617–565–8415
Augusta, ME (DO)	Rm. 512, 68 Sewall St., 04330	Maurice Dube	207–622–8378
Boston, MA (DO)	Suite 265, 10 Causeway St., 02222	Robert Nelson	617–565–5561
Concord, NH (DO)	Suite 3101, 55 Pleasant St., 03301	Witmer Jones	603–225–1400
Hartford, CT (DO)	2d Fl., 330 Main St., 06106	Bernard Sweeney	860–240–4700
Montpelier, VT (DO)	Suite 205, 87 State St., 05602	Darcy Carter, *Acting*	802–828–4422
Providence, RI (DO)	5th Fl., 380 Westminster Mall, 02903	Mark Hayward	401–528–4561
Springfield, MA (BO)	One Federal St., Bldg. 101, 01105	Edgardo Tarrats	413–785–0484
CHICAGO, IL (RO)	Suite 1240, 500 W. Madison St., 60661	Judith Roussel, *Acting*	312–353–4626
Chicago, IL (DO)	Suite 1250, 500 W. Madison St., 60661	Judith Roussel	312–353–4508
Cincinnati, OH (BO)	Rm. 2–522, JWP Federal Bldg., 550 Main St., 45202.	Ronald Carlson	513–684–2814
Cleveland, OH (DO)	Suite 211, 1315 Euclid Ave., 44115–1815	Gilbert Goldberg	216–522–4182
Columbus, OH (DO)	Suite 200, 401 N. Front St., 43215–2240	Tom Mueller	614–469–6860
Detroit, MI (DO)	Suite 515, 477 Michigan Ave., 48226	Richard Temkin	313–226–6075
Indianapolis, IN (DO)	Suite 400, 8500 Keystone Crossing, 46240–7336	Gail Gessell	317–226–7272
Milwaukee, WI (DO)	Suite 400, 310 W. Wisconsin Ave., 53203	Eric Ness	414–297–1471
Minneapolis, MN (DO)	Suite 210–C, 100 N. 6th St., 55403–1563	Ed Daum	612–370–2306
Springfield, IL (BO)	Suite B-East, 3330 Ginger Creek Rd., 62704	Valerie Ross	217–492–4416
DALLAS, TX (RO)	Suite 108, 4300 Amon Carter Blvd., Ft. Worth, TX 76155.	Dorothy Overal, *Acting*	817–684–5581
Albuquerque, NM (DO)	Suite 320, 625 Silver Ave. SW., 87102	John Woosley	505–248–8225

Field Offices—Small Business Administration—Continued

(RO: Regional Office; DO: District Office; BO: Branch Office)

Office	Address	Officer in Charge	Telephone
Corpus Christi, TX (BO)	Suite 411, 3649 Leopard St., 78408	Simon Castillo	361–879–0017
El Paso, TX (DO)	Suite 201, 211 N. Florence St., 79901	Phillip Silva, *Acting*	915–633–7001
Fort Worth, TX (DO)	Suite 114, 4300 Amon Carter Blvd., 76155	Herbert Austin	817–684–5500
Harlingen, TX (DO)	Rm. 500, 222 E. Van Buren St., 78550–6855	Michael Wilk, *Acting*	956–427–8533
Houston, TX (DO)	Suite 1200, 8701 S. Gessner Dr., 77074	Manuel Gonzalez	713–773–6500
Little Rock, AR (DO)	Suite 100, 2120 Riverfront Dr., 72202	Linda Nelson	501–324–5871
Lubbock, TX (DO)	Rm. 408, 1205 Texas Ave., 79401–2693	Herbert Johnston	806–472–7462
New Orleans, LA (DO)	Suite 2820, 365 Canal Pl., 70130	Michael W. Ricks	504–589–6685
Oklahoma City, OK (DO).	Suite 116, 301 N. 8th St., 73102	Dorothy Overal	405–231–5521
San Antonio, TX (DO)	Suite 200, 17319 San Pedro, Bldg. No. 2, 78232	Pamela Sapia	210–403–5900
DENVER, CO (RO)	Suite 400, 721 19th St., 80202–2599	Elton W. Ringsak	303–844–0503
Casper, WY (DO)	P.O. Box 4001, 100 E. B St., 82601	Steven Despain	307–261–6501
Denver, CO (DO)	Suite 426, 721 19th St., 80202–2599	Stanley Nakano, *Acting*	303–844–6500
Fargo, ND (DO)	Rm. 219, 657 2d Ave. N., 58108–3086	James L. Stai	701–239–5131
Helena, MT (DO)	Suite 1100, 10 W. 15th St., 59626	Michelle Johnston	406–441–1080
Salt Lake City, UT (DO)	Rm. 2237, 125 S. State St., 84138–1195	Stanley Nakano	801–524–3200
Sioux Falls, SD (DO)	Suite 105, 2329 N. Career Ave., 57107	John Brown	605–330–4243
KANSAS CITY, MO (RO)	Suite 530, 1000 Walnut St., 64106–1500	A. Dean Cotton, *Acting*	816–426–4840
Cedar Rapids, IA (BO)	Suite 350, 2750 1st Ave. NE., 52402–4831	Dennis Larkin	319–362–6405
Des Moines, IA (DO)	Rm. 749, 210 Walnut St., 50309–2186	Joe Folsom	515–284–4026
Kansas City, MO (DO)	Suite 500, 1000 Walnut St., 64106–1500	Gary Cook	816–426–4900
Omaha, NE (DO)	Suite 100, 10675 Bedford Ave., 68134–3613	Leon Milobar	402–221–4691
Springfield, MO (BO)	Suite 101, 830 E. Primrose, 65807–5254	Walter Cowart	417–890–8501
St. Louis, MO (DO)	Suite 1500, 200 N. Broadway, 63102	Dennis Melton	314–539–6600
Wichita, KS (DO)	Suite 2500, 271 W. 3d St. N., 67202–1212	Wayne Bell	316–269–6566
NEW YORK, NY (RO)	Rm. 31–08, 26 Federal Plz., 10278	Bernard J. Paprocki, *Acting.*	212–264–1450
Buffalo, NY (DO)	Suite 540, 130 S. Elmwood St., 14202	Franklin J. Sciortino	716–551–4301
Elmira, NY (BO)	333 E. Water St., 14901	Brian Qualey	607–734–1571
Hato Rey, PR (DO)	252 Ponce de Leon Ave., 00918	Jose Sifontes	787–766–5002
Melville, NY (BO)	Suite 207, 35 Pinelawn Rd., 11747	Al Titone	631–454–0750
New York, NY (DO)	Suite 3100, 26 Federal Plz., 10278	Al Titone, *Acting*	212–264–2454
Newark, NJ (DO)	15th Fl., 2 Gateway Ctr., 07102	James Kocsi, *Acting*	973–645–3580
Rochester, NY (BO)	Suite 410, 100 State St., 14614	Victoria Reynolds	716–263–6700
St. Croix, VI (BO)	Rm. 167, Americ L. Christian Fed. Bldg., 00820	Carl Christensen	340–778–5380
St. Thomas, VI (BO)	3800 Crown Bay St., 00802	(vacancy)	809–774–8530
Syracuse, NY (DO)	5th Fl., 401 S. Salina St., 13202	Bernard J. Paprocki	315–471–9393
KING OF PRUSSIA, PA (RO).	Suite 1001, 1150 First Ave., 19406	Bridget Bean, *Acting*	610–382–3073
Baltimore, MD (DO)	Suite 6220, 10 S. Howard St., 21201–2525	Stephen D. Umberger	410–962–6195
Charleston, WV (BO)	Suite 412, 405 Capitol St., 25301	(vacancy)	304–347–5220
Clarksburg, WV (DO)	320 W. Pike St., 26301	Judy McCauley	304–623–5631
Harrisburg, PA (BO)	Suite 850, 228 Walnut St., 17101	(vacancy)	717–782–3840
King of Prussia, PA (DO).	Suite 1001, 1150 First Ave., 19406	David Dickson	610–382–3073
Pittsburgh, PA (DO)	Suite 1450, 411 7th Ave., 15219	Carl Knoblock	412–395–6560
Richmond, VA (DO)	11th Fl., 400 N. 8th St., 23240	Ron Bew	804–771–2400
Washington, DC (DO)	740 15th St. NW., 20005	Eugene Cornelius, Jr.	202–606–4000
Wilmington, DE (DO)	Suite 1200, 1007 N. Orange St., 19801–1232	Jayne Armstrong	302–573–6294
GLENDALE, CA (RO)	Suite 1200, 330 N. Brand Blvd., 91203	Alberto Alvarado, *Acting*	818–552–3434
Citrus Heights, CA (BO)	Suite 100, 6501 Sylvan Rd., 95610	James O'Neal	916–735–1700
Fresno, CA (DO)	Suite 200, 2719 N. Air Fresno Dr., 93727–1547	Carlos G. Mendoza	559–487–5791
Glendale, CA (DO)	Suite 1200, 330 N. Brand Blvd., 91203–2304	Alberto Alvarado	818–552–3201
Mongmong, GU (BO)	Suite 302, 400 Rt. 8, 96927	Kenneth Lujan	671–472–7419
Honolulu, HI (DO)	Box 50207, Rm. 2–235, 300 Ala Moana Blvd., 96850–4981.	Karen Sakihama	808–541–2990
Las Vegas, NV (DO)	Suite 250, 400 S. 4th St., 89101	John E. Scott	702–388–6611
Phoenix, AZ (DO)	Suite 800, 2828 N. Central Ave., 85004–1025	Robert J. Blaney	602–745–7200
San Diego, CA (DO)	Suite 550, 550 W. C St., 92101	Ruben Garcia	619–557–7250
San Francisco, CA (DO)	6th Fl., 455 Market St., 94105	Mark Quinn	415–744–6820
Santa Ana, CA (DO)	Suite 700, 200 W. Santa Ana Blvd., 92701	Adalberto Quijada	714–550–7420
SEATTLE, WA (RO)	Suite 400, 2401 4th Ave., 98121	Nancy Porzio, *Acting*	206–553–5676
Anchorage, AK (DO)	Suite 310, 510 L St., 99501	Karen Forsland	907–271–4022
Boise, ID (DO)	Suite 330, 380 E. Parkcenter Blvd., 83702–3965	Norman Proctor, *Acting*	208–334–9004
Portland, OR (DO)	Suite 950, 601 SW. 2d Ave., 97201–6695	Harry L. DeWolf	503–326–5221
Seattle, WA (DO)	Suite 450, 2401 4th Ave., 98121	Nancy Porzio	206–553–7040
Spokane, WA (BO)	Suite 200, 801 W. Riverside, 99201	Ted Schinzel, *Acting*	509–353–2806

Disaster Area Offices

Office	Address	Telephone
Atlanta, GA	Suite 700, 101 Marietta St., 30303	404–331–0333
Buffalo, NY	120 S. Elmwood Ave., 14202	716–843–4100
Citrus Heights, CA	6501 Sylvan Rd. 95610	916–566–7246
Fort Worth, TX	14925 Kingsport Rd., 76155	817–886–2300

Sources of Information

Electronic Access Information on the Small Business Administration is available electronically by various means. Internet, www.sba.gov. FTP, ftp.sbaonline.sba.gov.

Access the U.S. Business Adviser through the Internet at www.business.gov.

Access the Administration's electronic bulletin board by modem at 800–697–4636 (limited access), 900–463–4636 (full access), or 202–401–9600 (Washington, DC, metropolitan area).

General Information Contact the nearest Small Business Administration field office listed in the preceding text, or call the SBA answer desk. Phone, 800–827–5722. Fax, 202–205–7064. TDD, 704–344–6640.

Public Affairs For public inquiries and small business advocacy affairs, contact the Office of Public Communications and Public Liaison, 409 Third Street SW., Washington, DC 20416. Phone, 202–205–6740. Internet, www.sba.gov.

Publications A free copy of *The Resource Directory for Small Business Management,* a listing of for-sale publications and videotapes, is available from any local SBA office or the SBA answer desk.

For further information, contact the Office of Public Communications and Public Liaison, Small Business Administration, 409 Third Street SW., Washington, DC 20416. Phone, 202–205–6740. Internet, www.sba.gov.

SOCIAL SECURITY ADMINISTRATION

6401 Security Boulevard, Baltimore, MD 21235
Phone, 410–965–1234. Internet, www.socialsecurity.gov.

COMMISSIONER OF SOCIAL SECURITY	MICHAEL J. ASTRUE
DEPUTY COMMISSIONER	(VACANCY)
Chief of Staff	JAMES A. WINN
Deputy Chief of Staff	JO TITTEL
Senior Advisor to the Deputy Commissioner	LINDA D. MAXFIELD
Special Advisor for Health IT	JAMES C. BORLAND
Executive Secretary	ROBIN F. KAPLAN
International Programs	DIANE K. BRAUNSTEIN, *Acting*
Chief Actuary	STEPHEN C. GOSS
Deputy Chief Actuary (Short Range)	ELI N. DONKAR
Deputy Chief Actuary (Long Range)	ALICE H. WADE
Chief Information Officer	GREGORY C. PACE, *Acting*
Deputy Chief Information Officer	GREGORY C. PACE
Deputy Commissioner for Communications	JAMES J. COURTNEY

Assistant Deputy Commissioner for Communications	PHILIP A. GAMBINO
Deputy Commissioner for Budget, Finance, and Management	MARY E. GLENN-CROFT
Assistant Deputy Commissioner for Budget, Finance, and Management	MICHAEL G. GALLAGHER
Deputy Commissioner for Disability Adjudication and Review	DAVID V. FOSTER
Assistant Deputy Commissioner for Disability Adjudication and Review	RONALD T. RABORG
Senior Advisor for the Deputy Commissioner for Disability Adjudication and Review	LISA DE SOTO
General Counsel	DAVID F. BLACK
Deputy General Counsel	THOMAS W. CRAWLEY
Deputy Commissioner for Human Resources	REGINALD F. WELLS
Assistant Deputy Commissioner for Human Resources	NANCY A. BERRYHILL, *Acting*
Inspector General	PATRICK P. O'CARROLL
Deputy Inspector General	JAMES A. KISSKO
Deputy Commissioner for Legislative and Regulatory Affairs	MARGARET A. HOSTETLER
Assistant Deputy Commissioner for Legislative and Regulatory Affairs	ANGELA J. ARNETT
Deputy Commissioner for Operations	LINDA S. MCMAHON
Assistant Deputy Commissioner for Operations	ROGER P. MCDONNELL
Deputy Commissioner for Quality Performance	G. KELLY CROFT
Assistant Deputy Commissioner for Quality Performance	(VACANCY)
Deputy Commissioner for Retirement and Disability Policy	DAVID A. RUST
Assistant Deputy Commissioners for Retirement and Disability Policy	MARIANA E. LACANFORA, (VACANCY)
Deputy Commissioner for Systems	WILLIAM E. GRAY
Assistant Deputy Commissioner for Systems	JERRY L. BERSON

[For the Social Security Administration statement of organization, see the Code of Federal Regulations, Title 20, Part 422]

The Social Security Administration manages the Nation's social insurance program—consisting of retirement, survivors, and disability insurance programs—commonly known as Social Security; administers the Supplemental Security Income program for the aged, blind, and disabled; assigns Social Security numbers to U.S. citizens; and maintains earnings records for workers under their Social Security numbers.

The Social Security Administration (SSA) was established by Reorganization Plan No. 2 of 1946 (5 U.S.C. app.), effective July 16, 1946. It became an independent agency in the executive branch by the Social Security Independence and Program Improvements Act of 1994 (42 U.S.C. 901), effective March 31, 1995.

The Administration is headed by a Commissioner, appointed by the President with the advice and consent of the Senate.

In administering the programs necessary to carry out the Administration's mission, by law the Commissioner is assisted by a Deputy Commissioner who performs duties assigned or delegated by the Commissioner, a Chief Financial Officer, a Chief Information Officer, a General

SOCIAL SECURITY ADMINISTRATION

Counsel, a Chief Actuary, and an Inspector General.

Programs and Activities

Old-Age, Survivors, and Disability Insurance   The agency administers social insurance programs, which provide monthly benefits to retired and disabled workers, their spouses and children, and to survivors of insured workers. Financing is under a system of contributory social insurance, whereby employees, employers, and the self-employed pay contributions that are pooled in special trust funds. When earnings stop or are reduced because the worker retires, dies, or becomes disabled, monthly cash benefits are paid to partially replace the earnings the family has lost.

Supplemental Security Income   The agency administers this needs-based program for the aged, blind, and disabled. A basic Federal monthly payment is financed out of general revenue, rather than a special trust fund. Some States, choosing to provide payments to supplement the benefits, have agreements with the Administration under which it administers the supplemental payments for those States.

Medicare   While the administration of Medicare is the responsibility of the Centers for Medicare and Medicaid Services, the Social Security Administration provides Medicare assistance to the public through SSA field offices and call centers, and adjudicates requests for hearings and appeals of Medicare claims.

Black Lung   By agreement with the Department of Labor, SSA is involved in certain aspects of the administration of the black lung benefits provisions of the Federal Coal Mine Health and Safety Act of 1969, as amended (30 U.S.C. 901).

Regional Offices   Social Security Administration operations are decentralized to provide services at the local level. Each of the 10 SSA regions, under the overall direction of its Regional Commissioner, contains a network of field offices and call centers, which serve as the contacts between SSA and the public. The Administration operates over 1200 field offices, 35 call centers, 7 Social Security card centers, and 7 processing centers. These installations are responsible for the following:

—informing the public of the purposes and provisions of Social Security programs and their rights and responsibilities;

—assisting with claims filed for retirement, survivors, disability, or health insurance benefits, black lung benefits, or Supplemental Security Income;

—developing and adjudicating claims;

—assisting certain beneficiaries in claiming reimbursement for medical expenses;

—developing cases involving earnings records, coverage, and fraud-related questions;

—making rehabilitation service referrals; and

—assisting claimants in filing appeals on SSA determinations of benefit entitlement or amount.

Hearing Offices   SSA also administers a nationwide hearings and appeals program which provides a mechanism for individuals dissatisfied with determinations affecting their rights to and amounts of benefits or their participation in programs under the Social Security Act. The act allows for administrative appeals of these determinations in accordance with the requirements of the Administrative Procedure and Social Security Acts. SSA has approximately 140 hearing offices located in the 10 SSA regions.

For further information, contact the Social Security Administration. Phone, 800–772–1213. TTY, 800–325–0778.

Sources of Information

Inquiries on the following subjects may be directed to the appropriate office, Social Security Administration, 6401 Security Boulevard, Baltimore, MD 21235.

Contracts and Small Business Activities Contact the Office of Acquisitions and Grants. Phone, 410–965–7467.

Electronic Access Information regarding the Social Security Administration may be obtained through the Internet at www.socialsecurity.gov.

Employment For information about careers with the Social Security Administration, go to www.socialsecurity.gov/careers. For current vacancies, go to www.jobsearch.usajobs.opm.gov.

General Information The Office of the Deputy Commissioner for Operations manages SSA's toll-free public service telephone. Phone, 800–772–1213. TTY, 800–325–0778.

Inspector General The Office of the Inspector General maintains a toll-free hotline that operates between the hours of 10 a.m. and 4 p.m. e.s.t. (phone, 800–269–0271; TTY, 866–501–2101) to receive allegations of fraud. Persons may submit allegations by fax at 410–597–0118, by Web site at www.socialsecurity.gov/oig, or by mail at Social Security Fraud Hotline, P.O. Box 17768, Baltimore, MD 21235–7768.

Publications The Office of the Deputy Commissioner for Communications publishes numerous pamphlets concerning SSA programs. SSA also collects a substantial volume of economic, demographic, and other data in furtherance of its program mission. Basic data on employment, payments, and other items of program interest are published regularly in the *Social Security Bulletin,* its *Annual Statistical Supplement,* and in special releases and reports that appear periodically on selected topics of interest to the public. Single copies may be obtained at any local office or by calling 800–772–1213. Requests for bulk orders of publications should be sent to the Social Security Administration, Office of Supply and Warehouse Management, 239 Supply Building, 6301 Security Boulevard, Baltimore, MD 21235. In addition, over 150 publications are available online in English, Spanish, and other languages at www.socialsecurity.gov.

Reading Room Requests for information, for copies of records, or to inspect records may be made at any local office or the Headquarters Contact Unit, Room G–44, Altmeyer Building.

Speakers and Films SSA makes speakers, films, and exhibits available to public or private organizations, community groups, schools, etc., throughout the Nation. Requests for this service should be directed to the local Social Security office.

For further information, contact the Office of Public Inquiries, Social Security Administration, 6401 Security Boulevard, Windsor Park Building, Baltimore, MD 21235. Phone, 800–772–1213. TTY, 800–325–0778. Internet, www.socialsecurity.gov.

TENNESSEE VALLEY AUTHORITY

400 West Summit Hill Drive, Knoxville, TN 37902
Phone, 865–632–2101. Internet, www.tva.com.

One Massachusetts Avenue NW., Washington, DC 20444–0001
Phone, 202–898–2999

CHAIRMAN   ROBERT M. DUNCAN

Directors	DENNIS BOTTORFF, THOMAS GILLILAND, WILLIAM GRAVES, WILLIAM B. SANSOM, HOWARD A. THRAILKILL, (2 VACANCIES)
President and Chief Operating Officer	TOM D. KILGORE
Chief Administrative Office and Executive Vice President, Administrative Services	JOHN E. LONG, JR.
Senior Vice President, Communications, Government and Valley Relations	EMILY J. REYNOLDS
Chief Operating Officer	WILLIAM R. McCOLLUM, JR.
Chief Nuclear Officer	PRESTON D. SWAFFORD
Chief Financial Officer and Executive Vice President, Financial Services	KIMBERLY S. GREENE

The Tennessee Valley Authority conducts a unified program of resource development for the advancement of economic growth in the Tennessee Valley region.

The Tennessee Valley Authority (TVA) is a wholly owned Government corporation created by act of May 18, 1933 (16 U.S.C. 831–831dd). All functions of the Authority are vested in its nine-member Board of Directors, the members of which are appointed by the President with the advice and consent of the Senate. The Board designates one member as Chairman.

Programs and Activities

TVA's program and activities includes flood control, navigation, electric power production and transmission, recreation improvement, water supply, water quality, environmental stewardship, and economic development.

TVA's electric power program is financially self-supporting and operates as part of an independent system with TVA's system of dams on the Tennessee River and its larger tributaries. These dams provide flood regulation on the Tennessee River and contribute to regulation of the lower Ohio and Mississippi Rivers. The system maintains a continuous 9-foot-draft navigation channel for the length of the 650-mile Tennessee River main stream, from Paducah, KY, to Knoxville, TN. The dams harness the power of the rivers to produce electricity. They also provide other benefits, notably outdoor recreation and water supply.

TVA operates the river management system and provides assistance to State and local governments in reducing local flood problems. It also works with other agencies to encourage full and effective use of the navigable waterway by industry and commerce.

TVA is the wholesale power supplier for 158 local municipal and cooperative electric systems serving customers in parts of 7 States. It supplies power to 60 industries and Federal installations whose power requirements are large or unusual. Power to meet these demands is supplied from dams, coal-fired power plants, nuclear power plants, combustion turbine and diesel installations, solar energy sites, wind turbines, a methane gas facility, and a pumped-storage hydroelectric plant; U.S. Corps of Engineers dams in the Cumberland Valley; and Aluminum Company of America dams, whose operation is coordinated with TVA's system.

Economic development is at the heart of TVA's mission of making the Tennessee Valley a better place to live. A healthy economy means quality jobs, more investment in the region, sustainable growth, and opportunities for residents in the southeastern region to build more prosperous lives. TVA Economic Development takes a regional approach on economic growth by partnering with power distributors and both public and private organizations to attract new investments and quality jobs, supporting retention and growth of existing businesses and industries, preparing communities for leadership and economic growth, and providing financial and technical services.

Sources of Information

Citizen Participation   TVA Communications, 400 West Summit Hill Drive, Knoxville, TN 37902–1499. Phone, 865–632–2101.

Contracts   Purchasing, WT 3A, 400 West Summit Hill Drive, Knoxville, TN 37902–1499. Phone, 865–632–4796. This office will direct inquiries to the appropriate procurement officer.

Economic Development   OCP 2A–NST, One Century Place, 26 Century Boulevard., Suite 100, Nashville, TN 37214. Mailing address: P.O. Box 292409, Nashville, TN 37229–2409. Phone, 615–232–6051.

Electric Power Supply   1101 Market Street, Chattanooga, TN 37402. Phone, 423–751–6000.

Electric Rates   One Century Plaza, 26 Century Boulevard, Suite 100, Nashville, TN 37214–3685.

Employment   For employment inquiries, visit www.tva.com.

Library Services   TVA Research Library, 400 West Summit Hill Drive, Knoxville, TN 37902–1499. Phone, 865–632–3464. Chattanooga Office Complex, LP4A–C, 1101 Market Street, Chattanooga, TN 37402–2791. Phone, 423–751–4913. P.O. Box 1010, CTR 1E–M, Muscle Shoals, AL 35662. Phone, 256–386–2872.

Maps   Maps Information and Photo Records, HV 1C–C, 2837 Hickory Valley Road, Chattanooga, TN 37421. Phone, 423–499–6285; 800–627–7882.

Publications   TVA Communications, WT 7D, 400 West Summit Hill Drive, Knoxville, TN 37902–1499. Phone, 865–632–6000.

For further information, contact the Tennessee Valley Authority at either 400 West Summit Hill Drive, Knoxville, TN 37902–1499, phone, 865–632–3199; or One Massachusetts Avenue NW., Washington, DC 20044, phone, 202–898–2999. Internet, www.tva.com.

TRADE AND DEVELOPMENT AGENCY

1000 Wilson Boulevard, Suite 1600, Arlington, VA 22209–3901
Phone, 703–875–4357. Fax, 703–875–4009. Email, info@ustda.gov. Internet, www.ustda.gov.

DIRECTOR	LEOCADIA I. ZAK, *Acting*
General Counsel	JAMES A. WILDEROTTER
Chief of Staff	THOMAS R. HARDY
Director for Policy and Programs	GEOFFREY JACKSON
Resource Advisor	MICHAEL HILLIER
Communications/Policy Advisor	DONNA THIESSEN
Congressional Relations Liaison	AMY LORENZINI
Regional Directors:	
East Asia	GEOFFREY JACKSON
Europe and Eurasia	DANIEL D. STEIN
Latin America and Caribbean	NATHAN YOUNGE
Middle East and North Africa	CARL B. KRESS
South and Southeast Asia	HENRY D. STEINGASS
Sub-Saharan Africa	PAUL MARIN
Economist/Evaluation Officer	DAVID DENNY
Financial Manager	NOREEN ST. LOUIS
Contracts Manager	RICHARD SALLEE

Administrative Officer CAROLYN HUM
Grants Administrator PATRICIA DAUGHETEE

---

*The Trade and Development Agency advances economic development and U.S.
commercial interest in developing and middle-income countries in the following
regions of the world: East Asia, Europe and Eurasia, Latin America and the
Caribbean, Middle East and North Africa, South and Southeast Asia, and Sub-Saharan
Africa.*

The Trade and Development Program
was established on July 1, 1980, as a
component organization of the
International Development Cooperation
Agency. Section 2204 of the Omnibus
Trade and Competitiveness Act of 1988
(22 U.S.C. 2421) made it a separate
component agency. The organization
was renamed the Trade and
Development Agency (USTDA) and
made an independent agency within the
executive branch of the Federal
Government on October 28, 1992, by
the Jobs Through Exports Act of 1992
(22 U.S.C. 2421).

USTDA is a foreign assistance agency
that delivers its program commitments
through overseas grants, contracts with
U.S. firms, and the use of trust funds at
several multilateral development bank
groups. The projects supported by
USTDA activities represent strong and
measurable development priorities in
host countries and offer opportunities for
commercial participation by U.S. firms.
Public and private sector project
sponsors, in developing and middle-
income countries, request USTDA
support to assist them in implementing
their development priorities.

USTDA helps countries establish a
favorable trading environment and a
modern infrastructure that promotes
sustainable economic development. To
this end, USTDA funds overseas projects
and sponsors access to U.S. private
sector expertise in the areas of project
definition and investment analysis and
trade capacity building and sector
development. Project definition and
investment analysis involves activities
that support large capital investments
that contribute to overseas infrastructure
development. Trade capacity building
and sector development supports the
establishment of industry standards, rules
and regulations, trade agreements,
market liberalization, and other policy
reform.

USTDA works with other U.S.
Government agencies to bring their
particular expertise and resources to a
development objective. These agencies
include the Departments of State, the
Treasury, Commerce, Transportation,
Energy, Agriculture, and Homeland
Security; the Office of the U.S. Trade
Representative; the Export-Import Bank
of the United States; and the Overseas
Private Investment Corporation.

Activities

USTDA funds various forms of technical
assistance, training, early investment
analysis, orientation visits, and business
workshops that support the development
of a modern infrastructure and a fair and
open trading environment. Working
closely with a foreign project sponsor,
USTDA makes its funds available on the
condition that the foreign entity contract
with a U.S. firm to perform the activity
funded. This affords American firms
market entry, exposure, and information,
thus helping them to establish a position
in markets that are otherwise difficult to
penetrate. USTDA is involved in many
sectors, including transportation, energy,
telecommunications, environment,
health care, mining and minerals
development, biotechnology, and
agriculture.

USTDA-funded studies evaluate the
technical, economic, and financial
aspects of a development project. They
also advise the host nation about the
availability of U.S. goods and services
and can be used by financial institutions
in assessing the creditworthiness of an
undertaking. Grants are based on an
official request for assistance made by
the sponsoring government or private
sector organization of a developing or
middle-income nation. Study costs
typically are shared between USTDA
and the U.S. firm developing the project.

TRADE AND DEVELOPMENT AGENCY

DIRECTOR

CHIEF OF STAFF

OFFICE OF EXTERNAL RELATIONS

GENERAL COUNSEL

DEPUTY DIRECTOR

FINANCIAL MANAGER

CONTRACTING OFFICER

ADMINISTRATIVE OFFICER

ECONOMIST/ EVALUATION OFFICER

GRANTS ADMINISTRATOR

POLICY AND PROGRAM DIRECTOR

REGIONAL DIRECTOR EAST ASIA

REGIONAL DIRECTOR EUROPE AND EURASIA

REGIONAL DIRECTOR LATIN AMERICA AND CARIBBEAN

REGIONAL DIRECTOR MIDDLE EAST AND NORTH AFRICA

REGIONAL DIRECTOR SOUTH AND SOUTHEAST ASIA

REGIONAL DIRECTOR SUB-SAHARAN AFRICA

The Agency makes decisions on funding requests based on the recommendations contained in definitional mission or desk study reports, the advice of the U.S. Embassy, and its own internal analysis.

Sources of Information

Requests for proposals to conduct USTDA-funded technical assistance and feasibility studies, or definitional missions involving review of projects under consideration for USTDA support are listed on the Federal Business Opportunities (FBO) Web site. Links to the FBO postings can be found at www.ustda.gov.

Small and minority U.S. firms that wish to be considered for future USTDA desk study solicitations should register with the Agency's online Consultant Database at www.ustda.gov/consultantdb.

In an effort to provide timely information on Agency-supported activities, USTDA sends out an eNewsletter with current business opportunities and a calendar of events on a biweekly basis. A free email subscription is available at www.ustda.gov. The Agency's printed newsletter, *USTDA Update,* contains current items of interest on a variety of program activities. Region- or sector-specific factsheets and case studies are also available. An annual report summarizes the Agency's activities.

Agency news, reports, and lists of current business opportunities and upcoming events are available at www.ustda.gov.

USTDA's library maintains final reports on the Agency's activities. The reports are available for public review Monday through Friday from 8:30 a.m. to 5:30 p.m. Copies of completed studies may be purchased through the Department of Commerce's National Technical Information Service at www.ntis.gov.

Regional program inquiries should be directed to the assigned Country Manager. Phone, 703–875–4357. Fax, 703–875–4009. Email, info@ustda.gov.

For further information, contact the Trade and Development Agency, Suite 1600, 1000 Wilson Boulevard, Arlington, VA 22209–3901. Phone, 703–875–4357. Fax, 703–875–4009. Email, info@ustda.gov. Internet, www.ustda.gov.

UNITED STATES AGENCY FOR INTERNATIONAL DEVELOPMENT

1300 Pennsylvania Avenue NW., Washington, DC 20523
Phone, 202–712–0000. Internet, www.usaid.gov.

ADMINISTRATOR	ALONZO FULGRAM, *Acting*
DEPUTY ADMINISTRATOR	(VACANCY)
Counselor	JAMES MICHEL
Chief Operating Officer	ALONZO FULGHAM
Assistant Administrator for Africa	EARL GAST
Assistant Administrator for Asia	MARGOT ELLIS, *Acting*
Assistant Administrator for Middle East	GEORGE LAUDATO, *Acting*
Assistant Administrator for Democracy, Conflict and Humanitarian Assistance	SHARON L. CROMER, *Acting*
Assistant Administrator for Economic Growth, Agriculture and Trade	MICHAEL YATES, *Acting*
Assistant Administrator for Europe and Eurasia	KEN YAMASHITA, *Acting*
Assistant Administrator for Global Health	GLORIA STEEL, *Acting*

Assistant Administrator for **Latin America and the Caribbean**	DEBBIE KENNEDY-IRAHETA, *Acting*
Assistant Administrator for **Legislative and Public Affairs**	CHRIS MILLIGAN, *Acting*
Assistant Administrator for **Management**	DREW LUTEN, *Acting*
Director of Office of Development Partners	KAREN TURNER
Director of Security	RANDY STREUFERT
Director of Equal Opportunity Programs	JESSALYN L. PENDARVIS
Director of Small and Disadvantaged Business Utilization/Minority Resource Center	MAURICIO VERA
General Counsel	ALAN SWENDIMAN
Inspector General	DONALD A. GAMBATESA

[For the Agency for International Development statement of organization, see the *Federal Register* of Aug. 26, 1987, 52 FR 32174]

The U.S. Agency for International Development administers U.S. foreign economic and humanitarian assistance programs worldwide in the developing world, Central and Eastern Europe, and Eurasia.

The United States Agency for International Development (USAID) is an independent Federal agency established by 22 U.S.C. 6563. Its principal statutory authority is the Foreign Assistance Act of 1961, as amended (22 U.S.C. 2151 *et seq.*). USAID serves as the focal point within the Government for economic matters affecting U.S. relations with developing countries. USAID administers international economic and humanitarian assistance programs. The Administrator is under the direct authority and foreign policy guidance of the Secretary of State.

Programs

The Agency meets its post-cold war era challenges by utilizing its strategy for achieving sustainable development in developing countries. It supports programs in four areas: population and health, broad-based economic growth, environment, and democracy. It also provides humanitarian assistance and aid to countries in crisis and transition.

Population and Health   The Agency contributes to a cooperative global effort to stabilize world population growth and support women's reproductive rights. The types of population and health programs supported vary with the particular needs of individual countries and the kinds of approaches that local communities initiate and support. Most USAID resources are directed to the following areas: support for voluntary family planning systems, reproductive health care, needs of adolescents and young adults, infant and child health, and education for girls and women.

Economic Growth   The Agency promotes broad-based economic growth by addressing the factors that enhance the capacity for growth and by working to remove the obstacles that stand in the way of individual opportunity. In this context, programs concentrate on strengthening market economies, expanding economic opportunities for the disadvantaged in developing countries, and building human skills and capacities to facilitate broad-based participation.

Environment   The Agency's environmental programs support two strategic goals: reducing long-term threats to the global environment, particularly loss of biodiversity and climate change; and promoting sustainable economic growth locally, nationally, and regionally by addressing environmental, economic, and developmental practices that impede development and are unsustainable. Globally, Agency programs focus on reducing sources and enhancing sinks of greenhouse gas emissions and on promoting innovative approaches to the conservation and sustainable use of the planet's biological diversity. The approach to national environmental

UNITED STATES AGENCY FOR INTERNATIONAL DEVELOPMENT

problems differs on a country-by-country basis, depending on a particular country's environmental priorities. Country strategies may include improving agricultural, industrial, and natural resource management practices that play a central role in environmental degradation; strengthening public policies and institutions to protect the environment; holding dialogs with country governments on environmental issues and with international agencies on the environmental impact of lending practices and the design and implementation of innovative mechanisms to support environmental work; and environmental research and education.

Democracy The Agency's strategic objective in the democracy area is the transition to and consolidation of democratic regimes throughout the world. Programs focus on such problems as human rights abuses; misperceptions about democracy and free-market capitalism; lack of experience with democratic institutions; the absence or weakness of intermediary organizations; nonexistent, ineffectual, or undemocratic political parties; disenfranchisement of women, indigenous peoples, and minorities; failure to implement national charter documents; powerless or poorly defined democratic institutions; tainted elections; and the inability to resolve conflicts peacefully.

Humanitarian Assistance and Post-Crisis Transitions The Agency provides humanitarian assistance that saves lives, reduces suffering, helps victims return to self-sufficiency, and reinforces democracy. Programs focus on disaster prevention, preparedness, and mitigation; timely delivery of disaster relief and short-term rehabilitation supplies and services; preservation of basic institutions of civil governance during disaster crisis; support for democratic institutions during periods of national transition; and building and reinforcement of local capacity to anticipate and handle disasters and their aftermath.

Overseas Organizations

U.S. Agency for International Development country organizations are located in countries where a bilateral program is being implemented. The in-country organizations are subject to the direction and guidance of the chief U.S. diplomatic representative in the country, usually the Ambassador. The organizations report to the Agency's Assistant Administrators for the four geographic bureaus: the Bureaus for Africa, Asia and Near East, Europe and the New Independent States, and Latin America and the Caribbean.

The overseas program activities that involve more than one country are administered by regional offices. These offices may also perform country organizational responsibilities for assigned countries. Generally, the offices are headed by a regional development officer.

Development Assistance Coordination and Representative Offices provide liaison with various international organizations and represent U.S. interests in development assistance matters. Such offices may be only partially staffed by Agency personnel and may be headed by employees of other U.S. Government agencies.

Country Organizations—U.S. Agency for International Development

Country	Officer in Charge[1]
Afghanistan	Robin Phillips (MD)
Albania	Ted Landau (MD)
Angola	Diana Swain (MD)
Armenia	Robin Phillips (MD)
Azerbaijan	Scott Taylor (CPO)
Bangladesh	Denise Rollins (MD)
Barbados	Jim Goggin (MD)
Belarus	Peter Argo (CPO)
Benin	(vacancy) (MD)
Bolivia	Peter Natiello (MD)
Bosnia	Jane Nandy (MD)
Brazil	Jennifer Adams (MD)
Bulgaria	Michael Fritz (MD)
Cambodia	Erin Soto (MD)
Colombia	Susan Reichle (MD)
Croatia	Rebecca Latorraca, Acting (MD)
Cyprus	(vacancy) (MD)
Democratic Republic of the Congo.	Stephen Haykin (MD)
Dominican Republic	Richard Goughnour (MD)
East Timor	Mark White (AIDR)
Ecuador	Alexandra Panehal (MD)
Egypt	Hilda Arellano (MD)
El Salvador	Lawrence Brady (MD)
Eritrea	Jatinder Cheema (MD)
Ethiopia	Glenn Anders (MD)

Country Organizations—U.S. Agency for International Development—Continued

Country	Officer in Charge [1]
Georgia	Bob Wilson (MD)
Ghana	Robert Helleyer (MD)
Guatemala	Wayne Nilsestuen (MD)
Guinea	Cliff Brown (MD)
Guyana	Fenton Sands (MD)
Haiti	Beth Cypser (MD)
Honduras	William Brands (MD)
India	George Deikun (MD)
Indonesia	William Frej (MD)
Iraq	Christopher Crowley (MD)
Jamaica	Karen Hilliard (MD)
Jordan	Jay Knott (MD)
Kenya	Cheryl Anderson (MD)
Kosovo	Paricia Radar (MD)
Kyrgyzstan	Ken McNamara (CPO)
Lebanon	Denise Herbol (AID R)
Liberia	Pamela White (MD)
Macedonia	(vacancy) (MD)
Madagascar	Gerald Cashion (MD)
Malawi	Roger Yochelson (MD)
Mali	Alexander Newton (MD)
Mexico	Rodger Garner (MD)
Moldova	Gary Linden (CPO)
Mongolia	Barry Primm (MD)
Montenegro	Joseph Taggart (CPO)
Morocco	Monica Stein-Olson (MD)
Mozambique	Jay Knott (MD)
Namibia	Gary Newton (MD)
Nepal	Beth Paige (MD)
Nicaragua	Alexander Dickie (MD)

Country Organizations—U.S. Agency for International Development—Continued

Country	Officer in Charge [1]
Nigeria	Sharon Coromer (MD)
Panama	Littleton Tazewell (AID R)
Pakistan	Anne Aarnes (MD)
Paraguay	John Beed (MD)
Peru	Paul Weisenfeld (MD)
Philippines	Edward Birgells (MD)
Romania	Rodger Garner (MD)
Russia	Leon Waskin (MD)
Rwanda	Dennis Weller (MD)
Senegal	Kevin Mullally (MD)
Serbia	Michael Harvey (MD)
Sri Lanka	Rebecca Cohn (MD)
Sudan	Pat Fleure (MD)
Tajikistan	Carolyn Bryan (MD)
Tanzania	Robert Cunnane (MD)
Thailand	Olivier Carduner (MD)
Turkmenistan	Ashley Moretz (CPO)
Uganda	David Eckerson (MD)
Ukraine	Earl Gast (MD)
Uzbekistan	James Bonner (CPO)
Vietnam	Roger Carlson (CPO)
West Bank/Gaza in Israel	Howard Sumka (MD)
Yemen	Mike Sarhan (AIDR)
Zambia	James Bednar (MD)
Zimbabwe	Karen Freeman (MD)

[1] MD: Mission Director; CPO: Country Program Officer; RD: Regional Director; AAO: AID Affairs Officer for Section of Embassy; CO: Coordinator in Washington; AID R: USAID Representative; FFP: Food for Peace Officer

International Organizations—U.S. Agency for International Development
(Selected Regional Organizations)

(A: Adviser; C: Counselor; D: Director; ED: Executive Director; MD: Mission Director; AID R: USAID Representative; RD: Regional Director)

Office	Officer in Charge
Regional Offices	
Regional Center for Southern Africa—Gaborone, Botswana	Gerald Cashion (RD)
Regional Economic Development Services Offices—Nairobi, Kenya	Andrew Sission (RD)
Regional Mission to Central Asia—Almaty, Kazakhstan	Chris Crowley (RD)
Regional Mission to Ukraine, Belarus and Moldova—Kiev, Ukraine	Chuck Howell (RD)
Regional Support Center—Budapest, Hungary	James Ray Kirkland (RD)
USAID Mission to Southern Africa	Carleene Dei (RD)
West Africa Regional Program	Henderson M. Patrick (MD)
International Organizations and USAID Contacts	
Office for Humanitarian Assistance, World Food Program Affairs—Rome, Italy	Richard Newberg (FFP)
Office of the U.S. Representative to the Development Assistance Committee of the Organization for Economic Cooperation and Development—Paris, France.	George Carner (AID R)
U.S. Mission to the European Office of the United Nations and Other International Organizations—Geneva, Switzerland.	(vacancy) (AID R)
AID Office for Development Cooperation—Tokyo, Japan	Charles Aaenenson (AID R)
Office of AID Coordination Representative—Brussels, Belgium	Patricia Lerner (AID R)

Sources of Information

General Inquiries Inquiries may be directed to the Bureau for Legislative and Public Affairs, USAID/LPA, Washington, DC 20523–0001. Phone, 202–712–4810. Fax, 202–216–3524.

Congressional Affairs Congressional inquiries may be directed to the Bureau for Legislative and Public Affairs, USAID/LPA, Washington, DC 20523–0001. Phone, 202–712–4810.

Contracting and Small Business Inquiries For information regarding contracting opportunities, contact the Office of Small and Disadvantaged Business Utilization,

U.S. Agency for International Development, Washington, DC 20523–0001. Phone, 202–712–1500. Fax, 202–216–3056.

Employment For information regarding employment opportunities, contact the Workforce Planning, Recruitment, and Personnel Systems Division, Office of Human Resources, U.S. Agency for International Development, Washington, DC 20523–0001. Internet, www.usaid.gov.

General Inquiries General inquiries may be directed to the Bureau for Legislative and Public Affairs, USAID/LPA, Washington, DC 20523–0001. Phone, 202–712–4810. Fax, 202–216–3524.

News Media Inquiries from the media only should be directed to the Press Relations Division, Bureau for Legislative and Public Affairs, USAID/LPA, Washington, DC 20523–0001. Phone, 202–712–4320.

For further information, contact the United States Agency for International Development, 1300 Pennsylvania Avenue NW., Washington, DC 20523–0001. Phone, 202–712–0000. Internet, www.usaid.gov.

UNITED STATES COMMISSION ON CIVIL RIGHTS

624 Ninth Street NW., Washington, DC 20425
Phone, 202–376–8177. TTY, 202–376–8116. Internet, www.usccr.gov.

CHAIRMAN	GERALD A. REYNOLDS
VICE CHAIR	ABIGAIL THERNSTROM
Commissioners	TODD GAZIANO, GAIL HERIOT, PETER KIRSANOW, ARLAN D. MELENDEZ, ASHLEY TAYLOR, MICHAEL YAKI
Staff Director	(VACANCY)
Deputy Staff Director	(VACANCY)
Associate Deputy Staff Director	DEBRA A. CARR
General Counsel	DAVID BLACKWOOD
Deputy General Counsel	(VACANCY)
Assistant Staff Director for Civil Rights Evaluation	ROBERT LERNER
Assistant Staff Director for Congressional Affairs	(VACANCY)
Assistant Staff Director for Management	(VACANCY)
Chief, Public Affairs Unit	(VACANCY)
Chief, Regional Programs Coordination	CHRIS BYRNES

[For the Commission on Civil Rights statement of organization, see the *Code of Federal Regulations*, Title 45, Part 701]

The Commission on Civil Rights collects and studies information on discrimination or denials of equal protection of the laws because of race, color, religion, sex, age, disability, national origin, or in the administration of justice in such areas as voting rights, enforcement of Federal civil rights laws, and equal opportunity in education, employment, and housing.

The Commission on Civil Rights was first created by the Civil Rights Act of 1957, as amended, and reestablished by the United States Commission on Civil Rights Act of 1994, as amended (42 U.S.C. 1975).

UNITED STATES COMMISSION ON CIVIL RIGHTS

Activities

The Commission makes findings of fact but has no enforcement authority. Findings and recommendations are submitted to the President and Congress, and many of the Commission's recommendations have been enacted, either by statute, Executive order, or regulation. The Commission evaluates Federal laws and the effectiveness of Government equal opportunity programs. It also serves as a national clearinghouse for civil rights information.

Regional Programs The Commission maintains six regional divisions.

Regional Divisions

Region (Address/Telephone)	Director
Central (Suite 908, 400 State Ave., Kansas City, KS 66101–2406. Phone, 913–551–1400) ..	Farella Robinson
Eastern (Rm. 500, 624 9th St. NW., Washington, DC 20425. Phone, 202–376–7533)	Ivy Davis
Midwestern (Suite 410, 55 W. Monroe St., Chicago, IL 60603. Phone, 312–353–8311)	David Mussatt
Rocky Mountain (Suite 710, 1700 Broadway, Denver, CO 80290. Phone, 303–866–1040)	Malee Craft
Southern (Suite 1840T, 61 Forsyth St. SW., Atlanta, GA 30303. Phone, 404–562–7000)	Peter Minarik
Western (Suite 2010, 300 N. Los Angeles, Los Angeles, CA 90012. Phone, 213–894–3437)	(vacancy)

Sources of Information

Complaints Complaints alleging denials of civil rights may be reported to Complaints Referral, 624 Ninth Street NW., Washington, DC 20425. Phone, 202–376–8513 or 800–552–6843. Internet, www.usccr.gov.

Employment Human Resources Office, Room 510, 624 Ninth Street NW., Washington, DC 20425. Phone, 202–376–8364.

Publications Commission publications are made available upon request from the Administrative Services and Clearinghouse Division, Room 550, 624 Ninth Street NW., Washington, DC 20425. Phone, 202–376–8105. A catalog of publications may be obtained from this office.

Reading Room The National Civil Rights Clearinghouse Library is located in Room 602, 624 Ninth Street NW., Washington, DC 20425. Phone, 202–376–8110.

For further information, contact the Office of the Staff Director, United States Commission on Civil Rights, Room 730, 624 Ninth Street NW., Washington, DC 20425. Phone, 202–376–7700. TTY, 202–376–8116. Internet, www.usccr.gov.

UNITED STATES INTERNATIONAL TRADE COMMISSION

500 E Street SW., Washington, DC 20436
Phone, 202–205–2000. Internet, www.usitc.gov.

CHAIRMAN	SHARA L. ARANOFF
VICE CHAIRMAN	DANIEL R. PEARSON
Commissioners	CHARLOTTE R. LANE, DEANNA TANNER OKUN, DEAN A. PINKERT, IRVING A. WILLIAMSON
Chief Administrative Law Judge	PAUL J. LUCKERN

Administrative Law Judges	CHARLES E. BULLOCK, CARL C. CHARNESKI, THEODORE R. ESSEX, JAMES E. GILDEA, ROBERT K. ROGERS, JR.
Director, Office of Administration/Chief Information Officer	STEPHEN MCLAUGHLIN
Deputy Chief Information Officer	PAMELA C. DYSON
Director, Office of Economics	ROBERT B. KOOPMAN
Director, Office of External Relations	LYN M. SCHLITT
Congressional Relations Officer	DOMINIC L. BIANCHI
Public Affairs Officer	MARGARET M. O'LAUGHLIN
Trade Remedy Assistance Program Manager	JOHN J. GREER
Director, Office of Equal Employment Opportunity	JACQUELINE A. WATERS
Director, Office of Industries	KAREN LANEY-CUMMINGS
Division Chief, Agriculture and Fisheries	JONATHAN COLEMAN
Division Chief, Natural Resources and Metals	ROBERT CARR
Division Chief, Chemicals and Textiles	DENNIS RAPKINS
Division Chief, Advanced Technology and Machinery	MICHAEL ANDERSON
Division Chief, Services	RICHARD W. BROWN
Director, Office of Investigations	JOHN ASCIENZO, *Acting*
Director, Office of Operations	ROBERT ROGOWSKY
Director, Office of Tariff Affairs and Trade Agreements	DAVID BECK
Director, Office of Unfair Import Investigations	LYNN LEVINE
General Counsel	JAMES M. LYONS
Inspector General	JUDITH GWYNN, *Acting*
Secretary	MARILYN R. ABBOTT

The United States International Trade Commission furnishes studies, reports, and recommendations involving international trade and tariffs to the President, the U.S. Trade Representative, and congressional committees. The Commission also conducts a variety of investigations pertaining to international trade relief.

The United States International Trade Commission is an independent agency created by the Revenue Act (39 Stat. 795) and originally named the United States Tariff Commission. The name was changed to the United States International Trade Commission by section 171 of the Trade Act of 1974 (19 U.S.C. 2231).

Six Commissioners are appointed by the President with the advice and consent of the Senate for 9-year terms, unless appointed to fill an unexpired term. The Chairman and Vice Chairman are designated by the President for 2-year terms, and succeeding Chairmen may not be of the same political party. The Chairman generally is responsible for the administration of the Commission. Not more than three Commissioners may be members of the same political party (19 U.S.C. 1330).

Activities

The Commission performs a number of functions pursuant to the statutes referred to above. Under the Tariff Act of 1930, the Commission is given broad powers of investigation relating to the customs laws of the United States and foreign countries; the volume of importation in comparison with domestic production and consumption; the conditions, causes, and effects relating to competition of foreign industries with those of the United States; and all other factors affecting competition between articles of the United States and imported articles. The Commission is

UNITED STATES INTERNATIONAL TRADE COMMISSION

required, whenever requested, to make available to the President, the House Committee on Ways and Means, and the Senate Committee on Finance all information at its command, and is directed to make such investigations and reports as may be requested by the President, said committees, or Congress.

In order to carry out these responsibilities, the Commission is required to engage in extensive research, conduct specialized studies, and maintain a high degree of expertise in all matters relating to the commercial and international trade policies of the United States.

Imported Articles Subsidized or Sold at Less Than Fair Value   The Commission conducts preliminary-phase investigations to determine whether imports of foreign merchandise allegedly being subsidized or sold at less than fair value injure or threaten to injure an industry in the United States. If the Commission's determination is affirmative, and the Secretary of Commerce determines there is reason to believe or suspect such unfair practices are occurring, then the Commission conducts final-phase investigations to determine the injury or threat of injury to an industry because of such imports.

Under the Uruguay Round Agreements Act, the Commission also conducts sunset reviews. In these reviews, the Commission evaluates whether material injury to a U.S. industry would continue or recur if the antidumping duty or countervailing duty order under review was revoked. Such injury reviews must be conducted on all antidumping duty and countervailing duty orders every 5 years as long as the orders remain in effect.

Unfair Practices in Import Trade   The Commission applies U.S. statutory and common law of unfair competition to the importation of products into the United States and their sale. If the Commission determines that there is a violation of law, it is to direct that the articles involved be excluded from entry into the United States, or it may issue cease-and-desist orders directing the person engaged in such violation to cease and desist from engaging in such unfair methods or acts.

Trade Negotiations   The Commission advises the President as to the probable economic effect on the domestic industry and consumers of modification of duties and other barriers to trade that may be considered for inclusion in any proposed trade agreement with foreign countries.

Generalized System of Preferences   The Commission advises the President with respect to every article that may be considered for preferential removal of the duty on imports from designated developing countries as to the probable economic effect the preferential removal of duty will have on the domestic industry and on consumers.

Industry Adjustment to Import Competition (Global Safeguard Actions)   The Commission conducts investigations upon petition on behalf of an industry, a firm, a group of workers, or other entity representative of an industry to determine whether an article is being imported in such increased quantities as to injure or threaten to injure the domestic industry producing an article like or directly competitive with the imported article. If the Commission's finding is affirmative, it recommends to the President the action that would address such a threat and be most effective in facilitating positive adjustment by the industry to import competition. The President determines if import relief is appropriate.

The Commission reports with respect to developments within an industry that has been granted import relief and advises the President of the probable economic effect of the reduction or elimination of the tariff increase that has been granted. The President may continue, modify, or terminate the import relief previously granted.

Imports From NAFTA Countries (Bilateral Safeguard Actions)   The Commission conducts investigations to determine whether, as a result of the reduction or elimination of a duty provided for under the North American Free Trade Agreement (NAFTA), a Canadian article or a Mexican article, as the case may be, is being imported into the United States in such increased quantities and under such conditions so that imports of the article constitute a substantial cause of serious injury or (except in the case of a Canadian article) a threat of serious injury to the domestic industry producing an article that is like or directly competitive with the imported article. If the Commission's determination is in the affirmative, the Commission recommends to the President the relief which is necessary to prevent or remedy serious injury. Commission investigations under these provisions are similar procedurally to those conducted under the global safeguard action provisions.

Imports from China (Bilateral Safeguard Actions)   The Commission conducts investigations to determine whether products from China are being imported into the United States in such increased quantities or under such conditions as to cause or threaten to cause market disruption to the domestic producers of like or directly competitive products. If the Commission makes an affirmative determination, it proposes a remedy. The Commission sends its reports to the President and the U.S. Trade Representative. The President makes the final remedy decision.

Market Disruption From Communist Countries   The Commission conducts investigations to determine whether increased imports of an article produced in a Communist country are causing market disruption in the United States. If the Commission's determination is in the affirmative, the President may take the same action as in the case of serious injury to an industry, except that the action would apply only to imports of the article from the Communist country. Commission investigations conducted under this provision are similar procedurally to those conducted under the global safeguard action provisions.

Import Interference With Agricultural Programs   The Commission conducts investigations, at the direction of the President, to determine whether any articles are being or are practically certain to be imported into the United

States under such conditions and in such quantities as to render or tend to render ineffective or to materially interfere with programs of the Department of Agriculture for agricultural commodities or products thereof, or to substantially reduce the amount of any product processed in the United States from such commodities or products, and makes findings and recommendations. The President may restrict the imports in question by imposition of either import fees or quotas. Such fees or quotas may be applied only against countries that are not members of the World Trade Organization.

Uniform Statistical Data   The Commission, in cooperation with the Secretary of the Treasury and the Secretary of Commerce, establishes for statistical purposes an enumeration of articles imported into the United States and exported from the United States, and seeks to establish comparability of such statistics with statistical programs for domestic production.

Harmonized Tariff Schedule of the United States, Annotated   The Commission issues a publication containing the U.S. tariff schedules and related matters and considers questions concerning the arrangement of such schedules and the classification of articles.

International Trade Studies   The Commission conducts studies, investigations, and research projects on a broad range of topics relating to international trade, pursuant to requests of the President, the House Ways and Means Committee, the Senate Finance Committee, either branch of the Congress, or on its own motion. Public reports of these studies, investigations, and research projects are issued in most cases.

The Commission also keeps informed of the operation and effect of provisions relating to duties or other import restrictions of the United States contained in various trade agreements. Occasionally the Commission is required by statute to perform specific trade-related studies.

Industry and Trade Summaries The Commission prepares and publishes a series of summaries of trade and tariff information. These summaries contain descriptions (in terms of the Harmonized Tariff Schedule of the United States) of the thousands of products imported into the United States, methods of production, and the extent and relative importance of U.S. consumption, production, and trade, together with certain basic factors affecting the competitive position and economic health of domestic industries.

Sources of Information

Inquiries should be directed to the specific organizational unit or to the Secretary, United States International Trade Commission, 500 E Street SW., Washington, DC 20436. Phone, 202–205–2000.

Contracts The Procurement Executive has responsibility for contract matters. Phone, 202–205–2745.

Electronic Access Commission publications, news releases, *Federal Register* notices, scheduling information, the Commission's interactive Trade and Tariff DataWeb, and general information about ITC are available for electronic access. Investigation-related public inspection files are available through the Electronic Document Imaging System (EDIS). Internet, www.usitc.gov.

Employment Information on employment can be obtained from the Director, Office of Human Resources. The Agency employs international economists, attorneys, accountants, commodity and industry specialists and analysts, and clerical and other support personnel. Phone, 202–205–2651.

Publications The Commission publishes results of investigations concerning various commodities and subjects. Other publications include *Industry and Trade Summaries*, an annual report to the Congress on the operation of the trade agreements program, and an annual review of Commission activities. Specific information regarding these publications can be obtained from the Office of the Secretary.

Reading Rooms Reading rooms are open to the public in the Office of the Secretary and the ITC Main Library. The ITC Law Library is available to individuals who make prior arrangements by calling 202–205–3287.

For further information, contact the Secretary, United States International Trade Commission, 500 E Street SW., Washington, DC 20436. Phone, 202–205–2000. Internet, www.usitc.gov.

UNITED STATES POSTAL SERVICE

475 L'Enfant Plaza SW., Washington, DC 20260
Phone, 202–268–2000. Internet, www.usps.gov.

Board of Governors:

CHAIRMAN	CAROLYN LEWIS GALLAGHER
VICE CHAIRMAN	LOUIS J. GIULIANO
Governors	MICKEY D. BARNETT, JAMES H. BILBRAY, ALAN C. KESSLER, THURGOOD MARSHALL, JR., JAMES C. MILLER III, KATHERINE C. TOBIN, ELLEN C. WILLIAMS
Postmaster General, Chief Executive Officer	JOHN E. POTTER
Deputy Postmaster General, Chief Operating Officer	PATRICK R. DONAHOE
Secretary	JULIE S. MOORE
Inspector General	DAVID C. WILLIAMS

Officers:

Postmaster General, Chief Executive Officer	JOHN E. POTTER
Deputy Postmaster General, Chief Operating Officer	PATRICK R. DONAHOE
Managing Director and Vice President, Global Business	PRANAB SHAH
Operations Senior Vice President	WILLIAM GALLIGAN
Retail Operations Vice President	KATHLEEN AINSWORTH
Network Operations Management Vice President	TONY PAJUNAS
Delivery Operations Vice President	JORDAN SMALL
Engineering Vice President	WALT O'TORMEY
Facilities Vice President	TOM SAMRA
Sustainability Vice President	SAM PULCRANO
Intelligent Mail and Address Quality Senior Vice President	TOM DAY
Business Mail Entry and Payment Technologies Vice President	PRITHA MEHRA
Eastern Area Vice President	MEGAN BRENNAN
Great Lakes Area Vice President	JO ANN FEINDT
New York Metro Area Vice President	STEVEN FORTE
Northeast Area Vice President	TIM HANEY
Pacific Area Vice President	MICHAEL DALEY
Southeast Area Vice President	TERRY WILSON
Southwest Area Vice President	ELLIS BURGOYNE
Western Area Vice President	SYLVESTER BLACK
Capitol Metro Area Vice President	JERRY LANE
Mailing and Shipping Services President	ROBERT BERNSTOCK
Expedited Shipping Vice President	GARY REBLIN
Ground Shipping Vice President	JAMES COCHRANE
Sales Vice President	SUSAN PLONKEY
Retail Products and Services Vice President	TIMOTHY C. HEALY
Chief Information Officer, Executive Vice President	ROSS PHILO
Information Technology Operations Vice President	GEORGE WRIGHT
Chief Financial Officer, Executive Vice President	JOSEPH CORBETT
Supply Management Vice President	SUSAN BROWNELL
Controller Vice President	VINCENT DEVITO
Chief Human Resources Officer, Executive Vice President	ANTHONY VEGLIANTE
Employee Resource Management Vice President	DEBORAH GIANNONI-JACKSON
Employee Development and Diversity Vice President	SUSAN LACHANCE
Labor Relations Vice President	DOUG TULINO
Customer Relations Senior Vice President	STEPHEN KEARNEY
Consumer Advocate, Vice President	DELORES KILLETTE
Corporate Communications Vice President	MITZI BETMAN
Pricing Vice President	MAURA ROBINSON
General Counsel, Senior Vice President	MARY ANNE GIBBONS
Strategy and Transition Senior Vice President	LINDA KINGSLEY
Government Relations Vice President	MARIE THERESE DOMINGUEZ

Chief Postal Inspector	WILLIAM GILLIGAN, *Acting*
Judicial Officer	WILLIAM CAMPBELL

[For the United States Postal Service statement of organization, see the *Code of Federal Regulations,* Title 39, Part 221]

The United States Postal Service provides mail processing and delivery services to individuals and businesses within the United States.

The Postal Service was created as an independent establishment of the executive branch by the Postal Reorganization Act (39 U.S.C. 101 *et seq.*), approved August 12, 1970. The present United States Postal Service commenced operations on July 1, 1971.

The Postal Service has approximately 705,000 career employees and handles about 212 billion pieces of mail annually. The chief executive officer of the Postal Service, the Postmaster General, is appointed by the nine Governors of the Postal Service, who are appointed by the President with the advice and consent of the Senate. The Governors and the Postmaster General appoint the Deputy Postmaster General, and these 11 people constitute the Board of Governors.

In addition to the national headquarters, there are area and district offices supervising more than 37,000 post offices, branches, stations, and community post offices throughout the United States.

Activities

In order to expand and improve service to the public, the Postal Service is engaged in customer cooperation activities, including the development of programs for both the general public and major customers. The Consumer Advocate, a postal ombudsman, represents the interest of the individual mail customer in matters involving the Postal Service by bringing complaints and suggestions to the attention of top postal management and solving the problems of individual customers. To provide postal services responsive to public needs, the Postal Service operates its own planning, research, engineering, real estate, and procurement programs specially adapted to postal requirements, and maintains close ties with international postal organizations.

The Postal Service is the only Federal agency whose employment policies are governed by a process of collective bargaining under the National Labor Relations Act. Labor contract negotiations, affecting all bargaining unit personnel, as well as personnel matters involving employees not covered by collective bargaining agreements, are administered by Labor Relations or Human Resources.

The U.S. Postal Inspection Service is the Federal law enforcement agency which has jurisdiction in criminal matters affecting the integrity and security of the mail. Postal Inspectors enforce more than 200 Federal statutes involving mail fraud, mail bombs, child pornography, illegal drugs, mail theft, and other postal crimes, as well as being responsible for the protection of all postal employees.

Postal Service customers and employees can contact the Postal Inspection Service online at www.usps.gov/postalinspectors or by calling 1–877–876–2455 to reach the appropriate Inspection Service office.

Postal Inspection Service—United States Postal Service

Division	Address	Telephone
Atlanta	P.O. Box 16489, Atlanta, GA 30321–0489	404–608–4500
Boston	495 Summer St., Boston, MA 02210–2214	617–556–4400
Charlotte	2901 Scott Futrell Dr., Charlotte, NC 28228–3000	704–329–9120
Chicago	Fl. 6, 433 W. Harrison St., Chicago, IL 60669–2201	312–983–7900
Denver	Suite 900, 1745 Stout St., Denver, CO 80202–3034	303–313–5320
Detroit	P.O. Box 330119, Detroit, MI 48232–6119	313–226–8184
Fort Worth	14800 Trinity Blvd., Fort Worth, TX 76161–2929	817–359–2700

Postal Inspection Service—United States Postal Service—Continued

Division	Address	Telephone
Houston	650 N. Sam Houston Pkwy., Houston, TX 77251–1276	713–238–4400
Los Angeles	P.O. Box 2000, Pasadena, CA 91102–2000	626–405–1200
Miami	6th Fl., 3400 Lakeside Dr., Miramar, FL 33027–3242	954–436–7200
New Jersey/Caribbean	P.O. Box 509, Newark, NJ 07101–0509	973–693–5400
New York	P.O. Box 555, New York, NY 10116–0555	212–330–3844
Philadelphia	Rm. 400, 2970 Market St., Philadelphia, PA 19101–9000	215–895–8450
Pittsburgh	Rm. 2101, 1001 California Ave., Pittsburgh, PA 15290–9000	412–359–7900
San Francisco	P.O. Box 882528, San Francisco, CA 94188–2528	415–778–5800
Seattle	P.O. Box 400, Seattle, WA 98111–4000	206–442–6300
St. Louis	1106 Walnut St., St. Louis, MO 63199–2201	314–539–9300
Washington, DC	Suite 200, 10500 Little Patuxent Pkwy., Columbia, MD 21044–3509	410–715–7700

Sources of Information

Consumer Information   Customers may check shipping rates, buy stamps, print postage, track packages, locate ZIP codes, shop at the Postal Store, change addresses, or obtain answers to frequently asked questions by visiting www.usps.com. For general information 24 hours a day, call 1–800–ASK–USPS (1–800–275–8777). For the Express Mail, Priority Mail, and Package Support Line, call 1–800–222–1811. Information on past and present schemes used to defraud the public is available at www.usps.com/postalinspectors. Reports of fraudulent activity involving the mail may be made to the Mail Fraud Hotline, 1–800–372–8347.

Contracts and Small Business Activities Contact Supplier Diversity. Phone, 202–268–4633.

Employment   General information about jobs such as clerk, letter carrier, etc., including information about programs for veterans, may be obtained by contacting the nearest post office or from the Postal Service Web site at www.usps.gov/employment.

Information about Postal Inspector Service employment may be obtained online at www.usps.com/postalinspectors.

Inspector General   The Office of Inspector General maintains a toll-free hotline as a means for individuals to report activities involving fraud, waste, or mismanagement. Such reports may be made by email to hotline@uspsoig.gov, by telephone at 1–888–USPS–OIG (1–888–877–7644), by fax at 1–866–756–6741, or by mail to the United States Postal Service, Office of Inspector General Hotline, 10th Floor, 1735 North Lynn Street, Arlington, VA 22209–2020. Publicly available documents and information on the Office of Inspector General and some Freedom of Information Act documents are available electronically at www.uspsoig.gov.

Philatelic Sales   Contact Stamp Fulfillment Services, Kansas City, MO 64179–1009. Phone, 800–782–6724.

Publications   Pamphlets on mailability, postage rates and fees, and many other topics may be obtained free of charge from the nearest post office.

Most postal regulations are contained in Postal Service manuals covering domestic mail, international mail, postal operations, administrative support, and employee and labor relations. These manuals and other publications including the *National Five-Digit ZIP Code and Post Office Directory* (Publication 65) may be purchased from the Superintendent of Documents, Government Printing Office, Washington, DC 20402–0001. The *National Five-Digit ZIP Code and Post Office Directory* is also available through local post offices.

Reading Rooms   Located on 11th Floor North, Library. Phone, 202–268–2900.

For further information, contact the U.S. Postal Service, 475 L'Enfant Plaza SW., Washington, DC 20260. Phone, 202–268–2000. Internet, www.usps.gov.

Boards, Commissions, and Committees

Note: This is a listing of Federal boards, commissions, councils, etc., not listed elsewhere in the *Manual*, which were established by congressional or Presidential action, whose functions are not strictly limited to the internal operations of a parent department or agency and which are authorized to publish documents in the *Federal Register*. While the editors have attempted to compile a complete and accurate listing, suggestions for improving coverage of this guide are welcome. Please address your comments to the Office of the Federal Register, National Archives and Records Administration, Washington, DC 20408. Phone, 202–741–6040. Internet, www.federalregister.gov.

Federal advisory committees, as defined by the Federal Advisory Committee Act, as amended (5 U.S.C. app.), have not been included here. Information on Federal advisory committees may be obtained from the Committee Management Secretariat, General Services Administration, General Services Building (MC), Room G–230, Washington, DC 20405. Phone, 202–273–3556. Internet, www.gsa.gov/committeemanagement.

Administrative Committee of the Federal Register

Office of the Federal Register, National Archives and Records Administration, 8601 Adelphi Road, College Park, MD 20740-6001. Phone, 202–741–6010. Email, fedreg.info@nara.gov. Internet, www.federalregister.gov

Advisory Council on Historic Preservation

1100 Pennsylvania Avenue NW., Suite 803, Washington, DC 20004. Phone, 202–606–8503. Fax, 202–606–5073. Email, achp@achp.gov. Internet, www.achp.gov.

American Battle Monuments Commission

2300 Clarendon Boulevard, Court House Plaza 2, Suite 500, Arlington, VA 22201. Phone, 703–696–6900. Fax, 703–696–6666. Email, info@abmc.gov. Internet, www.abmc.gov.

Appalachian Regional Commission

1666 Connecticut Avenue NW., Suite 700, Washington, DC 20009–1068. Phone, 202–884–7700. Email, info@arc.gov. Internet, www.arc.gov.

Architectural and Transportation Barriers Compliance Board [1]

1331 F Street NW., Suite 1000, Washington, DC 20004–1111. Phone, 202–272–0080 or TTY, 202–272–0082. Fax, 202–272–0081. Internet, www.access-board.gov.

Arctic Research Commission

4350 North Fairfax Drive, Suite 510, Arlington, VA 22203. Phone, 703–525–

---

[1] Also known as the Access Board.

0111. Fax, 703–525–0114. Internet, www.arctic.gov.

Arthritis and Musculoskeletal Interagency Coordinating Committee
National Institutes of Health/NIAMS, Building 31, Room 4C02, 31 Center Drive, Bethesda, MD 20892–2350. Phone, 301–496–8190. Internet, www.niams.nih.gov.

Barry M. Goldwater Scholarship and Excellence in Education Foundation
6225 Brandon Avenue, Suite 315, Springfield, VA 22150–2519. Phone, 703–756–6012. Fax, 703–756–6015. Email, goldh2o@vacoxmail.com. Internet, www.act.org/goldwater.

Chemical Safety and Hazard Investigation Board
2175 K Street NW., Suite 400, Washington, DC 20037–1809. Phone, 202–261–7600. Fax, 202–261–7650. Email, info@csb.gov. Internet, www.csb.gov.

Citizens' Stamp Advisory Committee
United States Postal Service, 1735 N. Lynn Street, Suite 5013, Arlington, VA 22209–6432. Phone, 703–292–3810. Fax, 703–292–3634. Internet, www.usps.com/communications/organization/csac.htm

Commission of Fine Arts
National Building Museum, 401 F Street NW., Suite 312, Washington, DC 20001–2728. Phone, 202–504–2200. Fax, 202–504–2195. Email, staff@cfa.gov. Internet, www.cfa.gov.

Committee on Foreign Investment in the United States
Department of the Treasury, 1500 Pennsylvania Avenue NW., Room 5221, Washington, DC 20220. Phone, 202–622–1860. Fax, 202–622–0391. Email, cfius@do.treas.gov. Internet, www.treas.gov/offices/international-affairs/cfius/.

Committee for the Implementation of Textile Agreements
Department of Commerce, Office of Textiles and Apparel, Fourteenth Street

and Constitution Avenue NW., Room 3001A, Washington, DC 20230. Phone, 202–482–3737. Fax, 202–482–2331. Email, otexa@mail.doc.gov. Internet, http://otexa.ita.doc.gov/cita.htm.

Committee for Purchase From People Who Are Blind or Severely Disabled
1421 Jefferson Davis Highway, Jefferson Plaza 2, Suite 10800, Arlington, VA 22202–3259. Phone, 703–603–7740. Email, info@abilityone.gov. Internet, www.abilityone.gov.

Coordinating Council on Juvenile Justice and Delinquency Prevention
Department of Justice, Office of Juvenile Justice and Delinquency Prevention, 810 7th Street NW., Washington, DC 20531. Phone, 202–307–5911. Fax, 202–307–2093. Internet, www.juvenilecouncil.gov.

Delaware River Basin Commission
25 State Police Drive, P.O. Box 7360, West Trenton, NJ 08628–0360. Phone, 609–883–9500. Fax, 609–883–9522. Internet, www.drbc.net.

Endangered Species Program
4401 N. Fairfax Drive, Room 420, Arlington, VA 22203. Phone, 703–358–2390. Fax, 703–358–1735. Internet, http://endangered.fws.gov.

Export Administration Operating Committee
Department of Commerce, Bureau of Industry and Security, 1401 Constitution Avenue, NW., Herbert C. Hoover Building, Room 3889, Washington, DC 20230. Phone, 202–482–5863. Fax, 202–501–2815.

Federal Financial Institutions Examination Council
3501 Fairfax Drive, Suite B3030, Arlington, VA 22226. Phone, 703–516–5588. Fax, 703–516–5487. Internet, www.ffiec.gov.

Federal Financing Bank
Department of the Treasury, 1500 Pennsylvania Avenue NW., Washington, DC 20220. Phone, 202–622–2470. Fax,

202–622–0707. Email, ffb@do.treas.gov. Internet, www.ustreas.gov/ffb.

Federal Interagency Committee on Education

Department of Education, 400 Maryland Avenue SW., Federal Office Building 6, Room 5E222, Washington, DC 20202–3572. Phone, 202–401–3673. Fax, 202–260–7465.

Federal Laboratory Consortium for Technology Transfer

1001 Connecticut Avenue NW., Suite 735, Washington, DC 20036. Phone, 202–296–7201. Fax, 202–296–7203. Internet, www.federallabs.org.

Federal Library and Information Center Committee

Library of Congress, 101 Independence Avenue SE., Adams Building, Room 217, Washington, DC 20540–4935. Phone, 202–707–4800. Fax, 202–707–4818. Internet, www.loc.gov/flicc/.

Harry S. Truman Scholarship Foundation

712 Jackson Place NW., Washington, DC 20006. Phone, 202–395–4831. Fax, 202–395–6995. Email, office@truman.gov. Internet, www.truman.gov.

Indian Arts and Crafts Board

Department of the Interior, Room MS 2528–MIB, 1849 C Street NW., Washington, DC 20240. Phone, 202–208–3773. Email, iacb@ios.doi.gov. Internet, www.iacb.doi.gov.

J. William Fulbright Foreign Scholarship Board

Dpeartment of State, Bureau of Educational and Cultural Affairs, 301 Fourth Street SW., State Annex 44, Washington, DC 20547. Phone, 202–453–8189. Fax, 202–453–8183. Email, fulbright@state.gov. Internet, http://fulbright.state.gov.

James Madison Memorial Fellowship Foundation

2000 K Street NW., Suite 303, Washington, DC 20006–1809. Phone, 202–653–8700. Fax, 202–653–6045. Email, madison@act.org. Internet, www.jamesmadison.com.

Japan-United States Friendship Commission

1201 15th Street NW., Suite 330, Washington, DC 20005. Phone, 202–653–9800. Fax, 202–653–9802. Email, jusfc@jusfc.gov. Internet, www.jusfc.gov.

Joint Board for the Enrollment of Actuaries

Internal Revenue Service, SE: OPR, 1111 Constitution Avenue NW., Washington, DC 20224. Phone, 202–622–8229. Fax, 202–622–8300. Email, nhqjbea@irs.gov. Internet, www.irs.gov/taxpros/actuaries/index.html.

Marine Mammal Commission

4340 East-West Highway, Suite 905, Bethesda, MD 20814. Phone, 301–504–0087. Fax, 301–504–0099. Email, mmc@mmc.gov. Internet, www.mmc.gov.

Medicare Payment Advisory Commission

601 New Jersey Avenue NW., Suite 9000, Washington, DC 20001. Phone, 202–220–3700. Internet, www.medpac.gov.

Migratory Bird Conservation Commission

United States Fish and Wildlife Service, Division of Realty, Mail Code: ARLSQ-622, 4401 North Fairfax Drive, Arlington, VA 22203–1610. Phone, 703–358–1716. Fax, 703–358–2223. Internet, www.fws.gov/realty/mbcc.html.

Mississippi River Commission

United States Army Corps of Engineers, Mississippi Valley Division, 1400 Walnut Street, Vicksburg, MS 39180–0080. Phone, 601–634–5760. Fax, 601–634–7110. Email, cenvd-pa@usace.army.mil. Internet, www.mvd.usace.army.mil.

Morris K. Udall Scholarship and Excellence in National Environmental Policy Foundation

130 South Scott Avenue, Tucson, AZ 85701–1922. Phone, 520–901–8500.

Fax, 520–670–5530. Internet, www.udall.gov.

National Council on Disability
1331 F Street NW., Suite 850, Washington, DC 20004. Phone, 202–272–2004. TTY, 202–272–2074. Fax, 202–272–2022. Email, ncd@ncd.gov. Internet, www.ncd.gov.

National Indian Gaming Commission
1441 L Street NW., Suite 9100, Washington, DC 20005. Phone, 202–632–7003. Fax, 202–632–7066. Email, info@nigc.gov. Internet, www.nigc.gov.

National Park Foundation
1201 I Street NW., Suite 550B, Washington, DC 20005. Phone, 202–354–6460. Fax, 202–371–2066. Email, ask-npf@nationalparks.org. Internet, www.nationalparks.org.

Northwest Power and Conservation Council
851 SW. Sixth Avenue, Suite 1100, Portland, OR 97204. Phone, 503–222–5161 or 800–452–5161. Fax, 503–820–2370. Internet, www.nwcouncil.org.

Office of Navajo and Hopi Indian Relocation
201 East Birch Avenue, Flagstaff, AZ 86001. Phone, 928–779–2721 or 800–321–3114. Fax, 928–774–1977.

Permanent Committee for the Oliver Wendell Holmes Devise
Library of Congress, Manuscript Division, Washington, DC 20540–4680. Phone, 202–707–1082.

President's Intelligence Advisory Board
New Executive Office Building, Room 5020, Washington, DC 20502. Phone, 202–456–2352. Fax, 202–395–3403.

Presidio Trust
34 Graham Street, P.O. Box 29052, San Francisco, CA 94129–0052. Phone, 415–561–5300. TTY, 415–561–5301. Fax, 415–561–5315. Email,

presidio@presidiotrust.gov. Internet, www.presidio.gov.

Social Security Advisory Board
400 Virginia Avenue SW., Suite 625, Washington, DC 20024. Phone, 202–475–7700. Fax, 202–475–7715. Email, info@ssab.gov. Internet, www.ssab.gov.

Susquehanna River Basin Commission
1721 North Front Street, Harrisburg, PA 17102–2391. Phone, 717–238–0423. Fax, 717–238–2436. Email, srbc@srbc.net. Internet, www.srbc.net.

Trade Policy Staff Committee
Office of the United States Trade Representative, 1724 F Street NW., Washington, DC 20508. Phone, 202–395–3475. Fax, 202–395–5141.

United States Holocaust Memorial Museum
100 Raoul Wallenberg Place SW., Washington, DC 20024–2126. Phone, 202–488–0400. TTY, 202–488–0406. Internet, www.ushmm.org.

United States Nuclear Waste Technical Review Board
2300 Clarendon Boulevard, Suite 1300, Arlington, VA 22201. Phone, 703–235–4473. Fax, 703–235–4495. Internet, www.nwtrb.gov.

Veterans Day National Committee
Department of Veterans Affairs, 810 Vermont Avenue NW., Mail Code 002C, Washington, DC 20420. Phone, 202–273–4849. Fax, 202–273–5717. Email, vetsday@va.gov. Internet, www1.va.gov/opa/vetsday.

White House Commission on Presidential Scholars
Department of Education, 400 Maryland Avenue SW., Washington, DC 20202–8173. Phone, 202–401–0961. Fax, 202–260–7464. Email, presidential.scholars@ed.gov. Internet, www.ed.gov/programs/psp/index.html.

QUASI–OFFICIAL AGENCIES

Note: This section contains organizations that are not executive agencies under the definition in 5 U.S.C. 105 but that are required by statute to publish certain information on their programs and activities in the *Federal Register.*

LEGAL SERVICES CORPORATION *

3333 K Street NW., Washington, DC 20007
Phone, 202–295–1500. Fax, 202–337–6797. Internet, www.lsc.gov.

President	HELAINE M. BARNETT
Vice President for Legal Affairs, General Counsel, and Corporate Secretary	VICTOR M. FORTUNO
Vice President for Programs and Compliance	KAREN J. SARJEANT
Director, Office of Compliance and Enforcement	DANILO CARDONA
Director, Office of Information Management	JOHN MEYER
Director, Office of Program Performance	MICHAEL GENZ
Chief Administrative Officer	CHARLES JEFFRESS
Comptroller/Treasurer	DAVID L. RICHARDSON
Director, Office of Human Resources	ALICE DICKERSON
Director, Office of Information Technology	JEFF MORNINGSTAR
Director, Government Relations and Public Affairs	JOHN CONSTANCE
Inspector General	JEFFREY E. SCHANZ

[For the Legal Services Corporation statement of organization, see the *Code of Federal Regulations,* Title 45, Part 1601]

The Legal Services Corporation's mission is to promote equal access to justice in our Nation and to provide high-quality civil legal assistance to low-income persons.

The Legal Services Corporation (LSC) is a private, nonprofit corporation established by the Legal Services Act of 1974, as amended (42 U.S.C. 2996), to seek to ensure equal access to justice under the law for all Americans.

LSC is headed by an 11-member Board of Directors, appointed by the President and confirmed by the Senate. By law, the Board is bipartisan; no more than six members may be of the same political party. LSC is funded through

---

*EDITORIAL NOTE: The Legal Services Corporation did not meet the publication deadline for submitting updated information of its activities, functions, and sources of information.

LEGAL SERVICES CORPORATION

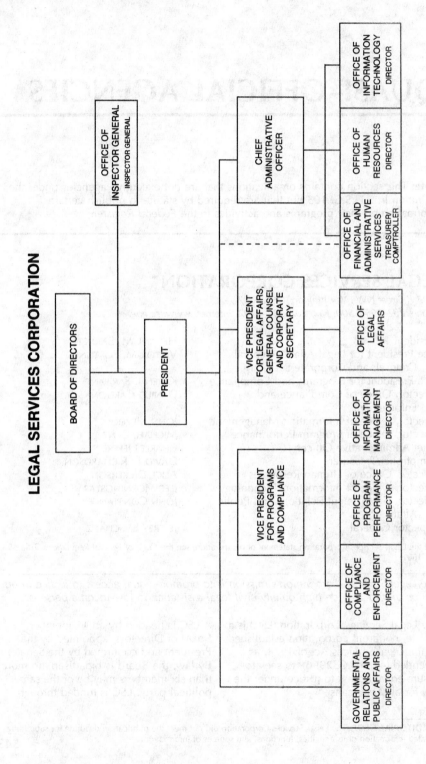

congressional appropriations and provides legal services through grants to independent local programs selected through a system of competition. In 2005, LSC funded 138 programs. Together they serve every county and congressional district in the Nation, as well as the U.S. territories. Special service areas also address the needs of Native Americans and migrant farmworkers.

The legal services delivery is based on several principles: local priorities, national accountability, competition for grants, and a strong public-private partnership. Local programs are governed by their own boards of directors, which set priorities and determine the types of cases that will be handled subject to restrictions set by Congress. A majority of each local board is appointed by local bar associations and one-third of each local board is composed of client representatives appointed by client groups. Each board hires its own executive director. Programs may supplement their LSC grants with additional funds from State and local governments and other sources. They further leverage Federal funds by involving private attorneys in the delivery of legal services for the poor, mostly through volunteer pro bono work.

LSC-funded programs do not handle criminal cases, nor do they accept fee-generating cases that private attorneys are willing to accept on a contingency basis. In addition, in 1996 a series of new limitations were placed upon activities in which LSC-funded programs may engage on behalf of their clients, even with non-LSC funds. All Legal Services programs must comply with laws enacted by Congress and the implementing regulations promulgated by the Legal Services Corporation.

For further information, contact the Office of Government Relations and Public Affairs, Legal Services Corporation, 3333 K Street NW., Washington, DC 20007–3522. Phone, 202–295–1500. Fax, 202–337–6797. Internet, www.lsc.gov.

SMITHSONIAN INSTITUTION *

1000 Jefferson Drive SW., Washington, DC 20560
Phone, 202–633–1000. TDD, 202–357–1729. Internet, www.smithsonian.org.

Board of Regents:

The Chief Justice of the United States (*Chancellor*)	JOHN G. ROBERTS, JR.
The Vice President of the United States	JOSEPH R. BIDEN, JR.
Members of the Senate	THAD COCHRAN, CHRISTOPHER DODD, PATRICK J. LEAHY
Members of the House of Representatives	XAVIER BECERRA, SAMUEL JOHNSON, DORIS MATSUI
Citizen Members	ELI BROAD, PHILLIP FROST, SHIRLEY ANN JACKSON, ROBERT P. KOGOD, JOHN W. MCCARTER, JR., ROGER SANT, ALAN G. SPOON, PATTY STONESIFER, (VACANCY)

*EDITORIAL NOTE: The Smithsonian Institution did not meet the publication deadline for submitting updated information of its activities, functions, and sources of information.

Officials:

SECRETARY	G. WAYNE CLOUGH
Inspector General	A. SPRIGHTLEY RYAN
Director, Communications and Public Affairs	EVELYN LIEBERMAN
Director, Equal Employment and Minority Affairs	ERA MARSHALL
Director, External Affairs	VIRGINIA B. CLARK
Director, Government Relations	NELL PAYNE
General Counsel	JUDITH E. LEONARD
Undersecretary for Finance and Administration	ALISON MCNALLY
Chief Financial Officer	ALICE C. MARONI
Chief Information Officer	ANN SPEYER
Director, Accessibility Program	ELIZABETH ZIEBARTH
Director, Exhibits Central	MICHAEL HEADLEY
Director, Facilities Engineering and Operations	CLAIR GILL, Acting
Director, Human Resources	JAMES DOUGLAS
Director, Investments	AMY CHEN
Director, National Collections	BILL THOMPKINS
Director, Policy and Analysis	CAROLE P. NEVES
Director, Smithsonian Institution Archives	ANNE VAN CAMP
Director, Special Events and Protocol	NICOLE L. KRAKORA
Ombudsman	CHANDRA HEILMAN
Undersecretary for History, Art, and Culture	RICHARD KURIN
Director, Anacostia Community Museum	CAMILE AKEJU
Director, Archives of American Art	JOHN W. SMITH
Director, Asian Pacific American Program	FRANKLIN ODO
Director, Center for Folklife and Cultural Heritage	DANIEL SHEEHY, Acting
Director, Cooper-Hewitt National Design Museum	PAUL W. THOMPSON
Director, Freer Gallery of Art and Arthur M. Sackler Gallery	JULIAN RABY
Director, Hirshorn Museum and Sculpture Garden	RICHARD KOSHALEK
Director, National Museum of African American History and Culture	LONNIE BUNCH
Director, National Museum of African Art	JOHNNETTA B. COLE
Director, National Museum of American History	BRENT GLASS
Director, National Museum of the American Indian	KEVIN GOVER
Director, National Portrait Gallery	MARTIN SULLIVAN
Director, National Postal Museum	ALLEN KANE
Director, National Programs	RICHARD KURIN, Acting
Director, Smithsonian Affiliations	HAROLD CLOSTER
Director, Smithsonian Associates	BARBARA TUCELING
Director, Smithsonian American Art Museum and Renwick Gallery	ELIZABETH BROUN
Director, Smithsonian Center for Education and Museum Studies	STEPHANIE NORBY
Director, Smithsonian Latino Center	EDUARDO DIAZ
Director, Smithsonian Institution Traveling Exhibition Service (SITES)	ANNA R. COHN
Undersecretary for Science	CHARLES ALCOCK, Acting
Director, National Air and Space Museum	JOHN R. DAILEY

Director, National Museum of Natural History	CRISTIAN SAMPER
Director, National Science Resources Center	SALLY SHULER
Director, Fellowships	CATHERINE HARRIS
Director, National Zoological Park	STEVEN MONFORT, *Acting*
Director, Smithsonian Astrophysical Observatory	CHARLES ALCOCK
Director, Smithsonian Environmental Research Center	ANSON H. HINES
Director, Smithsonian Institution Libraries	NANCY E. GWINN
Director, Smithsonian Marine Station	VALERIE PAUL
Director, Smithsonian Museum Conservation Institute	ROBERT KOESTLER
Director, Smithsonian Tropical Research Institute	ELDREDGE BERMINGHAM
President, Smithsonian Enterprises and Smithsonian Publishing	TOM OTT
Editor-in-Chief, Smithsonian Magazine	CAREY WINFREY
Group Publisher, Smithsonian Publishing	KERRY BIANCHI

The John F. Kennedy Center for the Performing Arts [1]

| Chairman | STEPHEN A. SCHWARZMAN |
| President | MICHAEL M. KAISER |

National Gallery of Art [1]

| President | VICTORIA P. SANT |
| Director | EARL A. POWELL III |

Woodrow Wilson International Center for Scholars [1]

Director	LEE H. HAMILTON
Deputy Director	MICHAEL VAN DUSEN
Chairman, Board of Trustees	JOSEPH B. GILDENHORN

The Smithsonian Institution is an independent trust instrumentality of the United States which comprises the world's largest museum and research complex; includes 19 museums and galleries, the National Zoo, and research facilities in several States and the Republic of Panama; and is dedicated to public education, national service, and scholarship in the arts, sciences, history, and culture.

The Smithsonian Institution was created by an act of Congress on August 10, 1846 (20 U.S.C. 41 *et seq.*), to carry out the terms of the will of British scientist James Smithson (1765–1829), who in 1826 had bequeathed his entire estate to the United States "to found at Washington, under the name of the Smithsonian Institution, an establishment for the increase and diffusion of knowledge among men." On July 1, 1836, Congress accepted the legacy and pledged the faith of the United States to the charitable trust.

In September 1838, Smithson's legacy, which amounted to more than 100,000 gold sovereigns, was delivered to the mint at Philadelphia. Congress vested responsibility for administering the trust in the Secretary of the Smithsonian and the Smithsonian Board of Regents, composed of the Chief Justice, the Vice President, three Members of the Senate, three Members of the House of Representatives, and nine citizen members appointed by joint resolution of Congress. To carry out Smithson's

---

[1] Administered under a separate Board of Trustees.

SMITHSONIAN INSTITUTION

mandate, the Institution executes the following functions:

—conducts scientific and scholarly research;

—publishes the results of studies, explorations, and investigations;

—preserves for study and reference more than 136 million artifacts, works of art, and scientific specimens;

—organizes exhibits representative of the arts, the sciences, and American history and culture;

—shares Smithsonian resources and collections with communities throughout the Nation; and

—engages in educational programming and national and international cooperative research.

Smithsonian activities are supported by its trust endowments and revenues; gifts, grants, and contracts; and funds appropriated to it by Congress. Admission to the museums in Washington, DC, is free.

Activities

Anacostia Community Museum The Museum, located in the historic Fort Stanton neighborhood of southeast Washington, serves as a national resource for exhibitions, historical documentation, and interpretive and educational programs relating to African-American history and culture.

For further information, contact the Anacostia Community Museum, 1901 Fort Place SE., Washington, DC 20020. Phone, 202–633–1000. Internet, www.si.edu/anacostia.

Archives of American Art The Archives contains the Nation's largest collection of documentary materials reflecting the history of visual arts in the United States. On the subject of art in America, it is the largest archives in the world, holding more than 16 million documents. The Archives gathers, preserves, and microfilms the papers of artists, craftsmen, collectors, dealers, critics, and art societies. These papers include manuscripts, letters, diaries, notebooks, sketchbooks, business records, clippings, exhibition catalogs, transcripts of tape-recorded interviews, and photographs of artists and their work. The Archives is

located at 750 Ninth Street NW., in Washington, DC.

For further information, contact the Archives of American Art, Smithsonian Institution, Washington, DC 20560. Phone, 202–275–2156. Internet, http:// archivesofamericanart.si.edu/askus.htm.

Cooper-Hewitt National Design Museum The Museum is the only museum in the country devoted exclusively to historical and contemporary design. Collections include objects in such areas as applied arts and industrial design, drawings and prints, glass, metalwork, wallcoverings, and textiles. Changing exhibits and public programs seek to educate by exploring the role of design in daily life. The Museum is open daily, except Mondays and holidays. The general admission fee is $12, $7 for students and senior citizens with ID, and free for members and children under 12.

For further information, contact Cooper-Hewitt National Design Museum, 2 East Ninety-First Street, New York, NY 10128. Phone, 212–849–8400. Internet, www.si.edu/ndm.

Freer Gallery of Art The building, the original collection, and an endowment were the gift of Charles Lang Freer (1854–1919). The Gallery houses one of the world's most renowned collections of Asian art, an important group of ancient Egyptian glass, early Christian manuscripts, and works by 19th and early 20th century American artists. The objects in the Asian collection represent the arts of East Asia, the Near East, and South and Southeast Asia, including paintings, manuscripts, scrolls, screens, ceramics, metalwork, glass, jade, lacquer, and sculpture. Members of the staff conduct research on objects in the collection and publish results in scholarly journals and books for general and scholarly audiences.

For further information, contact the Freer Gallery of Art, Jefferson Drive at Twelfth Street SW., Washington, DC 20560. Phone, 202–633–1000. Internet, www.asia.si.edu.

Hirshhorn Museum and Sculpture Garden From cubism to minimalism, the Museum houses major collections of modern and contemporary art. The nucleus of the collection is the gift and bequest of Joseph H. Hirshhorn (1899–1981). Supplementing the permanent collection are loan exhibitions. The Museum houses a collection research facility, a specialized art library, and a photographic archive, available for consultation by prior appointment. The outdoor sculpture garden is located nearby on the National Mall. There is an active program of public service and education, including docent tours, lectures on contemporary art and artists, and films of historic and artistic interest.

For further information, contact the Hirshhorn Museum and Sculpture Garden, Seventh Street and Independence Avenue SW., Washington, DC 20560. Phone, 202–633–1000. Internet, www.hirshhorn.si.edu.

National Air and Space Museum Created to memorialize the development and achievements of aviation and space flight, the Museum collects, displays, and preserves aeronautical and space flight artifacts of historical significance as well as documentary and artistic materials related to air and space. Among its artifacts are full-size planes, models, and instruments. Highlights of the collection include the Wright brothers' *Flyer*, Charles Lindbergh's *Spirit of St. Louis*, a Moon rock, and Apollo spacecraft. The exhibitions and study collections record human conquest of the air from its beginnings to recent achievements. The principal areas in which work is concentrated include flight craft of all types, space flight vehicles, and propulsion systems. Recent blockbuster exhibitions at this most popular museum have included "Star Wars: The Magic of Myth" and "Star Trek." The Museum's IMAX Theater and the 70-foot domed Einstein Planetarium are popular attractions. The Museum's Steven F. Udvar-Hazy Center, at Washington Dulles International Airport, opened in December 2003. Its featured artifacts include a space shuttle and the *Enola Gay* B–29 World War II bomber.

For further information, contact the National Air and Space Museum, Sixth Street and Independence Avenue SW., Washington, DC 20560. Phone, 202–633–1000. Internet, www.nasm.si.edu.

National Museum of African Art This is the only art museum in the United States dedicated exclusively to portraying the creative visual traditions of Africa. Its research components, collection, exhibitions, and public programs establish the Museum as a primary source for the examination and discovery of the arts and culture of Africa. The collection includes works in wood, metal, fired clay, ivory, and fiber. The Eliot Elisofon Photographic Archives includes slides, photos, and film segments on Africa. There is also a specialized library.

For further information, contact the National Museum of African Art, 950 Independence Avenue SW., Washington, DC 20560. Phone, 202–633–1000. Internet, www.nmafa.si.edu.

National Museum of African American History and Culture The Museum was established in 2003 and will be the only national museum devoted exclusively to the documentation of African American life, art, history, and culture.

For further information, contact the National Museum of African American History and Culture, 470 L'Enfant Plaza SW., Washington, DC 20560. Phone, 202–633–1000. Internet, www.nmaahc.si.edu.

Smithsonian American Art Museum The Museum's art collection spans centuries of American painting, sculpture, folk art, photography, and graphic art. A major center for research in American art, the Museum has contributed to such resources as the Inventory of American Paintings Executed Before 1914; the Smithsonian Art Index; and the Inventory of American Sculpture. The library, shared with the National Portrait Gallery, contains volumes on art, history, and biography, with special emphasis on the United States. The Donald W. Reynolds Center for American Art and Portraiture is home to both the Smithsonian American Art Museum and the National Portrait Gallery. Hundreds of images from the collection and extensive information on its collections, publications, and activities are available electronically at www.saam.si.edu.

For further information, contact the Smithsonian American Art Museum, Eighth and G Streets NW., Washington, DC 20560. Phone, 202–633–1000. Internet, www.americanart.si.edu.

Renwick Gallery The Gallery is dedicated to exhibiting crafts of all periods and to collecting 20th century American crafts. It offers changing exhibitions of American crafts and decorative arts, both historical and contemporary, and a rotating selection from its permanent collection. The Gallery's grand salon is elegantly furnished in the Victorian style of the 1860s and 1870s.

For further information, contact the Renwick Gallery, Seventeenth Street and Pennsylvania Avenue NW., Washington, DC 20560. Phone, 202–633–1000. Internet, www.saam.si.edu/collections/exhibits/renwick25.

National Museum of American History In pursuit of its fundamental mission to inspire a broader understanding of the United States and its people, the Museum provides learning opportunities, stimulates the imagination of visitors, and presents challenging ideas about the Nation's past. The Museum's exhibits provide a unique view of the American experience. Emphasis is placed upon innovative individuals representing a wide range of cultures, who have shaped our heritage, and upon science and the remaking of our world through technology. Exhibits draw upon strong collections in the sciences and engineering, agriculture, manufacturing, transportation, political memorabilia, costumes, musical instruments, coins, Armed Forces history, photography, computers, ceramics, and glass. Classic cars, icons of the American Presidency, First Ladies' gowns, musical instruments, the Star-Spangled Banner flag, Whitney's cotton gin, Morse's telegraph, the John Bull locomotive, Dorothy's ruby slippers from "The Wizard of Oz," and other American icons are highlights of the collection. The Museum is currently closed for renovations and will reopen in summer 2008.

For further information, contact the National Museum of American History, Fourteenth Street and Constitution Avenue NW., Washington, DC 20560. Phone, 202–633–1000. Internet, www.americanhistory.si.edu.

National Museum of the American Indian The Museum was established in 1989, and the building on the National Mall opened September 2004. The collection of the Museum is comprised of the collection of the Museum of the American Indian, Heye Foundation, in New York City. It is an institution of living cultures dedicated to the collection, preservation, study, and exhibition of the life, languages, literature, history, and arts of the Native peoples of the Americas. Highlights include Northwest Coast carvings; dance masks; pottery and weaving from the Southwest; painted hides and garments from the North American Plains; goldwork of the Aztecs, Incas, and Maya; and Amazonian featherwork.

For further information, contact the National Museum of the American Indian, Fourth Street and Independence Avenue SW., Washington, DC 20560. Phone, 202–633–1000. Internet, www.nmai.si.edu.

National Museum of Natural History Dedicated to understanding the natural world and the place of humans in it, the Museum's permanent exhibits focus on human cultures, Earth sciences, biology, and anthropology, with the most popular displays featuring gemstones such as the Hope diamond, dinosaurs, insects, marine ecosystems, birds, and mammals. To celebrate the millennial anniversary of the journey of Leif Ericson to America, the Museum mounted a special exhibition titled Vikings: The North Atlantic Saga; the exhibition is now traveling around the Nation. A new IMAX theater offers large-format nature films. The Museum's encyclopedic collections comprise nearly 126 million specimens, making the Museum one of the world's foremost facilities for natural history research. The Museum's four departments are anthropology, mineral sciences, paleobiology, and systematic biology. Doctorate-level staff researchers ensure the continued growth and value of the collection by conducting studies in the field and laboratory.

For further information, contact the National Museum of Natural History, Tenth Street and Constitution Avenue NW., Washington, DC 20560. Phone, 202–633–1000. Internet, www.mnh.si.edu.

National Portrait Gallery The Gallery was established in 1962 for the exhibition and study of portraiture depicting men and women who have made significant contributions to the history, development, and culture of the United States. The Gallery contains more than 19,000 works, including photographs and glass negatives. The first floor of the Gallery is devoted to changing exhibitions from the Gallery's collection of paintings, sculpture, prints, photographs, and drawings as well as to special portrait collections. Featured on the second floor are the permanent collection of portraits of eminent Americans and the Hall of Presidents, including the famous Gilbert Stuart portrait-from-life of George Washington. The two-story American Victorian Renaissance Great Hall on the third floor of the Gallery houses a Civil War exhibit, and is used for special events and public programs. The Gallery shares a large library with the Smithsonian American Art Museum and the Archives of American Art. The education department offers public programs; outreach programs for schools, senior adults, hospitals, and nursing homes; and walk-in and group tours. For further information, contact the National Portrait Gallery, Eighth and F Streets NW., Washington, DC 20560. Phone, 202–633–1000. Internet, www.npg.si.edu.

National Postal Museum The Museum houses the Nation's postal history and philatelic collection, the largest of its kind in the world, with more than 13 million objects. The Museum is devoted to the history of America's mail service, and major galleries include exhibits on mail service in colonial times and during the Civil War, the Pony Express, modern mail service, automation, mail transportation, and the art of letters, as well as displays of the Museum's priceless stamp collection. Highlights include three mail planes, a replica of a railway mail car, displays of historic letters, handcrafted mail boxes, and rare U.S. and foreign issue stamps and covers.

For further information, contact the National Postal Museum, 2 Massachusetts Avenue NE., Washington, DC 20560. Phone, 202–633–1000. Internet, www.si.edu/postal.

National Zoological Park The National Zoo encompasses 163 acres along Rock Creek Park in Northwest Washington, DC. Established in 1889, the Zoo is developing into a biopark with live animals, botanic gardens and aquaria, and artworks with animal themes. Currently, the collection has animals ranging in size and diversity from leaf-cutter ants to giraffes. The zoo recently acquired a new pair of young giant pandas, Mei Xiang and Tian Tian. In July 2005, Mei Xiang gave birth to a cub named "Tai Shan." Recent exhibits include "Amazonia," a simulated tropical rain forest; the "Pollinarium" exhibit; the Reptile Discovery Center, featuring the world's largest lizards, Komodo dragons; and the Fujifilm Giant Panda Habitat and Asia Trail. Research on genetics, animal behavior, and reproductive studies has given the National Zoo a leadership role among the Nation's conservation institutions.

For further information, contact the National Zoo, 3000 Connecticut Avenue NW., Washington, DC 20008. Phone, 202–673–4717. Internet, www.si.edu/natzoo.

Center for Folklife and Cultural Heritage The Center is responsible for research, documentation, and presentation of grassroots cultural traditions. It maintains a documentary collection and produces Smithsonian Folkways Recordings, educational materials, documentary films, publications, and traveling exhibits, as well as the annual Smithsonian Folklife Festival on the National Mall. Recent Folklife festivals have featured a range of American music styles, a number of State tributes, and performers from around the world. Admission to the festival is free. The 2-

week program includes Fourth of July activities on the National Mall.

For further information, contact the Center for Folklife and Cultural Heritage, Suite 4100, 750 Ninth Street NW., Washington, DC 20560. Phone, 202–633–1000. Internet, www.folklife.si.edu.

International Center The International Center supports Smithsonian activities abroad and serves as liaison for the Smithsonian's international interests. The Smithsonian seeks to encourage a broadening of public understanding of the histories, cultures, and natural environments of regions throughout the world. The International Center provides a meeting place and an organizational channel to bring together the world's scholars, museum professionals, and the general public, to attend and participate in conferences, public forums, lectures, and workshops.

For further information, contact the Office of International Relations, MRC 705, 1100 Jefferson Drive SW., Washington, DC 20560. Phone, 202–633–1000.

Arthur M. Sackler Gallery This Asian art museum opened in 1987 on the National Mall. Changing exhibitions drawn from major collections in the United States and abroad, as well as from the permanent holdings of the Sackler Gallery, are displayed in the distinctive below-ground museum. The Gallery's growing permanent collection is founded on a group of art objects from China, South and Southeast Asia, and the ancient Near East that was given to the Smithsonian by Arthur M. Sackler (1913–1987). The Museum's current collection features Persian manuscripts; Japanese paintings; ceramics, prints, and textiles; sculptures from India; and paintings and metalware from China, Korea, Japan, and Southeast Asia. The Sackler Gallery is connected by an underground exhibition space to the neighboring Freer Gallery.

For further information, contact the Arthur M. Sackler Gallery, 1050 Independence Avenue SW., Washington, DC 20560. Phone, 202–633–1000. Internet, www.asia.si.edu.

Smithsonian Institution Archives The Smithsonian Institution Archives acquires, preserves, and makes available for research the official records of the Smithsonian Institution and the papers of individuals and organizations associated with the Institution or with its work. These holdings document the growth of the Smithsonian and the development of American science, history, and art.

For further information, contact the Smithsonian Institution Archives, MRC 414, 900 Jefferson Drive SW., Washington, DC 20560. Phone, 202–633–1000.

Smithsonian Astrophysical Observatory The Smithsonian Astrophysical Observatory and the Harvard College Observatory have coordinated research activities under a single director in a cooperative venture, Harvard-Smithsonian Center for Astrophysics. The Center's research activities are organized in the following areas of study: atomic and molecular physics, radio and geoastronomy, high-energy astrophysics, optical and infrared astronomy, planetary sciences, solar and stellar physics, and theoretical astrophysics. Research results are published in the *Center Preprint Series* and other technical and nontechnical bulletins, and distributed to scientific and educational institutions around the world.

For more information, contact the Smithsonian Astrophysical Observatory, 60 Garden Street, Cambridge, MA 02138. Phone, 617–495–7461. Internet, www.cfa.harvard.edu/saohome.

Smithsonian Museum Conservation Institute The Institute researches preservation, conservation, and technical study and analysis of collection materials. Its researchers investigate the chemical and physical processes that are involved in the care of art, artifacts, and specimens, and attempt to formulate conditions and procedures for storage, exhibit, and stabilization that optimize the preservation of these objects. In interdisciplinary collaborations with archeologists, anthropologists, and art historians, natural and physical scientists study and analyze objects from the collections and related materials to expand knowledge and understanding of their historical and scientific context.

For further information, contact the Museum Conservation Institute, Museum Support Center, Suitland, MD 20746. Phone, 301–238–1240.

Smithsonian Environmental Research Center (SERC)

The Center is the leading national research center for understanding environmental issues in the coastal zone. SERC is dedicated to increasing knowledge of the biological and physical processes that sustain life on Earth. The Center, located near the Chesapeake Bay, trains future generations of scientists to address ecological questions of the Nation and the globe.

For further information, contact the Smithsonian Environmental Research Center, 647 Contees Wharf Road, Edgewater, MD 21037. Phone, 443–482–2200. Internet, www.serc.si.edu.

Smithsonian Institution Libraries

The Smithsonian Institution Libraries include more than one million volumes (among them 40,000 rare books) with strengths in natural history, art, science, humanities, and museology. Many volumes are available through interlibrary loan.

For further information, contact the Smithsonian Institution Libraries, Tenth Street and Constitution Avenue NW., Washington, DC 20560. Phone, 202–633–2240. Internet, www.sil.si.edu. Email, libhelp@sil.si.edu.

Smithsonian Institution Traveling Exhibition Service (SITES)

Since 1952, SITES has been committed to making Smithsonian exhibitions available to millions of people who cannot view them firsthand at the Smithsonian museums. Exhibitions on art, history, and science (including such exhibits as "Full Deck Art Quilts," "Red, Hot, and Blue: A Salute to American Musicals," and "Hubble Space Telescope") travel to more than 250 locations each year.

For further information, contact the Smithsonian Institution Traveling Exhibition Service, Suite 7103, 470 L'Enfant Plaza SW., Washington, DC 20024. Phone, 202–633–1000. Internet, www.si.edu/organiza/offices/sites.

Smithsonian Marine Station

The research institute features a state-of-the-art laboratory where Station scientists catalog species and study marine plants and animals. Among the most important projects being pursued at the site is the search for possible causes of fish kills including *pfiesteria* and other organisms.

For further information, contact the Smithsonian Marine Station, 701 Seaway Drive, Fort Pierce, FL 34946. Phone, 772–465–6630. Internet, www.sms.si.edu.

Smithsonian Tropical Research Institute (STRI)

The Institute is a research organization for advanced studies of tropical ecosystems. Headquartered in the Republic of Panama, STRI maintains extensive facilities in the Western Hemisphere tropics. It is the base of a corps of tropical researchers who study the evolution, behavior, ecology, and history of tropical species of systems ranging from coral reefs to rain forests.

For further information, contact the Smithsonian Tropical Research Institute, 1100 Jefferson Drive SW., Suite 3123, Washington, DC 20560. Phone, 202–633–4016. Phone (Panama), 011–507–212–8000. Internet, www.stri.org.

The John F. Kennedy Center for the Performing Arts

The Kennedy Center is the only official memorial to President Kennedy in Washington, DC. Since its opening in 1971, the Center has presented a year-round program of the finest in music, dance, and drama from the United States and abroad. The Kennedy Center box offices are open daily, and general information and tickets may be obtained by calling 202–467–4600 or 202–416–8524 (TTY). A limited number of half-price tickets are available for some attractions to eligible partrons, including senior citizens over the age of 65, enlisted military personnel of grade E–1 through E–4, persons with fixed low incomes, full time students, and persons with permanent disabilities. Visitor services are provided by the Friends of the Kennedy Center volunteers. Tours are available free of charge between 10 a.m. and 5 p.m. on weekdays and between 10 a.m. and 1 p.m. on weekends. Free performances are given every day at 6 p.m. on the Millennium Stage in the Grand Foyer.

For further information, contact the Kennedy Center. Phone, 202–467–4600. Internet, www.kennedy-center.org.

National Gallery of Art The Gallery houses one of the finest collections in the world, illustrating Western man's achievements in painting, sculpture, and the graphic arts. The West Building includes European (13th–early 20th century) and American (18th–early 20th century) works. An extensive survey of Italian painting and sculpture, including the only painting by Leonardo da Vinci in the Western Hemisphere, is presented here. Rich in Dutch masters and French impressionists, the collection offers superb surveys of American, British, Flemish, Spanish, and 15th and 16th century German art, as well as Renaissance medals and bronzes, Chinese porcelains, and about 97,000 works of graphic art from the 12th to the 20th centuries. The East Building collections and Sculpture Garden include important works by major 20th century artists. The Gallery represents a partnership of Federal and private resources. Its operations and maintenance are supported through Federal appropriations, and all of its acquisitions of works of art, as well as numerous special programs, are made possible through private donations and funds. Graduate and postgraduate research is conducted under a fellowship program; education programs for schoolchildren and the general public are conducted daily; and an extension service provides slide teaching and multimedia programs, videocassettes, CD ROMs, DVDs, and videodiscs to millions of people each year.

For further information, contact the National Gallery of Art. Phone, 202–737–4215. TTY, 202–842–6176. Internet, www.nga.gov.

Woodrow Wilson International Center for Scholars The Center was established by Congress in 1968 as the Nation's official memorial to its 28th President. The Center is a nonpartisan institution of advanced study that promotes scholarship in public affairs. The Center convenes scholars and policymakers, businesspeople, and journalists in a neutral forum for open, serious, and informed dialogue. The Center supports research in social sciences and humanities, with an emphasis on history, political science, and international relations.

For further information, contact the Scholar Administration Office, Woodrow Wilson Center, One Woodrow Wilson Plaza, 1300 Pennsylvania Avenue NW., Washington, DC 20004–3027. Phone, 202–691–4170. Fax, 202–691–4001. Internet, www.wilsoncenter.org.

Sources of Information

Smithsonian Institution

Contracts and Small Business Activities Information regarding procurement of supplies, property management and utilization services for Smithsonian Institution organizations, and contracts for construction, services, etc., may be obtained from the Director, Office of Contracting, Smithsonian Institution, Washington, DC 20560. Phone, 202–275–1600.

Education and Research Write to the Directors of the following offices at the Smithsonian Institution, Washington, DC 20560: Office of Fellowships and Grants, Center for Folklife and Cultural Heritage, National Science Resources Center; and Smithsonian Center for Education and Museum Studies.

Electronic Access Information about the Smithsonian Institution is available electronically through the Internet at www.si.edu or www.smithsonian.org.

Employment Employment information for the Smithsonian is available from the Office of Human Resources, Smithsonian Institution, Suite 6100, 750 Ninth Street NW., Washington, DC 20560. Phone, 202–275–1102. Recorded message, 202–287–3102.

Media Affairs Members of the press may contact the Smithsonian Office of Public Affairs, 1000 Jefferson Drive SW., Washington, DC 20560. Phone, 202–633–2400. Internet, http://newsdesk.si.edu.

Memberships For information about Smithsonian membership (Resident Program), write to the Smithsonian Associates, MRC 701, 1100 Jefferson Drive SW., Washington, DC 20560. Phone, 202–357–3030. For information about Smithsonian membership (National Program), call 202–357–4800. For information about the Contributing

Membership, call 202–357–1699. For information about the Young Benefactors, call 202–786–9049.

Information about activities of the Friends of the National Zoo and their magazine, *The Zoogoer,* is available by writing to FONZ, National Zoological Park, Washington, DC 20008. Phone, 202–673–4950.

Photographs   Color and black-and-white photographs and slides are available to Government agencies, research and educational institutions, publishers, and the general public from the Smithsonian photographic archives. A searchable database of images is available through the Internet. Information, order forms, and price lists may be obtained from the Office of Imaging, Printing, and Photographic Services, MAH CB–054, Smithsonian Institution, Washington, DC 20560. Internet, http://photos.si.edu. Email, psdmx@sivm.si.edu.

Publications   To purchase the Smithsonian Institution's annual report, *Smithsonian Year,* call 202–633–2400. The Smithsonian Institution Press publishes a range of books and studies related to the sciences, technology, history, culture, air and space, and the arts. A book catalog is available from Publications Sales, Smithsonian Books or Smithsonian Institution University Press, 1111 North Capitol Street, Washington, DC 20002. Phone, 800–782–4612. To purchase a recording of the *Smithsonian Folkways Recordings,* call 800–410–9815. Internet, www.si.edu/folkways.

A free brochure providing a brief guide to the Smithsonian Institution is published in English and several foreign languages. For a copy, call Visitor Information at 202–633–1000, or pick up a copy at the information desks in the museums. A visitor's guide for individuals with disabilities is also available.

Smithsonian Institution Research Reports, containing news of current research projects in the arts, sciences, and history that are being conducted by Smithsonian staff, is produced by the Smithsonian Office of Public Affairs, Smithsonian Institution Building, 1000 Jefferson Drive SW., Washington, DC 20560. Phone, 202–633–2400.

To request a copy of *Smithsonian Runner,* a newsletter about Native American-related activities at the Smithsonian, contact the National Museum of the American Indian, Smithsonian Institution, Washington, DC 20560. Phone, 800–242–NMAI.

For the newsletter *Art to Zoo* for teachers of fourth through eighth graders, write to the Smithsonian Center for Education and Museum Studies, Room 1163, MRC 402, Arts and Industries Building, Washington, DC 20560. Phone, 202–357–2425.

Telephone   *Dial-A-Museum,* 202–633–1000, provides a taped message with daily announcements on new exhibits and special events. For a Spanish listing of Smithsonian events, call 202–633–9126.

Tours   For information about museum and gallery tours, contact the Smithsonian Information Center, 1000 Jefferson Drive SW., Washington, DC 20560. Phone, 202–633–1000. School groups are welcome. Special behind-the-scenes tours are offered through the various memberships.

Visitor Information   The Smithsonian Information Center, located in the original Smithsonian building, commonly known as "The Castle," provides general orientation, through films, computer interactive programs, and visitor information specialists, to help members and the public learn about the national collections, museum events, exhibitions, and special programs. Write to the Smithsonian Information Center, 1000 Jefferson Drive SW., Washington, DC 20560. Phone, 202–633–1000. TTY, 202–633–5285.

Volunteer Service Opportunities   The Smithsonian Institution welcomes volunteers and offers a variety of interesting service opportunities. For information, write to the Visitor Information and Associates' Reception Center, 1000 Jefferson Drive SW., Washington, DC 20560. Phone, 202–633–1000. TTY, 202–633–5285.

John F. Kennedy Center for the Performing Arts

Contracts and Small Business Activities Contact the John F. Kennedy Center for the Performing Arts, Washington, DC 20566.

Education and Research For information regarding Kennedy Center education programs, contact the John F. Kennedy Center for the Performing Arts, Washington, DC 20566. Phone, 202–416–8000.

Electronic Access Information on the John F. Kennedy Center for the Performing Arts is available through the Internet at www.kennedy-center.org.

Employment For information on employment opportunities at the John F. Kennedy Center for the Performing Arts, contact the Human Resources Department, Washington, DC 20566. Phone, 202–416–8610.

Memberships Information about the national and local activities of Friends of the Kennedy Center (including the bimonthly *Kennedy Center News* for members) is available at the information desks within the Center or by writing to Friends of the Kennedy Center, Washington, DC 20566.

Special Functions Inquiries regarding the use of Kennedy Center facilities for special functions may be directed to the Office of Special Events, John F. Kennedy Center for the Performing Arts, Washington, DC 20566. Phone, 202–416–8000.

Theater Operations Inquiries regarding the use of the Kennedy Center's theaters may be addressed to the Booking Coordinator, John F. Kennedy Center for the Performing Arts, Washington, DC 20566. Phone, 202–416–8000.

Volunteer Service Opportunities For information about volunteer opportunities at the Kennedy Center, write to Friends of the Kennedy Center, Washington, DC 20566. Phone, 202–416–8000.

National Gallery of Art

Calendar of Events The Calendar of Events is available through the Internet at www.nga.gov/calendar.htm. To receive email notices when new calendars go online, send your name, street address, and email address to calendar@nga.gov.

Concerts Concerts by world-renowned musicians are presented Sunday evenings from October through June. For information, call the Concert Line at 202–842–6941. Internet, www.nga.gov/programs/music.htm.

Contracts and Small Business Activities Contact National Gallery of Art, Office of Procurement and Contracts, 2000B South Club Drive, Landover, MD 20785. Phone, 202–842–6745.

Educational Resources The National Gallery of Art provides slide teaching and multimedia programs, videocassettes, CD ROMs, DVDs, and videodiscs at no charge to individuals, schools, and civic organizations throughout the country. Contact the Department of Education Resources, National Gallery of Art, 2000B South Club Drive, Landover, MD 20785. Phone, 202–842–6273. Internet, www.nga.gov/education/classroom/loanfinder. Please write or email EdResources@nga.gov to request a free catalog of programs.

Electronic Access Information on the National Gallery of Art is available through the Internet at www.nga.gov. NGAkids (www.nga.gov/kids) includes interactive activities and adventures with works of art in the Gallery's collection and an animated tale set in the Gallery's Sculpture Garden.

Employment For information on employment opportunities at the National Gallery, contact the Personnel Office, National Gallery of Art, 601 Pennsylvania Avenue South NW., Second Floor, Washington, DC 20004. Phone, 202–842–6282. TDD, 202–842–6176. Internet, www.nga.gov/resources/employ.htm.

Family Programs The Gallery offers a full range of free family programs suitable for children ages 4 and up, including workshops, children's films, music performances, and storytelling. Phone, 202–789–3030. Internet, www.nga.gov/kids.

Fellowships For information about research fellowship programs, contact the Center for Advanced Study in the Visual Arts. Phone, 202–842–6482. Fax, 202–842–6733. Internet, www.nga.gov/resources/casva.htm.

Films An ongoing free program of independent films, major retrospectives, classic cinema, and area premieres are presented. Visiting filmmakers and scholars are often invited to discuss films with the audience following screenings. The auditorium is equipped with an FM wireless listening system for the hearing impaired. Receivers, ear phones, and neck loops are available at the East Building Art Information Desk near the main entrance. Phone, 202–842–6799. Internet, www.nga.gov/programs/film.htm.

Internships For information about National Gallery internship programs for college graduates, master's degree students, and Ph.D. candidates, contact the Department of Academic Programs, National Gallery of Art, 2000B South Club Drive, Landover, MD 20785. Email, intern@nga.gov. Phone, 202–842–6257. Fax, 202–842–6935.

Lectures An ongoing schedule of lectures, symposia, and works in progress are free and open to the public on a first-come, first-serve basis. Internet, www.nga.gov/programs/lectures.htm.

Library The Gallery's collection of more than 330,000 books and periodicals on the history, theory, and criticism of art and architecture emphasizes Western art from the Middle Ages to the present, and American art from the colonial era to the present. The library is open by appointment on Mondays from 12 noon to 4:30 p.m. and Tuesday through Friday from 10 a.m. to 4:30 p.m. It is closed on all Federal holidays. Adult researchers may gain access to the library by calling 202–842–6511. Internet, www.nga.gov/resources/dldesc.htm.

Library Image Collections The Department of Image Collections is the study and research center for images of Western art and architecture at the National Gallery of Art. The collection now numbers nearly 10 million photographs, slides, negatives, and microform images, making it one of the

largest resources of its kind. The Department serves the Gallery's staff, members of the Center for Advanced Study in the Visual Arts, visiting scholars, and serious adult researchers. The library is open by appointment on Mondays from 12 noon to 4:30 p.m. and Tuesday through Friday from 10 a.m. to 4:30 p.m. It is closed on all Federal holidays. Phone, 202–842–6026. Internet, www.nga.gov/resources/dldesc.htm.

Memberships The Circle of the National Gallery of Art is a membership program which provides support for special projects for which Federal funds are not available. For more information about membership in the Circle of the National Gallery of Art, please write to The Circle, National Gallery of Art, Washington, DC 20565. Phone, 202–842–6450. Internet, www.nga.gov/ginfo/involved.htm.

Publications The National Gallery shop makes available quality reproductions and publications about the Gallery's collections. To order, call 202–842–6002. Select items are also available for sale on the Web site at www.nga.gov/shop. The Office of Press and Public Information offers a free bimonthly calendar of events, which can be ordered by calling 202–842–6662, or through email at calendar@nga.gov. The calendar and *Brief Guide to the National Gallery of Art* are also available at art information desks throughout the Gallery or by calling Visitor Services at 202–842–6691.

Tours The Education Division of the National Gallery of Art offers gallery talks and lectures. Phone, 202–842–6247. Internet, www.nga.gov/education/school.htm or www.nga.gov/programs/tours.htm.

Visitor Services The Visitor Services Office of the National Gallery of Art provides individual assistance to those with special needs, responds to written and telephone requests, and provides information to those planning to visit the Washington, DC, area. For more information, write to the National Gallery of Art, Office of Visitor Services, Washington, DC 20565. Phone, 202–

842–6691. Internet, www.nga.gov/ginfo/disabled.htm.

Volunteer Opportunities   For information about volunteering as a docent or as an Art Information Desk volunteer, please call Volunteer Opportunities at 202–789–3013. Internet, www.nga.gov/education/volunteer.htm.

Library Volunteering   Phone, 202–842–6510. Internet, www.nga.gov/ginfo/involved.htm.

Horticulture Volunteers   Phone, 202–842–6844.

Works on Paper   Works of art on paper that are not on view may be seen by appointment on weekdays by calling 202–842–6380. The Matisse cutouts are on view in the East Building, Concourse from 10 a.m. to 3 p.m., Monday through Saturday, and from 11 a.m. to 4 p.m. on Sunday.

Woodrow Wilson Center for International Scholars

Electronic Access   Information on the Woodrow Wilson Center for International Scholars is available through the Internet at www.wilsoncenter.org.

Employment   For information on employment opportunities at the Woodrow Wilson Center, contact the Office of Human Resources, One Woodrow Wilson Plaza, 1300 Pennsylvania Avenue NW., Washington, DC 2004–3027. Internet, www.wilsoncenter.org/hr/index.htm.

Fellowships and Internships   The Woodrow Wilson Center offers residential fellowships that allow academics, public officials, journalists, business professionals, and others to pursue their research and writing at the Center, while interacting with policymakers in Washington. The Center also invites public policy scholars and senior scholars from a variety of disciplines to conduct research for varying lengths of time in residence. For more information, call 202–691–4213. The Center also has a year-round need for interns to assist the program and projects staff and to act as research assistants for scholars and fellows. For more information, call 202–691–4053.

Media Affairs   Members of the press may contact the Woodrow Wilson Center at 202–691–4016.

Publications   The Woodrow Wilson Center publishes the monthly newsletter *Centerpoint,* and books written by staff and visiting scholars and fellows, through the Wilson Center Press. It also produces *Dialogue,* a weekly radio and television program about national and international affairs, history, and culture. For more information, call 202–691–4016.

Visitor Services   To hear a listing of events at the Woodrow Wilson Center, call 202–691–4188. All events, unless otherwise noted, are free and open to the public. Please note that a photo identification is required for entry.

For further information, contact the Smithsonian Information Center, 1000 Jefferson Drive SW., Washington, DC 20560. Phone, 202–633–1000. TDD, 202–357–1729. Internet, www.smithsonian.org.

STATE JUSTICE INSTITUTE

Suite 600, 1650 King Street, Alexandria, VA 22314
Phone, 703–684–6100. Internet, www.sji.gov.

Board of Directors:

CHAIRMAN	ROBERT A. MILLER
VICE CHAIRMAN	JOSEPH F. BACA
Secretary	SANDRA A. O'CONNOR
Executive Committee Member	KEITH MCNAMARA

| Members | TERRENCE B. ADAMSON, ROBERT N. BALDWIN, CARLOS R. GARZA, SOPHIA H. HALL, TOMMY JEWELL, ARTHUR McGIVERIN, (VACANCY) |

Officers:
Executive Director — JANICE MUNSTERMAN
Deputy Director — JONATHAN MATTIELLO

The State Justice Institute awards grants to improve judicial administration in the State courts of the United States.

The State Justice Institute was created by the State Justice Institute Act of 1984 (42 U.S.C. 10701) as a private, nonprofit corporation to further the development and improvement of judicial administration in the State courts.

The Institute is supervised by a Board of Directors consisting of 11 members appointed by the President with the advice and consent of the Senate. The Board is statutorily composed of six judges, a State court administrator, and four members of the public, of whom no more than two can be of the same political party.

The goals of the Institute are to fulfill the following duties:

—direct a national program of assistance to ensure that all U.S. citizens have ready access to a fair and effective judicial system;

—foster coordination and cooperation with the Federal judiciary;

—serve as a clearinghouse and information center for the dissemination of information regarding State judicial systems; and

—encourage education for judges and support personnel of State court systems.

To accomplish these broad objectives, the Institute is authorized to provide funds, through grants, cooperative agreements, and contracts, to State courts and organizations that can assist in the achievement of improving judicial administration of the State courts.

Sources of Information

Inquiries concerning grants, publications, consumer information, speakers, or Privacy Act/Freedom of Information Act requests should be directed to the Executive Director or Deputy Director, State Justice Institute, Suite 600, 1650 King Street, Alexandria, VA 22314. Phone, 703–684–6100.

Information regarding the programs and services of the State Justice Institute is also available through the Internet at www.sji.gov.

For further information, contact the State Justice Institute, Suite 600, 1650 King Street, Alexandria, VA 22314. Phone, 703–684–6100. Internet, www.sji.gov.

UNITED STATES INSTITUTE OF PEACE

Suite 200, 1200 Seventeenth Street NW., Washington, DC 20036
Phone, 202–457–1700. Fax, 202–429–6063. Internet, www.usip.org.

Board of Directors:
Public Members:
CHAIRMAN — J. ROBINSON WEST
VICE CHAIRMAN — GEORGE E. MOOSE

| Members | ANNE H. CAHN, CHESTER A. CROCKER, KERRY KENNEDY, IKRAM U. KHAN, KATHLEEN MARTINEZ, JEREMY A. RABKIN, JUDY VAN REST, NANCY ZIRKIN |

Ex Officio Members:

Secretary of State	HILLARY R. CLINTON
Secretary of Defense	ROBERT M. GATES
President, National Defense University	FRANCES C. WILSON
President, U.S. Institute of Peace	RICHARD H. SOLOMON

Officials:

President	RICHARD H. SOLOMON
Executive Vice President	TARA D. SONESHINE
Vice President, Headquarters Project	CHARLES E. NELSON
Vice President, Management	MICHAEL B. GRAHAM
Vice President, Grants and Fellowships	STEVEN HEYDEMANN
Vice President, Center for Conflict Analysis and Prevention	ABIODUN WILLIAMS
Vice President, Domestic Education and Training Center	PAMELA AALL
Vice President, International Education and Training Center	MICHAEL LEKSON
Vice President, Center for Post-conflict Peace and Stability Operations	DANIEL P. SERWER
Vice President, Center for Mediation and Conflict Resolution	DAVID R. SMOCK
Vice President, Planning and Outreach	TARA D. SONENSHINE
Director, Administration	CHRISTOPHER DE PAOLA
Chief Information Officer	DOUGLAS LEINS
Director, Human Resources	PAULA KING
Director, Library Services and Knowledge Management	ELLEN ENSEL
Director, Congressional Relations	LAURIE SCHULTZ-HEIM
Director, Public Affairs and Communications	LAUREN SUCHER, *Acting*
Director, Publications	VALERIE NORVILLE

Centers of Innovation:

Associate Vice President, Rule of Law	NEIL J. KRITZ
Associate Vice President, Religion and Peacemaking	DAVID R. SMOCK
Associate Vice President, Sustainable Economies	RAYMOND GILPIN
Associate Vice President, Media, Conflict and Peacebuilding/Technology and Peacebuilding	SHELDON HIMELFARB

The United States Institute of Peace promotes research, policy analysis, education, and training on international peace and conflict resolution.

The United States Institute of Peace (USIP) is an independent institution, established by Congress pursuant to title XVII of the Defense Authorization Act of 1985, as amended (22 U.S.C. 4601-4611). USIP's mission is to help prevent and resolve violent conflicts, promote post-conflict stablility and development, and increase peacebuilding capacity, tools, and intellectual capital worldwide. The Institute achieves this by empowering others with knowledge, skills, and resources, as well as by directly engaging in peacebuilding throughout the world.

The Institute is governed by a bipartisan board of directors appointed by the President and confirmed by the Senate. The board is comprised of members from outside the Federal service, the Secretary of State, the Secretary of Defense, and the President of the National Defense University. The board appoints the President of the Institute.

Programs and Activities

In carrying out its mission, USIP operates on the ground in conflict zones, providing services that include:
—mediating and facilitating dialog among parties in conflict;
—building conflict management skills and capacity;
—indentifying and disseminating best practices in conflict management;
—promoting the rule of law;
—reforming and strengthening education systems;
—strengthening civil society and state-building; and
—educating the public through film, radio, the Internet, special events, and other outreach activities.

The Institute conducts and sponsors relevant research on causes of and solutions to violent conflict. Drawing on this intellectual capital, USIP identifies promising models and innovative approaches and practices. USIP shares these tools with others through its publications, the Internet, and training programs. Tools developed by USIP include book series on international mediation and cultural negotiating behavior, resources on religious peacemaking, a toolkit for promoting the rule of law in fragile states, guidelines for civilian and military interactions in hostile environments, and textbooks on international conflict management.

USIP works in partnership with non-governmental organizations, higher and secondary educational institutions, and internatinoal organizations to promote collaborative problem-solving through conferences, standing working groups, Track II diplomacy, and special events. The Institute offers training on conflict management, including mediation and negotiating skills, for government and military personnel, civil society leaders, and staff of non-governmental and international organizations.

As part of its efforts to strengthen and professionalize the field of international conflict management, the Institute shares the resources and tools it has developed with the larger conflict management community. In conflict zones, USIP works in partnership with local organizations to build their capacity and promote sustainability. The Institute also extends its reach by investing in nonprofit organizations in the United States and overseas. Recent efforts include Afghanistan, Cote d'Ivoire, the Democratic Republic of the Congo, Haiti, Iran, Iraq, Korea, Liberia, Syria, and Sudan.

Strategic Centers

The Institute includes strategic centers focused on preventing violent conflicts before they occur, mediating and resolving conflicts when they do occur, and promoting post-conflict stability once the fighting ends. The efforts of these cross-disciplinary centers focus on education, training, grantmaking, fellowships, scholarships, and innovation in peacebuilding (e.g. rule of law; religon and peacemaking; science and technology in peacebuilding; media and conflict; and sustainable economies).

Sources of Information

Electronic access to the Institute is available through the Internet at www.usip.org.

For further information, contact the Office of Public Affairs and Communications, United States Institute of Peace, 1200 Seventeenth Street NW., Suite 200, Washington, DC 20036–3011. Phone, 202–457–1700. Fax, 202–429–6063. Internet, www.usip.org.

SELECTED MULTILATERAL ORGANIZATIONS

MULTILATERAL INTERNATIONAL ORGANIZATIONS IN WHICH THE UNITED STATES PARTICIPATES

Explanatory note: The United States participates in the organizations named below in accordance with the provisions of treaties, other international agreements, congressional legislation, or executive arrangements. In some cases, no financial contribution is involved.

Various commissions, councils, or committees subsidiary to the organizations listed here are not named separately on this list. These include the international bodies for drugs and crime, which are subsidiary to the United Nations.

This listing is provided for reference purposes and should not be considered exhaustive. For more information on international organizations and United States participation in them, contact the State Department's Bureau of International Organizations. Phone, 202–647–9326. Internet, www.state.gov/p/io.

I. Specialized Agencies of the United Nations

Food and Agricultural Organization
International Atomic Energy Agency
International Civil Aviation Organization
International Fund for Agriculture Development
International Labor Organization
International Maritime Organization
International Telecommunication Union
United Nations Educational, Scientific and Cultural Organization
Universal Postal Union
World Health Organization
World Intellectual Property Organization
World Meteorological Organization

II. Peacekeeping

African Union/United Nations Hybrid Mission in Darfur
United Nations Interim Administration Mission in Kosovo
United Nations Mission in Ethiopia/ Eritrea
United Nations Mission in Liberia
United Nations Mission in Sudan
United Nations Observer Mission in Georgia
United Nations Stabilization Mission in Haiti
United Nations Truce Supervision Organization (Middle East)

III. Inter-American Organizations

Caribbean Postal Union
Inter-American Center of Tax Administrators
Inter-American Indian Institute
Inter-American Institute for Cooperation on Agriculture
Inter-American Institute for Global Change Research
Inter-American Tropical Tuna Commission
Pan American Health Organization
Pan American Institute of Geography and History
Pan American Railway Congress Association
Postal Union of the Americas and Spain and Portugal

IV. Regional Organizations

Antarctic Treaty System
Arctic Council
Asia-Pacific Economic Cooperation
Asia Pacific Energy Research Center
Colombo Plan for Cooperative Economic
    and Social Development in Asia and
    the Pacific
Commission for Environmental
    Cooperation
Commission for Labor Cooperation
International Commission for the
    Conservation of Atlantic Tunas
North Atlantic Assembly
North Atlantic Treaty Organization
North Atlantic Salmon Conservation
    Organization
North Pacific Anadromous Fish
    Commission
North Pacific Coast Guard Forum
North Pacific Marine Science
    Organization
Northwest Atlantic Fisheries
    Organization
Secretariat of the Pacific Community
South Pacific Regional Environment
    Program
Western and Central Pacific Fisheries
    Commission

V. Other International Organizations

Center for International Forestry
    Research
Commission for the Conservation of
    Antarctic Marine Living Resources
Consultative Group on International
    Agricultural Research
COPAS-SARSAT (Search and Rescue
    Satellite System)
Global Biodiversity Information Facility
Integrated Ocean Drilling Program
    Council
International Bureau for the Permanent
    Court of Arbitration
International Bureau of Weights and
    Measures
International Center for Agricultural
    Research in the Dry Areas
International Center for Migration Policy
    Development
International Center for the Study of the
    Preservation and the Restoration of
    Cultural Property
International Coffee Organization
International Committee of the Red Cross

International Cotton Advisory Committee
International Council for the Exploration
    of the Seas
International Criminal Police
    Organization (INTERPOL)
International Customs Tariffs Bureau
International Development Law
    Organization
International Energy Agency
International Energy Forum Secretariat
International Fertilizer Development
    Center
International Grains Council
International Hydrographic Organization
International Institute for Applied
    Systems Analysis
International Institute for Cotton
International Institute for the Unification
    of Private Law
International Mobile Satellite
    Organization
International North Pacific Fisheries
    Commission
International Organization for Legal
    Metrology
International Organization of Supreme
    Audit Institutions
International Rubber Study Group
International Science and Technology
    Center
International Seed Testing Association
International Service for National
    Agriculture Research
International Sugar Council
International Telecommunications
    Satellite Organization
International Tropical Timber
    Organization
International Union of Credit and
    Investment Insurers (Berne Union)
International Whaling Commission
Inter-Parliamentary Union
Iran-United States Claims Tribunal
Hague Conference on Private
    International Law
Human Frontier Science Program
    Organization
Multinational Force and Observers
Nuclear Energy Agency
Organization for Economic Cooperation
    and Development
Organization for the Prohibition of
    Chemical Weapons
Pacific Aviation Safety Office
Permanent International Association of
    Navigation Congresses

Preparatory Commission for the Comprehensive Nuclear Test-Ban Treaty

Regional Environmental Center for Central and Eastern Europe

Science and Technology Center in Ukraine

Sierra Leone Special Court

World Heritage Fund

World Customs Organization

World Trade Organization

VI. Special Voluntary Programs

Asian Vegetable Research and Development Center

Convention on International Trade in Endangered Species of Wild Fauna and Flora (CITES)

Global Fund to Fight HIV/AIDS, Tuberculosis, and Malaria

International Council for Science

International Crop Research Institute for Semi-Arid Tropics

International Federation of the Red Cross and Red Crescent Societies

International Food Policy Research Institute

International Fund for Agricultural Development

International Institute of Tropical Agriculture

Joint United Nations Program on HIV/AIDS (UNAIDS)

Korean Peninsula Energy Development Organization

Multilateral Fund for the Implementation of the Montreal Protocol

Permanent Interstate Committee for Drought Control in the Sahel

Ramsar Convention on Wetlands

United Nations Children's Fund (UNICEF)

United Nations Development Fund for Women (UNIFEM)

United Nations Development Program

United Nations Environment Program

United Nations World Food Program

United Nations High Commissioner for Refugees Programs

United Nations Relief and Works Agency

United Nations Voluntary Fund for the Victims of Torture

World Agroforestry Center

World Health Organization Special Programs

African Development Bank

Headquarters (temporary): Angle des Trois Rues, Avenue Du Ghana, Rue Pierre De Coubertin, Rue Hedi Nouira, BP. 323, 1002 Tunis Belvédère, Tunisia. Internet, www.afdb.org. Email, afdb@afdb.org.

President: Donald Kaberuka

The African Development Bank (AFDB) was established in 1964 and, by charter amendment, opened its membership to non-African countries in 1982. Its mandate is to contribute to the economic development and social progress of its regional members. Bank members total 77, including 53 African countries and 24 nonregional countries. With the September 1999 ratification of the agreement on the fifth general capital increase, Bank ownership is 60 percent African and 40 percent nonregional.

The African Development Fund (AFDF), the concessional lending affiliate, was established in 1973 to complement AFDB operations by providing concessional financing for high-priority development projects in the poorest African countries. The Fund's membership consists of 25 nonregional member countries, South Africa, and AFDB, which represents its African members and is allocated half of the votes.

In February 2003, security concerns resulted in AFDB headquarters temporarily relocating to Tunis, Tunisia.

Asian Development Bank

Headquarters: 6 ADB Avenue, Mandaluyong City, 1550 Metro Manila, Philippines. Phone, 632-632-4444. Fax, 632-636-2444. Internet, www.adb.org.

President: Haruhiko Kuroda

The Asian Development Bank commenced operations on December 19, 1966. It now has 67 member countries: 48 from Asia and 19 from outside the region.

The purpose of the Bank is to foster sustainable economic development, poverty alleviation, and cooperation among its developing member countries in the Asia/Pacific region.

For further information, contact the Asian Development Bank, P.O. Box 789, 0980 Manila, Philippines. Email, information@adb.org. Or contact the ADB North American Representative Office, 815 Connecticut Avenue NW., Washington, DC 20006. Phone, 202–728–1500. Email, adbnaro@adb.org.

Inter-American Defense Board

2600 Sixteenth Street NW., Washington, DC 20441. Phone, 202–939–6041. Fax, 202–387–2880. Internet, www.jid.org. Email, protocol1@jid.org.

Chairman: Rear Adm. Elis Treidler Oberg

The Inter-American Defense Board is the oldest permanently constituted, international military organization in the world. It was founded by Resolution XXXIX of the Meeting of Foreign Ministers at Rio de Janeiro in January 1942. Senior army, navy, and air force officers from 25 member nations staff the various agencies of the Board. Its three major components are the Council of Delegates, the decisionmaking body; the International Staff; the Inter-American Defense College; and the Secretariat, which provides administrative and logistical support.

The Board studies and recommends to member governments measures it feels are necessary for the safety and security of the hemisphere. It also acts as a technical military adviser for the Organization of American States and is involved in projects such as disaster preparedness and humanitarian demining programs in Central and South America.

The Inter-American Defense College, founded in 1962, prepares senior military officers and civilian functionaries for positions in their respective governments. The College's multidisciplinary program uses four annual seminars to focus on the Western Hemisphere's most pressing defense and security issues.

Inter-American Development Bank

Headquarters: 1300 New York Avenue NW., Washington, DC 20577. Phone, 202–623–1000. Internet, www.iadb.org.

President: Luis Alberto Moreno

The Inter-American Development Bank (IDB) was established in 1959 to help accelerate economic and social development in Latin America and the Caribbean. It is based in Washington, DC.

The Bank has 47 member countries, 26 of which are borrowing members in Latin America and the Caribbean.

Inter-American Investment Corporation

Headquarters: 1350 New York Avenue NW., Washington, DC 20577. Phone, 202–623–3900. Internet, www.iic.int.

Chairman of Board of Directors: Luis Alberto Moreno
General Manager: Jacques Rogozinski

The Inter-American Investment Corporation (IIC), an affiliate of the Inter-American Development Bank based in Washington, DC, began operations in 1989 to promote the economic development of its Latin American and Caribbean members by financing small- and medium-size private enterprises. IIC provides project financing in the form of direct loans and equity investments, lines of credit to local financial intermediaries, and investments in local and regional investment funds. IIC has 43 member countries, of which 27 are in the Western Hemisphere, including the United States, and 16 are outside the region.

International Bank for Reconstruction and Development

Headquarters: 1818 H Street NW., Washington, DC 20433. Phone, 202–473–1000

President: Robert Zoellick

The International Bank for Reconstruction and Development (IBRD), also known as the World Bank, officially came into existence on December 27, 1945.

The Bank's purpose is to promote economic, social, and environmental progress in developing nations by reducing poverty so that their people may live better and fuller lives. The Bank lends funds at market-determined interest rates, provides advice, and serves as a catalyst to stimulate outside investments. Its resources come primarily from funds raised in the world capital markets, its retained earnings, and repayments on its loans.

International Development Association
The International Development Association (IDA) came into existence on September 24, 1960, as an affiliate of IBRD. The Association's resources consist of subscriptions and supplementary resources in the form of general replenishments, mostly from its more industrialized and developed members; special contributions by its richer members; repayments on earlier credits; and transfers from IBRD's net earnings.

The Association promotes economic development, reduces poverty, and raises the standard of living in the least developed areas of the world. It does this by financing their developmental requirements on concessionary terms, which are more flexible and bear less heavily on the balance of payments than those of conventional loans, thereby furthering the objectives of IBRD and supplementing its activities.

International Finance Corporation

Headquarters: 2121 Pennsylvania Avenue NW., Washington, DC 20433. Phone, 202–473–3800. Internet, www.ifc.org.
President: Robert Zoellick
Executive Vice President: Lars Thunell

The International Finance Corporation (IFC), an affiliate of the World Bank, was established in July 1956 to promote productive private enterprise in developing member countries.

The Corporation pursues its objective principally through direct debt and equity investments in projects that establish new businesses or expand, modify, or diversify existing businesses. It also encourages cofinancing by other investors and lenders.

Additionally, advisory services and technical assistance are provided by IFC to developing member countries in areas such as capital market development,

privatization, corporate restructuring, and foreign investment.

International Monetary Fund

700 Nineteenth Street NW., Washington, DC 20431. Phone, 202–623–7000. Fax, 202–623–4661. Internet, www.imf.org.
Managing Director and Chairman of the Executive Board: Dominique Strauss-Kahn
First Deputy Managing Director: John Lipsky
Deputy Managing Directors: Murilo Portugal, Takatoshi Kato

The Final Act of the United Nations Monetary and Financial Conference, signed at Bretton Woods, NH, on July 22, 1944, set forth the original Articles of Agreement of the International Monetary Fund (IMF). The Agreement became effective on December 27, 1945, when the President, authorized by the Bretton Woods Agreements Act (22 U.S.C. 286), accepted membership for the United States in IMF, the Agreement having thus been accepted by countries whose combined financial commitments (quotas) equaled approximately 80 percent of IMF's original quotas. The inaugural meeting of the Board of Governors was held in March 1946, and the first meeting of the Executive Directors was held May 6, 1946.

On May 31, 1968, the Board of Governors approved an amendment to the Articles of Agreement for the establishment of a facility based on Special Drawing Rights (SDR) in IMF and for modification of certain IMF rules and practices. The amendment became effective on July 28, 1969, and the Special Drawing Account became operative on August 6, 1969. United States acceptance of the amendment and participation in the Special Drawing Account were authorized by the Special Drawing Rights Act (22 U.S.C. 286 *et seq.*).

On April 30, 1976, the Board of Governors approved a second amendment to the Articles of Agreement, which entered into force on April 1, 1978. This amendment gave members the right to adopt exchange arrangements of their choice while placing certain obligations on them regarding their exchange rate policies, over which IMF was to exercise firm surveillance. The official price of gold was abolished, and the SDR account was promoted as the principal reserve asset of the international monetary system. United States acceptance of this amendment was authorized by the Bretton Woods Agreements Act Amendments (22 U.S.C. 286e–5).

On June 28, 1990, the Board of Governors approved a third amendment to the Articles of Agreement, which became effective on November 11, 1992. Under this amendment, a member's voting rights and certain related rights may be suspended by a 70-percent majority of the executive board if the member, having been declared ineligible to use the general resources of the Fund, persists in its failure to fulfill any of its obligations under the Articles.

As of December 31, 2007, IMF had 185 member countries. Total quotas at the end of December 2007 were SDR 217.3 billion (about $343.4 billion).

The IMF promotes international monetary cooperation through a permanent forum for consultation and collaboration on international monetary problems; facilitates the expansion and balanced growth of international trade; promotes exchange rate stability; assists in the establishment of an open multilateral system of payments for current transactions among members; and gives confidence to members by making IMF resources temporarily available to them under adequate safeguards.

IMF helps its members correct imbalances in their international balances of payments. It periodically examines the economic developments and policies of its member countries, offers policy advice, and at member's request and upon executive board approval, provides financial assistance through a variety of financial facilities designed to address specific problems. These financing mechanisms provide access to the Fund's general resources to offer short-term assistance during crises of market confidence, compensatory financing to countries suffering declines in export earnings, emergency assistance for countries recovering from natural disasters or armed conflict, and low-interest rate resources to support structural adjustment and promote growth in the poorest countries. IMF also provides technical assistance and training to its members. As of December 31, 2007, IMF usable resources were SDR 165.4 billion ($261.4 billion), and 1-year forward commitment capacity was SDR 127.7 billion ($201.7 billion).

For further information, contact the Chief, Public Affairs Division, External Relations Department, International Monetary Fund, 700 Nineteenth Street NW., Washington, DC 20431. Phone, 202–623–7300. Fax, 202–623–6278. Email, publicaffairs@imf.org. Internet, www.imf.org.

International Organization for Migration

Headquarters: 17 Route des Morillons, Grand-Saconnex, Geneva. Mailing address, P.O. Box 71, CH–1211, Geneva 19, Switzerland. Phone, 011–41–22–717–9111. Fax, 011–41–22–798–6150. Internet, www.iom.int.

Director General: William Lacy Swing (United States)

Deputy Director General: Ndioro Ndiaye (Senegal)

Washington Office: Suite 700, 1752 N Street NW., Washington, DC 20036. Phone, 202–862–1826. Fax, 202–862–1879. Email, MRFWashington@iom.int.

Regional Representative: Richard Scott (United States)

New York Office: Suite 1610, 122 E. 42d Street, New York, NY 10168. Phone, 212–681–7000. Fax, 212–867–5887. Email, newyork@iom.int

Chief of Mission: Michael Gray (United States)

Permanent Observer to the United Nations: Luca Dall'Oglio (Italy)

The International Organization for Migration (IOM) was formed in 1951 as the Intergovernmental Committee for European Migration (ICEM) to help solve the postwar problems of refugees and displaced persons in Europe and to assist in orderly transatlantic migration. It adopted its current name in 1989 to reflect its progressively global outreach. Since its creation, IOM has assisted more than 12 million refugees and migrants in over 125 countries. As of April 2009, 125 governments are members of IOM, and 18 others have observer status. IOM has observer status at the United Nations.

IOM's guiding principle is that humane and orderly migration benefits migrants and societies. In carrying out its mandate, IOM helps migrants, governments, and civil society plan and operate international and national migration programs at the request of its member states and in cooperation with other international organizations. Its major objectives are the processing and movement of migrants and refugees to countries offering them permanent resettlement opportunities; the promotion of orderly migration to meet the needs of both emigration and immigration communities; counter-trafficking activities; the transfer of technology through migration in order to promote the economic, educational, and social advancement of developing countries; the provision of a forum for states and other partners to exchange views; the promotion of cooperation and coordination on migration issues; and technical cooperation and advisory services on migration policies and legislation.

Multilateral Investment Guarantee Agency

Headquarters: 1818 H Street NW., Washington, DC 20433. Phone, 202–458–9292. Internet, www.miga.org.

President: Robert Zoellick
Executive Vice President: Izumi Kobayashi

The Multilateral Investment Guarantee Agency (MIGA), an affiliate of the World Bank, was formally constituted in April 1988.

Its basic purpose is to facilitate the flow of foreign private investment for productive purposes to developing member countries by offering long-term political risk insurance in the areas of expropriation, transfer restriction, breach of contract, and war and civil disturbance; and by providing advisory and consultative services. The Agency cooperates with national investment insurance schemes, such as OPIC, and with private insurers.

Organization of American States *

Headquarters: Seventeenth Street and Constitution Avenue NW., Washington, DC 20006. Phone, 202–458–3000. Fax, 202–458–3967. Internet, www.oas.org.

Secretary General: José Miguel Insulza
Assistant Secretary General: Albert R. Ramdin

The Organization of American States (OAS) brings together the countries of the Western Hemisphere to strengthen cooperation and advance common interests. At the core of the OAS mission is a commitment to democracy. Building on this foundation, OAS works to promote good governance, strengthen human rights, foster peace and security, expand trade, and address the complex problems caused by poverty, drugs, and corruption. Through decisions made by its political bodies and programs carried out by its General Secretariat, OAS promotes greater inter-American cooperation and understanding.

OAS member states have intensified their cooperation since the end of the cold war, taking on new and important challenges. In 1994, the region's 34 democratically elected presidents and prime ministers met in Miami for the First Summit of the Americas, where they established broad political, economic, and social development goals. They have continued to meet periodically since then to examine common interests and priorities. Through the ongoing Summits of the Americas process, the region's leaders have entrusted the OAS with a growing number of responsibilities to help advance the countries' shared vision.

With four official languages—English, Spanish, Portuguese, and French—the OAS reflects the rich diversity of peoples and cultures across the Americas. The

---

*EDITORIAL NOTE: The Organization of American States did not meet the publication deadline for submitting updated information of its activities, functions, and sources of information.

OAS has 35 member states; the independent nations of North, Central and South America; and the Caribbean. Since 1962, Cuba has been barred from participation by resolution of the Eight Meeting of Ministers of Foreign Affairs. Countries from all around the world are permanent observers, closely following the issues that are critical to the Americas and often providing key financial support for OAS programs.

Member states set major policies and goals through the General Assembly, which gathers the hemisphere's foreign ministers once a year in regular session. The Permanent Council, made up of ambassadors appointed by member states, meets regularly at OAS headquarters in Washington, DC, to guide ongoing policies and actions. The chairmanship of the Permanent Council rotates every 3 months, in alphabetical order of countries. Each member state has an equal voice, and most decisions are made through consensus.

Also under the OAS umbrella are several specialized agencies that have considerable autonomy. Those agencies are the Pan American Health Organization in Washington, DC; the Inter-American Children's Institute in Montevideo, Uruguay; the Inter-American Institute for Cooperation on Agriculture in San José, Costa Rica; and the Pan American Institute of Geography and History and the Inter-American Indian Institute, both in Mexico City.

In 1948, 21 nations of the hemisphere signed the OAS Charter at the Ninth International Conference of American States. They were Argentina, Bolivia, Brazil, Chile, Colombia, Costa Rica, Cuba (barred from participation), Dominican Republic, Ecuador, El Salvador, Guatemala, Haiti, Honduras, Mexico, Nicaragua, Panama, Paraguay, Peru, United States of America, Uruguay, and Venezuela.

Subsequently, 14 other countries joined the OAS by signing and ratifying the Charter. They were Barbados, Trinidad and Tobago, Jamaica, Grenada, Suriname, Dominica, Saint Lucia, Antigua and Barbuda, Saint Vincent and the Grenadines, the Bahamas, Saint Kitts and Nevis, Canada, Belize, and Guyana.

This brings the number of member states to 35.

For further information, contact the Director, Department of Press and Communications, OAS, 1889 F Street NW., Washington, DC 20006. Phone, 202–458–3760. Fax, 202–458–6421.

United Nations

United Nations, New York, NY 10017. Phone, 212–963–1234. Internet, www.un.org.
Secretary-General: Ban Ki-moon

United Nations Office at Geneva: Palais des Nations, 1211 Geneva 10, Switzerland
Director-General: Sergei Ordzhonikidze

United Nations Office at Vienna: Vienna International Centre, P.O. Box 500, A–1400, Vienna, Austria
Director-General: Antonio Maria Costa

Washington, DC, Office: U.N. Information Centre, Suite 400, 1775 K Street NW., Washington, DC 20006. Phone, 202–331–8670. Fax, 202–331–9191. Internet, www.unicwash.org. Email, unicdc@unicwas.org
Director: Will Davis

The United Nations is an international organization that was set up in accordance with the Charter [1] drafted by governments represented at the Conference on International Organization meeting at San Francisco. The Charter was signed on June 26, 1945, and came into force on October 24, 1945, when the required number of ratifications and accessions had been made by the signatories. Amendments increasing membership of the Security Council and the Economic and Social Council came into effect on August 31, 1965.

The United Nations now consists of 191 member states, of which 51 are founding members.

The purposes of the United Nations set out in the Charter are to maintain

---

[1] Charter of the United Nations, together with the Statute of the International Court of Justice (Department of State Publication No. 2353, International Organization and Conference Series III, 21), June 26, 1945. Available for sale from the Superintendent of Documents, Government Printing Office, Washington, DC 20402. Phone, 202–512–1800.

international peace and security; to develop friendly relations among nations; to achieve international cooperation in solving international problems of an economic, social, cultural, or humanitarian character and in promoting respect for human rights; and to be a center for harmonizing the actions of nations in the attainment of these common ends.

The principal organs of the United Nations are as follows:

General Assembly   All states that are members of the United Nations are members of the General Assembly. Its functions are to consider and discuss any matter within the scope of the Charter of the United Nations and to make recommendations to the members of the United Nations and other organs. It approves the budget of the organization, the expenses of which are borne by the members as apportioned by the General Assembly.

The General Assembly may call the attention of the Security Council to situations likely to endanger international peace and security, may initiate studies, and may receive and consider reports from other organs of the United Nations. Under the "Uniting for Peace" resolution adopted by the General Assembly in November 1950, if the Security Council fails to act on an apparent threat to or breach of the peace or act of aggression because of lack of unanimity of its five permanent members, the Assembly itself may take up the matter within 24 hours—in emergency special session—and recommend collective measures, including, in case of a breach of the peace or act of aggression, use of armed force when necessary to maintain or restore international peace and security.

The General Assembly normally meets in regular annual session from September through December. It also has met in special sessions and emergency special sessions.

Security Council   The Security Council consists of 15 members, of which 5—the People's Republic of China, France, Russia, the United Kingdom, and the United States of America—are permanent members. The 10 nonpermanent members are elected for 2-year terms by the General Assembly. The primary responsibility of the Security Council is to act on behalf of the members of the United Nations in maintenance of international peace and security. Measures that may be employed by the Security Council are outlined in the Charter.

The Security Council, together with the General Assembly, also elects the judges of the International Court of Justice and makes a recommendation to the General Assembly on the appointment of the Secretary-General of the organization.

The Security Council first met in London on January 17, 1946, and is so organized as to be able to function continuously.

Economic and Social Council   This organ is responsible, under the authority of the General Assembly, for the economic and social programs of the United Nations. Its functions include making or initiating studies, reports, and recommendations on international economic, social, cultural, educational, health, and related matters; promoting respect for and observance of human rights and fundamental freedoms for all; calling international conferences and preparing draft conventions for submission to the General Assembly on matters within its competence; negotiating agreements with the specialized agencies and defining their relationship with the United Nations; coordinating the activities of the specialized agencies; and consulting with nongovernmental organizations concerned with matters within its competence. The Council consists of 54 members of the United Nations elected by the General Assembly for 3-year terms; 18 are elected each year.

The Council usually holds two regular sessions a year. It has also held a number of special sessions.

Trusteeship Council   The Trusteeship Council was initially established to consist of any member states that administered trust territories, permanent members of the Security Council that did not administer trust territories, and enough other nonadministering countries elected by the General Assembly for 3-year terms to ensure that membership would be equally divided between administering and nonadministering members. Under authority of the General Assembly, the Council considered reports from members administering trust territories, examined petitions from trust territory inhabitants, and provided for periodic inspection visits to trust territories.

With the independence of Palau, the last remaining U.N. trust territory, the Trusteeship Council formally suspended operations after nearly half a century. The council will henceforth meet only on an extraordinary basis, as the need may arise.

International Court of Justice The International Court of Justice is the principal judicial organ of the United Nations. It has its seat at The Hague, the Netherlands. All members of the United Nations are *ipso facto* parties to the Statute of the Court. Nonmembers of the United Nations may become parties to the Statute of the Court on conditions prescribed by the General Assembly on the recommendation of the Security Council.

The jurisdiction of the Court comprises all cases that the parties refer to it and all matters specially provided for in the Charter of the United Nations or in treaties and conventions in force.

The Court consists of 15 judges known as "members" of the Court. They are elected for 9-year terms by the General Assembly and the Security Council, voting independently, and may be reelected.

Secretariat The Secretariat consists of a Secretary-General and "such staff as the Organization may require." The Secretary-General, who is appointed by the General Assembly on the recommendation of the Security Council, is the chief administrative officer of the United Nations. He acts in that capacity for the General Assembly, the Security Council, the Economic and Social Council, and the Trusteeship Council. Under the Charter, the Secretary-General "may bring to the attention of the Security Council any matter that in his opinion may threaten the maintenance of international peace and security."

SELECTED BILATERAL ORGANIZATIONS

Border Environment Cooperation Commission
United States Section: P.O. Box 221648, El Paso, TX 79913. Internet, www.becc.org.
Mexican Section: Bulevar Tomás Fernádez 8069, Ciudad Juárez, Chihuahua, 32470. Phone, 011–52–656–688–4600. Fax, 011–52–915–975–8280. Internet, www.cocef.org.

Great Lakes Fishery Commission
2100 Commonwealth Boulevard, Suite 100, Ann Arbor, MI 48105. Telephone, 734–662–3209. Fax, 734–741–2010. Email, info@glfc.org. Internet, www.glfc.org.

International Boundary Commission, United States and Canada
United States Section: 2401 Pennsylvania Avenue NW., Suite 475, Washington, DC 20037. Phone, 202–736–9102. Fax, 202–254–4562. Internet, www.internationalboundary commission.org.
Canadian Section: 575–615 Booth Street, Ottawa, Ontario K1A 0E9. Phone, 613–995–2604. Fax, 613–947–1337.

International Boundary and Water Commission, United States and Mexico
United States Section: Building C, Suite 100, 4171 North Mesa Street, El Paso, TX 79902. Phone, 800–262–8857 or 915–832–4100. Fax, 915–832–4190. Internet, www.ibwc.state.gov.
Mexican Section: Avenue Universidad 2180, Zona Chamizal, Ciudad Juárez,

Chihuahua, 32310. Phone, 011–52–656–613–7311 or 011–52–656–613–7363. Fax, 011–52–656–613–9943. Internet, www.sre.gob.mx/cila.

International Joint Commission—United States and Canada
United States Section: 2401 Pennsylvania Avenue NW., 4th Floor, Washington, DC 20440. Phone, 202–736–9024. Fax, 202–254–4562. Internet, www.ijc.org.
Canadian Section: 234 Laurier Avenue West, 22d Floor, Ottawa, Ontario K1P 6K6. Phone, 613–947–1420. Fax, 613–993–5583.
Great Lakes Regional Office: 100 Ouellette Avenue, 8th Floor, Windsor, Ontario N9A 6T3. Phone, 519–257–6714. Fax, 519-257-6740.

Joint Mexican-United States Defense Commission
United States Section: 5134 Joint Staff, Room 2E773, The Pentagon, Washington, DC 20318. Phone, 703–695–8164.
Mexican Section: 6th Floor, 1911 Pennsylvania Avenue NW., Mexican Embassy, Washington, DC 20006. Phone, 202–728–1748.

Permanent Joint Board on Defense—United States and Canada
United States Section: Room 2E773, The Pentagon, Washington, DC 20318. Phone, 703–695–4477. Fax, 703–614–8945.

Canadian Section: National Defense Headquarters, 101 Colonel By Drive, Ottawa, ON K1A 0K2. Phone, 613–992–4423.

Appendices

APPENDIX A: Commonly Used Abbreviations and Acronyms

ADA   Americans with Disabilities Act of 1990

ADB   Asian Development Bank

AFDF   African Development Fund

AFDB   African Development Bank

AFIS   American Forces Information Service (Defense)

AGRICOLA   Agricultural Online Access

AHRQ   Agency for Healthcare Research and Quality

AmeriCorps*NCCC   National Civilian Community Corps

AmeriCorps*VISTA   Volunteers in Service to America

AMS   Agricultural Marketing Service

Amtrak   National Railroad Passenger Corporation

APH   American Printing House for the Blind (Education)

APHIS   Animal and Plant Health Inspection Service

ARS   Agricultural Research Service

ATF   Bureau of Alcohol, Tobacco, Firearms, and Explosives

BBG   Broadcasting Board of Governors

BEA   Bureau of Economic Analysis

BIA   Bureau of Indian Affairs

BIC   Business Information Center (SBA)

BIF   Bank Insurance Fund

BIS   Bureau of Industry and Security (Commerce)

BLM   Bureau of Land Management

BLS   Bureau of Labor Statistics

BRS   Biotechnology Regulatory Services (Agriculture)

BTA   Business Transformation Agency (Defense)

BTS   Bureau of Transportation Statistics Directorate of Border and Transportation Security (Homeland Security)

BVA   Board of Veterans' Appeals

CBO   Congressional Budget Office

CBP   Customs and Border Protection

CCC   Commodity Credit Corporation

CDBG   Community Development Block Grant

CDC   Centers for Disease Control and Prevention

CEA   Council of Economic Advisers

CEQ   Council on Environmental Quality

CFR   *Code of Federal Regulations*

CFTC   Commodity Futures Trading Commission

COPS   Office of Community Oriented Policing Services (Justice)

CRS   Congressional Research Service

CSR   Center for Scientific Review (HHS)

CSREES   Cooperative State Research, Education, and Extension Service

CSS *See* NSA/CSS

DAU Defense Acquisition University

DDESS Department of Defense Domestic Dependent Elementary and Secondary Schools

DEA Drug Enforcement Administration

DHS Department of Homeland Security

DIA Defense Intelligence Agency

DISA Defense Information Systems Agency

DLA Defense Logistics Agency

DNFSB Defense Nuclear Facilities Safety Board

DNI Director of National Intelligence

DOD Department of Defense

DODDS Department of Defense Dependent Schools

DODEA Department of Defense Education Activity

DODHRA Department of Defense Human Resources Activity

DOE Department of Energy

DOI Department of the Interior

DOL Department of Labor

DOT Department of Transportation

DPMO Defense Prisoner of War/Missing Personnel Office

DRL Bureau of Democracy, Human Rights, and Labor (State)

DSS Defense Security Service

DTIC Defense Technical Information Center

DTRA Defense Threat Reduction Agency

DTSA Defense Technology Security Administration

EBSA Employee Benefits Security Administration

EDA Economic Development Administration

EEOC Equal Employment Opportunity Commission

EO Executive order

EPA Environmental Protection Agency

EP&R Emergency Preparedness and Response Directorate

ERS Economic Research Service (Agriculture)

ESA Economics and Statistics Administration (Commerce)

Employee Standards Administration (Labor)

ETA Employment Training Administration (Labor)

EUCOM U.S. European Command

EUROPOL European Police Office

Ex-Im Bank Export-Import Bank of the United States

FAA Federal Aviation Administration

Fannie Mae Federal National Mortgage Association

Farmer Mac Federal Agricultural Mortgage Corporation

FAS Foreign Agricultural Service

Federal Acquisition Service (GSA)

FBI Federal Bureau of Investigation

FCA Farm Credit Administration

FCC Federal Communications Commission

FCIC Federal Crop Insurance Corporation

FDA Food and Drug Administration

FDIC Federal Deposit Insurance Corporation

FEB Federal Executive Boards

FEMA Federal Emergency Management Agency

FERC Federal Energy Regulatory Commission

FFB Federal Financing Bank

FHFA Federal Housing Finance Agency

FHWA Federal Highway Administration

FICO Financing Corporation

FMCS Federal Mediation and Conciliation Service

FMS Financial Management Service

FNS Food and Nutrition Service

FOIA Freedom of Information Act

FR *Federal Register*

Freddie Mac Federal Home Loan Corporation

FSA Farm Service Agency

FSIS   Food Safety and Inspection Service

FSS   Federal Supply Service

FTA   Federal Transit Administration

FTS   Federal Technology Service

GAO   Government Accountability Office

GATT   General Agreement on Tariffs and Trade

GC   Office of Government Contracting (SBA)

Ginnie Mae   Government National Mortgage Association

GIPSA   Grain Inspection, Packers, and Stockyards Administration

GNMA   Government National Mortgage Association

GPO   Government Printing Office

GPS   Global Positioning System

GSA   General Services Administration

HHS   Department of Health and Human Services

HIV/AIDS   Human Immunodeficiency Virus/Acquired Immunodeficiency Syndrome

HRSA   Health Resources and Services Administration

HUD   Department of Housing and Urban Development

IAF   Inter-American Foundation

IAIP   Information Analysis and Infrastructure Protection Directorate

IBRD   International Bank for Reconstruction and Development (World Bank)

IDA   International Development Association

IDB   Inter-American Development Bank

IFC   International Finance Corporation

IHA   Indian Housing Authority

IIC   Inter-American Investment Corporation

IMF   International Monetary Fund

IMLS   Institute of Museum and Library Services

INTERPOL   International Criminal Police Organization

IOM   International Organization for Migration

IRS   Internal Revenue Service

ISN   Bureau of International Security and Nonproliferation (State)

ISOO   Information Security Oversight Office (NARA)

IT   Information technology

ITA   International Trade Administration

JAG   Judge Advocate General

LSC   Legal Services Corporation

MBDA   Minority Business Development Agency

MDA   Missile Defense Agency

MDW   U.S. Military District of Washington

MIGA   Multilateral Investment Guarantee Agency

MSHA   Mine Safety and Health Administration

NAFTA   North American Free Trade Agreement

NAL   National Agricultural Library

NARA   National Archives and Records Administration

NASA   National Aeronautics and Space Administration

NASS   National Agricultural Statistics Service

NATO   North Atlantic Treaty Organization

NCA   National Cemetery Administration

NCCC   See AmeriCorps*NCCC

NCR   National Capital Region

NCUA   National Credit Union Administration

NEH   National Endowment for the Humanities

NESDIS   National Environmental Satellite, Data, and Information Service

NGA   National Geospatial-Intelligence Agency

NGO   Non-Governmental Organization

NHPRC   National Historical Publications and Records Commission

NHTSA	National Highway Traffic Safety Administration
NIC	National Institute of Corrections
NIH	National Institutes of Health
NIST	National Institute of Standards and Technology
NLRB	National Labor Relations Board
NMAO	NOAA Marine and Aviation Operations
NMB	National Mediation Board
NMFS	National Marine Fisheries Service (Commerce)
NNSA	National Nuclear Security Administration
NOAA	National Oceanic and Atmospheric Administration
NOS	National Ocean Service (Commerce)
NPS	National Park Service
NRC	Nuclear Regulatory Commission
NRCS	Natural Resources Conservation Service
NSA/CSS	National Security Agency/Central Security Service
NSF	National Science Foundation
NTI	National Transit Institute (Transportation)
NTIA	National Telecommunications and Information Administration
NTID	National Technical Institute for the Deaf
NTIS	National Technical Information Service (Commerce)
NTSB	National Transportation Safety Board
NWS	National Weather Service (Commerce)
OAR	Office of Oceanic and Atmospheric Research (Commerce)
OAS	Organization of American States
OBCI	Office of Business and Community Initiatives (SBA)
OBO	Bureau of Overseas Building Operations
OCB	Office of Cuba Broadcasting
OCSC	Office of Citizen Services and Communications
ODEP	Office of Disability Employment Policy (Labor)
OECA	Office of Enforcement and Compliance Assurance (EPA)
OECD	Organization for Economic Cooperation and Development
OES	Bureau of Oceans and International Environmental and Scientific Affairs (State)
OFAM	Office of Financial and Administrative Management
OFCCP	Office of Federal Contract Compliance Programs (Labor)
OFM	Office of Foreign Missions (State)
OFO	Office of Field Operations (Labor)
OGP	Office of Governmentwide Policy
OIE	World Organization for Animal Health (Office International des Epizooties)
OIG	Office of Inspector General
OIT	Office of International Trade (SBA)
OJP	Office of Justice Programs
OMB	Office of Management and Budget
OPDR	Office of Policy Development and Research (Labor)
OPE	Office of Postsecondary Education
OPIC	Overseas Private Investment Corporation
OPM	Office of Personnel Management
OPS	Office of Pipeline Safety (Transportation)
ORD	Office of Research and Development (EPA)
OSC	Office of Special Counsel

OSDBU	Office of Small and Disadvantaged Business Utilization
OSDFS	Office of Safe and Drug-Free Schools
OSERS	Office of Special Education and Rehabilitative Services
OSHA	Occupational Safety and Health Administration
OSM	Office of Surface Mining Reclamation and Enforcement
OSO	Office of Space Operations
OST	Office of the Special Trustee for American Indians (Interior)
OTP	Office of Technology Policy (Commerce)
OTS	Office of Thrift Supervision
OVBD	Office of Veterans Business Development (SBA)
OWBO	Office of Women's Business Ownership (SBA)
PBGC	Pension Benefit Guaranty Corporation
PBS	Public Buildings Service
PFPA	Pentagon Force Protection Agency
PHA	Public Housing Agency
PHMSA	Pipeline and Hazardous Materials Administration
POW/MIA	Prisoner of War/Missing in Action
PPQ	Plant Protection and Quarantine
PROTECH	Office of Performance, Results, and Training (Labor)
PUASP	Postal Union of the Americas and Spain and Portugal
RFA	Radio Free Asia
RFE/RL	Radio Free Europe/Radio Liberty
RHS	Rural Housing Service
RITA	Research and Innovative Technology Administration (Transportation)
RMA	Risk Management Agency (Agriculture)
RSVP	Retired and Senior Volunteers Program

SAIF	Savings Association Insurance Fund
SAMHSA	Substance Abuse and Mental Health Services Administration
SBA	Small Business Administration
SCORE	Service Corps of Retired Executives
SEC	Securities and Exchange Commission
SFH	Single Family Homes
SERC	Smithsonian Environmental Research Center
SES	Senior Executive Service
SITES	Smithsonian Institution Traveling Exhibit Service
SSA	Social Security Administration
S&T	Science and Technology Directorate (DHS)
Stat.	*United States Statutes at Large*
STRI	Smithsonian Tropical Research Institute
TA	Technology Administration (Commerce)
TBIC	Tribal Business Information Centers (SBA)
TDA	Trade and Development Agency
TIGTA	Treasury Inspector General for Tax Administration
TMA	TRICARE Management Activity (Defense)
TTB	Alcohol and Tobacco Tax and Trade Bureau
TVA	Tennessee Valley Authority
U.N.	United Nations [1]
UNAIDS	Joint United Nations Programme on HIV/AIDS
UNESCO	United Nations Educational, Scientific and Cultural Organization
UNHCR	United Nations High Commissioner for Refugees Program

---

[1] Acronyms for U.N. agencies can be found under *Selected Multilateral Organizations* in the preceding text.

UNICEF	United Nations Children's Fund (formerly United Nations International Children's Emergency Fund)
UNICOR	Federal Prison Industries
UNSCEAR	United Nations Scientific Committee on the Effects of Atomic Radiation
USA	United States Army
USACE	United States Army Corps of Engineers
USAF	United States Air Force
USAID	United States Agency for International Development
USAREUR	U.S. Army Europe
USARPAC	U.S. Army Pacific
U.S.C.	United States Code
USCG	United States Coast Guard
USCIS	U.S. Citizenship and Immigration Services (Homeland Security)
USDA	United States Department of Agriculture
USEAC	United States Export Assistance Centers (SBA)
USGS	United States Geological Survey
USMC	United States Marine Corps
USMS	United States Maritime Service
USN	United States Navy
USNCB	U.S. National Central Bureau (Justice)
USPTO	U.S. Patent and Trademark Office
VA	Department of Veterans Affairs
VETS	Veterans' Employment and Training Service
VISTA	See AmeriCorps*VISTA
VOA	Voice of America
WBC	Women's Business Center (SBA)
WFP	United Nations/Food and Agricultural Organization World Food Program
WHS	Washington Headquarters Services (DOD)
WIC	Special Supplemental Food Program for Women, Infants, and Children
WMD	Weapons of Mass Destruction
WNET	Women's Network for Entrepreneurial Training (SBA)
World Bank	See IBRD
WSP	Federal Witness Security Program
WTO	World Trade Organization

APPENDIX B: Federal Executive Agencies Terminated, Transferred, or Changed in Name Subsequent to March 4, 1933

NOTE: Italicized terms indicate obsolete agencies, organizations, and entities. In most instances, explanatory remarks are written at those terms elsewhere in this appendix. Dates prior to March 4, 1933, are included to provide additional information about the agencies.

This appendix is indexed in a format considered to be useful to the reader. Entries are carried at the most significant term in their titles, or when there is more than one significant term, the entry is carried at the first significant term. Thus, **Bureau of the Budget** is found at **Budget, Bureau of the,** and **Annual Assay Commission** is found at **Assay Commission, Annual.** Reader comments on the format are encouraged and should be sent to the address shown on page iv of the *Manual.*

Accounting Office, General Established by act of June 10, 1921 (42 Stat. 20). Renamed Government Accountability Office by act of July 7, 2004 (118 Stat. 814).

ACTION Established by Reorg. Plan No. 1 of 1971 (5 U.S.C. app.), effective July 1, 1971. Reorganized by act of Oct. 1, 1973 (87 Stat. 405). Functions relating to SCORE and ACT programs transferred to Small Business Administration by EO 11871 of July 18, 1975 (40 FR 30915). Functions exercised by the Director of ACTION prior to Mar. 31, 1995, transferred to the Corporation for National and Community Service (107 Stat. 888 and Proclamation 6662 of Apr. 4, 1994 (57 FR 16507)).

Acts of Congress *See* **State, Department of**

Administrative Conference of the United States Established by act of Aug. 30, 1964 (78 Stat. 615). Terminated by act of Nov. 19, 1995 (109 Stat. 480).

Advanced Research Projects Agency *See* Defense Advanced Research Projects Agency

Advisory Board. *See other part of title*

Aeronautical Board Organized in 1916 by agreement of *War* and Navy Secretaries. Placed under supervision of President by military order of July 5, 1939. Dissolved by Secretary of Defense letter of July 27, 1948, and functions transferred to *Munitions Board* and *Research and Development Board.* Military order of July 5, 1939, revoked by military order of Oct. 18, 1948.

Aeronautics, Bureau of Established in the Department of the Navy by act of July 12, 1921 (42 Stat. 140). Abolished by act of Aug. 18, 1959 (73 Stat. 395) and functions transferred to *Bureau of Naval Weapons.*

Aeronautics, National Advisory Committee for Established by act of Mar. 3, 1915 (38 Stat. 930).

Terminated by act of July 29, 1958 (72 Stat. 432), and functions transferred to National Aeronautics and Space Administration, established by same act.

Aeronautics Administration, Civil *See* **Aeronautics Authority, Civil**

Aeronautics Authority, Civil Established under act of June 23, 1938 (52 Stat. 973). Renamed *Civil Aeronautics Board* and Administrator transferred to the Department of Commerce by Reorg. Plan Nos. III and IV of 1940, effective June 30, 1940. Office of Administrator designated *Civil Aeronautics Administration* by Department Order 52 of Aug. 29, 1940. *Administration* transferred to *Federal Aviation Agency* by act of Aug. 23, 1958 (72 Stat. 810). Functions of *Board* under act of Aug. 23, 1958 (72 Stat. 775), transferred to National Transportation Safety Board by act of Oct. 15, 1966 (80 Stat. 931). Functions of *Board* terminated or transferred—effective in part Dec. 31, 1981; in part Jan. 1, 1983; and in part Jan. 1, 1985—by act of Aug. 23, 1958 (92 Stat. 1744). Most remaining functions transferred to Secretary of Transportation, remainder to U.S. Postal Service. Termination of *Board* finalized by act of Oct. 4, 1984 (98 Stat. 1703).

Aeronautics Board, Civil *See* **Aeronautics Authority, Civil**

Aeronautics Branch Established in the Department of Commerce to carry out provisions of act of May 20, 1926 (44 Stat. 568). Renamed *Bureau of Air Commerce* by Secretary's administrative order of July 1, 1934. Personnel and property transferred to *Civil Aeronautics Authority* by EO 7959 of Aug. 22, 1938.

Aeronautics and Space Council, National Established by act of July 29, 1958 (72 Stat. 427). Abolished by Reorg. Plan No. 1 of 1973, effective June 30, 1973.

Aging, Administration on Established by *Secretary of Health, Education, and Welfare* on Oct. 1, 1965, to carry out provisions of act of July 14, 1965 (79 Stat. 218). Reassigned to *Social and Rehabilitation Service* by Department reorganization of Aug. 15, 1967. Transferred to Office of Assistant Secretary for Human Development by Secretary's order of June 15, 1973. Transferred to the Office of the Secretary of Health and Human Services by Secretary's reorganization notice dated Apr. 15, 1991.

Aging, Federal Council on Established by Presidential memorandum of Apr. 2, 1956. Reconstituted at Federal level by Presidential letter of Mar. 7, 1959, to *Secretary of Health, Education, and Welfare.* Abolished by EO 11022 of May 15, 1962, which established *President's Council on Aging.*

Aging, Office of Established by *Secretary of Health, Education, and Welfare* June 2, 1955, as *Special Staff on Aging.* Terminated Sept. 30, 1965, and functions assumed by Administration on Aging.

Aging, President's Council on Established by EO 11022 of May 14, 1962. Terminated by EO 11022, which was revoked by EO 12379 of Aug. 17, 1982.

Agricultural Adjustment Administration Established by act of May 12, 1933 (48 Stat. 31). Consolidated into *Agricultural Conservation and Adjustment Administration* as *Agricultural Adjustment Agency,* Department of Agriculture, by EO 9069 of Feb. 23, 1942. Grouped with other agencies to form *Food Production Administration* by EO 9280 of Dec. 5, 1942. Transferred to *War Food Administration* by EO 9322 of Mar. 26, 1943. Administration terminated by EO 9577 of June 29, 1945, and functions transferred to Secretary of Agriculture. Transfer made permanent by Reorg. Plan No. 3 of 1946, effective July 16, 1946. Functions of *Agricultural Adjustment Agency* consolidated with *Production and Marketing Administration* by Secretary's Memorandum 1118 of Aug. 18, 1945.

Agricultural Adjustment Agency *See* **Agricultural Adjustment Administration**

Agricultural Advisory Commission, National Established by EO 10472 of July 20, 1953. Terminated Feb. 4, 1965, on resignation of members.

Agricultural Chemistry and Engineering, Bureau of *See* **Agricultural Engineering, Bureau of**

Agricultural Conservation and Adjustment Administration Established by EO 9069 of Feb. 23, 1942, consolidating *Agricultural Adjustment Agency, Sugar Agency, Federal Crop Insurance Corporation,* and *Soil Conservation Service.* Consolidated into *Food Production Administration* by EO 9280 of Dec. 5, 1942.

Agricultural Conservation Program Service Established by Secretary of Agriculture Jan. 21, 1953, from part of *Production and Marketing Administration.* Merged with *Commodity Stabilization Service* by Secretary's Memorandum 1446, supp. 2, of Apr. 19, 1961.

Agricultural Developmental Service, International Established by Secretary of Agriculture memorandum of July 12, 1963. Functions and delegations of authority transferred to Foreign Agricultural Service by Secretary's memorandum of Mar. 28, 1969. Functions transferred by Secretary to *Foreign Economic Development Service* Nov. 8, 1969.

Agricultural Economics, Bureau of Established by act of May 11, 1931 (42 Stat. 532). Functions transferred to other units of the Department of Agriculture, including *Consumer and Marketing Service* and Agricultural Research Service, under Secretary's Memorandum 1320, supp. 4, of Nov. 2, 1953.

Agricultural Engineering, Bureau of Established by act of Feb. 23, 1931 (46 Stat. 1266). Merged with *Bureau of Chemistry and Soils* by Secretarial order of Oct. 16, 1938, to form *Bureau of Agricultural Chemistry and Engineering.*

Agricultural and Industrial Chemistry, Bureau of *Bureau of Chemistry* and *Bureau of Soils,* created in 1901, combined into *Bureau of Chemistry and Soils* by act of Jan. 18, 1927 (44 Stat. 976). Soils units transferred to other agencies of the Department of Agriculture and remaining units of *Bureau of Chemistry and Soils* and *Bureau of Agricultural Engineering* consolidated with *Bureau of Agricultural Chemistry and Engineering* by Secretary's order of Oct. 16, 1938. In February 1943 agricultural engineering research made part of *Bureau of Plant Industry, Soils, and Agricultural Engineering,* and organization for continuing agricultural chemistry research relating to crop utilization named *Bureau of Agricultural and Industrial Chemistry,* in accordance with *Research Administration* Memorandum 5 issued pursuant to EO 9069 of Feb. 23, 1942, and in conformity with Secretary's Memorandums 960 and 986. Functions transferred to *Agricultural Research Service* under Secretary's Memorandum 1320, supp. 4, of Nov. 2, 1953.

Agricultural Library, National Established by Secretary of Agriculture Memorandum 1496 of Mar. 23, 1962. Consolidated into *Science and Education Administration* by Secretary's order of Jan. 24, 1978. Reestablished as National Agricultural Library by Secretary's order of June 16, 1981. Became part of Agricultural Research Service in 1994 under Department of Agriculture reorganization.

Agricultural Marketing Administration Established by EO 9069 of Feb. 23, 1942, consolidating *Surplus Marketing Administration, Agricultural Marketing Service,* and *Commodity Exchange Administration. Division of Consumers' Counsel* transferred to *Administration* by Secretary's memorandum of Feb. 28, 1942. Consolidated into *Food Distribution Administration* in the Department of Agriculture by EO 9280 of Dec. 5, 1942.

Agricultural Marketing Service Established by the Secretary of Agriculture pursuant to act of June 30, 1939 (53 Stat. 939). Merged into *Agricultural Marketing Administration* by EO 9069 of Feb. 23, 1942. Renamed *Consumer and Marketing Service* by Secretary's Memorandum 1567, supp. 1, of Feb. 8, 1965. Reestablished as Agricultural Marketing Service by the Secretary of Agriculture on Apr. 2,

1972, under authority of Reorg. Plan No. 2 of 1953 (67 Stat. 633).

Agricultural Relations, Office of Foreign *See* **Agricultural Service, Foreign**

Agricultural Research Administration Established by EO 9069 of Feb. 23, 1942. Superseded by Agricultural Research Service.

Agricultural Research Service Established by Secretary of Agriculture Memorandum 1320, supp. 4, of Nov. 2, 1953. Consolidated into *Science and Education Administration* by Secretary's order of Jan. 24, 1978. Reestablished as Agricultural Research Service by Secretarial order of June 16, 1981.

Agricultural Service, Foreign Established by act of June 5, 1930 (46 Stat. 497). Economic research and agricultural attaché activities administered by *Foreign Agricultural Service Division, Bureau of Agricultural Economics,* until June 29, 1939. Transferred by Reorg. Plan No. II of 1939, effective July 1, 1939, from the Department of Agriculture to the Department of State. Economic research functions of *Division* transferred to *Office of Foreign Agricultural Relations* June 30, 1939. Functions of *Office* transferred to Foreign Agricultural Service Mar. 10, 1953. Agricultural attachés placed in the Department of Agriculture by act of Aug. 28, 1954 (68 Stat. 908).

Agricultural Stabilization and Conservation Service Established June 5, 1961, by the Secretary of Agriculture under authority of revised statutes (5 U.S.C. 301) and Reorg. Plan No. 2 of 1953 (5 U.S.C. app.). Abolished and functions assumed by the *Farm Service Agency* by Secretary's Memorandum 1010–1 dated Oct. 20, 1994 (59 FR 60297, 60299).

Agricultural Statistics Division Transferred to *Bureau of Agricultural Economics* by EO 9069 of Feb. 23, 1942.

Agriculture, Division of *See* **Farm Products, Division of**

Air Commerce, Bureau of *See* **Aeronautics Branch**

Air Coordinating Committee Established Mar. 27, 1945, by interdepartmental memorandum; formally established by EO 9781 of Sept. 19, 1946. Terminated by EO 10883 of Aug. 11, 1960, and functions transferred for liquidation to *Federal Aviation Agency.*

Air Force Management Engineering Agency Established in 1975 in Air Force as separate operating unit. Made subordinate unit of Air Force Military Personnel Center (formerly Air Force Manpower and Personnel Center) in 1978. Reestablished as separate operating unit of Air Force, effective Mar. 1, 1985, by Secretarial order.

Air Force Manpower and Personnel Center Certain functions transferred on activation of Air Force Management Engineering Agency, which was made separate operating unit from Air Force Manpower and Personnel Center (later Air Force Military Personnel Center) in April 1985 by general order of Chief of Staff.

Air Force Medical Service Center Renamed Air Force Office of Medical Support by Program Action Directive 85–1 of Mar. 6, 1985, approved by Air Force Vice Chief of Staff.

Air Mail, Bureau of Established in Interstate Commerce Commission to carry out provisions of act of June 12, 1934 (48 Stat. 933). Personnel and property transferred to *Civil Aeronautics Authority* by EO 7959 of Aug. 22, 1938.

Air Patrol, Civil Established in *Civilian Defense Office* by Administrative Order 9 of Dec. 8, 1941. Transferred to *Department of War* as auxiliary of Army Air Forces by EO 9339 of Apr. 29, 1943. Transferred to the Department of the Air Force by Secretary of Defense order of May 21, 1948. Established as civilian auxiliary of U.S. Air Force by act of May 26, 1948 (62 Stat. 274).

Air Safety Board Established by act of June 23, 1938 (52 Stat. 973). Functions transferred to *Civil Aeronautics Board* by Reorg. Plan No. IV of 1940, effective June 30, 1940.

Airways Modernization Board Established by act of Aug. 14, 1957 (71 Stat. 349). Transferred to *Federal Aviation Agency* by EO 10786 of Nov. 1, 1958.

Alaska, Board of Road Commissioners for Established in *Department of War* by act of Jan. 27, 1905 (33 Stat. 616). Functions transferred to the Department of Interior by act of June 30, 1932 (47 Stat. 446), and delegated to *Alaska Road Commission.* Functions transferred to the Department of Commerce by act of June 29, 1956 (70 Stat. 377), and terminated by act of June 25, 1959 (73 Stat. 145).

Alaska, Federal Field Committee for Development Planning in Established by EO 11182 of Oct. 2, 1964. Abolished by EO 11608 of July 19, 1971.

Alaska, Federal Reconstruction and Development Planning Commission for Established by EO 11150 of Apr. 2, 1964. Abolished by EO 11182 of Oct. 2, 1964, which established *President's Review Committee for Development Planning in Alaska* and *Federal Field Committee for Development Planning in Alaska.*

Alaska, President's Review Committee for Development Planning in Established by EO 11182 of Oct. 2, 1964. Superseded by *Federal Advisory Council on Regional Economic Development* established by EO 11386 of Dec. 28, 1967. EO 11386 revoked by EO 12553 of Feb. 25, 1986.

Alaska Communication System Operational responsibility vested in Secretary of the Army by act of May 26, 1900 (31 Stat. 206). Transferred to Secretary of the Air Force by Secretary of Defense reorganization order of May 24, 1962.

Alaska Engineering Commission *See* **Alaska Railroad**

Alaska Game Commission Established by act of Jan. 13, 1925 (43 Stat. 740). Expired Dec. 31, 1959, pursuant to act of July 7, 1958 (72 Stat. 339).

Alaska International Rail and Highway Commission
Established by act of Aug. 1, 1956 (70 Stat. 888).
Terminated June 30, 1961, under terms of act.

**Alaska Natural Gas Transportation System, Office
of Federal Inspector of Construction for the**
Established by Reorg. Plan No. 1 of 1979 (5 U.S.C.
app.), effective July 1, 1979. Abolished by act of
Oct. 24, 1992 (106 Stat. 3128) and functions and
authority vested in the Inspector transferred to the
Secretary of Energy. Functions vested in the
Secretary of Energy transferred to the Federal
Coordinator, Office of the Federal Coordinator for
Alaska Natural Gas Transportation Projects by act of
Oct. 13, 2004 (118 Stat. 1261).

Alaska Power Administration Established by the
Secretary of the Interior in 1967. Transferred to the
Department of Energy by act of Aug. 4, 1977 (91
Stat. 578).

Alaska Railroad Built pursuant to act of Mar. 12,
1914 (38 Stat. 305), which created *Alaska
Engineering Commission.* Placed under the Secretary
of the Interior by EO 2129 of Jan. 26, 1915, and
renamed Alaska Railroad by EO 3861 of June 8,
1923. Authority to regulate tariffs granted to
Interstate Commerce Commission by EO 11107 of
Apr. 25, 1963. Authority to operate Railroad
transferred to the Secretary of Transportation by act
of Oct. 15, 1966 (80 Stat. 941), effective Apr. 1,
1967. Railroad purchased by State of Alaska,
effective Jan. 5, 1985.

Alaska Road Commission *See* **Alaska, Board of
Road Commissioners for**

Alcohol, Bureau of Industrial Established by act of
May 27, 1930 (46 Stat. 427). Consolidated into
Bureau of Internal Revenue by EO 6166 of June 10,
1933. Consolidation deferred until May 11, 1934, by
EO 6639 of Mar. 10, 1934. Order also transferred to
Internal Revenue Commissioner certain functions
imposed on Attorney General by act of May 27,
1930, with relation to enforcement of criminal laws
concerning intoxicating liquors remaining in effect
after repeal of 18th amendment; personnel of, and
appropriations for, *Bureau of Industrial Alcohol;* and
necessary personnel and appropriations of *Bureau of
Prohibition,* Department of Justice.

**Alcohol, Drug Abuse, and Mental Health
Administration** Established by the *Secretary of
Health, Education, and Welfare* by act of May 21,
1972 (88 Stat. 134). Redesignated as an agency of
the Public Health Service from the *National Institute
of Mental Health* Sept. 25, 1973, by the Secretary of
Health, Education, and Welfare. Functions
transferred to the Department of Health and Human
Services by act of Oct. 17, 1979 (93 Stat. 695).
Established as an agency of the Public Health
Service by act of Oct. 27, 1986 (100 Stat. 3207–
106). Renamed Substance Abuse and Mental Health
Services Administration by act of July 10, 1992 (106
Stat. 325).

**Alcohol Abuse and Alcoholism, National Institute
on** Established within the National Institute of
Mental Health, *Department of Health, Education,
and Welfare* by act of Dec. 31, 1970 (84 Stat. 1848).
Removed from within the National Institute of

Mental Health and made an entity within the
Alcohol, Drug Abuse, and Mental Health
Administration by act of May 14, 1974 (88 Stat.
1356). Functions transferred to the Department of
Health and Human Services by act of Oct. 17, 1979
(93 Stat. 695). (*See also* act of Oct. 27, 1986; 100
Stat. 3207–106.) Abolished by act of July 10, 1992
(106 Stat. 331). Reestablished by act of July 10,
1992 (106 Stat. 359).

Alcohol Administration, Federal *See* **Alcohol
Control Administration, Federal**

Alcohol Control Administration, Federal
Established by EO 6474 of Dec. 4, 1933. Abolished
Sept. 24, 1935, on induction into office of
Administrator, *Federal Alcohol Administration,* as
provided in act of Aug. 29, 1935 (49 Stat. 977).
Abolished by Reorg. Plan No. III of 1940, effective
June 30, 1940, and functions consolidated with
activities of Internal Revenue Service.

Alcohol, Tobacco, and Firearms, Bureau of
Established within Treasury Department by Treasury
Order No. 221, eff. July 1, 1972. Transferred to
Bureau of Alcohol, Tobacco, Firearms, and
Explosives in Justice Department by act of Nov. 25,
2002, except some authorities, functions, personnel,
and assets relating to administration and
enforcement of certain provisions of the Internal
Revenue Code of 1986 and title 27 of the U.S. Code
(116 Stat. 2275).

Alexander Hamilton Bicentennial Commission
Established by act of Aug. 20, 1954 (68 Stat. 746).
Terminated Apr. 30, 1958.

Alien Property Custodian Appointed by President
Oct. 22, 1917, under authority of act of Oct. 6,
1917 (40 Stat. 415). Office transferred to *Alien
Property Division,* Department of Justice, by EO
6694 of May 1, 1934. Powers vested in President by
act delegated to Attorney General by EO 8136 of
May 15, 1939. Authority vested in Attorney General
by EO's 6694 and 8136 transferred by EO 9142 of
Apr. 21, 1942, to *Office of Alien Property
Custodian, Office for Emergency Management,* as
provided for by EO 9095 of Mar. 11, 1942.

American Forces Information Service Established
by Secretary of Defense Directive 5122.10 of March
13, 1989. Dissolved by Secretary's Directive
5105.74 of Dec. 18, 2007 and functions transferred
to Defense Media Activity effective Oct. 1, 2008.

**American Republics, Office for Coordination of
Commercial and Cultural Relations between the**
Established by *Council of National Defense* order
approved by President Aug. 16, 1940. Succeeded by
*Office of the Coordinator of Inter-American Affairs,
Office for Emergency Management,* established by
EO 8840 of July 30, 1941. Renamed *Office of Inter-
American Affairs* by EO 9532 of Mar. 23, 1945.
Information functions transferred to the Department
of State by EO 9608 of Aug. 31, 1945. Terminated
by EO 9710 of Apr. 10, 1946, and functions
transferred to the Department of State, functioning as
Institute of Inter-American Affairs. Transferred to
Foreign Operations Administration by Reorg. Plan
No. 7, effective Aug. 1, 1953.

American Revolution Bicentennial Administration
See **American Revolution Bicentennial Commission**

American Revolution Bicentennial Commission
Established by act of July 4, 1966 (80 Stat. 259).
American Revolution Bicentennial Administration
established by act of Dec. 11, 1973 (87 Stat. 697),
to replace *Commission. Administration* terminated
June 30, 1977, pursuant to terms of act. Certain
continuing functions transferred to the Secretary of
the Interior by EO 12001 of June 29, 1977.

Anacostia Neighborhood Museum   Renamed
Anacostia Museum by Smithsonian Institution
announcement of Apr. 3, 1987.

Animal Industry, Bureau of   Established in the
Department of Agriculture by act of May 29, 1884
(23 Stat. 31). Functions transferred to Agricultural
Research Service by Secretary's Memorandum 1320,
supp. 4, of Nov. 2, 1953.

Apprenticeship, Federal Committee on   Previously
known as *Federal Committee on Apprentice
Training,* established by EO 6750–C of June 27,
1934. Functioned as part of *Division of Labor
Standards,* Department of Labor, pursuant to act of
Aug. 16, 1937 (50 Stat. 664). Transferred to *Office
of Administrator, Federal Security Agency,* by EO
9139 of Apr. 18, 1942. Transferred to *Bureau of
Training, War Manpower Commission,* by EO 9247
of Sept. 17, 1942. Returned to the Department of
Labor by EO 9617 of Sept. 19, 1945.

Archive of Folksong   Renamed Archive of Folk
Culture by administrative order of Deputy Librarian
of Congress, effective Sept. 21, 1981.

Archives Council, National   Established by act of
June 19, 1934 (48 Stat. 1122). Transferred to
General Services Administration by act of June 30,
1949 (63 Stat. 378). Terminated on establishment of
Federal Records Council by act of Sept. 5, 1950 (64
Stat. 583).

Archives Establishment, National   *Office of
Archivist of the U.S.* and *National Archives* created
by act of June 19, 1934 (48 Stat. 1122). Transferred
to General Services Administration by act of June
30, 1949 (63 Stat. 381), and incorporated as
National Archives and Records Service by order of
General Services Administrator, together with
functions of *Division of the Federal Register,
National Archives Council, National Historical
Publications Commission,* National Archives Trust
Fund Board, *Trustees of the Franklin D. Roosevelt
Library,* and Administrative Committee of the Federal
Register. Transferred from General Services
Administration to National Archives and Records
Administration by act of Oct. 19, 1984 (98 Stat.
2283), along with certain functions of Administrator
of General Services transferred to Archivist of the
United States, effective Apr. 1, 1985.

Archives and Records Service, National   *See*
Archives Establishment, National

Archives Trust Fund Board, National   *See* **Archives
Establishment, National**

Area Redevelopment Administration   Established
May 8, 1961, by the Secretary of Commerce

pursuant to act of May 1, 1961 (75 Stat. 47) and
Reorg. Plan No. 5 of 1950, effective May 24, 1950.
Terminated Aug. 31, 1965, by act of June 30, 1965
(79 Stat. 195). Functions transferred to Economic
Development Administration in the Department of
Commerce by Department Order 4–A, effective Sept.
1, 1965.

Arlington Memorial Amphitheater Commission
Established by act of Mar. 4, 1921 (41 Stat. 1440).
Abolished by act of Sept. 2, 1960 (74 Stat. 739), and
functions transferred to the Secretary of Defense.

Arlington Memorial Bridge Commission
Established by act of Mar. 4, 1913 (37 Stat. 885;
D.C. Code (1951 ed.) 8–158). Abolished by EO
6166 of June 10, 1933, and functions transferred to
*Office of National Parks, Buildings, and
Reservations.*

Armed Forces, U.S. Court of Appeals for the   *See*
Military Appeals, United States Court of

Armed Forces Medical Library   Founded in 1836 as
Library of the Surgeon General's Office, U.S. Army.
Later known as *Army Medical Library,* then *Armed
Forces Medical Library* in 1952. Personnel and
property transferred to National Library of Medicine
established in Public Health Service by act of Aug.
3, 1956 (70 Stat. 960).

Armed Forces Museum Advisory Board, National
Established by act of Aug. 30, 1961 (75 Stat. 414).
Functions discontinued due to lack of funding.

Armed Forces Staff College   Renamed Joint Forces
Staff College by act of Oct. 30, 2000 (144 Stat.
165A–230).

Armed Services Renegotiation Board   Established
by Secretary of Defense directive of July 19, 1948.
Abolished by Secretary's letter of Jan. 18, 1952, and
functions transferred to *Renegotiation Board.*

Arms Control and Disarmament Agency, U.S.
Established by act of Sept. 26, 1961 (75 Stat. 631).
Abolished by act of Oct. 21, 1998 (112 Stat. 2681–
767) and functions transferred to the Secretary of
State.

Army Communications Command, U.S.   Renamed
U.S. Army Information Systems Command by
Department General Order No. 26 of July 25, 1984.

**Army Materiel Development and Readiness
Command, U.S.**   Renamed U.S. Army Materiel
Command by Department General Order No. 28 of
Aug. 15, 1984.

Army and Navy, Joint Board   Placed under
direction of President by military order of July 5,
1939. Abolished Sept. 1, 1947, by joint letter of
Aug. 20, 1947, to President from Secretaries of *War*
and Navy.

Army and Navy Staff College   Established Apr. 23,
1943, and operated under Joint Chiefs of Staff.
Redesignated the National War College, effective
July 1, 1946.

Army Specialist Corps   Established in *Department
of War* by EO 9078 of Feb. 26, 1942. Abolished by

the *Secretary of War* Oct. 31, 1942, and functions merged into central *Officer Procurement Service.*

Arts, National Collection of Fine   Established within Smithsonian Institution by act of Mar. 24, 1937 (50 Stat. 51). Renamed *National Museum of American Art* in Smithsonian Institution by act of Oct. 13, 1980 (94 Stat. 1884).

Arthritis, Diabetes, and Digestive and Kidney Diseases, National Institute of   See **Arthritis, Metabolism, and Digestive Diseases, National Institute of**

Arthritis, Metabolism, and Digestive Diseases, National Institute of   Renamed *National Institute of Arthritis, Diabetes, and Digestive and Kidney Diseases* by Secretary's order of June 15, 1981, pursuant to act of Dec. 19, 1980 (94 Stat. 3184). Renamed National Institute of Diabetes and Digestive and Kidney Diseases and National Institute of Arthritis and Musculoskeletal and Skin Diseases by act of Nov. 20, 1985 (99 Stat. 820).

Arts, Advisory Committee on the   Established under authority of act of Sept. 20, 1961 (75 Stat. 527). Terminated July 1973 by act of Oct. 6, 1972. Formally abolished by Reorg. Plan No. 2 of 1977, effective Apr. 1, 1978.

Arts, National Council on the   Established in Executive Office of the President by act of Sept. 3, 1964 (78 Stat. 905). Transferred to National Foundation on the Arts and the Humanities by act of Sept. 29, 1965 (79 Stat. 845).

Assay Commission, Annual   Established initially by act of Apr. 2, 1792 (1 Stat. 250) and by act of Feb. 12, 1873 (Revised Statute sec. 3647; 17 Stat. 432). Terminated and functions transferred to the Secretary of the Treasury by act of Mar. 14, 1980 (94 Stat. 98).

Assistance, Bureau of Public   Renamed *Bureau of Family Services* by order of the *Secretary of Health, Education, and Welfare,* effective Jan. 1, 1962. Functions redelegated to *Social and Rehabilitation Service* by Secretary's reorganization of Aug. 15, 1967.

Assistance Coordinating Committee, Adjustment   Established by act of Jan. 3, 1975 (88 Stat. 2040). Inactive since 1981.

Assistance Payments Administration   Established by *Secretary of Health, Education, and Welfare* reorganization of Aug. 15, 1967. Transferred by *Secretary's* reorganization of Mar. 8, 1977 (42 FR 13262), from *Social and Rehabilitation Service* to Social Security Administration.

Athletics, Interagency Committee on International   Established by EO 11117 of Aug. 13, 1963. Terminated by EO 11515 of Mar. 13, 1970.

Atlantic-Pacific Interoceanic Canal Study Commission   Established by act of Sept. 22, 1964 (78 Stat. 990). Terminated Dec. 1, 1970, pursuant to terms of act.

Atomic Energy Commission   Established by act of Aug. 1, 1946 (60 Stat. 755). Abolished by act of Oct. 11, 1974 (88 Stat. 1237) and functions

transferred to *Energy Research and Development Administration* and Nuclear Regulatory Commission.

Aviation, Interdepartmental Committee on Civil International   Established by Presidential letter of June 20, 1935. Terminated on organization of *Civil Aeronautics Authority.*

Aviation Agency, Federal   Established by act of Aug. 23, 1958 (72 Stat. 731). Transferred to Secretary of Transportation by act of Oct. 15, 1966 (80 Stat. 931). *Agency* reestablished as Federal Aviation Administration by act of Jan 12, 1983 (96 Stat. 2416).

Aviation Commission, Federal   Established by act of June 12, 1934 (48 Stat. 938). Terminated Feb. 1, 1935, under provisions of act.

Beltsville Research Center   Established to operate with other agencies of the Department of Agriculture under *Agricultural Research Administration.* Consolidated into *Agricultural Research Administration,* the Department of Agriculture, by EO 9069 of Feb. 23, 1942.

Bilingual Education and Minority Languages Affairs, Office of   Renamed Office of English Language Acquisition, Language Enhancement, and Academic Achievement for Limited English Proficient Students by act of Jan. 8, 2002 (115 Stat. 2089).

Biobased Products and Bioenergy, Advisory Committee on   Established by EO 13134 of June 3, 1999. Abolished by EO 13423 of Jan. 24, 2007.

Biobased Products and Bioenergy, Interagency Council on   Established by EO 13134 of June 3, 1999. Abolished by EO 13423 of Jan. 24, 2007.

Biobased Products and Bioenergy Coordination Office, National   Established by EO 13134 of June 3, 1999. Abolished by EO 13423 of Jan. 24, 2007.

Biological Service, National   Established in the Department of the Interior in 1995 by Secretarial order. Transferred to U.S. Geological Survey as new Biological Resources Division by Secretarial Order No. 3202, Sept. 30, 1996.

Biological Survey, Bureau of   Established by Secretary's order July 1, 1885, as part of *Division of Entomology,* Department of Agriculture. Made separate bureau by act of Apr. 23, 1904 (33 Stat. 276). Transferred to the Department of the Interior by Reorg. Plan No. II of 1939, effective July 1, 1939. Consolidated with *Bureau of Fisheries* into *Fish and Wildlife Service* by Reorg. Plan No. III of 1940, effective June 30, 1940.

Biological Survey, National   Established in the the Department of the Interior by Secretarial Order 3173 of Sept. 29, 1993. Renamed *National Biological Service* by Secretarial order in 1995.

Blind, Inc., American Printing House for the   Established in 1858 as privately owned institution in Louisville, KY. Functions of the Secretary of the Treasury, except that relating to perpetual trust funds, transferred to *Federal Security Agency* by Reorg. Plan No. II of 1939, effective July 1, 1939. Functions performed by *Department of Health,*

Education, and Welfare transferred to the Department of Education.

Blind-made Products, Committee on Purchases of Established by act of June 25, 1938 (52 Stat. 1196). Renamed *Committee for Purchase of Products and Services of the Blind and Other Severely Handicapped* by act of June 23, 1971 (85 Stat. 77). Renamed *Committee for Purchase from the Blind and Other Severely Handicapped* by act of July 25, 1974 (88 Stat. 392). Renamed Committee for Purchase From People Who Are Blind or Severely Disabled by act of Oct. 29, 1992 (106 Stat. 4486).

Blind and Other Severely Handicapped, Committee for Purchase of Products and Services of the *See* **Blind-made Products, Committee on Purchases of**

Board. *See other part of title*

Bond and Spirits Division Established as *Taxes and Penalties Unit,* as announced by Assistant to Attorney General in departmental circular of May 25, 1934, pursuant to EO 6639 of May 10, 1934. Abolished by administrative order of October 1942, and functions transferred to Tax, Claims, and Criminal Divisions, Department of Justice.

Bonneville Power Administration Established by the Secretary of the Interior pursuant to act of Aug. 20, 1937 (50 Stat. 731). Transferred to the Department of Energy by act of Aug. 4, 1977 (91 Stat. 578).

Boston National Historic Sites Commission Established by joint resolution of June 16, 1955 (69 Stat. 137). Terminated June 16, 1960, by act of Feb. 19, 1957 (71 Stat. 4).

Brazil-U.S. Defense Commission, Joint Established in May 1942 by agreement between the U.S. and Brazil. Terminated in September 1977 at direction of Brazilian Government.

Broadcast Bureau Merged with *Cable Television Bureau* to form Mass Media Bureau by Federal Communications Commission order, effective Nov. 30, 1982.

Broadcast Intelligence Service, Foreign *See* **Broadcast Monitoring Service, Foreign**

Broadcast Monitoring Service, Foreign Established in Federal Communications Commission by Presidential directive of Feb. 26, 1941. Renamed *Foreign Broadcast Intelligence Service* by FCC order of July 28, 1942. Transferred to *Department of War* by Secretarial order of Dec. 30, 1945. Act of May 3, 1945 (59 Stat. 110), provided for liquidation 60 days after Japanese armistice. Transferred to *Central Intelligence Group* Aug. 5, 1946, and renamed *Foreign Broadcast Information Service.*

Budget, Bureau of the Established by act of June 10, 1921 (42 Stat. 20), in the Department of the Treasury under immediate direction of President. Transferred to Executive Office of the President by Reorg. Plan No. I of 1939, effective July 1, 1939. Reorganized by Reorg. Plan No. 2 of 1970, effective July 1, 1970, and renamed Office of Management and Budget.

Buildings Administration, Public Established as part of *Federal Works Agency* by Reorg. Plan No. I of 1939, effective July 1, 1939. Abolished by act of June 30, 1949 (63 Stat. 380), and functions transferred to General Services Administration.

Buildings Branch, Public Organized in *Procurement Division,* established in the Department of the Treasury by EO 6166 of June 10, 1933. Consolidated with *Branch of Buildings Management,* National Park Service, to form *Public Buildings Administration, Federal Works Agency,* under Reorg. Plan No. I of 1939, effective July 1, 1939.

Buildings Commission, Public Established by act of July 1, 1916 (39 Stat. 328). Abolished by EO 6166 of June 10, 1933, and functions transferred to *Office of National Parks, Buildings, and Reservations,* Department of the Interior. Functions transferred to *Public Buildings Administration, Federal Works Agency,* under Reorg. Plan No. I of 1939, effective July 1, 1939.

Buildings Management, Branch of Functions of National Park Service (except those relating to monuments and memorials) consolidated with *Public Buildings Branch, Procurement Division,* Department of the Treasury, to form *Public Buildings Administration, Federal Works Agency,* in accordance with Reorg. Plan No. I of 1939, effective July 1, 1939.

Buildings and Public Parks of the National Capital, Office of Public Established by act of Feb. 26, 1925 (43 Stat. 983), by consolidation of *Office of Public Buildings and Grounds* under Chief of Engineers, U.S. Army, and *Office of Superintendent of State, War, and Navy Department Buildings.* Abolished by EO 6166 of June 10, 1933, and functions transferred to *Office of National Parks, Buildings, and Reservations,* Department of the Interior.

Bureau. *See other part of title*

Business, Cabinet Committee on Small Established by Presidential letter of May 31, 1956. Dissolved January 1961.

Business Administration, Domestic and International *See* **Business and Defense Services Administration**

Business and Defense Services Administration Established by the Secretary of Commerce Oct. 1, 1953, and operated under Department Organization Order 40–1. Abolished by Department Organization Order 40–1A of Sept. 15, 1970, and functions transferred to *Bureau of Domestic Commerce.* Functions transferred to *Domestic and International Business Administration,* effective Nov. 17, 1972. *Administration* terminated by Secretary's order of Dec. 4, 1977, and functions assumed by *Industry and Trade Administration.*

Business Economics, Office of Established by the Secretary of Commerce Jan. 17, 1946. Renamed *Office of Economic Analysis* Dec. 1, 1953. Transferred to the *Administration of Social and Economic Statistics* along with Bureau of the Census and renamed Bureau of Economic Analysis on Jan. 1, 1972.

Business Operations, Bureau of International Established by the Secretary of Commerce Aug. 8, 1961, by Departmental Orders 173 and 174. Abolished by Departmental Order 182 of Feb. 1, 1963, which established *Bureau of International Commerce.* Functions transferred to *Domestic and International Business Administration,* effective Nov. 17, 1972.

Cable Television Bureau Merged with *Broadcast Bureau* by Federal Communications Commission order to form Mass Media Bureau, effective Nov. 30, 1982.

California Debris Commission Established by act of Mar. 1, 1893 (27 Stat. 507). Abolished by act of Nov. 17, 1986 (100 Stat. 4229), and functions transferred to the Secretary of the Interior.

Canal Zone Government Established by act of Aug. 24, 1912 (37 Stat. 561). Abolished by act of Sept. 27, 1979 (93 Stat. 454).

Capital Housing Authority, National Established by act of June 12, 1934 (48 Stat. 930). Made agency of District of Columbia government by act of Dec. 24, 1973 (87 Stat. 779), effective July 1, 1974.

Capital Park Commission, National Established by act of June 6, 1924 (43 Stat. 463). *National Capital Park and Planning Commission* named successor by act of Apr. 30, 1926 (44 Stat. 374). Functions transferred to National Capital Planning Commission by act of July 19, 1952 (66 Stat. 781).

Capital Park and Planning Commission, National *See* **Capital Park Commission, National**

Capital Regional Planning Council, National Established by act of July 19, 1952 (66 Stat. 785). Terminated by Reorg. Plan No. 5 of 1966, effective Sept. 8, 1966.

Capital Transportation Agency, National Established by act of July 14, 1960 (74 Stat 537). Authorized to establish rapid rail transit system by act of Sept. 8, 1965 (79 Stat. 663). Functions transferred to Washington Metropolitan Area Transit Authority by EO 11373 of Sept. 20, 1967.

Career Executive Board Established by EO 10758 of Mar. 4, 1958. Terminated July 1, 1959, and EO 10758 revoked by EO 10859 of Feb. 5, 1960.

Caribbean Organization Act of June 30, 1961 (75 Stat. 194), provided for acceptance by President of Agreement for the Establishment of the Caribbean Organization, signed at Washington, June 21, 1960. Article III of Agreement provided for termination of *Caribbean Commission,* authorized by Agreement signed Oct. 30, 1946, on first meeting of Caribbean Council, governing body of *Organization.* Terminated, effective Dec. 31, 1965, by resolution adopted by Council.

Cemeteries and Memorials in Europe, National Supervision transferred from *Department of War* to American Battle Monuments Commission by EO 6614 of Feb. 26, 1934, which transfer was deferred to May 21, 1934, by EO 6690 of Apr. 25, 1934.

Cemeteries and Parks, National *Department of War* functions regarding National Cemeteries and Parks located in continental U.S. transferred to *Office of National Parks, Buildings, and Reservations,* Department of the Interior, by EO 6166 of June 10, 1933.

Cemetery System, National Established in the *Veterans' Administration* by act of June 18, 1973 (87 Stat. 75). Redesignated as the National Cemetery Administration by act of Nov. 11, 1998 (112 Stat. 3337).

Censorship, Office of Established by EO 8985 of Dec. 19, 1941. Terminated by EO 9631 of Sept. 28, 1945.

Censorship Policy Board Established by EO 8985 of Dec. 19, 1941. Terminated by EO 9631 of Sept. 28, 1945.

Census, Bureau of the *See* **Census Office**

Census Office Established temporarily within the the Department of the Interior in accordance with act of Mar. 3, 1899. Established as a permanent office by act of Mar. 6, 1902. Transferred from the Department of the Interior to *Department of Commerce and Labor* by act of Feb. 14, 1903. Remained in the Department of Commerce under provisions of Reorganization Plan No. 5 of May 24, 1950, effective May 24, 1950.

Center. *See other part of title*

Central. *See other part of title*

Chemistry and Soils, Bureau of *See* **Agricultural and Industrial Chemistry, Bureau of**

Chesapeake Bay Center for Environmental Studies Established in 1965 in Annapolis, MD, as part of Smithsonian Institution by Secretarial order. Merged with *Radiation Biology Laboratory* by Secretarial Order July 1, 1983, to form Smithsonian Environmental Research Center.

Chief Information Officers Council Established by EO 13011 of July 16, 1996. Abolished by EO 13403 of May 12, 2006.

Chief People Officer, Office of the Renamed Office of the Chief Human Capital Officer by administrative order 5440.597 of June 16, 2006.

Chief Strategic Officer, Office of the Established by the Commissioner of Social Security Dec. 20, 2002. Abolished by Commissioner's memorandum of Jan. 14, 2008, and functions transferred to the Office of the Deputy Commissioner for Budget, Finance, and Management.

Child Development, Office of *See* **Children's Bureau**

Children's Bureau Established by act of Apr. 9, 1912 (37 Stat. 79). Placed in the Department of Labor by act of Mar. 4, 1913 (37 Stat. 737). Transferred, with exception of child labor functions, to *Social Security Administration, Federal Security Agency,* by Reorg. Plan No. 2 of 1946, effective July 16, 1946. Continued under *Administration* when *Agency* functions assumed by the *Department of*

Health, Education, and Welfare. Reassigned to *Welfare Administration* by Department reorganization of Jan. 28, 1963. Reassigned to *Social and Rehabilitation Service* by Department reorganization of Aug. 15, 1967. Reassigned to *Office of Child Development* by Department reorganization order of Sept. 17, 1969.

Child Health and Human Development, National Institute of Established by act of Oct. 17, 1962 (76 Stat. 1072). Renamed Eunice Kennedy Shriver National Institute of Child Health and Human Development by act of Dec. 21, 2007 (121 Stat. 1826).

China, U.S. Court for Established by act of June 30, 1906 (34 Stat. 814). Transferred to the Department of Justice by EO 6166 of June 10, 1933, effective Mar. 2, 1934. Act of June 30, 1906, repealed effective Sept. 1, 1948 (62 Stat. 992).

Christopher Columbus Quincentenary Jubilee Commission Established by act of Aug. 7, 1984 (98 Stat. 1257). Terminated pursuant to terms of act.

Civil defense. *See* **Defense**

Civil Rights, Commission on Established by act of Sept. 9, 1957 (71 Stat. 634). Terminated in 1983 and reestablished by act of Nov. 30, 1983 (97 Stat. 1301). Renamed United States Commission on Civil Rights by act of Nov. 2, 1994 (108 Stat. 4683).

Civil Service Commission, U.S. Established by act of Jan. 16, 1883 (22 Stat. 403). Redesignated as Merit Systems Protection Board and functions transferred to Board and Office of Personnel Management by Reorg. Plan No. 2 of 1978, effective Jan. 1, 1979.

Civil War Centennial Commission Established by act of Sept. 7, 1957 (71 Stat. 626). Terminated May 1, 1966, pursuant to terms of act.

Civilian Conservation Corps Established by act of June 28, 1937 (50 Stat. 319). Made part of *Federal Security Agency* by Reorg. Plan No. I of 1939, effective July 1, 1939. Liquidation provided for by act of July 2, 1942 (56 Stat. 569), not later than June 30, 1943.

Civilian Health and Medical Program of the United States, Office of Established as field activity in the Department of Defense in 1974. Functions consolidated into the TRICARE Management Activity in November 1997 by Defense Reform Initiative.

Civilian Production Administration Established by EO 9638 of Oct. 4, 1945. Consolidated with other agencies to form *Office of Temporary Controls, Office for Emergency Management,* by EO 9809 of Dec. 12, 1946.

Civilian Service Awards Board, Distinguished Established by EO 10717 of June 27, 1957. Terminated by EO 12014 of Oct. 19, 1977, and functions transferred to *U.S. Civil Service Commission.*

Claims, U.S. Court of Established Feb. 25, 1855 (10 Stat. 612). Abolished by act of Apr. 2, 1982 (96 Stat. 26) and trial jurisdiction transferred to *U.S.*

Claims Court and appellate functions merged with those of *U.S. Court of Customs and Patent Appeals* to form U.S. Court of Appeals for the Federal Circuit. U.S. Claims Court renamed U.S. Court of Federal Claims by act of Oct. 29, 1992 (106 Stat. 4516).

Claims Commission of the United States, International Established in the Department of State by act of Mar. 10, 1950 (64 Stat. 12). Abolished by Reorg. Plan No. 1 of 1954, effective July 1, 1954, and functions transferred to Foreign Claims Settlement Commission of the United States.

Claims Settlement Commission of the United States, Foreign Established by Reorg. Plan No. 1 of 1954, effective July 1, 1954. Transferred to the Department of Justice by act of Mar. 14, 1980 (94 Stat. 96).

Clark Sesquicentennial Commission, George Rogers Established by Public Resolution 51 (45 Stat. 723). Expenditures ordered administered by the Department of the Interior by EO 6166 of June 10, 1933.

Classification Review Committee, Interagency Established by EO 11652 of Mar. 8, 1972. Abolished by EO 12065 of June 28, 1978.

Clemency Board, Presidential Established in Executive Office of the President by EO 11803 of Sept. 16, 1974. Final recommendations submitted to President Sept. 15, 1975, and *Board* terminated by EO 11878 of Sept. 10, 1975.

Coal Commission, National Bituminous Established under authority of act of Aug. 30, 1935 (49 Stat. 992). Abolished by Reorg. Plan No. II of 1939, effective July 1, 1939, and functions transferred to *Bituminous Coal Division,* Department of the Interior.

Coal Consumers' Counsel, Office of the Bituminous Established by act of Apr. 11, 1941 (55 Stat. 134), renewing provisions of act of Apr. 23, 1937 (50 Stat. 72) for 2 years to continue functions of *Consumers' Counsel Division,* Department of the Interior. Functions continued by acts of Apr. 24, 1943 (57 Stat. 68), and May 21, 1943 (57 Stat. 82). Terminated Aug. 24, 1943.

Coal Division, Bituminous Established July 1, 1939, by Secretary of the Interior Order 1394 of June 16, 1939, as amended by Order 1399, of July 5, 1939, pursuant to act of Apr. 3, 1939 (53 Stat. 562) and Reorg. Plan No. II of 1939, effective July 1, 1939. Administered functions vested in *National Bituminous Coal Commission* by act of Apr. 23, 1937 (50 Stat. 72). Act extended to Aug. 24, 1943, on which date it expired.

Coal Labor Board, Bituminous Established by act of July 12, 1921 (42 Stat. 140). Abolished as result of U.S. Supreme Court decision, May 18, 1936, in case of *Carter* v. *Carter Coal Company et al.*

Coal Mine Safety Board of Review, Federal Established by act of July 16, 1952 (66 Stat. 697). Inactive after Mar. 30, 1970, pursuant to act of Dec. 30, 1969 (83 Stat. 803).

Coal Mines Administration Established by the Secretary of the Interior July 1, 1943. Abolished by

Secretary's Order 1977 of Aug. 16, 1944, as amended by Order 1982 of Aug. 31, 1944, and functions assumed by *Solid Fuels Administration for War. Administration* reestablished in the Department of the Interior by EO 9728 of May 21, 1946. Terminated June 30, 1947, by act of Mar. 27, 1942 (56 Stat. 176).

Coal Research, Office of Established in the Department of the Interior by act of July 7, 1960 (74 Stat. 336). Functions transferred to *Energy Research and Development Administration* by act of Oct. 11, 1974 (88 Stat. 1237).

Coalition Provisional Authority, Inspector General of the Established by act of Nov. 6, 2003 (117 Stat. 1234). Renamed Special Inspector General for Iraq Reconstruction by act of Oct. 28, 2004 (118 Stat. 2078.)

Coalition Provisional Authority, Office of the Inspector General of the Established by act of Nov. 6, 2003 (117 Stat. 1234). Renamed Office of the Special Inspector General for Iraq Reconstruction by act of Oct. 28, 2004 (118 Stat. 2078).

Coast and Geodetic Survey *See* **Coast Survey**

Coast Guard, U.S. Established by act of Jan. 28, 1915 (38 Stat. 800) as a military service and branch of the U.S. Armed Forces at all times and as a service in Treasury Department, except when operating as a service in the Navy. Transferred from the Department of the Treasury to the Department of the Navy by EO 8929 of Nov. 1, 1941. Returned to the Department of the Treasury by EO 9666 of Dec. 28, 1945. Transferred to the Department of Transportation by act of Oct. 15, 1966 (80 Stat. 931). Transferred to Homeland Security Department by act of Nov. 25, 2002 (116 Stat. 2249) with related authorities and functions of the Secretary of Transportation.

Coast Survey Established by act of Feb. 10, 1807 (2 Stat. 413). Redesignated as *Coast and Geodetic Survey* by act of June 20, 1878 (20 Stat. 206). Transferred to *Environmental Science Services Administration* by Reorg. Plan No. 2 of 1965, effective July 13, 1965.

Codification Board Established by act of June 19, 1937 (50 Stat. 304). Abolished by Reorg. Plan No. II of 1939, effective July 1, 1939, and functions transferred to *Division of the Federal Register.*

Coinage, Joint Commission on the Established by act of July 23, 1965 (79 Stat. 258). Expired Jan. 4, 1975, pursuant to act of Oct. 6, 1972 (88 Stat. 776).

Columbia Institution for the Instruction of the Deaf and Dumb, and the Blind Established by act of Feb. 16, 1857 (11 Stat. 161). Renamed *Columbia Institution for the Instruction of the Deaf and Dumb* by act of Feb. 23, 1865 (13 Stat. 436). Renamed *Columbia Institution for the Deaf* by act of Mar. 4, 1911 (36 Stat. 1422). Renamed *Gallaudet College* by act of June 18, 1954 (68 Stat. 265). Functions of the *Department of Health, Education, and Welfare* transferred to the Department of Education by act of Oct. 17, 1979 (93 Stat. 695). Renamed Gallaudet University by act of Aug. 4, 1986 (100 Stat. 781).

Commander in Chief, U.S. Fleet, and Chief of Naval Operations Duties of two positions prescribed by EO 8984 of Dec. 18, 1941. Combined under one officer by EO 9096 of Mar. 12, 1942.

Commerce, Bureau of Domestic *See* **Business and Defense Services Administration**

Commerce, Bureau of Foreign Established by the Secretary of Commerce Oct. 12, 1953, by Reorg. Plan No. 5 of 1950, effective May 24, 1950. Abolished by department order of Aug. 7, 1961, and functions vested in *Bureau of International Programs* and *Bureau of International Business Operations.*

Commerce, Bureau of Foreign and Domestic Established by act of Aug. 23, 1912 (37 Stat. 407). Functions reassigned to other offices of the Department of Commerce due to internal reorganizations.

Commerce, Bureau of International *See* **Business Operations, Bureau of International**

Commerce Service, Foreign Established in *Bureau of Foreign and Domestic Commerce,* Department of Commerce, by act of Mar. 3, 1927 (44 Stat. 1394). Transferred to the Department of State as part of Foreign Service by Reorg. Plan No. II of 1939, effective July 1, 1939.

Commercial Company, U.S. Established Mar. 27, 1942, as subsidiary of *Reconstruction Finance Corporation.* Transferred to *Office of Economic Warfare* by EO 9361 of July 15, 1943. *Office* consolidated into *Foreign Economic Administration* by EO 9380 of Sept. 25, 1943. Functions returned to *Corporation* by EO 9630 of Sept. 27, 1945, until June 30, 1948.

Commercial Policy, Executive Committee on Established by Presidential letter of Nov. 11, 1933, to Secretary of State. Abolished by EO 9461 of Aug. 7, 1944.

Commercial Standards Division Transferred with *Division of Simplified Trade Practice* from *National Bureau of Standards* to the Secretary of Commerce by Reorg. Plan No. 3 of 1946, effective July 16, 1946, to permit reassignment to *Office of Domestic Commerce.* Functions transferred to *National Bureau of Standards* by the Department of Commerce Order 90, June 7, 1963, pursuant to Reorg. Plan No. 5 of 1950, effective May 24, 1950.

Commission. *See other part of title*

Committee. *See also other part of title*

Committee Management Secretariat Established in the Office of Management and Budget Jan. 5, 1973, by act of Oct. 6, 1972 (86 Stat. 772). Functions transferred to General Services Administrator by Reorg. Plan No. 1 of 1977, effective Apr. 1, 1978. Reassigned to the *National Archives and Records Service* by GSA order of Feb. 22, 1979. Transferred in Archives to Office of the Federal Register by GSA order of Oct. 14, 1980. Transferred to Office of the Archivist of the United States by GSA order of Sept. 24, 1982. Reassigned to Office of Program Initiatives, GSA, by GSA order of May 18, 1984.

Transferred to Office of Management Services, GSA, by GSA order of Apr. 7, 1986.

Commodities Corporation, Federal Surplus *See* **Relief Corporation, Federal Surplus**

Commodity Credit Corporation   Organized by EO 6340 of Oct. 16, 1933, and managed in close affiliation with *Reconstruction Finance Corporation.* Transferred to the Department of Agriculture by Reorg. Plan No. I of 1939, effective July 1, 1939.

Commodity Exchange Administration   *See* **Grain Futures Administration**

Commodity Exchange Authority   *See* **Grain Futures Administration**

Commodity Exchange Commission   Established by act of Sept. 21, 1922 (42 Stat. 998). Functions transferred to Commodity Futures Trading Commission by act of Oct. 23, 1974 (88 Stat. 1414).

Commodity Stabilization Service   Established in the Department of Agriculture Nov. 2, 1953, by Secretary's Memorandum 1320, supp. 4. Renamed Agricultural Stabilization and Conservation Service by Secretary's Memorandum 1458 of June 14, 1961, effective June 5, 1961.

Communication Agency, International   *See Information Agency, U.S.*

Communications Program, Joint Tactical
Combined with *Joint Interoperability of the Tactical Command and Control Systems Programs* to form Joint Tactical Command, Control, and Communications Agency in July 1984, pursuant to DOD Directive 5154.28.

Community Development Corporation   Established in the Department of Housing and Urban Development by act of Dec. 31, 1970 (84 Stat. 1791). Renamed *New Community Development Corporation* by act of Aug. 22, 1974 (88 Stat. 725). Abolished Nov. 30, 1983, by act of Nov. 30, 1983 (97 Stat. 1238), and functions transferred to Assistant Secretary for Community Planning and Development, Department of Housing and Urban Development.

Community Development Corporation, New   *See* **Community Development Corporation**

Community Facilities, Bureau of   Established in 1945 by *Federal Works Administrator.* Transferred by act of June 30, 1949 (63 Stat. 380), to General Services Administration, functioning as *Community Facilities Service.* Certain functions transferred to various agencies, including the Department of the Interior, *Housing and Home Finance Agency,* and *Federal Security Agency* by Reorg. Plans Nos. 15, 16, and 17 of 1950, effective May 24, 1950.

Community Facilities Administration   Established in *Housing and Home Finance Agency* by Administrator's Organizational Order 1 of Dec. 23, 1954. Terminated by act of Sept. 9, 1965 (79 Stat. 667), and functions transferred to the Department of Housing and Urban Development.

Community Organization, Committee on
Established in *Office of Defense Health and Welfare*

Services Sept. 10, 1941. Functions transferred to *Federal Security Agency* by EO 9338 of Apr. 29, 1943.

Community Relations Service   Established in the Department of Commerce by act of July 2, 1964 (78 Stat. 241). Transferred to the Department of Justice by Reorg. Plan No. 1 of 1966, effective Apr. 22, 1966.

Community Service, Commission on National and
Established by act of Nov. 16, 1990 (104 Stat. 3168). Abolished by act of Sept. 21, 1993, and functions vested in the Board of Directors or the Executive Director prior to Oct. 1, 1993, transferred to the Corporation for National and Community Service (107 Stat. 873, 888).

Community Services Administration   Established by act of Jan. 4, 1975 (88 Stat. 2291) as successor to *Office of Economic Opportunity.* Abolished as independent agency through repeal of act of Aug. 20, 1964 (except titles VIII and X of such act) by act of Aug. 13, 1981 (95 Stat. 519).

Community Services Administration   Functions concerning Legal Services Program transferred to Legal Services Corporation by act of July 25, 1974 (88 Stat. 389). Renamed *Public Services Administration* by *Health, Education, and Welfare* departmental notice of Nov. 3, 1976. Transferred to *Office of Human Development* by Secretary's reorganization of Mar. 8, 1977 (42 FR 13262).

Community War Services   Established in *Office of the Administrator* under EO 9338 of Apr. 29, 1943, and *Federal Security Agency* order. Terminated Dec. 31, 1946, by act of July 26, 1946 (60 Stat. 695).

Conciliation Service, U.S.   Established by act of Mar. 4, 1913 (37 Stat. 738). Functions transferred to Federal Mediation and Conciliation Service, established by act of June 23, 1947 (61 Stat. 153).

Conference on Security and Cooperation in Europe
Renamed Organization for Security and Cooperation in Europe by EO 13029, Dec. 3, 1996 (61 FR 64591).

Consolidated Farm Service Agency   Established by act of Oct. 13, 1994 (108 Stat. 3214). Renamed Farm Service Agency (61 FR 1109), effective Jan. 16, 1996.

Constitution, Commission on the Bicentennial of the United States   Established by act of Sept. 29, 1983, as amended (97 Stat. 722). Terminated by act of Dec. 3, 1991 (105 Stat. 1232).

Constitution, transfer of functions   *See* **Statutes at Large and other matters**

Construction, Collective Bargaining Committee in
Established by EO 11849 of Apr. 1, 1975. Inactive since Jan. 7, 1976. Formally abolished by EO 12110 of Dec. 28, 1978.

Construction, Equipment and Repairs, Bureau of
Established in the Department of the Navy by act of Aug. 31, 1842 (5 Stat. 579). Abolished by act of July 5, 1862 (12 Stat. 510), and functions distributed among *Bureau of Equipment and Recruiting, Bureau*

of Construction and Repair, and *Bureau of Steam Engineering.*

Construction Branch   Established in the Department of the Treasury in 1853 and designated *Bureau of Construction* under control of *Office of Supervising Architect* by Sept. 30, 1855. *Office* incorporated into *Public Buildings Branch, Procurement Division,* by EO 6166 of June 10, 1933. Transferred to *Federal Works Agency* by Reorg. Plan No. I of 1939, effective July 1, 1939, when *Public Buildings Branch* of *Procurement Division, Bureau of Buildings Management,* National Park Service, Department of the Interior—so far as latter concerned with operation of public buildings for other departments or agencies—and *U.S. Housing Corporation* consolidated with *Public Buildings Administration, Federal Works Agency.*

Construction Industry Stabilization Committee   Established by EO 11588 of Mar. 29, 1971. Abolished by EO 11788 of June 18, 1974.

Construction and Repair, Bureau of   Established by act of July 5, 1862 (12 Stat. 510), replacing *Bureau of Construction, Equipment and Repairs.* Abolished by act of June 20, 1940 (54 Stat. 492), and functions transferred to *Bureau of Ships.*

Consumer Advisory Council   Established by EO 11136 of Jan. 3, 1964. *Office of Consumer Affairs* established in Executive Office of the President by EO 11583 of Feb. 24, 1971, and Council reestablished in *Office.*

Consumer Affairs, Office of   Established by EO 11583 of Feb. 24, 1971. Transferred to the *Department of Health, Education, and Welfare* by EO 11702 of Jan. 25, 1973.

Consumer Affairs Staff, National Business Council for   Established in the Department of Commerce by departmental organization order of Dec. 16, 1971. Terminated by departmental order of Dec. 6, 1973, due to lack of funding.

Consumer agencies   Consumer agencies of *National Emergency Council* and *National Recovery Administration* reorganized and functions transferred, together with those of *Consumers' Advisory Board, NRA,* and *Cabinet Committee on Price Policy,* to *Consumers' Division, NRA,* by EO 7120 of July 30, 1935. *Division* transferred to the Department of Labor by EO 7252 of Dec. 21, 1935. Transferred to *Division of Consumers' Counsel, Agricultural Adjustment Administration,* Department of Agriculture, by Secretary of Labor letter of Aug. 30, 1938, to the Secretary of Agriculture. Continued as *Consumer Standards Project* until June 30, 1941. Research on consumer standards continued by *Consumer Standards Section, Consumers' Counsel Division,* transferred to *Agricultural Marketing Administration* by administrative order of Feb. 28, 1942. Other project activities discontinued.

Consumer Cooperative Bank, National   Established by act of Aug. 20, 1978 (92 Stat. 499). Removed from mixed-ownership, Government corporation status by acts of Sept. 13, 1982 (96 Stat. 1062) and Jan. 12, 1983 (96 Stat. 2478).

Consumer Interests, President's Committee on   Established by EO 11136 of Jan. 3, 1964. Abolished by EO 11583 of Feb. 24, 1971.

Consumer and Marketing Service   Established by the Secretary of Agriculture Feb. 2, 1965. Renamed *Agricultural Marketing Service* Apr. 2, 1972, by Secretary's order and certain functions transferred to Animal and Plant Health Inspection Service.

Consumers' Counsel   Established in *National Bituminous Coal Commission* by act of Aug. 30, 1935 (49 Stat. 993). Office abolished by Reorg. Plan No. II of 1939, effective July 1, 1939, and functions transferred to Office of Solicitor, Department of the Interior, to function as *Consumers' Counsel Division* under direction of the Secretary of the Interior. Functions transferred to *Office of the Bituminous Coal Consumers' Counsel* June 1941 by act of Apr. 11, 1941 (55 Stat. 134).

Consumers' Counsel Division   *See* **Consumers' Counsel**

Consumers' Counsel, Division of   Established by act of May 12, 1933 (48 Stat. 31). Transferred by order of the Secretary of Agriculture from *Agricultural Adjustment Administration* to supervision of *Director of Marketing,* effective Feb. 1, 1940. Transferred to *Agricultural Marketing Administration* by administrative order of Feb. 28, 1942.

Consumers' Problems, Adviser on   *See* **Consumer agencies**

Contract Committee Government   *See* **Contract Compliance, Committee on Government**

Contract Compliance, Committee on Government   Established by EO 10308 of Dec. 3, 1951. Abolished by EO 10479 of Aug. 13, 1953, which established successor *Government Contract Committee.* Abolished by EO 10925 of Mar. 6, 1961, and records and property transferred to *President's Committee on Equal Employment Opportunity.*

Contract Settlement, Office of   Established by act of July 1, 1944 (58 Stat. 651). Transferred to *Office of War Mobilization and Reconversion* by act of Oct. 3, 1944 (58 Stat. 785). Terminated by EO 9809 of Dec. 12, 1946, and Reorg. Plan No. 1 of 1947, effective July 1, 1947, and functions transferred to the Department of the Treasury. Functions transferred to General Services Administration by act of June 30, 1949 (63 Stat. 380).

Contract Settlement Advisory Board   Established by act of July 1, 1944 (58 Stat. 651). Transferred to the Department of the Treasury by EO 9809 of Dec. 12, 1946, and by Reorg. Plan No. 1 of 1947, effective July 1, 1947. Transferred to General Services Administration by act of June 30, 1949 (63 Stat. 380) and established as *Contract Review Board.* Renamed Board of Contract Appeals in 1961 by Administrator's order. Board established as independent entity within General Services Administration Feb. 27, 1979, pursuant to act of Nov. 1, 1978 (92 Stat. 2383).

Contract Settlement Appeal Board, Office of   Established by act of July 1, 1944 (58 Stat. 651). Transferred to the Department of the Treasury by EO

9809 of Dec. 12, 1946, and by Reorg. Plan No. 1 of 1947, effective July 1, 1947. Functions transferred to General Services Administration by act of June 30, 1949 (63 Stat. 380). Abolished by act of July 14, 1952 (66 Stat. 627).

Contract Termination Board, Joint   Established Nov. 12, 1943, by *Director of War Mobilization.* Functions assumed by *Office of Contract Settlement.*

Contracts Division, Public   Established in the Department of Labor to administer act of June 30, 1936 (49 Stat. 2036). Consolidated with Wage and Hour Division by Secretarial order of Aug. 21, 1942. Absorbed by Wage and Hour Division by Secretarial order of May 1971.

Cooperation Administration, International   Established by Department of State Delegation of Authority 85 of June 30, 1955, pursuant to EO 10610 of May 9, 1955. Abolished by act of Sept. 4, 1961 (75 Stat. 446), and functions redelegated to Agency for International Development pursuant to Presidential letter of Sept. 30, 1961, and EO 10973 of Nov. 3, 1961.

Cooperative State Research Service   Established in the Department of Agriculture. Incorporated into Cooperative State, Research, Education, and Extension Service under Department of Agriculture reorganization in 1995.

Coordinating Service, Federal   *Office of Chief Coordinator* created by Executive order promulgated in *Bureau of the Budget* Circular 15, July 27, 1921, and duties enlarged by other *Bureau* circulars. Abolished by EO 6166 of June 10, 1933. Contract form, Federal traffic, and surplus property functions transferred to *Procurement Division* by order of the Secretary of the Treasury, approved by President Oct. 9, 1933, issued pursuant to EO's 6166 of June 10, 1933, and 6224 of July 27, 1933.

Copyright Arbitration Royalty Panels   Established by act of Dec. 17, 1993 (107 Stat. 2304). Replaced by Copyright Royalty Judges under act of Nov. 30, 2004 (118 Stat. 2351).

Copyright Royalty Tribunal   Established as an independent entity within the legislative branch by act of Oct. 19, 1976 (90 Stat. 2594). Abolished by act of Dec. 17, 1993 (107 Stat. 2304), and functions transferred to copyright arbitration royalty panels.

Copyrighted Works, National Commission on New Technological Uses of   Established by act of Dec. 31, 1974 (88 Stat. 1873). Terminated Sept. 29, 1978, pursuant to terms of act.

Corporate Payments Abroad, Task Force on Questionable   Established by Presidential memorandum of Mar. 31, 1976. Terminated Dec. 31, 1976, pursuant to terms of memorandum.

Corporation, Federal Facilities   Established in the Department of the Treasury by EO 10539 of June 22, 1954. Placed under supervision of Director appointed by General Services Administrator by EO 10720 of July 11, 1957. Dissolved by act of Aug. 30, 1961 (75 Stat. 418), and functions transferred to Administrator of General Services.

Corregidor-Bataan Memorial Commission   Established by act of Aug. 5, 1953 (67 Stat. 366). Terminated May 6, 1967, by act of Dec. 23, 1963 (77 Stat. 477).

Cost Accounting Standards Board   Established by act of Aug. 15, 1970 (84 Stat. 796). Terminated Sept. 30, 1980, due to lack of funding. Reestablished by act of Nov. 17, 1988 (102 Stat. 4059).

Cost of Living Council   Established by EO 11615 of Aug. 15, 1971. Abolished by EO 11788 of June 18, 1974.

Cotton Stabilization Corporation   Organized June 1930 under laws of Delaware by *Federal Farm Board* pursuant to act of June 15, 1929 (46 Stat. 11). Certificate of dissolution filed with Corporation Commission of Delaware Dec. 27, 1934.

Cotton Textile Industry, Board of Inquiry for the   Established by EO 6840 of Sept. 5, 1934. Abolished by EO 6858 of Sept. 26, 1934.

Council.   *See other part of title*

Counterespionage Section Transferred from the Criminal Division to the National Security Division by act of Mar. 9, 2006 (120 Stat. 249).

Counterintelligence, Office of   Established within the Department of Energy by Public Law 106–65 of Oct. 5, 1999 (113 Stat. 955). Merged with *Office of Intelligence* to form *Office of Intelligence and Counterintelligence* by memorandum of March 9, 2006 of the Secretary of Energy.

Counterterrorism Section   Transferred from the Criminal Division to the National Security Division by act of Mar. 9, 2006 (120 Stat. 249).

Courts   Under act of Aug. 7, 1939 (53 Stat. 1223), and revised June 25, 1948 (62 Stat. 913), to provide for administration of U.S. courts, administrative jurisdiction over all continental and territorial courts transferred to Administrative Office of the U.S. Courts, including U.S. courts of appeals and district courts, District Court for the Territory of Alaska, U.S. District Court for the District of the Canal Zone, District Court of Guam, District Court of the Virgin Islands, Court of Claims, Court of Customs and Patent Appeals, and Customs Courts.

Credit Unions, Bureau of Federal   *See* **Credit Union System, Federal**

Credit Union System, Federal   Established by act of June 26, 1934 (48 Stat. 1216), to be administered by *Farm Credit Administration.* Transferred to Federal Deposit Insurance Corporation by EO 9148 of Apr. 27, 1942, and Reorg. Plan No. 1 of 1947, effective July 1, 1947. Functions transferred to *Bureau of Federal Credit Unions, Federal Security Agency,* established by act of June 29, 1948 (62 Stat. 1091). Functions transferred to the *Department of Health, Education, and Welfare* by Reorg. Plan No. 1 of 1953, effective Apr. 11, 1953. Functions transferred to National Credit Union Administration by act of Mar. 10, 1970 (84 Stat. 49).

Crime, National Council on Organized Established by EO 11534 of June 4, 1970. Terminated by EO 12110 of Dec. 28, 1978.

Critical Materials Council, National Established within Executive Office of the President by act of July 31, 1984 (98 Stat. 1250). *Office* abolished in September 1993 due to lack of funding and functions transferred to the Office of Science and Technology Policy.

Crop Insurance Corporation, Federal Established by act of Feb. 16, 1938. Consolidated with the *Agricultural Stabilization and Conservation Service* and *Farmers' Home Administration* in 1995 to form the *Farm Service Agency* pursuant to act of Oct. 13, 1994 (108 Stat. 3178).

Crop Production Loan Office Authorized by Presidential letters of July 26, 1918, and July 26, 1919, to the Secretary of Agriculture. Further authorized by act of Mar. 3, 1921 (41 Stat. 1347). Transferred to Farm Credit Administration by EO 6084 of Mar. 27, 1933.

Cultural Center, National Established in Smithsonian Institution by act of Sept. 2, 1958 (72 Stat. 1698). Renamed John F. Kennedy Center for the Performing Arts by act of Jan. 23, 1964 (78 Stat. 4).

Customs, Bureau of Established under sec. 1 of act of Mar. 3, 1927 (19 U.S.C. 2071) in Treasury Department. Functions relating to award of numbers to undocumented vessels, vested in *Collectors of Customs,* transferred to Commandant of Coast Guard by EO 9083 of Feb. 27, 1942. Transfer made permanent by Reorg. Plan No. 3 of 1946, effective July 16, 1946. Redesignated U.S. Customs Service by the Department of the Treasury Order 165–23 of Apr. 4, 1973. Functions transferred to and agency established within Homeland Security Department by act of Nov. 25, 2002 (116 Stat. 2178).

Customs Court, U.S. Formerly established as Board of General Appraisers by act of June 10, 1890 (26 Stat. 136). Renamed *U.S. Customs Court* by act of May 26, 1926 (44 Stat. 669). Renamed U.S. Court of International Trade by act of Oct. 10, 1980 (94 Stat. 1727).

Customs and Patent Appeals, U.S. Court of Established by act of Mar. 2, 1929 (45 Stat. 1475). Abolished by act of Apr. 2, 1982 (96 Stat. 28) and functions merged with appellate functions of *U.S. Court of Claims* to form U.S. Court of Appeals for the Federal Circuit.

Dairy Industry, Bureau of *Bureau of Dairying* established in the Department of Agriculture by act of May 29, 1924 (43 Stat. 243). *Bureau of Dairy Industry* designation first appeared in act of May 11, 1926 (44 Stat. 499). Functions transferred to Agricultural Research Service by Secretary's Memorandum 1320, supp. 4, of Nov. 2, 1953.

Defense, Advisory Commission to the Council of National *See* **Defense, Council of National**

Defense, Council of National Established by act of Aug. 29, 1916 (39 Stat. 649). *Advisory Commission*—composed of Advisers on Industrial Production, Industrial Materials, Employment, Farm Products, Price Stabilization, Transportation, and Consumer Protection—established by *Council* pursuant to act and approved by President May 29, 1940. *Commission* decentralized by merging divisions with newly created national defense units. Agencies evolved from *Commission,* except *Office of Agricultural War Relations* and *Office of Price Administration,* made units of *Office for Emergency Management. Council* inactive.

Defense, Office of Civilian Established in *Office for Emergency Management* by EO 8757 of May 20, 1941. Terminated by EO 9562 of June 4, 1945.

Defense Administration, Federal Civil Established in *Office for Emergency Management* by EO 10186 of Dec. 1, 1950; subsequently established as independent agency by act of Jan. 12, 1951 (64 Stat. 1245). Functions transferred to *Office of Defense and Civilian Mobilization* by Reorg. Plan No. 1 of 1958, effective July 1, 1958.

Defense Advanced Research Projects Agency Established as a separate agency of the Department of Defense by DOD Directive 5105.41 dated July 25, 1978. Renamed *Advanced Research Projects Agency* by order of the Secretary of Defense dated July 13, 1993. Reestablished by act of Feb. 10, 1996 (110 Stat. 406).

Defense Advisory Council, Civil Established by act of Jan. 12, 1951 (64 Stat. 1245). Transferred to *Office of Defense and Civilian Mobilization* by Reorg. Plan No. 1 of 1958, effective July 1, 1958.

Defense Aid Reports, Division of Established in *Office for Emergency Management* by EO 8751 of May 2, 1941. Abolished by EO 8926 of Oct. 28, 1941, which created *Office of Lend-Lease Administration.*

Defense Air Transportation Administration Established Nov. 12, 1951, by Department of Commerce Order 137. Abolished by Amendment 3 of Sept. 13, 1962, to Department Order 128 (revised) and functions transferred to *Office of the Under Secretary of Commerce for Transportation.*

Defense Atomic Support Agency Renamed *Defense Nuclear Agency* by General Order No. 1 of July 1, 1971.

Defense Audiovisual Agency Established by DOD Directive 5040.1 of June 12, 1979. Abolished by Secretary's memorandum of Apr. 19, 1985, and functions assigned to the military departments.

Defense Audit Service Established by DOD Directive of Oct. 14, 1976. Abolished by Deputy Secretary's memorandum of Nov. 2, 1982, and functions transferred to Office of the Inspector General.

Defense Civil Preparedness Agency Functions transferred from the Department of Defense to the Federal Emergency Management Agency by EO 12148 of July 20, 1979.

Defense and Civilian Mobilization Board Established by EO 10773 of July 1, 1938. Redesignated *Civil and Defense Mobilization Board* by act of Aug. 26, 1958 (72 Stat. 861). Abolished by

Office of Emergency Preparedness Circular 1200.1 of Oct. 31, 1962.

Defense Communications Agency   Established by direction of the Secretary of Defense on May 12, 1960. Renamed Defense Information Systems Agency by DOD Directive 5105.19 dated June 25, 1991.

Defense Communications Board   Established by EO 8546 of Sept. 24, 1940. Renamed *Board of War Communications* by EO 9183 of June 15, 1942. Abolished by EO 9831 of Feb. 24, 1947, and property transferred to Federal Communications Commission.

Defense Coordinating Board, Civil   Established by EO 10611 of May 11, 1955. EO 10611 revoked by EO 10773 of July 1, 1958.

Defense Electric Power Administration   Established by Order 2605 of Dec. 4, 1950 of the Secretary of the Interior. Abolished June 30, 1953, by Secretary's Order 2721 of May 7, 1953. Reestablished by Departmental Manual Release No. 253 of Aug. 6, 1959. Terminated by Departmental Manual Release No. 1050 of Jan. 10, 1977.

Defense Fisheries Administration   Established by Order 2605 of Dec. 4, 1950 of the Secretary of the Interior. Abolished June 30, 1953, by Secretary's Order 2722 of May 13, 1953.

Defense Health and Welfare Services, Office of   Established by EO 8890 of Sept. 3, 1941. Terminated by EO 9338 of Apr. 29, 1943, and functions transferred to *Federal Security Agency.*

Defense Homes Corporation   Incorporated pursuant to President's letter to the Secretary of the Treasury of Oct. 18, 1940. Transferred to *Federal Public Housing Authority* by EO 9070 of Feb. 24, 1942.

Defense Housing Coordinator   Office established July 21, 1940, by *Advisory Commission to Council of National Defense.* Functions transferred to *Division of Defense Housing Coordination, Office for Emergency Management,* by EO 8632 of Jan. 11, 1941.

Defense Housing Division, Mutual Ownership   Established by Administrator of *Federal Works Agency* under provisions of act of June 28, 1941 (55 Stat. 361). Functions transferred to *Federal Public Housing Authority, National Housing Agency,* by EO 9070 of Feb. 24, 1942.

Defense Intelligence College.   Established by DOD Directive 3305.1 of January 28, 1983. Renamed Joint Military Intelligence College by DOD Directive 3305.1 of January 14, 1998. *See also Defense Intelligence School.*

Defense Intelligence School.   Established by DOD Directive 5105.25 of November 2, 1962. Renamed Defense Intelligence College by DOD Directive 3305.1 of January 28, 1983.

Defense Investigative Service   Established by the Secretary of Defense Jan. 1, 1972. Renamed Defense Security Service in November 1997 by Defense Reform Initiative.

Defense Manpower Administration   Established by the Secretary of Labor by General Order 48, pursuant to EO 10161 of Sept. 9, 1950, and Reorg. Plan No. 6 of 1950, effective May 24, 1950. General Order 48 revoked by General Order 63 of Aug. 25, 1953, which established *Office of Manpower Administration* in Department.

Defense Mapping Agency   Established as a the Department of Defense agency in 1972. Functions transferred to the National Imagery and Mapping Agency by act of Sept. 23, 1996 (110 Stat. 2677).

Defense Materials Procurement Agency   Established by EO 10281 of Aug. 28, 1951. Abolished by EO 10480 of Aug. 14, 1953, and functions transferred to General Services Administration.

Defense Materials Service   See Emergency Procurement Service

Defense Mediation Board, National   Established by EO 8716 of Mar. 19, 1941. Terminated on creation of *National War Labor Board, Office for Emergency Management* by EO 9017 of Jan. 12, 1942. Transferred to the Department of Labor by EO 9617 of Sept. 19, 1945. *Board* terminated by EO 9672 of Dec. 31, 1945, which established *National Wage Stabilization Board* in the Department of Labor. Terminated by EO 9809 of Dec. 12, 1946, and functions transferred to the Secretary of Labor and the Department of the Treasury, effective Feb. 24, 1947.

Defense Medical Programs Activity   Functions consolidated into the TRICARE Management Activity in November 1997 by Defense Reform Initiative.

Defense Minerals Administration   Established by Order 2605 of Dec. 4, 1950 of the Secretary of the Interior. Functions assigned to *Defense Materials Procurement Agency.* Functions of exploration for critical and strategic minerals redelegated to the Secretary of the Interior and administered by *Defense Minerals Exploration Administration* by Secretary's Order 2726 of June 30, 1953. Termination of program announced by Secretary June 6, 1958. Certain activities continued in *Office of Minerals Exploration,* Department of the Interior.

Defense Minerals Exploration Administration   See Defense Minerals Administration

Defense Mobilization, Office of   Established in Executive Office of the President by EO 10193 of Dec. 16, 1950. Superseded by *Office of Defense Mobilization* established by Reorg. Plan No. 3 of 1953, effective June 12, 1953, which assumed functions of former *Office, National Security Resources Board,* and critical materials stockpiling functions of Army, Navy, Air Force, and Interior Secretaries and of *Army and Navy Munitions Board.* Consolidated with *Federal Civil Defense Administration* into *Office of Defense and Civilian Mobilization* by Reorg. Plan No. 1 of 1958, effective July 1, 1958, and offices of Director and Deputy Director terminated.

Defense Mobilization Board   Established by EO 10200 of Jan. 3, 1951, and restated in EO 10480 of

Aug. 14, 1953. Terminated by EO 10773 of July 1, 1958.

Defense Nuclear Agency   Established in 1971. Renamed *Defense Special Weapons Agency* by DOD Directive 5105.31 of June 14, 1995.

Defense Nuclear Counterintelligence, Office of Established by act of Oct. 5, 1999 (113 Stat. 960). Abolished by act of Oct. 17, 2006 (120 Stat. 2507) and functions transferred to the Secretary of Energy.

Defense Plant Corporation   Established by act of June 25, 1940 (54 Stat. 572). Transferred from *Federal Loan Agency* to the Department of Commerce by EO 9071 of Feb. 24, 1942. Returned to *Federal Loan Agency* pursuant to act of Feb. 24, 1945 (59 Stat. 5). Dissolved by act of June 30, 1945 (59 Stat. 310), and functions transferred to *Reconstruction Finance Corporation.*

Defense Plants Administration, Small   Established by act of July 31, 1951 (65 Stat. 131). Terminated July 31, 1953, by act of June 30, 1953 (67 Stat. 131). Functions relating to liquidation transferred to Small Business Administration by EO 10504 of Dec. 1, 1953.

Defense Production Administration   Established by EO 10200 of Jan. 3, 1951. Terminated by EO 10433 of Feb. 4, 1953, and functions transferred to *Office of Defense Mobilization.*

Defense Property Disposal Service   Renamed Defense Reutilization and Marketing Service by Defense Logistics Agency General Order 10–85, effective July 1, 1985.

Defense Prisoner of War/Missing in Action Office Established by DOD Directive 5110.10, July 16, 1993. Renamed Defense Prisoner of War/Missing Personnel Office by Secretary of Defense memorandum of May 30, 1996.

Defense Public Works Division   Established in *Public Works Administration.* Transferred to *Office of Federal Works Administrator* by administrative order of July 16, 1941. Abolished by administrative order of Mar. 6, 1942, and functions transferred to *Office of Chief Engineer, Federal Works Agency.*

Defense Purchases, Office for the Coordination of National   Established by order of *Council of National Defense,* approved June 27, 1940. Order revoked Jan. 7, 1941, and records transferred to Executive Office of the President.

Defense Research Committee, National   Established June 27, 1940, by order of *Council of National Defense.* Abolished by order of *Council* June 28, 1941, and reestablished in *Office of Scientific Research and Development* by EO 8807 of June 28, 1941. *Office* terminated by EO 9913 of Dec. 26, 1947, and property and records transferred to *National Military Establishment.*

Defense Resources Committee   Established by Administrative Order 1496 of June 15, 1940. Replaced by *War Resources Council* by Administrative Order 1636 of Jan. 14, 1942. Inactive.

Defense Security Assistance Agency   Established on Sept. 1, 1971. Renamed the Defense Security Cooperation Agency by DOD Directive 5105.38.

Defense Solid Fuels Administration   Established by Order 2605 of Dec. 4, 1950 of the Secretary of the Interior. Abolished June 29, 1954, by Secretary's Order 2764.

Defense Special Weapons Agency   Established by General Order No. 1 of July 1, 1971. Functions transferred to the Defense Threat Reduction Agency by DOD Directive 5105.62 of Sept. 30, 1998.

Defense Stockpile Manager, National   Established by act of Nov. 14, 1986 (100 Stat. 4067). Functions transferred from the Administrator of General Services to the Secretary of Defense by EO 12626 of Feb. 25, 1988.

Defense Supplies Corporation   Established under act of June 25, 1940 (54 Stat. 572). Transferred from *Federal Loan Agency* to the Department of Commerce by EO 9071 of Feb. 24, 1942. Returned to *Federal Loan Agency* by act of Feb. 24, 1945 (59 Stat. 5). Dissolved by act of June 30, 1945 (59 Stat. 310), and functions transferred to *Reconstruction Finance Corporation.*

Defense Supply Agency   Renamed Defense Logistics Agency by DOD Directive 5105.22 of Jan. 22, 1977.

Defense Supply Management Agency   Established in the Department of Defense by act of July 1, 1952 (66 Stat. 318). Abolished by Reorg. Plan No. 6 of 1953, effective June 30, 1953, and functions transferred to the Secretary of Defense.

Defense Technology Security Administration Established on May 10, 1985. Functions transferred to the Defense Threat Reduction Agency by DOD Directive 5105.62 of Sept. 30, 1998.

Defense Transport Administration   Established Oct. 4, 1950, by order of Commissioner of *Interstate Commerce Commission* in charge of *Bureau of Service,* pursuant to EO 10161 of Sept. 9, 1950. Terminated by DTA Commissioner's order, effective July 1, 1955, and functions transferred to *Bureau of Safety and Service, Interstate Commerce Commission.*

Defense Transportation, Office of   Established in *Office for Emergency Management* by EO 8989 of Dec. 18, 1941. Terminated by EO 10065 of July 6, 1949.

Director.   *See other part of title*

Disarmament Administration, U.S.   Established in the Department of State. Functions transferred to *U.S. Arms Control and Disarmament Agency* by act of Sept. 26, 1961 (75 Stat. 638).

Disarmament Problems, President's Special Committee on   Established by President Aug. 5, 1955. Dissolved in February 1958.

Disaster Assistance Administration, Federal Functions transferred from the Department of Housing and Urban Development to the Federal

Emergency Management Agency by EO 12148 of July 20, 1979.

Disaster Loan Corporation   Grouped with other agencies to form *Federal Loan Agency* by Reorg. Plan No. I of 1939, effective July 1, 1939. Transferred to the Department of Commerce by EO 9071 of Feb. 24, 1942. Returned to *Federal Loan Agency* by act of Feb. 24, 1945 (59 Stat. 5). Dissolved by act of June 30, 1945 (59 Stat. 310), and functions transferred to *Reconstruction Finance Corporation.*

Disease Control, Center for   Established within the Public Health Service by the *Secretary of Health, Education, and Welfare* on July 1, 1973. Renamed *Centers for Disease Control* by Health and Human Services Secretary's notice of Oct. 1, 1980 (45 FR 67772). Renamed Centers for Disease Control and Prevention by act of Oct. 27, 1992 (106 Stat. 3504).

Displaced Persons Commission   Established by act of June 25, 1948 (62 Stat. 1009). Terminated Aug. 31, 1952, pursuant to terms of act.

District of Columbia   Established by acts of July 16, 1790 (1 Stat. 130), and Mar. 3, 1791. *Corporations of Washington and Georgetown* and *levy court of Washington County* abolished in favor of territorial form of government in 1871. Permanent commission government established July 1, 1878. District Government created as municipal corporation by act of June 11, 1878 (20 Stat. 102). Treated as branch of U.S. Government by various statutory enactments of Congress. District Government altered by Reorg. Plan No. 3 of 1967, effective Nov. 3, 1967. Charter for local government in District of Columbia provided by act of Dec. 24, 1973 (87 Stat. 774).

District of Columbia, Highway Commission of the   Established by act of Mar. 2, 1893 (27 Stat 532). *National Capital Park and Planning Commission* named successor by act of Apr. 30, 1926 (44 Stat. 374). Functions transferred to National Capital Planning Commission by act of July 19, 1952 (66 Stat. 781).

District of Columbia, Reform-School of the   Established by act of May 3, 1876 (19 Stat. 49). Renamed *National Training School for Boys* by act of May 27, 1908 (35 Stat. 380). Transferred to the Department of Justice by Reorg. Plan No. II of 1939, effective July 1, 1939, to be administered by Director of Bureau of Prisons.

District of Columbia Auditorium Commission   Established by act of July 1, 1955 (69 Stat. 243). Final report submitted to Congress Jan. 31, 1957, pursuant to act of Apr. 27, 1956 (70 Stat. 115).

District of Columbia Redevelopment Land Agency   Established by act of Aug. 2, 1946 (60 Stat. 790). Agency established as instrumentality of District Government by act of Dec. 24, 1973 (87 Stat. 774), effective July 1, 1974.

District of Columbia-Virginia Boundary Commission   Established by act of Mar. 21, 1934 (48 Stat. 453). Terminated Dec. 1, 1935, to which date it had been extended by Public Resolution 9 (49 Stat. 67).

Division.   *See other part of title*

Domestic Council   Established in Executive Office of the President by Reorg. Plan No. 2 of 1970, effective July 1, 1970. Abolished by Reorg. Plan No. 1 of 1977, effective Mar. 26, 1978, and functions transferred to President and staff designated as *Domestic Policy Staff.* Pursuant to EO 12045 of Mar. 27, 1978, *Staff* assisted President in performance of transferred functions. Renamed Office of Policy Development in 1981. Abolished in February 1992 by President's reorganizational statement, effective May 1992.

Domestic Policy Staff   *See* **Domestic Council**

Dominican Customs Receivership   Transferred from *Division of Territories and Island Possessions,* Department of the Interior, to the Department of State by Reorg. Plan No. IV of 1940, effective June 30, 1940.

Drug Abuse, National Institute on   Established within the National Institute of Mental Health, *Department of Health, Education, and Welfare* by act of Mar. 21, 1972 (86 Stat. 85). Removed from within the National Institute of Mental Health and made an entity within the Alcohol, Drug Abuse, and Mental Health Administration by act of May 14, 1974 (88 Stat. 136). Functions transferred to the Department of Health and Human Services by act of Oct. 17, 1979 (93 Stat. 695). (*See also* act of Oct. 27, 1986; 100 Stat. 3207–106.) Abolished by act of July 10, 1992 (106 Stat. 331). Reestablished by act of July 10, 1992 (106 Stat. 361).

Drug Abuse, President's Advisory Commission on Narcotic and   Established by EO 11076 of Jan. 15, 1963. Terminated November 1963 under terms of order.

Drug Abuse Control, Bureau of   Established in Food and Drug Administration, Department of Health and Human Services, to carry out functions of act of July 15, 1965 (79 Stat. 226). Functions transferred to *Bureau of Narcotics and Dangerous Drugs,* Department of Justice, by Reorg. Plan No. 1 of 1968, effective Apr. 8, 1968. Abolished by Reorg. Plan No. 2 of 1973, effective July 1, 1973, and functions transferred to Drug Enforcement Administration.

Drug Abuse Law Enforcement, Office of   Established by EO 11641 of Jan. 28, 1972. Terminated by EO 11727 of July 6, 1973, and functions transferred to Drug Enforcement Administration.

Drug Abuse Policy, Office of   Established in Executive Office of the President by act of Mar. 19, 1976 (90 Stat. 242). Abolished by Reorg. Plan No. 1 of 1977, effective Mar. 26, 1978, and functions transferred to President.

Drug Abuse Prevention, Special Action Office for   Established by EO 11599 of June 17, 1971, and act of Mar. 21, 1972 (86 Stat. 65). Terminated June 30, 1975, pursuant to terms of act.

Drug Abuse Prevention, Treatment, and Rehabilitation, Cabinet Committee on   Established Apr. 27, 1976, by Presidential announcement. Terminated by Presidential memorandum of Mar. 14, 1977.

Drug Law Enforcement, Cabinet Committee for
Established Apr. 27, 1976, pursuant to Presidential
message to Congress of Apr. 27, 1976. Abolished by
Presidential memorandum of Mar. 14, 1977.

Drugs, Bureau of Narcotics and Dangerous See
Drug Abuse Control, Bureau of

Drugs and Biologics, National Center for Renamed
Center for Drugs and Biologics by Food and Drug
Administration notice of Mar. 9, 1984 (49 FR
10166). Reestablished as Center for Drug Evaluation
and Research and Center for Biologics Evaluation
and Research by Secretary's notice of Oct. 6, 1987
(52 FR 38275).

Drunk Driving, Presidential Commission on
Established by EO 12358 of Apr. 14, 1982.
Terminated Dec. 31, 1983, by EO 12415 of Apr. 5,
1983.

Dryden Research Center, Hugh L. Formerly
separate field installation of National Aeronautics
and Space Administration. Made component of
Ames Research Center by NASA Management
Instruction 1107.5A of Sept. 3, 1981.

Economic Administration, Foreign Established in
Office for Emergency Management by EO 9380 of
Sept. 25, 1943. Functions of *Office of Lend-Lease
Administration, Office of Foreign Relief and
Rehabilitation Operations, Office of Economic
Warfare* (together with *U.S. Commercial Company,
Rubber Development Corporation, Petroleum
Reserves Corporation,* and *Export-Import Bank of
Washington* and functions transferred thereto by EO
9361 of July 15, 1943), and foreign economic
operations of *Office of Foreign Economic
Coordination* transferred to *Administration*. Foreign
procurement activities of *War Food Administration*
and Commodity Credit Corporation transferred by
EO 9385 of Oct. 6, 1943. Terminated by EO 9630
of Sept. 27, 1945, and functions redistributed to the
Departments of State, Commerce, and Agriculture
and the *Reconstruction Finance Corporation.*

Economic Analysis, Office of See *Business
Economics, Office of*

Economic Cooperation Administration Established
by act of Apr. 3, 1948 (62 Stat. 138). Abolished by
act of Oct. 10, 1951 (65 Stat. 373), and functions
transferred to *Mutual Security Agency* pursuant to
EO 10300 of Nov. 1, 1951.

Economic Coordination, Office of Foreign See
Board of Economic Operations

Economic Defense Board Established by EO 8839
of July 30, 1941. Renamed *Board of Economic
Warfare* by EO 8982 of Dec. 17, 1941. *Board*
terminated by EO 9361 of July 15, 1943, and *Office
of Economic Warfare* established in *Office for
Emergency Management. Office of Economic
Warfare* consolidated with *Foreign Economic
Administration* by EO 9380 of Sept. 25, 1943.

Economic Development, Office of Regional
Established by the Secretary of Commerce Jan. 6,
1966, pursuant to act of Aug. 26, 1965 (79 Stat.
552). Abolished by Department Order 5A, Dec. 22,

1966, and functions vested in Economic
Development Administration.

Economic Development Service, Foreign
Established by order of the Secretary of Agriculture
Nov. 8, 1969. Abolished by order of Secretary Feb.
6, 1972, and functions transferred to Economic
Research Service.

Economic Growth and Stability, Advisory Board on
Established by Presidential letter to Congress of June
1, 1953. Superseded by *National Advisory Board on
Economic Policy* by Presidential direction Mar. 12,
1961. *Cabinet Committee on Economic Growth*
established by President Aug. 21, 1962, to succeed
Board.

Economic Management Support Center Established
by Secretary of Agriculture Memorandum 1836 of
Jan. 9, 1974. Consolidated with other Department
units into *Economics, Statistics, and Cooperatives
Service* by Secretary's Memorandum 1927, effective
Dec. 23, 1977.

Economic Operations, Board of Established by
Department of State order of Oct. 7, 1941.
Abolished by departmental order of June 24, 1943,
and functions transferred to *Office of Foreign
Economic Coordination* established by same order.
Office abolished by departmental order of Nov. 6,
1943, pursuant to EO 9380 of Sept. 25, 1943.

Economic Opportunity, Office of Established in
Executive Office of the President by act of Aug. 20,
1964 (78 Stat. 508). All OEO programs except three
transferred by administrative action to the
Departments of *Health, Education, and Welfare,*
Labor, and Housing and Urban Development July 6,
1973. Community Action, Economic Development,
and Legal Services Programs transferred to
Community Services Administration by act of Jan. 4,
1975 (88 Stat. 2310).

Economic Policy, Council on Established by
Presidential memorandum of Feb. 2, 1973.
Functions absorbed by *Economic Policy Board* Sept.
30, 1974.

Economic Policy, Council on Foreign Established
Dec. 22, 1954, by Presidential letter of Dec. 11,
1954. Abolished by President Mar. 12, 1961, and
functions transferred to Secretary of State.

Economic Policy, Council on International
Established in Executive Office of the President by
Presidential memorandum of January 1971.
Reestablished by act of Aug. 29, 1972 (86 Stat. 646).
Terminated Sept. 30, 1977, on expiration of statutory
authority.

Economic Policy, National Advisory Board on See
Economic Growth and Stability, Advisory Board on

Economic Policy Board, President's Established by
EO 11808 of Sept. 30, 1974. Terminated by EO
11975 of Mar. 7, 1977.

Economic Research Service Established by
Secretary of Agriculture Memorandum 1446, supp.
1, of Apr. 3, 1961. Consolidated with other
Department of Agriculture units into *Economics,
Statistics, and Cooperatives Service* by Secretary's

Memorandum 1927, effective Dec. 23, 1977. Redesignated as Economic Research Service by Secretarial order of Oct. 1, 1981.

Economic Security, Advisory Council on Established by EO 6757 of June 29, 1934. Terminated on approval of act of Aug. 14, 1935 (49 Stat. 620) Aug. 14, 1935.

Economic Security, Committee on Established by EO 6757 of June 29, 1934. Terminated as formal agency in April 1936, as provided in act, but continued informally for some time thereafter.

Economic Stabilization, Office of Established in *Office for Emergency Management* by EO 9250 of Oct. 3, 1942. Terminated by EO 9620 of Sept. 20, 1945, and functions transferred to *Office of War Mobilization and Reconversion.* Reestablished in *Office for Emergency Management* by EO 9699 of Feb. 21, 1946. Transferred by EO 9762 of July 25, 1946, to *Office of War Mobilization and Reconversion.* Consolidated with other agencies to form *Office of Temporary Controls* by EO 9809 of Dec. 12, 1946.

Economic Stabilization Agency Established by EO 10161 of Sept. 9, 1950, and EO 10276 of July 31, 1951. Terminated, except for liquidation purposes, by EO 10434 of Feb. 6, 1953. Liquidation completed Oct. 31, 1953, pursuant to EO 10480 of Aug. 14, 1953.

Economic Stabilization Board Established by EO 9250 of Oct. 3, 1942. Transferred to *Office of War Mobilization and Reconversion* by EO 9620 of Sept. 20, 1945. Returned to *Office of Economic Stabilization* on reestablishment by EO 9699 of Feb. 21, 1946. *Board* returned to *Office of War Mobilization and Reconversion* by EO 9762 of July 25, 1946. Functions terminated by EO 9809 of Dec. 12, 1946.

Economic Warfare, Board of *See* **Economic Defense Board**

Economic Warfare, Office of *See* **Economic Defense Board**

Economics, Bureau of Industrial Established by the Secretary of Commerce Jan. 2, 1980, in conjunction with Reorg. Plan No. 3 of 1979, effective Oct. 1, 1980, and operated under Department Organization Order 35–5B. Abolished at bureau level by Secretarial order, effective Jan. 22, 1984 (49 FR 4538). Industry-related functions realigned and transferred from Under Secretary for Economic Affairs to Under Secretary for International Trade. Under Secretary for Economic Affairs retained units to support domestic macroeconomic policy functions.

Economics, Statistics, and Cooperatives Service Renamed *Economics and Statistics Service* by Secretary of Agriculture Memorandum 2025 of Sept. 17, 1980. Redesignated as Economic Research Service and *Statistical Reporting Service* by Secretarial order of Oct. 1, 1981.

Economy Board, Joint Placed under direction of President by military order of July 5, 1939. Abolished Sept. 1, 1947, by joint letter of Aug. 20, 1947, from Secretaries of *War* and Navy to President.

Education, Federal Board for Vocational Established by act of Feb. 23, 1917 (39 Stat. 929). Functions transferred to the Department of the Interior by EO 6166 of June 10, 1933. Functions assigned to *Commissioner of Education* Oct. 10, 1933. *Office of Education* transferred from the Department of the Interior to the *Federal Security Agency* by Reorg. Plan No. I of 1939, effective July 1, 1939. *Board* abolished by Reorg. Plan No. 2 of 1946, effective July 16, 1946.

Education, National Institute of Established by act of June 23, 1972 (86 Stat. 327). Transferred to Office of Educational Research and Improvement, Department of Education, by act of Oct. 17, 1979 (93 Stat. 678), effective May 4, 1980.

Education, Office of Established as independent agency by act of Mar. 2, 1867 (14 Stat. 434). Transferred to the Department of the Interior by act of July 20, 1868 (15 Stat. 106). Transferred to *Federal Security Agency* by Reorg. Plan No. I of 1939, effective July 1, 1939. Functions of *Federal Security Administrator* administered by *Office of Education* relating to student loans and defense-related education transferred to *War Manpower Commission* by EO 9247 of Sept. 17, 1942.

Education, Office of Bilingual Abolished by act of Oct. 17, 1979 (93 Stat. 675), and functions transferred to Office of Bilingual Education and Minority Languages Affairs, Department of Education.

Education Beyond the High School, President's Committee on Established by act of July 26, 1956 (70 Stat. 676). Terminated Dec. 31, 1957. Certain activities continued by *Bureau of Higher Education, Office of Education.*

Education Division Established in the *Department of Health, Education, and Welfare* by act of June 23, 1972 (86 Stat. 327). Functions transferred to the Department of Education by act of Oct. 17, 1979 (93 Stat. 677).

Education Goals Panel, National Terminated by Congressional mandate, March 15, 2002.

Education Statistics, National Center for Established in the Office of the Assistant Secretary, Department of Health and Human Services, by act of Aug. 21, 1974 (88 Stat. 556). Transferred to the Office of Educational Research and Improvement, Department of Education, by act of Oct. 17, 1979 (93 Stat. 678), effective May 4, 1980. Renamed *Center for Education Statistics* by act of Oct. 17, 1986 (100 Stat. 1579). Renamed National Center for Education Statistics by act of Apr. 28, 1988 (102 Stat. 331).

Educational and Cultural Affairs, Bureau of Established by Secretary of State in 1960. Terminated by Reorg. Plan No. 2 of 1977, effective July 1, 1978, and functions transferred to *International Communication Agency*, effective Apr. 1, 1978.

Educational and Cultural Affairs, Interagency Council on International   Established Jan. 20, 1964, by Foreign Affairs Manual Circular, under authority of act of Sept. 21, 1961 (75 Stat. 527). Terminated Oct. 1973 following creation of Subcommittee on International Exchanges by National Security Council directive.

Educational Exchange, U.S. Advisory Commission on   Established by act of Jan. 27, 1948 (62 Stat. 10). Abolished by act of Sept. 21, 1961 (75 Stat. 538), and superseded by U.S. Advisory Commission on International Educational and Cultural Affairs.

Efficiency, Bureau of   Organized under act of Feb. 28, 1916 (39 Stat. 15). Abolished by act of Mar. 3, 1933 (47 Stat. 1519), and records transferred to *Bureau of the Budget.*

Elderly, Committee on Mental Health and Illness of the   Established by act of July 29, 1975 (89 Stat. 347). Terminated Sept. 30, 1977.

Electoral votes for President and Vice President, transfer of functions   See **State, Department of**

Electric Home and Farm Authority   Incorporated Aug. 1, 1935, under laws of District of Columbia. Designated as U.S. agency by EO 7139 of Aug. 12, 1935. Continued by act of June 10, 1941 (55 Stat. 248). Grouped with other agencies in *Federal Loan Agency* by Reorg. Plan. No. I of 1939, effective July 1, 1939. Functions transferred to the Department of Commerce by EO 9071 of Feb. 24, 1942. Terminated by EO 9256 of Oct. 13, 1942.

Electric Home and Farm Authority, Inc.   Organized Jan. 17, 1934, under laws of State of Delaware by EO 6514 of Dec. 19, 1933. Dissolved Aug. 1, 1935, and succeeded by *Electric Home and Farm Authority.*

Electricity Delivery and Energy Reliability, Office of   Established by Secretary of Energy announcement of June 9, 2005. Position of director elevated to Assistant Secretary of Electricity Delivery and Energy Reliability by Secretary's memorandum EXEC-2007-010607 of Oct. 24, 2007.

Electricity Transmission and Distribution, Office of   Renamed *Office of Electricity Delivery and Energy Reliability* by the Secretary of Energy's memo of Feb. 15, 2005.

Emergency Administration of Public Works, Federal   Established by act of June 16, 1933 (48 Stat. 200). Operation continued by subsequent legislation, including act of June 21, 1938 (52 Stat. 816). Consolidated with *Federal Works Agency* as *Public Works Administration* by Reorg. Plan No. I of 1939, effective July 1, 1939. Functions transferred to *Office of Federal Works Administrator* by EO 9357 of June 30, 1943.

Emergency Conservation Work   Established by EO 6101 of Apr. 5, 1933. Succeeded by *Civilian Conservation Corps.*

Emergency Council, National   Established by EO 6433–A of Nov. 17, 1933. Consolidated with *Executive Council* by EO 6889–A of Oct. 29, 1934. Abolished by Reorg. Plan No. II of 1939, effective

July 1, 1939, and functions (except those relating to *Radio Division* and *Film Service*) transferred to Executive Office of the President.

Emergency Council, Office of Economic Adviser to National   Established by EO 6240 of Aug. 3, 1933, in connection with *Executive Council,* which later consolidated with *National Emergency Council.* Records and property used in preparation of statistical and economic summaries transferred to *Central Statistical Board* by EO 7003 of Apr. 8, 1935.

Emergency Management, Office for   Established in Executive Office of the President by administrative order of May 25, 1940, in accordance with EO 8248 of Sept. 8, 1939. Inactive.

Emergency Management Agency, Federal   Established in EO 12127 of Mar. 31, 1979. Functions transferred to Department of Homeland Security by act of Nov. 25, 2002 (116 Stat. 2213). Established as a distinct entity with the Department of Homeland Security by act of Oct. 4, 2006 (120 Stat. 1400).

Emergency Mobilization Preparedness Board   Established Dec. 17, 1981, by the President. Abolished by Presidential directive of Sept. 16, 1985.

Emergency Planning, Office of   Established as successor to *Office of Civil and Defense Mobilization* by act of Sept. 22, 1961 (75 Stat. 630). Renamed *Office of Emergency Preparedness* by act of Oct. 21, 1968 (82 Stat. 1194). Terminated by Reorg. Plan No. 2 of 1973, effective July 1, 1973, and functions transferred to the the Departments of the Treasury and Housing and Urban Development and the General Services Administration.

Emergency Preparedness, Office of   See **Emergency Planning, Office of**

Emergency Procurement Service   Established Sept. 1, 1950, by Administrator of General Services. Renamed *Defense Materials Service* Sept. 7, 1956. Functions transferred to *Property Management and Disposal Service* July 29, 1966. *Service* abolished July 1, 1973, and functions transferred to Federal Supply Service, Public Buildings Service, and Federal Property Resources Service.

Emergency Relief Administration, Federal   Established by act of May 12, 1933 (48 Stat. 55). Expired June 30, 1938, having been liquidated by *Works Progress Administrator* pursuant to act of May 28, 1937 (50 Stat. 352).

Employee-Management Relations Program, President's Committee on the Implementation of the Federal   Established by EO 10988 of Jan. 17, 1962. Terminated upon submission of report to President June 21, 1963.

Employees' Compensation, Bureau of   Transferred from *Federal Security Agency* to the Department of Labor by Reorg. Plan No. 19 of 1950, effective May 24, 1950. Functions absorbed by Employment Standards Administration Mar. 13, 1972.

Employees' Compensation Appeals Board
Transferred from *Federal Security Agency* to the
Department of Labor by Reorg. Plan No. 19 of 1950,
effective May 24, 1950.

Employees' Compensation Commission, U.S.
Established by act of Sept. 7, 1916 (39 Stat. 742).
Abolished by Reorg. Plan No. 2 of 1946, effective
July 16, 1946, and functions transferred to *Federal
Security Administrator.*

Employment Board, Fair   Established by *U.S. Civil
Service Commission* pursuant to EO 9980 of July 26,
1948. Abolished by EO 10590 of Jan. 18, 1955.

**Employment of People With Disabilities, President's
Committee on**   Created by EO 12640 of May 10,
1988. Duties subsumed by the Office of Disability
Employment within the Department of Labor as
directed by Public Law 106–554 of Dec. 21, 2000.

**Employment of the Physically Handicapped,
President's Committee on**   Established by EO
10640 of Oct. 10, 1955, continuing *Committee*
established by act of July 11, 1949 (63 Stat. 409).
Superseded by President's Committee on
Employment of the Handicapped established by EO
10994 of Feb. 14, 1962.

**Employment Policy, President's Committee on
Government**   Established by EO 10590 of Jan. 18,
1955. Abolished by EO 10925 of Mar. 6, 1961, and
functions transferred to *President's Committee on
Equal Employment Opportunity.*

Employment Practice, Committee on Fair
Established in *Office of Production Management* by
EO 8802 of June 25, 1941. Transferred to *War
Manpower Commission* by Presidential letter
effective July 30, 1942. Committee terminated on
establishment of *Committee on Fair Employment
Practice, Office for Emergency Management,* by EO
9346 of May 27, 1943. Terminated June 30, 1946,
by act of July 17, 1945 (59 Stat. 743).

Employment Security, Bureau of   Transferred from
Federal Security Agency to the Department of Labor
by Reorg. Plan No. 2 of 1949, effective Aug. 20,
1949. Abolished by order of Mar. 14, 1969 of the
Secretary of Labor, and functions transferred to
Manpower Administration.

Employment Service, U.S.   Established in the
Department of Labor in 1918 by departmental order.
Abolished by act of June 6, 1933 (48 Stat. 113), and
created as bureau with same name. Functions
consolidated with unemployment compensation
functions of *Social Security Board, Bureau of
Employment Security,* and transferred to *Federal
Security Agency* by Reorg. Plan No. I of 1939,
effective July 1, 1939. *Service* transferred to *Bureau
of Placement, War Manpower Commission,* by EO
9247 of Sept. 17, 1942. Returned to the Department
of Labor by EO 9617 of Sept. 19, 1945. Transferred
to *Federal Security Agency* by act of June 16, 1948
(62 Stat. 443), to function as part of *Bureau of
Employment Security,* Social Security Administration.
Bureau, including *U.S. Employment Service,*
transferred to the Department of Labor by Reorg.
Plan No. 2 of 1949, effective Aug. 20, 1949.
Abolished by reorganization of *Manpower*

Administration, effective Mar. 17, 1969, and
functions assigned to *U.S. Training and Employment
Service.*

Employment Stabilization Board, Federal
Established by act of Feb. 10, 1931 (46 Stat. 1085).
Abolished by EO 6166 of June 10, 1933. Abolition
deferred by EO 6623 of Mar. 1, 1934, until
functions of *Board* transferred to *Federal
Employment Stabilization Office,* established in the
Department of Commerce by same order. *Office*
abolished by Reorg. Plan No. I of 1939, effective
July 1, 1939, and functions transferred from the
Department of Commerce to *National Resources
Planning Board,* Executive Office of the President.

Employment Stabilization Office, Federal.   *See*
Employment Stabilization Board, Federal

Employment and Training, Office of Comprehensive
Established in the Department of Labor. Terminated
due to expiration of authority for appropriations after
fiscal year 1982. Replaced by *Office of Employment
and Training Programs.*

Employment and Training Programs, Office of
Renamed Office of Job Training Programs by
Employment and Training Administration
reorganization in the Department of Labor, effective
June 1984.

Endangered Species Scientific Authority
Established by EO 11911 of Apr. 13, 1976.
Terminated by act of Dec. 28, 1979 (93 Stat. 1228),
and functions transferred to the Secretary of the
Interior.

Energy Administration, Federal   Established by act
of May 7, 1974 (88 Stat. 96). Assigned additional
responsibilities by acts of June 22, 1974 (88 Stat.
246), Dec. 22, 1975 (89 Stat. 871), and Aug. 14,
1976 (90 Stat. 1125). Terminated by act of Aug. 4,
1977 (91 Stat. 577), and functions transferred to the
Department of Energy.Energy Advisory Support
Office, Secretary of Abolished by secretarial decision
of Feb. 6, 2006.

Energy Assurance, Office of   Abolished pursuant to
Conference Report No. 108-729 on H.R. 4818,
Consolidated Appropriations Act. Functions merged
with *Office of Electricity Delivery and Energy
Reliability.*

Energy Conservation, Office of   Established by
Interior Secretarial Order 2953 May 7, 1973.
Functions transferred to *Federal Energy
Administration* by act of May 7, 1974 (88 Stat. 100).

Energy Data and Analysis, Office of   Established by
Interior Secretarial Order 2953 of May 7, 1973.
Functions transferred to *Federal Energy
Administration* by act of May 7, 1974 (88 Stat. 100).

Energy Policy Office   Established in Executive
Office of the President by EO 11726 of June 29,
1973. Abolished by EO 11775 of Mar. 26, 1974.

Energy Programs, Office of   Established by
Department of Commerce Organization Order 25–
7A, effective Sept. 24, 1975. Terminated by act of
Aug. 4, 1977 (91 Stat. 581), and functions
transferred to the Department of Energy.

Energy Research and Development Administration
Established by act of Oct. 11, 1974 (88 Stat. 1234).
Assigned responsibilities by acts of Sept. 3, 1974 (88
Stat. 1069, 1079), Oct. 26, 1974 (88 Stat. 1431),
and Dec. 31, 1974 (88 Stat. 1887). Terminated by
act of Aug. 4, 1977 (91 Stat. 577), and functions
transferred to the Department of Energy.

Energy Resources Council   Established in Executive
Office of the President by act of Oct. 11, 1974 (88
Stat. 1233). Establishing authority repealed by act of
Aug. 4, 1977 (91 Stat. 608), and *Council* terminated.

**Energy Supplies and Resources Policy, Presidential
Advisory Committee on**   Established July 30, 1954,
by President. Abolished Mar. 12, 1961, by President
and functions transferred to the Secretary of the
Interior.

Enforcement Commission, National   Established by
General Order 18 of *Economic Stabilization
Administrator,* effective July 30, 1952. Functions
transferred to Director, *Office of Defense
Mobilization,* and Attorney General by EO 10494 of
Oct. 14, 1953.

Engineering, Bureau of   *See* **Steam Engineering,
Bureau of**

Entomology, Bureau of   *See* **Entomology and Plant
Quarantine, Bureau of**

Entomology and Plant Quarantine, Bureau of
Bureau of Entomology and *Bureau of Plant
Quarantine* created by acts of Apr. 23, 1904 (33
Stat. 276), and July 7, 1932 (47 Stat. 640),
respectively. Consolidated with disease control and
eradication functions of *Bureau of Plant Industry* into
Bureau of Entomology and Plant Quarantine by act
of Mar. 23, 1934 (48 Stat. 467). Functions
transferred to Agricultural Research Service by
Secretary's Memorandum 1320, supp. 4, of Nov. 2,
1953.

Environment, Cabinet Committee on the   *See*
Environmental Quality Council

Environmental Financing Authority   Established by
act of Oct. 18, 1972 (86 Stat. 899). Expired June 30,
1975, pursuant to terms of act.

Environmental Quality Council   Established by EO
11472 of May 29, 1969. Renamed *Cabinet
Committee on the Environment* by EO 11514 of
Mar. 5, 1970. EO 11514 terminated by EO 11541
of July 1, 1970.

Environment, Safety, and Health, Office of
Established by act of Aug. 4, 1977 (91 Stat. 570).
Abolished by Secretary of Energy memorandum
2006-007929 of Aug. 30, 2006, and functions
transferred to Office of Health, Safety, and Security.

Environmental Science Services Administration
Established in the Department of Commerce by
Reorg. Plan No. 2 of 1965, effective July 13, 1965,
by consolidating *Weather Bureau* and *Coast and
Geodetic Survey.* Abolished by Reorg. Plan No. 4 of
1970, effective Oct. 3, 1970, and functions
transferred to National Oceanic and Atmospheric
Administration.

**Equal Employment Opportunity, President's
Committee on**   Established by EO 10925 of Mar. 6,
1961. Abolished by EO 11246 of Sept. 24, 1965,
and functions transferred to the Department of Labor
and *U.S. Civil Service Commission.*

Equal Opportunity, President's Council on
Established by EO 11197 of Feb. 5, 1965. Abolished
by EO 11247 of Sept. 24, 1965, and functions
transferred to the Department of Justice.

Equipment, Bureau of   Established as *Bureau of
Equipment and Recruiting* by act of July 5, 1862 (12
Stat. 510), replacing *Bureau of Construction,
Equipment and Repairs.* Designated as *Bureau of
Equipment* in annual appropriation acts commencing
with fiscal year 1892 (26 Stat. 192) after cognizance
over enlisted personnel matters transferred, effective
July 1, 1889, to *Bureau of Navigation.* Functions
distributed among bureaus and offices in the
Department of the Navy by act of June 24, 1910 (61
Stat. 613). Abolished by act of June 30, 1914 (38
Stat. 408).

Ethics, Office of Government   Established in the
Office of Personnel Management by act of Oct. 26,
1978 (92 Stat. 1862). Became a separate executive
agency status by act of Nov. 3, 1988 (102 Stat.
3031).

**European Migration, Intergovernmental Committee
for**   Renamed Intergovernmental Committee for
Migration by Resolution 624, passed by
Intergovernmental Committee for European
Migration Council, effective Nov. 11, 1980.

Evacuation, Joint Committee on   *See* **Health and
Welfare Aspects of Evacuation of Civilians, Joint
Committee on**

Exchange Service, International   Established in
1849 in Smithsonian Institution. Renamed Office of
Publications Exchange by Secretary's internal
directive of Jan. 11, 1985.

**Executive Branch of the Government, Commission
on Organization of the**   Established by act of July
7, 1947 (61 Stat. 246). Terminated June 12, 1949,
pursuant to terms of act. Second *Commission on
Organization of the Executive Branch of the
Government* established by act of July 10, 1953 (67
Stat. 142). Terminated June 30, 1955, pursuant to
terms of act.

Executive Council   Established by EO 6202–A of
July 11, 1933. Consolidated with *National
Emergency Council* by EO 6889–A of Oct. 29, 1934.

Executive Exchange, President's Commission on
See **Personnel Interchange, President's Commission
on**

Executive orders   *See* **State, Department of**

**Executive Organization, President's Advisory
Council on**   Established by President Apr. 5, 1969.
Terminated May 7, 1971.

Executive Protective Service   *See* **Secret Service
Division**

Executives, Active Corps of   Established in ACTION
by act of Oct. 1, 1973 (87 Stat. 404). Transferred to

Small Business Administration by EO 11871 of July 18, 1975.

Export Administration, Bureau of   Established as a separate agency within the Department of Commerce on Oct. 1, 1987 (50 USC app. 2401 *et seq.*). Renamed Bureau of Industry and Security by Department of Commerce internal organization order of Apr. 18, 2002 (67 FR 20630).

Export Control, Administrator of   Functions delegated to Administrator by Proc. 2413 of July 2, 1940, transferred to *Office of Export Control, Economic Defense Board,* by EO 8900 of Sept. 15, 1941. Renamed *Board of Economic Warfare* by EO 8982 of Dec. 17, 1941. *Board* terminated by EO 9361 of July 15, 1943.

Export Control, Office of   *See* **Export Control, Administrator of**

Export-Import Bank of Washington   Organization of District of Columbia banking corporation directed by EO 6581 of Feb. 2, 1934. Certificate of incorporation filed Feb. 12, 1934. Grouped with other agencies to form *Federal Loan Agency* by Reorg. Plan No. I of 1939, effective July 1, 1939. Transferred to the Department of Commerce by EO 9071 of Feb. 24, 1942. Functions transferred to *Office of Economic Warfare* by EO 9361 of July 15, 1943. Established as permanent independent agency by act of July 31, 1945 (59 Stat. 526). Renamed Export-Import Bank of the U.S. by act of Mar. 13, 1968 (82 Stat. 47).

Export-Import Bank of Washington, DC, Second   Authorized by EO 6638 of Mar. 9, 1934. Abolished by EO 7365 of May 7, 1936, and records transferred to *Export-Import Bank of Washington,* effective June 30, 1936.

Export Marketing Service   Established by the Secretary of Agriculture Mar. 28, 1969. Merged with Foreign Agricultural Service by Secretary's memorandum of Dec. 7, 1973, effective Feb. 3, 1974.

Exports and Requirements, Division of   Established in *Office of Foreign Economic Coordination* by the Department of State order of Feb. 1, 1943. Abolished by departmental order of Nov. 6, 1943, pursuant to EO 9380 of Sept. 25, 1943.

Extension Service   Established by act of May 14, 1914 (38 Stat. 372). Consolidated into *Science and Education Administration* by Secretary's order of Jan. 24, 1978. Reestablished as *Extension Service* by Secretarial order of June 16, 1981. Became part of Cooperative State, Research, Education, and Extension Service under Department of Agriculture's reorganization in 1995.

Facts and Figures, Office of   Established in *Office for Emergency Management* by EO 8922 of Oct. 24, 1941. Consolidated with *Office of War Information* in *Office for Emergency Management* by EO 9182 of June 13, 1942.

Family Security Committee   Established in *Office of Defense Health and Welfare Services* Feb. 12, 1941, by administrative order. Terminated Dec. 17, 1942.

Family Services, Bureau of   *See* **Assistance, Bureau of Public**

Family Support Administration   Established on Apr. 4, 1986, in the Department of Health and Human Services under authority of section 6 of Reorganization Plan No. 1 of 1953, effective Apr. 11, 1953 (*see also* 51 FR 11641). Merged into Administration for Children and Families by Secretary's reorganization notice dated Apr. 15, 1991.

Farm Board, Federal   Established by act of June 15, 1929 (46 Stat. 11). Renamed Farm Credit Administration and certain functions abolished by EO 6084 of Mar. 27, 1933. Administration placed under the Department of Agriculture by Reorg. Plan No. I of 1939, effective July 1, 1939. Made independent agency in the executive branch of the Government, to be housed in the Department of Agriculture, by act of Aug. 6, 1953 (67 Stat. 390). Removed from the Department of Agriculture by act of Dec. 10, 1971 (85 Stat. 617).

Farm Credit Administration   *See* **Farm Board, Federal**

Farm Loan Board, Federal   Established in the Department of the Treasury to administer act of July 17, 1916 (39 Stat. 360). Offices of appointed members of *Board,* except member designated as *Farm Loan Commissioner,* abolished by EO 6084 of Mar. 27, 1933, and *Board* functions transferred to *Farm Loan Commissioner,* subject to jurisdiction and control of Farm Credit Administration. Title changed to *Land Bank Commissioner* by act of June 16, 1933. Abolished by act of Aug. 6, 1953 (67 Stat. 393).

Farm Loan Bureau, Federal   Established in the Department of the Treasury under supervision of *Federal Farm Loan Board* and charged with execution of act of July 17, 1916 (39 Stat. 360). Transferred to *Farm Credit Administration* by EO 6084 of Mar. 27, 1933.

Farm Loan Commissioner   *See* **Farm Loan Board, Federal**

Farm Mortgage Corporation, Federal   Established by act of Jan. 31, 1934 (48 Stat. 344). Transferred to the Department of Agriculture by Reorg. Plan No. I of 1939, effective July 1, 1939, to operate under supervision of Farm Credit Administration. Abolished by act of Oct. 4, 1961 (75 Stat. 773).

Farm Products, Division of   (Also known as *Division of Agriculture*) Established by *Advisory Commission to Council of National Defense* pursuant to act of Aug. 29, 1916 (39 Stat. 649). *Office of Agricultural Defense Relations* (later known as *Office for Agricultural War Relations*) established in the Department of Agriculture by Presidential letter of May 5, 1941, which transferred to the Secretary of Agriculture functions previously assigned to *Division of Agriculture.* Functions concerned with food production transferred to *Food Production Administration* and functions concerned with food distribution transferred to *Food Distribution Administration* by EO 9280 of Dec. 5, 1942.

Farm Security Administration *See* **Resettlement Administration**

Farm Service Agency Established by Secretary's Memorandum 1010–1 dated Oct. 20, 1994, under authority of the act of Oct. 13, 1994 (7 U.S.C. 6901), and assumed certain functions of the *Agricultural Stabilization and Conservation Service,* the *Farmers' Home Administration,* and the *Federal Crop Insurance Corporation.* Renamed *Consolidated Farm Service Agency* by Acting Administrator on Dec. 19, 1994.

Farmer Cooperative Service Established by Secretary of Agriculture Memorandum 1320, supp. 4, of Dec. 4, 1953. Consolidated with other Department of Agriculture units into *Economics, Statistics, and Cooperatives Service* by Secretary's Memorandum 1927, effective Dec. 23, 1977.

Farmers' Home Administration. *See* **Resettlement Administration**

Federal. *See also other part of title*

Federal Advisory Council Established in *Federal Security Agency* by act of June 6, 1933 (48 Stat. 116). Transferred to the Department of Labor by Reorg. Plan No. 2 of 1949, effective Aug. 20, 1949.

Federal Register, Administrative Committee of the *See* **Archives Establishment, National**

Federal Register, Division of the Established by act of July 26, 1935 (49 Stat. 500). Transferred to General Services Administration as part of *National Archives and Records Service* by act of June 30, 1949 (63 Stat. 381). Renamed Office of the Federal Register by order of General Services Administrator, Feb. 6, 1959. Transferred to National Archives and Records Administration by act of Oct. 19, 1984 (98 Stat. 2283).

Federal Register, Office of the *See* **Federal Register, Division of the**

Federal Reserve Board Renamed Board of Governors of the Federal Reserve System, and Governor and Vice Governor designated as Chairman and Vice Chairman, respectively, of Board by act of Aug. 23, 1935 (49 Stat. 704).

Federal Tax Reform, President's Advisory Panel on Established by EO 13369 of Jan. 7, 2005. Abolished by EO 13446 of Sept. 28, 2007.

Field Services, Office of Established by the Secretary of Commerce Feb. 1, 1963, by Department Organization Order 40–3. Terminated by Department Organization Order 40–1A of Sept. 15, 1970, and functions transferred to *Bureau of Domestic Commerce.*

Filipino Rehabilitation Commission Established by act of June 29, 1944 (58 Stat. 626). Inactive pursuant to terms of act.

Film Service, U.S. Established by *National Emergency Council* in September 1938. Transferred to *Office of Education, Federal Security Agency,* by Reorg. Plan No. II of 1939, effective July 1, 1939. Terminated June 30, 1940.

Films, Coordinator of Government Director of *Office of Government Reports* designated *Coordinator of Government Films* by Presidential letter of Dec. 18, 1941. Functions transferred to *Office of War Information* by EO 9182 of June 13, 1942.

Financial Operations, Bureau of Government Renamed Financial Management Service by Order 145–21 of the Secretary of the Treasury, effective Oct. 10, 1984.

Fire Administration, U.S. *See* **Fire Prevention and Control Administration, National**

Fire Council, Federal Established by EO 7397 of June 20, 1936. Transferred July 1, 1939, to *Federal Works Agency* by EO 8194 of July 6, 1939, with functions under direction of *Federal Works Administrator.* Transferred with *Federal Works Agency* to General Services Administration by act of June 30, 1949 (63 Stat. 380). Transferred to the Department of Commerce by EO 11654 of Mar. 13, 1972.

Fire Prevention and Control, National Academy for Established in the Department of Commerce by act of Oct. 29, 1974 (88 Stat. 1537). Transferred to Federal Emergency Management Agency by Reorg. Plan No. 3 of 1978, effective Apr. 1, 1979.

Fire Prevention and Control Administration, National Renamed U.S. Fire Administration by act of Oct. 5, 1978 (92 Stat. 932). Transferred to Federal Emergency Management Agency by Reorg. Plan No. 3 of 1978, effective Apr. 1, 1979.

Fish Commission, U.S. *Commissioner of Fish and Fisheries* established as head of *U.S. Fish Commission* by joint resolution of Feb. 9, 1871 (16 Stat. 594). *Commission* established as *Bureau of Fisheries* in *Department of Commerce and Labor* by act of Feb. 14, 1903 (32 Stat. 827). Department of Labor created by act of Mar. 4, 1913 (37 Stat. 736), and *Bureau* remained in the Department of Commerce. Transferred to the Department of the Interior by Reorg. Plan No. II of 1939, effective July 1, 1939. Consolidated with *Bureau of Biological Survey* into *Fish and Wildlife Service* by Reorg. Plan No. III of 1940, effective June 30, 1940.

Fish and Wildlife Service Established by Reorg. Plan No. III of 1940, effective June 30, 1940, consolidating *Bureau of Fisheries* and *Bureau of Biological Survey.* Succeeded by U.S. Fish and Wildlife Service.

Fisheries, Bureau of *See* **Fish Commission, U.S.**

Fisheries, Bureau of Commercial Organized in 1959 under U.S. Fish and Wildlife Service, the Department of the Interior. Abolished by Reorg. Plan No. 4 of 1970, effective Oct. 3, 1970, and functions transferred to National Oceanic and Atmospheric Administration.

Fishery Coordination, Office of Established in the Department of the Interior by EO 9204 of July 21, 1942. Terminated by EO 9649 of Oct. 29, 1945.

Flood Indemnity Administration, Federal Established in *Housing and Home Finance Agency* by Administrator's Organizational Order 1, effective Sept. 28, 1956, redesignated as Administrator's Organizational Order 2 on Dec. 7, 1956, pursuant to act of Aug. 7, 1956 (70 Stat. 1078). Abolished by Administrator's Organizational Order 3, effective July 1, 1957, due to lack of funding.

Food, Cost of Living Council Committee on Established by EO 11695 of Jan. 11, 1973. Abolished by EO 11788 of June 18, 1974.

Food, Drug, and Insecticide Administration Established by act of Jan. 18, 1927 (44 Stat. 1002). Renamed Food and Drug Administration by act of May 27, 1930 (46 Stat. 422). Transferred from the Department of Agriculture to *Federal Security Agency* by Reorg. Plan No. IV of 1940, effective June 30, 1940. Transferred to *Department of Health, Education, and Welfare* by Reorg. Plan No. 1 of 1953, effective Apr. 11, 1953.

Food Distribution Administration Established in the Department of Agriculture by EO 9280 of Dec. 5, 1942, consolidating *Agricultural Marketing Administration, Sugar Agency,* distribution functions of *Office for Agricultural War Relations,* regulatory work of *Bureau of Animal Industry,* and food units of *War Production Board.* Consolidated with other agencies by EO 9322 of Mar. 26, 1943, to form *Administration of Food Production and Distribution.*

Food and Drug Administration See **Food, Drug, and Insecticide Administration**

Food Industry Advisory Committee Established by EO 11627 of Oct. 15, 1971. Abolished by EO 11781 of May 1, 1974.

Food and Nutrition Service Established Aug. 8, 1969, by Secretary of Agriculture under authority of 5 U.S.C. 301 and Reorg. Plan No. 2 of 1953 (5 U.S.C. app.). Abolished by Secretary's Memorandum 1010–1 dated Oct. 20, 1994. Functions assumed by Food and Consumer Service.

Food Production Administration Established in the Department of Agriculture by EO 9280 of Dec. 5, 1942, which consolidated *Agricultural Adjustment Agency,* Farm Credit Administration, *Farm Security Administration,* Federal Crop Insurance Corporation, Soil Conservation Service, and food production activities of *War Production Board, Office of Agricultural War Relations,* and *Division of Farm Management and Costs, Bureau of Agricultural Economics.* Consolidated with other agencies by EO 9322 of Mar. 26, 1943, to form *Administration of Food Production and Distribution.*

Food Production and Distribution, Administration of Established by consolidation of *Food Production Administration, Food Distribution Administration,* Commodity Credit Corporation, and Extension Service, Department of Agriculture, by EO 9322 of Mar. 26, 1943, under direction of Administrator, directly responsible to President. Renamed *War Food Administration* by EO 9334 of Apr. 19, 1943. Terminated by EO 9577 of June 29, 1945, and functions transferred to the Secretary of Agriculture. Transfer made permanent by Reorg. Plan No. 3 of 1946, effective July 16, 1946.

Food Safety and Quality Service Renamed Food Safety and Inspection Service by Agriculture Secretary's memorandum of June 19, 1981.

Foods, Bureau of Renamed Center for Food Safety and Applied Nutrition by Food and Drug Administration notice of Mar. 9, 1984 (49 FR 10166).

Foreign. *See also other part of title*

Foreign Aid, Advisory Committee on Voluntary Established by President May 14, 1946. Transferred from the Department of State to the Director of the *Mutual Security Agency,* and later to Director of the *Foreign Operations Administration,* by Presidential letter of June 1, 1953.

Foreign Intelligence Advisory Board, President's Established by EO 12863 of Sept. 13, 1993. Abolished by EO 13462 of Feb. 29, 2008.

Foreign Operations Administration Established by Reorg. Plan No. 7 of 1953, effective Aug. 1, 1953, and functions transferred from *Office of Director of Mutual Security, Mutual Security Agency, Technical Cooperation Administration, Institute of Inter-American Affairs.* Abolished by EO 10610 of May 9, 1955, and functions and offices transferred to the Departments of State and Defense.

Foreign Scholarships, Board of Renamed J. William Fulbright Foreign Scholarship Board by act of Feb. 16, 1990 (104 Stat. 49).

Forest Reservation Commission, National Established by act of Mar. 1, 1911 (36 Stat. 962). Terminated by act of Oct. 22, 1976 (90 Stat. 2961), and functions transferred to the Secretary of Agriculture.

Forests, Director of Established by Administrative Order 1283 of May 18, 1938. Made part of *Office of Land Utilization,* Department of the Interior, by Administrative Order 1466 of Apr. 15, 1940.

Freedmen's Hospital Established by act of Mar. 3, 1871 (16 Stat. 506; T. 32 of D.C. Code). Transferred from the Department of the Interior to *Federal Security Agency* by Reorg. Plan No. IV of 1940, effective June 30, 1940.

Fuel Yards Established by act of July 1, 1918 (40 Stat. 672). Transferred from *Bureau of Mines,* Department of Commerce, to *Procurement Division,* Department of the Treasury, by EO 6166 of June 10, 1933, effective Mar. 2, 1934.

Fuels Coordinator for War, Office of Solid *See* **Fuels Administration for War, Solid**

Fuels Corporation, U.S. Synthetic Established by act of June 30, 1980 (94 Stat. 636). Terminated Apr. 18, 1986, by act of Dec. 19, 1985 (99 Stat. 1249), and functions transferred to the Secretary of the Treasury.

Fund-Raising Within the Federal Service, President's Committee on Established by EO 10728 of Sept. 6, 1957. Abolished by EO 10927 of Mar. 18, 1961, and functions transferred to *U.S. Civil Service Commission.*

Gallaudet College *See* **Columbia Institution for the Instruction of the Deaf and Dumb, and the Blind**

General Programs, Office of Renamed Office of Public Programs by the Chairman, National Endowment for the Humanities, in January 1991.

Geographic Board, U.S. Established by EO 27–A of Sept. 4, 1890. Abolished by EO 6680 of Apr. 17, 1935, and duties transferred to *U.S. Board on Geographical Names,* Department of the Interior, effective June 17, 1934. *Board* abolished by act of July 25, 1947 (61 Stat. 457), and duties assumed by *Board on Geographic Names.*

Geographical Names, U.S. Board on *See* **Geographic Board, U.S.**

Geography, Office of Function of standardizing foreign place names placed in the Department of the Interior conjointly with the *Board on Geographic Names* by act of July 25, 1947 (61 Stat. 456). Functions transferred to the Department of Defense by memorandum of understanding by the Departments of the Interior and Defense and the *Bureau of the Budget* Mar. 9, 1968.

Geological Survey Established in the the Department of the Interior by act of Mar. 3, 1879 (20 Stat. 394). Renamed United States Geological Survey by acts of Nov. 13, 1991 (105 Stat. 1000) and May 18, 1992 (106 Stat. 172).

Germany, Mixed Claims Commission, U.S. and Established by agreement of Aug. 10, 1922, between U.S. and Germany. Duties extended by agreement of Dec. 31, 1928. Time limit for filing claims expired June 30, 1928. All claims disposed of by Oct. 30, 1939. Terminated June 30, 1941.

Global Communications, Office of Established within the White House Office by EO 13283 of Jan. 21, 2003. Abolished by EO 13385 of Sept. .

Goethals Memorial Commission Established by act of Aug. 4, 1935 (49 Stat. 743). Placed under jurisdiction of *Department of War* by EO 8191 of July 5, 1939.

Government. *See other part of title*

Grain Futures Administration Established in the Department of Agriculture under provisions of act of Sept. 21, 1922 (42 Stat. 998). Superseded by *Commodity Exchange Administration* by order of Secretary, effective July 1, 1936. Consolidated with other agencies into *Commodity Exchange Branch, Agricultural Marketing Administration,* by EO 9069 of Feb. 23, 1942. Functions transferred to the Secretary of Agriculture by EO 9577 of June 29, 1945. Transfer made permanent by Reorg. Plan No. 3 of 1946, effective July 16, 1946. Functions transferred to *Commodity Exchange Authority* by Secretary's Memorandum 1185 of Jan. 21, 1947. Functions transferred to Commodity Futures Trading Commission by act of Oct. 23, 1974 (88 Stat. 1414).

Grain Inspection Service, Federal Established in the Department of Agriculture by act of Oct. 21, 1976 (90 Stat. 2868). Abolished by Secretary's Memorandum 1010–1 dated Oct. 20, 1994, and program authority and functions transferred to the

Grain Inspection, Packers and Stockyards Administration.

Grain Stabilization Corporation Organized as Delaware corporation to operate in connection with *Federal Farm Board* pursuant to act of June 15, 1929 (46 Stat. 11). Terminated by filing of certificate of dissolution with Corporation Commission of State of Delaware Dec. 14, 1935.

Grant Administration, Office of Transferred from the Office of the General Council to the Deputy Director, U.S. Trade and Development Agency by administrative order of Apr. 25, 2007.

Grants and Program Systems, Office of Abolished and functions transferred to Cooperative State Research Service, Department of Agriculture, by Secretarial Memorandum 1020–26 of July 1, 1986.

Grazing Service Consolidated with *General Land Office* into Bureau of Land Management, Department of the Interior, by Reorg. Plan No. 3 of 1946, effective July 16, 1946.

Great Lakes Basin Commission Established by EO 11345 of Apr. 20, 1967. Terminated by EO 12319 of Sept. 9, 1981.

Great Lakes Pilotage Administration Established in the Department of Commerce to administer act of June 30, 1960 (74 Stat. 259). Administration of act transferred to the Secretary of Transportation by act of Oct. 15, 1966 (80 Stat. 931).

Greening the Government through Waste Prevention and Recycling, Steering Committee Established by EO 13101 of Sept. 14, 1998. Abolished by EO 13423 of Jan. 24, 2007.

Handicapped, National Center on Education Media and Materials for the Established by agreement between the *Secretary of Health, Education, and Welfare* and Ohio State University, pursuant to acts of Aug. 20, 1969 (83 Stat. 102) and Apr. 13, 1970 (84 Stat. 187). Authorization deleted by act of Nov. 29, 1975 (89 Stat. 795), and the Secretary was authorized to enter into agreements with non-Federal organizations to establish and operate centers for handicapped.

Handicapped, National Council on the Established in the *Department of Health, Education, and Welfare* by act of Nov. 6, 1978 (92 Stat. 2977). Transferred to the Department of Education by act of Oct. 17, 1979 (93 Stat. 677). Reorganized as independent agency by act of Feb. 22, 1984 (98 Stat. 26).

Handicapped Employees, Interagency Committee on Alternately renamed Interagency Committee on Employment of People with Disabilities by EO 12704 of Feb. 26, 1990.

Handicapped Individuals, White House Conference on Established by act of Dec. 7, 1974 (88 Stat. 1617). Terminated Dec. 30, 1977, pursuant to terms of act.

Handicapped Research, National Institute of Renamed National Institute on Disability and Rehabilitation Research by act of Oct. 21, 1986 (100 Stat. 1820).

Health, Cost of Living Council Committee on
Established by EO 11695 of Jan. 11, 1973.
Abolished by EO 11788 of June 18, 1974.

Health, Education, and Welfare, Department of
Established by Reorganization Plan No. 1 of 1953 (5
U.S.C. app.), effective Apr. 11, 1953. Renamed
Department of Health and Human Services by act of
Oct. 17, 1979 (93 Stat. 695).

**Health, Welfare, and Related Defense Activities,
Office of the Coordinator of** *Federal Security
Administrator* designated as Coordinator of health,
welfare, and related fields of activity affecting
national defense, including aspects of education
under *Federal Security Agency*, by *Council of
National Defense*, with approval of President, Nov.
28, 1940. Office of Coordinator superseded by
Office of Defense Health and Welfare Services,
established in *Office for Emergency Services* by EO
8890 of Sept. 3, 1941.

Health Care Technology, National Council on
Established by act of July 1, 1944, as amended (92
Stat. 3447). Renamed *Council on Health Care
Technology* by act of Oct. 30, 1984 (98 Stat. 2820).
Name lowercased by act of Oct. 7, 1985 (99 Stat.
493). Terminated by act of Dec. 19, 1989 (103 Stat.
2205).

**Health Facilities, Financing, Compliance, and
Conversion, Bureau of** Renamed Bureau of Health
Facilities by Department of Health and Human
Services Secretarial order of Mar. 12, 1980 (45 FR
17207).

Health Industry Advisory Committee Established
by EO 11695 of Jan. 11, 1973. Abolished by EO
11781 of May 1, 1974.

Health Manpower, Bureau of Renamed Bureau of
Health Professions by Department of Health and
Human Services Secretarial order of Mar. 12, 1980
(45 FR 17207).

Health and Medical Committee Established by
Council of National Defense order of Sept. 19,
1940. Transferred to *Federal Security Agency* by
Council order approved by President Nov. 28, 1940.
Reestablished in *Office of Defense Health and
Welfare Services, Office for Emergency
Management*, by EO 8890 of Sept. 3, 1941.
Committee transferred to *Federal Security Agency* by
EO 9338 of Apr. 29, 1943.

Health Resources Administration Established in
Public Health Service. Abolished by Department of
Health and Human Services Secretarial
reorganization of Aug. 20, 1982 (47 FR 38409), and
functions transferred to Health Resources and
Services Administration.

Health Service, Public Originated by act of July
16, 1798 (1 Stat. 605). Transferred from the
Department of the Treasury to the *Federal Security
Agency* by Reorg. Plan No. I of 1939, effective July
1, 1939.

Health Services Administration Established in
Public Health Service. Abolished by Department of
Health and Human Services Secretarial
reorganization of Aug. 20, 1982 (47 FR 38409), and

functions transferred to Health Resources and
Services Administration.

Health Services Industry, Committee on the
Established by EO 11627 of Oct. 15, 1971.
Abolished by EO 11695 of Jan. 11, 1973.

Health Services and Mental Health Administration
Established in Public Health Service Apr. 1, 1968.
Abolished by *Department of Health, Education, and
Welfare* reorganization order and functions
transferred to *Centers for Disease Control, Health
Resources Administration*, and *Health Services
Administration*, effective July 1, 1973.

Health Services Research, National Center for
Established by act of July 23, 1974 (88 Stat. 363).
Transferred from *Health Resources Administration* to
Office of the Assistant Secretary for Health by
Department of Health, Education, and Welfare
reorganization, effective Dec. 2, 1977. Renamed
*National Center for Health Services Research and
Health Care Technology Assessment* by Secretary's
order, pursuant to act of Oct. 30, 1984 (98 Stat.
2817). Terminated by act of Dec. 19, 1989 (103
Stat. 2205).

Health Statistics, National Center for Established
by act of July 23, 1974 (88 Stat. 363). Transferred
from *Health Resources Administration* to Office of
the Assistant Secretary for Health by the *Department
of Health, Education, and Welfare* reorganization,
effective Dec. 2, 1977. Transferred to *Centers for
Disease Control* by Secretary's notice of Apr. 2,
1987 (52 FR 13318).

**Health and Welfare Activities, Interdepartmental
Committee to Coordinate** Appointed by President
Aug. 15, 1935, and reestablished by EO 7481 of
Oct. 27, 1936. Terminated in 1939.

**Health and Welfare Aspects of Evacuation of
Civilians, Joint Committee on** Established August
1941 as joint committee of *Office of Defense Health
and Welfare Services* and *Office of Civilian Defense*.
Reorganized in June 1942 and renamed *Joint
Committee on Evacuation*. *Office of Defense Health
and Welfare Services* abolished by EO 9388 of Apr.
29, 1943, and functions transferred to *Federal
Security Agency*. *Committee* terminated.

Heart and Lung Institute, National Renamed
National Heart, Lung, and Blood Institute by act of
Apr. 22, 1976 (90 Stat. 402).

Heritage Conservation and Recreation Service
Established by the Secretary of the Interior Jan. 25,
1978. Abolished by Secretarial Order 3060 of Feb.
19, 1981, and functions transferred to National Park
Service.

Hemispheric Defense Studies, Center for
Established by Department of Defense Directive
3200.12 of Sept. 3, 1997. Abolished by act of Oct.
17, 2006 (120 Stat. 2353).

Highway Safety Agency, National Established in
the Department of Commerce by act of Sept. 9,
1966 (80 Stat. 731). Functions transferred to the
Department of Transportation by act of Oct. 15,
1966 (80 Stat. 931). Functions transferred to
National Highway Safety Bureau by EO 11357 of

June 6, 1967. *Bureau* renamed National Highway Traffic Safety Administration by act of Dec. 31, 1970 (84 Stat. 1739).

Highway Safety Bureau, National *See* **Highway Safety Agency, National**

Home Economics, Bureau of Human Nutrition and *See* **Home Economics, Office of**

Home Economics, Office of Renamed *Bureau of Home Economics* by Secretary's Memorandum 436, effective July 1, 1923, pursuant to act of Feb. 26, 1923 (42 Stat. 1289). Redesignated *Bureau of Human Nutrition and Home Economics* February 1943 in accordance with *Research Administration* Memorandum 5 issued pursuant to EO 9069 of Feb. 23, 1942, and in conformity with Secretary's Memorandums 960 and 986. Functions transferred to Agricultural Research Service by Secretary's Memorandum 1320, supp. 4, of Nov. 2, 1953.

Home Loan Bank Administration, Federal *See* **Home Loan Bank Board, Federal**

Home Loan Bank Board *See* **Home Loan Bank Board, Federal**

Home Loan Bank Board, Federal Established by acts of July 22, 1932 (47 Stat. 725), June 13, 1933 (48 Stat. 128), and June 27, 1934 (48 Stat. 1246). Grouped with other agencies to form *Federal Loan Agency* by Reorg. Plan No. I of 1939, effective July 1, 1939. Functions transferred to *Federal Home Loan Bank Administration, National Housing Agency,* by EO 9070 of Feb. 24, 1942. Abolished by Reorg. Plan No. 3, effective July 27, 1947, and functions transferred to *Home Loan Bank Board, Housing and Home Finance Agency.* Renamed *Federal Home Loan Bank Board* and made independent agency by act of Aug. 11, 1955 (69 Stat. 640). Abolished by act of Aug. 9, 1989 (103 Stat. 354, 415), and functions transferred to Office of Thrift Supervision, Resolution Trust Corporation, Federal Deposit Insurance Corporation, and Federal Housing Finance Board.

Home Loan Bank System, Federal Grouped with other agencies to form *Federal Loan Agency* by Reorg. Plan No. I of 1939, effective July 1, 1939. Functions transferred to *Federal Home Loan Bank Administration, National Housing Agency,* by EO 9070 of Feb. 24, 1942. Transferred to *Housing and Home Finance Agency* by Reorg. Plan No. 3 of 1947, effective July 27, 1947.

Home Mortgage Credit Extension Committee, National Voluntary Established by act of Aug. 2, 1954 (68 Stat 638). Terminated Oct. 1, 1965, pursuant to terms of act.

Home Owners' Loan Corporation Established by act of June 13, 1933 (48 Stat. 128), under supervision of *Federal Home Loan Bank Board.* Grouped with other agencies to form *Federal Loan Agency* by Reorg. Plan No. I of 1939, effective July 1, 1939. Transferred to *Federal Home Loan Bank Administration, National Housing Agency,* by EO 9070 of Feb. 24, 1942. Board of Directors abolished by Reorg. Plan No. 3 of 1947, effective July 27, 1947, and functions transferred, for liquidation of assets, to *Home Loan Bank Board, Housing and Home Finance Agency.* Terminated by order of

Secretary of the Home Loan Bank Board, effective Feb. 3, 1954, pursuant to act of June 30, 1953 (67 Stat. 121).

Homesteads, Division of Subsistence Established by act of June 16, 1933 (48 Stat. 205). Secretary of the Interior authorized to administer section 208 of act by EO 6209 of July 21, 1933. *Federal Subsistence Homesteads Corporation* created by Secretary's order of Dec. 2, 1933, and organization incorporated under laws of Delaware. Transferred to *Resettlement Administration* by EO 7041 of May 15, 1935.

Homesteads Corporation, Federal Subsistence *See* **Homesteads, Division of Subsistence**

Hospitalization, Board of Federal Organized Nov. 1, 1921. Designated as advisory agency to *Bureau of the Budget* May 7, 1943. Terminated June 30, 1948, by Director's letter of May 28, 1948.

Housing, President's Committee on Equal Opportunity in Established by EO 11063 of Nov. 20, 1962. Inactive as of June 30, 1968.

Housing Administration, Federal Established by act of June 27, 1934 (48 Stat. 1246). Grouped with other agencies to form *Federal Loan Agency* by Reorg. Plan No. I of 1939, effective July 1, 1939. Functions transferred to *Federal Housing Administration, National Housing Agency,* by EO 9070 of Feb. 24, 1942. Transferred to *Housing and Home Finance Agency* by Reorg. Plan No. 3, effective July 27, 1947. Functions transferred to the Department of Housing and Urban Development by act of Sept. 9, 1965 (79 Stat. 667).

Housing Administration, Public Established as constituent agency of *Housing and Home Finance Agency* by Reorg. Plan No. 3 of 1947, effective July 27, 1947. Functions transferred to the Department of Housing and Urban Development by act of Sept. 9, 1965 (79 Stat. 667).

Housing Agency, National Established by EO 9070 of Feb. 24, 1942, to consolidate housing functions relating to *Federal Home Loan Bank Board, Federal Home Loan Bank System, Federal Savings and Loan Insurance Corporation, Home Owners' Loan Corporation, U.S. Housing Corporation, Federal Housing Administration, U.S. Housing Authority, Defense Homes Corporation, Division of Defense Housing Coordination, Central Housing Committee, Farm Security Administration* with respect to nonfarm housing, *Public Buildings Administration, Division of Defense Housing, Mutual Ownership Defense Housing Division, Office of Administrator of Federal Works Agency,* and the Departments of *War* and the Navy with respect to housing located off military installations. Agency dissolved on creation of *Housing and Home Finance Agency* by Reorg. Plan No. 3 of 1947, effective July 27, 1947.

Housing Authority, Federal Public Established by EO 9070 of Feb. 24, 1942. Public housing functions of *Federal Works Agency, the Departments of War* and the Navy (except housing located on military installations), and *Farm Security Administration* (nonfarm housing) transferred to *Authority,* and *Defense Homes Corporation* administered by the

Commissioner of the *Authority'*. Functions transferred to *Public Housing Administration, Housing and Home Finance Agency,* by Reorg. Plan No. 3 of 1947, effective July 27, 1947.

Housing Authority, U.S. Established in the Department of the Interior by act of Sept. 1, 1937 (50 Stat. 888). Transferred to *Federal Works Agency* by Reorg. Plan No. I of 1939, effective July 1, 1939. Transferred to *Federal Public Housing Authority, National Housing Agency,* by EO 9070 of Feb. 24, 1942. Office of Administrator abolished by Reorg. Plan No. 3 of 1947, effective July 27, 1947, and functions transferred to *Public Housing Administration, Housing and Home Finance Agency.*

Housing Corporation, U.S. Incorporated July 10, 1918, under laws of New York. Transferred from the Department of Labor to the Department of the Treasury by EO 7641 of June 22, 1937. Transferred from the Department of the Treasury to the *Public Buildings Administration, Federal Works Agency,* by EO 8186 of June 29, 1939. Functions transferred for liquidation to *Federal Home Loan Bank Administration, National Housing Agency,* by EO 9070 of Feb. 24, 1942. Terminated Sept. 8, 1952, by the *Secretary of the Home Loan Bank Board.*

Housing Council, National Established in *Housing and Home Finance Agency* by Reorg. Plan No. 3 of 1947, effective July 27, 1947. Terminated by Reorg. Plan No. 4 of 1965, effective July 27, 1965, and functions transferred to President.

Housing Division Established in *Public Works Administration* by act of June 16, 1933 (48 Stat. 195). Functions transferred to *U.S. Housing Authority* by EO 7732 of Oct. 27, 1937.

Housing Enterprise Oversight, Office of Federal Office and positions of Director and Deputy Director established within the Department of Housing and Urban Development by the act of October 28, 1992 (106 Stat. 3944). Abolished by the act of July 30, 2008 (122 Stat. 2794), and functions, personnel, and property transferred to Federal Housing Finance Agency.

Housing Expediter, Office of the Established in *Office of War Mobilization and Reconversion* by Presidential letter of Dec. 12, 1945, to *Housing Expediter.* Functions of *Housing Expediter* defined by EO 9686 of Jan. 26, 1946. *Housing Expediter* confirmed in position of *National Housing Administrator* Feb. 6, 1946. *Office of the Housing Expediter* established by act of May 22, 1946 (60 Stat. 208). Functions of *Office* and *National Housing Administrator* segregated by EO 9820 of Jan. 11, 1947. Housing functions of *Civilian Production Administration* transferred to *Office* by EO 9836 of Mar. 22, 1947, effective Apr. 1, 1947. Rent control functions of *Office of Temporary Controls* transferred to *Office* by EO 9841 of Apr. 23, 1947. *Office* terminated by EO 10276 of July 31, 1951, and functions transferred to *Economic Stabilization Agency.*

Housing Finance Board, Federal Established by the act of August 9, 1989 (103 Stat. 354, 415), and certain functions transferred from Federal Home Loan Bank Board. Abolished by the act of July 30,

2008 (122 Stat. 2797), and functions, personnel, and property transferred to Federal Housing Finance Agency.

Housing and Home Finance Agency Established by Reorg. Plan No. 3 of 1947, effective July 27, 1947. Terminated by act of Sept. 9, 1965 (79 Stat. 667), and functions transferred to the Department of Housing and Urban Development.

Howard University Established by act of Mar. 2, 1867 (14 Stat. 438). Functions of the Department of the Interior transferred to *Federal Security Agency* by Reorg. Plan No. IV of 1940, effective June 30, 1940. Functions of the *Department of Health, Education, and Welfare* transferred to the Department of Education by act of Oct. 17, 1979 (93 Stat. 678).

Human Development, Office of Established in *Department of Health, Education, and Welfare.* Renamed Office of Human Development Services and component units transferred to or reorganized under new administrations in Office by Secretary's reorganization order of July 26, 1977. Merged into the Administration for Children and Families by Secretary of Health and Human Services reorganization notice dated Apr. 15, 1991.

Human Development Services, Office of See **Human Development, Office of**

Human Embryo Stem Cell Registry Approved by Presidential announcement of Aug. 9, 2001 and established through National Institute of Health's Departmental Notice NOT-OD-01-058 of Aug. 27, 2001. Renamed Human Pluripotent Stem Cell Registry by EO 13435 of June 20, 2007.

Hydrographic Office Jurisdiction transferred from *Bureau of Navigation* to Chief of Naval Operations by EO 9126 of Apr. 8, 1942, and by Reorg. Plan No. 3 of 1946, effective July 16, 1946. Renamed U.S. Naval Oceanographic Office by act of July 10, 1962 (76 Stat. 154).

Imagery and Mapping Agency, National Established by act of Sept. 23, 1996 (110 Stat. 2677). Renamed National Geospatial-Intelligence Agency by act of Nov. 24, 2003 (117 Stat. 1568).

Imagery Office, Central Established as a Department of Defense agency on May 6, 1992. Functions transferred to National Imagery and Mapping Agency by act of Sept. 23, 1996 (110 Stat. 2677).

Immigration, Bureau of Established as branch of the Department of the Treasury by act of Mar. 3, 1891 (26 Stat. 1085). Transferred to *Department of Commerce and Labor* by act of Feb. 14, 1903 (34 Stat. 596). Made *Bureau of Immigration and Naturalization* by act of June 29, 1906 (37 Stat. 736). Made separate division after the Department of Labor created by act of Mar. 4, 1913 (37 Stat. 736). Consolidated into Immigration and Naturalization Service, Department of Labor, by EO 6166 of June 10, 1933. Transferred to the Department of Justice by Reorg. Plan No. V of 1940, effective June 14, 1940. Abolished by act of Nov. 25, 2002 (116 Stat. 2205) and functions transferred to Homeland Security Department.

Immigration, Commissioners of Offices of commissioners of immigration of the several ports created by act of Aug. 18, 1894 (28 Stat. 391). Abolished by Reorg. Plan No. III of 1940, effective June 30, 1940, and functions transferred to *Bureau of Immigration and Naturalization,* Department of Labor.

Immigration and Naturalization, Bureau of *See* **Immigration, Bureau of**

Immigration and Naturalization, District Commissioner of Created by act of Aug. 18, 1894 (28 Stat. 391). Abolished by Reorg. Plan No. III of 1940, effective June 30, 1940. Functions administered by the Commissioner of Immigration and Naturalization, Department of Justice, through district immigration and naturalization directors.

Immigration and Naturalization Service *See* **Immigration, Bureau of**

Import Programs, Office of Established by the Secretary of Commerce Feb. 14, 1971. Functions transferred to *Domestic and International Business Administration,* effective Nov. 17, 1972.

Indian Claims Commission Established by act of Aug. 13, 1946 (60 Stat. 1049). Terminated by act of Oct. 8, 1976 (90 Stat. 1990), and pending cases transferred to *U.S. Court of Claims* Sept. 30, 1978.

Indian Commissioners, Board of Established by section 2039, Revised Statutes. Abolished by EO 6145 of May 25, 1933.

Indian Education Programs, Office of Established within the Bureau of Indian Affairs, Department of the Interior, by act of June 23, 1972 (86 Stat. 343). Renamed Bureau of Indian Education by Departmental Manual Release No. 3721 of Aug. 29, 2006.

Indian Medical Facilities Functions transferred from the Department of the Interior to the *Department of Health, Education, and Welfare,* to be administered by the Surgeon General of Public Health Service, by act of Aug. 5, 1954 (68 Stat. 674).

Indian Opportunity, National Council on Established by EO 11399 of Mar. 6, 1968. Terminated Nov. 26, 1974, by act of Nov. 26, 1969 (83 Stat. 220).

Indian Policy Review Commission, American Established by act of Jan. 2, 1975 (88 Stat. 1910). Terminated June 30, 1977, pursuant to terms of act.

Industrial Analysis, Committee of Established by EO 7323 of Mar. 21, 1936. Terminated Feb. 17, 1937.

Industrial Cooperation, Coordinator for Established by EO 7193 of Sept. 26, 1935. Continued by EO 7324 of Mar. 30, 1936. Terminated June 30, 1937.

Industrial Emergency Committee Established by EO 6770 of June 30, 1934. Consolidated with *National Emergency Council* by EO 6889–A of Oct. 29, 1934.

Industrial Pollution Control Council Staff, National Established by Department of Commerce Organization Order 35–3 of June 17, 1970. *Staff* abolished by departmental organization order of Sept. 10, 1973. Council inactive.

Industrial Recovery Board, National Established by EO 6859 of Sept. 27, 1934. Terminated by EO 7075 of June 15, 1935.

Industrial Recovery Board, Special Established by EO 6173 of June 16, 1933. Functions absorbed by *National Emergency Council* under terms of EO 6513 of Dec. 18, 1933.

Industrial Relations, Office of Activated in the Department of the Navy Sept. 14, 1945. Superseded June 22, 1966, by creation of *Office of Civilian Manpower Management.*

Industry and Trade Administration *See* **Business and Defense Services Administration**

Information, Committee for Reciprocity Established by EO 6750 of June 27, 1934; reestablished by EO 10004 of Oct. 5, 1948, which revoked EO 6750. Superseded by EO 10082 of Oct. 5, 1949; abolished by EO 11075 of Jan. 15, 1963, which revoked EO 10082.

Information, Coordinator of Established by Presidential order of July 11, 1941. Functions exclusive of foreign information activities transferred by military order of June 13, 1942, to jurisdiction of Joint Chiefs of Staff, War Department, as *Office of Strategic Services.* Foreign information functions transferred to *Office of War Information* by EO 9182 of June 13, 1942.

Information, Division of Established pursuant to Presidential letter of Feb. 28, 1941, to *Liaison Officer, Office of Emergency Management.* Abolished by EO 9182 of June 13, 1942. Functions relating to public information on war effort transferred and consolidated with *Office of War Information,* and publication services relating to specific agencies of OEM transferred to those agencies.

Information, Office of Coordinator of Transferred, exclusive of foreign information activities, to *Office of War Information* by EO 9182 of June 13, 1942. Designated *Office of Strategic Services* and transferred to jurisdiction of Joint Chiefs of Staff by military order of June 13, 1942. Terminated by EO 9621 of Sept. 20, 1945, and functions distributed to the Departments of State and *War.*

Information Administration, International Transferred from the Department of State to the *U.S. Information Agency* by Reorg. Plan No. 8 of 1953, effective Aug. 1, 1953.

Information Agency, U.S. Established by Reorg. Plan No. 8 of 1953, effective Aug. 1, 1953. Abolished by Reorg. Plan No. 2 of 1977, effective Apr. 1, 1978; replaced by and functions transferred to *International Communication Agency.* Redesignated *U.S. Information Agency* by act of Aug. 24, 1982 (96 Stat. 291). Abolished by act of Oct. 21, 1998 (112 Stat. 2681–761), and functions transferred to the Department of State, effective Oct. 1, 1999.

Information and Public Affairs, Office of Merged with *Office of Intergovernmental Affairs* to form Office of Public and Intergovernmental Affairs by Order 1–85 of June 5, 1985 of the Secretary of Labor.

Information Resources Management, Office of *See* **Telecommunications Service, Automated Data**

Information Resources Management Service Established in the General Services Administration. Renamed Information Technology Service in 1995.

Information Security Committee, Interagency Established by EO 12065 of June 28, 1978. Abolished by EO 12356 of Apr. 2, 1982.

Information Security Oversight Office Established in General Services Administration by EO 12065 of June 28, 1978. EO 12065 revoked by EO 12356 of Apr. 2, 1982, which provided for continuation of Office.

Information Service, Government *See* **Information Service, U.S.**

Information Service, Interim International Established in the Department of State by EO 9608 of Aug. 31, 1945. Abolished Dec. 31, 1945, pursuant to terms of order.

Information Service, U.S. Established in March 1934 as division of *National Emergency Council.* Transferred to *Office of Government Reports* by Reorg. Plan No. II of 1939, effective July 1, 1939. Consolidated, along with other functions of *Office,* into *Division of Public Inquiries, Bureau of Special Services, Office of War Information,* by EO 9182 of June 13, 1942. *Bureau of Special Services* renamed *Government Information Service* and transferred to *Bureau of the Budget* by EO 9608 of Aug. 31, 1945. *Service* transferred to *Office of Government Reports* by EO 9809 of Dec. 12, 1946.

Information Systems Council Established by EO 13356 of Aug. 27, 2004. Abolished by EO 13388 of Oct. 25, 2005 (70 FR 62025).

Information Technology Service Established in General Services Administration. Abolished by General Services Administrative Order No. 5440.492, Aug. 21, 1996, and functions transferred to Federal Telecommunications Service.

Insane, Government Hospital for the Established by act of Mar. 3, 1855 (10 Stat. 682). Renamed Saint Elizabeth's Hospital by act of July 1, 1916 (39 Stat. 309). Transferred from the Department of the Interior to *Federal Security Agency* by Reorg. Plan No. IV of 1940, effective June 30, 1940. Transferred to *Department of Health, Education, and Welfare* by Reorg. Plan No. 1 of 1953, effective Apr. 11, 1953. Functions redelegated to National Institute of Mental Health by Secretary's reorganization order of Aug. 9, 1967. Property and administration transferred to District of Columbia Government by act of Nov. 8, 1984 (98 Stat. 3369).

Installations, Director of Established in the Department of Defense by act of July 14, 1952 (66 Stat. 625). Abolished by Reorg. Plan No. 6 of 1953, effective June 30, 1953, and functions transferred to the Secretary of Defense.

Insular Affairs, Bureau of Transferred from *Department of War* to *Division of Territories and Island Possessions,* the Department of the Interior, by Reorg. Plan No. II of 1939, effective July 1, 1939.

Insurance Administrator, Federal Established by act of Aug. 1, 1968 (82 Stat. 567). Functions transferred to Federal Emergency Management Agency by Reorg. Plan No. 3 of 1978, effective Apr. 1, 1979.

Integrity and Efficiency, President's Council on Established by EO 12301 of Mar. 26, 1981 (46 FR 19211). Abolished and reestablished by EO 12625 of Jan 27, 1988 (53 FR 2812). Abolished and reestablished by EO 12805 of May 11, 1992 (57 FR 20627).

Intelligence, Office of Established within the Department of Energy by Public Law 106–65 of Oct. 5, 1999 (113 Stat. 955). Merged with *Office of Counterintelligence* to form Office of Intelligence and Counterintelligence by memorandum of March 9, 2006 of the Secretary of Energy.

Intelligence Activities, President's Board of Consultants on Foreign Established by EO 10656 of Feb. 6, 1956. EO 10656 revoked by EO 10938 of May 4, 1961, and *Board* terminated. Functions transferred to President's Foreign Intelligence Advisory Board.

Intelligence Advisory Board, President's Foreign Established by EO 11460 of Mar. 20, 1969. Abolished by EO 11984 of May 4, 1977. Reestablished by EO 12331 of Oct. 20, 1981.

Intelligence Authority, National Established by Presidential directive of Jan. 22, 1946. Terminated on creation of Central Intelligence Agency under National Security Council by act of July 26, 1947 (61 Stat. 497).

Intelligence Group, Central Terminated on creation of Central Intelligence Agency by act of July 26, 1947 (61 Stat. 497).

Intelligence Policy and Review, Office of Transferred from the Criminal Division to the National Security Division by act of Mar. 9, 2006 (120 Stat. 249).

Inter-American Affairs, Institute of *See* **American Republics, Office for Coordination of Commercial and Cultural Relations between the**

Inter-American Affairs, Office of *See* **American Republics, Office for Coordination of Commercial and Cultural Relations between the**

Inter-American Affairs, Office of the Coordinator of *See* **American Republics, Office for Coordination of Commercial and Cultural Relations between the**

Interagency. *See other part of title*

Interdepartmental. *See also other part of title*

Interdepartmental Advisory Council   Established January 1941 to advise *Coordinator of Health, Welfare, and Related Defense Activities.* Terminated on creation of *Office of Defense Health and Welfare Service* Sept. 3, 1941.

Interest and Dividends, Committee on   Established by EO 11695 of Jan. 11, 1973. Abolished by EO 11781 of May 1, 1974.

Intergovernmental Affairs, Office of   Merged with *Office of Information and Public Affairs* to form Office of Public and Intergovernmental Affairs by Order 1–85 of June 5, 1985 of the Secretary of Labor.

Intergovernmental and Interagency Affairs, Office of   Abolished by decision of March 21, 2005 of the Secretary of Education under authority of section 413 of the Department of Education Organization Act.

Intergovernmental Relations, Advisory Commission on   Established by act of Sept. 24, 1959 (73 Stat. 703). Terminated pursuant to act of Nov. 19, 1995 (109 Stat. 480). Continued in existence by act of Oct. 19, 1996 (110 Stat. 4004).

Intergovernmental Relations, Commission on   Established by act of July 10, 1953 (67 Stat. 145). Final report submitted to Congress by June 30, 1955, pursuant to act of Feb. 7, 1955 (69 Stat. 7).

Intergovernmental Relations, Office of   Established by EO 11455 of Feb. 14, 1969. Functions transferred to *Domestic Council* by EO 11690 of Dec. 14, 1972.

Interim Compliance Panel   Established by Dec. 30, 1969 (83 Stat. 774). Terminated June 30, 1976, pursuant to terms of act.

Internal Revenue Service   Functions relating to alcohol, tobacco, firearms, and explosives transferred to Bureau of Alcohol, Tobacco, and Firearms by Department of Treasury order of July 1, 1972.

Internal Security Division   Established July 9, 1945, by transfer of functions from Criminal Division. Abolished Mar. 22, 1973, and functions transferred to Criminal Division, Department of Justice.

International.   *See also other part of title*

International Activities, Office of   Renamed *Office of Service and Protocol* by Secretary of the Smithsonian Institution internal directive of Jan. 11, 1985.

International Development, Agency for   Transferred from the Department of State to *U.S. International Development Cooperation Agency* by Reorg. Plan No. 2 of 1979, effective Oct. 1, 1979. Continued as agency within *IDCA* by IDCA Delegation of Authority No. 1 of Oct. 1, 1979. By act of Oct. 21, 1998 (112 Stat. 2681–790), became independent agency.

International Development Cooperation Agency, U.S.   Established by Reorg. Plan No. 2 of 1979, effective Oct. 1, 1979. Abolished by act of Oct. 21, 1998 (112 Stat. 2681–790) and functions transferred

to the Department of State, U.S. Agency for International Development, and Overseas Private Investment Corporation.

Interstate Commerce Commission   Created by act of Feb. 4, 1887 (24 Stat. 379). Certain functions as cited in act of Oct. 15, 1966 (80 Stat. 931) transferred to the Secretary of Commerce. Functions relating to railroad and pipeline safety transferred to Federal Railroad Administrator and motor carrier safety to Federal Highway Administrator by act. Abolished by act of Dec. 29, 1995 (109 Stat. 932) and many functions transferred to the newly created Surface Transportation Board within the Department of Transportation.

Investigation, Bureau of   Established by act of May 22, 1908 (35 Stat. 235). Functions consolidated with investigative functions of *Bureau of Prohibition, Division of Investigation,* Department of Justice, by EO 6166 of June 10, 1933, effective Mar. 2, 1934.

Investigation, Division of   Designated as Federal Bureau of Investigation in the Department of Justice by act of Mar. 22, 1935 (49 Stat. 77).

Investigation and Research, Board of   Established by act of Sept. 18, 1940 (54 Stat. 952). Extended to Sept. 18, 1944, by Proc. 2559 of June 26, 1942.

Investigations, Division of   Established by administrative order of Apr. 27, 1933. Abolished Jan. 17, 1942, by administrative order and functions transferred to *Branch of Field Examination, General Land Office,* Department of the Interior.

Investments, Office of Foreign Direct   Established in the Department of Commerce Jan. 2, 1968, by Departmental Organization Order 25–3 to carry out provisions of EO 11387 of Jan. 1, 1968. Controls on foreign investments terminated Jan. 29, 1974.

Iraq Reconstruction, Office of the Inspector General for   Established by act of Nov. 6, 2003 (117 Stat. 1234). Abolished by act of Oct. 17, 2006 (120 Stat. 2397).

Jamestown-Williamsburg-Yorktown National Celebration Commission   Established by act of Aug. 13, 1953 (67 Stat. 576). Terminated upon submission of final report to Congress Mar. 1, 1958.

Job Corps, Office of   Transferred from the Employment and Training Administration to the Office of the Secretary, U.S. Department of Labor by act of Dec. 30, 2005 (119 Stat. 2842).

Joint.   *See also other part of title*

Joint Resolutions of Congress   *See State, Department of*

Judicial Procedure, Commission on International Rules of   Established by act of Sept. 2, 1958 (72 Stat. 1743). Terminated Dec. 31, 1966, by act of Aug. 30, 1964 (78 Stat. 700).

Justice Assistance, Research, and Statistics, Office of   Established in the Department of Justice by act of Dec. 27, 1979 (93 Stat. 1201). Abolished by act of Oct. 12, 1984 (98 Stat. 2091).

Kennedy, Commission To Report Upon the Assassination of President John F. Established by EO 11130 of Nov. 29, 1963. Report submitted Sept. 24, 1964, and *Commission* discharged by Presidential letter of same date.

Labor, President's Committee on Migratory Appointed by Presidential letter of Aug. 26, 1954. Formally established by EO 10894 of Nov. 15, 1960. Terminated Jan. 6, 1964, by the Secretary of Labor in letter to members, with approval of President.

Labor and Commerce, Department of Established by act of Feb. 14, 1903 (32 Stat. 825). Reorganized into separate Departments of Labor and Commerce by act of Mar. 4, 1913 (37 Stat. 736).

Labor Department, Solicitor for Transferred from the Department of Justice to the Department of Labor by EO 6166 of June 10, 1933.

Labor-Management Advisory Committee Established by EO 11695 of Jan. 11, 1973. Abolished by EO 11788 of June 18, 1974.

Labor-Management Policy, President's Advisory Committee on Established by EO 10918 of Feb. 16, 1961. Abolished by EO 11710 of Apr. 4, 1973.

Labor-Management Relations Services, Office of Established by Order 3–84 of May 3, 1984 of the Secretary of Labor. Renamed Bureau of Labor-Management Relations and Cooperative Programs by Secretarial Order 7–84 of Sept. 20, 1984 (49 FR 38374).

Labor-Management Services Administration *Office of Pension and Welfare Benefit Programs* transferred from *Administration* and constituted as separate unit by Order 1–84 of Jan. 20, 1984 of the Secretary of Labor (49 FR 4269). Remaining labor-management relations functions reassigned by Secretarial Order 3–84 of May 3, 1984.

Labor Organization, International Established in 1919 by Treaty of Versailles with U.S. joining in 1934. U.S. membership terminated Nov. 1, 1977, at President's direction.

Labor Relations Council, Federal Established by EO 11491 of Oct. 29, 1969. Abolished by Reorg. Plan No. 2 of 1978, effective Jan. 1, 1979, and functions transferred to Federal Labor Relations Authority.

Labor Standards, Apprenticeship Section, Division of Transferred to *Federal Security Agency* by EO 9139 of Apr. 18, 1942, functioning as *Apprentice Training Service.* Transferred to *War Manpower Commission* by EO 9247 of Sept. 17, 1942, functioning in *Bureau of Training.* Returned to the Department of Labor by EO 9617 of Sept. 19, 1945.

Labor Standards, Bureau of Established by Labor departmental order in 1934. Functions absorbed by Occupational Safety and Health Administration in May 1971.

Land Bank Commissioner *See* **Farm Loan Board, Federal**

Land Law Review Commission, Public Established by act of Sept. 19, 1964 (78 Stat. 982). Terminated Dec. 31, 1970, pursuant to terms of act.

Land Office, General Consolidated with *Grazing Service* into Bureau of Land Management, Department of the Interior, by Reorg. Plan No. 3 of 1946, effective July 16, 1946.

Land Office, Office of Recorder of the General Created in the Department of the Interior by act of July 4, 1836 (5 Stat. 111). Abolished by Reorg. Plan No. III of 1940, effective June 30, 1940, and functions transferred to *General Land Office.*

Land Policy Section Established in 1934 as part of *Program Planning Division, Agricultural Adjustment Administration.* Personnel taken over by *Resettlement Administration* in 1935.

Land Problems, Committee on National Established by EO 6693 of Apr. 28, 1934. Abolished by EO 6777 of June 30, 1934.

Land Program, Director of Basis of program found in act of June 16, 1933 (48 Stat. 200). *Special Board of Public Works* established by EO 6174 of June 16, 1933. Land Program established by *Board* by resolution passed Dec. 28, 1933, and amended July 18, 1934. *Federal Emergency Relief Administration* designated to administer program Feb. 28, 1934. Land Program transferred to *Resettlement Administration* by EO 7028 of Apr. 30, 1935. Functions of *Administration* transferred to the Secretary of Agriculture by EO 7530 of Dec. 31, 1936. Land conservation and land-utilization programs administered by *Administration* transferred to *Bureau of Agricultural Economics* by Secretary's Memorandum 733. Administration of land programs placed under Soil Conservation Service by Secretary's Memorandum 785 of Oct. 6, 1938.

Land Use Coordination, Office of Established by Secretary of Agriculture Memorandum 725 of July 12, 1937. Abolished Jan. 1, 1944, by General Departmental Circular 21 and functions administered by *Land Use Coordinator.*

Land Use and Water Planning, Office of Established in the Department of the Interior by Secretarial Order No. 2953 of May 7, 1973. Abolished by Secretarial Order No. 2988 of Mar. 11, 1976.

Law Enforcement Assistance Administration Established by act of June 19, 1968 (82 Stat. 197). Operations closed out by the Department of Justice due to lack of appropriations and remaining functions transferred to *Office of Justice Assistance, Research, and Statistics.*

Law Enforcement Training Center, Federal *See* **Law Enforcement Training Center, Consolidated Federal**

Law Enforcement Training Center, Consolidated Federal Established by Treasury Order No. 217, Mar. 2, 1970. Renamed Federal Law Enforcement Training Center by Amendment No. 1 to Treasury Order No. 217 on Aug. 14, 1975. Transferred to Department of Homeland Security by act of Nov. 25, 2002 (116 Stat. 2178).

Legislative Affairs, Office of Renamed Office of Intergovernmental and Legislative Affairs Feb. 24, 1984, by Attorney General's Order 1054–84 (49 FR 10177).

Lend-Lease Administration, Office of Established by EO 8926 of Oct. 28, 1941, to replace *Division of Defense Aid Reports.* Consolidated with *Foreign Economic Administration* by EO 9380 of Sept. 25, 1943.

Lewis and Clark Trail Commission Established by act of Oct. 6, 1964 (78 Stat. 1005). Terminated October 1969 by terms of act.

Libraries and Information Science, National Commission on Established by act of July 20, 1970 (84 Stat. 440). As per close out activities, the Commission was abolished by act of Dec. 26, 2007 (121 Stat. 2204), and functions transferred to the Institute of Museum and Library Services pursuant to instructions set forth in House Report 110–231 and Senate Report 110–107.

Library of Congress Police Established by act of Aug. 4, 1950 (64 Stat. 411). Personnel transferred to United States Capitol Police by acts of Dec. 26, 2007 (121 Stat. 2228) and Jan. 7, 2008 (121 Stat. 2546).

Lighthouses, Bureau of Established in the Department of Commerce by act of Aug. 7, 1789 (1 Stat. 53). Consolidated with U.S. Coast Guard by Reorg. Plan No. II of 1939, effective July 1, 1939.

Lincoln Sesquicentennial Commission Established by joint resolution of Sept. 2, 1957 (71 Stat. 587). Terminated Mar. 1, 1960, pursuant to terms of joint resolution.

Liquidation, Director of Established in *Office for Emergency Management* by EO 9674 of Jan. 4, 1946. Terminated by EO 9744 of June 27, 1946.

Liquidation Advisory Committee Established by EO 9674 of Jan. 4, 1946. Terminated by EO 9744 of June 27, 1946.

Loan Agency, Federal Established by Reorg. Plan No. I of 1939, effective July 1, 1939, by consolidating *Reconstruction Finance Corporation*— including subordinate units of *RFC Mortgage Company, Disaster Loan Corporation, Federal National Mortgage Association, Defense Plant Corporation, Defense Homes Corporation, Defense Supplies Corporation, Rubber Reserve Company, Metals Reserve Company,* and *War Insurance Corporation* (later known as *War Damage Corporation*)—with *Federal Home Loan Bank Board, Home Owners' Loan Corporation, Federal Savings and Loan Insurance Corporation, Federal Housing Administration, Electric Home and Farm Authority,* and *Export-Import Bank of Washington. Federal Home Loan Bank Board, Federal Savings and Loan Insurance Corporation, Home Owners' Loan Corporation, Federal Housing Administration,* and *Defense Homes Corporation* transferred to *National Housing Agency* by EO 9070 of Feb. 24, 1942. *Reconstruction Finance Corporation* and its units (except *Defense Homes Corporation*), *Electric Home and Farm Authority,* and *Export-Import Bank of Washington* transferred to the Department of

Commerce by EO 9071 of Feb. 24, 1942. *RFC* and units returned to *Federal Loan Agency* by act of Feb. 24, 1945 (59 Stat. 5). *Agency* abolished by act of June 30, 1947 (61 Stat. 202), and all property and records transferred to *Reconstruction Finance Corporation.*

Loan Fund, Development Established in *International Cooperation Administration* by act of Aug. 14, 1957 (71 Stat. 355). Created as independent corporate agency by act of June 30, 1958 (72 Stat. 261). Abolished by act of Sept. 4, 1961 (75 Stat. 445), and functions redelegated to Agency for International Development.

Loan Policy Board Established by act of July 18, 1958 (72 Stat. 385). Abolished by Reorg. Plan No. 4 of 1965, effective July 27, 1965, and functions transferred to Small Business Administration.

Longshoremen's Labor Board, National Established in the Department of Labor by EO 6748 of June 26, 1934. Terminated by Proc. 2120 of Mar. 11, 1935.

Low-Emission Vehicle Certification Board Established by act of Dec. 31, 1970 (84 Stat. 1701). Terminated by act of Mar. 14, 1980 (94 Stat. 98).

Lowell Historic Canal District Commission Established by act of Jan. 4, 1975 (88 Stat. 2330). Expired January 1977 pursuant to terms of act.

Loyalty Review Board Established Nov. 10, 1947, by *U.S. Civil Service Commission,* pursuant to EO 9835 of Mar. 21, 1947. Abolished by EO 10450 of Apr. 27, 1953.

Management, Budget and Evaluation, Office of Established within the Department of Energy pursuant to the Conference Report No. 107–258 on H.R. 2311, Energy and Water Development Appropriations Act, 2002. Abolished by memorandum of July 28, 2005 of the Secretary of Energy, and various functions transferred within the Department of Energy to the *Office of Management, Office of Chief Financial Officer,* and *Office of Human Capital Management.*

Management Improvement, Advisory Committee on Established by EO 10072 of July 29, 1949. Abolished by EO 10917 of Feb. 10, 1961, and functions transferred to *Bureau of the Budget.*

Management Improvement, President's Advisory Council on Established by EO 11509 of Feb. 11, 1970. Inactive as of June 30, 1973.

Manpower, President's Committee on Established by EO 11152 of Apr. 15, 1964. Terminated by EO 11515 of Mar. 13, 1970.

Manpower Administration Renamed Employment and Training Administration by Order 14–75 of Nov. 12, 1975 of the Secretary of Labor.

Manpower Management, Office of Civilian Renamed Office of Civilian Personnel by Notice 5430 of Oct. 1, 1976 of the Secretary of the Navy.

Marine Affairs, Office of Established by the Secretary of the Interior Apr. 30, 1970, to replace *Office of Marine Resources,* created by Secretary Oct. 22, 1968. Abolished by Secretary Dec. 4, 1970.

Marine Corps Memorial Commission, U.S.
Established by act of Aug. 24, 1947 (61 Stat. 724).
Terminated by act of Mar. 14, 1980 (94 Stat. 98).

Marine Debris Coordinating Committee Renamed
Interagency Marine Debris Coordinating Committee
by act of Dec. 22, 2006 (120 Stat. 3337).

Marine Inspection and Navigation, Bureau of *See*
Navigation and Steamboat Inspection, Bureau of

Marine Resources and Engineering Development,
National Council on Established in Executive
Office of the President by act of June 17, 1966 (80
Stat. 203). Terminated Apr. 30, 1971, due to lack of
funding.

Maritime Administration Established in the
Department of Commerce by Reorg. Plan No. 21 of
1950, effective May 24, 1950. Transferred to the
Department of Transportation by act of Aug. 6, 1981
(95 Stat. 151).

Maritime Advisory Committee Established by EO
11156 of June 17, 1964. Terminated by EO 11427
of Sept. 4, 1968.

Maritime Board, Federal *See* **Maritime**
Commission, U.S.

Maritime Commission, U.S. Established by act of
June 29, 1936 (49 Stat. 1985), as successor agency
to *U.S. Shipping Board* and *U.S. Shipping Board*
Merchant Fleet Corporation. Training functions
transferred to Commandant of Coast Guard by EO
9083 of Feb. 27, 1942. Functions further transferred
to *War Shipping Administration* by EO 9198 of July
11, 1942. Abolished by Reorg. Plan No. 21 of 1950,
effective May 24, 1950, which established *Federal*
Maritime Board and *Maritime Administration* as
successor agencies. *Board* abolished, regulatory
functions transferred to Federal Maritime
Commission, and functions relating to subsidization
of merchant marine transferred to the Secretary of
Commerce by Reorg. Plan No. 7 of 1961, effective
Aug. 12, 1961.

Maritime Labor Board Authorized by act of June
23, 1938 (52 Stat. 968). Mediatory duties abolished
by act of June 23, 1941 (55 Stat. 259); title expired
June 22, 1942.

Marketing Administration, Surplus Established by
Reorg. Plan No. III of 1940, effective June 30, 1940,
consolidating functions vested in *Federal Surplus*
Commodities Corporation and *Division of Marketing*
and Marketing Agreements, Agricultural Adjustment
Administration. Consolidated with other agencies
into *Agricultural Marketing Administration* by EO
9069 of Feb. 23, 1942.

Marketing and Marketing Agreements, Division of
Established in the Department of Agriculture by act
of June 3, 1937 (50 Stat. 246). Consolidated with
Federal Surplus Commodities Corporation into
Surplus Marketing Administration by Reorg. Plan No.
III of 1940, effective June 30, 1940.

Mediation, U.S. Board of Established by act of
May 20, 1926 (44 Stat. 577). Abolished by act of
June 21, 1934 (48 Stat. 1193), and superseded by
National Mediation Board, July 21, 1934.

Medical Information Systems Program Office, Tri-
Service Renamed Defense Medical Systems Support
Center by memorandum of the Assistant Secretary of
Defense (Health Affairs) May 3, 1985.

Medical Services Administration Established by the
Secretary of Health, Education, and Welfare
reorganization of Aug. 15, 1967. Transferred from
Social and Rehabilitation Service to Health Care
Financing Administration by Secretary's
reorganization of Mar. 8, 1977 (42 FR 13262).

Medicine and Surgery, Department of Established
in the *Veterans Administration* by act of Sept. 2,
1958 (72 Stat. 1243). Renamed *Veterans Health*
Services and Research Administration in the the
Department of Veterans Affairs by act of Oct. 25,
1988 (102 Stat. 2640). Renamed Veterans Health
Administration by act of May 7, 1991 (105 Stat.
187).

Memorial Commission, National Established by
Public Resolution 107 of Mar. 4, 1929 (45 Stat.
1699). Terminated by EO 6166 of June 10, 1933,
and functions transferred to *Office of National Parks,*
Buildings, and Reservations, Department of the
Interior.

Mental Health, National Institute of Established by
act of July 3, 1946 (60 Stat. 425). Made entity within
the Alcohol, Drug Abuse, and Mental Health
Administration by act of May 14, 1974 (88 Stat.
135). Functions transferred to the Department of
Health and Human Services by act of Oct. 17, 1979
(93 Stat. 695). (*See also* act of Oct. 27, 1986; 100
Stat. 3207–106.) Abolished by act of July 10, 1992
(106 Stat. 331). Reestablished by act of July 10,
1992 (106 Stat. 364).

Metals Reserve Company Established June 28,
1940, by act of Jan. 22, 1932 (47 Stat. 5).
Transferred from *Federal Loan Agency* to the
Department of Commerce by EO 9071 of Feb. 24,
1942. Returned to *Federal Loan Agency* by act of
Feb. 24, 1945 (59 Stat. 5). Dissolved by act of June
30, 1945 (59 Stat. 310), and functions transferred to
Reconstruction Finance Corporation.

Metric Board, U.S. Established by act of Dec. 23,
1975 (89 Stat. 1007). Terminated Oct. 1, 1982, due
to lack of funding.

Mexican-American Affairs, Interagency Committee
on Established by Presidential memorandum of June
9, 1967. Renamed *Cabinet Committee on*
Opportunities for Spanish-Speaking People by act of
Dec. 30, 1969 (83 Stat. 838). Terminated Dec. 30,
1974, pursuant to terms of act.

Mexican Claims Commission, American
Established by act of Dec. 18, 1942 (56 Stat. 1058).
Terminated Apr. 4, 1947, by act of Apr. 3, 1945 (59
Stat. 59).

Mexican Claims Commission, Special Established
by act of Apr. 10, 1935 (49 Stat. 149). Terminated
by EO 7909 of June 15, 1938.

Mexico Commission for Border Development and
Friendship, U.S.- Established through exchange of
notes of Nov. 30 and Dec. 3, 1966, between U.S.
and Mexico. Terminated Nov. 5, 1969.

Micronesian Claims Commission Established by act of July 1, 1971 (85 Stat. 92). Terminated Aug. 3, 1976, pursuant to terms of act.

Migration, Intergovernmental Committee for European Renamed Intergovernmental Committee for Migration by Resolution 624, passed by *Intergovernmental Committee for European Migration Council,* effective Nov. 11, 1980.

Migration, International Committee for Created in 1951. Renamed International Organization for Migration pursuant to article 29, paragraph 2, of the ICM constitution, effective Nov. 14, 1989.

Migratory Bird Conservation Commission Chairmanship transferred from the Secretary of Agriculture to the Secretary of the Interior by Reorg. Plan No. II of 1939, effective July 1, 1939.

Military Air Transport Service Renamed *Military Airlift Command* in U.S. Air Force by HQ MATS/ MAC Special Order G–164 of Jan. 1, 1966.

Military Airlift Command Inactivated June 1, 1992.

Military Appeals, United States Court of Established under Article I of the Constitution of the United States pursuant to act of May 5, 1950, as amended. Renamed United States Court of Appeals for the Armed Forces by act of Oct. 5, 1994 (108 Stat. 2831).

Military Establishment, National Established as executive department of the Government by act of July 26, 1947 (61 Stat. 495). Designated Department of Defense by act of Aug. 10, 1949 (63 Stat. 579).

Military Intelligence College, Joint Established by DoD Directive 3305.1 of January 14, 1998. Renamed *National Defense Intelligence College by DOD Instruction 3305.01 of Dec. 22, 2006. See also* Defense Intelligence College.

Military Purchases, Interdepartmental Committee for Coordination of Foreign and Domestic Informal liaison committee created on Presidential notification of Dec. 6, 1939, to the Secretaries of the Treasury and *War* and the Acting Secretary of the Navy. Committee dissolved in accordance with Presidential letter to the Secretary of the Treasury Apr. 14, 1941, following approval of act of Mar. 11, 1941 (55 Stat. 31).

Military Renegotiation Policy and Review Board Established by directive of the Secretary of Defense July 19, 1948. Abolished by Secretary's letter of Jan. 18, 1952, which transferred functions to *Renegotiation Board.*

Military Sea Transportation Service Renamed Military Sealift Command in U.S. Navy by COMSC notice of Aug. 1, 1970.

Militia Bureau Established in 1908 as *Division of Militia Affairs, Office of the Secretary of War.* Superseded in 1933 by National Guard Bureau.

Mine Health and Safety Academy, National Transferred from the Department of the Interior to the Department of Labor by act of July 25, 1979 (93 Stat. 111).

Minerals Exploration, Office of Established by act of Aug. 21, 1958 (72 Stat. 700). Functions transferred to *Geological Survey* by Order 2886 of Feb. 26, 1965 of the Secretary of the Interior.

Minerals Mobilization, Office of Established by the Secretary of the Interior pursuant to act of Sept. 8, 1950 (64 Stat. 798) and EO 10574 of Nov. 5, 1954, and by order of *Office of Defense Mobilization.* Succeeded by *Office of Minerals and Solid Fuels* Nov. 2, 1962. *Office of Minerals Policy Development* combined with *Office of Research and Development* in the Department of the Interior May 21, 1976, under authority of Reorg. Plan No. 3 of 1950, to form *Office of Minerals Policy and Research Analysis.* Abolished Sept. 30, 1981, by Secretarial Order 3070 and functions transferred to Bureau of Mines.

Minerals Policy and Research Analysis, Office of *See* **Minerals Mobilization, Office of**

Minerals and Solid Fuels, Office of Established by the Secretary of the Interior Oct. 26, 1962. Abolished and functions assigned to Deputy Assistant Secretary—Minerals and Energy Policy, Office of the Assistant Secretary—Mineral Resources, effective Oct. 22, 1971.

Mines, Bureau of Established in the Department of the Interior by act of May 16, 1910 (36 Stat. 369). Transferred to the Department of Commerce by EO 4239 of June 4, 1925. Transferred to the Department of the Interior by EO 6611 of Feb. 22, 1934. Renamed United States Bureau of Mines by act of May 18, 1992 (106 Stat. 172). Terminated pursuant to act of Jan. 26, 1996 (110 Stat. 32). Certain functions transferred to Secretary of Energy by act of Apr. 26, 1996 (110 Stat. 1321–167).

Mining Enforcement and Safety Administration Established by Order 2953 of May 7, 1973 of the Secretary of the Interior. Terminated by departmental directive Mar. 9, 1978, and functions transferred to Mine Safety and Health Administration, Department of Labor, established by act of Nov. 9, 1977 (91 Stat. 1319).

Minority Business Enterprise, Office of Renamed Minority Business Development Agency by Commerce Secretarial Order DOO–254A of Nov. 1, 1979.

Mint, Bureau of the Renamed U.S. Mint by Treasury Secretarial order of Jan. 9, 1984 (49 FR 5020).

Missile Sites Labor Commission Established by EO 10946 of May 26, 1961. Abolished by EO 11374 of Oct. 11, 1967, and functions transferred to Federal Mediation and Conciliation Service.

Missouri Basin Survey Commission Established by EO 10318 of Jan. 3, 1952. Final report of *Commission* submitted to President Jan. 12, 1953, pursuant to EO 10329 of Feb. 25, 1952.

Missouri River Basin Commission Established by EO 11658 of Mar. 22, 1972. Terminated by EO 12319 of Sept. 9, 1981.

Mobilization, Office of Civil and Defense *See* **Mobilization, Office of Defense and Civilian**

Mobilization, Office of Defense and Civilian Established by Reorg. Plan No. 1 of 1958, effective July 1, 1958. Redesignated as *Office of Civil and Defense Mobilization* by act of Aug. 26, 1958 (72 Stat. 861), consolidating functions of *Office of Defense Mobilization* and *Federal Civil Defense Administration.* Civil defense functions transferred to the Secretary of Defense by EO 10952 of July 20, 1961, and remaining organization redesignated *Office of Emergency Planning* by act of Sept. 22, 1961 (75 Stat. 630).

Mobilization Policy, National Advisory Board on Established by EO 10224 of Mar. 15, 1951. EO 10224 revoked by EO 10773 of July 1, 1958.

Monetary and Financial Problems, National Advisory Council on International Established by act of July 31, 1945 (59 Stat. 512). Abolished by Reorg. Plan No. 4 of 1965, effective July 27, 1965, and functions transferred to President. Functions assumed by National Advisory Council on International Monetary and Financial Policies, established by EO 11269 of Feb. 14, 1966.

Monument Commission, National Established by act of Aug. 31, 1954 (68 Stat. 1029). Final report submitted in 1957, and audit of business completed September 1964.

Monuments in War Areas, American Commission for the Protection and Salvage of Artistic and Historic Established by President June 23, 1943; announced by Secretary of State Aug. 20, 1943. Activities assumed by the Department of State Aug. 16, 1946.

Mortgage Association, Federal National Chartered Feb. 10, 1938, by act of June 27, 1934 (48 Stat. 1246). Grouped with other agencies to form *Federal Loan Agency* by Reorg. Plan No. I of 1939, effective July 1, 1939. Transferred to the Department of Commerce by EO 9071 of Feb. 24, 1942. Returned to *Federal Loan Agency* by act of Feb. 24, 1945 (59 Stat. 5). Transferred to *Housing and Home Finance Agency* by Reorg. Plan No. 22 of 1950, effective July 10, 1950. Rechartered by act of Aug. 2, 1954 (68 Stat. 590) and made constituent agency of *Housing and Home Finance Agency.* Transferred with functions of *Housing and Home Finance Agency* to the Department of Housing and Urban Development by act of Sept. 9, 1965 (79 Stat. 667). Made Government-sponsored, private corporation by act of Aug. 1, 1968 (82 Stat. 536).

Motor Carrier Claims Commission Established by act of July 2, 1948 (62 Stat. 1222). Terminated Dec. 31, 1952, by acts of July 11, 1951 (65 Stat. 116), and Mar. 14, 1952 (66 Stat. 25).

Mount Rushmore National Memorial Commission Established by act of Feb. 25, 1929 (45 Stat. 1300). Expenditures ordered administered by the Department of the Interior by EO 6166 of June 10, 1933. Transferred to National Park Service, Department of the Interior, by Reorg. Plan No. II of 1939, effective July 1, 1939.

Mounted Horse Unit Transferred from the United States Capitol Police to the United States Park Police by Public Law 109–55 of Aug. 2, 2005 (119 Stat. 572).

Munitions Board Established in the Department of Defense by act of July 26, 1947 (61 Stat. 499). Abolished by Reorg. Plan No. 6 of 1953, effective June 30, 1953, and functions vested in the Secretary of Defense.

Munitions Board, Joint Army and Navy Organized in 1922. Placed under direction of President by military order of July 5, 1939. Reconstituted Aug. 18, 1945, by order approved by President. Terminated on establishment of *Munitions Board* by act of July 26, 1947 (61 Stat. 505).

Museum of American Art, National Renamed Smithsonian American Art Museum by Act of October 27, 2000 (114 Stat. 1463).

Museum of History and Technology, National Renamed National Museum of American History in Smithsonian Institution by act of Oct. 13, 1980 (94 Stat. 1884).

Museum Services, Institute of Established by act of June 23, 1972 (86 Stat. 327). Transferred to Office of Educational Research and Improvement, Department of Education, by act of Oct. 17, 1979 (93 Stat. 678), effective May 4, 1980. Transferred to National Foundation on the Arts and the Humanities by act of Dec. 23, 1981 (95 Stat. 1414). Functions transferred to the Institute of Museum and Library Services by act of Sept. 30, 1996 (110 Stat. 3009–307).

Narcotics, Bureau of Established in the Department of the Treasury by act of June 14, 1930 (46 Stat. 585). Abolished by Reorg. Plan No. 1 of 1968, effective Apr. 8, 1968, and functions transferred to *Bureau of Narcotics and Dangerous Drugs,* Department of Justice.

Narcotics, President's Council on Counter- Renamed President's Drug Policy Council by EO 13023, Nov. 6, 1996 (61 FR 57767).

Narcotics Control, Cabinet Committee on International Established by Presidential memorandum of Aug. 17, 1971. Terminated by Presidential memorandum of Mar. 14, 1977.

National. *See other part of title*

Naval Material, Office of Established by act of Mar. 5, 1948 (62 Stat. 68). Abolished by the Department of Defense reorg. order of Mar. 9, 1966, and functions transferred to the Secretary of the Navy (31 FR 7188).

Naval Material Command *See* **Naval Material Support Establishment**

Naval Material Support Establishment Established by Department of the Navy General Order 5 of July 1, 1963 (28 FR 7037). Replaced by *Naval Material Command* pursuant to General Order 5 of Apr. 29, 1966 (31 FR 7188). Functions realigned to form Office of Naval Acquisition Support, and termination of *Command* effective May 6, 1985.

Naval Observatory   Jurisdiction transferred from *Bureau of Navigation* to Chief of Naval Operations by EO 9126 of Apr. 8, 1942, and by Reorg. Plan No. 3 of 1946, effective July 16, 1946.

Naval Oceanography Command   Renamed Naval Meteorology and Oceanography Command in 1995.

Naval Petroleum and Oil Shale Reserves, Office of   Established by the Secretary of the Navy, as required by law (70A Stat. 457). Jurisdiction transferred to the Department of Energy by act of Aug. 4, 1977 (91 Stat. 581).

Naval Reserve   Established by act of Mar. 3, 1915 (38 Stat. 940). Redesignated Navy Reserve by Public Law 109–163 of Jan. 6, 2006 (119 Stat. 3233).

Naval Weapons, Bureau of   Established by act of Aug. 18, 1959 (73 Stat. 395), to replace *Bureau of Ordnance and Aeronautics.* Abolished by Department of Defense reorg. order of Mar. 9, 1966, and functions transferred to the Secretary of the Navy (31 FR 7188), effective May 1, 1966.

Navigation, Bureau of   Created by act of July 5, 1884 (23 Stat. 118), as special service under the Department of the Treasury. Transferred to the *Department of Commerce and Labor* by act of Feb. 4, 1903 (32 Stat. 825). Consolidated with *Bureau of Navigation and Steamboat Inspection* by act of June 30, 1932 (47 Stat. 415).

Navigation, Bureau of   Renamed Bureau of Naval Personnel by act of May 13, 1942 (56 Stat. 276).

Navigation and Steamboat Inspection, Bureau of   Renamed *Bureau of Marine Inspection and Navigation* by act of May 27, 1936 (49 Stat. 1380). Functions transferred to *Bureau of Customs,* Department of the Treasury, and U.S. Coast Guard by EO 9083 of Feb. 28, 1942. Transfer made permanent and *Bureau* abolished by Reorg. Plan. No. 3 of 1946, effective July 16, 1946.

Navy, Department of   Defense housing functions transferred to *Federal Public Housing Authority, National Housing Agency,* by EO 9070 of Feb. 24, 1942.

Navy Bureau of Medicine and Surgery, Dental Division of   Renamed Dental Corps of the Navy Bureau of Medicine and Surgery by act of Oct. 17, 2006 (120 Stat. 2234).

Navy Commissioners, Board of   Established by act of Feb. 7, 1815 (3 Stat. 202). Abolished by act of Aug. 31, 1842 (5 Stat. 579).

Neighborhoods, National Commission on   Established by act of Apr. 30, 1977 (91 Stat. 56). Terminated May 4, 1979, pursuant to terms of act.

Neighborhoods, Voluntary Associations and Consumer Protection, Office of   Abolished and certain functions transferred to Office of the Assistant Secretary for Housing—Federal Housing Commissioner and Office of the Assistant Secretary for Community Planning and Development. Primary enabling legislation, act of Oct. 31, 1978 (92 Stat. 2119), repealed by act of Aug. 13, 1981 (95 Stat. 398). Abolishment of *Office* and transfer of functions carried out by Housing and Urban Development Secretarial order.

New England River Basins Commission   Established by EO 11371 of Sept. 6, 1967. Terminated by EO 12319 of Sept. 9, 1981.

Nicaro Project   Responsibility for management of Nicaro nickel producing facilities in Oriente Province, Cuba, transferred from *Office of Special Assistant to the Administrator (Nicaro Project)* to *Defense Materials Service* by General Services Administrator, effective July 7, 1959. Facilities expropriated by Cuban Government and nationalized Oct. 26, 1960.

Noble Training Center   Transferred from Public Health Service to the Center for Domestic Preparedness, Department of Homeland Security by act of Oct. 4, 2006 (120 Stat. 1433).

Northern Mariana Islands Commission on Federal Laws   Created by joint resolution of Mar. 24, 1976 (90 Stat. 263). Terminated upon submission of final report in August 1985.

Nursing Research, National Center for   Renamed National Institute of Nursing Research by act of June 10, 1993 (107 Stat. 178).

Nutrition Division   Functions transferred from *Department of Health, Education, and Welfare* to the Department of Agriculture by EO 9310 of Mar. 3, 1943.

Ocean Mining Administration   Established by Interior Secretarial Order 2971 of Feb. 24, 1975. Abolished by Department Manual Release 2273 of June 13, 1980.

Oceanography, Interagency Committee on   Established by *Federal Council for Science and Technology* pursuant to EO 10807 of Mar. 13, 1959. Absorbed by *National Council on Marine Resources and Engineering Development* pursuant to Vice Presidential letter of July 21, 1967.

Office.   *See also other part of title*

Office Space, President's Advisory Commission on Presidential   Established by act of Aug. 3, 1956 (70 Stat. 979). Terminated June 30, 1957, by act of Jan. 25, 1957 (71 Stat. 4).

Official Register   Function of preparing *Official Register* vested in Director of the Census by act of Mar. 3, 1925 (43 Stat. 1105). Function transferred to *U.S. Civil Service Commission* by EO 6166 of June 10, 1933. Yearly compilation and publication required by act of Aug. 28, 1935 (49 Stat. 956). Act repealed by act of July 12, 1960 (74 Stat. 427), and last *Register* published in 1959.

Ohio River Basin Commission   Established by EO 11578 of Jan. 13, 1971. Terminated by EO 12319 of Sept. 9, 1981.

Oil and Gas, Office of   Established by the Secretary of the Interior May 6, 1946, in response to Presidential letter of May 3, 1946. Transferred to *Federal Energy Administration* by act of May 7, 1974 (88 Stat. 100).

Oil Import Administration Established in the Department of the Interior by Proc. 3279 of Mar. 10, 1959. Merged into *Office of Oil and Gas* Oct. 22, 1971.

Oil Import Appeals Board Established by the Secretary of Commerce Mar. 13, 1959, and made part of Office of Hearings and Appeals Dec. 23, 1971.

On-Site Inspection Agency Established on Jan. 26, 1988. Functions transferred to the Defense Threat Reduction Agency by DOD Directive 5105.62 of Sept. 30, 1998.

Operations Advisory Group Established by EO 11905 of Feb. 18, 1976. Abolished by Presidential Directive No. 2 of Jan. 20, 1977.

Operations Coordinating Board Established by EO 10483 of Sept. 2, 1953, which was superseded by EO 10700 of Feb. 25, 1957. EO 10700 revoked by EO 10920 of Feb. 18, 1961, and *Board* terminated.

Ordnance, Bureau of *See* **Ordnance and Hydrography, Bureau of**

Ordnance and Hydrography, Bureau of Established in the Department of the Navy by act of Aug. 31, 1842 (5 Stat. 579). Replaced under act of July 5, 1862 (12 Stat. 510), by *Bureau of Ordnance* and *Bureau of Navigation.* Abolished by act of Aug. 18, 1959 (73 Stat. 395), and functions transferred to *Bureau of Naval Weapons.*

Organization, President's Advisory Committee on Government Established by EO 10432 of Jan. 24, 1953. Abolished by EO 10917 of Feb. 10, 1961, and functions transferred to *Bureau of the Budget* for termination.

Organizations Staff, International Functions merged with Foreign Agricultural Service by memorandum of Dec. 7, 1973 of , effective Feb. 3, 1974.

Overseas Private Investment Corporation Transferred as separate agency to *U.S. International Development Cooperation Agency* by Reorg. Plan No. 2 of 1979, effective Oct. 1, 1979. Became an independent agency following the abolition of *IDCA* by act of Oct. 21, 1998 (112 Stat. 2681–790).

Oversight Board (for the Resolution Trust Corporation) Established by act of Aug. 9, 1989 (103 Stat. 363). Renamed *Thrift Depositor Protection Oversight Board* by act of Dec. 12, 1991 (105 Stat. 1767). Abolished by act of July 29, 1998 (112 Stat. 908). Authority and duties transferred to the Secretary of the Treasury.

Pacific Northwest River Basins Commission Established by EO 11331 of Mar. 6, 1967. Terminated by EO 12319 of Sept. 9, 1981.

Packers and Stockyards Administration Established by Memorandum 1613, supp. 1, of May 8, 1967 of the Secretary of Agriculture. Certain functions consolidated into Agricultural Marketing Service by Secretary's Memorandum 1927 of Jan. 15, 1978. Remaining functions incorporated into the Grain Inspection, Packers and Stockyards Administration

by Secretary's Memorandum 1010–1 dated Oct. 20, 1994.

Panama Canal Operation of piers at Atlantic and Pacific terminals transferred to *Panama Railroad Company* by EO 7021 of Apr. 19, 1935. Panama Canal reestablished as *Canal Zone Government* by act of Sept. 26, 1950 (64 Stat. 1038).

Panama Canal Commission Established by act of Oct. 1, 1979, as amended (22 U.S.C. 3611). U.S. responsibility terminated by stipulation of the Panama Canal Treaty of 1977, which transferred responsibility for the Panama Canal to the Republic of Panama, effective Dec. 31, 1999. Commission terminated by act of Sept. 30, 2004 (118 Stat. 1140).

Panama Canal Company Established by act of June 29, 1948 (62 Stat. 1076). Abolished and superseded by *Panama Canal Commission* (93 Stat. 454).

Panama Railroad Company Incorporated Apr. 7, 1849, by New York State Legislature. Operated under private control until 1881, when original *French Canal Company* acquired most of its stock. *Company* and its successor, *New Panama Canal Company,* operated railroad as common carrier and also as adjunct in attempts to construct canal. In 1904 their shares of stock in *Panama Railroad Company* passed to ownership of U.S. as part of assets of *New Panama Canal Company* purchased under act of June 28, 1902 (34 Stat. 481). Remaining shares purchased from private owners in 1905. *Panama Railroad Company* reincorporated by act of June 29, 1948 (62 Stat. 1075) pursuant to requirements of act of Dec. 6, 1945 (59 Stat. 597). Reestablished as *Panama Canal Company* by act of Sept. 26, 1950 (64 Stat. 1038). The Secretary of the Army was directed to discontinue commercial operations of *Company* by Presidential letter of Mar. 29, 1961.

Paperwork, Commission on Federal Established by act of Dec. 27, 1974 (88 Stat. 1789). Terminated January 1978 pursuant to terms of act.

Park Service, National Functions in District of Columbia relating to space assignment, site selection for public buildings, and determination of priority in construction transferred to *Public Buildings Administration, Federal Works Agency,* under Reorg. Plan No. I of 1939, effective July 1, 1939.

Park Trust Fund Board, National Established by act of July 10, 1935 (49 Stat. 477). Terminated by act of Dec. 18, 1967 (81 Stat. 656), and functions transferred to National Park Foundation.

Parks, Buildings, and Reservations, Office of National Established in the Department of the Interior by EO 6166 of June 10, 1933. Renamed National Park Service by act of Mar. 2, 1934 (48 Stat. 362).

Parole, Board of Established by act of June 25, 1948 (62 Stat. 854). Abolished by act of Mar. 15, 1976 (90 Stat. 219), and functions transferred to U.S. Parole Commission.

Patent Office Provisions of first patent act administered by the Department of State, with authority for granting patents vested in board comprising Secretaries of State and *War* and Attorney General. Board abolished, authority transferred to Secretary of State, and registration system established by act of Feb. 21, 1793 (1 Stat. 318). *Office* made bureau in the Department of State in October 1802, headed by *Superintendent of Patents. Office* reorganized in 1836 by act of June 4, 1836 (5 Stat. 117) under *Commissioner of Patents. Office* transferred to the Department of the Interior in 1849. *Office* transferred to the Department of Commerce by EO 4175 of Mar. 17, 1925.

Patents Board, Government   Established by EO 10096 of Jan. 23, 1950. Abolished by EO 10930 of Mar. 24, 1961, and functions transferred to the Secretary of Commerce.

Pay Board   Established by EO 11627 of Oct. 15, 1971. Abolished by EO 11695 of Jan. 11, 1973.

Payment Limitations, Commission on Application of   Established by act of May 13, 2002 (116 Stat. 216). Abolished by acts of May 22, 2008 (122 Stat. 1025) and June 18, 2008 (122 Stat. 1753).

Peace Corps   Established in the Department of State by EO 10924 of Mar. 1, 1961, and continued by act of Sept. 22, 1961 (75 Stat. 612), and EO 11041 of Aug. 6, 1962. Functions transferred to ACTION by Reorg. Plan No. 1 of 1971, effective July 1, 1971. Made independent agency in executive branch by act of Dec. 29, 1981 (95 Stat. 1540).

Pennsylvania Avenue, Temporary Commission on   Established by EO 11210 of Mar. 25, 1956. Inactive as of Nov. 15, 1969, due to lack of funding.

Pennsylvania Avenue Development Corporation   Established by act of Oct. 27, 1972 (86 Stat. 1266). Terminated pursuant to act of Jan. 26, 1996 (110 Stat. 32) and act of Apr. 26, 1996 (110 Stat. 1321–198). Functions transferred to General Services Administration, National Capital Planning Commission, and National Park Service (61 FR 11308), effective Apr. 1, 1996.

Pension and Welfare Benefit Programs, Office of   *See* **Labor-Management Services Administration**

Pensions, Commissioner of   Provided for by act of Mar. 2, 1833 (4 Stat. 668). Continued by act of Mar. 3, 1835 (4 Stat. 779), and other acts as *Office of the Commissioner of Pensions.* Transferred to the Department of the Interior as bureau by act of Mar. 3, 1849 (9 Stat. 395). Consolidated with other bureaus and agencies into *Veterans Administration* by EO 5398 of July 21, 1930.

Pensions, Office of the Commissioner of   *See* **Pensions, Commissioner of**

Perry's Victory Memorial Commission   Created by act of Mar. 3, 1919 (40 Stat. 1322). Administration of Memorial transferred to National Park Service by act of June 2, 1936 (49 Stat. 1393). *Commission* terminated by terms of act and membership reconstituted as advisory board to the Secretary of Interior.

Personal Property, Office of   *See* **Supply Service, Federal**

Personnel, National Roster of Scientific and Specialized   Established by *National Resources Planning Board* pursuant to Presidential letter of June 18, 1940, to the Secretary of the Treasury. After Aug. 15, 1940, administered jointly by *Board* and *U.S. Civil Service Commission.* Transferred to *War Manpower Commission* by EO 9139 of Apr. 18, 1942. Transferred to the Department of Labor by EO 9617 of Sept. 19, 1945. Transferred with *Bureau of Employment Security* to *Federal Security Agency* by act of June 16, 1948 (62 Stat. 443). Transferred to the Department of Labor by Reorg. Plan No. 2 of 1949, effective Aug. 20, 1949, and became inactive. Roster functions transferred to National Science Foundation by act of May 10, 1950 (64 Stat. 154). Reactivated in 1950 as *National Scientific Register* by *Office of Education, Federal Security Agency,* through *National Security Resources Board* grant of funds, and continued by National Science Foundation funds until December 1952, when *Register* integrated into Foundation's National Register of Scientific and Technical Personnel project in Division of Scientific Personnel and Education.

Personnel Administration, Council of   Established by EO 7916 of June 24, 1938, effective Feb. 1, 1939. Made unit in *U.S. Civil Service Commission* by EO 8467 of July 1, 1940. Renamed *Federal Personnel Council* by EO 9830 of Feb. 24, 1947. Abolished by act of July 31, 1953 (67 Stat. 300), and personnel and records transferred to *Office of Executive Director, U.S. Civil Service Commission.*

Personnel Council, Federal   *See* **Personnel Administration, Council of**

Personnel Interchange, President's Commission on   Established by EO 11451 of Jan. 19, 1969. Continued by EO 12136 of May 15, 1979, and renamed *President's Commission on Executive Exchange.* Continued by EO 12493 of Dec. 5, 1984. Abolished by EO 12760 of May 2, 1991.

Personnel Management, Liaison Office for   Established by EO 8248 of Sept. 8, 1939. Abolished by EO 10452 of May 1, 1953, and functions transferred to *U.S. Civil Service Commission.*

Petroleum Administration for Defense   Established under act of Sept. 8, 1950 (64 Stat. 798) by Order 2591 of Oct. 3, 1950 of the Secretary of the Interior, pursuant to EO 10161 of Sept. 9, 1950. Continued by Secretary's Order 2614 of Jan. 25, 1951, pursuant to EO 10200 of Jan. 3, 1951, and PAD Delegation 1 of Jan. 24, 1951. Abolished by Secretary's Order 2755 of Apr. 23, 1954.

Petroleum Administration for War   *See* **Petroleum Coordinator for War, Office of**

Petroleum Administrative Board   Established Sept. 11, 1933, by the Secretary of the Interior. Terminated Mar. 31, 1936, by EO 7076 of June 15, 1935. The Secretary of the Interior was authorized to execute functions vested in President by act of Feb. 22, 1935 (49 Stat. 30) by EO 7756 of Dec. 1, 1937. Secretary also authorized to establish *Petroleum Conservation Division* to assist in administering act. Records of *Petroleum Administrative Board* and *Petroleum Labor Policy Board* housed with

Petroleum Conservation Division, Office of Oil and Gas, acting as custodian for the Secretary of the Interior.

Petroleum Coordinator for War, Office of
Secretary of the Interior designated *Petroleum Coordinator for National Defense* pursuant to Presidential letter of May 28, 1941, and approved *Petroleum Coordinator for War* pursuant to Presidential letter of Apr. 20, 1942. *Office* abolished by EO 9276 of Dec. 2, 1942, and functions transferred to *Petroleum Administration for War,* established by same EO. *Administration* terminated by EO 9718 of May 3, 1946.

Petroleum Labor Policy Board Established by the Secretary of the Interior, as *Administrator of Code of Fair Competition for Petroleum Industry,* on recommendation of Planning and Coordination Committee Oct. 10, 1933. Reorganized by Secretary Dec. 19, 1933, and reorganization confirmed by order of Mar. 8, 1935. Terminated Mar. 31, 1936, when *Petroleum Administrative Board* abolished by EO 7076 of June 15, 1935.

Petroleum Reserves Corporation Established June 30, 1943, by *Reconstruction Finance Corporation.* Transferred to *Office of Economic Warfare* by EO 9360 of July 15, 1943. *Office* consolidated into *Foreign Economic Administration* by EO 9380 of Sept. 25, 1943. Functions transferred to *Reconstruction Finance Corporation* by EO 9630 of Sept. 27, 1945. *RFC's* charter amended Nov. 9, 1945, to change name to *War Assets Corporation. Corporation* designated by *Surplus Property Administrator* as disposal agency for all types of property for which *Reconstruction Finance Corporation* formerly disposal agency. Domestic surplus property functions of *Corporation* transferred to *War Assets Administration* by EO 9689 of Jan. 31, 1946. *Reconstruction Finance Corporation Board of Directors* ordered by President to dissolve *War Assets Corporation* as soon after Mar. 25, 1946, as practicable.

Philippine Alien Property Administration
Established in *Office for Emergency Management* by EO 9789 of Oct. 14, 1946. Abolished by EO 10254 of June 15, 1951, and functions transferred to the Department of Justice.

Philippine War Damage Commission Established by act of Apr. 30, 1946 (60 Stat. 128). Terminated Mar. 31, 1951, by act of Sept. 6, 1950 (64 Stat. 712).

Photographic Interpretation Center, National
Functions transferred to the National Imagery and Mapping Agency by act of Sept. 23, 1996 (110 Stat. 2677).

Physical Fitness, Committee on Established in *Office of Federal Security Administrator* by EO 9338 of Apr. 29, 1943. Terminated June 30, 1945.

Physical Fitness, President's Council on *See* **Youth Fitness, President's Council on**

Physician Payment Review Commission
Established by act of Apr. 7, 1986 (100 Stat. 190). Terminated by act of Aug. 5, 1997 (111 Stat. 354). Assets, staff, and continuing responsibility for reports transferred to the Medicare Payment Advisory Commission.

Planning Board, National Established by *Administrator of Public Works* July 30, 1933. Terminated by EO 6777 of June 30, 1934.

Plant Industry, Bureau of Established by act of Mar. 2, 1902 (31 Stat. 922). Soil fertility and soil microbiology work of *Bureau of Chemistry and Soils* transferred to *Bureau* by act of May 17, 1935. Soil chemistry and physics and soil survey work of *Bureau of Chemistry and Soils* transferred to *Bureau* by Secretary's Memorandum 784 of Oct. 6, 1938. In February 1943 engineering research of *Bureau of Agricultural Chemistry and Engineering* transferred to *Bureau of Plant Industry, Soils, and Agricultural Engineering* by Research Administration Memorandum 5 issued pursuant to EO 9069 of Feb. 23, 1942, and in conformity with Secretary's Memorandums 960 and 986. Functions transferred to Agricultural Research Service by Secretary's Memorandum 1320, supp. 4, of Nov. 2, 1953.

Plant Industry, Soils, and Agricultural Engineering, Bureau of *See* **Plant Industry, Bureau of**

Plant Quarantine, Bureau of *See* **Entomology and Plant Quarantine, Bureau of**

Policy Development, Office of *See* **Domestic Council**

Post Office, Department of *See* **Postal Service**

Postal Rate Commission Renamed Postal Regulatory Commission by act of Dec. 20, 2006 (120 Stat. 3241).

Postal Savings System Established by act of June 25, 1910 (36 Stat. 814). System closed by act of Mar. 28, 1966 (80 Stat. 92).

Postal Service Created July 26, 1775, by Continental Congress. Temporarily established by Congress by act of Sept. 22, 1789 (1 Stat. 70), and continued by subsequent acts. *Department of Post Office* made executive department under act of June 8, 1872 (17 Stat. 283). Offices of First, Second, Third, and Fourth Assistant Postmasters General abolished and Deputy Postmaster General and four Assistant Postmasters General established by Reorg. Plan No. 3 of 1949, effective Aug. 20, 1949. Reorganized as U.S. Postal Service in executive branch by act of Aug. 12, 1970 (84 Stat. 719), effective July 1, 1971.

Power Commission, Federal Established by act of June 10, 1920 (41 Stat. 1063). Terminated by act of Aug. 4, 1977 (91 Stat. 578), and functions transferred to the Department of Energy.

Preparedness, Office of Renamed *Federal Preparedness Agency* by General Services Administrator's order of June 26, 1975.

Preparedness Agency, Federal Functions transferred from General Services Administration to Federal Emergency Management Agency by EO 12148 of July 20, 1979.

Presidential. *See other part of title*

President's.   *See other part of title*

Press Intelligence, Division of   Established in August 1933. Made division of *National Emergency Council* July 10, 1935. Continued in *Office of Government Reports* by Reorg. Plan No. II of 1939, effective July 1, 1939. Transferred to *Office of War Information* by EO 9182 of June 13, 1942, functioning in *Bureau of Special Services. Office* abolished by EO 9608 of Aug. 31, 1945, and *Bureau* transferred to *Bureau of the Budget.* Upon reestablishment of *Office of Government Reports,* by EO 9809 of Dec. 12, 1946, *Division of Press Intelligence* made unit of *Office.*

Price Administration, Office of   Established by EO 8734 of Apr. 11, 1941, combining *Price Division* and *Consumer Division* of *National Defense Advisory Commission.* Renamed *Office of Price Administration* by EO 8875 of Aug. 28, 1941, which transferred *Civilian Allocation Division* to *Office of Production Management.* Consolidated with other agencies into *Office of Temporary Controls* by EO 9809 of Dec. 12, 1946, except *Financial Reporting Division,* transferred to Federal Trade Commission.

Price Commission   Established by EO 11627 of Oct. 15, 1971. Abolished by EO 11695 of Jan. 11, 1973.

Price Decontrol Board   Established by act of July 25, 1946 (60 Stat. 669). Effective period of act of Jan. 30, 1942 (56 Stat. 23), extended to June 30, 1947, by joint resolution of June 25, 1946 (60 Stat. 664).

Price Stability for Economic Growth, Cabinet Committee on   Established by Presidential letter of Jan. 28, 1959. Abolished by Presidential direction Mar. 12, 1961.

Price Stabilization, Office of   Established by General Order 2 of *Economic Stabilization Administrator* Jan. 24, 1951. *Director of Price Stabilization* provided for in EO 10161 of Sept. 9, 1950. Terminated Apr. 30, 1953, by EO 10434 of Feb. 6, 1953, and provisions of acts of June 30, 1952 (66 Stat. 296) and June 30, 1953 (67 Stat. 131).

Prices and Costs, Committee on Government Activities Affecting   Established by EO 10802 of Jan. 23, 1959. Abolished by EO 10928 of Mar. 23, 1961.

Priorities Board   Established by order of *Council of National Defense,* approved Oct. 18, 1940, and by EO 8572 of Oct. 21, 1940. EO 8572 revoked by EO 8629 of Jan. 7, 1941.

Prison Industries, Inc., Federal   Established by EO 6917 of Dec. 11, 1934. Transferred to the Department of Justice by Reorg. Plan No. II of 1939, effective July 1, 1939.

Prison Industries Reorganization Administration   Functioned from Sept. 26, 1935, to Sept. 30, 1940, under authority of act of Apr. 8, 1935 (49 Stat. 115), and of EO's 7194 of Sept. 26, 1935, 7202 of Sept. 28, 1935, and 7649 of June 29, 1937. Terminated due to lack of funding.

Private Sector Programs, Office of   Functions transferred to the Office of Citizen Exchanges within the Bureau of Educational and Cultural Affairs, USIA, by act of Feb. 16, 1990 (104 Stat. 56).

Processing tax   *Agricultural Adjustment Administration's* function of collecting taxes declared unconstitutional by U.S. Supreme Court Jan. 6, 1936. Functions under acts of June 28, 1934 (48 Stat. 1275), Apr. 21, 1934 (48 Stat. 598), and Aug. 24, 1935 (49 Stat. 750) discontinued by repeal of these laws by act of Feb. 10, 1936 (49 Stat. 1106).

Processing Tax Board of Review   Established in the Department of the Treasury by act of June 22, (49 Stat. 1652). Abolished by act of Oct. 21, 1942 (56 Stat. 967).

Proclamations   *See* **State, Department of**

Procurement, Commission on Government   Established by act of Nov. 26, 1969 (83 Stat. 269). Terminated Apr. 30, 1973, due to expiration of statutory authority.

Procurement and Assignment Service   Established by President Oct. 30, 1941. Transferred from *Office of Defense Health and Welfare Services* to *War Manpower Commission* by EO 9139 of Apr. 18, 1942. Transferred to *Federal Security Agency* by EO 9617 of Sept. 19, 1945, which terminated *Commission.*

Procurement Division   Established in the Department of the Treasury by EO 6166 of June 10, 1933. Renamed *Bureau of Federal Supply* by Department of the Treasury Order 73 of Nov. 19, 1946, effective Jan. 1, 1947. Transferred to General Services Administration as Federal Supply Service by act of June 30, 1949 (63 Stat. 380).

Procurement Policy, Office of Federal   Established within Office of Management and Budget by act of Aug. 30, 1974 (88 Stat. 97). Abolished due to lack of funding and functions transferred to Office of Management and Budget by act of Oct 28, 1993 (107 Stat. 1236).

Product Standards Policy, Office of   Formerly separate operating unit under Assistant Secretary for Productivity, Technology, and Innovation, Department of Commerce. Transferred to *National Bureau of Standards* by departmental reorganization order, effective Apr. 27, 1982.

Production Areas, Committee for Congested   Established in Executive Office of the President by EO 9327 of Apr. 7, 1943. Terminated Dec. 31, 1944, by act of June 28, 1944 (58 Stat. 535).

Production Authority, National   Established in the Department of Commerce Sept. 11, 1950, by EO's 10161 of Sept. 9, 1950, 10193 of Dec. 16, 1950, and 10200 of Jan. 3, 1951. Abolished by order of Oct. 1, 1953 of the Secretary of Commerce, and functions merged into *Business and Defense Services Administration.*

Production Management, Office of   Established in *Office for Emergency Management* by EO 8629 of Jan. 7, 1941. Abolished by EO 9040 of Jan. 24,

1942, and personnel and property transferred to *War Production Board.*

Production and Marketing Administration
Established by Secretary of Agriculture Memorandum 1118 of Aug. 18, 1945. Functions transferred under Department reorganization by Secretary's Memorandum 1320, supp. 4, of Nov. 2, 1953.

Productivity Council, National Established by EO 12089 of Oct. 23, 1978. EO 12089 revoked by EO 12379 of Aug. 17, 1982.

Programs, Bureau of International Established by the Secretary of Commerce Aug. 8, 1961, by Departmental Orders 173 and 174. Abolished by Departmental Order 182 of Feb. 1, 1963, which established *Bureau of International Commerce.* Functions transferred to *Domestic and International Business Administration,* effective Nov. 17, 1972.

Programs, Office of Public Established in the National Archives and Records Administration. Reorganized by Archivist under Notice 96–260, Sept. 23, 1996, effective Jan. 6, 1997. Functions restructured and transferred to Office of Records Services—Washington, DC.

Prohibition, Bureau of Established by act of May 27, 1930 (46 Stat. 427). Investigative functions consolidated with functions of *Bureau of Investigation* into *Division of Investigation,* Department of Justice. by EO 6166 of June 10, 1933, which set as effective date Mar. 2, 1934, or such later date as fixed by President. All other functions performed by *Bureau of Prohibition* ordered transferred to such division in the Department of Justice as deemed desirable by Attorney General.

Property, Office of Surplus Established in *Procurement Division,* Department of the Treasury, by EO 9425 of Feb. 19, 1944, and act of Oct. 3, 1944 (58 Stat. 765), under general direction of *Surplus Property Board* established by same legislation. Transferred to the Department of Commerce by EO 9541 of Apr. 19, 1945. Terminated by EO 9643 of Oct. 19, 1945, and activities and personnel transferred to *Reconstruction Finance Corporation.*

Property Administration, Surplus *See* **War Property Administration, Surplus**

Property Board, Surplus *See* **War Property Administration, Surplus**

Property Council, Federal Established by EO 11724 of June 25, 1973, and reconstituted by EO 11954 of Jan. 7, 1977. Terminated by EO 12030 of Dec. 15, 1977.

Property Management and Disposal Service *See* **Emergency Procurement Service**

Property Office, Surplus Established in *Division of Territories and Island Possessions,* Department of the Interior, under Regulation 1 of *Surplus Property Board,* Apr. 2, 1945. Transferred to *War Assets Administration* by EO 9828 of Feb. 21, 1947.

Property Review Board Established by EO 12348 of Feb. 25, 1982. EO 12348 revoked by EO 12512 of Apr. 29, 1985.

Protective Service, Federal Functions established in the *Federal Works* Agency by act of June 1, 1948 (62 Stat. 281). Functions transferred to General Services Administrator by act of June 30, 1949 (63 Stat. 380). Established as an agency within General Services Administration by GSA Administrator on Jan. 11, 1971 (ADM. 5440.46). Transferred to Homeland Security Department by act of Nov. 25, 2002 (116 Stat. 2178).

Prospective Payment Assessment Commission Established by act of Apr. 20, 1983 (97 Stat. 159). Terminated by act of Aug. 5, 1997 (111 Stat. 354). Assets, staff, and continuing responsibility for reports transferred to the Medicare Payment Advisory Commission.

Provisions and Clothing, Bureau of Established by acts of Aug. 31, 1842 (5 Stat. 579), and July 5, 1862 (12 Stat. 510). Designated *Bureau of Supplies and Accounts* by act of July 19, 1892 (27 Stat. 243). Abolished by Department of Defense reorg. order of Mar. 9, 1966, and functions transferred to the Secretary of the Navy (31 FR 7188).

Public. *See other part of title*

Publications Commission, National Historical Established by act of Oct. 22, 1968 (82 Stat. 1293). Renamed National Historical Publications and Records Commission by act of Dec. 22, 1974 (88 Stat. 1734).

Puerto Rican Hurricane Relief Commission Established by act of Dec. 21, 1928 (45 Stat. 1067). No loans made after June 30, 1934, and *Commission* abolished June 3, 1935, by Public Resolution 22 (49 Stat. 320). Functions transferred to *Division of Territories and Island Possessions,* Department of the Interior. After June 30, 1946, collection work performed in *Puerto Rico Reconstruction Administration.* Following termination of *Administration,* remaining collection functions transferred to the Secretary of Agriculture by act of July 11, 1956 (70 Stat. 525).

Puerto Rico, U.S.-Puerto Rico Commission on the Status of Established by act of Feb. 20, 1964 (78 Stat. 17). Terminated by terms of act.

Puerto Rico Reconstruction Administration Established in the Department of the Interior by EO 7057 of May 28, 1935. Terminated Feb. 15, 1955, by act of Aug. 15, 1953 (67 Stat. 584).

Radiation Biology Laboratory *See* **Radiation and Organisms, Division of**

Radiation Council, Federal Established by EO 10831 of Aug. 14, 1959, and act of Sept. 23, 1959 (73 Stat. 688). Abolished by Reorg. Plan No. 3 of 1970, effective Dec. 2, 1970, and functions transferred to Environmental Protection Agency.

Radiation and Organisms, Division of Established by Secretarial order of May 1, 1929, as part of Smithsonian Astrophysical Observatory. Renamed *Radiation Biology Laboratory* by Secretarial order of

Feb. 16, 1965. Merged with *Chesapeake Center for Environmental Studies* by Secretarial order of July 1, 1983, to form Smithsonian Environmental Research Center.

Radio Commission, Federal Established by act of Feb. 23, 1927 (44 Stat. 1162). Abolished by act of June 19, 1934 (48 Stat. 1102), and functions transferred to Federal Communications Commission.

Radio Division Established by *National Emergency Council* July 1, 1938. Transferred to *Office of Education, Federal Security Agency,* by Reorg. Plan No. II of 1939, effective July 1, 1939. Terminated June 30, 1940, by terms of act of June 30, 1939 (53 Stat. 927).

Radio Propagation Laboratory, Central Transferred from *National Bureau of Standards* to *Environmental Science Services Administration* by the Department of Commerce Order 2–A, effective July 13, 1965.

Radiological Health, National Center for Devices and Renamed Center for Devices and Radiological Health by Food and Drug Administration notice of Mar. 9, 1984 (49 FR 10166).

Rail Public Counsel, Office of Established by act of Feb. 5, 1976 (90 Stat. 51). Terminated Dec. 1, 1979, due to lack of funding.

Railroad Administration, U.S. *See* **Railroads, Director General of**

Railroad and Airline Wage Board Established by *Economic Stabilization Administrator's* General Order 7 of Sept. 27, 1951, pursuant to act of Sept. 8, 1950 (64 Stat. 816). Terminated Apr. 30, 1953, by EO 10434 of Feb. 6, 1953, and acts of June 30, 1952 (66 Stat. 296), and June 30, 1953 (67 Stat. 131).

Railroads, Director General of Established under authority of act of Aug. 29, 1916 (39 Stat. 645). Organization of *U.S. Railroad Administration* announced Feb. 9, 1918. Office abolished by Reorg. Plan No. II of 1939, effective July 1, 1939, and functions transferred to the Secretary of the Treasury.

Railway Association, U.S. Established by act of Jan. 2, 1974 (87 Stat. 985). Terminated Apr. 1, 1987, by act of Oct. 21, 1986 (100 Stat. 1906).

Railway Labor Panel, National Established by EO 9172 of May 22, 1942. EO 9172 revoked by EO 9883 of Aug. 11, 1947.

Real Estate Board, Federal Established by EO 8034 of Jan. 14, 1939. Abolished by EO 10287 of Sept. 6, 1951.

Reclamation, Bureau of *See* **Reclamation Service**

Reclamation Service Established July 1902 in *Geological Survey* by the Secretary of the Interior, pursuant to act of June 17, 1902 (32 Stat. 388). Separated from Survey in 1907 and renamed *Bureau of Reclamation* June 1923. Power marketing functions transferred to the Department of Energy by act of Aug. 4, 1977 (91 Stat. 578). *Bureau* renamed *Water and Power Resources Service* by Secretarial Order 3042 of Nov. 6, 1979. Renamed Bureau of

Reclamation by Secretarial Order 3064 of May 18, 1981.

Reconciliation Service Established by Director of Selective Service pursuant to EO 11804 of Sept. 16, 1974. Program terminated Apr. 2, 1980.

Reconstruction Finance Corporation Established Feb. 2, 1932, by act of Jan. 22, 1932 (47 Stat. 5). Grouped with other agencies to form *Federal Loan Agency* by Reorg. Plan No. I of 1939, effective July 1, 1939. Transferred to the Department of Commerce by EO 9071 of Feb. 24, 1942. Returned to *Federal Loan Agency* by act of Feb. 24, 1945 (59 Stat. 5). *Agency* abolished by act of June 30, 1947 (61 Stat. 202), and functions assumed by *Corporation*. Functions relating to financing houses or site improvements, authorized by act of Aug. 10, 1948 (61 Stat. 1275), transferred to *Housing and Home Finance Agency* by Reorg. Plan No. 23 of 1950, effective July 10, 1950. *Corporation* Board of Directors, established by act of Jan. 22, 1932 (47 Stat. 5), abolished by Reorg. Plan No. 1 of 1951, effective May 1, 1951, and functions transferred to Administrator and *Loan Policy Board* established by same plan, effective Apr. 30, 1951. Act of July 30, 1953 (67 Stat. 230), provided for *RFC* succession until June 30, 1954, and for termination of its lending powers Sept. 28, 1953. Certain functions assigned to appropriate agencies for liquidation by Reorg. Plan No. 2 of 1954, effective July 1, 1954. *Corporation* abolished by Reorg. Plan No. 1 of 1957, effective June 30, 1957, and functions transferred to *Housing and Home Finance Agency,* General Services Administration, Small Business Administration, and the Department of the Treasury.

Records Administration, Office of Established in the National Archives and Records Administration. Reorganized by Archivist under Notice 96–260, Sept. 23, 1996, effective Jan. 6, 1997. Functions restructured and transferred to Office of Records Services—Washington, DC.

Records Centers, Office of Federal Established in the National Archives and Records Administration. Reorganized by Archivist under Notice 96–260, Sept. 23, 1996, effective Jan. 6, 1997. Functions restructured and transferred to Office of Regional Records Services.

Records and Information Management, Office of Functions transferred from *National Archives and Records Service* to *Automated Data and Telecommunications Service* by General Services Administrator's decision, effective Jan. 10, 1982, regionally and Apr. 1, 1982, in Washington, DC.

Recovery Administration, Advisory Council, National Established by EO 7075 of June 15, 1935. Transferred to the Department of Commerce by EO 7252 of Dec. 21, 1935, and functions ordered terminated not later than Apr. 1, 1936, by same order. *Committee of Industrial Analysis* created by EO 7323 of Mar. 21, 1936, to complete work of *Council*.

Recovery Administration, National Established by President pursuant to act of June 16, 1933 (48 Stat. 194). Provisions of title I of act repealed by Public Resolution 26 of June 14, 1935 (49 Stat. 375), and extension of *Administration* in skeletonized form authorized until Apr. 1, 1936. *Office of Administrator, National Recovery Administration,* created by EO 7075 of June 15, 1935. *Administration* terminated by EO 7252 of Dec. 21, 1935, which transferred *Division of Review, Division of Business Corporation,* and *Advisory Council* to the Department of Commerce for termination of functions by Apr. 1, 1936. *Consumers' Division* transferred to the Department of Labor by same order.

Recovery Review Board, National   Established by EO 6632 of Mar. 7, 1934. Abolished by EO 6771 of June 30, 1934.

Recreation, Bureau of Outdoor   Established in the Department of the Interior by act of May 28, 1963 (77 Stat. 49). Terminated by Secretary's order of Jan. 25, 1978, and functions assumed by *Heritage Conservation and Recreation Service.*

Recreation and Natural Beauty, Citizens' Advisory Committee on   Established by EO 11278 of May 4, 1966. Terminated by EO 11472 of May 29, 1969.

Recreation and Natural Beauty, President's Council on   Established by EO 11278 of May 4, 1966. Terminated by EO 11472 of May 29, 1969.

Recreation Resources Review Commission, Outdoor Established by act of June 28, 1958 (72 Stat. 238). Final report submitted to President January 1962 and terminated Sept. 1, 1962.

Regional Action Planning Commissions   Authorized by act of Aug. 26, 1965 (79 Stat. 552). Federal role abolished through repeal by act of Aug. 13, 1981 (95 Stat. 766). At time of repeal, eight commissions—Coastal Plains, Four Corners, New England, Old West Ozarks, Pacific Northwest, Southwest Border, Southwest Border Region, and Upper Great Lakes—affected.

Regional Archives, Office of Special and Established in the National Archives and Records Administration. Reorganized by Archivist under Notice 96–260, Sept. 23, 1996, effective Jan. 6, 1997. Functions restructured and transferred between Office of Records Services—Washington, DC and Office of Regional Records Services.

Regional Councils, Federal   Established by EO 12314 of July 22, 1981. Abolished by EO 12407 of Feb. 22, 1983.

Regional Operations, Executive Director of Established in Food and Drug Administration by order of May 20, 1971 of the *Secretary of Health, Education, an.' Welfare.* Merged into Office of Regulatory Affairs by order of Nov. 5, 1984 of the Secretary of Health and Human Services.

Regulations and Rulings, Office of   Established in the U.S. Customs and Border Protection. Abolished by act of Oct. 13, 2006 (120 Stat. 1924) and functions transferred to the Office of International Trade.

Regulatory Council, U.S.   Disbanded by Vice Presidential memorandum of Mar. 25, 1981. Certain

functions continued in Regulatory Information Service Center.

Regulatory Relief, Presidential Task Force on Establishment announced in President's remarks Jan. 22, 1981. Disbanded and functions transferred to Office of Management and Budget in August 1983.

Rehabilitation Services Administration   Functions transferred from *Department of Health, Education, and Welfare* to Office of Special Education and Rehabilitative Services, Department of Education, by act of Oct. 17, 1979 (93 Stat. 678), effective May 4, 1980.

Relief Corporation, Federal Surplus   Organized under powers granted to President by act of June 16, 1933 (48 Stat. 195). Charter granted by State of Delaware Oct. 4, 1933, and amended Nov. 18, 1935, changing name to *Federal Surplus Commodities Corporation* and naming the Secretary of Agriculture, *Administrator of Agricultural Adjustment Administration,* and *Governor of Farm Credit Administration* as Board of Directors. Continued as agency under the Secretary of Agriculture by acts of June 28, 1937 (50 Stat. 323) and Feb. 16, 1938 (52 Stat. 38). Consolidated with *Division of Marketing and Marketing Agreements* into *Surplus Marketing Administration* by Reorg. Plan No. III of 1940, effective June 30, 1940. Merged into *Agricultural Marketing Administration* by EO 9069 of Feb. 23, 1942.

Relief and Rehabilitation Operations, Office of Foreign   Established in the Department of State as announced by White House Nov. 21, 1942. Consolidated with *Foreign Economic Administration* by EO 9380 of Sept. 25, 1943.

Renegotiation Board   Established by act of Mar. 23, 1951 (65 Stat. 7). Terminated Mar. 31, 1979, by act of Oct. 10, 1978 (92 Stat. 1043).

Rent Advisory Board   Established by EO 11632 of Nov. 22, 1971. Abolished by EO 11695 of Jan. 11, 1973.

Rent Stabilization, Office of   Established by General Order 9 of *Economic Stabilization Administrator* July 31, 1951, pursuant to act of June 30, 1947 (61 Stat. 193), and EO' s 10161 of Sept. 9, 1950, and 10276 of July 31, 1951. Abolished by EO 10475 of July 31, 1953, and functions transferred to *Office of Defense Mobilization. Office of Research and Development* combined with *Office of Minerals Policy Development* in the Department of the Interior May 21, 1976, under authority of Reorg. Plan No. 3 of 1950, effective May 24, 1950, to form *Office of Minerals Policy and Research Analysis.* Abolished Sept. 30, 1981, by Secretarial Order 3070 and functions transferred to *Bureau of Mines.*

Reports, Office of Government   Established July 1, 1939, to perform functions of *National Emergency Council* abolished by Reorg. Plan No. II of 1939, effective July 1, 1939. Established as administrative unit of Executive Office of the President by EO 8248 of Sept. 8, 1939. Consolidated with *Office of War Information, Office for Emergency Management,* by EO 9182 of June 13, 1942. Reestablished in

Executive Office of the President by EO 9809 of Dec. 12, 1946, which transferred to it functions of *Media Programming Division* and *Motion Picture Division, Office of War Mobilization and Reconversion,* and functions transferred from *Bureau of Special Services, Office of War Information,* to *Bureau of the Budget* by EO 9608 of Aug. 31, 1945. Subsequent to enactment of act of July 30, 1947 (61 Stat. 588), functions of *Office* restricted to advertising and motion picture liaison and operation of library. Terminated June 30, 1948.

Research, Office of University Transferred from *Office of Program Management and Administration,* Research and Special Programs Administration, to Office of Economics, Office of the Assistant Secretary for Policy and International Affairs, under authority of the Department of Transportation appropriation request for FY 1985, effective Oct. 1, 1984.

Research and Development Board Established in the Department of Defense by act of July 26, 1947 (61 Stat. 499). Abolished by Reorg. Plan No. 6 of 1953, effective June 30, 1953, and functions vested in the Secretary of Defense.

Research and Development Board, Joint Established June 6, 1946, by charter of Secretaries of *War* and Navy. Terminated on creation of *Research and Development Board* by act of July 26, 1947 (61 Stat. 506).

Research and Intelligence Service, Interim Established in the Department of State by EO 9621 of Sept. 20, 1945. Abolished Dec. 31, 1945, pursuant to terms of order.

Research and Special Programs Administration Established by act of Oct. 24, 1992 (106 Stat. 3310). Abolished and certain duties and powers transferred to both the Pipeline Hazardous Materials Safety Administration and the Administrator of the Research and Innovative Technology Administration, Department of Transportation, by act of Nov. 30, 2004 (118 Stat. 2424–2426).

Research Resources, Division of Established in National Institutes of Health, Department of Health and Human Services. Renamed National Center for Research Resources by Secretarial notice of Feb. 23, 1990 (55 FR 6455) and act of June 10, 1993 (107 Stat. 178).

Research Service, Cooperative State Established by Secretary of Agriculture Memorandum 1462, supp. 1, of Aug. 31, 1961. Consolidated into *Science and Education Administration* by Secretary's order of Jan. 24, 1978. Reestablished as Cooperative State Research Service by Secretarial order of June 16, 1981.

Research and Service Division, Cooperative Functions transferred to the Secretary of Agriculture in *Farmer Cooperative Service* by act of Aug. 6, 1953 (67 Stat. 390).

Resettlement Administration Established by EO 7027 of Apr. 30, 1935. Functions transferred to the Department of Agriculture by EO 7530 of Dec. 31, 1936. Renamed *Farm Security Administration* by Secretary's Memorandum 732 of Sept. 1, 1937.

Abolished by act of Aug. 14, 1946 (60 Stat. 1062) and functions incorporated into the *Farmers' Home Administration,* effective Jan. 1, 1947. *Farmers' Home Administration* abolished, effective Dec. 27, 1994, under authority of Secretary's Memorandum 1010–1 dated Oct. 20, 1994 (59 FR 66441). Functions assumed by the *Consolidated Farm Service Agency* and the *Rural Housing and Community Development Service.*

Resolution Trust Corporation Established by act of Aug. 9, 1989 (103 Stat. 369). Board of Directors of the Corporation abolished by act of Dec. 12, 1991 (105 Stat. 1769). Corporation functions terminated pursuant to act of Dec. 17, 1993 (107 Stat. 2369).

Resources Board and Advisory Committee, National Established by EO 6777 of June 30, 1934. Abolished by EO 7065 of June 7, 1935, and functions transferred to *National Resources Committee.*

Resources Committee, National Established by EO 7065 of June 7, 1935. Abolished by Reorg. Plan No. I of 1939, effective July 1, 1939, and functions transferred to *National Resources Planning Board* in Executive Office of the President. *Board* terminated by act of June 26, 1943 (57 Stat. 169).

Resources Planning Board, National *See* **Resources Committee, National**

Retired Executives, Service Corps of Established in ACTION by act of Oct. 1, 1973 (87 Stat. 404). Transferred to Small Business Administration by EO 11871 of July 18, 1975.

Retraining and Reemployment Administration Established by EO 9427 of Feb. 24, 1944, and act of Oct. 3, 1944 (58 Stat. 788). Transferred from *Office of War Mobilization and Reconversion* to the Department of Labor by EO 9617 of Sept. 19, 1945. Terminated pursuant to terms of act.

Revenue Sharing, Office of Established by the Secretary of the Treasury to administer programs authorized by acts of Oct. 20, 1972 (86 Stat. 919), and July 22, 1976 (90 Stat. 999). Transferred from the Office of the Secretary to Assistant Secretary (Domestic Finance) by Department of the Treasury Order 242, rev. 1, of May 17, 1976.

Review, Division of Established in *National Recovery Administration* by EO 7075 of June 15, 1935. Transferred to the Department of Commerce by EO 7252 of Dec. 21, 1935, and functions terminated Apr. 1, 1936. *Committee of Industrial Analysis* created by EO 7323 of Mar. 21, 1936, to complete work of *Division.*

RFC Mortgage Company Organized under laws of Maryland Mar. 14, 1935, pursuant to act of Jan. 22, 1932 (47 Stat. 5). Grouped with other agencies to form *Federal Loan Agency* by Reorg. Plan No. I of 1939, effective July 1, 1939. Transferred to the Department of Commerce by EO 9071 of Feb. 24, 1942. Returned to *Federal Loan Agency* by act of Feb. 24, 1945 (59 Stat. 5). Assets and liabilities transferred to *Reconstruction Finance Corporation* by act of June 30, 1947 (61 Stat. 207).

River Basins, Neches, Trinity, Brazos, Colorado, Guadalupe, San Antonio, Nueces, and San Jacinto,

and Intervening Areas, U.S. Study Commission on
Established by act of Aug. 28, 1958 (72 Stat. 1058).
Terminated June 30, 1962.

**River Basins, Savannah, Altamaha, Saint Marys,
Apalachicola-Chattahoochee, and Perdido-
Escambia, and Intervening Areas, U.S. Study
Commission on** Established by act of Aug. 28,
1958 (72 Stat. 1090). Terminated Dec. 23, 1962.

Road Inquiry, Office of Established by the
Secretary of Agriculture under authority of act of
Aug. 8, 1894 (28 Stat. 264). Federal aid for
highways to be administered by the Secretary of
Agriculture through *Office of Public Roads and Rural
Engineering* authorized by act of July 11, 1916 (39
Stat. 355), known as *Bureau of Public Roads* after
July 1918. Transferred to *Federal Works Agency* by
Reorg. Plan No. I of 1939, effective July 1, 1939,
and renamed *Public Roads Administration.*
Transferred to General Services Administration as
Bureau of Public Roads by act of June 30, 1949 (63
Stat. 380). Transferred to the Department of
Commerce by Reorg. Plan No. 7 of 1949, effective
Aug. 20, 1949. Transferred to the Secretary of
Transportation by act of Oct. 15, 1966 (80 Stat.
931), and functions assigned to Federal Highway
Administration.

Roads, Bureau of Public *See* **Road Inquiry, Office
of**

Roads Administration, Public *See* **Road Inquiry,
Office of**

Roads and Rural Engineering, Office of Public *See*
Road Inquiry, Office of

Rock Creek and Potomac Parkway Commission
Established by act of Mar. 14, 1913 (37 Stat. 885).
Abolished by EO 6166 of June 10, 1933, and
functions transferred to *Office of National Parks,
Buildings, and Reservations,* Department of the
Interior.

Roosevelt Centennial Commission, Theodore
Established by joint resolution of July 28, 1955 (69
Stat. 383). Terminated Oct. 27, 1959, pursuant to
terms of act.

Roosevelt Library, Franklin D. Functions assigned
to National Park Service by Reorg. Plan No. 3 of
1946, effective July 16, 1946, transferred to General
Services Administration by Reorg. Plan No. 1 of
1963, effective July 27, 1963.

Roosevelt Library, Trustees of the Franklin D.
Established by joint resolution of July 18, 1939 (53
Stat. 1063). Transferred to General Services
Administration by act of June 30, 1949 (63 Stat.
381). Abolished by act of Mar. 5, 1958 (72 Stat. 34),
and Library operated by *National Archives and
Records Service,* General Services Administration.

Roosevelt Memorial Commission, Franklin Delano
Established by joint resolution of Aug. 11, 1955 (69
Stat. 694). Terminated by act of Nov. 14, 1997 (111
Stat. 1601).

Rubber Development Corporation Establishment
announced Feb. 20, 1943, by the Secretary of
Commerce. Organized under laws of Delaware as

subsidiary of *Reconstruction Finance Corporation.*
Assumed all activities of *Rubber Reserve Company*
relating to development of foreign rubber sources
and procurement of rubber therefrom. Functions
transferred to *Office of Economic Warfare* by EO
9361 of July 15, 1943. *Office* consolidated into
Foreign Economic Administration by EO 9380 of
Sept. 25, 1943. *Office* returned to *Reconstruction
Finance Corporation* by EO 9630 of Sept. 27, 1945.
Certificate of incorporation expired June 30, 1947.

Rubber Producing Facilities Disposal Commission
Established by act of Aug. 7, 1953 (67 Stat. 408).
Functions transferred to *Federal Facilities
Corporation* by EO 10678 of Sept. 20, 1956.

Rubber Reserve Company Established June 28,
1940, under act of Jan. 22, 1932 (47 Stat. 5).
Transferred from *Federal Loan Agency* to the
Department of Commerce by EO 9071 of Feb. 24,
1942. Returned to *Federal Loan Agency* by act of
Feb. 24, 1945 (59 Stat. 5). Dissolved by act of June
30, 1945 (59 Stat. 310), and functions transferred to
Reconstruction Finance Corporation.

Rural Areas Development, Office of Established by
Secretary of Agriculture memorandum in 1961
(revised Sept. 21, 1962). Renamed *Rural Community
Development Service* by Secretary's Memorandum
1570 of Feb. 24, 1965.

**Rural Business and Cooperative Development
Service** Established within the Department of
Agriculture by Secretary's Memorandum 1020–34
dated Dec. 31, 1991. Renamed Rural Business-
Cooperative Service (61 FR 2899), effective Jan. 30,
1996.

Rural Community Development Service
Established by Secretary of Agriculture Memorandum
1570 of Feb. 25, 1965, to supersede *Office of Rural
Areas Development.* Abolished Feb. 2, 1970, by
Secretary's Memorandum 1670 of Jan. 30, 1970,
and functions transferred to other agencies in the
Department of Agriculture.

Rural Development Administration Established
within the Department of Agriculture by Secretary's
Memorandum 1020–34 dated Dec. 31, 1991.
Abolished Dec. 27, 1994 (59 FR 66441) under
authority of Secretary's Memorandum 1010–1 dated
Oct. 20, 1994. Functions assumed by the Rural
Business and Cooperative Development Service.

Rural Development Committee *See* **Rural
Development Program, Committee for**

Rural Development Policy, Office of Established
initially as *Office of Rural Development Policy
Management and Coordination,* Farmers Home
Administration, by Secretary of Agriculture
Memorandum 1020–3 of Oct. 26, 1981. Abolished
in 1986 due to lack of funding.

Rural Development Program, Committee for
Established by EO 10847 of Oct. 12, 1959.
Abolished by EO 11122 of Oct. 16, 1963, which
established *Rural Development Committee.*
Committee superseded by EO 11307 of Sept. 30,
1966, and functions assumed by the Secretary of
Agriculture.

Rural Development Service Established by Agriculture Secretarial order in 1973. Functions transferred to *Office of Rural Development Coordination and Planning, Farmers Home Administration,* by Secretarial order in 1978.

Rural Electrification Administration Established by EO 7037 of May 11, 1935. Functions transferred by EO 7458 of Sept. 26, 1936, to *Rural Electrification Administration* established by act of May 20, 1936 (49 Stat. 1363). Transferred to the Department of Agriculture by Reorg. Plan No. II of 1939, effective July 1, 1939. Abolished by Secretary's Memorandum 1010–1 dated Oct. 20, 1994, and functions assumed by Rural Utilities Service.

Rural Housing and Community Development Service Established by act of Oct. 13, 1994 (108 Stat. 3219). Renamed Rural Housing Service (61 FR 2899), effective Jan. 30, 1996.

Rural Rehabilitation Division Established April 1934 by act of May 12, 1933 (48 Stat. 55). Functions transferred to *Resettlement Administration* by *Federal Emergency Relief Administrator's* order of June 19, 1935.

Saint Elizabeth's Hospital *See* **Insane, Government Hospital for the**

Saint Lawrence Seaway Development Corporation Established by act of May 13, 1954 (68 Stat. 92). Secretary of Commerce given direction of general policies of *Corporation* by EO 10771 of June 20, 1958. Transferred to the Department of Transportation by act of Oct. 15, 1966 (80 Stat. 931).

Salary Stabilization, Office of *See* **Salary Stabilization Board**

Salary Stabilization Board Established May 10, 1951, by *Economic Stabilization Administrator's* General Order 8. Stabilization program administered by *Office of Salary Stabilization.* Terminated Apr. 30, 1953, by EO 10434 of Feb. 6, 1953, and acts of June 30, 1952 (66 Stat. 296), and June 30, 1953 (67 Stat. 131).

Sales Manager, Office of the General Established by the Secretary of Agriculture Feb. 29, 1976. Consolidated with Foreign Agricultural Service by Secretary's Memorandum 2001 of Nov. 29, 1979.

Savings Bonds, Interdepartmental Committee for the Voluntary Payroll Savings Plan for the Purchase of U.S. Established by EO 11532 of June 2, 1970. Superseded by EO 11981 of Mar. 29, 1977, which established Interagency Committee for the Purchase of U.S. Savings Bonds.

Savings and Loan Advisory Council, Federal Established by act of Oct. 6, 1972 (86 Stat. 770). Continued by act of Dec. 26, 1974 (88 Stat. 1739). Terminated by act of Aug. 9, 1989 (103 Stat. 422).

Savings and Loan Insurance Corporation, Federal Established by act of June 27, 1934 (48 Stat. 1246). Grouped with other agencies to form *Federal Loan Agency* by Reorg. Plan No. I of 1939, effective July 1, 1939. Transferred to *Federal Home Loan Bank Administration, National Housing Agency,* by EO 9070 of Feb. 24, 1942. Board of Trustees abolished by Reorg. Plan No. 3 of 1947, effective July 27, 1947, and functions transferred to *Home Loan Bank Board.* Abolished by act of Aug. 9, 1989 (103 Stat. 354).

Savings Bonds Division, United States Established by Departmental Order 62 of Dec. 26, 1945, as successor to the War and Finance Division, War Savings Staff, and Defense Savings Staff. Functions transferred to Bureau of Public Debt by Departmental Order 101–05 of May 11, 1994, and *Division* renamed Savings Bond Marketing Office.

Science, Engineering, and Technology, Federal Coordinating Council for Established by act of May 11, 1976 (90 Stat. 471). Abolished by Reorg. Plan No. 1 of 1977, effective Feb. 26, 1978, and functions transferred to President. Functions redelegated to Director of the Office of Science and Technology Policy and Federal Coordinating Council for Science, Engineering, and Technology, established by EO 12039 of Feb. 24, 1978.

Science, Engineering, and Technology Panel, Intergovernmental Established by act of May 11, 1976 (90 Stat. 465). Abolished by Reorg. Plan No. 1 of 1977, effective Feb. 26, 1978, and functions transferred to President. Functions redelegated to Director of Office of Science and Technology Policy by EO 12039 of Feb. 24, 1978, which established Intergovernmental Science, Engineering, and Technology Advisory Panel.

Science Advisory Committee, President's Established by President Apr. 20, 1951, and reconstituted Nov. 22, 1957. Terminated with *Office of Science and Technology,* effective July 1, 1973.

Science Exhibit-Century 21 Exposition, U.S. Established Jan. 20, 1960, by Department of Commerce Order 167. Abolished by revocation of order on June 5, 1963.

Science and Technology, Federal Council for *See* **Scientific Research and Development, Interdepartmental Committee on**

Science and Technology, Office of Established by Reorg. Plan No. 2 of 1962, effective June 8, 1962. *Office* abolished by Reorg. Plan No. 1 of 1973, effective June 30, 1973, and functions transferred to National Science Foundation.

Science and Technology, President's Committee on Established by act of May 11, 1976 (90 Stat. 468). Abolished by Reorg. Plan No. 1 of 1977, effective Feb. 26, 1978, and functions transferred to President.

Scientific and Policy Advisory Committee Established by act of Sept. 26, 1961 (75 Stat. 631). Terminated Apr. 30, 1996 under terms of act.

Scientific Research and Development, Interdepartmental Committee on Established by EO 9912 of Dec. 24, 1947. EO 9912 revoked by EO 10807 of Mar. 13, 1959, which established *Federal Council for Science and Technology.* Abolished by act of May 11, 1976 (90 Stat. 472).

Scientific Research and Development, Office of
Established in *Office for Emergency Management* by
EO 8807 of June 28, 1941. Terminated by EO 9913
of Dec. 26, 1947, and property transferred to
National Military Establishment for liquidation.

**Scientists and Engineers, National Committee for
the Development of** Established by President Apr.
3, 1956. Renamed *President's Committee on
Scientists and Engineers* May 7, 1957. Final report
submitted Dec. 17, 1958, and expired Dec. 31,
1958.

Scientists and Engineers, President's Committee on
See **Scientists and Engineers, National Committee
for the Development of**

Screw Thread Commission, National Established
by act of July 18, 1918 (40 Stat. 912). Terminated
by EO 6166 of June 10, 1933, and records
transferred to the Department of Commerce,
effective Mar. 2, 1934. Informal Interdepartmental
Screw Thread Committee established on Sept. 14,
1939, consisting of representatives of the
Departments of *War*, the Navy, and Commerce.

Sea Grant Review Panel, National Established by
act of Oct. 8, 1976 (90 Stat. 1967). Renamed
National Sea Grant Advisory Board by act of Oct.
13, 2008 (122 Stat. 4207.

Secret Service, United States *See* **Secret Service
Division**

Secret Service Division Established July 5, 1865, as
a Bureau under Treasury Department.
Acknowledged as distinct agency within Treasury
Department in 1883. *White House Police Force*
created on October 1, 1922, and placed under
supervision of *Secret Service Division* in 1930.
White House Police Force renamed *Executive
Protective Service* by act of June 30, 1970 (84 Stat.
358). *Executive Protective Service* renamed U.S.
Secret Service Uniformed Division by act of Nov.
15, 1977 (91 Stat. 1371). *Treasury Police Force*
merged into Secret Service on Oct. 5, 1986. U.S.
Secret Service transferred to Homeland Security
Department by act of Nov. 25, 2002 (116 Stat.
2224).

**Security and Safety Performance Assurance, Office
of** Established by Secretary of Energy memorandum
of December 2, 2003. Abolished by Secretary's
Memorandum 2006-007929 of Aug. 30, 2006 and
functions transferred to the Office of Health, Safety
and Security.

Security, Commission on Government Established
by act of Aug. 9, 1955 (69 Stat. 595). Terminated
Sept. 22, 1957, pursuant to terms of act.

Security, Office of the Director for Mutual *See*
Security Agency, Mutual

Security Agency, Federal Established by Reorg.
Plan No. I of 1939, effective July 1, 1939, grouping
under one administration *Office of Education, Public
Health Service, Social Security Board, U.S.
Employment Service, Civilian Conservation Corps,*
and *National Youth Administration.* Abolished by
Reorg. Plan No. 1 of 1953, effective Apr. 11, 1953,

and functions and units transferred to *Department of
Health, Education, and Welfare.*

Security Agency, Mutual Established and
continued by acts of Oct. 10, 1951 (65 Stat. 373)
and June 20, 1952 (66 Stat. 141). *Agency* and *Office
of Director for Mutual Security* abolished by Reorg.
Plan No. 7 of 1953, effective Aug. 1, 1953, and
functions transferred to *Foreign Operations
Administration,* established by same plan.

**Security and Individual Rights, President's
Commission on Internal** Established by EO 10207
of Jan. 23, 1951. Terminated by EO 10305 of Nov.
14, 1951.

Security Resources Board, National Established by
act of July 26, 1947 (61 Stat. 499). Transferred to
Executive Office of the President by Reorg. Plan No.
4 of 1949, effective Aug. 20, 1949. Functions of
Board transferred to Chairman and *Board* made
advisory to him by Reorg. Plan No. 25 of 1950,
effective July 10, 1950. Functions delegated by
Executive order transferred to *Office of Defense
Mobilization* by EO 10438 of Mar. 13, 1953. *Board*
abolished by Reorg. Plan No. 3 of 1953, effective
June 12, 1953, and remaining functions transferred
to *Office of Defense Mobilization.*

Security Training Commission, National
Established by act of June 19, 1951 (65 Stat. 75).
Expired June 30, 1957, pursuant to Presidential letter
of Mar. 25, 1957.

Seed Loan Office Authorized by Presidential letters
of July 26, 1918, and July 26, 1919, to the Secretary
of Agriculture. Further authorized by act of Mar. 3,
1921 (41 Stat. 1347). Office transferred to Farm
Credit Administration by EO 6084 of Mar. 27, 1933.

Selective Service Appeal Board, National
Established by EO 9988 of Aug. 20, 1948. Inactive
as of Apr. 11, 1975.

Selective Service Records, Office of *See* **Selective
Service System**

Selective Service System Established by act of Sept.
16, 1940 (54 Stat. 885). Placed under jurisdiction of
War Manpower Commission by EO 9279 of Dec. 5,
1942, and designated *Bureau of Selective Service.*
Designated Selective Service System, separate
agency, by EO 9410 of Dec. 23, 1943. Transferred
for liquidation to *Office of Selective Service Records*
established by act of Mar. 31, 1947 (61 Stat. 31).
Transferred to Selective Service System by act of
June 24, 1948 (62 Stat. 604).

**Self-Help Development and Technical
Development, Office of** Established in *National
Consumer Cooperative Bank* by act of Aug. 20,
1978 (92 Stat. 499). Abolished by act of Aug. 13,
1981 (95 Stat. 437), and assets transferred to
Consumer Cooperative Development Corporation,
Department of Commerce, Dec. 30, 1982.

Services, Bureau of Special *See* **Office of War
Information**

Services, Division of Central Administrative
Established by *Liaison Officer for Emergency
Management* pursuant to Presidential letter of Feb.

28, 1941. Terminated by EO 9471 of Aug. 25, 1944, and functions discontinued or transferred to constituent agencies of *Office for Emergency Management* and other agencies.

Shipbuilding Stabilization Committee Originally organized by *National Defense Advisory Commission* in 1940. Established August 1942 by *War Production Board.* Transferred to the Department of Labor from *Civilian Production Administration,* successor agency to *Board,* by EO 9656 of Nov. 15, 1945. Terminated June 30, 1947.

Shipping Board, U.S. Established by act of Sept. 7, 1916 (39 Stat. 729). Abolished by EO 6166 of June 10, 1933, and functions, including those with respect to *U.S. Shipping Board Merchant Fleet Corporation,* transferred to *U.S. Shipping Board Bureau,* Department of Commerce, effective Mar. 2, 1934. Separation of employees deferred until Sept. 30, 1933, by EO 6245 of Aug. 9, 1933. Functions assumed by *U.S. Maritime Commission* Oct. 26, 1936, pursuant to act of June 29, 1936 (49 Stat. 1985).

Shipping Board Bureau, U.S. *See* **Shipping Board, U.S.**

Shipping Board Emergency Fleet Corporation, U.S. Established Apr. 16, 1917, under authority of act of Sept. 7, 1916 (39 Stat. 729). Renamed *U.S. Shipping Board Merchant Fleet Corporation* by act of Feb. 11, 1927 (44 Stat. 1083). Terminated Oct. 26, 1936, under provisions of act of June 29, 1936 (49 Stat. 1985), and functions transferred to *U.S. Maritime Commission.*

Shipping Board Merchant Fleet Corporation, U.S. *See* **Shipping Board Emergency Fleet Corporation, U.S.**

Ships, Bureau of Established by act of June 20, 1940 (54 Stat. 493), to replace *Bureau of Engineering* and *Bureau of Construction and Repair.* Abolished by Department of Defense reorg. order of Mar. 9, 1966, and functions transferred to the Secretary of the Navy (31 FR 7188).

Simpson Historical Research Center, Albert F. Renamed Headquarters USAF Historical Research Center by special order of Dec. 16, 1983 of the Secretary of Defense.

Small and Disadvantaged Business Utilization, Office of Established within certain Defense Departments by act of Oct. 24, 1978 (92 Stat. 1770). Renamed Office of Small Business Programs by Public Law 109–163 of Jan. 6, 2006 (119 Stat. 3399).

Smithsonian Symposia and Seminars, Office of Renamed Office of Interdisciplinary Studies by Smithsonian Institution announcement of Mar. 16, 1987.

Social Development Institute, Inter-American Established by act of Dec. 30, 1969 (83 Stat. 821). Renamed Inter-American Foundation by act of Feb. 7, 1972 (86 Stat. 34).

Social Protection, Committee on Established in *Office of Defense Health and Welfare Services* by

administrative order June 14, 1941. Functions transferred to *Federal Security Agency* by EO 9338 of Apr. 29, 1943.

Social and Rehabilitation Service Established by the *Secretary of Health, Education, and Welfare* reorganization of Aug. 15, 1967. Abolished by Secretary's reorganization of Mar. 8, 1977 (42 FR 13262), and constituent units—*Medical Services Administration, Assistance Payments Administration, Office of Child Support Enforcement,* and *Public Services Administration*—transferred.

Social Security Administration *See* **Social Security Board**

Social Security Board Established by act of Aug. 14, 1935 (49 Stat. 620). Incorporated into *Federal Security Agency* by Reorg. Plan No. I of 1939, effective July 1, 1939. *Social Security Board* abolished and Social Security Administration established by Reorg. Plan No. 2 of 1946 (5 U.S.C. app.), effective July 16, 1946, and functions of the *Board* transferred to *Federal Security Administrator.* Social Security Administration transferred from the *Federal Security Agency* by Reorganization Plan No. 1 of 1953 (5 U.S.C. app.), effective Apr. 11, 1953, to the *Department of Health, Education, and Welfare.* Social Security Administration became an independent agency in the executive branch by act of Aug. 15, 1994 (108 Stat. 1464), effective Mar. 31, 1995.

Soil Conservation Service *See* **Soil Erosion Service**

Soil Erosion Service Established in the Department of the Interior following allotment made Aug. 25, 1933. Transferred to the Department of Agriculture by Secretary of Interior administrative order of Mar. 25, 1935. Made *Soil Conservation Service* by order of the Secretary of Agriculture, Apr. 27, 1935, pursuant to provisions of act of Apr. 27, 1935 (49 Stat. 163). Certain functions of *Soil Conservation Service* under jurisdiction of the Department of the Interior transferred from the Department of Agriculture to the Department of the Interior by Reorg. Plan No. IV of 1940, effective June 30, 1940. *Soil Conservation Service* abolished by act of Oct. 13, 1994 (108 Stat. 3225) and functions assumed by the Natural Resources Conservation Service.

Soils, Bureau of *See* **Agricultural and Industrial Chemistry, Bureau of** and **Plant Industry, Bureau of**

Solicitor General, Office of Assistant Established in the Department of Justice by act of June 16, 1933 (48 Stat. 307). Terminated by Reorg. Plan No. 2 of 1950, effective May 24, 1950.

Southeastern Power Administration Established by the Secretary of the Interior in 1943 to carry out functions under act of Dec. 22, 1944 (58 Stat. 890). Transferred to the Department of Energy by act of Aug. 4, 1977 (91 Stat. 578).

Southwestern Power Administration Established by the Secretary of the Interior in 1943 to carry out functions under act of Dec. 22, 1944 (58 Stat. 890). Transferred to the Department of Energy by act of Aug. 4, 1977 (91 Stat. 578).

Space Access and Technology, Office of
Established in the National Aeronautics and Space Administration. Abolished by Administrator's order of Feb. 24, 1997.

Space Communications, Office of Established in the National Aeronautics and Space Administration. Abolished by Administrator's order of Feb. 24, 1997.

Space Payload Technology Organization, Joint Operationally Responsive Established by act of Jan. 6, 2006 (119 Stat. 3408). Abolished by acts of Oct. 17, 2006 (120 Stat. 2358) and Dec. 20, 2006 (120 Stat. 3286).

Space Science, Office of See **Space and Terrestrial Applications, Office of**

Space Science Board Renamed Space Studies Board by authority of the National Research Council, National Academy of Sciences, effective May 8, 1989.

Space Station, Office of Established in the National Aeronautics and Space Administration. Abolished in 1990 and remaining functions transferred to the Office of Space Flight.

Space Technology Laboratories, National Renamed John C. Stennis Space Center by EO 12641 of May 20, 1988.

Space and Terrestrial Applications, Office of Combined with *Office of Space Science* to form Office of Space Science and Applications by National Aeronautics and Space Administrator's announcement of Sept. 29, 1981.

Space Tracking and Data Systems, Office of Renamed Office of Space Operations by National Aeronautics and Space Administrator's announcement of Jan. 9, 1987.

Space Transportation Operations, Office of Combined with *Office of Space Transportation Systems* to form Office of Space Transportation Systems, National Aeronautics and Space Administration, effective July 1982.

Space Transportation Systems, Office of See **Space Transportation Operations, Office of**

Spanish-Speaking People, Cabinet Committee on Opportunities for See **Mexican-American Affairs, Interagency Committee on**

Special. *See other part of title*

Specifications Board, Federal Established by *Bureau of the Budget* Circular 42 of Oct. 10, 1921. Transferred from *Federal Coordinating Service* to *Procurement Division* by order of Oct. 9, 1933 of the Secretary of the Treasury. *Board* superseded by *Federal Specifications Executive Committee,* set up by *Director of Procurement* under Circular Letter 106 of July 16, 1935.

Sport Fisheries and Wildlife, Bureau of Established in the Department of the Interior by act of Aug. 8, 1956 (70 Stat. 1119). *Bureau* replaced by U.S. Fish and Wildlife Service pursuant to act of Apr. 22, 1974 (88 Stat. 92).

Standards, National Bureau of See **Weights and Measures, Office of Standard**

State, Department of Duty of Secretary of State of procuring copies of all statutes of the States, as provided for in act of Sept. 28, 1789 (R.S. 206), abolished by Reorg. Plan No. 20 of 1950, effective May 24, 1950. Functions of numbering, editing, and distributing proclamations and Executive orders transferred from the Department of State to the *Division of the Federal Register, National Archives,* by EO 7298 of Feb. 18, 1936. Duty of Secretary of State of publishing Executive proclamations and treaties in newspapers in District of Columbia, provided for in act of July 31, 1876 (19 Stat. 105), abolished by Reorg. Plan No. 20 of 1950, effective May 24, 1950. Functions concerning publication of U.S. Statutes at Large, acts and joint resolutions in pamphlet form known as slip laws, and amendments to the Constitution; electoral votes for President and Vice President; and Territorial papers transferred from the Department of State to the Administrator of the General Services Administration by Reorg. Plan No. 20 of 1950. (*See also* **Archives Establishment, National**)

State and Local Cooperation, Division of Established by *Advisory Commission to Council of National Defense* Aug. 5, 1940. Transferred to *Office of Civilian Defense.*

State and Local Government Cooperation, Committee on Established by EO 11627 of Oct 15, 1971. Abolished by EO 11695 of Jan. 11, 1973.

State Technical Services, Office of Established by the Secretary of Commerce Nov. 19, 1965, pursuant to act of Sept. 14, 1965 (79 Stat. 697). Abolished by Secretary, effective June 30, 1970.

Statistical Board, Central Organized Aug. 9, 1933, by EO 6225 of July 27, 1933. Transferred to *Bureau of the Budget* by Reorg. Plan No. I of 1939, effective July 1, 1939. Expired July 25, 1940, and functions taken over by *Division of Statistical Standards, Bureau of the Budget.*

Statistical Committee, Central Established by act of July 25, 1935 (49 Stat. 498). Abolished by Reorg. Plan No. I of 1939, effective July 1, 1939, and functions transferred to *Bureau of the Budget.*

Statistical Policy Coordination Committee Established by EO 12013 of Oct. 7, 1977. Abolished by EO 12318 of Aug. 21, 1981.

Statistical Reporting Service Established by Memorandum 1446, supp. 1, part 3, of 1961 of the Secretary of Agriculture. Consolidated with other departmental units into *Economics, Statistics, and Cooperatives Service* by Secretary's Memorandum 1927, effective Dec. 23, 1977. Redesignated as *Statistical Reporting Service* by Secretary's order of Oct. 1, 1981. Renamed National Agricultural Statistics Service.

Statistics Administration, Social and Economic Established Jan. 1, 1972, by the Secretary of Commerce. Terminated by Department of Commerce Organization Order 10–2, effective Aug. 4, 1975 (40 FR 42765). Bureau of Economic Analysis and Bureau of the Census restored as primary operating units of the Department of Commerce by Organization Orders 35–1A and 2A, effective Aug. 4, 1975.

Statutes at Large   *See* **State, Department of**

Statutes of the States   *See* **State, Department of**

Steam Engineering, Bureau of   Established in the Department of the Navy by act of July 5, 1862 (12 Stat. 510). Redesignated as *Bureau of Engineering* by act of June 4, 1920 (41 Stat. 828). Abolished by act of June 20, 1940 (54 Stat. 492), and functions transferred to *Bureau of Ships.*

Steamboat Inspection Service   President authorized to appoint *Service* by act of June 28, 1838 (5 Stat. 252). Secretary of Treasury authorized to establish boards of local inspectors at enumerated ports throughout the U.S. by act of Feb. 28, 1871 (16 Stat. 440). Authority to appoint boards of local inspectors delegated to *Secretary of Commerce and Labor* by act of Mar. 4, 1905 (33 Stat. 1026). Consolidated with *Bureau of Navigation and Steamboat Inspection* by act of June 30, 1932 (47 Stat. 415).

Stock Catalog Board, Federal Standard   Originated by act of Mar. 2, 1929 (45 Stat. 1461). Transferred from *Federal Coordinating Service* to *Procurement Division* by order of Oct. 9, 1933 of the Secretary of the Treasury.

Strategic Defense Initiative Organization   Established in 1986 as a separate agency of the Department of Defense. Renamed Ballistic Missile Defense Organization by Deputy Secretary's memorandum in May 1993.

Strategic Posture of the United States, Commission on the Implementation of the New   Established by act of Jan. 6, 2006 (119 Stat. 3431). Terminated by act of Jan. 28, 2009 (122 Stat. 328)

Strategic Services, Office of   *See* **Information, Office of Coordinator of**

Strategic Trade, Office of   Established in the U.S. Customs and Border Protection pursuant to Customs Service Reorganization plan, effective Sept. 30, 1995. Abolished by act of Oct. 13, 2006 (120 Stat. 1924) and functions transferred to the Office of International Trade.

Subversive Activities Control Board   Established by act of Sept. 23, 1950 (64 Stat. 987). Terminated June 30, 1973, due to lack of funding.

Sugar Division   Created by act of May 12, 1933 (48 Stat. 31), authorized by act of Sept. 1, 1937 (50 Stat. 903). Taken from *Agricultural Adjustment Administration* and made independent division of the Department of Agriculture by Secretary's Memorandum 783, effective Oct. 16, 1938. Placed under *Agricultural Conservation and Adjustment Administration* by EO 9069 of Feb. 23, 1942, functioning as *Sugar Agency.* Functions transferred to *Food Distribution Administration* by EO 9280 of Dec. 5, 1942.

Sugar Rationing Administration   Established by Memorandum 1190 of Mar. 31, 1947, of the Secretary of Agriculture under authority of act of

Mar. 31, 1947 (61 Stat. 35). Terminated Mar. 31, 1948, on expiration of authority.

Supplies and Accounts, Bureau of   *See* **Provisions and Clothing, Bureau of**

Supplies and Shortages, National Commission on   Established by act of Sept. 30, 1974 (88 Stat. 1168). Terminated Mar. 31, 1977, pursuant to terms of act.

Supply, Bureau of Federal   *See* **Procurement Division**

Supply, Office of   Renamed Office of Procurement and Property by Smithsonian Institution announcement of Nov. 4, 1986.

Supply Committee, General   Established by act of June 17, 1910 (36 Stat. 531). Abolished by EO 6166 of June 10, 1933, effective Mar. 2, 1934, and functions transferred to *Procurement Division,* the Department of the Treasury.

Supply Priorities and Allocations Board   Established in *Office for Emergency Management* by EO 8875 of Aug. 28, 1941. Abolished by EO 9024 of Jan. 16, 1942, and functions transferred to *War Production Board.*

Supply Service, Federal   Renamed *Office of Personal Property* by General Services Administration (GSA) order, effective Sept. 28, 1982; later renamed *Office of Federal Supply and Services* by GSA order of Jan. 22, 1983; then redesignated *Federal Supply Service.* Merged with *Federal Technology Service* to form Federal Acquisition Service by GSA Order No. 5440.591 of Sept. 9, 2005. *See also* act of Oct. 6, 2006 (120 Stat. 1735).

Surveys and Maps, Federal Board of   *See* **Surveys and Maps of the Federal Government, Board of**

Surveys and Maps of the Federal Government, Board of   Established by EO 3206 of Dec. 30, 1919. Renamed *Federal Board of Surveys and Maps* by EO 7262 of Jan. 4, 1936. Abolished by EO 9094 of Mar. 10, 1942, and functions transferred to Director, *Bureau of the Budget.*

Space System Development, Office of   Established in the National Aeronautics and Space Administration. Renamed Office of Space Access and Technology in 1995.

Tariff Commission, U.S.   Established by act of Sept. 8, 1916 (39 Stat. 795). Renamed U.S. International Trade Commission by act of Jan. 3, 1975 (88 Stat. 2009).

Tax Appeals, Board of   Established as an independent agency within the executive branch by act of June 2, 1924 (43 Stat. 336). Continued by acts of Feb. 26, 1926 (44 Stat. 105) and Feb. 10, 1939 (53 Stat. 158). Renamed *Tax Court of the United States* by act of Aug. 16, 1954 (68A Stat. 879). Renamed United States Tax Court by act of Dec. 30, 1969 (83 Stat. 730).

Technical Cooperation Administration   Transferred from the Department of State to *Mutual Security Agency* by EO 10458 of June 1, 1953. Transferred to *Foreign Operations Administration* by Reorg. Plan No. 7 of 1953, effective Aug. 1, 1953.

Technical Services, Office of Designated unit of Office of the Secretary of Commerce by Department Order 179, July 23, 1962. Functions transferred to *National Bureau of Standards* by Order 90 of Jan. 30, 1964.

Technology Administration Established by act of Oct. 24, 1988 (102 Stat. 2593). Abolished by act of Aug. 9, 2007 (121 Stat. 587) and functions absorbed by National Institute of Standards and Technology, Department of Commerce.

Technology Assessment, Office of Created by act of Oct. 13, 1972 (86 Stat. 797). Office inactive as of Sept. 30, 1995.

Technology, Automation, and Economic Progress, National Commission on Established by act of Aug. 19, 1964 (78 Stat. 463). Terminated January 1966 pursuant to terms of act.

Technology Service, Federal Merged with *Federal Supply Service* to form Federal Acquisition Service by General Services Administration Order No. 5440.591 of Sept. 9, 2005. *See also* act of Oct. 6, 2006 (120 Stat. 1735).

Telecommunications Adviser to the President Established in Executive Office of the President by EO 10297 of Oct. 9, 1951. EO 10297 revoked by EO 10460 of June 16, 1953, and functions transferred to Director of *Office of Defense Mobilization.*

Telecommunications Management, Director of Established in *Office of Emergency Planning* by EO 10995 of Feb. 16, 1962. Assignment of radio frequencies delegated to Government agencies and foreign diplomatic establishments by EO 11084 of Feb. 16, 1963. Abolished by Reorg. Plan No. 1 of 1970, effective Apr. 20, 1970.

Telecommunications Policy, Office of Established in Executive Office of the President by Reorg. Plan No. 1 of 1970, effective Apr. 20, 1970. Abolished by Reorg. Plan No. 1 of 1977, effective Mar. 26, 1978, and certain functions transferred to President with all other functions transferred to the Department of Commerce.

Telecommunications Service, Automated Data Renamed *Office of Information Resources Management* by General Services Administration order of Aug. 17, 1982. Later renamed Information Resources Management Service.

Temporary Controls, Office of Established in *Office for Emergency Management* by EO 9809 of Dec. 12, 1946, consolidating *Office of War Mobilization and Reconversion, Office of Economic Stabilization, Office of Price Administration,* and *Civilian Production Administration.* Functions with respect to Veterans' Emergency Housing Program transferred to *Housing Expediter* by EO 9836 of Mar. 22, 1947. Functions with respect to distribution and price of sugar products transferred to the Secretary of Agriculture by act of Mar. 31, 1947 (61 Stat. 36). Office terminated by EO 9841 of Apr. 23, 1947, and remaining functions redistributed.

Temporary Emergency Court of Appeals Established by act of Dec. 22, 1971 (85 Stat. 749).

Abolished by act of Oct. 29, 1992, effective Apr. 30, 1993 (106 Stat. 4507). Court's jurisdiction and pending cases transferred to the United States Court of Appeals for the Federal Circuit.

Territorial Affairs, Office of Established by Interior Secretarial Order 2951 of Feb. 6, 1973. Abolished by Departmental Manual Release 2270 of June 6, 1980, and functions transferred to Office of Assistant Secretary for Territorial and International Affairs.

Territorial papers *See* **State, Department of**

Territories, Office of Established by the Secretary of the Interior July 28, 1950. Functions reassigned to *Deputy Assistant Secretary for Territorial Affairs* in *Office of the Assistant Secretary—Public Land Management,* Department of the Interior, by Secretarial Order 2942, effective July 1, 1971.

Terrorism, Cabinet Committee To Combat Established by Presidential memorandum of Sept. 25, 1972. Terminated by National Security Council memorandum of Sept. 16, 1977.

Terrorist Threat Integration Center Established on May 1, 2003, pursuant to Presidential initiative. Transferred to the National Counterterrorism Center by act of Dec. 17, 2004 (118 Stat. 3697).

Textile National Industrial Relations Board Established by administrative order of June 28, 1934. Abolished by EO 6858 of Sept. 26, 1934, which created *Textile Labor Relations Board* in connection with the Department of Labor. *Board* terminated July 1, 1937, and functions absorbed by *U.S. Conciliation Service,* Department of Labor.

Textile National Industrial Relations Board, Cotton Established by original Code of Fair Competition for the Cotton Textile Industry, as amended July 10, 1934. Abolished by EO 6858 of Sept. 26, 1934.

Textile Work Assignment Board, Cotton Amendments to Code of Fair Competition for Cotton Textile Industry approved by EO 6876 of Oct. 16, 1934, and *Cotton Textile Work Assignment Board* appointed by *Textile Labor Relations Board. Board* expired June 15, 1935.

Textile Work Assignment Board, Silk Appointed by *Textile Labor Relations Board* following President's approval of amendments to Code of Fair Competition for Silk Textile Industry by EO 6875 of Oct. 16, 1934. Terminated June 15, 1935.

Textile Work Assignment Board, Wool Established by EO 6877 of Oct. 16, 1934. Terminated June 15, 1935.

Textiles, Office of Established by the Secretary of Commerce Feb. 14, 1971. Functions transferred to *Domestic and International Business Administration,* effective Nov. 17, 1972.

Thrift Depositor Protection Oversight Board. *See* **Oversight Board (of the Resolution Trust Corporation).**

Trade, Special Adviser to the President on Foreign Established by EO 6651 of Mar. 23, 1934. Terminated on expiration of *National Recovery Administration.*

Trade Administration, International *See* **Business and Defense Services Administration**

Trade Agreements, Interdepartmental Committee on Established by Secretary of State in 1934 and reestablished by EO 9832 of Feb. 25, 1947. Abolished by EO 11075 of Jan. 15, 1963.

Trade and Development Program Established by act of Sept. 4, 1961, as amended (88 Stat. 1804). Designated separate entity within the *U.S. International Development Cooperation Agency* by act of Sept. 4, 1961, as amended (102 Stat. 1329). Renamed Trade and Development Agency by act of Oct. 28, 1992 (106 Stat. 3657).

Trade Expansion Act Advisory Committee Established by EO 11075 of Jan. 15, 1963. Abolished by EO 11846 of Mar. 27, 1975, and records transferred to Trade Policy Committee established by same EO.

Trade Negotiations, Office of the Special Representative for Renamed Office of the U.S. Trade Representative by EO 12188 of Jan. 4, 1980.

Trade Policy Committee Established by EO 10741 of Nov. 25, 1957. Abolished by EO 11075 of Jan. 15, 1963.

Traffic Safety, President's Committee for Established by Presidential letter of Apr. 14, 1954. Continued by EO 10858 of Jan. 13, 1960. Abolished by EO 11382 of Nov. 28, 1967.

Traffic Safety Agency, National Established in the Department of Commerce by act of Sept. 9, 1966 (80 Stat. 718). Activity transferred to the Department of Transportation by act of Oct. 15, 1966 (80 Stat. 931). Responsibility placed in *National Highway Safety Bureau* by EO 11357 of June 6, 1967.

Training and Employment Service, U.S. Established in *Manpower Administration,* Department of Labor, Mar. 17, 1969. Abolished by Secretary's letter of Dec. 6, 1971, and functions assigned to *Office of Employment Development Programs* and *U.S. Employment Service.*

Training School for Boys, National *See* **District of Columbia, Reform-School of the**

Transportation, Federal Coordinator of Established by act of June 16, 1933 (48 Stat. 211). Expired June 16, 1936, under provisions of Public Resolution 27 (49 Stat. 376).

Transportation, Office of Established in the Department of Agriculture by Secretary's Memorandum 1966 dated Dec. 12, 1978. Abolished by Secretary's Memorandum 1030–25 dated Dec. 28, 1990.

Transportation and Communications Service Established by General Services Administrator Oct. 19, 1961. Abolished by Administrator's order, effective July 15, 1972. Motor equipment, transportation, and public utilities responsibilities assigned to Federal Supply Service; telecommunications function assigned to *Automated Data Telecommunications Service.*

Transportation and Public Utilities Service Abolished by General Services Administration order of Aug. 17, 1982. Functions transferred to various GSA organizations.

Transportation Safety Board, National Established in the Department of Transportation by act of Oct. 15, 1966 (80 Stat. 935). Abolished by act of Jan. 3, 1975 (88 Stat. 2156), which established independent National Transportation Safety Board.

Transportation Security Administration Established by act of Nov. 19, 2001 (115 Stat. 597). Functions transferred from Department of Transportation to Department of Homeland Security by act of Nov. 25, 2002 (116 Stat. 2178).

Transportation Statistics, Bureau of Established by act of Dec. 18, 1991 (105 Stat. 2172). Transferred to Research and Innovative Technology Administration, Transportation Department, by act of Nov. 30, 2004 (118 Stat. 2424).

Travel Service, U.S. Replaced by *U.S. Travel and Tourism Administration,* Department of Commerce, pursuant to act of Oct. 16, 1981 (95 Stat. 1014).

Travel and Tourism Administration, U.S. Established by act of Oct. 16, 1981 (95 Stat. 1014). Abolished by act of Oct. 11, 1996 (110 Stat. 3407).

Travel and Tourism Advisory Board Established by act of Oct. 16, 1981 (95 Stat. 1017). Abolished by act of Oct. 11, 1996 (110 Stat. 3407).

Treasury, Office of the Assistant Secretary of the— Electronics and Information Technology Established by Secretary's Order 114–1 of Mar. 14, 1983. Abolished by Secretary's Order 114–3 of May 17, 1985, and functions transferred to Office of the Assistant Secretary for Management. Certain provisions effective Aug. 31, 1985 (50 FR 23573).

Treasury, Solicitor of the Position established when certain functions of *Solicitor of the Treasury* transferred to the Department of Justice by EO 6166 of June 10, 1933. *Solicitor of the Treasury* transferred from the Department of Justice to the Department of the Treasury by same order. *Office of Solicitor of the Treasury* abolished by act of May 10, 1934 (48 Stat. 758), and functions transferred to General Counsel, the Department of the Treasury.

Treasury Police Force *See* **Secret Service Division**

Treasury Secretary, Assistant Office abolished by Reorg. Plan No. III of 1940, effective June 30, 1940, and functions transferred to Fiscal Assistant Secretary, Department of the Treasury.

Treasury Under Secretary for Enforcement, Office of Established by act of Oct. 28, 1993 (107 Stat. 1234). Office abolished by act of Dec. 8, 2004 (118 Stat. 3245), and functions transferred to the Office of the Under Secretary for Terrorism and Financial Crimes, Department of the Treasury.

Treaties *See* **State, Department of**

Typhus Commission, U.S. of America Established in *Department of War* by EO 9285 of Dec. 24, 1942. Abolished June 30, 1946, by EO 9680 of Jan. 17, 1946.

U.S.   *See other part of title*

Uniformed Services University of the Health Sciences, School of Medicine of the   Renamed F. Edward Hébert School of Medicine by act of Sept. 24, 1983 (97 Stat. 704).

United Nations Educational, Scientific and Cultural Organization   U.S. membership in UNESCO authorized by act of July 30, 1946 (60 Stat. 712). Announcement of U.S. intention to withdraw made Dec. 28, 1983, in accordance with UNESCO constitution. Official U.S. withdrawal effective Dec. 31, 1984, by Secretary of State's letter of Dec. 19, 1984. U.S. maintains status as observer mission in UNESCO.

Upper Mississippi River Basin Commission Established by EO 11659 of Mar. 22, 1972. Terminated by EO 12319 of Sept. 9, 1981.

Urban Affairs, Council for   Established in Executive Office of the President by EO 11452 of Jan. 23, 1969. Terminated by EO 11541 of July 1, 1970.

Urban Mass Transportation Administration Functions regarding urban mass transportation established in the Department of Housing and Urban Development by act of July 9, 1964 (78 Stat. 302). Most functions transferred to the Department of Transportation by Reorg. Plan No. 2 of 1968, effective June 30, 1968 (82 Stat. 1369), and joint responsibility assigned to the Departments of Transportation and Housing and Urban Development for functions relating to research, technical studies, and training. Transportation and Housing and Urban Development Under Secretaries agreed in November 1969 that the Department of Transportation should be focal point for urban mass transportation grant administration; at which time functions transferred to the Department of Transportation. Renamed Federal Transit Administration by act of Dec. 18, 1991 (105 Stat. 2088).

Urban Renewal Administration   Established in *Housing and Home Finance Agency* by Administrator's Organizational Order 1 of Dec. 23, 1954. Functions transferred to the Department of Housing and Urban Development by act of Sept. 9, 1965 (78 Stat. 667), and *Administration* terminated.

Utilization and Disposal Service   Established July 1, 1961, by Administrator of General Services and assigned functions of Federal Supply Service and Public Buildings Service. Functions transferred to *Property Management and Disposal Service* July 29, 1966.

Veterans Administration   Legal work in defense of suits against the U.S. arising under act of June 7, 1924 (43 Stat. 607), transferred to the Department of Justice by EO 6166 of June 10, 1933. Transfer deferred to Sept. 10, 1933, by EO 6222 of July 27, 1933. Established as an independent agency under the President by Executive Order 5398 of July 21, 1930, in accordance with the act of July 3, 1930 (46 Stat. 1016) and the act of Sept. 2, 1958 (72 Stat. 1114). Made an executive department in the executive branch and redesignated the Department

of Veterans Affairs by act of Oct. 25, 1988 (102 Stat. 2635).

Veterans Appeals, U.S. Court of   Established by act of Nov. 18, 1988 (102 Stat. 4113). Renamed U.S. Court of Appeals for Veterans Claims by act of Nov. 11, 1998 (112 Stat. 3341).

Veterans Education Appeals Board   *See* **Veterans Tuition Appeals Board**

Veterans Employment and Training, Advisory Committee on   Renamed Advisory Committee on Veterans Employment, Training, and Employer Outreach by act of June 15, 2006 (120 Stat. 403).

Veterans Employment Service   Renamed Veterans' Employment and Training Service by Order 4–83 of Mar. 24, 1983 of the Secretary of Labor (48 FR 14092).

Veterans Health Administration   *See* **Medicine and Surgery, Department of**

Veterans Health Services and Research Administration   *See* **Medicine and Surgery, Department of**

Veterans Placement Service Board   Established by act of June 22, 1944 (58 Stat. 293). Abolished by Reorg. Plan No. 2 of 1949, effective Aug. 20, 1949, and functions transferred to the Secretary of Labor.

Veterans Tuition Appeals Board   Established by act of Aug. 24, 1949 (63 Stat. 654). Functions assumed by *Veterans Education Appeals Board* established by act of July 13, 1950 (64 Stat. 336). *Board* terminated by act of Aug. 28, 1957 (71 Stat. 474).

Veterinary Medicine, Bureau of   Established in Food and Drug Administration, *Department of Health, Education, and Welfare.* Renamed Center for Veterinary Medicine by FDA notice of Mar. 9, 1984 (49 FR 10166).

Virgin Islands   Public works programs under act of Dec. 20, 1944 (58 Stat. 827), transferred from General Services Administrator to the Secretary of the Interior by Reorg. Plan No. 15 of 1950, effective May 24, 1950.

Virgin Islands Company   Established in 1934. Reincorporated as Government corporation by act of June 30, 1949 (63 Stat. 350). Program terminated June 30, 1965, and *Corporation* dissolved July 1, 1966.

Virgin Islands Corporation   *See* **Virgin Islands Company**

Visitor Facilities Advisory Commission, National Established by act of Mar. 12, 1968 (82 Stat. 45). Expired Jan. 5, 1975, pursuant to act of Oct. 6, 1972 (86 Stat. 776).

Vocational Rehabilitation, Office of   Established to administer provisions of act of July 6, 1943 (57 Stat. 374). Other duties delegated by acts of Aug. 3, 1954 (68 Stat. 652), Nov. 8, 1965 (79 Stat. 1282), July 12, 1960 (74 Stat. 364), and July 10, 1954 (68 Stat. 454). Redesignated *Vocational Rehabilitation Administration* Jan. 28, 1963. Made component of newly created *Social and Rehabilitation Service* as

Rehabilitation Services Administration by Department of Health, Education, and Welfare reorganization of Aug. 15, 1967.

Vocational Rehabilitation Administration *See* **Vocational Rehabilitation, Office of**

Voluntary Citizen Participation, State Office of Renamed State Office of Volunteerism in ACTION by notice of Apr. 18, 1986 (51 FR 13265), effective May 18, 1986.

Volunteer Service, International, Secretariat for Established in 1962 by International Conference on Middle Level Manpower called by President. Terminated Mar. 31, 1976, due to insufficient funding.

Volunteers in Service to America Established by act of Nov. 8, 1966 (80 Stat. 1472). *Service* administered by *Office of Economic Opportunity* and functions transferred to ACTION by Reorg. Plan No. 1 of 1971, effective July 1, 1971.

Wage Adjustment Board Established May 29, 1942, by the Secretary of Labor at Presidential direction of May 14, 1942, to accomplish purpose of act of Mar. 3, 1931 (46 Stat. 1494), as amended by acts of Aug. 30, 1935 (49 Stat. 1011), and Jan. 30, 1942 (56 Stat. 23). Disbanded on termination of *National Wage Stabilization Board.*

Wage and Price Stability, Council on Established in Executive Office of the President by act of Aug. 24, 1974 (88 Stat. 750). Abolished by EO 12288 of Jan. 29, 1981. Funding ceased beyond June 5, 1981, by act of June 5, 1981 (95 Stat. 74), and authorization for appropriations repealed by act of Aug. 13, 1981 (95 Stat. 432).

Wage and Price Stability Program *See* **Wage and Price Stability, Council on**

Wage Stabilization Board Established by EO 10161 of Sept. 9, 1950. Reconstituted by EO 10377 of July 25, 1952. Terminated Apr. 30, 1953, by EO 10434 of Feb. 6, 1953, and acts of June 30, 1952 (66 Stat. 296), and June 30, 1953 (67 Stat. 131).

Wage Stabilization Board, National *See* **Defense Mediation Board, National**

Wallops Flight Center, Wallops Island, VA Formerly separate field installation of National Aeronautics and Space Administration. Made component of Goddard Space Flight Center by NASA Management Instruction 1107.10A of Sept. 3, 1981.

War, Solid Fuels Administration for Established in the Department of the Interior by EO 9332 of Apr. 19, 1943. Absorbed *Office of Solid Fuels Coordinator for War* (originally established as *Office of Solid Fuels Coordinator for National Defense*) pursuant to Presidential letter of Nov. 5, 1941; later changed by Presidential letter of May 25, 1942. Terminated by EO 9847 of May 6, 1947.

War Assets Administration Established in *Office for Emergency Management* by EO 9689 of Jan. 31, 1946. Functions transferred to *Surplus Property Administration* by Reorg. Plan No. 1 of 1947,

effective July 1, 1947, and agency renamed *War Assets Administration.* Abolished by act of June 30, 1949 (63 Stat. 738), and functions transferred for liquidation to General Services Administration.

War Assets Corporation *See* **Petroleum Reserves Corporation**

War Claims Commission Established by act of July 3, 1948 (62 Stat. 1240). Abolished by Reorg. Plan No. 1 of 1954, effective July 1, 1954, and functions transferred to Foreign Claims Settlement Commission of the U.S.

War Commodities Division Established in *Office of Foreign Economic Coordination* by Department of State Order of Aug. 27, 1943. *Office* abolished by departmental order of Nov. 6, 1943, pursuant to EO 9380 of Sept. 25, 1943, which established *Foreign Economic Administration* in *Office for Emergency Management.*

War Communications, Board of *See* **Defense Communications Board**

War Contracts Price Adjustment Board Established by act of Feb. 25, 1944 (58 Stat. 85). Abolished by act of Mar. 23, 1951 (65 Stat. 7), and functions transferred to *Renegotiation Board,* established by same act, and General Services Administrator.

War Damage Corporation *See* **War Insurance Corporation**

War, Department of Established by act of Aug. 7, 1789 (1 Stat. 49), succeeding similar department established prior to adoption of the Constitution. Three military departments—Army; Navy, including naval aviation and U.S. Marine Corps; and Air Force—reorganized under *National Military Establishment* by act of July 26, 1947 (61 Stat. 495).

War Finance Corporation Established by act of Apr. 5, 1918 (40 Stat. 506). Functions and obligations transferred by Reorg. Plan No. II of 1939, effective July 1, 1939, to the Secretary of the Treasury for liquidation not later than Dec. 31, 1939.

War Food Administration *See* **Food Production and Distribution, Administration of**

War Information, Office of Established in *Office of Emergency Management* by EO 9182 of June 13, 1942, consolidating *Office of Facts and Figures; Office of Government Reports; Division of Information, Office for Emergency Management;* and *Foreign Information Service—Outpost, Publications, and Pictorial Branches, Coordinator of Information.* Abolished by EO 9608 of Aug. 31, 1945. *Bureau of Special Services* and functions with respect to review of publications of Federal agencies transferred to *Bureau of the Budget.* Foreign information activities transferred to the Department of State.

War Insurance Corporation Established Dec. 13, 1941, by act of June 10, 1941 (55 Stat. 249). Charter filed Mar. 31, 1942. Renamed *War Damage Corporation* by act of Mar. 27, 1942 (56 Stat. 175). Transferred from *Federal Loan Agency* to the Department of Commerce by EO 9071 of Feb. 24, 1942. Returned to *Federal Loan Agency* by act of

Feb. 24, 1945 (59 Stat. 5). *Agency* abolished by act of June 30, 1947 (61 Stat. 202), and functions assumed by *Reconstruction Finance Corporation*. Powers of *War Damage Corporation*, except for purposes of liquidation, terminated as of Jan. 22, 1947.

War Labor Board, National *See* **Defense Mediation Board, National**

War Manpower Commission Established in *Office for Emergency Management* by EO 9139 of Apr. 18, 1942. Terminated by EO 9617 of Sept. 19, 1945, and functions, except *Procurement and Assignment Service,* transferred to the Department of Labor.

War Mobilization, Office of Established by EO 9347 of May 27, 1943. Transferred to *Office of War Mobilization and Reconversion* by EO 9488 of Oct. 3, 1944.

War Mobilization and Reconversion, Office of Established by act of Oct. 3, 1944 (58 Stat. 785). Consolidated with other agencies by EO 9809 of Dec. 12, 1946, to form *Office of Temporary Controls. Media Programming Division* and *Motion Picture Division* transferred to *Office of Government Reports,* reestablished by same order. Certain other functions transferred to President and the Secretary of Commerce.

War Mobilization and Reconversion Advisory Board, Office of Established by act of Oct. 3, 1944 (58 Stat. 788). Transferred to *Office of Temporary Controls* by EO 9809 of Dec. 12, 1946.

War Plants Corporation, Smaller Established by act of June 11, 1942 (56 Stat. 351). Functions transferred by EO 9665 of Dec. 27, 1945, to *Reconstruction Finance Corporation* and the Department of Commerce. Abolished by act of June 30, 1947 (61 Stat. 202), and functions transferred for liquidation to General Services Administration by Reorg. Plan No. 1 of 1957, effective July 1, 1957.

War and Post War Adjustment Policies, Advisory Unit on Established in *Office of War Mobilization* by Presidential direction Nov. 6, 1943. Report submitted Feb. 15, 1944, and Unit Director and Assistant Director submitted letter to Director of *War Mobilization* ending their work May 12, 1944.

War Production Board Established in *Office for Emergency Management* by EO 9024 of Jan. 16, 1942. *Board* terminated and successor agency, *Civilian Production Administration,* established by EO 9638 of Oct. 4, 1945.

War Property Administration, Surplus Established in *Office of War Mobilization* by EO 9425 of Feb. 19, 1944. Terminated on establishment of *Surplus Property Board* by act of Oct. 3, 1944 (58 Stat. 768). *Surplus Property Administration* established in *Office of War Mobilization and Reconversion* by act of Sept. 18, 1945 (59 Stat. 533), and *Board* abolished. Domestic functions of *Administration* merged into *War Assets Corporation, Reconstruction Finance Corporation,* by EO 9689 of Jan. 31, 1946. Foreign functions transferred to the Department of State by same order. Transfers made permanent by Reorg. Plan No. 1 of 1947, effective July 1, 1947.

War Refugee Board Established in Executive Office of the President by EO 9417 of Jan. 22, 1944. Terminated by EO 9614 of Sept. 14, 1945.

War Relations, Agricultural, Office for *See* **Farm Products, Division of**

War Relief Agencies, President's Committee on Established by Presidential letter of Mar. 13, 1941. *President's War Relief Control Board* established by EO 9205 of July 25, 1942, to succeed *Committee. Board* terminated by EO 9723 of May 14, 1946, and functions transferred to the Department of State.

War Relief Control Board, President's *See* **President's Committee on War Relief Agencies**

War Relocation Authority Established in *Office for Emergency Management* by EO 9102 of Mar. 18, 1942. Transferred to the Department of the Interior by EO 9423 of Feb. 16, 1944. Terminated by EO 9742 of June 25, 1946.

War Resources Board Established in August 1939 as advisory committee to work with *Joint Army and Navy Munitions Board.* Terminated by President Nov. 24, 1939.

War Resources Council *See* **Defense Resources Committee**

War Shipping Administration Established in *Office for Emergency Management* by EO 9054 Feb. 7, 1942. Terminated by act of July 8, 1946 (60 Stat. 501), and functions transferred to *U.S. Maritime Commission,* effective Sept. 1, 1946.

Water, Office of Saline Established to perform functions vested in the Secretary of the Interior by act of July 29, 1971 (85 Stat. 159). Merged with *Office of Water Resources Research* to form *Office of Water Research and Technology* by Secretary's Order 2966 of July 26, 1974.

Water Commission, National Established by act of Sept. 26, 1968 (82 Stat. 868). Terminated Sept. 25, 1973, pursuant to terms of act.

Water Policy, Office of Established by Department of the Interior Manual Release 2374 of Dec. 29, 1981, under authority of Assistant Secretary. Abolished by Secretarial Order No. 3096 of Oct. 19, 1983, and functions transferred to *Geological Survey* and *Office of Policy Analysis.*

Water Pollution Control Administration, Federal Established under the *Secretary of Health, Education, and Welfare* by act of Oct. 2, 1965 (79 Stat. 903). Transferred to the Department of the Interior by Reorg. Plan No. 2 of 1966, effective May 10, 1966. Renamed *Federal Water Quality Administration* by act of Apr. 3, 1970. Abolished by Reorg. Plan No. 3 of 1970, effective Dec. 2, 1970, and functions transferred to Environmental Protection Agency.

Water and Power Resources Service Renamed Bureau of Reclamation May 18, 1981, by Interior Secretarial Order 3064.

Water Quality Administration, Federal *See* **Water Pollution Control Administration, Federal**

Water Research and Technology, Office of
Established by Interior Secretarial Order 2966 of July
26, 1974. Abolished by Secretarial order of Aug. 25,
1982, and functions transferred to Bureau of
Reclamation, Geological Survey, and *Office of
Water Policy.*

Water Resources Council   Established by act of July
22, 1965 (89 Stat 575). Inactive as of Oct. 1, 1982.

Water Resources Research, Office of   Established
to perform functions vested in the Secretary of the
Interior by act of July 17, 1964 (78 Stat. 329).
Merged with *Office of Saline Water* to form *Office
of Water Research and Technology* by Secretary's
Order 2966 of July 26, 1974.

Watergate Special Prosecution Force   Established
by Attorney General order, effective May 25, 1973.
Terminated by Attorney General order, effective June
20, 1977.

Waterways Corporation, Inland   Incorporated
under act of June 3, 1924 (43 Stat. 360). Transferred
from the *Department of War* to the Department of
Commerce by Reorg. Plan No. II of 1939, effective
July 1, 1939. *Corporation* sold to *Federal Waterways
Corporation* under contract of July 24, 1953.
Renamed *Federal Barge Lines, Inc.* Liquidated by act
of July 19, 1963 (77 Stat. 81).

Weather Bureau   Established in the Department of
Agriculture by act of Oct. 1, 1890 (26 Stat. 653).
Transferred to the Department of Commerce by
Reorg. Plan No. IV of 1940, effective June 30, 1940.
Functions transferred to *Environmental Science
Services Administration* by Reorg. Plan No. 2 of
1965, effective July 13, 1965.

Weather Control, Advisory Committee on
Established by act of Aug. 13, 1953 (67 Stat. 559).
Act of Aug. 28, 1957 (71 Stat. 426), provided for
termination by Dec. 31, 1957.

Weed and Seed, Executive Office of   Abolished by
Public Law 109–162 of Jan. 5, 2006 (119 Stat.
3107). Functions transferred to Office of Weed and
Seed Strategies, Office of Justice Programs, within
the Department of Justice.

Weights and Measures, Office of Standard
Renamed *National Bureau of Standards* by act of
Mar. 3, 1901 (31 Stat. 1449). *Bureau* transferred
from the Department of the Treasury to the
Department of Commerce and Labor by act of Feb.
14, 1903 (32 Stat. 825). *Bureau* established within
the Department of Commerce by act of Mar. 4,
1913 (37 Stat. 736). Renamed National Institute of
Standards and Technology by act of Aug. 23, 1988
(102 Stat. 1827).

Welfare Administration   Established by the
Secretary of Health, Education, and Welfare
reorganization of Jan. 28, 1963. Components
consisted of *Bureau of Family Services, Children's
Bureau, Office of Juvenile Delinquency and Youth
Development,* and *Cuban Refugee Staff.* These
functions reassigned to *Social and Rehabilitation
Service* by Department reorganization of Aug. 15,
1967.

White House Police Force   *See* **Secret Service
Division**

Wilson Memorial Commission, Woodrow
Established by act of Oct. 4, 1961 (75 Stat. 783).
Terminated on submittal of final report to President
and Congress Sept. 29, 1966.

**Women, Interdepartmental Committee on the
Status of**   Established by EO 11126 of Nov. 1,
1963. Terminated by EO 12050 of Apr. 4, 1978.

Women, President's Commission on the Status of
Established by EO 10980 of Dec. 14, 1961.
Submitted final report to President Oct. 11, 1963.

Women's Army Auxiliary Corps   Established by act
of May 14, 1942 (56 Stat. 278). Repealed in part
and superseded by act of July 1, 1943 (57 Stat. 371),
which established *Women's Army Corps. Corps*
abolished by the Secretary of Defense Apr. 24,
1978, pursuant to provisions of 10 U.S.C. 125A.

Women's Business Enterprise Division   Renamed
Office of Women's Business Enterprise by Small
Business Administrator's reorganization, effective
Aug. 19, 1981. Renamed Office of Women's
Business Ownership Aug. 19, 1982.

Women's Reserve   Established in U.S. Coast Guard
by act of Nov. 23, 1942 (56 Stat. 1020).

**Women's Year, 1975, National Commission on the
Observance of International**   Established by EO
11832 of Jan. 9, 1975. Continued by act of Dec. 23,
1975 (89 Stat. 1003). Terminated Mar. 31, 1978,
pursuant to terms of act.

Wood Utilization, National Committee on
Established by Presidential direction in 1925.
Abolished by EO 6179–B of June 16, 1933.

Work Projects Administration   *See* **Works Progress
Administration**

Work-Training Programs, Bureau of   Abolished by
reorganization of *Manpower Administration* and
functions assigned to *U.S. Training and Employment
Service,* effective Mar. 17, 1969.

**Working Life, Productivity and Quality of, National
Center for**   Established by act of Nov. 28, 1975 (89
Stat. 935). Authorized appropriations expired Sept.
30, 1978, and functions assumed by *National
Productivity Council.*

Works, Advisory Committee on Federal Public
Established by President Oct. 5, 1955. Abolished by
President Mar. 12, 1961, and functions assigned to
Bureau of the Budget.

Works Administration, Federal Civil   Established by
EO 6420–B of Nov. 9, 1933. Function of
employment expired March 1934. Function of
settling claims continued under *Works Progress
Administration.*

Works Administration, Public   *See* **Emergency
Administration of Public Works, Federal**

Works Agency, Federal   Established by Reorg. Plan
No. I of 1939, effective July 1, 1939. Functions
relating to defense housing transferred to *Federal*

Public Housing Authority, National Housing Agency, by EO 9070 of Feb. 24, 1942. Abolished by act of June 30, 1949 (63 Stat. 380), and functions transferred to General Services Administration.

Works Emergency Housing Corporation, Public Established by EO 6470 of Nov. 29, 1933. Incorporated under laws of State of Delaware. Abolished and liquidated as of Aug. 14, 1935, by filing of certificate of surrender of corporate rights.

Works Emergency Leasing Corporation, Public Incorporated Jan. 3, 1934, under laws of Delaware by direction of Administrator of Public Works. Terminated with filed certificate of dissolution with secretary of state of Delaware Jan. 2, 1935.

Works Progress Administration Established by EO 7034 of May 6, 1935, and continued by subsequent yearly emergency relief appropriation acts. Renamed *Work Projects Administration* by Reorg. Plan No. I of 1939, effective July 1, 1939, which provided for consolidation of *Works Progress Administration* into *Federal Works Agency.* Transferred by President to *Federal Works Administrator* Dec. 4, 1942.

Works, Special Board of Public   *See* **Land Program, Director of**

Yards and Docks, Bureau of Established by acts of Aug. 31, 1842 (5 Stat. 579), and July 5, 1862 (12 Stat. 510). Abolished by Department of Defense reorg. order of Mar. 9, 1966, and functions transferred to the Secretary of the Navy (31 FR 7188).

Youth Administration, National Established in *Works Progress Administration* by EO 7086 of June 26, 1935. Transferred to *Federal Security Agency* by Reorg. Plan No. I of 1939, effective July 1, 1939. Transferred to *Bureau of Training, War Manpower Commission,* by EO 9247 of Sept. 17, 1942. Terminated by act of July 12, 1943 (57 Stat. 539).

Youth Crime, President's Committee on Juvenile Delinquency and Established by EO 10940 of May 11, 1961. Terminated by EO 11529 of Apr. 24, 1970.

Youth Fitness, President's Council on Established by EO 10673 of July 16, 1956. Renamed *President's Council on Physical Fitness* by EO 11074 of Jan. 8, 1963. Renamed President's Council on Physical Fitness and Sports by EO 11398 of Mar. 4, 1968. Abolished and reestablished by EO 13265 of June 6, 2002.

Youth Opportunity, President's Council on Established by EO 11330 of Mar. 5, 1967. Inactive as of June 30, 1971; EO 11330 revoked by EO 12379 of Aug. 17, 1982.

Youth Programs, Office of Established in the Department of the Interior by Secretarial Order No. 2985 of Jan. 7, 1965. Functions moved to Office of Historically Black College and University Programs and Job Corps, Office of the Secretary, by Departmental Manual Release 2788 of Mar. 22, 1988.

APPENDIX C: Agencies Appearing in the Code of Federal Regulations

NOTE: This section contains an alphabetical listing of agencies appearing in the *Code of Federal Regulations* (CFR). The listing was revised as of January 1, 2009.

Agency	CFR Title, Subtitle or Chapter
Administrative Committee of the Federal Register	1, I
Advanced Research Projects Agency	32, I
Advisory Council on Historic Preservation	36, VIII
African Development Foundation	22, XV
Federal Acquisition Regulation	48, 57
Agency for International Development	22, II
Federal Acquisition Regulation	48, 7
Agricultural Marketing Service	7, I, IX, X, XI
Agricultural Research Service	7, V
Agriculture Department	5, LXXIII
Agricultural Marketing Service	7, I, IX, X, XI
Agricultural Research Service	7, V
Animal and Plant Health Inspection Service	7, III; 9, I
Chief Financial Officer, Office of	7, XXX
Commodity Credit Corporation	7, XIV
Cooperative State Research, Education, and Extension Service	7, XXXIV
Economic Research Service	7, XXXVII
Energy, Office of	2, IX; 7, XXIX
Environmental Quality, Office of	7, XXXI
Farm Service Agency	7, VII, XVIII
Federal Acquisition Regulation	48, 4
Federal Crop Insurance Corporation	7, IV
Food and Nutrition Service	7, II
Food Safety and Inspection Service	9, III
Foreign Agricultural Service	7, XV
Forest Service	36, II
Grain Inspection, Packers and Stockyards Administration	7, VIII; 9, II
Information Resources Management, Office of	7, XXVII
Inspector General, Office of	7, XXVI
National Agricultural Library	7, XLI
National Agricultural Statistics Service	7, XXXVI
Natural Resources Conservation Service	7, VI
Operations, Office of	7, XXVIII
Procurement and Property Management, Office of	7, XXXII
Rural Business-Cooperative Service	7, XVIII, XLII, L
Rural Development Administration	7, XLII
Rural Housing Service	7, XVIII, XXXV, L
Rural Telephone Bank	7, XVI
Rural Utilities Service	7, XVII, XVIII, XLII, L
Secretary of Agriculture, Office of	7, Subtitle A
Transportation, Office of	7, XXXIII
World Agricultural Outlook Board	7, XXXVIII
Air Force Department	32, VII
Federal Acquisition Regulation Supplement	48, 53
Air Transportation Stabilization Board	14, VI
Alcohol and Tobacco Tax and Trade Bureau	27, I
Alcohol, Tobacco, Firearms, and Explosives, Bureau of	27, II
AMTRAK	49, VII
American Battle Monuments Commission	36, IV
American Indians, Office of the Special Trustee	25, VII

Agency	CFR Title, Subtitle or Chapter
Animal and Plant Health Inspection Service	7, III; 9, I
Appalachian Regional Commission	5, IX
Architectural and Transportation Barriers Compliance Board	36, XI
Arctic Research Commission	45, XXIII
Armed Forces Retirement Home	5, XI
Army Department	32, V
Engineers, Corps of	33, II; 36, III
Federal Acquisition Regulation	48, 51
Benefits Review Board	20, VII
Bilingual Education and Minority Languages Affairs, Office of	34, V
Blind or Severely Disabled, Committee for Purchase From People Who Are	41, 51
Broadcasting Board of Governors	22, V
Federal Acquisition Regulation	48, 19
Census Bureau	15, I
Centers for Medicare & Medicaid Services	42, IV
Central Intelligence Agency	32, XIX
Chief Financial Officer, Office of	7, XXX
Child Support Enforcement, Office of	45, III
Children and Families, Administration for	45, II, III, IV, X
Civil Rights, Commission on	5, LXVIII; 45, VII
Civil Rights, Office for	34, I
Coast Guard	33, I; 46, I; 49, IV
Coast Guard (Great Lakes Pilotage)	46, III
Commerce Department	44, IV
Census Bureau	15, I
Economic Affairs, Under Secretary	37, V
Economic Analysis, Bureau of	15, VIII
Economic Development Administration	13, III
Emergency Management and Assistance	44, IV
Federal Acquisition Regulation	48, 13
Fishery Conservation and Management	50, VI
Foreign-Trade Zones Board	15, IV
Industry and Security, Bureau of	15, VII
International Trade Administration	15, III; 19, III
National Institute of Standards and Technology	15, II
National Marine Fisheries Service	50, II, IV, VI
National Oceanic and Atmospheric Administration	15, IX; 50, II, III, IV, VI
National Telecommunications and Information Administration	15, XXIII; 47, III
National Weather Service	15, IX
Patent and Trademark Office, United States	37, I
Productivity, Technology and Innovation, Assistant Secretary for	37, IV
Secretary of Commerce, Office of	15, Subtitle A
Technology, Under Secretary for	37, V
Technology Administration	15, XI
Technology Policy, Assistant Secretary for	37, IV
Commercial Space Transportation	14, III
Commodity Credit Corporation	7, XIV
Commodity Futures Trading Commission	5, XLI; 17, I
Community Planning and Development, Office of Assistant Secretary for	24, V, VI
Community Services, Office of	45, X
Comptroller of the Currency	12, I
Construction Industry Collective Bargaining Commission	29, IX
Consumer Product Safety Commission	5, LXXI; 16, II
Cooperative State Research, Education, and Extension Service	7, XXXIV
Copyright Office	37, II
Copyright Royalty Board	37, III
Corporation for National and Community Service	2, XXII; 45, XII, XXV
Cost Accounting Standards Board	48, 99
Council on Environmental Quality	40, V
Court Services and Offender Supervision Agency for the District of Columbia	28, VIII
Customs and Border Protection Bureau	19, I
Defense Contract Audit Agency	32, I

Agency	CFR Title, Subtitle or Chapter
Defense Department	5, XXVI; 32, Subtitle A; 40, VII
Advanced Research Projects Agency	32, I
Air Force Department	32, VII
Army Department	32, V; 33, II; 36, III; 48, 51
Defense Acquisition Regulations System	48, 2
Defense Intelligence Agency	32, I
Defense Logistics Agency	32, I, XII; 48, 54
Engineers, Corps of	33, II; 36, III
Human Resources Management and Labor Relations Systems	5, XCIX
National Imagery and Mapping Agency	32, I
Navy Department	32, VI; 48, 52
Secretary of Defense, Office of	2, XI; 32, I
Defense Contract Audit Agency	32, I
Defense Intelligence Agency	32, I
Defense Logistics Agency	32, XII; 48, 54
Defense Nuclear Facilities Safety Board	10, XVII
Delaware River Basin Commission	18, III
District of Columbia, Court Services and Offender Supervision Agency for the	28, VIII
Drug Enforcement Administration	21, II
East-West Foreign Trade Board	15, XIII
Economic Affairs, Under Secretary	37, V
Economic Analysis, Bureau of	15, VIII
Economic Development Administration	13, III
Economic Research Service	7, XXXVII
Education, Department of	5, LIII
Bilingual Education and Minority Languages Affairs, Office of	34, V
Civil Rights, Office for	34, I
Educational Research and Improvement, Office of	34, VII
Elementary and Secondary Education, Office of	34, II
Federal Acquisition Regulation	48, 34
Postsecondary Education, Office of	34, VI
Secretary of Education, Office of	34, Subtitle A
Special Education and Rehabilitative Services, Office of	34, III
Vocational and Adult Education, Office of	34, IV
Educational Research and Improvement, Office of	34, VII
Election Assistance Commission	11, II
Elementary and Secondary Education, Office of	34, II
Emergency Oil and Gas Guaranteed Loan Board	13, V
Emergency Steel Guarantee Loan Board	13, IV
Employee Benefits Security Administration	29, XXV
Employees' Compensation Appeals Board	20, IV
Employees Loyalty Board	5, V
Employment and Training Administration	20, V
Employment Standards Administration	20, VI
Endangered Species Committee	50, IV
Energy, Department of	5, XXIII; 10, II, III, X
Federal Acquisition Regulation	48, 9
Federal Energy Regulatory Commission	5, XXIV; 18, I
Property Management Regulations	41, 109
Energy, Office of	7, XXIX
Engineers, Corps of	33, II; 36, III
Engraving and Printing, Bureau of	31, VI
Environmental Protection Agency	2, XV; 5, LIV; 40, I, IV, VII
Federal Acquisition Regulation	48, 15
Property Management Regulations	41, 115
Environmental Quality, Office of	7, XXXI
Equal Employment Opportunity Commission	5, LXII; 29, XIV
Equal Opportunity, Office of Assistant Secretary for	24, I
Executive Office of the President	3, I
Administration, Office of	5, XV
Environmental Quality, Council on	40, V

Agency	CFR Title, Subtitle or Chapter
Management and Budget, Office of	5, III, LXXVII; 14, VI; 48, 99
National Drug Control Policy, Office of	21, III
National Security Council	32, XXI; 47, 2
Presidential Documents	3
Science and Technology Policy, Office of	32, XXIV; 47, II
Trade Representative, Office of the United States	15, XX
Export-Import Bank of the United States	2, XXXV; 5, LII; 12, IV
Family Assistance, Office of	45, II
Farm Credit Administration	5, XXXI; 12, VI
Farm Credit System Insurance Corporation	5, XXX; 12, XIV
Farm Service Agency	7, VII, XVIII
Federal Acquisition Regulation	48, 1
Federal Aviation Administration	14, I
Commercial Space Transportation	14, III
Federal Claims Collection Standards	31, IX
Federal Communications Commission	5, XXIX; 47, I
Federal Contract Compliance Programs, Office of	41, 60
Federal Crop Insurance Corporation	7, IV
Federal Deposit Insurance Corporation	5, XXII; 12, III
Federal Election Commission	11, I
Federal Emergency Management Agency	44, I
Federal Employees Group Life Insurance Federal Acquisition Regulation	48, 21
Federal Employees Health Benefits Acquisition Regulation	48, 16
Federal Energy Regulatory Commission	5, XXIV; 18, I
Federal Financial Institutions Examination Council	12, XI
Federal Financing Bank	12, VIII
Federal Highway Administration	23, I, II
Federal Home Loan Mortgage Corporation	1, IV
Federal Housing Enterprise Oversight Office	12, XVII
Federal Housing Finance Agency	12, XII
Federal Housing Finance Board	12, IX
Federal Labor Relations Authority, and General Counsel of the Federal Labor Relations Authority	5, XIV; 22, XIV
Federal Law Enforcement Training Center	31, VII
Federal Management Regulation	41, 102
Federal Maritime Commission	46, IV
Federal Mediation and Conciliation Service	29, XII
Federal Mine Safety and Health Review Commission	5, LXXIV; 29, XXVII
Federal Motor Carrier Safety Administration	49, III
Federal Prison Industries, Inc.	28, III
Federal Procurement Policy Office	48, 99
Federal Property Management Regulations	41, 101
Federal Railroad Administration	49, II
Federal Register, Administrative Committee of	1, I
Federal Register, Office of	1, II
Federal Reserve System	12, II
Board of Governors	5, LVIII
Federal Retirement Thrift Investment Board	5, VI, LXXVI
Federal Service Impasses Panel	5, XIV
Federal Trade Commission	5, XLVII; 16, I
Federal Transit Administration	49, VI
Federal Travel Regulation System	41, Subtitle F
Fine Arts, Commission on	45, XXI
Fiscal Service	31, II
Fish and Wildlife Service, United States	50, I, IV
Fishery Conservation and Management	50, VI
Food and Drug Administration	21, I
Food and Nutrition Service	7, II
Food Safety and Inspection Service	9, III
Foreign Agricultural Service	7, XV
Foreign Assets Control, Office of	31, V
Foreign Claims Settlement Commission of the United States	45, V
Foreign Service Grievance Board	22, IX
Foreign Service Impasse Disputes Panel	22, XIV
Foreign Service Labor Relations Board	22, XIV

Agency	CFR Title, Subtitle or Chapter
Foreign-Trade Zones Board	15, IV
Forest Service	36, II
General Services Administration	5, LVII; 41, 105
Contract Appeals, Board of	48, 61
Federal Acquisition Regulation	48, 5
Federal Management Regulation	41, 102
Federal Property Management Regulations	41, 101
Federal Travel Regulation System	41, Subtitle F
General	41, 300
Payment From a Non-Federal Source for Travel Expenses	41, 304
Payment of Expenses Connected With the Death of Certain Employees	41, 303
Relocation Allowances	41, 302
Temporary Duty (TDY) Travel Allowances	41, 301
Geological Survey	30, IV
Government Accountability Office	4, I
Government Ethics, Office of	5, XVI
Government National Mortgage Association	24, III
Grain Inspection, Packers and Stockyards Administration	7, VIII; 9, II
Harry S. Truman Scholarship Foundation	45, XVIII
Health and Human Services, Department of	2, III; 5, XLV; 45, Subtitle A,
Centers for Medicare & Medicaid Services	42, IV
Child Support Enforcement, Office of	45, III
Children and Families, Administration for	45, II, III, IV, X
Community Services, Office of	45, X
Family Assistance, Office of	45, II
Federal Acquisition Regulation	48, 3
Food and Drug Administration	21, I
Human Development Services, Office of	45, XIII
Indian Health Service	25, V
Inspector General (Health Care), Office of	42, V
Public Health Service	42, I
Refugee Resettlement, Office of	45, IV
Homeland Security, Department of	2, XXX; 6, I
Coast Guard	33, I; 46, I; 49, IV
Coast Guard (Great Lakes Pilotage)	46, III
Customs and Border Protection Bureau	19, I
Federal Emergency Management Agency	44, I
Human Resources Management and Labor Relations Systems	5, XCVII
Immigration and Customs Enforcement Bureau	19, IV
Immigration and Naturalization	8, I
Transportation Security Administration	49, XII
HOPE for Homeowners Program, Board of Directors of	24, XXIV
Housing and Urban Development, Department of	2, XXIV; 5, LXV; 24, Subtitle B
Community Planning and Development, Office of Assistant Secretary for	24, V, VI
Equal Opportunity, Office of Assistant Secretary for	24, I
Federal Acquisition Regulation	48, 24
Federal Housing Enterprise Oversight, Office of	12, XVII
Government National Mortgage Association	24, III
Housing—Federal Housing Commissioner, Office of Assistant Secretary for	24, II, VIII, X, XX
Housing, Office of, and Multifamily Housing Assistance Restructuring, Office of	24, IV
Inspector General, Office of	24, XII
Public and Indian Housing, Office of Assistant Secretary for	24, IX
Secretary, Office of	24, Subtitle A, VII
Housing—Federal Housing Commissioner, Office of Assistant Secretary for	24, II, VIII, X, XX
Housing, Office of, and Multifamily Housing Assistance Restructuring, Office of	24, IV
Human Development Services, Office of	45, XIII
Immigration and Customs Enforcement Bureau	19, IV

Agency	CFR Title, Subtitle or Chapter
Immigration and Naturalization	8, I
Immigration Review, Executive Office for	8, V
Independent Counsel, Office of	28, VII
Indian Affairs, Bureau of	25, I, V
Indian Affairs, Office of the Assistant Secretary	25, VI
Indian Arts and Crafts Board	25, II
Indian Health Service	25, V
Industry and Security, Bureau of	15, VII
Information Resources Management, Office of	7, XXVII
Information Security Oversight Office, National Archives and Records Administration	32, XX
Inspector General	
Agriculture Department	7, XXVI
Health and Human Services Department	42, V
Housing and Urban Development Department	24, XII
Institute of Peace, United States	22, XVII
Inter-American Foundation	5, LXIII; 22, X
Interior Department	
American Indians, Office of the Special Trustee	25, VII
Endangered Species Committee	50, IV
Federal Acquisition Regulation	48, 14
Federal Property Management Regulations System	41, 114
Fish and Wildlife Service, United States	50, I, IV
Geological Survey	30, IV
Indian Affairs, Bureau of	25, I, V
Indian Affairs, Office of the Assistant Secretary	25, VI
Indian Arts and Crafts Board	25, II
Land Management, Bureau of	43, II
Minerals Management Service	30, II
National Indian Gaming Commission	25, III
National Park Service	36, I
Reclamation, Bureau of	43, I
Secretary of the Interior, Office of	2, XIV; 43, Subtitle A
Surface Mining and Reclamation Appeals, Board of	30, III
Surface Mining Reclamation and Enforcement, Office of	30, VII
Internal Revenue Service	26, I
International Boundary and Water Commission, United States and Mexico, United States Section	22, XI
International Development, United States Agency for	22, II
Federal Acquisition Regulation	48, 7
International Development Cooperation Agency, United States	22, XII
International Fishing and Related Activities	50, III
International Joint Commission, United States and Canada	22, IV
International Organizations Employees Loyalty Board	5, V
International Trade Administration	15, III; 19, III
International Trade Commission, United States	19, II
Interstate Commerce Commission	5, XL
Investment Security, Office of	31, VIII
James Madison Memorial Fellowship Foundation	45, XXIV
Japan–United States Friendship Commission	22, XVI
Joint Board for the Enrollment of Actuaries	20, VIII
Justice Department	2, XXVII; 5, XXVIII; 28, I, XI; 40, IV
Alcohol, Tobacco, Firearms, and Explosives, Bureau of	27, II
Drug Enforcement Administration	21, II
Federal Acquisition Regulation	48, 28
Federal Claims Collection Standards	31, IX
Federal Prison Industries, Inc.	28, III
Foreign Claims Settlement Commission of the United States	45, V
Immigration Review, Executive Office for	8, V
Offices of Independent Counsel	28, VI
Prisons, Bureau of	28, V
Property Management Regulations	41, 128
Labor Department	5, XLII
Benefits Review Board	20, VII
Employee Benefits Security Administration	29, XXV
Employees' Compensation Appeals Board	20, IV

Agency	CFR Title, Subtitle or Chapter
Employment and Training Administration	20, V
Employment Standards Administration	20, VI
Federal Acquisition Regulation	48, 29
Federal Contract Compliance Programs, Office of	41, 60
Federal Procurement Regulations System	41, 50
Labor-Management Standards, Office of	29, II, IV
Mine Safety and Health Administration	30, I
Occupational Safety and Health Administration	29, XVII
Public Contracts	41, 50
Secretary of Labor, Office of	29, Subtitle A
Veterans' Employment and Training Service, Office of the Assistant Secretary for	41, 61; 20, IX
Wage and Hour Division	29, V
Workers' Compensation Programs, Office of	20, I
Labor-Management Standards, Office of	29, II, IV
Land Management, Bureau of	43, II
Legal Services Corporation	45, XVI
Library of Congress	36, VII
Copyright Office	37, II
Copyright Royalty Board	37, III
Local Television Loan Guarantee Board	7, XX
Management and Budget, Office of	5, III, LXXVII; 14, VI; 48, 99
Marine Mammal Commission	50, V
Maritime Administration	46, II
Merit Systems Protection Board	5, II, LXIV
Micronesian Status Negotiations, Office for	32, XXVII
Millenium Challenge Corporation	22, XIII
Mine Safety and Health Administration	30, I
Minerals Management Service	30, II
Minority Business Development Agency	15, XIV
Miscellaneous Agencies	1, IV
Monetary Offices	31, I
Morris K. Udall Scholarship and Excellence in National Environmental Policy Foundation	36, XVI
Museum and Library Services, Institute of	2, XXXI
National Aeronautics and Space Administration	2, XVIII; 5, LIX; 14, V
Federal Acquisition Regulation	48, 18
National Agricultural Library	7, XLI
National Agricultural Statistics Service	7, XXXVI
National and Community Service, Corporation for	45, XII, XXV
National Archives and Records Administration	2, XXVI; 5, LXVI; 36, XII
Information Security Oversight Office	32, XX
National Capital Planning Commission	1, IV
National Commission for Employment Policy	1, IV
National Commission on Libraries and Information Science	45, XVII
National Council on Disability	34, XII
National Counterintelligence Center	32, XVIII
National Credit Union Administration	12, VII
National Crime Prevention and Privacy Compact Council	28, IX
National Drug Control Policy, Office of	21, III
National Endowment for the Arts	2, XXXII
National Endowment for the Humanities	2, XXXIII
National Foundation on the Arts and the Humanities	45, XI
National Highway Traffic Safety Administration	23, II, III; 49, V
National Imagery and Mapping Agency	32, I
National Indian Gaming Commission	25, III
National Institute for Literacy	34, XI
National Institute of Standards and Technology	15, II
National Intelligence, Office of Director of	32, XVII
National Labor Relations Board	5, LXI; 29, I
National Marine Fisheries Service	50, II, IV, VI
National Mediation Board	29, X
National Oceanic and Atmospheric Administration	15, IX; 50, II, III, IV, VI
National Park Service	36, I
National Railroad Adjustment Board	29, III
National Railroad Passenger Corporation (AMTRAK)	49, VII

Agency	CFR Title, Subtitle or Chapter
National Science Foundation	2, XXV; 5, XLIII; 45, VI
Federal Acquisition Regulation	48, 25
National Security Council	32, XXI
National Security Council and Office of Science and Technology Policy	47, II
National Telecommunications and Information Administration	15, XXIII; 47, III
National Transportation Safety Board	49, VIII
Natural Resources Conservation Service	7, VI
Navajo and Hopi Indian Relocation, Office of	25, IV
Navy Department	32, VI
Federal Acquisition Regulation	48, 52
Neighborhood Reinvestment Corporation	24, XXV
Northeast Interstate Low-Level Radioactive Waste Commission	10, XVIII
Nuclear Regulatory Commission	5, XLVIII; 10, I
Federal Acquisition Regulation	48, 20
Occupational Safety and Health Administration	29, XVII
Occupational Safety and Health Review Commission	29, XX
Offices of Independent Counsel	28, VI
Oklahoma City National Memorial Trust	36, XV
Operations Office	7, XXVIII
Overseas Private Investment Corporation	5, XXXIII; 22, VII
Patent and Trademark Office, United States	37, I
Payment From a Non-Federal Source for Travel Expenses	41, 304
Payment of Expenses Connected With the Death of Certain Employees	41, 303
Peace Corps	22, III
Pennsylvania Avenue Development Corporation	36, IX
Pension Benefit Guaranty Corporation	29, XL
Personnel Management, Office of	5, I, XXXV; 45, VIII
Human Resources Management and Labor Relations Systems, Department of Defense	5, XCIX
Human Resources Management and Labor Relations Systems, Department of Homeland Security	5, XCVII
Federal Acquisition Regulation	48, 17
Federal Employees Group Life Insurance Federal Acquisition Regulation	48, 21
Federal Employees Health Benefits Acquisition Regulation	48, 16
Pipeline and Hazardous Materials Safety Administration	49, I
Postal Regulatory Commission	5, XLVI; 39, III
Postal Service, United States	5, LX; 39, I
Postsecondary Education, Office of	34, VI
President's Commission on White House Fellowships	1, IV
Presidential Documents	3
Presidio Trust	36, X
Prisons, Bureau of	28, V
Procurement and Property Management, Office of	7, XXXII
Productivity, Technology and Innovation, Assistant Secretary	37, IV
Public Contracts, Department of Labor	41, 50
Public and Indian Housing, Office of Assistant Secretary for	24, IX
Public Health Service	42, I
Railroad Retirement Board	20, II
Reclamation, Bureau of	43, I
Recovery Accountability and Transparency Board	4, II
Refugee Resettlement, Office of	45, IV
Relocation Allowances	41, 302
Research and Innovative Technology Administration	49, XI
Rural Business-Cooperative Service	7, XVIII, XLII, L
Rural Development Administration	7, XLII
Rural Housing Service	7, XVIII, XXXV, L
Rural Telephone Bank	7, XVI
Rural Utilities Service	7, XVII, XVIII, XLII, L
Saint Lawrence Seaway Development Corporation	33, IV
Science and Technology Policy, Office of	32, XXIV
Science and Technology Policy, Office of, and National Security Council	47, II
Secret Service	31, IV
Securities and Exchange Commission	17, II

Agency	CFR Title, Subtitle or Chapter
Selective Service System	32, XVI
Small Business Administration	2, XXVII; 13, I
Smithsonian Institution	36, V
Social Security Administration	2, XXIII; 20, III; 48, 23
Soldiers' and Airmen's Home, United States	5, XI
Special Counsel, Office of	5, VIII
Special Education and Rehabilitative Services, Office of	34, III
State Department	2, VI; 22, I; 28, XI
Federal Acquisition Regulation	48, 6
Surface Mining and Reclamation Appeals, Board of	30, III
Surface Mining Reclamation and Enforcement, Office of	30, VII
Surface Transportation Board	49, X
Susquehanna River Basin Commission	18, VIII
Technology Administration	15, XI
Technology Policy, Assistant Secretary for	37, IV
Technology, Under Secretary for	37, V
Tennessee Valley Authority	5, LXIX; 18, XIII
Thrift Supervision Office, Department of the Treasury	12, V
Trade Representative, United States, Office of	15, XX
Transportation, Department of	2, XII; 5, L
Commercial Space Transportation	14, III
Contract Appeals, Board of	48, 63
Emergency Management and Assistance	44, IV
Federal Acquisition Regulation	48, 12
Federal Aviation Administration	14, I
Federal Highway Administration	23, I, II
Federal Motor Carrier Safety Administration	49, III
Federal Railroad Administration	49, II
Federal Transit Administration	49, VI
Maritime Administration	46, II
National Highway Traffic Safety Administration	23, II, III; 49, V
Pipeline and Hazardous Materials Safety Administration	49, I
Saint Lawrence Seaway Development Corporation	33, IV
Secretary of Transportation, Office of	14, II; 49, Subtitle A
Surface Transportation Board	49, X
Transportation Statistics Bureau	49, XI
Transportation, Office of	7, XXXIII
Transportation Security Administration	49, XII
Transportation Statistics Bureau	49, XI
Travel Allowances, Temporary Duty (TDY)	41, 301
Treasury Department	5, XXI; 12, XV; 17, IV; 31, IX
Alcohol and Tobacco Tax and Trade Bureau	27, I
Community Development Financial Institutions Fund	12, XVIII
Comptroller of the Currency	12, I
Customs and Border Protection Bureau	19, I
Engraving and Printing, Bureau of	31, VI
Federal Acquisition Regulation	48, 10
Federal Claims Collection Standards	31, IX
Federal Law Enforcement Training Center	31, VII
Fiscal Service	31, II
Foreign Assets Control, Office of	31, V
Internal Revenue Service	26, I
Investment Security, Office of	31, VIII
Monetary Offices	31, I
Secret Service	31, IV
Secretary of the Treasury, Office of	31, Subtitle A
Thrift Supervision, Office of	12, V
Truman, Harry S. Scholarship Foundation	45, XVIII
United States and Canada, International Joint Commission	22, IV
United States and Mexico, International Boundary and Water Commission, United States Section	22, XI
Utah Reclamation Mitigation and Conservation Commission	43, III
Veterans Affairs Department	2, VIII; 38, I
Federal Acquisition Regulation	48, 8
Veterans' Employment and Training Service, Office of the Assistant Secretary for	41, 61; 20, IX

Agency	CFR Title, Subtitle or Chapter
Vice President of the United States, Office of	32, XXVIII
Vocational and Adult Education, Office of	34, IV
Wage and Hour Division	29, V
Water Resources Council	18, VI
Workers' Compensation Programs, Office of	20, I
World Agricultural Outlook Board	7, XXXVIII

NAME INDEX

NOTE: Separate listings of Senators and Representatives can be found beginning on pages 32 and 34, respectively. Any other references to said persons can be found in this index.

A

Aaenenson, Charles — 526
Aall, Pamela — 561
Aarnes, Anne — 526
Abbenhaus, Colleen — 322
Abbot, Mark C. — 461
Abbott, James — 395
Abbott, Marilyn R. — 530
Abbott, Shere — 97
Abramson, Jeffrey Alan — 377
Acheson, Eleanor D. — 460
Ackerman, Jean — 280
Acosta, Marcel — 440
Acosta, Maria — 137
Acton, Mark — 492
Adams, David J. — 307
Adams, Jennifer — 525
Adams, Millie B. — 70
Adams, Patricia C. — 170
Adams, Susan — 44
Adamson, Terrence B. — 560
Adcock, Judith — 511
Addleman, Katherine — 500
Adkins, Charles — 283
Adler, Robert — 359
Agee, G. Steven — 68
Agnello, Gino J. — 69
Aguilar, Luis A. — 496
Aguirre, Eduardo, Jr. — 299, 301
Agwunobi, John O. — 351
Ahearn, Richard L. — 454
Ahern, Jayson — 226
Ahern, Paul T. — 493
Aikin, Jane — 447
Ainsworth, Kathleen — 535
Akeju, Camile — 546
Alcalde, Nancy — 307
Alcock, Charles — 546, 547
Alexander, Elizabeth — 88
Alexander, Fiona — 129
Alexander, Keith B. — 189
Ali, Russlynn — 194
Alito, Samuel A., Jr. — 65, 68, 69
Allen, Bernadette M. — 300
Allen, George — 172
Allen, Jean Cottam — 97
Allen, Kenneth — 286
Allen, Rosemary G. — 485
Allen, Thad W. — 226
Allgeier, Peter F. — 98
Allison, Herbert M. — 328
Almanza, Alfred V. — 103
Alston, C. Donald — 156
Altshuler, Ruth — 53
Altwegg, David — 188
Alvarado, Alberto — 512
Alvarez, Scott D. — 405, 406
Ambro, Thomas L. — 68
Ames, Fred — 98

Ames, Herbert F. — 440
Amoni, Marilena — 306
Amoroso, Frank — 254
Amos, James — 172
Anchondo, Teresa — 375
Anderegg, Clarence R. — 156
Anders, Glenn — 525
Anderson, Cheryl — 526
Anderson, Frank J., Jr. — 191
Anderson, Howard — 486
Anderson, Julie — 344
Anderson, Karen L. — 89
Anderson, Michael — 530
Anderson, William — 362
Andrezze, Christopher — 183
Andrion, Elizabeth — 382
Andross, Susan — 352
Angel, James H., Jr. — 389
Aniello, JoAnna — 235
Aoki, Steven — 203
App, Steven O. — 388
Appel, Peter H. — 308
Aramaki, Suzan J. — 127
Aranoff, Shara L. — 529
Arberg, Kathleen L. — 65
Arbit, Terry S. — 356
Arbuthnot, Richard E. — 426
Architzel, David — 171
Archuleta, Deanna — 237
Archuleta, Katherine — 273
Arellano, Hilda — 525
Argo, Peter — 525
Arlook, Martin M. — 454
Armey, Scott — 421
Armstrong, Jayne — 512
Arnett, Angela J. — 514
Arnold, Kay Kelley — 422
Arnolie, Anthony A. — 462
Arny, Louis W., III — 146
Arreola, Philip — 254
Arthur, Bruce — 43
Artilles, Joseph H. — 455
Arvizu, Dan E. — 461
Ascienzo, John — 530
Ash, Darren B. — 470
Ashe, Victor Henderson — 301
Ashtianie, Susan M. — 431
Ashton, Billie — 375
Asin, Steven G. — 75
Askew, John B. — 371
Astrue, Michael J. — 513
Atha, Ken — 283
Atkins, Hae Jung — 376
Augustine, John — 308
Augustyn, Noel J. — 75
Austin, Danforth W. — 352
Austin, Herbert — 512
Austin-Diggs, Carolyn M. — 417
Avery, Napoleon — 504
Axelrod, David M. — 86
Ayalde, Liliana — 301

Ayers, Stephen T. — 43, 44, 45
Ayers, Steve — 511
Aytes, Michael — 226
Azzaro, Richard A. — 366

B

Babers, C. Donald — 235
Baca, Joseph F. — 559
Bach, Kenneth — 362
Bachmann, Michael L. — 172
Baden, Laurence M. — 445
Bader, Joseph F. — 366
Baer, Kenneth — 92
Bagnati, David — 188
Bailey, Catherine Todd — 300
Bailey, Chester — 376
Bailey, Teresa — 43
Bair, Sheila C. — 388
Baker, Alan — 173
Baker, C. Steven — 414
Baker, Diane — 492
Baker, Elizabeth A. — 318
Baker, Kenneth E. — 203
Baker, Meredith Attwell — 382
Baldonado, Michael — 376
Baldwin, Robert N. — 560
Bale, Mary — 104
Ball, Theresa — 277
Balsiger, James W. — 129
Bange, Gerald — 104
Banks, Sharon J. — 421
Banks-Dubose, Inez — 231
Bansal, Preeta — 92
Baptiste-Kalaris, Mark — 454
Barab, Jordan — 273
Barber, Stephen E. — 489
Barish, Barry C. — 461
Barker, Constance S. — 372
Barker, Joseph A. — 454
Barkett, Rosemary — 71
Barkley, Timothy — 305
Barlow, Ralph M. — 385
Barnes, Bert — 337
Barnes, Melody C. — 96
Barnett, Helaine M. — 543
Barnett, Mickey D. — 534
Barr, Michael S. — 328
Barrett, Mason — 376
Barringer, Martha M. — 494
Barrios, Melissa — 375
Barron, David — 253
Barry, Maryanne Trump — 68
Bartell, Michael E. — 388
Bartholow, Steven A. — 493
Barton, Mike — 443
Bassett, Leslie — 300
Batchelder, Alice M. — 69
Bates, Carol — 43
Bathurst, Donald G. — 225

Batten, Katherine M. — 237
Battles, Thomas — 254
Batts, Rebecca Anne — 490
Bauerly, Cynthia L. — 392
Baukol, Andy — 328
Baumann, Paul — 280
Baumgaertner, Martin W. — 425
Bautch, Doris J. — 321
Baxter, Greg — 283
Baxter, John R. — 305
Bazzle, Diane N. — 368
Bea, Carlos T. — 70
Beal, William F. — 286
Bean, Bridget — 512
Beard, Daniel — 25
Beaver, Billy — 280
Becerra, Xavier — 545
Bechtol, Ted — 44
Beck, David — 530
Beck, Richard T. — 238
Beck, Thomas M. — 395
Beckenbaugh, Scot L. — 401
Becker, David — 496
Becker, Lou — 426
Bednar, James — 526
Beecroft, Robert S. — 300
Beed, John — 526
Beering, Steven C. — 461
Beers, Rand — 225
Beets, Gary — 336
Belcher, Roger — 282
Belinkski, Betty — 336
Belisle, Philip — 336
Beliveau, Emmett S. — 87
Bell, Hubert T., Jr. — 470
Bell, Wayne — 512
Bellamy, Thomas — 486
Bement, Arden L., Jr. — 461
Benavides, Fortunado P. — 69
Benbow, Camilla P. — 461
Benkert, Joseph — 146
Bennett, Cynthia — 43
Bennett, Edgar — 489
Bennett, Margareth — 503
Benson, Martha — 416
Benton, William Duane — 70
Beresford, Lynne G. — 130
Bergers, David — 500
Bergey, Barry — 445
Berman, Ken — 352
Bermingham, Eldredge — 547
Bernanke, Ben S. — 404, 405
Bernard, Jeremy — 447
Berner, Kevin J. — 161
Bernicat, Marcia S. — 300
Berning, Michael — 362
Bernstein, Jared — 88
Bernstein, Sheldon — 447
Bernstock, Robert — 535
Berrick, Cathleen — 47
Berry, David P. — 452
Berry, Dennis — 194
Berry, John — 479
Berryhill, Nancy A. — 514
Bersin, Alan — 225
Berson, Jerry L. — 514
Berzon, Marsha S. — 70
Betman, Mitzi — 535
Betro, Thomas A. — 170
Bevan, Larry P. — 351
Bew, Ron — 512
Beyer, Wayne C. — 273
Beyrle, Jon Ross — 300
Bhagowalia, Sanjeer — 238
Bianchi, Dominic L. — 530
Bianchi, Kerry — 547
Bibeault, James — 282

Biddick, Dennis — 171
Biden, Joseph R., Jr. — 25, 85, 90, 545
Bilbray, James H. — 534
Billington, James H. — 53
Birch, Stanley F., Jr. — 71
Birgells, Edward — 526
Biro, Susan L. — 368
Bishop, Beverly — 235
Bishop, Clyde — 300
Bittner, Mamie — 450
Black, Barry — 25
Black, David F. — 514
Black, Scott C. — 161
Black, Steven W. — 237
Black, Susan H. — 71
Black, Sylvester — 535
Blackadar, Edward A., Jr. — 501
Blackman, Anita K. — 307
Blackwell, Edith — 237
Blackwood, David — 527
Blackwood, R. Duke — 436
Blair, Dan G. — 492
Blair, Dennis C. — 90, 476
Blake, Robert O., Jr. — 300, 301
Blanchard, Charles A. — 156
Blanchard, Laricke D. — 405
Blaney, Robert J. — 512
Blank, Rebecca M. — 128
Blaszkowsky, David M. — 497
Blau, Robert — 300
Blaya, Joaquin F. — 352
Blickstein, Jill — 92
Blinken, Tony — 88
Bliss, Christine — 99
Block, Steve — 489
Bloom, Thomas R. — 329
Blumenthal, David — 212
Blyer, Alvin B. — 455
Boardman, Joseph H. — 459
Bobley, Brett — 447
Bodde, Peter W. — 300
Boehm, Martin — 490
Boehne, Kenneth P. — 494
Boehne, Kevin — 322
Boesz, Christine C. — 461
Boggs, Danny J. — 69
Bolden, Charles F., Jr. — 425
Boling, Edward A. — 89
Bolinger, Madge — 356
Bolle, Thomas — 308
Bolls, William — 286
Bond, Elizabeth — 280
Bonner, James — 526
Booth, Donald E. — 301
Boots, Michael — 89
Borbeau, Sharie — 225
Borchardt, R. William — 470
Bordoff, Jason — 89
Bordonaro, Molly Hering — 300
Borgia, Stanley — 203
Borinsky, Susan — 306
Borland, James C. — 513
Borman, Matthew S. — 127
Bosanko, William J. — 431
Boswell, Eric J. — 290
Boswell, June — 276
Bottorff, Dennis — 518
Boucher, Charles — 497
Boucher, Richard A. — 290
Boudin, Michael — 68
Boulden, William L. — 425
Boulware, Mark — 300
Bourgeois, Douglas — 238
Bovenzi, John F. — 388
Bowen, David M. — 304
Bowen, Ray M. — 461
Bowers, Pamela S. — 377

Bowling, David — 469
Bowling, Timothy — 47
Bowman, Charles — 44
Bowman, John E. — 331
Bowman, Linda — 308
Boyce, Ralph Leo, Jr. — 301
Boyd, April S. — 127
Boyd, Lisa M. — 402
Boyer, Kimber H., Jr. — 415
Boynton, Doug — 352
Bozin, Stanley D. — 170
Brachfeld, Paul — 432
Bradford-Washington, Linda — 231
Bradley, James C. — 50
Bradley, Kim — 504
Bradtke, Robert A. — 300
Brady, Barbara — 352
Brady, Lawrence — 525
Brady, Michael — 50
Brady, Roger A. — 158
Brainard, Lael — 328
Brambilla, Janice H. — 352
Brand, Lauren K. — 321
Brands, William — 526
Brasseux, Barnaby L. — 415
Bratcher, Rita — 329
Braun, Jacob H. — 226
Braunstein, Diane K. — 513
Braunstein, Sandra F. — 405
Brazel, Susan M. — 80
Brecht-Clark, Jan — 308
Breen, Barry N. — 368
Breese, Terry — 300
Brennan, Anne M. — 170
Brennan, John O. — 86
Brennan, Joseph E. — 398
Brennan, Megan — 535
Brenner, Eliot B. — 470
Brereton, Peter — 393
Bress, Joseph M. — 459
Brettell, Richard — 282
Breuer, Lanny A. — 253
Brewster, Lawrence — 277
Breyer, Stephen G. — 65, 68, 70
Breyman, Terrence — 89
Bridge, Shirley — 282
Bridgeman, Jimmy H. — 421
Bridgewater, James A. — 385
Briggs, Xavier — 92
Brill, Kenneth — 476
Brimmer, Esther — 290
Brinkley, Paul A. — 146
Brinkman, William — 203
Brinza, Daniel — 98
Briscoe, Mary Beck — 70
Broad, Eli — 545
Broadbent, Alfred — 127
Broadus, Barbi — 486
Brockbank, Dale — 286
Brogan, Michael — 173
Broglie, William F. — 129
Brooks, Dave — 316
Brooks, Laurie — 450
Brooks, Vicki — 344
Brooks-LaSure, M. Allyn — 366
Broun, Elizabeth — 546
Broun, Laurence — 238
Brown, Aletha L. — 372
Brown, Bruce L. — 277
Brown, Bryan D. — 151
Brown, Cliff — 526
Brown, Darrol — 286
Brown, Elizabeth M. — 86
Brown, Gayleatha B. — 300
Brown, Herbert — 376
Brown, Janice Rogers — 67
Brown, Jeanette L. — 368

Brown, John — 512
Brown, Larry W. — 366
Brown, Laura B. — 237
Brown, Laura J. — 305
Brown, Mary Patrice — 254
Brown, Reginald — 479
Brown, Richard W. — 530
Brown, Wayne — 445
Brownell, Susan — 535
Browner, Carol M. — 87
Brownfield, William R. — 300
Browning, Steven A. — 301
Bruce, Lucia — 277
Bruer, John T. — 461
Bruininks, R. Todd — 282
Brunger, Deborah — 282
Brunhart, Andrew — 330
Brunner, Teresa — 313
Bryan, Carolyn — 526
Bryner, Gary C. — 422
Bryson, Sharon — 466
Bryson, William C. — 71
Buccigrosso, Alfred — 187
Buck, Jennifer C. — 146
Buffa, Nicole — 89
Bullard, James B. — 405
Bullen, Roland — 300
Buller, Kathy — 486
Bullock, Charles E. — 530
Bumpus, Jeanne — 411
Bunch, Lonnie — 546
Bundick, Bruce — 104
Bungard, B. Chad — 423
Burchill, William R., Jr. — 75
Buren, David M. Van — 156
Burgess, David — 486
Burgess, Ronald L., Jr. — 185
Burgoyne, Ellis — 535
Burke, Michael — 445
Burnett, Bryan — 452
Burns, Stephen G. — 470
Burns, William J. — 290, 301
Burt, Robert — 171
Burton, Faith — 253
Buswell, Bradley — 225
Butler, J. Dudley — 104
Buttrey, Kathleen V. — 359
Butts, Cassandra Q. — 87
Buzzi, Frank J. — 493
Bybee, Jay S. — 70
Bydume, Doreen G.B. — 75
Bye, Kermit E. — 70
Byerly, Chet H., Jr. — 454
Byrd, Rick — 330
Byrd, Robert C. — 25
Byrne, Joseph A. — 307
Byrnes, Chris — 527

C

Cabana, Robert D. — 426
Cabot, Daniel — 375
Cabranes, Jose A. — 68
Cadagin, Mary — 362
Cadle, Elizabeth — 375
Cahn, Anne H. — 561
Cain, James — 300
Calatrello, Frederick — 454
Caliendo, Madeline C. — 415
Callahan, Consuelo Maria — 70
Callahan, Mary Ellen — 226
Callahan, Robert — 300
Callender, John F. — 492
Calvery, Steven E. — 190
Cameron, Jon J. — 329
Campbell, Charles C. — 162
Campbell, Kevin T. — 162

Campbell, Rachel D. — 309
Campbell, Scott V. — 501
Campbell, Stacia — 455
Campbell, William — 536
Canales, Judy — 103
Canning, John A., Jr. — 405
Capolongo, Mabel — 280
Caponiti, James E. — 307
Cara, Joseph — 306
Cardona, Danilo — 543
Carduner, Olivier — 526
Carey, Robert J. — 170
Carfine, Kenneth — 328
Carlisle, Herbert J. — 156
Carlson, Roger — 526
Carlson, Ronald — 511
Carlton, Dennis P. — 385
Carner, George — 526
Carnes, Edward E. — 71
Carney, Jay — 88
Carns, Fred S. — 389
Carpenter, Wendi B. — 172
Carper, Tom — 459
Carr, Debra A. — 527
Carr, Florence A. — 398
Carr, Nevin P., Jr. — 171
Carr, Robert — 530
Carr, William B., Jr. — 80
Carr, William J. — 146
Carra, Joseph — 306
Carrion, Adolfo, Jr. — 87
Carroll, Suzie — 486
Carson, John — 89
Carter, Ashton B. — 146
Carter, Darcy — 511
Carter, David W. — 377
Carter, Gary — 226
Cartwright, James E. — 147
Carver, Douglas L. — 161
Carver, Jonathan — 503
Casey, George W., Jr. — 147, 161
Casey, Kathleen L. — 496
Cashion, Gerald — 526
Casias, Lisa — 127
Cassidy, Jeremiah — 425
Cassil, Dan — 43
Castellano, Joseph A. — 400
Castillo, Ruben — 80
Castillo, Simon — 512
Castro, Randal R. — 188
Catterson, Cathy A. — 70
Caughman, Bruce E. — 416
Caulfield, John — 301
Center, Charles — 395
Cestare, Thomas W. — 454
Chadwick, Kristine — 496
Chagares, Michael A. — 68
Chaikin, Karen — 281
Chakiris, Georgia S. — 318
Chalmers, Jane H. — 129
Champoux, Bernard — 161
Chan, Tony F. — 461
Chandler, Carrol H. — 158
Chao, Kelu — 352
Chappell, D. Michael — 411
Charles, John Frant — 127
Charneski, Carl C. — 530
Chasek, Daniel — 277
Cheatham, James A. — 305
Cheema, Jatinder — 525
Chen, Amy — 546
Chen, Nancy — 277
Chero, Linda L. — 421
Cherry, Schroeder — 450
Chester, Robert W. — 454
Chiarelli, Peter W. — 161
Chiari, Jeannette — 104

Childs, Robert D. — 192
Chilton, Bartholomew H. — 356
Chilton, Kevin P. — 151
Chinni, Benjamin — 277
Chipkevich, Robert J. — 466
Chopra, Aneesh — 97
Christensen, Carl — 512
Chu, Steven — 203
Chute, Mary L. — 449
Cianchette, Peter — 300
Clancy, Carolyn — 212
Clapper, James R., Jr. — 147
Clark, Cynthia — 103
Clark, David — 47
Clark, Donald S. — 411
Clark, John F. — 253
Clark, Oliver E. — 400
Clark, Virginia B. — 546
Clark, Willie L., Jr. — 454
Clarke, Bruce M. — 79
Clay, Colleen — 362
Clay, Eric L. — 69
Clement, Donna — 65
Clement, Edith Brown — 69
Clifton, Richard R. — 70
Clinefelter, Carl A. — 379
Clinton, Hillary Rodham — 90, 289,
  352, 561
Closter, Harold — 546
Cloud, John A., Jr. — 300
Clough, G. Wayne — 461, 546
Clyburn, Mignon — 382
Coats, Michael — 426
Cober, Gail — 375
Cochran, Thad — 545
Cochrane, James — 535
Cofer, Jonathan H. — 190
Coffey, Georgia — 344
Cogan, Phillip S. — 378
Cogbill, John V., III — 440
Cohen, David S. — 328
Cohen, Kenneth P. — 80
Cohen, Robert F., Jr. — 402
Cohn, Anna R. — 546
Cohn, Rebecca — 526
Colangelo, Brook — 91
Colclough, Thomas — 376
Cole, Gerald M. — 397
Cole, Johnnetta B. — 546
Cole, Owen — 443
Cole, Ransey Guy, Jr. — 69
Cole, Roger T. — 405
Coleman, Casey — 415
Coleman, Elizabeth A. — 405
Coleman, Jonathan — 530
Coleman, Maryruth — 301
Coleman, Neill — 231
Coleman, Ronald — 173
Coleman, S. Robert — 379
Coleman, Ted E. — 79
Coles, Julius E. — 351
Collins, D. Michael — 389
Collins, James — 461
Colloton, Steven M. — 70
Collotta, Mike — 329
Colon, Isabel — 280
Comer, Robert D. — 237
Comstock, Douglas A. — 426
Concannon, Kevin — 103
Coneway, Peter R. — 301
Conlin, Linda Mysliwy — 377
Conniff, Brian T. — 353
Connor, Michael — 237
Connor, Patricia S. — 68
Connors, Michael — 283
Conrad, Roger — 486
Constance, John — 543

Conway, James T. — 147, 172
Conway, Roger — 104
Cook, Deborah L. — 69
Cook, Gary — 512
Cook, Kamil P. — 377
Cooke, Douglas — 425
Cooke, Jacqueline — 277
Cooke, John S. — 79
Cooks, Romell W. — 318
Cooley, Thomas N. — 461
Cooper, Barry — 313
Cooper, Elliott — 511
Cooper, Susan — 431
Cooper, Tiffani — 503
Coppess, Jonathan — 103
Copps, Michael J. — 382
Corbett, Amy Lind — 313
Corbett, Joseph — 535
Cordova, France A. — 461
Cordova, Lu M. — 405
Corley, John D.W. — 158
Cornelison, Lee — 511
Cornelius, Eugene, Jr. — 512
Corr, William — 212
Costa, Anthony — 416
Cothron, Tony L. — 171
Cotton, A. Dean — 512
Coughlin, Daniel P. — 25
Courlander, Michael — 80
Courtney, James J. — 513
Cousins, Lynn E. — 493
Cowart, Walter — 512
Cowen, William B. — 452
Cowhey, Peter — 98
Cox, Edwin L. — 53
Cox, Margaret — 44
Cox, Maurice — 445
Craft, Malee — 529
Cragg, Scott — 343
Craig, B.B. — 330
Craig, Elizabeth — 368
Craig, Gregory B. — 86, 90
Crane, Tanny B. — 405
Crawley, Thomas W. — 514
Crean, Sean — 171
Creel, Rob — 286
Cretz, Gene — 300
Crew, John — 104
Crocker, Chester A. — 561
Croft, David — 337
Croft, G. Kelly — 514
Cromer, Sharon L. — 522
Crosbie, William L. — 459
Cross, Gerald M. — 343
Cross, Meredith — 496
Cross, Stephen M. — 393
Crowder, William Douglas — 171, 172
Crowley, Christopher — 526
Cruden, John — 253
Crum, John — 423
Crumpacker, Jill M. — 104
Cruse, James C. — 378
Crutchfield, Danielle M. — 87
Cullum, Blanquita Walsh — 352
Culp, James — 277
Culver, Mike — 43
Cummings, Julie Fisher — 362
Cunnane, Robert — 526
Cunningham, Daniel — 75
Cunningham, James B. — 300
Cunningham, Peter — 194
Cunningham, Sarah B. — 445
Curran, Lori K. — 307
Curry, Thomas J. — 388
Curtin, Jeremy — 290
Curtis, George — 500
Cushing, Michael — 377

Cusick, Robert I. — 478
Cutler, Wendy — 98
Cypser, Beth — 526
Czech, Barbara — 466

D

D'Agostino, Thomas P. — 203
Daher, Brian — 276
Dahm, Werner J.A. — 156
Dailey, John R. — 546
Daisey, Susan — 447
Daley, Michael — 535
Dall'Oglio, Luca — 568
Dallachie, Charles A. — 173
Dalton, Patricia — 47
Danello, Mary Ann — 359
Daniels, Reuben — 375
Daniels, Stephen M. — 415
Danker, Deborah — 406
Darling, Ray H., Jr. — 473
Darnell, Daniel J. — 156
Daugherty, Linda — 323
Daughetee, Patricia — 520
Daum, Ed — 511
Davenport, Heyward — 137
Davidson, Janine — 146
Davidson, Linda L. — 454
Davidson, William A. — 156
Davie, Mary A. — 416
Davila, Robert R. — 199
Davis, D. Scott — 405
Davis, Edward — 60
Davis, Lula Johnson — 25
Davis, Michael L. — 273
Davis, Mike — 273
Davis, Morgan M. — 351
Davis, Patricia — 489
Davis, Paul — 362
Davis, Richard G. — 50
Davis, W. Eugene — 69
Davis, Will — 570
Dawn, Ralph — 47
Dawsey, Toni — 426
Dawson, Tom — 173
Day, Barbara K. — 485
Day, Tom — 535
Dayton, Daniel — 226
de Paola, Christopher — 561
de Soto, Lisa — 514
De Vos, Elisabeth — 53
Dean, James L. — 417
Debbink, Dirk — 171
Deboer, Joan — 304
DeCarlo, Linda — 282
Decker, Anita — 445
Decker, Jo A. — 170
Deikun, George — 526
Delaney, Michael — 98
DeLeo, Wanda — 393
DeLeon, Rafael — 368
Delgado, Glenn A. — 426
DeLisi, John — 466
Delli-Colli, Kevin — 127
DelNegro, Elizabeth L. — 416
DeMarco, Edward J. — 393
Dempsey, L. Antoinette — 281
Dempsey, Martin E. — 162
Deneen, Terrence M. — 490
Denison, Terri — 511
Dennin, Fred, II — 194
Dennis, James L. — 69
Dennis, Robert A. — 60
Denniston, Robert W. — 95
Denny, David — 519
Dentel, Christopher W. — 359
Deptula, David A. — 156

Der, Victor — 203
DeRosa, Mary B. — 87
Derse, Anne E. — 299
Desai, Monica — 382
DeSanti, Susan — 411
DeSarno, William — 443
DeSio, Henry F., Jr. — 87
Desmond, Paul — 286
Desmukes, LaJuene — 127
Despain, Steven — 512
Destafano, Stacy — 286
Destler, William W. — 201
DeSutter, R. Joseph — 192
DeTrani, Joseph — 476
Devaney, Earl E. — 237
Devine, Daniel C. — 344
Devine, Michael — 436
DeVine, Stephen — 496
DeVito, Vincent — 535
DeWolf, Harry L. — 512
Diaz, Eduardo — 546
DiCarlo, Rosemary — 291
DiCicco, John — 253
Dickerson, Alice — 543
Dickerson, Chris — 393
Dickie, Alexander — 526
Dickman, Martin J. — 493
Dickson, David — 512
Didier, Elaine K. — 436
DiEullis, Diane — 97
Diffily, J.A. — 300
Digregorio, Evon — 286
Dillaman, Kathy — 479
Dillard, Stephen — 343
Dillingham, Steven — 308
Dilts, Martha — 235
Dinger, Larry Miles — 300, 301
Dinwiddie, Carl — 469
Dioguardi, Paul — 212
Dixey, B. Michele — 377
Dixon, Arrington — 440
Doane, Margaret M. — 470
Dobyne, Eric — 137
Dodaro, Gene L. — 47
Dodd, Christopher — 545
Dodd, Thomas J. — 422
Dohner, Robert S. — 328
Dolder, Nancy S. — 273
Doll, John J. — 130
Dolphin, Tene — 127
Dominguez, Marie Therese — 535
Dominguez, Olga — 426
Domzal, Teresa — 476
Donahoe, Patrick R. — 534, 535
Donald, Kirkland H. — 171, 203
Donilon, Mike — 88
Donkar, Eli N. — 513
Donley, Michael B. — 156
Donlion, Thomas E. — 86, 91
Donohue, Andrew J. — 496
Donohue, Kenneth M., Sr. — 231
Donovan, Richard C. — 68
Donovan, Shaun — 231
Doone, Alison — 330
Dorch, Rebecca — 385
Dorris, Martha A. — 415
Dorsett, David J. — 172
Doss, Antonio — 503
Dougherty, Elizabeth — 456
Douglas, Cynthia — 308
Douglas, James — 546
Dowd, William G. — 441
Downe, William — 406
Drabkin, David A. — 415
Drake, David — 435
Dribinsky, Leonard — 484
Droegemeier, Kelvin K. — 461

Drumheller, Robert B. — 485
Dube, Maurice — 511
Dubina, Joel F. — 70
Duckworth, L. Tammy — 344
Duda, Robert J. — 494
Dudley, William C. — 405
Duff, James C. — 75
Duffy, Michael F. — 402
Duffy, Mike — 327
Duffy, Terrence A. — 409
Dugan, John C. — 328, 388
Dugan, Regina E. — 181
Duhon, David A. — 282
Duke, Elaine C. — 225
Duke, Elizabeth — 404
Duma, David W. — 147
Dunaway, David — 171
Duncan, Allyson K. — 68
Duncan, Arne — 194
Duncan, Robert M. — 517
Duncan, Thomasenia P. — 392
Dunford, Joseph, F., Jr. — 173
Dunn, Anita B. — 86
Dunn, Michael V. — 356
Dunn, Timothy J. — 300
Dunne, Patrick — 343
Dunnigan, John H. — 129
Dunning, Amy — 425
Dunston, Jerri U. — 254
Durham, Mario Garcia — 445
Durst, Steven — 286
Dwyer, Molly — 70
Dwyer, Timothy — 366
Dybul, Mark — 289
Dye, Rebecca F. — 398
Dyer, James E. — 470
Dyk, Timothy B. — 71
Dyke, Landon Van — 89
Dyson, Pamela C. — 530

E

Eaglin, James B. — 79
Earley, Keith B. — 493
Easterbrook, Frank H. — 69
Eastham, Alan W. — 300
Easton, John — 194
Easton, Mark E. — 170
EchoHawk, Larry — 237
Eck, David — 183
Eckerman, Larry — 337
Eckerson, David — 526
Eckert, Dennis — 281
Eckrote, Debra — 469
Edmondson, James Larry — 70
Edwards, Bret D. — 388
Edwards, Kathleen M. — 445
Edwards, Lynn — 125
Egelman, Glenn — 487
Eichler, Francine C. — 395
Eischen, Steve — 280
Eisenman, Ross — 75
Eissenstat, Everett — 99
Elachi, Charles — 426
Elbein, Bradley — 414
Elder, Jacqueline — 359
Elias, Carlos — 44
Elias, Karen — 445
Eller, Sharon — 238
Ellis, Margot — 522
Ellis, Raymond J. — 377
Ellison, Michele — 382
Elmendorf, Douglass W. — 60
Elmore, William — 503
Elrod, Jennifer Walker — 69
Elton, Kim S. — 237
Eltrich, Katherine — 92

Ely, Kay T. — 479
Elzy, Nadine L. — 50
Emanuel, Rahm I. — 86, 90
Emerson, Catherine V. — 395
Emmons, Terrell — 43
Emswiler, Thomas K. — 410
English, Charles L. — 300
Ensel, Ellen — 561
Erb, Karl A. — 461
Ereli, J. Adam — 300
Erickson, Nancy — 25
Erickson, Paul — 50
Ericsson, Sally — 92
Erikson, Byron — 286
Ernst, Mark A. — 330
Erwin, Jenny — 277
Espinosa, Michael — 286
Esquivel, Pedro — 376
Essex, Theodore R. — 530
Etheridge, Arrie — 489
Evans, Charles L. — 405
Evans, Terence T. — 69
Everest, Shirley — 486
Ezerski, Beatrice E. — 493

F

Fagel, Marc J. — 500
Fagnoni, Cynthia M. — 47
Falcone, Jim — 330
Falvey, Cheryl A. — 359
Fanning, Fred E. — 127
Farmer, Lisa F. — 304
Farquhar, Edward — 238
Farrell, Claudia — 411
Farrell, Diana L. — 96
Farrell, Diane — 377
Farrell, Ellen A. — 452
Farrell, Joe — 410
Faubion, Michael — 445
Faulkner, John W. — 187
Favreau, Jonathan E. — 86
Fawcett, Sharon K. — 431
Fazio, Anthony — 313
Federici, Gary A. — 171
Feeley, William F. — 343
Feindt, Jo Ann — 535
Feinstein, Rich — 410
Feit, Gary — 416
Felder, Wilson — 314
Feldman, Eric — 281
Felix, Larry R. — 329
Felson, Michael — 277
Feltman, Jeffrey D. — 290
Fenn, Michael — 43
Fenner, Robert M. — 443
Fenton, Carol A. — 307
Fenty, Adrian M. — 440
Ferguson, David — 43
Ferguson, John H. — 452
Ferguson, Mark E., III — 171, 172
Fernandez, Alberto M. — 301
Fernandez, Magdalena — 282
Fernstrom, Kate — 450
Ferriter, Olivia — 238
Ferry, Kelli H. — 80
Fetler, Steve — 97
Fetzer, Michael — 375
Fiely, Lisa — 273
Figueroa, Marta — 455
Fil, Joseph F., Jr. — 162
Finch, Warren L., Jr. — 436
Fine, Glenn A. — 253
Fink, Thomas A. — 409
Finley, Julie — 301
Fiorenzo, Les — 316
Fisher, Ann — 492

Fisher, D. Michael — 68
Fisher, David M. — 181
Fisher, Raymond C. — 70
Fisher, Richard W. — 405
Fisher, Steven — 410
Fiske, David — 383
Fites, Jeanne — 146
Fitts, Catherine E. — 65
Fitzgerald, Mark — 172
Fitzgerald, Patrick J. — 161
Fitzpatrick, Collins T. — 69
Flahavan, Richard S. — 501
Flatau, Warren — 305
Flaum, Joel M. — 69
Fletcher, Daniel — 238
Fletcher, William A. — 70
Fleure, Pat — 526
Flippen, Deidre — 372
Flom, Ronald — 479
Flournoy, Michele — 146
Flowers, Richard — 226
Flynn, George — 173
Focarino, Margaret A. — 130
Foden, Lynn — 486
Foley, April H. — 300
Folsom, Joe — 512
Fong, Ivan K. — 226
Fong, Phyllis K. — 104
Fontaine, Pete — 60
Fontenot, Keith — 92
Ford, Charles — 300
Ford, Delorice — 503
Foreman, Timothy — 170
Forgione, C. Michael — 377
Fornarotto, Christa — 304
Forrest, Christopher — 187
Forsland, Karen — 512
Forsythe, Jack — 426
Forte, Steven — 535
Fortuno, Victor M. — 543
Foster, Bill — 328
Foster, David V. — 514
Foster, Dwight — 466
Fountain, Carey — 487
Fowler, William E., Jr. — 466
Fox, Don W. — 478
Fox, Rosemary — 375
Fox, Sam — 300
Foye, Kristine — 235
Fraker, Ford M. — 301
Frank, Joyce — 366
Frankel, Robert — 445
Franklin, Mark D. — 170
Franklin, Rita — 203
Franklin-Thomas, Delner — 375
Franz, Anna — 43
Franzel, Jeanette M. — 47
Fraser, Douglas M. — 151
Fraser, William M., III — 156
Frazier, T. Michael — 50
Fredriksen, Amanda G. — 416
Freeman, Carmelita — 254
Freeman, Karen — 526
Freis, James — 328
Frej, William — 526
Fremaux, Emmett — 460
Friday, George, Jr. — 281
Fried, Daniel — 290
Frieden, Thomas — 213
Friedman, Gregory H. — 203
Friedman, Stephen — 405
Friedrich, Dabney L. — 80
Fritz, Michael — 525
Froehlich, Maryann — 368
Frost, Phillip — 545
Frye, Jan R. — 343
Frye, Jocelyn C. — 87

Fuentes, Julio M. — 68
Fugate, W. Craig — 225
Fulbruge, Charles R., III — 69
Fulgham, Alonzo — 522
Fuller, Patricia — 375
Fulton, Scott — 366
Furgione, Laura — 129
Furth, David — 382

G

Gade, Mary A — 371
Gaffney, Glenn A. — 476
Gagne, Martha — 94
Gainer, Terrance — 25
Gajarsa, Arthur J. — 71
Gallagher, Carolyn Lewis — 534
Gallagher, Michael F. — 300
Gallagher, Michael G. — 514
Gallagher, Patrick D. — 129
Gallaway, Chuck — 226
Galligan, William — 535
Gallo, Carmine — 313
Galloway, Patricia D. — 461
Gallup, Bryan — 286
Gallups, Vivian B. — 352
Gambatesa, Donald A. — 523
Gambino, Philip A. — 514
Gambrell, Donna — 328
Gandji, Sheila — 352
Gangloff, Joseph E. — 478
Gans, Michael Ellis — 70
Gant, Jon — 231
Garcia, Ernest E. — 501
Garcia, Frances — 47
Garcia, Lisa — 98
Garcia, Rick — 50
Garcia, Ruben — 512
Gardella, Wayne L. — 377
Gardiner, Pamela J. — 329
Gardner, Janice — 328
Gardner, Leland L. — 309
Gardner, Nadina — 447
Garibaldi, Vielka — 362
Garland, Merrick B. — 67
Garner, Rodger — 526
Garner, Terri — 436
Garnett, Patsy A. — 489
Garratt, David — 225
Garvelink, William J. — 300
Garver, Lori B. — 425
Gary, Arthur E. — 237
Garza, Carlos R. — 560
Garza, David T. — 454
Garza, Emilio M. — 69
Gaskell, Judith — 65
Gaspard, Patrick H. — 86
Gast, Earl — 522, 526
Gates, M. Catherine — 351
Gates, Robert M. — 90, 146, 440, 561
Gaudio, Rocco — 362
Gaziano, Todd — 527
Gearan, Mark D. — 362
Gedmin, Jeffrey — 353
Gee, King W. — 305
Geisel, Harold W. — 289
Geiser, David — 203
Geithner, Timothy F. — 53, 90, 327, 489
Genachowski, Julius — 382
Gensler, Gary — 356
Genz, Michael — 543
George, J. Russell — 327
George, Jonathan — 203
Geren, Preston M. — 161
Germain, Danielle M. — 415
German, Bobby — 426

Gerstenlauer, James P. — 71
Gerstenmaier, William — 426
Gessell, Gail — 511
Gestrin, Joan — 277
Getter, James — 43
Gfoeller, Tatiana — 300
Giambalvo, John — 352
Giannasi, Robert A. — 452
Giannoni-Jackson, Deborah — 535
Gibbons, Julia Smith — 69
Gibbons, Larry — 456
Gibbons, Mary Anne — 535
Gibbs, Robert L. — 86
Gibbs Thibodeau, Sharon — 434
Gibson, Calvin — 306
Gibson, Ventris C. — 305
Gidner, Jerold — 237
Gigante, Corrado — 376
Gildea, James E. — 530
Gildenhorn, Joseph B. — 547
Gill, Clair — 546
Gill, John — 91
Gillan, Kayla J. — 496
Gillette, Merri Jo — 500
Gilligan, Margaret — 305
Gilligan, William — 536
Gilliland, Thomas — 518
Gilman, Ronald Lee — 69
Gilmore, J. Michael — 60
Gilmore, Keith I. — 398
Gilpin, Raymond — 561
Gingrich, John R. — 343
Ginsburg, Douglas H. — 67
Ginsburg, Ruth Bader — 65, 68
Gips, Donald H. — 86
Girod, Olivier A. — 50
Girton, Maribeth — 282
Giuliano, Louis J. — 534
Giusti, John — 382
Glackin, Mary M. — 129
Glaser, Danny — 328
Glass, Brent — 546
Glasser, Stephen M. — 454
Glassman, Mitchell L. — 388
Glassman, Stuart — 282
Glauber, Joseph — 104
Glenn-Croft, Mary E. — 514
Glickman, Rhoda — 362
Glisson, Patricia — 376
Glunz, Christine — 89
Godec, Robert F. — 301
Goggin, Jim — 525
Gold, Wayne R. — 454
Goldberg, Gilbert — 511
Goldberg, Steven — 466
Goldman, Arthur E. — 426
Goldowitz, Israel — 490
Goldsmith, Stephen — 362
Goldway, Ruth Y. — 492
Gomez, Anna M. — 129
Gomez, Gabriella — 194
Gonzales, Milton — 286
Gonzalez, Elena — 238
Gonzalez, Manuel — 512
Gonzalez, Wilfredo — 511
Goodwin, Robert G., Jr. — 321
Goodwin, Roderick — 60
Goolsbee, Austan D. — 89
Goolsby, Charles — 352
Gorcowski, Susan — 306
Gordon, Leonard — 414
Gordon, Robert — 92
Gordon, Robert M. — 238
Goren, Nicola — 362
Gorenflo, Mark — 344
Gortney, William E. — 172
Gorusch, Neil M. — 70

Goss, Stephen C. — 513
Gottemoeller, Rose — 289
Gottlieb, Michael K. — 94
Gottschalk, Irving E. — 455
Goughnour, Richard — 525
Gould, Michael C. — 160
Gould, Ronald M. — 70
Gould, W. Scott — 343
Gover, Kevin — 546
Graber, Richard W. — 300
Graber, Susan P. — 70
Grace, Donna — 352
Graf, Robin G. — 421
Graham, Michael B. — 561
Graham, Wilmer — 490
Granat, Rochelle — 327
Grandier, Howard J. — 75
Grandmaison, J. Joseph — 377
Grant, David — 330
Grappo, Gary — 300
Graves, Margie — 225
Graves, William — 518
Gray, Andrew S. — 389
Gray, John — 129
Gray, Michael — 568
Gray, Richard — 286
Gray, Vincent C. — 440
Gray, William E. — 514
Greczmiel, Horst — 89
Green, Leonard — 69
Green, Lorraine A. — 459
Greenberg, John H. — 490
Greene, Kimberly S. — 518
Greene, Richard E. — 371
Greenert, Jonathan W. — 172
Greenfield, Deborah — 273
Greer, Chris — 97
Greer, John J. — 530
Gregoire, Courtney O. — 127
Gregory, Karen V. — 398
Gregory, Roger L — 68
Greiner, Patricia M. — 330
Gresham, Dana — 304
Gresham, Ed — 286
Griffin, Christine M. — 372
Griffin, Richard A. — 69
Griffis, Kevin — 127
Griffith, Thomas B. — 67
Griffith, Vincent — 186
Griffiths, José-Marie — 461
Grigsby, Sharlyn — 238
Grimes, John G. — 147
Grimm, Robert — 362
Grippo, Gary — 328
Griswold, Deborah — 235
Groeneveld, David B. — 282
Groff, Peter — 194
Grosner, Brian — 366
Grosof, Eric — 466
Gruenberg, Martin J. — 388
Gruender, Raymond W. — 70
Guay, Jon — 286
Guerin, William J. — 416
Gulari, Esin — 461
Gunderson, Richard — 225
Gunlicks, James B. — 161
Gur-Arie, Mira — 79
Gustafson, David — 489
Gustafson, Richard — 184
Gute, William — 323
Guthridge, Clay G. — 398
Guthrie, Carol — 99
Guthrie, Priscilla — 476
Guzman, Augusto — 137
Guzzetti, Jeff — 466
Gwinn, Nancy E. — 547
Gwynn, Judith — 530

H

Habersham, Myrtle S. — 394
Hackett, Edwin M. — 470
Hackett, James T. — 405
Hadden, Carlton M. — 372
Hadley, Mark P. — 60
Haeyman, David — 225
Hagans, Bennie L. — 490
Hage, Curtis L. — 406
Hagenbeck, Franklin L. — 162
Hagerty, Mark A. — 410
Haggstrom, Glenn D. — 343
Haghighat, Nader — 385
Hagin, Helen — 308
Hairston, Darryl — 504
Hakes, Jay E. — 436
Halbert, Gary — 466
Hale, Robert F. — 146
Hall, Garry — 192
Hall, Keith — 273
Hall, Peter W. — 68
Hall, Sophia H. — 560
Hall, Thomas — 286
Hall, Tony P. — 301
Hall, Walt — 276
Hall-Craig, Marcia — 375
Hallman, Janet M. — 494
Hallmark, Shelby — 273
Hallock, Michael — 305
Ham, Carter F. — 162
Hamburg, Margaret — 213
Hamilton, Jill — 307
Hamilton, John — Jr.
Hamilton, Lee H. — 547
Hammond, Tony — 492
Hampel, Karen J. — 416
Hancher, Kimberly — 372
Handley, James C. — 421
Hanes, Patricia — 137
Haney, Tim — 535
Hanley, John — 489
Hanna, Richard — 282
Hannan, Maureen — 405
Hanratty, Dennis — 53
Hanretta, Kevin — 344
Hanson, Ellen D. — 309
Harbour, Pamela Jones — 410
Hardiman, Joseph — 376
Hardiman, Thomas M. — 68
Hardt, Brent — 299, 300, 301
Hardy, Thomas R. — 519
Harnish, Reno L., III — 289
Harper, Sallyanne — 47
Harris, Brenda Valentine — 452
Harris, Catherine — 547
Harris, Donald — 395
Harris, Harry B., Jr. — 171
Harris, Ondray T. — 253
Harris, Scott Blake — 203
Harris, Scott S. — 05
Harris, Seth D. — 273
Harris, William T. — 50
Hart, Christopher A. — 466
Hart, John M. — 440
Hartman, Dan — 309
Hartz, Harris L. — 70
Harvey, John C., Jr. — 171
Harvey, Michael — 526
Harwood, Charles A. — 414
Hastings, James — 434
Hastings, Robert L. — 147
Hasvold, Laurence A. — 316
Hattix, Larry — 329
Haueter, Thomas E. — 466
Haugen, Steve — 280
Hawes, William M. — 426

Hawke, Daniel M. — 500
Hawkens, E. Roy — 470
Hawkins, Karen L. — 330
Hawkins, Michael Daly — 70
Hawkins, Patricia M. — 301
Hayashi, Minoru N. — 454
Hayes, David — 237
Hayes, Denise — 104
Hayes, John L. — 129
Haykin, Stephen — 525
Haynes, Catharina — 69
Hayward, Mark — 511
Haze, Pamela K. — 238
Headley, Michael — 546
Healy, Timothy C. — 535
Hecht, William F. — 405
Heckmann, Cynthia C. — 47
Hecox, Doug R. — 305
Heddell, Gordon S. — 147, 273
Hedgespeth, Grady — 503
Hefferan, Colien — 103
Heilman, Chandra — 546
Hellert, William E. — 378
Helleyer, Robert — 526
Hellman, Karl — 187
Heltzer, Lester A. — 452
Henderson, Karen LeCraft — 67
Hennemuth, Jeffrey A. — 75
Henningsen, Jacqueline R. — 156
Henriquez, Sandra B. — 231
Henry, Robert H. — 70
Henry, Sudafi — 88
Hensley, Willie L. — 344
Herbol, Denise — 526
Herbold, Patricia Louise — 301
Herbst, Ellen — 127, 129
Heriot, Gail — 527
Herman, Steven — 53
Hermanson, John — 283
Hernandez, Jorge — 353
Herrington, Mikel — 362
Hershey, Cheryl — 307
Hersman, Deborah A.P. — 466
Hess, Karl — 461
Heybey, Berta M. — 485
Heydemann, Steven — 561
Hickey, Robert A. — 392
Hicks, Alan T. — 321
Hicks, Kathleen — 146
Higginbotham, Karen D. — 368
Higginbottom, Heather A. — 96
Higgins, Heather — 286
Higgins, James — 385
Higgins, John E., Jr. — 452
Hight, Elizabeth — 184
Hightower, Dennis F. — 127
Hilburn, Roger — 280
Hildebrandt, Betsey J. — 237
Hilding, Suzanne E. — 127
Hill, Daniel O. — 127
Hill, Keith — 376
Hill, Vern W. — 398
Hill, Walter, Jr. — 377
Hilliard, Karen — 526
Hillier, Michael — 519
Hillman, Richard J. — 47
Hillson, Marc — 104
Himelfarb, Sheldon — 561
Hindman, Ronald L. — 435
Hines, Anson H. — 547
Hines, Billy — 322
Hines, Debra — 331
Hinkhouse, Paul — 286
Hinojosa, Ricardo H. — 80
Hire, Elisabeth — 88
Hirsch, Pat — 368
Hirschberg, D. Jeffrey — 352

Hoagland, Richard — 300
Hoban-Moore, Pat — 235
Hodge, David — 97
Hodge, James L. — 162
Hodge, Michelle — 281
Hodges, Jennifer — 422
Hoefer, Michael — 225
Hoenig, Thomas M. — 405
Hoffman, Alan — 88
Hoffman, Donald J. — 158
Hoffman, Elizabeth — 461
Hoffman, Patricia — 203
Hoffman, William J. — 379
Hogan, Cynthia — 88
Hoglander, Harry R. — 456
Hogue, Robert D. — 173
Hohenstein, William — 104
Hoidal, Chris — 323
Holden, Richard — 285
Holder, Cornel A. — 186
Holder, Eric — 253
Holdren, John — 97
Holian, Thomas P., III — 305
Holladay, Jon — 104
Holliday, Scott — 344
Hollis, Tricia — 492
Holmes, Jerome A. — 70
Honnoll, Liz A. — 362
Hontz, Karen — 504
Hood, Rodney E. — 441
Hooks, Craig E. — 368
Hooks, Ronald K. — 455
Hope, Brian — 368
Hopewell, Luz — 503
Horbaly, Jan — 71
Horn, Joseph A., Jr. — 188
Horne, Timothy — 421
Horner, John — 359
Horowitz, Barnett — 454
Horowitz, Michael E. — 80
Hortiz, Joseph W., Jr. — 286
Hoskin, Charles T. — 454
Hostetler, Margaret A. — 514
Houck, James W. — 170, 172
Houle, David — 286
House, Joseph — 490
Houston, Tina — 436
Howard, Jeffrey R. — 68
Howard, Tom — 426
Howell, Beryl A. — 80
Howell, Chuck — 526
Howell, Robert J. — 359
Hsing, Helen — 48
Hubbel, Daniel L. — 454
Huber, Keith M. — 162
Huff, Preston — 435
Hughes, John M. — 75
Hughes, Lisa Bobbie Schreiber — 301
Hughes, Miriam K. — 300
Hull, Frank Mays — 71
Hum, Carolyn — 520
Hume, Cameron R. — 300
Hummer, John — 321
Hunter, Caroline — 392
Hunter, Denise — 47
Hunter, Glenn S., Jr. — 416
Hunter, Robert P. — 397
Huntley, Kim — 186
Huntoon, David H. — 161
Huntoon, Ivan — 323
Hurdle, Lana — 304
Hurley, Charles — 306
Hurst, Kevin — 97
Hurvcombe, Helen M. — 127
Hurwitz, T. Alan — 201
Huso, Ravic Rolf — 300
Hutter, Victoria — 445

Hwang, Tommy — 423
Hyatt, Amy J. — 300
Hyland, Gigi — 441
Hylton, Stacia — 254
Hynes, James J. — 405

I

Iannicola, Dan — 327
Ice, Jerry — 125
Iglehart, John — 137
Im, Hyepin — 362
Inglis, John C. — 189
Ingram, Sarah H. — 330
Insulza, José Miguel — 569
Intrepidi, Lynn — 276
Inzeo, Nicholas — 372
Isaac, Linda — 486
Isakowitz, Steven J. — 203
Isherwood, Dorothy A. — 494
Ishimaru, Stuart J. — 372
Israel, Kenneth D., Jr. — 500
Iudicello, Fay — 237
Iyengar, Sunil — 445

J

Jackson, Alfonso — 137
Jackson, Frederick R. — 344
Jackson, Geoffrey — 519
Jackson, Herbert — 50
Jackson, Lisa — 366
Jackson, Sharon F. — 425
Jackson, Shirley Ann — 545
Jacob, Andrew D. — 379
Jacobs, Bob — 426
Jacobs, Dennis G. — 68
Jacobs, Janice L. — 289
Jacobs, Joanna M. — 253
Jacobs, Nicki — 445
Jacobs, Stephen — 128
Jacobs-Simmons, Lenita — 279
Jacobson, Tracey — 301
Jaczko, Gregory B. — 470
Jaffe, Ira F. — 289
Jagadesan, Dev — 485
James, Kathleen — 452
James, Ronald J. — 161
James, Tawana Y. — 443
Jarrett, H. Marshall — 253
Jarrett, Valerie B. — 87
Jarvinen, Matthew — 397
Javey, Wilma L. — 375
Jedrey, Chris — 426
Jefferson, Deborah — 127
Jefferson, Frances — 277
Jeffress, Charles — 543
Jeffries, Richard R. — 173
Jenkins, Jo Ann C. — 53
Jennings, Kevin — 194
Jennis, Wendy — 75
Jenson, Nancy — 282
Jenson, William G. — 104
Jeu, Joseph H. — 416
Jew, Robert — 431
Jewell, Linda — 300
Jewell, Tommy — 560
Jodice, Ralph J., II — 160
Joel, Alexander W. — 476
John, Richard — 308
Johns, Raymond E., Jr. — 156
Johnson, Bart — 226
Johnson, Bruce N., Sr. — 400
Johnson, Christy — 97
Johnson, Christyl — 425
Johnson, Collister, Jr. — 307
Johnson, Crisanta — 280

Johnson, David — 290
Johnson, Deborah — 308
Johnson, Delia L. — 352
Johnson, Donald C. — 300
Johnson, Esther R. — 273
Johnson, Jeh Charles — 147, 185
Johnson, Jennifer J. — 405
Johnson, Kristina — 203
Johnson, Mary — 456
Johnson, Peter O. — 329
Johnson, Rodney L. — 161, 162
Johnson, Samuel — 545
Johnson, Scott — 329
Johnson, Stephen E. — 172
Johnston, Herbert — 512
Johnston, Michelle — 512
Jolly, E. Grady — 69
Jones, Anthony — 89
Jones, Auvonett — 445
Jones, Deborah K. — 300
Jones, Edith Hollan — 69
Jones, Gary — 172
Jones, James — 368
Jones, James L., Jr. — 86, 90
Jones, John Melvin — 300
Jones, Kevin — 187, 253
Jones, Mickey J. — 286
Jones, Paul — 290
Jones, Richard S. — 397
Jones, Taylor E., II — 307
Jones, Witmer — 511
Jones-Brown, Patrease — 378
Jordan, Jon A. — 416
Jordan, Joseph — 504
Jordan, Kent A. — 68
Jordan, Mary Lucille — 402
Joseph, Arthur S. — 425
Joseph, Gloria J. — 452
Josserand, Michael W. — 455
Juarez, Joseph C. — 279
Judson, Richard — 431
Jukes, James J. — 92

K

Kaberuka, Donald — 565
Kaczmarczyk, Stanley F. — 416, 417
Kadeli, Lek — 368
Kaepplein, Kristi J. — 496
Kagan, Elena — 253
Kahn, Thomas K. — 71
Kaidanow, Tina S. — 300
Kaiser, Michael M. — 547
Kaloi, Kaiini — 238
Kaminski, Todd — 286
Kane, Allen — 546
Kang, C.S. Eliot — 289
Kanne, Michael S. — 69
Kanoff, Marjorie — 47
Kanovsky, Helen R. — 231
Kanter, Martha — 194
Kaplan, Elaine — 479
Kaplan, Robin F. — 513
Kapos, Ervin — 226
Karesh, Lewis — 99
Karrh, Thomas M. — 286
Kasun, Katherine P. — 192
Kato, Takatoshi — 567
Kavanaugh, Brett M. — 67
Kavanaugh, David — 328
Kawa, Patrick — 280
Kay, Donna — 276
Kay, Jonathan — 280
Kayyem, Juliette — 225
Kea, Arleas Upton — 388
Keable, Edward — 237
Kearney, Barry J. — 452

Kearney, Stephen — 535
Keating, Timothy J. — 151
Keefer, Timothy J. — 226
Keegan, Richard J. — 426
Keen, Stanley E. — 276
Kehler, Robert C. — 158
Keith, Frank M. — 330
Keller, Burl — 44
Keller, Steve L. — 343
Kelly, Ian — 290
Kelly, J. Michael — 104
Kelly, Jennifer C. — 329
Kelly, John — 362
Kelly, Patricia — 490
Kelly, Paul J., Jr. — 70
Kelly, Suedeen G. — 204
Kelly, Thomas E., III — 161
Kelvington, Areon — 286
Kempf, Steven J. — 416
Kendall, Mary — 237
Kenealy, Timi E. — 352
Kennedy, Anthony M. — 65, 70
Kennedy, Brian — 273
Kennedy, Jeff — 468, 469
Kennedy, Kerry — 561
Kennedy, Louis — 286
Kennedy, Patrick F. — 289
Kennedy-Iraheta, Debbie — 523
Kennelly, Mary Estelle — 450
Kenney, Justin — 129
Kenney, Kristie A. — 301
Kent, Carlton — 172
Kent, Marthe — 283
Kentov, Rochelle — 454
Kepplinger, Gary L. — 47
Kerlikowske, R. Gil — 94
Kerr, T. Michael — 273
Kerry, Cameron F. — 127
Kerwin, Mary D. — 426
Kessler, Alan C. — 534
Kethledge, Raymond M. — 69
Kever, Jerome F. — 493
Khan, Ikram U. — 561
Khuzami, Robert — 496
Ki-moon, Ban — 570
Kian, Bijan R. — 377
Kichak, Nancy H. — 479
Kicza, Mary E. — 129
Kiel, Gerald — 375
Kientiz, Roy — 304
Kikla, Rich — 226
Kilbane, Grace A. — 279
Kile, Joseph — 60
Kiley, Bradley J. — 87
Kilgore, Tom D. — 518
Killeen, Timothy L. — 461
Killette, Delores — 535
Kilner, Scott F. — 299
Kimbell, Abigail — 103
Kimmons, John F. — 476
Kinard, Martha — 454
King, Carolyn Dineen — 69
King, June — 456
King, Letitia — 352
King, Loretta — 253
King, Paula — 561
King, Peter J. — 398
King, Robert B — 68
Kingsbury, Nancy — 47
Kingsley, Linda — 535
Kinsey, Mark — 394
Kipen, David — 445
Kipsen, Janet — 282
Kirby, Michael D. — 300
Kireilis, Althea — 91
Kirk, Ronald — 98
Kirkland, James Ray — 526

Kirsanow, Peter — 527
Kirsch, Kevin — 226
Kissko, James A. — 514
Klain, Ron — 88
Klein, Aaron — 327
Klein, Dale E. — 470
Kleinfeld, Andrew J. — 70
Kleinman, Samuel D. — 146
Klemm, Hans G. — 300
Kluge, John W. — 53
Klurfeld, Jeffrey A. — 414
Klurfeld, Roger J. — 104
Knapp, Julius — 382
Knapp, Lindy — 304
Knipling, Edward B. — 103
Knoblock, Carl — 512
Knott, Jay — 526
Kobayashi, Izumi — 569
Koch, Cynthia M. — 436
Kocsi, James — 512
Kodalen, Keith — 186
Kodlick, Les A. — 156
Koestler, Robert — 547
Kogod, Robert P. — 545
Koh, Harold — 289
Kohlenberger, Jim — 97
Kohn, Donald L. — 404
Koizumi, Kei — 97
Kolb, Ingrid — 203
Kolko, Linda B. — 422
Kolly, Joseph — 466
Konove, Elissa K. — 305
Konwinski, Lisa M. — 87
Koonin, Steven — 203
Koopman, Robert B. — 530
Kopec, John — 329
Koppel, Rosa M. — 395
Kores, Katherine — 375
Koromilas, Alec J. — 273
Kort, John — 103
Kosciow, Walter — 377
Koshalek, Richard — 546
Kosiak, Steve — 92
Koster, Julia A. — 441
Kotz, H. David — 497
Kouts, Christopher A. — 203
Kovacic, William E. — 410
Kovar, Peter — 231
Kozinski, Alex — 70
Krakora, Nicole L. — 546
Krakowski, Henry P. — 304
Kramer, Alan — 434
Kramlich, Richard — 172
Kratzke, Stephen R. — 306
Kraus, Joseph — 47
Kress, Carl B. — 519
Krewson, Caroline H. — 235
Kris, David — 253
Kritz, Neil J. — 561
Kroeker, James L. — 497
Krohmer, Jon R. — 226
Kroloff, Noah — 225
Kronopolus, Cathleen C. — 416
Krueger, Alan B. — 327
Kuehl, David E. — 435
Kuester, Michele A. — 378
Kulik, Robert — 283
Kundra, Vivek — 92
Kurin, Richard — 546
Kuroda, Haruhiko — 565
Kurtz, Michael J. — 431
Kurtz, William — 50
Kushner, Peter — 44
Kusnitz, Len — 301
Kusumoto, Sandra L. — 398
Kutz, Gregory D. — 47

L

La'Cour, Erika — 376
Laackman, Allyson — 91
LaBelle, James — 469
LaCanfora, Mariana E. — 514
LaChance, Susan — 535
Lacker, Jeffery M. — 405
Lacquement, David P. — 162
LaFleur, Christopher J. — 300
Lafreniere, Steven — 309
LaHood, Ray — 304, 459
Lake, Richard — 173
Lalumiere, Frank — 503
Lambright, James H. — 377
Landau, Ted — 525
Landefeld, J. Steven — 128
Lander, Eric — 97
Landesman, Rocco — 445
Landry, Marc — 337
Lane, Charlotte R. — 529
Lane, Jerry — 535
Laney-Cummings, Karen — 530
Lang, Catherine M. — 304
Langer, Mark J. — 67
Langford, Dale — 286
Langford, Timothy — 476
Langley, Nanci E. — 492
Lanphear, Thomas J. — 425
Lanzerotti, Louis J. — 461
Lappin, Harley G. — 253
Larkin, Dennis — 512
Lartigue, Laura — 486
Laseter, Cindy Coe — 283
Latorraca, Rebecca — 525
Laudato, George — 522
Laurent, Janet St. — 47
Laux, Thomas — 171
Lavigne, Carrie — 307
Lavigne, Thomas A. — 307
Lavoy, Peter — 476
Lawler, Patrick J. — 394
Lawrence, Michael — 352
Lawrence, Susan — 162
Leach, Jim — 447
Leach, Richard A. — 170
Leahy, Patrick J. — 545
LeBaron, Joseph — 301
LeBlanc, Diane — 435
LeBlanc, Mike — 97
LeBlanc, Stephen G. — 50
Lebryk, David A. — 329
Lee, Charles — 282
Lee, David A. — 394
Leech, John — 226
Lefevre, Maria S. — 50
Leheny, Robert — 181
Lehman, Ronald — 281
Lehman, William J. — 75
Leibowitz, Jonathan — 410
Lein-Hayes, Candace — 435
Leins, Douglas — 561
Leiss, Wayne G. — 331
Leistikow, Dan — 203
Leiter, Michael — 476
Lekson, Michael — 561
Lemaitre, Rafael — 95
Lemkin, Bruce S. — 156
Lennon, John — 352
Lennon, Marie — 352
Leonard, Joe — 104
Leonard, Judith E. — 546
Leonard, Rachael — 97
Leonard, Robert — 444
Leone, Kelly — 308
Leonhart, Michele — 254
Lerner, Patricia — 526

Lerner, Robert — 527
Lesher, Jan — 225
Leshner, Alan I. — 461
Leslie, John W. — 351
Lesnick, H. Keith — 307
Lesnick, Robert J. — 402
Lettice, Paula — 44
Levey, Stuart — 328
Levine, Lynn — 530
Levinson, Daniel R. — 212
Levonian, Mark — 329
Levy, David W. — 441
Lew, Ginger — 503
Lew, Jacob J. — 289
Lewis, Lemuel E. — 405
Lewis, Paula — 305
Lewis, Paulette N. — 277
Lewis, Robert N. — 313
Lewis, Spencer H., Jr. — 376
Ley, Jane S. — 478
Ley, Rhonda P. — 454
Leyser, Catherine A. — 494
Libbey, Ted — 445
Lichte, Arthur J. — 158
Lidinsky, Richard A., Jr. — 398
Lidz, Theodore J. — 75
Lieber, Margery E. — 452
Lieberman, Evelyn — 546
Lieberman, Joseph I. — 440
Liebman, Jeffrey — 92
Liebman, Wilma B. — 451
Lightbourne, James H. — 461
Lightfoot, David W. — 461
Lightfoot, Robert M. — 426
Lightner, J. Michael — 455
Limon, Raymond — 362
Linden, Gary — 526
Lindley, Jeffrey A. — 305
Lindsey, S. Mark — 306
Lindsley, Margaret A. — 493
Lineback, Rik — 455
Linn, Richard — 71
Linnertz, Ann — 306
Linscott, Mark — 98
Lintner, W. James, Jr. — 199
Linton, Mark — 231
Lipez, Kermit V. — 68
Lippert, Mark W. — 87
Lipscomb, Gene — 235
Lipscomb, Sara — 503
Lipsitz, Rochelle — 128
Lipsky, John — 567
Lipstein, Steven H. — 405
Lira, Jose A. — 273
Liser, Florie — 98
Litt, Robert S. — 476
Littles, Nadine — 454
Liu, Libby — 353
Livingood, Wilson L. — 25
Livingston, Debra Ann — 68
Livingston, Karl J. — 307
Llewellyn, Stephen — 372
LoBue, Nancy — 305
Lock, Betty — 277
Locke, Gary F. — 127, 489
Lockhart, Dennis P. — 405
Loddo, Joseph — 504
Loeb, Richard C. — 473
Loesche, Robert K. — 75
Loewentritt, Lennard S. — 415
Loftin, Melinda J. — 237
Loftus, Lee — 253
Loken, James B. — 69
Long, Gregory T. — 409
Long, John E., Jr. — 518
Long, Letitia A. — 185
Long, Timothy M. — 329

Loose, Michael K. — 171
Lopatkiewicz, Ted — 466
Lopez, Mara — 372
Lorenz, Stephen R. — 158
Lorenzini, Amy — 519
Loria, Dennis — 385
Lotz, R. David — 282
Louis, Noreen St. — 519
Louizou, Thomas M. — 318
Lourie, Alan D. — 71
Love, Melinda — 443
Love, William — 466
Lovelace, Gail T. — 415
Lovelace, James J. — 162
Lowder, Michael — 304
Lowe, Stanley — 410
Lu, Christopher P. — 86
Lubchenco, Jane — 128
Lucero, Carlos F. — 70
Lucero, Luis — 376
Luckern, Paul J. — 529
Luedtke, Thomas S. — 425
Lujan, Kenneth — 512
Lupovitz, Joni — 410
Lute, Jane Holl — 225
Luten, Drew — 523
Lyden, Michael J. — 172
Lyle, Beverly — 277
Lynch, Lisa M. — 405
Lynch, Sandra L. — 68
Lynn, William, III — 146
Lyons, James M. — 530

M

Ma, Ana — 503
MacDonald, Bruce — 170
MacDonald, W. Larry — 328
Mach, L. Frank — 321
MacIntosh, Robert — 466
Macklin, Renee — 128
MacSpadden, Lisa N. — 441
Macy, Richard — 490
Maddox, Clarence G., II — 69
Maddox, John — 306
Madigan, Brian — 405, 406
Madison, George W. — 327
Madzelan, Daniel T. — 194
Maes, Denise — 91
Magladry, Bruce — 466
Magyar, Theresa — 282
Maher, Jessica — 89
Maher, Shawn P. — 87
Mahoney, James A., Jr. — 377
Mahoney, Kevin E. — 479
Maier, Harold — 454
Malecki, Eva — 43
Mallett, Bruce S. — 470
Malphrus, Stephen R. — 405
Mancini, Nadine N. — 473
Manclark, John T. — 156
Manfreda, John — 328
Mange, Robert — 336
Manning, David — 318
Manning, Timothy — 225
Manno, Claudia — 305
Mansfield, John E. — 366
Mansour, Christopher — 237
Manuel, Brenda R. — 425
Manza, Edythe — 447
Marantis, Demetrios — 98
Marchbanks, Georgia — 375
Marcum, Deanna — 53
Marcus, Stanley — 71
Margolis, Andrew — 400
Maria Costa, Antonio — 570
Marin, Paul — 519

Marine, Michael W. — 301
Markison, Marlene — 306
Marmolejo, Linda — 137
Marmolejos, Poli A. — 203
Maroni, Alice C. — 546
Marquardt, R. Niles — 300
Marquette, Margaret — 329
Marquez, Mercedes M. — 231
Marquez, Pascal — 254
Marquis, David M. — 443
Marrero, Francisco — 511
Marrett, Cora B. — 461
Marsh, William — 352
Marshall, C. Douglas — 454
Marshall, Era — 546
Marshall, Rebecca — 280
Marshall, Thurgood, Jr. — 534
Marsteller, William A. — 377
Martin, Boyce F., Jr. — 69
Martin, Carmel — 194
Martin, Doris Mason — 351
Martin, Pam — 487
Martinez, Adair — 344
Martinez, Kathleen — 273, 561
Martinez, Steve E. — 454
Marx, Michele C. — 95
Mas, Alexandre — 273
Mascetti, Rom — 344
Mastromonaco, Alyssa M. — 86
Masuda, Alan — 305
Mather, Chris — 104
Mathiasen, Karen — 328
Mathieu, Gail Dennise — 300
Matsuda, David — 304
Matsui, Doris — 545
Matthewman, Robin — 301
Mattiello, Jonathan — 560
Mattina, Celeste J. — 454
Mattis, James N. — 151
Mauk, Rosie — 487
Mauldin, Angela — 286
Maxfield, Linda D. — 513
Maxwell, Lois — 282
Maxwell, Raymond D. — 301
May, Kennie — 309
Maybus, Raymond E. — 170
Mayer, Eileen — 330
Mayer, Haldane Robert — 71
Maynes, Barry — 447
Mayock, Andrew — 327
Mazer, Roslyn A. — 476
Mazur, Mark J. — 330
McAdams, John A. — 377
McBride, David D. — 426
McCabe, Cathy — 368
McCabe, Peter G. — 75
McCaffery, Benjamin — 286
McCallum, Robert M. — 299
McCammon, Thomas — 376
McCarter, John W., Jr. — 545
McCarthy, Natasha — 377
McCarver, Bill — 186
McCauley, Judy — 512
McClenney, Lucretia — 343
McClintock, Peter — 503
McCloud, Edith J. — 128
McCluskey, Sue — 395
McCollum, William R., Jr. — 518
McConnell, Michael W. — 70
McConnell, Mitch — 25
McCord, Craig M., Sr. — 445
McCord, Michael A. — 402
McCord, Michael J. — 147
McCormick, William Paul — 300, 301
McCoy, Kevin M. — 172
McCoy, Kimberly A. — 331
McCoy, Stanford — 99

McCullom, Ellen — 337
McCullough, Bernard — 171
McCully, Ruth — 368
McDaniel, Dean — 283
McDermott, James J. — 455
McDonald, Michael — 447
McDonnell, Erin M. — 484
McDonnell, Roger P. — 514
McDonough, Denis R. — 87
McDowell, Robert M. — 382
McDowell, Vicky — 328
McFarland, Lynne A. — 392
McFarland, Patrick E. — 479
McFarland, Stephen — 300
McGahn, Donald F., II — 392
McGaw, Bridger — 225
McGee, James D. — 301
McGibbon, Shawne — 503
McGill, Rebecca A. — 307
McGinn, Gail H. — 146
McGinnis, David L. — 146
McGinnis, Roger — 226
McGiverin, Arthur — 560
McGlaughlin, Pat — 171
McGowan, Kristine — 385
McGrath, Toby — 503
McGuire-Rivera, Bernadette A. — 129
McHale, Alvina A. — 329
McHugh, Joseph H. — 459
McInerney, Roberta — 388
McIssac, Karen — 300
McKay, Teresa A. — 184
McKeague, David W. — 69
McKechnie, John J., III — 441
McKee, Theodore A. — 68
McKeever, Jean E. — 307
McKenna, Jack — 282
McKenzie, Thomas G. — 379
McKeon, Robert F. — 321
McKeown, M. Margaret — 70
McKinley, Craig R. — 156, 161
McKinley, P. Michael — 301
McKinney, M. Kathleen — 454
McKinney, Robert C. — 385
McKinny, John — 286
McLaughlin, Brian — 306
McLaughlin, Stephen — 530
McLaurin, Hugh M. — 359
McLean, Donna — 459
McLellan, A. Thomas — 94
McMahon, Linda S. — 514
McMenamin, Rebecca — 352
McMullen, Ronald K. — 300
McMurray, Rose A. — 309
McNabb, Duncan J. — 151
McNair, Jacqueline — 375
McNair, John W., Jr. — 170
McNally, Alison — 546
McNally, Bill — 426
McNamara, Keith — 559
McNamara, Ken — 526
McNamara, Phil — 226
McNamara, Thomas E. — 476
McNulty, David — 286
McPhie, Neil A.G. — 423
McQueary, Charles E. — 147
McQuistion, Patricia E. — 186
McSwain, Kristin — 362
McSweeney, Denis S. — 285
McSweeney, James — 435
McSweeny, Terrell — 88
Medford, Ronald — 306
Medveckis, John — 53
Mehra, Pritha — 535
Meiburg, Stan — 371
Meisburg, Ronald — 452
Meldonian, Ron — 183

Melendez, Arlan D. — 527
Melendez, Rosa — 254
Melendez, Thelma — 194
Melloy, Michael J. — 70
Melson, Kenneth E. — 253
Melton, Dennis — 512
Meltzer, Daniel J. — 87
Memmolo, Frances — 282
Mendenhall, John — 414
Mendoza, Carlos G. — 512
Mendoza, Felipe — 415
Merrigan, Kathleen — 103
Merson, Melissa — 60
Mesenbourg, Thomas — 128
Meske, Jerry — 286
Messenger, Michael — 352
Messerschmidt, John G. — 172
Messina, James A. — 86
Messner, Kevin A. — 415, 416
Metts, Christopher — 313
Meyer, Ben — 50
Meyer, Eric — 328
Meyer, John — 543
Michael, Jeffrey — 306
Michael, M. Blane — 68
Michel, James — 522
Michel, Paul R. — 71
Michner, Michael — 103
Middlebrook, Craig H. — 307
Mihm, J. Christopher — 47
Milan, Noel — 447
Mildrew, Sean M. — 416
Miles, Richard — 301
Milholland, Terry V. — 330
Milks, Thomas E. — 182
Miller, Brian D. — 415
Miller, Daniel — 201
Miller, Douglas — 385
Miller, Elin D. — 371
Miller, James — 103
Miller, James C., II — 534
Miller, James N., Jr. — 146
Miller, Jillian L. — 445
Miller, Lorraine C. — 25
Miller, Matthew — 253
Miller, Michael H. — 170
Miller, Robert A. — 559
Miller, Robert E. — 440
Miller, Stephen J. — 160
Miller, Steven T. — 330
Miller, Tony — 194
Miller, Warren F., Jr. — 203
Millette, James — 290
Millies, Richard — 187
Milligan, Chris — 523
Millings, Bernadette — 306
Mills, Alberta — 359
Mills, Cheryl — 289
Mills, Karen — 503
Mills, Thomas E. -- 431
Milobar, Leon — 512
Milovanovic, Gillian Arlette — 300
Milstead, Robert E., Jr. — 173
Milton, Karen Greve — 68
Milton, Wanda — 375
Minarik, Peter — 529
Minear, Jeffrey P. — 65
Mingione, Emanuel J. — 400
Miniace, Joseph N. — 313
Minor, Larry — 309
Minor, Laura C. — 75
Minton, Mark Clements — 300
Mintz, Eric O. — 400
Miron, Deborah — 423
Miserendino, C. Richard. — 452
Mitchell, Anthony — 447
Mitchell, Herbert — 503

Mitchell, Sharon — 286
Mitchelson, Mary — 194
Mixon, Benjamin R. — 162
Moazed, Shirine — 484
Moeller, Philip D. — 204
Moffat, John — 318
Moffitt, G. Michael — 385
Mojica, Angel — 286
Moller, Patricia — 300
Moneck, Michael A. — 400
Monfort, Steven — 547
Monniere, Robert — 308
Monteith, Kris — 382
Montgomery, Kathy — 308
Montgomery, Pamela G. — 80
Montoya, Elizabeth — 479
Montpellier, Rick — 486
Moore, Julie S. — 534
Moore, Karen Nelson — 69
Moore, Kimberly — 71
Moore, Thomas H. — 359
Moore-Duncan, Dorothy L. — 454
Moose, George E. — 560
Morales, Hector E., Jr. — 290, 301
Morales, Susan — 282
Moran, Ellen — 127
Moran, Pamela-Jeanne — 410
More, Robert S. — 238
Moreno, Luis Alberto — 566
Moretz, Ashley — 526
Morey, Robin — 44
Morgan, Barry — 286
Morgan, Terri S. — 493
Moriarty, James — 300
Morin, Jamie M. — 156
Morin, Robert A. — 377
Morningstar, Jeff — 543
Morphy, Martha — 431
Morrill, Arthur B., III — 186
Morris, Rod — 485
Morris, Samuel J., III — 416
Morrison, Judith — 422
Morrow, Joyce E. — 161
Morrow, Sheryl — 329
Mortensen, Royal — 173
Morton, C. Keith — 444
Morton, John T. — 226
Mosley, Raymond A. — 431
Motz, Diana Gribbon — 68
Mousa, Jay — 285
Mower, Joan — 352
Moy, Edmund C. — 330
Mozena, Dan W. — 299
Mueller, Robert S., III — 253
Mueller, Tom — 511
Muffley, Gary — 454
Mulhollan, Daniel P. — 53
Mulholland, John F., Jr. — 162
Mulkey, Marcia — 368
Mullally, Kevin — 526
Mullan, John Gibson — 359
Mullen, Michael G. — 90, 147
Mulvey, Francis P. — 309
Mundaca, Michael — 327
Muñoz, Cecilia — 87
Munson, Alden — 476
Munsterman, Janice — 560
Munter, Cameron P. — 301
Murin, Joseph J. — 231
Muro, Steve L. — 343
Murphy, Bonnie — 316
Murphy, Catherine O. — 277
Murphy, Diana E. — 70
Murphy, Douglas R. — 313
Murphy, Elizabeth M. — 496
Murphy, James — 98
Murphy, James J. — 321

Murphy, Janet — 394
Murphy, Michael R. — 70
Murphy, Ronald D. — 398
Murphy, William — 103
Murray, Brenda P. — 497
Murray, Chris — 301
Murray, David W. — 95
Murray, Edward J. — 343
Murrett, Robert B. — 189
Murton, Arthur J. — 388
Mussatt, David — 529
Mussomeli, Joseph A. — 300
Muzio, David — 468
Myers, Arthur J. — 146
Myers, David R. — 316
Myers, Judith Diaz — 329
Myers, Larry — 447
Myles, Marianne M. — 300

N

Nabors, Robert — 92
Nadeau, Roger A. — 162
Naftali, Timothy — 436
Nagel, Kevin — 286
Nakano, Stanley — 512
Nandy, Jane — 525
Naples, Nancy — 459
Napolitano, Janet — 225
Nardella, Michelle — 376
Nash, Elson — 362
Nash, Paul — 388
Nastri, Wayne H. — 371
Natiello, Peter — 525
Ndiaye, Ndioro — 568
Neal, Jeff — 225
Nebbia, Karl — 129
Neely, James, Jr. — 376
Neely, Jeffrey E. — 421
Neimeyer, Charles P. — 173
Nelson, Charles E. — 561
Nelson, David — 289
Nelson, David P. — 500
Nelson, Ed — 183
Nelson, Linda — 512
Nelson, Robert — 511
Nembhard, Lois — 362
Nesbit, Jeff — 461
Nesbitt, Wanda L. — 300
Ness, Eric — 511
Nester, John — 496
Netherton, Charles R. — 286
Neuberger, Anne — 170
Neves, Carole P. — 546
Newberg, Richard — 526
Newell, Richard — 203
Newman, Gary — 280
Newman, Pauline — 71
Newton, Alexander — 526
Newton, Gary — 526
Newton, Richard Y., III — 156
Nield, George — 304
Niemeyer, Paul V. — 68
Nigro, Louis J., Jr. — 300
Nilsestuen, Wayne — 526
Nilsson, Kent — 382
Nisanci, Didem A. — 496
Noble, David L. — 425
Noel, Daniel W. — 385
Nolan, Elizabeth A. — 203
Nolan, Robert B. — 300
Nolan, Stephen J. — 300
Norby, Stephanie — 546
Nord, Nancy — 359
Norelli, Joseph P. — 454
Norland, Richard — 301
Northup, Anne — 359

Norville, Valerie — 561
Nottingham, Charles D. — 309
Nuland, Victoria — 301
Nussel, Gregory A. — 69
Nwachuku, Frances I. — 377

O

O'Boyle, Barbara A. — 377
O'Brien, Bill — 445
O'Brien, Michael F. — 425
O'Brien, Richard — 359
O'Brien, Terrence L. — 70
O'Carroll, Patrick P. — 514
O'Connor, Bryan — 426
O'Connor, Dennis — 330
O'Connor, Sandra A. — 559
O'Hare, Edward J. — 416
O'Laughlin, Margaret M. — 530
O'Malley, Kevin P. — 307
O'Neal, James — 512
O'Neill, Michelle — 128
O'Reilly, Patrick J. — 188
O'Scannlain, Diarmuid F. — 70
O'Sullivan, Kathleen — 309
O'Tormey, Walt — 535
Obama, Barack H. — 85, 90
Oberg, Elis Treidler — 566
Obie, Stephen — 356
Obsitnik, Vincent — 301
Odo, Franklin — 546
Ogden, David W. — 253
Ogden, J. Anthony — 50
Ohanesian, Nicholas — 454
Ohlson, Kevin A. — 253
Ojeda, Pennie — 445
Okun, Deanna Tanner — 529
Olaimey, N. Anne — 127
Olavarria, Esther — 225
Olijar, Leonard R. — 329
Oliver, Louise V. — 301
Oliver, Mark — 238
Olson, Nina E. — 330
Olson, Richard — 301
Opfer, George J. — 343
Ordzhonikidze, Sergei — 570
Orloff, Nancy — 88
Orndoff, Donald H. — 343
Orszag, Peter — 92
Orta, Lucy — 375
Osmus, Lynne A. — 304
Osterman, Joseph G. — 466
Ostrout, John — 445
Ostrowski, Nancy — 327
Ott, Tom — 547
Overal, Dorothy — 511, 512
Overdahl, James — 497
Overstreet, Cornele A. — 455
Owen, Priscilla Richman — 69

P

Pace, Gregory C. — 513
Paez, Richard A. — 70
Paige, Beth — 526
Pajunas, Tony — 535
Pallone, Michael — 353
Palman, Glen K. — 75
Palmer, James — 362
Palmer, Larry L. — 422
Palou, George — 371
Pane, Karen W. — 344
Panehal, Alexandra — 525
Panetta, Leon — 355
Paniati, Jeffery F. — 305
Paprocki, Bernard J. — 512
Paradis, Julie — 103

Paredes, Troy A. — 496
Paret, Elizabeth H. — 67
Parker, Barrington D., Jr. — 68
Parker, David B. — 452
Parker, Helen N. — 279
Parker, Maurice S. — 301
Parkinson, Larry R. — 238
Parmenter, Lester — 286
Parmly, Michael E. — 300
Parsons, D. Scott — 327
Patillo, Jackie — 304
Patrick, Connie L. — 226
Patrick, Henderson M. — 526
Patterson, Anne W. — 300
Patterson, Clara — 91
Patterson, Mark — 327
Paul, Bajinder N. — 329
Paul, Valerie — 547
Paustenbach, Mark — 306
Payne, Nell — 546
Pearce, David D. — 299
Pearce, Hardy — 90
Pearson, Daniel R. — 529
Pearson, Tom — 286
Peddicord, Charlotte G. — 75
Peebles, Oliver, III — 281
Peede, Jon P. — 445
Pegg, Rayne — 103
Pellett, Nancy C. — 379
Pelosi, Nancy — 25
Pendarvis, Jessalyn L. — 523
Penn, B.J. — 171
Pennington, Joseph — 299
Pennington, Rebecca — 306
Peoples, Darlene — 306
Pepin, Andy — 194
Perez, Paul — 377
Perko, Michael J. — 383
Perna, Gus — 186
Perrelli, Thomas J. — 253
Perry, June Carter — 301
Perry, Olophius — 375
Peters, H. Fay — 405
Peters, Joseph R., Jr. — 75
Peters, Marybeth — 53
Petersen, Daniel R. — 95
Petersen, Matthew S. — 392
Peterson, Duane — 280
Peterson, George P. — 461
Peterson, Richard — 330
Petraeus, David H. — 151
Petrick, James B. — 410
Petrou, Laura — 212
Petruccelli, Kathy — 368
Petrucci, James — 397
Pfeiffer, Howard D. — 87
Pfeiffer, W. Dean — 170
Phelann, John J., III — 127
Phelps, Thomas — 447
Phillips, John — 308
Phillips, Paul — 183
Phillips, Robin — 525
Phillips, Samuel W. — 68
Phillips, Stanley Davis — 300
Philo, Ross — 535
Pianalto, Sandra — 405
Pickett, Penny — 503
Pierce, Catherine — 253
Pierson, Lloyd O. — 351
Pinkert, Dean A. — 529
Pinson, Tracey L. — 161
Pisani, Salvatore L. — 307
Pitra, Mark — 378
Plonkey, Susan — 535
Plowden, William C., Jr. — 286
Podonsky, Glenn S. — 203
Poindexter, Robert J. — 452

Polakoff, Scott N. — 331
Polan, James C. — 485
Polaski, Sandra — 273
Pollard, Alfred M. — 393
Pollett, Carroll F. — 184
Poneman, Daniel — 203
Poole, Brooke D. — 470
Pooler, Rosemary S. — 68
Pope, Carol Waller — 395
Popps, Dean G. — 161
Porter, Lisa — 476
Portugal, Murilo — 567
Porzio, Nancy — 512
Posner, Richard A. — 69
Posser, Charles L. — 405
Post, Robert — 103
Potter, Clarissa — 330
Potter, John E. — 534, 535
Poussard, Ronald A. — 156
Powell, Earl A., III — 547
Powell, Nancy J. — 300
Powell, Patrice Walker — 445
Prado, Edward C. — 69
Prahl, Mark L. — 353
Pregerson, Harry — 70
Preston, Phyllis — 314
Price, Geoffrey — 356
Primm, Barry — 526
Prindle, Annette — 282
Proctor, Charlene — 423
Proctor, Norman — 512
Prosperi, Patricia A. — 305
Prost, Sharon — 71
Protos, Grace — 277
Prouty, Paul F. — 415, 440
Pryor, William H., Jr. — 71
Pugh, Elizabeth — 53
Pula, Nikolao — 238
Pulcrano, Sam — 535
Punwani, Ramesh K. — 304
Purcell, Anne G. — 452
Pustay, Melanie Ann — 253
Putnam, Thomas J. — 436
Pyatt, Fred — 331
Pye, Rosemary — 454
Pyke, Thomas N. — 203

Q

Quade, William — 309
Qualey, Brian — 512
Quijada, Adalberto — 512
Quinlan, Anne K. — 309
Quinn, Mark — 512
Quinn, Timothy — 253
Quist, Edward E. — 359

R

Rabkin, Jeremy A. — 561
Raborg, Ronald T. — 514
Raby, Julian — 546
Radar, Paricia — 526
Rader, Randall R. — 71
Radhakrishnan, Ananda — 356
Radice, Anne-Imelda M. — 449
Rae, Karen — 305
Raggi, Reena — 68
Ragsdale, Bruce A. — 79
Rainey, Daniel — 456
Ramdin, Albert R. — 569
Ramirez, Lilia — 226
Randall, Douglas D. — 461
Randt, Clark T., Jr. — 300
Rankin, Janet S. — 285
Ranneberger, Michael E. — 300
Rapkins, Dennis — 530

Rapoport, Bernard — 53
Rardain, Lorraine — 282
Rawlinson, Johnnie B. — 70
Rawls, Charles R. — 379
Ray, Charlie — 226
Ray, James D. — 305
Ray, Joyce — 450
Ray, Tracey A. — 409
Read, James — 423
Rebich, David — 329
Reblin, Gary — 535
Reddick, Eunice S. — 300, 301
Redisch, Steve — 352
Reed, Jeff — 44
Reed, Pearlie — 104
Reed, Richard A. — 415
Reed, Rita A. — 343
Reger, Mark — 479
Regners, Michael R. — 173
Reich, Edward — 368
Reich, Jay — 127
Reichard, Alan B. — 455
Reichle, Susan — 525
Reid, Harry — 25
Reid, Peggy — 305
Reid, Robert N. — 328
Reif, Timothy — 98
Reilly, Arthur K. — 461
Reilly, Edward F., Jr. — 80, 254
Reilly, Robert D., Jr. — 172
Reimold, Di — 305
Reinhardt, Stephen — 70
Reischman, Michael M. — 461
Reitinger, Phillip — 225
Rendell, Marjorie O. — 68
Renkiewicz, Martin — 254
Reno, Loren M. — 156
Renuart, Victor E. — 151
Rest, Judy Van — 561
Reukauf, William — 483
Reyes, Juan — 368
Reynolds, Emily J. — 518
Reynolds, Gerald A. — 527
Reynolds, Victoria — 512
Rhodes, Michael L. — 147
Rhodes, Rebecca R. — 417
Ribeau, Sidney A. — 200
Rice, Charles L. — 194
Rice, Jon E. — 94
Rice, Kevin — 329
Rice, Susan E. — 291, 301
Rice, William Craig — 447
Rich, David — 286
Rich, Jeff — 469
Richards, Lori A. — 497
Richardson, Angelia — 445
Richardson, Cecil R. — 156
Richardson, David L. — 543
Richardson, Eric — 282
Richter, John — 377
Ricks, Michael W. — 512
Riddle, Kim — 308
Rider, Christine — 503
Riera, Timothy — 375
Riggin, E. Philip — 343
Riley, Emma — 282
Riley, William Jay — 70
Ringsak, Elton W. — 512
Rios, Rosie — 327
Risinger, Jeffrey — 496
Ritter, James — 466
Ritz, Lindy — 314
Rivait, David J. — 307
Rivera, Fanny — 304
Rivera, Raymond — 237
Rivera, Reinaldo — 254
Rives, Jack L. — 156

Roberts, Angela — 362
Roberts, Craig — 300
Roberts, John G., Jr. — 65, 67, 68, 71, 545
Roberts, Philip T. — 397
Robilotti, Richard V. — 282
Robinette, Steven W. — 160
Robinson, Adam M., Jr. — 171, 172
Robinson, Aleda — 362
Robinson, Craig R. — 461
Robinson, David M. — 128
Robinson, Elizabeth M. — 92
Robinson, John M. — 289
Robinson, Laurie — 253
Robinson, Maura — 535
Robinson, R. Townsend — 75
Roche, Charlie — 423
Rochelle, Michael D. — 161
Rodenhausen, Patricia M. — 277
Roderick, Bill — 368
Rodgers, Gregory B. — 359
Rodgers, Ronald L. — 254
Rodriguez, Alta — 497
Rodriquez, Steven J. — 289
Roe, Lesa — 426
Roeber, Danielle — 466
Roeder, Douglas W. — 329
Roegner, Russell H. — 359
Rogers, Anita J. — 493
Rogers, John — 352
Rogers, John M. — 69
Rogers, Judith W. — 67
Rogers, Marc E. — 156
Rogers, Margot — 194
Rogers, Randall D. — 321
Rogers, Robert K., Jr. — 530
Rogers, T. Gary — 405
Rogers, Thomasina V. — 473
Roggero, Frederick F. — 156
Rogowsky, Robert — 530
Rogozinski, Jacques — 566
Rohde, Matthew — 99
Roig, Pedro V. — 353
Rolf, Joan — 97
Rollins, Denise — 525
Rollow, Thomas A. — 171
Roman, Leonardo San — 304
Romer, Christina D. — 89
Romero, Rose — 500
Rondeau, Ann E. — 192
Rooney, Francis — 300
Rooney, William — 460
Roop, James — 385
Rosch, J. Thomas — 410
Rose, Charles P. — 194
Rose, Mary M. — 423
Rosecrans, Michael — 466
Rosel, Joan — 282
Roseman, Louise L. — 405
Rosenberg, Jose — 375
Rosengren, Eric S. — 405
Rosenswike, Tom — 286
Ross, Stephen M. — 447
Ross, Valerie — 511
Rossides, Gale — 226
Roth, Barry — 237
Rothstein, Barbara J. — 79
Rotondo, Glenn C. — 421
Roubideaux, Yvette — 213
Roudebush, James G. — 156
Roughead, Gary — 147, 171
Rouse, Cecilia E. — 89
Rouse, Peter M. — 86
Roussel, Judith — 511
Rovner, Ilana Diamond — 69
Row, Shelly — 308
Rowdabaugh, Kirk — 238

Rowe, John P. — 375
Rowe, Leslie V. — 301
Rowe, Richard A., Jr. — 162
Rowe, William A., III — 329, 388
Rowland, Lloyd B. — 189
Rowland, Matthew — 75
Roy, James A. — 156
Roy, Lisa — 388
Roy, Robie Samanta — 97
Rubenstein, Irvin — 353
Rudolph, Lawrence — 461
Rufe, Roger T., Jr. — 226
Ruff, Roy J. — 375
Ruggerio, Steve — 421
Ruggiero, Frank J. — 289
Ruiz, Carl-Martin — 104
Ruiz, Diego T. — 496
Rulon, Kathy — 486
Rundlet, Peter F. — 87
Runnels, Al — 327
Rush, Scott L. — 493
Rushin, Carol — 371
Russell, Cathy — 88
Russell, Jim — 183
Russo, Ronald — 494
Rust, David A. — 514
Ryan, A. Sprightley — 546
Ryan, Barbara A. — 388
Ryan, Diane — 330
Ryan, Evan — 88
Ryan, JoAnn — 194
Ryan, Mary — 328
Ryckman, Mary — 99
Rymer, John T. — 389
Rymer, Pamela Ann — 70
Ryschkewitsch, Michael — 426

S

Sachen-Gute, Kathy — 443
Sakihama, Karen — 512
Sakowitz, Philip E., Jr. — 182
Salas, Brian F. — 173
Salazar, John P. — 422
Salazar, Kenneth L. — 237, 440
Sallee, Richard — 519
Salt, Terrence — 161
Salzman, Amelia — 90
Sammartino, Frank — 60
Samper, Cristian — 547
Sampsel, Laura — 186
Samra, Tom — 535
Sanchez, Alejandro M. — 409
Sanchez, Alfred — 187
Sanchez, Rudy G., Jr. — 501
Sanchez, William — 376
Sandalow, David — 203
Sanders, Robert L. — 375
Sanders, Ronald P. — 476
Sanderson, Janet A. — 300
Sands, Fenton — 526
Sanford, James — 98
Sansom, William B. — 518
Sansone, Janet — 50
Sant, Roger — 545
Sant, Victoria P. — 547
Santamorena, Lori — 330
Sapia, Pamela — 512
Sapir, Zev — 282
Sarandos, Chris — 487
Sargeant, Stephen T. — 160
Sarhan, Mike — 526
Sarjeant, Karen J. — 543
Saul, Andrew M. — 409
Saul, B. Francis, II — 53
Saum, Christine — 441
Saunders, Mary — 128

Sawady, Edna R. — 406
Sayenga, Jill C. — 75
Scales, Charles — 425
Scalia, Antonin — 65, 69
Schafer, George H. — 75
Schaffer, Gregory — 225
Schall, Alvin A. — 71
Schanz, Jeffrey E. — 543
Schapiro, Mary L. — 496
Schaub, James — 104
Schaumber, Peter C. — 452
Scheel, Donna — 286
Schelbert, J. Kenneth — 416
Schiappa, David J. — 25
Schiavone, Terrance D. — 318
Schick, Holly — 503
Schieffer, John Thomas — 300
Schiffer, Lois J. — 441
Schiliro, Philip M. — 86
Schimansky, H. Joseph — 395
Schinasi, Katherine — 47
Schinzel, Ted — 512
Schlicher, Ronald L. — 300
Schlichting, Jim — 382
Schlitt, Lyn M. — 530
Schmelzer, Ranit — 362
Schmid, Julie — 376
Schmidt, Rebecca L. — 470
Schmitt, Austin L. — 398
Schmitt, Glenn R. — 80
Schmitz, Dan — 286
Schmitz, Diane — 238
Schneider, Charles — 410
Schoem, Marc J. — 359
Schonfeld, Mark K. — 500
Schoomaker, Eric B. — 161, 162
Schornagel, Karl — 53
Schregardus, Donald — 171
Schroeder, Mary M. — 70
Schruth, Susan E. — 306
Schuda, Paul — 466
Schuerch, William E. — 351
Schultz, Earl R. — 285
Schultz-Heim, Laurie — 561
Schulz, William — 496
Schulze, Dana — 466
Schwartz, Michael S. — 493
Schwartz, Norton A. — 147, 156
Schwarzman, Stephen A. — 547
Schweickhardt, Reynold — 50
Sciortino, Franklin J. — 512
Scirica, Anthony J. — 68
Scobey, Margaret — 300
Scolese, Christopher — 425
Scott, Bradley — 421
Scott, John E. — 512
Scott, Richard — 568
Scott, Wilma — 375
Scovel, Cal — 304
Screnar, Brian — 237
Seaman, Dara — 331
Sebelius, Kathleen — 212
Seche, Stephen — 301
Secor, Kevin — 343
Seeba, John — 411
Seeley, Rodrick M. — 323
Seidel, Cathy — 382
Seidel, Edward — 461
Seidel, Stan — 286
Selfridge, Pete — 88
Selfridge, Psrits Shah — 127
Sellers, Corlis L. — 281
Sellers, David A. — 75
Semansky, Joe — 276
Semmel, Marsha — 449, 450
Semple, Patricia M. — 359
Sena, David — 377

Sentelle, David Bryan — 67
Sepulveda, Daniel — 98
Sepulveda, Juan — 194
Serwer, Daniel P. — 561
Sessions, William K., III — 80
Sessoms-Ford, Joan — 281
Settje, Alvin — 316
Shaffner, Lawrence — 383
Shafroth, William G. — 237
Shah, Pranab — 535
Shah, Sonal R. — 96
Shand, Tania — 479
Shandor, Anita — 330
Shannon, Thomas A., Jr. — 290, 422
Shapiro, Micheal N. — 368
Shapiro, Neil K. — 127
Sharfman, Stephen L. — 492
Shark, David — 99
Sharp, Rebecca — 225
Sharpe, Tom — 327
Shaub, Walter M., Jr. — 478
Shaver, Dan — 330
Shea, Kevin — 103
Shear, Wayne, Jr. — 172
Shears, Nikki — 385
Shedd, David R. — 476
Shedd, Dennis W. — 68
Shedd, Steven T. — 50
Sheehan, Raymond — 104
Sheehan, Sharon — 496
Sheehy, Daniel — 546
Sheets, D. Nathan — 405, 406
Sheigekawa, Joan — 445
Shelton, James H. — 194
Shelton, Terry — 309
Shelton, William L. — 156
Sheon, Judith W. — 80
Shepherd, Bobby E. — 70
Shepherd, Gloria M. — 305
Shepherd, Leslie L. — 416
Sher, Susan S. — 87
Sherman, Andrew M. — 50
Sherman, Bruce — 352
Sherman, Michael — 441
Sherman, Stephen — 186
Sherry, Peggy — 225
Sheth, Darshan — 484
Shilts, Richard — 356
Shimizu, Holly H. — 44, 45
Shin, Jaiwon — 425
Shinnick, Richard — 290
Shinseki, Eric K. — 343
Shonka, David C. — 411
Shuler, Sally — 547
Shulman, Douglas H. — 330
Shumaker, Elisabeth A. — 70
Shycoff, Barbara L. — 331
Shyshka, Jeff — 344
Siegel, Richard A. — 452
Sienko, Nancy — 375
Sifontes, Jose — 512
Siger, Frederick C. — 127
Siggerud, Katherine — 47
Sikora, Garry — 492
Silva, Phillip — 512
Silverman, Barry G. — 70
Simmons, Gregory — 44
Simmons, Scott — 322
Simmons, Steven J. — 352
Simons, Paul E. — 300
Simonson, John F. — 377
Simpson, Donna M. — 359
Sims, Roy — 231
Sinha, Ajoy — 504
Sippel, Richard L. — 382
Sirri, Erik R. — 496
Sison, Michelle — 300

Sission, Andrew — 526
Skelly, Thomas — 194
Skibine, George — 237
Skidmore, David — 406
Skinner, David — 447
Skinner, Richard L. — 226
Skodon, Emil M. — 300
Skud, Timothy E. — 328
Slaughter, Anne-Marie — 289
Slawsky, Toby D. — 68
Sloviter, Dolores Korman — 68
Small, James F. — 455
Small, Jordan — 535
Smalley, Colleen — 282
Smith, Chris — 104
Smith, Clint — 511
Smith, D. Brooks — 68
Smith, Daniel — 306
Smith, Daniel B. — 289
Smith, Derek — 186
Smith, Douglas M. — 226
Smith, Elizabeth S. — 87
Smith, Emily — 344
Smith, Jeffrey — 372
Smith, Jerry Edwin — 69
Smith, John W. — 546
Smith, Kathy D. — 129
Smith, Lauri — 44
Smith, Lavenski R. — 70
Smith, Michele — 88
Smith, Michelle A. — 405
Smith, Milan D., Jr. — 70
Smith, Nancy Kegan — 436
Smith, Richard — 194
Smith, Roger — 171
Smith, Roland E. — 379
Smith, Sarah — 376
Smith, Sean — 226
Smith, Stephen G. — 379
Smith, Steven — 308
Smith, V. Chapman — 435
Smith-Heimbrock, Sydney — 480
Smithart, Anthony — 286
Smitherman, William D. — 281
Smock, David R. — 561
Smoot, Julianna — 98
Smyth, Paul — 237
Snow, Howard — 171
Snow, Thomas G. — 253
Snowbarger, Vincent K. — 489
Snyder, James — 225
Sobel, Clifford M. — 300
Sobel, Mark — 328
Sobel, Sylvan A. — 79
Socks, Barry S. — 440
Sokobin, Jonathan S. — 497
Solis, Hilda L. — 273, 489
Solomon, Lafe E. — 452
Solomon, Richard H. — 561
Solomont, Alan — 362
Soloway, Stan — 362
Sommer, Irving — 473
Sommers, Jill E. — 356
Sonderman, Debra — 238
Sonenshine, Tara D. — 561
Sonntag, Douglas — 445
Sorbera, Joseph — 377
Sorensen, Steven J. — 455
Sorenson, Jeffrey A. — 161
Sosebee, Carl — 486
Soshea, Brad — 282
Sotelo, John — 445
Soto, Erin — 525
Sotomayor, Sonia — 65
Soukup, Benjamin J., Jr. — 199
Southwick, Leslie H. — 69
Southworth, James — 466

Souvaine, Diane L. — 461
Spalding, Drew — 50
Speakes, Stephen M. — 161
Speakman, V.M., Jr. — 493
Speckhard, Daniel P. — 300
Spence, Karen — 282
Spencer, John — 466
Spencer, William D. — 423
Speyer, Ann — 546
Spinelli, Lawrence — 484
Spinrad, Richard W. — 129
Spisak, Craig — 162
Spitler, Eric J. — 389
Spitzer, Marc L. — 204
Spoehel, Ronald R. — 426
Spogli, Ronald — 300
Spohn, Jeffrey — 393
Spoon, Alan G. — 545
Spooner, David — 128
Sprague, Mary G. — 392
Springer, Cynthia Z. — 331
Staats, Karen — 282
Stabler, Michael A. — 277
Stackley, Sean J. — 171
Stadnik, Andrew G. — 359
Stadtler, D.J. — 459
Stagner, Randall K. — 344
Stai, James L. — 512
Stanberry, Garry — 487
Stanbro, Gene — 385
Stanton, Robert — 238
Stapleton, Craig Roberts — 300
Starek, Mildred — 466
Starling, H. Denby, II — 172
Starr, Judith — 490
Stavridis, James G. — 151
Stebbins, Mike — 97
Steel, Gloria — 522
Steel, Robert — 192
Steele, Scott — 104
Stein, Daniel D. — 519
Stein-Olson, Monica — 526
Steinberg, James B. — 289
Steingass, Henry D. — 519
Stenner, Charles E., Jr. — 156, 158
Stephenson, April — 182
Stephenson, Barbara — 300
Stephenson, Thomas F. — 301
Stern, Gary H. — 405
Stern, Gary M. — 432
Stevens, David — 231
Stevens, John Paul — 65, 69
Stevenson, Mitchell — 161
Stevenson, Todd A. — 359
Stewart, Carl E. — 69
Stewart, Janita — 511
Stewart, Karen B. — 289, 300
Stiff, Linda — 330
Still, Christopher — 286
Stiller, Allison — 171
Stine, Deborah — 97
Stockton, David J. — 405, 406
Stokke, Michael A. — 379
Stone, R. Renee — 237
Stonesifer, Patty — 545
Stores, Charles — 286
Stormes, Janet K. — 352
Strader, George — 47
Strain, Robert D. — 426
Strang, Jo — 305
Stratford, Timothy — 98
Strauss, Jon C. — 461
Strawn, George O. — 462
Streufert, Randy — 523
Strickland, Thomas — 237
Strom, Cordia A. — 75
Strom, Leland A. — 379

Stubbs, Bruce — 170
Stueckler, Sandra — 445
Stultz, Jack C. — 161, 162
Sturgill, D. James — 329
Sucher, Lauren — 561
Suchman, Stan — 285
Suh, Rhea S. — 238
Sullivan, Kathryn D. — 461
Sullivan, Mark J. — 226
Sullivan, Martin — 546
Sullivan, Robert — 282
Sullivan, Travis — 127
Sumka, Howard — 526
Summers, Francis P., Jr. — 182
Summers, Lawrence H. — 90, 96
Sumwalt, Robert L. — 466
Sunshine, Robert A. — 60
Suro-Bredie, Carmen — 99
Suter, William K. — 65
Sutley, Nancy — 89
Sutphen, Mona K. — 86
Sutter, Leonard — 307
Sutton, Jeffrey S. — 69
Sutton, Peter A. — 397
Svinicki, Kristine L. — 470
Swafford, Preston D. — 518
Swain, Diana — 525
Swales, John R., III — 331
Swan, James C. — 300
Swann, Alonzo A., III — 444
Swart, Jim L. — 304
Swart, Susan — 290
Sweeney, Bernard — 511
Swendiman, Alan — 523
Swing, William Lacy — 568
Sykes, Diane S. — 69
Symington, W. Stuart, IV — 301

T

Tacha, Deanell Reece — 70
Tafara, Ethiopis — 497
Taggart, Joseph — 526
Taggart, William J. — 194
Talkin, Pamela — 65
Talleri, Peter — 186
Tallman, Richard C. — 70
Tamargo, Mauricio J. — 254
Tanenblatt, Eric J. — 362
Tangherlini, Daniel — 327
Tankersley, Michael W. — 378
Tapella, Robert C. — 50
Tapia, Marcus — 282
Tarrats, Edgardo — 511
Tarullo, Daniel K. — 404
Tatel, David S. — 67
Taubman, Nicholas F. — 301
Taylor, Ashley — 527
Taylor, Carolyn — 47
Taylor, Derek — 286
Taylor, Jesse — 254
Taylor, Patricia T. — 476
Taylor, Rhonda — 362
Taylor, Robert S. — 185
Taylor, Scott — 525
Taylor, Thomas N. — 461
Taylor, William B. — 301
Taylor, Willie R. — 238
Tazewell, Littleton — 526
Tchen, Christina M. — 87
Teague, Clayton — 97
Teague, Evelyn Y. — 280
Tefft, John F. — 300
Tegnelia, James A. — 188
Teitelbaum, Donald — 300
Temkin, Richard — 511
Tenebaum, Inez — 358

Terrill, Richard — 283
Terry, James P. — 343
Terry, Paula — 445
Terwilliger, Thom H. — 389
Teti, Catherine — 47
Tharp, Andrew — 282
Thatcher, Gary — 352
Thernstrom, Abigail — 527
Thiessen, Donna — 519
Thisen, Duane — 173
Thomas, Adrienne C. — 431
Thomas, Clarence — 65, 70
Thomas, Harry K., Jr. — 290
Thomas, Jeff — 447
Thomas, John C. — 417
Thomas, Sidney R. — 70
Thomas-Greenfield, Linda — 300
Thompkins, Bill — 546
Thompson, Alan S. — 186
Thompson, Horace A. — 473
Thompson, John H. — 343
Thompson, Paul W. — 546
Thompson, Sandra L. — 389
Thomsen, Jim — 171
Thorpe, Frank, IV — 170
Thorsen, Kimberly — 238
Thorson, Eric — 327
Thrailkill, Howard A. — 518
Thrasher, Ellen M. — 503
Thunell, Lars — 567
Thurman, James D. — 161
Tibbits, Paul — 344
Tighe, David J. — 70
Tighe, Tony — 445
Timken, William Robert, Jr. — 300
Timofeyev, Igor V. — 225
Tinder, John Daniel — 69
Tinsley, Kenneth M. — 377
Tinsley, Tuck, III — 199
Tisak, Francis — 171
Tiscione, Frank — 44
Tiscione, Rebecca — 43
Tisor, Darrell J. — 316
Titley, David W. — 172
Titone, Al — 512
Tittel, Jo — 513
Tjoflat, Gerald B. — 70
Tobey, William — 395
Tobias, Constance B. — 212
Tobiassen, Robert — 328
Tobin, Katherine C. — 534
Tochen, Dave — 309
Todt, Thomas — 511
Tokarski, Kevin M. — 307
Tolliver, Candice — 309
Tomasso, Marie — 376
Tonsager, Dallas P. — 379
Toole, Joseph S. — 305
Torborg, Dick — 137
Torres, Guy — 504
Torres, Rafael A. — 343, 344
Torruella, Juan R. — 68
Towns, Edolphus — 440
Trabucco, Thomas J. — 410
Trainor, Ed — 460
Trainor, Robert — 466
Tran, Dat — 344
Tran, Oanh — 352
Trasviña, John — 231
Trautman, George J. — 173
Travers, Linda — 368
Traxler, William B., Jr. — 68
Treat, Kim — 330
Treichel, Mark A. — 443, 444
Tremain, Ralph R. — 454
Trentacoste, Michael F. — 305
Triay, Ines R. — 203

Trigg, Richard — 279
Trimble, Jeffrey N. — 352
Trinity, Frank — 362
Tritell, Randolph W. — 411
Trowell-Harris, Irene — 343
Trujillo, Rose — 306
Trzeciak, Adam R. — 398
Tuccillo, Robert J. — 306
Tuceling, Barbara — 546
Tucker, Daniel A. — 343
Tulino, Doug — 535
Turco, Kathleen M. — 415
Turnbull, Michael G. — 43
Turnbull, Nate — 304
Turner, Karen — 523
Turner, Stacie S. — 440
Turner, Thomas R., II — 162
Turton, Daniel A. — 87
Tuttle, Robert H. — 301
Tyler, Gary — 286
Tyler, Sharon — 282
Tymkovich, Timothy M. — 70
Tyson, Rosalind — 500

U

Umberger, Stephen D. — 512
Urs, Krishna R. — 300
Usher, Edward G., III — 173

V

Vacca, Marilyn A. — 476
Valdes, Vincent — 306
Valiulis, Henry M. — 493
Van Antwerp, Robert L., Jr. — 161, 162
Van Camp, Anne — 546
Van Dusen, Michael — 547
Vance, Will — 454
Vance-Cooks, Davita — 50
Vanderwagen, W. Craig — 212
VanStavern, Thomas N. — 385
Varmus, Harold — 97
Varnado, Tyree — 416
Varney, Christine A. — 253
Varney, Robert W. — 371
Vasquez, Jack — 376
Vaughn, Clyde A. — 162
Vaughn, Jack C., Jr. — 422
Vavrichek, Bruce — 60
Veach, Julie — 382
Veer, Gretchen Van der — 362
Vegliante, Anthony — 535
Vela, Moe — 88
Venlet, David J. — 172
Vera, Mauricio — 523
Verble, Sedelta — 479
Verdino, Carlo — 501
Verenes, Constantine G. — 344
Verga, Peter — 146
Verma, Richard R. — 289
Verner, Doug — 443
Vernon, Kathryn — 313
Vershbow, Alexander R. — 146, 300
Vickers, Michael — 146
Vietti-Cook, Annette L. — 470
Villalobos, Veronica — 372
Villarosa, Sharon E. — 300
Villarreal, Jesse O., Jr. — 388
Vilsack, Tom — 103
Vincent, Alan — 129
Viola, Dennis — 286
Virgilio, Martin T. — 470
Vitale, Michael C. — 172
Vittone, John M. — 273
Vladeck, David — 410
Voetsch, Stephen S. — 171, 172

Voorst, Carol Van — 300
Voss, Barbara — 435
Vu, Vanessa T. — 368

W

Wade, Alice H. — 513
Wade, Rick — 127
Wagner, Ann Louise — 300
Wagner, Christopher — 330
Wagner, Frank D. — 65
Wakabayashi, Ron — 254
Wakefield, Mary K. — 213
Walch, Timothy G. — 436
Walcoff, Mike — 343
Walcott, Sheila — 104
Waldron, Marcia M. — 68
Walke, James W. — 225
Walker, Deborah J. — 95
Walker, E. Martin — 282
Walker, Starnes — 226
Wall, Debra — 431
Wallace, Kim N. — 327
Wallace, Roger W. — 422
Wallen, Matthew T. — 309
Waller, John D. — 492
Walsh, Helene — 378
Walsh, John G. — 329
Walsh, Mary U. — 304
Walsh, Patrick M. — 171
Walter, Elisse B. — 496
Walter, Gregory — 306
Walters, David A. — 98
Walters, Jane — 444
Walters, Sandra — 128
Walther, Michael F. — 254
Walther, Steven T. — 392
Ward, Laysha — 362
Ward, Lisa A. — 416
Ward, Nancy E. — 75
Ward, Patrick M. — 94
Ward, Timothy T. — 331
Ward, Wanda E. — 461
Ward, William E. — 151
Wardlaw, Kim M. — 70
Warren, Stephen — 343
Warsh, Kevin M. — 404, 405
Wash, Michael — 50
Washington, Albert A. — 173
Washington, Linda J. — 304
Waskin, Leon — 526
Watada, Bill — 318
Water, Read Van de — 456
Waters, Jacqueline A. — 530
Watkins, Roland — 456
Watkins, Sheila — 285
Watkins, Tracey D. — 423
Watson, Carole — 447
Watson, Cynthia — 281
Watson, Kathleen — 187
Watts, Michael G. — 104
Wayne, Earl Anthony — 299
Weber, Larry H. — 461
Webster, Cottrell L. — 389
Webster, Douglas W. — 181
Webster, William F. — 416
Weddle, Patrick D. — 359
Wegner, Gail L. — 343
Weiderhold, Fred E. — 460
Weiler, Ed — 426
Weinstein, Elaine — 466
Weinstein, Mindy — 376
Weintraub, Ellen L. — 392
Weisel, Barbara — 98
Weisenfeld, Paul — 526
Weiser, Philip J. — 318
Weiss, Mark — 44

Weiss, Nancy E. — 450
Weiss, Rick — 97
Weissenbach, Karl — 436
Welbes, Matthew J. — 306
Welch, John — 352
Weller, Dennis — 526
Wellinghoff, John — 204
Wells, Barry L. — 300
Wells, James D. — 385
Wells, Reginald F. — 514
Wells, Sandra — 238
Welsh, Donald S. — 371
Welters, Anthony — 53
Wente, Gary — 68
Werfel, Daniel I. — 92
Wesley, Richard C. — 68
West, D. Anthony — 253
West, J. Robinson — 560
Westfield, Richard — 452
Whatley, Annie — 203
Wheeler, Jill — 422
Wheeler, Kathleen J.H. — 238
Wheeler, Seth — 328
Whelihan, Alice M. — 445
Whitaker, Cheryl — 47
Whitaker, R. Reed — 435
Whitcomb, R. Steven — 161
White, Clifford J., III — 253
White, David — 103
White, Douglas N. — 277
White, Helene N. — 69
White, Kim — 128
White, Mark — 525
White, Pamela — 526
Whiteside, Ruth A. — 290
Whiting, Gordon J. — 409
Whitlock, Steve A. — 330
Whitlow, James W. — 304
Whitlow, Woodrow — 426
Whitney, Benson K. — 300
Wholley, Michael C. — 426
Wieringa, Jeffrey — 187
Wiese, Jeffrey — 308
Wiggins, Chani — 226
Wigham-Jones, Mary — 304
Wilder, Renee — 410
Wilderotter, James A. — 519
Wilk, Michael — 512
Wilkinson, James Harvie, III — 68
Willard, Robert F. — 172
Willemssen, Joel — 47
Williams, Aaron S. — 486
Williams, Abiodun — 561
Williams, Andrew — 327
Williams, Ann C. — 69
Williams, Carolyn Fleming — 383
Williams, Carwile — 225
Williams, Charlene — 329
Williams, Charles E., Jr. — 183
Williams, David C. — 534
Williams, Ellen C. — 534
Williams, James A. — 416
Williams, Jerry — 225
Williams, Jerry E. — 231
Williams, Julie L. — 329
Williams, Kathleen M. — 431
Williams, Lester L., Jr. — 286
Williams, Richard — 226
Williams, Richard S. — 426
Williams, Stanley — 286
Williams, Steven W. — 492
Williams, Theodore J. — 156
Williams-Bennett, Kenneth F. — 87
Williams-Bridgers, Jacquelyn — 47
Williams-Kimbrough, Bernice — 375
Williamson, Dave — 231
Williamson, Irving A. — 529

Willke, Theodore — 308
Wilson, Bob — 526
Wilson, Charles R. — 71
Wilson, Christopher — 98
Wilson, Frances C. — 561
Wilson, John — 194
Wilson, Robert — 161, 162
Wilson, Ross — 301
Wilson, Scott — 329
Wilson, Terry — 535
Winfrey, Carey — 547
Winfrey, Patrick — 286
Wing, Jeannette M. — 461
Winkler, Kevin — 394
Winn, James A. — 513
Winns, Anthony L. — 170
Winokur, Peter S. — 366
Winstead, David L. — 416
Winter, Theodore J., Jr. — 490
Winters, Edward G. — 172
Winterton, Joyce L. — 426
Withers, John — 299
Witherspoon, Dorothy A. — 277
Withycombe, William C. — 313
Witkin, Maxanne — 425
Witten, Samuel M. — 289
Witter, Michael — 318
Wohlfeld, Anne — 484
Wolanin, Barbara — 43
Wolf, Deborah G. — 330
Wolfe, Catherine O'Hagan — 68

Wolff, Alejandro Daniel — 291
Wolfson, Adam — 447
Wolfteich, Paul — 330
Wolin, Neal S. — 327
Wollman, Roger L. — 69
Wood, Diane P. — 69
Wood, Michael M. — 301
Wood, William B. — 299
Woodka, Janet — 226
Woodson, Mary Ann — 443
Woosley, John — 511
Worden, S. Pete — 426
Work, Robert O. — 170
Worley, Allen B. — 307, 321
Worth, John — 327
Wright, George — 535
Wright, Kenneth R. — 173
Wright, Lauren E. — 92
Wright, Randall — 286
Wurster, Donald C. — 158
Wyatt, Harry M., III — 156
Wylie, Maureen E. — 129

Y

Yachmetz, Mark — 305
Yaki, Michael — 527
Yamamoto, Donald Y. — 300
Yamashita, Ken — 522
Yates, Michael — 522
Yellen, Janet L. — 405

Yellman, James — 44
Yochelson, Roger — 526
Young, Charles — 47
Young, Deborah B. — 441
Young, Fernanda F. — 377
Young, Michael G. — 402
Younge, Nathan — 519
Yun, Thomas W. — 290

Z

Zahner, Richard P. — 161
Zak, Leocadia I. — 519
Zapata, Jaime — 273
Zarnikow, Eric — 503
Zears, Bill — 385
Zeck, Van — 330
Zeigler, Sandra S. — 280
Zeller, Randall — 226
Zezima, Debra A. — 401
Zichal, Heather R. — 87
Ziebarth, Elizabeth — 546
Zinser, Todd J. — 127
Zirkin, Nancy — 561
Zoellick, Robert — 566, 567, 569
Zoi, Cathy — 203
Zuckman, Jill — 304
Zudiema, Byron — 279
Zuniga-Brown, Timothy — 300
Zurita, Manuel — 376

AGENCY/SUBJECT INDEX

NOTE: This index does not include material appearing in Appendixes A–C.

A

Accounting — 47, 135, 182, 184, 333, 335, 337
Acquisition Service, Federal — 420
Actuaries, Joint Board for the Enrollment of — 541
Administration, Office of — 91
Advisory Council, Federal — 406
Aeronautics and Space Administration, National — 425
African American History and Culture, National Museum — 550
African Americans — 451
African Art, National Museum of — 550
African Development Bank — 565
African Development Foundation — 351
Aged — 115, 122, 214, 219, 232, 234, 318, 490, 494, 514, 516
Aging, Administration on — 214
Agricultural Library, National — 119
Agricultural Marketing Service — 109
Agricultural Mortgage Corporation, Federal — 381
Agricultural Research Service — 119
Agricultural Statistics Service, National — 120
Agriculture, Department of — 103
Agriculture and agricultural commodities — 103, 379, 533
Air Force, Department of the — 156
Air Force Academy, U.S. — 160
Air and Space Museum, National — 550
Air quality — 120, 122, 123
Air transportation — 156, 176, 258, 294, 311, 312, 425, 456, 468, 550
Airport development — 312
Alcohol, Tobacco, Firearms and Explosives, Bureau of — 267
Alcohol and alcohol abuse — 219, 222, 267, 311, 333, 334
Alcohol and Tobacco Tax and Trade Bureau — 334
Aliens — 281
AmeriCorps — 364
AmeriCorps*National Civilian Community Corps — 364
AmeriCorps*VISTA — 364
American Forces Information Service — 151
American Indian, National Museum of the — 551
American States, Organization of — 569
Ames Research Center — 429
Amtrak — 459
Anacostia Community Museum — 549
Animal and Plant Health Inspection Service — 111
Antitrust — 113, 256, 311, 410, 413, 497, 532
Appalachian Regional Commission — 539
Architect of the Capitol — 43
Archives and Records Administration, National — 431
Archives of American Art — 549
Archives Trust Fund Board, National — 437
Arctic Research Commission — 539
Armed forces — 73, 146, 156, 161, 170, 191, 192, 194, 270, 297, 501
Arms and munitions — 146, 156, 161, 170, 181, 186, 188, 189, 204, 207, 261, 267, 296, 299, 366
Army, Department of the — 161
Army Staff — 163
Art, National Gallery of — 555
Art Museum, Smithsonian American — 550
Arthritis and Musculoskeletal Interagency Coordinating Committee — 540

Arts and humanities — 53, 445, 540, 541, 545, 549, 551, 553, 554
Arts and Humanities, National Foundation on the — 445
Arts, National Endowment for the — 445
Asian Development Bank — 565
Audits — 47, 182, 281, 295
Aviation Administration, Federal — 312

B

Bankruptcy — 76, 256, 257, 263
Banks and banking — 257, 260, 333, 334, 338, 377, 379, 388, 393, 404, 441, 540, 565–567
Battle Monuments Commission, American — 539
Biologics — 112, 124, 219, 267
Blind — 58, 199, 514, 540
Blind or Severely Disabled, Committee for Purchase From People Who Are — 540
Book, Center for the — 57
Border Environment Cooperation Commission — 573
Botanic Garden, U.S. — 45
Boundary rights and demarcation — 573
Broadcasting Board of Governors — 352
Budget, Federal — 60, 92, 333
Buildings and facilities, Federal — 44, 158, 159, 163, 176, 415, 420, 440
Bush Award, Vannevar — 464
Business and industry — 106, 107, 109, 127, 130, 137, 139, 141, 256, 294, 356, 422, 451, 456, 473, 484, 496, 529

C

COPS — 269
Cabinet — 85
California Institute of Technology — 430
Campaign funds — 392
Canada International Boundary Commission, United States and — 573
Canada International Joint Commission, United States and — 573
Canada, Permanent Joint Board on Defense — 573
Cancer — 219
Capital Planning Commission, National — 440
Cemetery Administration, National — 346
Census — 121, 134
Census, Bureau of the — 134
Central Bureau, U.S. National — 265
Central Intelligence Agency — 355
Central Security Service — 189
Chemical Safety and Hazard Investigation Board — 540
Children and Families, Administration for — 216
China — 533
Citizens' Stamp Advisory Committee — 540
Citizenship and Immigration Services — 229
Civil rights — 232, 234, 258, 280, 372, 527
Civil Rights, U.S. Commission on — 527
Claims — 73, 257, 263, 270, 347, 348
Clemency and pardons — 254
Coast Guard, U.S. — 176, 229
Colleges and universities — 110, 123, 139, 198, 199, 232, 267, 365, 462
Commerce, Department of — 127

Commodity Futures Trading Commission — 356
Common carriers — 304, 315, 318, 383, 398
Communications — ,58, 159, 177, 184, 220, 243, 244, 294, 352, 382, 419
Communications Commission, Federal — 382
Community development — 106–108, 124, 133, 232, 267, 269, 362, 422, 519
Community Oriented Policing Services, Office of — 269
Community Service, Corporation for National and — 362
Comptroller of the Currency, Office of the — 334
Computer technology — 158, 176, 260
Congress — 25
Congressional Budget Office — 60
Congressional Research Service — 56
Conservation — 116, 117, 120–124, 138, 139, 203, 204, 237, 540, 541, 553, 554
Constitution of the United States — 5
Constitutional amendments — 31
Consular affairs — 293
Consumer Advisory Council — 406
Consumer Product Safety Commission — 358
Consumer protection — 109, 110, 112–114, 234, 257, 338, 358, 389, 411, 413, 444
Cooper-Hewitt National Design Museum — 549
Cooperative State Research, Education, and Extension Service — 119
Cooperatives — 106, 119, 123, 381
Copyrights — 55, 58, 175, 257, 260
Correctional facilities — 264, 267
Corrections, National Institute of — 264
Court of Appeals for the Armed Forces, U.S. — 73
Court of Appeals for the Federal Circuit, U.S. — 67
Court of Appeals for Veterans Claims, U.S. — 74
Court of Federal Claims, U.S. — 73
Court of International Trade, U.S. — 72
Courts — 65, 75, 559
Courts, Administrative Office of the U.S. — 75
Courts of Appeals, U.S. — 66
Credit — 116, 117, 338, 347, 377, 379, 406, 441
Credit Union Administration, National — 441
Crime — 259, 230, 264, 268, 281
Criminal Police Organization, International — 265
Crop Insurance Corporation, Federal — 117
Cuba Broadcasting, Office of — 355
Cultural exchange programs — 294, 486, 549
Currency — 331, 334, 335, 337, 406, 409
Customs and Border Protection — 229
Customs duties and inspections — 72, 99, 230, 398, 530

D

Dairy products — 109, 110, 115, 117, 120
Deaf, Model Secondary School for the — 200
Deaf, National Technical Institute for the — 201
Declaration of Independence — 1
Defense, Department of — 146
Defense, national — 90, 138, 146, 156, 161, 170, 181–192, 194, 206, 207, 228, 257, 311, 355, 366, 476, 501, 542, 566, 573,
Defense Acquisition University — 191
Defense Advanced Research Projects Agency — 181
Defense Business Transformation Agency — 181
Defense Commissary Agency — 182
Defense Contract Audit Agency — 182
Defense Contract Management Agency — 183
Defense Finance and Accounting Service — 184
Defense Information Systems Agency — 184
Defense Intelligence Agency — 185
Defense Intelligence College, National — 191
Defense Legal Services Agency — 185
Defense Logistics Agency — 186
Defense Nuclear Facilities Safety Board — 366
Defense policy — 149
Defense Security Cooperation Agency — 187
Defense Security Service — 187
Defense Threat Reduction Agency — 188
Defense unified combatant commands — 151
Defense University, National — 192
Delaware River Basin Commission — 540

Deposit Insurance Corporation, Federal — 388
Developing countries — 118, 333, 351, 422, 485, 487, 520, 522, 565–567, 569
Development, U.S. Agency for International — 522
Digital Humanities — 449
Disability, National Council on — 542
Disability Employment Policy, Office of — 284
Disaster assistance — 115, 116, 118, 123, 138, 226, 370, 506, 525
Disease Control and Prevention, Centers for — 216
Diseases — 111, 112, 122, 216, 219–221, 258, 281
District courts, U.S. — 71
District of Columbia Court of Appeals — 74
District of Columbia Superior Court — 74
Domestic Policy Council — 96
Drug Control Policy, Office of National — 94
Drug Enforcement Administration — 266
Drugs and drug abuse — 94, 220, 222, 229, 260, 264–267, 295, 311
Dryden Flight Research Center — 429

E

Economic Advisers, council of — 89
Economic Analysis, Bureau of — 135
Economic Council, National — 96
Economic Development Administration — 133
Economic Research Service — 120
Economic policy — 60, 89, 96, 134, 135, 327, 331, 333, 356, 400, 406
Economics and Statistics Administration — 134
Education — 109, 111, 115, 116, 119, 120, 123, 125, 152, 158, 176, 195, 258, 267, 347, 365, 438, 449, 555
Education, Department of — 195
Education, Federal Interagency Committee on — 541
Educational facilities — 119, 160, 178, 191, 192, 194, 199–201, 431
Einstein Planetarium — 550
Election Commission, Federal — 392
Electric power — 108, 109, 208, 209, 518, 542
Elisofon Photographic Archives, Eliot — 550
Emergency preparedness — 158, 163, 165, 217, 265, 267
Employee Benefits Security Administration — 279
Employees' Compensation Appeals Board — 274
Employment — 273, 276, 278, 284, 347, 372, 423, 451, 479
Employment and Training Administration — 278
Employment Standards Administration — 280
Empowerment zones — 106, 107, 234
Endowments — 445
Energy — 106, 176, 203, 244, 247, 257, 312, 325, 333
Energy, Department of — 203
Energy Regulatory Commission, Federal — 208
Energy Technology Laboratory, National — 206
Engineering — 158, 163, 176, 177, 243, 313
English Second Language — 196
Engraving and Printing, Bureau of — 335
Environmental Health and Injury Prevention, Coordinating Centers for — 216
Environmental protection — 89, 107–109, 111, 112, 117, 119, 120, 123, 124, 138, 139, 141, 149, 158, 176, 207, 220, 229, 234, 237, 239, 244, 258, 261, 297, 312, 322, 323, 333, 366, 470, 523, 540, 541, 554
Environmental Protection Agency — 366
Environmental Quality, Council on — 89
Environmental Satellite, Data, and Information Service, National — 138
Equal Employment Opportunity Commission — 372
Executive Boards, Federal — 483
Export Administration Operating Committee — 540
Export-Import Bank of the United States — 377
Exports and imports — 110, 112, 113, 118, 132, 136, 377, 529, 540

F

Farm Credit Administration — 379
Farm Service Agency — 116
Federal Law Enforcement Training Center — 229

Film Preservation Board, National — 57
Finance Corporation, International — 567
Financial Institutions Examination Council, Federal — 540
Financial Management Service — 335
Financing Bank, Federal — 109, 540
Fine Arts, Commission of — 540
Fire prevention — 122, 141, 247
Fish and Wildlife Service, U.S. — 241
Fisheries — 138, 242
Flood control — 122–124, 518
Fogarty International Center — 220
Folklife and Cultural Heritage, Center for — 552
Folklife Center, American — 56
Folklife programs — 56, 552
Food and Drug Administration — 217
Food and food safety — 217, 218
Food and Nutrition Service — 114
Food grades and standards — 109, 110, 112
Food safety — 109, 111, 114, 119, 120
Food Safety and Inspection Service — 114
Foreign Agricultural Service — 118
Foreign assistance — 118, 351, 422, 487, 522
Foreign Claims Settlement Commission of the United States
   — 270
Foreign Intelligence Advisory Board, President's — 542
Foreign Investment in the United States, Committee on —
   540
Foreign relations — 242, 261, 277, 289, 311, 333, 400,
   519, 522, 541, 553, 560, 563, 573
Foreign service — 293, 298, 299, 397, 525
Foreign Service Institute — 294
Foreign Service Labor Relations Board — 397
Forest Service — 121
Forests and forest products — 121–123
Fossil fuels — 206
Fraud — 230, 246, 257, 260, 295, 334
Freer Gallery of Art — 549
Fulbright Foreign Scholarship Board, J. William — 541

G

Gallaudet University — 199
General Service Administration — 415
Generalized System of Preferences — 532
Genetics — 220, 221
Geological Survey, U.S. — 243
Geospatial-Intelligence Agency, National — 189
Glenn Research Center, John H. — 429
Global Health, Coordinating Office for — 217
Goddard Space Flight Center — 429
Goldwater Scholarship and Excellence in Education
   Foundation, Barry M. — 540
Government Accountability Office — 47
Government contracts — 73, 182, 183, 257, 280, 417, 506
Government employees — 257, 258, 261, 263, 281, 299,
   395, 409, 423, 478, 479, 483
Government Ethics, Office of — 478
Government Printing Office — 50
Government property management — 415
Graduate School, Department of Agriculture — 125
Grain Inspection, Packers, and Stockyards Administration
   — 112
Grants — 106–108, 133, 140, 196, 196, 198, 220, 221,
   232, 234, 258, 269, 318, 347, 348, 364, 365, 422, 438,
   446, 447, 449, 450, 462, 464, 520
Great Lakes Fishery Commission — 573
Gross domestic product — 135

H

Harmonized Tariff Schedule of the United States — 533
Hazardous substances — 216, 234, 258, 322, 370, 468,
   472, 540
Hazardous waste — 207, 370, 540, 542
Health, National Institutes of — 218
Health and health care — 109, 111, 115, 116, 141, 149,
   153, 157, 159, 165, 177, 194, 212, 216, 261, 281, 297,
   313, 346–348, 480, 494, 516, 523, 540, 541
Health care facilities — 346–348

Health and Human Services, Department of — 212
Health Information Service, Coordinating Center for — 217
Health Promotion, Coordinating Center for — 217
Health Resources and Services Administration — 218
Healthcare Research and Quality, Agency for — 216
Hearing impaired — 200, 201, 220
Hebert School of Medicine, F. Edward — 194
Highway Administration, Federal — 314
Highway Traffic Safety Administration, National — 316
Highways and roads — 314, 316, 440, 468
Hirshhorn Museum and Sculpture Garden — 549
Historic preservation — 44, 55, 57, 58, 159, 163, 244, 431,
   434, 437, 447, 449, 451, 539, 549, 553
Historic Preservation, Advisory Council on — 539
Historical Publications and Records Commission, National
   — 437
History, National Museum of American — 551
History, National Museum of Natural — 551
Holmes Devise, Permanent Committee for the Oliver
   Wendell — 542
Holocaust Memorial Museum, United States — 542
Home Loan Mortgage Corporation, Federal — 234
Homeland Security, Department of — 225
Homeless — 108, 232, 348
House of Representatives — 25, 34–43
Housing — 107, 108, 231, 258, 259, 338, 347, 393
Housing and Urban Development, Department of — 231
Housing Finance Agency, Federal — 393
Howard University — 200
Humanities, National Endowment for the — 447
Humanities, National Foundation on the Arts and — 445
Hydroelectric power — 209

I

IMAX Theater — 550
INTERPOL — 265
Immigration — 226, 228–230, 257, 259, 261, 268, 293, 298,
   568
Immigration and Customs Enforcement, U.S. — 230
Immigration and naturalization — 229
Immigration Review, Executive Office for — 268
Imports — 533
Indian Affairs, Bureau of — 245
Indian Arts and Crafts Board — 541
Indian Education, Bureau of — 245
Indian Gaming Commission, National — 542
Indian Health Service — 218
Individuals with disabilities — 58, 198, 232, 234, 258, 259,
   280, 281, 318, 347, 348, 482, 514, 516, 540, 542
Industrial College of the Armed Forces — 192
Industry and Security, Bureau of — 132
Infants and children — 114, 115, 196, 216, 219, 260, 281,
   347, 523, 541
Infectious Diseases, Coordinating Center for — 217
Information Resources Management College — 192
Information Security Oversight Office, National Security —
   437
Information technology — 119, 141, 184, 219, 260, 294
Infrastructure, critical — 260, 297
Insurance — 116, 117, 257, 313, 347, 378, 388, 443, 480,
   485, 490, 494, 516, 541, 542
Intelligence — 91, 149, 152, 159, 165, 175, 177, 185, 189,
   191, 204, 228, 230, 257, 263, 264, 266, 293, 295, 311,
   476, 542
Inter-American Defense Board — 566
Inter-American Development Bank — 566
Inter-American Foundation — 422
Inter-American Investment Corporation — 566
Interagency relations — 541
Interior, Department of the — 237
Internal Revenue Service — 336
International Broadcasting Bureau — 353
International organizations, U.S. participation — 333, 563
International Trade Administration — 136
Inventions and patents — 67, 141, 142, 257
Investigation, Federal Bureau of — 263
Investigations — 47, 253, 263, 265, 266, 281, 293, 385,
   400, 468, 472, 480, 540

Investments — 333, 337, 381, 389, 409, 437, 484, 496, 508, 540, 566, 567, 569

J

Japan-United States Friendship Commission — 541
Jet Propulsion Laboratory — 430
Johnson Space Center, Lyndon B. — 429
Joint Chiefs of Staff — 150
Joint Forces Staff College — 192
Joint Staff — 151
Judges — 65, 78, 264
Judicial Center, Federal — 79
Judicial Conference of the United States — 67
Judicial Panel on Multidistrict Litigation — 72
Justice, Department of — 253
Justice Programs, Office of — 266
Juvenile Justice and Delinquency Prevention, Coordinating Council on — 540

K

Kendall Demonstration Elementary School — 200
Kennedy Center for the Performing Arts, John F. — 554
Kennedy Space Center, John F. — 429

L

Labor, Department of — 273
Labor-management relations — 281, 395, 401, 451, 456, 482
Labor Relations Authority, Federal — 395
Labor Relations Board, National — 451
Labor Statistics, Bureau of — 284
Laboratories — 109, 140, 206, 218–220, 430, 541
Laboratory Consortium for Technology Transfer, Federal — 541
Land Management, Bureau of — 246
Langley Research Center — 430
Laurent Clerc National Deaf Education Center — 200
Law, international — 265
Law enforcement — 65, 79, 112, 141, 175, 185, 230, 242, 244, 253, 263–269, 295, 331, 336, 358, 371, 374, 385, 392, 402, 413, 497, 499, 508, 540
Lawyers — 65, 78, 253
Learn and Serve America — 365
Legal services — 48, 65, 175, 185, 253, 333, 338, 543
Legal Services Corporation — 543
Legislative procedure — 31
Libraries — 53, 119, 221, 436, 541, 554
Libraries, Presidential — 436
Library and Information Center Committee, Federal — 541
Library of Congress — 53
Licensing — 311, 383, 400, 468, 472
Literacy, National Institute for — 201
Loans — 106–109, 116, 232, 234, 257, 347, 348, 377, 381, 406, 410, 443, 484, 506, 511

M

Madison Memorial Fellowship Foundation, James — 541
Management and Budget, Office of — 92
Manpower training — 79, 149, 153, 158, 165, 176, 177, 218, 219, 278, 285, 294, 320, 480, 482, 487
Maps and mapping — 123, 139, 177, 243, 244, 312
Marine and Aviation Operations, Office of — 139
Marine Corps, U.S. — 178
Marine Fisheries Service, National — 138
Marine life — 261, 554
Marine Mammal Commission — 541
Maritime activities — 138, 170, 229, 258, 281, 294, 311, 312, 320, 398, 468
Maritime Administration — 320
Maritime Commission, Federal — 398
Marketing — 109, 112, 116, 118, 209
Marshall Space Flight Center, George C. — 430
Marshals Service, U.S. — 264
Marshals Service Training Academy, U.S. — 265
Measurements and standards — 112, 113, 140, 280, 281

Meat and meat products — 109, 110, 112, 114, 120
Mediation and Conciliation Service, Federal — 401
Mediation Board, National — 456
Medicaid — 217
Medicare — 217, 516
Medicare and Medicaid Services, Centers for — 217
Medicare Payments Advisory Commission — 541
Merchant marine — 320
Merit Systems Protection Board — 423
Mexican-U.S. Defense Commission, Joint — 573
Mexico International Boundary and Water Commission, United States and — 573
Middle East Broadcasting Networks — 355
Migration, International Organization for — 568
Migratory Bird Conservation Commission — 541
Mine Safety and Health Administration — 283
Mine Safety and Health Review Commission, Federal — 402
Minerals Management Service — 246
Mining and minerals — 124, 244, 246, 247, 281, 283, 402
Minorities — 137, 140, 196, 232, 278, 280, 346, 348, 482
Minority Business Development Agency — 137
Mint, U.S. — 337
Missile Defense Agency — 188
Missing personnel — 153
Mississippi River Commission — 541
Monetary Fund, International — 567
Montgomery GI Bill — 347
Monuments and memorials — 243, 261, 346, 347, 440, 539, 542
Mortgage Association, Federal National — 234
Mortgage Association, Government National — 234
Mortgages — 232, 234, 257, 381
Motor Carrier Safety Administration, Federal — 323
Motor vehicles — 316, 323, 347
Multilateral Investment Guarantee Agency — 569
Museum and Library Services, Institute of — 449
Museums — 438, 451, 542, 545, 549–553

N

National Security Council — 90
Native Americans — 106, 115, 123, 196, 218, 235, 239, 244, 245, 260, 261, 267, 346, 347, 450, 451, 508, 541, 542, 551
Natural gas — 208, 247
Natural Resources Conservation Service — 123
Navajo and Hopi Relocation Commission — 542
Naval Academy, U.S. — 178
Naval Observatory — 177
Navy, Department of the — 170
North American Free Trade Agreement — 532
Northwest Power Planning Council — 542
Nuclear energy — 159, 204, 206, 207, 366, 470, 542
Nuclear Regulatory Commission — 470
Nuclear Security Agency, National — 206
Nuclear Waste Technical Review Board, United States — 542
Nursing, Graduate School of — 194
Nutrition — 114–117, 119, 120
Nutrition Policy and Promotion, Center for — 116

O

Occupational safety and health — 141, 217, 258, 283, 402, 473
Occupational Safety and Health Administration — 283
Occupational Safety and Health, National Institute — 217
Occupational Safety and Health Review Commission — 473
Ocean Service, National — 139
Oceanic and Atmospheric Administration, National — 138
Oceanic and Atmospheric Research, Office of — 139
Ombudsman — 276
Organic Standards Board, National — 110
Overseas Private Investment Corporation — 484

P

Park Foundation, National — 542

Park Service, National — 243
Parole Commission, U.S. — 269
Passports and visas — 257, 260, 293
Patent and Trademark Office — 141
Peace, United States Institute of — 560
Peace Corps — 486
Pension Benefit Guaranty Corporation — 489
Pensions — 279, 347, 480, 489, 493
Pentagon Force Protection Agency — 190
Personnel Management, Office of — 479
Pests and pesticides — 109, 111, 112, 122, 370
Petroleum — 208, 247, 261, 323
Pipeline and Hazardous Materials Safety Administration — 322
Pipelines — 209, 312, 322, 323, 325, 468
Plants — 45, 109–113, 116, 120, 123, 124, 242
Policy Development, Office of — 96
Portrait Gallery, National — 550, 552
Ports — 229
Postal Inspection Service — 536
Postal Museum, National — 552
Postal Regulatory Commission — 492
Postal Service, U.S. — 534
Power administrations — 209
President of the United States — 85, 86, 90
Presidential Emergency Boards — 458
Presidio Trust — 542
Price controls — 120
Price supports — 109, 110, 117
Printing — 50, 335
Printing House for the Blind, American — 199
Prison Industries, Federal — 264
Prisoners of war — 153, 270
Prisons, Bureau of — 264
Probation and parole — 76, 80, 269
Protective services — 160, 230, 259, 260, 263–265, 293
Public assistance programs — 114, 115, 232, 245, 254, 267, 318, 319
Public Buildings Service — 420
Public debt — 331, 335, 337
Public Debt, Bureau of the — 337
Public health and safety — 120, 214, 216–218
Public lands — 121, 237, 239, 243, 246, 247, 261, 542
Public Law Boards — 458
Public Service Award — 464

R

Racketeering — 260
Radiation protection — 258, 370
Radio Free Asia — 355
Radio Free Europe/Radio Liberty — 353
Radio Marti — 355
Railroad Adjustment Board, National — 458
Railroad Administration, Federal — 315
Railroad Passenger Corporation, National — 459
Railroad Retirement Board — 493
Railroads — 315, 325, 456, 459, 468, 493
Rates and fares — 492
Reclamation, Bureau of — 247
Reconstruction and Development, International Bank for — 566
Records management — 270, 431, 432, 434, 439
Recreation and recreation areas — 122, 243, 246, 247, 261, 518, 542
Refugees — 298, 568
Register, Administrative Committee of the Federal — 539
Register, Office of the Federal — 436
Renwick Gallery — 551
Research and Innovative Technology Administration — 323
Reserve Banks, Federal — 408
Reserve System, Federal — 404
Retirement Thrift Investment Board, Federal — 409
Risk Management Agency — 117
Rochester Institute of Technology — 201
Rural areas — 106, 108–110, 119, 120, 133, 231, 319
Rural Business-Cooperative Programs — 106
Rural development — 106, 107, 119, 120
Rural Housing — 107

Rural Utilities Service — 108

S

Sackler Gallery, Arthur M. — 553
Safety — 313, 315, 316, 320, 322, 323, 358, 366, 466, 470, 472, 540
Saint Lawrence Seaway Development Corporation — 321
Savings bonds — 337
Scholars, White House Commission on Presidential — 542
Scholarships and fellowships — 294, 365, 446, 449, 464, 540–542
Schools — 109, 115, 125, 195, 200, 365, 487
Science and technology — 97, 106–110, 112, 113, 119–124, 130, 133, 139–141, 149, 152, 157–159, 175, 177, 181, 196, 198, 201, 206, 208, 214, 218–221, 228, 234, 239, 244, 266, 267, 283, 295, 297, 313, 315, 316, 319, 320, 323, 324, 333, 371, 428–430, 461, 510, 539, 541, 553, 554
Science and Technology Policy, Office of — 97
Science Board, National — 462
Science Foundation, National — 461
Secret Service, U.S. — 230
Securities and Exchange Commission — 496
Security, international — 149
Security Agency, National — 189
Selective Service System — 501
Senate — 25, 32–34
Senior Corps — 364
Sentencing Commission, U.S. — 80
Small Business Administration — 503
Small Business Centers — 420
Small Business Development Centers — 509
Small businesses — 274, 420, 503
Smithsonian Astrophysical Observatory — 553
Smithsonian Environmental Research Center — 554
Smithsonian Institution — 545
Smithsonian Institution Archives — 553
Smithsonian Institution International Center — 553
Smithsonian Institution Libraries — 554
Smithsonian Institution Traveling Exhibition Service (SITES) — 554
Smithsonian Marine Station — 554
Smithsonian Museum Conservation Institute — 553
Smithsonian Tropical Research Institute — 554
Social Security Administration — 513
Social Security Advisory Board — 542
Solicitor of Labor — 276
Sound Recording Preservation Board, National — 57
Space shuttle — 428, 429
Space transportation and exploration — 156, 167, 297, 313, 425, 429, 550
Special Boards of Adjustment — 458
Special Council, Office of — 483
Standards and Technology, National Institute of — 140
State, Department of — 289
State Justice Institute — 559
Statistics — 120, 134, 141, 267, 284, 533
Stennis Space Center, John C. — 430
Substance Abuse and Mental Health Services Administration — 222
Supplemental Security Income — 516
Supreme Court of the United States — 65
Surface Mining Reclamation and Enforcement, Office of — 244
Surface transportation — 324
Surface Transportation Board — 324
Surplus property and commodities — 420
Susquehanna River Basin Commission — 542

T

TV Marti — 355
Tax Court, U.S. — 73
Taxes — 73, 263, 327, 333–336
Technical Information Service, National — 141
Telecommunications — 108, 109, 140, 176, 382, 420
Telecommunications and Information Administration, National — 140

Tennessee Valley Authority — 517
Territorial courts — 71
Terrorism — 217, 226, 228, 229, 261, 264, 265, 267
Terrorism Prepardness and Emergency Response, Coordinating Office for — 217
Textile Agreements, Committee for the Implementation of — 540
Textiles — 540
Thrift Institutions Advisory Council — 406
Thrift Savings Plan — 410
Thrift Supervision, Office of — 338
Tobacco — 109, 116, 267, 333, 334
Toxic Substances and Disease Registry, Agency for — 216
Trade — 98, 112, 118, 127, 130, 134, 136, 139–141, 226, 229, 230, 256, 257, 294, 311, 322, 333, 356, 377, 398, 410, 507, 519, 529, 540, 542
Trade and Development Agency — 519
Trade Commission, Federal — 410
Trade Commission, United States International — 529
Trade Policy Staff Committee — 542
Trace Representative, Office of the U.S. — 98
Trademarks — 67, 142, 175, 257
Transit Administration, Federal — 318
Transportation — 110, 167, 177, 230, 243, 304, 456, 459, 466
Transportation, Department of — 304
Transportation Safety Board, National — 466
Transportation Security Administration — 230
Travel — 459
Treasury, Department of the — 327
Truman Scholarship Foundation, Harry S. — 541
Trusts and trustees — 256, 333, 437

U

Udall Scholarship and Excellence in National Environmental Policy Foundation, Morris K. — 541
Udvar-Hazy Center, Steven F. — 550
Uniformed Services University of the Health Sciences — 194
United Nations — 563, 570
Urban areas — 108, 133, 231
Utilities — 108, 204, 210, 518

V

Veterans — 74, 280, 285, 343, 480, 482, 510, 542

Veterans Affairs, Department of — 343
Veterans Day National Committee — 542
Veterans' Employment and Training Service — 285
Veterinary services — 112
Vice President of the United States — 25, 28, 85, 88, 90
Vocational rehabilitation — 198, 278, 347, 348
Voice of America — 353
Volunteer programs — 122, 362, 440, 487

W

Wages — 280, 452
War College, National — 192
Waste management — 108
Water pollution control — 108, 122, 139, 370
Water supply — 108, 117, 120, 122–124, 163, 239, 243, 244, 247, 261, 573
Waterman Award, Alan T. — 464
Waterways — 123, 124, 138, 139, 177, 281, 297, 321, 325, 518, 540–542, 573
Weather — 124, 138, 159, 177
Weather Service, National — 138
Welfare — 279
Wetlands — 247
Whistleblowing — 257, 484
White House Office — 86
Wildlife — 111, 112, 117, 122–124, 139, 239, 241, 242, 247, 261, 540, 541, 552
Wilson International Center for Scholars, Woodrow — 555
Witness Security Program, Federal — 260, 265
Women — 115, 140, 277, 278, 280, 346, 348, 482, 510, 523
World Bank — 566
World Wise Schools — 487

Y

Youth — 122, 199, 234, 267, 278, 281, 347, 364, 523, 540, 541

Z

Zoological Park, National — 552